Gathering Time

Dating the Early Neolithic Enclosures of Southern Britain and Ireland

Volume 2

Alasdair Whittle, Frances Healy and Alex Bayliss

With contributions by

Michael J. Allen, Tim Allen, Christopher Bronk Ramsey, Lydia Cagney, Gabriel Cooney, Ed Danaher, Timothy Darvill, Philip Dixon, Peter Dorling, Mark Edmonds, Christopher Evans, Steve Ford, Charles French, Mark Germany, Seren Griffiths, Derek Hamilton, Julie Hamilton, Robert Hedges, Gill Hey, Tom Higham, Andy M. Jones, Thomas Kador, Richard Lewis, Jim Mallory, Gerry McCormac, John Meadows, Roger Mercer, Muiris O'Sullivan, Francis Pryor, Mick Rawlings, Keith Ray, Reay Robertson-Mackay, Grant Shand, Niall Sharples, Jessica Smyth, Simon Stevens, Nicholas Thomas, Malcolm Todd, Johannes van der Plicht, Geoffrey Wainwright and *Michael Wysocki*

Principal illustrator

Ian Dennis

OXBOW BOOKS
Oxford and Oakville

Published in the United Kingdom in 2011. Reprinted in 2015 by
OXBOW BOOKS
10 Hythe Bridge Street, Oxford OX1 2EW

and in the United States by
OXBOW BOOKS
1950 Lawrence Road, Havertown, PA 19083

ISBN 978-1-84217-425-8

Cover design by Ian Dennis

A CIP record of this book is available from the British Library

Library of Congress Cataloging-in-Publication Data

Whittle, Alasdair.
Gathering time : dating the early Neolithic enclosures of southern Britain and Ireland / Alasdair Whittle, Frances Healy and Alex Bayliss ; with contributions by Michael J. Allen... [et.al.].
v.1-2. cm.
Includes bibliographical references and index.
ISBN 978-1-84217-425-8 (vols 1 & 2)
1. Neolithic period--Great Britain. 2. Neolithic period--Ireland. 3. Dwellings, Prehistoric--Great Britain. 4. Dwellings, Prehistoric--Ireland. 5. Roads, Prehistoric--Great Britain. 6. Roads, Prehistoric--Ireland. 7. Archaeological dating--Great Britain. 8. Archaeological dating--Ireland. 9. Great Britain--Antiquities. 10. Ireland--Antiquities. I. Healy, Frances. II. Bayliss, Alex. III. Allen, Michael J. IV. Title.
GN776.22.G7W444 2011
936.1--dc22
2011012525

Printed and bound in Great Britain by
Short Run Press, Exeter

For a complete list of Oxbow titles, please contact:

UNITED KINGDOM
Oxbow Books
Telephone (01865) 241249, Fax (01865) 794449
Email: oxbow@oxbowbooks.com
www.oxbowbooks.com

UNITED STATES OF AMERICA
Oxbow Books
Telephone (800) 791-9354, Fax (610) 853-9146
Email: queries@casemateacademic.com
www.casemateacademic.com/oxbow

Oxbow Books is part of the Casemate Group

Contents

VOLUME II

11 The Marches, south Wales and the Isle of Man

Alex Bayliss, Alasdair Whittle, Frances Healy, Keith Ray, Peter Dorling, Richard Lewis, Timothy Darvill, Geoffrey Wainwright and Michael Wysocki

The area covered in this chapter (Fig. 11.1) ranges from the west Midlands to the Preseli Hills in south-west Wales. It encompasses the low-lying areas of the Avon, Severn and Wye valleys and the south-east Welsh coast, all of them rich in prehistoric settlement, as well as the uplands to the north and west, where stone-built monuments are often well preserved. Neolithic enclosures currently seem markedly less numerous in the Marches and south and west Wales than in southern England (Fig. 1.1), although this may change with future research, as more enclosures of all kinds are recognised as Neolithic. We also consider one site, Billown, in the south of the Isle of Man.

Research histories have been varied, although much of the fieldwork has been quite recent. Hill Croft Field, in Herefordshire, was discovered from aerial photographs in 2006 and evaluated in the course of a broader assessment of the Lugg valley. Aerial photography in 2006 revealed a double-ditched causewayed enclosure at Womaston in the Walton basin, Powys (Chris Musson, pers. comm.; Toby Driver, pers. comm.), extending the history of a monument complex in which the earliest component had previously seemed to be a cursus (Gibson 1999); preliminary excavation followed in 2008.[1] The earthworks at Beech Court Farm, in the Vale of Glamorgan, were already known, although relocated by aerial photography in 1988, and were investigated from 1999 in advance of limestone quarrying. Banc Du, in Pembrokeshire, was first identified by aerial photography in 1990, photographed again under better conditions in 2002, and investigated through field evaluation as part of a research project on ancient communities in the Strumble-Preseli area. Billown, on the Isle of Man, was discovered in 1995 through quarrying and geophysical survey.

Several other probably and possibly Neolithic enclosures are known, including earth- and stone-built segmented earthworks on Dorstone Hill, Herefordshire, which have yielded early Neolithic material (Oswald *et al.* 2001, fig. 4.13; Pye 1967; 1968; 1969) and a possible causewayed site at Woolston, near Oswestry in Shropshire, known through aerial photography since 1971 (Oswald *et al.* 2001, 154). The rate of recent discoveries suggests that many more could remain to be discovered across the area. Three further sites are suspected on hilltops in Herefordshire, one close to Hereford and two to the north-east of the Black Mountains. In south-east Wales, two probably Neolithic enclosures with interrupted ditches have been recognised by aerial photography at Corntown and Norton, both in the Ogmore valley. The surface of the Corntown site yielded a lithic collection including 30 leaf arrowheads (Burrow *et al.* 2001), and evaluation of the Norton enclosure in 2006 established the presence of two ditches and recovered a considerable amount of animal and possibly human bone from a back-filled basal deposit. Diagnostic artefacts were absent and radiocarbon dates are awaited (Richard Lewis, pers. comm.). A third possible site, with a layout like the Corntown example, made up of two close-set, concentric interrupted ditches and a third, incomplete circuit some way outside them, was seen from the air some 12 km to the south-east in the summer drought of 2006 at Flemingston, near St Athan, in the Vale of Glamorgan (Toby Driver, pers. comm.; Pitts 2006).

11.1 Hill Croft Field, Bodenham, Herefordshire, SO 5405 4995

Location and topography

The enclosure in Hill Croft Field lies at 112 m OD, surrounding a natural knoll on the end of a small ridge above the Lugg valley, surrounded by ranges of hills, all visible from the enclosure (Fig. 11.1). The area of the entrance is on Bishop's Frome Limestone, while most of the enclosure is on the Raglan Mudstone Formation, both parts of the Lower Old Red Sandstone system. The solid geology is overlain by glacial clays. The Lugg and other small streams rise in the hills to the north and then run south to join the Wye.

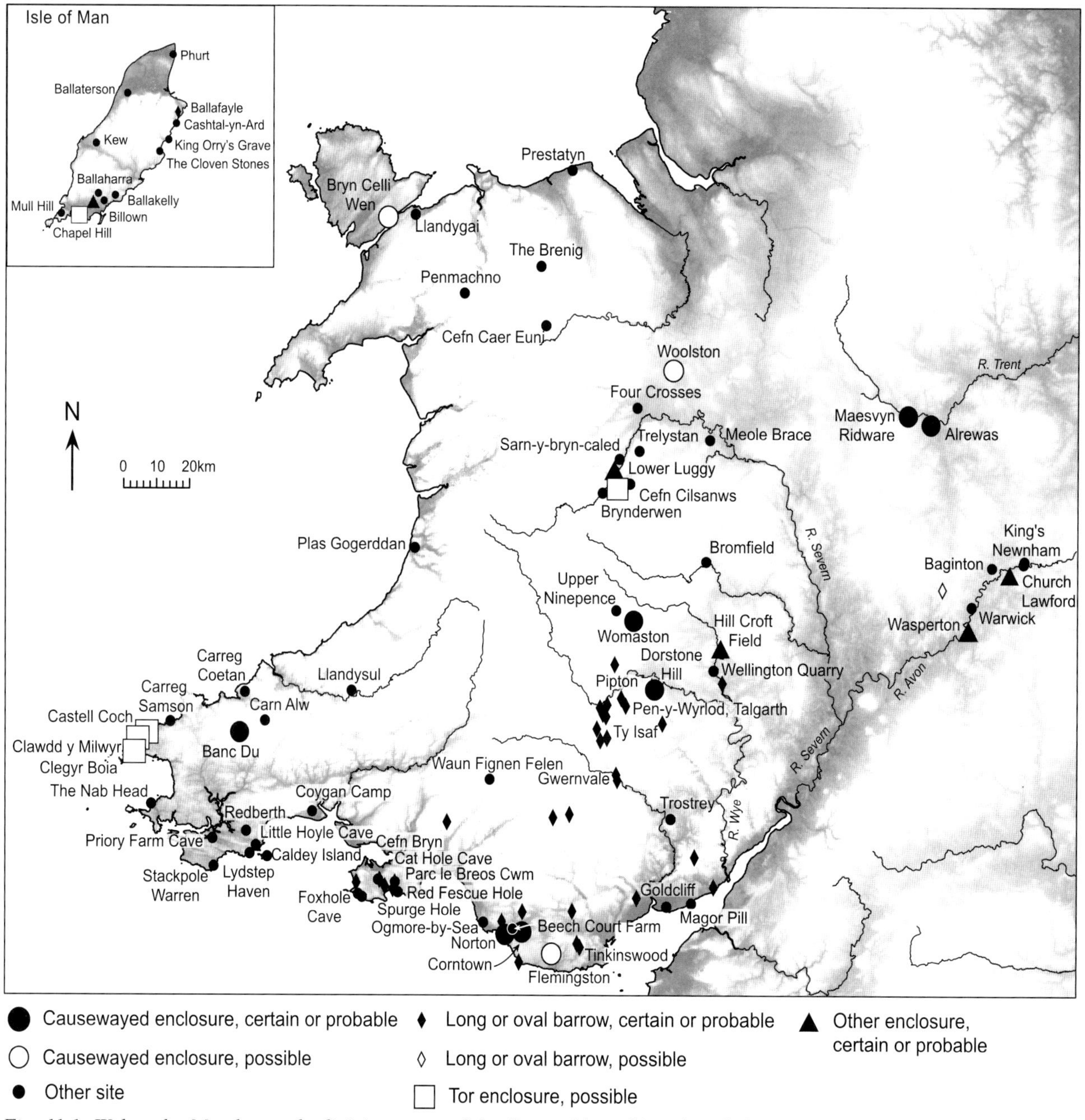

Fig. 11.1. Wales, the Marches and adjoining parts of the Cotswolds and North Wiltshire, showing causewayed enclosures, long barrows and cairns and other sites mentioned in Chapter 11. The Isle of Man is shown as an inset.

History of investigation

The site was first recognised from the vertical aerial photographic coverage (taken in 2001) in the county GIS in 2006, as an ovoid ditched enclosure, *c.* 180 m in maximum dimension, with one apparent entrance to the north. It was investigated by Herefordshire Archaeology as part of the Lugg Valley Archaeology, Landscape Change and Conservation Project, which was partly funded by the European Union and DEFRA through the Herefordshire Rivers LEADER+ Programme and English Heritage. Selective geophysical survey led to test excavation in three trenches. Two encountered no significant archaeology. A third trench, 10 m by 5 m, was positioned to investigate the entrance and located two terminals, 4.50 m apart, one of which was excavated (Fig. 11.2). Here the ditch was 3.30 m wide and 0.85 m deep. A primary fill of red-brown silty clay (context 30) contained plain Neolithic Bowl pottery with struck flint, animal and human bone, and numerous snail shells. Above this, compact silts and clays appeared to have been backfilled from the inside of the ditch, followed by a layer of silt with charcoal flecks. This in turn was overlain by a band of charcoal (context 23), and then a mixed, substantial upper fill.

Objectives of the dating programme

The main aim was to confirm and refine the Neolithic date indicated by the artefacts.

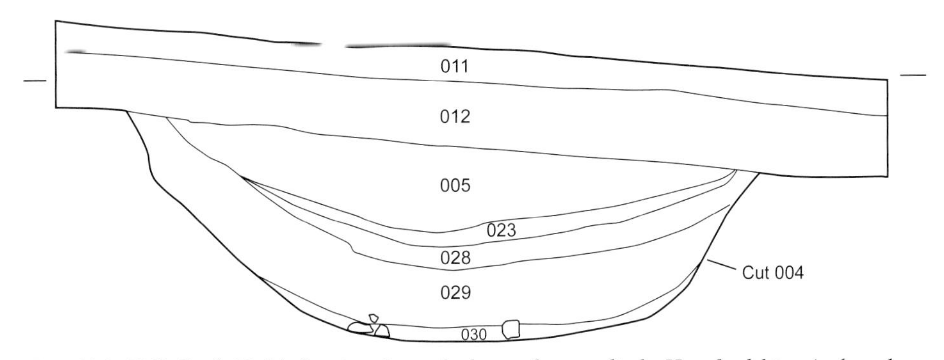

Fig. 11.2. Hill Croft Field. Section through the enclosure ditch. Herefordshire Archaeology.

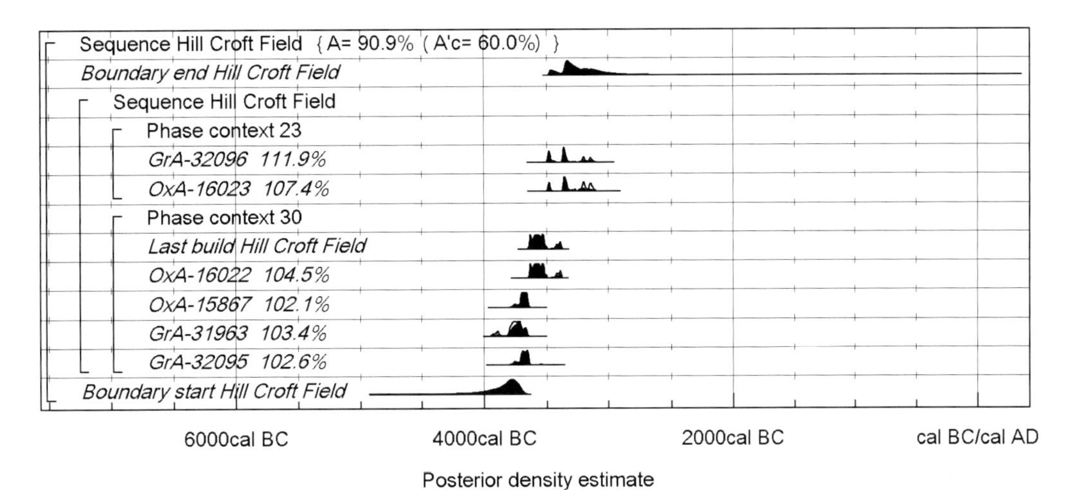

Fig. 11.3. Hill Croft Field. Probability distributions of dates from the enclosure. Each distribution represents the relative probability that an event occurred at a particular time. For each of the dates two distributions have been plotted, one in outline which is the result produced by the scientific evidence alone, and a solid one which is based on the chronological model used. The other distributions correspond to aspects of the model. For example, the distribution 'start Hill Croft Field' is the estimated date for the start of Neolithic activity on the site. The large square brackets down the left-hand side of the diagram, along with the OxCal keywords, define the overall model exactly.

Sampling

Samples were restricted to disarticulated human and animal bone and scattered short-life charcoal from the lowest layer (context 30) and to short-life charcoal from the band of charcoal (context 23).

Results and calibration

Full details of the results are shown in Table 11.1.

Analysis and interpretation

A chronological model is shown in Fig. 11.3. Four samples from context 30 provided statistically inconsistent radiocarbon determinations (T'=16.3; T'(5%)=7.8; ν=3). Since all these samples were of disarticulated bone or scattered charcoal, the latest of them provides the best estimate for construction, in *3640–3500 cal BC* (*92% probability*; Fig. 11.3: *build Hill Croft Field*) or *3415–3380 cal BC* (*3% probability*), probably in *3635–3620 cal BC* (*9% probability*) or *3605–3520 cal BC* (*59% probability*). The two bone samples are older than the two charcoal samples. However, since the two measurements on charcoal samples are themselves statistically inconsistent (T'=6.0; T'(5%)=3.8; ν=1), it seems that this context contained redeposited material, with the connotation of previous Neolithic activity in the area.

Context 23 yielded two statistically consistent measurements on single fragments of oak sapwood charcoal (T'=0.1; T'(5%)=3.8; ν=1). This band of charred material was separated from context 30 by apparent backfill followed by silting. A century or two may have intervened before context 23 was deposited in the later fourth millennium (Fig. 11.3).

Implications

The mid-fourth millennium cal BC date of the monument confirms that in this region, as in others, enclosures of the period included forms other than the readily recognised causewayed plans of, for example, Dorstone Hill or Womaston. Now that the date of the site is established,

Table 11.1 Radiocarbon dates from Hill Croft Field, Herefordshire. Posterior density estimates derive from the model defined in Fig. 11.3.

Laboratory number	Sample reference	Material	Context	Radiocarbon age (BP)	$\delta^{13}C$ (‰)	Calibrated date range (cal BC) (95% confidence)	*Posterior density estimate (cal BC) (95% probability)*
GrA-32095	HC06 30/C	Single fragment *Corylus* sp. charcoal	Trench 1, feature 4, context 30. On base of ditch, in thin layer of silt sealed by apparent backfill, scattered in deposit of sherds, probably from one pot, and human and animal bone with numerous macroscopic snail shells clustered around bones	4895±40	−26.1	3770–3630	*3765–3635*
OxA-16022	HC06 30/A	Single fragment *Prunus* sp. charcoal	From the same context as GrA-32095	4762±37	−26.0	3640–3370	*3640–3500 (92%)* or *3415–3380 (3%)*
OxA-15867	HC06 30/B	Human. From robust R femur shaft fragment, weighing 114 g	From the same context as GrA-32095	4911±29	−19.5	3760–3640	*3760–3740 (4%)* or *3735–3720 (2%)* or *3715–3640 (89%)*
GrA-31963	HC06 30/D	Cattle. From distal R femur fragment weighing 173 g	From the same context as GrA-32095	4970±40	−22.5	3930–3650	*3805–3650*
GrA-32096	HC06 23/A	Single fragment *Quercus* sp. sapwood charcoal	Trench 1, feature 4, context 23. Charcoal lens, not burnt *in situ*, above apparent backfill sealing context 30 and above subsequent silt	4585±35	−23.9	3500–3120	*3505–3425 (36%)* or *3380–3315 (49%)* or *3220–3175 (6%)* or *3160–3120 (4%)*
OxA-16023	HC06 23/B	Single fragment *Quercus* sp. sapwood charcoal	From the same context as GrA-32096	4568±35	−23.3	3490–3110	*3500–3445 (22%)* or *3380–3280 (55%)* or *3275–3260 (1%)* or *3240–3170 (11%)* or *3160–3120 (6%)*

its roles and functions call for elucidation by further investigation.

11.2 Beech Court Farm, Ewenny, Vale of Glamorgan, SS 9040 7660

Location and topography

The enclosure at Beech Court Farm lies at 84 m OD at the west end of the Vale of Glamorgan, encircling a low rise, to the south and west of which the ground drops sharply to the valley of the Afon Alun, one of several rivers running into the sea close by (Fig. 11.1).

History of investigation

Earthworks on the site were first noted by Rev. William Harris in 1773. Cyril and Aileen Fox noted additional earthworks in 1935, though a further visit in 1957 found none. A chance over-flight by RCHAMW in 1988 showed that the sub-circular enclosure was still visible from the air. Ground and geophysical survey from 1998 onwards, in advance of the threat of quarrying, established the presence of two circuits of ditch and bank, some 190 m across in maximum dimension (Fig. 11.4). According to survey, these circuits were incomplete, though the ditches were apparently continuous in long stretches; they were only doubled for one stretch on the east side. The inner bank was more extensive, with an overlapping entrance to the north-west and an outer bank roughly coinciding with the portion of observable outer ditch.

Test trenches showed that the inner ditch was up to 3.5 m across and under 1 m deep from the present surface; the outer ditch was of similar depth but as seen in the excavated portion very slightly narrower. Evaluation was followed by extensive excavation in 2002 of a substantial portion of the western part of the site then closest to the quarry. This showed that the single ditch here was discontinuous, with segments averaging 20 m long with enlarged terminals, and with a probable bank immediately on the inner side (Fig. 11.4). There were virtually no finds from the ditch segments. Very few features were found in the interior, though struck flint and other finds were recovered. A double posthole contained Collared Urn sherds.

Previous dating

A bulk sample of oak charcoal was dated by LSC at Beta Analytic Inc during the assessment (A. Caseldine *et al.* 2001), using methods described at http://radiocarbon.com/analytic.htm. The sample was recovered from a double posthole and may have derived from an oak post or posts burnt *in situ*. The section, however, perhaps suggests that this material was tipped in from the west. If this was the case, the sample may have included fragments of diverse ages and/or charcoal with a considerable age offset. The date would then provide a *terminus post quem* for its context. This date falls within the currency of Collared Urn pottery

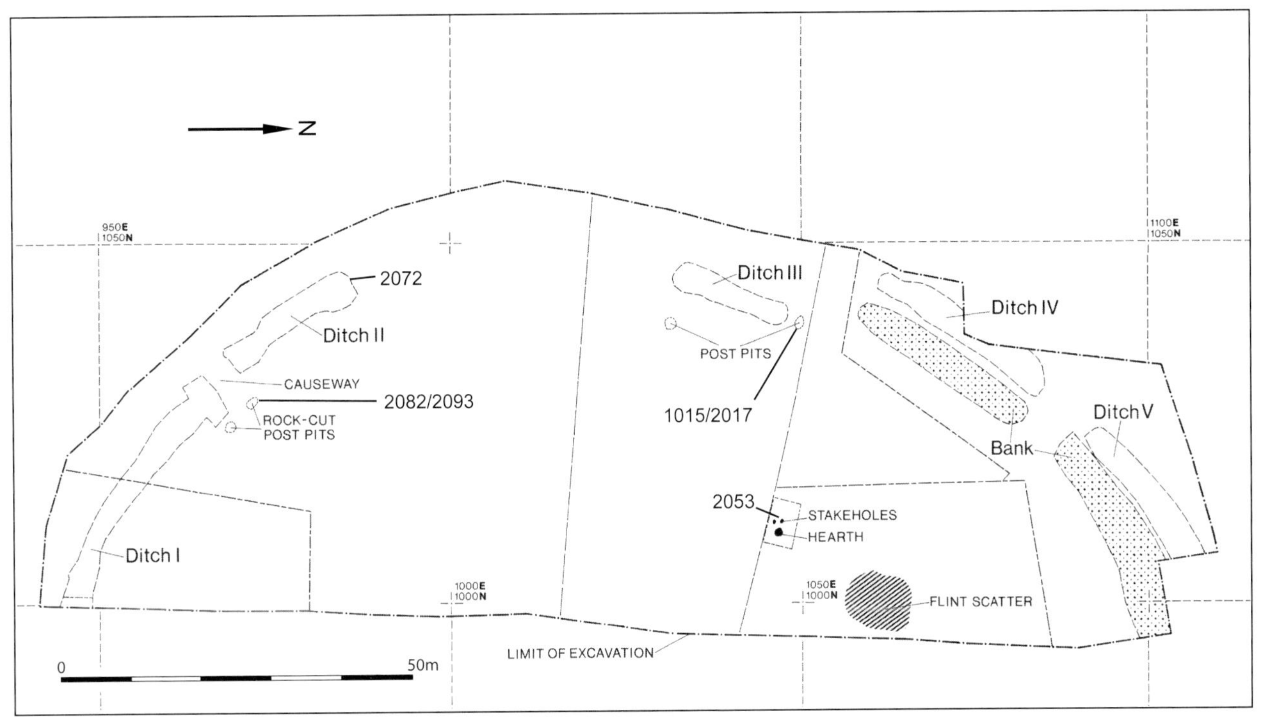

Fig. 11.4. Beech Court Farm, Ewenny. Plan of the excavated area. © GGAT 2003.

(Needham 1996), and sherds of this type were found within the feature. If the charcoal did derive from a post or posts, then, since the sockets were approximately 0.18 m in diameter, it may have derived from immature timber.

Objectives of the dating programme

This project aimed to determine whether the enclosure ditch was Neolithic. Further samples were submitted to determine the date of interior features.

Sampling

There was a severe shortage of datable material from the site. Bone was rarely preserved and there was no pottery in the ditch. One of two cattle molars from the base of the ditch was submitted for dating, the proximity of the two teeth suggesting that they may have been deposited as part of a jaw. Two single fragments of short-life charcoal were also submitted from an apparent dump of charcoal-rich material made in the butt of the same segment after some silt had accumulated.

In addition, Wessex Archaeology submitted samples from a stakehole associated with a hearth and from one of a pair of postholes framing a causeway.

Results and calibration

Full details of the five radiocarbon determinations from Beech Court Farm are provided in Table 11.2. The two samples processed at the Rafter Radiocarbon Laboratory, Lower Hutt, New Zealand, were dated by methods set out by Mook and Waterbolk (1985) and Zondervan *et al.* (2007).

Analysis and interpretation

A chronological model for the enclosure is shown in Fig. 11.5. Two episodes of activity are apparent, one in the early second millennium cal BC and one in the later first millennium cal BC.

Samples from the double posthole and from a stakehole adjacent to hearth 2047 produced statistically consistent measurements (T'=0.6; T'(5%)=3.8; ν=1), and suggest activity on the site in the Early Bronze Age (Fig. 11.5). The sample from one of the pair of postholes flanking a causeway in the enclosure was dated to *785–515 cal BC* (*95% probability*; Fig. 11.5: *NZA-21146*), although since it consisted of *Fraxinus* charcoal it may have an age offset of several centuries. Unfortunately, the cattle tooth from the base of the enclosure ditch contained no collagen and could not be dated. The two results from the charcoal fragments are in poor agreement with the stratigraphic sequence of the contexts from which these were recovered ($A_{overall}$=41.0%). It appears that GrA-27318 may be reworked from an earlier deposit, and so the best estimate for the date of the enclosure is provided by OxA-14142. This suggests that the enclosure was constructed in or before *195–50 cal BC* (*95% probability*; Fig. 11.5: *OxA-14142*), probably in or before *175–90 cal BC* (*66% probability*) or *70–60 cal BC* (*2% probability*).

Implications

This enclosure is not an early Neolithic one. This result may have considerable implications for our understanding and interpretation of other enclosures of similar form, which lack cultural material.

Table 11.2. Radiocarbon dates from Beech Court Farm, Ewenny, Vale of Glamorgan. Posterior density estimates derive from the model defined in Fig. 11.5.

Laboratory number	Sample reference	Material	Context	Radiocarbon age (BP)	$\delta^{13}C$ (‰)	Calibrated date range (cal BC) (95% confidence)	*Posterior density estimate (cal BC) (95% probability)*
Enclosure ditch							
GrA-27318	BCF sample 2016/A	Single fragment of *Prunus* sp. roundwood, charcoal	Ditch terminal 2072, lower-middle part of context 2085. In apparent dump of charcoal-rich material made in butt of segment after some silt had accumulated over the backfill covering BCF find 1578	2230±40	−25.5	400–190	*390–200*
OxA-14142	BCF sample 2019	Single fragment of *Prunus* sp. roundwood, charcoal	Ditch terminal 2072, context 2098. One of several charcoal fragments scattered in a layer (probably backfill) covering the base of the ditch, in the NW terminal of a ditch segment, beside an exceptionally large causeway, probably an entrance	2099±26	−25.0	200–40	*195–50*
Entrance							
NZA-21146	BCF sample 2009	*Fraxinus* charcoal, >1 fragment	Posthole 2082/2093. From unspecified layer in recut posthole at one side of entrance to enclosure. Only *Fraxinus* present, taken as remains of post	2500±30	−23.2	790–510	*785–515*
Beta-148233	BCF sample 1000	Bulk charcoal sample, mainly or entirely of *Quercus* sp.	Posthole 1015 in evaluation = posthole 2017 in subsequent excavation, context 1016. In postpipe which yielded 1 Early Bronze Age sherd. Since this was recovered from a double posthole, it may have derived from an oak post or posts burnt *in situ*. The section, however, shows a single fill without obvious postpipes and with scattered but dense charcoal fragments, perhaps tipped from the west	3490±60	−25.0 (assumed)	1960–1660	
Interior							
NZA-21145	BCF sample 2007	*Prunus* sp charcoal, >1 fragment	Stakehole 2053, layer 2054. Stakehole close to a hearth in interior of enclosure. Charcoal of >1 species present, thought to derive from hearth	3439±30	−24.5	1880–1680	

11.3 Banc Du, Casmael/Puncheston, Pembrokeshire, SN 0612 3065

Location and topography

The enclosure at Banc Du lies at *c.* 330 m OD on the south end of a ridge or promontory running from one of the series of rounded hills – Carn or Cerrig Lladron – which constitute the western part of the Preseli upland of south-west Wales (Fig. 11.1). There is a cragline to the south-east and steep sides to the south and west. The site overlooks the source of the Afon Syfynwy to the south-east and gives extensive views to south and west.

History of investigation

The site was discovered by Chris Musson during RCAHMW aerial reconnaissance in 1990, but at the time it was covered by scrub vegetation which obscured its unusual character. Further photography by Toby Driver of RCAHMW in December 2002 in better conditions prompted surface checking which revealed the presence of earthworks (Fig. 11.6). It appears to have been built against a steep ridge or cragline to the east. There is an inner earthwork, defining an area *c.* 200 m by 150 m with stretches of detectable bank and external ditch, in both of which interruptions can be seen (Darvill *et al.* 2003). On the south side, the line of earthworks is doubled, and this double earthwork continues from the west side clockwise round to the north-west, going on to the north-east again as a single line; further interruptions are visible, especially in one portion of the single earthwork to the south-east and in one stretch of the doubled earthwork to the north-west (Darvill *et al.* 2003; 2007a; 2007b). The outer earthwork defines an overall area some 300 m by 230 m.

Field evaluation involving geophysical and topographic surveys was undertaken as part of the Strumble-Preseli Ancient Communities and Environment Study (SPACES) in 2003, and a single cutting 1 m wide was made across the north side of the inner circuit in 2005 (Fig. 11.6; Darvill *et al.* 2006, 22–3; 2007a). It revealed a low earth and stone bank, some 4 m wide (Fig. 11.7). This had a large slate slab at its inner edge, a large stone at its outer face, and two substantial postholes some 2 m back from the outer face. Directly outside this apparently timber-framed bank or rampart, there was a large ditch of rounded V-profile, over 2.5 m wide and *c.* 1 m deep. This had a series of stony fills, seemingly naturally deposited, some of them rich in charred plant material.

Objectives of the dating programme

This project aimed to determine the date of the enclosure, in the light of suggestions that the segmented earthwork could be Neolithic.

Sampling

The local geological conditions are such that unburnt bone

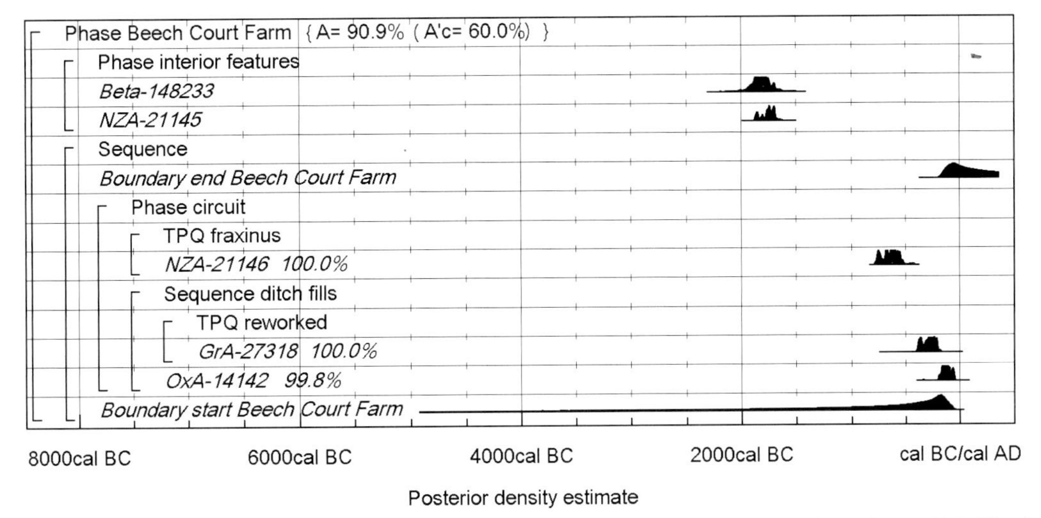

Fig. 11.5. Beech Court Farm. Probability distributions of dates. The format is identical to that of Fig. 11.3. The large square brackets down the left-hand side of the diagram, along with the OxCal keywords, define the overall model exactly.

would not have survived had it been present. There were no finds apart from charcoal and charred plant remains. Short-life samples of charred plant material were dated from three concentrations in the ditch fills.

Results and calibration

Full details of the radiocarbon measurements are given in Table 11.3.

Analysis and interpretation

A model for the chronology of the enclosure is shown in Fig. 11.8.

Two fragments of short-life material were dated from the primary fill of the ditch (context 21). These provided statistically inconsistent measurements (GrA-32006–7; T'=4.3; T'(5%)=3.8; v=1), although this difference is sufficiently subtle that it may simply be that one of the measurements is a statistical outlier. Above context 21, a substantial recut can be suggested. Two samples were dated from what appears to be the third layer within this recut (context 18) and provided statistically consistent radiocarbon measurements (GrA-32008, -31099; T'=0.7; T'(5%)=3.8; v=1). Towards the middle of the recut two samples were dated from another concentration of charred plant remains (context 15). Statistically consistent results were also obtained from this deposit (GrA-31186–7; T'=0.5; T'(5%)=3.8; v=1).

The chronology suggested from this series of samples, and on the basis of such selective excavation so far, can only be tentative. The available data, however, suggest that the ditch was cut in *3645–3490 cal BC* (*84% probability*; Fig. 11.8: *build Banc Du*) or *3470–3400 cal BC* (*11% probability*), probably in *3640–3620 cal BC* (*7% probability*) or *3610–3515 cal BC* (*61% probability*).

There may have been a significant gap between the original construction of the earthwork and the recut. This may have lasted *80–570 years* (*95% probability*; distribution not shown), and possibly for several centuries (*195–215 years at 2% probability* or *280–530 years at 66% probability*). Although there were several layers between the base of the recut and the lowest dated fill within it, a preliminary indication of the date of the recut may be obtained from the earlier material in context 18. This suggests that the recut dates to *3340–3205 cal BC* (*21% probability*; Fig. 11.8: *Banc Du recut?*) or *3195–3150 cal BC* (*5% probability*) or *3140–2905 cal BC* (*69% probability*), probably to *3310–3300 cal BC* (*1% probability*) or *3265–3240 cal BC* (*5% probability*) or *3105–2915 cal BC* (*62% probability*). The sequence of fills in the recut continued into the first half of the third millennium cal BC (Fig. 11.8).

Implications for the site

The fact that a search for short-life charcoal samples yielded Ericaceae from the fills of the recut but not from the initial fill suggests that heathland may have become established in the area during the third quarter of the fourth millennium cal BC.

11.4 The Marches and South Wales: discussion

A later Mesolithic presence, defined by narrow-blade industries and various associated microlith forms, can be widely documented in Wales, and extends into the English side of the Marches, perhaps best documented in the Forest of Dean and on the lower Wye (Darvill 2006). The better published Welsh material shows a broad distribution, from coasts to lowlands and uplands (Jacobi 1980; David and Walker 2004, fig. 17. 11; Olding 2000, fig. 3; Bell 2007a; 2007b). Clusters of sites, for example on the coast in Pembrokeshire or in the Glamorgan uplands, may reflect unusual archaeological visibility and concentrations of local collectors, so that we cannot claim to have anything

Table 11.3. Radiocarbon dates from Banc Du, Pembrokeshire. Posterior density estimates derive from the model defined in Fig. 11.8.

Laboratory number	Sample reference	Material	Context	Radiocarbon age (BP)	$\delta^{13}C$ (‰)	Calibrated date range (cal BC) (95% confidence)	*Posterior density estimate (cal BC) (95% probability)*
GrA-31187	BDE 05 ES <1> (b)	Single fragment Ericaceae charcoal	F1, Context 15. Upper of two layers rich in charred material (the lower being context 18) within a possible recut, stratified above context 18	4085±35	−26.9	2860–2490	*2865–2805 (27%) or 2760–2715 (9%) or 2710–2560 (55%) or 2525–2495 (4%)*
GrA-31186	BDE 05 ES <1> (a)	Single fragment Ericaceae charcoal	From the same context as GrA-31187	4120±35	−28.2	2880–2570	*2875–2800 (30%) or 2780–2575 (65%)*
GrA-32008	BDE 05 ES <12> (c)	Single fragment Ericaceae charcoal	F1, Context 18. Lower of two layers rich in charred material (the upper being context 15) within a possible recut, stratified above context 21	4390±80	−26.6	3350–2880	*3340–3205 (21%) or 3195–3145 (6%) or 3140–2890 (68%)*
GrA-31099	BDE 05 ES <12> (a)	Single fragment Ericaceae charcoal	From the same context as GrA-32008	4315±40	−26.3	3030–2880	*3025–2880*
GrA-32007	BDE 05 ES <14> (d)	Single fragment unidentified bark charcoal	F1, Context 21. Initial silt on floor of ditch, stratified below contexts 15 and 18	4775±40	−27.5	3650–3380	*3645–3505 (80%) or 3430–3375 (15%)*
GrA-32006	BDE 05 ES <14> (c)	Single fragment *Quercus* sapwood charcoal	From the same context as GrA-32007	4665±35	−23.3	3630–3360	*3620–3610 (1%) or 3525–3360 (94%)*

like the full picture. A wide range of site types can be envisaged. The sourcing of lithic raw materials suggests that territories embraced both coastal and inland landscapes, as at the repeatedly visited lakeside site of Waun Fignen Felen on the Black Mountain. Here, beach pebble flint, from at least 30 km away, and Greensand chert, from a distance of at least 80 km, were abundant in the early Mesolithic, and had in many cases been brought to the area as complete, unworked pebbles or nodules, suggesting frequent movement between upland and coast (Barton *et al.* 1995, 89–92, 105–7). Farther east, late Mesolithic assemblages from cave and rock shelter sites in the Wye valley, some 25 km inland from the Severn estuary, include imported flint and perforated cowrie shells (Barton and Roberts 2004, 352–3).

Figure 11.9 presents dates from the fifth millennium cal BC and the latter part of the Mesolithic sequence in south Wales. At Lydstep Haven, Pembrokeshire (Leach 1918; Jacobi 1980, 175; David and Walker 2004), a date of 4350–3940 cal BC (95% confidence; Fig. 11.9; Table 11.4: OxA-1412) was obtained on an articulated pig skeleton found in 1917 in foreshore peats with two broken rod microliths immediately above its neck vertebrae. This animal appears to be the prey of a late Mesolithic hunting episode; speculation that it could have been domesticated (M. Lewis 1992) has not been supported so far by further analysis.

At Goldcliff, Monmouthshire, on the inter-tidal foreshore of the Caldicot Levels on the north side of the upper Severn estuary, a later Mesolithic occupation west of Goldcliff Island resulted in the formation of a layer, in places more than 0.25 m thick and extending over at least 17 m by up to 8 m (Bell *et al.* 2000, figs 4.4–5). Spreads of charcoal, animal bone including dog, otter, red and roe deer, bird bone and fish bone, were characteristic. Lithics included waste from narrow blade production and there were a few microliths, including a scalene triangle (Barton 2000). Four other radiocarbon determinations (Bell *et al.* 2000; David and Walker 2004, fig. 17.12; not listed in Table 11.4 here) suggest that this activity goes back to the sixth millennium cal BC. A hazelnut from the surface of this deposit, however, provides a radiocarbon date of 4440–4040 cal BC (95% confidence; Fig. 11.9; Table 11.4: OxA-6682). East of Goldcliff Island, further work on comparable occupations has produced dates from sites A and B going back again to the sixth millennium cal BC (Bell 2007b, table 8.2). From Site J, an area of Holocene soil preserved beneath estuarine silt and peat, there was a concentration of heat-fractured stone, animal bone, including deer, aurochs and pig, some smashed and burnt and some cut-marked, and late Mesolithic lithics (Bell *et al.* 2003, 7–12; Bell 2007b, 68, 109–112, figs 6.8, 6.16). There are two dates for wooden artefacts, one from the palaeosol (95% confidence; 4940–4710 cal BC; Fig. 11.9; Table 11.4: OxA-15549), and another from the interface of the overlying estuarine clay and the peat which grew above it (95% confidence; 4910–4710 cal BC; Fig. 11.9: OxA-15550). A series of radiocarbon determinations from one location, where silts

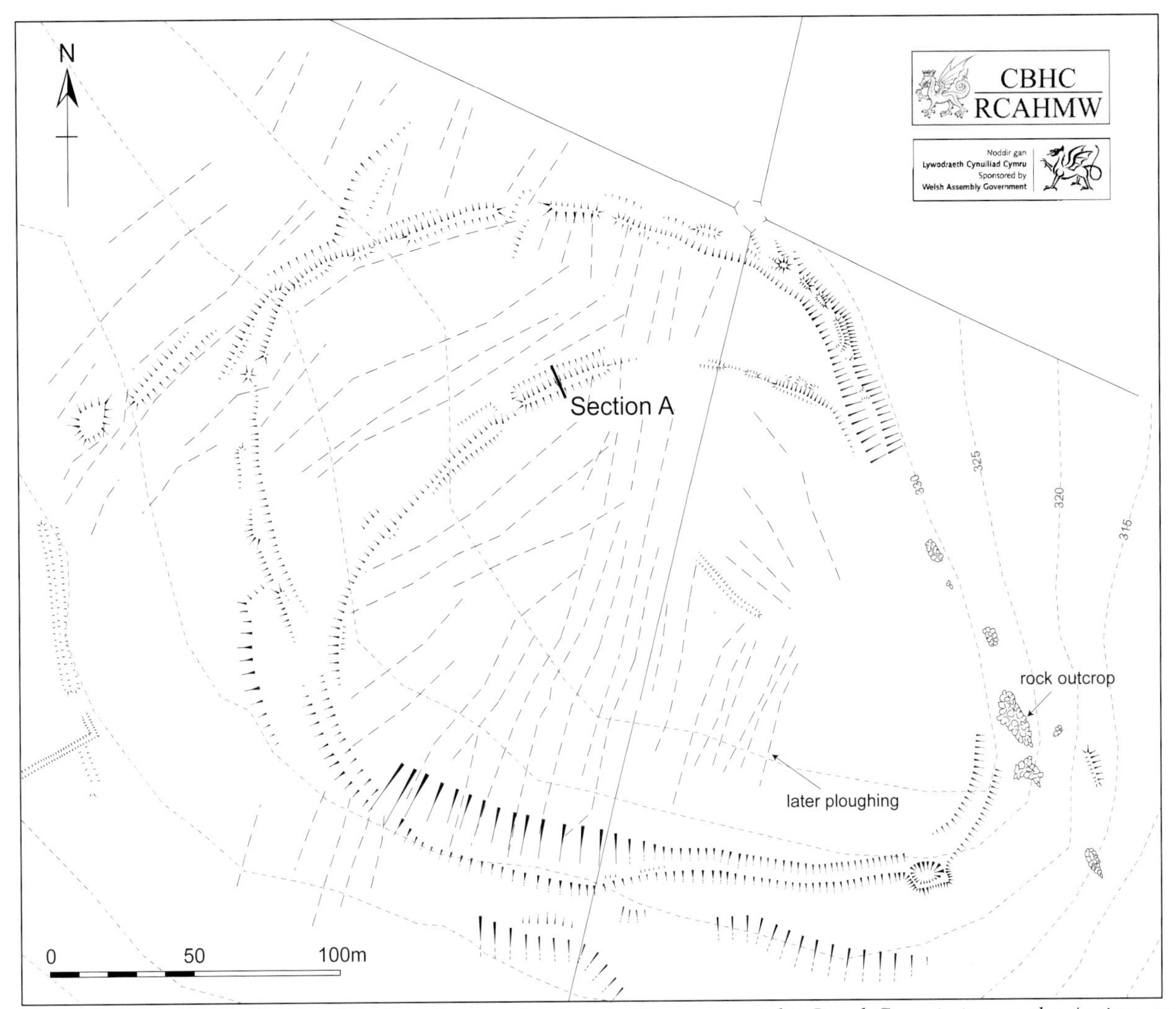

Fig. 11.6. Banc Du. Plan showing location of excavation trench. Crown copyright: Royal Commission on the Ancient and Historical Monuments of Wales.

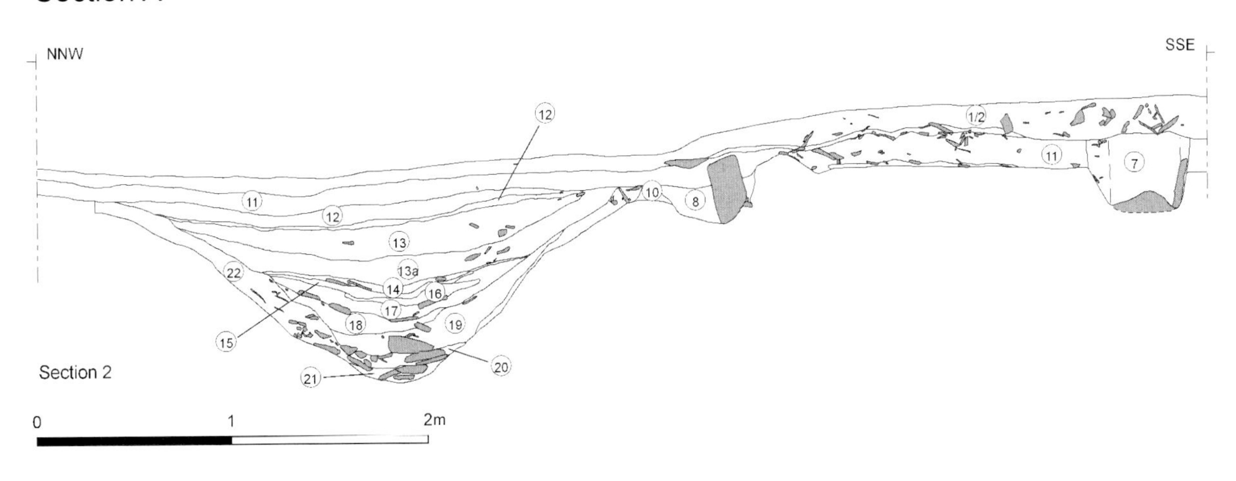

Fig. 11.7. Banc Du. Section showing ditch stratigraphy and bank revetment. SPACES project.

had been deposited before peat growth began (Table 11.4: OxA-13934, -12356, -13933, -13520, -13932, -12355), produced an environmental sequence running from the second quarter of the fifth millennium cal BC to the first quarter of the fourth millennium cal BC. These dates do not, however, refine the date of the Mesolithic occupation in the underlying palaeosol. A single date from the base of the peat at another location, where the peat directly overlay

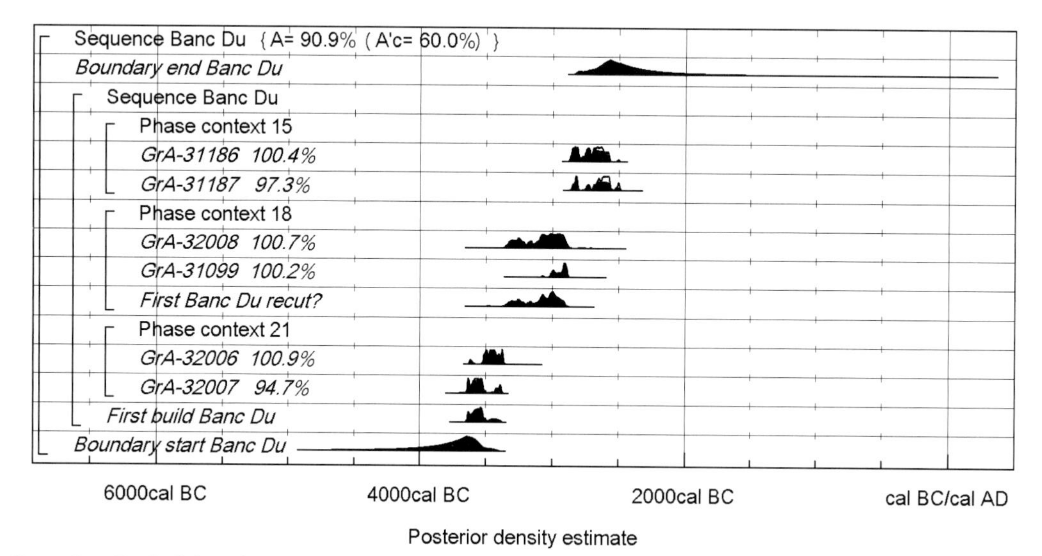

Fig. 11.8. Banc Du. Probability distributions of dates. The format is identical to that of Fig. 11.3. The large square brackets down the left-hand side of the diagram, along with the OxCal keywords, define the overall model exactly.

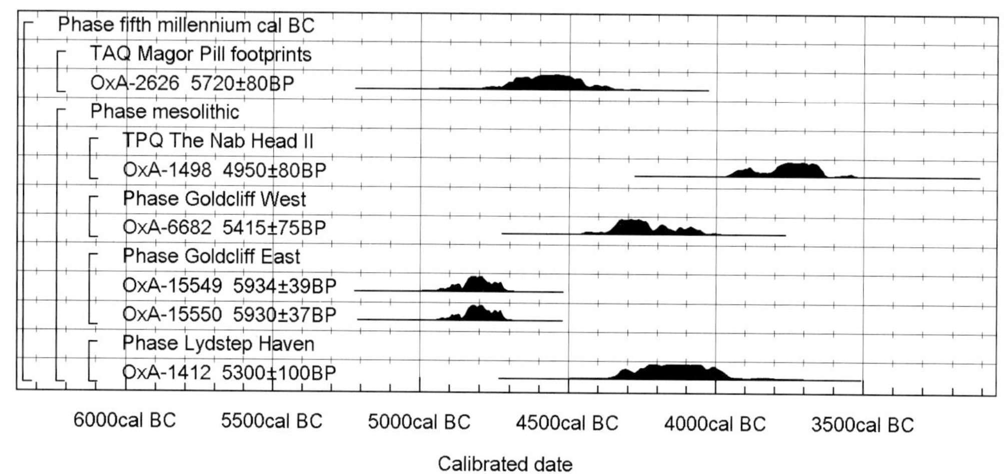

Fig. 11.9. South Wales. Probability distributions of calibrated radiocarbon dates (Stuiver and Reimer 1993) associated with late Mesolithic material or falling in the fifth millennium cal BC.

the palaeosol (Table 11.4: OxA-14023) falls in the earlier part of the fourth millennium cal BC.

The Nab Head, Pembrokeshire, has been one of the best documented coastal locations in south-west Wales (David 1989; 1990; David and Walker 2004). On site II there was a probable hearth area, with concentrations of material including debitage (some refitting), microliths dominated by narrow scalene triangles, a range of other retouched forms, and bevelled pebbles (David 1990, fig. 6.11). Despite their technological homogeneity, these accumulations may be the result of repeat visits, and three radiocarbon determinations (Table 11.4: OxA-860–1, and -1497; David and Walker 2004, fig. 17.12) suggest that this activity may have extended over a long period from the eighth or seventh to the fifth millennia cal BC. In a test trench beyond the main area a single fragment of *Quercus* charcoal from the base of a shallow soil, from which scalene triangles and refitting bladelet cores and debitage were also recovered, provided a date of 3960–3530 cal BC (95% confidence; Fig. 11.9: OxA-1498). It is unclear whether this sample is reliably associated with the flintwork, although no diagnostic Neolithic material was recovered from that trench (David 1990).

Figure 11.9 also shows the radiocarbon date (Fig. 11.9: OxA-2626) for peat overlying a trail of human footprints at Magor Pill, Monmouthshire, also on the inter-tidal foreshore of the upper Severn estuary. Since the footprints are not eroded, the deposits containing them were presumably fast-forming (Aldhouse-Green *et al.* 1992), and further fifth millennium cal BC activity is indicated, although the identity of the people in question cannot be directly determined since there is no associated cultural material.

It is worth noting Mesolithic sites in north Wales (Bell 2007b; Burrow 2006a, 9), though we have not modelled radiocarbon dates from any of them. The shell middens at Prestatyn had few stratified artefacts. Radiocarbon measurements on charcoal from site D at Nant Hall Road

Table 11.4. Radiocarbon dates from the Marches and Wales. Posterior density estimates derive from the models defined in Figs 11.10–11, 11.15 and 11.18–19.

Laboratory number	Sample reference	Material	Context	Radiocarbon age (BP)	$\delta^{13}C$ (‰)	Weighted mean (BP)	Calibrated date range (cal BC) (95% confidence)	*Posterior density estimate (cal BC) (95% probability)*
Lydstep Haven, Pembrokeshire								
OxA-1412	1970–3063	Pig. Bone	Articulated pig skeleton found in 1917 in foreshore peats with two broken rod microliths immediately above its neck vertebrae, apparently lodged in its neck when it died, and overlain by a fallen tree trunk (Leach 1918; Jacobi 1980, figs 4.25–6, pl. 4.V)	5300±100	−21.0		4350–3940	
Goldcliff West, Monmouthshire								
OxA-6682	4208	Hazelnut	From context 1202 , the surface of the late Mesolithic occupation layer exposed on the present inter-tidal foreshore of the Caldicot Levels in the upper Severn estuary (R. Hedges *et al.* 1998, 236; Bell *et al.* 2000, 37, figs 4.4–5)	5415±75	−23.3		4440–4040	
Goldcliff East, Monmouthshire								
OxA-15549	9199	Worked wood, unidentified species	Goldcliff J. Context 328 from palaeosol containing abundant late Mesolithic assemblage (almost all flint rather than chert), including geometric microliths, bones of deer, aurochs and pig, and a small amount of fish bone (Bell 2007b, 68, 109–112, table 8.11, figs 6.8, 6.16)	5934±39	−25.2		4940–4710	
OxA-15550	9224	Worked piece of *Quercus*	Goldcliff J. Context 331/327 at interface of estuarine clay (331) overlying palaeosol (328) and overlying upper peat (327), both containing technologically Mesolithic lithics (mainly chert in 331, flint in 327); bones of deer and pig in silt, of deer in peat (Bell 2007b, 69, 112, table 8.11, figs 6.8, 6.16)	5930±37	−25.7		4910–4710	
OxA-13934	5125/91	Waterlogged *Carex* fragment	Goldcliff J. Context 362. Pit J, monolith 5125. Thin reed peat overlying 331 and underlying 327. From sequence of samples through upper peat, stratified below OxA-12356 (Bell 2007b, table 8.2, fig. 6.8)	5730±33	−25.9		4690–4480	
OxA-12356	5125/82	Reed peat	Goldcliff J. Context 327. Pit J, monolith 5125. From sequence of samples through upper peat, overlying 331/327, stratified above OxA-13934 and below OxA-13933 (Bell 2007b, table 8.2, fig. 6.8)	5749± 23	−28.1		4690–4525	
OxA-13933	5125/50	Waterlogged *Rubus* seeds	Goldcliff J. Context 327. Pit J, monolith 5125. From sequence of samples through upper peat, overlying 331/327, stratified above OxA-12356 and below OxA-13520 (Bell 2007b, table 8.2, fig. 6.8)	5439±22	−29.8		4345–4255	
OxA-13520	5125/41	Waterlogged *Betula* seeds	Goldcliff J. Context 327. Pit J, monolith 5125. From sequence of samples through upper peat, overlying 331/327, stratified above OxA-13933 and below OxA-13932 (Bell 2007b, table 8.2, fig. 6.8)	5213±23	−26.4		4050–3965	

Laboratory number	Sample reference	Material	Context	Radiocarbon age (BP)	$\delta^{13}C$ (‰)	Weighted mean (BP)	Calibrated date range (cal BC) (95% confidence)	*Posterior density estimate (cal BC) (95% probability)*
OxA-13932	5125/34	Waterlogged *Alnus* catkin	Goldcliff J. Context 327. Pit J, monolith 5125. From sequence of samples through upper peat, overlying 331/327, stratified above OxA-13520 and below OxA-12355 (Bell 2007b, table 8.2, fig. 6.8)	5138±31	−27.9		3990–3810	
OxA-12355	5125/4	Peat/waterlogged wood	Goldcliff J. Context 327. Pit J, monolith 5125. From sequence of samples through upper peat, overlying 331/327, stratified above OxA-13932 (Bell 2007b, table 8.2, fig. 6.8)	5061±21	−29.3		3955–3785	
OxA-14023	5640/26	Charcoal	Goldcliff J. Context 327. Monolith 5640. From base of upper peat, overlying 328 (Bell 2007b, table 8.2, fig. 6.9)	4978±27	−26.7		3900–3690	
The Nab Head II, Pembrokeshire								
OxA-860	106	Unidentified charcoal fragments	Shallow pit in concentration of later Mesolithic artefacts, including numerous geometric microliths, in 0.10 m deep zone at base of soil profile (David 1989, 245–51; David 1990, ch. VI; Gowlett *et al.* 1987)	7360±90			6430–6030	
OxA-861	D9 NW	Single fragment of *Prunus* sp. charcoal	Hearth area in concentration of later Mesolithic artefacts, including numerous geometric microliths, at base of soil profile (David 1989, 245–51; David 1990, ch.VI; Gowlett *et al.* 1987)	6210±90			5370–4935	
OxA-1497	NH II 86 01	Single fragment of *Quercus* charcoal	From about 4.50 m SW of OxA-861 (David 1990, ch. VI; R. Hedges *et al.* 1989b)	8070±80	−26.0		7305–6695	
OxA-1498	NH II 86 02	Single fragment of *Quercus* charcoal	From a 2 m x 2 m test trench 14 m N of main excavation trench at the Nab Head Site II. Finds came from a very shallow soil (0.15–0.20 m) with a concentration of late Mesolithic flintwork, including bladelet cores, scalene triangles and debitage, some of which refits, as well as bevelled pebbles (David 1990, ch. VI; R. Hedges *et al.* 1989b)	4950±80	−26.0		3960–3530	
Magor Pill, Monmouthshire								
OxA-2626	MP/9.3.90	Peat	*Terminus ante quem* for human footprints stratified in deposits on the present inter-tidal foreshore (Aldhouse-Green *et al.* 1992)	5720±80	−26.5		4770–4360	
Nant Hall Road, Prestatyn, Denbighshire								
CAR-1424		Charcoal	Site D, context 24, soil layer just below shell midden (Bell 2007b, 272–75, figs 20.8–20.10)	5470±80			4460–4070	
CAR-1423		Charcoal	Site D, context 21, squares 32(lower) and 33. Midden on margin of wetland deposits, consisting mainly of mussel shells, with 2 bones of red deer (D. Thomas 1993; Bell 2007b, 272–75, 296, figs 20.8–20.10)	5270±80			4330–3950	

Laboratory number	Sample reference	Material	Context	Radiocarbon age (BP)	$\delta^{13}C$ (‰)	Weighted mean (BP)	Calibrated date range (cal BC) (95% confidence)	*Posterior density estimate (cal BC) (95% probability)*
CAR-1421		Worked wood	Site D, context 17, layer over shell midden, including 1 geometric microlith (D. Thomas 1993; Bell 2007b, 272–75, 299, figs 20.8–20.10)	4910±70			3930–3530	
CAR-1420		Charcoal	Site E, context 105, lower layer of shell midden. Midden on margin of wetland deposits, consisting mainly of mussel shells (D. Thomas 1993; Bell 2007b, 275, fig. 20.11)	5530±80			4530–4230	
CAR-1422		Charcoal	Site E, context 104, upper layer of midden, Midden on margin of wetland deposits, consisting mainly of mussel shells (D. Thomas 1993; Bell 2007b, 275, fig. 20.11)	5110±80			4050–3700	
CAR-1355		Charcoal	Site C, bottom layer of midden on margin of wetland deposits, consisting mainly of cockle shells (D. Thomas 1992; Bell 2007b, 271–72, fig. 20.7)	4890±90			3940–3380	
CAR-1356		Charcoal	Site B. Shell midden on margin of wetland deposits, consisting mainly of cockle shells (D. Thomas 1992; Bell 2007b, 270)	4700±70			3650–3350	
Prestatyn, Denbighshire								
OxA-16606	'Prestatyn woman' 4.903	R femur	Found 1924, 400 m W of Nant Hall Road, at interface of boulder clay and overlying peat. Bones of young adult female 'in a heap', skull about 0.60 m from rest (Bell 2007b, 303–305, 309)	4867±38	−19.4		3710–3530	
Wellington Quarry, Marden, Herefordshire, original permitted area								
OxA-12570	3852/1	Charred hazelnut shell	Pit 3852. One of a group of pits containing Neolithic Bowl pottery, struck flint, stone artefacts, animal bone and charred cereals (Bapty 2007; Bayliss *et al*. 2007d; Jackson and Miller forthcoming)	4762±31	−22.8		3640–3380	*3640–3510 (88%)* or *3425–3380 (7%)*
OxA-12547	3852/2	Single charred wheat grain	From the same context as OxA-12570	4850±31	−24.5		3700–3530	*3700–3630 (77%)* or *3580–3530 (18%)*
OxA-12568	3854/1	Charred hazelnut shell	Pit 3854. One of a group of pits containing Neolithic Bowl pottery, struck flint, stone artefacts, animal bone and charred cereals (Bapty 2007)	4823±32	−23.5		3660–3520	*3660–3620 (36%)* or *3605–3520 (59%)*
OxA-12569	3854/2	Single charred wheat grain	From the same context as OxA-12568	4810±33	−23.5		3660–3520	*3655–3620 (25%)* or *3605–3520 (70%)*
Wellington Quarry, Marden, Herefordshire, Moreton Camp extension								
Wk-12257	HSM 32268/2406	Single fragment of wood charcoal	Single pit identified during evaluation, containing a reworked fragment of a ground stone axe, a small assemblage of struck flint and a sherd of quartz-tempered pottery (Bapty 2007; Bayliss *et al*. 2007d; Jackson and Miller forthcoming)	5100±79	−25.0±0.2		4050–3700	*4050–3700*

Wellington Quarry, Marden, Herefordshire, new area, 2008								
Beta-245652		Charred hazelnut fragment	Single pit containing plain Neolithic Bowl pottery (Robin Jackson pers. comm.)	4730±40			3640–3370	*3635–3495* (*62%*) or *3460–3375* (*33%*)
Cwm Meudwy, Llandysul, Ceredigion								
Beta-185679		*Corylus avellana* charcoal	Pit 50. Small, shallow pit with sherds of at least five Bowls, including two with everted decorated rims (Murphy 2003; Murphy and Evans 2005; Caseldine and Griffiths 2005)	4840±40			3700–3520	*3700–3625* (*55%*) or *3600–3525* (*40%*)
Beta-185680		*Corylus avellana* charcoal	Pit 113. Pit with sherds of two Bowls, one shouldered (Murphy 2003; Murphy and Evans 2005; Caseldine and Griffiths 2005)	4870±50			3760–3530	*3710–3625* (*76%*) or *3590–3525* (*19%*)
Beta-185678		*Alnus glutinosa* charcoal	Pit 142. Small isolated pit with very charcoal-rich fill but no pottery, to south-west of later prehistoric palisade enclosure, on settlement where most of pottery assessed as early Neolithic (Murphy 2003; Murphy and Evans 2005; Caseldine and Griffiths 2005)	4800±40			3660–3510	*3660–3515* (*94%*) or *3400–3380* (*1%*)
Beta-189116		*Prunus* sp. charcoal	Posthole 64. Flanking north-east entrance of sub-trapezoid palisade enclosure, undoubtedly measured on redeposited sample because other entrance postholes of same enclosure yielded dates in second millennium cal BC and first millennium cal AD (Murphy 2003; Murphy and Evans 2005; Caseldine and Griffiths 2005)	5080±40			3970–3770	*3970–3785*
Coygan Camp, Carmarthenshire								
NPL-132		Charred hazelnut shells	Pit CXIX (3). Isolated pit containing sherds of a single heavy-rimmed plain Bowl, struck flint, animal bone, charcoal (Wainwright 1967, 14–20, figs 3, 6)	5000±95	−25.0		3980–3630	*3750–3625* (*84%*) or *3600–3520* (*11%*)
Bromfield, Shropshire								
HAR-3968	S163	Bulked charcoal sample	F247. From base of one of two Neolithic pits, overlain by sherds of 3 or 4 Bowls, one heavy-rimmed and one with simple linear decoration on the rim. Also present were charred hazelnut shells, and small amounts of charred cereals and struck flint (Stanford 1982, 282–7)	4680±80	−26.9		3650–3130	*3635–3350*
Plas Gogerddan, Ceredigion								
CAR-994		Unidentified charcoal	Pit 206, containing charred emmer wheat, barley, chaff, apple pips and fragments, hazelnut shells. No artefacts (Murphy 1992, 7, 24–6)	4700±80			3650–3340	*3640–3360*
Carreg Coetan portal dolmen, Pembrokeshire								
CAR-391	Sample 1	Bulked charcoal sample	Old ground surface sealed beneath mound material (Dresser 1985, 381)	4560±80	−28.2		3620–3020	*3625–3600* (*2%*) or *3525–3290* (*93%*)
CAR-392	Sample 2	Bulked charcoal sample	F36. Area of burning sealed beneath stone kerb	4830±80	−27.8		3780–3370	*3780–3495* (*84%*) or *3460–3375* (*11%*)

Laboratory number	Sample reference	Material	Context	Radiocarbon age (BP)	$\delta^{13}C$ (‰)	Weighted mean (BP)	Calibrated date range (cal BC) (95% confidence)	*Posterior density estimate (cal BC) (95% probability)*
CAR-393	Sample 3	Bulked charcoal sample	Within material of the mound	4470±80	−26.8		3490–2900	*3505–3425 (14%)* or *3385–3270 (81%)*
CAR-394	Sample 4	Bulked charcoal sample	F44. Socket of orthostat framing chamber	4700±80	−27.6		3650–3340	*3640–3360*
Sarn-y-bryn-caled cursus, Powys								
OxA-3997	SYBC 92:1	Fast-grown *Quercus* sp. charcoal	Patch of small charcoal fragment immediately above primary silt of east ditch (Gibson 1994)	4960±70	−25.2		3960–3630	*3945–3635*
Fronddyrys, Powys								
HAR-1330		Unidentified charcoal fragments	Cutting 1. In layer below topsoil in small exploratory trench containing much charcoal, flint, a fragment of agate, and pottery including 1 Mortlake Ware sherd (Pye 1975; 1976). Mesolithic and early Neolithic lithics in same field	4530±260			3910–2490	
BM-2953		*Prunus avium* and *Frangula alnus* charcoal	From the same context as HAR-1330 (Gibson 1995; Gibson and Kinnes 1997; Ambers and Bowman 1998) Both dates deemed rejected and/or unusable by Gibson and Kinnes on ground of admixture of earlier material, and both excluded here for the same reason	5480±45	−24.0		4450–4250	
Penywyrlod, Talgarth, long cairn, Powys								
HAR-674		Human. Bulked sample of broken small bone	Bone from chamber NEII (Britnell and Savory 1984, 19–20)	4970±80	−21.5		3960–3630	*3950–3640*
Gwernvale long cairn, Powys								
CAR-118		Unidentified bulk charcoal sample	Pit F308. Lower fill of pit partly sealed by A horizon of pre-cairn soil. No contained artefacts (Britnell and Savory 1984, 50)	6900±80	−26.4		5990–5630	
CAR-113		Unidentified bulk charcoal sample	Pit F68. Dark ashy soil forming upper layer of pre-cairn pit containing struck flint and some sherds of Carinated Bowl pottery and Mesolithic and early Neolithic lithics (Britnell and Savory 1984, 55, 101)	5050±75	−26.0		3990–3650	*3980–3690 (94%)* or *3685–3660 (1%)*
CAR-114		Unidentified bulk charcoal sample	Pit F58. Pit outside cairn and sealed by blocking, containing sherds of a Peterborough Ware bowl (Britnell and Savory 1984, 88–9, 104)	4390±70	−26.2		3340–2880	
CAR-116		Unidentified bulk charcoal sample	Pit F47. Pit outside cairn outside cairn and sealed by blocking, adjacent to F58 and containing a sherd of the same Peterborough Ware vessel as was found in F58 and in surrounding area (Britnell and Savory 1984, 88–9, 103–4)	4590±75	−25.8		3630–3090	

Laboratory number	Sample reference	Material	Context	Radiocarbon age (BP)	$\delta^{13}C$ (‰)	Weighted mean (BP)	Calibrated date range (cal BC) (95% confidence)	*Posterior density estimate (cal BC) (95% probability)*
Lower Luggy long barrow, Powys								
BM-2954		Fast-grown *Quercus* sp. charcoal	Trench 1. Outer rings of partly charred post *c.* 0.10 m in diameter, closely set in palisade trench along SE side of barrow and extracted from NE section of trench mid-way along its length (Gibson 2000, 6–11; 2003)	4830±45	−24.1		3640–3360	*3705–3520*
BM-2955		Fast-grown *Quercus* sp. charcoal	Trench 2. Outer rings of post *c.* 0.20 m in diameter, burnt *in situ* near proximal end of palisade trench along SE side of barrow (Gibson 2000, 10–11; 2003)	4710±40	−23.8		3640–3360	*3635–3555 (28%)* or *3540–3485 (21%)* or *3475–3370 (46%)*
Pipton long cairn, Powys								
OxA-14396	P14/99.5 H/12	Human. Adult L ulna	Entrance passage to chamber I	4653±34	−18.7		3620–3350	*3520–3360*
OxA-12083	P15/99.5 H/11	Human. Adult R mandible	Inner passage, chamber I (Savory 1956)	4601±33	−20.3		3500–3190	*3500–3430 (50%)* or *3380–3335 (45%)*
OxA-14254	P21/99.5 H/19	Human. Skull fragment	Under floor slab, in S annex of chamber I	4742±34	−20.5		3640–3370	*3640–3495 (74%)* or *3435–3375 (21%)*
OxA-14251	P19/99.5 H/4[2]	Human. R femur	Group C, chamber II	4866±32	−20.4		3710–3540	*3705–3630 (91%)* or *3555–3535 (4%)*
OxA-14252	P18/99.5 H/2	Human. R femur	Group D, chamber II	4906±33	−20.6		3770–3630	*3710–3640*
OxA-14253	P20/99.5 H/21	Cattle. Horncore	Forecourt	4658±33	−21.3		3630–3360	*3520–3360*
Parc le Breos Cwm long cairn, Swansea								
OxA-6487	PC#1	Human. Adult L humerus	SE chamber (Whittle and Wysocki 1998)	4685±65	−21.2		3640–3340	*3635–3550 (22%)* or *3540–3360 (73%)*
OxA-6496	PC#11	Human. L humerus	SE chamber (Whittle and Wysocki 1998)	4850±65	−21.5		3770–3510	*3715–3510 (92%)* or *3425–3380 (3%)*
OxA-6641	PC#2	Human. Adult. L humerus	SE chamber (Whittle and Wysocki 1998)	4690±55	−20.4		3640–3350	*3635–3555 (21%)* or *3540–3360 (74%)*
OxA-6488	PC#3	Human. Adult L humerus	SW chamber (Whittle and Wysocki 1998)	4780±60	−20.7		3660–3370	*3660–3495 (77%)* or *3460–3375 (18%)*
OxA-6489	PC#4	Human. Adult L humerus	SW chamber (Whittle and Wysocki 1998)	4445±60	−21.3		3360–2910	
OxA-6493	PC#8	Human. Adult. L humerus	NE chamber (Whittle and Wysocki 1998)	4875±55	−21.8		3780–3530	*3715–3620 (74%)* or *3600–3520 (21%)*

Laboratory number	Sample reference	Material	Context	Radiocarbon age (BP)	$\delta^{13}C$ (‰)	Weighted mean (BP)	Calibrated date range (cal BC) (95% confidence)	*Posterior density estimate (cal BC) (95% probability)*
OxA-6494	PC#9	Human. Adult L humerus	NE chamber (Whittle and Wysocki 1998)	4645±60	−21.4		3630–3130	*3630–3580 (9%)* or *3535–3335 (86%)*
OxA-6490	PC#5	Human. Adult L humerus	NW chamber (Whittle and Wysocki 1998)	4660±60	−21.2		3640–3340	*3635–3575 (12%)* or *3535–3345 (83%)*
OxA-6491	PC#6	Human. Adult L humerus	NW chamber (Whittle and Wysocki 1998)	4710±60	−21.2		3640–3360	*3635–3365*
OxA-6495	PC#10	Human. Subadult skull	Passage (Whittle and Wysocki 1998)	3705±55	−21.4		2290–1940	
OxA-6492	PC#7	Human. L humerus	Passage (Whittle and Wysocki 1998)	4805±55	−21.3		3700–3380	*3695–3500 (87%)* or *3430–3380 (8%)*
OxA-6497	PC#12	Human. Occipital	Passage (Whittle and Wysocki 1998)	3750±55	−21.6		2340–1980	
Ty Isaf long cairn, Powys								
OxA-12055	9/39.190/315	Human. Adult cranium, ?female	C compartment of rotunda, lower level (Grimes 1939, 128–9, 142)	4529±31	−20.4		3370–3090	*3370–3295*
OxA-14248	TI 1/39.190/316.1	Human. Cranium (Individual a)	C compartment of rotunda, lower level (Grimes 1939, 128–9, 142)	4202±31	−20.5		2900–2670	
OxA-14393	TI 2/39.190/316.2	Human. Cranium (Individual b)	C compartment of rotunda, lower level (Grimes 1939, 128–9, 142)	4523±35	−18.9		3370–3090	*3370–3290*
OxA-14250	TI 9/39.190/200	Human. Cranium	C compartment of rotunda, upper level (Grimes 1939, 128–9, 142)	4082±30	−20.8		2860–2490	
OxA-14394	TI 5/39.190/54	Human. Adult R humerus	Passage of rotunda (17.9) (Grimes 1939, 128–9, 142)	4658±32	−18.9		3620–3360	*3520–3360*
OxA-14249	TI 7/39.190/56	Human. Adult R humerus. Replicate of OxA-14395	Passage of rotunda (17.9) (Grimes 1939, 128–9, 142)	4545±50	−20.6	4550±29 T'=0.0; T'(5%)=3.8; ν=1	3370–3100	*3485–3475 (1%)* or *3370–3310 (94%)*
OxA-14395	TI 7 repeat	Replicate of OxA-14249	From the same context as OxA-14249 (Grimes 1939, 128–9, 142)	4552±35	−19.5			
Llandygai house B1, Gwynedd								
NPL-223		Bulk sample of mature *Quercus* sp. charcoal	Posthole 9. Within stone packing, probably parts of post (Lynch and Musson 2001, 27–36, 116–18)	5240±150	−25.7±1.0		4360–3700	
GrN-26824	Sample B98	45 g of *Quercus* sp. charcoal	Posthole 12. Among stone packing. Sample included large fragments from core of post post (Lynch and Musson 2001, 27–36, 116–18)	5055±25	−26.6		3960–3770	
GrN-26823	Sample B77	60 g of charcoal, 38 fragments *Quercus* sp., 3 too incinerated for identification	Posthole 2. Among stone packing, probably from post pipe (Lynch and Musson 2001, 27–36, 116–18)	5040±30	−24.3		3960–3710	
GrA-20012	Sample B72	Single charred hazelnut shell fragment	Posthole 5. Among stone packing for post (Lynch and Musson 2001, 27–36, 116–18)	4860±50	−25.7		3720–3520	

Laboratory number	Sample reference	Material	Context	Radiocarbon age (BP)	$\delta^{13}C$ (‰)	Weighted mean (BP)	Calibrated date range (cal BC) (95% confidence)	*Posterior density estimate (cal BC) (95% probability)*
Lower Luggy enclosure, Powys								
Beta-177037		*Corylus* sp. twigs, charcoal	Charcoal deposit on ditch terminal floor (100SW) immediately below primary silts (Gibson 2006)	4760±50			3650–3370	*3640–3495 (71%)* or *3455–3375 (24%)*
Beta-206282		*Corylus* sp. twigs, charcoal	From the same context as Beta-177037	4690±40			3640–3360	*3630–3580 (11%)* or *3535–3365 (84%)*
Beta-206283		*Corylus* sp. charcoal	Middle silts of ditch, redeposited (Gibson 2006)	4980±40			3940–3650	*3940–3870 (14%)* or *3810–3655 (81%)*
Church Lawford , Warwickshire								
SUERC-3385		Single fragment of *Alnus/Corylus* charcoal	304/8/1. Charcoal-rich fill of shallow scoop cut into the third and most substantial fill of enclosure ditch, overlain by a layer rich in Peterborough and Grooved Ware. Interpreted by excavator as *terminus post quem* for context (S. Palmer 2003; forthcoming)	4520±45	−24.8		3370–3020	*3370–3105*
Wk-14819 (conventional)	TR99:C:304/8/2	Bulk sample of *Alnus/Corylus* charcoal	304/8/2. From the same context as SUERC-3385	4834±88	−25.0±0.2		3790–3370	*3710–3485 (75%)* or *3475–3370 (20%)*
Brynderwen, Powys								
OxA-4409		Carbonised residue from sherd	Single sherd of Fengate Ware retrieved by cleaning section of pit exposed in pipe trench within undated sub-rectangular enclosure *c.* 100 m across (Gibson and Musson 1990; Gibson and Kinnes 1997)	4440±70	−28.8		3370–2900	*3330–2915*
OxA-5317		Charred hazelnut shell fragment	From the same context as OxA-4409	4550±50	−23.4		3500–3090	*3375–3085*
A477 Sageston-Redberth bypass, Pembrokeshire								
Wk-10153	SR01-026	'small charcoal sample', of *Corylus avellana*	Context 026. Secondary fill of linear pit 025 on west end of 'settlement of early to late Neolithic date' covering 100 m of easement and extending to either side of it (Page 2001; 2002; Gale 2002)	4656±67	−26.9±0.2		3640–3130	*3635–3555 (14%)* or *3540–3345 (81%)*
Wk-10156	SR01-517	'small charcoal sample', of *Corylus avellana*	Context 517. Spread of burnt material on east end of 'settlement of early to late Neolithic date' covering 100 m of easement and extending to either side of it (Page 2001; 2002; Gale 2002)	4553±62	−25.0±0.2		3500–3020	*3520–3420 (32%)* or *3385–3295 (63%)*
Wk-10158	SR01-537	'small charcoal sample', of *Corylus avellana*	Context 537. Fill of posthole 536 in posthole row 552 on west end of 'settlement of early to late Neolithic date' covering 100 m of easement and extending to either side of it (Page 2001; 2002; R. Gale 2002)	4965±57	−27.3±0.2		3950–3640	*3740–3635*

Laboratory number	Sample reference	Material	Context	Radiocarbon age (BP)	δ^{13}C (‰)	Weighted mean (BP)	Calibrated date range (cal BC) (95% confidence)	*Posterior density estimate (cal BC) (95% probability)*
Wk-10159	SR01-554	'small charcoal sample', of *Corylus avellana*	Context 554. Fill of posthole 553, one of a pair west of row 552, on west end of 'settlement of early to late Neolithic date' covering 100 m of easement and extending to either side of it (Page 2001; 2002; Gale 2002)	4791±57	−24.9±0.2		3700–3370	*3695–3680 (1%)* or *3665–3495 (82%)* or *3440–3375 (12%)*
Ogmore-by-Sea, Bridgend								
HAR-1140		Charred hazel nutshells	Occupation layer in sand dunes. Webley (1976, 35), Savory (1980, 228) and Gibson (1998, fig. 1) attribute it to the upper of two layers associated with Mortlake Ware. Hamilton and Aldhouse-Green state that this sample came from the lower of two layers (1998, 113), as does Peterson (2003, 115)	4320±80			3640–3090	*3320–3215 (6%)* or *3185–3155 (1%)* or *3130–2855 (88%)*
BM-1112		Unidentified bulk charcoal sample	Occupation layer in sand dunes. Webley (1976, 35), Savory (1980, 228) and Gibson (1998, fig 1) attribute it to the lower of two layers associated with Mortlake Ware. Hamilton and Aldhouse-Green state that this sample came from the upper (1998, 113), as does Peterson (2003, 115)	4659±52	−25.4		3630–3340	*3635–3575 (10%)* or *3535–3345 (85%)*
OxA-5318		Carbonised residue	From Mortlake Ware. Sample very small and carbon content very low (Gibson 1995b, 38). Excluded from model	5870±90	−29.3		4950–4610	
Sarn-y-bryn-caled II, Powys								
BM-2820		*Quercus* sp. charcoal	Recut in penannular ring ditch, containing cremations and some small Mortlake Ware sherds (Gibson 1994, 159–61, 171–3)	4400±45	−23.7		3330–2900	*3325–3230 (11%)* or *3175–3155 (1%)* or *3120–2905 (83%)*
BM-2819		*Quercus* sp. charcoal	From the same context as BM-2819	4220±40	−23.8		2910– 2670	*2920–2835 (86%)* or *2815–2755 (9%)*
Upper Ninepence, Powys								
BM-2967	17	Bulk sample of 'mixed short-lived wood charcoal' (Ambers and Bowman 1998, 427)	Pit 16. Containing Mortlake Ware sherds, struck flint, charred hazelnut shells, *Corylus*, Pomoideae and *Prunus* charcoal (Gibson 1999, 33–8, 84–7, 143, 150–3)	4400±50	−24.8		3330–2900	*3320–3225 (10%)* or *3180–3155 (2%)* or *3125–2900 (83%)*
BM-2966	21	Bulk sample of *Corylus avellana* and *Populus* sp. charcoal	Pit 20. Containing Peterborough Ware sherds, struck flint (Gibson 1999, 33–8, 84–7)	4410±35	−24.6		3320–2910	*3310–3290 (1%)* or *3265–3235 (4%)* or *3120–2910 (90%)*
SWAN-23	U9D I: Context 66	Bulk sample of *Corylus avellana* charcoal	Pit 65. Containing a Mortlake Ware sherd and struck flint (Gibson 1999, 33–8, 84–7)	4470±80	−26.1		3490–2900	*3340–2920*

Laboratory number	Sample reference	Material	Context	Radiocarbon age (BP)	δ^{13}C (‰)	Weighted mean (BP)	Calibrated date range (cal BC) (95% confidence)	*Posterior density estimate (cal BC) (95% probability)*
BM-3071		Bulk sample of *Corylus avellana* charcoal	Pit 200. Containing Fengate Ware sherds, charred hazelnut shells, a few charred wheat grains, *Quercus* (only one fragment), *Corylus*, Pomoideae and *Prunus* charcoal (Gibson 1999, 33–8, 84–7, 143, 150–3)	4590±60	−24.2		3520–3090	*3495–3430*.(4%) or *3385–3085* (91%)
BM-3070		Bulk sample of *Corylus avellana* charcoal	Pit 500. Containing Fengate Ware sherds, charred hazelnut shells, *Corylus*, Pomoideae and *Prunus* charcoal (Gibson 1999, 33–8, 84–7, 143, 150–3)	4490±60	−24.7		3370–2920	*3355–3005* (93%) or *2980–2955* (2%)
Cefn Bryn, Great Carn, Gower, Swansea								
Birm-1235		Charcoal	Pit containing Mortlake Ware and struck flint, sealed beneath pre-cairn ground surface (Ward 1987; Gibson 1995)	4230±95			3090–2500	
Birm-1236		Charcoal	Hearth associated with Mortlake Ware and struck flint, sealed beneath pre-cairn ground surface (Ward 1987; Gibson 1995b)	3960±100			2870–2140	
Birm-1237		Charcoal	Posthole associated with Mortlake Ware and struck flint, sealed beneath pre-cairn ground surface (Ward 1987; Gibson 1995b)	4340±100			3350–2670	
Birm-1238		Charred hazelnut shell	From the same context as Birm-1237 (Ward 1987; Gibson 1995b)	3990±100			2880–2200	
Four Crosses, Powys, site 5								
CAR-670		Charcoal (other charcoal from same context identified as *Quercus*)	Charcoal concentration in one part of base of burial pit, overlying one of two slots bracketing inhumation accompanied by pear-shaped stone, animal jaw and undecorated bag-shaped, round-based bowl with flaring neck of profile and fabric compatible with Ebbsfleet Ware (Warrilow *et al*. 1986, 64–5, 71; Gibson 1995b)	4440±70			3370–2900	*3340–2920*
Meole Brace, Shropshire								
OxA-4206	3-F10 (1013)	*Quercus* stem, *Corylus* stem and Pomoideae charcoal (small fragments recovered by dry sieving)	Pit F10, context 1024. Pit containing Mortlake Ware sherds. One of a group outside ring ditch (Hughes and Woodward 1995)	4570±85	−24.3		3630–3020	*3390–3005* (92%) or *2990–2930* (3%)
Trostrey Castle, Monmouthshire								
Beta-169094	C476	Charcoal	Base of post 0.40 m in diameter, rotted *in situ*. One of 3 large postholes S of ovoid stone mound (Mein 2002)	5050±50			3970–3700	*3960–3755* (89%) or *3745–3710* (6%)
Beta-173357	C532	Charcoal. Undated remainder mainly scrubby and short-lived, identified by Rowena Gale	Pyre 3 (Mein 2002, 107–8; Mein 2003, 67)	4800±90			3770–3360	*3760–3735* (1%) or *3715–3365* (94%)

Laboratory number	Sample reference	Material	Context	Radiocarbon age (BP)	$\delta^{13}C$ (‰)	Weighted mean (BP)	Calibrated date range (cal BC) (95% confidence)	*Posterior density estimate (cal BC) (95% probability)*
GU-4414	C278	Charcoal	Pyre 1. Later series of firings in linear hearth seen as pyre and including pottery described as Grimston Ware (Mein 1996, 65; 2003, 67)	4930±70	−25.4		3940–3530	*3945–3850 (12%)* or *3825–3630 (81%)* or *3560–3535 (2%)*
GU-2559	C91	Charcoal	Hearth in flint-working area including leaf arrowheads (Mein 1994, 50; 1996, 65)	4820±80	−23.4		3770–3370	*3770–3490 (82%)* or *3465–3370 (13%)*
GU-2634		Charcoal	From a firepit (Mein 1992, 11)	5340±60	−27.5		4340–3990	*4330–4040*
Nanna's Cave, Caldey Island, Pembrokeshire								
OxA-7740	63.335/61.1	Human. Patella	From a cave containing scatters of fragmentary human bone, as well as Upper Palaeolithic, Mesolithic and Neolithic artefacts, including a rim fragment from a plain Bowl (Lacaille and Grimes 1955, 96–120; 1961, 36–7; van Nedervelde 1977)	4520±45	−21.2		3370–3020	*3495–3465 (6%)* or *3375–3185 (89%)*
OxA-7739	91.9H/4	Human. Femur	From the same cave as OxA-7740	4560±45	−21.1		3500–3090	*3500–3425 (21%)* or *3380–3260 (69%)* or *3245–3180 (5%)*
Ogof-yr-Benlog, Caldey Island, Pembrokeshire								
OxA-7743	88.71H/2	Human. Female vertebra	From a cave (Schulting and Richards 2002a)	4660±45	−19.8		3630–3350	*3630–3590 (6%)* or *3530–3355 (89%)*
Foxhole Cave, Gower								
OxA-8318	FX177	Human. Adult phalange	Layer 3. Soliflucted scree, yielding early Mesolithic artefacts and late glacial fauna, much disturbed by badger set. Stratified below layer 2 (Aldhouse-Green 2000, 14–18; Pettitt 2000)	4840±45	−20.3		3710–3520	*3710–3620 (54%)* or *3605–3520 (41%)*
OxA-8315	FX32	Human. Adult phalange	Layer 2. Humic scree, yielding modern and early Mesolithic artefacts, much disturbed by badger set. Stratified above layer 3 (Aldhouse-Green 2000, 14–18; Pettitt 2000)	4940±45	−20.3		3900–3640	*3775–3640*
OxA-8317	FX59	Human. Adult tooth	Layer 1. Modern topsoil, overlying layer 2 (Aldhouse-Green 2000, 14–18; Pettitt 2000)	4625±40	−20.6		3520–3340	*3520–3345*
Little Hoyle Cave, Pembrokeshire								
OxA-3304	1983.2376/2	Human. Adult mandible	From a group of human remains representing c. 17 individuals found in 19th century excavations in the infill of a shaft or 'chimney' connecting Little Hoyle Cave system to surface of ridge above, where two stakeholes, Neolithic Bowl pottery and a lithic scatter have been found (Green *et al.* 1986; R. Hedges *et al.* 1993, 151)	4930±80	−21.2		3950–3530	*3800–3625 (85%)* or *3600–3525 (10%)*
OxA-3306	1983.2435/9	Human. Adult mandible	From the same group as OxA-3304	4880±90	−20.4		3940–3380	*3785–3500 (91%)* or *3430–3380 (4%)*
OxA-3305	1983.2376/11	Human. Adult mandible	From the same group as OxA-3304	4750±75	−19.9		3660–3360	*3655–3365*
OxA-3303	1983.2375/5	Human. Adult mandible	From the same group as OxA-3304	4660±80	−19.4		3640–3120	*3635–3335*

Laboratory number	Sample reference	Material	Context	Radiocarbon age (BP)	$\delta^{13}C$ (‰)	Weighted mean (BP)	Calibrated date range (cal BC) (95% confidence)	*Posterior density estimate (cal BC) (95% probability)*
Priory Farm Cave, Monkton, Pembrokeshire								
OxA-10647	09.18/101.4	Human. Adult mandible	From among the disarticulated, fragmented remains from several individuals, recovered from a cave that had seen intermittent activity from the upper Palaeolithic to the historical period (Grimes 1933). Measurement probably anomalously old (Bronk Ramsey *et al.* 2004a; Bayliss et al. 2007a, fig. 25)	4950±45	−20.6			
Red Fescue Hole, Rhosili, Swansea								
OxA-10649	2001.5H/4	Human. Adult fibula	Found in limited excavation in entrance of coastal cave with fragmentary human femur, animal bones, limpet and mussel shells (M. Davies 1986a; Schulting and Richards 2002a). Measurement probably anomalously old (Bronk Ramsey *et al.* 2004a; Bayliss *et al.* 2007a, fig. 25)	4880±40	−19.9			
Spurge Hole, Southgate, Swansea								
OxA-3815		Human. Adult femur, probably male	Articulated burial found in limited excavation, lying across cave entrance, demarcated by boulders on outer side (M. Davies 1986b; Aldhouse-Green *et al.* 1996; Schulting and Richards 2002a)	4830±100	−19.8		3900–3360	*3760–3490 (79%) or 3470–3370 (16%)*

may suggest fifth millennium cal BC activity (Table 11.4), and one context overlying the midden there has a radiocarbon date (Table 11.4: CAR-1421) suggesting fourth millennium activity as well (Bell 2007b). A similar pattern is suggested by dates on charcoal samples from sites E, C and B (Table 11.4; Bell 2007b), and not far away, an unassociated adult female has been dated to the earlier fourth millennium cal BC (Table 11.4: OxA-16606; Bell 2007b).

An early Neolithic presence can be widely documented throughout the area covered by this chapter, though recovery of evidence, as for the Mesolithic, has had an uneven history. In the Marches, early Neolithic settlement has been identified in river valleys and on the terraces above them, as have cursus monuments (Ray 2007; Gibson 1999; 2002b). This has been given fresh focus by the new project 'Beneath Hay Bluff', led by Keith Ray and Julian Thomas, including investigation of a megalith in the Olchon valley. On the east side of the Black Mountains, flint collectors have provided abundant evidence for early Neolithic activity in the Golden Valley, which runs south from Dorstone Hill (Olding 2000, fig. 5), and farther west, pollen analysis of the upper levels of the lake sequence at Waun Fignen Felen may suggest early Neolithic clearance (Smith and Cloutman 1988; Barton *et al.* 1995, 84). On the south-west of the Black Mountains an inland presence is documented in greater detail in the occupation under the Gwernvale long cairn, in the upper Usk valley (Britnell 1984).

The settlement evidence from lowland and coastal south-east Wales is scattered and of variable quality. At Goldcliff, early Neolithic clearance may be suggested by pollen analysis (A. Caseldine 2000, 219–20; Bell 2007b), although there are very few early Neolithic artefacts (Bell 2007b). Lithics from all stages of the Neolithic are plentiful, for example, near the coast at the west end of the Ogmore valley at Ogmore-by-Sea and close by at Merthyr-Mawr Warren, both long established collecting grounds (Burrow 2006b, fig. 16; Webley 1976; Hamilton and Aldhouse-Green 1998). Farther west, the evidence remains diffuse. A pit at Coygan Camp, Carmarthenshire (Wainwright 1967), has recently been augmented by others near Redberth (Page 2001; 2002) and, farther north, at Llandysul, Ceredigion (Murphy 2003; Murphy and Evans 2005). On the Pembrokeshire coast, an early Neolithic presence is attested by lithic scatters, most of them multi-period (C. Barker 1992; Tilley 1994). Excavation within one of these, at Stackpole Warren, recovered fragments of three Bowls, one with a pronounced, decorated rim (Benson *et al.* 1990; Darvill 1990). Overall, we are probably at the stage of research where quite widespread activity of probable fourth millennium cal BC date can be identified over this broad area, but where clear patterns have not yet been established.

Monuments other than enclosures are represented, broadly speaking, by the long cairns of the Black Mountains, the south-east Welsh coastal lowland and the Gower peninsula (Corcoran 1969; Cummings and Whittle 2004; F. Lynch 2000), and the portal dolmens and related constructions of south-west Wales (F. Lynch 1972; C. Barker 1992;

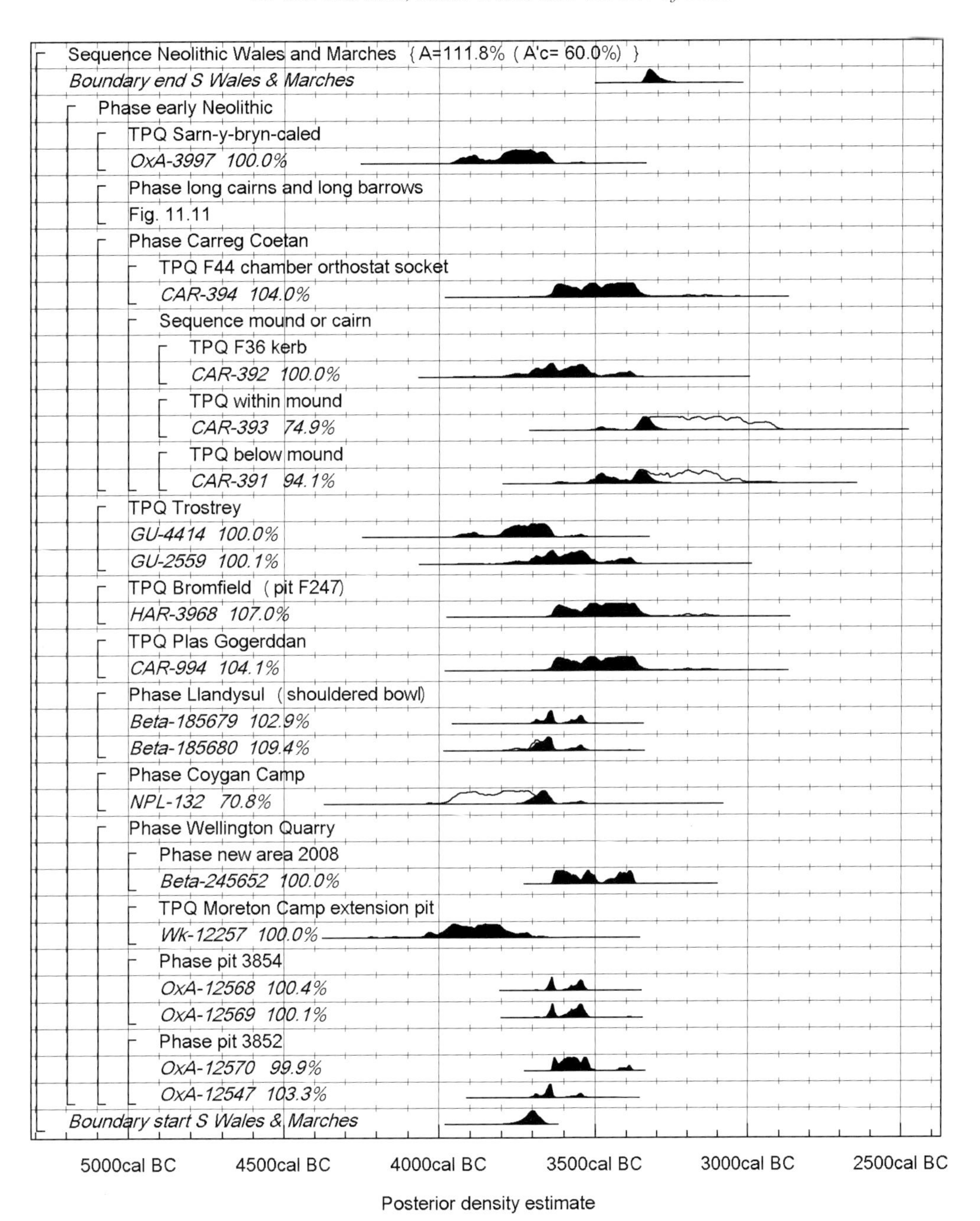

Fig. 11.10. South Wales and the Marches. Overall structure of the chronological model for the date of the early Neolithic. The component section of this model relating to long cairns is shown in detail in Fig. 11.11. The large square brackets down the left-hand side of Figs 11.10–11, along with the OxCal keywords, define the overall model exactly.

Cummings and Whittle 2004; Cummings 2009). Cursus monuments have been confidently identified in Powys, in the Walton basin (Gibson 1999) and in the upper Severn valley at Sarn-y-bryn-caled (Gibson 1994), but not so far in south or west Wales. Farther east such monuments are more abundant in the catchment of the Warwickshire Avon (Loveday 1989; Hughes and Crawford 1995; Hingley 1996; W. Ford 2003). There is a long enclosure attached to a sub-trapezoid enclosure at Church Lawford, Warwickshire, and the layout as a whole (though not the smaller size) recalls that of Godmanchester in the Great Ouse valley of eastern England (McAvoy 2000; and see Chapter 6).

A model which estimates the chronology of the early Neolithic in the Marches and south Wales is shown in Figs 11.10–11. Figure 11.10 shows the overall form of the model, with the component section relating to long cairns given in Fig. 11.11. This model includes radiocarbon determinations from samples directly associated with diagnostic material culture.

Turning first to occupation sites, in the Lugg valley, some 4 km downstream from the Hill Croft Field enclosure, excavation in advance of gravel extraction at Wellington Quarry, Marden, Herefordshire, has revealed a group of 13 pits, containing decorated and plain Neolithic Bowl pottery, lithics, animal bone, charred cereals and hazelnut shells (Bapty 2007; Jackson and Miller forthcoming). Single-entity

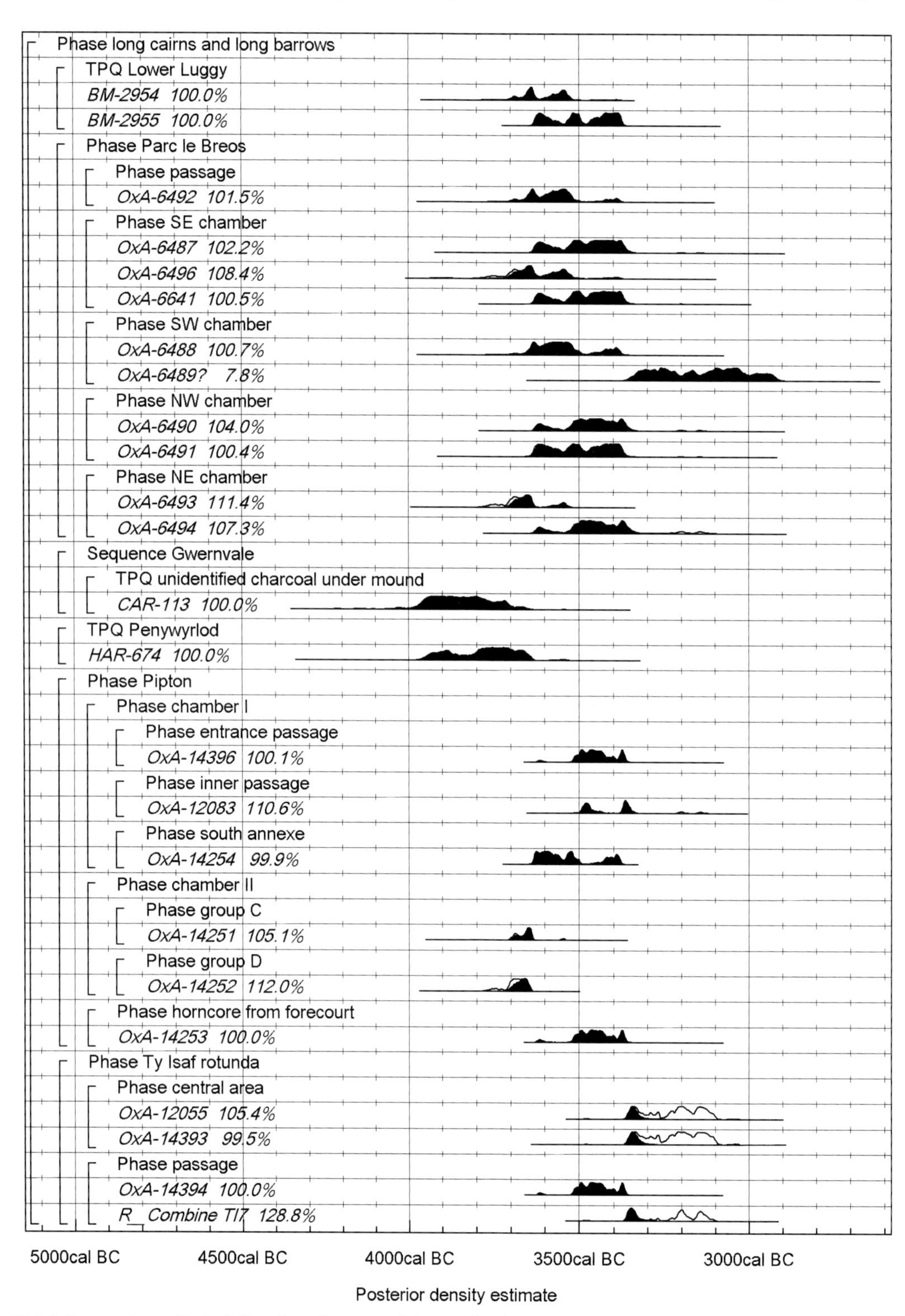

Fig. 11.11. Welsh long cairns. Probability distributions of dates. The format is identical to that of Fig. 11.3. The overall structure of this model is shown in Fig. 11.10.

short-life samples have been dated from two pits (3852, 3854) which were probably open at the same time on the evidence of conjoining sherds (Fig. 11.10: *OxA-12547, -12568–70*). The four measurements are statistically consistent (T'=1.2; T'(5%)=3.8; v=3). An apparently isolated pit in another part of the quarry contained a reworked fragment of a ground stone axehead, a small assemblage of struck flint, and a sherd of quartz-tempered pottery, and unidentified charcoal (Bapty 2007). One charcoal fragment has been dated (Fig. 11.10: Wk-12257). A charred hazelnut fragment has been dated from a further pit, containing plain Neolithic pottery, in a newly evaluated part of the site (Fig. 11.10: Beta-245652; Robin Jackson, pers. comm.). This activity is broadly contemporary with the nearby enclosure at Hill Croft Field.

One of the best preserved and fully investigated occupation

sites is at Gwernvale in the upper Usk valley on the south-west side of the Black Mountains, where the terrace on which a long cairn was eventually built was occupied intermittently from the upper Palaeolithic onwards (Britnell 1984). This is thus among the many sites where late Mesolithic and early Neolithic remains occur at the same location, and its history invites comparison with those of Hazleton and Ascott-under-Wychwood in the Cotswolds (Chapter 9). The late Mesolithic industry is characterised by scalene triangle and rod microliths. It is impossible to tell if it was associated with a pit some 25 m away from the main concentration of Mesolithic material which contained no artefacts but yielded charcoal dated to 5990–5630 cal BC (95% confidence; Table 11.4: CAR-118; Britnell 1984, figs 13, 58). There may have been an interval between the last two pre-cairn occupations. The early Neolithic assemblage had a virtually identical distribution to its predecessor (Britnell 1984, figs 43, 58) and was focussed on one or two rectangular timber structures, represented by bedding trenches and stone-packed postholes (Britnell 1984, 50–4, 139–41, figs 14, 23). If there was a single building, it would have measured 5.50 m by at least 10 m, on the scale of the better preserved rectangular structures of the early fourth millennium elsewhere in Britain and Ireland (F. Lynch 2000, 52, fig. 2.2). The pottery assemblage, all of potentially local clays (Darvill 1984c), was completely undecorated and included both open, light-rimmed Carinated Bowls and heavier-rimmed, unshouldered vessels (Britnell 1984, 97–105; F. Lynch 1984). There were also a few pits, and an unidentified bulk charcoal sample was dated from one of them, which contained struck flint and sherds of a Carinated Bowl (Table 11.4; Britnell and Savory 1984, 101). This date (*CAR-113*; Fig. 11.11) provides a *terminus post quem* for the contents of the pit and, by implication, the rest of the occupation and the raising of the cairn.

A pit within Coygan Camp, an Iron Age and later promontory fort overlooking Carmarthen Bay, contained a large block of sandstone, 24 sherds from a single heavy-rimmed plain Bowl, struck flint and small animal bone fragments (among which the long bone shafts were cattle- and caprine-sized), charcoal and charred hazelnut shells. A sample of hazelnut shells was dated in the mid-1960s (Fig. 11.10; Table 11.4: *NPL-132*; Wainwright 1967, 14–20, 128–9, 191). Although this was a bulk sample, it is treated as close in age to its context, since it consisted entirely of short-lived material, the components of which were probably not redeposited because the pit itself was an isolated one and because Mesolithic and Neolithic remains on the promontory were spatially distinct (Wainwright 1967, 12–14, 175–7). Two samples of short-life charcoal have been dated from pits containing Bowl pottery, some of it decorated and shouldered, at Llandysul, Ceredigion (Fig. 11.10; Table 11.4: *Beta-185679–80*; Murphy and Evans 2005). At Plas Gogerddan, Ceredigion, a pit containing charred emmer wheat, barley, chaff, apple pips and fragments and hazelnut shells, but no artefacts, yielded a bulk charcoal sample which provides a *terminus post quem* of the mid-fourth millennium cal BC for the cereals (Fig. 11.10: *CAR-994*; Murphy 1992, 7, 24–6). At Bromfield, Shropshire, a sample of unidentified bulk charcoal was dated from a pit containing sherds of three or four Bowls and small amounts of charred cereals (Fig. 11.10; Table 11.4: *HAR-3968*; Stanford 1982, 282–7), although this measurement only provides a *terminus post quem* for the context.

Excavations at Trostrey Castle, Monmouthshire, have been summarised so far only in interim reports by the late Geoffrey Mein. They produced among other features (further described below) a post-built façade at one end of which cremation deposits were buried in five pits. All included pottery described as Grimston Ware, each initially marked by a post, and, when they had gone out of use, by a stone cairn (Mein 2003, 67–8). Beyond the façade, two rows of posts led to cremation pyres, charcoal from two of which is dated (Table 11.4: Beta-173357, GU-4414). *GU-4414* (Fig. 11.10) a bulk sample of unidentified charcoal, provides a *terminus post quem* for Pyre 1, which included a leaf-shaped arrowhead and a sherd described as Grimston Ware. Charcoal from two further features has also yielded fourth millennium dates (Table 11.4: GU-2559, -2624), as has a posthole seen as forming the corner of a hurdle-walled rectangular house (Beta-155430), although the actual result is not cited (Mein 2003, 110). *GU-2559* (Fig. 11.10), another bulk sample of unidentified charcoal, provides a *terminus post quem* for a hearth in a flint-working area which included leaf arrowheads (Mein 1994, 50; 1996, 65).

Among the monuments, a series of unidentified bulk charcoal samples were dated from the Carreg Coetan portal dolmen, Pembrokeshire (Rees 1992, 15–16; C. Barker 1992, 19–21; Cummings and Whittle 2004, 141). Each of these measurements therefore provides a *terminus post quem* for the context from which it was recovered. Our understanding of stratigraphy is based on interim information provided in advance of full publication (Dresser 1985; Rees 1992, 15–16; C. Barker 1992, 19–21; Cummings and Whittle 2004, 141). Three samples (CAR-391–3) come from the small, low, surrounding mound or cairn and its 'kerb', but these features need not be directly associated with the chamber. From the chamber there is one sample, CAR-394, from the socket of one of the orthostatic uprights (Table 11.4).[2] This sample provides a *terminus post quem* for the erection of this orthostat, whereas the building of the mound or cairn may be best dated by the *terminus post quem* provided by CAR-393. The model shown in Fig. 11.10 suggests that the dolmen was erected after *3640–3360 cal BC* (*95% probability*; Fig. 11.10: *CAR-394*), probably after *3630–3585 cal BC* (*15% probability*) or *3530–3490 cal BC* (*15% probability*) or *3470–3370 cal BC* (*38% probability*). The surrounding mound or cairn may have been built somewhat later, after *3505–3425 cal BC* (*14% probability*; Fig. 11.10: *CAR-393*) or *3385–3270 cal BC* (*81% probability*), probably after *3370–3310 cal BC* (*68% probability*). Although other monuments of this general kind contain typologically early pottery (F. Lynch 1976), we may have to question long-held assumptions, based on their architectural simplicity, that portal dolmens have all to be early in the Neolithic sequence.

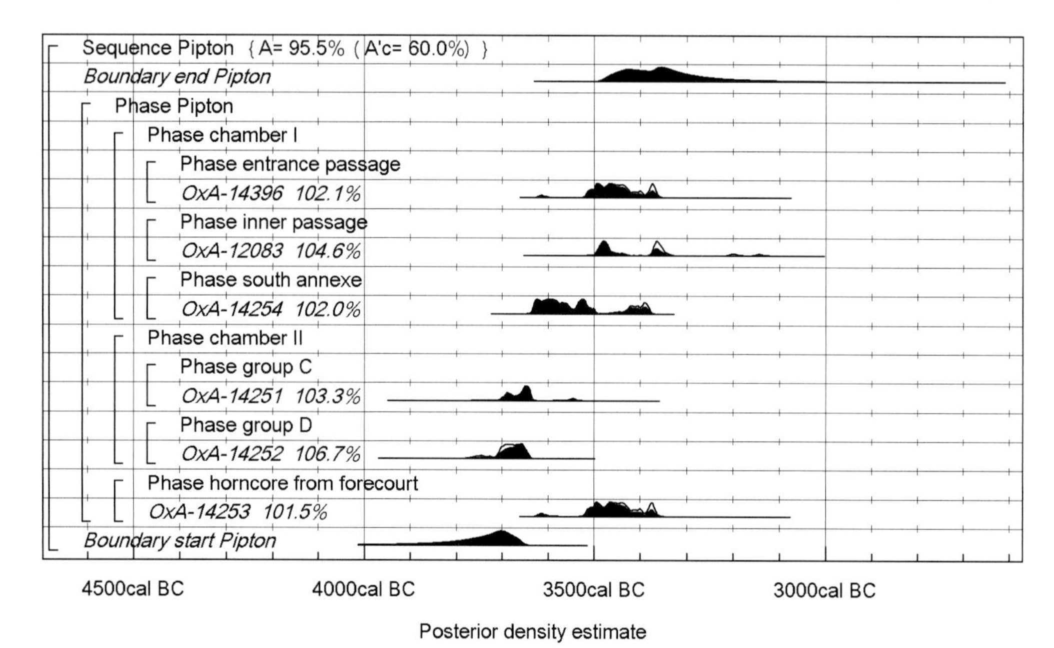

Fig. 11.12. Pipton. Probability distributions of dates. The format is identical to that of Fig. 11.3. The large square brackets down the left-hand side of the diagram, along with the OxCal keywords, define the overall model exactly.

Among the Welsh long cairns and barrows, a bulk sample of broken small bones, probably from a variety of individuals, was dated from the NEII chamber of Penywyrlod, Talgarth, Powys (Fig. 11.11; Table 11.4: *HAR-674*; Britnell and Savory 1984). The mixed derivation of this material suggests that it simply provides a *terminus post quem* for deposition in the monument. Further samples are being dated for this site (by Alasdair Whittle and Michael Wysocki). Occupation beneath the cairn at Gwernvale, some 15 km to the south-east, has already been dealt with above, and provides a *terminus post quem* for the tomb (Fig. 11.11: *CAR-113*). At Lower Luggy long barrow, Powys, the outer rings of two charred oak posts were dated from the ditch forming the south-east long side of the barrow, probably part of a flanking revetment (Fig. 11.11: *BM-2954–5*; Gibson 2000, 6–11; 2003). This oak is described as fast-grown, but sapwood was not identified. On the other hand, the posts were slight (0.10 m and 0.20 m in diameter respectively), although no indication is given of the methods of timber conversion. If these posts were whole timbers, then this material may be only a few decades older than the construction of the barrow and may provide a date reasonably close to the actual date of construction.

Dates have also been obtained from other monuments in a programme stemming from a project to investigate human remains from the long cairns (Wysocki and Whittle 2000). At Pipton, Powys (Savory 1956), six samples have been dated: five disarticulated human bones from different individuals and a cattle horncore from the forecourt. These relate to the use rather than the construction of the monument. At Parc le Breos Cwm, on the Gower peninsula, 12 measurements have been obtained from different individuals deposited in the chambers and passage (Whittle and Wysocki 1998). Two of these (OxA-6495 and -6497) relate to later deposition in the passage and so are not included in the model. There may be some grounds for thinking that they may have been excavated from Cat Hole Cave, which is nearby, and reburied in the tomb with the other human remains by its Victorian excavators. The other results form a coherent group, with perhaps one later outlier from the SW chamber (OxA-6489). This measurement has not been included here as part of the primary phase of burial in the cairn. At Ty Isaf, Powys (Grimes 1939), seven radiocarbon determinations have been obtained on human bone (Table 11.4). Statistically consistent replicate measurements were obtained on an adult right humerus from the passage of the rotunda (T'=0.0; T'(5%)=3.8; v=1). The other five dates were obtained from different individuals. Two of these (Table 11.4: OxA-14250 from the upper level of the central compartment of the rotunda, and OxA-14248, from the lower level of the same area) seem to relate to later use of the rotunda in the first half of the third millennium cal BC. They have therefore been excluded from the modelling.

The model shown in Figs 11.10–11 treats each date from different individuals deposited in these three long cairns as information contributing to the overall chronology of the early Neolithic in the Marches and south Wales. It does not attempt to estimate the dates of use of each of these monuments. Separate models have been constructed to estimate these specific chronologies (Figs 11.12–14). At Pipton, the dated samples suggest that deposition in the chambers began in *3920–3645 cal BC* (*95% probability*; Fig. 11.12: *start Pipton*), probably in *3775–3660 cal BC* (*68% probability*). This deposition ended in *3490–3090 cal BC* (*95% probability*; Fig. 11.12: *end Pipton*), probably in *3460–3300 cal BC* (*68% probability*). When considering these results, it is important to note the possibility, raised by examination of the remains by Michael Wysocki, that bone groups C and D in chamber II could have been curated or

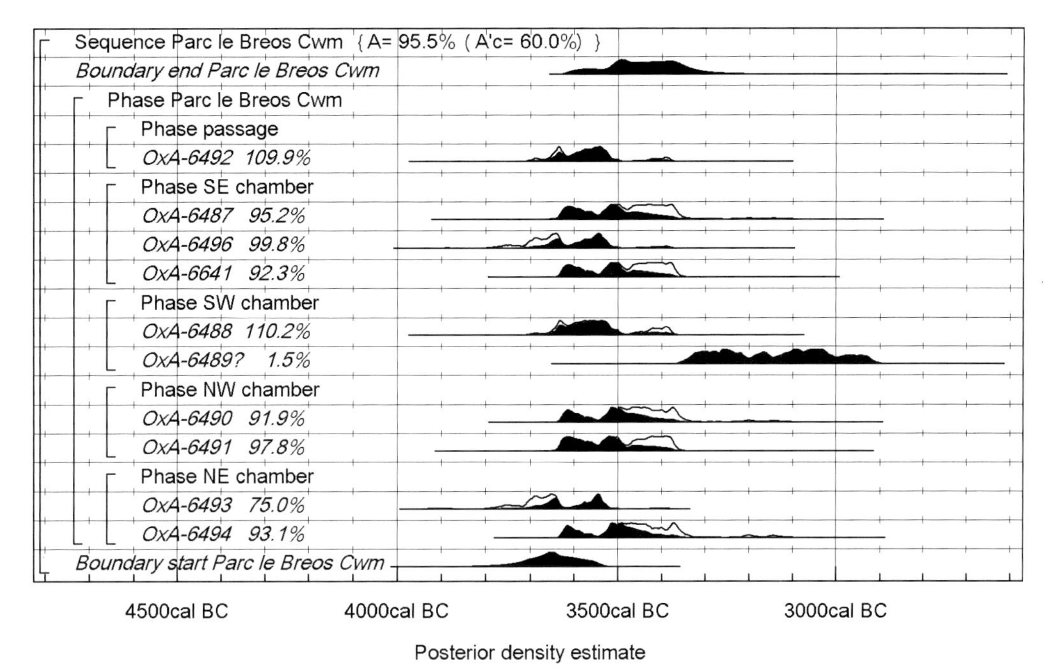

Fig. 11.13. Parc le Breos Cwm. Probability distributions of dates for the primary burials. The format is identical to that of Fig. 11.3. The large square brackets down the left-hand side of the diagram, along with the OxCal keywords, define the overall model exactly.

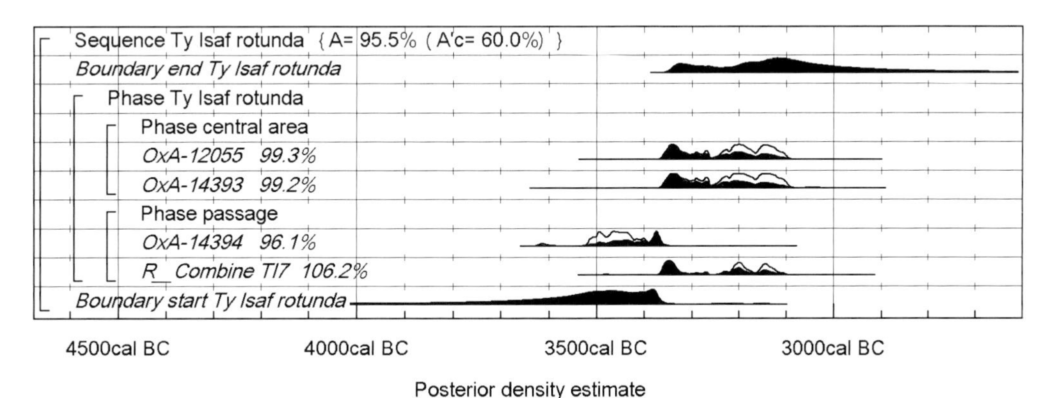

Fig. 11.14. Ty Isaf. Probability distributions of dates from the rotunda. The format is identical to that of Fig. 11.3. The large square brackets down the left-hand side of the diagram, along with the OxCal keywords, define the overall model exactly.

collected from elsewhere. At Parc le Breos Cwm, the model suggests that deposition began in *3780–3530 cal BC* (*95% probability*; Fig. 11.13: *start Parc le Breos Cwm*), probably in *3705–3580 cal BC* (*68% probability*). The principal phase of deposition appears to have ended in *3615–3295 cal BC* (*95% probability*; Fig. 11.13: *end Parc le Breos Cwm*), probably in *3515–3350 cal BC* (*68% probability*). At Ty Isaf, burial in the rotunda began in *3855–3355 cal BC* (*95% probability*; Fig. 11.14: *start Ty Isaf rotunda*), probably in *3575–3365 cal BC* (*68% probability*). The principal phase of deposition appears to have ended in *3355–2765 cal BC* (*95% probability*; Fig. 11.14: *end Ty Isaf rotunda*), probably in *3340–3260 cal BC* (*13% probability*) or *3210–2995 cal BC* (*55% probability*).

It is worth remembering that 'rotunda' is a term first applied to this monument in the 1930s (Grimes 1939), and it has remained in the literature ever since, with important connotations for some authors (e.g. Darvill 2004a; Pailler and Sheridan 2009) of possible early date. For Ty Isaf itself, Timothy Darvill has proposed the term 'simple passage grave' rather than rotunda (2004a, 59–60), and floats the possibility that this is another potentially early form of construction. The results presented here, however, do not suggest a particularly early date in the Neolithic sequence of the region, though we have dated use rather than construction of the monument and, in this particular case, the chamber in the rotunda would have remained accessible after the construction of the long cairn, if, indeed, they were built sequentially (Grimes 1939, fig. 3). Other dates are pending from Tinkinswood, in the Vale of Glamorgan.

A single sample of oak charcoal from immediately above the primary silt of the east ditch of the Sarn-y-bryn-caled cursus, Powys (Gibson 1994), yielded a date of *3945–3635 cal BC* (Fig. 11.10: *OxA-3997*), probably of *3895–3880 cal BC* (*2% probability*) or of *3800–3650 cal BC* (*66% probability*). This sample provides a *terminus post quem* for the early use of the monument. Radiocarbon dates for the Hindwell cursus in the Walton basin, Powys, were obtained too recently for inclusion in this project.[3]

For this project, we have not modelled radiocarbon measurements from early Neolithic sites in north Wales, but it is worth briefly noting some of the salient ones. The Bryn Celli Wen enclosure on Anglesey may be of early Neolithic date (Edmonds and Thomas 1993; J. Thomas 2001). Unfortunately, no suitable samples could be located to help this project (thanks are due to Julian Thomas for searching). A few more radiocarbon dates from pits in north Wales also indicate a fourth millennium cal BC inland presence, for example at the Brenig (F. Lynch 1993, 17–32, 214–5). Two early Neolithic houses, as well as various hollows and pits, have now been discovered at Llandygai, just outside Bangor at the east end of the Menai Strait (Lynch and Musson 2001; Kenney and Davidson 2006; cf. Kenney 2009). Radiocarbon measurements on oak charcoal from the tripartite, 13 m-long House B1, associated with plain Bowl pottery, some shouldered and with fairly heavy rims (Lynch and Musson 2001, 27–36) provide *termini post quos*, possibly for the second phase of the structure, since there was evidence for post replacement (Lynch and Musson 2001, 121–3). A charred hazelnut shell from the packing of one post, however, is dated to 3720–3520 cal BC (95% confidence; Table 11.4: GrA-20012). If the shell was neither redeposited nor intrusive, its age could be close to that of the building. Wider excavation in advance of further planned development has led to the discovery of the second, 12-m long, house at Parc Bryn Cegin, some 500 m distant, where Group VII rock from Graig Llwyd was worked (Kenney and Davidson 2006; Kenney 2009).[4] A further early Neolithic house, 16 m long, has come to light at Parc Cybi near Holyhead (Jane Kenney, pers. comm.).

A model incorporating all the radiocarbon dates (with the exception of those from Womaston which came too late to be modelled in this project) from the Marches and south Wales which are associated with diagnostically Neolithic material or architecture is defined in Figs 11.10–11. This suggests that the Neolithic in this region began in *3765–3655 cal BC* (*95% probability*; Fig. 11.10: *start S Wales & Marches*), probably in *3725–3675 cal BC* (*68% probability*). The model estimates that this phase of activity, associated for example with Bowl pottery, ended in *3350–3260 cal BC* (*95% probability*; Fig. 11.10: *end S Wales & Marches*), probably in *3340–3300 cal BC* (*68% probability*).

The extent of enclosure building in the region under discussion here is made particularly uncertain by the fourth millennium cal BC date of the apparently single-entranced enclosure at Hill Croft Field, which on the evidence of its plan was considered later prehistoric, and the first millennium cal BC date of the enclosure with causeways at Beech Court Farm, which on the evidence of its plan was considered Neolithic. There are, furthermore, other indications that earlier fourth millennium cal BC enclosures in the region took many forms, in addition to the largely uninvestigated causewayed enclosures listed above. A small sub-trapezoid enclosure, 40 m across and with a single entrance giving on to the Lower Luggy long barrow, is dated by measurements on two fragments of hazel twig charcoal from a deposit on the base of one terminal (Table 11.4: Beta-177037, -206282; Gibson 2006). A third sample, from the middle silts of the ditch, was redeposited (Table 11.4: Beta-206283). These dates suggest that the Lower Luggy enclosure was constructed in *3640–3490 cal BC* (*81% probability*; Fig. 11.15: *build Lower Luggy*) or *3470–3395 cal BC* (*14% probability*), probably in *3635–3510 cal BC* (*68% probability*). It is one of several morphologically similar sites in the Marches.

Farther east, in the valley of the Warwickshire Avon at Church Lawford, a larger two-entranced sub-trapezoid enclosure, of almost 0.80 ha, may also belong to this period (Palmer forthcoming). There is a single Neolithic Bowl sherd from a lower fill, and others from pits. From an upper fill came two statistically inconsistent measurements (Table 11.4: SUERC-3385, Wk-14819; T'=10.3; T'(5%)=3.8; ν=1). The later of these provides a *terminus ante quem* for construction of *3370–3105 cal BC* (*95% probability*; Fig. 11.15: *taq Church Lawford*), probably of *3365–3260 cal BC* (*54% probability*) or *3240–3195 cal BC* (*14% probability*). The significance of the Avon and its tributaries is reinforced by finds of plain Bowl pottery, some of it carinated, from a gully and pits at two different sites in King's Newnham, Warwickshire (S. Palmer 2003; forthcoming), in one of several pits at Baginton, Warwickshire (Hobley 1971), and of plain and decorated Bowl in Warwick itself (Woodward 1992).

Also on the Avon terraces, an open, C-plan enclosure with a few causeways at Wasperton, Warwickshire, yielded Ebbsfleet Ware and probably dates to the later fourth millennium cal BC (Hughes and Crawford 1995). Much farther west, there are other candidates in the Preselis for enclosures of Neolithic date, tentatively identified by their interrupted earthworks (Darvill and Wainwright 2002, 623). Farther west again, near St David's, Clegyr Boia is another candidate for a small, stone-walled, early Neolithic enclosure. The evidence is uncertain; early Neolithic occupation directly underlies an enclosure rampart of small stone rubble and soil within a revetment of stone blocks, but two charcoal samples, thought to be from the Neolithic occupation, were radiocarbon dated to the first millennium cal BC (Vyner 2001). The enclosure is, however, smaller than probable Iron Age examples in the area. On this basis of size, nearby Clawdd y Milwyr, on St David's Head, and Castell Coch, Trevine, might also be Neolithic (Vyner 2001; and see Chapter 10 for potentially comparable sites in Cornwall). There could thus be an even greater diversity of fourth millennium cal BC enclosures in the region than that established by the dating presented here.

A chronological model for the enclosures in this region is shown in Fig. 11.15. This suggests that the first enclosure here was constructed in *3710–3515 cal BC* (*95%

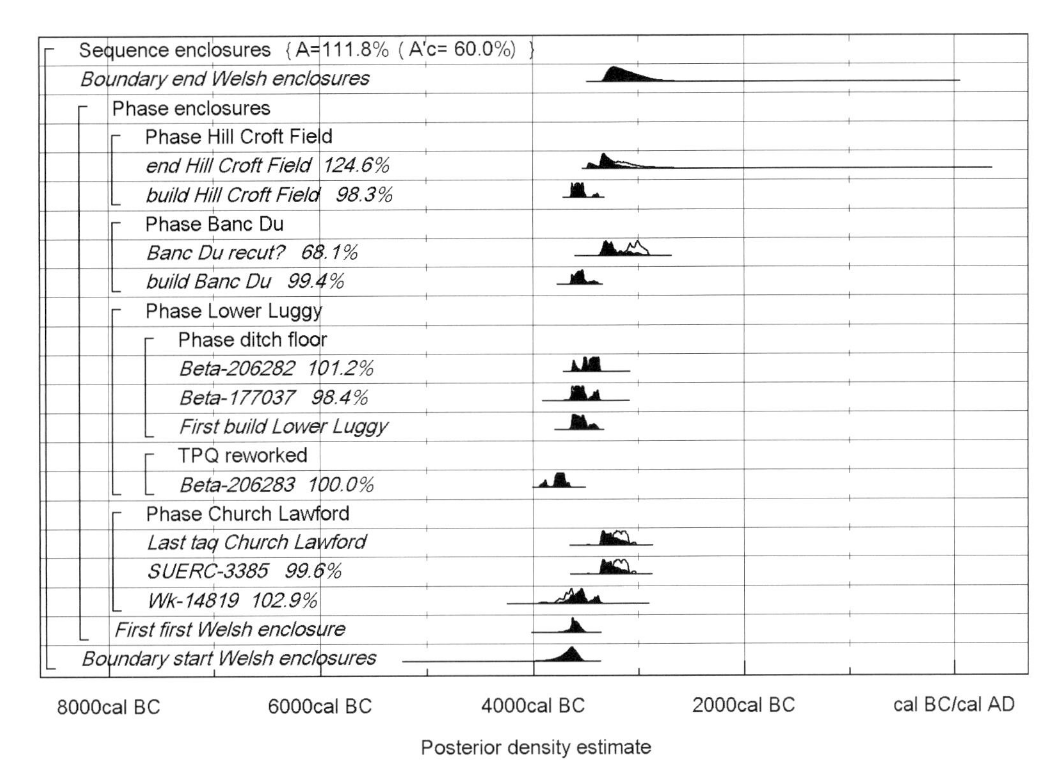

Fig. 11.15. South Wales and the Marches. Probability distributions of dates from Neolithic enclosures. Distributions for Hill Croft Field derive from the model defined in Fig. 11.3; those for Banc Du derive from the model defined in Fig. 11.8. The format is identical to that of Fig. 11.3. The large square brackets down the left-hand side of the diagram, along with the OxCal keywords, define the overall model exactly.

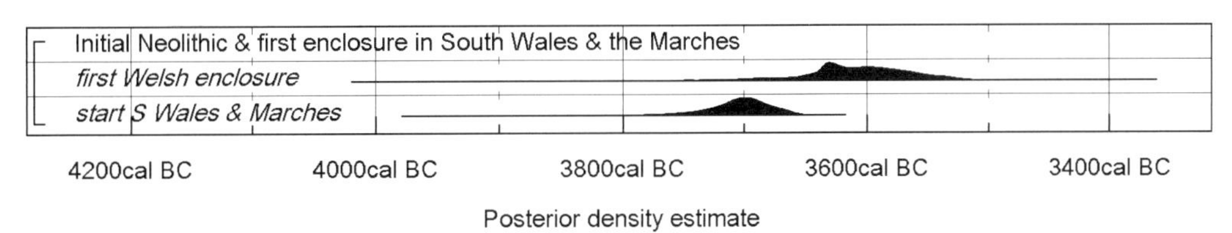

Fig. 11.16. South Wales and the Marches. Probability distributions of dates of the first dated Neolithic enclosure and of the start of Neolithic activity in this region. The distributions are taken from the models defined in Fig. 11.15 and Figs 11.10–11 respectively. The format is identical to that of Fig. 11.3.

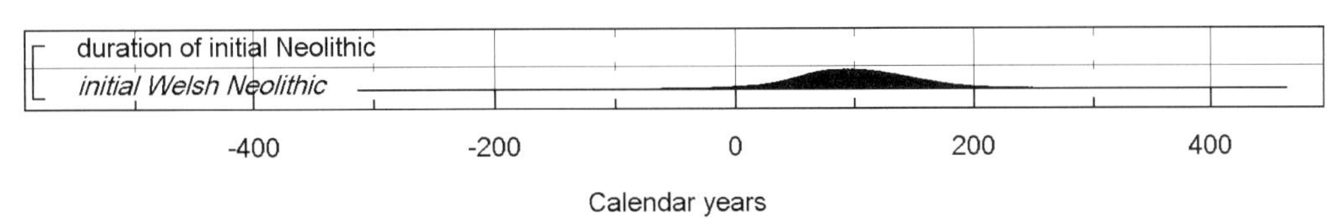

Fig. 11.17. South Wales and the Marches. Probability distribution of the number of years between the start of the Neolithic and the date of the first enclosure in this region (derived from the difference between the two distributions shown in Fig. 11.16). The format is identical to that of Fig. 11.3.

probability; Fig. 11.15: *first Welsh enclosure*), probably in *3645–3560 cal BC* (*68% probability*).

It should be stressed that the estimates for the date when the Neolithic began in the Marches and south Wales (Figs 11.10–11) and for the date when the first enclosure appeared (Fig. 11.15) are entirely independent of each other. Figure 11.16 shows these two distributions. It is *96% probable* that the Neolithic in this region as defined above had begun before the first enclosure was built. The first enclosure was constructed *−20–215 years* (*95% probability*; Fig. 11.17: *initial Welsh Neolithic*) after the initiation of the Neolithic in this region, probably *50–150 years* (*68% probability*) – two to six generations later.

Dates for other potentially Neolithic samples do not change these estimates substantively. Figure 11.18 shows other dates falling in the fourth millennium cal BC from south Wales and the Marches, measured on samples which were not associated with diagnostically Neolithic material

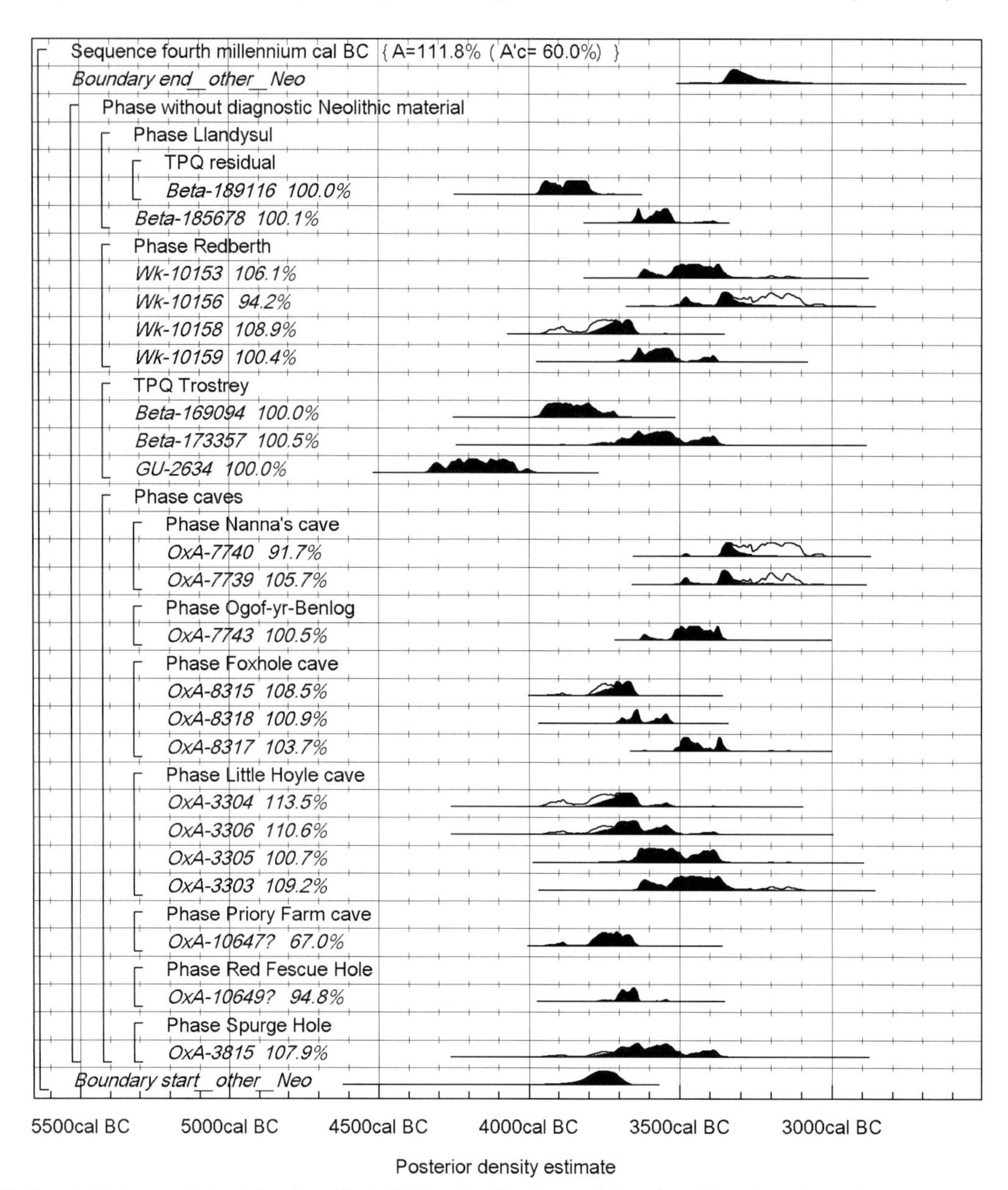

Fig. 11.18. South Wales and the Marches. Probability distributions of fourth millennium dates from contexts not directly associated with diagnostic Neolithic material. The format is identical to that of Fig. 11.3. The large square brackets down the left-hand side of the diagram, along with the OxCal keywords, define the overall model exactly.

or architecture as defined above. From Llandysul, already discussed above, two further fourth millennium dates were obtained. Beta-185678 came from a small isolated pit, without pottery, and Beta-189116 was redeposited in a posthole which is otherwise dated to the second millennium cal BC (Fig. 11.18; Table 11.4). Investigation in advance of bypass construction at Redberth, Pembrokeshire, revealed a series of prehistoric features. Pits, postholes and areas of burning could be identified (Page 2001). Little diagnostic material has so far been reported. Four radiocarbon dates were obtained on hazel charcoal from such contexts (Fig. 11.18; Table 11.4).

The interim reports on excavations at Trostrey Castle, Monmouthshire, summarised by Mein (2003), suggest that it included Neolithic constructions. These seem to have included a row of three posts each about 0.40 m in diameter, charcoal from one of which provided the sample for Beta-169094 (Mein 2002). North of the row was a pear-shaped, stone-kerbed mound or platform some 10 m long, twig charcoal from beneath which is reported as yielding a date in the first quarter of the fourth millennium cal BC, although the actual radiocarbon result is not cited (Mein 2003: Beta-184103). Embedded in this feature were a central post-built structure, seen as an excarnation table, and a lateral cluster of five posts, charcoal from one of which is reported to date to the first quarter of the fourth millennium cal BC (Beta-155429; no actual radiocarbon result cited; Mein 2001; 2002). North of the mound or platform was the post-built façade and two post rows leading to cremation pyres described above. Identification of the undated part of the sample for Beta-173357, from Pyre 3, as narrow roundwood from shrub species by

Rowena Gale (Mein 2003, 67), suggests that the date may be close in age to its context. Charcoal from another pyre, on top of which was a sherd described as Grimston Ware, is reported as dating to the mid-fourth millennium (Beta-184101), although the actual measurement is again not reported (Mein 2003). The three radiocarbon dates for which we have radiocarbon ages and which are not certainly associated with diagnostic Neolithic material are included in the model shown in Fig. 11.18 as *termini post quos* for their contexts (Beta-169094 and -173357, and GU-2634). This may prove an overly conservative interpretation, but is forced on us by the currently limited information available about this potentially important site.

A series of fourth millennium radiocarbon dates have been obtained on human remains from caves along the south Welsh coast (Schulting and Richards 2002a). Unfortunately, two of these samples were affected by a technical difficulty in laboratory processing (OxA-10647 and -10649), and these results are probably anomalously old (Bronk Ramsey *et al.* 2004a; Bayliss *et al.* 2007a, fig. 25). For this reason, they have been excluded from the analysis.

None of the above results have been included in the model for the early Neolithic of this region, because of the lack of diagnostic associations. There is, however, good circumstantial evidence that much of this activity may indeed be Neolithic. At Llandysul there were numerous finds of Bowl pottery; and, although the same cannot be said of Redberth, there is so far no reported Mesolithic material there. The isotope values of the human remains from the south Welsh coast have terrestrial signatures (Richards and Hedges 1999; Schulting 1998; Schulting and Richards 2002a), and accepting for the sake of argument here that this may reflect a dietary shift proposed as associated with the initiation of farming and other practices, there is some reason to assume that the people in question can meaningfully be classed as Neolithic.

Although we do not consider these dates to be sufficiently securely Neolithic to be included in the main model (Figs 11.10–11), if they are assumed to be part of a continuous phase of activity, analogous to but separate from that defined in the main model, then this started in *3880–3665 cal BC* (*95% probability*; Fig 11.18: *start_other_Neo*), probably in *3800–3700 cal BC* (*68% probability*). This estimate is compatible with the estimate for the start of the Neolithic here produced by the main model, and may provide additional supporting evidence for a relatively late start to the Neolithic here. Further, but more ambitiously, if these results are included in the main model as Neolithic without qualification, then the Neolithic in the Marches and south Wales is estimated to have begun in *3770–3670 cal BC* (*95% probability*; distribution not shown), probably in *3735–3685 cal BC* (*68% probability*). This estimate is based on more measurements and so is slightly more precise than that provided by the main model, and is entirely compatible with it. For the reasons given above, however, we prefer the model given in Figs 11.10–11.

Our evidence for the time when the enclosures in this region went out of primary use is limited. As set out above, the ditch at Hill Croft Field may have largely infilled by the later fourth millennium cal BC (Fig. 11.3). In contrast, the ditch at Banc Du appears to have been substantially recut at this time, with activity continuing into the third millennium cal BC (Fig. 11.8). We know nothing about the later use of Lower Luggy since the two non-residual dated samples are from the ditch base. At Church Lawford, activity within the enclosure ditch appears to have continued into the later fourth millennium cal BC on the basis of the later of the two dated samples (SUERC-3385) and Peterborough Ware in the overlying layer. Radiocarbon dates for other finds of Peterborough and related wares in this region are given in Fig. 11.19 and Table 11.4. Modelling these results as part of a simple continuous phase of activity suggests that Peterborough Ware began to be used in this region in *3615–3140 cal BC* (*95% probability*; Fig. 11.19: *start Welsh Peterborough Ware*), probably in *3435–3215 cal BC* (*68% probability*). The latest deposits of this style occurred in *2915–2670 cal BC* (*95% probability*; Fig. 11.19: *end Welsh Peterborough Ware*), probably in *2900–2810 cal BC* (*68% probability*). It should be noted that the results from Cefn Bryn, Gower (Table 11.4; Ward 1987; Gibson 1995b), have not been included in this model. Some at least of these appear to be anomalously late (Birm-1238 and Birm-1236, with probabilities of 4.7% and 2.9% respectively of lying within this phase of deposition). The samples in question came from beneath a Bronze Age cairn, and it is possible that later material was incorporated into these bulk samples. Two results from Fronddyrys, Powys, have also been excluded from the model, having been earlier deemed unusable by Gibson and Kinnes (1997). These samples are from a deposit immediately below the topsoil where the taphonomy of the dated material is uncertain (Table 11.4).

Turning, finally, to other aspects of the early Neolithic in the Marches and south Wales, it is striking that, in comparison especially to Ireland (Chapter 12), and perhaps also to the south-west of England (Chapter 10), there is little definite evidence for rectangular timber structures, in addition to those at Gwernvale and Llandygai, noted above. Regardless of whether the stone-built enclosure on Clegyr Boia in Pembrokeshire is Neolithic (Vyner 2001), the hill was the site of at least two post-built structures, one of them rectangular and each associated with Neolithic artefacts, including largely open, and fairly light-rimmed shouldered bowls with rare decoration and horizontal lugs (A. Williams 1952; F. Lynch 2000, 49–51). It is possible that some of the postholes at Redberth (Page 2001; 2002) could be all that survives of such structures, but that remains to be established in more detail. Rhos-y-Clegyrn, Pembrokeshire, is another candidate, but is of uncertain date, and the excavator's identification of seven separate small structures seems sanguine (J. Lewis 1974; Page 2001). Other known structures date, with varying degrees of certainty, to later in the Neolithic sequence, such as at Cefn Caer Euni, Cefn Cilsanws, Trelystan, and Upper Ninepence in the Walton basin, and are of varied form (F. Lynch 1986; Webley 1958, Britnell 1982; Gibson 1999; Page 2001).

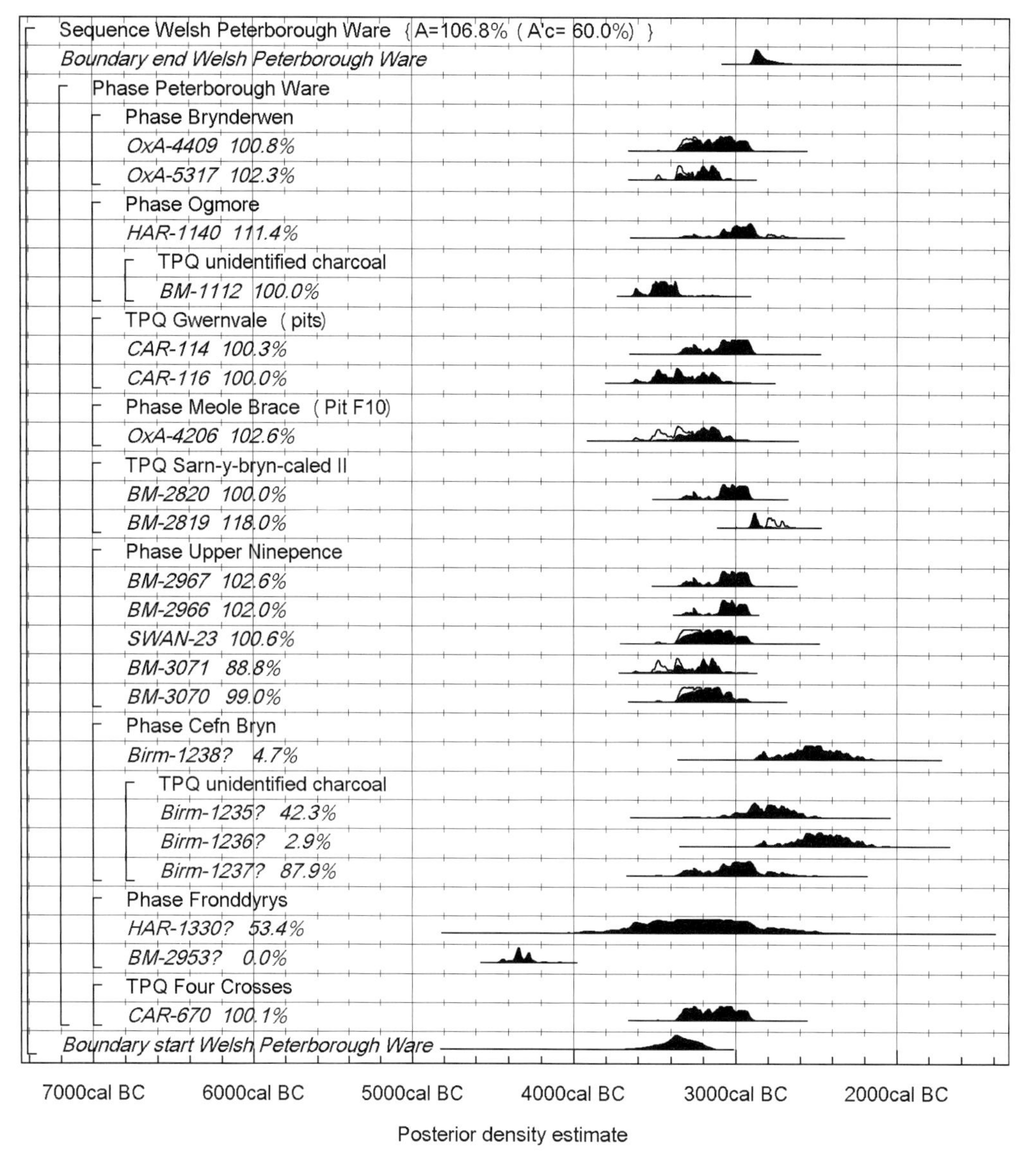

Fig. 11.19. South Wales and the Marches. Probability distributions of dates associated with Peterborough Ware. The format is identical to that of Fig. 11.3. The large square brackets down the left-hand side of the diagram, along with the OxCal keywords, define the overall model exactly.

This situation may of course change with further research. Two recent linear watching briefs appear, however, to have yielded no further evidence of this kind, which would now be an unusual result in Ireland. Observation of road improvements to the A55 across Anglesey did not find early Neolithic houses, despite their known presence at Llandygai on the adjacent mainland, and watching briefs in 2006 on the major gas pipeline running east from from Milford Haven to near Gloucester had a similar negative result (A. Barber *et al.* 2006).

The date estimates presented in this chapter help, as in Chapter 10, further to define the chronology of use of material culture in the early Neolithic, though with less impact than was the case for the south-west of England. Fine-grained, rhyolitic tuffs attributed to petrological Group VIII were worked in the Preselis. So far, there is evidence for the manufacture of axeheads and other products from erratics at two locations, rather than at the nearby *in situ* source of Carn Alw. The two identified working areas are unlikely to be the only ones, and the rocks worked at them showed some petrological diversity. It is possible to envisage a number of working sites, where various materials were modified (David and Williams 1995).

Most Group VIII axeheads are found around the source area of the Preselis and in eastern Wales, although small numbers have been found as far afield as eastern England; these rocks were far less extensively worked and transported than the augite granophores of Group VII, quarried in the Penmaenmawr area of north Wales (Burrow 2006a 45). Contexted Group VIII implements within the region are few. There are two axehead fragments from post-Neolithic contexts at Coygan Camp (Wainwright 1967, 161–2), although their relation to the dated pit is unknown. Another Group VIII fragment came from the Dorstone Hill causewayed enclosure in Herefordshire, but its context is unclear (cf. Olding 2000, 99). An axe-polishing slab possibly of group VIII was placed in a pit with a cremation deposit opposite the entrance of henge A at Llandygai, the cremated bone itself dating to 3370–2930 cal BC (95% confidence; 4480±50 BP; GrA-22954). Two cord-impressed sherds, perhaps of Peterborough Ware, were also present (Lynch and Musson 2001, 43–6).

Farther afield, more confidently identified examples also tend to occur in later fourth or even third millennium cal BC contexts (I. Smith 1979). At Windmill Hill (Chapter 3), axehead fragments and flakes found by Alexander Keiller came from upper spits, in which Peterborough Ware and later pottery traditions were present, as well as from a round barrow (I. Smith 1965a, 113–14; Davis *et al.* 1988; David and Williams 1995, 453; Whittle *et al.* 1999, table 193). At Hambledon Hill, a flake came from a slot-like recut in an almost fully silted segment of the outer east cross-dyke which, although its contained artefacts were early Neolithic in character, may have been one of the last Neolithic earthworks to be built on the site (Chapter 4; I. Smith 2008b). At Downton, a complete axehead was found in an occupied area on a silt-covered terrace of the Wiltshire Avon, where the nearby pottery was mainly Peterborough Ware (Rahtz and ApSimon 1962); and, in Cranborne Chase, an axehead came from the upper fill of a pit of the early third millennium cal BC at Wyke Down henge (Barrett *et al.* 1991, 101).

Lithics were transported into the region as well as out of it (Darvill 1989). Stephen Burrow (2006b, fig. 37) has pointed out that most flint axeheads found in Wales, the majority of them from the south and east, must have been brought from areas with larger and better-quality flint than is locally available, and the most likely source area is the southern English Chalk. It is noteworthy that, as in other regions, axeheads are often of different flints from the bulk of the assemblages in which they occur, for example in the pre-cairn assemblage from Gwernvale, where some arrowheads were also of distinctive material and may, like the axeheads, have been imported as finished artefacts (Healey and Green 1984, 114). The distinction between the raw material of axeheads and other artefacts persists in the predominantly later Neolithic and Early Bronze Age collections from the Walton Basin (P. Bradley 1999, 50–1, 73). Again as in other regions, there is also evidence of the transport of flint for knapping. This was often from secondary sources rather than directly from the Chalk, as at Gwernvale (Healey and Green 1984, 114), although some of the Walton Basin lithics seem to have been made on Chalk flint (P. Bradley 1999, 50–1), as does a hoard of blade-like flakes and an edge-polished knife from Penmachno, Conwy (F. Lynch 2000, 110, pl. 6).

The model presented here (Fig. 11.10) suggests that the early Neolithic in the Marches and south Wales probably began in the late 38th or early 37th century cal BC. On this basis, we can now define the chronology of Bowl pottery in this region with greater precision. The situation may be comparable to that in the south-west of England. Most of the pottery consists of plain shouldered or unshouldered Bowls with relatively unpronounced rims (F. Lynch 2000; Peterson 2003). Some may have more accentuated shoulders and more open mouths, as at Carreg Samson portal dolmen (F. Lynch 1972), but this element appears to be in the minority and is so far at least not demonstrably earlier in this area than the dominant style.

It is clear from this review that, despite the recent discoveries reported here, there is much still to do on the early Neolithic in the Marches and south Wales in general. Overall it appears, however, that in this region too, as in south-west England (Chapter 10) and elsewhere, enclosures came later than the initiation of the Neolithic. The date of their appearance in this region conforms to that seen elsewhere in southern Britain, while the initiation of the Neolithic is not quite as early as often supposed, on the basis of the dataset modelled here, since no recognisably Neolithic activity can yet be shown definitely to belong very early in the fourth millennium cal BC.

Both results are important, and we will return to them in the wider contexts and perspectives discussed in Chapters 14 and 15.

11.5 Billown, Malew, Rushen, Isle of Man, SC 2674 7018

Location and topography

Billown lies on a low, gently rounded hilltop *c.* 40 m OD, a little inland from Castletown at the southern end of the Isle of Man (Fig. 1.1), on up to 4 m of glacial till with granite, quartzite, slate, mudstone and other erratics, which overlies Carboniferous Limestone. This is within the expanse of lower though undulating land in the south-eastern portion of the island, much of the rest of which, apart from the northern end, is dominated by upland. It lies on a narrow interfluve between the Silver Burn to the east and a stream from Chibbyr Unjin to the west, both of which run south to the sea. The longest view is to the south-west, over the coastal plain to the Irish Sea (Darvill 2001a).

History of investigation

Billown was investigated between 1995 and 2004 as a joint research, rescue and training venture by Bournemouth University and Manx National Heritage, following discoveries of Neolithic finds and features within an area designated for an expansion of limestone quarrying. Quarrying, perhaps over centuries (Darvill 2001a, 158), had clearly already impinged on the remains, truncating an extensive series of ditches (Darvill 2001a, fig. 12.2; 2003a, fig. 12.2). Excavation over eight seasons has revealed a substantial number of features (Fig. 11.20). Scattered across the excavated area of roughly 300 m by 200 m are a series of Neolithic pits, scoops and shafts of varying sizes. Some are extremely large, one reaching 6 m in diameter (Darvill 2001a, fig. 12.3). Most show evidence for lighting fires and perhaps also for cooking and eating; the model is of occasional, episodic, use (Darvill 2001a, 161). There are also undated postholes, gullies, a small stone cairn and, nearby, a large white quartz standing stone, the Boolievane Stone. One or two Mesolithic pits have also been found. Further large scoops or hollows, earthfast jars, a 'mini-henge', and a more substantial class I henge have been assigned to the local late Neolithic Ronaldsway culture. A substantial settlement comprising at least five houses dating to *c.* 1000 cal BC lay within the excavated area, associated with a field system set out on a co-axial arrangement with some fields and paddocks in excess of 100 m across. At the north end of the site was a group of circular structures dating to the late first millennium cal BC, one certainly associated with metalworking, and the whole area is criss-crossed by early modern field boundaries which in places follow earlier alignments.

The general age of the Mesolithic and Neolithic pits does not seem problematic; they are dated by the finds they contain. Dating the ditch systems has been more of a challenge. Some contain early Neolithic material: pottery and leaf arrowheads. Another contains Ronaldsway material. Most, however, are quite narrow and shallow (Fig. 11.20), and some of this material may be residual from areas of early activity. Ongoing post-excavation analysis of the ditch fills and contents shows that the Bronze Age settlement and field system were more extensive than was appreciated during fieldwork. Interim accounts of the project used the results of geophysical surveys and available excavation results to propose the existence of a substantial D-shaped Neolithic enclosure, at least 240 m north to south and more than 220 m east to west, encompassing more than 4 ha (Darvill 2001a, 158; 2003a, 113–14). The western boundary of this enclosure can now be recognised as wholly or substantially Bronze Age in date, and by implication the same also applies to the southern boundary which is known only through geophysical survey. It is also now clear that a ditch intersection that was critical to the provisional phasing of the enclosure boundaries contains a previously unrecognised Bronze Age element.

Previous dating

Thirty radiocarbon determinations were available at the start of this project for Bronze Age and earlier material at Billown. Twelve single-entity samples were dated by AMS at the Oxford Radiocarbon Accelerator Unit using methods described by R. Hedges *et al.* (1989a) and Bronk Ramsey and Hedges (1997). The remaining 18 samples were measured by Beta Analytic Inc, using methods outlined at http://radiocarbon.com/analytic.htm. Seven samples were measured by AMS, denoted by an asterisk against the laboratory number in Table 11.5. The remainder were bulk samples dated by LSC.

Twenty-four determinations are available from discrete features, most frequently pits (Table 11.5). The dates demonstrate that pit digging and filling span the fourth to second millennia cal BC (Fig. 11.21). The two samples of fifth millennium date were of unidentified charcoal or from long-lived species of wood. These results may therefore have a significant age offset and do not confirm archaeological activity of this date; Mesolithic lithics, however, have been recovered from the site. Beta-110691 at least derived from a feature which appears to date from the second half of the fourth millennium cal BC, on the evidence of OxA-10300 from an overlying fill (Table 11.5).

Six radiocarbon measurements were available from the fills of ditches at Billown before this project (Fig. 11.22). Four of these are on unidentified charcoal or charcoal from long-lived wood species. The other two samples (OxA-11084, -10127), from F127 and F475 (Fig. 11.22), are on short-life material. If interpreted as non-residual, they suggest that this activity dates to the late third or second millennium cal BC. With single grains of cereals, on a site with considerable activity and recutting, however, there can be no certainty that these samples are not residual, and in that case they would therefore only be *termini post quos* for their contexts. We discuss this further below.

Objectives of the dating programme

The existing radiocarbon dates cast doubt on the initial interpretation, formed when the excavated area was much smaller than it finally became, of the interrupted ditches as part of an earlier Neolithic causewayed enclosure (Darvill 2001a; 2003a). Further samples of short-lived charcoal were submitted from the fills of selected features on the south-western and north-eastern sides of the putative enclosure in an attempt to clarify this interpretation.

Sampling

Six single fragments of charcoal were dated, two from each of three fills from different stretches of ditch. All the charcoal was comminuted and dispersed within the fills. GrA-31541–2 were from the lowest fill of F14, on the north-eastern boundary of the enclosure as originally proposed. The other samples were from single fills in F5206 and F5209, elements of the south-western side of the enclosure.

Results and calibration

Full details of the radiocarbon determinations from Billown considered in this chapter are provided in Table 11.5.

Analysis and interpretation

The calibrated dates from the ditches at Billown are shown in Fig. 11.23. Since all the charcoal was dispersed within the fills rather than occurring in concentrations, all the samples strictly provide *termini post quos* for the fills from which they were recovered. It is therefore difficult to estimate when particular ditch systems were laid out, especially since ditches of this small size may have been cleaned out with ease. Single dates of many periods are represented in this series, almost certainly from material reworked from the lengthy period of activity on the site

Fig. 11.20. Billown. Plan and sections. Bournemouth University School of Conservation Sciences.

Table 11.5. Radiocarbon dates from Billown, Isle of Man.

* = AMS date measured by Beta Analytic Inc.

Laboratory number	Sample reference	Material	Context	Radiocarbon age (BP)	$\delta^{13}C$ (‰)	Calibrated date range (cal BC) (95% confidence)
Discrete pre-first millennium features						
OxA-10203		Carbonised residue on decorated pottery	1993/C214. Pit	4510±45	−27.3	3370–3020
Beta-89312		*Quercus* stickwood charcoal	Site D, F47. One of several lenses of charcoal-rich soil above clay ?hearth in pit (Darvill 1996a, 26)	5650±80	−25.0	4690–4340
Beta-110690		Substantial pieces of burnt timber, all oak	Site H, F224. Charcoal layer in shaft fill 0.90 m from top. Grain and nutshell also present	3980±60	−25.0	2830–2290
OxA-10301	ES177	Grain of *Hordeum vulgare*	Site J, F360, context 425. Large hollow/pit	3120±55	−23.5	1500–1260
Beta-129973		Stickwood charcoal	Site J, F360, context 709. Hearth in large hollow/pit pre-dating Neolithic pottery	4650±150	−25.0	3710–2910
Beta-110691		*Quercus* charcoal from one of a series of charred planks	Site K, F376. Planks overlay 2.5 m deep shaft extending from base of pit. They underlay a hearth with sherds of 3 bowls, charred cereals and hazelnut shells which provided samples for OxA-10300, -10202, -10222	5910±70	−25.0	4950–4610
OxA-10300	ES132	Charred grain of *Hordeum vulgare*	Site K, F376, context 491. Hearth in upper fill of shaft, with Neolithic Bowl pottery, charred cereals and hazelnuts stratified above sample for Beta-110691	4570±65	−23.1	3520–3090
OxA-10202		Carbonised residue from decorated pottery	From the same context as OxA-10300	4600±45	−27.8	3510–3120
OxA-10222	ES132	Charred grain of *Hordeum vulgare*	From the same context as OxA-10300	4575±55	−23.2	3500–3090
OxA-10141	ES266	Charred grain of *Hordeum vulgare*	Site K, F541, context 724. Pit	4650±39	−25.3	3630–3350
Beta-129019		Unidentified charcoal	Site L, F431, context 802. From hearth in central part of 25 m x 15 m scoop, 1.2 m from surface, cut by later pits, etc. Finds from lower levels (inc. hearth) all Neolithic	4170±90	−25.0	2930–2480
Beta-140098*		Stickwood charcoal	Site O, F605, context 1034. Central fills of scoop, charcoal associated with fragments of a polished stone axe and sherds of plain Bowl	4980±40	−26.1	3940–3650
Beta-140097		Unidentified charcoal	Site O, F623, context 1120. Hearth in 1 of series of coalescing scoops. Leaf arrowheads, scraper, flakes & blades	4600±70	−25.0	3630–3090
Beta-125767*		?unidentified charcoal fragment	F526, pit cut by ditch F496=F28=F17=F14	5680±40	−25.0	4610–4410
OxA-10140	ES192	Grain of *Hordeum vulgare*	F526, pit cut by ditch F496=F28=F17=F14	4495±40	−23.2	3360–3020
OxA-10182	ES138	Grain of *Hordeum vulgare*	F472, context 608. Scoop or pit containing early/middle Neolithic pottery, cut by ditch F68 (Darvill 1998, 11–12), upper part of fill	4930±55	−23.9	3910–3630
OxA-10245	ES133	Grain of *Hordeum vulgare*	From the same context as OxA-10182	4440±45	−23.5	3340–2910
OxA-10244	ES122	Grain of *Hordeum vulgare*	From the same context as OxA-10182	4465±45	−22.4	3360–2920
Beta-110692		Unidentified charcoal	Site K, F418. Charcoal lining of hearth/oven	2910±70	−25.0	1370–900
Beta-178341	ES939	*Alnus* charcoal	Site P, F1100, context 2001. From fill of a drain beneath structure 1, a Bronze Age round house	2810±40	−26.1	1060–840
Beta-178338	DPS 205	*Corylus*	Site P, F676, context 1553. From area of burning or temporary hearth on floor of a Bronze Age structure, a possible animal byre, next to structure 1	2780±40	−26.2	1020–820
Beta-154616*	DPS 198	*Quercus*	Site P, F694, context 1354. From pit or posthole of possible shrine next to BA settlement and approached by path from it	3010±40	−23.5	1400–1120
Beta-178339	DPS543	*Alnus*	Site P, F805, context 1915. From a lower fill of pit with large numbers of ash-rich fills, in intercutting cluster SW of Bronze Age settlement	2820±40	−27.5	1120–850

Laboratory number	Sample reference	Material	Context	Radiocarbon age (BP)	$\delta^{13}C$ (‰)	Calibrated date range (cal BC) (95% confidence)
Beta-178340	ES777	*Betula*	Site P, F817, context 1661. From pit containing basally retouched flake of Mesolithic type in intercutting cluster SW of Bronze Age settlement	2900±40	−25.4	1260–940
Ditches						
OxA-11084		Grain of *Hordeum* sp.	F127, context 325. Middle fill of ditch F127, stratified below sample for Beta-125766	3855±40		2470–2150
Beta-125766*		Unidentified charcoal	F127, context 163. Latest recut of ditch, with stone setting, stratified above sample for OxA-11084	3590±40	−25.2	2040–1780
Beta-125768*		Unidentified charcoal	F68, 'Earliest ditch fill'. Ditch sealed beneath cobbled surface. Cereals present	5780±40	−25.4	4730–4530
GrA-31542	DPS 21 BIL04 F14 (8)	Single fragment *Corylus avellana* roundwood charcoal, radius 10 mm, 5 growth rings	Site H, F14, context 18. Lowest fill of ditch parallel to F68 and continuing E from F28=F17 (Darvill 1998, ill. 4). Assessment of two samples (61 and 65) yielded 150 identifications, mainly of indeterminate tuber fragments but including Cerealia awns and miscellaneous seeds (Fairbairn 1999b)	3170±35	−26.0	1510–1390
GrA-31541	ES62 BIL04 F14 (8)	Single fragment *Corylus avellana* charcoal	From the same context as GrA-31542	3300±35	−24.9	1690–1490
OxA-10127	ES192	Grain of *Hordeum vulgare*	F475, context 607. Fill of ditch	3150±55	−23.2	1530–1300
GrA-31360	ES5536	*Ulex* sp. (gorse) or *Cytisus scoparius* (broom)	Site R, F5206, context 5740. Single fill of ditch, forming W boundary of enclosure N side of which is formed by F5209, F68, F28=F14, F496	1950±40	−24.9	50 cal BC–cal AD 130
GrA-31359	ES5544	Single fragment *Betula* sp. charcoal	Site R, F5206, context 5747. Single fill of ditch, forming W boundary of enclosure N side of which is formed by F5209, F68, F28=F14, F496	2415±40	−25.9	760–390
GrA-31537	ES5395 BIL04 (5314)	Single fragment *Betula* sp. charcoal	Site R, F5209, context 5314. Single fill of ditch, forming part of N boundary of enclosure with F68, F28=F14, F496	2220±35	−26.3	390–190
GrA-31540	ES5434 BIL04 Tr R F[5209] (5334)	Single fragment *Betula* sp. charcoal	Site R, F5209, context 5334. Single fill of ditch, forming part of N boundary of enclosure with F68, F28=F14, F496	2045±35	−26.3	170 cal BC–cal AD 50
Beta-154614*		*Quercus* charcoal	Site O, F619, context 1186. Ditch	4190±40	−26.1	2900–2630
Beta-154615*	ES515	Mixed charcoal	Site O, F662, context 1253. From upper fill of ditch with small amounts of struck flint but no pottery	3060±40	−24.4	1430–1210
Other contexts						
Beta-89310		Unidentified charcoal	F19. Burnt planks in IA palisade	2310±90	−25.0	750–170
Beta-89311		Unidentified charcoal	F19. Burnt planks in IA palisade	2200±90	−25.0	410–1
Beta-110689		Unidentified charcoal	F288. Fill of IA furnace or kiln	1560±60	−25.0	cal AD 380–640
Beta-140095		Unidentified charcoal	F630. Fill of IA ring ditch	2360±60	−25.0	750–260
Beta-140096		Unidentified charcoal	F647. From IA furnace	2250±40	−26.2	400–200
OxA-10128	ES276	Charred grain of *Triticum dicoccum*	Site K, F541, context 725. Pit	70±45	−23.3	cal AD 1680–1960

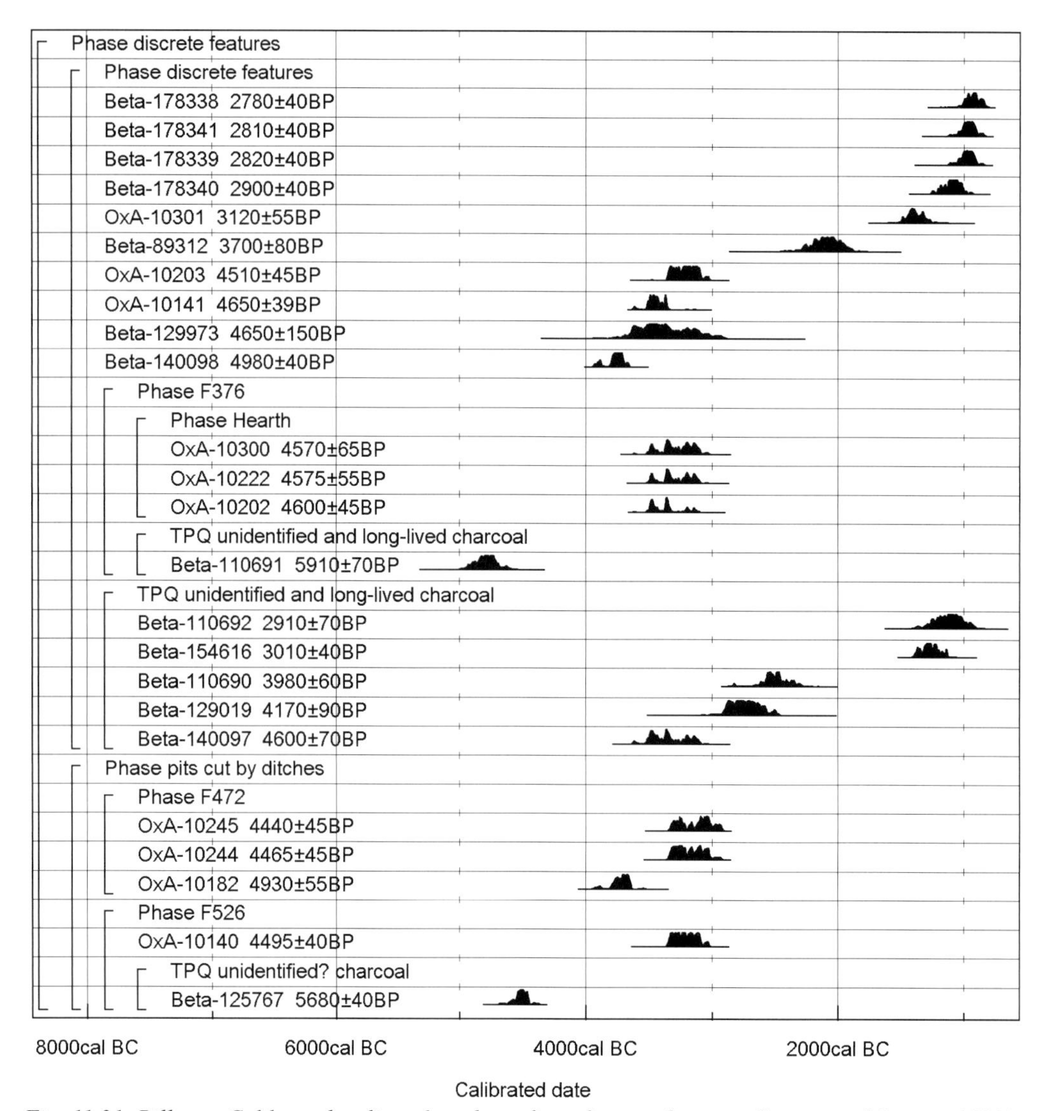

Fig. 11.21. Billown. Calibrated radiocarbon dates from discrete features (Stuiver and Reimer 1993).

evidenced by the discrete features (Fig. 11.21). Perhaps the four samples falling in the middle of the second millennium cal BC (GrA-31541–2, OxA-10127, and the *terminus post quem* Beta-154615) provide an indication of when the field system was first laid out. It may have been maintained until the end of the first millennium cal BC, as evidenced from samples from ditches F5206 and F5209.

A series of lengths of ditch which share similarities of profile and size appear to define three sides of a D-shaped block some 140 m by more than 160 m, one side of which is aligned with part of the Bronze Age system (Fig. 11.20). This is not a conventional causewayed enclosure, although the excavator feels it should be seen as an enclosure of sorts, the ditches of which surround most of the fourth millennium cal BC features revealed by excavation. All recognised sections of the ditch system in question have yielded leaf-shaped arrowheads, though these occur across the whole site in great abundance and might well be redeposited.

As now defined, the north-east side of the ditch system is represented by F1052, F400, F297, F272 and F17, all of which were shallow, less than 0.6 m deep. None of these yielded material suitable for radiocarbon dating (Darvill 1997, ill. 11; 1998, ill. 4; 2003b, ill. 3). The southern terminal of F17, however, cuts a pit, F526, a short-lived grain sample from which is dated to 3360–3020 cal BC (95% confidence; Fig. 11.22; Table 11.5: OxA-10140). This sample is a *terminus post quem* both for the pit and the ditch F17, which cuts it.

In turn, F17 is later cut by ditch F127 which itself shows several phases of recutting, the first of which is dated by a measurement, already noted above, on a short-lived grain sample to 2470–2150 cal BC (95% confidence; Fig. 11.23: OxA-11084). This can be seen as either dating the context in question or be taken as a *terminus post quem*, as discussed above. Higher in F127, in its latest recut, there is another sample, of bulk unidentified charcoal, which provides a *terminus post quem* for its context of 2040–1780 cal BC (95% confidence; Fig. 11.23: Beta-125766).

Finally in this rather packed area, the Bronze Age field boundary ditch F28/F14, short-lived samples from which are dated to 1510–1390 cal BC and 1690–1490 cal BC (95% confidence; Fig 11.23: GrA-31541–2), terminates on the edge of F127.

The south side of the ditch system in question here

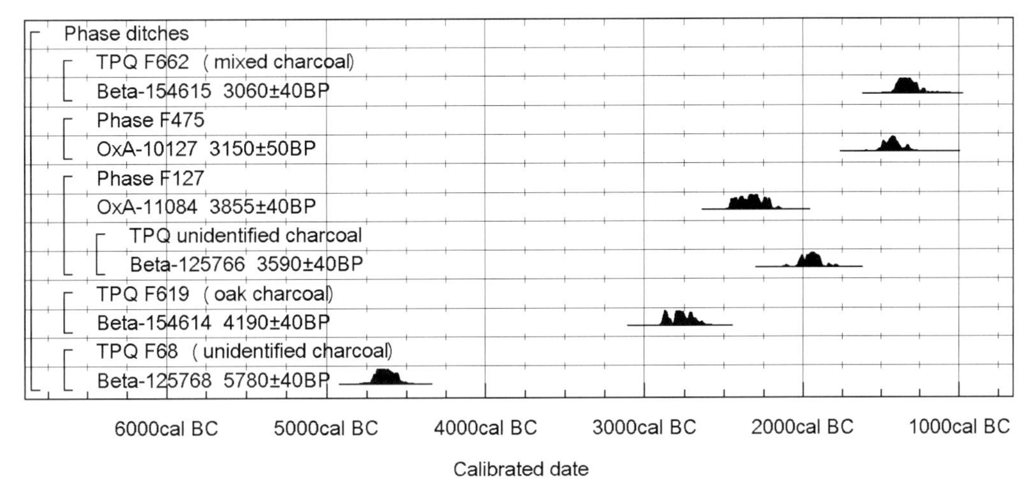

Fig. 11.22. Billown. Calibrated radiocarbon dates from ditches (Stuiver and Reimer 1993), obtained before 2005.

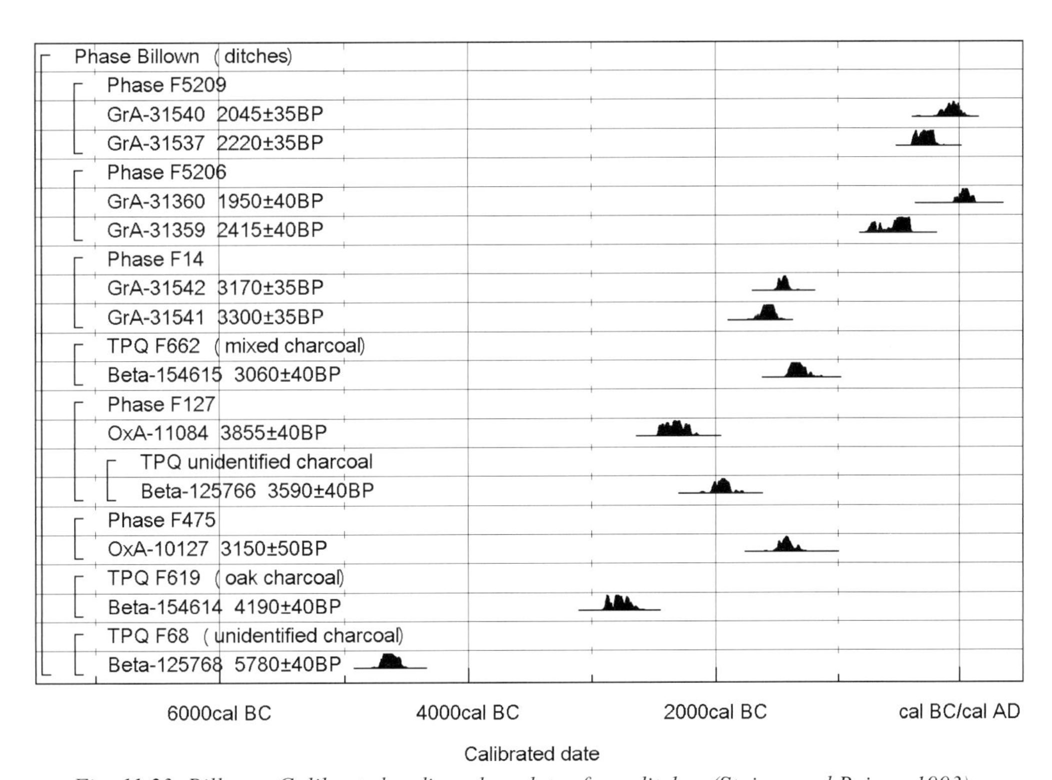

Fig. 11.23. Billown. Calibrated radiocarbon dates from ditches (Stuiver and Reimer 1993).

is represented at the eastern end by F68, securely sealed by later surfaces and, like F17, cutting pit F526, which contained the sample for OxA-10140 discussed above. A *terminus post quem* for F68 of 4730–4530 cal BC (95% confidence) is provided by Beta-125768, a sample of bulk unidentified charcoal (Fig. 11.23; Darvill 1998, ill. 4). The central section of the south side, excavated in 2004, is heavily disturbed by the presence of later Bronze Age and early modern field boundaries following more or less the same line. F5218 represents the western side of the ditch system in question, but is again fairly slight for much of its length.

Ongoing post-excavation analysis will in due course resolve some of the outstanding questions about the construction and phasing of the ditches and boundaries, and further dates may eventually be obtained when work on the environmental samples is complete. OxA-10140 (95% confidence; 3360–3020 cal BC) from F526 provides a *terminus post quem* for F17, but we simply cannot tell at present whether F17 belongs to the late fourth millennium cal BC or considerably later. If OxA-11084 (95% confidence; 2470–2150 cal BC; Table 11.5) from F127, which cuts F17, is taken as non-residual, this ditch system could have been in place by the later third millennium cal BC. But, in the absence of certainty on this point, the ditch system may be little earlier than or coeval with the Bronze Age ditch system, and could represent one of its earliest phases on the site.

The presence of a seemingly quite separate and more substantial ditch perhaps forming the south-western edge of a second ditch system at the north end of the excavated area must also be considered a part of the overall complex (Darvill 2004c, 11–17). It contained Ronaldsway style pottery and so far only has a *terminus post quem* of 2890–2620 cal BC (95% confidence; Fig. 11.23: Beta-154614).

The Isle of Man in its fourth millennium cal BC context

The Neolithic of the Isle of Man has been, until fairly recently, comparatively under-researched (reviewed in Davey 1999; Darvill 2000a; 2004d), but a synthesis by Steven Burrow (1997), the inception of the Billown Project (Darvill 1996a), other work on settlements (Davey and Woodcock 2003), studies of rock art (Darvill and O'Connor 2005) and detailed palynological investigations (Davey and Innes 2003; Innes *et al.* 2003), especially in the north of the island, have all served to change this situation, and the island has figured prominently in recent interpretive literature (e.g. Cooney 2000a, 227; Darvill 2000a; 2003a; 2004d; C. Fowler 2001; 2002; 2004b; Cummings and Fowler 2004; Cummings 2009; Davey 2004). There is still much to do, however, including on two issues of particular concern for this volume: the nature of the Mesolithic-Neolithic transition, and the character of subsequent development. The Billown Project has made substantial contributions to both.

Mesolithic occupation of the island is well documented. An earlier microlithic industry is known, dating to as late perhaps as the seventh millennium cal BC (McCartan 1999; Davey and Innes 2003, 126). A circular post-framed structure or house dating to the seventh millennium cal BC has recently been excavated at Ronaldsway (Pitts 2009). The later Mesolithic industry is based on heavy blades, with notched butted artefacts, and relates clearly to contemporary industries in northern Ireland (Woodman 1978a; 1978b; McCartan 1994; 2000; Davey and Innes 2003). The heavy-blade site of Rhendoo, Jurby, is probably of fifth millennium date (McCartan 1994; Davey and Innes 2003, 123). The development from the earlier microlithic industry to the heavy-blade one is unclear; it has even been mooted that there could have been a break in occupation between the two phases (Davey and Innes 2003, 126). On the basis of claimed pre-elm decline cereal-type pollen and other indicators of slight vegetational disturbances at Ballachrink in the north of the island, radiocarbon dated to the early fifth millennium cal BC (Innes *et al.* 2003), the radical hypothesis has been formulated that 'heavy-bladed Mesolithic people' were arable farmers, 'possibly from the beginning' (Davey and Innes 2003, 125). The claim of very early cereal cultivation is discussed in more detail in Chapter 15, in the wider context of western Britain and Ireland. Suffice it to say here that this interpretation of the evidence seems unconvincing, both in the north of the Isle of Man and elsewhere. There are serious questions of identification and stratigraphic integrity, and then there is the issue of why, if experimentation with cereals had begun in the early fifth millennium cal BC, it was not continued, and with other, more visible palynological and archaeological effects through the fifth millennium.

In more conventional terms, there is no certain sign of the earliest Neolithic on the Isle of Man. No pottery related to the Achnacreebeag type (Sheridan 2003a; 2004; and Chapters 1, 14 and 15) has been found on the island, and no classic Carinated Bowl pottery has yet been discovered (Burrow 1997, 9). Does this just reflect the current state of still under-developed research? At present the Mull Hill (also Meayll Hill) tradition of round-based, shouldered pottery, with decorated rims, is the earliest known ceramic style on the island and can be compared with traditions in both Ireland and south-west Scotland (Burrow 1997, 11–18; Piggott 1932; Davey and Woodcock 2003). Other earlier Neolithic features such as leaf arrowheads, ground stone axes (of local, northern Irish, northern English and northern Welsh origin: Cooney 2000a, 227), long barrows or court cairns, and passage graves, are also not so far closely dated. Davey and Innes have argued (2003, 127), drawing on Burrow (1997, 9–17; 1999), that 'the cultural package that included megalithic tomb building, distinctive pottery and lithic forms cannot easily be derived from insular prototypes'. This in turn raises the question of whether a 'package' is appropriate, not least because none of the megalithic forms have been dated (Chiverrell *et al.* 1999). At this stage, one could posit either much influence and introduction from the outside, or, maintaining the importance of local continuity, a strong sense of connectedness with the outside world – or indeed both.

Herein lies perhaps the true significance of the Billown Project. Although the site has earlier been seen as an enclosure, and even compared in plan with Haddenham (Darvill 2000a, 376), our review here cannot support the existence of an earlier fourth millennium cal BC enclosure, but rather suggests a ditch system, probably a field system, mainly of second millennium date, which grew up in a place which had long been used for occupation and deposition, some, perhaps much of it, of special character. This is not to say that the Isle of Man could not have supported an earlier fourth millennium enclosure, though given the rarity of the form both in western Britain – exemplified by Banc Du in south-west Wales (this chapter), Bryn Celli Wen on Anglesey, of uncertain date and character (Edmonds and Thomas 1993), and the possible site of Green How in Cumbria (Horne *et al.* 2002) – and in Ireland as a whole (Chapter 12), the presence of one on the island would be interesting. Chapel Hill in the south of the island is a possible tor enclosure, though we know little about this site; excavations by Bersu in 1944–5 produced plentiful Neolithic flintwork, and survey by Darvill has traced the heavily eroded stone wall (Darvill 2001a, 166). But Billown remains highly significant in many other ways. Though the samples principally provide *termini post quos* for their contexts, they probably indicate a period from the earlier fourth millennium cal BC when activity became established at the site, probably in the 38th or 37th century cal BC (Figs 11.21 and 14.148: *Beta-140098, OxA-10182*). In general, the position of Billown in the centre of the Southern Plain suggests that it was a focal point for communities occupying the fertile lands in south-western part of the island. Periodic visits involving pit digging and the veneration and elaboration of natural hollows are represented over a long period. But the evidence for early activity is slight. Beta-140098 was associated with fragments of a polished stone axe and sherds of plain Bowl which could be taken as early in the Mull Hill tradition. OxA-10182 appears to be a residual early Neolithic barley grain in a later fourth millennium pit.

What of other evidence? Environmental evidence suggests that, throughout the fourth millennium cal BC, the Isle of Man was fairly well wooded except for the higher hills; cultivation phases represented by cereal pollen and clearance indicators increase 'in frequency and intensity' in the fourth and third millennia (Davey and Innes 2003, 121). Other settlements are so far absent from the archaeological record, although pits at Phurt on the north-eastern coast (Davey and Woodcock 2003) may either be traces of occupation places or an example of a ceremonial site. Quartz mounds, a minority of which date to the fourth millennium cal BC, as at Rheast Buigh (Davey and Woodcock 2003), and about 50 panels of rock art, mainly comprising cup-marks (Darvill and O'Connor 2005), make up the majority of the remaining archaeological evidence for the period, although a fair scatter of stone axes imported from the Lake District (Group VI) and North Wales (Group VII) suggests eastward contacts with Britain (Burrow 1997; Darvill forthcoming); there are also Group IX axes from Ireland, and one jadeitite axe from Onchan, Glencrutchery, in the east-centre of the island (Cooney 2000a, 227; Coope and Garrard 1988).

Long barrows or, perhaps better, court cairns (the terminology varies: Darvill 2000a; 2003a; Davey and Woodcock 2003; Davey 2004) are known on the north-eastern part of the Island: Cashtal-yn-Ard; King Orry's Grave; Ballafayle; and The Cloven Stones. Passage graves and other related kinds of chambered tomb are more widely scattered, for example at Mull or Meayll Hill, Kew, Ballaharra, Ballaterson and Ballakelly (Darvill 2010). Chris Fowler (2001; 2002; 2004b) has drawn attention in a series of papers to the assembly of relationships that inhumed and cremated remains in these sites may project, the cremations at Mull Hill, for example, being seen as 'citations of a type of personal relationship which stressed the integration of different selves' (C. Fowler 2001, 152. At Mull Hill, 'the geography of place, path and event may have been intended to connect the deposits...with the wider world' (C. Fowler 2001, 153–4), and such deposits may also have been designed to 'keep the dead, the past and spiritual powers within the present community' (C. Fowler 2004b, 91). The views out from Mull Hill and other sites are extensive (Cummings and Fowler 2004). That wider world included the broader Irish Sea setting (Burrow 1999; Darvill 2004d, 52–3), and it has even been suggested that the island had a central role in that context, famed for its creation myths and rituals (Davey 2004, 133, 142). We know very little of the chronology of such developments. Billown, and imported axes, indicate that connections are not only to be seen in the megalithic monuments, and Billown, again, contributes significantly to the task of the construction of more reliable timeframes.

Notes

1 After this chapter was first drafted, small-scale excavations have been carried out by Clwyd-Powys Archaeological Trust in 2008, and three radiocarbon dates on charred material (in at least two cases on hazel charcoal) have been obtained from basal fills and recuts in the basal fills in the ditches (Nigel Jones, pers. comm.). These are 3650–3380 cal BC (95% confidence; 4780±40 BP; Beta-25492), 3630–3350 cal BC (95% confidence; 4650±40 BP; Beta-25493), and 3630–3350 cal BC (95% confidence; 4650±40 BP; Beta-25494). Further note added in press: see now N. Jones (2010).

2 Since this analysis, a fragment of cremated bone from the south-west part of the cairn, between the kerbstones, has been dated to 3100–2890 cal BC (95% confidence; 4361±36 BP; UB-6751; Kytmannow 2008, table 7.1).

3 Trial work was carried out by Clwyd-Powys Archaeological Trust early in 2009, and three dates obtained from different fills of the southern ditch (3950–3710 cal BC (95% confidence, 5030±30 BP: SUERC-24618; 3780–3630 cal BC (95% confidence), 4900±45 BP: SUERC-24834; and 3660–3520 cal BC (95% confidence), 4815±35 BP: SUERC-24619) (CPAT Annual Report 08/09), but at the time of writing, in 2010, details of sample composition and taphonomy are not available.

4 Chronological modelling of an extensive series of radiocarbon dates from this structure suggests that it was constructed in *3800–3670 cal BC* (*95% probability*; *start*; P. Marshall 2008, fig. 4), probably in *3760–3700 cal BC* (*68% probability*). This house was abandoned in *3690–3610 cal BC* (*95% probability*; *end*; P. Marshall 2008, fig. 4), probably in *3670–3620 cal BC* (*68% probability*). Full details of the radiocarbon dates can be found in Kenney (2009, 123–32).

12 Ireland

Gabriel Cooney, Alex Bayliss, Frances Healy, Alasdair Whittle, Ed Danaher, Lydia Cagney, Jim Mallory, Jessica Smyth, Thomas Kador and Muiris O'Sullivan

The Neolithic in Ireland is distinctive, and recent years have seen many exciting new discoveries and changes in understanding. Questions of the date when and the processes whereby the Neolithic was introduced into Ireland have been the subject of considerable discussion (e.g. Woodman 2000; Sheridan 2003a; 2003b; 2005; 2010; Cooney 2007a; Pailler and Sheridan 2009) but much remains unclear. There are relatively few known early Neolithic enclosure sites or indeed candidates for this kind of site, despite the greatly expanded spread and scale of investigation provided by the fieldwork boom of recent years. The scope of this chapter is therefore both narrower and broader than that of the others in this volume. So far, individual regions within southern Britain have been covered, as far west as south-west Wales. The Isle of Man was briefly considered as part of Chapter 11. This chapter begins with just two enclosures: Donegore Hill in Co. Antrim in the north-east of Ireland and Magheraboy in Co. Sligo in the north-west. To make sense of our date estimates for these sites, however, we turn not only to their local contexts, but also to varied aspects and features of the early Neolithic in Ireland as a whole, thereby encompassing a broader geographical sweep than has been attempted in the other regional chapters (Fig 12.1). Moreover, in order to constrain our chronological models for the early Neolithic in Ireland, we offer a model for the initiation of the middle Neolithic of the island, represented by Linkardstown burials and dated passage tombs. Although it has been suggested that the earliest passage tombs themselves form part of an initial phase of the Neolithic in Ireland and western Britain (e.g. Sheridan 2003a; 2003b), our models will suggest otherwise. These analyses represent a first attempt at providing formal, statistical models for the chronology of the early Neolithic in Ireland, using data gathered in the winter of 2006–7. Further relevant radiocarbon dates have been published since that time, but we do not believe that so far these change the patterns presented here substantively. Currently the *Cultivating Societies* project is assessing the evidence for the arrival of farming in Ireland (McClatchie *et al.* 2009), and obtaining a new series of radiocarbon dates on cereal remains.[1]

The island of Ireland is characterised by marked regional diversity, encompassing both major biogeographical differences and considerable variation at a more detailed, local level (Cooney 2000b). Our enclosure case studies belong to two such local settings, detailed further below: Donegore in upland Antrim, part of the catchment of Lough Neagh, Magheraboy on the Cúil Irra peninsula and its hinterland in coastal Sligo. The other evidence drawn on this chapter comes from many parts of Ireland, including well known areas such as the Céide Fields, Co. Mayo, The Burren, Co. Clare and the Bend of the Boyne, Co. Meath, as well as from a range of development-led projects.

In incorporating such a wide range of evidence, we are drawing on a long and varied history of research on the Neolithic in Ireland as a whole (Cooney 2000a, with bibliography). The range of enclosures of all kinds in Ireland is extensive (Sheridan 2001; Cooney 2002), and there is the possibility that more could be recognised as Neolithic in the future. For the present, after all the surveys, investigations and excavations to date, causewayed enclosures seemingly remain very scarce, the only certain examples being Donegore Hill (Mallory and Hartwell 1984; Mallory 1993; Mallory *et al.* forthcoming) and Magheraboy (Danaher 2004; Danaher and Cagney 2005; Danaher 2007). Palisade enclosures of varied kinds, known since the work at Knowth in the 1960s and 1970s (Eogan 1984) and dramatically extended at Thornhill, Co. Londonderry (Sheridan 2001; Logue 2003), may in fact be more common. A significant addition to the repertoire of enclosure forms is represented by Tullahedy, Co. Limerick (McConway 1998; Kelleher 2009).

It remains to be seen whether other, smaller earthwork- or stone-defined enclosures can be recognised in Ireland as being of Neolithic date, as seen for example in south-west England and south-west Wales (Chapters 10 and 11). The embanked enclosure at Lyles Hill, Co. Antrim, was thought by the original excavator to be Neolithic (E. Evans 1953) but was subsequently shown to be of second millennium cal BC date (Sheridan 2001, 178; Simpson and Gibson 1989). It has been suggested that the hill-top

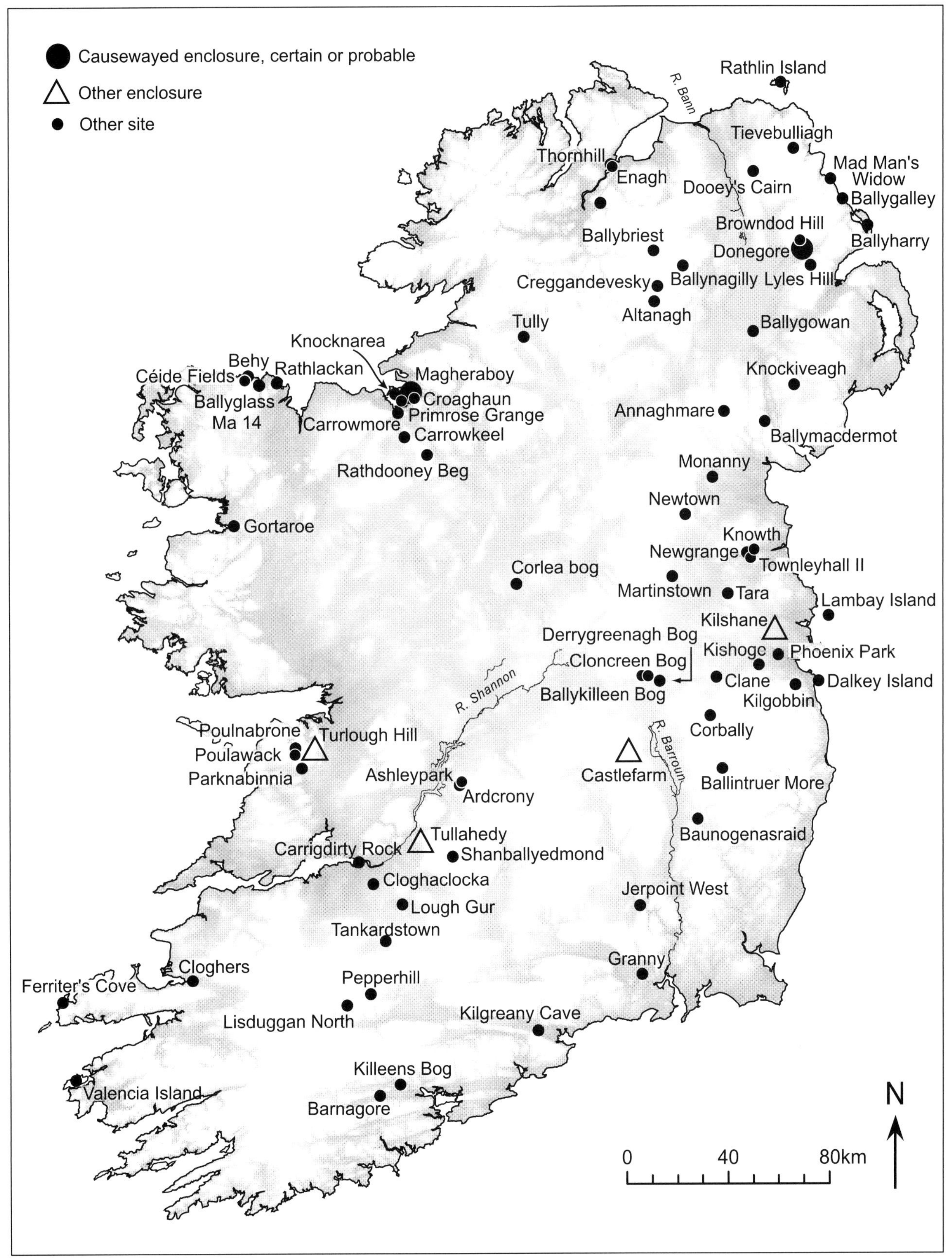

Fig. 12.1. Ireland showing causewayed enclosures and other sites mentioned in Chapter 12.

stone-walled enclosure on Turlough Hill on the northern edge of the Burren could be of Neolithic date, since its massive single circuit, 225 m in diameter, has several interruptions (Cooney 2002; C. Jones 2004, 42–5), and aerial photographs indicate a possible causewayed enclosure west of the Knockadoon peninsula at Lough Gur (see Danaher 2007, 121). There are a number of instances where excavation has revealed Neolithic enclosures.

These include Kilshane, Co. Meath (Moore 2004; 2009) and potentially Castlefarm, Co. Kildare. Kilshane was an irregular shaped ditched enclosure, 45m in maximum external diameter. It was composed of 14 inter-connecting segments. After initial silting a series of articulated and disarticulated cattle bone deposits comprising the remains of at least 58 cattle were placed in the ditch. Further infilling and silting were followed by the placement of a middle Neolithic globular bowl in two different segments over the earlier deposits (one of them from just above and on the cattle bone).[2] A stretch of an outer segmented ditch with at least two causeways was revealed to the north-west of the enclosure (Moore 2009). At Castlefarm, limited excavation prior to development revealed three concentric ditches continuing beyond the area of excavation. They were exposed for a maximum length of 30 m and could, if part of an enclosure, have enclosed an area some 100 m across (Mullins 2000). There were a number of charcoal-rich pits with tiny fragments of burnt bone, some of them cutting the ditches. Ash charcoal from one of these, located between the middle and outer ditches, provided a date of 3970–3700 cal BC (95% confidence; 5040±45 BP; Table 12.13: OxA-7955).[3]

Donegore Hill was discovered by a combination of fieldwalking, excavation and aerial photography in the early 1980s, while Magheraboy was discovered by test trenches in 2001 and then fuller excavation in 2003, in advance of road construction. Donegore is in the kind of hill top setting which has not been much affected by the developments in infrastructure, transport and housing which have produced so many other significant discoveries in recent years, not least of early Neolithic rectangular houses (Cooney 2000a; Grogan 2004; Smyth 2006; 2007; cf. Cooney *et al.* 2006). Both the numbers and the geographical distribution of those houses have been greatly expanded. Some 80 are now known from 49 sites, and they are now scarce in only the under-researched midlands (Smyth 2006; 2007; 2011). Magheraboy, in a lowland setting, close to Sligo town, indicates the potential for further discoveries of enclosures.

12.1 Donegore Hill, Freemanstown, Co. Antrim, Irish grid reference 321440 389150

Location and topography

Donegore Hill rises to 234 m OD in the rolling country north-east of Lough Neagh in Co. Antrim (Fig. 12.1). It lies between streams which run south to join the Six Mile Water, as it flows west into the north-east corner of Lough Neagh at Antrim. Like many other early Neolithic sites, it is well inland, and locally speaking, in an upland rather than a lowland setting. There is a court tomb on the top of Browndod Hill to the north (Evans and Davies 1935).

The basalt hill itself is rounded, falling away steeply to the east and south sides; it is more stepped on the west and linked to other high ground to the north (Mallory and Hartwell 1984, 272; Sheridan 2001, fig. 13.2). The enclosure lies on a south-east-facing slope, 'tilted' off the top of the hill. Parts of the circuit follow the contours; others ignore them, and there is a marked disjunction in the line of the double circuit on the west side of the hill, seemingly coinciding with a step in the hillside (Fig. 12.2; Sheridan 2001, 174).

History of investigation

The enclosure was discovered through a research programme set up in 1981 to investigate the catchment of the Six Mile Water between Lyles Hill and Donegore Hill, in the first instance through aerial photography and field walking. Pottery and flint were found in a ploughed field on the top of Donegore Hill, which led in 1982 to more systematic collection of a considerable density of finds, and then to phosphate and magnetic survey. Excavation began in 1983, and during this season, in an unusually dry spell, aerial reconnaissance, which until then had revealed nothing on the hill, suddenly showed a series of interrupted ditches surrounding the summit; the outermost ditch was confirmed by excavation (Mallory and Hartwell 1984). A further two seasons of excavation followed (Mallory 1993).

These established that the enclosure is a circuit formed by two quite closely spaced interrupted ditches, about 3 m wide and 1 m deep, partly rock-cut, and traceable for some three-quarters of the circumference, but so far not visible on the steep south-east portion of the hill (Fig. 12.2; Mallory *et al.* forthcoming). Internal banks were detectable from the air under snow cover, though they were largely invisible on the ground except in one stretch on the north-east side. The area enclosed by the outer ditch measured some 220 by 175 m and occupied some 2.6 ha. A palisade slot usually not more than *c.* 0.5 m wide and 0.6 m deep was encountered inside the inner ditch in sectors E1, E2 and E5, and continued in sector E6 on the steepest side of the hill where no ditches or banks were identified. In sector E1, the site of a probable entrance, the palisade was double. In sector E4, exceptionally, the only palisade slot encountered was between the ditches (Figs 12.2–3; Mallory *et al.* forthcoming). A portion of an outer palisade was found in sector E1, on the west side, but it was located in only one cutting, although the outer ditch was investigated in several. In that one cutting it ran at an oblique angle to the ditch; and it may have been continuous with a linear feature observed on air photographs (Mallory *et al.* forthcoming).

A variety of ditch fills were found (Fig. 12.3), with different sequences in different parts of the circuit. Natural, probably rapid, infilling was recurrent, followed by slower silting, with some recuts and charcoal-rich lenses. In sector E2 the inner ditch had been almost completely filled with rapidly accumulated basalt rubble before it was recut (Mallory *et al.* forthcoming).

While the ditches and palisade slots contained Neolithic material, the bulk of the vast assemblage came from the ploughsoil in cuttings in the interior, which had clearly been badly damaged (Sheridan 2001, 174; Nelis 2003).

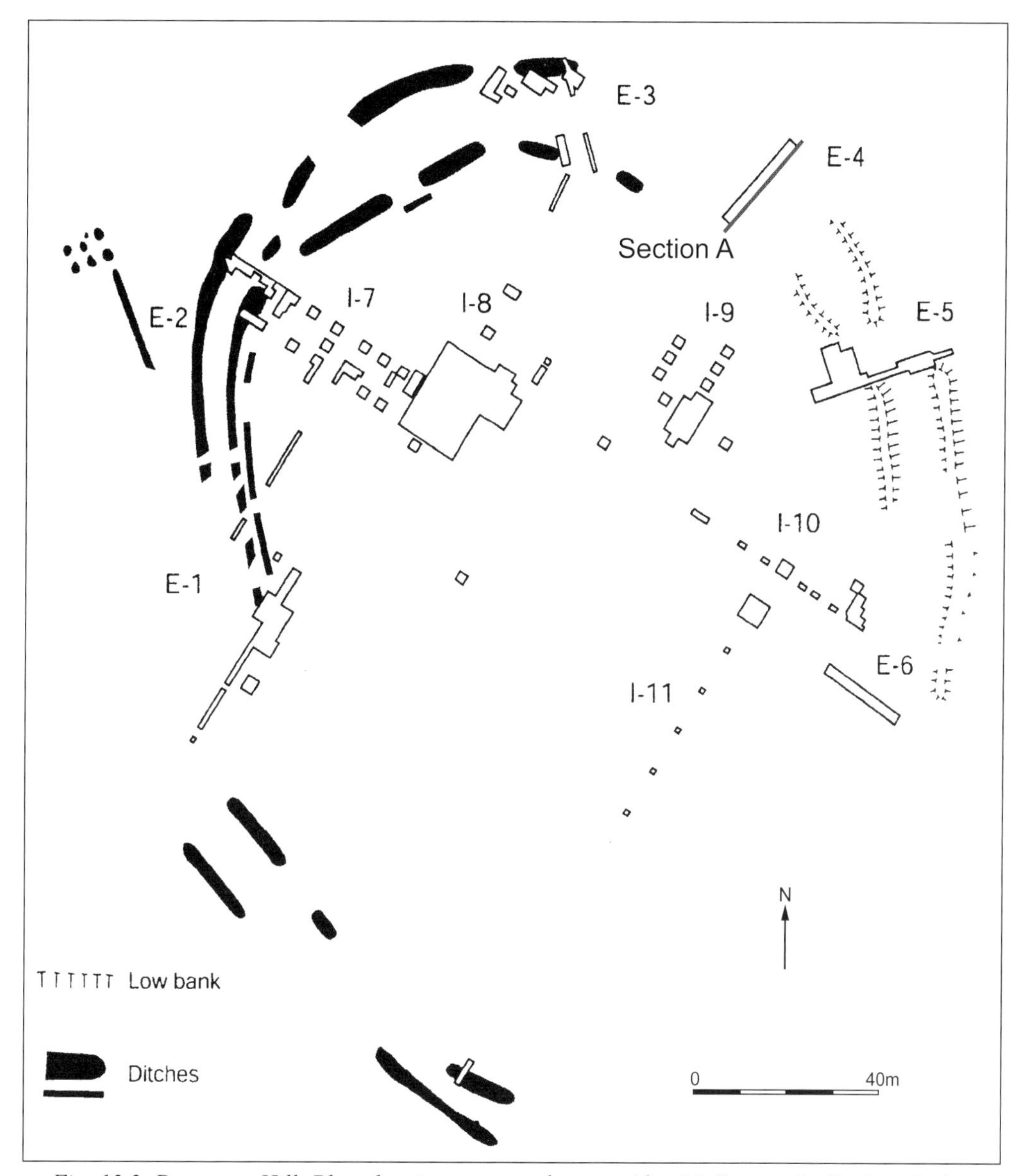

Fig. 12.2. Donegore Hill. Plan showing excavated areas. After Mallory et al. *(forthcoming).*

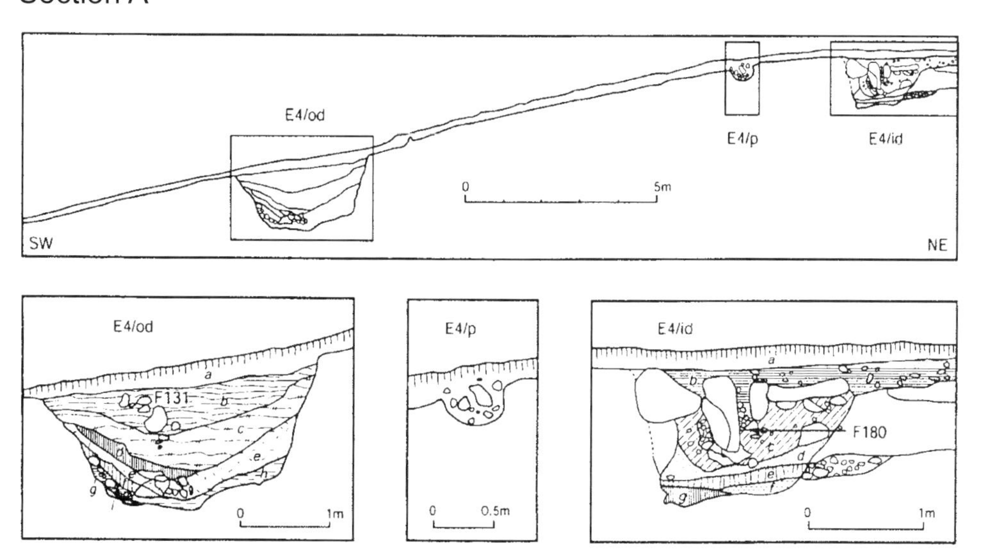

Fig. 12.3. Donegore Hill. Sections through, from left to right, the outer ditch, outer palisade and inner ditch in sector E4. After Mallory et al. *(forthcoming).*

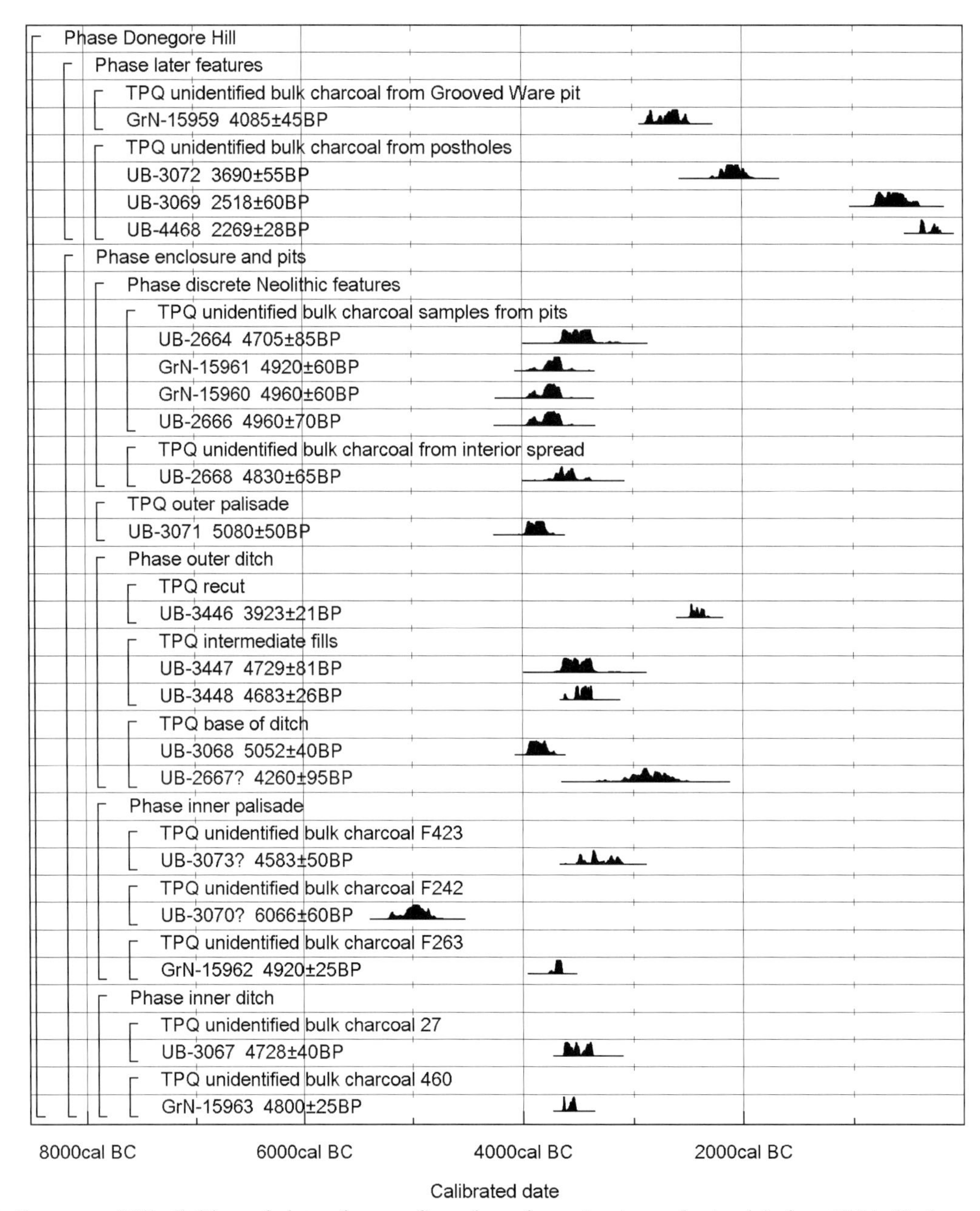

Fig. 12.4. Donegore Hill. Calibrated dates from radiocarbon determinations obtained before 2004 (Stuiver and Reimer 1993).

Several hundred postholes, pits, hearths and other features were found, some post-early Neolithic, but some of early Neolithic date. It has been estimated that least 1500 Neolithic vessels were present, represented by *c.* 45,000 sherds/*c.* 1350 kg of pottery; axeheads included examples of porcellanite from the known sources over 35 km away to the north-east (Sheridan 1995, 7; 2001, 174); and the flaked lithic assemblage amounts to 23,849 pieces (Nelis 2003). Both Carinated and unshouldered plain Bowl pottery, some of it ripple-burnished, was found in the ditches of both circuits and in pits in the interior. Charcoal, carbonised hazelnuts, cereal grains, chaff and weeds were recovered. No unburnt animal bone survived.

Previous dating

Twenty radiocarbon measurements were available before this project, all made on bulk samples of unidentified charcoal. Fifteen samples were dated at the Belfast Radiocarbon Laboratory using methods described by Mook and Waterbolk (1985) and Pearson (1984). The other five samples were similarly pretreated and dated at the University of Groningen by GPC of carbon dioxide as described by Mook and Streurman (1983).

Because the samples were unidentified bulk charcoal, all may have contained material of diverse ages and with significant old wood offsets. Each sample therefore provides a *terminus post quem* for its context. In these circumstances, the results provide only the most general

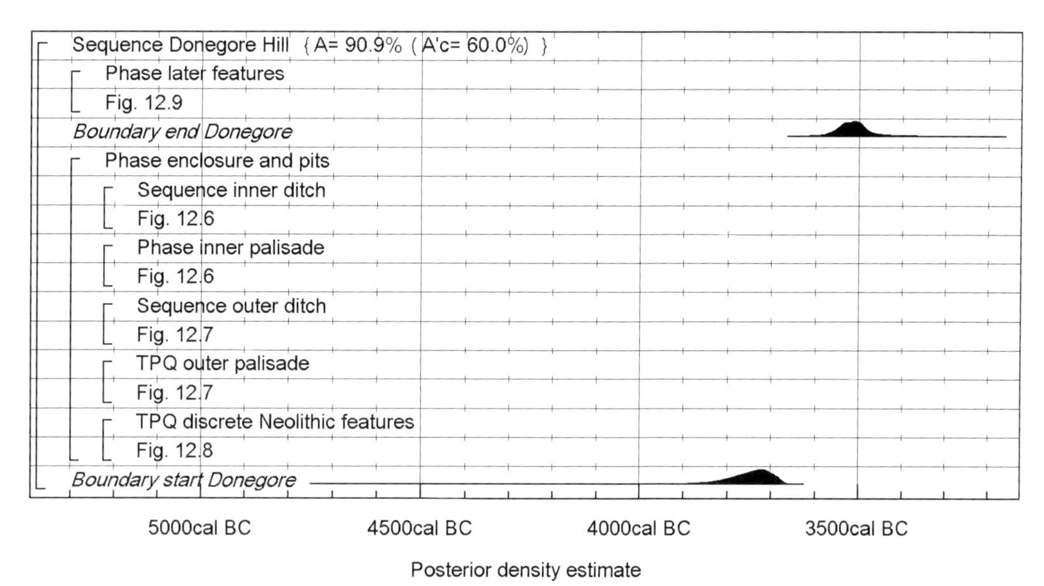

Fig. 12.5. Donegore Hill. Overall structure of the chronological model. The component sections of this model are shown in detail in Figs 12.6–9. The large square brackets down the left-hand side of Figs 12.5–9, along with the OxCal keywords, define the overall model exactly.

indication of the date of the monument. Four pits in the interior yielded fourth millennium cal BC dates (Table 12.1: UB-2664, -2666, GrN-15960–1), as did a spread of material (UB-2668). The inner ditch provided two dates (UB-3067 and GrN-15963) which fall in the mid-fourth millennium cal BC (Fig. 12.4), although neither context is primary. These have been interpreted as providing a *terminus ante quem* of *c.* 3700–3400 cal BC for construction (Mallory *et al.* forthcoming). Three dates from the inner palisade (Table 12.1: GrN-15962, UB-3070, -3073) are widely spaced in time, UB-3073 possibly suggesting a date for this structure in the later fourth millennium cal BC (Fig. 12.4). All three samples were of mixed charcoal, rather than the burnt stumps of posts. Five determinations were obtained from the fills of the outer ditch. From its base, UB-3068 and UB-2667 provided widely divergent ages. UB-2667 was probably from a recut. This recut was identified in a contiguous cutting in the year following its first excavation and was dated by UB-3446 (Mallory *et al.* forthcoming). UB-3068 is thus the only measurement from the base of the outer ditch, the remaining measurements (Table 12.1: UB-3446–8) coming from higher levels. The five have been interpreted as dating the ditch to *c.* 3800–3400 cal BC (Mallory *et al.* forthcoming). A single fourth millennium cal BC date came from the outer palisade (Table 12.1: UB-3071).

The excavator's conclusion, based on a combination of the archaeological evidence and the radiocarbon dates, was that a first phase consisted of the construction of an outer linear palisade (F272, dated by UB-3071 and more extensively traced from air photographs), soon followed by the digging of both ditches and the construction of the inner palisade. Once the ditches were infilled, a second much later phase of activity consisted of recuts and some internal features (Mallory *et al.* forthcoming).

On their own, the radiocarbon dates obtained before 2004 support the division of the site into two principal phases of activity separated by some centuries (Fig. 12.4). The suggested sequence of outer palisade and enclosure construction is, however, based on the spatial relationship of these elements, and cannot be derived from the radiocarbon dates. Because all the samples are *termini post quos* for their contexts, all the activity to which they relate may have occurred within a restricted period in the mid-fourth millennium cal BC (Fig. 12.4).

Objectives of the dating programme

The project sought to refine the existing dating of the site, by obtaining further radiocarbon measurements on short-life material.

Sampling

The relative scarcity of pottery in well stratified ditch deposits and the non-survival of unburnt bone meant that sampling was restricted to charcoal and charred plant remains, which were available thanks to large-scale flotation. It was not possible to find further samples from the outer ditch or the possible outer palisade, or from the lowest levels of the inner ditch.

Results and calibration

Details of all the radiocarbon determinations from Donegore are listed in Table 12.1.

Analysis and interpretation

The overall chronological model for the site is shown in Fig. 12.5, with its components relating to the inner ditch and palisade shown in Fig. 12.6, to the outer ditch and

Table 12.1. Radiocarbon dates from Donegore Hill, Co. Antrim. Posterior density estimates derive from the model defined in Figs 12.5–9.

Laboratory number	Sample reference	Material	Context	Radiocarbon age (BP)	δ^{13}C (‰)	Calibrated date range (cal BC) (95% confidence)	*Posterior density estimate (cal BC) (95% probability)*
Discrete Neolithic features							
UB-2664		Unidentified bulk charcoal sample	Sector I10, Tr 34, F20. Pit	4705±85		3660–3340	*3665–3480*
GrN-15961		Unidentified bulk charcoal sample	Sector I8, Tr 66, F237. Pit	4920±60		3910–3540	*3935–3870 (5%)* or *3810–3630 (89%)* or *3560–3535 (1%)*
GrN-15960		Unidentified bulk charcoal sample	Sector I8, Tr 62, F61. Pit	4960±60		3950–3640	*3945–3855 (16%)* or *3820–3640 (79%)*
UB-2668		Unidentified bulk charcoal sample	Sector I9, Tr 20. Spread in interior of enclosure	4830±65		3710–3380	*3760–3740 (2%)* or *3715–3515 (93%)*
UB-2666		Unidentified bulk charcoal sample	Sector I9, Tr 25, F14. Pit	4960±70		3960–3630	*3945–3635*
GrN-15959		Unidentified bulk charcoal sample	Sector I8, Tr 62, F56. Pit containing 2 Grooved Ware pots	4085±45		2870–2480	
Inner ditch							
GrN-15963		Unidentified bulk charcoal sample	Sector E1, Tr 77, F460. Very dark grey silt 0.22 m thick with large amounts of charcoal mixed with gravel and a small quantity of pottery, deposited when ditch more than half full	4800±25		3650–3520	*3645–3620 (23%)* or *3600–3525 (72%)*
GrA-31328	SQ 46 /A	Single fragment *Corylus avellana* charcoal	Sector E2, Tr 46, F27. Circumscribed charcoal spread 0.12 m thick, and measuring *c.* 0.75 m x 0.30 m, in base of probable recut in segment butt. Neolithic pottery and abundant charred sheep sorrel seeds present. In segment butt opposed to that containing F77, F37, F39, F76	4785±45	−25.8	3660–3380	*3650–3520*
GrA-31330	SQ 46 /B	Single fragment *Corylus avellana* charcoal	From the same context as GrA-31328	4770±35	−26.4	3650–3380	*3640–3520*
UB-3067		Unidentified bulk charcoal sample	From the same context as GrA-31328	4728±40		3640–3370	*3640–3505*
GrA-31331	Ft 29/A	Single fragment *Betula* sp. charcoal	Sector E2, Tr 55, F29. Pit cut into fully silted inner ditch, next to and at same level as F28. South of and stratified above other samples from segment	2210±35	−26.3	390–170	
GrA-31332	Ft 29/B	Single fragment *Corylus avellana* narrow roundwood charcoal	From the same context as GrA-31331	2250±35	−26.7	400–200	
GrA-31337	AG 47 (3)/B	Single fragment *Betula* sp. charcoal	Sector E2, Tr 46, F39 (3). Small pit cut into fill of inner ditch in segment butt opposed to that containing F27. Stratified below F28–F30	2205±35	−25.4	390–170	
GrA-31336	AG 47 (3)/A	Single fragment *Betula* sp. charcoal	From the same context as GrA-31337	2230±35	−26.1	400–190	
GrA-31341	SQ 46 (3)/B	Single fragment *Corylus avellana* charcoal	Sector E2, Tr 46, F76 (3). Charcoal spread beneath large stone (F76), containing Neolithic Bowl pottery, in recut in segment butt opposed to that containing F27. Stratified below F77 and F39	4855±35	−25.5	3710–3530	*3705–3630 (81%)* or *3580–3535 (14%)*
GrA-31339	SQ 46 (3)/A	Single fragment *Corylus avellana* charcoal	From the same context as GrA-31341	4935±40	−26.0	3800–3640	*3750–3640*

Laboratory number	Sample reference	Material	Context	Radiocarbon age (BP)	$\delta^{13}C$ (‰)	Calibrated date range (cal BC) (95% confidence)	*Posterior density estimate (cal BC) (95% probability)*
GrA-31334	SQ 46 /A	Single fragment Pomoideae charcoal	Sector E2, Tr 46, F77. Circumscribed charcoal spread in segment butt opposed to that containing F27. Stratified below F28–F30 and above F76	3995±35	−27.7	2580–2460	
GrA-31335	SQ 46 /B	Single fragment *Corylus avellana* charcoal	From the same context as GrA-31334	4020±35	−25.0	2830–2460	
GrA-31324	SQ 37 /B	Single fragment *Corylus avellana* charcoal	Sector E4, Tr 37, F180, ko 10. Fill of steep-sided ?recut	4955±35	−27.5	3800–3650	*3760–3645*
GrA-31322	SQ 37 /A	Single fragment *Corylus avellana* charcoal	From the same context as GrA-31324	4930±35	−26.0	3790–3640	*3750–3640*
Inner palisade							
UB-3070		Unidentified bulk charcoal sample	Sector E1, Tr 77, F242. One of 2 palisade slots upslope from inner ditch	6066±60		5210–4800	
UB-3073		Unidentified bulk charcoal sample	Sector E1, Tr 86, F423. Palisade slot upslope from inner ditch	4583±50		3500–3100	
GrA-31320	TR 78 (2)/A	Single fragment *Corylus avellana* charcoal	Sector E5, Tr 78, F263. Basal layer of palisade slot packed with stones and a large assemblage of Neolithic pottery, sealed by 0.10 m of silt washed down from upslope	4780±35	−25.9	3650–3380	*3640–3520*
GrA-31321	TR 78 (2)/B	Single fragment *Corylus avellana* charcoal	From the same context as GrA-31320	4790±35	−25.1	3650–3510	*3645–3520*
GrN-15962		Unidentified bulk charcoal sample	From the same context as GrA-31320	4920±25		3770–3640	*3765–3720 (10%)* or *3715–3645 (85%)*
GrA-31326	SQ 50 (3)/B	Single fragment *Corylus avellana* charcoal	Sector E6, F22 (3). Stone-packed palisade trench on E side of hill, where no ditches identified	4805±35	−27.0	3660–3520	*3655–3615 (27%)* or *3610–3520 (68%)*
GrA-31325	SQ 50 (3)/A	Single fragment *Corylus avellana* charcoal	From the same context as GrA-31326	4775±35	−26.7	3650–3380	*3640–3520*
Outer ditch							
UB-3447		Unidentified bulk charcoal sample	Sector E1, Tr 77, F280. Dark brown silt with charcoal 0.10 m thick, descending on to layer of stones with a few Neolithic sherds, an upper fill of the ditch, *c.* 0.80 m above ditch base	4729±81		3660–3350	*3695–3680 (1%)* or *3665–3490 (94%)*
UB-2667		Unidentified bulk charcoal sample	Sector E3, Tr 24. Layer c on base of ditch, 0.20 m of orange-brown gravel, some charcoal and Neolithic bowl pottery, in cutting later extended as Tr 61. Trench 24 was opened and backfilled in 3 days in the final week of the first season's excavation, and nothing corresponding to F34, found in Tr 61 the following year, was recognised	4260±95		3100–2570	
UB-3446		Unidentified bulk charcoal sample	Sector E3, Tr 61, F34. Narrow, slot-like recut into intermediate fill extending to base of ditch, containing dark soil, charcoal and medium to large stones	3923±21		2475–2340	
UB-3068		Unidentified bulk charcoal sample	Sector E3, Tr 61, F51. Charcoal from base of ditch, below stones and gravels of lowest layer	5052±40		3970–3710	*3960–3760 (94%)* or *3725–3710 (1%)*

Laboratory number	Sample reference	Material	Context	Radiocarbon age (BP)	$\delta^{13}C$ (‰)	Calibrated date range (cal BC) (95% confidence)	*Posterior density estimate (cal BC) (95% probability)*
UB-3448		Unidentified bulk charcoal sample	Sector E5, Tr 78, F301. Charcoal lens containing porcellanite axehead in layer of darker grey silt with coarse basalt stones overlying lowest layer of ditch	4683±26		3630–3360	*3635–3575 (63%)* or *3535–3485 (32%)*
Outer palisade							
UB-3071		Unidentified bulk charcoal sample	Sector E1, Tr 77, F272. Palisade trench converging with outer ditch	5080±50		3980–3710	*3980–3760*
Later contexts							
UB-3072		Unidentified bulk charcoal sample	Sector I8st, Tr 80, F296. Posthole of stockade on summit	3690±55		2280–1920	
UB-3069		Unidentified bulk charcoal sample	Sector I8cs, Tr 62, F130. Posthole of penannular post-built structure on summit	2518±60		810–400	
UB-4468		Unidentified bulk charcoal sample	Sector I8cs, Tr 62, F111. Posthole of penannular post-built structure on summit	2269±28		400–210	

possible palisade in Fig. 12.7, to discrete interior features in Fig. 12.8 and to later features in Fig. 12.9.

The inner ditch. There were neither suitable samples nor pre-existing measurements from the lowest levels. The dated samples are from upper fills and recuts, most of them scattered around the circuit without stratigraphic relation to each other. In sector E1, an unidentified bulk charcoal sample (Fig. 12.6: *GrN-15963*) comes from the charcoal-rich layer F460, deposited when the ditch was more than half full. This result is treated as a *terminus post quem* for the layers above it. In sector E4, two statistically consistent measurements (Fig. 12.6: *GrA-31322, -31324*; T'=0.3; T'(5%)=3.8; ν=1) were made on short-life samples from a probable recut, F180, made when the ditch was almost fully silted (Fig. 12.3). In trench 46 of sector E2, the opposed butts of two segments were excavated. F27, a discrete charcoal spread in a recut made into a rapid accumulation of basalt rubble in one butt, yielded two short-life samples (Fig. 12.6: *GrA-31328, -31330*) and an unidentified bulk sample (Fig. 12.6: *UB-3067*). These provide statistically consistent measurements (T'=1.0; T'(5%)=6.0; ν=2). Because the unidentified sample is statistically consistent with the two short-life samples, the model treats it as close in age to this deposit. In the butt of the other segment, which was also more than half-filled with rapidly accumulated basalt fragments, a sequence of samples was dated from a further recut. The lowest of these was a charcoal spread, F76(3), from which there were two short-life samples which provided further statistically consistent measurements dating to the second quarter of the fourth millennium cal BC (Fig. 12.6: *GrA-31339, -31341*; T'=2.3; T'(5%)=3.8; ν=1). Samples from overlying contexts were submitted in the expectation that they too would date to the fourth millennium cal BC. In the event, however, two short-life samples from F77, a charcoal spread overlying F76, provided statistically consistent measurements in the early third millennium cal BC (Fig. 12.9: GrA-31334–5; T'=0.3; T'(5%)=3.8; ν=1); and two further short-life samples from pit F39, which was cut into the ditch, dated to the first millennium cal BC (Fig. 12.9: GrA-31336–7; T'=0.3; T'(5%)=3.8; ν=1). In Trench 55 in the same sector, 5 m to the south-west, two further short-life samples from F29, a scoop cut into the top of the silted ditch, also dated to the first millennium cal BC (Fig. 12.9: GrA-31331–2; T'=0.7; T'(5%)=3.8; ν=1). These later features do not form part of the initial construction and use of the enclosure but demonstrate that its earthworks remained visible and were a focus for later activity.

On this basis, the construction date for the inner ditch can be estimated as *3810–3660 cal BC* (*95% probability*; Fig. 12.6: *build inner ditch*), probably *3750–3675 cal BC* (*68% probability*). As no samples have been dated from the base of the ditch, it is possible that the circuit was dug slightly earlier than this. It would be difficult to argue for an extended interval, since both sector E2 F27 (the source of the samples for UB-3067, GrA-31328 and -31330) and sector E2 F76 (the source of the samples for GrA-31339 and -31341) directly succeeded undifferentiated fills of basalt rubble which had accumulated rapidly on the ditch base.

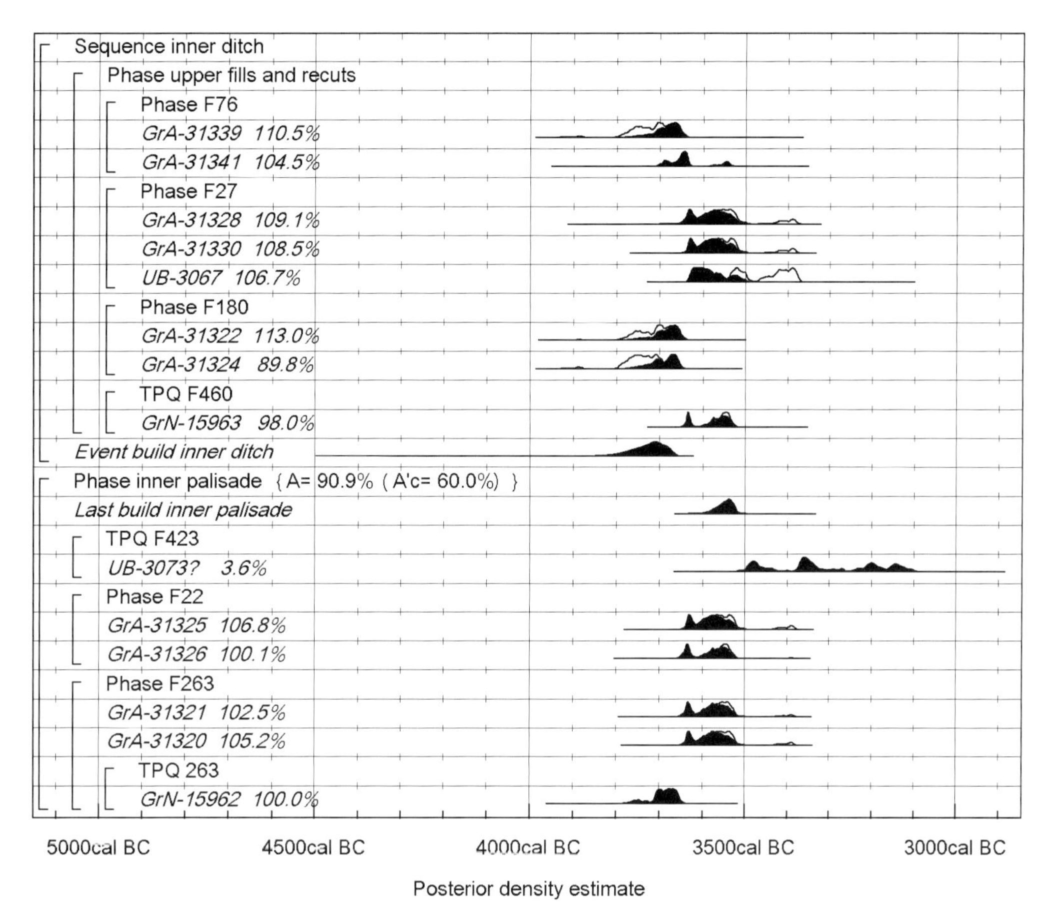

Fig. 12.6. Donegore Hill. Probability distributions of dates from the inner ditch and palisade. Each distribution represents the relative probability that an event occurred at a particular time. For each of the dates two distributions have been plotted, one in outline which is the result produced by the scientific evidence alone, and a solid one which is based on the chronological model used. The other distributions correspond to aspects of the model. For example, the distribution 'build inner ditch' is the estimated date when the inner ditch at Donegore was dug. Dates followed by a question mark have been calibrated (Stuiver and Reimer 1993), but not included in the chronological model for reasons explained in the text. The overall structure of this model is shown in Fig. 12.5, and its other components in Figs 12.7–9.

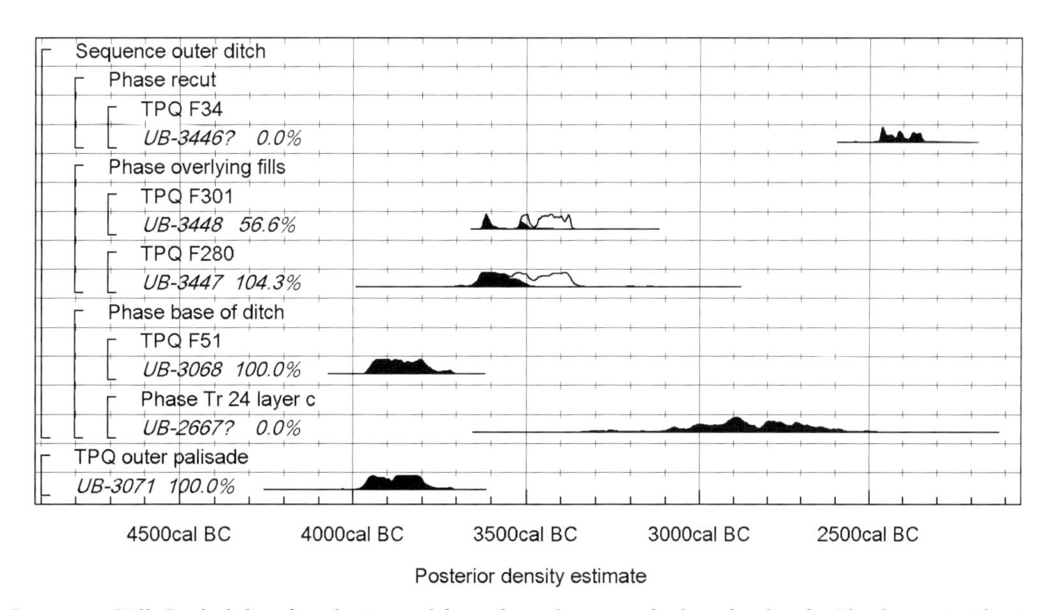

Fig. 12.7. Donegore Hill. Probability distributions of dates from the outer ditch and palisade. The format is identical to that of Fig. 12.6. The overall structure of this model is shown in Fig. 12.5, and its other components in Figs 12.6 and 12.8–9.

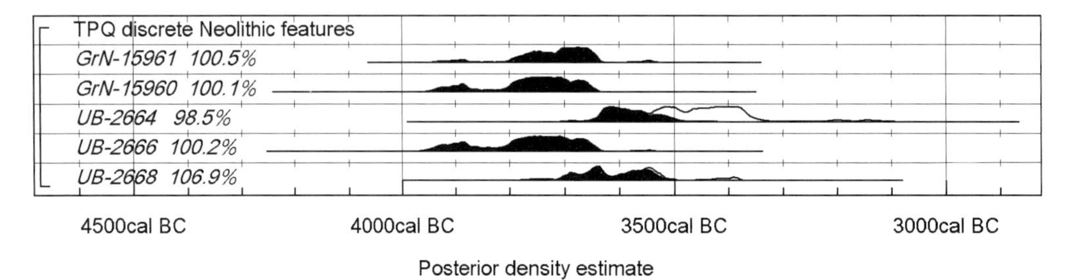

Fig. 12.8. Donegore Hill. Probability distributions of dates from discrete interior features. The format is identical to that of Fig. 12.6. The overall structure of this model is shown in Fig. 12.5, and its other components in Figs 12.6–7 and 12.9.

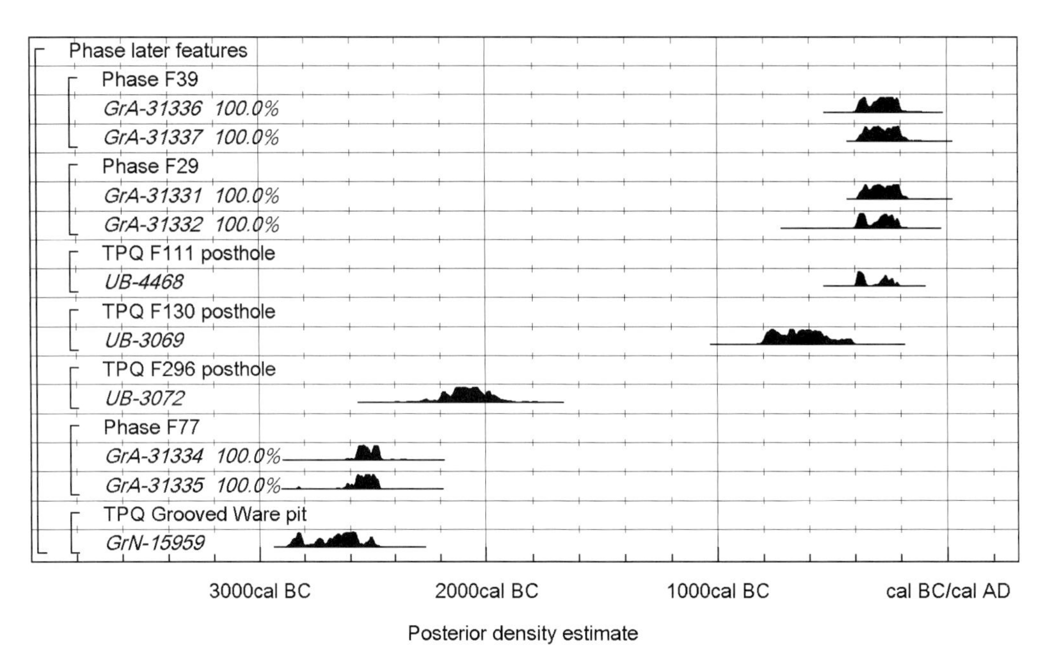

Fig. 12.9. Donegore Hill. Probability distributions of dates from later features. The format is identical to that of Fig. 12.6. The overall structure of this model is shown in Fig. 12.5, and its other components in Figs 12.6–8.

The inner palisade. In sector E5, palisade trench F263 provided two statistically consistent measurements (Fig. 12.6: *GrA-31320–1*; T'=0.0; T'(5%)=3.8; ν=1). A measurement on an unidentified bulk charcoal sample from the same context (Fig. 12.6: *GrN-15962*) is inconsistent with these (T'=14.8; T'(5%)=6.0; ν=2), and is treated as a *terminus post quem* for the feature. In sector E6, where no ditch accompanied the palisade, F22 provided two further short-life samples (Fig. 12.6: *GrA-31325–6*), results from which are statistically consistent with each other (T'=0.4; T'(5%)=3.8; ν=1) and with those for the short-life samples from F263 (T'=0.4; T'(5%)=7.8; ν=3). In sector E1, an unidentified bulk charcoal sample from F242, the outer of two converging palisade slots, provided a date in the late sixth to early fifth millennium cal BC (Table 12.1: UB-3070). This is excluded from the model on the grounds that the sample must have included already old charcoal, although a preliminary account of the lithics gives no indication that Mesolithic artefacts were present (Nelis 2003). Twenty-five metres to the north, an unidentified bulk charcoal sample from F423, the only palisade slot in Trench 86 in the same sector, provided a date in the second half of the fourth millennium cal BC (Fig. 12.6: UB-3073). This is statistically inconsistent with, and more recent than, all four dates on short-life samples from the inner palisade (T'=15.0; T'(5%)=9.5; ν=4). F423 was extremely shallow (Mallory *et al.* forthcoming, fig. 3.7). Given this and the statistical inconsistency with the short-life material, there must be some possibility that this sample contained later, intrusive, material. For this reason, it has been excluded from the model.

On this basis, the date of the inner palisade can be estimated as *3600–3515 cal BC* (*95% probability*; Fig. 12.6: *build inner palisade*), probably *3565–3520 cal BC* (*68% probability*).

The outer ditch. This provided no new samples. The existing measurements on bulk charcoal samples are all treated as *termini post quos*. In sector E3, *UB-3068* (Fig. 12.7) was measured on a sample from F51 on the base of the ditch in Trench 61. UB-2667 (Fig. 12.7), from Trench 24 in the same sector, is excluded from the model because it probably came from a late Neolithic recut, as discussed above. From a contiguous cutting, UB-3446 (Fig. 12.7) also seems to derive from a later recut. This sample has been excluded from the model since it appears to relate to a later third millennium cal BC phase of activity on the site rather

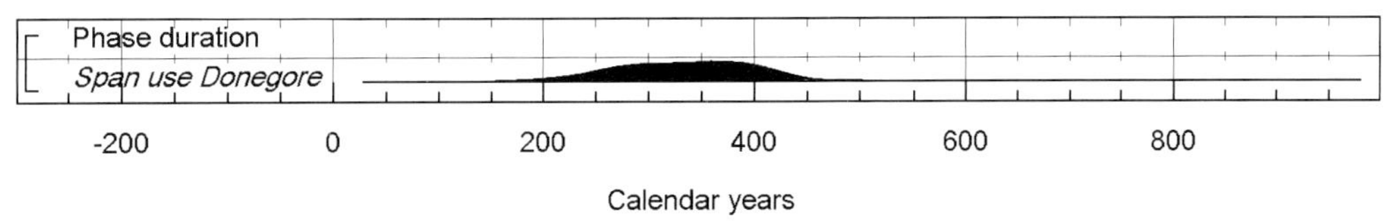

Fig. 12.10. Donegore Hill. Probability distribution of the number of years during which the enclosure was in primary use, derived from the model shown in Figs 12.5–9.

than the main Neolithic use. If it is included, the model has poor overall agreement ($A_{overall}$=55.6%). *UB-3448*, from the charcoal lens F301 in sector E5, and *UB-3447*, from the silt and charcoal layer F280 in sector E1, provide further measurements from the upper levels (Fig. 12.7).

These results do not provide a robust estimate for the date when the outer ditch was constructed. *UB-3068* (Fig. 12.7) provides a *terminus post quem* of *3960–3760 cal BC (94% probability)* or *3725–3710 cal BC (1% probability)*, probably *3960–3855 cal BC (49% probability)* or *3845–3830 cal BC (5% probability)* or *3825–3790 cal BC (14% probability)*, although the actual ditch construction could be several centuries later than this.

The outer palisade. This remains dated only by the *terminus post quem* provided by *UB-3071* (*95% probability*; *3980–3760 cal BC*; probably *3955–3905 cal BC, 24% probability* or *3880–3800 cal BC, 44% probability*; Fig. 12.7), although again the actual construction of the palisade may be some centuries later than this.

Five samples of unidentified bulk charcoal provide *termini post quos* for features in the interior of the enclosure (four pits and an occupation spread; Fig. 12.8; Table 12.1). All these features appear to belong to the fourth millennium cal BC use of the site.

Overall, the model defined in Figs 12.5–9 suggests that the early Neolithic activity on Donegore Hill began in *3855–3665 cal BC* (*95% probability*; Fig. 12.5: *start Donegore*), probably in *3780–3685 cal BC* (*68% probability*). This primary activity ended in *3590–3430 cal BC* (*95% probability*; Fig. 12.5: *end Donegore*), probably in *3545–3485 cal BC* (*68% probability*). Early Neolithic activity on the hill spanned a period of *200–455 years* (*95% probability*; Fig. 12.10: *use Donegore*), probably *270–410 years* (*68% probability*).

Some later activity has been dated on the hill (Fig. 12.9). There may be two discrete episodes of later activity. The first fell in the middle centuries of the third millennium cal BC, perhaps associated with Grooved Ware (GrN-15959, from F56, a pit in the interior) and with recutting of parts of the enclosure ditches (F77, in the inner ditch; and F34, Fig. 12.7, in the outer ditch). A second episode of activity took place in the third quarter of the first millennium cal BC (here dated by GrA-31331–2, from F29 and GrA-31336–7, from F39 (3), both pits cut into the silted up inner ditch, and by UB-4468 and UB-3069, bulk samples of unidentified charcoal from postholes providing *termini post quos* for this activity: Fig. 12.9).

Implications for the site

In the area of roughly 30 km by 30 km around Donegore Hill – between Lough Neagh to the west and Larne on the Irish Sea coast to the east, and from the Glencloy River to the north and the Lagan River to the south – eleven houses of the early Neolithic rectangular tradition have been discovered. These are at Ballygalley (*c.* 4; D. Simpson 1993; 1996; John Ó Néill, pers. comm.), Ballyharry (2; Moore 2003), Ballyharry Farm (1; Ó Néill *et al.* 2004), Mullaghbuoy (1; McManus 2004), Broughshane (1; Paul Logue, pers. comm.), Ballymacoss (1; Warren Bailie, pers. comm.) and Aghalislane (1; Ruairí Ó Baoill, pers. comm.). The dated examples are discussed below. While the scale of and evidence from the timber houses suggest the activities of individual family groups, Mallory, in pointing out that construction of the ditches at Donegore would have required about 18,000 labour hours, has proposed a workforce for the enclosure composed of several such family groups (Mallory and McNeill 1991, 78). The sheer quantity of material from the Donegore excavation also suggests the activities of a considerable number of people. For example, whether the partially excavated enclosure was permanently settled or only occasionally used and occupied on a periodic basis, it should be noted that it has produced an artefact assemblage that is vastly different to the size of the average assemblage from early Neolithic houses.

On the evidence of antiquarian collections, especially that of W. J. Knowles, large early Neolithic assemblages seem to have been present in some parts of the Antrim plateau to the north and in the valleys of the rivers that flow east from the plateau watershed through the Antrim Glens into the Irish Sea and those flowing west from it to form tributaries of the Bann. The floor of the Bann valley itself has also produced Neolithic material but there is a particularly Mesolithic character to the collections from there (Woodman *et al.* 2006, 297–304). It seems likely that people living in these areas, those using the Donegore enclosure and those using the houses were connected through social ties, reflected in the archaeological record as distribution or exchange networks, which also extended across the Irish Sea to south-west Scotland (Cooney 2000a, 227). County Antrim has yielded numerous caches of flint artefacts, especially scrapers (Woodman *et al.* 2006, 201–42) and has the highest numbers of flint and stone axeheads in the island (Cooney and Mandal 1998, figs 3.3, 4.29). Some of the coastal house sites, such as Ballygalley (Simpson 1995) and Ballyharry (Moore 2003), have yielded substantial lithic assemblages of both imported and locally sourced artefacts. Derek Simpson (1996, 132), referring particularly to the presence of pitchstone from Arran, suggested that Ballygalley played a role in the circulation of lithics along the coast and across the Irish Sea. Donegore may have had a role in the movement of materials from the Antrim coast inland along river routes such as the Six Mile Water into the Lough Neagh basin.

In terms of sites that may have had a similar role to Donegore, on Lyles Hill, on the opposite side of the Six Mile Water valley and 7 km south-east from Donegore Hill, there is another well known hill top enclosed Neolithic site. However, as discussed in detail below, the palisades there may be no earlier than the third millennium cal BC and the embanked enclosure (E. Evans 1953) may be of second millennium cal BC date. While the date of the cairn within the enclosure is unclear, Alison Sheridan (2006a) has argued that it is one of a number of examples of a non-megalithic early Neolithic funerary tradition (see also discussion in Nelis 2004, 164). The Lyles Hill lithic assemblage has characteristics that indicate activity both in the early and middle Neolithic (Nelis 2004, 158, 164). There were differences between Lyles Hill and Donegore Hill in the amounts and types of tools produced, some of which may reflect the greater extent of later activity at Lyles Hill. Modified tools counted for 11% of the Lyles Hill assemblage but just 1% of the Donegore material. A greater proportion of hollow scrapers (which appear to develop at some point in the early Neolithic and to be dominant in middle Neolithic assemblages) were recovered at Lyles Hill than at Donegore Hill: 20 in *c.* 5500 pieces, compared with 1 in *c.* 25,000 (Nelis 2003, 216). Much effort appears to have gone into the production of projectiles and knives at Donegore Hill (Nelis 2003, 216). At Lyles Hill it is projectiles and hollow scrapers that stand out in the assemblage. The two enclosures are roughly equidistant from a small Cretaceous flint outcrop at Templepatrick in the Six Mile Water valley (Paul Logue, pers. comm.).

At Squires Hill, a hilltop site 7 km south-east of Lyles Hill and Donegore Hill (E. Evans 1938), a very large Neolithic biface and arrowhead assemblage was recovered, but only one finished arrowhead. Technologically, the assemblages from all these three sites were similar (Nelis 2004, 158) but at Donegore, Lyles Hill, and at the coastal promontory flint extraction and occupation site at Ballygalley Hill (A. Collins 1978), smaller leaf-shaped bifaces were dominant.

The Donegore enclosure thus can be set in local and regional contexts with considerable early Neolithic evidence. Whatever doubt there may be about the dating of the enclosing elements at Lyles Hill, it seems likely that particular hilltops were chosen as the focus of communal activity.

12.2 Magheraboy, Magheraboy townland, Co. Sligo, Irish grid reference 168690 335180

Location and topography

The Magheraboy enclosure is on the Cúil Irra peninsula, between Ballysadare Bay and Sligo Harbour. It is located 2 km north-east of the Carrowmore passage tomb cemetery, *c.* 50 m above sea level, off the summit of a domed south-west to north-east ridge (Figs 12.1 and 12.11). The highest point on the peninsula is Knocknarea at its western end, crowned by the passage tomb of Maeve's Cairn or Grave and smaller tombs. Carns Hill at the eastern end of the peninsula, with further passage tombs, is the next highest point (Bergh 1995; Cooney 2000a, with references). The Magheraboy ridge is intervisible with both these hills, as well as affording panoramic views of the surrounding countryside. The underlying geology is limestone, with overlying morainic deposits (Danaher 2004; Danaher and Cagney 2005; Danaher 2007, 91–3). Further indications of the complexity of the peninsula's prehistory are given by the recognition of a discontinuous stone-built bank, locally tripled, around the north and east of Knocknarea (Bergh 2000; 2002) and by discoveries in the Caltragh valley to the south of Magheraboy, including a possible megalithic tomb and an arc of stone wall built along the margin of marsh and drier ground, subsequently covered by peat and underlying two *fulachta fiadh*. The wall was formed of large upright stones with smaller stones packed between them and incorporated three stone axeheads (two of mudstone and one of gabbro) and two deposits of burnt animal bone. The wall, in which there was an entrance, continued beyond the excavated area, and it may have formed part of an enclosure or of a field system. The incorporated axeheads may indicate a Neolithic date or have been incorporated from nearby Neolithic occupation (Danaher 2007, 61–70).

Magheraboy is also near to other well known Neolithic sites and complexes (Fig. 12.1). To the west along the north Mayo coast there are areas of pre-peat field systems, notably at the Céide Fields (Caulfield 1983; Caulfield *et al.* 1998; Cooney 2000a, 25–9), about 50 km west of Magheraboy.

History of investigation

The Magheraboy enclosure was excavated in 2003 in advance of the construction of a new relief road running south from Sligo town (Danaher 2004; Danaher and Cagney 2005; Danaher 2007). Known archaeology in the immediate vicinity included a ringfort, and test excavation of this revealed a palisade trench cut by the ringfort ditch and running inside two segments of discontinuous ditch. More extensive topsoil stripping along the ridge revealed further stretches of palisade and further ditch segments. Excavation was widened within the area of the road-take. Over 1 ha of the eastern portion of the site was excavated. This showed an incomplete circuit, of irregular shape, possibly open on the east side, with a maximum dimension of 150 m and an estimated total area of 2.02 ha (Figs 12.11–12). The single segmented ditch circuit was generally accompanied by an internal palisade; but no ditch was seen at the north of the site in the north-west part of zone 2 where the palisade went on as a near-continuous line, nor in zone 4 to the east, where the palisade was formed of staggered, unconnected, short stretches. A possible entrance was marked by two opposed

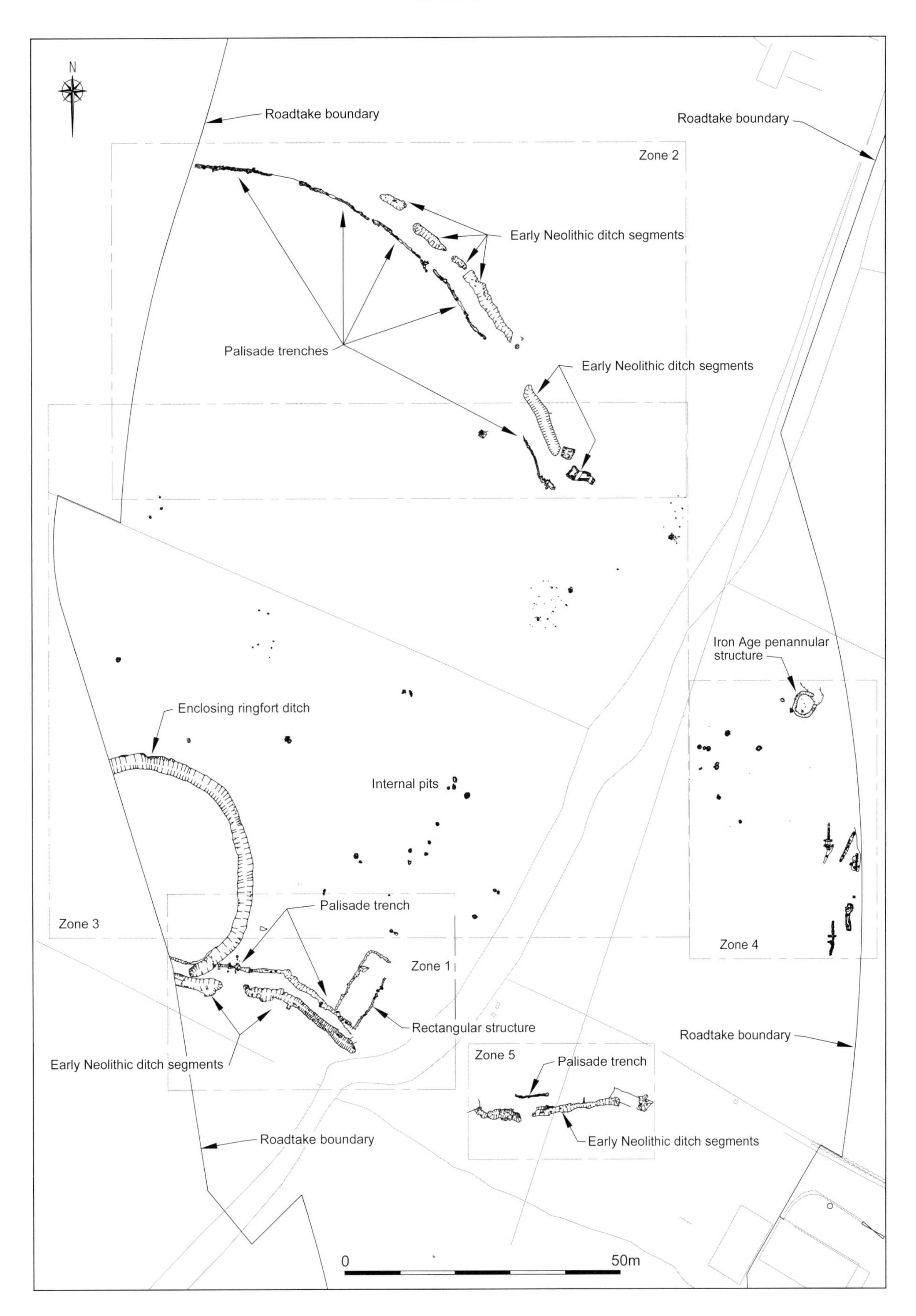

Fig. 12.11. Magheraboy. Plan showing Neolithic features; the later ring fort; and the extent of the landtake. After Danaher and Cagney 2005. © Archaeological Consultancy Services Ltd.

Fig. 12.12. Magheraboy. The ditch under excavation in zone 2 (location shown in Fig. 12.11). © Archaeological Consultancy Services Ltd.

inturned segment butts in the north-east, and there was a concave stretch in the south, where a 14 m-long rectangular timber structure was built at right-angles to and continuous with the palisade on its inner side. This structure survived as shallow, stone-packed slots, with no indication of any load-bearing posts, and is thus likely to have been open rather than roofed (Danaher 2007, 104–6).

Ditch segments varied in size, from over 20 m long, over 1.5 m wide and 0.7 m deep, with U-profiles and flat bases, to what were little more than shallow, elongated pits (Fig. 12.13). Carinated Bowl sherds and a small number of lithics were recovered from the ditch fills. These included three axeheads. One made from mudstone was found in segment 1 in zone 5, surrounded by some 30 quartz crystals. The butt of a porcellanite (Group IX) axehead that appeared to have been deliberately broken before deposition (Mandal 2007) was found with pottery and other lithics on the base of the ditch towards the north-west terminal of segment 3 in zone 2. There was also the butt of a limestone axehead in the same context. Farther to the south-east, on the base of the segment were fragments of a charred oak plank or planks. The segment was then backfilled but later recut, the recut avoiding the earlier placed deposit. Further deposition took place, with subsequent backfilling.

Much of the palisade was built in short stretches and was formed by post-pits and split timber planks, with stone packing (and early Neolithic Carinated Bowl sherds). In zone 5 at the south-east end of the site, the palisade was formed by close-set postholes, *c.* 0.25 m wide and deep.

Fifty-five pits were identified in the interior of the enclosure, along with some postholes. The majority of pits were small, from 0.4 to 0.9 m in diameter, and mainly only 0.2 m deep. These contained early Neolithic material, including deliberately broken sherds of pottery, some leaf-shaped arrowheads, scrapers and blades, lumps of fired clay, scraps of burnt bone and carbonised cereals (Danaher 2004; Danaher and Cagney 2005; Danaher 2007).

The artefact assemblage of 303 struck lithics (mainly chert) and 1229 Neolithic sherds, representing at least 36 vessels, from this extensively excavated site contrasts, as Danaher points out (2007, 117), with that of 23,849 struck lithics (mainly flint) and *c.* 45,000 Neolithic sherds from Donegore, which is of comparable size but of which only some 3% was excavated. The ratios of sherds to struck lithics are also different: 4:1 and 2:1 respectively. Several factors may contribute to this, not least the abundance of flint in Antrim, the fact that almost all of the Donegore assemblage came from topsoil and disturbed contexts (Nelis 2003, 208), while topsoil was removed by machine at Magheraboy, and the fact that later lithics were present at Donegore. Nonetheless, some of these differences could derive from distinct uses of the two enclosures.

Previous dating

Sixteen radiocarbon results were available from Neolithic contexts at Magheraboy before the start of this project. All samples were dated by Beta Analytic Inc according to

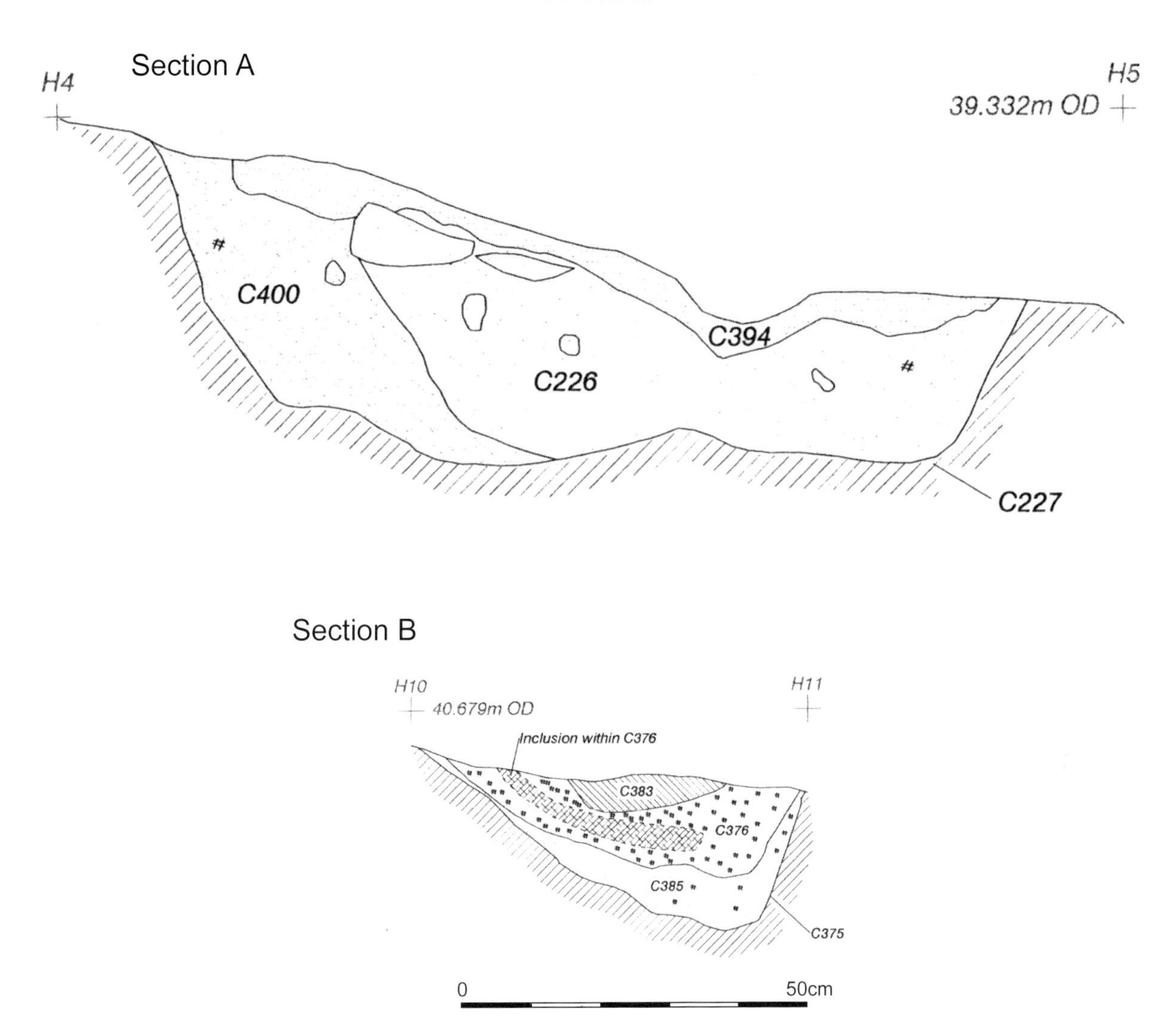

Fig. 12.13. Magheraboy. Sections of zone 2 segment 6 and zone 5 segment 2 (locations shown in Fig. 12.11). After Danaher and Cagney 2005. © Archaeological Consultancy Services Ltd.

methods outlined at http://radiocarbon.com/analytic.htm. Ten samples were measured by AMS and are denoted by an asterisk in Table 12.2; the other six samples were dated by LSC (Chapter 2.4).

A chronological model integrating the stratigraphic information from the site with these radiocarbon results is shown in Fig. 12.14. Three sequences are available from the enclosure ditch. In zone 2, segment 3 a sample of oak charcoal was dated from a plank lying on the base of the ditch (Fig. 12.14: *Beta-186488*). Because of the potential for an age offset in this sample it has been treated as a *terminus post quem* for its context. An AMS measurement on mixed short-life species of charcoal came from a stratigraphically later context also close to the base of the ditch (*Beta-199989*). In zone 5, segment 1, several fragments of *Corylus avellana* were dated from a context on the base of the segment (*Beta-199986*). This short-life sample was stratigraphically earlier than a bulk sample of *Corylus avellana* dated from the main fill of the segment (*Beta-199988*). In zone 5, segment 2, *Beta-199987*, an AMS determination on more than one fragment of *Corylus* charcoal came from a tip of charred material lying directly on the bottom of the ditch and occupying the entire depth of the ditch butt. Probably later than this is *Beta-199985*, from a middle fill further along the segment. This was overlain by *Beta-199984*, an AMS measurement on short-life charcoal. This evidence suggests that the enclosure ditch was constructed in *4050–3925 cal BC* (*95% probability*; Fig. 12.14: *build Magheraboy enclosure*), probably in *4040–4015 cal BC* (*30% probability*) or *3995–3960 cal BC* (*38% probability*).

Nine more dates were obtained from discrete features within the enclosure. These may provide an indication for the period in which the enclosure was in use (Fig. 12.14). There were a further six dates from later features (Table 12.2).

Objectives of the dating programme

The project aimed to refine the dating of the enclosure ditch and to confirm the early construction date suggested by the previous dating programme.

Table 12.2. Radiocarbon dates from Magheraboy, Co. Sligo. Posterior density estimates derive from the model defined in Figs 12.15.

Laboratory number	Sample reference	Material	Context	Radiocarbon age (BP)	$\delta^{13}C$ (‰)	Weighted mean (BP)	Calibrated date range (cal BC) (95% confidence)	*Posterior density estimate (cal BC) (95% probability)*
Enclosure ditch								
OxA-16037	03E538F226S135/C	Single fragment *Corylus avellana* charcoal	Zone 2 segment 6. Context 226. Lower fill of F227, below 394, sometimes on base, sometimes above 400 (Danaher and Cagney 2005, figs 12, 20)	5014±37	−24.9		3950–3700	*3945–3705*
GrA-31959	03E538F226S135/A	Single fragment Pomoideae charcoal	From the same context as OxA-16037	4915±40	−25.4		3780–3630	*3775–3640*
Beta-199989*	03E538C169S159	Pomoideae and *Corylus* sp. charcoal	Zone 2 segment 3. Context 169. On base of NW butt of segment F82, over 203 at its SE end (Danaher and Cagney 2005, fig. 21)	5090±40	−25.9		3975–3785	*3920–3765*
Beta-186488	03E538F203S119	*Quercus* sp. charcoal, from the same plank as GrA-319161, OxA-X-2173-16	Zone 2 segment 3. Context 203. One of two fragments of charred plank on base of SE of segment F82, there underlying 169 (Danaher and Cagney 2005, fig. 21)	5060±70	−26.0	5085±35 T'=0.0; T'(5%)=3.8; v=1	3970–3780	*3990–3800*
GrA-31961	Context 290/A	Single fragment *Quercus* sp. sapwood charcoal. Replicate of OxA-X-2173-16	Zone 2 segment 3. Context 290. From one of two fragments of charred plank on base of F82 (Danaher and Cagney 2005, fig. 21)	5085±40	−24.8			*3965–3810*
OxA-X-2173-16	Context 290/B	Single fragment *Quercus* sp. sapwood charcoal. Replicate of GrA-319161	From the same plank fragment as GrA–319161	5270±40	−25.1		4240–3970	
Beta-199986*	03E538C371S195	>1 fragment *Corylus avellana* charcoal	Zone 5 segment 1. Context 371. Within context 370 on base of segment F320, under 321 (Danaher and Cagney 2005, fig. 55)	5030±40	−25.5		3955–3705	*3955–3760*
Beta-199988	03E538C321S176	Bulk sample of *Corylus avellana* charcoal	Zone 5 segment 1. Context 321. Main fill of segment F320, overlying 370 (Danaher and Cagney 2005, figs 54, 55)	5080±90	−26.1		4045–3655	*3910–3655*
Beta-199987*	03E538C323S203	*Corylus* sp. charcoal, probably >1 fragment	Zone 5 segment 2. Context 323. Fill of W butt of segment F322. ?tipped in, lying directly on bottom and occupying entire depth of butt (Danaher and Cagney 2005, figs 54, 56)	5150±40	−26.2		4040–3805	*4045–3925* (73%) or *3880–3815* (22%)
GrA-31960	03E538C376S226/C	Single fragment *Corylus avellana* charcoal	Zone 5 segment 2. Context 376. A middle fill of segment F375, with oxidised clay and many charcoal flecks. Dump? Below 383 and above 385 (Danaher and Cagney 2005, figs 54, 56)	4860±40	−25.5		3710–3530	*3715–3625* (82%) or *3590–3530* (13%)
OxA-16021	03E538C376S226/D	Single fragment *Corylus avellana* charcoal	Zone 5 segment 2. Context 376. A middle fill of segment F375, with oxidised clay and many charcoal flecks. Dump? Below 383 and above 385 (Danaher and Cagney 2005, figs 54, 56)	4870±37	−25.4		3710–3540	*3715–3630* (91%) or *3565–3535* (4%)
Beta-199985*	03E538C382S231	>1 fragment *Corylus avellana* charcoal	Zone 5 segment 2. Context 382. A middle fill of segment F375, beneath 378 and above 418 (Danaher and Cagney 2005, figs 54, 56)	5230±60	−25.0		4235–3950	*4030–3925* (48%) or *3880–3795* (47%)

Laboratory number	Sample reference	Material	Context	Radiocarbon age (BP)	$\delta^{13}C$ (‰)	Weighted mean (BP)	Calibrated date range (cal BC) (95% confidence)	*Posterior density estimate (cal BC) (95% probability)*
Beta-199984*	03E538C425S236	*Corylus avellana*, charcoal, probably >1 fragment	Zone 5 segment 2. Context 425. Fill of recut in top of segment F375 (Danaher and Cagney 2005, fig. 56)	5160±60	−25.7		4055–3795	*4225–4205 (1%)* or *4165–4130 (3%)* or *4075–3790 (91%)*
Discrete Neolithic features								
Beta-197649*	03E0536F3S5	>1 fragment charred hazelnut shell	F3. Pit containing Carinated Bowl pottery (O'Neil 2005a, figs 4, 7; pl. 15)	4910±40	−22.3		3780–3630	*3775–3635*
Beta-197653*	03E0536F69S36	> 1 fragment *Corylus* sp. charcoal	F69. Stray charcoal in postpit of one posthole among several forming an arc within the ringfort, inside the causewayed enclosure (O'Neil 2005a, figs 3, 7). Sub-circular, 0.56 m x 0.40 m, 0.13 m deep, probably truncated. Contained fragment of rock crystal	4790±40	−25.2		3650–3380	*3650–3520*
Beta-186486	03E538F126S90	Bulk sample of *Quercus* sp. charcoal	Context 126. Fill of pit F125 within enclosure, containing Neolithic Bowl pottery	5150±110	−25.0		4240–3700	*4240–3705*
Beta-186487	03E538F148S92	Bulk sample of *Quercus* sp. charcoal	Context 148. 1 of 3 fills of pit F147 within enclosure, containing Neolithic Bowl pottery	4880±70	−26.3		3800–3520	*3895–3880 (1%)* or *3800–3520 (94%)*
Beta-196298*	03E538C230S123	>1 grain charred hexaploid wheat	Context 230. Fill of pit F221	4660±40	−24.1		3630–3350	*3635–3575 (42%)* or *3535–3415 (53%)*
Beta-196299*	03E538C249S138	>1 fragment charred hazelnut shell	Context 249. Fill of pit F248. Much root disturbance	4670±40	−23.8		3630–3350	*3635–3555 (46%)* or *3535–3415 (49%)*
Beta-199990	03E538C93S38	>1 fragment *Corylus avellana* charcoal	Context 93. Fill of pit F93	5080±70	−24.9		4040–3700	*3975–3705*
Beta-186483	03E538F29S23	Bulk sample of *Alnus glutinosa* charcoal	Context 29. Fill of pit F28 within enclosure, containing Neolithic Bowl pottery	5130±100	−25.6		4230–3700	*4035–3700*
Beta-186484*	03E538F41S17	> 1 fragment *Corylus* sp. charcoal	Context 41. Base of pit F40 within enclosure, containing Neolithic Bowl pottery and some lithics	4770±50	−25.2		3650–3370	*3660–3495*
Later contexts								
Beta-197650	03E0536F10S1	Barley grains	F10. Pit within ringfort	1170±40	−24.4		cal AD 720–980	
Beta-197651	03E0536F12S3	Barley grains	F12. Spread within ringfort	1240±40	−23.9		cal AD 660–890	
Beta-197655	03E0536F121S34	*Corylus* sp./*Alnus* sp. charcoal	F16. Pit within ringfort	830±60	−26.0		cal AD 1030–1290	
Beta-197654	03E0536F75S29	*Fraxinus* sp. charcoal	F75. A fill of section D of ringfort	1340±80	−24.4		cal AD 560–890	
Beta-197652	03E0536F57S32	*Corylus* sp. charcoal	F57. Spread of burnt material overlying hearth within ringfort	1150±70	−26.6		cal AD 680–1030	
Beta-186485	03E538F72S97	Charred split *Quercus* sp. plank	F72. Charred plank from foundation trench of small, circular structure. No sign of burning *in situ*	2140±60	−26.2		390–40	

* AMS date measured by Beta Analytic Inc.

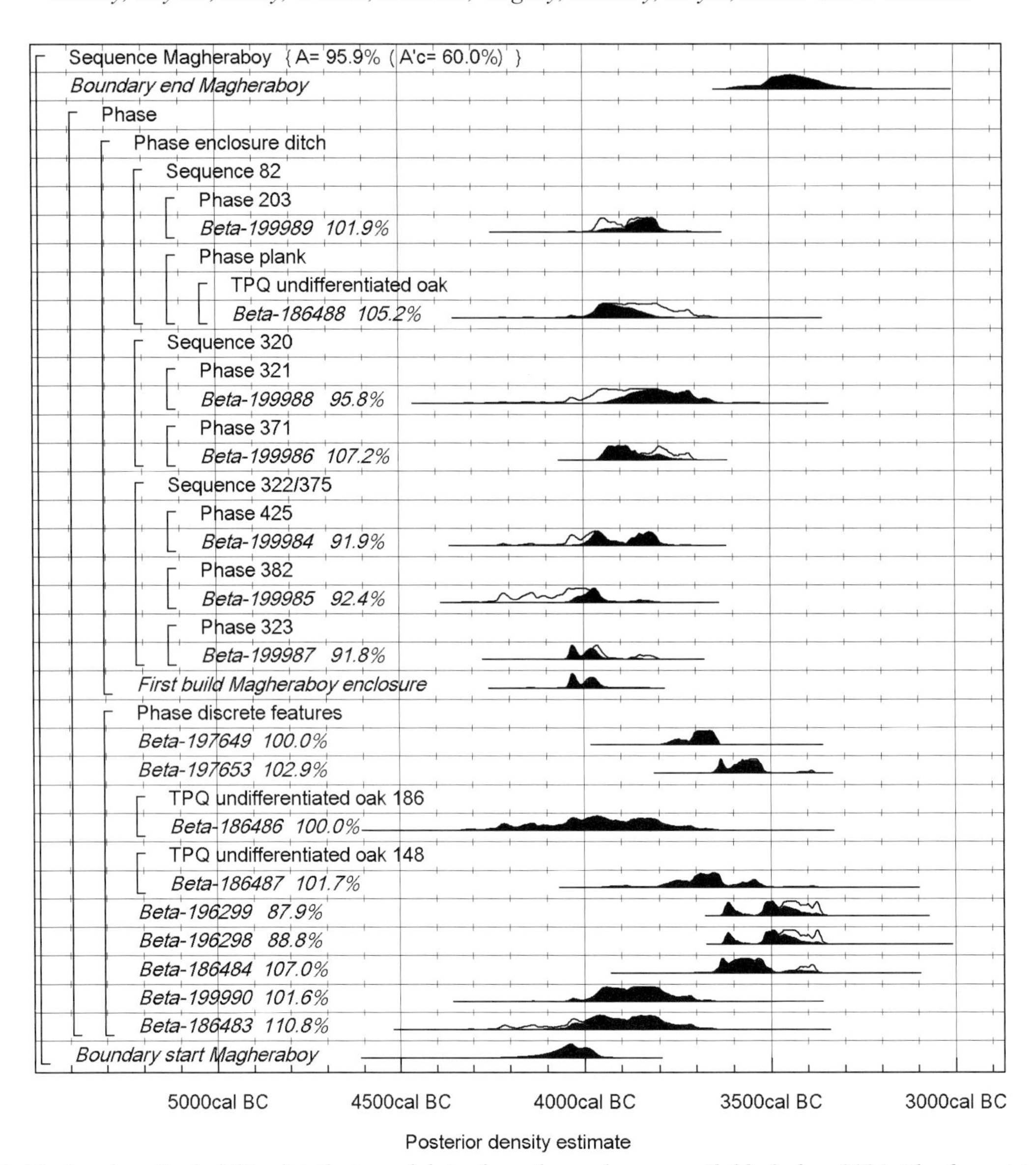

Fig. 12.14. Magheraboy. Probability distribution of dates from the enclosure available before 2004. The format is identical to that of Fig. 12.6. The large square brackets down the left-hand side of the diagram, along with the OxCal keywords, define the overall model exactly.

Sampling

Six fragments of short-life charcoal were submitted for dating: two from zone 2, segment 6, from a lower fill on the base or near the base of the segment; two replicate measurements of sapwood from the oak plank from zone 2, segment 3, previously dated by Beta-186488; and two samples from context 376, a middle fill of zone 5, segment 2, which was dated to provide a longer sequence of samples in this segment. No samples were available at any stage from the palisade or the rectangular structure, probably reflecting the fact that neither had burnt down.

Results and calibration

Full details of all the radiocarbon determinations from the Neolithic contexts at Magheraboy are provided in Table 12.2.

Analysis and interpretation

A chronological model for the Neolithic enclosure at Magheraboy is shown in Fig. 12.15. The two replicate samples on sapwood charcoal from the plank from zone 2, segment 3, contexts 203 and 290 (GrA-31961, OxA-X-2173-16), are not statistically consistent with the original measurement (Fig. 12.15: *Beta-186488*; T'=12.4; T'(5%)=6.0; ν=2). OxA-X-2173-16, an experimental measurement on a target which produced only 457 μg, produced a result which was significantly earlier than the other two measurements. It appears that this sample contained sediment carbon in addition to the charcoal. This measurement is therefore regarded as providing an inaccurate date for the plank and has been excluded from the model. The other two determinations are statistically consistent (T'=0.0; T'(5%)=3.8; ν=1), although *Beta-186488* is still treated as a *terminus post quem* as it may

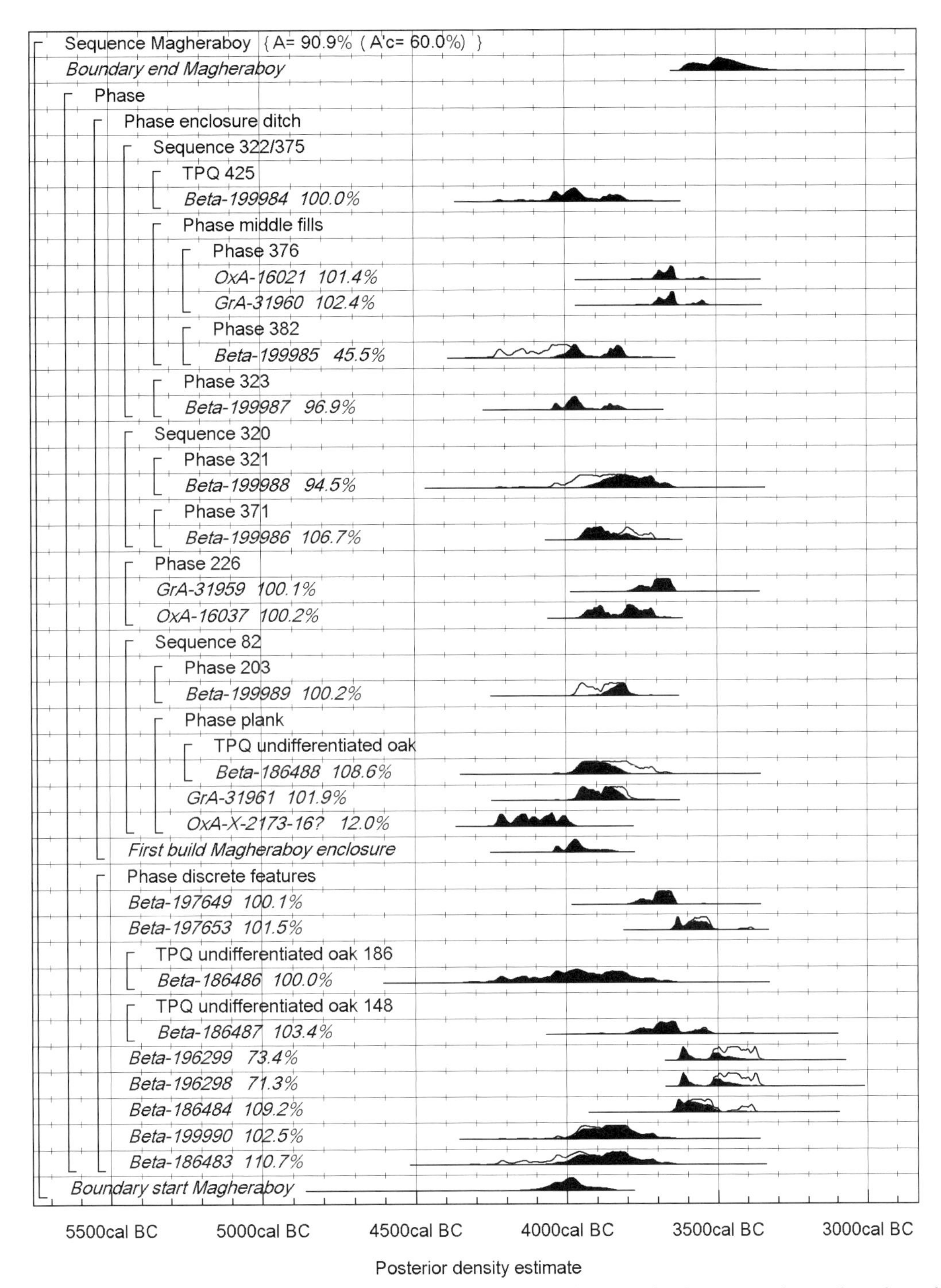

Fig. 12.15. Magheraboy. Probability distributions of dates from the enclosure. The format is identical to that of Fig. 12.6. The large square brackets down the left-hand side of the diagram, along with the OxCal keywords, define the overall model exactly.

have contained charcoal from the interior part of the dated tree. *Beta-199989* (Fig. 12.15), a mixed charcoal sample of short-lived species from a context overlying 203, produced a measurement which is in good agreement with this sequence.

The two samples from context 226 in zone 2 segment 6, provided determinations which are statistically consistent (Fig. 12.15: *OxA-16037, GrA-31959*; T'=3.3; T'(5%)=3.8; ν=1). These samples are rather later than those from some of the other dated segments and the section across the segment (Fig. 12.13: section A) may suggest that the ditch had been cleaned out, at least in this area. In zone 5 segment 1, short-lived samples were dated from context 371, a charcoal lens within context 370 which lay on the base of the ditch (Fig. 12.15: *Beta-199986*) and from the overlying layer, context 321 (Fig. 12.15: *Beta-199988*). The two measurements are in good agreement with this stratigraphic relationship.

In zone 5, segment 2, context 323, tipped into a segment butt on to the base of the ditch, provided a date on short-

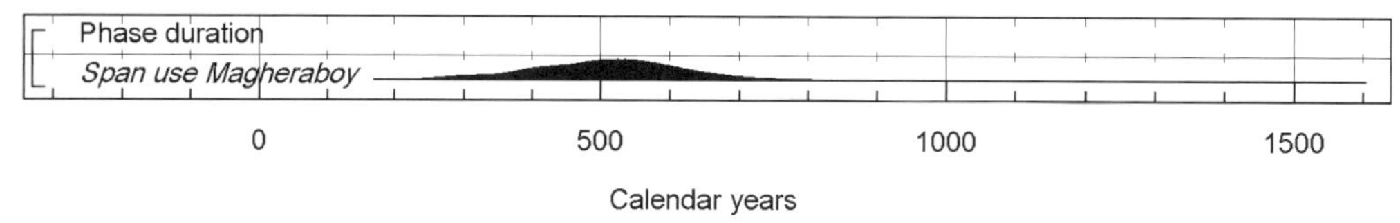

Fig. 12.16. Magheraboy. Probability distribution of the number of years during which the enclosure was in primary use, derived from the model shown in Fig. 12.15.

lived charcoal (Fig. 12.15: *Beta-199987*), and context 382, a middle fill of the same segment, provided another (Fig. 12.15: *Beta-199985*). Another middle fill, context 376 (Fig. 12.13: section B), provided two statistically consistent measurements on short-life samples (Fig. 12.15: *OxA-16021, GrA-31960*; T'=0.0; T'(5%)=3.8; v=1). These measurements, however, are substantially later than *Beta-199984,* measured on more than one fragment of short-lived charcoal from a recut into the top of the same segment. It seems most likely that the sample for *Beta-199984* included already reworked charcoal, and so this date is modelled as a *terminus post quem* for its context; alternatively, context 376 may have been the fill of an otherwise unidentified recut.

Samples were also dated from eight pits and a posthole within the enclosure (Fig. 12.15), the posthole forming part of an arc. Of these, *Beta-186486* and *-186487* were of oak charcoal and may be rather older than the contexts from which they were recovered. All these features are treated as part of the phase of use of the enclosure.

The model shown in Fig. 12.15 suggests that the Neolithic enclosure at Magheraboy was constructed in *4040–3850 cal BC* (*95% probability*; Fig. 12.15: *build Magheraboy enclosure*), probably *4040–4015 cal BC* (*11% probability*) or *4000–3935 cal BC* (*57% probability*). Including the discrete features in the interior, overall activity at Magheraboy started in *4115–3850 cal BC* (*95% probability*; Fig. 12.15: *start Magheraboy*), probably in *4065–3945 cal BC* (*68% probability*). Neolithic activity continued until *3615–3355 cal BC* (*95% probability*; Fig. 12.15: *end Magheraboy*), probably until *3595–3545 cal BC* (*15% probability*) or *3520–3410 cal BC* (*53% probability*). The site was in use for *285–715 years* (*95% probability*; Fig. 12.16: *use Magheraboy*), probably for *405–620 years* (*68% probability*).

Sensitivity analysis: an alternative model

An alternative model for the chronology of the enclosure at Magheraboy is shown in Fig. 12.17. In this reading, all bulk samples, whether measured by LSC or by AMS, and even if composed of short-life material, are interpreted as *termini post quos* for the contexts from which they were recovered. This accounts for the potential for such samples to include redeposited fragments of charred plant remains.

This model suggests that the enclosure at Magheraboy was constructed in *3965–3780 cal BC* (*95% probability*; Fig. 12.17: *build Magheraboy enclosure*), probably in *3910–3795 cal BC* (*68% probability*). If the discrete features within the enclosure are interpreted as part of the phase of its use, then activity on the site began in *4320–3775 cal BC* (*95% probability*; Fig. 12.17: *start Magheraboy*), probably in *4030–3815 cal BC* (*68% probability*). The primary Neolithic use of the site ended in *3610–3335 cal BC* (*95% probability*; Fig. 12.17: *end Magheraboy*), probably in *3520–3370 cal BC* (*68% probability*). In this case, we estimate that the site was in use for *220–895 years* (*95% probability*; Fig. 12.18: *use Magheraboy*), probably for *330–620 years*.

Key parameters from both models (Figs 12.15 and 12.17) are shown in Fig. 12.19. It is apparent that our estimates for the time when the enclosure went out of use are robust against our alternative interpretations. This is largely because in both readings all the radiocarbon dates provide *termini post quos* for the end of the primary Neolithic use of the site. In contrast, our estimates for the date when the enclosure was constructed and when early Neolithic activity on the site began are more variable. In the first model, this activity began in the 40th or 41st centuries cal BC, within a few generations of 4000 cal BC. The second model provides less precise estimates because it depends on fewer radiocarbon dates. In this case, activity probably began rather later, in the 39th or 40th centuries cal BC.

The first model is preferred for two reasons. First, it uses the same criteria by which to determine whether dates are dismissed as *termini post quos* as are employed elsewhere in this project, while the second model is based on different and more stringent ones. Secondly, in the absence of definitely Mesolithic lithics from the assemblage (Danaher and Cagney 2005, 234–5), it is difficult to invoke the extensive presence of earlier, redeposited charcoal, for example as the result of some kind of extensive land-use including clearance and burning by hunter-gatherers, to account for all the measurements on bulk short-life material.

Implications for the site

At Magheraboy, Carinated Bowl pottery occurs from the base of the ditch segments onwards. The ditch also contained a mudstone axehead, probably of local origin, in segment 1, zone 5, dated by *Beta-199986* to *3955–3760 cal BC* (*95% probability*; Fig. 12.15: *Beta-199986*), probably to *3945–3855 cal BC* (*64% probability*) or *3805–3790 cal BC* (*4% probability*). A porcellanite axehead broken by a series of controlled blows before deposition was recovered from the base of segment 3 in zone 2. This is best dated by sapwood from the burnt plank on the base of the ditch (presumably non-residual because of its integrity as a single piece), to

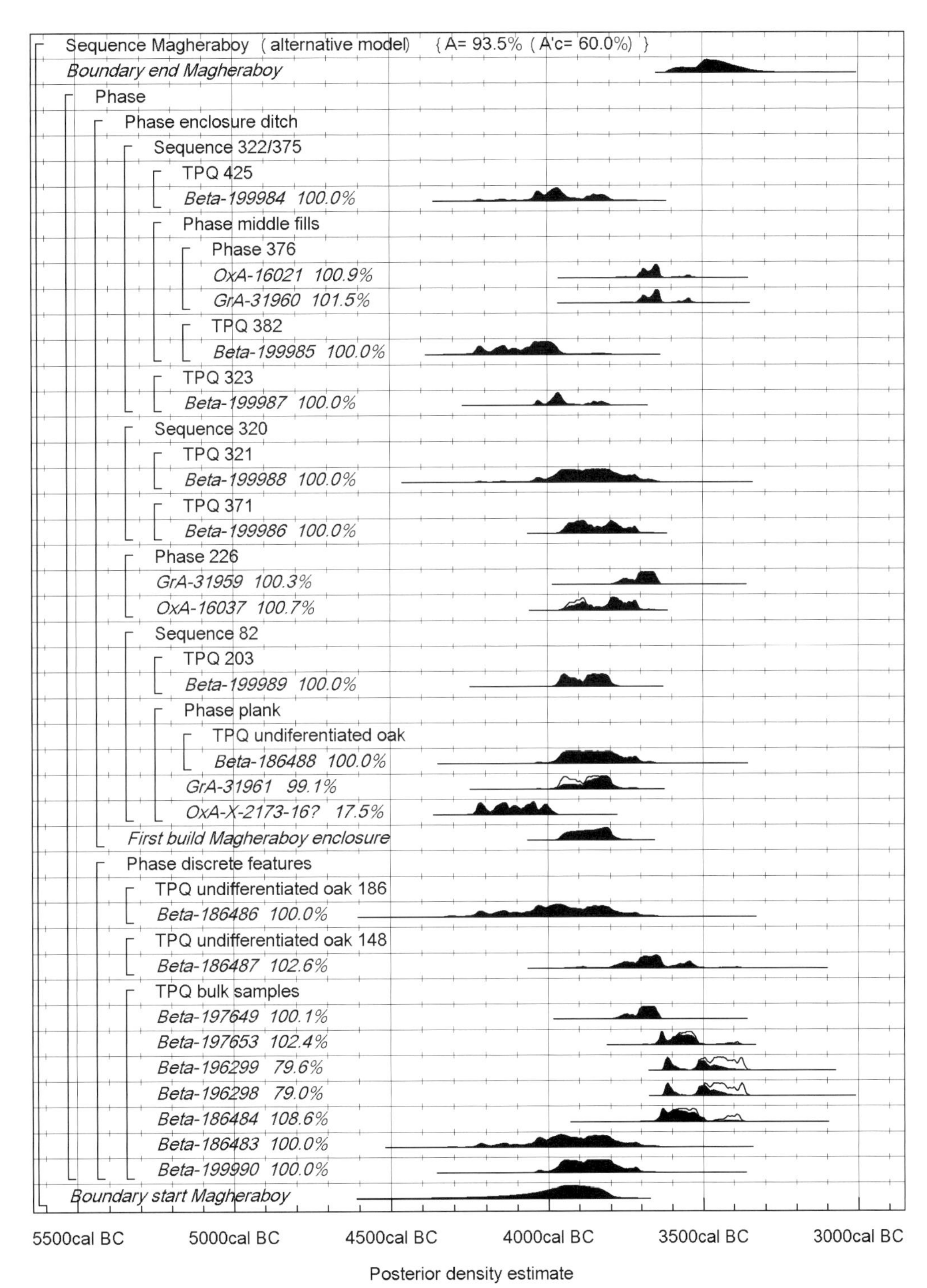

Fig. 12.17. Magheraboy. Probability distributions of dates from the enclosure according to the alternative chronological model. The format is identical to that of Fig. 12.6. The large square brackets down the left-hand side of the diagram, along with the OxCal keywords, define the overall model exactly.

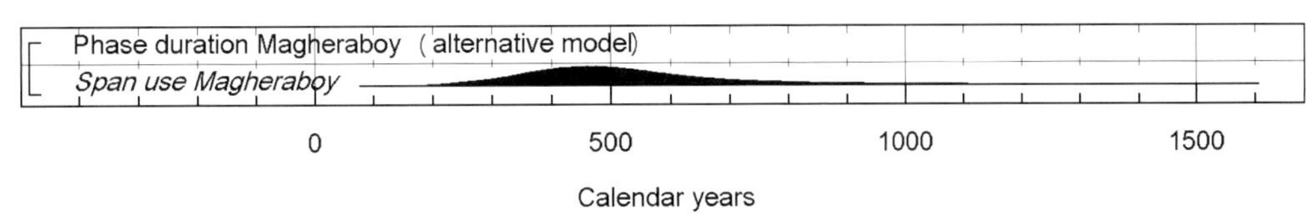

Fig. 12.18. Magheraboy. Probability distribution of the number of years during which the enclosure was in primary use, derived from the alternative model shown in Fig. 12.17.

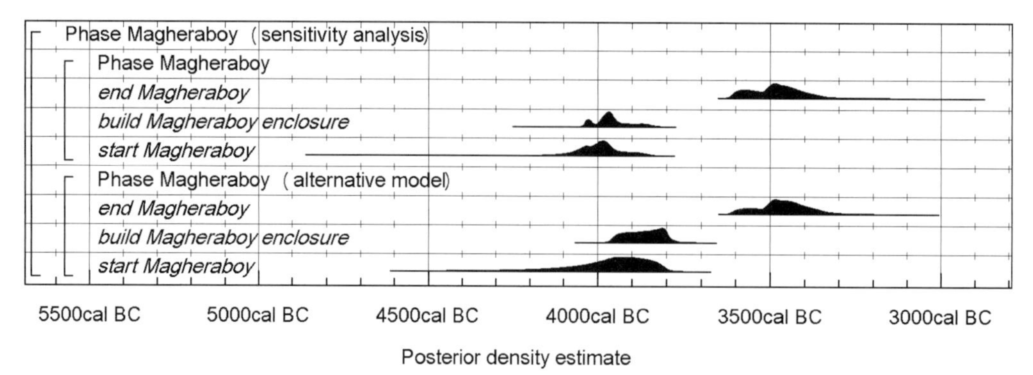

Fig. 12.19. Magheraboy. Key parameters from the chronological models defined in Figs 12.15 and 12.17.

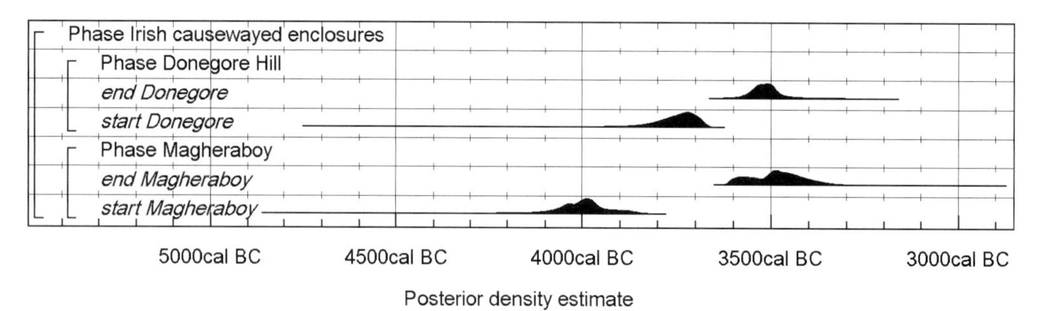

Fig. 12.20. Donegore Hill and Magheraboy. Probability distributions for the dates for construction and disuse, derived from the models defined in Figs 12.5–9 and 12.15.

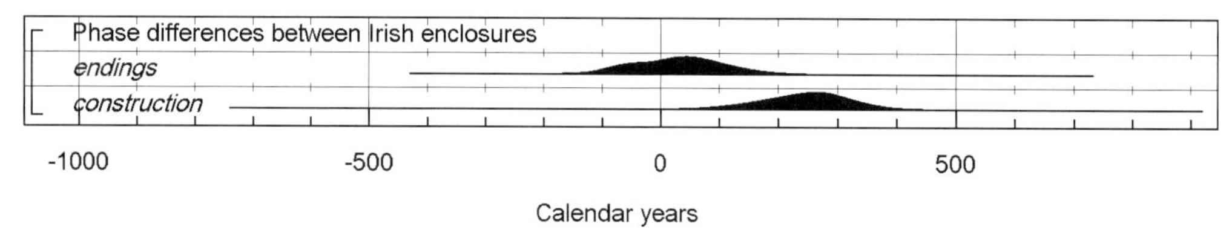

Fig. 12.21. Donegore Hill and Magheraboy. Differences between dates of construction and disuse for the causewayed enclosures at Donegore and Magheraboy, calculated from the distributions shown in Fig. 12.20.

3965–3810 cal BC (*95% probability*; Fig. 12.15: *GrA-31961*), probably to *3960–3905 cal BC* (*35% probability*) or *3880–3830 cal BC* (*33% probability*). This in turn appears to demonstrate that porcellanite was in circulation across the northern part of Ireland by the 40th or 39th centuries cal BC (see Sheridan *et al.* 1992; Cooney and Mandal 1998; Cooney 2000a). Hexaploid wheat was dated from pit F221 in the interior, although more than one grain was bulked together for AMS dating. This dates to *3635–3575 cal BC* (*42% probability*; Fig. 12.15: *Beta-196298*) or *3535–3415 cal BC* (*53% probability*), probably to *3630–3595 cal BC* (*34% probability*) or *3520–3480 cal BC* (*31% probability*) or *3475–3460 cal BC* (*3% probability*).

The undated palisade and rectangular timber structure could be earlier, contemporary with or, indeed, later than the ditch.

We will not go on in this instance to discuss the implications of these date estimates for our understanding of the local region around Magheraboy. At this point, given the early date of the site, that first requires the assessment of a very wide body of evidence for the rest of the early Neolithic in the area and in Ireland as a whole. This poses fundamental questions about the date of the start of the Neolithic in Ireland, and is a major challenge, raising several difficult, unresolved issues. We return to Magheraboy, however, at intervals and in the concluding discussion of this chapter.

Preliminary discussion of the two dated enclosures

The two causewayed enclosures dated in Ireland were built at very different times. Magheraboy began in *4115–3850 cal BC* (*95% probability*; Fig. 12.20: *start Magheraboy*), probably in *4065–3945 cal BC* (*68% probability*); see also the concluding section of the chapter (12.4) for a discussion of the issues raised by this date estimate. Donegore began in *3855–3665 cal BC* (*95% probability*; Fig. 12.20: *start Donegore*), probably in *3780–3685 cal BC* (*68% probability*). No short-life material has been dated from the base of the ditch circuits at Donegore, and so the actual date of construction could be slightly earlier than the estimates presented here. On the basis of the consistency of the dates from recuts F76 and F180 in the inner ditch (Fig. 12.6: *GrA-31339*, *-31341*, *-32322*, and

-31324), and the comparable *terminus post quem* provided by *UB*-3068 from the base of the outer ditch, however, it is improbable that Donegore is as early as Magheraboy, and it is perfectly possible that the estimates presented here are close to the actual age of the enclosure. The enclosures were constructed *70–405 years apart* (*95% probability*; Fig. 12.21: *construction*), probably *170–330 years apart* (*68% probability*). Activity still seems to have been continuing at Magheraboy at the time when Donegore was constructed, as both sites seem to have gone out of use within a relatively restricted span of time in the 36th or earlier 35th centuries cal BC (Fig. 12.21: *endings*; Fig. 12.20: *end Donegore* and *end Magheraboy*).

12.3 Donegore and Magheraboy in context: the early Neolithic and the start of the middle Neolithic in Ireland

In order to put our estimates for the dates of the enclosures at Donegore Hill and Magheraboy in context, we have to consider the chronology of other aspects of the early Neolithic in Ireland. Several alternative models are presented for the introduction of Neolithic practices into the island (Figs 12.53–7). These express different views of what defines the early Neolithic in Ireland and distinguishes it from the middle Neolithic. This is critical because, in order to provide a reliable estimate for the start of the Neolithic, it is necessary to impose a statistical distribution on the overall phase of activity sampled for radiocarbon dating, and so this has to be explicitly defined (see Chapter 2.4.1 and 2.8 for fuller discussion). In the analyses presented here we have used a uniform distribution as the uninformative prior information for our models (Buck *et al.* 1992; Bronk Ramsey 1995). This is required to counteract the statistical scatter on the radiocarbon dates (Steier and Rom 2000; Bronk Ramsey 2000; Chapter 2.2). If this scatter is not explicitly taken into account, such assemblages of dates can be erroneously interpreted as suggesting a start date for the activity in question which is anomalously early, an end date that is anomalously late and a duration that is anomalously long (Bayliss *et al.* 2007a). A uniform distribution has been chosen because this is comparatively uninformative, meaning that the results of the models change little if the dated activity was actually not distributed uniformly. Research is now underway which will allow other forms of distribution to be implemented for such analyses (Karlsberg 2006; Bronk Ramsey 2009). In due course, therefore, it will be possible to compare estimates from models with different forms of distribution to assess the sensitivity of results to this input. In this chapter, however, we will compare models which impose different archaeological definitions of the uniform phase. Differences between the results can therefore be used to assess how far the date estimates depend on the archaeological and scientific information put into the models, and how far on the statistical assumptions which underpin them.

All our models for the early Neolithic in Ireland exclude dates from causewayed enclosures, since the purpose of this analysis is to provide independent date estimates for comparison with the dated enclosures. The models include components relating to houses and other occupation evidence and forms of activity associated with diagnostically early Neolithic material. Dates from portal tombs and court tombs, and from two round mounds and Neolithic field systems, also form components of the models, although these are treated in different ways: either as by definition early Neolithic, or as potentially early and middle Neolithic in date. In either case, these sites must date to after the introduction of Neolithic practices into Ireland. In all models, dates made on samples of domesticated animals and plants must also post-date this boundary. Dates from Linkardstown burials and passage tombs, regarded here as elements of the middle Neolithic because of their different practices and associated material, have been included in the models as providing a *terminus ante quem* for the end of the early Neolithic phase of activity. The difficulties with the early Neolithic dating of passage tombs that has been proposed (e.g. Sheridan 2003a; 2003b; 2004; 2005) are discussed in the relevant section below. It should be stressed that no formal attempt has been made to model the chronology of the middle Neolithic as a whole.

It should also be noted that other radiocarbon dates which fall into the fourth millennium cal BC but which are not associated with diagnostically Neolithic activity have not been included in our preferred models: principally dates on trackways and unaccompanied burials. Dates for late Mesolithic contexts have not been systematically included. Radiocarbon dates falling in the fifth millennium cal BC and associated with diagnostically Mesolithic material are still, unfortunately, too few to enable a chronological model for the dating of the terminal Mesolithic in Ireland to be constructed which can bear comparison with our models for the introduction of Neolithic practices (see discussion in Woodman 2009; Bayliss and Woodman 2009). Some relevant dates, such as those from Ferriter's Cove (Woodman *et al.* 1999), are modelled and discussed as appropriate.

The components of the overall models for the chronology of the early Neolithic in Ireland are first discussed one by one. Individual models have been constructed to estimate independently the dating of different aspects of the early Neolithic on the island. So, for example, Figs 12.22–7 define a model for the chronology of early Neolithic houses. This enables us to compare the chronology of houses with that of enclosures. Neolithic houses are, however, associated with diagnostic early Neolithic material culture, as are other occupation and activity sites (such as for axehead production and burial; Fig. 12.30), portal tombs (Fig. 12.31) and court tombs (Figs 12.32–4). Consequently, if we wish to date the introduction of early Neolithic material into Ireland, then a model which includes the dates from all these sites is to be preferred (Figs 12.53–7). The component sections of the overall model, however, serve two purposes. First, they provide independent date

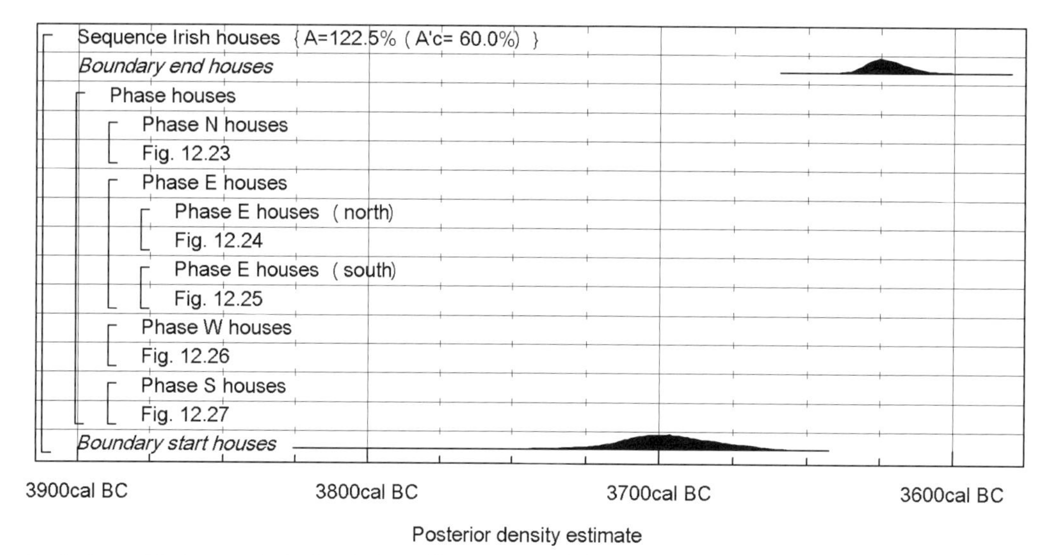

Fig. 12.22. Early Neolithic houses in Ireland. Overall structure of the chronological model. The component sections of this model are shown in detail in Figs 12.23–7. The large square brackets down the left-hand side of Figs 12.22–7, along with the OxCal keywords, define the overall model exactly.

estimates for particular aspects of the early Neolithic in Ireland. Secondly, comparison of their results allows us to assess the robustness of the overall model and to consider questions such as whether all these elements were introduced at the same time.

The assemblage of radiocarbon dates associated with Irish Neolithic material has a particularly high proportion of results from samples which consisted of bulked, unidentified, or mature charcoal, or were in uncertain relation to their contexts, or both (Woodman *et al.* 1999, 145–6; Woodman 2000, 225–9). This is partially a consequence of the poor survival of unburnt bone in many parts of the island, although too often even today samples of oak are submitted for dating without the isolation of sapwood (Ashmore 1999a; McSparron 2003). It is also a function of the accessibility of megalithic tombs over long periods and the timing of many excavations of tombs which took place in the early days of radiocarbon dating when large samples were necessary.

Houses

The boom in numbers of known Irish early Neolithic houses has already been discussed in detail elsewhere (Cooney 1999; Grogan 2004; Smyth 2006; 2007; McSparron 2008). Smyth (2011) notes some 80 structures from 49 sites and publication of discoveries has continued after the modelling for this project was carried out, for example the houses at Russellstown and Busherstown, Co. Carlow (O'Connell and O'Neill 2009). Dated early Neolithic houses are described here for the sake of presentation in five regional groupings: a northern group, with Enagh, Ballygalley, Ballyharry and Ballynagilly; an eastern (north) grouping, with Monanny, Newtown, and Knowth; an eastern (south) grouping, with Corbally, Kishoge and Kilgobbin; Ballyglass and Gortaroe in the west; and a southern group from Granny in the east to Cloghers in the west (Fig. 12.1). Full details of the dated samples and radiocarbon measurements are given in Table 12.3.

The overall form of the model for the chronology of early Neolithic houses in Ireland is given in Fig. 12.22, with the component sections relating to the northern group being given in Fig. 12.23, to the eastern (north) group in Fig. 12.24, to the eastern (south) group in Fig. 12.25, to the western group in Fig. 12.26, and to the southern group in Fig. 12.27.

In the northern group, a basically rectangular structure at Enagh, Co. Derry, was partially excavated in advance of housing development (McSparron 2003). This was some 6.2 by 4.3 m, defined by a foundation trench, two corner postholes and a central internal posthole. Only coarse pottery and a single flint blade were directly associated with the structure. Two radiocarbon determinations were obtained. A sample of unidentified charcoal from the wall slot (*Beta-152195*) produced a result which is statistically significantly earlier than that from hazelnut shells from posthole F207 of the same structure (Fig. 12.23: *Beta-188378*; T'=13.1; T'(5%)=3.8; ν=1).

Four structures were excavated at Ballygalley, Co. Antrim (D. Simpson 1996; John Ó Néill, pers. comm.), a site remarkable for the large-scale working of flint from the adjacent beach and from an extraction site on Ballygalley Hill (A. Collins 1978) as well as for the largest concentration in Ireland of imported Arran pitchstone (Ballin 2009). These, together with other non-local materials, including porcellanite (Group IX) and tuff (Group VI) axeheads, have led to the interpretation of the site as a redistribution centre for both local and imported materials (D. Simpson 1996, 132). In the north of the excavated area, on site 1, a large number of pits with some postholes, stakeholes and slot trenches were found, as well as House 1, a sub-rectangular structure 8 m by 4 m defined by beam slots (which contained large quantities of charred grain), and containing two parallel rows of three postholes, with a partly open 'annexe' at one

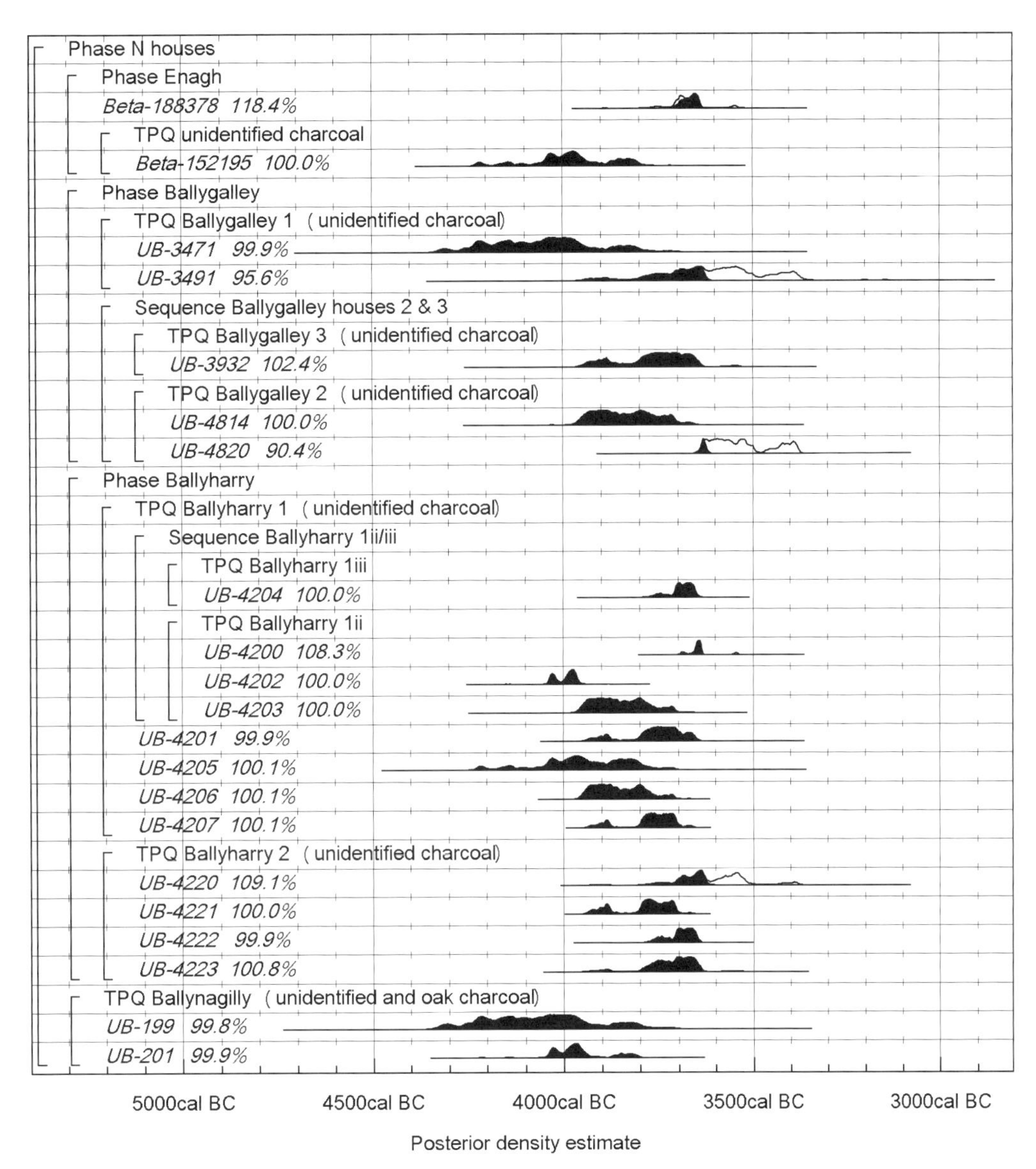

Fig. 12.23. Early Neolithic houses in Ireland (northern). Probability distributions of dates. The format is identical to that of Fig. 12.6. The overall structure of this model is shown in Fig. 12.22 and its other components are shown in Figs 12.24–7.

end (D. Simpson 1996, 123–7). The pottery from these features and adjacent pits is provisionally described as 'western Neolithic', with decoration confined to finger-tip fluting and occasional incised lines (D. Simpson 1995, 41; cf. Simpson *et al.* 1990, fig. 7:1–3, 5, 18–20), i.e. modified Carinated Bowl as defined by Sheridan (1995). The area was sealed by a cobbled surface, which included sherds of coarse and more elaborately decorated globular bowls. This also occurred in the topsoil (D. Simpson 1993, 62; 1995, 41; cf. Simpson *et al.* 1990, fig. 7:21–2, 25–6). To the south, across a palaeochannel, on site 2, were further features, including Structure 4 (2.70 m by 2.20 m) and Houses 2 (6.60 m by 5.20 m) and 3 (5 m by 3 m), all defined by wall slots and posts. House 2 preceded House 3 on the stratigraphic evidence of ard marks which cut the wall slots of House 2 (Simpson *et al.* 1995, 4) and were cut by one of the postholes of House 3. Site 2 was also covered by a stone layer.

Bulk samples of unidentified charcoal were dated from the foundation trenches of Houses 1–3, all the samples providing *termini post quos* for construction (Fig. 12.23). Seventeen other unidentified bulk charcoal samples from discrete features, principally pits, were dated to the fourth millennium cal BC. These are listed in Table 12.13, but are not included in the overall model for early Neolithic activity presented here because, at the present stage of post-excavation analysis, it is not clear which were associated with the earlier phases of Neolithic activity at the site, and which with the later.

Two houses were revealed in advance of gas pipeline installation at Ballyharry, on the Islandmagee peninsula, Co. Antrim (Moore 2003; 2004). House 1 showed a complex sequence. Phase 1 consisted of a sub-rectangular arrangement, some 13 m by 6.50 m, of stone-packed postholes, from which posts had been removed. There was little associated material. Phase 2 was a trapezoidal

Table 12.3. Radiocarbon dates for rectangular buildings in Ireland. Posterior density estimates derive from the model defined in Figs 12.22–7.

Laboratory number	Sample reference	Material	Context	Radiocarbon age (BP)	$\delta^{13}C$ (‰)	Weighted mean (BP)	Calibrated date range (cal BC) (95% confidence)	*Posterior density estimate (cal BC) (95% probability)*
Enagh, Co. Derry								
Beta-152195		Charcoal (unidentified)	Site 2, F205, context 204. Charcoal-rich fill of foundation trench (McSparron 2003)	5170±70			4230–3790	*4230–4195 (3%)* or *4170–4125 (6%)* or *4120–4085 (2%)* or *4080–3790 (84%)*
Beta-188378		Charred hazelnut shell fragments	Site 2, F207, context 208. Basal fill of corner posthole of house (McSparron 2003)	4880±40	−24.9		3720–3540	*3700–3635*
Ballygalley house 1, Co. Antrim								
UB-3471	BG 91 F22	Charcoal (unidentified, 'a bulk sample from sieving many kilos of soil' — Simpson 1996, 129)	Ballygalley 1. Foundation trench	5219±104	−26.6		4330–3780	*4325–4290 (2%)* or *4270–3790 (93%)*
UB-3491	BG 91 22/2	Charcoal (unidentified, 'from a more concentrated sample [than UB-3471]' — Simpson 1996, 129)	Ballygalley 1. North slot trench (F1022)	4830±117	−24.8		3940–3360	*3945–3850 (11%)* or *3815–3615 (84%)*
Ballygalley house 2, Co. Antrim								
UB-4814	Grid 5 Context 2374	Charcoal (unidentified)	Ballygalley 2. South slot trench, joining 2041 (F2374; Dermot Moore pers comm.)	5035±60	−26.4		3970–3660	*3965–3700*
UB-4820	Tr S Context 2041	Charcoal (unidentified)	Ballygalley 2. South slot trench (F2041)	4749±51	−26.9		3650–3370	*3660–3610*
Ballygalley house 3, Co. Antrim								
UB-3932	BG 94 427	Charcoal (unidentified)	Ballygalley 3. South slot trench (F2427; Dermot Moore pers comm.)	4953±74	−26.8		3960–3630	*3945–3850 (19%)* or *3825–3635 (76%)*
Ballyharry 1, Co. Antrim								
UB-4201	BTP4 (A)	Charcoal (unidentified)	Context 97 (fill)	4968±48	−25.9		3940–3640	*3940–3870 (13%)* or *3815–3645 (82%)*
UB-4200	BTP4 (A)	Charcoal (unidentified)	Context 79 (fill). Phase ii of structure	4854±25	−25.9		3700–3630	*3695–3630*
UB-4202	BTP4 (B)	Charcoal (unidentified)	Context 37 (fill). South wall slot (F37). Phase ii of structure	5184±25	−25.3		4050–3950	*4045–4010 (31%)* or *4005–3955 (64%)*
UB-4203	BTP4 (B)	Charcoal (unidentified)	Context 118 (fill) of north wall slot (F117). Phase ii of structure	5047±48	−25.6		3970–3700	*3960–3755 (89%)* or *3745–3710 (6%)*
UB-4204	BTP4 (C)	Charcoal (unidentified)	Deposit F67, context 66. Phase iii of structure	4921±27	−26.2		3770–3640	*3765–3720 (14%)* or *3715–3645 (81%)*
UB-4205	BTP4 (C)	Charcoal (unidentified)	Context 201 (fill)	5149±87	−26.2		4230–3710	*4230–4195 (3%)* or *4175–3760 (91%)* or *3735–3710 (1%)*
UB-4206	BTP4 (D)	Charcoal (unidentified)	Context 66 (fill)	5044±39	−25.9		3960–3710	*3955–3755 (92%)* or *3740–3710 (3%)*
UB-4207	BTP4 (D)	Charcoal (unidentified)	Context 125 (fill)	4988±33	−25.9		3940–3690	*3935–3870 (15%)* or *3810–3690 (78%)* or *3680–3660 (2%)*
Ballyharry 2, Co. Antrim								
UB-4220	BTP5	Charcoal (unidentified)	Context 3 (fill)	4840±67	−25.8		3770–3380	*3775–3620*

Laboratory number	Sample reference	Material	Context	Radiocarbon age (BP)	δ^{13}C (‰)	Weighted mean (BP)	Calibrated date range (cal BC) (95% confidence)	*Posterior density estimate (cal BC) (95% probability)*
UB-4221	BTP5	Charcoal (unidentified)	Slot fill (F11)	4998±32	−26.0		3940–3700	*3940–3855 (23%)* or *3815–3695 (72%)*
UB-4222	BTP5 context 13 (fill)	Charcoal (unidentified)	Slot fill (F13)	4922±32	−25.6		3780–3640	*3770–3645*
UB-4223	BTP5	Charcoal (unidentified)	Context 19 (fill)	4929±51	−25.7		3900–3630	*3895–3880 (1%)* or *3800–3635 (94%)*
Ballynagilly, Co. Tyrone								
UB-199		Charcoal (unidentified)	F(L) 149. Posthole of house	5230±125			4340–3770	*4330–3795*
UB-201		*Quercus* sp. charcoal	F (L) 158. Remains of split oak planking, compressed in wall-slot of house (A. Smith *et al.* 1970)	5165±50			4050–3800	*4155–4130 (1%)* or *4055–3900 (75%)* or *3885–3795 (19%)*
Monanny house A, Co. Monaghan								
Wk-17338	C245 S65	*Quercus* sp. charcoal	Burnt post in west wall of House A (Fintan Walsh pers. comm.)	5037±40	−24.4		3960–3700	*3955–3755 (88%)* or *3745–3710 (7%)*
UB-7595	C110 S26	Charred hazelnut shell fragments recovered by flotation	House A context 110. Primary packing deposit in foundation trench	4897±37	−22.0		3770–3630	*3705–3635*
Monanny house B, Co. Monaghan								
Wk-17341	C555 S324	*Quercus* sp. charcoal	Internal wall of House B (Fintan Walsh pers. comm.)	5048±40	−24.0		3960–3710	*3960–3760 (93%)* or *3740–3730 (1%)* or *3725–3710 (1%)*
Wk-17342	C542 S170	*Quercus* sp. charcoal	Burnt timber in south wall of House B (Fintan Walsh pers. comm.)	5082±64	−25.3		4040–3700	*3990–3710*
UB-7594	C592 S270	Charred hazelnut shell fragments recovered by flotation	House B context 592. Occupation deposit within internal wall of structure, containing over 200 sherds of early Neolithic pottery	4836±37	−21.0		3700–3530	*3695–3625*
Monanny house C, Co. Monaghan								
Wk-17343	C765 S320	*Quercus* sp. charcoal	Burnt post in south wall of House C (Fintan Walsh pers. comm.)	5043±43	−25.0		3960–3700	*3955–3755 (90%)* or *3745–3710 (5%)*
Wk-17344	C1050 S470	*Quercus* sp. charcoal	Burnt post in NW corner of House C	4991±47	−25.2		3950–3650	*3945–3855 (24%)* or *3845–3830 (1%)* or *3820–3655 (70%)*
UB-7596	C948 S420	Charred hazelnut shell fragments recovered by flotation	House C context 948. Part of main burnt horizon within north wall foundation trench	4970±37	−22.0		3910–3650	*3715–3645*
Newtown, Co. Meath								
UB-3521	F30 E633: 41	Charcoal (unidentified)	Foundation trench of rectangular structure (E. Halpin pers. comm.)	5033±42	−26.0		3960–3700	*3950–3710*
UB-3522	F30 E633: 42	Charcoal (unidentified)	Foundation trench of rectangular structure (E. Halpin pers. comm.)	4978±32	−25.7		3910–3660	*3910–3875 (6%)* or *3805–3655 (89%)*
Knowth, Co. Meath, zone A								
GrN-20179	15.90:1666	Charcoal (unidentified)	From the fill of Foundation Trench 1, under NE part of main tomb (Eogan and Roche 1997)	5080±20	−25.2		3960–3790	*3960–3895 (30%)* or *3885–3795 (65%)*

Laboratory number	Sample reference	Material	Context	Radiocarbon age (BP)	$\delta^{13}C$ (‰)	Weighted mean (BP)	Calibrated date range (cal BC) (95% confidence)	*Posterior density estimate (cal BC) (95% probability)*
GrN-20180	K90:179	Charcoal (unidentified)	From the fill of Foundation Trench 1, under NE part of main tomb (Eogan and Roche 1997)	5040±15	−24.9		3950–3780	*3945–3855 (72%)* or *3845–3830 (1%)* or *3825–3780 (22%)*
Knowth, Co. Meath, zone B								
GrN-20181	K92:72	Charcoal (unidentified)	From the fill of Foundation Trench 6, on the east side of main tomb (Eogan and Roche 1997)	5345±20	−24.7		4320–4050	*4315–4295 (3%)* or *4265–4220 (20%)* or *4210–4145 (37%)* or *4135–4050 (35%)*
Knowth tomb 8, Co. Meath								
BM-1076	Sample 2/1970	Charcoal (unidentified)	Pit 6 in sub-rectangular House 1, associated with Neolithic pot sherds, under kerbstone 10 of tomb 8 (Eogan 1984, 215, 241; 1986, 199; Burleigh *et al.* 1976)	4852±71			3780–3380	*3790–3620*
Kishoge, Co. Dublin								
GrN-26770	01E0061:125–6	*Quercus* sp. charcoal	Charred oak planking within 104, the upper fill of F196, the eastern slot trench (O'Donovan 2003, 126)	4880±40	−23.9		3720–3540	*3760–3740 (3%)* or *3715–3630 (92%)*
GrN-26771	01E0061:140–17	*Quercus* sp. charcoal	Burnt post within F135, upper fill of north-western slot trench F192 (O'Donovan 2003, 126)	5020±40	−24.7	5008±31	3950–3700	*3945–3855 (33%)* or *3820–3700 (62%)*
GrN-26789	01E0061:140–17	Replicate of GrN-26671	From the same context as GrN-26770	4990±50	−24.7	T'=0.2; T'(5%)=3.8; v=1		
Kilgobbin, Co. Dublin								
UB-6199	03E0306 Area 6 Sample 85 F404	*Quercus* sp. charcoal	F404. Wall footing (Ines Hagen pers. comm.)	4842±45	−25.6		3710–3520	*3710–3625*
UB-6200	03E0306 Area 6 Sample 119 F985	Charred hazelnut shells	F985. Basal fill of internal posthole (Ines Hagen pers. comm.)	4914±42	−25.5		3790–3630	*3705–3635*
Corbally 1, Co. Kildare								
GrA-13701	F13/SS2	Single fragment *Corylus avellana* (unclear if nut or wood)	From internal posthole (F13; Purcell 2002, 46)	4930±50	−25.6		3900–3630	*3710–3635*
GrA-13702	F3/SS59	Single grain *Triticum dicoccum*	From external trench (F3; Purcell 2002, 46)	4880±50	−24.9		3770–3530	*3705–3630*
Beta-118361		Charcoal (unidentified)	From a corner posthole in foundation trench (F23; Purcell 2002, 46)	5220±80			4260–3800	*4260–3925 (88%)* or *3880–3800 (7%)*
Corbally 2, Co. Kildare								
GrA-13698	F148/SS177	*Corylus avellana* fragments (unclear if nut or wood)	From an internal posthole (F148; Purcell 2002, 57)	4900±50	−28.9		3790–3540	*3705–3635*
GrA-13700	F53/SS70	Single grain *Triticum dicoccum*	From an internal posthole (F53; Purcell 2002, 57)	4900±50	−23.6		3790–3540	*3705–3635*

Laboratory number	Sample reference	Material	Context	Radiocarbon age (BP)	$\delta^{13}C$ (‰)	Weighted mean (BP)	Calibrated date range (cal BC) (95% confidence)	*Posterior density estimate (cal BC) (95% probability)*
Beta-118362		Charcoal (unidentified)	From an internal posthole (F53; Purcell 2002, 57)	4910±80			3940–3520	*3940–3855 (11%)* or *3815–3625 (84%)*
Corbally 3, Co. Kildare								
GrA-13695	F249/SS285	*Corylus avellana* fragments (unclear if nut or wood)	From an internal posthole (F249; Purcell 2002, 67)	4920±50	−25.4		3800–3630	*3705–3635*
GrA-13697	F208/SS265	Single grain *Triticum dicoccum*	From an internal posthole (F208; Purcell 2002, 67)	4910±50	−24.5		3800–3630	*3705–3635*
Corbally 4, Co. Kildare								
GrA-24234	F47-30	Charred hazelnut	From the eastern wall of the foundation trench (Redmond Tobin pers. comm.)	4905±45	−23.2		3780–3630	*3705–3635*
Corbally 5, Co. Kildare								
GrA-24212	F2061.1-286	Cereal remains	From foundation trench (Redmond Tobin pers. comm.)	4885±45	−23.4		3770–3540	*3705–3635*
GrN-28255	F2098-285	Hazelnut and cereal remains	From one of the roof support postholes (Redmond Tobin pers. comm.)	4770±60	−25.8		3660–3370	*3695–3610*
Corbally 6, Co. Kildare								
GrA-24213	F2536-262	Hazelnut and cereal remains	From foundation trench (Redmond Tobin pers. comm.)	4840±45	−25.9		3710–3520	*3695–3625*
Ballyglass Ma 13, Co. Mayo								
SI-1450	E83:432/3	Charcoal (unidentified)	North wall trench (Ó Nualláin *et al.* forthcoming)	4680±95			3650–3100	
SI-1451	E83:436-8	Charcoal (unidentified)	South wall trench (Ó Nualláin *et al.* forthcoming)	4575±90			3630–3010	
SI-1452	E83:446-8	Charcoal (unidentified)	East wall trench (Ó Nualláin *et al.* forthcoming)	4480±90			3500–2900	
SI-1453	E83:442-5	Charcoal (unidentified)	Partition wall trench (Ó Nualláin *et al.* forthcoming)	4530±95			3620–2910	
SI-1454	E83:456	*Quercus* charcoal	Posthole 29 (F62), house (Ó Nualláin *et al.* forthcoming)	4575±105			3640–2920	
Gortaroe, Co. Mayo								
GrN-27799	II 90-34	*Quercus* charcoal	From an internal posthole (Richard Gillespie pers. comm.)	4940±50	−25.3		3910–3630	*3910–3875 (4%)* or *3805–3635 (91%)*
GrN-27800	II 109-5	*Alnus* charcoal	From the foundation trench (C5; Richard Gillespie pers. comm.)	4620±50	−27.1		3620–3130	*3640–3610*
Granny 2, Co. Kilkenny								
UB-6315	Context 27314 : Context 179	*Quercus* sp. charcoal	C27314. NE corner posthole of irregular setting of foundation trenches and postholes (Hughes 2005, 148)	5054±38	−26.6		3970–3710	*3960–3765*
Barnagore, Co. Cork								
Beta-171411	02E384F27S16	*Quercus* stake, charred	Remains of *in situ* stake within eastern slot trench but not cutting it (Ed Danaher pers. comm.)	4880±70	−23.4		3950–3630	*3895–3880 (1%)* or *3800–3620 (94%)*

Laboratory number	Sample reference	Material	Context	Radiocarbon age (BP)	$\delta^{13}C$ (‰)	Weighted mean (BP)	Calibrated date range (cal BC) (95% confidence)	*Posterior density estimate (cal BC) (95% probability)*
Beta-171412	02E384F88S65	*Quercus* split timber, charred	Vertical grain, on south-facing side of southern slot trench (Ed Danaher pers. comm.)	4950±70	−25.1		3950–3630	*3945-3855 (17%)* or *3815–3635 (78%)*
Pepperhill, Co. Cork								
GrN-15476		Charcoal (unidentified, organic fraction measured)	Fragmentary, irregular setting of foundation trench, postholes and gully with early Neolithic artefacts (Gowen 1988, 44–51)	4860±70	−24.0		3790–3510	*3795–3620*
Tankardstown 1, Co. Limerick								
GrN-14713	Tankardstown 42	*Quercus* planking, charred	Foundation trench of sub-quadrangular house with early Neolithic artefacts (Gowen 1988, 26–43; Gowen and Tarbett 1989)	5105±45	−24.2		3990–3780	*3985–3785*
GrN-15386	Tankardstown 44	*Quercus* planking, charred	From the same context as GrN-14713	5005±25	−24.9		3940–3700	*3935–3870 (25%)* or *3810–3705 (70%)*
GrN-15387	Tankardstown 46	*Quercus* planking, charred	From the same context as GrN-14713	4880±110	−24.1		3960–3370	*3945–3855 (15%)* or *3845–3830 (1%)* or *3825–3620 (79%)*
OxA-1476	F23 fill 35 1/2	Emmer grain	F23, context 35. Foundation trench (Monk 2000, 76)	4890±80	−26.0		3930–3520	*3705–3625*
OxA-1477	F23 fill 35 2/2	Emmer grain	F23, context 35. Foundation trench (Monk 2000, 76)	4840±80	−26.0		3790–3370	*3705–3620*
Tankardstown 2, Co. Limerick								
GrN-16557	Tankardstown 332	*Quercus* timber, charred	From E wall of central compartment (Gowen and Tarbett 1989; 1990)	4995±20	−25.7		3910–3700	*3905–3875 (7%)* or *3805–3705 (88%)*
GrN-16558	Tankardstown 334	*Quercus* timber, charred	From E wall of central compartment (Gowen and Tarbett 1989; 1990)	5070±20	−26.7		3960–3790	*3955–3890 (34%)* or *3885–3795 (61%)*
Lough Gur, Co. Limerick								
D-40		Charcoal (unidentified)	First phase of central house at circle L. 'Thin layer of habitation soil defined on the south-western side by a line of large post-pits', confused by another structure elsewhere. Early Neolithic and later pottery present (McAulay and Watts 1961; Grogan and Eogan 1987, 391–415, figs 34–5)	4410±240			3660–2460	
D-41		Charcoal (unidentified)	Posthole of house dated by D-40 (McAulay and Watts 1961; Grogan and Eogan 1987, 391–415, figs 34–5)	4690±240			3980–2870	
Cloghers, Co. Kerry								
Beta-134226	98E0238:138	Charred hazelnut shell(s)	From basal fill of posthole in western internal wall (Kiely and Dunne 2005, 41)	4850±40			3710–3530	*3695–3630*
Beta-134227	98E0238:153	Charred hazelnut shell(s)	From fill in eastern section of northern wall (Kiely and Dunne 2005, 41)	4900±40			3770–3630	*3705–3635*

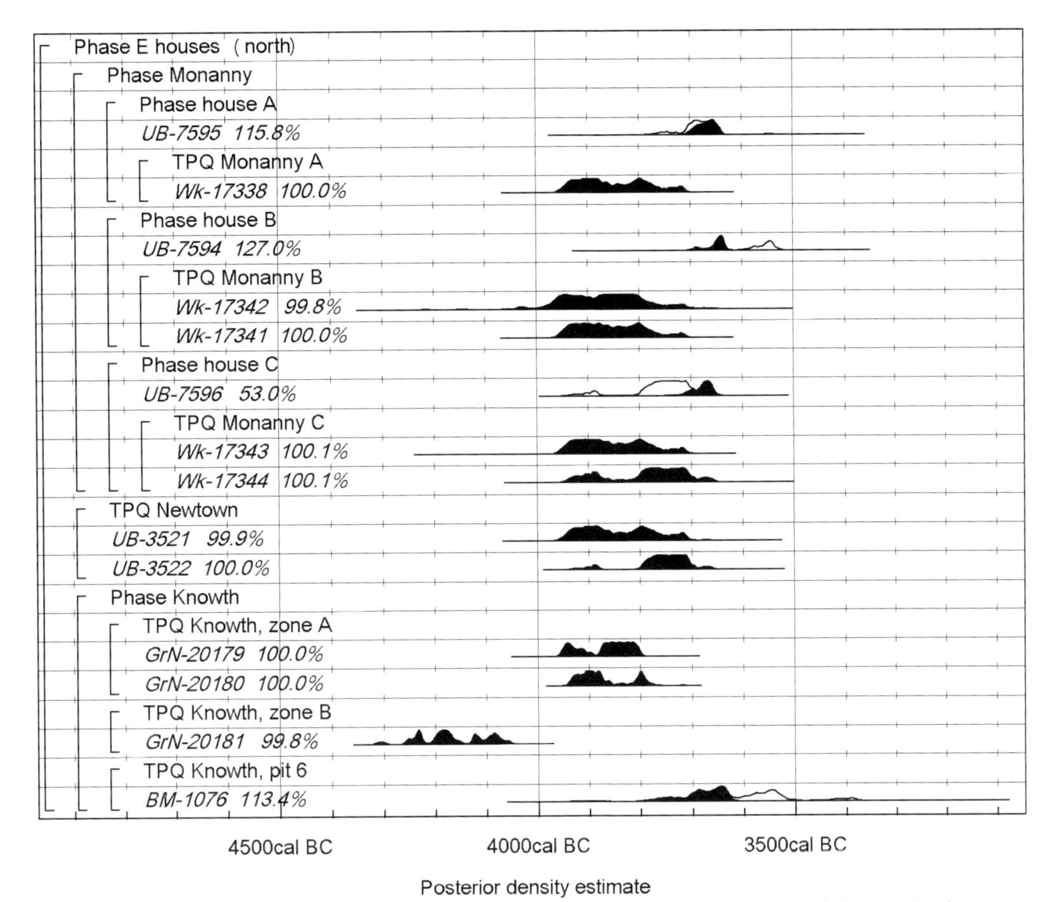

Fig. 12.24. Early Neolithic houses in Ireland (eastern (north)). Probability distributions of dates. The format is identical to that of Fig. 12.6. The overall structure of this model is shown in Fig. 12.22 and its other components are shown in Figs 12.23 and 12.25–7.

structure, some 7 m by 5 m, defined by wall slots containing posts and planks, and with a later annexe; a further ancillary rectangular structure was located to the north, though the full layout of this was not revealed. There was a wide variety of associated lithics, including porcellanite. These phase 2 structures were burnt and 34 leaf-shaped arrowheads, some burnt and broken, have been associated with this episode. Phase 3 saw some reconstruction and deliberate deposition of finds, and Phase 4 consisted of a series of large shallow pits, containing among other things flakes of tuff (Group VI) axeheads. Plain Carinated and uncarinated Bowl pottery was found. There were carbonised remains of cereals and charred hazelnut shells, and there were also finds of burnt animal bone. Eight radiocarbon measurements were obtained from unidentified charcoal providing *termini post quos* for their contexts. Four of these samples can be assigned only to House 1, although a further three have been assigned to its Phase 2 and one to its Phase 3 (Dermot Moore and Cormac McSparron, pers. comm.). This relative dating has been incorporated into the chronological model (Fig. 12.23).

House 2 at Ballyharry was only partially revealed, as a rectangular structure some 5.70 m wide but of uncertain length, defined by foundation trenches. Four radiocarbon measurements were obtained on unidentified charcoal samples (Table 12.3), and so are treated as *termini post quos* for the construction and use of the structure (Fig. 12.23).

A rectangular house was excavated at Ballynagilly, Co. Tyrone, in advance of gravel quarrying (ApSimon 1969; 1976). This measured some 6.50 m by 6 m, defined by foundation trenches on the long sides, containing principally split oak planks, and internal postholes and two hearths. Associated material included plain Carinated Bowl pottery (ApSimon 1969, 167). A broader area around the house was excavated but no further early Neolithic structures were found, although several pits were recorded. Two radiocarbon measurements were obtained from charcoal samples directly associated with the house but which potentially contained long-lived timber. Both have been treated as *termini post quos* for the construction of the house (Fig. 12.23).

Turning to the eastern (north) group, three rectangular houses, two very close together, were excavated at Monanny, Co. Monaghan, in advance of road construction (Walsh 2004). All three were defined by foundation trenches. House C measured some 12 m by 7 m, and its near neighbour House B some 13.50 m by 8 m, with an internal cross-division. House A was some 10 m by 7 m; its foundation trench was not found on one long side, perhaps because of erosion. From the foundation trenches of all three structures came substantial quantities of fine, plain, Carinated Bowl pottery, some worked lithics, including a polished stone axehead of porphyritic andesite from House B and hazelnut shells. There were also pits and gullies containing Carinated Bowl pottery. Eight radiocarbon determinations were obtained from oak charcoal and charred hazelnut shells from the Neolithic houses (Table 12.3). In House A, a measurement on a burnt post in the west wall (*Wk-17338*) is statistically inconsistent with another result from charred hazelnut shell from the same structure (Fig. 12.24; Table 12.3: *UB-7595*; T'=0.6.1; T'(5%)=3.8; ν=1). Similarly, a date on charred hazelnut shell from House B (*UB-7594*) is significantly later than those from structural oak charcoal (*Wk-17341–2*; T'=18.1; T'(5%)=6.0.8; ν=2). In contrast, measurements on two burnt posts, one estimated as 0.15 m in diameter, from House C (*Wk-17343–4*) are statistically consistent with a result on charred hazelnut shell from the same building (*UB-7596*; T'=1.7; T'(5%)=6.0; ν=2). The five dates on oak charcoal have been included in the model as *termini post quos* for the construction of the houses, with the measurements on nutshells providing dates for the use of the structures. In two of the houses the old wood effect introduced by the dating of oak charcoal is demonstrably significant. This bias may, however, amount to no more than a few decades for House C. This is suggested by the consistency of the radiocarbon determinations from this house and by the relatively slight diameter of one of the posts.

The partial remains of a rectangular house were excavated at Newtown, Co. Meath, along with an associated ancillary structure of less regular form, and pits and finds (E. Halpin 1995). The house was some 7 m wide and at least 10 m long, defined by foundation trenches (containing stone packing and some postholes) and some internal postholes. Little detailed information is available on associated material, but there are finds of pottery. Two radiocarbon measurements were obtained on unidentified bulk charcoal samples from the foundation trenches (*UB-3521–2*), providing *termini post quos* for the use of the structure (Fig. 12.24). Two other radiocarbon measurements were obtained on charcoal samples from one of the pits (Table 12.13: UB-3568–9), but as we could not ascertain what the associated material was, these have not been included in the model. Cereals have been noted from the site (Monk 2000), but we are uncertain from which specific contexts.

The remains of at least three structures were identified in the first two phases of occupation at Knowth, Co. Meath (Eogan 1984, 211–44; Eogan and Roche 1997). From what was defined as the first stage of occupation, on the north-east (Zone A) and east side (Zone B) of the main mound, site 1 (Eogan and Roche 1997, fig. 1), two structures, represented by foundation trenches 1–3 (Zone A) and 4–6 (Zone B), were identified from the partially excavated features. Others can be suspected on the basis of further but incomplete foundation trenches (Eogan and Roche 1997, 7–21). In Zone A, two statistically consistent radiocarbon measurements (*GrN-20179*, *-20180*; T'=2.6; T'(5%)=3.8; ν=1) were obtained from charcoal from Foundation Trench 1 (Eogan and Roche 1997, 9). In Zone B, a single radiocarbon measurement (*GrN-20181*) was obtained from charcoal from Foundation Trench 6 (Eogan and Roche 1997, 18). All three dates have been treated as *termini post quos* for their contexts (Fig. 12.24). A further measurement (GrN-18773) was obtained on another sample of bulk charcoal from zone A, but has not been included in the model because there were no associated artefacts in Zone A (Eogan and Roche 1997, 7).

On the west side of the main mound, (Eogan 1984, 211–19; Eogan and Roche 1997, 43–4), a sub-rectangular structure, House B, measuring some 12.30 by 10.10 m and defined by a foundation trench was assigned to the second phase ('developed Western') of occupation on the site. This underlay the outer of two arcs of palisade, and both the structure and the palisade trench were beneath the small passage tomb mound 8 (Eogan 1984, 211–19; 1986; Eogan and Roche 1997, 43–4). Within the structure was Pit 6, which contained slightly modified Carinated Bowl (Eogan 1984, 218, figs 765–7, 804–21; Sheridan 1995, 7), a flake retouched to a point and other lithics (Eogan 1984, 218, fig. 77: 823–6), as well as unidentified charcoal which provided a bulk sample for *BM-1076*, which has been treated as a *terminus post quem* for its context (Fig. 12.24). Part of a further, undated, rectangular structure (House A) was found during the excavation of the western tomb of the main mound (Eogan and Roche 1998).

In the eastern (south) group, a roughly rectangular house was excavated at Kishoge, Co. Dublin, in advance of development (O'Donovan 2003; 2004). This measured some 6 m by 4.50 m, defined by foundation trenches holding oak posts and planks. There were two internal postholes. Minor modifications had taken place in a short use-life which ended in the burning of the structure (O'Donovan 2003; 2004, 5). Only one pottery sherd was found, in a pit outside the house, and some scrapers and flakes were recovered. Three samples of oak charcoal were dated from wall planks, two of the samples being replicate measurements on the same post (GrN-26771, -26789; *F135*). These are statistically consistent (T'=0.2; T'(5%)=3.8; ν=1). A third measurement (*GrN-26770*) is significantly later (T'=6.6; T'(5%)=6.0; ν=2). These results are treated as *termini post quos* for their contexts (Fig. 12.25).

A rectangular house, Structure 3, was excavated at Kilgobbin, Co. Dublin (Ines Hagen, pers. comm.). This was some 9 m by 7 m, defined by foundation trenches (containing evidence for both posts and planks) and both internal and external postholes. Postholes and pits were also found nearby. Associated material included some Carinated Bowl sherds and a leaf-shaped arrowhead. A radiocarbon determination (*UB-6199*) was obtained on an oak charcoal sample from the foundation trench, and another (*UB-6200*) on hazelnut shells from one of the internal postholes. The first of these samples provides a *terminus post quem* for its context, while the second may date the use of the structure (Fig. 12.25).

Three rectangular houses (Houses 1–3) were excavated

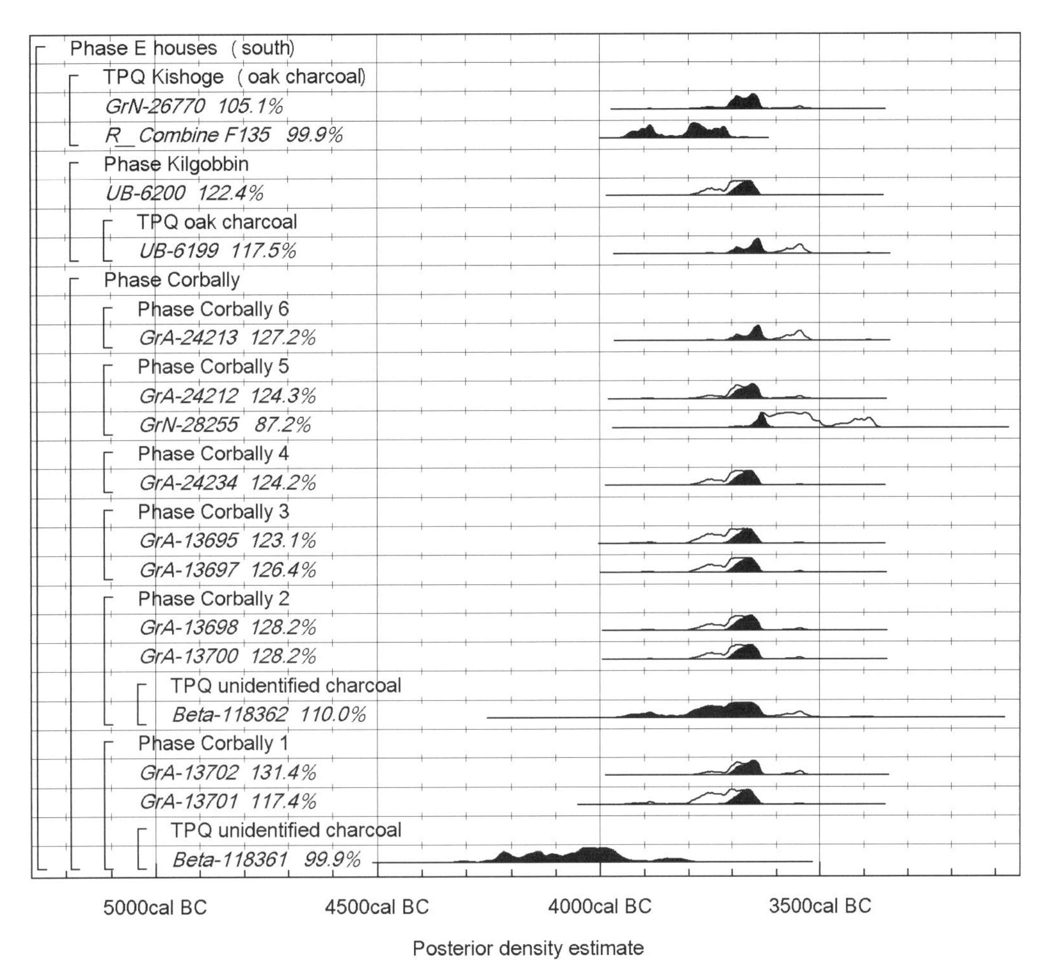

Fig. 12.25. Early Neolithic houses in Ireland (eastern (south)). Probability distributions. The format is identical to that of Fig. 12.6. The overall structure of this model is shown in Fig. 12.22 and its other components are shown in Figs 12.23–4 and 12.26–7.

close together in advance of gravel quarrying at Corbally, Kilcullen, Co. Kildare (Purcell 2002), and a further three, and a possible fourth (Houses 4–7), have been recorded 60–100 m to the south-west (Purcell 2002, 33; Tobin 2002; Redmond Tobin, pers. comm.; Smyth 2007, fig. 6). House 1 measured some 11 m by 6.70 m, with an internal division and, like both its neighbours, was defined by foundation trenches and internal and external postholes; a sequence of modifications could be suggested. Associated material included Carinated Bowl sherds, two flint leaf-shaped arrowheads and scrapers, a slate spearhead and a dolerite axehead. Small quantities of charred hazelnut shells, wheat and barley were also found. Three radiocarbon measurements were obtained. *GrA-13702* came from a single grain of *Triticum dicoccum* from the external foundation trench, and produced a measurement statistically consistent with that from *GrA-13701* (T'=0.5; T'(5%)=3.8; ν=1), on *Corylus avellana* from an internal posthole, F13, assigned to Phase 3 modifications (Purcell 2002, 43). *Beta-118361*, on unidentified charcoal, is significantly earlier than the other two measurements (T'=13.8; T'(5%)=6.0; ν=2). It came from a corner posthole in the foundation trench, F23, and has been treated as a *terminus post quem* for the construction of the house (Fig. 12.25).

House 2 measured 10.70 m by some 5 m, defined like House 1 by foundation trenches and also like it with an internal cross-division. A sequence of modifications can again be suggested. Finds included lithics (one a leaf-shaped arrowhead) and Carinated Bowl sherds. Carbonised plant remains included cereal grains and chaff. Three radiocarbon measurements were obtained. *GrA-13700* came from a single grain of *Triticum dicoccum* from one of the central internal postholes, F53; *Beta-118362* was measured on unidentified charcoal from the same feature; and *GrA-13698* on *Corylus avellana* from another internal posthole, F148, assigned to the second building phase (Purcell 2002, 54). The three measurements are statistically consistent (T'=0.0; T'(5%)=6.0; ν=2), although *Beta-118362* is treated as a *terminus post quem* for its context as it may incorporate a slight age offset (Fig. 12.25).

House 3 was a simpler, sub-rectangular, single-phase construction, measuring some 7.30 m by 6.40 m, its foundation trench containing evidence for plank walls. Carinated Bowl sherds, lithics, including a leaf-shaped arrowhead, grain and chaff were found in the foundation trench. Two statistically consistent radiocarbon measurements were obtained (T'=0.0; T'(5%)=3.8; ν=1). *GrA-13697* came from a single grain of *Triticum dicoccum*

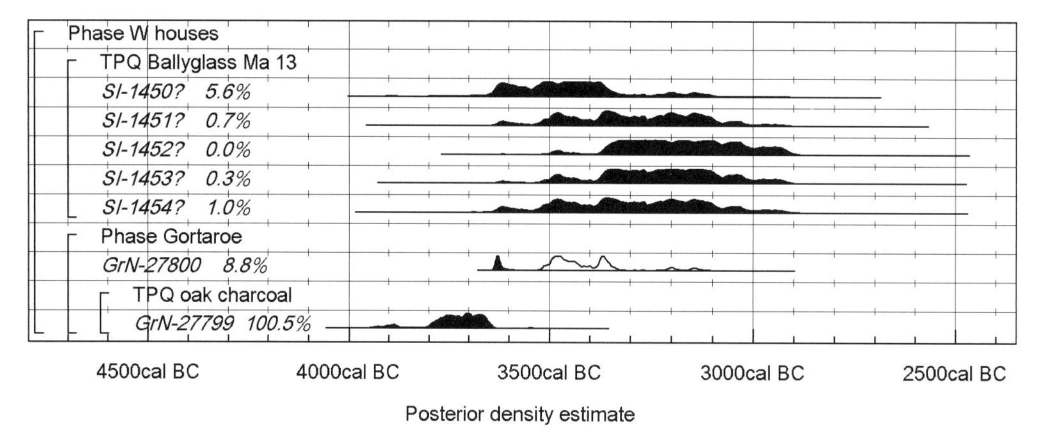

Fig. 12.26. Early Neolithic houses in Ireland (western). Probability distributions of dates. The format is identical to that of Fig. 12.6. The overall structure of this model is shown in Fig. 12.22 and its other components are shown in Figs 12.23–5 and 12.27.

from an internal posthole, F208; and *GrA-13695* on *Corylus avellana* came from another internal posthole, F249. These provide dates for the use of the structure (Fig. 12.25).

Further radiocarbon measurements were obtained from Houses 4–6 (Redmond Tobin, pers. comm.). House 4 measured some 10 m by 7 m and was defined by a bedding trench containing the burnt remains of upright oak planks which had been replaced by flimsier panels. Finds included large quantities of pottery and lithics, as well as a stone axehead which had been placed in the foundation trench and charred seeds, chaff and hazelnut shells. One hazelnut shell fragment from the eastern foundation trench was the sample for *GrA-24234* (Fig. 12.25). House 5, at right-angles to House 4, was much poorer in finds, and measured only 7 m by 5 m. It too was defined by a bedding trench, the oak planks in which had burnt along the west side (Tobin 2002, 186). *GrA-24212* was measured on cereal remains from the foundation trench and *GrN-28255* on hazelnut and cereal remains from an internal posthole. The two results are statistically consistent (T'=2.3; T'(5%)=3.8; ν=1). House 6, on the same axis as House 5 and to the west of it, was identified more tentatively and yielded a high density of seeds and chaff (Tobin 2002, 186–7). *GrA-24213* was measured on hazelnut and cereal remains from the foundation trench. The samples from all of these three houses date their use (Fig. 12.25).

Turning to the west (Fig. 12.26), a rectangular house, some 13 m by 6 m, defined by foundation trenches and postholes, was found underlying the court tomb (Ma 13) at Ballyglass, Co. Mayo (Ó Nualláin 1972; Ó Nualláin *et al.* forthcoming). The excavator has suggested that the house may have been deliberately demolished (Ó Nualláin 1972, 54–5). Plain Carinated Bowl pottery was associated with it. Five samples of bulk charcoal were obtained from the house and produced statistically consistent radiocarbon measurements (Fig. 12.26; T'=2.5; T'(5%)=9.5; ν=4). Of these, one (SI-1454) was identified as oak. These dates should provide *termini post quos* for construction, but are excluded from the model because, like Smithsonian Institution dates for samples from the other Ballyglass court tomb (Ma 14; see Ó Nualláin 1998) and the Céide Fields (Tables 12.5–6), they seem anomalously recent for their contexts. It has not been possible to establish how the samples were prepared and measured, although other samples dated by the Smithsonian Institution were prepared as described by Stuckenrath and Mielke (1973) and dated by GPC of methane (Mielke and Long 1969). Further radiocarbon dates recently obtained from Ma 13 confirm that the Smithsonian measurements are anomalous.[4]

A rectangular house was excavated at Gortaroe, just north of Westport, Co. Mayo (Gillespie 2002; Richard Gillespie, pers. comm.). Measuring some 9.80 m by 6.60 m, it was defined by a foundation trench with packing stones, suggesting a split plank wall and internal postholes and stakeholes. Associated finds included flint and chert leaf-shaped arrowheads and scrapers and one body sherd. Charred hazelnuts and one grain of *Hordeum vulgare* were recovered. Two statistically inconsistent radiocarbon measurements (T'=20.5; T'(5%)=3.8; ν=1) were obtained from samples directly associated with the structure. *GrN-27799* came from oak charcoal from an internal posthole (context 34) and has been treated as a *terminus post quem* for the use of the structure; *GrN-27800* came from alder charcoal from the foundation trench (context 5) and dates the construction of the house (Fig. 12.26).

Turning finally to the southern grouping (Fig. 12.27), two structures were excavated in advance of road construction just outside Waterford at Granny, Co. Kilkenny (Hughes 2005). Structure 1 was rectangular, over 6 m by 5 m, defined by foundation trenches and perhaps by external postholes. Finds included a possible leaf-shaped arrowhead and sherds of Carinated Bowl pottery. Structure 2, 9 m to the south-east, was less regular, consisting of an L-shaped foundation trench, and other postholes, very short foundation trenches and a pit. Associated material included a chert leaf-shaped arrowhead and a small quantity of Carinated Bowl pottery. A single radiocarbon measurement (*UB-6315*) was obtained on oak charcoal from one of the postholes, and has been treated as a *terminus post quem* for the construction of Structure 2 (Fig. 12.27).

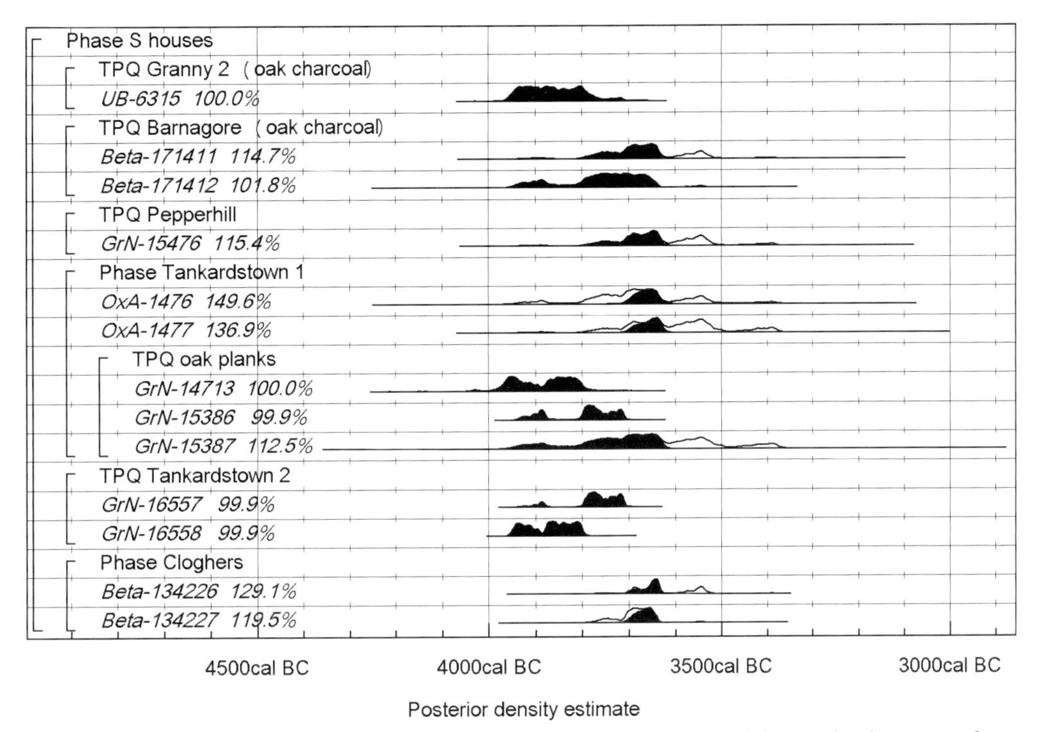

Fig. 12.27. Early Neolithic houses in Ireland (southern). Probability distributions of dates. The format is identical to that of Fig. 12.6. The overall structure of this model is shown in Fig. 12.22 and its other components are shown in Figs 12.23–6.

A rectangular house was excavated in advance of road construction at Barnagore, west of Cork, Co. Cork (Danaher 2003; 2009). This measured 6.40 m by 5.40 m, defined by foundation trenches, which had held split timber planks on one long and one short side, and panels of wickerwork or wattle and daub on the others. No artefacts or animal bones were recovered. The structure appeared to have been burnt down. Two statistically consistent radiocarbon measurements (T'=0.5; T'(5%)=3.8; ν=1) were obtained from the structure. *Beta-171411* was measured on a charred oak stake from within the east foundation trench, and *Beta-171412* on a charred split timber from the southern foundation trench. Both have been treated as *termini post quos* for the construction of the house (Fig. 12.27). It is possible, however, that *Beta-171411*, from a stake, may have been a relatively slight timber with an age offset of only a few decades.

A probable but severely truncated house was found at Pepperhill, Co. Cork, in advance of gas pipeline construction (Gowen 1988). A length of foundation trench and associated postholes were associated with plain Carinated Bowl pottery. A single radiocarbon measurement (*GrN-15476*) was obtained on unidentified charcoal from the foundation trench and is treated as a *terminus post quem* for the construction of the structure (Fig. 12.27)

Excavation in advance of a gas pipeline at Tankardstown, Co. Limerick (Gowen 1988, 30), revealed the rectangular foundation trench of a burnt plank house (House 1), 7.40 m by 6.40 m, with two main internal postholes and other small internal features. The foundation trench had held split planks, with stone packing and posts at the corners and midway on the long sides. Associated finds, mainly from the upper fill of the foundation trench, included a lozenge-shaped flint arrowhead, worked quartz and chert, and some small sherds of plain fine Carinated Bowl pottery (Gowen 1988, 34, figs 8–9). Carbonised remains of *Triticum dicoccum* were recovered in some quantity (Gowen 1988, 41). Five radiocarbon measurements were obtained, three on samples from charred oak planks (*GrN-14713*, -15386–7), and two on wheat grains (*OxA-1476–7*). The measurements on the wheat grains are statistically consistent (T'=0.2; T'(5%)=3.8; ν=1), and may date the use of the structure (Fig. 12.27). They are significantly later than those on the oak planks (T'=12.5; T'(5%)=9.5; ν=4), which have been used as *termini post quos* for their contexts (Fig. 12.27). Further excavations revealed a second, larger, rectangular structure (House 2), some 20 m to the north-west (Gowen 1988; Gowen and Tarbett 1988; 1989; 1990). This too was defined by a foundation trench, measuring some 15.50 by 7.50 m, with two internal cross-divisions. Associated material includes plain, fine 'classic' Carinated Bowl pottery. Two statistically inconsistent radiocarbon measurements (*GrN-16557-8*; T'=7.0; T'(5%)=3.8; ν=1) were obtained on charred oak timbers from the east wall of the central compartment, and have been treated as *termini post quos* for the construction of the house (Fig. 12.27).

To the north-east of Tankardstown is the well known site of Lough Gur with the focus of Neolithic settlement activity on Knockadoon, for long the key site for Irish Neolithic settlement. Ó Ríordáin's major report on his campaign of excavation in the 1940s and 1950s (Ó Ríordáin 1954) was followed by the later publication of other unpublished sites (Grogan and Eogan 1987). Recent excavation has demonstrated the extent of Bronze

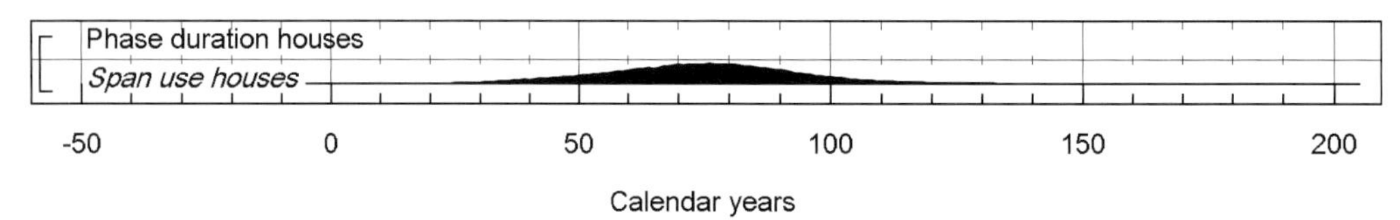

Fig. 12.28. Early Neolithic houses in Ireland. Probability distribution of the number of years during which they were constructed and used, derived from the model shown in Figs 12.22–7.

Age activity there (Cleary 1993; 1995; 2003) and has suggested that some structures previously thought of as Neolithic may be of Bronze Age date. This has given rise to debate about the initiation and significance of Neolithic settlement at Knockadoon, the ceramic sequence and the date of the settlement structures (Grogan 2005; Cooney 2007b). Resolution is not advanced by the fact that there are a limited number of radiocarbon dates covering the Neolithic period here, and that two of them (Table 12.3: D-40–1), from the central house at circle L, were measured in the very early days of the method. In this context, while there is clearly early Neolithic activity at Lough Gur, the site cannot add much to the present discussion, and the dates are not included in the model.

At Cloghers, just outside Tralee, Co. Kerry, a rectangular house was revealed by excavation in advance of housing development (Kiely 2003; Kiely and Dunne 2005). The structure, defined by foundation trenches (containing postholes and split planks) and postholes, was some 7.8 m by 13 m. It was associated with Carinated Bowl pottery, worked lithics of various materials, and remains of hazelnuts, bread wheat, barley, oats and perhaps spelt; some calcined bones of cattle and sheep came from a pit outside the house. Two statistically consistent radiocarbon measurements (T'=0.8; T'(5%)=3.8; ν=1) were obtained on hazelnuts directly associated with pottery (*Beta-134227*, *-134226*), from the northern wall of the house and the basal fill of a posthole in the west internal wall, respectively. They date the use of the house (Fig. 12.27).

Chronologies for early Neolithic houses in Ireland

The model defined in Figs 12.22–7 suggests that the construction and use of early Neolithic houses in Ireland began in *3730–3660 cal BC* (*95% probability*; Fig. 12.22: *start houses*), probably in *3715–3680 cal BC* (*68% probability*). These structures were in use until *3640–3605 cal BC* (*95% probability*; Fig. 12.22: *end houses*), probably until *3635–3615 cal BC* (*68% probability*). This model suggests that the activity represented by the use of these rectangular structures lasted for a relatively restricted period of time: *30–115 years* (*95% probability*; Fig. 12.28: *use houses*), probably for *55–95 years* (*68% probability*). In social and human terms this represents perhaps only three or four generations.[5]

Sixty-eight radiocarbon determinations are included in this model, from 30 different structures. At first sight, this seems an impressive assemblage, but only 20 of the measurements are on short-life material which provides more than a *terminus post quem* for the construction or demolition of the structure concerned. These 20 dates on short-life material come from 14 houses. Again these appear to provide a representative sample, but six of these houses and ten of the short-life samples come from the single site of Corbally. Given this, it is necessary to examine the robustness of this model.

As previously observed (McSparron 2003; 2008), the dates on short-life material form a highly coherent group. The model shows good overall agreement ($A_{overall}$=122.5%; Fig. 12.22) and all the dates which provide *termini post quos* are in good agreement with the end date for the use of rectangular houses calculated by the model. The only outlier is the bulk sample of alder charcoal from Gortaroe (Fig. 12.26: *GrN-27800*; A=9.9%), which falls rather later than the rest. This determination may simply be a statistical outlier, not unexpected in a series of this size.

To investigate further the sensitivity of our results to the existing limited suite of short-life samples, we have to assess the possibility that the model defined in Figs 12.22–12.27 is unduly influenced by the number of dates from Corbally. If Corbally happened to be of short overall life within a longer-lasting phenomenon of house construction and use this site may be biasing the sample. For this reason, an alternative model has been constructed (Fig. 12.29). This is of identical form to that shown in Fig. 12.22, but in this case the two oak samples from Monanny House C (Fig. 12.24) and *Beta-171411* from Barnagore (Fig. 12.27) have been interpreted as close in age to the construction of the structures from which they derive. This could be the case since the undifferentiated oak samples in question appear to have come from relatively slight timbers. This model suggests that houses may have begun perhaps a generation earlier, in *3770–3675 cal BC* (*95% probability*; Fig. 12.29: *start houses* (sensitivity analysis)), probably in *3740–3695 cal BC* (*68% probability*). The estimate for the time when houses went out of use in this reading changes little and is *3635–3600 cal BC* (*95% probability*; Fig. 12.29: *end houses* (sensitivity analysis)), probably *3630–3615 cal BC* (*68% probability*). In this case, houses were in use for *45–155 years* (*95% probability*; distribution not shown), probably for *70–125 years*.

This analysis demonstrates once again the importance of submitting short-life, single-entity samples for radiocarbon dating (Ashmore 1999a). The precision of the date estimates and the apparently short duration of this phenomenon mean that even a relatively small old-wood offset (say, from a timber that was 50 years-old when felled) is of significance in our statistical modelling and archaeological interpretation.

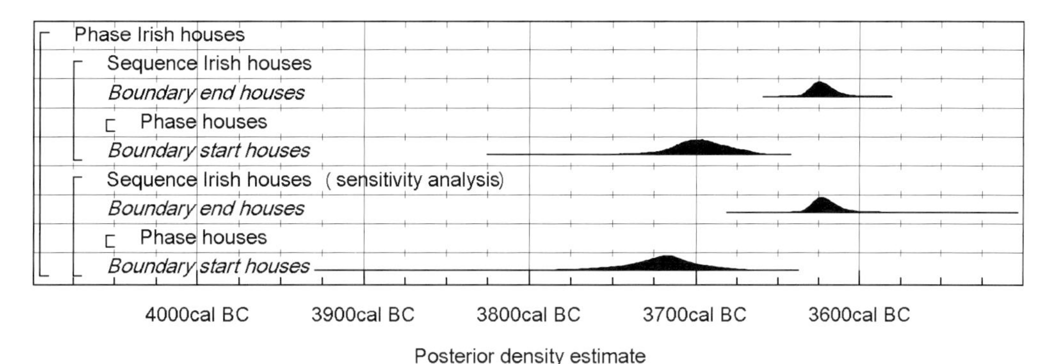

Fig. 12.29. Early Neolithic houses in Ireland. Probability distributions for the dates when they were constructed and used, derived from the model shown in Figs 12. 22–7 and the alternative model described in the text.

It emerges from this analysis as of the outmost importance to date a more representative selection of houses – with short-life, single-entity samples. On present evidence, we prefer the shorter chronology suggested by the first model (Figs 12.22–7), because it relies only on samples that are known to be short-life. A very slightly longer chronology, however, cannot be ruled out at this stage.

It is hard to over-emphasise the significance of these chronologies for understanding both early Neolithic rectangular houses in their own right and the early Neolithic in Ireland as a whole, as already argued by Cormac McSparron (2003; 2008). The numbers of these structures have increased dramatically over recent years, and they have been taken as a powerful icon of the different nature of the early Neolithic in Ireland as compared with southern Britain, denoting a sedentary existence based around house-based residential units, and very possibly also the expression of a different process of initiation of the Neolithic in Ireland, involving colonisation (Cooney 2000a; Cooney 2007a; Grogan 2003; Rowley-Conwy 2004; R. Bradley 2007; among many other references). On the basis of the chronological models proposed above, a radically different perspective emerges. These structures cannot be seen as belonging necessarily to the whole of the Irish early Neolithic, but to a tightly defined horizon within it, probably confined to a duration of three to four, or four to five, generations. This use centres on the first three quarters of the 37th century cal BC (Fig. 12.29, upper). So why did these buildings suddenly become fashionable and can their social role be recast?

Are these generations when houses were current also the first generations of the Irish Neolithic as a whole? We come back to this question when models for the start of the Neolithic in Ireland are presented below (Chapter 12.4).

Do the models also affect our view of whether these structures were part of a sedentary existence? Size is one argument that the houses have a residential function. The Irish structures cluster between 5 m and 11 m in length and include no examples comparable with large, hall-like British buildings like those at White Horse Stone (Chapter 7), Yarnton (Chapter 8) or in Scotland (Chapter 14), although at Mullaghbuoy on the Islandmagee peninsula, Co. Antrim, in the north-east (McManus 2004) two structures tacked onto one another give a total length of *c.* 24 m. It is possible that form and location here indicate a link with the contemporary Scottish hall tradition (see Chapter 14.7). If houses were bases for sedentary existence, however, why were they in use for such a short period of time? The brief timescales involved might still be compatible with a style of living rooted in particular places, with people using as a residential base structures which could have endured for at least a generation, extended by rebuilding in some cases. As a variant on this, this particular expression of attachment to place could have emerged at a particular historical moment as a chosen social strategy on the part of what have been termed house societies (Cooney 2003; R. Bradley 2007; Borić 2008).

In either case, there are other dimensions of houses to consider, where again the brief currency of the phenomenon is central. Cross (2003) has proposed that they could have been loci for feasting, although the food remains from them have not yet been published in sufficient detail to support or refute this particular interpretation. A recent review of the totality of the evidence for Irish early Neolithic settlement has emphasised how the houses fit into a wider pattern of varied occupation and activity in the landscape. Both the foundation and ending of many were marked by series of placed deposits and their use was diverse and variable (Smyth 2006; 2007; 2011). Smyth argues persuasively that the burning which ended the histories of many of these structures was the result of sustained, purposeful effort, perhaps linked to turning points in individual or group life cycles. She sees a shared house 'template' and tradition in island-wide similarities in materials, methods of construction and size (Smyth 2006; 2007; 2011).

Is it coincidental that the brief currency of houses in Ireland was contemporary with the introduction and most intensive period of construction of enclosures in southern Britain? More directly in the Irish context, it is *85% probable* that both the enclosures at both Magheraboy and Donegore were built before the start of the Irish house tradition, and *99.8% probable* that both enclosures continued in use after the house tradition. The obvious distinctions between houses and enclosures are those of scale and brevity. Most enclosures would have encompassed more people and some had longer sequences of use. But episodes of

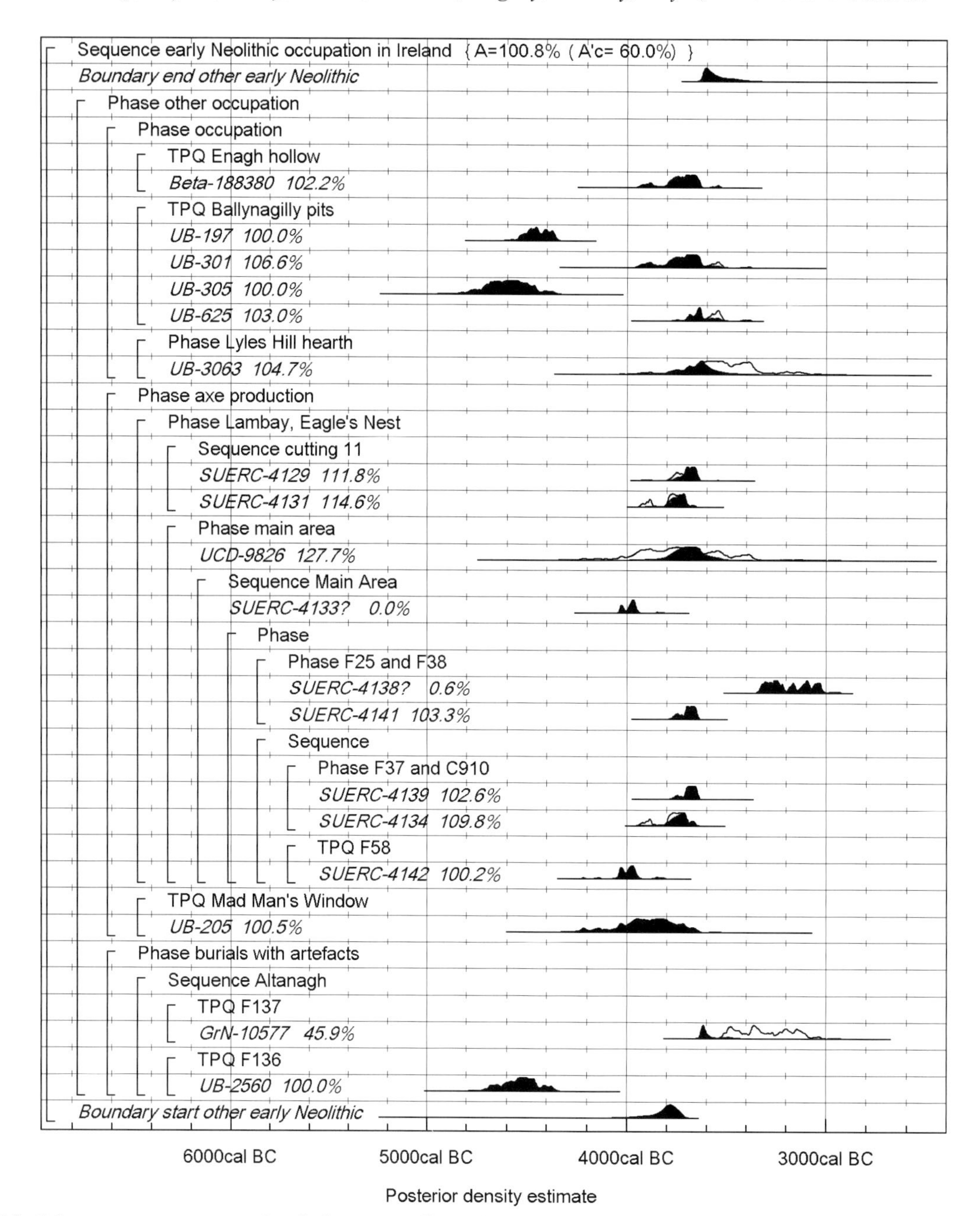

Fig. 12.30. Other contexts associated with diagnostically early Neolithic cultural material. Probability distributions of dates. The format is identical to that of Fig. 12.6. The large square brackets down the left-hand side, along with the OxCal keywords, define the overall model exactly.

activity at some enclosures can be broken down in terms of both temporality and scale, so that the differences may be relative rather than absolute. Indeed Smyth (2006, 243) has noted the similarities between open house sites like Ballygalley and those set within the palisaded enclosure at Thornhill, Co. Derry (Logue 2003). Houses and enclosures shared certain roles. Houses may have brought numbers of people together for both construction and very possibly for ending by demolition or burning as well. The births and deaths, as well as the lives, of houses were accompanied by purposeful depositions (Smyth 2006; 2007). At least some houses can be seen as nodes in systems of movement and exchange of materials across the landscape, as argued by Derek Simpson for Ballygalley (1996), a role also attributed to the Thornhill settlement. Houses marked place, and gave meaning to chosen parts of the landscape. Their use involved repetition, and to some extent rebuildings, for example as seen at Ballyharry and Corbally.

Given this degree of overlap, if we think in terms of social strategies that emerge at particular historical moments, could there be a link between the appearance of rectangular houses in Ireland and the appearance of causewayed enclosures, principally in southern Britain? Do both reflect a similar kind of sociality, expressed in different forms and distributed differently through their respective landscapes, both social forms that respect a physical template but are used in quite varied ways? Or did different kinds of more complex interaction take place at and through enclosures? We discuss the Irish houses further in relation to other evidence for the Irish early Neolithic below, and again in relation to southern British and Scottish evidence in Chapters 14.8–9 and 15; and the scarcity of enclosures in Ireland is also considered in a broader perspective in Chapter 15.9.

Other early Neolithic occupation and activity

Houses are not the only manifestation of settlement in the early Neolithic in Ireland, though they have attracted much recent coverage. Other features including spreads of artefacts, pits, hearths and scattered postholes and stakeholes are also known, some in the general vicinity of houses, and others on their own (Cooney 2000a; Grogan 2004, 103; Smyth 2007; McQuade *et al.* 2009). In addition to the houses and features within them containing diagnostically early Neolithic material culture presented above, some other early Neolithic occupation sites have also been dated (Table 12.4). We also present dating for other activity, including axehead production.

A hollow 200 m east of the house at Enagh produced five small body sherds of what appears to be Carinated Bowl pottery and unidentified charcoal, which provides a *terminus post quem* for this activity (Fig. 12.30: *Beta-188380*).

At Ballynagilly, four samples of charcoal were dated from various pit contexts around the house, all associated with early Neolithic material. Three of the samples (*UB-301*, *-305*, *-625*) are unidentified and so provide *termini post quos* for the features from which they were recovered (Fig. 12.30). Two of these samples (*UB-301*, *-625*) provide *termini post quos* in the second quarter of the fourth millennium cal BC. The third (*UB-305*) is of mid-fifth millennium cal BC date. A fourth sample (UB-197) consisted of pine charcoal, providing a date of 4550–4350 cal BC (95% confidence; Table 12.4). These two fifth millennium dates, along with four other unidentified charcoal samples of similar age but unassociated with diagnostic material (Table 12.13), were first taken to support a very early date for the start of the Neolithic in Ireland (ApSimon 1976), but were subsequently interpreted as probably old wood (Kinnes 1988; Sheridan 1995, 7; Cooney 2000a, 13). Pine generally does not live as long as oak (Mitchell 1974) and an old-wood offset of more than a few hundred years at the outside is improbable. Either, therefore, we must revive the idea that Ballynagilly is by far the earliest Neolithic settlement in Ireland and Britain, or the charcoal dated by UB-197 must have been redeposited from an earlier feature, or derived from a bog pine. We strongly incline to the view that the sample was older than its context, because UB-197 is at least several hundred years earlier than any other sample relating to Neolithic artefacts in Ireland, and because it seems too much to base such a radical argument on a single date.

At Lyles Hill, although there is no doubting the quantities of early Neolithic material (E. Evans 1953; Sheridan 1995, 7; Cooney 2000a, 113; Nelis 2003, 216), it is now, as noted above, unlikely that the enclosure is of Neolithic date. Several radiocarbon dates have been obtained from the site (Simpson and Gibson 1989). *UB-3063*, on barley from a hearth associated with 'modified' Carinated Bowl pottery (Sheridan 2001), provides a date for some of this early Neolithic activity (Fig. 12.30). Two other samples are associated with unweathered Carinated Bowl, but are on unidentified charcoal, from the inner and outer palisades respectively (UB-3074, -3062). The date of these palisades is uncertain, although, given these *termini post quos,* they appear to be of third millennium cal BC date or later (Table 12.4). Two other samples, also on unidentified charcoal, came from the top of the buried soil under the enclosure bank and from the core of the bank respectively (UB-3061, -3060), and post-date the Neolithic (Table 12.4). In these circumstances, it seems most plausible to interpret the palisades as part of a later enclosure of the hilltop, whether or not it was the same episode as that represented by the earthwork, and the early Neolithic pottery from them as redeposited.

Dates are available for two axehead production sites. Excavations at Eagle's Nest, Lambay Island, Co. Dublin, recovered evidence for the extraction and working of porphyry (porphyritic andesite; Cooney 2005). This is a medium-grained volcanic lithology which was worked by hammering and pecking with some flaking. Excavation took place in two small adjoining valleys defined by porphyry outcrops. All stages of axehead production, from quarrying to grinding or polishing, took place at the production site, where there is also evidence for formal, structured deposition. Four samples of short-life charcoal were submitted from debitage layers in one of the excavated quarry areas (Cutting 11). Two of these (SUERC-4130, -4132) produced dates falling in the eighth and seventh millennia cal BC and must have been redeposited (Table 12.4). The other two samples (*SUERC-4129*, *-4131*) produced measurements which are statistically consistent (T'=1.5; T'(5%)=3.8; ν=1), and are in good agreement with the stratigraphic sequence (Fig. 12.30).

From the main area of depositional activity on the floor of the eastern valley, a sample of oak charcoal (*SUERC-4142*) from pit F58 provides a *terminus post quem* for the overlying deposits, including F37 and context C910. Feature 37, a polygonal slab setting placed over a pit concentration (of which pit F58 forms a part), produced a radiocarbon measurement on *Prunus* sp. charcoal (*SUERC-4139*). Context C910, a dark brown loam deposit with a rich artefact assemblage including flint and jasper artefacts, produced another measurement (*SUERC-4134*) on a fragment of alder charcoal. These last two samples provided statistically consistent radiocarbon determinations (T'=1.7; T'(5%)=3.8; ν=1), which are in good agreement with the measurement from pit F58 below (Fig. 12.30). Samples have been dated from two other features. F38, a deposit of porphyry debitage and sediment in a hollow, produced a measurement on a fragment of alder charcoal (*SUERC-4141*), and the fill of F25, a linear cut, produced

Table 12.4. Radiocarbon dates for other early Neolithic activity in Ireland. Posterior density estimates derive from the model defined in Fig. 12.30.

Laboratory number	Sample reference	Material	Context	Radiocarbon age (BP)	$\delta^{13}C$ (‰)	Calibrated date range (cal BC) (95% confidence)	*Posterior density estimate (cal BC) (95% probability)*
Enagh, Co. Derry							
Beta-188380		Charcoal (unidentified)	Site 3, F305, context 302. Upper fill of depression containing early Neolithic pottery, 200 m away from site 2 (McSparron 2003)	5170±70		4230–3790	*3945–3855 (12%)* or *3825–3630 (83%)*
Ballynagilly, Co. Tyrone, discrete features							
UB-197	L67.32	*Pinus* sp. charcoal	Pit (F135). Pit containing hearth debris and Carinated Bowl sherds, 7 m south of house in Square L (A. Smith *et al.* 1970)	5625±50		4550–4350	*4550–4350*
UB-301	L67.11, L67.12	Charcoal (unidentified)	Pit F (L) 134) with early Neolithic pottery, 30 m E of house (A. Smith *et al.* 1971)	4910±90		3950–3520	*3950–3620 (92%)* or *3590–3535 (3%)*
UB-305	L67.48	Charcoal (unidentified)	Pit F (L) 16. Hearth pit with early Neolithic pottery, 15 m SE of house (A. Smith *et al.* 1971)	5745±90		4800–4360	*4790–4440 (91%)* or *4425–4370 (4%)*
UB-625	L67.40-43, 67.50-1, 67.65	Charcoal (unidentified)	F162. Pit with early Neolithic pottery, isolated (Arthur ApSimon pers. comm.)	4835±55	−24.8	3710–3510	*3760–3740 (1%)* or *3715–3520 (94%)*
Lyles Hill, Co. Antrim							
UB-3063		*Hordeum* sp.	Hearth with modified Carinated Bowl pottery (Sheridan 2001; Simpson and Gibson 1989). Measurement communicated by Queen's University, Belfast	4765±135	−30.6	3900–3110	*3800–3475*
UB-3074		Charcoal (unidentified)	Inner palisade, with unweathered Carinated Bowl pottery (Sheridan 2001; Simpson and Gibson 1989). Measurement communicated by Queen's University, Belfast	4433±40	−26.1	3340–2910	
UB-3062		Charcoal (unidentified)	Outer palisade, with unweathered Carinated Bowl pottery (Sheridan 2001; Simpson and Gibson 1989). Measurement communicated by Queen's University, Belfast	3974±165	−23.5	2910–1980	
UB-3061		Charcoal (unidentified)	Top of buried soil beneath enclosure bank (Simpson and Gibson 1989). Measurement communicated by Queen's University, Belfast	3386±100	−26.6	1940–1440	
UB-3060		Charcoal (unidentified)	Core of bank (Simpson and Gibson 1989). Measurement communicated by Queen's University, Belfast	3229±115	−26.4	1760–1260	
UB-3058		Charcoal (unidentified)	Gravel capping of bank (Simpson and Gibson 1989). Measurement communicated by Queen's University, Belfast	1958±130	−26.8	360 cal BC–cal AD 380	
UB-3059		Charcoal (unidentified)	Posthole (Simpson and Gibson 1989). Measurement communicated by Queen's University, Belfast	1796±55	−27.0	cal AD 80–390	
Eagle's Nest, Lambay Island, Co. Dublin							
SUERC-4130		*Prunus* sp. charcoal	C1108. Porphyry debitage layer associated with the production of stone axeheads	8070±40	−24.7	7140–6840	
SUERC-4132		*Prunus* sp. charcoal	C1112. Porphyry debitage layer associated with the production of stone axeheads	7965±40	−24.8	7050–6680	
SUERC-4131		*Prunus* sp. charcoal	C1109. Debitage layer, stratified below sample for SUERC-4129	4990±35	−24.4	3940–3660	*3810–3665*
SUERC-4129		*Corylus avellana* charcoal	C1106. Debitage layer, stratified above sample for SUERC-4131	4925±40	−25.3	3790–3640	*3755–3640*
SUERC-4138		*Prunus* sp. charcoal	Main area, F25. Linear cut	4460±35	−26.2	3350–3010	
SUERC-4141		*Alnus glutinosa* charcoal	Main area, F38. Deposit of porphyry debitage and associated sediment in a hollow	4920±35	−29.3	3780–3640	*3765–3640*

Laboratory number	Sample reference	Material	Context	Radiocarbon age (BP)	δ¹³C (‰)	Calibrated date range (cal BC) (95% confidence)	*Posterior density estimate (cal BC) (95% probability)*
SUERC-4142		*Quercus* sp. charcoal	Main area, F58. Pit	5180±45	−25.3	4050–3940	*4225–4205* (*1%*) or *4160–4130* (*2%*) or *4070–3930* (*85%*) or *3875–3805* (*7%*)
SUERC-4139		*Prunus* sp. charcoal	Main area, F37. Polygonal slab setting, stratigraphically later than context of SUERC-4142	4910±35	−25.3	3770–3630	*3765–3640*
SUERC-4134		*Alnus glutinosa* charcoal	Main area, C910. Deliberate deposit of worked flint, charcoal, jasper and other cultural material, stratigraphically later than context of SUERC-4142	4980±40	−25.9	3940–3650	*3800–3655*
SUERC-4133		*Corylus avellana* charcoal	Main area, C904. Deliberate deposit of worked flint, charcoal, jasper and other cultural material	5170±35	−25.1	4050–3940	
UCD-9826		*Prunus* sp. charcoal	Main area pit F1. Stratigraphically isolated pit containing rich artefact assemblage	4930±175		4070–3340	*3875–3510*
Mad Man's Window, Co. Antrim							
UB-205		Charcoal (unidentified)	Site 1. Spread of charcoal in soil formed on large slab of rock and preserved under basalt scree, associated with Carinated Bowl, a scatter of flint debitage and several roughouts for flint axeheads (Woodman 1992, 78)	5095±120		4240–3540	*4230–4195* (*2%*) or *4170–4125* (*3%*) or *4120–4090* (*2%*) or *4080–3645* (*88%*)
Altanagh, Co. Tyrone							
UB-2560		Charcoal (unidentified)	Irregular pit, F136, with Carinated Bowl sherds, polished stone axeheads etc., overlain by burial F137 (context of GrN-10557)	5685±70	−26.3	4710–4350	*4690–4365*
GrN-10577		Charcoal (unidentified)	F137. Oval, stone-lined pit containing bones of two individuals, Bowl pottery and lithics. Overlay pit F136 (context of UB-2560) On same hilltop as badly damaged megalith, possibly a court tomb (B. Williams 1986)	4590±80	−23.7	3630–3020	*3655–3545* (*78%*) or *3540–3430* (*17%*)

a result from a fragment of *Prunus* sp. charcoal (*SUERC-4138*). Both of these samples, along with those from Feature 37 and context C910, are stratigraphically earlier than a fragment of short-life, hazel charcoal (*SUERC-4133*) from context C904. This measurement, however, has poor agreement with the samples from the contexts beneath (A=6.7%) and must be reworked. A bulk sample of *Prunus* sp. charcoal (*UCD-9826*) was also dated from F1, a stratigraphically isolated pit that contained a rich artefact assemblage including porphyry debitage and associated hammerstones, struck flint and middle Neolithic pottery, which raises the probability that the charcoal was derived from earlier activity at the site.

When the eighth to seventh millennium cal BC dates (SUERC-4130, -4132) are disregarded, six of the seven remaining measurements of single-entity short-life charcoal samples are statistically consistent (T'=4.2; T'(5%)=11.1; v=5). These dates may suggest a fairly short period of porphyry exploitation for axe production falling in the 38th or 37th centuries cal BC (Fig. 12.30). SUERC-4138 may date a later episode of activity falling in the third quarter of the fourth millennium cal BC, perhaps relating to the middle Neolithic pottery from F1, and so has been excluded from the model for early Neolithic activity at Lambay. It is an open question whether there may have been earlier exploitation of the porphyry source. There is obviously residual charcoal on the site, evidenced by the eighth and seventh millennia cal BC dates. There are no Mesolithic lithics on the site but there is definite evidence for Mesolithic activity on the island (Dolan and Cooney 2010). The sample for SUERC-4133 was redeposited in the context from which it was recovered, and the depositional activity could have disturbed charcoal from earlier deposits. It does, however, provide a measurement on a short-life charcoal sample dating to the decades around 4000 cal BC. Whether this can be taken as an indicator of the beginning of the working of the porphyry source is debatable.

At Mad Man's Window, Co. Antrim (Woodman 1992), a small area of Neolithic activity (Site 1) was preserved under a basalt scree where soil had developed on a rock-cut platform. This was one of a number of Neolithic chipping floors investigated during the rebuilding of the Antrim coast road. Within the soil and on top of a large slab of rock, there was a spread of charcoal associated with Carinated Bowl, a scatter of flint debitage and several roughouts for flint axeheads (Woodman 1992, 78). Unidentified charcoal produced a date of 4240–3540 cal BC (95% confidence; Table 12.4: UB-205). This date provides a *terminus post quem* for the artefacts and axe production. It should be noted that Site 1 stands out from the other sites at Mad Man's Window where flint axe production was more dispersed (Woodman 1992, 84–6).

An early Neolithic burial from Altanagh, Co. Tyrone (Williams 1986) can be included here. Unidentified charcoal (*UB-2560*) from an irregular pit, F136, with finds including Carinated Bowl sherds and polished stone axeheads, provides a *terminus post quem* for a feature above it. This was an oval, stone-lined pit (F137), containing the bones of two individuals, Bowl pottery and lithics. In turn, this produced another sample of unidentified charcoal (*GrN-10577*), which provides a *terminus post quem* for this secondary activity (Fig. 12.30).

A chronology for early Neolithic occupation and other activity

The model for occupation and other activity associated with culturally diagnostic early Neolithic material is shown in Fig. 12.30. This suggests that this activity began in *4000–3700 cal BC* (*95% probability*; Fig. 12.30: *start other early Neolithic*), probably in *3840–3725 cal BC* (*68% probability*). It ended in *3645–3360 cal BC* (*95% probability*; Fig. 12.30: *end other early Neolithic*), probably in *3630–3520 cal BC* (*68% probability*). These estimates are independent of those derived from dates associated with the early Neolithic rectangular houses, so that this sample is not biased by a disproportionate number of dates derived from an intense but short period of house construction in the 37th century cal BC. Consequently, this model provides an independent indication of the appearance of early Neolithic activity and its associated material culture in Ireland. Further radiocarbon dates associated with other, diagnostic Neolithic practices in Ireland are considered below.

Portal, court and related tombs

Generally dispersed across the landscape (Cummings 2009, chapter 6), and with greater concentrations in the northern and eastern parts of the island, portal tombs and court tombs are a striking feature of the Irish Neolithic (e.g. Cody 2002; C. Jones 2007). The architecture of portal tombs appears to emphasise the prominently raised, often tilted, capstone, whether or not that was above a surrounding platform or a more substantial cairn (Ó Nualláin 1983; Shee Twohig 1990; cf. Whittle 2005). The architecture of court tombs combines the frontal (in some cases central) arena of the court with a linear arrangement of stone chambers, within a cairn which in some instances may not have fully covered the chamber (de Valera 1960; Cody 2002). Human remains have been found in both kinds of monument, with burnt or charred bones more common in court tombs (Herity 1987; Cooney and Grogan 1994, fig. 4.14; A. Powell 2005). Both kinds of monument are now generally assigned to the early Neolithic (e.g. ApSimon 1986; Waddell 1998; F. Lynch 2000; Cooney 2000a; Cummings and Whittle 2004), though previously the finds from portal tombs had encouraged a dating to later in the Neolithic (e.g. Herity 1982; cf. Herity 1987). It has been long recognised that there are structural affinities between portal and court tombs, with chambers of portal tomb form occurring in court tombs (see discussion in Waddell 1998, 91–2). The court tomb at Ballymacaldrack provides a clear link with a non-megalithic monumental funerary tradition in the early Neolithic in Ireland (Sheridan 2006a). Two sites within this non-megalithic tradition are discussed below.

Portal tombs

The dating of portal tombs is challenging because their chambers could have remained accessible for an extended period after construction. Finds include early Neolithic artefacts, but also later ones (Herity 1982; Shee Twohig 1990; Waddell 1998; Kytmannow 2008). Many have been investigated, though few by modern excavation, and Poulnabrone is the only one site with a sequence of radiocarbon dates. Ballykeel, Co. Armagh, produced a date in the first half of the second millennium cal BC from charcoal in the cairn (95% confidence; 3350±45 BP; 1750–1510 cal BC; UB-239; A. Collins 1965), and single dates on human bone have been obtained from three other sites as part of a programme of research on portal tombs, which was published after the modelling reported here was undertaken (Kytmannow 2008, 100–12).[6] Of these, only Ballynacloghy, Co. Galway has produced a radiocarbon date which falls in the Neolithic period, although in the face of the taphonomic complexities of these monuments, it is hard to assess how this single date may relate to the construction and use of the tomb.

At Poulnabrone, on the Burren in Co. Clare, excavation took place in 1985 because of threats to the structural integrity of the monument (A. Lynch 1988; Cooney 2000a; C. Jones 2004). The artefacts from the chamber could be early or middle Neolithic in date (C. Jones 2004, fig. 4). The remains of over 20 people were found in the chamber as a jumbled mass of disarticulated bones, some scorched and burnt after flesh had gone, and many found in cracks in the natural limestone floor (A. Lynch 1988; A. Lynch and Ó Donnabhain 1994; C. Jones 2004, 30).

In interim reports, the excavator, Ann Lynch, has suggested that the disarticulated bones came from corpses originally kept elsewhere, perhaps in caves (Cooney 2000a, 94–7; O'Dowd 2008). One articulated neonate (dated by OxA-1904; Fig. 12.31; Table 12.5) was a significantly later insertion (A. Lynch 1988; 1990; cf. C. Jones 2004, 30). According to an interim statement on the human bone assemblage, a minimum of 22 individuals are represented by 4755 identified bones, including four articulated bone groups; less than 50% of all skeletal elements are present, with an over-representation of carpals and tarsals and discrepancies between upper and lower body elements, especially long bones. These observations all tend to support the original interpretation of secondary burial (Beckett and Robb 2006, 62–3). It remains, however, difficult to assess this interpretation in advance of a full osteological report.

There are three main possibilities. The presence of human bones in cracks in the chamber floor may support the suggestion that some of this material was placed in the chamber soon after its construction and before any sediment had accumulated. If this is the case, then a *terminus ante quem* for the construction of Poulnabrone may be provided by the latest human remains recovered from the deposit of disarticulated bone. The model shown in Fig. 12.31 would then suggest that construction occurred in or after *3290–2520 cal BC* (*95% probability*; Fig. 12.31:

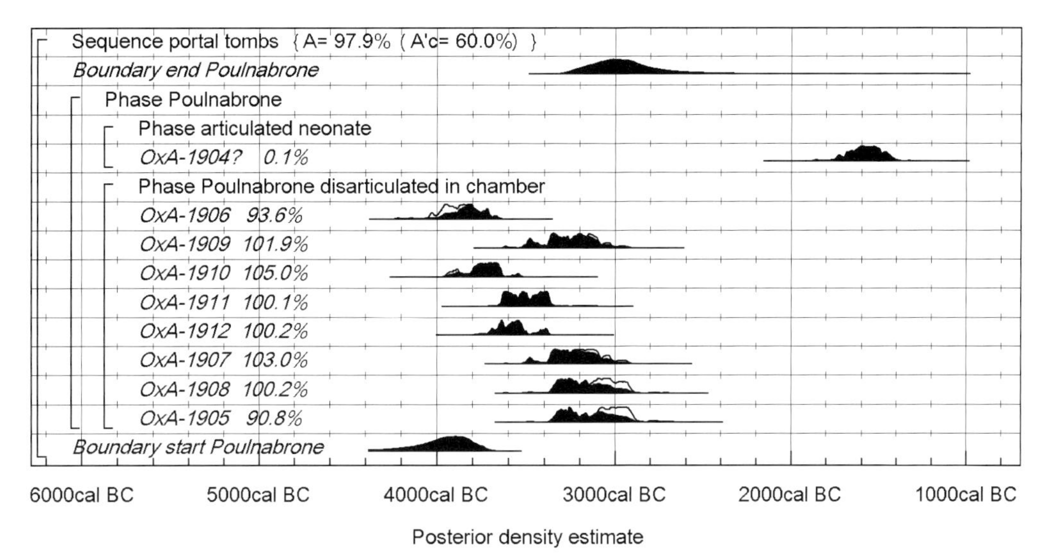

Fig. 12.31. Poulnabrone portal tomb. Probability distributions of dates. The format is identical to that of Fig. 12.6. The large square brackets down the left-hand side, along with the OxCal keywords, define the overall model exactly.

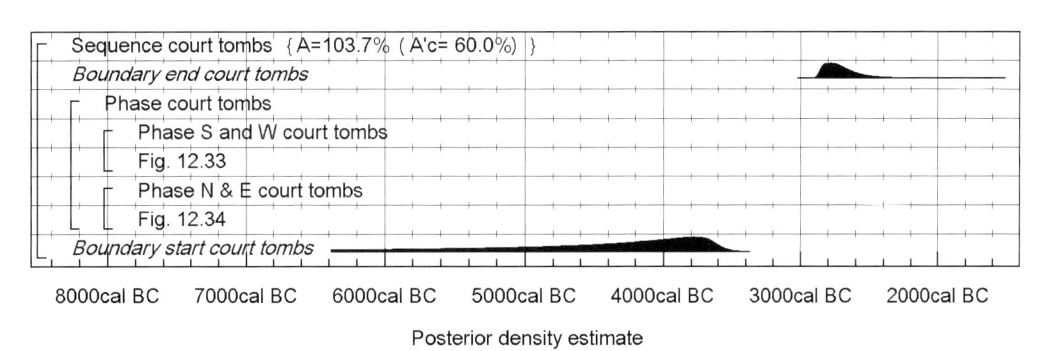

Fig. 12.32. Court tombs and related forms. Overall structure of the chronological model. The component sections are shown in detail in Figs 12.33–4. The large square brackets down the left-hand side of Figs 12.32–4, along with the OxCal keywords, define the overall model exactly.

end Poulnabrone), probably in or after *3165–2830 cal BC* (*68% probability*). If, however, this is not the case, for example if some other formation process, such as later solution, was at play in introducing the bones into the cracks in the limestone, then this estimate simply dates the deposition of the human remains in the chamber, not the construction of the monument itself. Least plausibly, given the uneven representation of skeletal elements, the deposit might be reinterpreted as being made up of individuals interred progressively as fleshed corpses and subsequently rearranged. In this case, the construction of the monument may be dated by the first individual deposited in it, to *4270–3715 cal BC* (*95% probability*; Fig. 12.31: *start Poulnabrone*), probably in *4055–3785 cal BC* (*68% probability*). Better informed readings of the taphonomy must await full publication of the site, and radiocarbon dating of the articulated bone groups. At present, the first interpretation, that of both Lynch, and Beckett and Robb, seems the most probable, with its concomitant late construction date for the monument.

Court tombs

Numerous court tombs have been excavated. Most, however, were investigated in or before the mid-twentieth century, so that, where radiocarbon dates have been obtained, they are mainly on bulk charcoal samples, often unidentified. There are thus *termini post quos* for several monuments (Figs 12.32–4; Table 12.5). Herity's survey of the finds from court tombs (1987) concluded that the Carinated Bowl pottery from pre-cairn contexts was all undecorated, while subsequent contexts, including the burial chambers, also contained decorated Bowl and sometimes vessels in later traditions. The same repertoire of early Neolithic lithics was shared by pre-cairn and chamber contexts.

The most extensive and most recently obtained series of dates is from Parknabinnia on the Burren, Co. Clare, where research excavations took place in 1998–2001 (Table 12.5; C. Jones 2004, 46–51; pers. comm.; in prep.). Here, a sub-ovoid cairn covered an elongated, bipartite chamber like those of court tombs, although there was a narrow entrance passage rather than the more usual expanded court. The associated artefacts are comparable with those from court

Table 12.5. Radiocarbon dates for portal tombs, court tombs and other related monuments in Ireland. Posterior density estimates derive from the models defined in Figs 12.31, 12.32–4 and 12.35.

Laboratory number	Sample reference	Material	Context	Radiocarbon age (BP)	$\delta^{13}C$ (‰)	Calibrated date range (cal BC) (95% confidence)	*Posterior density estimate (cal BC) (95% probability)*
Poulnabrone portal tomb, Co. Clare							
OxA-1905		Human. R talus, disarticulated	F24. From among disarticulated bone in soil on chamber floor and in natural fissures in limestone beneath it (A. Lynch 1988; R. Hedges *et al.* 1990)	4390±90	−21.0 (assumed)	3360–2870	*3355–2915*
OxA-1906		Human. R talus, disarticulated	F15/F16. As OxA-1905	5100±80	−21.0 (assumed)	4050–3700	*3985–3690 (93%)* or *3685–3655 (2%)*
OxA-1907		Human. R talus, disarticulated	F15. As OxA-1905	4520±80	−21.0 (assumed)	3500–2920	*3510–3425 (7%)* or *3385–3005 (88%)*
OxA-1908		Human. R talus, disarticulated	F28A. As OxA-1905	4440±80	−21.0 (assumed)	3370–2890	*3360–2940*
OxA-1909		Human. R talus, disarticulated	F28C. As OxA-1905	4550±80	−21.0 (assumed)	3520–3010	*3520–3025*
OxA-1910		Human. R talus, disarticulated	F28C. As OxA-1905	4940±80	−21.0 (assumed)	3960–3530	*3940–3630 (93%)* or *3565–3535 (2%)*
OxA-1911		Human. R talus, disarticulated	F15/F16. As OxA-1905	4720±70	−21.0 (assumed)	3650–3350	*3640–3365*
OxA-1912		Human. R talus, disarticulated	F15/F16. As OxA-1905	4810±70	−21.0 (assumed)	3710–3370	*3710–3490 (82%)* or *3465–3370 (13%)*
OxA-1904		Human. Bone of neonate	F18A. Undisturbed in a fissure in the natural limestone close to the sill stone at entrance to chamber (A. Lynch 1988, 106; R. Hedges *et al.* 1990)	3290±80	−21.0 (assumed)	1750–1410	
Parknabinnia court tomb-like monument, Co. Clare							
AA-53131	Find 305	Human. Distal R femur	Context 305. Monument of court tomb-like affinities, with bipartite chamber. Samples from chamber (C. Jones 2004)	4645±55	−21.4	3630–3340	*3630–3575 (6%)* or *3540–3335 (89%)*
AA-53132	Find 373	Human. Proximal R tibia	Context 335	4235±55	−22.1	2920–2640	*3015–2830 (80%)* or *2820–2745 (15%)*
AA-53133	Find 471	Human. Distal R tibia	Context 379	4455±60	−21.4	3360–2910	*3350-3000 (86%)* or *2995–2925 (9%)*
AA-53134	Find 549	Human. Skull fragments	Context 388	4640±75	−21.2	3640–3100	*3635–3550 (8%)* or *3540–3305 (73%)* or *3240–3100 (14%)*
AA-53135	Find 555	Human. L scapula fragment	Context 388	4455±60	−21.3	3360–2910	*3350–3000 (86%)* or *2995–2925 (9%)*
AA-53136	Find 625	Human. L tibia fragment	Context 389	4195±55	−21.0 (assumed)	2910–2580	*2920–2730*
AA-53137	Find 961	Human. Skull fragments	Context 443	4535±60	−21.4	3500–3020	*3495–3460 (3%)* or *3375–3075 (88%)* or *3070–3020 (4%)*
AA-53138	Find 1725	Human. R pelvis fragment	Context 565	4705±60	−20.7		*3630–3550 (19%)* or *3545–3365 (76%)*
AA-53139	Find 1933	Human. Complete L humerus	Context 583	4785±60	−21.0	3700–3370	*3650–3495 (67%)* or *3465–3370 (28%)*

Laboratory number	Sample reference	Material	Context	Radiocarbon age (BP)	$\delta^{13}C$ (‰)	Calibrated date range (cal BC) (95% confidence)	*Posterior density estimate (cal BC) (95% probability)*
AA-53140	Find 998	Human. Femur shaft	Context 490	4315±55	−20.5	3090–2870	*3095–2870*
AA-53141	Find 1958	Human. Complete R femur	Context 584	4725±60	−21.2	3650–3360	*3635–3485 (48%)* or *3475–3370 (47%)*
AA-53142	Find 2133	Human. R tibia fragments	Context 614	4550±60	−21.6	3500–3020	*3500–3435 (7%)* or *3380–3085 (86%)* or *3060–3025 (2%)*
Primrose Grange court tomb-like monument (no court, but bipartite chamber), 2 km S of Carrowmore, Co. Sligo							
Ua-16969	ID 60337	Bone	From a tomb containing mainly inhumed rather than cremated bone. Leaf arrowheads also present. Samples described as from central chamber, but precise contexts unknown (Burenhult 2001, 12)	4545±80	−22.0	3520–2940	*3520–3010*
Ua-12738	ID 60305	Charcoal	As Ua-16969	4360±80	−27.85	3340–2870	*3340–3205 (15%)* or *3195–3145 (4%)* or *3140–2875 (76%)*
Ua-16967	ID 60354	Charcoal	As Ua-16969	5230±75	−24.9	4260–3810	*4260–3935 (92%)* or *3865–3810 (3%)*
Ua-16968	ID 60355	Charcoal	As Ua-16969	5145±75	−26.2	4230-3770	*4230–4200 (2%)* or *4170–4125 (3%)* or *4120–4095 (1%)* or *4080–3760 (89%)*
Ua-11582	ID 60006	Charcoal	As Ua-16969	5140±65	−24.8	4050–3780	*4160–4130 (1%)* or *4070–3765 (94%)*
Ua-12739	ID 60314	Charcoal1[1]	As Ua-16969	4645±70	−21.5	3640–3120	*3635–3320 (87%)* or *3220–3170 (4%)* or *3165–3115 (4%)*
Annaghmare court tomb, Co. Armagh							
UB-241		Charcoal (unidentified)	Court tomb. Sealed behind primary blocking of court (Waterman 1965, fig. 11, fig. 5; A. Smith *et al.* 1970; corrected by A. Smith *et al.* 1971)	4397±55		3340–2890	*3330–3215 (16%)* or *3185–3155 (2%)* or *3125–2900 (77%)*
Ballybriest court tomb, Co. Derry							
UB-534	CH2	Charcoal, unidentified, but deposit described as including hazelnuts and *Corylus* charcoal (E. Evans 1939, 9)	Black layer below cairn of court tomb, associated with Carinated Bowl pottery (A. Smith *et al.* 1973)	4930±80	−25.7	3950–3530	*3950–3630 (92%)* or *3570–3530 (3%)*
UB-535	CH5/6	Charcoal	Black layer 4 around Neolithic pot (A. Smith *et al.* 1973)	5045±95	−24.9	4040–3640	*4040–4015 (1%)* or *3995–3645 (94%)*
Ballymacdermot court tomb, Co. Armagh							
UB-207		Charcoal (unidentified)	Black deposit (3) 'below stone blocking' of inner court (Collins and Wilson 1964, 11, fig. 4; Herity 1987, 158; A. Smith *et al.* 1973)	3660±60		2210–1880	

Laboratory number	Sample reference	Material	Context	Radiocarbon age (BP)	$\delta^{13}C$ (‰)	Calibrated date range (cal BC) (95% confidence)	*Posterior density estimate (cal BC) (95% probability)*
UB-695	Sample 5	Charcoal (unidentified)	Brown earth (layer 8) in northern part of western half of Chamber 3, butted against orthostats and overlying charcoal-rich layer (7), with numerous Neolithic sherds at interface of the two (Collins and Wilson 1964, 15, fig. 4, f; A. Smith *et al.* 1974). Could date funerary use of chamber but possibly a mixture of charcoal of different ages	4295±90	−25.7	3270–2630	
UB-694	Sample 4	Charcoal (unidentified)	Brown earth in north part of Chamber 3 together with charcoal from same layer containing Carinated Bowl pottery under flat stone (A. Smith *et al.* 1974). Could possibly date funerary use of chamber	4830±95	−25.1	3800–3370	*3800–3365*
UB-705	Sample 2	Charcoal (unidentified)	Dark soil (3) below stones blocking forecourt (Collins and Wilson 1964, 11, fig. 4; Herity 1987, 158; A. Smith *et al.* 1974)	3515±85	−24.4	2120–1620	
UB-702	Sample 10	Charcoal (unidentified)	Low levels in cracks between lowest cairn stone in cutting 9 (Collins and Wilson 1964, fig. 5	6925±95	−25.1	6010–5630	*5990–5655*
UB-698	Sample 3	Charcoal (unidentified)	Under fill of tightly packed granite blocks and on scattered flat slabs (=continuation of forecourt blocking) in chamber 1 of gallery (Collins and Wilson 1964, 14, fig. 4; A. Smith *et al.* 1974)	4715±190	−24.0	3950–2910	*3935–3870 (2%)* or *3810–2925 (93%)*
UB-693	Sample 6	Charcoal (unidentified)	S end of Chamber 3, from dark brown soil (layer 8) containing Carinated Bowl sherds and a little burnt bone	1180±75	−25.7	AD 660–1020	
UB-697	Sample 7	Charcoal (unidentified)	Deposit under large stone in SW corner of chamber 3	940±75	−25.6	AD 970–1260	
UB-700	Sample 8	Charcoal (unidentified)	Among stones and soil overlying pre-cairn soil in cutting 9 through body of cairn (Collins and Wilson 1964, figs 3, 5)	1025±40	−25.2	AD 890–1150	
UB-703	Sample 9	Charcoal (unidentified)	Among stones and soil overlying pre-cairn soil in cutting 9	975±70	−25.3	AD 890–1220	
Creggandevesky court tomb, Co. Tyrone							
UB-2539		Charcoal (unidentified)	'Gallery deposit' in tomb with cremations, flint arrowheads, other lithics, 112 stone beads, 7 fragmentary Carinated Bowls (Foley 1988; Sheridan 1995, 8)	4740±85	−26.8	3700–3350	*3665–3350*
UB-2540		Charcoal (unidentified)	'Gallery deposit' in tomb with cremations, flint arrowheads, other lithics 112 stone beads, 7 fragmentary Carinated Bowls (Foley 1988; Sheridan 1995, 8)	4825±80	−26.2	3780–3370	*3775–3495 (83%)* or *3465–3375 (12%)*
Dooey's Cairn, Ballymacaldrack, Co. Antrim							
UB-2045		Charcoal (unidentified)	Forecourt blocking deposit (A. Collins 1976, 2–3, 5, fig. 2)	4630±130		3660–2920	*3655–3005*

Laboratory number	Sample reference	Material	Context	Radiocarbon age (BP)	$\delta^{13}C$ (‰)	Calibrated date range (cal BC) (95% confidence)	*Posterior density estimate (cal BC) (95% probability)*
UB-2030		Charcoal (unidentified)	From wall crevices and just above till floor of 'cremation passage' (A. Collins 1976)	5150±90	−23.8	4230–3710	*4230–4195* (*3%*) or *4175–3755* (*91%*) or *3745–3725* (*1%*)
UB-2029		*Quercus* charcoal	Inner end of narrow 'cremation passage', extending beyond chamber, in which were 3 large postpits, possibly from a pre-mound structure. Charcoal probably under paving of passage, which had been removed during 1935 excavations (A. Collins 1976)	4940±50	−23.6	3910–3630	*3915–3875* (*4%*) or *3805–3635* (*91%*)
Tully court tomb, Co. Fermanagh							
UB-2120		Charcoal (unidentified)	Charcoal from Chamber 1, under stone filling (Waterman 1978, fig.5)	4785±85	−23.7	3710–3360	*3710–3365*
UB-2119		Charcoal (unidentified)	Charcoal from Chamber 1 under stone filling (Waterman 1978)	4890±65	−24.2	3800–3520	*3910–3875* (*2%*) or *3805–3620* (*81%*) or *3605–3520* (*12%*)
UB-2116		Charcoal (unidentified). Combined with UB-2118, sample from northern half of chamber	Charcoal from southern half of Chamber 2. UB-2116 sealed by stone filling, but addition to it of UB-2118, from an area lacking stone filling 'must introduce a suspicion of error' (Waterman 1978, 12)	4445±130	−28.8	3520–2780	
UB-2115		Charcoal (unidentified)	Charcoal from surface of forecourt to E of gallery portal, where blocking best preserved (Waterman 1978)	4960±85	−24.5	3960–3530	*3960–3630*
UB-2114		Charcoal (unidentified)	Charcoal under blocking, centre of forecourt (Waterman 1978)	4575±50		3500–3090	*3505–3425* (*16%*) or *3380–3260* (*36%*) or *3255–3095* (*43%*)
Ballyglass Ma 13 court tomb, Co. Mayo							
GrN-24991	E83:468	*Quercus* charcoal	From ash spread (F63), east of house (Ó Nualláin *et al.* forthcoming)	4990±110	−24.2	4040–3530	*4000–3625* (*92%*) or *3585–3530* (*3%*)
Ballyglass, Ma 14 court tomb, Co. Mayo							
SI-1463		Charcoal (unidentified)	Dark layer immediately under cairn of tomb (Ó Nualláin 1998, 128, 141, 143)	4270±90		3100–2620	
Shanballyedmond court tomb, Co. Tipperary							
GrN-11431	Shanballeyedmond no 3	Charcoal (unidentified).	Fragments from postholes in setting of 34, connecting with forecourt horns and running along facade and around entire monument, 0.22 to 0.40 m in diameter (most 0.25 m to 0.30 m; O'Kelly 1958, 40–41, fig. 1; ApSimon 1986). Material from postholes originally identified as 7 fragments of *Corylus* and 4 fragments of *Quercus* (O'Kelly 1958, 72)	4930±60	−25.3	3930–3630	*3940–3870* (*7%*) or *3810–3630* (*88%*)
D-52		Charcoal (unidentified)	From chamber (Herity 1987, 158). Excavator commented that there was doubt as to whether sample was in primary position (McAulay and Watts 1961, 34)	4000±130		2900–2130	

Laboratory number	Sample reference	Material	Context	Radiocarbon age (BP)	$\delta^{13}C$ (‰)	Calibrated date range (cal BC) (95% confidence)	*Posterior density estimate (cal BC) (95% probability)*
Rathdooney Beg ovoid mound, Co. Sligo							
Beta-110614		Waterlogged seeds. Plant remains from this context were identified as *Urtica dioica*, *Ranunculus* sub-genus *Batrachium*, *Rubus fructicosus*, *Sonchus asper*, *Potamogeton* sp.and Gramineae (B. Collins 1999)	Context 116 (29–31 cm). Waterlogged clay about half way up ditch fill, probably eroded from mound, with fragments of hazel and willow rods, animal bone, charcoal (Mount 1999, fig. 7). Stratified above context 117 (source of sample for Beta-109607). Ditch surrounded large, uninvestigated oval mound, pollen *c.* 70% grass in all three dated contexts	4990±40	−23.8	3940–3660	
Beta-109607		Waterlogged seeds. Plant remains from this context were identified as *Urtica dioica*, *Rumex* sp., *Ranunculus repens/acris*, *Ranunculus* sub-genus *Batrachium, Torilis japonica, Sonchus asper* and Gramineae (B. Collins 1999)	Context 117 (56–58 cm). Waterlogged clay with animal bone, hazel and willow rods and charcoal, immediately below context 116 (source of sample for Beta-110614; Mount 1999, fig. 7)	4940±40	−24.6	3800–3640	*3740–3635*
Beta-109608		Waterlogged seeds. Plant remains from this context were identified as *Rumex* sp., *Stellaria media*, *Ranunculus* sub-genus *Batrachium* and *Torilis* cf. *nododa* (B. Collins 1999)	Context 118 (67–70 cm) Waterlogged clay filling lower part of ditch and underlying context 117 (source of sample for Beta-109607; Mount 1999, fig. 7)	4840±50	−23.7	3710–3520	*3775–3645*
Knockiveagh round mound, Co. Down							
D-37		Charcoal	From surface beneath round mound. Thick brown soil, much charcoal (including hazel, birch, oak and willow), charred hazelnut shells, some burnt bone (at least some human), numerous artefacts including abundant Carinated Bowl, some fluted. Traces of *in situ* burning limited to patch *c.* 0.30 m across. Further spreads of burnt bone (at least some also human) at various levels in mound, central cist disturbed (A. Collins 1957; McAulay and Watts 1961). Interpreted by Alison Sheridan as cremation pyre (2003b)	5020±170		4240–3370	*4240–3615*

[1] Kytmannow (2008, table 7.3) states that this result was produced on a human femur from a young adult in cist A, citing Burenhult (1998) as her authority. This contradicts Burenhult (2001) who states that this sample is charcoal. In the light of these uncertainties, we have taken the conservative course and modelled this result as a *terminus post quem*.

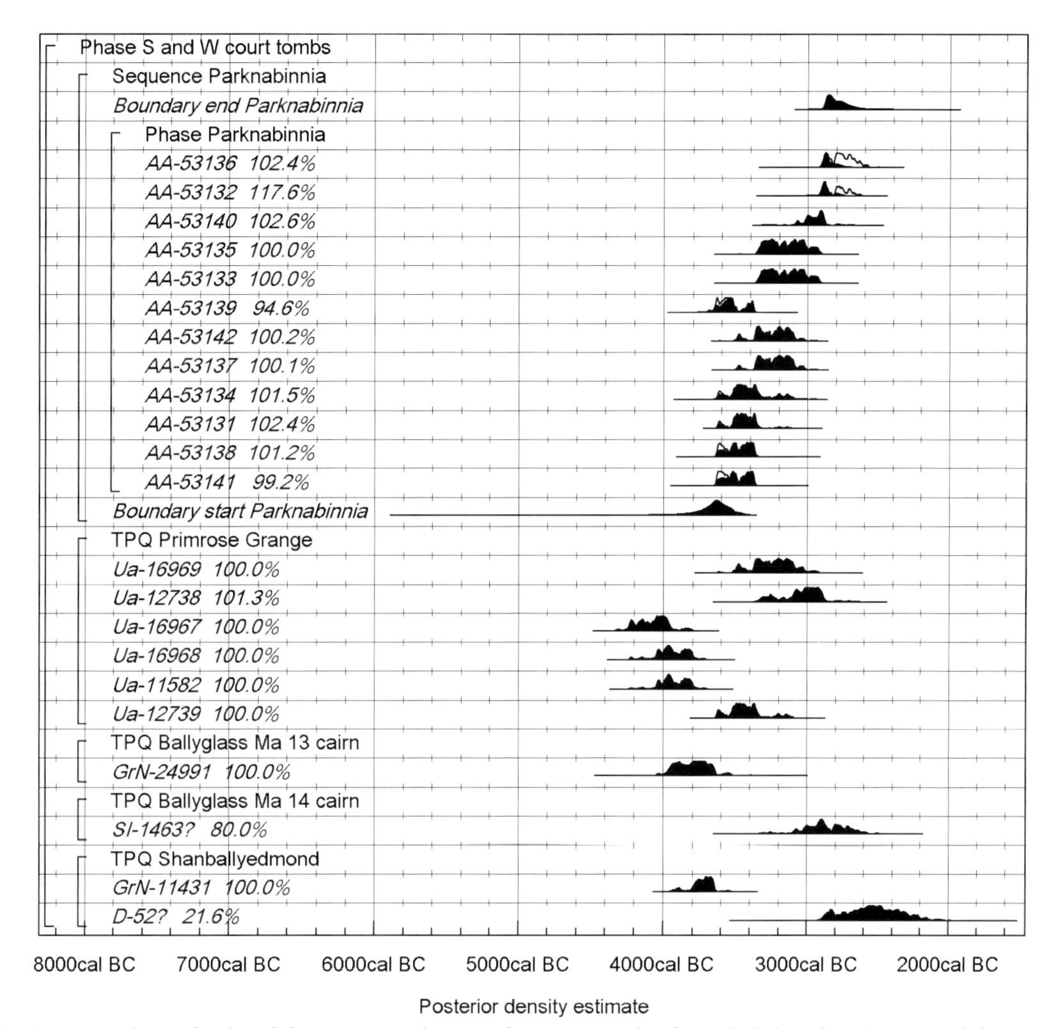

Fig. 12.33. Court tombs and related forms in southern and western Ireland. Probability distributions of dates. The format is identical to that of Fig. 12.6. The overall structure of this model is shown in Fig. 12.32 and its other component in Fig. 12.34.

tombs. In the chamber were the fragmented remains of at least 20 people, most of them inhumed, represented by 6084 identified bones including 25 articulating groups and one articulated group. All skeletal elements were present, but there was better preservation of the more robust bones, observations interpreted as reflecting primary inhumations disturbed in the course of successive interments (Beckett and Robb 2006, 62–3). Refits showed extensive and complex rearrangement (Beckett and Robb 2006, fig. 4.8). The piling up of bones in the front chamber against the blocking slabs separating it from the back chamber indicated that the back chamber had gone out of use first. In both chambers, the bottom layer of stone and bones seemed to stabilise the upright slabs and thus to have been part of the original construction (C. Jones 2004, 48). The earliest of the human remains might thus be close in age to the building of the tomb. Post-excavation analysis is still in progress, full contextual information is not yet available and, although each sample was a single bone, it is not yet clear whether each was from a separate individual and crucially whether any of the dated samples derive from articulated remains (see Chapter 2.5.2).

On the basis of the information available so far, we present a provisional model for the chronology of Parknabinnia, shown in Fig. 12.33. According to this, the monument was constructed in *3885–3440 cal BC* (*95% probability*; Fig. 12.33: *start Parknabinnia*), probably in *3715–3530 cal BC* (*68% probability*). The deposition of human remains continued until *2900–2640 cal BC* (*95% probability*; Fig. 12.33: *end Parknabinnia*), probably until *2880–2760 cal BC* (*68% probability*).

Another series of measurements come from a court tomb-like monument at Primrose Grange in Co. Sligo (Ó Nualláin 1989, 31), 2 km from the Carrowmore passage tomb cemetery, excavated in 1996–98 (Burenhult 2001; 2003). Like Parknabinnia, this had a bipartite chamber but lacked a court. According to the interim information available, its contents included predominantly inhumed, with very few cremated, bones together with chert leaf-shaped arrowheads. Six measurements were made (Table 12.5), five on unidentified charcoal and one on bone; although these are described as from the central chamber, their precise contexts are unknown (Burenhult 2001, 12; 2003, 68). At this stage, therefore, they can probably only

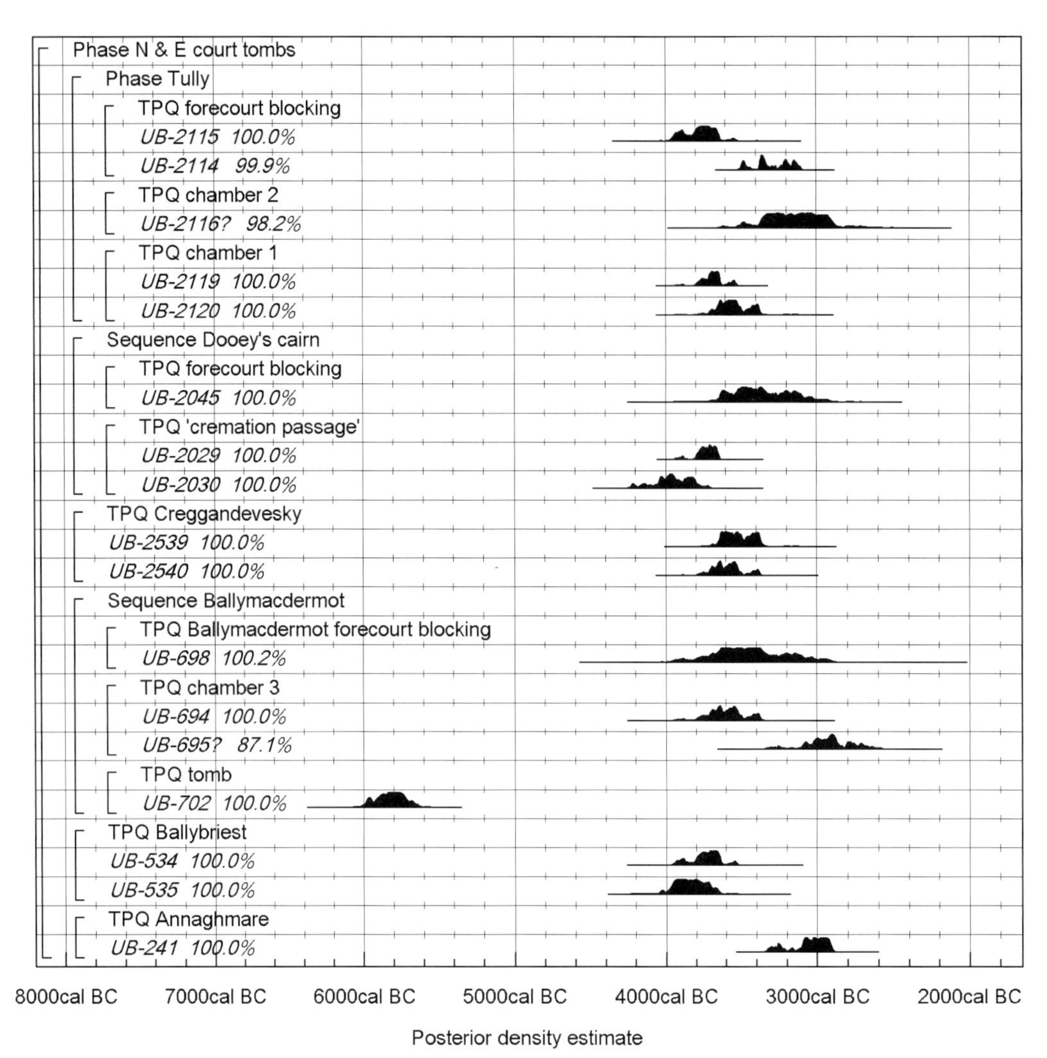

Fig. 12.34. Court tombs and related forms in northern and eastern Ireland. Probability distributions of dates. The format is identical to that of Fig. 12.6. The overall structure of this model is shown in Fig. 12.32 and its other component in Fig. 12.33.

be interpreted as providing *termini post quos* for the use of the chamber (Fig. 12.33).

A radiocarbon measurement (*GrN-24991*) was obtained on oak charcoal from an ash spread (F63) under the central court tomb at Ballyglass (Ma 13), close to the east wall of the underlying house (see above: Ó Nualláin 1972; Ó Nualláin *et al.* forthcoming). A large piece of struck chert and fragments of Carinated Bowl pottery were associated with this feature. The date is treated a *terminus post quem* for the construction of the tomb (Fig. 12.33), while the five Smithsonian dates for samples from the house which also pre-dated the tomb are not included in the model because they seem to be anomalously young, as discussed above. SI-1463, measured on unidentified charcoal from a dark layer immediately under the other court tomb nearby at Ballyglass (Ma 14; Ó Nualláin 1998), provides a *terminus post quem* for its construction but is excluded from the model for the same reason.

Two samples are available from the court tomb at Shanballyedmond, Co. Tipperary, excavated in 1958 (O'Kelly 1958; ApSimon 1986). A sample of unidentified charcoal bulked from a number of postholes surrounding the monument provides a *terminus post quem* for construction of 3930–3630 cal BC (95% confidence; Table 12.5: GrN-11431).[7] Another sample of unidentified charcoal described simply as from the chamber was dated (D-52), but appears anomalously young (McAulay and Watts 1961, 34), and so has been excluded from the model.

A court tomb at Annaghmare, Co. Armagh, with additional lateral chambers behind those entered from the court, was excavated in 1963–4 (Waterman 1965). A single sample of unidentified charcoal was dated and provides a *terminus post quem* for the primary blocking of the court and thus the disuse of the monument (Fig. 12.34: *UB-241*).[8]

A court tomb at Ballybriest, Co. Derry, was excavated in 1937 (E. Evans 1939). Two samples of unidentified charcoal were dated from a black layer containing early Neolithic material beneath the cairn of the monument. This deposit, however, was described as containing hazelnuts and hazel charcoal, so it is possible that these samples do not have a significant age offset. Strictly, however, they provide *termini post quos* for the construction of the monument and they have been incorporated in the model on that basis (Fig. 12.34: *UB-534–5*).

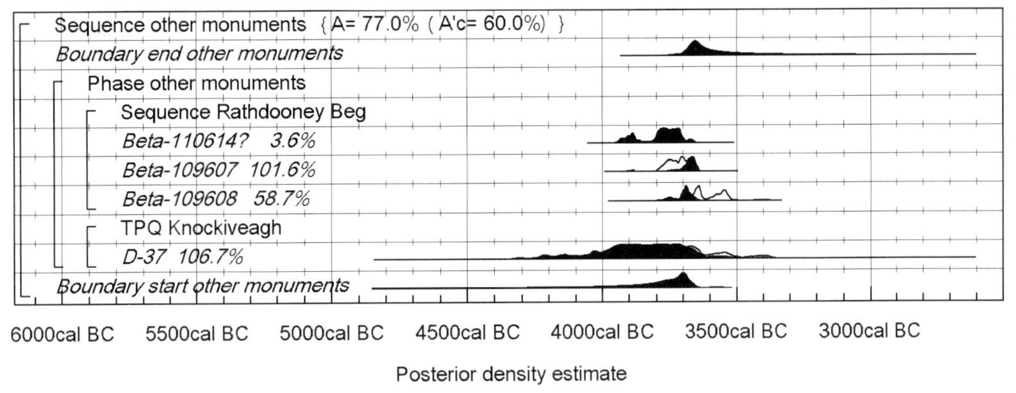

Fig. 12.35. Other monuments. Probability distributions of dates. The format is identical to that of Fig. 12.6. The large square brackets down the left-hand side, along with the OxCal keywords, define the overall model exactly.

A court tomb at Ballymacdermot, Co. Armagh, was excavated in 1962 (A. Collins and Wilson 1964). Ten samples of unidentified charcoal were dated (Table 12.5). *UB-702* provides a *terminus post quem* for the building of the cairn, although the sample clearly derived from earlier activity (Fig. 12.34). Two samples (*UB-694*, -695) come from layers relating to the use of chamber 3. They therefore provide *termini post quos* for the end of the primary use of this chamber. UB-695, however, has been excluded from the model because it may have included intrusive charcoal (A. Smith *et al.* 1974). *UB-698* provides a *terminus post quem* for the blocking of the forecourt (Fig. 12.34), although this does not appear to have occurred until the Bronze Age (UB-207, -705), and material appears to have been deposited in the chambers in the Viking period (UB-693, -697, -700, -703). There was clearly much post-Neolithic use and disturbance of the monument.

A court tomb at Creggandevesky, Co. Tyrone, was excavated in 1977 (Foley 1988; Sheridan 1995). Two radiocarbon determinations on unidentified bulk charcoal are available (Table 12.5: *UB-2539, -2540*). Both samples are from within the chamber, from a context associated with Carinated Bowl pottery. In advance of full publication, these dates have been included in the model as *termini post quos* for the end of the primary Neolithic use of the monument (Fig. 12.34).

A court tomb (Dooey's Cairn) at Ballymacaldrack, Co. Antrim, was excavated in 1935 and 1975 (E. Evans 1938; A. Collins 1976). It provides the only definite example of a timber mortuary structure in Ireland (Sheridan 2006a, 27) followed by a stone cremation passage and then one of the best sequences for the construction and development of a court tomb, and a rich assemblage of Neolithic finds (A. Collins 1976; Herity 1987; Cooney 2000a, fig. 4.3). Only three radiocarbon determinations are available. A sample of oak charcoal (*UB-2029*) may provide a *terminus post quem* for the construction of the stone cremation passage (Phase II: Cooney 2000a, fig. 4.3), and a sample of unidentified charcoal (*UB-2030*) may do likewise. A third sample (*UB-2045*) of unidentified charcoal provides a *terminus post quem* for the final blocking of the forecourt (Phase IV) (Fig. 12.34).

A court tomb at Tully, Co. Fermanagh, was excavated in 1976 (Waterman 1978). Five dates were obtained on bulk samples of unidentified charcoal. Two samples from chamber 1 provide *termini post quos* for its disuse (*UB-2119–20*). A date from a similar deposit in chamber 2 (UB-2116) has been excluded from the model, since it contained charcoal that was not sealed by the stone filling and may be intrusive (Waterman 1978, 12). Two samples provide *termini post quos* for the blocking of the forecourt (Fig. 12.34: *UB-2114–5*).

Further series of radiocarbon dates from the court tombs at Behy and Rathlackan, Co. Mayo, two results from Aghanaglack, Co. Fermanagh, and single dates from two further sites reported by Kytmannow (2008, table 7.3), appeared after the modelling here was completed but do not substantially alter our date estimates for the currency of court tombs.[9]

Round mounds

At Rathdooney Beg, Co. Sligo, some 17 km south of Magheraboy, a section was cut across the ditch surrounding an otherwise uninvestigated, slightly ovoid mound surviving to 6.1 m high and with a maximum dimension of 24.5 m (Mount 1999). The mound was sited on a drumlin, affording views of Sligo Bay and the surrounding landscape. Pollen from throughout the dated layers reflected grassland, with indicators of disturbed, bare ground confined to the base of the sequence, suggesting that clearance immediately preceded mound building. Low levels of cereal-type pollen were present throughout. Tree pollen did not exceed 15%, although the small area of the ditch probably means that these results relate to the vegetation of the hilltop and that the wider area was more heavily wooded (Weir 1999).

The lower fills of the ditch consisted of clays which had remained waterlogged. Charcoal was present in all three layers. The basal fill of the ditch (context 118) preserved seeds of wild plants, dated by *Beta-109608* (Fig. 12.35). The overlying layer (context 117) contained badly preserved animal bone including a cattle humerus fragment, hazel and willow rods, insect remains, molluscs, and further seeds of wild plants, dated by *Beta-109607*. The clay above

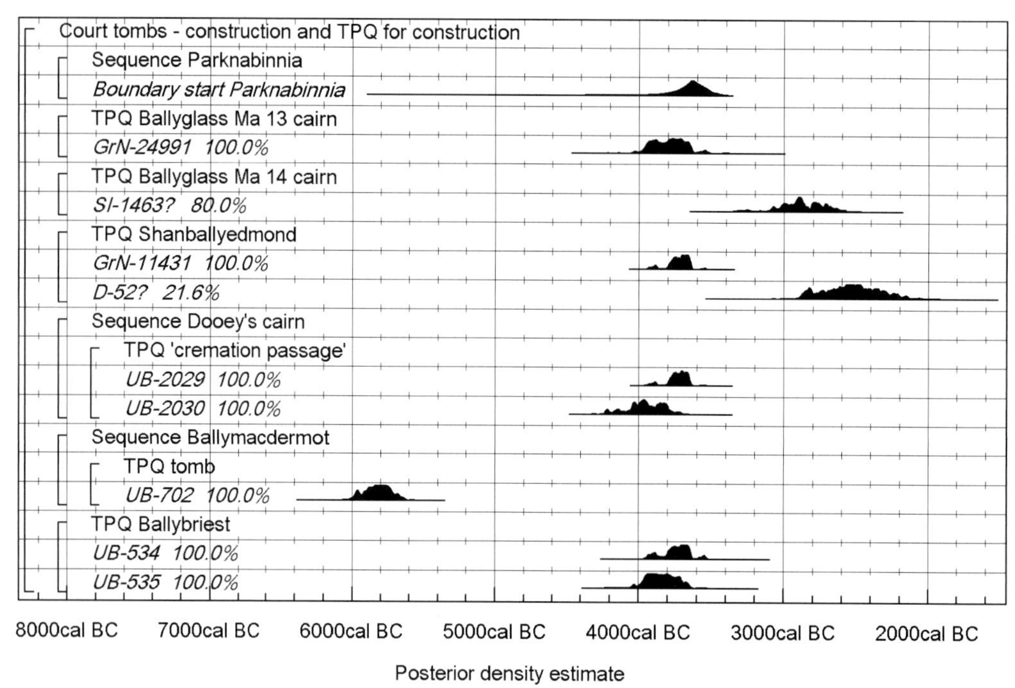

Fig. 12.36. Court tombs and related forms. Key parameters for dates relating to construction, derived from the chronological model defined in Figs 12.32–4. All dates provide termini post quos for construction, except the estimate from Parknabinnia.

this (context 116) was confined to the inner edge of the ditch, and had probably eroded from the mound. It too contained hazel and willow rods, as well as charcoal, animal bone including goose limb fragments, and further seeds of wild plants, dated by Beta-110614. The measurements are statistically consistent (T'=5.5; T'(5%)= 6.0; ν=2). Given that turf may have formed on the surface of context 118 (Mount 1999, 342), this sequence may have taken some time to accumulate, so that the sample for Beta-110614 may well have formed part of the mound before silting into the ditch. For this reason, we have interpreted the material for Beta-110614 as redeposited, and it has been excluded from the model. On the basis of the basal sample, we estimate that the monument was constructed in *3775–3645 cal BC* (*95% probability*; Fig. 12.35: *Beta-109608*), probably in *3710–3660 cal BC* (*68% probability*).

A round mound containing a central cist at Knockiveagh, Co. Down, was excavated in 1956. It was built over a soil containing much charcoal, numerous artefacts including Carinated Bowl sherds, and cremated bone, some of it human (A. Collins 1957), a deposit interpreted as a cremation pyre (Sheridan 2003b; 2006a). An unidentified bulk charcoal sample provides a *terminus post quem* for the construction of the mound (Fig. 12.35; Table 12.5: *D-37*; McAulay and Watts 1961).

It is clear from the models shown in Figs 12.31–5 that our understanding of the chronology of early Neolithic megalithic tombs in Ireland is sadly inadequate. Of the portal tombs, at the time of modelling only Poulnabrone had radiocarbon dates, and until further analysis and publication of that assemblage are undertaken it is unclear how its dates should be interpreted. They can be read to suggest that the orthostats at Poulnabrone were raised in the first quarter of the fourth millennium cal BC, or alternatively that they were raised in the centuries around 3000 cal BC (an interpretation that we feel more plausible on the available evidence). All we can say for certain at present is that the mortuary deposit was placed in the monument sometime within the fourth millennium cal BC.[10]

Our understanding of the chronology of court tombs, based on their radiocarbon dating, is even more depressing (Fig. 12.36). Thirty-nine radiocarbon dates are available, all of which only provide *termini post quos* for the contexts from which they were recovered, except for the series of dates on human bone from Parknabinnia. Only samples from Ballyglass Ma 13 (*GrN-24991*), Ballyglass Ma 14 (SI-1463, considered unreliable on scientific grounds), Shanballyedmond (*GrN-11431*, and D-52, also considered unreliable on scientific grounds), Dooey's Cairn (*UB-2029–30*), Ballymacdermot (*UB-702*) and Ballybriest (*UB-534–5*) seem to provide *termini post quos* for construction of the monuments. All the other dates provide only *termini post quos* either for the final use of the chambers or for the blocking of their forecourts.[11]

Preliminary analysis of the series of dates from Parknabinnia suggests, more positively, that this monument may have been constructed in the second quarter of the fourth millennium cal BC (Fig. 12.33: *start Parknabinnia*). The available *termini post quos* for the construction of other court tombs, though the sample is small, as shown in Fig. 12.36, do not contradict the inference that this kind of monument may have been built in the first half of the fourth millennium cal BC, and the dates shown in Fig. 12.36 are also not inconsistent with the possibility of a shorter horizon of construction within that time period. Although court tombs are contexts which may have remained open

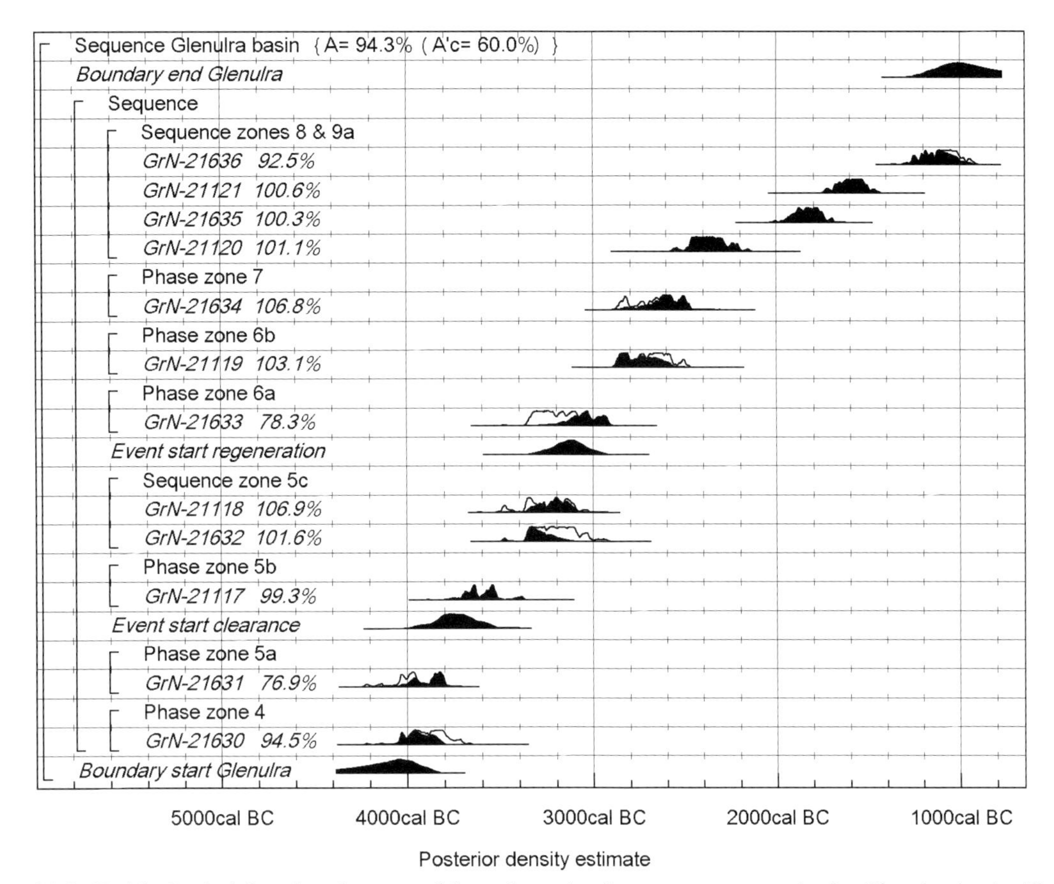

Fig. 12.37. Céide Fields. Probability distributions of dates from the deep peat sequence in the Glenulra basin. The format is identical to that of Fig. 12.6. The large square brackets down the left-hand side, along with the OxCal keywords, define the overall model exactly.

for many centuries, demonstrably into the Bronze Age and even the Viking period (as at Ballymacdermot), in general the blocking of forecourts and the end of primary use appear to have occurred in or before the first quarter of the third millennium cal BC. Some tombs may have remained in use for relatively short periods of time.

The two round mounds which we have considered, Rathdooney Beg and Knockiveagh (Fig. 12.35), may also date to the second quarter of the fourth millennium cal BC. The potential for providing further reliable suites of measurements, which might confirm or contradict the tentative suggestions for the chronology of court tombs given here, is good. The now routine availability of AMS and new methods for dating cremated bone should allow existing archives to be mined for short-life samples associated with the construction and primary use of these monuments. A start has now been made on this task with a series of new measurements on human and animal bone from court tombs (Rick Schulting, pers. comm.).

Field systems

Stone-built field walls extend intermittently for some 50 km along the north Mayo coast, where the best known system is the Céide Fields, investigated over many seasons from the 1970s to the 1990s by Seamas Caulfield. They are preserved beneath blanket bog which began to grow after they had ceased to be built, since, where the walls have been excavated, they generally stand on mineral soil, without intervening peat (Caulfield 1978; Molloy and O'Connell 1995). The few artefacts that have been recovered are Neolithic (Byrne 1991; Caulfield 1978). Settlement enclosures lie among the fields, in the case of the western part of the Céide Fields forming an irregular line two or three fields inland from the northern, coastal edge of the system (Cooney 2000a, 28). Court and portal tombs, of which there is a major concentration locally, also lie within and close to the fields (Caulfield 1983, fig. 1). One court tomb, at Behy, is abutted and post-dated by a wall (de Valera and Ó Nualláin 1964, 4–6), which forms part of an enclosure surrounding the tomb and occupying the junction of four field walls (Caulfield 1978, fig. 19.1). This does not mean that the fields post-date the tomb, since the enclosure, which is not aligned with the others in the area, post-dates the field walls (Caulfield 1978, 141). The way in which the field walls converge on the tomb, however, strongly suggests that it was already present when they were laid out.

Ten kilometres east of the Céide Fields and separated from them by the valley of the Ballinglen River is another complex of field and tombs at Rathlackan. A court tomb within the fields here pre-dated a small enclosure, which was itself independent of the field walls (Byrne 1990; 1992; 1993).

The dating of the north Mayo fields is bound up with that of local vegetation change and peat growth. Neither history need be uniform over so large an area, but certain patterns emerge. In the 1970s, a measurement on unidentified charcoal from a hearth in one of the settlement enclosures at Glenulra in the Céide Fields provided a *terminus post quem* for the settlement and for the start of peat growth in the later fourth or early third millennium cal BC (Table 12.6: SI-1464). This impression was reinforced by an early third millennium cal BC date for the outer five rings of a pine stump estimated to have been about 100 years old at death, within further fields at Belderg Beg to the west. This tree must have started growing after some peat had formed, since its lateral roots ran along the surface of mineral soil (Table 12.6: SI-1470; Caulfield 1978, 141). Consistent with this time scale was a third millennium cal BC date for peat from near the base of a monolith taken from close to the Behy court tomb (Fig. 12.38; Table 12.6: *UB-158F*; A. Smith *et al.* 1973, 223). Given the possibility that radiocarbon ages measured by the Smithsonian Institution at this time may have been anomalously young (see above), this chronology may now be in doubt.

In the early 1990s palynological analysis of deposits from a deep basin at Glenulra, close to the Céide Fields, where peat had begun to accumulate early in the Holocene, provided a vegetation record extending to the early medieval period (Molloy and O'Connell 1995; O'Connell and Molloy 2001). A series of conventional radiocarbon determinations were provided by the Rijksuniversiteit Groningen on the acid- and alkali-insoluble residue of bulk peat samples (Table 12.6). These were pretreated as described by Mook and Waterbolk (1985) and dated by GPC of carbon dioxide as described by Mook and Streurman (1983). The first significant event here is an episode of woodland burning and soil erosion, without obvious diminution of woodland cover, in local pollen zone 4, a peat sample from which has been dated to the early fourth millennium cal BC (*4070–3805 cal BC*; *95% probability*; Fig. 12.37: *GrN-21630*; or *4040–4015 cal BC* (*9% probability*) or *3995–3890 cal BC* (*47% probability*) or *3885–3850 cal BC* (*12% probability*)).

The second event is major forest clearance accompanied by the development of herb-rich grassland, beginning in local pollen zone 5a and reaching its peak in zone 5b. Grasses and herbs continued to be represented to the end of zone 5c, alongside regenerating mixed tree cover. This period can be modelled as starting in *3960–3540 cal BC* (*95% probability*; Fig. 12.37: *start clearance*), probably in *3845–3635 cal BC* (*68% probability*), and ending in *3300–2960 cal BC* (*95% probability*; Fig. 12.37: *start regeneration*), probably in *3210–3040 cal BC* (*68% probability*). The difference between these two date estimates suggests that the major clearance episode lasted for *335–880 years* (*95% probability*; distribution not shown), probably *475–745 years* (*68% probability*). After this, grasses and herbs fell to a low level, tree cover, including prominently pine in subzone 6b, regenerated, and bog and heath species increased. The authors interpret this sequence as resulting from a period of pastoral farming, at its most intensive in zone 5b. Following Caulfield's view that the field system was laid out as a single entity, which could have been done only in open conditions (1983), they conclude that the fields were laid out during zone 5b. They argued that there was no necessary link between the abandonment of the fields and the spread of blanket bog, which may have been separated by some time. Abandonment may have coincided with a period of unstable climate and increasing storminess, as argued by C. Caseldine *et al.* (2005) and Verrill (2006); the potential links between climate change and Neolithic agriculture in this region are currently being re-assessed (Graeme Warren, pers. comm.).

In the course of the same investigation, dates for peat from five of seven short monoliths taken from within the Céide Fields themselves provided further indications of when peat growth had extended beyond the basin, thus providing a series of *termini ante quos* for the disuse of the fields and supplementing work already done (A. Smith *et al.* 1973, 223). In the area of the Behy court tomb, peat did not begin to grow until the mid-third millennium cal BC. A sequence of two radiocarbon measurements obtained in the 1970s on the fine particulate fraction of peat from a core close to the tomb itself is in good agreement with the stratigraphy (Fig. 12.38: *UB-153F, -158F*). The radiocarbon ages obtained from the humic acid fraction of this material (Table 12.6: UB-158C, -153C, -155) appear to be anomalously young (A. Smith *et al.* 1973, 223) and are not included in the model.

Profile BHY III, 60 m west of the Behy court tomb, produced a series of seven radiocarbon dates (Table 12.6; Molloy and O'Connell 1995). Two samples have replicate determinations, in both cases statistically consistent (Table 12.6: GrN-23497 and Gd-6693; Gd-7147 and -7148). All the samples consisted of the acid- and alkali- insoluble residue of bulk peat samples and were dated by GPC of carbon dioxide (Mook and Streurman 1983; Pazdur and Pazdur 1986). Two measurements are also available for each of three further peat sections around the court tomb (Table 12.6: BHY IV, V and VI). In each case the dates are in good agreement with the stratigraphic sequence (Fig. 12.38). To the north, in the area of the Visitor Centre, peat growth did not begin until the turn of the second and first millennia (Table 12.6: GrN-20631).

Also in the 1990s, radiocarbon dates were obtained for 29 pine stumps growing in the peat over and around the field walls at Céide Fields as well as for a peat sample from beneath one of the stumps; and for further stumps and a further peat sample from the Erris region to the west (Caulfield *et al.* 1998). Those which relate to the fields are shown in Fig. 12.39. The trees are unlikely to have age offsets of more than 100 years, if reliance is placed on dendrochronological investigation of a group of pine stumps 200 m from the archaeological site at Belderg Beg, which established that the lifespan of the individual trees was *c.* 100 years (Caulfield 1988; Molloy and O'Connell 1995, 194). Most were rooted in peat, and can have grown

Table 12.6. Radiocarbon dates relating to field walls in Ireland. Posterior density estimates derive from the models defined in Figs 12.37–9.

Laboratory number	Sample reference	Material	Context	Radiocarbon age (BP)	$\delta^{13}C$ (‰)	Weighted mean (BP)	Calibrated date range (cal BC) (95% confidence)	*Posterior density estimate (cal BC) (95% probability)*
Céide Fields, Co. Mayo: Glenulra pollen core								
GrN-21636	GLU IV-12	Peat	2.55–2.58 m from surface. Zone 9a (top). Tree pollen low, grasses and herbs briefly high, following rise in hazel and alder between GrN-21121 and this	2890±50	−28.0		1260–920	*1270–970*
GrN-21121	GLU IV-5	Peat	2.89–2.93 m from surface. Zone 8/zone 9a boundary. Pine falling, total tree pollen low, grasses and herbs briefly high	3310±60	−27.8		1750–1440	*1740–1705 (4%)* or *1700–1450 (91%)*
GrN-21635	GLU IV-11	Peat	3.19–3.22 m from surface. Zone 8. Grasses high, tree and scrub species fairly low, moorland species fairly constant (Molloy and O'Connell 1995, fig. 6)	3510±50	−27.4		1960–1690	*1965–1725 (92%)* or *1720–1690 (3%)*
GrN-21120	GLU IV-4	Peat	3.51–3.55 m from surface. Base of zone 8. Grasses increasing, tree and scrub species decreasing (Molloy and O'Connell 1995, fig. 6)	3890±60	−27.0		2570–2150	*2550–2535 (1%)* or *2495–2195 (94%)*
GrN-21634	GLU IV-10	Peat	3.87–3.90 m from surface. Zone 7. Pine falling, other tree species and moorland species increasing, grass low (Molloy and O'Connell 1995, fig. 6)	4070±60	−27.8		2880–2460	*2835–2810 (1%)* or *2755–2465 (94%)*
GrN-21119	GLU IV-3	Peat	4.02–4.06 m. Zone 6b. Grass pollen low, pine peak, scrub and moorland species declining (Molloy and O'Connell 1995, fig. 6)	4110±60	−28.0		2890–2480	*2880–2580*
GrN-21633	GLU IV-9	Peat	4.40–4.44 m from surface Zone 6a. Grass pollen low; pine, scrub and moorland species spreading; developing moorland with pine spreading (Molloy and O'Connell 1995, fig. 6)	4470±60	−28.1		3370–2910	*3195–2910*
GrN-21118	GLU IV-2	Peat	4.48–4.52 m from surface. Zone 5c. Falling but still high levels of grass pollen accompanied by some woodland regeneration (Molloy and O'Connell 1995, fig. 6)	4550±60	−27.6		3500–3020	*3355–3095*
GrN-21632	GLU IV-8	Peat	4.59–4.62 m from surface. Zone 5c. Falling but still high levels of grass pollen accompanied by some woodland regeneration (Molloy and O'Connell 1995, fig. 6)	4500±60	−26.9		3370–2930	*3495–3465 (3%)* or *3375–3145 (92%)*
GrN-21117	GLU IV-1	Peat	4.86–4.90 m from surface. Base of zone 5b. Major decrease in pine and other arboreal pollen and increase in grass (Molloy and O'Connell 1995, fig. 6)	4840±60	−28.2		3710–3510	*3715–3500 (89%)* or *3430–3375 (6%)*
GrN-21631	GLU IV-7	Peat	4.94–4.97 m from surface. Zone 5a. Post-elm decline, clearance beginning (Molloy and O'Connell 1995, fig. 6)	5170±60	−27.5		4230–3800	*4030–3790*
GrN-21630	GLU IV-6	Peat	5.15–5.18 m from surface. Zone 4. Pre-elm decline, largely wooded, pine decreasing, oak and hazel increasing (Molloy and O'Connell 1995, fig. 6)	5100±80	−28.5		4050–3700	*4070–3805*
Céide Fields, Co. Mayo: peat beside Behy court tomb								
UB-158F		Fine particulate fraction of peat	0.36–0.38 m (A. Smith *et al.* 1973, 223)	3930±105	−29.1		2860–2130	*2840–2810 (1%)* or *2700–2200 (94%)*
UB-158C		Humic acid fraction peat	0.36–0.38 m 'difference between fine-particulate and humic acid fractions of UB-153 indicates considerable movement of humic substances in profile' (A. Smith *et al.* 1973, 223)	3750±85	−28.0		2470–1920	
UB-155		Combined fine particulate and humic acid fractions of blanket peat	0.30–0.34 m 'difference between fine-particulate and humic acid fractions of UB-153 indicates considerable movement of humic substances in profile. Result from combined sample, UB-155, is therefore, possibly largely erroneous' (A. Smith *et al.* 1973, 223)	3630±70	−27.5		2130–1770	

Laboratory number	Sample reference	Material	Context	Radiocarbon age (BP)	$\delta^{13}C$ (‰)	Weighted mean (BP)	Calibrated date range (cal BC) (95% confidence)	*Posterior density estimate (cal BC) (95% probability)*
UB-153F		Fine particulate fraction of peat	0.24–0.28 m (A. Smith *et al.* 1973)	3890±110			2840–2030	*2565–2115 (92%)* or *2095–2040 (3%)*
UB-153C		Humic acid fraction of peat	0.24–0.28 m (A. Smith *et al.* 1973)	3245±70	−27.4		1690–1390	
Céide Fields, Co. Mayo: profile BHY III, 60 m W of Behy court tomb								
GrN-23497		Peat	0.01–0.00 m above base of peat. Start of peat accumulation, grasses declining, pine, other trees and heather beginning to increase (Molloy and O'Connell 1995; O'Connell and Molloy 2001)	4110±40	−29.2	4094±36 T'=0.8; T'(5%)=3.8; ν=1	2870–2490	*2860–2805 (12%)* or *2760–2715 (8%)* or *2710–2560 (67%)* or *2535–2490 (8%)*
Gd-6693	BHY III-1	Replicate of GrN-232497	As GrN-23497	4030±80	−25.0 (assumed)			
GrN-23498		Peat	0.06–0.05 m above base of peat. Pine and heather declining, birch increasing	3870±25	−29.3		2470–2210	*2465–2280 (93%)* or *2250–2230 (2%)*
Gd-7147	BHY III-2	Peat	0.07 to 0.06 m above base of peat. Birch dominant	3360±50	−25.0 (assumed)	3332±38 T'=1.0; T'(5%)=3.8; ν=1	1730–1510	*1735–1710 (4%)* or *1695–1530 (91%)*
Gd-7148	BHY III-2	Replicate of Gd-7147	As Gd-7147	3290±60	−25.0 (assumed)			
GrN-20031	BHY III (5)	Peat	0.14–0.16 m above base of peat. Grasses dominant	3290±30	−29.0		1640–1490	*1625–1495*
GrN-23499		Peat	0.165–0.175 m above base of peat. Grasses dominant	3090±30	−29.4		1430–1270	*1435–1290*
Céide Fields, Co. Mayo: profile BHY IV, 25 m N of Behy court tomb								
GrN-20029	BHY IV(3)	Peat	0.01–0.04 m above base of peat. Much tree cover (Molloy and O'Connell 1995, fig. 11)	3630±40	−29.4		2140–1880	*2135–2080 (12%)* or *2060–1885 (83%)*
GrN-20030	BHY IV(4)	Peat	0.07–0.10 above base of peat. Mainly grasses and herbs (Molloy and O'Connell 1995, fig. 11)	2940±40	−29.4		1300–1010	*1300–1025*
Céide Fields, Co. Mayo: profile BHY V, peat bank 35 m E of Behy Court tomb								
Gd-6694	BHY V-1	Peat	0–0.01 m below base of peat. Woodland, especially birch, some grasses and plants of bog and heath	3990±80	−25.0 (assumed)		2860–2280	*2855–2810 (3%)* or *2750–2720 (1%)* or *2700–2275 (88%)* or *2255–2205 (3%)*
Gd-6696	BHY V-2	Peat	0.70 m to 0.85 m above base of peat. Grasses and plants of bog and heath (Molloy and O'Connell 1995, fig. 13)	3450±80	−25.0 (assumed)		1960–1530	*2020–1995 (1%)* or *1980–1600 (94%)*
Céide Fields, Co. Mayo: profile BHY VI, *c.* 400 m NW of Behy court tomb								
GrN-20027	BHY VI (1)	Peat	0.05–0.08 m above base of peat. Pine, birch and other trees declining, grasses and plants of bog and heath increasing heath (Molloy and O'Connell 1995, fig. 14)	4080±50	−29.3		2880–2470	*2865–2805 (12%)* or *2760–2475 (83%)*
GrN-20028	BHY VI (2)	Peat	0.10–0.13 above base of peat. Grasses and plants of bog and heath dominant (Molloy and O'Connell 1995, fig. 14)	3540±50	−29.1		2030–1740	*2025–1990 (5%)* or *1985–1745 (90%)*
Céide Fields, Co. Mayo: monolith CFI, 30 m SW of visitor centre								
GrN-20631	CF I-1	Peat	0–0.01 m above base of peat, under tumble from wall. Grasses and plants of bog and heath dominant (Molloy and O'Connell 1995, figs 17, 18)	2760±40	−28.2		1010–810	
GrN-21116	CF-I-3	Peat	0.01–0.02 m above base of peat. Grasses and plants of bog and heath dominant (Molloy and O'Connell 1995, figs 17, 18)	2870±40	−29.3		1200–910	

Laboratory number	Sample reference	Material	Context	Radiocarbon age (BP)	$\delta^{13}C$ (‰)	Weighted mean (BP)	Calibrated date range (cal BC) (95% confidence)	*Posterior density estimate (cal BC) (95% probability)*
GrN-20632	CF-I-2	Peat	0.07–0.08 m above base of peat. Grasses and plants of bog and heath dominant (Molloy and O'Connell 1995, figs 17, 18)	2250±50	−28.9		410–190	
Céide Fields, Co. Mayo: Glenulra								
SI-1464		Charcoal	Hearth within the Glenulra enclosure (Caulfield 1978) Quoted as 4460±80 by Caulfield *et al.* (1998)	4460±115			3510–2880	
UCD-C45	G-050-404	Sub-fossil *Pinus sylvestris* stump	Growing on mineral soil at Behy, 1 m from wall of field system	4450±60			3360–2910	*3340–3000 (84%)* or *2995–2925 (11%)*
UCD-C51	G-050-404	Outer rings of sub-fossil *Pinus sylvestris* stump	Lying horizontally in bog which had grown over field system at Behy, near tomb, 0.05 m above mineral soil	4500±60			3370–2930	*3365–3010*
UCD-C57	G-047-405	Sub-fossil *Pinus sylvestris*. Outer remnant of very large trunk	Lying on mineral soil at Behy, 65 m W of tomb	4420±50			3340–2900	*3330–3210 (22%)* or *3190–3150 (5%)* or *3135–2910 (68%)*
UCD-C42	G-063-399	Sub-fossil *Pinus sylvestris* stump	Growing on bog which had grown over field system at Glenulra, 0.90 m above mineral soil, near edge of deep peat basin from which pollen core taken	4530±60			3500–3020	
UCD-C44	G-063-399	Sub-fossil *Pinus sylvestris* stump	At base of peat which had grown over peat at Glenulra, near edge of deep peat basin from which pollen core taken and in agreement with date for peat at just over 5 m in pollen core, where burnt pine fragments found	5370±70			4350–3990	
Céide Fields, Co. Mayo: Ballyknock								
UCD-C21	G-076-387	Sub-fossil *Pinus sylvestris* stump	Growing on bog which had grown over field system, at Ballyknock, 0.10 m above mineral soil	4490±60			3370–2920	*3365–3010 (94%)* or *2980–2960 (1%)*
UCD-C23	G-072-382	Sub-fossil *Pinus sylvestris* stump	Growing on bog which had grown over field system at Ballyknock, 0.75 m above mineral soil	4540±60			3500–3020	*3375–3080 (92%)* or *3065–3025 (3%)*
UCD-C28	G-072-382	Sub-fossil *Pinus sylvestris* stump	Growing on bog which had grown over field system at Ballyknock, 0.20 m above mineral soil	4230±60			2930–2630	*3010–2985 (1%)* or *2935–2615 (94%)*
UCD-C29	G-072-382	Sub-fossil *Pinus sylvestris* stump	Growing on bog which had grown over field system at Ballyknock, 0.30 m above mineral soil	4510±50			3370–3020	*3360–3085 (91%)* or *3065–3025 (4%)*
UCD-C34	G-073-382	Sub-fossil *Pinus sylvestris* stump	Growing on bog which had grown over field system at Ballyknock, 0.35 m above mineral soil	3950±60			2620–2280	*2590–2275 (94%)* or *2250–2230 (1%)*
UCD-C37	G-074-383	Sub-fossil *Pinus sylvestris* stump	Growing on bog which had grown over field system at Ballyknock, 0.30 m above mineral soil	4500±50			3370–3020	*3360–3080 (89%)* or *3070–3025 (6%)*
Céide Fields, Co. Mayo: Aghoo								
UCD-C22	G-086-354	Sub-fossil *Pinus sylvestris* stump	Growing on bog which had grown over field system at Aghoo, 0.25m above mineral soil	4210±60			2920–2610	*2920–2615*
UCD-C27	G-092-360	Sub-fossil *Pinus sylvestris* stump	Growing on bog which had grown over field system at Aghoo, 0.25m above mineral soil	4170±50			2900–2570	*2890–2615*
UCD-C30	G-089-357	Sub-fossil *Pinus sylvestris* stump	Growing on bog which had grown over field system at Aghoo, 0.20m above mineral soil	4190±50			2910–2600	*2900–2620*
UCD-C33	G-089-357	Sub-fossil *Pinus sylvestris* stump	Growing on bog which had grown over field system at Aghoo, 0.30 m above mineral soil	4100±60			2880–2470	*2875–2560 (88%)* or *2540–2490 (7%)*
Céide Fields, Co. Mayo: Belderg								
SI-1469	Belderg Beg 1	*Quercus* stump	Growing in peat E of site at Belderg Beg	3835±85			2570–2030	

Laboratory number	Sample reference	Material	Context	Radiocarbon age (BP)	$\delta^{13}C$ (‰)	Weighted mean (BP)	Calibrated date range (cal BC) (95% confidence)	*Posterior density estimate (cal BC) (95% probability)*
SI-1470	Belderg Beg 2	Outer 5 rings of large pine stump	15 m from wall at Belderg Beg. Lateral roots running along surface of mineral soil, i.e. bog already established when tree growing	4220±95			3080–2490	
SI-1471	Belderg Beg 3	Pointed *Quercus* stake	Driven into peat prolonging line of wall built on shallow encroaching peat	3220±85			1690–1310	
SI-1472	Belderg Beg 4	Pointed *Quercus* stake	Driven into peat prolonging line of wall built on shallow encroaching peat	3210±85			1690–1300	
SI-1473	Belderg Beg 5	Block of wood	In roundhouse	3170±85			1630–1260	
SI-1474	Belderg Beg 6	Charcoal	In roundhouse, 'impossible to reconcile with either the archaeological material or the radiocarbon dates from the site' (Caulfield 1978, 142)	2295±75			540–180	
SI-1475	Belderg Beg 7	Charcoal	Associated with scatter of flint scrapers 'impossible to reconcile with either the archaeological material or the radiocarbon dates from the site' (Caulfield 1978, 142)	2905±75			1380–900	
UCD-C04	F-997-412	Sub-fossil *Pinus sylvestris* stump	Growing on bog which had grown over field system at Belderg More, 0.30m above mineral soil and 2 m from a wall	4480±60			3370–2920	*3355–3005 (92%)* or *2980–2935 (3%)*
UCD-C11	G-008-408	Sub-fossil *Pinus sylvestris* stump	Growing on bog which had grown over field system at Belderg More, 0.50m above mineral soil and 55 m from a wall junction	4010±60			2840–2340	*2860–2810 (5%)* or *2750–2720 (1%)* or *2700–2340 (89%)*
UCD-C14	G-013-409	Sub-fossil *Pinus sylvestris* stump	Growing on bog which had grown over field system at Belderg More, 0.25m above mineral soil	4310±70			3100–2710	*3265–3235 (1%)* or *3110–2835 (84%)* or *2815–2690 (10%)*
UCD-C18	F-997-413	Sub-fossil *Pinus sylvestris* stump	In mineral soil 30 m E of a wall junction at Belderg More	4150±60			2900–2490	*2890–2575*
UCD-C49	F997-412	Sub-fossil *Pinus sylvestris* stump	Rooted in wall of field system at Belderg More, 9m south of wall junction close to UCD-C18	4580±60			3520–3090	*3495–3430 (4%)* or *3385–3085 (91%)*
UCD-C07	F-976-402	Sub-fossil *Pinus sylvestris* stump	Growing on bog which had grown over field system at Belderg Beg, 0.70m above mineral soil	3330±50			1750–1490	*1880–1840 (7%)* or *1770–1525 (88%)*
UCD-C31	F-984-406	Sub-fossil *Pinus sylvestris* stump	Growing at base of bog which had grown over field system at Belderg Beg	4510±50			3370–3020	*3360–3085 (91%)* or *3065–3025 (4%)*
UCD-C58	F-975-402	Sub-fossil *Pinus sylvestris* stump	Growing on bog which had grown over field system at Belderg Beg, 0.75m above mineral soil	3960±60			2620–2280	*2625–2280*
UCD-C60	F-985-405	Sub-fossil *Pinus sylvestris* stump	Growing on bog which had grown over field system at Belderg Beg, unknown distance above mineral soil	3930±50			2570–2240	*2575–2510 (11%)* or *2505–2285 (83%)* or *2250–2230 (1%)*
UCD-C47	F-983-409	Sub-fossil *Pinus sylvestris* stump	Growing on bog which had grown over field system at Geevraun, 0.45m above mineral soil and above sample for UCD-C46	4210±60			2920–2610	
UCD-C46	F-983-409	Peat	From bog which had grown over field system at Geevraun, on low ridge, 0.05m above mineral soil and below sample for UCD-C47	5710±90			3270–2880	
Excavations at Belderg, Co. Mayo, 2004–ongoing								
UB-7590		*Corylus* charcoal, Twig	BDG context 115. Hearth sealed by 'tumble' from a pre-bog field wall (Warren 2007)	4780±36	−23.1		3650–3380	

Laboratory number	Sample reference	Material	Context	Radiocarbon age (BP)	$\delta^{13}C$ (‰)	Weighted mean (BP)	Calibrated date range (cal BC) (95% confidence)	*Posterior density estimate (cal BC) (95% probability)*
UB-7591		*Betula* charcoal, twig	From the same context as UB-7590	4717±37	−23.1	4726±24	3635–3380	
UBA-7591		Replicate of UB-7591	From the same context as UB-7590	4732±30		T'=0.1 T'(5%)=3.8; ν=1		
Céide Fields, Co. Mayo: Annagh More/Annagh Beg								
UCD-C26	G-115-343	Sub-fossil *Pinus sylvestris* stump	Growing on wall of field system in bog which had grown over it at Annagh More	4350±60			3270–2880	*3320–3290 (1%)* or *3270–3235 (3%)* or *3120–2875 (91%)*
UCD-C50	G-115-343	Sub-fossil *Pinus sylvestris* stump	Rooted in mineral in mineral soil close to peat-covered field wall at Annagh More (Caulfield *et al.* 1998, 635)	4440±60			3360–2900	*3340–3205 (32%)* or *3195–2920 (63%)*
UCD-C24	G-118-323	Sub-fossil *Pinus sylvestris* stump	Growing on bog which had grown over field system at Annagh Beg, 1.80 m above mineral soil	4440±60			3360–2900	*3335–3205 (31%)* or *3195–2920 (64%)*
UCD-C38	G-119-323	Sub-fossil *Pinus sylvestris* stump	Growing on bog which had grown over field system at Annagh Beg, 1.40 m above mineral soil	3820±60			2470–2040	*2470–2130 (93%)* or *2085–2055 (2%)*
Erris region, Co. Mayo								
UCD-C01	F-784-338	Sub-fossil *Pinus sylvestris* stump	Growing on bog at Inver, 0.75 m above mineral soil	4240±60			2930–2630	
UCD-C02	F-857-351	Sub-fossil *Pinus sylvestris* stump	Growing on bog at Aghoos, 0.65 m above mineral soil	4340±60			3270–2870	
UCD-C12	F-854-356	Sub-fossil *Pinus sylvestris* stump	Growing on bog at Aghoos, 0.75 m above mineral soil	3950±60			2620–2280	
UCD-C05	F-824-356	Sub-fossil *Pinus sylvestris* stump	Growing on bog at Carnhill, 1.35 m above mineral soil	4250±60			3010–2670	
UCD-C13	F-781-309	Sub-fossil *Pinus sylvestris* stump	Growing on bog at Muings 2.00 m above mineral soil	3990±60			2840–2300	
UCD-C16	F-927-339	Sub-fossil *Pinus sylvestris* stump	Growing on bog at Bunalty, 0.65 m above mineral soil	4490±60			3370–2970	
UCD-C19	F-803-338	Sub-fossil *Pinus sylvestris* stump	Growing on bog at Gortmelia, 0.10 m above mineral soil	4530±60			3500–3020	
UCD-C20	F-817-314	Sub-fossil *Pinus sylvestris* stump	Growing on bog at Carrowmore, 0.65 m above mineral soil	4230±60			2930–2630	
UCD-C25	F-875-272	Sub-fossil *Pinus sylvestris* stump	Growing on bog at Glencullin, 0.15 m above mineral soil	4460±60			3370–2910	
UCD-C35	F-791-376	Sub-fossil *Pinus sylvestris* stump	Growing on bog at Graghil, 0.40 m above mineral soil	4440±50			3350–2910	
UCD-C36	F-815-356	Sub-fossil *Pinus sylvestris* stump	Growing on bog at Gortbrack North, 1.25 m above mineral soil	3090±50			1460–1210	
UCD-C43	F-848-318	Sub-fossil *Pinus sylvestris* stump	Growing on bog at Muingerron South, 0.30 m above mineral soil	4080±60			2880–2470	
UCD-C41	F-848-318	Sub-fossil *Pinus sylvestris* stump	Growing on bog at Muingerron South, on mineral soil	6720±90			5760–5480	
UCD-C52	F-753-149	Sub-fossil *Pinus sylvestris* stump	Growing on bog at Tullaghanbaun at unknown distance above mineral soil	4070±60			2880–2460	
UCD-C48	F-753-149	Sub-fossil *Pinus sylvestris* stump	On 0.80 m of peat in intertidal zone at Blacksod Bay, above sample for UCD-C54	7530±100			6600–6210	

Laboratory number	Sample reference	Material	Context	Radiocarbon age (BP)	$\delta^{13}C$ (‰)	Weighted mean (BP)	Calibrated date range (cal BC) (95% confidence)	*Posterior density estimate (cal BC) (95% probability)*
UCD-C54	F-753-149	Peat	Intertidal peat at Blacksod Bay, Tullaghanbaun, below sample for UCD-C48	8660±130			8210–7490	
Valencia Island, Co. Kerry								
I-14206		Waterlogged *Salix* twigs at base of wall	Sheet of willow twigs at base of wall provides *terminus post quem* for construction (F. Mitchell 1990)	4760±100			3710–3350	*3775–3340*

only after it began to develop. Thus, although in most cases it is not known which part of the tree was sampled for radiocarbon dating, all these dates should provide *termini ante quos* for the disuse of the field system that was covered by the peat in which the trees were rooted. The same applies to two trees (*UCD-C26, -C49*) which were actually rooted in field walls, where they could not have grown unless the walls were already peat-covered. Two further trees (*UCD-C18, -C50*) were rooted in the soil at the base of the peat, and may have started to grow before peat began to form. They must have died after or only shortly before this occurred locally, however, otherwise they would not have been preserved. As the parts of the trees that were dated are unknown, it is possible that the dated rings may have grown before peat initiation. These two measurements, therefore, provide only *termini post quos* for the end of the bog pine phase in this area and do not contribute to the estimate for the start of peat growth.

Four dates are excluded from the model because they seem to relate to early, localised pockets of peat growth (Table 12.6). UCD-C42 and -C44 date pine stumps from near the edge of the deep basin at Glenulra where one would expect peat to have spread early. UCD-C46 and -C47 from Geevraun in Belderrig also seem to be exceptionally early. SI-1469 and -1470, measured on pine stumps from Belderg (Table 12.6), are excluded from the model because dates measured at the same time on samples from the nearby Bronze Age settlement (Table 12.6: SI-1471–5) include two that appear to be anomalously recent (SI-1474–5; Caulfield 1978, 42). Given this and the anomalously recent dates for Ballyglass from the same laboratory (discussed above), caution seems appropriate.

Where it is possible to compare dates for stumps growing on or just above the mineral soil and dates for the base of the peat in a single area, that of the Behy court tomb, the stumps (Fig. 12.39: *UCD-C45, -C51, -C57*) are earlier than the base of the peat (Fig. 12.38: *UB-158F, 0.00–0.01 m above base, GrN-20029, Gd-6694, GrN-20027*), the two sets of dates being statistically inconsistent ($T'=259.1$; $T'(5\%)=14.1$; $\nu=7$). Pine thus started to grow before peat extended beyond the basin.

One of several other areas where pre-bog field walls occur is Valencia Island, Co. Kerry (Mitchell 1989, 75). *I-14206*, measured on a sample from a sheet of willow twigs at the base of one wall, provides a *terminus post quem* for its construction (Fig. 12.40).

An overall model for the chronology of the field systems of the Céide Fields and Valencia Island is provided in Fig. 12.40. The establishment of the Céide Fields is best dated by the start of the major clearance episode visible in the Glenulra pollen record, which suggests that they were laid out in *3960–3540 cal BC* (*95% probability*; Fig. 12.37: *start clearance*), probably in *3845–3635 cal BC* (*68% probability*). The fields seem to have gone out of use in the second half of the fourth millennium cal BC (Fig. 12.40), since pine woodland appears to have become established over the fields. We have two independent estimates for the date when this woodland became established. These

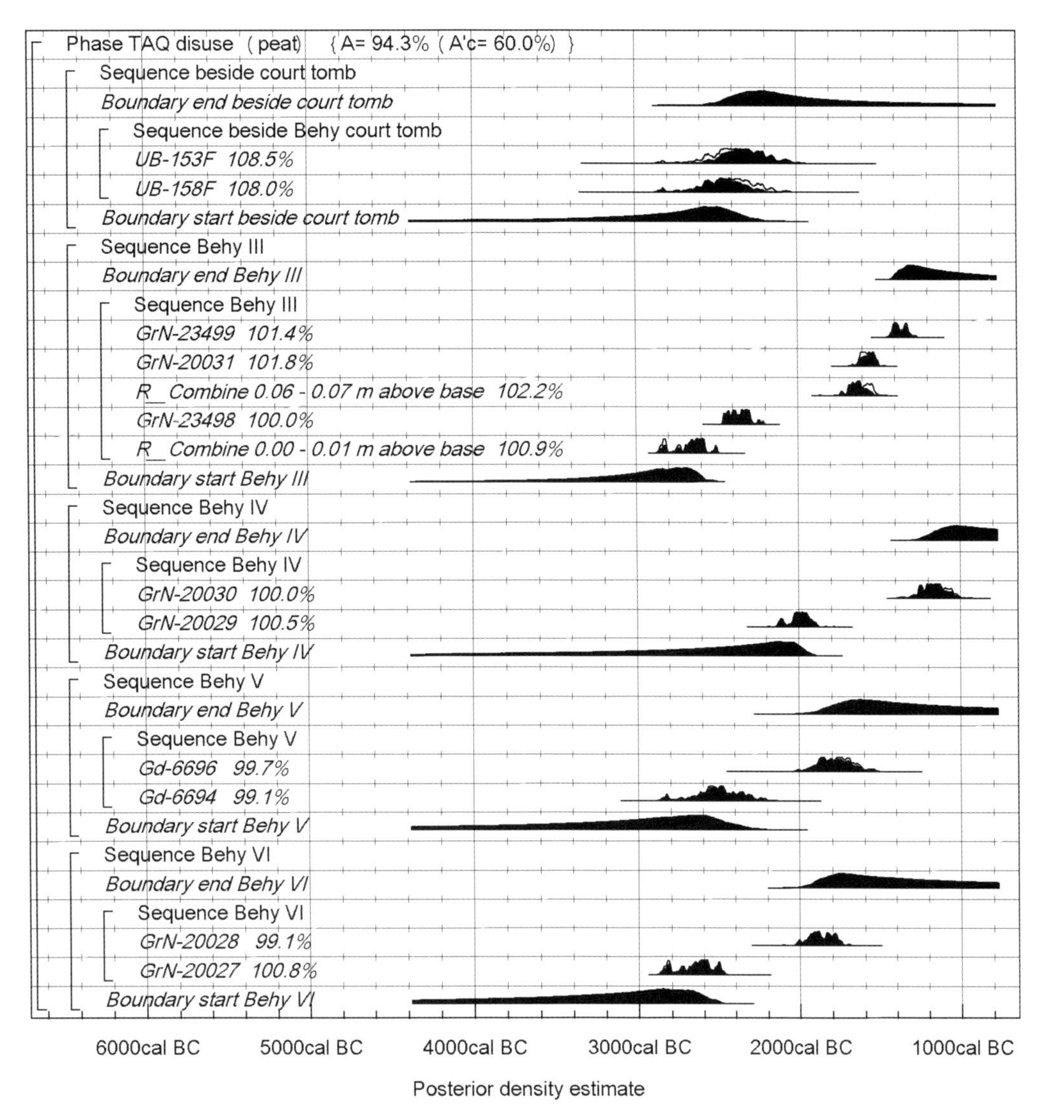

Fig. 12.38. Céide Fields. Probability distributions of dates from sequences through overlying peat. The format is identical to that of Fig. 12.6. The large square brackets down the left-hand side, along with the OxCal keywords, define the overall model exactly.

are divergent. On the basis of the waterlogged bog pines, pine became established from *3630–3245 cal BC* (*95% probability*; Fig. 12.39: *start stumps*), probably from *3465–3305 cal BC* (*68% probability*). The evidence for woodland regeneration, including a marked increase in pine pollen, in the Glenulra pollen record occurs slightly later, in *3300–2960 cal BC* (*95% probability*; Fig. 12.37: *start regeneration*), probably in *3210–3040 cal BC* (*68% probability*). A model which constrains the start of regeneration to be earlier than the first bog pine has poor overall agreement ($A_{overall}$=50.1%, and for *start regeneration*, A=20.2%). The difference between these two estimates for the initiation of the pine forest amounts to *40–515 years* (*95% probability*; distribution not shown), probably to *145–380 years* (*68% probability*). It may be that the two kinds of evidence do not relate to the same event; perhaps the local establishment of pine within the catchment of the pollen record at Glenulra was later than the very first growth of pine within the larger area of the field system. The estimate for this earliest establishment of pine forest provided by the bog pines is more spatially representative than that of the single pollen record from Glenulra. It seems plausible to suggest that the spread of pine across the field system was a process rather than a single event. The start of this process may therefore be most accurately dated by *start stumps*, with *start regeneration* reflecting its continuation in a particular locality. Similarly, it is conceivable that the abandonment of the Céide Fields was also a process rather than an event. Current evidence, however, indicates the establishment of the system in the first half, perhaps the second quarter, of the fourth millennium cal BC, and its disuse in the second half, probably from the third quarter of that millennium. Blanket bog encroached from the middle of the third millennium cal BC (Fig. 12.40). The single date for Valencia Island could be compatible with the use of that system in the mid-fourth millenium cal BC.

These models reinforce the original arguments of the excavator for a relatively early date for the Céide Fields (Caulfield 1978; 1983; Caulfield *et al.*1998). Further

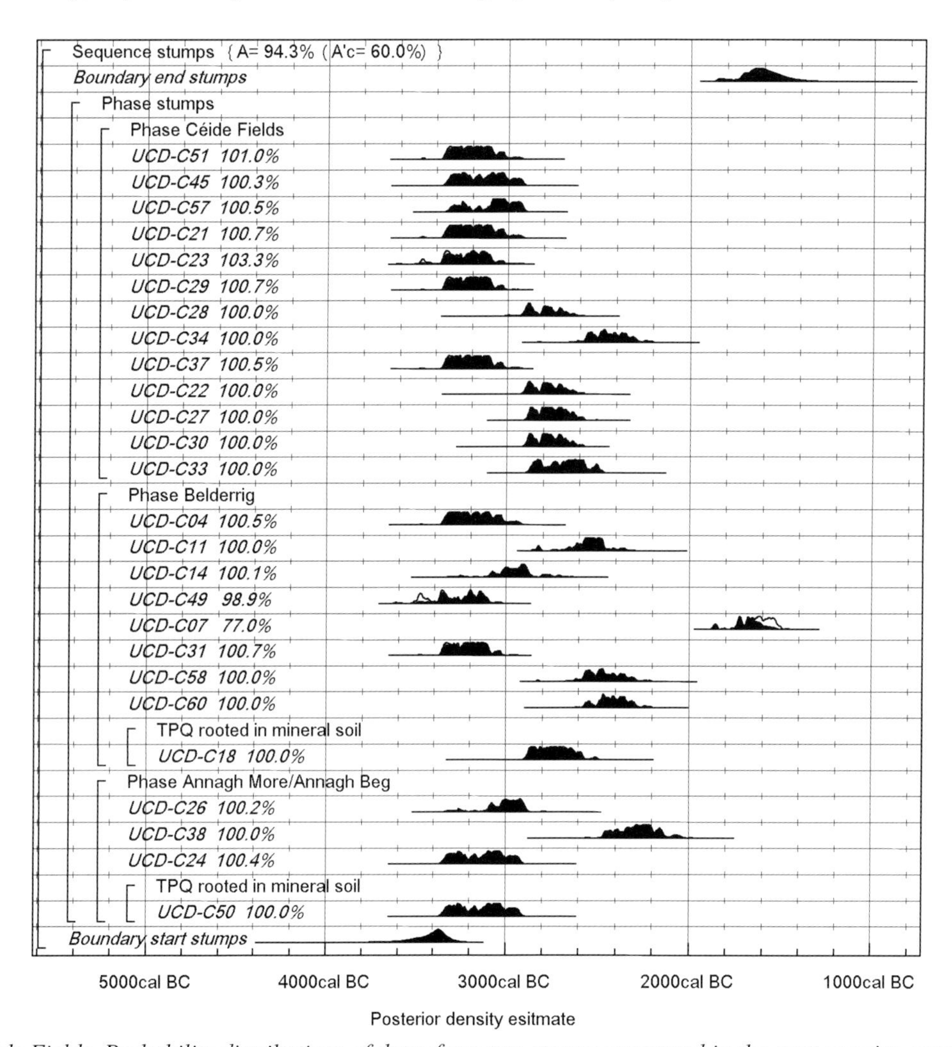

Fig. 12.39. Céide Fields. Probability distributions of dates from tree stumps preserved in the peat growing over the area. The format is identical to that of Fig. 12.6. The large square brackets down the left-hand side, along with the OxCal keywords, define the overall model exactly.

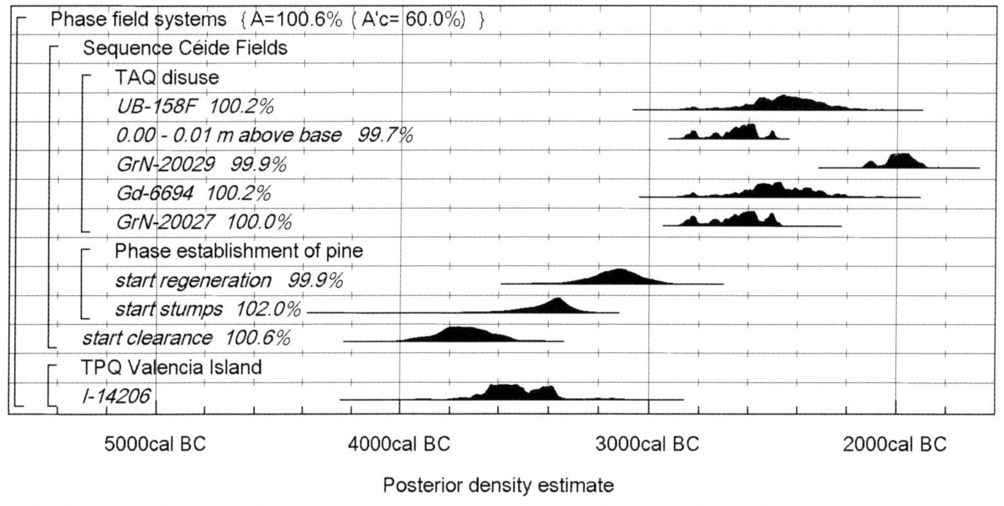

Fig. 12.40. Céide Fields and Valencia Island. Key parameters relating to the chronology of early fields, derived from the models defined in Figs 12.37–9.

dating evidence, not available when the models were built, is available from renewed work at Belderg More by Graeme Warren. Apart from documenting Mesolithic activity through the mid- to late fifth millennium cal BC, this project has demonstrated progressive local changes in the layout of the walls and obtained mid-fourth millennium cal BC dates on short-life samples from a hearth sealed by tumble from a nearby field wall which had accumulated before peat started to grow. While the relation of the hearth to the wall is unknown, the measurements provide *termini post quos* for the start of peat growth at this location (Table 12.6: UB-7590–1, UBA-7591; Warren 2009a; 2009b; Warren *et al.* 2009). Given other, comparable evidence from northern Co. Mayo (Cooney 2000a, 46), we can assert that this was at the very least a regional rather than a purely localised phenomenon (see also O'Connell and Molloy 2001). Summarising evidence from other parts of Ireland, it has been suggested (Cooney 2000a, 46–7) that the organisation of landscapes into fields was recurrent rather than exceptional. Other pre-bog examples include Valencia Island (G. Mitchell 1989, 75) and the walls on the Burren, for example at Roughan Hill, which appear on the surface as low grass-covered mounds. On the basis of the height of the limestone bedrock pedestals protected from erosion by the walls, C. Jones (2004, 63) argues that at Roughan Hill the majority are dated to the Final Neolithic/Early Bronze Age but points out that some mound walls have higher pedestals and are probably older.

The role of the fields within systems of production and tenure, in the context of an Atlantic setting seemingly ideally suited to grass growth, has already been explored by Seamas Caulfield (1978; 1983). The investment in stone wall construction is striking, on a cumulative scale probably exceeding the building of the later, major passage tombs. There is no inherent reason why even close management of herds should require stone walls. Perhaps, therefore, we can think in wider ways about their significance. Was this a distinctive way of signing the land, an expression of regional identity or identities, a means of aligning people with the substance of the earth and its mythic properties, and a medium through which community could be assembled and tied to place? This line of argument is supported by the location of the walls at Caltragh, south of the Magheraboy causewayed enclosure, separating areas of wet and dry ground (Danaher 2007, 65).

Following the conclusion of the pollen analysts that the abandonment of the field system at Céide had nothing directly to do with blanket bog encroachment (Molloy and O'Connell 1995), Caseldine *et al.* (2005) and Verrill (2006) have suggested that abandonment may have coincided with a period of unstable climate and increased storminess (see discussion above).

Trackways

The construction of wooden trackways could easily have been within the technological capabilities of foragers in Ireland, who after all possessed flint and stone axeheads, and Mesolithic wooden platforms have been found, as at Mitchelstowndown East, Co. Limerick (Brindley and Lanting 1998, 57), and Derragh on Lough Kinale in Co. Longford (Fredengren 2007). The possibility of a Mesolithic trackway in Lullymore Bog, Co. Kildare, is a real one, although doubt is raised by the disparity between late sixth/early fifth millennium cal BC dates for both bog pine below the track and peat above it and late seventh/early sixth millennium dates for the track itself (Brindley and Lanting 1998, 47, 57–8). This may mean that the track was built of bog pine older than that on which it lay. Brindley and Lanting see the Lullymore track as built to meet very specific local needs and can point to very few Mesolithic examples in north-west Europe, track building becoming more frequent from the start of the Neolithic. For this reason, we suggest that the construction and use of trackways are a kind of modification of the landscape which proliferated with the Neolithic. The earliest known dated example from Britain, the Sweet Track in the Somerset Levels, was already a substantial undertaking (see Chapter 4).

Trackways from five locations (four in the Irish midlands) have been dated to the fourth millennium cal BC (Fig. 12.41). At Corlea, Co. Longford (Raftery 1996), four brushwood trackways, numbers 8–11, have been dated, each by a sample of waterlogged hazel roundwood (Table 12.7: GrN-16830–1, -18375–6). At Derrygreenagh, Co. Westmeath, a timber from a trackway yielded a dendrochronological *terminus post quem* for felling of 3643±9 BC (Conor McDermott, pers. comm.). Brushwood trackways at Cloncreen Bog and at Ballykilleen, Co. Offaly, have been dated by Wk-11733 and Wk-11729 respectively, and at Killeens Bog, Co. Cork, trackway 2a is dated by UCD-0216 (Conor McDermott, pers. comm.).

'Undiagnostic' pottery

There are two further sites where pottery has been dated to the fourth millennium cal BC. At the time when the models in this chapter were constructed, we were uncertain about the character of this material. The pottery from these two sites was therefore modelled as 'undiagnostic' within the list of definitely Neolithic activity, though one find has since been attributed to a specific style, and it is referred to subsequently in this chapter in inverted commas.

At Lough Gur, the burial of a crouched juvenile in a pit (F101) was dated to 3640–3360 cal BC (95% confidence; Table 12.8: GrN-16825; Brindley and Lanting 1990; Cleary 1995). This forms part of a tradition of individual burial during the Neolithic at Lough Gur which seemed to be focused on children (Grogan and Eogan 1987), and included a burial of an adolescent with a decorated, bipartite bowl at Site C (Ó Ríordáin 1954; Herity 1982). The child in F101 overlay some patinated flint flakes and was accompanied by a chip of a stone axehead; there were also six sherds of corky-textured pottery in the fill of the grave (Cleary 1995). It is possible that this material was associated with the burial, although it is also possible that it is redeposited, and that the burial formed part of the same phase of activity as the decorated, bipartite Bowl (Herity 1982, 299, fig. 26:25). The radiocarbon date accords with either interpretation (Fig. 12.41).

Human bone from a skeleton in a pit at Clane, Co. Kildare, which it is now clear was associated with a simple decorated bowl of middle Neolithic style (Ryan 1980), has been dated by *GrN-12276* (Fig. 12.41).

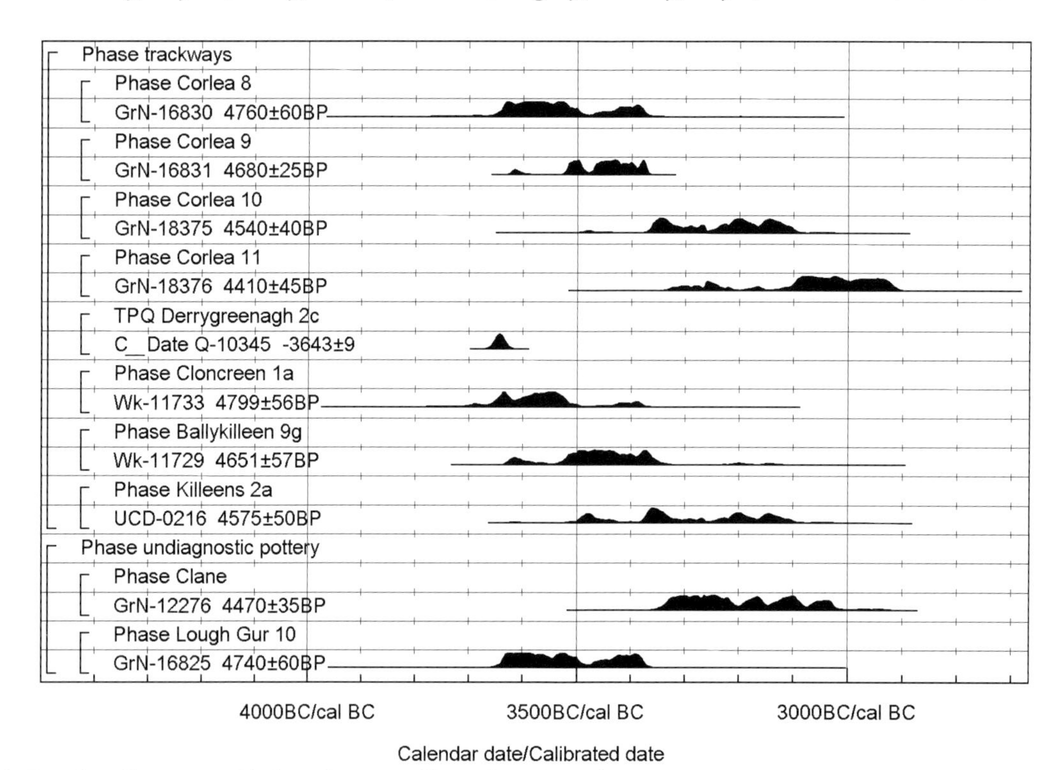

Fig. 12.41. Fourth millennium cal BC trackways and burials with 'undiagnostic' pottery. Calibrated dates (Stuiver and Reimer 1993).

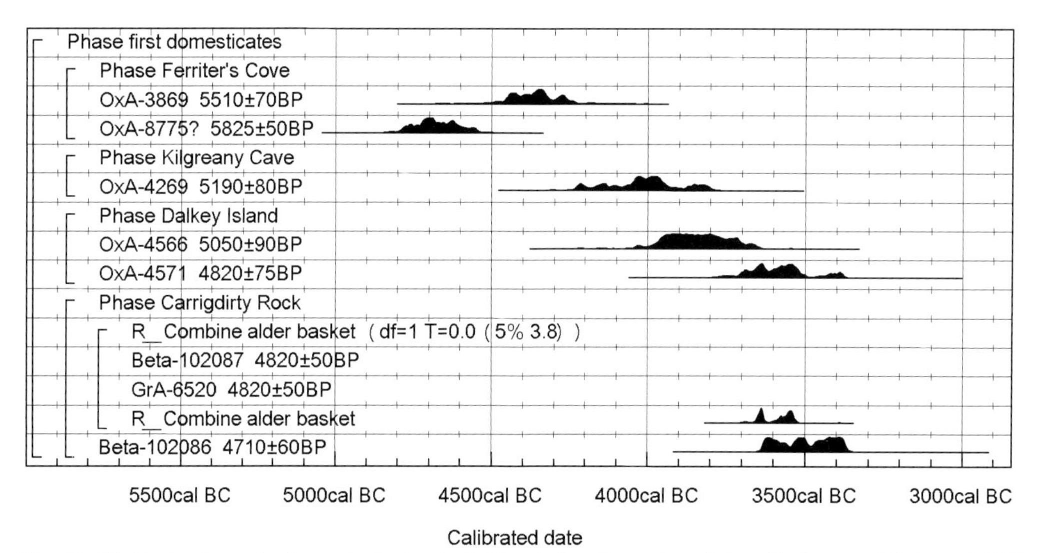

Fig. 12.42. Early domestic fauna in Ireland. Calibrated radiocarbon dates (Stuiver and Reimer 1993).

Domesticates

Seven cattle bones and a single sheep tooth (both species absent from Ireland in the early Holocene) came from a late Mesolithic milieu at Ferriter's Cove, Co. Kerry; two of the cattle bones have been dated to the fifth millennium cal BC (Fig. 12.42: OxA-3869, -8775; Woodman *et al.* 1999, 89–92, 144–51). These have been seen as the earliest evidence for the introduction of at least one element of Neolithic practice into the island and have been the subject of considerable discussion (e.g. Woodman and McCarthy 2003; Sheridan 2003a; Tresset 2003). In contrast to the variety and quantity of fish (and shellfish) resources, the remains of mammals and birds at Ferriter's Cove were scarce (Woodman *et al.* 1999, 92), and the stable isotope signatures of the human remains from the site, the two dated examples of whom died in the late fifth millennium cal BC (Table 12.9: OxA-4918, -5770; Woodman *et al.* 1999, 85–103), indicate a diet which included a large component of marine resources.

Woodman and McCarthy (2003, 33) suggest that the cattle and sheep represent little more than a dietary supplement to people who relied on marine sources,

Table 12.7. Radiocarbon dates relating to fourth millennium cal BC trackways in Ireland.

Laboratory number	Sample reference	Material	Context	Radiocarbon age (BP)	δ¹³C (‰)	Calibrated date range (cal BC) (95% confidence)
Corlea Bog, Co. Longford						
GrN-16830		Waterlogged *Corylus* roundwood, 22 mm diameter, 6 rings	Corlea 8.Trackway (B. Raftery 1996, 79–81; Brindley and Lanting 1998, 50)	4760±60	−28.5	3660–3370
GrN-16831		Waterlogged *Corylus* roundwood, 90 mm diameter, *c.* 20 rings	Corlea 9. Trackway (B. Raftery 1996, 81–91; Brindley and Lanting 1998, 50)	4680±125	−28.1	3630–3360
GrN-18375		Waterlogged *Corylus* roundwood, 65 mm diameter, 20–30 rings	Corlea 10. Trackway (B. Raftery 1996, 91; Brindley and Lanting 1998)	4540±40	−28.0	3370–3090
GrN-18376		Waterlogged *Corylus* roundwood, 40 mm diameter, 21 rings	Corlea 11. Trackway (B. Raftery 1996, 91–2; Brindley and Lanting 1998, 50)	4410±45	−29.3	3330–2900
Derrygreenagh Bog, Co. Westmeath						
Q10345	OF-DGH 0002c	Dendro date start 3988 BC, end 3675 BC, felling 3643±9 BC or later	Derrygreenagh 2c. Trackway			
Cloncreen Bog, Co. Offaly						
Wk-11733 (standard radiometric)	OF-CCR 001A	Waterlogged brushwood. 'I filtered the list to include only primary context dates where possible. For the most part there should be no issue regarding the 'old wood effect' or other anomalies as it is the general practice on such sites to choose a small piece of wood with a low ring count as there is usually an abundance of wood available to choose from. Where there was evidence of phasing identified by the excavator…I clearly indicate this in the label for the dates.' (Conor McDermott, pers. comm., Sept. 2006)	Cloncreen 1a .Trackway	4799±56	−28.9±0.2	3700–3370
Ballykilleen Bog, Co. Offaly						
Wk-11729 (standard radiometric)	OF-BKL 0009g	Waterlogged brushwood. Same comment from Conor McDermott above applies	Ballykilleen 9g. Trackway	4651±57	−27.1±0.2	3630–3340
Killeens Bog, Co. Cork						
UCD-0216	OF-KEN 0003a	Waterlogged wood. Same comment from Conor McDermott above applies	Killeens 2a. Trackway	4575±50		3500–3090

Table 12.8. Radiocarbon dates relating to burials with 'undiagnostic' pottery in Ireland.

Laboratory number	Sample reference	Material	Context	Radiocarbon age (BP)	δ¹³C (‰)	Calibrated date range (cal BC) (95% confidence)
Lough Gur, Co. Limerick						
GrN-16825	Lough Gur 10	Human. Bone	F101. From grave of 6–8 year-old child overlying patinated flint flakes and accompanied by a greenstone chip. 6 sherds of corky-textured ware in backfill, 1 of them shouldered (Cleary 1995; Brindley and Lanting 1990)	4740±60	−20.6	3640–3360
Clane, Co. Kildare						
GrN-12276		Human. Bone	Skeletons of 2 juveniles in small pit, accompanied by simple bowl with vertical and horizontal scores. One of a cemetery of 2 probably flat graves (Brindley and Lanting 1990; Herity 1982, 298, fig. 23:3; M. Ryan 1980)	4470±35	−20.9	3350–3010

Table 12.9. Radiocarbon dates for early occurrences of cattle and caprines in Ireland.

Laboratory number	Sample reference	Material	Context	Radiocarbon age (BP)	$\delta^{13}C$ (‰)	Weighted mean (BP)	Calibrated date range (cal BC) (95% confidence)
Dalkey Island, Co. Dublin							
OxA-4566	Humerus E 46	Sheep. Humerus	Southern basal midden Site II. Shell midden overlying cache of later Mesolithic artefacts but containing Neolithic artefacts and a Neolithic burial. Two other animal bone dates from this context fall in the sixth and second millennia cal BC (OxA-4567–8; D. Liversage 1968; Woodman *et al.* 1997, 137–8)	5050±90	−19.6		4040–3640
OxA-4571	Vertebra E-46	Cattle. Vertebra	Northern basal midden Site V. Shell midden containing later Mesolithic artefacts. Three other animal bone dates from this context fall in the seventh, sixth and fifth millennia cal BC; charcoal from inside limpet shells is dated to the late fifth/early fourth millennium (OxA-4569–70, -4572, D-38; D. Liversage 1968; Woodman *et al.* 1997, 137–8)	4820±75	−21.4		3760–3370
Kilgreany Cave, Co. Waterford							
OxA-4269	Tibia F20297	Cattle. Tibia	Context 8/lower stratum level KE1. Tufaceous stalagmite between C9, which contained a burial dated by Pta-2644 and C7, which contained a burial dated by BM-135 (Molleson 1986; Dowd 2002; 83; Woodman *et al.* 1997; R. Hedges *et al.* 1997)	5190±80	−22.5		4240–3790
Ferriter's Cove, Co. Kerry							
OxA-3869	Ulna E263	Cattle. Tibia	Context 302 (1992). One of six cattle bones found near each other in the southern area of the site (Woodman *et al.* 1997; Woodman *et al.* 1999, 21, 90)	5510±70	−20.5*		4490–4230
OxA-8775		Cattle. Lateral portion of charred metatarsus. Entire specimen used for dating	Recovered from bulk sample from silt near a hearth in the central area of the site (Woodman *et al.* 1999, 14, 90)	5825±50	−23.0		4800–4540
Carrigdirty Rock, Co. Limerick							
Beta-102087		Waterlogged basket woven from thin alder shoots	Carrigdirty Rock 5. Found in 3 fragments in scatter of worked and charred wood, a small slate axe, 2 chert flakes, possible pebble hammerstones, human, cattle and swan bone and hazelnut fragments (some charred) on foreshore of Shannon estuary, seen as a brief, small-scale episode (A. O'Sullivan 2001, 73–86)	4820±50		4820±35 T'=0.0; T'(5%)=3.8; ν=1	3660–3520
GrA-6520		Replicate of Beta-102087	From the same context as Beta-102087	4820±50	−24.9		
Beta-102086		Human. Skull fragment	From the same context as Beta-102087	4710±60			3640–3360

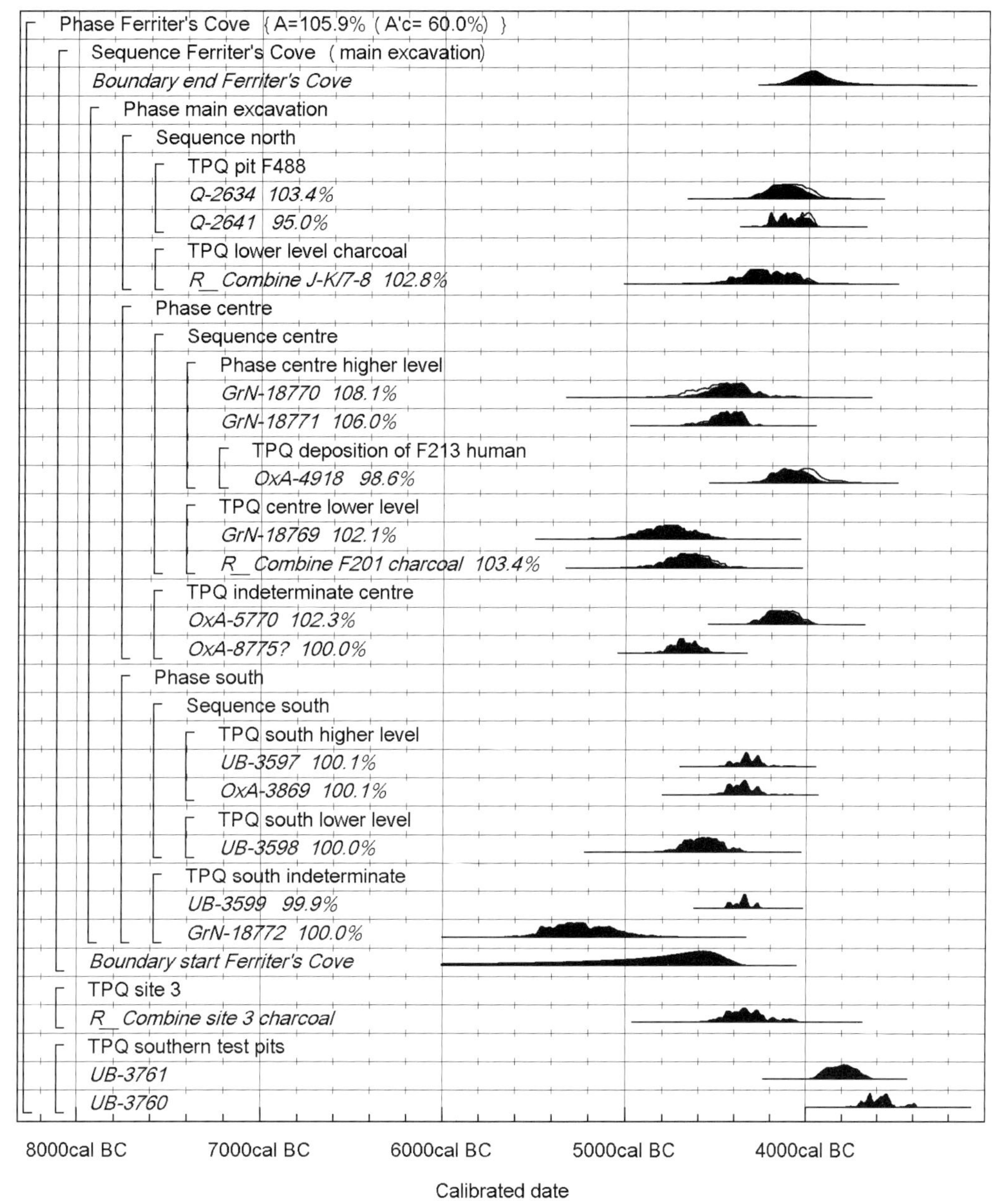

Fig. 12.43. Ferriter's Cove. Probability distributions of dates. The format is identical to that of Fig. 12.6. The large square brackets down the left-hand side, along with the OxCal keywords, define the overall model exactly.

but that the presence of domesticates may have had social consequences. The older of the two cattle bone measurements, OxA-8775, is excluded from the model because it was made on a bone which was charred and may thus have incorporated exogenous carbons of different age to itself (Gillespie 1989; Ambers *et al.* 1999, 331). This may be confirmed by the slightly enriched δ^{13}C value for this sample. The more recent date, OxA-3869, is earlier than any other for domestic fauna from Ireland, although its calibrated distribution overlaps with that for a cattle tibia from Kilgreany Cave, Co. Waterford (Table 12.9; Fig. 12.42: OxA-4269; Woodman *et al.* 1997; Dowd 2002). At Ferriter's Cove, the bone dated by OxA-3869 and the others near it were not closely associated with any specific focus of activity (Woodman and McCarthy 2003, 33) and the Kilgreany Cave tibia was clearly redeposited, since it pre-dates an articulated burial stratified below it (Table 12.13: Pta-2644); Neolithic artefacts were present in the cave, although their relation to the tibia or to the several burials there is uncertain (Dowd 2002, 82–4). At both Ferriter's Cove and Kilgreany it is the species that is significant, regardless of the context. These two specimens may be evidence for an initial introduction of cattle into Ireland in the later fifth millennium cal BC. This will be clarified only by further work.

The credibility of OxA-3869 from Ferriter's Cove is enhanced by the good agreement achieved when it is modelled with the other results from the site ($A_{overall}$=105.9%; Fig. 12.43; Table 12.10). Activity was clearly intermittent, since features occurred at varying levels in the silt which overlay the wave-cut platform occupied by the site; the density and composition of the lithics varied vertically and

Table 12.10. Radiocarbon dates from Ferriter's Cove, Co. Kerry. Posterior density estimates derive from the model defined in Fig. 12.43.

Laboratory number	Sample reference	Material	Context	Radiocarbon age (BP)	$\delta^{13}C$ (‰)	Weighted mean (BP)	Calibrated date range (cal BC) (95% confidence)	*Posterior density estimate (cal BC) (95% probability)*
North								
BM-2227R		'A general charcoal sample' (unidentified). NB most of the identified charcoal from adjacent 1 m squares was *Quercus* (McKeown 1999, 214–5)	1983 J–K/7–8. Patch of shells, charcoal and charcoal-rich soil, at edge of cliff, in lower level of silt (Woodman *et al.* 1999, 11–12, 108–110, figs 2.1–2, 7.1)	5400±220	−29.4	5414±124 T'=0.0; T'=(5%)=3.8; v=1	4500–3960	*4465–3990*
BM-2227AR		Replicate of BM-2227R	From the same context as the sample for BM-2227R	5420±150	−29.1			
Q-2641		Charcoal (unidentified)	Pit F488. Large pit with burnt basal layer and lens of unburnt shell, charcoal and burnt soil. In upper level of silt (Woodman *et al.* 1999, 12, 108–110, figs 2.1–2, 7.1)	5245±55			4240–3950	*4235–3975*
Q-2634		Marine shells	From the same context as sample for Q-2641. Both submitted as part of a project to compare dates on charcoal and marine shells from the same contexts	5680±70			4320–3925[1]	*4310–3970*
Centre								
GrN-18770		Charred hazelnut shells	F43. Small area of burnt hazelnut shells at N edge of F3 and at same level (Woodman *et al.* 1999, 20)	5620±130	−25.7		4770–4230	*4685–4225 (94%)* or *4200–4170 (1%)*
GrN-18771		Charred hazelnut shells	C132. Concentration of charred hazelnut shells near top of hearth overlying naturally silted hollow F133 (Woodman *et al.* 1999, 16–17, fig 2.4)	5620±80	−25.7		4690–4330	*4610–4325*
OxA-4918		Human. Probable femur fragment	C213. Lying W of and close to F5 but at a higher level (Woodman *et al.* 1999, 14–15, 110–1, figs 2.5, 7.2; Power 1999, 103)	5545±65	−13.9		4245–3805[2]	*4265–3930*
OxA-5770		Human. Tooth	K–L/3–4. From bulk sample taken from north of F5 (Woodman *et al.* 1999, 15, fig. 2.4; Power 1999, 103)	5590±60	−14.1		4330–3970[3]	*4315–4010*
OxA-8775		Cattle. Lateral portion of charred metatarsus. Entire specimen used for dating	Recovered in fragments from bulk sample from silt south of F5 (Woodman *et al.* 1999, 14, 90, fig. 2.5)	5825±50	−23.0		4800–4540	
BM-2228R		Charcoal (unidentified)	F201. Concentration of bone, artefacts and burnt rock, close to F5, on incipient soil, at base of silt (Woodman *et al.* 1999, 13–16, 110–1, figs 2.4, 7.2)	5750±140		5804±95 T'=0.3; T'=(5%)=3.8; v=1	4900–4450	*4900–4860 (2%)* or *4855–4480 (93%)*
BM-2228AR		Replicate of BM-2228R	From the same context as sample for BM-2228R	5850±140	−29.1			
GrN-18769		Charcoal (unidentified)	F5. Hearth, just NW of F201, on incipient soil, at base of silt (Woodman *et al.* 1999, 13–14, 110–11, figs 2.5, 7.2)	5900±110	−25.6		5050–4490	*5050–4525*
South								
OxA-3869	Ulna E263	Cattle. Tibia	C302. One of six cattle bones found near each other at relatively high level in silts (Woodman *et al.* 1997; Woodman *et al.* 1999, 21, 90, 111)	5510±70	−20.5[4]		4490–4230	*4500–4230*

Laboratory number	Sample reference	Material	Context	Radiocarbon age (BP)	$\delta^{13}C$ (‰)	Weighted mean (BP)	Calibrated date range (cal BC) (95% confidence)	*Posterior density estimate (cal BC) (95% probability)*
UB-3598		Charcoal (unidentified) and 'significant quantities of burnt hazelnut shells' (Woodman *et al.* 1999, 114)	C309. Layer underlying burnt surface F308, at a lower level than F303 (Woodman *et al.* 1999, 24, 113–14, fig. 2.15)	5727±81	−25.3		4780–4360	*4730–4435 (90%)* or *4430–4365 (5%)*
UB-3597		Charcoal (unidentified)	F303. Spread of burnt stone and shell close to F309 and at a higher level (Woodman *et al.* 1999, 24, 113–14, fig. 2.15)	5479±56			4450–4230	*4455–4230*
UB-3599		'Large lumps' of charcoal (unidentified; Woodman *et al.* 1999, 114)	C341. Charcoal-rich lens within pit F355 (Woodman *et al.* 1999, 21–2, fig. 2.11)	5503±45	−26.1		4450–4260	*4455–4315 (83%)* or *4300–4260 (12%)*
GrN-18772		Charcoal (unidentified)	Scatter of charcoal in area of shell midden F183, in extreme SW of main excavated area (Woodman *et al.* 1999, 26, figs 2.11, 2.27)	6300±140	−25.2		5530–4910	*5530–4930*
Site 3								
BM-2229R		Charcoal (unidentified)	Area of burnt soil surrounded by dark, char-coal-rich deposit, *c.* 20 m S of main excavation (Woodman *et al.* 1999, 173–4, figs 1.1, A.4)	5490±160	−28.3	5496±101 T'=0.0; T'(5%)=3.8; v=2	4540–4050	*4540–4145 (88%)* or *4135–4050 (7%)*
BM-2229AR		Replicate of BM-2229R	From the same context as sample for BM-2229R	5500±130	−29.1			
Southern test pits								
UB-3760		Charcoal (unidentified)	Shell midden exposed in cliff *c.* 60 m S of main excavation (Woodman *et al.* 1999, 170–2, fig. 1.1)	4820±67	−26.3		3710–3370	*3715–3495 (87%)* or *3440–3375 (8%)*
UB-3761		Marine shells	From the same context as sample for UB-3760	5402±24	+1.6		3950–3640[1]	*3935–3660*

1. Calibrated using marine data from Hughen *et al.* 2004 with a local reservoir correction of 22±54 BP (Harkness 1983)

2. Calibrated using a mixture of 84±8% marine data from Hughen *et al.* 2004 with a local reservoir correction of 22±54 BP (Harkness 1983) and 16±8% terrestrial data (Reimer *et al.* 2004)

3. Calibrated using a mixture of 74±8% marine data from Hughen *et al.* 2004 with a local reservoir correction of 22±54 BP (Harkness 1983) and 26±8% terrestrial data (Reimer *et al.* 2004)

4. −20.5 in monograph, −18.1 on Oxford Lab's website. Footnote on p 144 of monograph reads 'When first published . . . a $\delta^{13}C$ estimation of −18.1 ‰ was noted. The Oxford Accelerator Laboratory has since noted that $\delta^{13}C$ reading made at the time of the dating of this cattle bone lacked precision, and a recent estimate of −20.5‰ is more accurate'

horizontally; and there were discrete clusters of refitting artefacts (Woodman *et al.* 1999, 108–24). All the radiocarbon dates were measured either on bulk samples of unidentified charcoal, charred hazelnuts or marine shells, or on single fragments of disarticulated bone. The marine shell dates have been calibrated using the curve of Hughen *et al.* (2004), with a local ΔR correction of 22±54 BP (Stuiver and Braziunas 1993; Harkness 1983). The two human bone samples have $\delta^{13}C$ values of −13.9 and −14.1 and have therefore been calibrated using a mixture of the terrestrial calibration curve (Reimer *et al.* 2004) and the marine dataset with the same ΔR correction. The proportion of marine protein in each individual's diet has been estimated by linear interpolation based on the ranges of $\delta^{13}C$ values for terrestrial and marine food sources published by Mays (1998). OxA-5770 has therefore been calibrated using a figure for marine input of 74±8%; OxA-4198 has been calibrated using a figure for marine input of 84±8%.[12] All other determinations have been calibrated using the terrestrial dataset.

Two measurements are available on bulk samples of charred hazelnuts (Fig. 12.43: *GrN-18770–1*). Because the samples came from discrete concentrations, these are likely to have resulted from single events (Woodman *et al.* 1999, 16–17, 20). These are the only two short-life samples from Ferriter's Cove which are plausibly not residual. The charcoal dates are treated as *termini post quos*, since their samples could have comprised fragments of various ages, including some of mature wood, especially as most of the identified charcoal from the site was oak (McKeown 1999). Some such samples, such as *Q-2641* (Table 12.10), derived from discrete concentrations of charcoal which may represent single episodes, but they may still contain significant age offsets. Others, such as *GrN-18772*, come from general scatters of charcoal, which may include material of diverse ages. The two marine shell dates (Fig. 12.43: *Q-2634, UB-3761*) are treated as *termini post quos* because their samples too could have been heterogeneous. It should be noted, however, that in both cases where a pair of dates are available on marine shell and unidentified bulk charcoal from the same context, the calibrated dates are similar. This may suggest that in fact this material has not been significantly reworked. Dates on disarticulated bone (Fig. 12.43: *OxA-4918, -5770, -3869,* -8775) are treated as *termini post quos* because the creatures from which they came could have been long dead when the bones were finally buried. OxA-8775 is excluded from the model for the reason explained above.

On this basis, the use-life of the contiguous central, north and south parts of the main excavated area at Ferriter's Cove can be estimated as starting in *5780–4380 cal BC* (*95% probability*; Fig. 12.43: *start Ferriter's Cove*), probably in *5060–4420 cal BC* (*68% probability*). This distribution is imprecise because it depends on only the two samples of hazelnuts which are interpreted as deriving from discrete archaeological episodes. It is skewed towards the middle of the fifth millennium cal BC (Fig. 12.43). The occupation can be estimated as ending in *4175–3710 cal BC* (*95% probability*; Fig. 12.43: *end Ferriter's Cove*), probably in *4090–3895 cal BC* (*68% probability*). Although the dated activity probably occurred in the second half of the fifth millennium cal BC (Fig. 12.43), the imprecision of the dating estimates should be not be confused with persistence of archaeological activity. The radiocarbon dating would accord equally with an interpretation that this activity derived from a number of short-term occupation episodes at intervals during this period. On the evidence of two radiocarbon dates from testpits to the south of the main excavations, activity of similar character appears to continue into the first half of the fourth millennium cal BC (Fig. 12.43: *UB-3760–1*), the scant associated lithics being undiagnostic (Woodman *et al.* 1999, 170–2).

Ferriter's Cove highlights several important points. Activity at the site was probably episodic, as the character of the deposits strongly suggests. One date from the main excavated area indicates contact with elsewhere, in the form of cattle bone, in the later fifth millennium cal BC. This and a single sheep tooth, which failed to date (Woodman *et al.* 1999, 90), may genuinely represent a single event. The cattle bones in question are not sufficiently numerous or substantial to establish whether the animal or animals in question were alive or dead; even the transport of clean bones is not inconceivable, though the idea of a live animal or animals may be more appealing to the imagination. Whether the bones are sufficiently diagnostic to make it certain that they were from domesticated animal(s) is a question that should be raised for re-examination and re-confirmation. The movement of aurochs (as live animals, meat or bone) would still be of great interest, but it could entail only contact with western Britain rather than with continental areas where domesticated cattle were already present in the late fifth millennium (and see Chapter 15). The remaining cattle bones from Ferriter's Cove must be a high priority for further dating.

Dalkey Island, Co. Dublin, a small island 400 m off the east coast of Ireland, has also long been considered an important site in the discussion of the Mesolithic-Neolithic transition (e.g. Woodman 1976; 1978a; 1981). Excavations revealing multi-period activity on the island were carried out in the 1950s (Liversage 1968), Mesolithic and Neolithic activity being focused on a shell midden which extended for at least 10 m. The dating of the faunal remains (Woodman *et al.* 1997; Woodman 2009, 197), however, along with a re-consideration of the cultural material (Leon 2005), has indicated that there was activity on the island over a period of up to 4000 years from before 6000 cal BC down into the fourth millennium cal BC and beyond (Woodman *et al.* 1997, 137–8). The midden appears to have been the result of repeated visits to the island, and might have been subject to disturbance. In terms of the discussion of the date of the early occurrence of domesticated animal species, the two relevant dates from Dalkey are for sheep (Fig. 12.42: OxA-4566) and cattle (Fig. 12.42: OxA-4571). Falling in the first half of the fourth millennium cal BC, these no longer seem to represent an early introduction of domesticates, since, by the time these animals died, other elements of the Neolithic were already in place in Ireland.

Similar persistence of place is apparent from a culturally Mesolithic site at Derragh, on the shore of Lough Kinale, Co. Longford, where occupation on a man-made platform is described as dating from around 5500 cal BC (Fredengren 2007; 2009; 2010, 241). The site consists of layers of stone, brushwood, peat and habitation debris. There is a large assemblage of late Mesolithic lithics and worked wood, but occupation, including the presence of domesticated fauna, continued into the early fourth millennium cal BC (Fredengren 2010, 248).

From the south side of the estuary of the R. Shannon at Carrigdirty Rock 5, Co. Limerick, a waterlogged basket woven from alder shoots has been dated to the fourth millennium cal BC by Beta-102087 and GrA-6520; a human skull fragment from the same context was dated by Beta-102086 (Fig. 12.42; Table 12.9). Other material was associated with this find, including other worked wood, a small schist axehead, chert flakes, possible hammerstones, hazelnuts – and cattle bones. The scatter has been interpreted as reflecting ephemeral occupation in a probably estuarine, wetland setting (A. O'Sullivan 2001).

A sequence of activity from the Mesolithic to the Neolithic was revealed at Clowanstown 1, Co. Meath (E. O'Connor 2008). Here a low rise at the edge of a lake was used as the base for a small timber platform or structure. Finds included a cache of Later Mesolithic butt-trimmed flakes. In a hollow in the lakebed nearby there were a series of fish-baskets which provided later sixth and earlier fifth millennium BC radiocarbon dates.[13] Activity was renewed in the early Neolithic after the lake had infilled with peat. A series of mounds, the largest over the former hollow, were constructed of layers of burnt material, including cremated animal bone and redeposited lake marl (see Breen 2003 for comparable mounds at Cherryville, Co. Kildare). Finds included Carinated Bowl and burnt flint. All the mounds were sealed with a layer of unburnt stone including artefacts. A wooden container (alder) deposited in the centre of the main mound provided a date of 3710–3630 cal BC (95% confidence; 4880±40 BP; Beta-237056), and the fill of a second wooden container from the same mound provided a date of 3970–3710 cal BC (95% confidence; 5060±40 BP; Beta-237055).

The form of models for the early Neolithic and the beginning of the middle Neolithic

This discussion of introduced animal species concludes our review of radiocarbon dates relating to the early Neolithic in Ireland. We have defined this archaeological phase as encompassing houses, and other occupation and activity associated with diagnostic early Neolithic material culture. Provisionally the construction of at least certain classes of monument may also fall within this phase, including portal tombs, court tombs and other forms. The construction and use of early stone-walled field systems may also fall into this period.

As described earlier in this chapter (and more fully in Chapter 2.2), in order to counteract the statistical scatter of radiocarbon dates from an archaeological phase, it is necessary to impose a statistical distribution on the period. This demands that the end as well as the beginning of the early Neolithic in Ireland be defined. Defining what constitutes the beginning of the Neolithic in Ireland – and elsewhere – has not only been the focus of prolonged debate but has remained difficult. Defining what constitutes the end of the early Neolithic has attracted far less attention, although the methodology employed in this volume demands an ending if the introduction of Neolithic practices is to be dated accurately (Bayliss *et al.* 2007a).

Changes in material culture and classes of monument have, however, regularly been thought of as serving to mark out a middle phase of the Neolithic in Ireland. Although much of what is taken as characteristic of the early Neolithic remained current, innovations include Linkardstown burials and passage tombs; the development of decorated globular bowls, such as Carrowkeel and Goodland forms; and the manufacture of mushroom-headed bone or antler pins and beads (for general characteristics of the Middle Neolithic, see Sheridan 1995; Cooney 2000a). It can be debated whether or not this archaeological transition has any relation to the lived experience of Neolithic people. It could be argued, on the one hand, that changes may have been introduced so gradually that any one generation would scarcely have been able to perceive difference from what had gone before, and on the other, that material culture in general relies so much on non-discursive meanings that no one generation would have had to confront explicit reckoning of the significance of material changes. The question of the rate and coincidence of changes is a very real one, and some authors have strongly argued, for example, that there are early forms of passage tomb (e.g. Burenhult 2001; 2003; Sheridan 2003b). It seems unlikely, however, that people would have been unaware of the combination of changes in material culture and the architecture of monuments, especially as both Linkardstown burials and passage tombs involved different kinds of building, access and experience, and because repeated deposits of consistent selections of material culture were placed in them. On this basis, we believe that a case can be made for a meaningfully constituted middle Neolithic in Ireland, certainly as far as is required to provide a limit for the dating of the early Neolithic practices in Ireland.

So, for the purposes of this chapter, we only consider the middle Neolithic in Ireland as providing a *terminus ante quem* for the end of the early Neolithic, and our treatment of components of the middle Neolithic has been much more selective than for the early Neolithic. A sequence which suggests that Linkardstown burials are earlier than passage tombs (at least for the sample for which we currently have radiocarbon dates) is included in all the models for the chronology of the early Neolithic in Ireland which we present here. The available radiocarbon dates are in good agreement with this interpretation. The results of these models are, however, practically identical if Linkardstown burials and passage tombs are modelled as independent, potentially overlapping, phases of activity. So for the

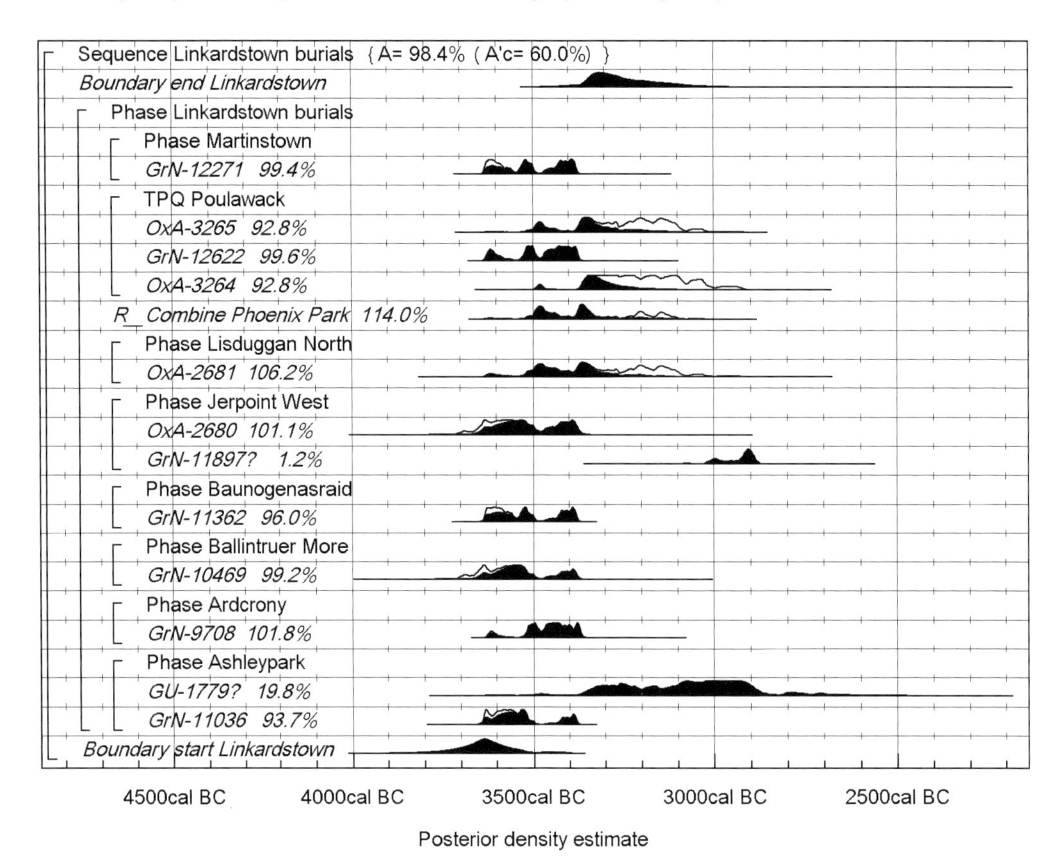

Fig. 12.44. Linkardstown burials. Probability distributions of dates. The format is identical to that of Fig. 12.6. The large square brackets down the left-hand side, along with the OxCal keywords, define the overall model exactly.

purposes of the models for the chronology of the early Neolithic in Ireland presented here, this interpretation is robust. It is not, however, based on stratigraphic evidence, and if the chronology of the middle Neolithic were the purpose of the study, this reading would certainly warrant further investigation.

Linkardstown burials

This group of inhumations in cists, accompanied by highly decorated bowls and generally under round mounds, has a distribution focussed in Munster and south Leinster (Herity 1982; Ryan 1981; Brindley and Lanting 1990; Sheridan 1995). A dozen examples have been excavated (Cooney 2000a), and they have been the subject of a dating programme (Brindley and Lanting 1990). The available measurements cover a large proportion of the known members of the class, but the samples were of variable integrity, and at least one, from Poulawack, Co. Clare (Table 12.11: GrN-12622), may have included bones from more than one individual. Others were disarticulated bones, from individuals who may have been dead for some time before their bones were deposited.

A femur from a disarticulated adult male skeleton was dated (Fig. 12.44: *GrN-11036*) from Ashleypark, Co. Tipperary (Manning 1985). Although disarticulated, the skeleton was more or less complete, so the individual was probably only recently dead when buried. A second measurement on cattle bones (GU-1779) from among the cairn stones of the outer part of the burial mound could relate to later activity on the site and has been excluded from the model.

A femur was dated (*GrN-9708*) from the younger of two disturbed, disarticulated but probably largely complete inhumations from the cist at Ardcrony, Co. Tipperary; a decorated bipartite bowl was placed between them in the middle of the cist (Wallace 1977).

Radiocarbon dates are available from the disarticulated bones of an adult male from Ballintruer More, Co. Wicklow (*GrN-10469*; J. Raftery 1973), and from a pile of disarticulated bones from a single individual from a cist at Baunogenasraid, Co. Carlow (*GrN-11362*; B. Raftery 1974). The former individual probably died shortly before burial, as most of the skeleton was represented. At Baunogenasraid, the bones were of a single individual. Although most of the small bones were missing, this loss can be accounted for by the soil conditions of the site (B. Raftery 1974, 283–4).

Two statistically inconsistent radiocarbon determinations (Table 12.11) are available from an articulated inhumation in the central cist at Jerpoint West, Co. Kilkenny (Ryan 1973; Herity 1982). The AMS determination (*OxA-2680*) is significantly earlier, and GrN-11897 appears to be aberrant, for reasons that are not clear (Brindley and Lanting 1990, 3). For this reason it has been excluded from the model.

Another date is available from an inhumation at Lisduggan North, Co. Cork, recorded in the 1940s (*OxA-2681*; Brindley and Lanting 1990, 2). It is not certain

Table 12.11. Radiocarbon dates for Linkardstown and related burials in Ireland. Posterior density estimates derive from the model defined in Fig. 12.44.

Laboratory number	Sample reference	Material	Context	Radiocarbon age (BP)	$\delta^{13}C$ (‰)	Weighted mean (BP)	Calibrated date range (cal BC) (95% confidence)	*Posterior density estimate (cal BC) (95% probability)*
Ashleypark, Co. Tipperary								
GU-1779		Cattle. Bone	Sample of cattle bones from among the cairn stones of outer part of burial mound, (Manning 1985, 69, fig. 6). Could post-date burial (Brindley and Lanting 1990)	4385±110	−20.4		3370–2700	
GrN-11036		Human. Femur of disarticulated adult male skeleton	More or less complete in one place in stone cist with disarticulated child and sherds of 1 plain Carinated Bowl bowl, 1 decorated, bipartite style bowl, 1 Goodland style bowl. Second child and animal bone immediately outside cist (Manning 1985, 68, fig. 3; Brindley and Lanting 1990)	4765±40	−21.5		3650–3370	*3640–3495* (*75%*) or *3435–3375* (*20%*)
Ardcrony, Co. Tipperary								
GrN-9708		Human. Femur from disarticulated bones of 17–18 year-old youth	Disarticulated bones of 17–18 year-old youth on W side of polygonal cist under mound, directly on paving, disturbed bones of older man on thin layer of silt on E side, decorated, bipartite style bowl in centre, between them. Excavators concluded that bones could not have reached their final positions if articulated; they were, however, kept separate from each other and each individual was well represented, including finger and toe bones, so that they would not have been long out of articulation (Wallace 1977; Brindley *et al.* 1983; Brindley and Lanting 1990, 2)	4675±35	−21.2		3630–3360	*3625–3600* (*3%*) or *3525–3365* (*92%*)
Ballintruer More, Co. Wicklow								
GrN-10469		Human. Bone from probable adult '30 to 40 pieces of adult skeleton (3–4 cm and 5–6 cm) probably male. Fairly large piece (22 cm) of shaft of tibia with a vertical post mortem crack and part of head which shows strong markings. Also part of sacrum, segments of which appear not to be completely fused. Pieces of innominate, fragments of long bones, axis and, of the skull, only fragments of maxilla, mandible and vault are present. Six teeth present which show moderate wear.' (J. Raftery 1973, 217)	In central polygonal cist under mound with decorated, bipartite style bowl, '. . . the remains of one individual. The grave had been rifled by vandals on the night of its discovery so that the bones were broken and mixed but all the evidence indicates that they had been deposited originally in a disarticulated position and were also broken before burial. There is, for example, no suggestion from any source that a complete skull had existed when the grave was first opened.' (J. Raftery 1973, 217).(J. Raftery 1973; Brindley *et al.* 1983; Brindley and Lanting 1990)	4800±70	−21.6		3710–3370	*3660–3490* (*68%*) or *3470–3370* (*27%*)

Baunogenasraid, Co. Carlow								
GrN-11362		Human. Bone from disarticulated inhumation of single adult male, most of skeleton represented, several teeth, only a few toe bones and rib fragments	Piled in one corner of polygonal cist under mound with 2 decorated, bipartite style bowls, lignite toggle, bone point (B. Raftery 1974; Brindley and Lanting 1990, 1)	4735±35	−21.2		3640–3370	*3635–3495 (59%)* or *3455–3375 (36%)*
Jerpoint West, Co. Kilkenny								
GrN-11897		Human. Inhumed bone from articulated inhumation of young adult male	Inhumation and cremation in central polygonal cist associated with decorated, bipartite style bowl, sherd of plain shouldered bowl, bone pin (M. Ryan 1973; Herity 1982, 298–9, fig. 24:1–4; Brindley and Lanting 1990)	4305±40	−21.9	4404±63 T'= 27.9; T'(5%)=3.8; ν=1	3020–2870	
OxA-2680	NMI E93:15	Replicate of GrN-11897	From the same context as GrN-11897 (R. Hedges *et al.* 1993)	4770±80	−21.9		3710–3360	*3645–3365*
Lisduggan North, Co. Cork								
OxA-2681	IA/500/47	Human bone	Inhumation and fragment of decorated, bipartite style bowl, collected in 1940s. No further information (Brindley and Lanting 1990, 2; R. Hedges *et al.* 1993)	4585±80	−23.3		3630–3020	*3630–3580 (3%)* or *3535–3170 (92%)*
Phoenix Park, Dublin								
OxA-2678	NMI W3	Human bone, unspecified, from one of 2 articulated adult male skeletons	2 articulated inhumations and small amount of bone from 3rd individual in cist under mound with shell necklace and bone object (Wilde 1857, 180–3; Herity 1982, 297, fig. 24: 5–6; Brindley and Lanting 1990; R. Hedges *et al.* 1993)	4650±70	−22.4	4594±53 T'=1.5; T'(5%)=3.8; ν=1	3520–3100	*3525–3260 (92%)* or *3220–3180 (3%)*
GrA-10970		Human. Carbonate from unburnt bone. Experimental replicate of OxA-2678	From the same context as OxA-2678 (Lanting and Brindley 1998)	4520±80				
Poulawack, Co. Clare								
GrN-12622		Human. From among disarticulated bones of middle-aged male and female, young adult female and infant. Probably a mixture of the bones of the 3 adults (Brindley and Lanting 1992, 13)	Grave 8/8a. Polygonal subdivided cist built on ground surface under cairn, accompanied by hollow scraper, boar tusk, 2 indeterminate sherds. Compartment 8A measured 0.70 m x 0.40 m x up to 0.90 m deep and contained scattered bones, a boar tusk and a flint hollow scraper. Compartment 8 measured 0.95 m x 0.40–0.50 m x 0.90 m deep and contained the disarticulated remains of the 4 individuals. Cairn enlarged and used for burial in early Bronze Age (Hencken 1935; M. Ryan 1981; Brindley and Lanting 1992)	4695±35	−22.1		3640–3360	*3630–3580 (16%)* or *3535–3365 (79%)*
OxA-3264	Poulawack 8/8a	Human. Single bone from different adult to that dated by OxA-3265	From the same context as GrN-12622 (Brindley and Lanting 1992; R. Hedges *et al.* 1993)	4485±60	−21.0 (assum ed)		3370–2920	*3500–3450 (8%)* or *3375–3135 (87%)*
OxA-3265	Poulawack 8/8a (2)	Human. Single bone from different adult to that dated by OxA-3264	From the same context as GrN-12622	4550±65	−21.0 (assum ed)		3500–3020	*3520–3395 (28%)* or *3385–3165 (66%)* or *3160–3140 (1%)*
Martinstown, Co. Meath								
GrN-12271		Human. Bone	Skeleton in pit associated with decorated, bipartite style bowl and lignite fragment (Hartnett 1951; Brindley and Lanting 1990)	4720±35	−21.9		3640–3370	*3635–3555 (25%)* or *3540–3490 (22%)* or *3470–3370 (48%)*

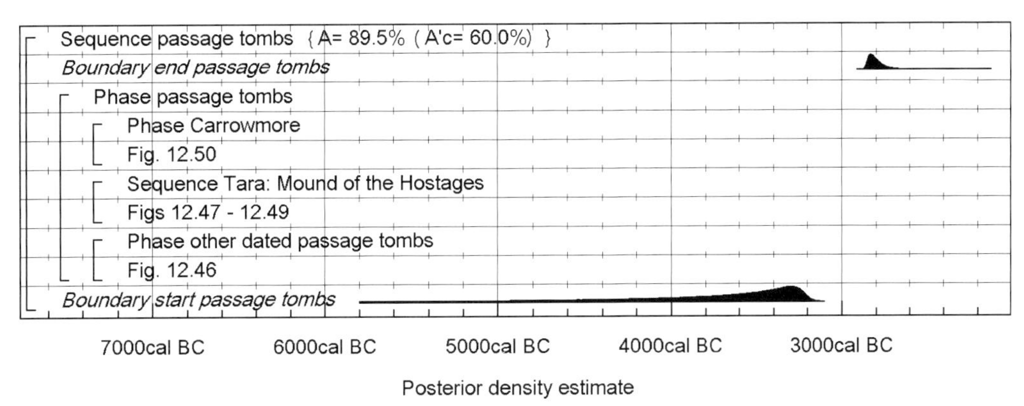

Fig. 12.45. Passage tombs. Overall structure of the chronological model. The component sections of this model are shown in detail in Figs 12.46–50. The large square brackets down the left-hand side of Figs 12.45–50, along with the OxCal keywords, define the overall model exactly.

whether this sample was from an articulated skeleton. Two statistically consistent measurements (Table 12.11: OxA-2678, GrA-10970) are also available from one of two articulated adult male skeletons found with a shell necklace and bone object in a cist under a mound at Phoenix Park, Dublin (Fig. 12.44: *Phoenix Park*: Wilde 1857, 180–3).

From Poulawack, Co. Clare (Hencken 1935), three dates are available from disarticulated bones. These provide *termini post quos* for the central burial. Although the sample for *GrN-12622* probably consisted of a mixture of bones from the adults in the cist, the date still provides a reliable *terminus post quem* for the last interment in the central cist. Fragile bones such as scapulae, pelves and vertebrae were well preserved in this deposit, but small bones were absent and crania slightly over-represented, suggesting that the remains of well preserved skeletons had been gathered up and placed in the cist (Beckett and Robb 2006, 63). *GrN-12271* provides a date from a skeleton associated with a decorated bipartite bowl from Martinstown, Co. Meath (Hartnett 1951).

The model for the currency of Linkardstown burials is shown in Fig. 12.44. Initially, this has been calculated without reference to the assumption that this tradition follows on from the early Neolithic. This model suggests that Linkardstown burials began in *3835–3500 cal BC* (*90% probability*; Fig. 12.44: *start Linkardstown*) or *3490–3410 cal BC* (*5% probability*), probably in *3710–3560 cal BC* (*68% probability*). It ended in *3425–3015 cal BC* (*95% probability*; Fig. 12.44: *end Linkardstown*), probably in *3355–3180 cal BC* (*68% probability*). These estimates are relatively imprecise because of the limited number of burials dated. Greater precision would require either site-specific dating of series of related samples (if available in archive) or the dating of a substantial number of further primary burials (which are not available in archive).[14]

Passage tombs

Passage tombs have long been excavated and analysed. The most extensive campaigns of the twentieth century were those of Michael J. O'Kelly at Newgrange and of George Eogan at Knowth, both in Brú na Bóinne or the Bend of the Boyne in Co. Meath (O'Kelly 1982; Eogan 1984; Eogan 1991; Eogan and Roche 1997), and those of Goran Burenhult at Carrowmore, in Co. Sligo (Burenhult 1980; 1984; 2001; 2003). A signal landmark is the recent publication by Muiris O'Sullivan (2005) of excavations at the Mound of the Hostages at Tara conducted by Seán P. Ó Ríordáin and Ruaidhrí de Valera in the 1950s. These monuments have long been recognised as linked by shared traditions of form, ritual, contents and imagery; their artefact repertoire places them after the early Neolithic, a chronological position emphasised by the construction of passage tombs over existing early Neolithic occupation at Knowth and Newgrange. Burenhult's assertion, based on radiocarbon dates obtained during the first years of his investigations at Carrowmore, that the passage tomb cemetery there had possibly Mesolithic origins (1980, 111–13; 1984) prompted contention and disbelief (Caulfield 1983, 206–3; Bergh 1995, 99–106; Woodman 2000, 234–5; Grogan 1991; Sheridan 2003a; and see Chapter 1.5). Some authors, however, have argued for the dating of closed polygonal chambers and simple passage tombs in Ireland to around 4000 cal BC (e.g. Sheridan 2003b; 2004; 2005; 2007a).

Dates from passage tombs are listed in Table 12.12. The overall form of the model for the chronology of passage tombs is shown in Fig. 12.45, with component sections relating to Townleyhall, Knowth, Newgrange and Carrowkeel given in Fig. 12.46, the component model for The Mound of the Hostages, Tara, in Figs 12.47–9, and the component for Carrowmore in Fig. 12.50. As for Linkardstown burials, initially the chronology of passage tombs has been modelled independently of their relationship to the early Neolithic. The Mound of the Hostages has been treated separately with a continuous phase of use incorporated into the model for that site alone. This means that in the overall model for passage tombs, only the start and end dates for The Mound of the Hostages are effective. This avoids the domination of the output of the model by the overwhelming number of dates from this single site. This is only partially successful, however, because no other

Table 12.12. Radiocarbon dates for passage tombs in Ireland. Posterior density estimates derive from the model defined in Figs 12.45–50.

Laboratory number	**Sample reference**	**Material**	**Context**	**Radiocarbon age (BP)**	**$\delta^{13}C$ (‰)**	**$\delta^{15}N$ (‰)**	**Weighted mean (BP)**	**Calibrated date range (cal BC) (95% confidence)**	***Posterior density estimate (cal BC) (95% probability)***
Townleyhall II, Co. Louth									
BM-170		Charcoal (unidentified)	Habitation layer beneath passage tomb	4680±150				3770–2930	*3765–3010*
Knowth I, Co. Meath									
UB-357	Samples 4 and 5, combined	Charcoal (unidentified)	Cuttings 29/30 and 36. Basal sod layer of mound	4745±165				3940–3020	*3940–3855* (*3%*) or *3820–3080* (*91%*) or *3070–3025* (*1%*)
UB-358	Sample 5	Humic acid	Cutting 36. Basal sod layer of mound	6835±110				5990–5550	
OxA-7786	UB-4090	Charcoal (unidentified)	Basal structural layer (Bronk Ramsey *et al.* 2002). Sample did not produce enough gas for LSC in Belfast. CO_2 graphitised and measured in Oxford	4890±40	−19.9			3760–3630	*3770–3630*
GrN-12357		Charcoal	From mound (Grogan 1991, 130; Bergh 1995)	4405±35				3310–2910	*3315–3270* (*2%*) or *3265–3235* (*4%*) or *3110–2910* (*89%*)
GrN-12827	Knowth 1984	Charcoal (unidentified)	Scattered fragments in sod layer at base of large mound below orthostat 75 of eastern tomb, possibly dates construction, Knowth 1	4465±40	−27.1			3350-2940	*3350–3010*
GrN-12358	Knowth 1983–4	Charcoal (unidentified)	Spread on old land surface beneath mound	4490±60	−25.1			3370–2920	*3365–3005* (*94%*) or *2980–2955* (*1%*)
Knowth 2, Co. Meath									
BM-785	Sample 3/1967	Charcoal (unidentified)	Spread of charcoal in mound, close to disturbed area with small amount of Beaker pottery (Grogan 1991, 129)	4158±126				3080–2450	
Knowth 9, Co. Meath									
GrN-11714[1]		Charcoal (unidentified)	Cremation deposit in end recess	4420±50				3340–2900	*3335–3210* (*23%*) or *3190–3150* (*5%*) or *3135–2910* (*67%*)
Knowth 16, Co. Meath									
BM-1078	Sample 4/1973	Charcoal (unidentified)	Spread sealed in mound of smaller tomb pre-dating main tomb (Eogan 1986, 83)	4399±67				3350–2890	*3335–3210* (*20%*) or *3190–3150* (*5%*) or *3140–2895* (*70%*)
Knowth 17, Co. Meath									
UB-318		Charcoal (unidentified)	Thin layer of dark material under mound	4873±150				3980–3350	*3995–3345*
UB-319		Charcoal (unidentified)	From the same context as UB-318	4797±185				3970–3020	*3970–3080*
Newgrange, Co. Meath									
GrN-5462-C	Sample 1	10.3 g of charcoal fragments from small twigs (organic fraction measured)	Soil caulking of roof slab 3 of passage, which could have been put in place only at time of construction (O'Kelly 1969), corrected from GrN-5462 (4500±45 BP) by O'Kelly (1972)	4425±45	−26.0			3340–2910	*3335–3210* (*25%*) or *3190–3155* (*4%*) or *3130–2915* (*66%*)

Laboratory number	Sample reference	Material	Context	Radiocarbon age (BP)	$\delta^{13}C$ (‰)	$\delta^{15}N$ (‰)	Weighted mean (BP)	Calibrated date range (cal BC) (95% confidence)	*Posterior density estimate (cal BC) (95% probability)*
GrN-5463	Sample 2	20 g of charcoal fragments from small twigs (organic fraction measured)	Soil caulking from under cross-lintel supporting boulder cap at junction of passage roof and chamber, which could have been put in place only at time of construction (O'Kelly 1969)	4415±40	−24.8			3330–2910	*3330–3230* (*15%*) or *3175–3155* (*2%*) or *3120–2915* (*78%*)
UB-360		Humic acid	Upper sod layer in mound, 0.60 to 0.90 above old ground surface	2250±45				400–190	
UB-361		Humic acid	Basal sod layer in mound, 0.05 to 0.20 m above old ground surface	4535±105				3630–2910	*3520–2920*
GrN-9057	Newgrange 6	Turves (described as peat by lab; organic fraction measured)	Sods possibly redeposited from structure predating main tomb	4480±60	−28.5			3370–2920	*3360–3005* (*92%*) or *2985–2935* (*3%*)
Mound of the Hostages, Tara, Co. Meath									
Pre-cairn									
D-42		Charcoal (unidentified)	Infill of pre-cairn ditch, but from beyond cairn (McAulay and Watts 1961; Newman 1997, 146; M. O'Sullivan 2005, 26)	4080±160					
GrA-17674	Sample 14	*Corylus* charcoal	Pre-cairn ditch, but from beyond cairn (M. O'Sullivan 2005, 27)	4525±40				3370–3090	*3365–3165*
GrN-26065	Sample 10	Unidentified charcoal fragments from sample in which all identified fragments *Corylus*	Pre-cairn ditch, but from beyond cairn (M. O'Sullivan 2005, 27)	4550±90				3630–2920	*3525–3155*
GrA-17676	Sample 9	*Corylus* charcoal	Pre-cairn ditch, Cutting L – near south edge of cutting 1959, actually sealed by cairn (M. O'Sullivan 2005, 27)	4485±40				3360–3020	*3350–3170*
D-44		Charcoal (unidentified)	Fire 3 or fire 4. Probably from horizon containing charcoal and burnt soil sealed by upcast from trench for orthostats of tomb; on old ground surface close to entry to passage (McAulay and Watts 1961; M. O'Sullivan 2005, 27–8, 63–5, fig. 19). Considered too recent by O'Sullivan	3880±150				2880–1920	
GrA-17675	Sample 11	*Quercus* charcoal	Fire 1. On flat stones, under cairn (M. O'Sullivan 2005, 27)	4900±50				3790–3540	*3795–3630* (*93%*) or *3555–3535* (*2%*)
D-43		Charcoal (unidentified)	Burnt ground surface under cairn (McAulay and Watts 1961; 7). Considered too recent by M. O'Sullivan (2005, 28)	4260±160					
GrA-17525	Sample 6	*Corylus* charcoal	Old ground surface under cairn at E edge of NE quadrant, 1959 (M. O'Sullivan 2005, 28)	4555±45				3500–3090	*3495–3460* (*7%*) or *3380–3165* (*88%*)
GrN-26064	Sample 8	Unidentified charcoal fragments from sample in which all identified fragments *Corylus*	Under cairn, NE quadrant 1959 (M. O'Sullivan 2005, 28)	4840±80				3790–3370	*3790–3495* (*86%*) or *3455–3375* (*9%*)

Laboratory number	Sample reference	Material	Context	Radiocarbon age (BP)	$\delta^{13}C$ (‰)	$\delta^{15}N$ (‰)	Weighted mean (BP)	Calibrated date range (cal BC) (95% confidence)	*Posterior density estimate (cal BC) (95% probability)*
Passage tomb									
GrA-17114	Sample 15	Human. Cremated bone	Fill of foundation trench dug into pre-tomb surface behind tomb backstone (M. O'Sullivan 2005, 63, 119, fig. 58)	4420±50				3340–2900	*3350–3210*
GrA-17274	Sample 43	Human. Cremated bone	Cremation in cist I. Sample taken from basal cleaning of cist. Under cairn, against exterior of chamber, on old land surface, coinciding with gap between orthostats, containing cremated remains of at least 8 individuals, unburnt infant and child bones, bone pins, tubular bone bead, biconical stone bead, Carrowkeel bowl, acorn husks and small animal bones (M. O'Sullivan 2005, 63–6, 69, figs 59, 61, 64–6)	4385±35				3270–2900	*3095–2915*
GrA-17272	Sample 44	Human. Cremated bone	Cremation in cist II. Under cairn, against exterior of N side of chamber, on old land surface, coinciding with gap between orthostats, containing cremated bones of at least 34 individuals, with some spillage from tomb fill including cremated bone, 3 or 4 unburnt adult skulls and infant bones. Sample taken from main fill of cist, but may have consisted of part of spillage from tomb. Also flint flake, stone bead, stone balls, bone pins, bone tubes, sherd (M. O'Sullivan 2005, 70–4, figs 59, 67–72)	4180±35			4187±29 T'=0.1; T'(5%)=3.8); v=1	2890–2660	*2895–2835*
GrA-17746	Sample 44*	Replicate of GrA-17272	From the same cremation deposit as GrA-17272	4200±50					
GrA-17747	Sample 45*	Human. Cremated bone	Cremation in cist III. Under cairn, against W side of S portal slab, in bedding trench for tomb orthostats, in gap between two orthostats, but isolated from tomb by its own slabs. Cremated and some unburnt bone of at least 3 adults in and around in a Carrowkeel Bowl lay on further cremated and unburnt bone of at least 5 adults and 1 child which lay on floor. Deposit including bowl overlain by silted clay. Also present were decorated bone pendants, stone beads, bone bead, bone and antler pins. Sample taken from in and under Carrowkeel bowl (M. O'Sullivan 2005, 75–9, figs 59, 73–8)	4530±60				3500–3020	*3275–3130*
GrA-17277	Sample 50	Human. Cremated bone	Inner compartment of tomb. Main cremation deposit, near large slab at sill stone 3, entering inner compartment of tomb. Mass of cremated bone from numerous individuals with some unburnt bone, disturbed by digging of pit for EBA inhumations 18 and 19, containing hammer pendant, mushroom-headed pin, sherds of Carrowkeel bowl (M. O'Sullivan 2005, 103–13, figs 100–110)	4390±35				3270–2900	*3095–2915*
GrA-17743	Sample 54	Human. Cremated bone	Gap between orthostat L1 and decorated orthostat L2 (M. O'Sullivan 2005, 119, fig. 58)	4480±50				3370–2930	*3250–3005 (90%)* or *2985–2930 (5%)*

Laboratory number	Sample reference	Material	Context	Radiocarbon age (BP)	$\delta^{13}C$ (‰)	$\delta^{15}N$ (‰)	Weighted mean (BP)	Calibrated date range (cal BC) (95% confidence)	*Posterior density estimate (cal BC) (95% probability)*
GrA-17678	Sample 65	Human. Unburnt, disarticulated bone	Deposit XLIX. Stony layer across passage in vicinity of sill stone 2, 1.2 m from east capstone, containing disarticulated unburnt bone from at least 11 individuals (1 of them ??more or less articulated), cremated bone from at least 5, bone pins, stone balls (M. O'Sullivan 2005, 100–103; fig. 97)	4390±45	−22.5	11.65		3310–2900	*3110–2900*
GrA-17669	Sample 66	Human. Unburnt, disarticulated bone	From the same context as GrA-17678, 1.2 m from east capstone	4415±40	−22.0			3330–2910	*3185–3155 (2%)* or *3130–2910 (93%)*
GrA-17668	Sample 67	Human. Unburnt, disarticulated bone	From the same context as GrA-17678. Junction of L1 and L2 near skull 4, 1.50 m depth from E end of capstone. Layer 2	4355±40	−22.3	11.43		3100–2890	*3090–3055 (9%)* or *3035–2895 (86%)*
GrA-17749	Sample 68	Human. Cremated bone	From the same context as GrA-17678. 1.20 m depth from E capstone, layer 1	4410±50				3340–2900	*3190–3150 (4%)* or *3140–2900 (91%)*
GrA-17682	Sample 70	Human. Unburnt bone	Deposit XXXVIII. Context problematical. Scatter of burnt and unburnt human bone close to fragments of two bowl Food Vessels against face of orthostat L2 in chamber (Brindley *et al.* 2005, 286; M. O'Sullivan 2005, 96–7, fig. 94)	4370±40	−22.3	11.57		3100–2890	*3090–2905*
GrA-18352	Sample 80	Human. Skull	Middle compartment. Skull 4, one of group of skulls between orthostat R2 and sill stone 2, in main cremation deposit on base, (M. O'Sullivan 2005, 113–16)	4370±50	−21.9	11.80		3270–2890	*3100–2895*
GrA-18353	Sample 81	Human. Skull	Middle compartment, Skull P. Unburnt adult cranium from group of skulls in main cremation deposit on base, in gap between sill stone 2 and orthostat R2, surrounded by calcined bone fragments (M. O'Sullivan 2005, 113–16)	4060±50	−22.1			2870–2470	*2880–2815*
GrA-18374	Sample 82	Human. Skull	Middle compartment, skull g (unburnt, probably adolescent or child). One of group of skulls between orthostat R2 and sill stone 2, in main cremation deposit on base; other disarticulated unburnt bones also present (M. O'Sullivan 2005, 113–16)	4230±50	−22.4	9.72		2920–2670	*3010–2985 (1%)* or *2930–2830 (94%)*
Perimeter burials									
GrA-17296	Sample 19	Human. Cremated bone	Burial 15. Cremated bone in stones, perimeter, overlying pre-cairn ditch, probably covered by earthen mound (M. O'Sullivan 2005, 31, 38, fig. 19)	4485±35				3360–3020	*3220–3020*
GrA-17295	Sample 20	Human. Cremated bone	Burial 2. Cremated bone associated with stone setting, perimeter, within limit of earthen mound (M. O'Sullivan 2005, 33, figs 19, 24, 25)	4550±50				3500–3090	*3220–3085 (91%)* *3460* or *3065–3025 (4%)*
GrA-17117	Sample 21	Human. Cremated bone	Burial 13. Cremated bone in stone setting, with fragmentary bone pin, perimeter, within limit of earthen mound (M. O'Sullivan 2005, 36, figs 19, 32, 55: 197)	4510±50				3370–3020	*3230–3015*

Laboratory number	Sample reference	Material	Context	Radiocarbon age (BP)	δ¹³C (‰)	δ¹⁵N (‰)	Weighted mean (BP)	Calibrated date range (cal BC) (95% confidence)	*Posterior density estimate (cal BC) (95% probability)*
GrA-17297	Sample 22	Human. Cremated bone	Burial 14. Comminuted cremated bone in stone setting, perimeter, outside limit of earthen mound (M. O'Sullivan 2005, 37, figs 19, 33, 34)	4515±35				3370–3090	*3215–3085 (92%)* or *3060–3030 (3%)*
GrA-17156	Sample 23	Human. Cremated bone	Burial 11. Small amount of ?human cremated bone, perimeter, outside limit of earthen mound (M. O'Sullivan 2005, 36)	4440±60				3360–2900	*3185–2915*
GrA-17157	Sample 24	Human. Cremated bone	Burial 4. Small amount of cremated bone with charcoal, perimeter, beneath yellow soil of mound (M. O'Sullivan 2005, 34, figs 19, 27)	4480±60				3370–2920	*3200–2925*
GrA-17158	Sample 25	Human. Cremated bone	Burial 9. Cremated bone with stone setting, perimeter, outside edge of earthen mound (M. O'Sullivan 2005, 35–6, fig. 31)	4470±70				3370–2910	*3195–2915*
GrA-17324	Sample 38	Human. Cremated bone	Burial 6. Small amount of cremated bone in stone setting, perimeter (M. O'Sullivan 2005, 35, fig. 29)	4530±35				3370–3090	*3220–3090*
GrA-17325	Sample 40	Human. Cremated bone	Burial 3. Cremated bone in stone setting, perimeter, within limit of earthen mound (M. O'Sullivan 2005, 33–4, figs 19, 26)	4470±35				3350–3010	*3225–3205 (1%)* or *3200–3010 (94%)*
GrA-17202	Sample 41	Human. Cremated bone	Burial 16. Cremated bone under shale slab, perimeter, about 9m west of mound (M. O'Sullivan 2005, 31, 38)	4460±60				3370–2910	*3190–2920*
GrA-17201	Sample 39	Human. Cremated bone	Burial 17. 3 scatters of cremated bone, some of it on large stone, perimeter, outside limit of mound (M. O'Sullivan 2005, 39, fig. 35)	4450±60				3360–2910	*3190–2915*
EBA burials in tomb and chamber									
GrA-17719	Sample 51	Human. Cremated bone	Inner compartment of tomb. Level of burial 18 (which was associated with a Food Vessel, a V-perforated button and a Copper alloy awl and lay in base of pit cut into floor of chamber (M. O'Sullivan 2005, 109–12, figs 100, 104)	3760±50				2340–2020	
GrA-18350	Sample 55	Human. Skull	Inner compartment of tomb. SE of chamber, main cremation deposit, context of GrA-17277 (M. O'Sullivan 2005, 111–12, figs 100–110). Seen by O'Sullivan as resulting from disturbance in course of insertion of EBA burials	3760±50	−22.0			2340–2020	
GrA-17680	Sample 62	Human. Inhumed bone	Inner compartment of tomb. Unspecified inhumation 'from basin in chamber' (M. O'Sullivan 2005, 103–12)	3665±35	−21.7			2150–1940	
GrA-17279	Sample 69	Human. Cremated bone	Burial 24. On S side of outer compartment, against orthostat L1, in cist. Cremation of 1 adult in inverted Encrusted Urn accompanied by vase Food Vessel, burnt flint knife, flint and ?chert flakes (M. O'Sullivan 2005, 90–4, figs 87–90)	3635±35				2140–1890	
EBA burials in mound									
GrA-17299	Sample 26	Human. Cremated bone	Burial 31. Cremation inserted into SE quadrant of mound, in cist, with 2 bone needles (M. O'Sullivan 2005, 182–3)	3475±35				1900–1690	

Laboratory number	Sample reference	Material	Context	Radiocarbon age (BP)	$\delta^{13}C$ (‰)	$\delta^{15}N$ (‰)	Weighted mean (BP)	Calibrated date range (cal BC) (95% confidence)	*Posterior density estimate (cal BC) (95% probability)*
GrA-17159	Sample 27	Human. Cremated bone	Burial 33. Cremation inserted into SE quadrant of mound. Small quantity of cremated bone beneath upright tripartite bowl Food Vessel (M. O'Sullivan 2005, 184–5)	3560±60				2120–1740	
GrA-17161	Sample 28	Human. Cremated bone	Burial 35. Cremation inserted into SE quadrant of mound beneath inverted enlarged Food Vessel and accompanied by inverted vase Food Vessel (M. O'Sullivan 2005, 186–90)	3470±60				1950–1620	
GrA-17162	Sample 29	Human. Cremated bone	Burial 34. Cremation inserted into SE quadrant of mound, within and around inverted Encrusted Urn, in cist (M. O'Sullivan 2005, 185–7)	3500±60				2020–1680	
GrA-17321	Sample 30	Human. Cremated bone	Burial 41. Cremation inserted into NE quadrant of mound. Beneath inverted Collared Urn with heat-damaged copper alloy dagger (M. O'Sullivan 2005, 201–3)	3445±35				1890–1660	
GrA-17539	Sample 31	Human. Cremated bone	Burial 45. In NE quadrant of mound, in cist, in two masses, with copper alloy fragments, flint fragment, possibly bone pinhead (M. O'Sullivan 2005, 209–10)	3550±45				2030–1740	
GrA-17193	Sample 32	Human. Cremated bone	Burial 40. Spread of cremated bone with burnt flint knife, close to an inverted bowl Food Vessel and a vase Food Vessel, association uncertain (M. O'Sullivan 2005, 197–201)	3600±60				2140–1770	
GrA-17195	Sample 33	Human. Cremated bone	Burial 43. In SW quadrant of mound, cremation of at least 1 adult beneath Encrusted Urn A, one of two adjacent inverted Encrusted Urns accompanied by two inverted vase Food Vessels (M. O'Sullivan 2005, 204–7)	3570±60				2130–1740	
GrA-17276	Sample 47	Human. Cremated bone	Burial 43. In SW quadrant of mound, cremation of at least 2 adults and a child beneath Encrusted Urn B, one of two adjacent inverted Encrusted Urns accompanied by two inverted vase Food Vessels (M. O'Sullivan 2005, 204–7)	3640±35				2140–1900	
GrA-17198	Sample 35	Human. Cremated bone	Burial 39. Cremation inserted into SE quadrant of mound, beneath inverted enlarged Food vessel with warped copper alloy dagger, burnt bone pin fragment, perforated pumice stone (M. O'Sullivan 2005, 195–7)	3500±60				2020–1680	
GrA-17232	Sample 36	Human. Cremated bone	Burial 38. Cremation inserted into SE quadrant of mound, beneath inverted Collared Urn with bronze dagger and stone battle-axe, both burnt, accompanied by inverted vase Food Vessel (M. O'Sullivan 2005, 186–90)	3430±35				1880–1630	
GrA-17196	Sample 34	Human. Cremated bone	Burial 42. Cremation of one or possibly two individuals in cist inserted into SW quadrant of mound, under inverted enlarged Food Vessel beside inverted Collared Urn (M. O'Sullivan 2005, 203–5)	3500±60				2020–1680	

Laboratory number	Sample reference	Material	Context	Radiocarbon age (BP)	$\delta^{13}C$ (‰)	$\delta^{15}N$ (‰)	Weighted mean (BP)	Calibrated date range (cal BC) (95% confidence)	*Posterior density estimate (cal BC) (95% probability)*
GrA-17199	Sample 37	Human. Cremated bone	Burial 42. Cremation under inverted Collared Urn with fragment of bone needle or pendant beside inverted enlarged Food Vessel in same cist as sample for GrA-17196. Impossible to tell if from a separate individual (M. O'Sullivan 2005, 203–5)	3410±60				1890–1530	
GrA-19180	Sample 83	Human. Articulated inhumation	Burial 30. Crouched inhumation inserted into NW quadrant of mound. Youth with bead necklace, including faience, amble jet, bone and copper alloy; razor near feet (M. O'Sullivan 2005, 177–82, figs 140–6)	3370±60	−21.5			1880–1500	
Miscellaneous features around perimeter									
GrN-26060	Sample 1	*Prunus spinosa* and *Corylus* charcoal	Pit F. Ash pit with some charcoal, at S edge of mound (M. O'Sullivan 2005, 43, fig. 19)	3480±50				1940–1680	
GrN-26061	Sample 2	*Corylus* charcoal	Pit O. Baulk between squares 14 and 15. Spread of charcoal, possibly in a shallow pit, perimeter, outside limit of mound (M. O'Sullivan 2005, 44, fig. 19)	3510±50				1960–1690	
GrN-26063	Sample 4	Mainly *Corylus* charcoal with some *Alnus*	Pit C. Square 26, pit containing dark soil and charcoal, perimeter, outside edge of mound (M. O'Sullivan 2005, 52, figs 15, 19)	3480±70				2010–1620	
GrA-17523	Sample 5	*Prunus spinosa* charcoal	Pit R. Square 66, pit containing dark soil, charcoal and burnt stones and/or clay, perimeter, outside limit of mound (M. O'Sullivan 2005, 45, fig. 19)	3610±50				2140–1780	
SE of mound									
GrN-26062	Sample 3	*Corylus* charcoal	Pit Z2. Square 35, perimeter, beyond south-east limit of mound, regarded as linked to palisade 3 (M. O'Sullivan 2005, 50–6, figs 19, 36, 47, 48)	3960±60				2620–2280	
GrA-17670	Sample 18	*Ulmus* charcoal	Palisade 2. Square 7, perimeter, north of mound (M. O'Sullivan 2005, 50, figs 19, 40, 47)	3925±40				2570–2290	
GrA-17113	Sample 12	Human. Cremated bone	Ring ditch beyond SE edge of mound. Small number of fragments of cremated bone, green bead and decayed sherds found together, perhaps at a lower level than sample for GrA-17294 (M. O'Sullivan 2005, 51–6)	2620±50					
GrA-17294	Sample 16	Human. Cremated bone	Cremation scatter on surface in interior of ring ditch, perhaps at a higher level than sample for GrA-17113 (M. O'Sullivan 2005, 53–6)	2255±30					
Mound									
GrA-17672	Sample 17	*Corylus* charcoal, *c.* 14 years old	From edge of cairn in original sod covering. May have been transported to site in turf (Brindley *et al.* 2005, 295)	4680±40				3630–3360	*3630–3585 (10%)* or *3530–3365 (85%)*
Carrowkeel M, Co. Sligo									
Ua-510	Sample 1	Human. Tooth	Between orthostats in end recess of passage grave, at different location to sample for Ua-511 (Bergh 1995, 105)	3770±100	−25.0			2480–1910	
Ua-511	Sample 2	Pomoideae (?) charcoal	Between orthostats in end recess, at different location to sample for Ua-510 (Bergh 1995, 105)	4530±100	−25.0			3630–2910	*3520–3420 (10%)* or *3385–2920 (85%)*

Laboratory number	Sample reference	Material	Context	Radiocarbon age (BP)	$\delta^{13}C$ (‰)	$\delta^{15}N$ (‰)	Weighted mean (BP)	Calibrated date range (cal BC) (95% confidence)	*Posterior density estimate (cal BC) (95% probability)*
Croaghaun, Glen, Co. Sligo									
Ua-713	C14:2	*Pinus sylvestris* charcoal	*In situ* cremation deposit between and partly under first and second chamber orthostats on L side of chamber. Including cremated bone, charcoal, coarse pottery and head of poppy-headed bone or antler pin (Bergh 1995, 105, 225)	6680±100	−25.0			5740–5470	
St-10453	C14:3	*Pinus sylvestris* charcoal	Charcoal spread with cremated bones in outer part of chamber (Bergh 1995, 105, 225)	5685±85				4720–4340	
St-10452	C14:1	Charcoal (unidentified)	In rift on bedrock beneath cairn (Bergh 1995, 105, 225)	4680±675				5220–1820	
St-10454	C14:5	Charcoal (unidentified)	Bedrock beneath cairn (Bergh 1995, 105, 225)	3280±295				2350–820	
St-10455	C14:6	Charcoal (unidentified)	Bedrock beneath cairn (Bergh 1995, 105, 225)	2025±285				800 BC–610 AD	
Carrowmore 1, Co. Sligo									
Ua-16970	ID 60106	Charcoal	Tomb 1. Sample from close to inner stone circle found when tomb sectioned 1995–6 (Burenhult 2001, 18). From stone socket (Burenhult 2003, 67)	5320±8	−26.2			4340–3960	*4330–3985*
Carrowmore 4, Co. Sligo									
Ua-16975	20/94	Charcoal	Tomb 4. 3rd phase, when 2nd inner stone circle and 2 cists built (Burenhult 2001, 19)	4425±80	−26.9			3370–2890	*3340–2905*
Ua-16976	24/94	Charcoal	Tomb 4. 3rd phase, when 2nd inner stone circle and 2 cists built (Burenhult 2001, 19).	4390±70	−25.2			3340–2880	*3335–3210 (19%)* or *3190–3150 (4%)* or *3135–2890 (72%)*
Ua-16972	14/94	Charcoal	Tomb 4. 3rd phase, when 2nd inner stone circle and 2 cists built (Burenhult 2001, 19)	4220±80	−26.0			3020–2570	*3085–3065 (1%)* or *3030–2750 (94%)*
Lu-1750	2:79	Charcoal	Tomb 4. Charcoal from just outside central stone packing (Bergh 1995, 102) or from secondary inner stone circle (Burenhult 1984, 131; Hakansson 1981). If this sample is that shown as 'C14 test 2' in Burenhult 1980, fig. 27, then Bergh's description of the context seems more accurate and the date should be a *terminus post quem* for the more extensive stone packing surrounding the chamber, i.e. for a secondary state of construction. No pretreatment; small sample; diluted; 50% sample. (3 1-day counts) (Hakansson 1981, 400)	4320±75	−24.3			3270–2710	*3330–3225 (6%)* or *3125–2855 (89%)*

Laboratory number	Sample reference	Material	Context	Radiocarbon age (BP)	$\delta^{13}C$ (‰)	$\delta^{15}N$ (‰)	Weighted mean (BP)	Calibrated date range (cal BC) (95% confidence)	*Posterior density estimate (cal BC) (95% probability)*
Lu-1840	4:79	Charcoal	Tomb 4. Charcoal from 'stone fundament to stone b in central cist'. Stone b was a large slab set in a bedding trench with others forming chamber of small passage Tomb. The sample came from a circumscribed concentration of charcoal in the soil at the base of the bedding trench, between the bases of two orthostats (Burenhult 1984, fig. 37). The contents of the chamber had been disturbed before excavation. It contained large amounts of displaced burnt human and animal bone and 4 fragmentary antler pins, more of which had been thrown out from the chamber (Burenhult 1980, 68–82; 1984, 128). The sample reference quoted here is that used by Burenhult (1984, 128). Previously, however, C14 sample 4-79 was attributed to Tomb 1 (Burenhult 1980, 47; Hakansson 1981)	5750±85	−30.2			4800–4370	*4795–4440 (94%)* or *4425–4395 (1%)*
Ua-16974	17/94	Charcoal	Tomb 4. 'May belong to' second phase, when passage and inner stone circle added (Burenhult 2001, 19). From stone socket (Burenhult 2003, 67)	5230±80	−25.6			4320–3800	*4265–3930 (90%)* or *3875–3805 (5%)*
Ua-13382	19/94	Charcoal?	Tomb 4. 'May belong to' second phase, when passage and inner stone circle added (Burenhult 2001, 19). From stone socket (Burenhult 2003, 67)	5180±90	−27.6			4240–3770	*4240–3770*
Ua-4486	7	*Corylus avellana* charcoal	Tomb 4. 'May belong to' second phase, when passage and inner stone circle added (Burenhult 2001, 19). From stone socket of passage (Burenhult 2003)	4945±100	−26.9			3970–3520	*3965–3625 (89%)* or *3600–3520 (6%)*
Ua-16973	16/94	Charcoal	Tomb 4. 3rd phase, when 2nd inner stone circle and 2 cists built (Burenhult 2001, 19)	4430±100	−26.1			3490–2880	*3360–2895*
Ua-16971	3/79	Charcoal	Tomb 4. Summary account suggests sample came from secondary cremation with barbed and tanged arrowhead (Burenhult 2001, 21)	3975±70	−25.7			2840–2280	
Ua-12736	26/94	Charcoal	Tomb 4. Summary account suggests sample was from bedding trench for stones of central cist, like Lu-1840 (Burenhult 2001, 19). Interim note describes sample as 'from the cist' (Burenhult 2000, 181)	6500±75	−26.1			5620–5310	*5615–5585 (4%)* or *5570–5320 (91%)*

Laboratory number	Sample reference	Material	Context	Radiocarbon age (BP)	$\delta^{13}C$ (‰)	$\delta^{15}N$ (‰)	Weighted mean (BP)	Calibrated date range (cal BC) (95% confidence)	*Posterior density estimate (cal BC) (95% probability)*
Carrowmore 7, Co. Sligo									
Lu-1441	I:77	Charcoal	Tomb 7. Charcoal partly from posthole at centre of central chamber of monument, within undisturbed bottom layer in chamber, partly from an indeterminate context in that layer, which included charred bark near the posthole (Bergh 1995, 104). Upper fills of chamber had been disturbed in recent times. Intact cremation deposits survived in corners of chamber, between orthostats, with burnt seashells, charcoal and, in one case, fragments of an antler pin (Burenhult 1980, 19–32, figs 5, 8, photo 8). Figs 5 and 8 show the posthole as *c.* 0.25 m in diameter. Photo 8, which lacks a scale, shows the truncated base of a dark postpipe occupying approximately 1/3 of the width of the posthole, suggesting that the post was *c.* 0.10 m in diameter. Described as dating construction (Burenhult 2001, 21). Mild pretreatment with NaOH and HCl (Hakansson 1981, 399)	5250±80	−26.2			4330–3940	*4325–4285* (*2%*) or *4270–3940* (*93%*)
Ua-16978	6/77	Charcoal	Tomb 7. No hint of context in summary account (Burenhult 2001, 20–1)	4405±70	−26.5			3350–2890	*3340–3205* (*23%*) or *3195–3145* (*6%*) or *3140–2900* (*66%*)
Carrowmore 19, Co. Sligo									
Ua-12734	ID 60207	Charcoal	Tomb 19. Rescue excavation recovered damaged central chamber. This and Ua-16981 described as dating use rather than construction (Burenhult 2001, 22)	4610±90	−24.9			3640–3020	*3635–3550* (*8%*) or *3540–3085* (*87%*)
Ua-16981	ID 60206	Charcoal	Tomb 19. Rescue excavation recovered damaged central chamber. This and Ua-12734 described as dating use rather than construction (Burenhult 2001, 22)	4915±75	−26.0			3940–3530	*3945–3855* (*10%*) or *3825–3625* (*78%*) or *3590–3525* (*7%*)
Carrowmore 27, Co. Sligo									
Lu-1698	4:79	Charcoal	Tomb 27. Charcoal from lower part of stone packing between central chamber and stone circle intermediate between it and outer kerb (Bergh 1995, 104; Burenhult 1980, 50–67; 1984, 128–31). Burenhult (1980, fig. 20) shows all three samples from this context (Lu-1698, -1808, -1810) at individual findspots close to each other near the entrance to the chamber. Chamber had been disturbed in recent times but contained cremated bone, fragmentary antler pins, walrus ivory rings, a stone bead, 2 chalk balls, sherds of Carrowkeel Ware. First millennium cal BC dates were obtained from charcoal in disturbed contexts in the chamber. Pretreated with HCl and NaOH (Hakansson 1981, 400)	5040±60	−22.9			3970–3670	*3965–3700*
Lu-1808	1:79	Charcoal	From the same context as and close to the sample for Lu-1698. Mild pretreatment with NaOH and HCl (Hakansson 1981, 401)	5000±65	−23.7			3960–3640	*3950–3655*

Laboratory number	Sample reference	Material	Context	Radiocarbon age (BP)	δ^{13}C (‰)	δ^{15}N (‰)	Weighted mean (BP)	Calibrated date range (cal BC) (95% confidence)	*Posterior density estimate (cal BC) (95% probability)*
Lu-1810	3:79	Charcoal	From the same context as and close to the sample for Lu-1698. No pretreatment; small sample; diluted; 48% sample (3 1-day counts) (Hakansson 1981, 401). Listed as Lu-1818 by Burenhult (1984, 131)	4940±85	−23.4			3960–3530	*3955–3630* (*92%*) or *3570–3535* (*3%*)
Carrowmore 51, Co. Sligo									
Ua-12731	ID 60102	Charcoal	Tomb 51. Outside E corner of central chamber, embedded in reddish, burnt area of brown/yellow layer with charcoal and artefacts above sterile limestone clay and below chamber and mound. Layer seen as deliberately deposited (Burenhult 1998, 18, 19, fig. 33)	4790±65	−26.4			3700–3370	*3695–3495* (*78%*) or *3460–3375* (*17%*)
Ua-12733	ID 60167	Charcoal	Tomb 51. Base of stone E at N corner of central chamber, between outer surfaces of stones E and F	1500±60	−26.6			AD 420–640	
Ua-12732	ID 60164	Charcoal	Tomb 51. Embedded in brown/yellow layer outside N corner of central chamber (Burenhult 1998, 18, fig. 39)	4655±65	−27.6			3640–3130	*3635–3330* (*92%*) or *3215–3185* (*2%*) or *3155–3130* (*1%*)
Ua-16108	ID 60165	Charcoal	Tomb 51. Embedded in stone packing inside structure VI, pit 48 cm diam, 35 cm deep, dug into brown/yellow layer, stone packing in bottom, much charcoal (Burenhult 1998, 18, 19, figs 22, 39–41, photos 52, 54, 55)	4740±70	−25.6			3660–3360	*3645–3365*
Ua-16110	ID 60186	Charcoal	Tomb 51. On top of sterile clay layer below brown/yellow layer, outside S limestone kerb (Burenhult 1998, 18)	5255±70	−26.3			4320–3950	*4315–4295* (*1%*) or *4265–3950* (*94%*)
Ua-11581		Human. Skull fragment with cut marks	Tomb 51. Partly excavated 1996–8. Just under the grass sod outside N corner of central chamber. Among other unburnt bone fragments and a little cremated bone apparently thrown out from chamber in course of recent disturbance (Burenhult 1998, 6, 17, 18)	4625±60	−22.7			3630–3120	
Ua-16107	ID 60074	Charcoal	Tomb 51. Structure I. ?Posthole 20 cm diam, 7.5 cm deep, cut into brown/yellow layer, outside E side of chamber, containing charcoal, flint scraper, bone fragments (Burenhult 1998, 9, figs 12, 21)	2510±70	−25.4			810–400	
Ua-11580	ID 60072	Charcoal	Tomb 51. Surface of brown/yellow layer close to stone C outside S corner of central chamber, beside Ua-1159	4775±60	−28.1			3660–3370	*3655–3490 75%*) or *3465–3370* (*20%*)
Ua-16111	ID 60193	Charcoal	Tomb 51. Surface of brown/yellow layer in E trench, directly under cairn filling (Burenhult 1998, 18, fig. 39)	4815±75	−26.7			3750–3370	*3760–3740* (*1%*) or *3715–3490* (*80%*) or *3470–3370* (*14%*)
Ua-11579	ID 60071	Charcoal	Tomb 51. Surface of brown/yellow layer near stone C, outside S corner of central chamber (Burenhult 1998, 17, fig. 40)	4830±60	−26.6			3710–3380	*3760–3740* (*1%*) or *3715–3500* (*89%*) or *3430–3380* (*5%*)

Laboratory number	Sample reference	Material	Context	Radiocarbon age (BP)	$\delta^{13}C$ (‰)	$\delta^{15}N$ (‰)	Weighted mean (BP)	Calibrated date range (cal BC) (95% confidence)	*Posterior density estimate (cal BC) (95% probability)*
Ua-11578	ID 600667	Charcoal	Tomb 51. Surface of brown/yellow layer outside chamber, near stone C (Burenhult 1998, 17, fig. 39)	4800±70	−27.2			3710–3370	*3705–3490 (79%)* or *3465–3375 (16%)*
Ua-16109	ID 60177	Charcoal	Tomb 51.Embedded in brown/yellow layer outside stone E of central chamber (Burenhult 1998, 18, figs 39–41)	4745±70	−26.4			3660–3360	*3650–3365*
Carrowmore 55, Co. Sligo									
Ua-13753	ID 60512	Charcoal	Tomb 55. Partly excavated 1998. Date described as relating to use, not construction (Burenhult 2001, 29)	4970±120	−25.2			4040–3520	*4000–3515*
Carrowmore 56, Co. Sligo									
Ua-10737	ID 60256	*Corylus avellana* charcoal	Tomb 56. Partly excavated 1994–5. Dates described as relating to use (Burenhult 2001, 29). A date or dates from this tomb is described as 'from stone packing outside central chamber' (Burenhult 2003, 67). It is unclear to which date(s) this refers	4620±70	−25.9			3630–3100	*3630–3575 (6%)* or *3535–3260 (70%)* or *3245–3100 (19%)*
Ua-10736	ID 60251	*Corylus avellana* charcoal	Tomb 56. Partly excavated 1994-5. Dates described as relating to use (Burenhult 2001, 29). A date or dates from this tomb is described as 'from stone packing outside central chamber' (Burenhult 2003, 67). It is unclear to which date(s) this refers	4525±80	−25.2			3500–2920	*3500–3430 (6%)* or *3380–3005 (86%)* or *2990–2930 (3%)*
Ua-10735	ID 60250	Pomoideae charcoal	Tomb 56. Partly excavated 1994-5. Dates described as relating to use (Burenhult 2001, 29). A date or dates from this tomb is described as 'from stone packing outside central chamber' (Burenhult 2003, 67). It is unclear to which date(s) this refers	4495±80	−26.3			3500–2910	*3370–2920*
Ua-4488	63	*Corylus avellana* charcoal	Tomb 56. Partly excavated 1994-5. Dates described as relating to use (Burenhult 2001, 29). A date or dates from this tomb is described as 'from stone packing outside central chamber' (Burenhult 2003, 67). It is unclear to which date(s) this refers	4480±75	−22.7			3490–2910	*3365–3000 (88%)* or *2995–2925 (7%)*
Ua-4487	35	*Corylus avellana* charcoal	Tomb 56. Partly excavated 1994-5. Dates described as relating to use (Burenhult 2001, 29). A date or dates from this tomb is described as 'from stone packing outside central chamber' (Burenhult 2003, 67). It is unclear to which date(s) this refers	4395±65	−26.7			3340–2890	*3335–3210 (19%)* or *3190–3150 (4%)* or *3135–2895 (72%)*

1. Previously published as GrN-(provisional) 4415±50 BP (e.g. Eogan 1986, 226)

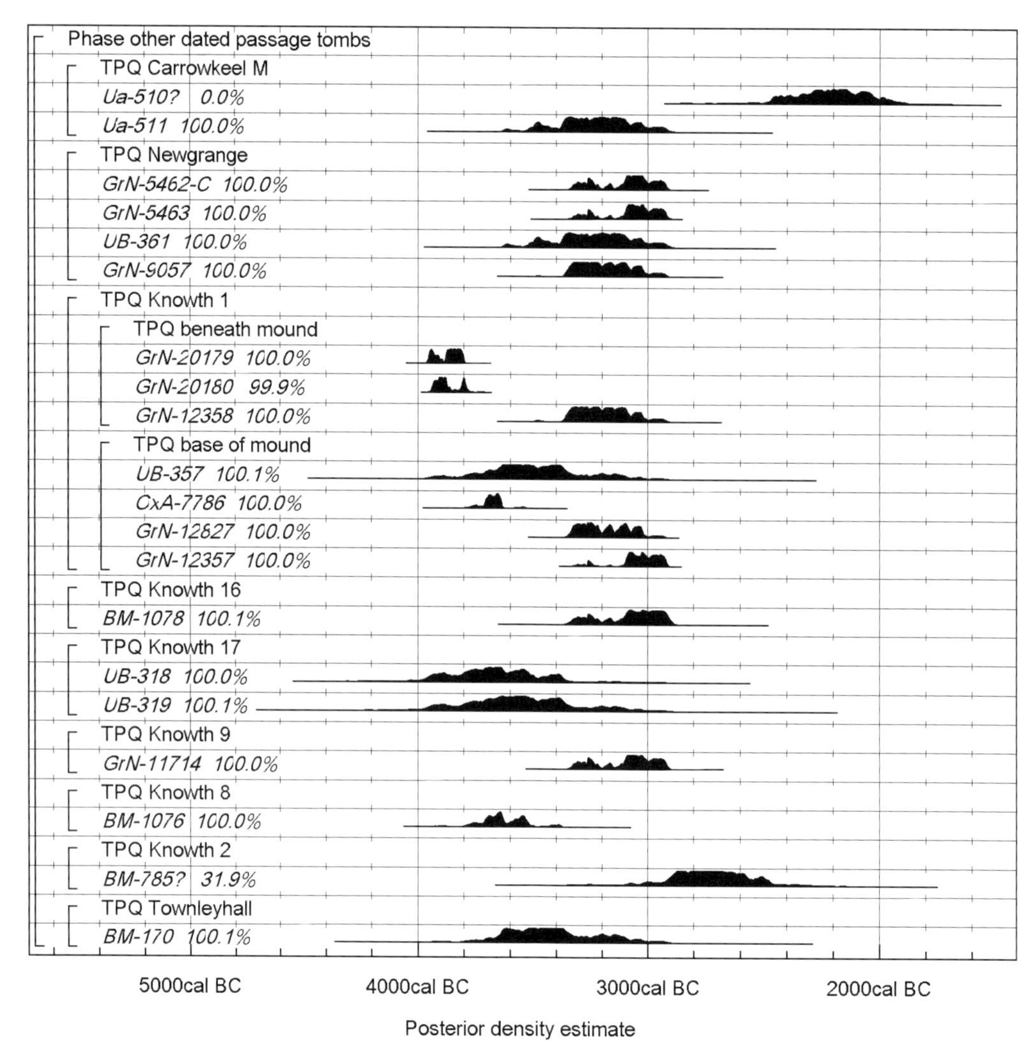

Fig. 12.46. Townleyhall, Knowth, Newgrange and Carrowkeel. Probability distributions of dates relating to passage tombs. The format is identical to that of Fig. 12.6. The overall structure of this model is shown in Fig. 12.45 and its other components in Figs 12.47–50.

passage tomb in Ireland currently has radiocarbon dates which unequivocally provide more than *termini post quos* for their contexts (and see further below).[15]

A bulk sample of unidentified charcoal was dated from beneath the passage tomb at Townleyhall II, Co. Louth, on the periphery of the Brú na Bóinne concentration. This measurement (Fig. 12.46: *BM-170*) thus provides a *terminus post quem* for the construction of the monument.

At Knowth, 20 smaller tombs surround the main mound, site 1. The evidence suggests that some of these 'satellites' may pre-date the enlarged, second phase of site 1, with a couple definitely post-dating it. Knowth site 16 is truncated by site 1, while the main mound appears to respect the position of sites 8 and 13. A bulk sample of unidentified charcoal (Table 12.12: BM-785) was dated from a spread within the mound of Knowth site 2, which has a cruciform chamber. At face value it should provide a *terminus post quem* for construction of the mound but, as it is close to a disturbed area with Beaker pottery, it is possible that the sample could have included some later material. Being cautious, we have therefore excluded this date from the model.

A *terminus post quem* for the construction of Knowth site 8 is provided by *BM-1076*, a bulk sample of unidentified charcoal from a pit in a sub-rectangular structure, underlying the sillstone of site 8. We have already noted this sample above (Fig. 12.46; Table 12.3). A *terminus post quem* for the end of use of Knowth site 9, with cruciform chamber, is provided by *GrN-11714*, on a sample of unidentified bulk charcoal from a cremation deposit in the end recess. Two statistically consistent radiocarbon determinations (*UB-318–9*; T'=0.2; T'(5%)=3.8; ν=1) for unidentified bulk charcoal from a thin layer under Knowth site 17, with cruciform chamber, provide *termini post quos* for its construction.

A further sample of bulk unidentified charcoal (*BM-1078*) has been dated from a spread sealed within the mound of site 16, with a simple chamber. This provides a *terminus post quem* for the construction of this mound, and also for that of site 1, which cuts this satellite. Further *termini post quos* (Table 12.3) for the construction of site 1 are provided by dates on bulk unidentified charcoal from the fill of Foundation Trench 1, under the north-east part of the main mound (*GrN-21079* and *GrN-21080*; and by a date

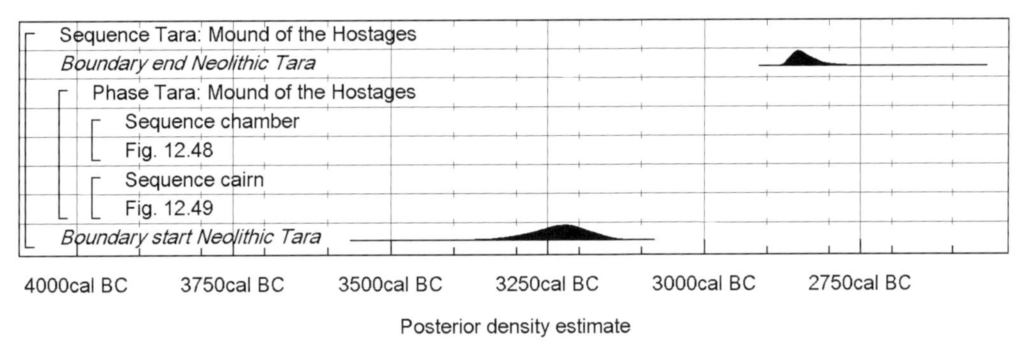

Fig. 12.47. The Mound of the Hostages, Tara. Overall structure of the component chronological model for this passage tomb. The two sub-components relating to the Mound of the Hostages are shown in Figs 12.48–9. The format is identical to that of Fig. 12.6. The overall structure of this model is shown in Fig. 12.45 and its other components in Figs 12.46 and 12.50.

on material from a charcoal spread on the old land surface beneath the main mound (*GrN-12358*). Five determinations are available from the material of the main mound of site 1 itself. Four (*UB-357, OxA-7786, GrN-12357, GrN-12827*) are of unidentified charcoal, and provide *termini post quos* for the construction of the main mound. A fifth determination on the humic acid fraction of the sod itself (UB-358) has not been included in the model because its result is so old that it is not relevant (Table 12.12).

Four dates provide *termini post quos* for the construction of Newgrange (Fig. 12.46; Table 12.12). *GrN-5462-C* and *GrN-5463* were measured on short-life charcoal fragments from soil caulking of the roof of the passage. Although this soil was almost certainly placed in this position when the tomb was constructed, it is unclear whether the charcoal derives from an earlier soil which has been redeposited. The samples can therefore only be treated as *termini post quos* for construction. The other two samples (*UB-361* and *GrN-9057*) are from turves forming the lower part of the mound. These again provide only *termini post quos* for construction. A date (UB-360) on the humic fraction of a turf layer, slightly higher than *UB-361*, is anomalously young and may have been affected by the penetration of younger material through the loose stone material of the mound (Table 12.12; A. Smith *et al.* 1971, 452).

Two dates (Fig. 12.46: Ua-510, *-511*) are available from Carrowkeel site M, Co. Sligo, both on short-life material from within the end recess of the chamber. Both provide *termini post quos* for the final use of the monument. Ua-510, however, appears to relate to Bronze Age re-use of the monument and so has been excluded from the present model.

Five radiocarbon dates are available from Croaghaun, Co. Sligo (Table 12.12: Ua-713, St-10452–5; Bergh 1995, 105, 225). None are modelled. The exceptionally large standard deviations (the greatest is 675 years) of measurements for samples from beneath the cairn would alone reduce their value as *termini post quos* and the fact that all three are of disparate ages (in one case extending into the historical period; T'=20.90; T'(5%)=6.0; ν=2) indicate that the cairn had been subjected to disturbance. The remaining two measurements (Ua-713, St-10453) have smaller standard deviations and are both from cremation deposits, one of them *in situ*. The samples for both were of pine charcoal, and pine does not normally live longer than two to three centuries, so that, other things being equal, one could regard both these samples as relatively close in age to the construction and use of the monument. They date, however, to the sixth and fifth millennia cal BC. It is plausible that these samples derive from bog pines, and we have therefore not included these dates in the current model.

The Mound of the Hostages, Tara, has a simple chamber and outer portal stones set within a small cairn but is distinguished by two features (M. O'Sullivan 2005). First, it has an extended sequence, which begins with pre-cairn features including pits, hearths and a segment of ditch, and extends to Early Bronze Age burials in the earthen capping over the cairn. Secondly, there are very substantial numbers of human remains, cremated and unburnt, from the compartments of the chamber, from three cists built against the backs of the chamber orthostats, and from the perimeter of the tomb. Nine dates are available on samples from beneath the tomb. There are 15 dates on human bone associated with the cists and chamber, and 11 on human bone from burials around the perimeter of the cairn; there is also one date from charcoal in the original turf covering directly over the stone cairn (Table 12.12). There are a further four dates on human bone from Early Bronze Age contexts in the chamber, 14 from Early Bronze Age cremations in the enlarged mound, and nine from Bronze Age and later activity around the tomb, but these are not considered here. This outstanding series constitutes not only the largest sample of radiocarbon measurements for an Irish passage tomb, but also one of the most complex sequences.

Nine radiocarbon dates have been obtained from material which probably pre-dates the stone cairn (Fig. 12.49). Four of these samples are from the pre-cairn ditch on the western side of the monument (M. O'Sullivan 2005, fig. 20). One consisted of unidentified bulk charcoal measured in the pioneering days of radiocarbon dating at Trinity College, Dublin (D-42). Three samples of short-life charcoal have been dated more recently (*GrA-17674, -17676, GrN-26065*). The latest of these samples may provide the best indication of the date of this feature.

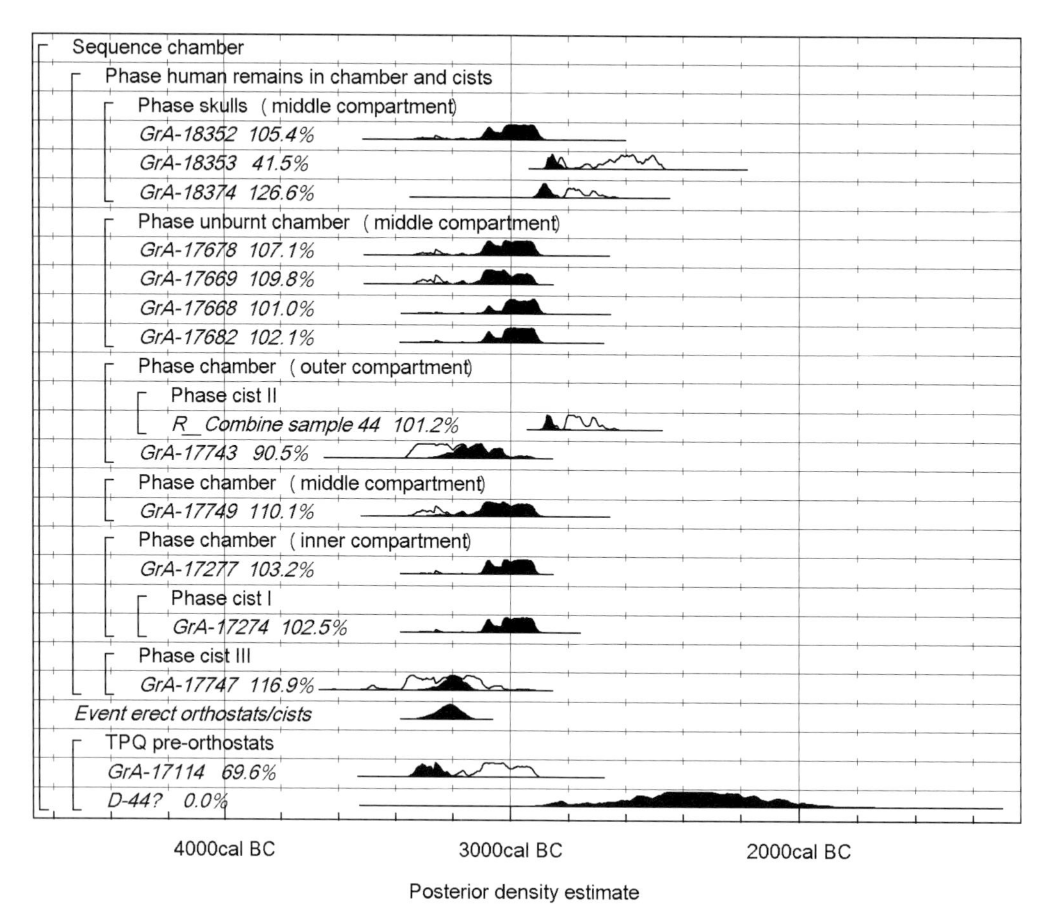

Fig. 12.48. The Mound of the Hostages, Tara. Probability distributions of dates relating to the chamber sequence. The format is identical to that of Fig. 12.6. The overall structure of this model is shown in Fig. 12.45 and its other components in Figs 12.46–7 and 12.49–50.

Of these samples, only *GrA-17676* came from a context which was actually sealed by the cairn; the other dates are interpreted as earlier than the stone cairn on the basis that the ditch is a single feature. Two further samples, one of unidentified bulk charcoal (D-44) and the other of oak charcoal (*GrA-17675*), also provide *termini post quos* for the construction of the cairn. D-44 probably also provides a *terminus post quem* for the erection of the portal stones (Fig. 12.48). Three further determinations are available from the old ground level under the cairn (Fig. 12.49). *GrA-17525* and *GrN-26064* seem to have comprised short-life species. D-43 was unidentified and so only provides a *terminus post quem* for its context. It is argued below that the turf covering was placed over the stone cairn very shortly after its construction. A sample of charcoal from a turf of the sod covering (*GrA-17672*) must therefore pre-date the construction of the cairn.

The process of constructing the chamber began with the excavation of a bedding trench for the orthostats. This was cut through the deposit which probably furnished the sample for D-44, and once the stones had been placed on the inner edge of the cut, the exterior part of the trench was filled with material that included cremated bone. A single fragment of cremated bone from behind the backstone has been dated from this deposit (Fig. 12.48: *GrA-17114*). Because of its inaccessible position behind a substantial orthostat, this sample cannot have been introduced from the chamber. Once the orthostats had been erected, three small stone cists were added to the exterior of the chamber (M. O'Sullivan 2005, figs 58–9). Human bone could now be deposited in both chamber and cists. One sample has been dated from the basal part of cist I (*GrA-17274*), which contained the cremated remains of at least eight adults and a range of finds including a complete miniature Carrowkeel bowl. Two statistically consistent replicate determinations (Table 12.12: GrA-17272 and -17746) were obtained from a cremated bone fragment from cist II (*sample 44*). This contained the cremated remains of at least 34 adults and a range of finds. A single determination is available from cist III (*GrA-17747*). This contained at least 13 cremated adults and numerous finds, including a large intact Carrowkeel bowl (M. O'Sullivan 2005, figs 77–8). The bulk of these deposits must have been placed in the cists before the cairn was constructed over them, but some fragments of cremated bone may have been introduced into them subsequently, since all three cists coincided with gaps between the orthostats of the chamber which were only incompletely sealed with smaller stones (M. O'Sullivan 2005, 66–68). It is, however, highly unlikely that complete Carrowkeel pots, such as the vessel from cist III, could have been so introduced. The presence of rodent-sized bones (M. O'Sullivan 2005, 69) may also suggest the possibility of

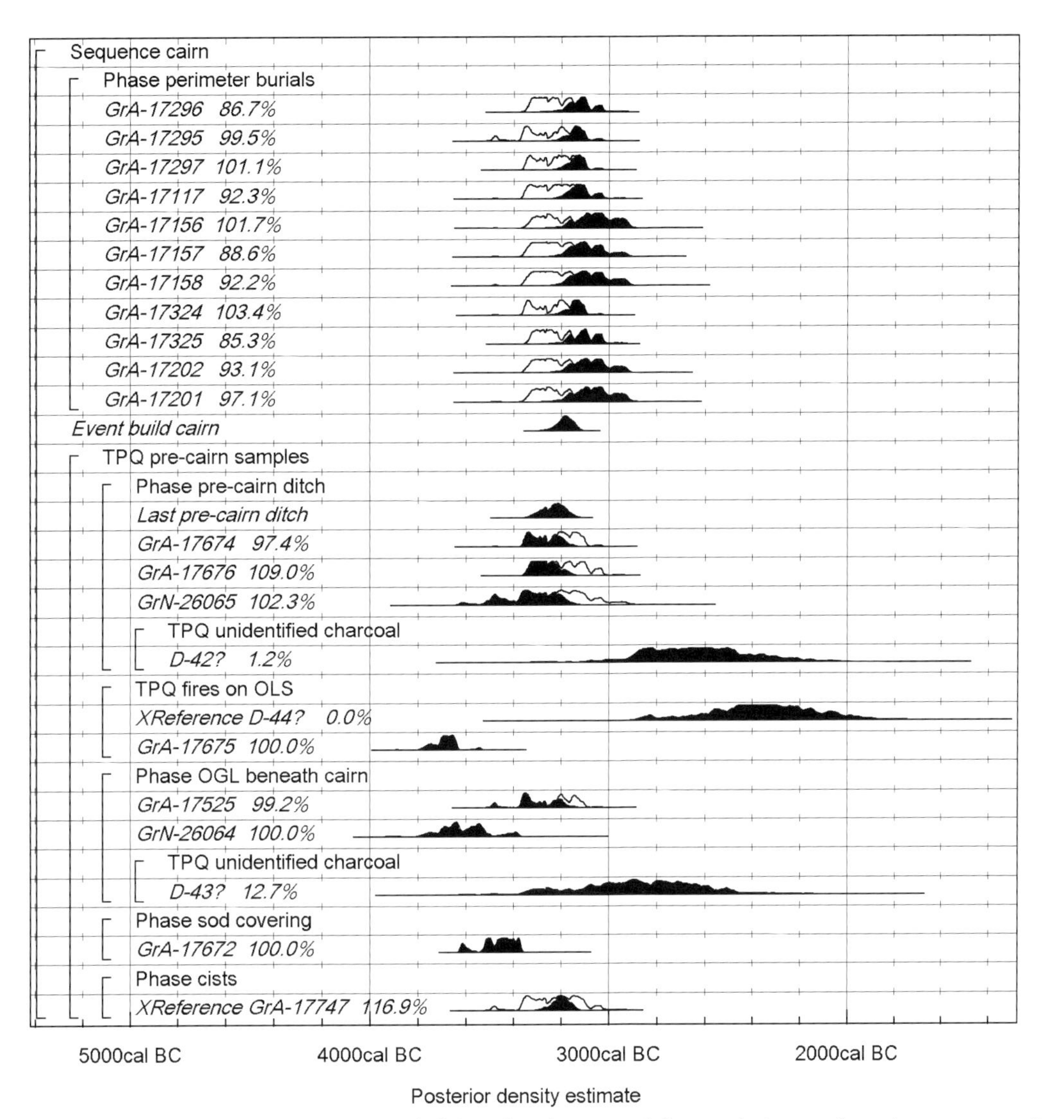

Fig. 12.49. The Mound of the Hostages, Tara. Probability distributions of dates relating to the cairn sequence. The format is identical to that of Fig. 12.6. The overall structure of this model is shown in Fig. 12.45 and its other components in Figs 12.46–8 and 12. 50.

later animal disturbance which could also have redeposited small fragments of material from chamber to cists. With these caveats, we have modelled the measurements from the cists as earlier than the construction of the cairn.

Ten radiocarbon determinations are available for Neolithic human remains in the chamber. Single fragments of cremated bone have been dated from the inner (Fig. 12.48: *GrA-17277*), middle (*GrA-17749*) and outer (*GrA-17743*) compartments. Probably none of these samples derive from an undisturbed deposit. Three measurements have been made on disarticulated unburnt human bone from deposit XLIX, a disturbed spread of mixed cremated and unburnt bone lying principally in the middle compartment (*GrA-17668–9*, *-17678*; M. O'Sullivan 2005, 100–3). A fourth sample (*GrA-17682*) of unburnt bone from this compartment is from a problematic context undoubtedly disturbed in the Bronze Age (deposit XXXVIII: M. O'Sullivan 2005, 96–7). Finally, three of probably 15 unburnt skulls from the middle compartment were dated (*GrA-18352–3*, *-18374*). It should be noted that although the human remains in the chamber were overwhelmingly dominated by cremated individuals (at least 73 adults), as opposed to perhaps nine inhumations and 15 unburnt skulls, the dated sample consists disproportionately of unburnt bone. This stemmed from the need to establish to what extent the unburnt human remains in the chamber were coeval with the cremated material and to what extent they were Early Bronze Age insertions.

After the human remains had been deposited in the cists, but not necessarily after all the human remains had been deposited in the chamber, a stone cairn was raised over both (M. O'Sullivan 2005, fig. 57). In the model presented here, we have placed the Neolithic cremations which follow the perimeter of the stone cairn after the construction of the cairn, since they respect it spatially. It is possible that they also post-date the earthen mound. This interpretation is supported by the fact that, unusually, the cairn had no kerb, but rather a rudimentary revetment (M. O'Sullivan 2005, fig. 127). Despite this, there does not seem to have been slippage of stones from the cairn, suggesting that the sod layer and earth mound followed on relatively swiftly (M. O'Sullivan 2005, 163). As excavated, some of the perimeter burials (e.g. nos 2, 3, 13 and 15) lay underneath the earthen mound, although none of them were so far from its edge that they could not have been covered by later earthen slippage. Other than this, the only stratigraphic relationships recorded for the perimeter burials are between undated burial 1 and the underlying pit B which contained sherds probably of both Carinated Bowl pottery and Grooved Ware (M. O'Sullivan 2005, 31–3, 42, 55); and between undated burials 5 and 6 and firepit I, which may have cut them (M. O'Sullivan 2005, 36 and 43). Of the 17 perimeter cremations, 11 have provided radiocarbon dates (Table 12.12).

A model which incorporates the radiocarbon dates and stratigraphic sequence described above has very poor agreement ($A_{overall}$=0.0%). This is accounted for by the anomalously young ages reported by the Dublin laboratory in the late 1950s and by surprisingly recent dates for samples from cists I and II (*GrA-17274* and *sample 44*). These results have poor agreement with the interpretation that the cists pre-date the raising of the cairn, and the samples appear to have been introduced from the deposits in the chamber, through gaps between the orthostats (M. O'Sullivan 2005, figs 70–1). This interpretation has been included in the model.

The overall structure of the model for the Neolithic use of the passage tomb of the Mound of the Hostages at Tara is shown in Fig. 12.47, with the components relating to the chamber and the cairn in Figs 12.48–9 respectively. This model suggests that the chamber and cists were constructed in *3295–3140 cal BC* (*95% probability*; Fig. 12.48: *erect orthostats/cists*), probably in *3250–3170 cal BC* (*68% probability*). The cairn was constructed in *3255–3120 cal BC* (*95% probability*; Fig. 12.49: *build cairn*), probably in *3210–3145 cal BC* (*68% probability*). The main phase of Neolithic burial ended in *2875–2790 cal BC* (*95% probability*; Fig. 12.47: *end Neolithic Tara*), probably in *2865–2825 cal BC* (*68% probability*). Pre-cairn activity occurred in the mid-fourth millennium cal BC (Fig. 12.49). Only the pre-cairn ditch has sufficient measurements to enable a formal estimate of its date. This suggests that the ditch may have been infilling by *3325–3150 cal BC* (*95% probability*; Fig. 12.49: *pre-cairn ditch*), probably by *3280–3260 cal BC* (*10% probability*) or *3255–3175 cal BC* (*58% probability*).

The model for the chronology of the Neolithic use of the Mound of the Hostages presented here is just one of a range of possible interpretations of what is a complex structural sequence. One alternative, for example, would be that the perimeter deposits were made to define this special place before the cairn was built, but possibly around the same time the tomb and cists were constructed. Human remains were introduced into the tomb and cists over time, and at some later stage the cairn and mound were constructed (M. O'Sullivan 2005, 222). In support of this view, the occurrence of cremated bone in the orthostat trench and of unburnt human bone on the surface underneath the cairn suggests that the construction of the cairn did not precede the Neolithic burial phase. In this case, the perimeter burials would pre-date the cairn and mound. Further discussion will be presented elsewhere (Bayliss and O'Sullivan forthcoming; Smyth forthcoming).

At Carrowmore, 37 samples have been measured from contexts related to passage tombs, one on human bone, five on short-life charcoal and the remainder on charcoal for which identifications are not available (Burenhult 1980, 114–5; 1984, 128–32; 2001; 2003; Håkansson 1981). Most of the more recently obtained results are available only with brief, generalised contextual information (Table 12.12; Burenhult 2001; 2003). Fuller contextual information, partly due to reassessment by Stefan Bergh (1995), is available from the first phase of work at Carrowmore 4 (Table 12.12: Lu-1750, -1840); from Carrowmore 7 (Table 12.12: Lu-1441); and from Carrowmore 27 (Table 12.12: Lu-1698, -1808, -1810); as well as from more recent work at Carrowmore 51, for which a detailed interim report is available (Burenhult 1998). The plans show that the samples were from single findspots (e.g. Burenhult 1980, fig. 27). The available contextual information is summarised in Table 12.12. The model shown in Fig. 12.50 treats all the unidentified charcoal samples as *termini post quos* for their contexts and treats samples attributed to tomb use by Göran Burenhult (2001; 2003) as coming from post-construction contexts. Given the limited availability of detailed contextual information, the models for the chronology of the Carrowmore tombs presented here are of necessity highly provisional. In contrast to our interpretation of these dates as *termini post quos* for the final Neolithic use of these monuments, Alison Sheridan (e.g. 2003a; 2003b) interprets the charcoal dates from the smaller, simpler tombs as showing them to be earlier than the large, central tomb (51), starting *c.* 4000 cal BC and echoing the forms of early Breton monuments. It is worth noting, however, that where finds have been recovered (such as from Carrowmore 4, 7 and 27), they are of very similar style to those in other Irish passage tombs, including Carrowkeel pottery and antler pins. It has been argued (e.g. Sheridan 2003a) that these represent re-use of sites during the development of the cemetery and the passage tomb tradition over the fourth millennium cal BC. However, given the number of passage tombs that have been excavated, the lack of demonstrably early Neolithic material in any of them makes it difficult to sustain the argument that all the middle Neolithic cultural material in them was inserted following the clearing out of earlier deposits. The antler pins are currently the subject of an AMS dating programme by Robert Hensey of the National University of Ireland, Galway.

In Carrowmore 4, there was more than one constructional phase, of which there are several possible interpretations. A central passage and chamber (known as the central cist) were surrounded and possibly blocked by two concentric circular stone settings, the outer of which incorporated two small cists (A and B). These features were covered by a cairn with a substantial kerb. One measurement (Fig. 12.50:

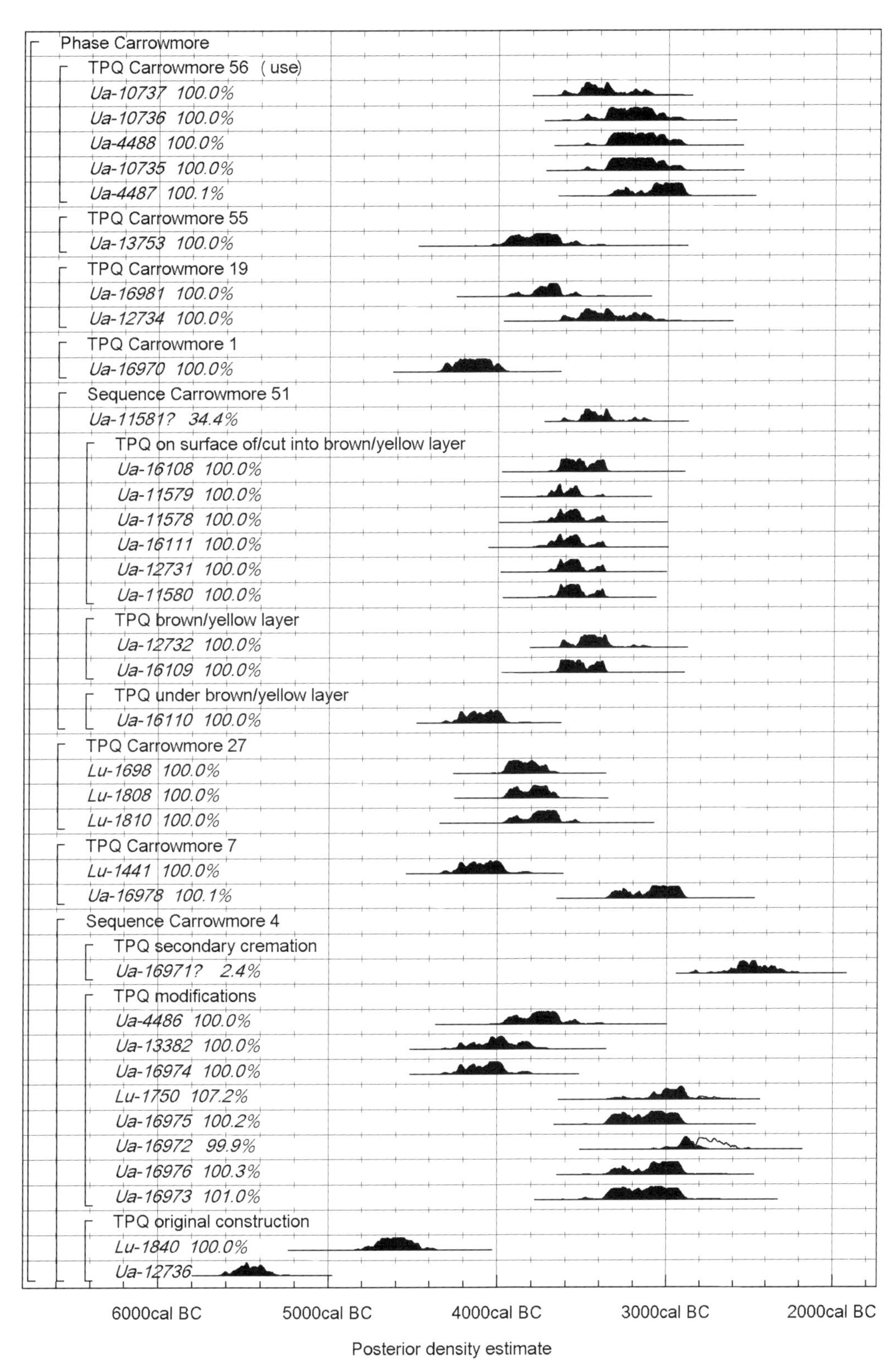

Fig. 12.50. Carrowmore. Probability distributions of dates from passage tombs. The format is identical to that of Fig. 12.6. The overall structure of this model is shown in Fig. 12.45 and its other components in Figs 12.46–9.

Lu-1840) provides a *terminus post quem* for the chamber; a second (Fig. 12.50: *Ua-12736*) may do the same. Of the remainder, *Lu-1750* provides a *terminus post quem* for the piling of a second, larger mass of stone packing around the chamber, and *Ua-4486*, *-13382*, and *-16972–6* all seem to be *termini post quos* for this or other modifications to the monument (Fig. 12.50). *Ua-4486* consisted of short-life charcoal, although the taphonomy of this sample is not clear. Ua-16971 provides a *terminus post quem* for a secondary cremation but is excluded from the model as it does not appear to relate to the main Neolithic use of the tomb.

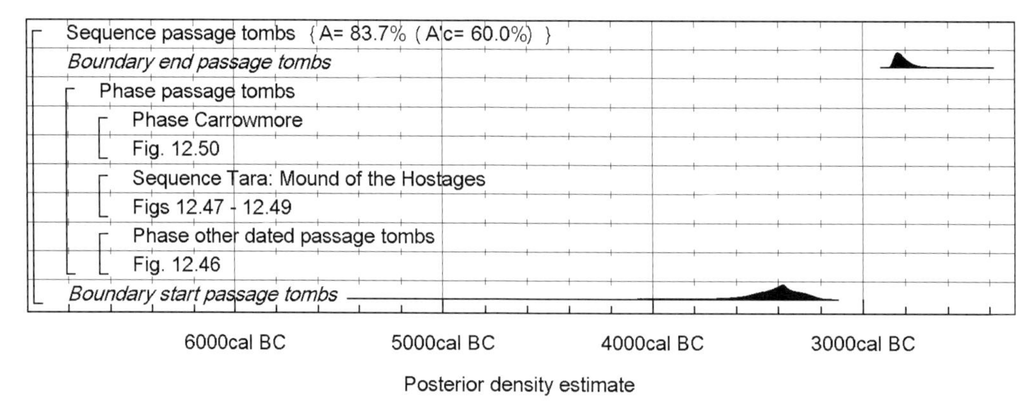

Fig. 12.51. Passage tombs. Overall structure of the alternative chronological model. The structures of the component sections of this model are shown in detail in Figs 12.46–50, with the modifications described in the text (although the posterior density estimates shown on these figures are not those relating to this model). The format is identical to that of Fig. 12.6. The large square brackets down the left-hand side of Figs 12.51 and 12.46–50 (with the modifications described in the text), along with the OxCal keywords, define the overall model exactly.

In Carrowmore 7, a bulk sample (Fig. 12.50; Table 12.12: *Lu-1441*) came from more than one context (Bergh 1995, 104), some of it from a posthole at the centre of the chamber from which the chamber was thought to have been laid out (Burenhult 1980, 21, photo 8, figs 5–8). The feature's relation to the chamber is questioned by Caulfield (1983, 207–8), on the grounds that it was sealed by a layer covering the chamber floor, at a level where no cremations were found, and may have been contemporary with postholes and concentrations of shells below and extending beyond the tomb. In either case, it provides a *terminus post quem* for the deposition of the 'culture layer' on the chamber floor. The context of a more recently measured sample of charcoal from the tomb (Fig. 12.50; Table 12.12: *Ua-16978*) remains unknown. In these circumstances, this only provides a *terminus post quem* for the end of use of the monument.

In Carrowmore 27 (Fig. 12.50), charcoal samples from three adjacent findspots, in the lower part of the stone packing between the central chamber and the stone circle intermediate between it and the outer kerb (Burenhult 1980, fig. 20) provide *termini post quos* for the construction of this part of the structure (Fig. 12.50: *Lu-1698, Lu-1808, Lu-1810*).

Carrowmore 51 (Listoghil), by far the largest of the passage tombs in the complex, was excavated in 1996–8 (Burenhult 1998). Before the tomb was built, a brown-yellow layer of morainic material appears to have been spread across the site. Within it were burnt areas and artefacts. One sample (Fig. 12.50: *Ua-16110*) lay beneath this layer, and provides a *terminus post quem* for its deposition. Seven samples came from within this layer (*Ua-12732* and *-16109*) or from its surface (*Ua-11580, -16111, -11579, -11578* and *-12731*, the last forming part of a burnt area). Charcoal from a stone-packed pit, structure VI, cut into this layer immediately outside the chamber, is dated by *Ua-16108*. All these samples probably provide *termini post quos* for construction. Caution, however, is in order, since a posthole also close to the chamber and cut into the same layer is dated by Ua-16107, again on unidentified charcoal, to the first millennium cal BC (Table 12.12). An unstratified human skull fragment with cutmarks found under the modern turf close to the chamber is dated by Ua-11581 to 3630–3120 cal BC (95% confidence); we have not included this in the model, because of the uncertainty over its derivation. A further charcoal sample from the stone cairn, just outside the north corner of the central chamber, is dated to the first millennium AD by Ua-12733 (Table 12.12). There was obviously disturbance in the area around the chamber, further evidenced by artefacts of later type (Burenhult 1998, 6–8).

In Carrowmore 1, a single charcoal sample provides a *terminus post quem* for one stage or another of construction (Fig. 12.50: *Ua-16970*). Two measurements (Fig. 12.50: *Ua-16981, -12734*) from unidentified charcoal samples described as dating the use of Carrowmore 19 (Burenhult 2001, 22) provide *termini post quos* for the end of its use. A similar sample (*Ua-13753*) provides a *terminus post quem* for the final use of Carrowmore 55.

Five radiocarbon dates are available on short-life charcoal from Carrowmore 56 (Fig. 12.50: Table 12.12: *Ua-10735–7, -4487–8*). Again, these are described only as deriving from the use of the tomb (Burenhult 2001, 29) and so at this stage of analysis can only be interpreted as providing *termini post quos* for the final use of the monument. It should be noted, however, that these measurements are statistically consistent (T'=5.7; $T'(5\%)$=9.5; ν=4) and so in fact they may provide accurate dates for the use of this monument.

The model for the date of the construction and primary Neolithic use of passage tombs in Ireland is shown in Figs 12.45–50. The form of this model is discussed above. It suggests that passage tombs in Ireland were first constructed in *5275–3160 cal BC* (*95% probability*; Fig. 12.45: *start passage tombs*), probably in *4005–3190 cal BC* (*68% probability*)! The first use of passage tombs ended in *2870–2715 cal BC* (*95% probability*; Fig. 12.45: *end passage tombs*), probably in *2855–2785 cal BC* (*68% probability*). This estimate for the time when the primary

Neolithic use of passage tombs ceased may be reasonably reliable, since it depends not only on the dated burials from Tara, but also on a large number of *termini post quos* from a range of other sites. Our estimate for the time when passage tombs were first constructed in Ireland, however, is obviously unsatisfactory as the Mound of the Hostages at Tara is the only site which has dates that are definitely not *termini post quos*. The existing *termini post quos* for tomb construction, however, seem more compatible with a currency for the passage tombs of Ireland falling in the second half of the fourth millennium cal BC (Figs 12.46 and 12.50). It is to be hoped that further research on surviving archives will enhance this dataset in the near future.[16]

Nonetheless, in an attempt to explore how limited our understanding of the chronology of Irish passage tombs is, given the data currently available, we have constructed a second model. In this we have adopted the most charitable interpretations of the taphonomy of the dated samples. In this alternative model, the following samples have been rehabilitated and are included as dating the use of the relevant tomb rather than as *termini post quos* for final use. GrN-5462-C and GrN-5463 from Newgrange are interpreted as deriving from activity contemporary with the construction of the tomb; Ua-11581 from Carrowmore 51 is interpreted as deriving from the use of the chamber (Burenhult 1998, 6, 17–19); and Ua-10735–7 and Ua-4487–8 from Carrowmore 56 are interpreted as relating to the use of the monument. The overall form of this alternative model is that shown in Fig. 12.51.

In this second model, we estimate that passage tombs began to be constructed in *3640–3205 cal BC* (*95% probability*; Fig. 12.51: *start passage tombs*), probably in *3495–3285 cal BC* (*68% probability*). Their first use ended in *2870–2735 cal BC* (*95% probability*; Fig. 12.51: *end passage tombs*), probably in *2860–2795 cal BC* (*68% probability*). This analysis demonstrates the limitations of our current understanding of the chronology of passage tombs in Ireland. Further samples of short-life material unequivocally associated with the primary use of these monuments are urgently required. Our estimates for when passage tombs were first built are extremely tentative at this stage, although a date within the third quarter of the fourth millennium cal BC is most plausible at present. In contrast, our estimates for when the initial use of these tombs ended are more robust. Both models suggest that this ending fell in the second half of the 29th century cal BC or a decade or two later.

Other fourth millennium cal BC activity

Further radiocarbon dates which fall in the fourth millennium cal BC have been obtained on archaeological material from Ireland. These are not, however, associated with diagnostically Neolithic material. They are therefore not included in the models for the chronology of the early Neolithic in Ireland presented below, although they undoubtedly reflect other aspects of contemporary life and are discussed here for completeness.

One of two burials from Kilgreany Cave, Co. Waterford, dated by *Pta-2644*, already noted above, lay some 7 m away from plain Carinated Bowl sherds, to which it may relate, although this is not demonstrable (Dowd 2002, 82, fig. 2b). The second, stratified above the first and dated by *BM-135* (Table 12.13), was tightly flexed, but not associated with any diagnostic cultural material (Fig. 12.52). Two further burials at the same sort of level were close to a stone axehead fragment, but also not directly associated with diagnostic material. A third individual from the cave has also been dated (GrA-21499; Table 12.13). The Kilgreany burials form part of a tradition of burial and deposition of human bone in caves in Neolithic Ireland which shows overlap in practice and material with other funerary traditions. A series of dates for other articulated burials and disarticulated human bone from caves span the fourth millennium cal BC, concentrated in the second and third quarters (Fig 12.52, and see note 11; Dowd 2008). The $\delta^{13}C$ values from these burials suggest that the dated individuals consumed a diet largely based on terrestrial resources, although it is debatable whether such signatures imply that the individuals concerned can be meaningfully classed as Neolithic (see Chapter 11.4). A crouched but unassociated inhumation was found in the south part of the midden at Dalkey Island, Co. Dublin (already discussed above) and dated by BM-78 (recalculated) to the end of the fourth millennium cal BC (Fig. 12.52; Brindley and Lanting 1990).

Fragments of a waterlogged oak logboat were dredged from the River Bann at Ballynagowan, Co. Armagh, in 1993 (Fry 2000, 106). The largest fragment, a 1.57m length of a floor rising to one of the original ends was dated by GrN-20550 (Fig. 12.52) to the fourth millennium cal BC (Lanting and Brindley 1996, 86). Further logboats with fourth-millennium dates have been dated from Rossfad, Co. Fermanagh, Ballylig, Co. Antrim, and Strangford Lough, Co. Down (Table 12.13; Fig. 12.52; O'Sullivan and Breen 2007, 74–8). Logboats are not, however, diagnostic of Neolithic material culture as Mesolithic examples are known from Europe (Lanting and Brindley 1996, 92, with references), including an example from Brookend, Co. Tyrone which has been dated to 5490–5350 cal BC (UB-4066; 6457±35BP; Fry 2000, 116; O'Sullivan and Breen 2007, 54–5).

At Cloghaclocka, Co. Limerick, one of three birch planks, thought to form the base of a trough in a damaged *fulacht fiadh*, was dated by GrN-15404 to the fourth millennium cal BC (Fig. 12.52; Table 12.13). This has been considered a surprisingly early date for a burnt mound (Brindley *et al.* 1990, 27); perhaps this is re-used bog birch.

12.4 Discussion

Dating the introduction of the Neolithic into Ireland

A wide range of forms of early Neolithic activity in Ireland that have scientific dates have now been discussed, along with dates from Linkardstown burials and passage tombs,

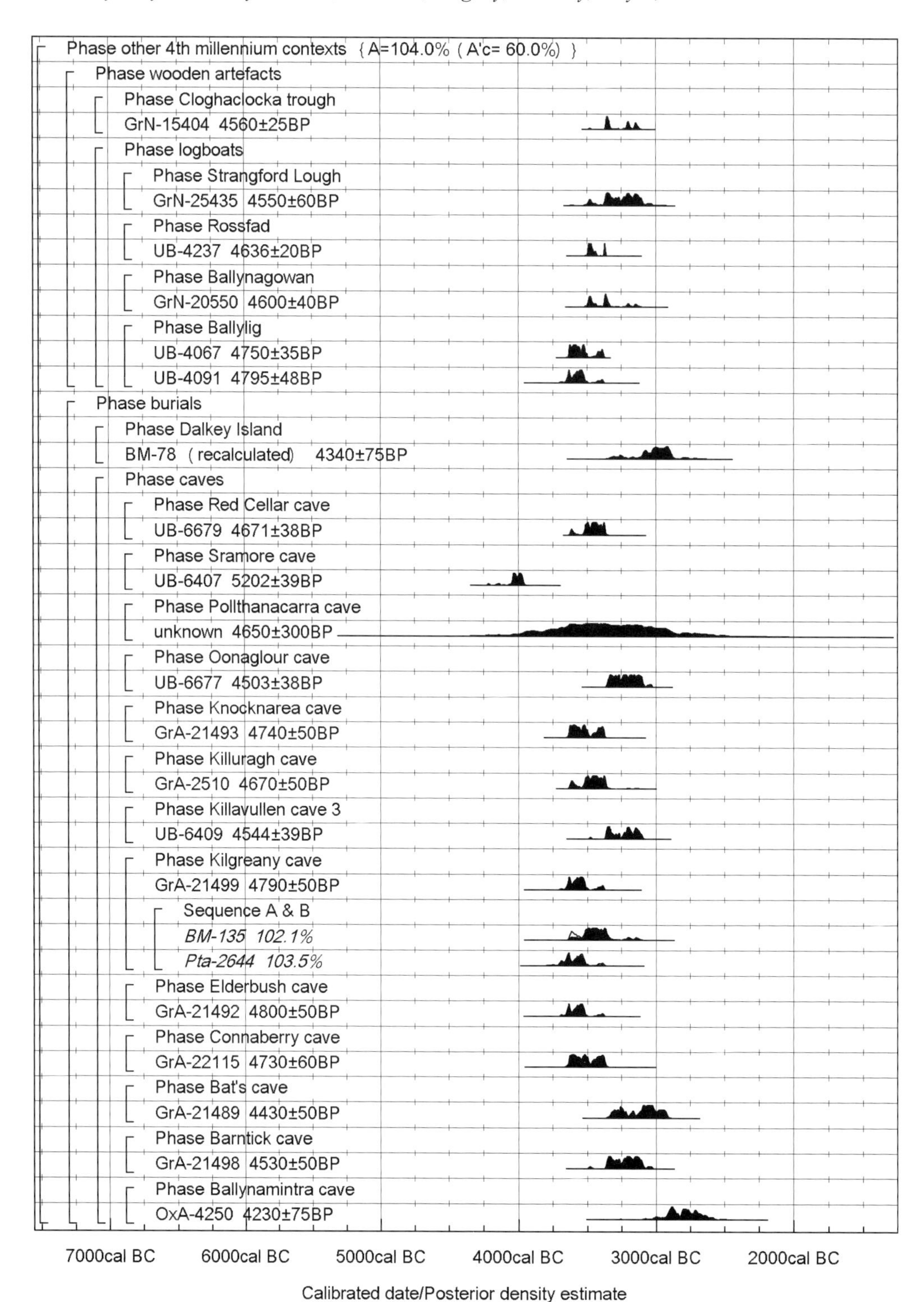

Fig. 12.52. Fourth millennium cal BC dates for contexts without diagnostic artefacts. Probability distributions of dates. Dates with laboratory numbers in normal type have been calibrated only (Stuiver and Reimer 1993).

the dated sample of which it is argued provides *termini ante quos* for the end of the early Neolithic period. It is now time to combine these elements into different models which estimate the date when the Neolithic came to Ireland. The purpose of these models is to put the Donegore and Magheraboy enclosures into context, and so the dates from those sites are not included in the models.

The first decision concerns which forms of activity to include in the early Neolithic period. The rectangular timber houses and other occupation associated with early Carinated Bowl pottery are certainly to be included. It has also often been suggested that portal tombs, court tombs, and other related monuments should fall in this period (Cooney 2000a), as might the Céide Fields and fields on Valencia Island (Caulfield 1978; 1983; Cooney 2000a). This range could be characterised as representing much of the character of a Carinated Bowl Neolithic tradition in Ireland (Cooney 2007a; Sheridan 2007a). Other forms of

Table 12.13. *Radiocarbon dates for other fourth millennium cal BC activity in Ireland.*

Laboratory number	Sample reference	Material	Context	Radiocarbon age (BP)	$\delta^{13}C$ (‰)	Calibrated date range (cal BC) (95% confidence)
Castlefarm, Co. Kildare						
OxA-7955		*Fraxinus* charcoal	F2. Bowl-shaped pit measuring 0.60 m x 0.40 m x 0.20 m deep. One of 15 charcoal-rich features within, cutting, and outside three concentric ditches, the outermost of which enclosed an area with an estimated diameter of 100 m. Little is known of any of these features because excavation was restricted to areas that would be destroyed by development. F2 was the only charcoal-rich features excavated and it is unclear whether it was one of those which cut the ditches. Small fragments of burnt bone were observed in the surfaces of other charcoal-rich features	5040±45		3970–3700
Newtown, Co. Meath						
UB-3568		Charcoal (unidentified)	Pit (Monk 2000, 76) uncertain if the same pit as source of UB-3569	4996±39	−26.2	3950–3660
UB-3569		Charcoal (unidentified)	Pit (Monk 2000, 76) uncertain if the same pit as source of UB-3568	5059±31	−26.4	3960–3770
Gortaroe, Co. Mayo						
GrN-27801	II 165-26	*Quercus* charcoal	External pit (C26) in scatter 10 m SE of house (Richard Gillespie pers. comm.)	4865±35	−25.2	
GrN-27798	II 1-2	*Corylus* charcoal	External pit with stone lining (C2), NE of house (Richard Gillespie pers. comm.)	4040±30	−26.5	2840–2470
Ballygalley, Co. Antrim, discrete features						
UB-3210		Charcoal (unidentified)	Site 1, tr D1, sq 12, hearth-pit 1002/2	5151±119		4310–3660
UB-3326		Charcoal (unidentified)	Site 1, main trench, sq K5, pit 1990	5046±101	−26.1	4050–3640
UB-3363		Charcoal (unidentified)	Site 1, main trench, sq K-M 6-7, pit 1026	5469±69	−26.3	4460–4170
UB-3374		Charcoal (unidentified)	Site 1, main trench, sq J9-10, pit 1030	5002±92	−26.4	3980–3630
UB-4818		Charcoal (unidentified)	Site 1, tr U, sq U17-18, pit 1107	4929±50	−26.3	3900–3630
UB-4839		Charcoal (unidentified)	Site 1, sq H-J 7-9, pit 1052	4493±60	−26.3	3370–2920
UB-4840		Charcoal (unidentified)	Site 1, sq AV-AT, 10- , cobbles 1164/1	4631±44	−27.0	3620–3340
UB-3368		Charcoal (unidentified)	Site 2, tr X, sq 13-14, pit 2002	4821±67	−26.8	3710–3370
UB-3925		Charcoal (unidentified)	Site 2, sq A3, deposit 202	5082±91	−26.3	4050–3650
UB-3926		*Pinus sylvestris* charcoal	Site 2 tr W sq 13-14, pit 2020/2	4881±62	−25.8	3970–3520
UB-4812		Charcoal (unidentified)	Site 2, tr W1, sq 4-5, 9-10, pit 2043	4563±41	−26.8	3500–3100
UB-4813		Charcoal (unidentified)	Site 2, sq K8, pit 2339	4690±42	−26.4	3640–3360
UB-4816		Charcoal (unidentified)	Site 2, sq L15–16, slot 2501	4876±56	−26.4	3780–3530
UB-4819		Charcoal (unidentified)	Site 2, sq M11–12, pit 2309	4684±58	−26.2	3650–3350
UB-4821		Charcoal (unidentified)	Site 2, tr S, sq P7–8, pit 2035	4575±59	−26.7	3520–3090
UB-4841		Charcoal (unidentified)	Site 2, tr T, sqs 2–5, pit 2044	4756±47	−26.1	3650–3370
UB-4843		Charcoal (unidentified)	Site 2, sq L9, pit 2347	4698±42	−25.3	3640–3360
Ballynagilly, Co. Tyrone, discrete features						
UB-304	L68.1, 68.2, 68.3	Charcoal (unidentified)	F (L) 211 layer 5b. Basal layer of large pit, 20 m E of house, without contents but sealed by layer containing Neolithic artefacts (A. Smith *et al.* 1971)	5370±85		4360–3980
UB-559	L67.14	Charcoal (unidentified)	F135a. Hearth overlying pit F135 (Arthur ApSimon pers. comm.)	5500±85	−23.2	4500–4170
UB-307	BG69 M3836; F46 51 54 53 + 67 16	Charcoal (unidentified)	Pit F (M) 46. In base of gully overlain by sterile sand and overlain by Beaker occupation material (A. Smith *et al.* 1971)	5640±90		4710–4330
UB-551	BG68 Ch3 + BG67 Ch25	Charcoal (unidentified)	F (M) 67. 'Cooking pit' (Arthur ApSimon pers. comm.)	5290±50	−25.3	4320–3970
Cloghaclocka, Co. Limerick						
GrN-15404	2/40/1	*Betula,* part of 1 of 3 waterlogged planks	Lying parallel to each other in damaged *fulacht fiadh*, probably base of trough (Gowen 1988, 133). Brindley *et al.* consider C_v value of 65.5% too high for wood though suggestive of charcoal and suspect that samples may have been confused (1990, 27)	4560±25	−27.3	3370–3120

Laboratory number	Sample reference	Material	Context	Radiocarbon age (BP)	$\delta^{13}C$ (‰)	Calibrated date range (cal BC) (95% confidence)
Ballynagowan, Co. Armagh						
GrN-20550		*Quercus* sp. wood from waterlogged logboat	Dredged from river Bann 1993 (Lanting and Brindley 1996; Fry 2000, 50)	4600±40	−24.1	3500–3130
Rossfad, Co. Fermanagh						
UB-4237		Unidentified waterlogged wood from incomplete logboat	Observed 1972 but remaining *in situ*, at least 8.65 m long with a beam 0.65-0.75 m wide (Fry 2000, 50)	4636±20	−25.8	3500–3360
Strangford Lough, Co. Down						
GrN-25435		Unidentified waterlogged wood from logboat	Substantially complete logboat recovered from the foreshore at Greyabbey Bay (McErlean *et al.* 2002, 404–6; Forsythe and Gregory 2007)	4550±60	−26.6	3500–3020
Ballylig, Co. Antrim						
UB-4607		*Quercus* sp. wood from waterlogged logboat	Largely complete oak logboat, 5.4 m long, 0.65 m wide, and 0.2 m high, which emerged from a layer of peat underlying marine mud on the edge of Larne Lough in 1996 (Fry 2000, 117)	4750±35	−24.2	3640–3370
UB-4091		*Quercus* sp. wood from waterlogged logboat	Fragmentary oak logboat which emerged from a layer of peat underlying marine mud on the edge of Larne Lough in 1996 (Fry 2000, 118)	4795±48	−24.1	3660–3380
Dalkey Island, Co. Dublin						
BM-78 (recalculated)	Burial 2	Human. Bone	Unprotected crouched inhumation in south midden (D. Liversage 1968, 103–4). Recalculated and corrected by Brindley and Lanting (1990)	4340±75		3330–2870
Ballynamintra Cave, Co. Waterford						
OxA-4250	Sample 61	Human. radius	Cave containing Pleistocene and later fauna and a few human bones (Woodman *et al.* 1997)	4230±75	−22.5	3020–2580
Barntick Cave, Co. Clare						
GrA-21498		Human. Adult male mandible	The Barntick, Bats' and Elderbush Caves formed part of a single complex, investigated 1902–4. Deposits seem to have been mixed, incorporating both early Holocene and recent fauna, artefacts ranging from prehistoric to medieval in date, and numerous disarticulated human bones (Scharff *et al.* 1906; Woodman *et al.* 1997; Dowd 2008)	4530±50	−21.6	3490–3020
Bats' Cave, Newhall, Co. Clare						
Gr-21489		Human. Scapula of child <10 yr	As GrA- 21498	4430±50	−21.8	3350–2910
Connaberry Cave, Co. Cork						
GrA-22115		Human. Adult R maxilla	Small chambered cavern with a thin floor deposit containing recent fauna, some human bone fragments and a 16th century coin (Gwynn *et al.* 1942, 371; Coleman 1947, 72; Dowd 2008)	4730±60	−22.1	3650–3360
Elderbush Cave, Newhall, Co. Clare						
GrA-21492		Human. Adult pelvis	As GrA- 21498	4800±50	−21.3	3660–3380
Kilgreany Cave, Co. Waterford						
BM-135	Kilgreany A	Human. Humerus and ribs of middle-aged woman. Standard acid pretreatment	Placed tightly flexed on charcoal-rich deposit (C7) with large stone slab on L shoulder. Two further relatively intact burials at same horizon, close to stone axehead fragment. Stratified above Pta-2644 and separated from it by stalagmite (Dowd 2002, 83; Molleson 1986; Barker and Mackey 1968)	4660±75		3640–3120
Pta-2644	Kilgreany B	Human. R femur from adult male	Placed on charcoal-rich deposit (C9), with large number of stones over skull and upper thorax. Stratified below BM-135 and separated from it by stalagmite (Dowd 2002, 82; Molleson 1986)	4820±60		3710–3380

Laboratory number	Sample reference	Material	Context	Radiocarbon age (BP)	$\delta^{13}C$ (‰)	Calibrated date range (cal BC) (95% confidence)
GrA-21499	Kilgreany 3+	Human. Adult ?male mandible	Publication does not specify context (Dowd 2008)	4790±50	−21.8	3660–3370
Killavullen Cave 3, Ballymacmoy, Co. Cork						
UB-6409		Human. Adult ?female R ilium	One of a group of caves excavated in 1934. No published report (Coleman 1947, 72; Dowd 2008)	4544±39	−22.7*	3490–3090
Killuragh Cave, Co. Limerick						
GrA-2510		Human. Metacarpal	Cave containing Late Glacial and recent fauna, Mesolithic and Neolithic artefacts, Mesolithic and Neolithic human remains (Woodman 1997; Dowd 2008)	4670±50	−22.4	3640–3350
Knocknarea Cave, Co. Sligo						
GrA-21493		Human. Occipital	Bone from floor of unexcavated cave (Dowd 2008, 307)	4740±50	−22.1	3650–3370
Oonaglour Cave, Bridgequarter, Co. Waterford						
UB-6677		Human. Adult L radius	Cave containing prehistoric and medieval artefacts (Dowd 2008)	4503±38	−21.0*	3370–3020
Pollthanacarra Cave, Legg, Co. Fermanagh						
Unknown		Human. Otherwise unknown	Swallowhole containing human remains with those of cattle, caprines, pigs, canids, red deer and hare (Dowd 2008)	4650±300		4050–2570
Red Cellar Cave, Knockfennel, Co. Limerick						
UB-6679		Human. Adult, R talus	Small fissure above Lough Gur, containing Late Glacial fauna (Woodman *et al.* 1997; Dowd 2008)	4671±38	−21.9*	3630–3360
Sramore Cave, Co. Leitrim						
UB-6407		Human. Adult ?male R femur	Bone from floor of unexcavated cave (Dowd 2008, 307)	5202±39	−20.1*	4150–3950

* $\delta^{13}C$ value measured by AMS at the Oxford Radiocarbon Accelerator Unit.

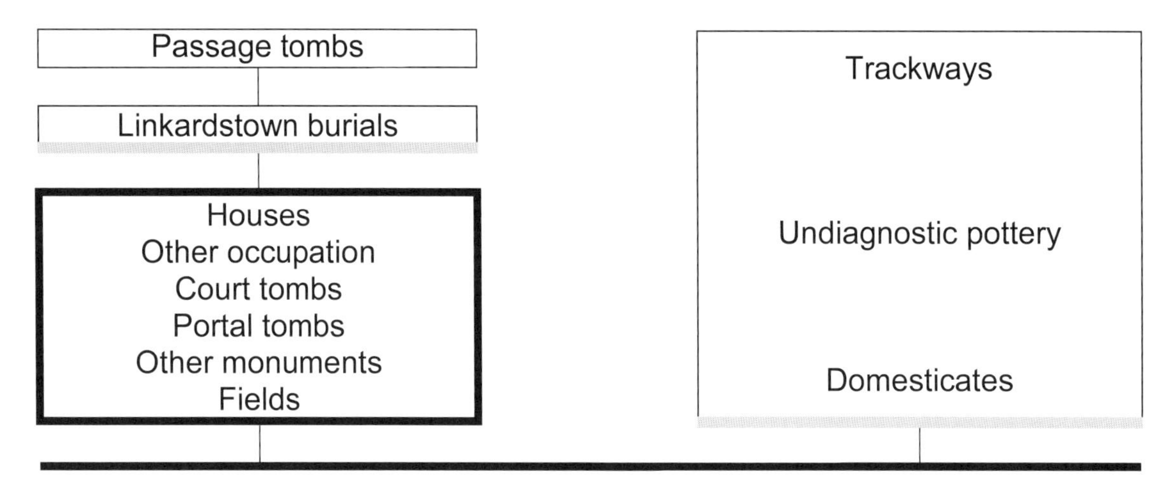

*Fig. 12.53. Model 1 of the early and middle Neolithic in Ireland. Outline of the overall model. The components of this model are the rectangular houses (Figs 12.22–7), other occupation (Fig. 12.30), portal tombs (Poulnabrone)(Fig. 12.31), court tombs (Figs 12.32–4), other monuments (Fig. 12.35), Linkardstown burials (Fig. 12.44) and passage tombs (Figs 12.45–50) – all without their surrounding uniform distributions. The trackway, undiagnostic pottery, and domesticate components are as shown in Figs 12.41–2. Three distributions for fields have been included from the models shown in Fig. 12.37 (*start clearance *and* start regeneration*) and Fig. 12.40 (*I-14206*). The heavy black line denotes the boundary 'start Neolithic', the heavy black box a uniform phase, and the grey lines* termini ante quos.

activity can be argued to be early Neolithic, but continue after the end of the period. These include trackways, activity associated with 'undiagnostic' forms of pottery, and plants and animals that were introduced into the island, notably cereals, cattle and sheep.

The second decision is technical. As already emphasised many times in this volume, in order to counteract the statistical scatter on a group of radiocarbon dates it is necessary to impose a distribution on the archaeological period under consideration. We have chosen to use a uniform distribution as this has been shown, both theoretically and empirically, to be 'uninformative' (Buck *et al.* 1992; Bayliss *et al.* 2007a). This means that the results of a model are relatively insensitive to a violation of this assumption.

The structure of the first model (model 1) is shown in Fig. 12.53. We have used a uniform distribution for the early Neolithic period in Ireland, shown as a box within the thick black line. Dates from trackways, 'undiagnostic' pottery and domesticates are used as *termini ante quos* for the start of the Irish Neolithic, and the sequence of Linkardstown and passage tombs has been used as a *terminus ante quem* for the end of the early Neolithic period in Ireland: indicated by the thick grey lines on the right and upper-left respectively of Fig. 12.53. The components of this model are rectangular houses (Figs 12.22–7), other occupation (Fig. 12.30), portal tombs (Poulnabrone) (Fig. 12.31), court tombs (Figs 12.32–4), other monuments (Fig. 12.35), Linkardstown burials (Fig. 12.44) and passage tombs (Figs 12.45–50) – all without their surrounding uniform distributions. The trackway, 'undiagnostic' pottery and domesticate components are as shown in Figs 12.41–2. Three distributions have been included here from the model shown in Fig. 12.37 (*start clearance* and *start regeneration*) and Fig. 12.40 (*I-14206*).

All versions of this model have extremely poor agreement ($A_{overall}$<0.5%): that is, versions which include or exclude dates on domesticates as diagnostically Neolithic activity, and models where Linkardstown burials and passage tombs are seen as sequential or overlapping periods of activity (see below). Examination of the indices of agreement for individual measurements included in this model suggests that this poor agreement arises because Parknabinnia and Primrose Grange continued in use until the middle Neolithic (as reflected in the artefacts from them). The fields may also have done so. The early measurement on cattle bone from Ferriter's Cove (OxA-3869) also has extremely poor individual agreement (A=0.6%). No graph is published for this model.

For this reason, a second model has been built (model 2). In this, houses and other occupation associated with Bowl pottery define the early Neolithic and form a uniformly distributed phase, shown as a box within the thick black line in Fig. 12.54. Portal tombs, court tombs and other related monuments, along with field systems, trackways, 'undiagnostic' pottery and domesticates provide *termini ante quos* for the start of the Irish Neolithic: indicated by the thick grey line on the lower right of Fig. 12.54. The sequence of Linkardstown burials and passage tombs again provides a *terminus ante quem* for the end of the early Neolithic: indicated by the thick grey line on the left of Fig. 12.54. The components of this model remain unaltered.

Model 2 also has poor overall agreement ($A_{overall}$=57.1% in the variant where Linkardstown burials and passage tombs are successive, and $A_{overall}$=56.6% when these traditions overlap). Examination of the indices of agreement suggests that this poor agreement arises almost entirely from the early date on a cattle bone from Ferriter's Cove (*OxA-3869*; A=0.5%). If this measurement is excluded from the model, the overall agreement goes up to 66.7% and

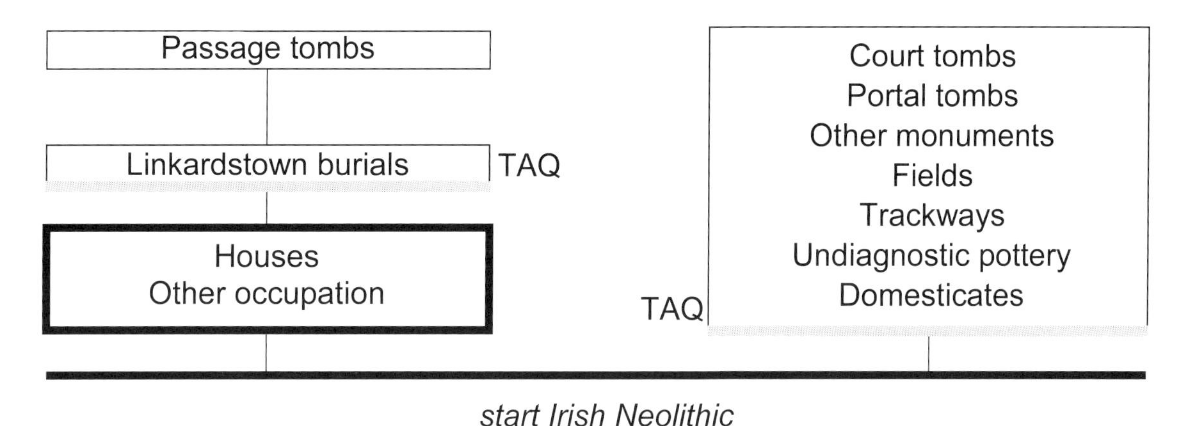

Fig. 12.54. Model 2 of the early and middle Neolithic in Ireland. Outline of an alternative overall model. The components of this model and the conventions used in the diagram are as Fig. 12.53.

66.2% respectively. However, we have seen above (Fig. 12.43) that OxA-3869 is compatible with the other dates from Ferriter's Cove. It seems special pleading, therefore, to exclude this measurement as inaccurate (although further dates from domestic fauna from Ferriter's Cove would be highly welcome). On this basis, we see no reason to accept domesticates *on their own*, without other diagnostic associations, as a sufficiently defining characteristic of the Neolithic (cf. Woodman *et al.* 1999, 144–51), and we therefore need to consider another variant of model 2, in which the dates on domestic fauna shown in Fig. 12.42 are not included in the analysis. These variants of model 2 without the domesticates and with Linkardstown burials and passage tombs as successive or overlapping phases have good overall agreement ($A_{overall}$=85.2% and 84.7% respectively). The estimates for the start of the Neolithic in Ireland for the three variants of model 2 (Fig. 12.54) where Linkardstown burials and passage tombs are successive are shown in Fig. 12.55: including (a) all the dates, (b) all the dates except for OxA-3869 from Ferriter's Cove, and (c) all the dates except those from domestic fauna. It is apparent that the results of the model are highly sensitive to the inclusion or exclusion of OxA-3869. In contrast, if this measurement is omitted, the inclusion or exclusion of the dates on other domestic fauna makes no appreciable difference. The early date from Ferriter's Cove is so radically different that either this single measurement must be appreciably inaccurate or the dated bone does not relate to wider processes of Neolithisation. Woodman and McCarthy (2003, 33) suggest that it may represent a situation where the cattle were little more than a food supplement to communities relying on marine resources but that eventually they may have had social consequences.

So, progress has been made in constructing a plausible chronological model for the introduction of the Neolithic to Ireland. Examination of the indices of agreement in alternative models has suggested that the use of court tombs, portal tombs, other related monuments and field systems continued into the middle Neolithic period, and cannot be seen as exclusively early Neolithic. This evidence also suggests that the early date on cattle from Ferriter's Cove (OxA-3869) is an extreme outlier, casting doubt on whether domesticates on their own may define the start of Neolithic practices in Ireland rather than contact with outside Neolithic communities. In contrast, all the models, whatever their other shortcomings, are in good agreement with a sequence that constrains Linkardstown burials to be later than houses and other occupation associated with diagnostic early Neolithic material, and Linkardstown burials to be earlier than passage tombs. Mathematically, this prior belief is highly informative, and so this good agreement renders the sequence inferred from associated material culture the more plausible. For these reasons, in the discussion from now on, the sequence between the end of the early Neolithic, Linkardstown burials and passage tombs remains constant. The dates on domesticates shown in Fig. 12.42 are also not included.

The form of the third model (model 3) is shown in Fig. 12.56. In this reading, houses and other occupation associated with diagnostic early Neolithic material are constrained to be earlier than Linkardstown burials and passage tombs, but all of these elements, along with court tombs, portal tombs, other related monuments, field systems, trackways and 'undiagnostic' pottery, form one uniformly distributed phase of activity which spans the early and middle Neolithic of Ireland. This is indicated on Fig. 12.56 by the box with a thick black line around it. This model has good overall agreement ($A_{overall}$=88.0%), so this interpretation of the data is plausible.

The estimates for when the Irish Neolithic began, derived from the variants of models 2 and 3 which do not include dates on domestic fauna, are shown in Fig. 12.57. According to model 2, Neolithic things and practices began in Ireland in *3750–3680 cal BC* (*95% probability*; Fig. 12.57: *start Irish Neolithic* (model 2)), probably in *3730–3695 cal BC* (*68% probability*). According to model 3, the Neolithic in Ireland started in *3850–3740 cal BC* (*95% probability*; Fig. 12.57: *start Irish Neolithic* (model 3)), probably in *3815–3760 cal BC* (*68% probability*). The difference between these two models relates basically to how we counteract the scatter on the radiocarbon dates. Model 2 postulates greater scatter, because a large

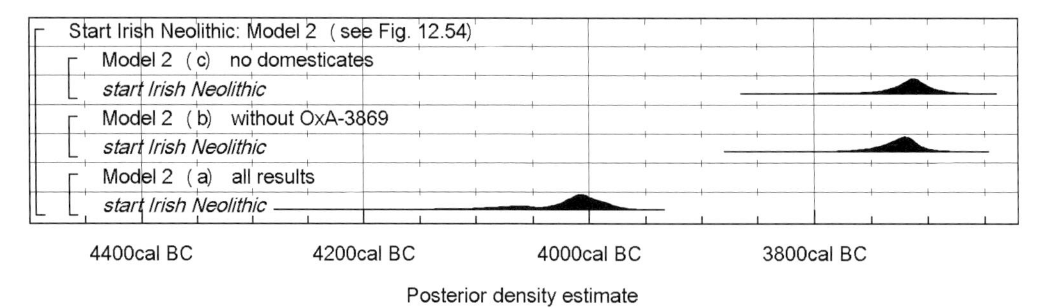

Fig. 12.55. The start of the Irish Neolithic. Posterior density estimates derived from three variants of model 2 (Fig. 12.54), (a) including all dates, (b) without OxA-3869 from Ferriter's Cove, and (c) without the domesticates shown in Fig. 12.42.

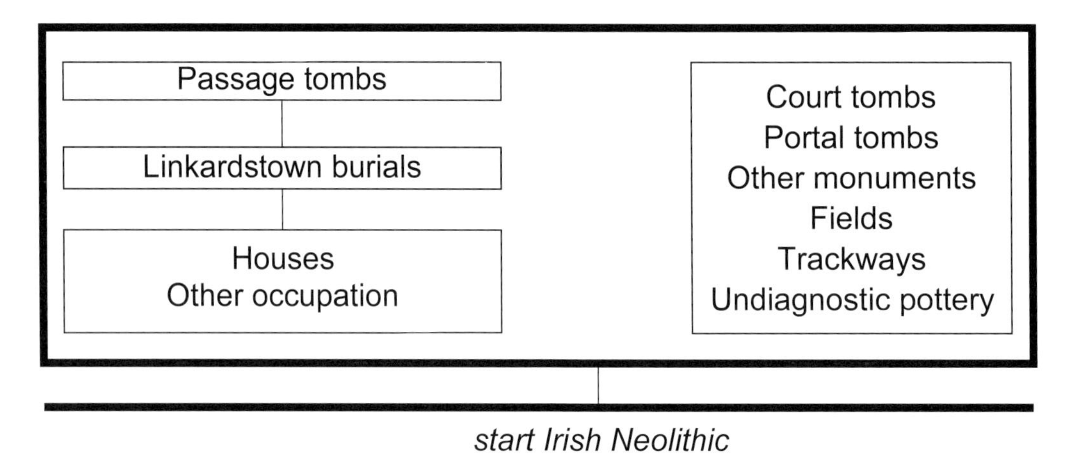

Fig. 12.56. Model 3 of the early and middle Neolithic in Ireland. Outline of another alternative overall model. The components of this model and the conventions used are as Fig. 12.53.

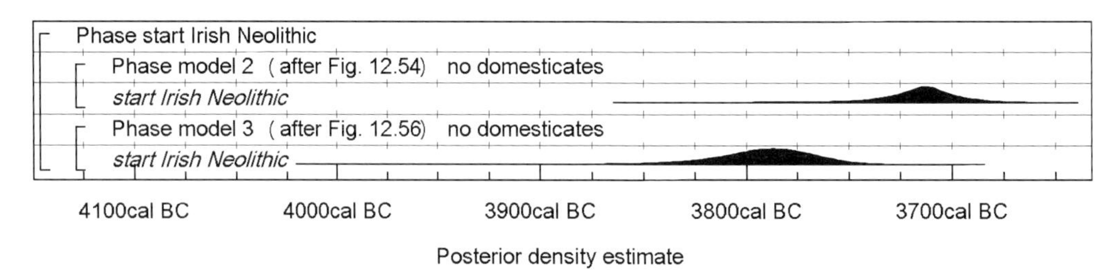

Fig. 12.57. The start of the Irish Neolithic. Posterior density estimates derived from model 2 (Fig. 12.54) and model 3 (Fig. 12.56), without the domesticates shown in Fig. 12.42.

number of dates are available over an extremely restricted chronological span. For this reason, the boundary estimates are more tightly constrained. In contrast, model 3 postulates proportionately less scatter and so these boundaries are pulled in less.

At this stage of research, it is not clear whether either of these models provides an accurate chronology for the introduction of Neolithic things and practices into Ireland. It is a concern that model 2 is biased by a disproportionate number of radiocarbon dates from rectangular houses, which provide more than half of the likelihoods in the uniform phase of early Neolithic activity in Ireland in this model. This could lead the model to over-estimate the scatter on the radiocarbon dates because of a large body of data from a restricted period within the overall phase of activity that is of interest, and thus to provide an estimate for the start of the Irish Neolithic that is too late. We have made no pretence, however, that our consideration of the chronology of the middle Neolithic in Ireland is comprehensive, and so its inclusion in the overall phase in model 3 may also introduce sampling bias, if later deposits are under-represented in our sample. In this case, the lack of a proportionate number of later dates would lead the model to under-estimate the actual statistical scatter at the start of the phase and provide an estimate for the start of the Irish Neolithic that is too early. It must be an urgent priority for Irish archaeology to obtain more dates on short-life samples associated with diagnostic early Neolithic material from contexts other than houses. This may resolve the disparity between the two models. In either case, on the basis of a single radiocarbon measurement on a cow from Kerry, it seems that domesticated fauna may have reached Ireland

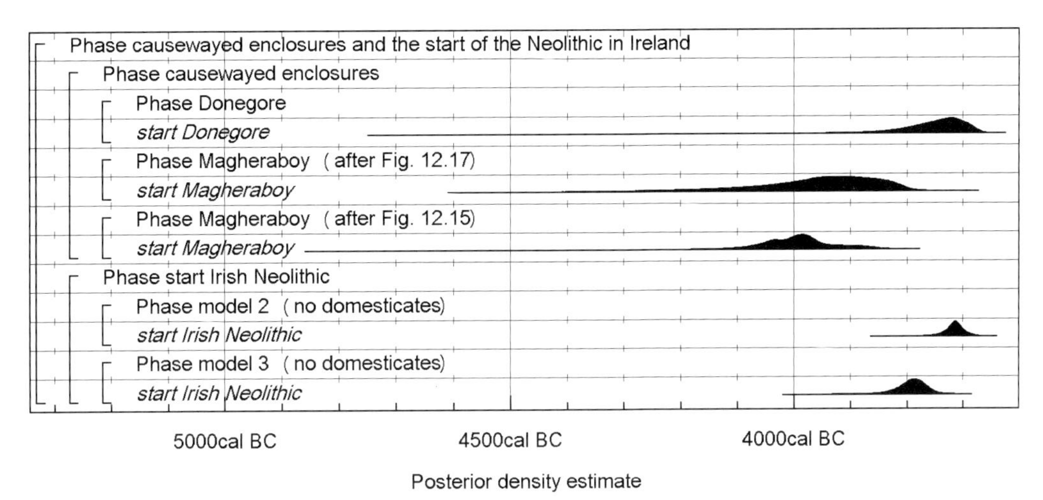

Fig. 12.58. Causewayed enclosures and the start of the Irish Neolithic. Posterior density estimates for the construction of Donegore (Figs 12.5–9) and Magheraboy (Fig. 12.15 and alternatively Fig. 12.17), and for the start of the Irish Neolithic, derived from model 2 (Fig. 12.54) and model 3 (Fig. 12.56), without the domesticates shown in Fig. 12.42.

sporadically for some centuries before Neolithic practices began.

The Magheraboy and Donegore enclosures in their early Neolithic context in Ireland

It is now time to consider the place of causewayed enclosures in the Irish Neolithic. The estimates for the start of the Neolithic in Ireland (models 2 and 3 discussed above) are shown on Fig. 12.58, along with our estimates for the dates when the enclosures at Donegore and Magheraboy were constructed.

It can be seen that the enclosure at Donegore was constructed within a century of the appearance of Neolithic material culture in Ireland. If model 3 is preferred, then enclosures may have appeared a few generations after the initial establishment of new practices. If, however, model 2 is preferred, then Donegore may form part of the first wave of the Neolithic, fitting in with the introduction of a 'Carinated Bowl Neolithic' tradition (Sheridan 2007a). The radiocarbon dates from this enclosure have good agreement with either interpretation. It should be noted again, however, that no short-life samples are available from the basal filling of this enclosure, and so a slightly earlier date is not out of the question.

According to the preferred model for Magheraboy (Fig. 12.15), the enclosure there was built in *4115–3850 cal BC* (*95% probability*; *start Magheraboy*), probably in *4065–3945 cal BC* (*68% probability*). This is significantly earlier than any other unequivocally diagnostic Neolithic element so far dated in Ireland. Although domesticates may have appeared sporadically from the second half of the fifth millennium cal BC, the ditch at Magheraboy is not just of Neolithic form. It also contains diagnostic Neolithic material: Carinated Bowl sherds and a small assemblage of lithics including leaf-shaped arrowheads and an axehead of Antrim porcellanite. The latter came from zone 2, segment 3, where oak sapwood from a charred plank lying on the base of the ditch has been dated (Fig. 12.15: *GrA-31961*). It is therefore difficult to argue that the enclosure at Magheraboy dates to before the introduction of wider Neolithic practices – the Carinated Bowl Neolithic – in the island. Clearly the material connections represented here were already extensive; but these, according to the models presented above, were not demonstrably in place before the 38th century cal BC.

For the reasons given earlier in this chapter, and on the criteria used throughout this volume, the model for the chronology of Magheraboy shown in Fig. 12.15 is to be preferred to the alternative chronological model shown in Fig. 12.17. When this is included as a component of the early Neolithic in model 2 here, however, that model has poor overall agreement ($A_{overall}$=52.2%). Further consideration of the individual indices of agreement indicates that this poor overall agreement is almost entirely caused by *Beta-199985* (A=6.2%). This is a bulk sample of hazel charcoal dated by liquid scintillation spectrometry. If this is interpreted as containing residual material, and the alternative model for the chronology of Magheraboy (Fig. 12.17) is incorporated as a component of the early Neolithic in model 2, then that model has good overall agreement ($A_{overall}$=61.7%). This reading suggests that the early Neolithic in Ireland began in *3840–3730 cal BC* (*95% probability*; Fig. 12.59: *start Irish Neolithic*, model 2), probably in *3810–3750 cal BC* (*68% probability*). Activity at Magheraboy began in *3830–3715 cal BC* (*95% probability*; Fig. 12.59: *start Magheraboy*, model 2 (Fig. 12.17)), probably in *3795–3730 cal BC* (*68% probability*).

If either model for the chronology of Magheraboy is included in model 3, the resultant models have good overall agreement ($A_{overall}$=71.6%: Fig 12.15; and $A_{overall}$=87.8%: Fig. 12.17), although *Beta-199985* still has poor agreement in the preferred interpretation (Fig. 12.15) of the chronology of Magheraboy (A=8.5%). The estimates for the beginning of the Irish Neolithic and the start of activity at Magheraboy calculated by these models are shown in Fig. 12.59. When

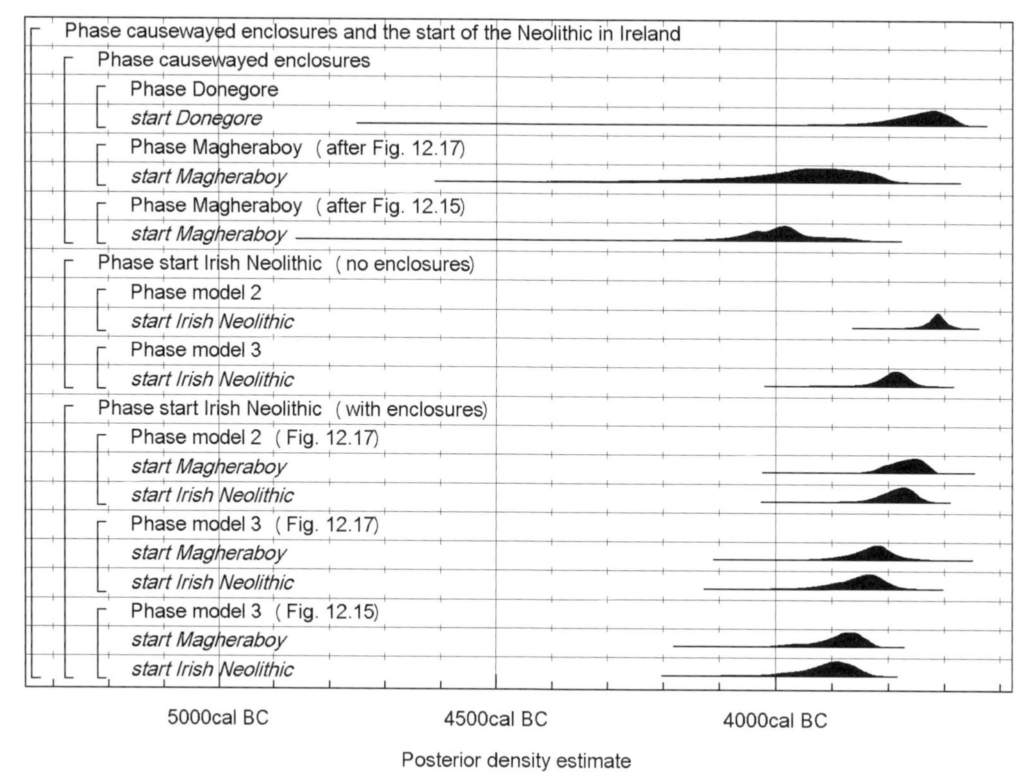

Fig. 12.59. Causewayed enclosures and the start of the Irish Neolithic. Posterior density estimates for the construction of Donegore (Figs 12.5–9) and Magheraboy (Fig. 12.15 and alternatively Fig. 12.17), and for the start of the Irish Neolithic, derived from model 2 (Fig. 12.54) and model 3 (Fig. 12.56), without the domesticates shown in Fig. 12.42. Alternative estimates for the date of the Magheraboy enclosure and for the start of the Irish Neolithic are provided by the version of model 2 (Fig. 12.54) which includes the model from Donegore and the alternative model for Magheraboy (Figs 12.5–9 and 12.17), and by versions of model 3 (Fig. 12.56), including models from Donegore and Magheraboy (Figs 12.5–9 and 12.15), or the model from Donegore and the alternative model for Magheraboy (Figs 12.5–9 and 12.17).

the preferred reading for the chronology of Magheraboy is included in model 3, we estimate that the Irish Neolithic began in *4000–3830 cal BC* (*95% probability*; Fig. 12.59: *start Irish Neolithic*, model 3 (Fig. 12.15)), probably in *3935–3850 cal BC* (*68% probability*). In this model, activity at Magheraboy began in *3980–3820 cal BC* (*95% probability*; Fig. 12.59: *start Magheraboy*, model 3 (Fig. 12.15)), probably in *3910–3835 cal BC* (*68% probability*). If the alternative reading of the chronology of Magheraboy is included in model 3, then the Irish Neolithic began in *3940–3780 cal BC* (*95% probability*; Fig. 12.59: *start Irish Neolithic*, model 3 (Fig. 12.17)), probably in *3880–3800 cal BC* (*68% probability*). In this model, activity at Magheraboy began in *3920–3745 cal BC* (*95% probability*; Fig. 12.59: *start Magheraboy*, model 3 (Fig. 12.17)), probably in *3865–3790 cal BC* (*68% probability*).

Figure 12.59 shows five different estimates for the date when the Neolithic in Ireland began — all derive from models that have good overall agreement, and so are statistically plausible. The estimated dates are, however, contradictory. Not all of these models can be right. Either the preferred chronology for Magheraboy is *importantly wrong* or our models for the introduction of Neolithic practices into Ireland are *importantly wrong* (Box 1979; Bayliss *et al.* 2007a). The basic problem is that the radiocarbon dates from Magheraboy are around 200 years earlier than any other dates for short-life material so far obtained on diagnostically Neolithic activity in the island. This lack of reliable radiocarbon dates falling in the first two centuries of the fourth millennium cal BC casts doubt on the reliability of the preferred chronology for Magheraboy and doubt on models for the Irish Neolithic that include this reading.

As previously noted by Peter Woodman (Woodman *et al.* 1999, 148), it is a real struggle to identify reliable radiocarbon determinations associated with the Irish Neolithic before 5000 BP (*c.* 3800 cal BC). One of the disarticulated bones from Poulnabrone (Fig. 12.31: OxA-1906) may be this early, as might a date on a redeposited cattle bone from Kilgreany Cave (Fig. 12.42: OxA-4269). Neither of these need be more than the expected statistical scatter on an assemblage of dates of this size, and doubts about whether domesticated fauna alone are enough to define the early Neolithic have already been expressed. The date on a person from Sramore Cave (UB-6407; Table 12.13; Fig 12.52) who has a probably largely terrestrial isotopic signature[17] – if such denotes a Neolithic lifeway – is also this early. At this point, early dates on pine charcoal should also be noted (Ballynagilly; Fig. 12.30: UB-197; Croaghaun; Table 12.12: Ua-713, St-10453), although these fall substantially earlier than the early fourth millennium cal BC, and our concerns about the possibility of re-used bog pine have been noted above.

It can also be noted that models 2 and 3 (in their variants excluding the measurements on domestic fauna shown in Fig. 12.42) include 292 radiocarbon dates; 144 are fully modelled, 149 are included as *termini post quos* only, and nine are included as *termini ante quos* only. Since these models were compiled in 2007, we have become aware of 33 further radiocarbon dates (listed in the other footnotes in this chapter) which are relevant to this study. Of these, 15 can be fully included in the models, five provide *termini post quos* for the end of the primary use of monuments, and 13 relate to later activity on the sites concerned. These results represent an increase of 10% in the most effective part of the dataset that can be fully modelled. The inclusion of these new data, however, alters the outputs of our models by only a decade at the most. The gap between Magheraboy and the other data for the early Neolithic stubbornly remains.

We have not considered the corpus of dated pollen sequences from Ireland at all in this chapter. That has been a task beyond the remit of this project, but it would now be highly informative to compare the radiocarbon dates from peat and other profiles for first, clearance activity, and secondly, reliably identified (if that is possible) cereal pollen, within Bayesian chronological models. OxCal v4 (Bronk Ramsey 2009a) and BPeat (Blaauw and Christen 2005) now allow more sophisticated modelling of processes such as peat accumulation rates (Blaauw *et al*. 2003; Christen *et al*. 1995), so that more robust models of the timescales of clearance and/or cultivation episodes should now be within reach. That is for the future. In the meantime, it is worth noting that dated pollen diagrams are skewed towards the north and west of Ireland. Appraisal of the available evidence tends to scepticism about most identifications of pre-elm decline cereal pollen (Monk 1993, 41–3; O'Connell and Molloy 2001, 117–18). Convincing cereal pollen from immediately below the elm decline (and a major clearance episode) at Lough Sheeauns, Connemara, is already within the early fourth millennium cal BC (Molloy and O'Connell 1987). Disturbances to woodland vegetation, not necessarily the outcome of activity by Neolithic people, occurred before the elm decline (taken by O'Connell and Molloy as a near-synchronous horizon in Ireland, occurring *c*. 3900 cal BC). Woodland disturbances were more numerous after the elm decline, when they are often associated with cultivation and/or pasture, and when the centuries-long duration of some *landnam* events, like that at the Céide Fields, suggests sustained settlement (O'Connell and Molloy 2001, 117–24). The informal chronologies for this evidence accord with all the varying start dates for the Irish early Neolithic presented here (Fig. 12.59).

For all these reasons, the dating model for Magheraboy must be re-examined. We have already suggested that *Beta-199985* and other bulk short-life samples from the ditch might have contained older, residual material (Fig. 12.17), and we might further suggest that the oak plank dated by *GrA-319161* could have been re-used. It should be noted that there are no dates on samples of cereals or domesticated animals from the ditch itself, and the one date on cereals from a pit in the interior (Table 12.2: Beta-196298), as well as some of those on charred hazelnut shell and hazel charcoal from other pits (Table 12.2: Beta-186484, -197649, -197653, -196299) are later than dates from ditch contexts and are in line with the date estimates for the Irish early Neolithic given in models 2 and 3 (Fig. 12.14). All these arguments could be made – and the need to date more samples from the site has already been emphasised. Compared with all the models considered throughout this volume, this may sound like special pleading, all the more so since the ditch dates are very consistent. At this point, however, we need to resolve a fundamental incompatibility between the Magheraboy dating and the weight of other evidence presented in this chapter. Special pleading which invokes some residual charcoal and a re-used plank may be the price to pay.

Alternatively, perhaps Magheraboy was an isolated, short-lived episode. Just as the first appearance of cattle in Ireland may have been sporadic and perhaps without immediate consequences (Woodman *et al*. 1999, 146–51; Woodman 2000, 230–43), so there is the possibility that the enclosure at Magheraboy represented a localised innovation in the context of wider cultural influences, perhaps with connections again to north-west France (and see Chapter 15.6), but again without longer-term effects.

The basic difficulty with this interpretation of Magheraboy is the evidence there for activity, material culture and connections of kinds typically represented elsewhere in the early Neolithic of Ireland. Ditch digging, palisade construction, and perhaps the building of a rectangular structure (Fig. 12.11); the use of leaf-shaped arrowheads and Carinated Bowl pottery; and the use of porcellanite from Antrim on the other side of the island; are all instances from the enclosure circuit itself of this typicality. One might make a more complicated case that leaf-shaped arrowheads and Carinated Bowl pottery might be sufficiently generic in character as to belong to other, wider cultural traditions, encompassing north-west France and perhaps beyond. The presence of a porcellanite axehead, however, as a distinctive feature of Neolithic practice and tradition, certainly in the northern part of the island, seems on the face of things to demand the existence of the rest of the early Neolithic in Ireland. This too, like every other element, has to be questioned. There has been more research in recent years on the Group IX sources, Brockley on Rathlin Island showing more extensive activity than previously known (Cooney *et al*. forthcoming), but the chronology of extraction and working can so far only be inferred from the contexts of the products elsewhere. In contrast, the working of the porphyry source at Eagle's Nest, Lambay, has been dated, apparently to a short period in the 38th to 37th centuries cal BC in the early Neolithic (Fig. 12.30). How key a role then did organised axehead production play in the process of Neolithisation (see Cooney 2008)? Further research on the porcellanite (and other) axehead sources must be another priority, but if Lambay is typical, they do not seem to have been active before the 38th century cal BC.

The discussion about Magheraboy has also to be set in the context of the wider issue of the date for the beginning of the early Neolithic in Ireland. We will follow the wider implications of these possibilities set out above in Chapters 14 and 15, when the chronological evidence from southern Britain is set alongside that from Ireland, Scotland and the European continent.

It should be clear from these discussions that there are still significant problems in deciding on when Neolithic practices in Ireland began. Leaving Magheraboy to one side, the evidence currently available may best be accommodated by a beginning in the 38th century cal BC. Models 2 and 3 estimate the start of the Irish Neolithic within this century, although they disagree as to when precisely this transition occurred (Fig. 12.59). The informal dating currently available for the pollen evidence does not contradict this suggested start date.

The models presented here represent a step forward. Despite their difficulties and uncertainties they represent formal, quantitative models for the chronology of one of the major social transitions in Ireland. Models 2 and 3 (Figs 12.54, 12.56, 12.59), which we feel are the least implausible, are contending between a few generations within a single century. But the fact remains that we still do not know when the Neolithic came to Ireland! And this matters.

Archaeologically, there are significant differences between these readings. If model 3 is correct, then the early Neolithic in Ireland began at the end of the 39th century cal BC or in the first half of the 38th century cal BC and, a few generations later, large numbers of substantial timber houses and perhaps enclosures were constructed. A few generations or a lifetime later again, these houses ceased to be built or used. In this reading, the introduction of the Neolithic to Ireland is a cumulative process, albeit a relatively rapid one. If model 2 is correct, however, then Neolithic practices were introduced into Ireland even more rapidly, with houses, enclosures, and other occupation associated with diagnostic early Neolithic material appearing all at once in the generation before 3700 cal BC. The differences between these chronologies are subtle – in human terms perhaps between the span of a lifetime and that of a generation – but the contrasting rates of change suggested have profound implications for explanations of how the Neolithic began in Ireland and the experience of those who lived through the transition.

This chapter has provided more questions than answers. It began with the task of providing date estimates for the enclosures at Donegore and Magheraboy (Fig. 12.59). Donegore appears to have been built in the 38th century cal BC, and Magheraboy in the 40th century cal BC in our preferred model (Fig. 12.15). To put both into context, we have used existing radiocarbon dates from a range of sites to model the early Neolithic in Ireland as a whole and selected features from the start of the middle Neolithic. That has suggested two principal models for the date of the start of the Irish Neolithic, in the first half and the second half respectively of the 38th century cal BC (Fig. 12.59). That presents interesting alternatives for the place of Donegore in the early generations of the Irish Neolithic, and thus the nature and rate of change. In its own right, however, its date is very interesting compared to those of enclosures in southern Britain: a theme which we will follow further in Chapters 14 and 15. It is the dating of the Magheraboy enclosure which raises fundamental problems.

Despite all these uncertainties, we would like to end on the positive note of key priorities for the future. This chapter has demonstrated not just how much we do not know about the chronology of the Irish Neolithic, but how much we do know. There is a substantial body of data already available and assessed in detail here, and more key sets of data are becoming available. Resolution of some key questions is within sight, if just beyond our immediate grasp. To resolve them, the agenda for the next decade of Neolithic research in Ireland must include: further dating of the enclosure and diagnostic Neolithic material culture at Magheraboy; the investigation of other possible enclosures; extensive dating of occupation and activity contexts other than houses; further dating of short-life samples from houses themselves; incorporation of environmental sequences into chronological models; further dating of short-life samples relating to the construction and primary use of monuments; and further investigation of the exploitation of porcellanite and other axehead sources. The list could go on: there is no shortage of things to do!

Notes

1 Note added in press: see now Whitehouse *et al.* (2010).

2 Since the modelling for this chapter was completed, a radiocarbon date has become available. Charcoal, identified as probably ash, from the sealing deposit has given a date of 3650–3510 cal BC at 95% confidence (4784±32 BP: Wk-18170) (D. Moore 2009).

3 Two further potential Neolithic enclosures are a sub-oval enclosure, approximately 40 m across, at Ballycreggy, Co. Antrim, revealed by top-soil stripping in advance of road widening by ADS Ltd in June 2009 (http://www.roadsni.gov.uk/m2link-archaeology-01.pdf), and a sub-D-shaped enclosure, approximately 100 m across, revealed by geophysics at Rossnaree, Co. Meath, during survey in the Brú na Bóinne World Heritage Site (Brady 2009).

4 Two samples of charred seeds from posthole F43 and the east end of the east wall trench respectively provided dates of 3950–3670 cal BC (95% confidence; UBA-8570; 5005±42BP) and 3800–3650 cal BC (95% confidence; UBA-8571; 4948±32BP) (Conor McDermott, pers. comm.).

5 These date estimates are basically compatible with those provided by McSparron (2008, figs 4–5), who produced a similar Bayesian model based on the measurements on short-life samples then available. His estimate for the time when the use of these structures came to an end is a few decades earlier than the estimate presented here, because he did not incorporate all the samples with potential age-offsets into his model as *termini post quos*.

6 A human phalanx from the surface in the open chamber of Ballynacloghy, Co. Galway, provided a date of 3700–3520 cal BC at 95% confidence (4835±39 BP; UB-6694). Cremated bone excavated from the back chamber II at Ballyrenan, Co. Tyrone (O. Davies 1937), was dated to 2290–2030 cal BC at 95% confidence (3743±36 BP; UB-6706). A piece of cremated human skull excavated from the disturbed eastern part of the chamber of the tomb at Drumanone, Co. Roscommon (Topp 1962), provided a date of 2140–1890 cal BC at 95% confidence (3639±37 BP; UB-6696) (Kytmannow 2008, table 7.1).

7 A further sample of unidentified charcoal from the base of the spread of cairn material on the north side of the monument (3475±40 BP; GrN-11432) provides a *terminus post quem* of 1900–1680 cal BC (95% confidence) for the slippage of the cairn (O'Kelly 1958, 40; 1989, 90–1) (Kytmannow 2008, table 7.3).

8 A further determination on human bone from this monument was reported after the modelling undertaken here (95% confidence; 4556±35 BP; 3490–3100 cal BC; UB-6741) (Kytmannow 2008, table 7.2). This falls comfortably within the currency of court tombs suggested here (Figs 12.32–4).

9 An, apparently otherwise unpublished, date on unidentified bulk charcoal from the façade at Dunloy, Co. Antrim (UB-3533; Kytmannow 2008, table 7.2), and a series of dates on unidentified bulk charcoal samples from Rathlackan, excavated by Gretta Byrne (Beta-48102, -63836, -76583–91; Kytmannow 2008, table 7.3; Byrne *et al.* 2009, 25), add little to our reported model. A date of 3640–3375 cal BC (95% confidence; 4737±35 BP; UB-6742), from Ballyedmond, Co. Down (Kytmannow 2008, table 7.3), again falls within the currency of court tombs suggested by our model (Figs 12.32–4). A series of seven measurements, five of them on short-life species of charcoal, from Behy, Co. Mayo are also consistent with a currency of court tombs including the middle centuries of the fourth millennium cal BC (the dates definitely on short-life charcoal samples are 3660–3370 cal BC (AA-43428; 4790±55BP), 3700–3380 cal BC (AA-43429; 4805±55BP), 3640–3350 cal BC (AA-43430; 4685±55BP), 3520–3090 cal BC (UCD-118; 4580±60BP), and 3640–3340 cal BC (UCD-142; 4680±70BP); AA-43416 (3970–3640 cal BC; 5005±75BP) was on oak charcoal, and UCD-141 (3630–3100 cal BC; 4610±60 BP) contained a component of oak and so could have an age-at-death offset from the contexts from which they derived). Two Early Bronze Age dates from Aghanaglack (UB-6730–1, 3433±39BP and 3446±38BP; Kytmannow 2008, table 7.3) presumably relate to the later use of the monument.

10 The date recently obtained from Ballynacloghy, Co. Galway (UB-6694; see note 6), does not change this interpretation substantively.

11 More recent work reported by Kytmannow (2008, 100–16) has perhaps added two further dates relating to the primary use of court tombs (UB-6741–2; see notes 7 and 8 above), the other additional dates reported by her either being *termini post quos* or relating to later use.

12 Given the strong evidence for the utilisation of marine fish and shellfish at Ferriter's Cove and the absence of practically any evidence for the exploitation of freshwater fish (99.8% of the fish bones were from marine species), we feel that this approach is reasonable (Woodman *et al.* 1999, chapter 6). Such simple linear interpolation of diet from stable isotopic values appears to be effective in cases where diet is dominated by a few extremely prominent components (Arneborg *et al.* 1999; Cook *et al.* 2001; Van Strydonck *et al.* 2009), although more complex mixing models may be required for mixed diets without a dominant protein source (e.g. Focken and Becker 1998; Phillips and Gregg 2003; Focken 2004; Bayliss *et al.* 2004; Beavan Athfield *et al.* 2008). It should be noted that seafood caught in the vicinity of Ferriter's Cove is likely to have a fully marine isotopic signature (unlike such resources from the Baltic which has more in common with a complex estuarine environment; cf. Brinch Petersen and Meiklejohn 2009).

13 The dates on the fish-baskets are 5040–4800 cal BC (Beta-231947, 6030±40BP), 5000–4720 cal BC (Beta-231948, 5970±50BP), 5000–4720 cal BC (Beta-231949, 5970±50BP), 5210–4800 cal BC (Beta-231950, 6060±50BP), 5060–4790 cal BC (Beta-231951, 6030±50BP), 5220–4940 cal BC (Beta-231952, 6130±40BP), 5060–4790 cal BC (Beta-231953, 6030±50BP), 5220–4950 cal BC (Beta-231954, 6140±40BP), 5000–4720 cal BC (Beta-231955, 5980±50BP), 5200–4800 cal BC (Beta-231956, 6050±50BP), 5310–4990 cal BC (Beta-231957, 6190±50BP), and 5220–4990 cal BC (Beta-231958, 6160±40BP). Further details, but no δ^{13}C values, are provided by E. O'Connor (2008, appendix 1).

14 Dates from Annagh Cave, Co. Limerick (Dowd 2008, 308; Ó Floinn 1992), may be relevant here, depending on the security of association between the five dated burials, some articulated and some disarticulated, and the two complete pots (a decorated bipartite bowl and a decorated hemispherical bowl), placed on a ledge above two of them. Right scapulae from five adult males provided radiocarbon dates of 3640–3190 cal BC (95% confidence; GrA-1703; 4670±70 BP, −20.9‰), 3660–3370 cal BC (GrA-1704; 4780±60 BP, −19.8‰), 3710–3370 cal BC (GrA-1707; 4810±60 BP, −20.1‰), 3630–3130 cal BC (GrA-1708; 4640±60 BP, −20.6‰) and 3710–3510 cal BC (GrA-1709; 4840±60 BP, −21.0‰). These results are statistically consistent (T'=8.1; T'(5%)=9.5; v=4), which suggests that this episode of burial may have been of limited duration.

15 A further dating programme for some of the Knowth passage tombs is currently underway (Rick Schulting, pers. comm.).

16 See again note 15.

17 The δ^{13}C value available for this burial is −20.1‰, which probably indicates a largely terrestrial-based diet. This valued was measured, however, by AMS, which means that it will include any fractionation induced in the graphitisation and measurement process as well as the natural isotopic ratio of the sample itself.

13 Carbon and nitrogen stable isotope values of animals and humans from causewayed enclosures

Julie Hamilton and Robert E.M. Hedges

13.1 Introduction

The analysis of stable isotopes in bone collagen is a well established technique in the study of palaeodiet (e.g. R. Hedges *et al.* 2007b; Jay and Richards 2006; 2007; Müldner and Richards 2007; Privat and O'Connell 2002). It is based on the principle that the isotopic composition of body tissues of animals and humans reflects the isotopic composition of their diets ('you are what you eat'). The isotopic composition of herbivore collagen will reflect that of the plants at the base of the food chain, which has not yet been directly measured for archaeological material, and the isotopic composition of carnivores will reflect that of their prey.

The relative abundance of the stable isotopes of carbon ^{13}C and ^{12}C ($\delta^{13}C$) differs clearly between plants with different photosynthetic pathways, and is clearly higher in marine than terrestrial ecosystems. Collagen $\delta^{13}C$ increases by *c.* 1‰ with each step up the food chain (trophic level) (Bocherens and Drucker 2003).

The ratio between the stable isotopes of nitrogen ^{15}N and ^{14}N ($\delta^{15}N$) increases with each trophic level by 3–5‰ (Bocherens and Drucker 2003; Hedges and Reynard 2007; Sponheimer *et al.* 2003). $\delta^{15}N$ values in plants depend on nitrogen cycling in the soil, and so are less predictable than $\delta^{13}C$ values, and in studies of human diet they are generally inferred from the herbivore values. Fish and mammals in marine ecosystems frequently have considerably higher $\delta^{15}N$ values than terrestrial herbivores, in part because of the longer food chains, so high values (i.e. enriched in the heavier isotope) for both $\delta^{13}C$ and $\delta^{15}N$ would be interpreted as indicating the use of marine resources. On the archaeological and isotopic evidence so far available, there was very little if any use of marine resources during the Neolithic in southern Britain (R. Hedges *et al.* 2007b; M. Richards 2000; M. Richards *et al.* 2003). A small amount of freshwater fish in the diet, however, might raise $\delta^{15}N$ values without much affecting $\delta^{13}C$, and cannot be discounted on isotopic grounds.

Because the trophic enrichment for ^{15}N is relatively large, it can be used to estimate the proportion of collagen protein that is derived from animal sources (assuming no fish in the diet). For omnivores such as humans, collagen $\delta^{15}N$ for someone who ate no animal products should be similar to herbivore values, while for someone who ate no plant protein it should be this plus 3–5‰. Values between these extremes reflect the relative amounts of protein from animal and plant sources. So far, values for the enrichment of $\delta^{15}N$ in human bone collagen ($\Delta^{15}N_{human\text{-}fauna}$) for the British Neolithic have been at least 4‰, which on the simplest assumptions suggests that at least 80% of collagen protein is from animal sources. This is unexpectedly high, and rather small adjustments in assumptions can change the estimate considerably (reviewed by Hedges and Reynard 2007). It is clearly interesting to see whether $\delta^{15}N$ for humans from causewayed enclosures is similarly high. Such a value would imply that about 50% of calories in the diet were from animal sources, either meat or dairy, which are isotopically indistinguishable.

There are also more subtle environmental influences on herbivore isotopic composition.

$\delta^{13}C$ of plants may be affected by climatic variation, both on a regional, long-term scale (Van Klinken *et al.* 1994; 2000) and at more local, shorter-term scales in response to temperature, water availability and altitude (Heaton 1999). Plants and tree leaves from the lower parts of closed-canopy forests commonly have $\delta^{13}C$ values 2–5‰ lower than vegetation in nearby open areas (Broadmeadow and Griffiths 1993; van der Merwe and Medina 1991), the 'canopy effect', and this has been suggested as an explanation of, for example, the generally lower $\delta^{13}C$ values for aurochs compared to domestic cattle in Denmark (Noe-Nygaard *et al.* 2005) and at Ascott-under-Wychwood (R. Hedges *et al.* 2007b; Stevens *et al.* 2006). However, most contemporary studies demonstrating a canopy effect have been in hotter environments and are often based on comparisons between rather than within species; a comparison of populations of red deer in various temperate environments (Stevens *et al.* 2006), did not find evidence of a canopy effect. As noted above, plant $\delta^{15}N$ values are affected by nitrogen cycling in the soil, and have also been shown to vary with environmental factors such as temperature and water availability (Ambrose 1991; Dawson *et al.* 2002; Sealy *et al.* 1987).

Variability in isotopic compositions of herbivore tissues will reflect these variations in plant isotopic composition via food and/or habitat selection by animals or by people managing them. There will also be inter-individual variation due to metabolic factors (e.g. genetics, growth, lactation, disease). The timescale of variation may also be important, ranging from centuries or decades to days or hours for both environmental and individual factors. Bone collagen has a relatively slow turnover time and probably averages the diet (and other variation) over a few seasons to several years in herbivores and humans (R. Hedges *et al.* 2007a; Stenhouse and Baxter 1979; Ubelaker *et al.* 2006).

Some of the variation in herbivore isotopic composition may be explicable by these effects, but the system is complex and not well characterised. Faunal data can best be used comparatively, looking for differences in (mean) values in large datasets that can be consistently related to environmental conditions or agricultural management. For the British Neolithic, where all plants are likely to use the C_3 photosynthetic pathway, the ranges of variation in $\delta^{13}C$ and $\delta^{15}N$ that we are trying to explain are around 1–3‰, not large in comparison with measurement and statistical errors. Interestingly, it is at least as wide in herbivores as in more omnivorous humans, which should perhaps make one cautious in attributing differences within human populations to different levels of carnivory.

When comparing and interpreting differences between sites in these sorts of ways, we are making several assumptions:

1. When comparing faunal and human values, we are assuming that the animals from the same site are more likely to be representative of those people's diets than animals from another site.
2. That the fauna at a site reflect 'local' conditions, while leaving the actual geographical scale rather vague – 5, 10, 20 km from the site? The causewayed enclosures may be sites of assembly rather than settlement, and the animals deposited there might represent a variety of management regimes.
3. Even where radiocarbon suggests relatively short phases of use of the sites, this could well be decades, and many animal generations, with potential for change over that time. At Ascott-under-Wychwood, for instance, the cattle from pre-barrow and barrow construction phases differed in mean $\delta^{13}C$ (R. Hedges *et al.* 2007b). The samples used here were selected to come from a relatively short timespan to avoid this problem, but it should be borne in mind when making comparisons with other sites which may have different dates and durations of use.

13.2 Aims

The aims of this project were:

1. To document animal C and N isotopic variation at causewayed enclosures as thoroughly as possible. Existing data suggest some patterns which may be common and may reflect environment and/or husbandry practices.
2. To get a measure of the average range of human $\delta^{15}N$ values from causewayed enclosures to compare with existing data from chambered tombs.
3. To measure the difference in human and animal $\delta^{15}N$ for the same site at as many sites as possible, to investigate trophic level.

13.3 Sampling strategy

To pursue these aims, we wished to sample from sites with both human and large collections of animal bone, and from the early phases of use of the enclosures to avoid confusion due to changes over time. Up to 20 samples per species of the major domestic animals (cattle, sheep, pig) and as many as possible human samples would be taken. The five sites that seemed to fulfil the criteria were Abingdon, Etton, Staines, Windmill Hill and Chalk Hill, Ramsgate. In the event no samples from Staines and only about a third of those from Etton yielded enough collagen, and there were no human samples from Abingdon. Pigs at Chalk Hill and sheep at Etton were relatively rare, so sample numbers for statistical analysis were rather unbalanced, limiting what could sensibly be inferred.

13.4 Methods

Samples were selected from a variety of contexts available from the appropriate phase of the site, preferably using cortical bone from different mature individuals, though it was not always possible to be certain of this. Collagen was extracted from up to 1 g of bone per sample using a standard protocol (O'Connell and Hedges 1999). Any superficial material was removed from the bone by shotblasting, then samples were demineralised in 0.5M HCl at 4°C, rinsed with distilled water, and gelatinised in a pH 3 solution for 48 h at 75°C. The solution was filtered, frozen and freeze-dried. Between 2.5 and 3.5 mg of dried collagen was loaded into a tin capsule for continuous flow combustion and isotopic analysis. Samples were isotopically analysed using an automated Carlo Erba carbon and nitrogen elemental analyser coupled with a continuous flow isotope ratio monitoring mass spectrometer (PDZ Europa Geo 20/20 mass spectrometer). Each sample was measured in at least duplicate and where possible triplicate runs, using internal secondary standards (nylon and alanine), giving an analytical error of ±0.2‰. The pooled estimate of standard deviation, including both measurement and random error, is 0.43‰ for $\delta^{13}C$ and 0.41‰ for $\delta^{15}N$, giving 95% confidence limits for any given sample mean of ±0.5‰. Results are reported in unit per mil (‰) and $\delta^{13}C$ and $\delta^{15}N$ values were measured relative to the VPDB and AIR standards respectively (Gonfiantini *et al.* 1990; Mariotti 1983). Samples with C:N ratios outside the range 3.1–3.4 or with less than 1% collagen yield (weight % of whole bone) were rejected; accepted samples with <2% collagen yield had acceptable weight % of nitrogen and carbon in their collagen as well as acceptable C:N ratios (Ambrose 1990; DeNiro 1985). Two samples were also excluded because they were not certainly from early phases of use or had been mislabelled, and one because it showed clear pathology (bone deposition in marrow cavity, possibly a response to infection).

A few additional isotope ratios were obtained during radiocarbon measurements. The details of sample preparation for radiocarbon measurement are slightly different, and these measurements are not replicated, so to avoid any possible systematic variation they have not been included in the overall analysis. Data were analysed using standard SPSS and Excel statistical packages.

13.5 Results

Results are shown in Tables 13.1–4 and summarised in Table 13.5 and Fig. 13.1. Each value is the mean of 2 or 3 measurements.

Collagen preservation

Collagen preservation differs between sites. None of the 25 samples from Staines yielded enough collagen. The range of collagen yields was greatest at Etton, where 45 of 65 samples failed, but 6 had yields >10%. This reflects the differential extent and continuity of waterlogging across the site. Only 2 of 58 samples from Abingdon, on river gravels, were rejected, but a higher proportion yielded only 1–2% collagen than at the two chalkland sites, Chalk Hill and Windmill Hill. C:N ratios were well within the accepted range (Tables 13.1–4), showing that collagen was well preserved, and results from replicate runs were in good agreement.

Fauna

Within-species variation

The range of animal $\delta^{13}C$ and $\delta^{15}N$ values is generally 1–3‰, and standard deviations of per-site means for each species were typically around 0.5 (*ns* 3–20; see Table 13.5), though rather higher for $\delta^{15}N$ of all fauna at Etton (with lower sample numbers) and $\delta^{15}N$ of sheep and pig at Windmill Hill. There are a few outliers with values >2 standard deviations from the mean: at Abingdon, one cattle individual with high $\delta^{15}N$ (AB34); at Chalk Hill, one sheep with high $\delta^{15}N$ (CH22); and at Windmill Hill, one sheep with both high $\delta^{13}C$ and $\delta^{15}N$ (WH6), one sheep with low $\delta^{15}N$ (WH3) and a pig with high $\delta^{15}N$ (WH57). WH57 was recorded as 'possibly juvenile', so the high $\delta^{15}N$ may represent a milk signal, but there are no obvious reasons for the other unusual values.

Between-species variation

There are consistent differences between the three major

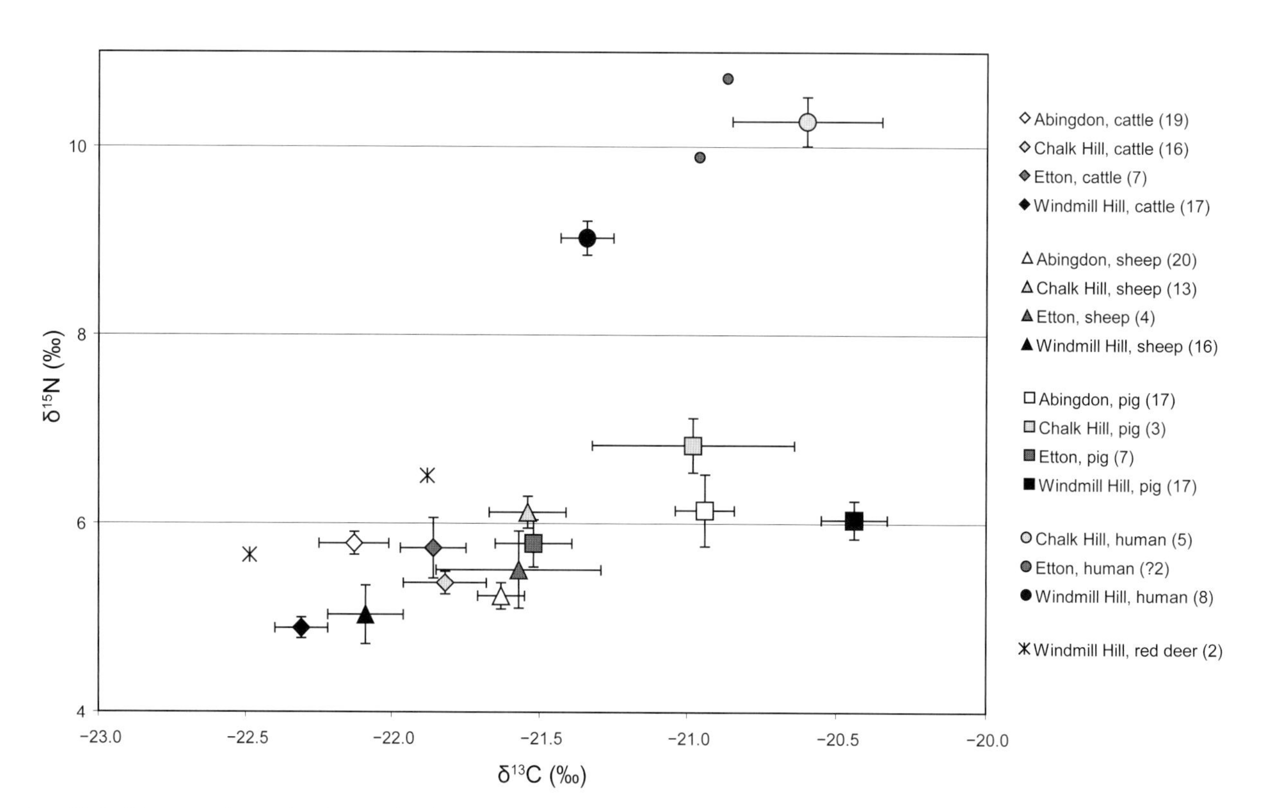

Fig. 13.1. Means ± 1 standard error for human and animal isotope values from causewayed enclosures (n in parentheses). Individual points are shown for Etton humans and Windmill Hill red deer.

Table 13.1. Stable isotope values from Abingdon causewayed enclosure.

RLAHA sample number	Site reference	Species	$\delta^{13}C$ (‰)	$\delta^{15}N$ (‰)	C:N ratio	Collagen (%)
AB1	AB C2 9 1	Sheep	−22.0	5.3	3.3	7.5
AB2	AB C2 9 8	Sheep	−21.2	5.0	3.2	5.6
AB3	AB C2 27 17	Sheep	−21.7	3.9	3.3	2.3
AB4	AB C2 29 19	Sheep	−21.7	5.2	3.3	3.5
AB5	AB C2 29 20	Sheep	−21.9	5.4	3.3	3.3
AB6	AB C2 24 33	Sheep	−21.6	4.5	3.2	3.3
AB7	AB C2 24 35	Sheep	−21.5	5.2	3.3	4.2
AB8	AB C2 24 37	Sheep	−22.0	5.2	3.3	4.6
AB9	AB C2 26+23N 42	Sheep	−21.1	4.6	3.3	2.3
AB10	AB C2 26+23N 43	Sheep	−20.9	5.6	3.3	6.2
AB11	AB C2 26+23N 44	Sheep	−21.4	5.1	3.3	11.4
AB12	AB C2 4 56	Sheep	−22.1	5.1	3.3	1.3
AB13	AB C2 4 57	Sheep	−21.8	5.9	3.3	3.1
AB14	AB C2 4 58	Sheep	−21.5	5.9	3.2	4.9
AB15	ABCE C2 5 6	Sheep	−21.3	4.5	3.2	3.3
AB16	AB B3 3 226	Sheep	−22.2	6.5	3.2	2.4
AB17	AB B3 3 226	Sheep	−21.7	6.1	3.3	2.2
AB18	AB C2 33A	Sheep	−21.5	5.0	3.3	6.0
AB19	AB C2 33A	Sheep	−21.5	4.9	3.2	3.9
AB20	AB C2 34	Sheep	−22.0	5.8	3.2	3.7
AB22	AB C2 4 27	Cattle	−22.0	5.4	3.2	2.3
AB23	AB C2 8 2	Cattle	−21.6	6.1	3.2	3.0
AB24	AB C2 9 1	Cattle	−22.6	5.2	3.3	3.4
AB25	AB C2 11 4	Cattle	−23.2	5.5	3.1	1.0
AB26	AB C2 24 21	Cattle	−22.2	5.7	3.2	1.3
AB27	AB C2 24 22	Cattle	−22.5	5.5	3.3	1.0
AB28	AB C2 24 16A	Cattle	−22.1	6.0	3.2	1.8
AB29	AB C2 26+33A 17	Cattle	−22.4	5.2	3.2	1.5
AB30	AB C2 29 11	Cattle	−22.6	5.9	3.2	1.1
AB31	AB C2 29 12	Cattle	−22.0	5.6	3.3	3.0
AB32	AB C2 33 5	Cattle	−22.1	5.6	3.2	1.3
AB33	AB C2 28+33B 8	Cattle	−21.7	6.1	3.3	3.3
AB34	AB C2 33+28 9	Cattle	−22.7	7.3	3.2	2.5
AB35	AB C2 51 5	Cattle	−21.0	5.4	3.3	7.4
AB36	AB C2 36 2	Cattle	−21.1	6.3	3.3	2.9
AB37	AB C2 41 4	Cattle	−22.3	5.4	3.2	2.0
AB38	AB B3 3 226	Cattle	−21.8	6.7	3.2	3.5
AB39	AB 26+23N C2 27	Cattle	−22.5	5.8	3.1	1.8
AB40	AB B3 3 226	Cattle	−22.2	5.4	3.2	2.0
AB41	AB 37 C2 1	Pig	−21.4	6.0	3.2	2.3
AB42	AB 27 C2 28	Pig	−20.6	6.0	3.2	3.1
AB43	AB B3 226 3	Pig	−21.9	6.0	3.2	3.7
AB45	AB C2 10 22	Pig	−20.7	6.3	3.2	1.6
AB46	AB 26+23N C2 27	Pig	−20.6	6.5	3.3	4.1
AB47	AB 26+23N C2 28	Pig	−21.2	6.4	3.2	2.3
AB48	AB C2 33+28 31	Pig	−20.7	6.0	3.4	1.3
AB49	AB C2 24 32	Pig	−20.9	6.2	3.2	3.0
AB50	AB 28+33B 40	Pig	−20.7	5.4	3.4	2.6
AB51	AB 28+33B C2 41	Pig	−20.7	5.5	3.2	2.2

AB52	AB C2 23A 42	Pig	−20.6	6.0	3.3	2.8
AB53	AB C2 24 50	Pig	−21.2	6.5	3.4	1.8
AB54	AB C2 24 51	Pig	−21.5	5.7	3.3	1.2
AB55	AB C2 24 53	Pig	−21.0	6.4	3.4	1.5
AB56	AB C2 24 54	Pig	−21.1	6.0	3.3	1.7
AB57	AB C2 4 73	Pig	−20.4	6.6	3.3	3.8
AB58	AB C2 4 74	Pig	−20.8	6.8	3.2	1.8

Table 13.2. Stable isotope values from Chalk Hill, Ramsgate, causewayed enclosure.

RLAHA sample number	**Site reference**	**Species**	**$\delta^{13}C$ (‰)**	**$\delta^{15}N$ (‰)**	**C:N ratio**	**Collagen (%)**
CH1	F968/1193	Cattle	−21.7	5.7	3.2	7.8
CH2	F968/1193	Cattle	−21.2	5.1	3.2	4.9
CH3	F968/1193	Cattle	−21.3	5.8	3.2	3.1
CH4	F1215/1450	Cattle	−21.5	6.0	3.2	7.1
CH5	D2 F1143/1256	Cattle	−22.5	4.3	3.2	5.0
CH6	D F1146/1273	Cattle	−21.0	5.4	3.2	6.4
CH7	D2 F1287/1262	Cattle	−21.5	5.1	3.3	6.8
CH8	Tr20 F65/59	Cattle	−22.4	5.8	3.2	5.6
CH9	Tr20 F74/63	Cattle	−22.0	5.2	3.2	4.5
CH10	F1421/1259	Cattle	−21.7	5.5	3.2	9.2
CH11	F1421/1259	Cattle	−22.8	6.3	3.2	3.6
CH12	F1421/1259	Cattle	−21.5	5.5	3.2	4.7
CH13	Tr20 F65/59	Cattle	−21.4	5.3	3.2	3.3
CH14	Tr20 F65/59	Cattle	−21.5	5.2	3.2	2.5
CH15	F1303/1473	Cattle	−22.5	4.8	3.2	1.9
CH20	D2 F1162/1259	Cattle	−22.7	5.1	3.2	1.2
CH21	Tr20 F55/45	Sheep	−21.2	5.8	3.3	3.1
CH22	Tr20 F57/57	Sheep	−22.5	7.5	3.3	4.5
CH23	Tr20 F68/61	Sheep	−21.9	5.6	3.3	3.1
CH24	D2 F968/1193	Sheep	−20.7	6.1	3.2	8.5
CH25	F1017/1217	Sheep	−21.7	6.4	3.3	1.7
CH26	F1354/1228	Sheep	−21.5	6.5	3.2	3.9
CH27	F1354/1228	Sheep	−21.7	6.3	3.3	3.5
CH28	D2 F1162/1259	Sheep	−21.8	6.3	3.2	3.0
CH29	F1166/1313	Sheep	−21.5	4.9	3.2	5.3
CH30	F1281/1334	Sheep	−21.8	5.8	3.3	3.9
CH31	F1289/1346	Sheep	−20.8	6.1	3.3	2.2
CH32	9802/1473	Sheep	−21.5	6.4	3.3	2.2
CH33	9802/1473	Sheep	−21.6	5.8	3.3	3.0
CH34	Tr20 F58/55	Pig	−20.3	7.2	3.3	3.2
CH35	Tr20 F58/55	Pig	−21.5	7.0	3.3	2.4
CH36	Seg7 F1574/1586	Pig	−21.1	6.3	3.3	3.5
CH37	Tr20 F68/61	Human	−20.2	10.8	3.3	6.3
CH38	D2A F1309/1538	Human	−20.1	10.7	3.3	3.0
CH39	D2 F1120/1232	Human	−21.0	9.6	3.2	4.5
CH40	D2A F1309/1538	Human	−21.3	9.7	3.2	3.8
CH41	D2 F1301/1336	Human	−20.3	10.5	3.2	2.6

Table 13.3. Stable isotope values from Etton causewayed enclosure.

RLAHA sample number	Site reference	Bone number	Species	$\delta^{13}C$ (‰)	$\delta^{15}N$ (‰)	C:N ratio	Collagen (%)
ET1	E85 F1[106-107] 3	6882	Cattle	−21.9	5.1	3.2	7.4
ET2	E85 F1[109-112]ext 2	6977	Cattle	−21.9	5.2	3.3	1.1
ET4	E85 F1[140-145] 2	7516	Cattle	−22.0	5.6	3.2	9.7
ET8	E86 F1[177-9] 3	9943	Cattle	−22.0	7.0	3.2	6.5
ET12	E87 F1[239-0] 6	12397	Cattle	−21.7	4.6	3.3	5.7
ET20	E87 F1[228-0] 5	15490	Cattle	−21.3	6.3	3.3	6.5
ET21	E87 F1[207-0]	15726	Cattle	−22.2	6.4	3.2	14.4
ET24	E83 F1[16-0] 4	5201	Pig	−21.7	5.7	3.3	4.1
ET30	E87 F1[199-0] 5	11560	Pig	−21.4	5.1	3.5	2.5
ET31	E87 F1[238-234] 3	12496	Pig	−21.4	6.3	3.4	1.3
ET32	E87 F1[227-0] 4	13310	Pig	−21.1	6.1	3.2	1.8
ET39	E87 F1[207-00]	15724	Pig	−22.0	5.6	3.4	4.7
ET40	E87 F1[207-00]	15735	Pig	−21.8	5.0	3.3	5.7
ET43	E87 F1[207-00]	16299	Pig	−21.2	6.8	3.3	7.5
ET46	E82 F1[11-12] 3	644	Sheep	−22.2	6.6	3.3	13.4
ET47	E83 F1[16-0] 4	5221	Sheep	−21.1	5.2	3.3	17.0
ET61	E87 F1[207-00]	15733	Sheep	−21.8	4.7	3.3	17.4
ET62	E87 F1[207-00]	16300	Sheep	−21.1	5.5	3.4	3.0
ETH2	E82 F1[5-6] 2	453	Human	−20.9	10.7	3.3	13.3
ETH6	E82 F1[5-6] 2	4530	Human	−21.0	9.9	3.4	15.7

domestic species in both $\delta^{13}C$ and $\delta^{15}N$ ratios (Fig. 13.1). At each site (excluding Etton for the moment), sheep mean $\delta^{13}C$ values are slightly higher than cattle, while pig values are considerably higher than cattle or sheep. Sheep and cattle $\delta^{15}N$ values are similar, while pig mean $\delta^{15}N$ values are always higher than both cattle and sheep values, by 0.3–1.4‰. At Etton the difference between the species means is so small and the errors so large that they are not statistically distinguishable, but they follow the same patterns as at the other sites. Because collagen preservation was much more variable here the sample numbers are much lower, and inadequate to test for small differences in the means of rather variable populations. The differences between means may be small, often within the statistical error for any particular pair of means compared, but they are consistent. Multivariate analysis (*post hoc* multiple comparisons, Scheffé test, *P*s<0.01) showed that mean $\delta^{13}C$ differs significantly between all three species, while cattle and sheep mean $\delta^{15}N$ values differ significantly from pig but not from each other.

The two values for red deer antler from Windmill Hill were not included in this analysis; they fall well within the cattle/sheep range for $\delta^{13}C$, and high within the cattle/sheep range for $\delta^{15}N$.

A few more measurements of animal isotope values from Windmill Hill were made during the dating programme (Table 13.6). They do not appear exceptional. The dog values are typical, with enriched $\delta^{15}N$ reflecting a more carnivorous diet than the other animals.

Variation between sites

Taking between-species variation into account, there is significant variation between sites in faunal $\delta^{15}N$ but not $\delta^{13}C$. Windmill Hill, with lowest mean $\delta^{15}N$, is significantly different from Chalk Hill, with the highest value (*post hoc* multiple comparisons, Scheffé test, *P*<0.05). This has obvious implications for interpretation of the human $\delta^{15}N$ values from these sites.

Humans

Results were obtained for eight humans from Windmill Hill, five from Chalk Hill and two from Etton. It is possible that the two from Etton are actually from the same skeleton (the question is not resolvable from the bag labelling and other records); the $\delta^{13}C$ values are very close though $\delta^{15}N$ differs by 0.8‰. No skeletal details were available for the humans from Chalk Hill. At Windmill Hill, all of the eight samples are described as adult (one 'young adult', WH26) or probably adult, and three are identified as male (WH20, WH22, WH27). The values from these are in no way exceptional. On such a limited sample, there is little isotopic evidence for dietary differentiation within the human population in relation to gender.

The single additional result from the dating programme (replicates OxA-14966, GrA-29711) for a human from Windmill Hill (Table 13.6) is considerably higher in $\delta^{15}N$ than those from the isotope study, and indeed than all the other humans measured during the dating programme; it

Table 13.4. Stable isotope values from Windmill Hill causewayed enclosure.

RLAHA sample number	Site reference	Bone number	Species	$\delta^{13}C$ (‰)	$\delta^{15}N$ (‰)	C:N ratio	Collagen (%)
WH1	B228	4342	Red Deer	−22.5	5.7	3.2	3.6
WH2	B228	4331	Red Deer	−21.9	6.5	3.2	8.1
WH3	E525	50	Sheep	−21.9	3.7	3.2	6.3
WH4	E525	73	Sheep	−21.8	6.3	3.2	5.3
WH5	MD XII 4	699	Sheep	−21.7	6.9	3.3	4.2
WH6	ID XVII 4	706	Sheep	−20.9	8.3	3.3	5.1
WH7	MD IB 4	711	Sheep	−22.4	3.9	3.3	4.9
WH8	MD IX 3	715	Sheep	−22.4	6.2	3.2	3.5
WH10	MD IB 3	1088	Sheep	−22.6	4.0	3.3	4.1
WH11	MD VII 3	1172	Sheep	−21.8	4.8	3.3	3.5
WH12	MD VII 4	1173	Sheep	−21.7	4.4	3.3	2.9
WH13	E508	1818	Sheep	−22.1	4.3	3.2	3.7
WH14	E504	1868	Sheep	−22.3	4.9	3.3	4.6
WH15	E504	1870	Sheep	−23.0	4.6	3.3	3.5
WH16	E508	1919	Sheep	−21.6	4.7	3.2	5.1
WH17	B228	4337	Sheep	−22.2	4.2	3.2	4.7
WH18	B228	4370	Sheep	−22.3	4.6	3.3	5.0
WH19	B228	4421	Sheep	−22.9	4.8	3.2	2.0
WH20	MD II ?4	10	Human	−21.2	9.8	3.3	3.0
WH21	ID I/II 3	50	Human	−21.1	9.6	3.4	2.1
WH22	MD IB 4	112	Human	−21.3	8.5	3.3	4.4
WH23	ID XI 3	158	Human	−21.7	8.8	3.3	2.4
WH24	MD XB 3	183	Human	−21.7	9.3	3.3	3.5
WH25	MD XIA /2 110	189	Human	−21.1	8.5	3.3	4.2
WH26	OD IIIC 6	220	Human	−21.4	8.7	3.3	2.8
WH27	Grave 707		Human	−21.2	9.0	3.3	1.4
WH28	E525	46	Cattle	−22.5	4.5	3.2	2.2
WH30	MD IX 3	271	Cattle	−22.7	5.1	3.3	1.7
WH31	ID VIII 3	273	Cattle	−21.9	4.7	3.2	1.6
WH32	MD XII 4	274	Cattle	−22.5	4.6	3.3	2.6
WH33	MD IB 5	277	Cattle	−22.5	5.0	3.3	3.3
WH34	MD VII 5	282	Cattle	−21.8	4.6	3.3	2.2
WH35	MD VII 4	283	Cattle	−22.0	5.1	3.3	4.3
WH36	MD VII 4	285	Cattle	−22.0	4.5	3.2	5.3
WH37	MD VI 5	908	Cattle	−21.8	4.6	3.2	4.7
WH38	MD IB 5	1307	Cattle	−22.5	5.9	3.3	4.4
WH39	MD IB 5	1313	Cattle	−22.8	5.2	3.3	2.7
WH40	MD VI 5	1491	Cattle	−22.3	4.9	3.2	6.8
WH41	E508	1800	Cattle	−22.3	4.5	3.3	2.7
WH42	E504	1854	Cattle	−22.3	5.2	3.2	4.3
WH43	B228	4374	Cattle	−23.0	5.9	3.2	5.4
WH44	B228	4382	Cattle	−22.1	4.6	3.2	4.2
WH45	E520	5872	Cattle	−22.2	4.3	3.2	2.7
WH46	E525	52	Pig	−20.6	6.1	3.2	8.8
WH47	E525	63	Pig	−20.8	6.1	3.2	4.4
WH48	E525	95	Pig	−21.1	5.9	3.2	3.8
WH49	ID VIII 3	739	Pig	−19.9	4.2	3.3	6.2
WH50	OD IB 6	740	Pig	−19.8	6.0	3.3	4.5
WH51	MD IX 4	743	Pig	−20.1	6.6	3.3	5.5

WH52	MD IB 4	744	Pig	−20.8	5.6	3.3	2.5
WH53	OD IV 5	745	Pig	−20.7	5.8	3.3	9.2
WH54	MD XII 4	755	Pig	−20.9	6.1	3.2	6.5
WH55	ID VIII 3	864	Pig	−20.9	6.4	3.3	5.5
WH56	D416	1416	Pig	−20.8	5.7	3.2	10.8
WH57	D416	1422	Pig	−20.6	8.5	3.2	5.6
WH58	D416	1741	Pig	−20.3	5.1	3.3	4.1
WH59	E510	1950	Pig	−20.1	6.0	3.2	5.5
WH60	E510	1964	Pig	−19.9	6.1	3.2	5.6
WH61	E510	1992	Pig	−20.8	6.4	3.3	5.1
WH62	B228	4339	Pig	−19.5	6.0	3.2	4.0

Table 13.5. Means and standard deviations of stable isotope values from each site.

Site	**Species**	**Mean $\delta^{13}C$ (‰)**	**SD**	**Mean $\delta^{15}N$ (‰)**	**SD**	**n**
Abingdon	Cattle	−22.1	0.5	5.8	0.5	19
	Pig	−20.9	0.4	6.1	0.4	17
	Sheep	−21.6	0.4	5.2	0.6	20
Chalk Hill	Cattle	−21.8	0.6	5.4	0.5	16
	Pig	−21.0	0.6	6.8	0.5	3
	Sheep	−21.5	0.5	6.1	0.6	13
	Human	−20.6	0.6	10.3	0.6	5
Etton	Cattle	−21.9	0.3	5.7	0.9	7
	Pig	−21.5	0.3	5.8	0.7	7
	Sheep	−21.6	0.6	5.5	0.8	4
	Human	−20.9	0.1	10.3	0.6	2
Windmill Hill	Cattle	−22.3	0.4	4.9	0.5	17
	Pig	−20.4	0.5	6.0	0.8	17
	Sheep	−22.1	0.5	5.0	1.2	16
	Red Deer	−22.2	0.4	6.1	0.6	2
	Human	−21.3	0.3	9.0	0.5	8

is from an individual 2–3 years-old, and probably reflects the higher trophic level of milk consumption during infancy. It is also probably more recent than the other individuals analysed from the site (*3490–3470 cal BC* (*9% probability*; Fig. 3.11: *WH29 B209*) or *3370–3330 cal BC* (*86% probability*)).

The humans from Chalk Hill and Windmill Hill differ significantly in both $\delta^{13}C$ and $\delta^{15}N$ (*t*-test, $P<0.05$, $P<0.01$ respectively, two-tailed). Both $\delta^{13}C$ and $\delta^{15}N$ are lower at Windmill Hill.

There are a few additional comparable results from the dating programme for humans from other causewayed enclosures, one each from Hill Croft Field and Offham Hill, two from Maiden Castle and three from Whitehawk (Table 13.6). While these are too few to look for systematic differences, Windmill Hill seems consistently most depleted in both $\delta^{13}C$ and $\delta^{15}N$; unfortunately there are no comparable faunal data from the other sites.

13.6 Discussion

Fauna

Within-species variation. The ranges of variation in the faunal data are similar to those found at other sites with large datasets. Many factors may contribute to this (see Introduction). There was no consistent difference between chalkland and other sites.

There were some outlying values (>2 standard deviations from the mean). These are consistent between replicates, identifications appear correct, as far as could be told the bones were from adult animals, and there was no apparent pathology. Occasional outlying values have been noted at other sites such as Ascott-under-Wychwood (R. Hedges *et al.* 2007b), and Wharram Percy (Müldner and Richards 2005). They may represent animals that for some reason were fed or treated differently from other stock, though apparently deposited similarly to other bone at the sites.

Table 13.6. Additional stable isotope values from the dating programme. Data from 'excluded' dates have been omitted.

Site	Sample reference	Material	Reference	$\delta^{13}C$ (‰)	$\delta^{15}N$ (‰)	Notes
Hill Croft Field	HC06 30/B	Human bone	OxA-15867	–19.5	8.1	
Maiden Castle	401 14577/A	Human bone	OxA-14832	–20.2	10.9	3–4 years
	401 2026	Human bone	OxA-14837	–20.6	9.2	3–5 years
Offham Hill	Burial 1. Barbican House Museum, Lewes 77.23	Human bone	GrA-27322	–20.9	10.5	20–25 years, male
Whitehawk	Brighton Museum R3162/169/N (1)	Red deer antler	GrA-26962	–23.8	5.7	
	Brighton Museum R3688/138/B	Cattle bone	GrA-26972	–21.8	5.5	
	Skeleton I. Brighton Museum R3688/128/S	Human bone	GrA-26971	–20.7	10.0	25–30 years, female
	Skeleton IIa. Brighton Museum R3688/129/T	Human bone	OxA-14063*	–20.6	9.9	20–25 years, female
	Skeleton IIa. Brighton Museum R3688/129/T	Human bone	GrA-26977*	–21.1	9.7	
	Skeleton III. Brighton Museum R 4100/139 221788/U	Human bone	OxA-14061	–20.3	10.0	Middle-aged male
Windmill Hill	WH26 B22.a	Dog bone	GrA-25558	–20.9	9.4	
	WH26 B22.c	Sheep bone	OxA-13715	–21.0	5.2	
	WH28 B106	Dog bone	OxA-13505	–20.4	7.3	
	WH28 B114	Red Deer antler	GrA-25554	–21.8	4.6	
	WH28 B369	Cattle bone	GrA-25555	–23.8	5.0	
	WH28 B370	Cattle bone	GrA-25545	–22.8	4.2	
	WH28 B372	Cattle bone	OxA-13679	–22.0	5.5	
	WH28 B374	Cattle bone	GrA-25559	–22.9	5.3	
	WH28 B671	Cattle bone	OxA-13501	–21.3	4.7	
	WH29 B209	Human bone	OxA-14966*	–21.1	11.9	2–3 years
	WH29 B209	Human bone	GrA-29711*	–21.7	11.8	
	WH88 12281 (B70)	Cattle bone	GrA-25707	–23.1	5.3	
	WH88 12301 (B54)	Cattle bone	OxA-13713	–22.1	5.3	
	WH88 1687 (B5338)	Large mammal bone	GrA-25546	–22.2	4.1	cf. cattle
	WH88 1688 (B5330)	Large mammal bone	OxA-13504	–21.3	4.7	cf. cattle
	WH88 1712 (B18)	Cattle bone	OxA-13503	–22.2	4.8	
	WH88 23207 (B4600)	Cattle bone	GrA-25553	–22.5	4.4	

	WH88 4225 (B1441)	Medium mammal bone	GrA-25556	−23.2	6.1	cf. sheep or pig
	WH88 4255 (B1458)	Medium mammal bone	OxA-13714	−22.0	6.4	cf. sheep or pig
	WH88 4330 (B1743)	Cattle bone	GrA-25706	−22.5	4.8	
	WH88 6419 (B1344)	Cattle bone	GrA-25560	−22.1	5.4	

* Immediately preceding/following measurement made at Oxford (OxA) or Groningen (GrA) on separate sample of same bone

Table 13.7. Correlations between human and faunal isotope values from Neolithic sites.

$\delta^{13}C$	Human	Cattle	Pig	Sheep
Human	1			
Cattle	0.62[2]	1		
Pig	−0.11	0.11	1	
Sheep	0.21	0.66[2]	0.12	1
$\delta^{15}N$				
Human	1			
Cattle	0.75[1]	1		
Pig	0.48	0.60[2]	1	
Sheep	0.72[2]	0.59[2]	0.89**	1
n	6	7	7	7

** $P<0.01$; [1]$0.10>P>0.05$; [2]$0.20>P>0.10$

Differences between species. The pattern of faunal values at the causewayed enclosures is consistent with that seen at other Neolithic sites for which there are enough data, e.g. the long barrows at Ascott-under-Wychwood (R. Hedges *et al*. 2007b) and Hazleton (R. Hedges *et al*. 2008), and Hambledon Hill (M. Richards 2000). Mean values for sheep and cattle are similar though cattle always have slightly more depleted values for $\delta^{13}C$ than sheep, and may have higher or lower $\delta^{15}N$ values, while pigs have clearly less depleted values for $\delta^{13}C$ and slightly enriched values for $\delta^{15}N$.

One obvious explanation might be that this reflects the different digestive physiologies of these animals, rather than isotopic differences in the diet; sheep and cattle are ruminants, with the foregut specialised to use bacterial fermentation to break down cellulose, while pigs are not. In support of this, red deer, also ruminants, group with sheep and cattle where data are available, while at Ascott-under-Wychwood isotope values from pigs identified as wild were not distinguishable from those of domestic pigs. It is not clear exactly why pig $\delta^{13}C$ values should be less depleted, but some physiological explanation might be possible. However, at later sites such as Thorpe Lea Nurseries and Yarnton (R. E. M. Hedges and J. Hamilton, unpublished work), Broxmouth, Trevelgue Head, Wetwang and Garton Slack, and Winnall Down (Jay and Richards 2006; 2007), and Roman York (Müldner and Richards 2007), pig values show an equally consistent but quite different relationship, with similar $\delta^{13}C$ values to sheep/cattle and higher $\delta^{15}N$s. It is unlikely that basic digestive physiology had changed over that time, but pig management may well have done, one probable explanation being a shift to feeding on human food waste giving pigs effectively a higher trophic level. In this case the enriched $\delta^{13}C$ values of Neolithic pigs would reflect a dietary difference. The slightly enriched $\delta^{15}N$ values in the Neolithic could plausibly be explained as due to a somewhat more omnivorous diet than sheep/cattle, or as a difference between ruminants and non-ruminants, but it is hard to explain the $\delta^{13}C$ values. One possibility to consider is the consumption of mycorrhizal and saprophytic fungi, which can have enriched $\delta^{13}C$ values compared to foliage (Hart *et al.* 2006; Trudell *et al.* 2004), reflecting more extensive use of wildwood resources by pigs in the Neolithic than in the Iron Age. This is not implausible, though it is generally assumed that Iron Age (and later) pigs also made considerable use of woodland resources (e.g. Grigson 1982b). Perhaps later woodlands were more intensively managed, with much less dead wood supporting saprophytic fungi with enriched $\delta^{13}C$ values (Hamilton *et al.* 2009).

The slight difference in mean $\delta^{13}C$ values between sheep and cattle seems to be consistent wherever prehistoric datasets are large enough to detect it. It is tempting to attribute it to a canopy effect, with sheep feeding in more open environments than cattle, by analogy with the difference between domestic cattle and aurochs seen at Ascott (Hedges *et al.* 2007b), and more generally in southern Scandinavia (Noe-Nygaard *et al.* 2005) and Britain (Lynch *et al.* 2008). However, a study of modern red deer populations feeding in open and forested environments (Stevens *et al.* 2006) was unable to demonstrate a canopy effect. If it does reflect a dietary difference, it might be to do with use of wetland resources rather than woodland. The ubiquity of the pattern (so far) might also suggest a metabolic rather than an environmental explanation, though it is not obvious what this might be.

Variation between causewayed enclosures. The patterns of faunal isotope ratios differ among the four sites, though as noted above, by rather small amounts compared with overall variability, and few of the differences are statistically significant. Many factors may contribute to this, and with only four sites it is unlikely that these can be distinguished. There is no clear pattern for this small set of sites in relation to obvious contrasts such as chalk (Windmill Hill, Chalk Hill) versus gravel (Abingdon) or wetter sites (Etton), species proportions at the sites, or the extent of forest clearance locally (as far as can be deduced from other environmental evidence).

Humans

The mean $\delta^{13}C$ and $\delta^{15}N$ values for humans from Chalk Hill are significantly less depleted than those from Windmill Hill. However, the mean values for the fauna also differ, with those from Chalk Hill also consistently less depleted (except pig $\delta^{13}C$, based on only 3 values at Chalk Hill). This will be discussed further below.

Comparing causewayed enclosures with other Early Neolithic sites

There are comparable data for humans and animals from the Cotswold long barrows at Ascott-under-Wychwood (R. Hedges *et al.* 2007b) and Hazleton (R. Hedges *et al.* 2008), and from the long barrow and enclosures at Hambledon (M. Richards 2000).

As discussed above, the pattern of values for cattle, sheep and pig from causewayed enclosures is consistent with that from the other sites. With all seven sites included, multivariate analysis showed that mean $\delta^{13}C$ differs significantly between all three species, while cattle and sheep mean $\delta^{15}N$ values differ significantly from pig but not from each other (*post hoc* multiple comparisons, Scheffé test, $Ps<0.01$), just as for causewayed enclosures alone. Including only domestic fauna, and analysing the two phases at Ascott-under-Wychwood separately, both $\delta^{13}C$ and $\delta^{15}N$ varied significantly between sites (*post hoc* multiple comparisons, Scheffé test, $Ps<0.05$, <0.01, respectively). For $\delta^{13}C$ this mainly reflected higher (less depleted) values at Hambledon, while for $\delta^{15}N$ it was the low values from Hazleton that stood out. Again, with this larger set of sites, there were no patterns that could clearly be related to environmental contrasts such as chalk or limestone geology versus low-lying, wetter sites, or to the site type.

Comparing humans and animals

The difference in $\delta^{15}N$ values between human and herbivore populations reflects their relative trophic level (ignoring fish for the moment). To estimate the difference, it seems reasonable to subtract the mean animal $\delta^{15}N$ value from the mean human value at a site, but there are some uncertainties in arriving at these figures. It is reasonable to omit juvenile humans and animals with high $\delta^{15}N$ values that are probably due to suckling (but see Jay and Richards 2006). One could take the mean of all herbivore values, but as we have shown that animal $\delta^{15}N$ values can differ between herbivore species, we would need to know how the different species are represented in human diets. We could weight the faunal means by relative abundance, but there are several alternative ways to express that, with differing results. We do not know how closely the relative quantities of bone deposited at a site, let alone the relative numbers of different species actually sampled, represent the diet of the humans at that site. Since cattle are much larger than sheep and pigs, it is likely that they supply the majority of meat and milk even at sites where they are relatively less represented, so one approach would be to look at the human-cattle difference ($\Delta^{15}N_{human-cattle}$). This is 4.9, 4.6 and 4.1‰ at Chalk Hill, Etton, and Windmill Hill respectively. For comparison, it is 4.5, 4.2 and 4.2 at Ascott-under-Wychwood (barrow construction phase), Hambledon and Hazleton, respectively. These are not significantly different between causewayed enclosures and other types of site (*t*-test), and are towards the high end of the expected range for humans eating meat and dairy products.

Is the difference between the high and low end of the range – in this case, between Chalk Hill and Windmill Hill – likely to represent a real difference in diet? Taken at face value, the figures would imply that >95% and >80%, respectively, of protein in collagen was from animal sources (taking $\Delta^{15}N_{collagen-diet}$ as 5‰), or a little less if pig made a significant contribution, but however calculated this remains surprisingly high. The issues raised have recently been thoroughly discussed (Hedges and Reynard 2007). The standard deviations of the estimate of $\Delta^{15}N_{human\text{-}cattle}$ are ±0.8‰ (Chalk Hill) and ±0.7‰ (Windmill Hill), so the difference is not statistically significant; at this level of error the difference would need to be about twice as great to be significant at α=0.05, though with larger samples of humans the error should be less, allowing finer discriminations. In any case, the causewayed enclosure results confirm the previous isotopic evidence from the Neolithic that a high proportion of human collagen protein came from animal sources. There is no evidence for the use of marine resources, either archaeologically or in the isotopes, though a small amount of freshwater fish in the diet cannot be ruled out on isotopic grounds.

If the standard interpretation of the human-faunal difference (Δ) holds (but see Hedges and Reynard 2007), at least 80% of collagen protein, implying about 50% of energy, in the diet comes from animal sources. There is little evidence that wild animals were important in the diet, while the relative importance of cultivated cereal versus gathered foods such as hazelnuts is still controversial (G. Jones 2000; Robinson 2000c; Rowley-Conwy 2004; Bogaard and Jones 2007). It is difficult to construct model human diets with very high values of Δ that are sustainable both nutritionally and agronomically, but including varying amounts of nuts as well as cereals, and particularly including dairy products, gives a more plausible range of possibilities. Some contemporary pastoralists may provide analogues of this kind of diet (see Hedges and Reynard 2007), though conditions may have been very different in southern Britain in the fourth millennium cal BC. A pastoralist economy need not imply reliance on wild plant foods as opposed to cultivated cereals, or any particular pattern of settlement mobility or sedentism; evidence from settlement sites, rather than sites of assembly such as causewayed enclosures, will be crucial in selecting among the various possibilities.

As noted above, both fauna and humans are more depleted in ^{13}C and ^{15}N at Windmill Hill than at the other sites. Are site means of faunal and human isotope ratios correlated when compared over all seven sites? Humans and cattle, and sheep and cattle (but not sheep and humans), show correlations of >0.6 in $\delta^{13}C$, though these are not significant ($0.20>P>0.10$) (Table 13.7). Correlations between $\delta^{15}N$ values are higher: >0.7 between humans and cattle or sheep (P= 0.09, 0.11 respectively), and 0.89 ($P<0.01$) between sheep and pig. Results from only a few more sites could confirm or falsify these apparent patterns, and if they turn out to be consistent would have important implications for understanding human palaeodiet. It would suggest that there is a real connection between animal and human values from the same site and that this is a valid scale of comparison; that measuring humans at a site without faunal measurements could be seriously misleading; and that the human-bovid dietary relationship is apparently similar over the range of sites studied.

13.7 Conclusions

The isotopic results for humans and animals from these four causewayed enclosures fit the emerging pattern for the earlier Neolithic in southern Britain. The $\delta^{13}C$ values of cattle, sheep and pig differ consistently, and pigs in particular show somewhat enriched $\delta^{13}C$ values relative to cattle and sheep, a pattern that is unusual at later sites. We suggest that this may be related to the use of wildwood resources. Pigs also have slightly enriched $\delta^{15}N$ values relative to cattle and sheep, but not to the extent seen at later sites, suggesting a different management regime in the earlier Neolithic. Mean faunal values can differ significantly between sites, and this needs to be taken into account when comparing human values.

The human-faunal difference ($\Delta^{15}N_{human\text{-}cattle}$) is over 4‰ at all the causewayed enclosures, in agreement with results from other earlier Neolithic sites. On the current interpretation, this implies a high proportion of animal protein (meat or dairy) in the diet. This could be interpreted as a pastoralist economy, but does not necessarily imply high reliance by people on wild plant foods as opposed to cultivated cereals, or any particular pattern of mobility.

Large comparable faunal samples are important when interpreting human isotopic values, and can also provide information on human interactions with the environment via agricultural systems, at geographical scales from site to landscape, and over archaeological time.

Acknowledgements

We would like to thank Ros Cleal of the Alexander Keiller Museum in Avebury, Arthur MacGregor and Alison Roberts of the Ashmolean in Oxford, Richard Sabin of the Natural History Museum and Pam Young of the British Museum in London, Grant Shand at Canterbury Archaeological Trust and Robin Bendrey for facilitating access to collections; Tony Lynch for permission to quote unpublished data; The Arts and Humanities Research Council for support of the Thames Valley project; and Frances Healy for her time, patience and company in the depths of the collections.

14 Neolithic narratives: British and Irish enclosures in their timescapes

Alex Bayliss, Frances Healy, Alasdair Whittle and Gabriel Cooney

14.1 Weaving narrative threads

If a 'landscape is time materializing' (Bender 2002, S103), a timescape is a dynamic land in which change materialises. It is a place accessed through the bare threads of chronology weaving together, crossing and connecting as warp and weft at particular points in space-time – 'events' in the parlance of relativist physics. But these 'events' and our chronological threads are not points and lines in Euclidean space (or even in some more curvaceous space-time metric). Both have areas, known to us only through the probability density functions of our posterior beliefs (Chapter 2.3), which reflect the varying resolution of our chronologies (Chapter 1.1).

We have already spun threads of chronology for selected sites in different regions of southern Britain. In some of those regions, and in Ireland, we have gone further and started to weave those threads into a cloth for the wider early Neolithic. In this chapter we will weave further sections of this material; the pattern of threads will be established by the sequences derived from our chronologies, the spacing of the threads will be set by the gaps and intervals between events in these sequences, and the ply of our yarns will be determined by the chronological resolution available to us. The resultant textile will, perforce, be rather uneven, but will reflect the structure of past events.

So, as we trace our chronological threads across the fabric of the insular early Neolithic, we are following not lines (Ingold 2007a, 84–90) but yarns of variable ply. Neighbouring threads may be near or far, the weave may be obscured by the thickness of our yarn, but, if we inhabit our thread, moving with space-time as a wayfarer (Mithen 2003), an event occurs, not as an unconnected point to be located in relation to our observer's position in the reference frame of our present, but as a happening in its context, deriving from past events and paving the way for future ones. Our observation can hope to come to not just a sense of this particular place at this particular time, but to reveal the history of the place as it moves forward through time.

This is surely what Paul Ricoeur meant when he wanted, in large part following on from Heidegger, to get away from time as a 'linear succession of instants', to explore the human experience of what he calls 'within-time-ness', and to investigate what he calls 'historicality', an emphasis on the weight of the past, and his view of temporality which he calls 'the plural unity of future, past and present' (Ricoeur 1980, 170–1). What is central for our purposes here is Ricoeur's insistence on the importance of narrative (1980; 1984). Narrative involves plot, 'the intelligible whole that governs a succession of events in any story' (Ricoeur 1980, 171). As his own account unfolds, it is clear that succession is important, as 'the episodic dimension' of narrative, alongside its 'configurational dimension, according to which the plot construes significant wholes out of scattered events' (Ricoeur 1980, 178); 'the humblest narrative is always more than a chronological series of events', since it elicits 'a configuration from a succession' (Ricoeur 1980, 178). In these circumstances, it is easy to disagree with his apparent dismissal of sequence, and what he calls, right from the beginning, the 'illusion of chronology' (Ricoeur 1980, 169). Chronology provides the succession which is required to elicit configuration. It relates scattered events and gives us access to the plot. It is not narrative, but a means to narrative.

Much, therefore, is at stake. We believe that we have to get succession right (and that the discipline has the means now to do this better), but that succession on its own is not enough; in narrative we can trace change, connection and causality. So far in this volume we have sought to exploit the now routine availability of Bayesian modelling to provide quantified, explicit, probabilistic date estimates for, first, a significant sample of early Neolithic enclosures in southern Britain and Ireland, and secondly, a variable sample of other forms of early Neolithic activity in those areas. We have proceeded region by region, and now it is time to bring the many models together, to provide generational narratives for the date, duration and character of the enclosures on the one hand and of other forms of early Neolithic activity on the other. In this way, as already seen in the regional chapters, we can provide estimates for the

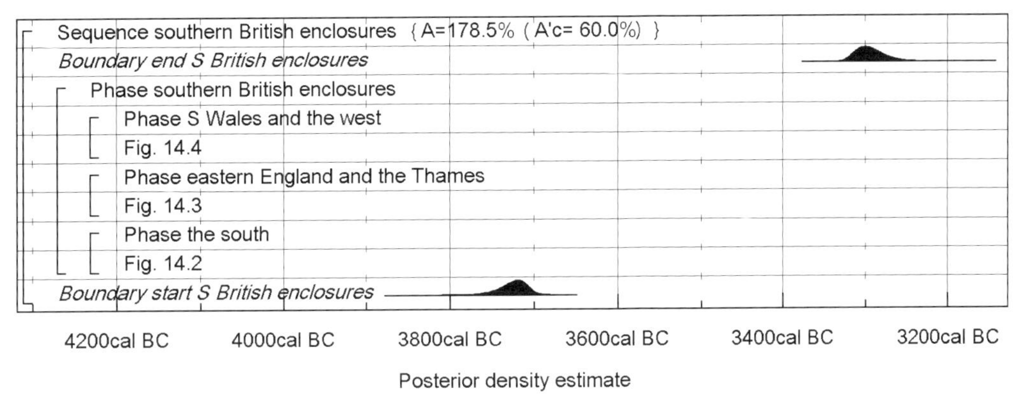

Fig. 14.1. Overall structure of the chronological model for the currency of causewayed and related enclosures in southern Britain. Each distribution represents the relative probability that an event occurred at a particular time. The distributions for the start and end of the use of each enclosure have been taken from the site models described in detail in Chapters 3–11 (and listed in the captions to Figs 14.2–4), and are shown in outline. Other distributions are based on the chronological model defined here, and shown in black. For example, the distribution 'start S British enclosures' is the estimated date when the first enclosure was constructed in this area. Distributions followed by a question mark are not included in the model for reasons explained in the text. The component sections of the model are shown in Figs 14.2–4. The large square brackets down the left-hand side of Figs 14.1–4, along with the OxCal keywords, define the overall model exactly.

place of enclosures within the history of the first centuries of the southern British and Irish Neolithic, and we can begin to use this control over the lapse of time to highlight some of the major issues concerning the use and character of these enclosures. We begin with southern Britain, starting with the enclosures themselves, and then comparing our date estimates for them with those separately derived for the start of the Neolithic. We then consider the place of some elements of early Neolithic things and practices individually. After this, we come back to Ireland and the Isle of Man, and briefly discuss some data from Scotland. There are many gaps in our coverage, and this chapter has to be regarded as a preliminary exercise in the wider task of constructing reliable chronologies and exploring narratives for the early Neolithic of Britain and Ireland as a whole. We will go on to discuss the many implications raised by our narratives in the final chapter.

14.2 Chronologies for enclosures in southern Britain

The currency of causewayed enclosures

A model for the construction and use of causewayed and related enclosures in southern Britain is shown in Figs 14.1–4. This has been constructed by taking the estimated dates for the start and, where appropriate, the end of the primary use of each site from the site models described in detail in Chapters 3–11. This constitutes the second twist of our hermeneutic spiral (Fig. 2.5), as the posterior density estimates provided by our site-based models now form the standardised likelihoods of this new model. The detail of the treatment of individual dates (for example why a particular measurement is treated as a *terminus post quem* or excluded) is given in the regional chapters. The prior information in this second round of modelling is now that enclosures were constructed and used continuously and relatively constantly over the period of their initial currency. We explore this assumption further below.

This model suggests that the first causewayed and related enclosure in southern Britain was constructed in *3765–3695 cal BC* (*95% probability*; Fig. 14.1: *start S British enclosures*), probably in *3740–3705 cal BC* (*68% probability*). It also suggests that the last enclosure in southern Britain went out of primary use in *3330–3255 cal BC* (*95% probability*; Fig. 14.1: *end S British enclosures*), probably in *3315–3280 cal BC* (*68% probability*). As discussed in the regional chapters, especially in relation to Windmill Hill (Chapter 3), endings are harder to define than beginnings.

The model shown in Figs 14.1–4 has good overall agreement ($A_{overall}$=178.5%). The endings of two sites, however, have been excluded from it. Although a model which includes all end dates has good overall agreement ($A_{overall}$=127.2%), in this interpretation *end Banc Du* has poor individual agreement (A=22.6%). It can be seen that the disuse of this enclosure falls more than half a millennium later than all the others considered in this volume (Fig. 14.4). This seems to relate to the late recut at this site (Chapter 11). When *end Banc Du* is excluded from the model, it again has good overall agreement ($A_{overall}$=135.9%), although now *end Haddenham* has extremely poor individual agreement (A=4.7%). For this reason, this distribution has also been excluded from the model (Fig. 14.3). The difficulties of dating Haddenham and the uncertain formation processes for the shell marl platform above the initial silts of its ditch, which provided the latest dates, have been discussed in Chapter 6.

The establishment of enclosures

Figure 14.5 investigates the period during which enclosures were constructed in southern Britain. In this case, a continuous and relatively constant period of enclosure

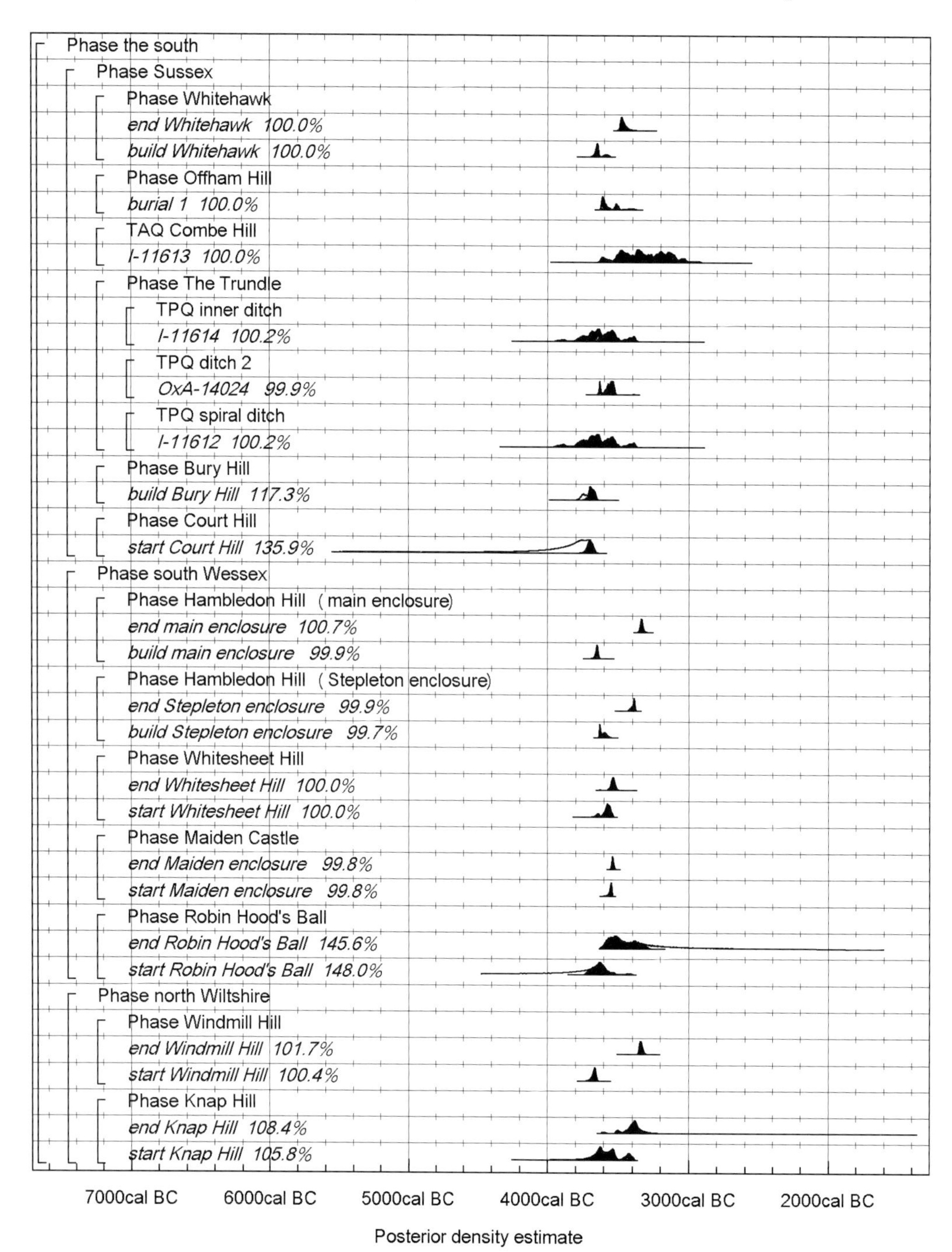

Fig. 14.2. Probability distributions of dates for causewayed and related enclosures from the south. The format is identical to that for Fig. 14.1. Distributions have been taken from the models defined in Figs 3.8–11 (Windmill Hill), Fig. 3.25 (Knap Hill), Fig. 4.51 (Robin Hood's Ball), Figs 4.41–5 (Maiden Castle), Fig. 4.26 (Whitesheet Hill), Figs 4.7–13 (Hambledon Hill), Fig. 5.28 (Court Hill), Fig. 5.25 (Bury Hill), Fig. 5.14 (Offham Hill), and Figs 5.5–9 (Whitehawk). Dates from The Trundle and Combe Hill have been calibrated (Stuiver and Reimer 1993). The overall structure of this model is shown in Fig. 14.1, and its other components in Figs 14.3–4.

construction is incorporated in the model along with the estimated start dates for each site provided by the site-based models defined in Chapters 3–11. This model suggests that new enclosures were established from *3750–3685 cal BC* (*95% probability*; Fig. 14.5: *start new S British enclosures*), probably from *3730–3700 cal BC* (*68% probability*). The last enclosure on virgin ground was constructed in *3595–3510 cal BC* (*95% probability*; Fig. 14.5: *end new S British enclosures*), probably in *3565–3525 cal BC* (*68% probability*). New enclosures were built for a period of *105–225 years* (*95% probability*; Fig. 14.6: *initiation S British enclosures*), probably for a period of *140–195 years* (*68% probability*).

A model which estimates the time when the circuits of the causewayed and related enclosures in southern Britain were dug is shown in Figs 14.7–10. This incorporates estimates for the dates of construction for all the circuits considered in Chapters 3–11. For Hambledon Hill the cross-

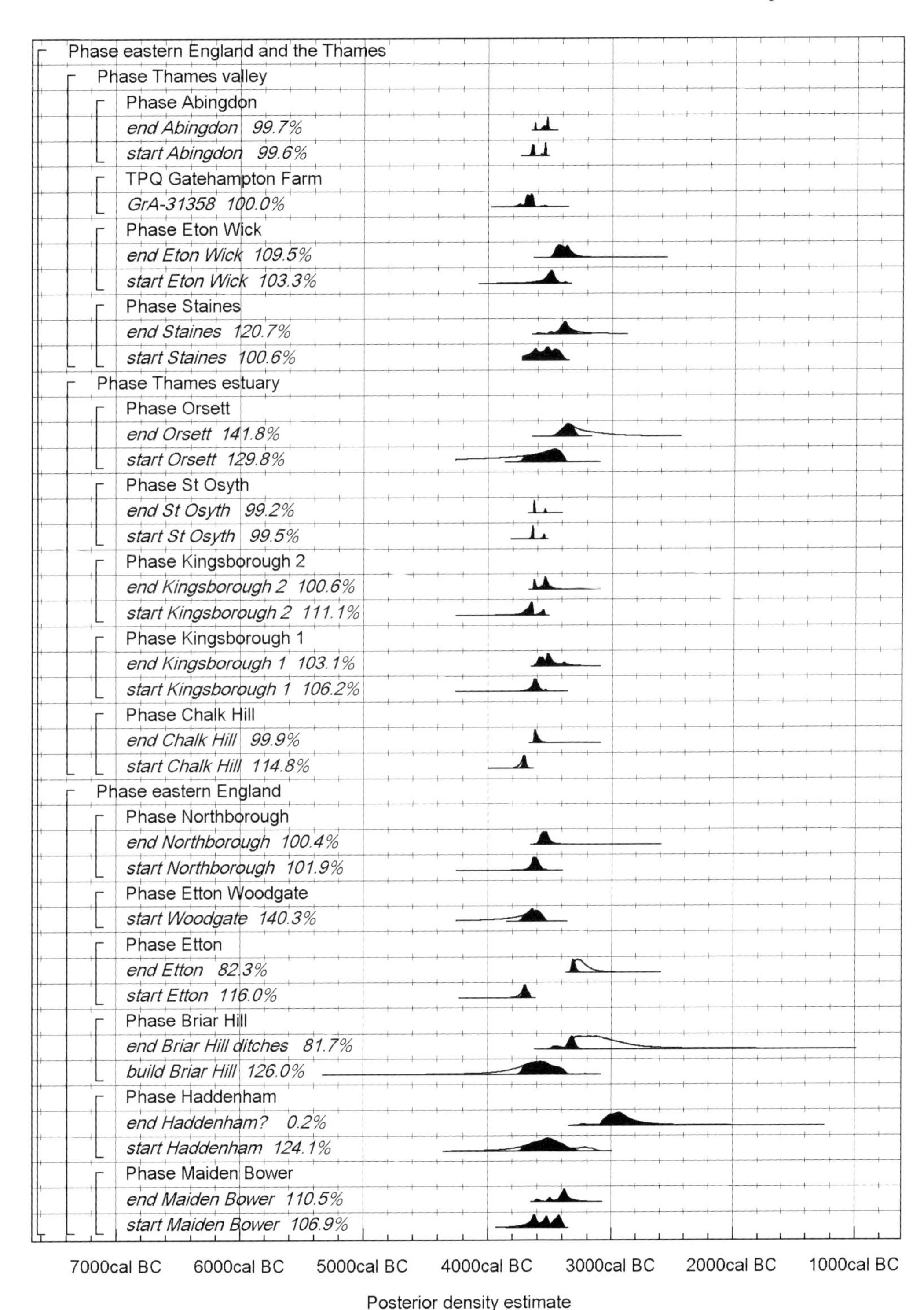

Fig. 14.3. Probability distributions of dates for causewayed and related enclosures from eastern England and the Thames valley. The format is identical to that for Fig. 14.1. Distributions have been taken from the models defined in Fig. 6.39 (Northborough), Fig. 6.36 (Etton Woodgate), Fig. 6.33 (Etton), Fig. 6.23 (Briar Hill), Fig. 6.11 (Haddenham), Fig. 6.4 (Maiden Bower), Fig. 7.21 (Chalk Hill), Figs 7.15 and 7.17 (Kingsborough 1 and 2), Fig. 7.10 (Orsett), Fig. 7.6 (St Osyth), Figs 8.18–8.21 (Abingdon), Fig. 8.5 (Eton Wick), and Fig. 8.3 (Staines). The date from Gatehampton Farm has been calibrated (Stuiver and Reimer 1993). The overall structure of this model is shown in Fig. 14.1, and its other components in Figs 14.2 and 14.4.

dykes are treated here as outer circuits of the enclosure; the outworks are not included in the model. This model is therefore different to that defined in Fig. 14.5, because now we are investigating whether further elaboration of existing sites continued once new monuments had ceased to be founded. Again, a continuous and relatively constant period of earthwork construction is assumed. *UB-4267*, from the outer east cross-dyke on Hambledon Hill (Chapter 4), has poor individual agreement if included in the model (A=4.7%), although the model as a whole has good overall

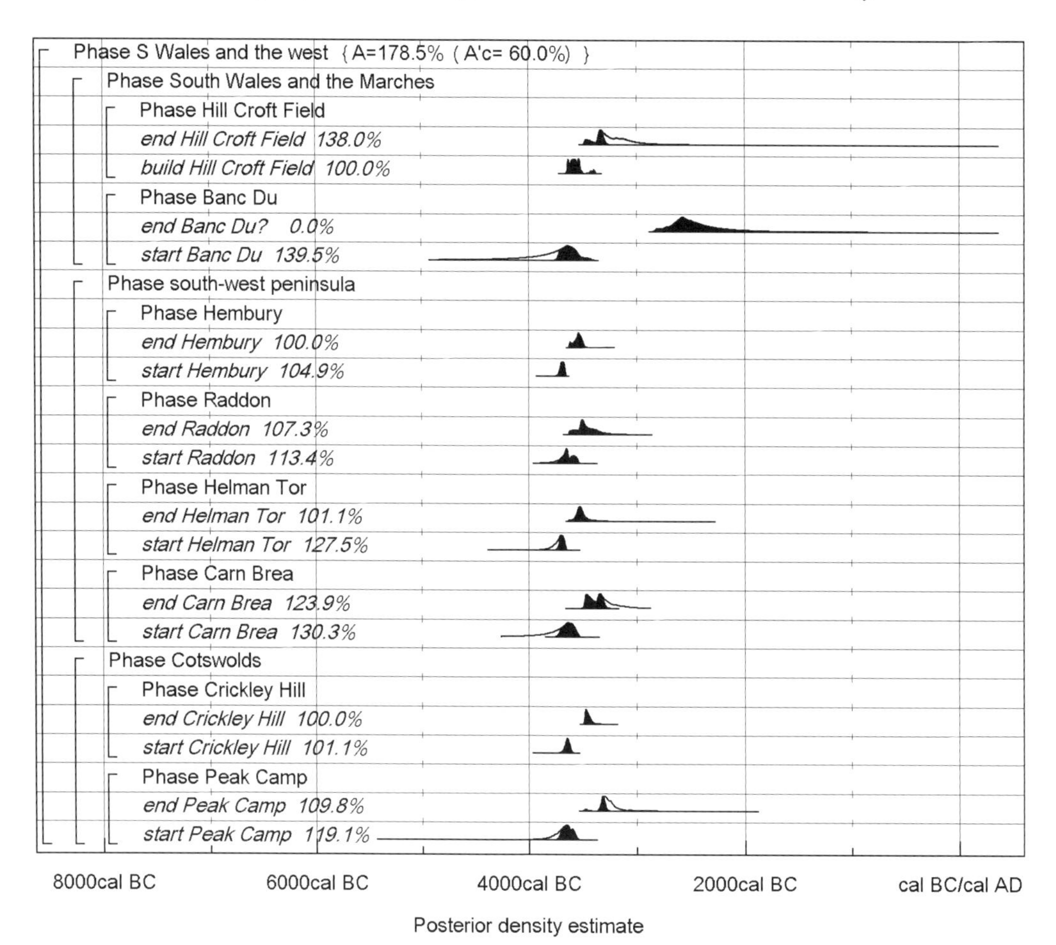

Fig. 14.4. Probability distributions of dates for causewayed and related enclosures from south Wales and the west. The format is identical to that for Fig. 14.1. Distributions have been taken from the models defined in Fig. 9.19 (Peak Camp), Figs 9.7–10 (Crickley Hill), Fig. 10.25 (Carn Brea), Fig. 10.22 (Helman Tor), Fig. 10.16 (Raddon), Figs 10.9–12 (Hembury), Fig. 11.15 (Church Lawford and Lower Luggy), Fig. 11.8 (Banc Du) and Fig. 11.3 (Hill Croft Field). The overall structure of this model is shown in Fig. 14.1, and its other components in Figs 14.2–3.

agreement in this reading ($A_{overall}$=77.7%). This date estimate may relate to a remodelling of the ditch segment in question (Chapter 4) and so may constitute continued use rather than fresh construction. If this distribution is excluded from the model, however, it then has poor overall agreement ($A_{overall}$=38.3%). Consideration of the individual indices of agreement clearly shows that it is the later circuits which have poor agreement (such as *build Orsett inner*, A=7.5%; *build Orsett entrance*, A=9.3%; *build Eton Wick inner*, A=29.4%). The construction dates for these three earthworks have therefore also been excluded from this model. It seems that the phase of construction of the circuits of southern British enclosures is not distributed uniformly, but rather that a few circuits continued to be built after an intensive period of circuit construction. In order to estimate the time when the first circuit was constructed, it is necessary, however, to define an ending for the period when circuits were dug. We have chosen to exclude the estimates for the construction of the dated circuits at Orsett and Eton Wick, and for the outer east cross-dyke at Hambledon Hill, from the model shown in Figs 14.7–10, which raises the overall agreement to an acceptable level ($A_{overall}$=84.0%). In effect, this approach estimates the end of the hey-day of circuit construction, rather than the end of all circuit construction. In this scenario, enclosure construction may have tailed off rather than come to a sudden halt. This approach is admittedly somewhat arbitrary, as we could, for example, have chosen to remove other potentially late constructions (such as Fig. 4.9: *build Knap Hill*; *build inner south cross-dyke*). In practice, however, these choices do not affect the outputs of the model importantly.[1] Although Eton Wick and Orsett are in the Thames valley and estuary respectively, it should be noted that other candidates for late circuits are to be found elsewhere.

This model suggests that the intensive construction of causewayed and related enclosure circuits in southern Britain began in *3715–3670 cal BC* (*95% probability*; Fig. 14.7: *intensify building circuits*), probably in *3705–3680 cal BC* (*68% probability*). The model suggests that this period of intensive circuit construction ended in *3555–3515 cal BC* (*95% probability*; Fig. 14.7: *end building new circuits*), probably in *the 3540s or 3530s cal BC* (*68% probability*). The hey-day of circuit construction spanned a period of *120–190 years* (*95% probability*; Fig. 14.11: *dig circuits*), probably of *135–170 years* (*68% probability*).

Figure 14.12 shows the estimated dates relating to

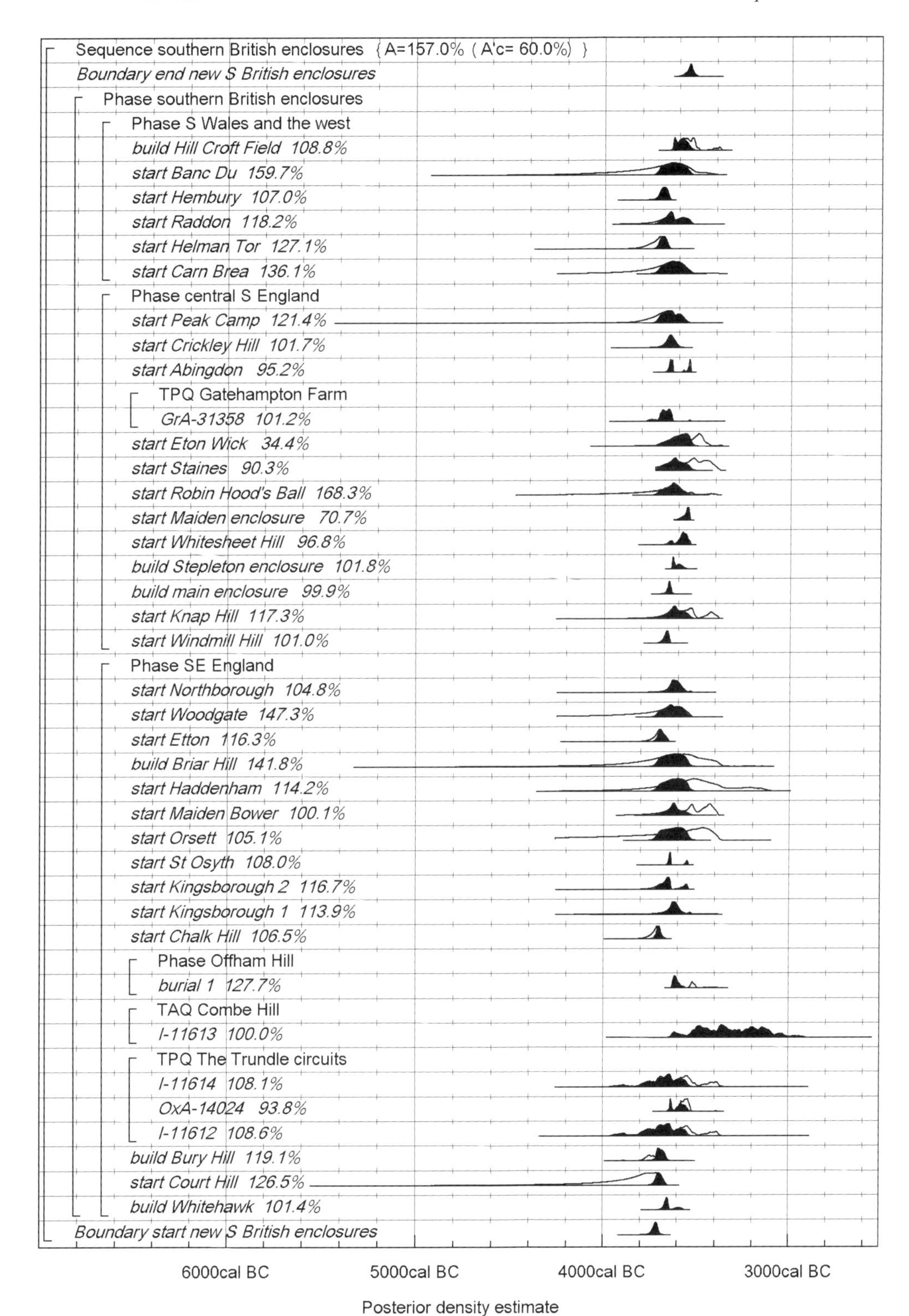

Fig. 14.5. Probability distributions of dates for the start of causewayed and related enclosures in southern Britain. Distributions have been taken from the models defined in Chapters 3–11, as detailed in the captions to Figs 14.2–4. The format is identical to that for Fig. 14.1. The large square brackets down the left-hand side, along with the OxCal keywords, define the overall model exactly.

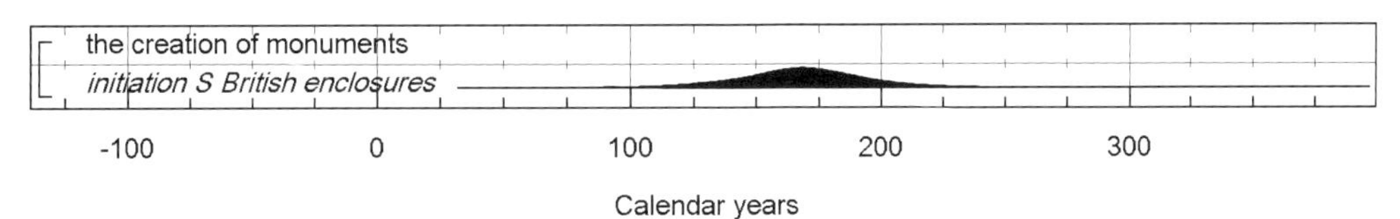

Fig. 14.6. Probability distribution of the number of years during which new causewayed and related enclosures were established in southern Britain, derived from the model defined in Fig. 14.5.

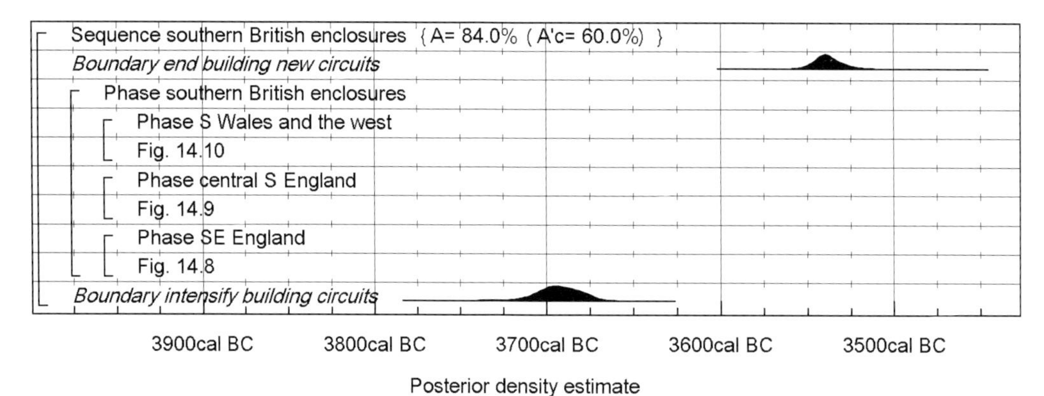

Fig. 14.7. Overall structure of the chronological model for the main period during which the circuits of the causewayed and related enclosures in southern Britain were constructed. Distributions have been taken from the models defined in Chapters 3–11, as detailed in the captions to Figs 14.2–4. The format is identical to that for Fig. 14.1. The large square brackets down the left-hand side of Figs 14.7–10, along with the OxCal keywords, define the overall model exactly.

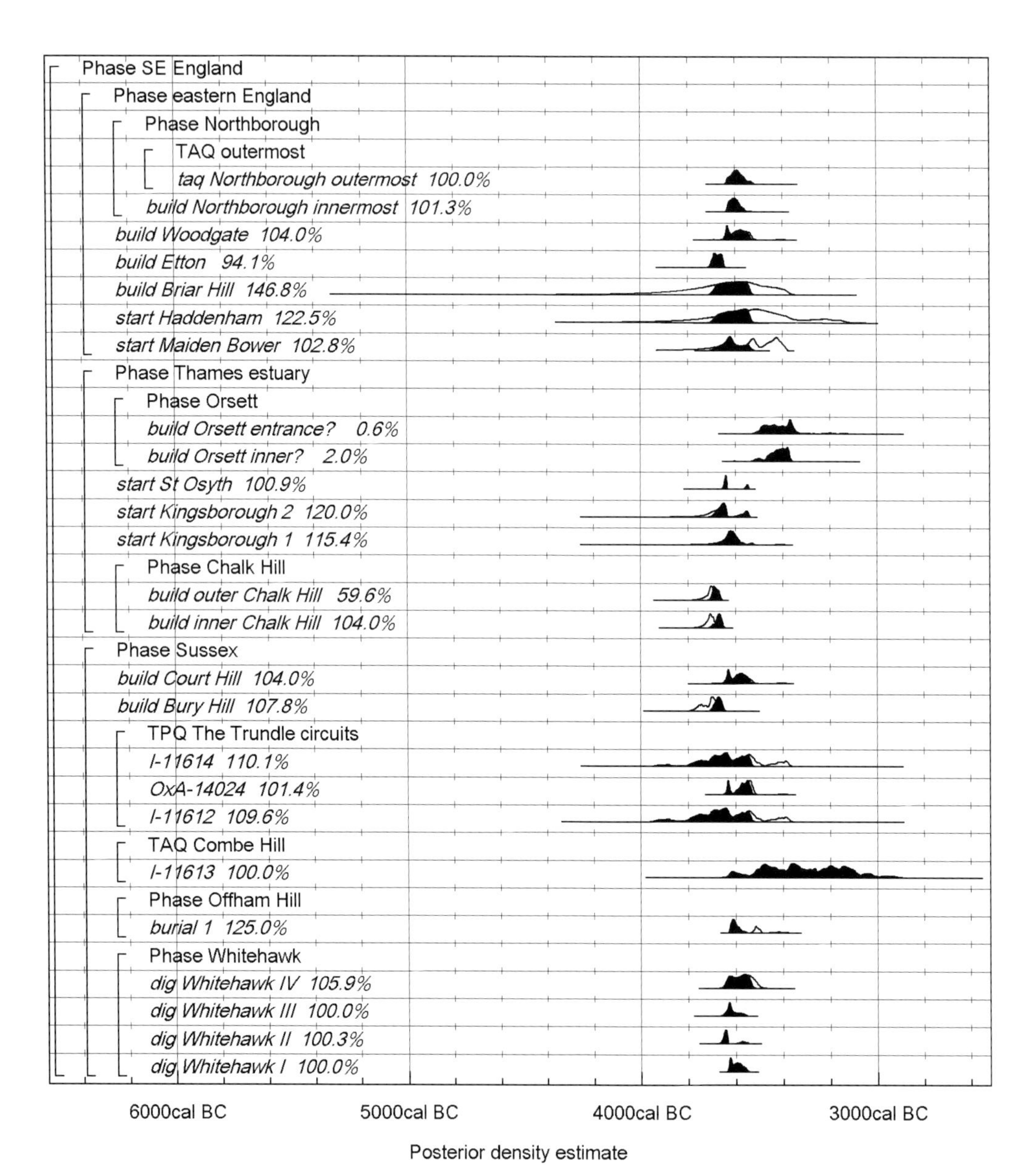

Fig. 14.8. Probability distributions of construction dates for circuits of causewayed and related enclosures from south-east England. The format is identical to that for Fig. 14.1. The overall structure of this model is shown in Fig. 14.7, and its other components in Figs 14.9–10.

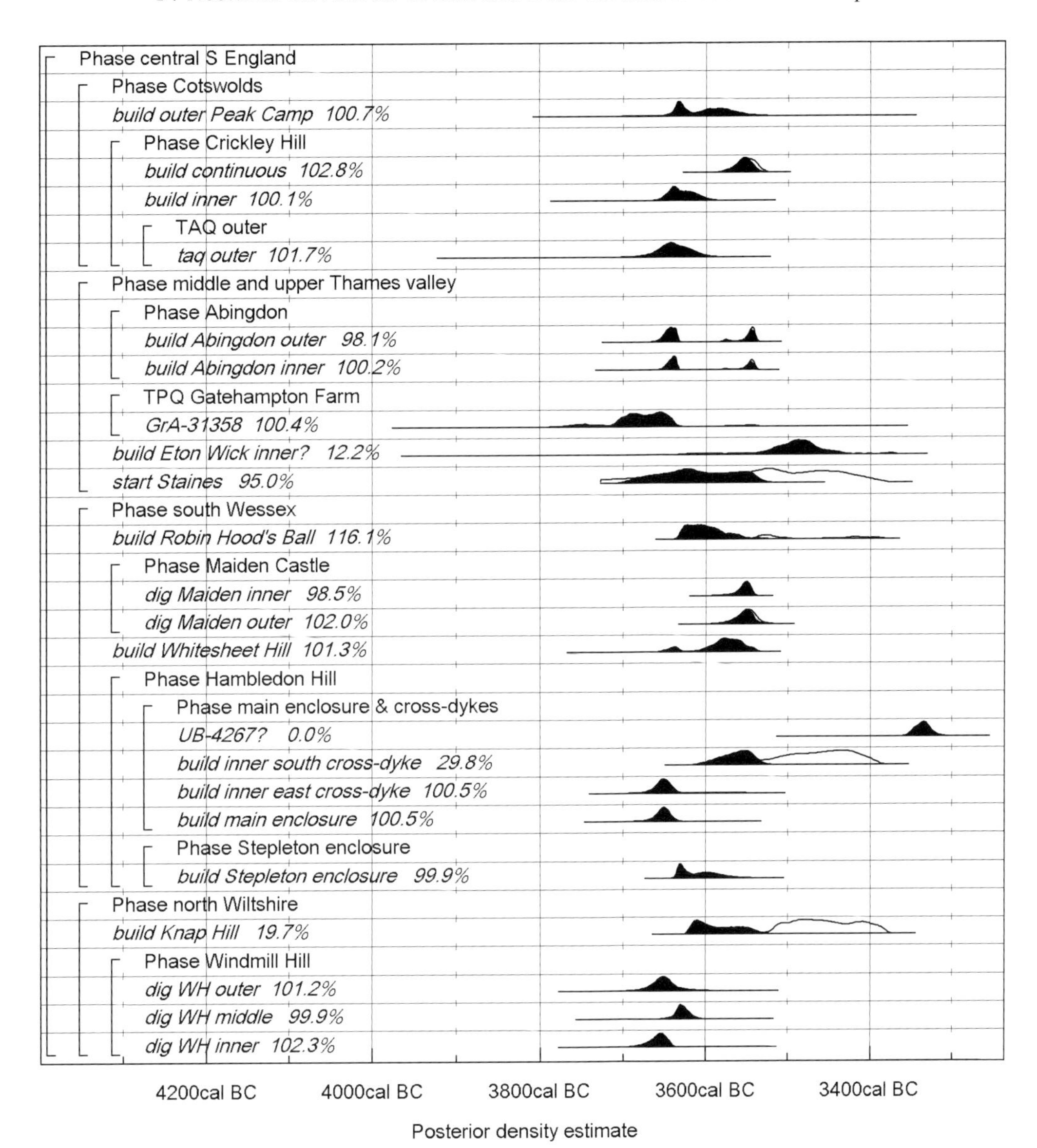

Fig. 14.9. Probability distributions of construction dates for circuits of causewayed enclosures from central-southern England. The format is identical to that for Fig. 14.1. The overall structure of this model is shown in Fig. 14.7, and its other components in Figs 14.8 and 4.10.

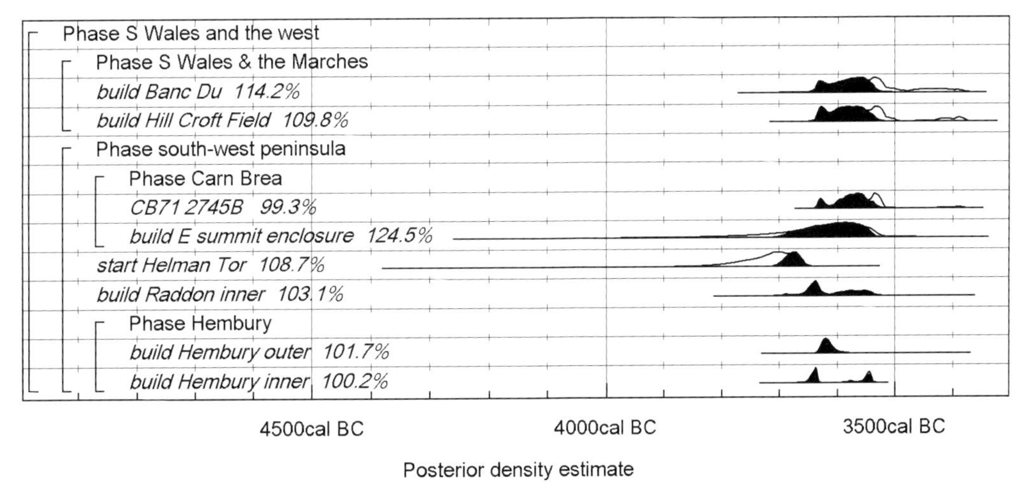

Fig. 14.10. Probability distributions of construction dates for circuits of causewayed and related enclosures from south Wales and the west. The format is identical to that for Fig. 14.1. The overall structure of this model is shown in Fig. 14.7, and its other components in Figs 14.8–9.

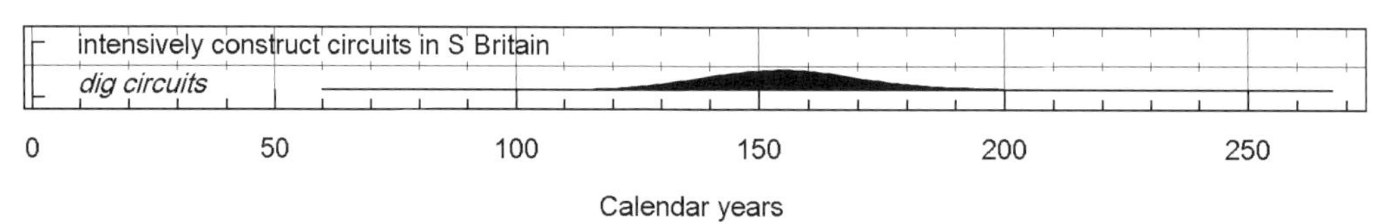

Fig. 14.11. Probability distribution of the number of years during which most of the circuits of the causewayed and related enclosures in southern Britain were constructed, derived from the model shown in Figs 14.7–10.

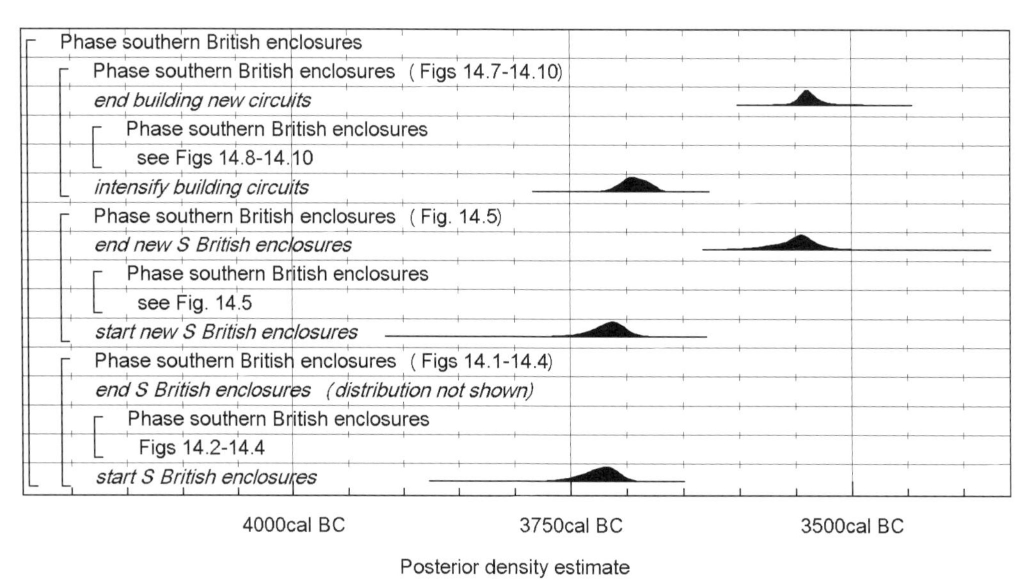

Fig. 14.12. Estimates for the date when the first causewayed and related enclosure was constructed in southern Britain, derived from the models defined in Figs 14.1–4, Fig. 14.5, and Figs 14.7–10, and for when the phase of construction ended according to the models shown in Fig. 14.5 and Figs 14.7–10.

the construction of causewayed and related enclosures in southern Britain. The models for the overall currency of southern British enclosures (Figs 14.1–4) and for the foundation of enclosures in this area (Fig. 14.5) agree in placing the construction of the first enclosure in the last quarter of the 38th century cal BC (Fig. 14.12: *start S British enclosures* and *start new S British enclosures*). The model for the intensive period of circuit construction provides an estimate which is significantly later, falling in the first quarter of the 37th century cal BC (Fig. 14.12: *intensify building circuits*). Each model estimates the dates of slightly different archaeological events (Fig. 14.13). The model shown in Fig. 14.5 estimates the time when the first enclosure was established, and the model defined in Figs 14.1–4 estimates the time when the first enclosure came into use. The times of these two events were presumably in reality very close, and the date estimates from these models are practically identical (Fig. 14.12). The third model (Figs 14.7–10) considers the period of intensive circuit building, and so *intensify building circuits* estimates the time when this more concentrated activity began. The difference between *start S British enclosures* and *intensify building circuits* therefore provides an indication of the tempo of the introduction of the enclosure phenomenon. This occurred within *−10–75 years* (*95% probability*; Fig. 14.14: *introduce enclosures*), probably within *10–50 years* (*68% probability*). From the shape of this probability distribution, it is apparent that it took a generation or so for this new practice to become more widely established.

The spread of enclosures

Turning now to the spatial dimension of the introduction of causewayed and related enclosures across southern Britain, the time when the first dated enclosure in each of our regional chapters was constructed, derived from the model shown in Figs 14.7–10, is shown in Fig. 14.15. It should be noted that this estimate does not relate to any particular dated enclosure in a region, but rather combines the earlier parts of the date estimates for each of the dated enclosures to produce a new estimate for the time when the first of the enclosures was established (and see Chapter 2.4.1). Enclosures do not seem to have appeared in all regions at the same time. They were established first in regions with south- or east-facing coastlines, in eastern England, the Thames estuary, Sussex and the south-west peninsula (Fig. 14.16), probably first on the Thames estuary. It is *more than 75% probable* that the first dated enclosure in the Thames estuary was earlier than the first dated enclosure in any other region. The idea of enclosure seems to have spread from the coast first to Wessex, perhaps in the second quarter of the 37th century cal BC, then to the Cotswolds and the middle and upper Thames valley, perhaps in the third quarter of the 37th century cal BC,

Table 14.1. Estimates of ditch length for the dated earthworks included in Figs 14.19–23.

Site	Ditch	Ditch length (m, rounded)	Worker days, where available (rounded)
A. Sites with resource estimates			
Abingdon	Inner	200	140 without turf revetment (Startin 1982a)
Abingdon	Outer	310	960 without turf revetment (Startin 1982a)
Haddenham		1110	2670 (Evans and Hodder 2006, 316)
Hambledon Hill	Main enclosure	1000	7015 with timber box frame 5520 earthmoving alone (Mercer 2008b)
Hambledon Hill	Inner E cross-dyke	280	1205 with timber box frame 500 earthmoving alone (Mercer 2008b)
Hambledon Hill	Inner S cross-dyke	170	1110 with timber box frame 700 earthmoving alone (Mercer 2008b)
Hambledon Hill	Shroton outwork	290	2685 with timber box frame 1960 earthmoving alone (Mercer 2008b)
Hambledon Hill	Stepleton enclosure	375	1795 with timber box frame 860 earthmoving alone (Mercer 2008b)
Hambledon Hill	Inner Stepleton outwork	300	2420 with timber box frame 1670 earthmoving alone (Mercer 2008b)
Hambledon Hill	Middle Stepleton outwork	500	2460 with timber box frame 1210 earthmoving alone (Mercer 2008b)
Hambledon Hill	Outer Stepleton outwork	500	2885 with timber box frame 1640 earthmoving alone (Mercer 2008b)
Windmill Hill	Inner	230	160 (Startin 1982b)
Windmill Hill	Middle	690	1310 (Startin 1982b)
Windmill Hill	Outer	1130	4810 (Startin 1982b)
B. Others			
Banc Du	Inner	700	
Bury Hill		430	
Chalk Hill	Inner	250, calculated from estimated maximum diameter by excavator (Shand 2001, 8)	
Chalk Hill	Outer	530, calculated from estimated maximum diameter (Shand 2001, 16)	
Court Hill		600	
Etton		530	
Hembury	Inner	150, if earthwork simply cuts off spur	
Kingsborough 2		270, if earthwork indeed open on steepest side	

Site	Ditch	Ditch length (m, rounded)	Worker days, where available (rounded)
Knap Hill		560	
Maiden Castle	Inner	980	
Maiden Castle	Outer	1110	
Northborough	Innermost	490	
Offham Hill	Outer	340, if complete (Oswald *et al.* 2001, fig. 4.8)	
Orsett	Inner	310	
Orsett	Middle	490, if complete	
Orsett	Outer	530, if complete	
Peak Camp	Outer	150, if earthwork simply cuts off spur	
Raddon	Inner	310	
Robin Hood's Ball	Inner	390	
Whitehawk	DI	320	
Whitehawk	DII	400	
Whitehawk	DIII	640	
Whitehawk	DIV	830	
Whitesheet Hill		370	

and then to south-west Wales and the Marches towards the end of the 37th century cal BC. Figure 14.17 shows the tempo of the spread of enclosures from a notional centre in the Thames estuary – to south Wessex within one or two generations, to the middle and upper Thames valley perhaps within two generations, and to south-west Wales and the Marches in three or four generations.

At this point it is necessary to highlight the limitations of the current dataset. On the one hand, Figure 14.15 represents a real step forward in our understanding of Neolithic chronology, since we are now able to consider change on a generational scale. On the other hand, the number of circuits which we have been able to date is limited, and if our sample is not representative, then even the relatively clear patterns shown in Fig. 14.15 may be spurious. We are conscious, for example, that for the upper Thames only Abingdon has been dated, and more than a dozen other enclosures are known only as cropmarks. It is obvious that Abingdon could simply be a late example within its regional sequence. A second reservation relates to the technical limitations of the model defined in Figs 14.7–10. We have already discussed the problem of defining the end of the phase of circuit construction, but are also concerned that the date estimates for different circuits within the same site are not statistically independent, since they derive from overall site-based models.

For these reasons, another model has been constructed which estimates the date when the first site was established in a number of areas in southern Britain (Fig. 14.18). This is of the form shown in Fig. 14.5. There are insufficient dated sites to enable this approach to be applied to each region covered by the individual chapters, and so, on the basis of the pattern shown in Fig. 14.15, we have amalgamated some regions into areas. The Thames estuary, eastern England and Sussex are grouped as south-east England for these purposes; the south-west peninsula stands as a region, though here dated sites are in particularly short supply; and south Wessex, north Wiltshire, the middle and upper Thames valley, and the Cotswolds have been combined to form central-southern England. There are too few dated sites in south-west Wales and the Marches for this region to do other than stand alone. The same spatial pattern is apparent in this analysis, with the enclosures in south-east England and the south-west peninsula being slightly earlier than those in central-southern England, and those in both being perhaps more substantially earlier than

Fig. 14.13. Illustration showing the archaeological differences between the date estimates for southern Britain shown in Fig. 14.12: (top) the time when the first enclosure was established (Fig. 14.5), (middle) the time when the first enclosure came into use (Figs 14.1–4) and (lower) the time when the intensive period of circuit construction began (Figs 14.7–10).

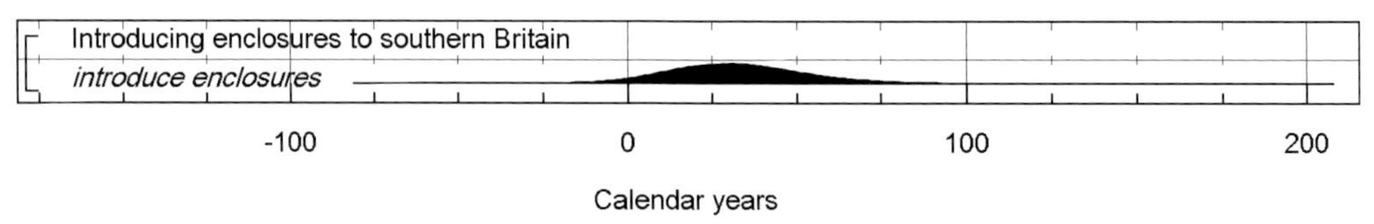

Fig. 14.14. Probability distribution for the speed of the introduction of causewayed and related enclosures to southern Britain (calculated as the difference between start S British enclosures *(Figs 14.1–4) and* intensify building circuits *(Fig. 14.7–10)).*

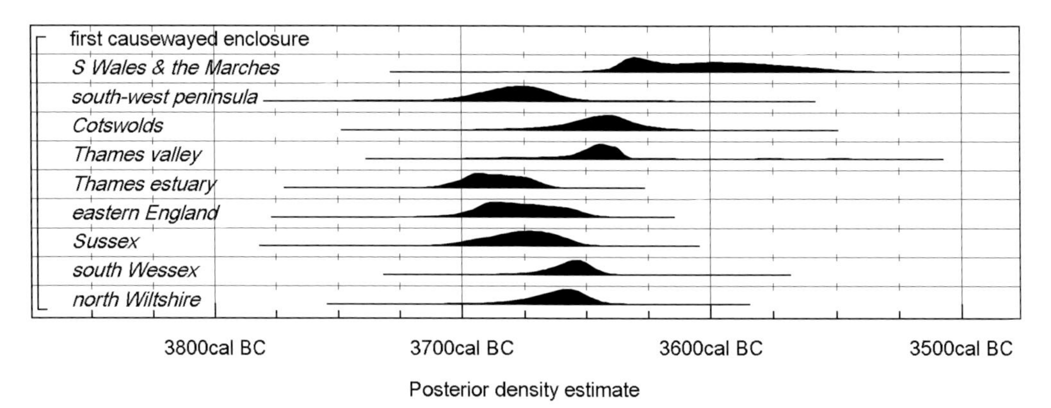

Fig. 14.15. Probability distributions for the first dated enclosure in each of our regional chapters, derived from the model shown in Figs 14.7–10.

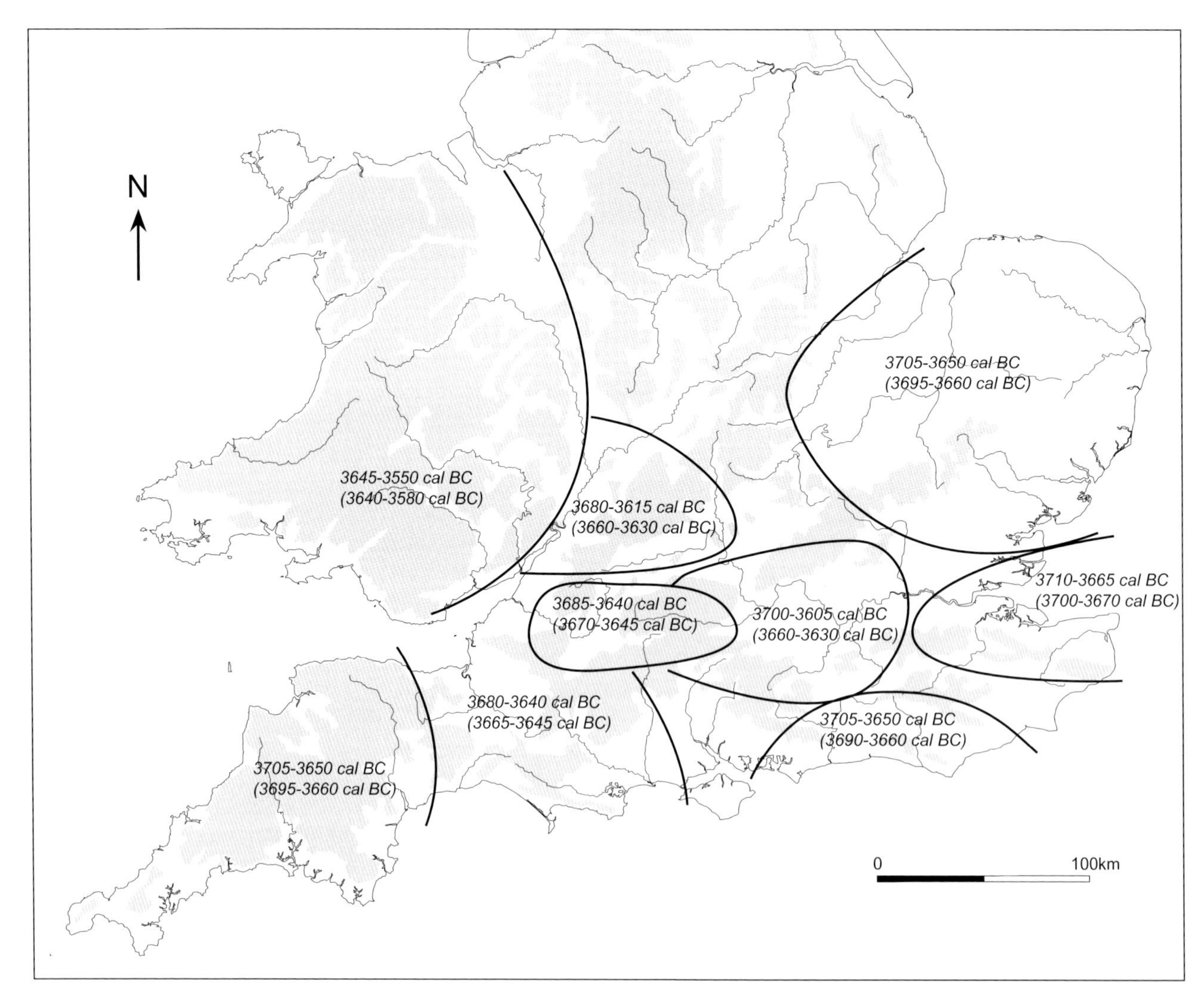

Fig. 14.16. Map showing the spread of causewayed and related enclosures across southern Britain, at 95% probability (68% probability in brackets).

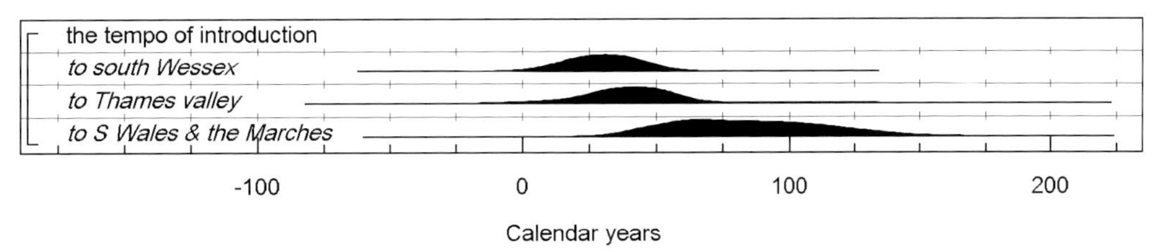

Fig. 14.17. Probability distributions for the number of years required for the spread of causewayed and related enclosures to selected regions of southern Britain (from a notional origin in the Thames estuary), derived from the model shown in Figs 14.7–10.

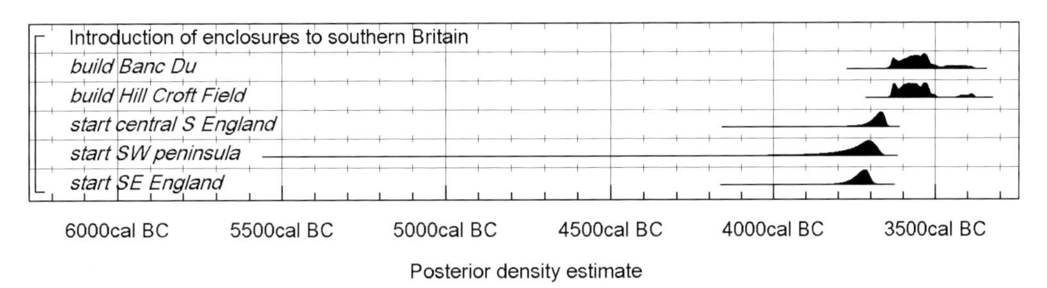

Fig. 14.18. Probability distributions for the start of enclosure by area, derived from the model shown in Fig. 14.5.

those in south-west Wales and the Marches (Fig. 14.18). This sensitivity analysis reassures us that the temporal and spatial trends which we have suggested for the introduction of enclosures across southern Britain are realistic.

The effort of construction

From the date estimates for the causewayed and related enclosures in southern Britain set out in Chapters 3–11, we are also now in a position to consider the effort expended by successive generations of people in the task of constructing ditch circuits. It is of course no easy matter to make calculations of labour requirements for enterprises of this kind. On the one hand, it is often far from straightforward to calculate both the total length of a circuit and the total volume of a given ditch segment, let alone that of a whole circuit. On the other, it is difficult to know how quickly Neolithic people could have dug a given volume of different subsoils such as chalk, greensand or gravel, with the tools available. The formulae most often employed (e.g. by Startin 1982a; 1982b; Startin and Bradley 1981; Mercer 2008b; A. Chapman 1985; Evans and Hodder 2006) are based on a combination of standard figures for manual labour in the eighteenth and nineteenth centuries, and of observations from recent experimental earthworks built without metal tools.

For calculating the effort of construction, we have used the estimated dates for the construction of ditch circuits provided by the site-based models detailed in Chapters 3–11. This means that we have avoided the problem of defining the end of the phase of circuit construction apparent in the model defined in Figs 14.7–10. We have used two approaches, the adoption of resource estimates already calculated for a minority of excavated enclosures by what are essentially the methods of a quantity surveyor and a simpler calculation based on ditch lengths alone, which applies to a wider sample of sites.

We have drawn on existing calculations of resource estimates for a small set of circuits, at Abingdon (Startin 1982a), Haddenham (Evans and Hodder 2006, 316), Hambledon Hill (Mercer 2008b), and Windmill Hill (Startin 1982b). In each case calculations have been made of the total volume of material extracted from the ditches and hence of the labour required to dig them and build the accompanying banks. In some cases this has been accompanied by estimates for other elements, notably timber rampart structures or palisades (Table 14.1). We then calculated for each circuit for which such estimates were available the probability that it was constructed in a given 25-year period, and multiplied this figure by the worker days required for the circuit (e.g. there is a 68.8% chance that the inner ditch at Windmill Hill was dug between 3650 and 3625 cal BC and, since the inner ditch required 160 days work, proportionately 110 worker days (68.8% of 160) were employed for this circuit in this time period). The figures for all the relevant circuits were totalled for the given time period and this figure divided by the total number of worker days required for the construction of all the relevant earthworks. So for example 7175 worker days were required for the earthworks constructed between 3650 and 3625 cal BC. As just over 27,000 worker days were required to construct all the relevant earthworks, 26.6% of the total effort was expended during this period.

The total effort expended in each 25-year period to construct these earthworks is shown in Fig. 14.19 (red line). It can be seen that there was a dramatic increase in building activity in the mid-37th century cal BC, which parallels the spread of the enclosure phenomenon at this time (Fig. 14.15). These estimates are practically identical whether the entire construction of the circuits is considered or just

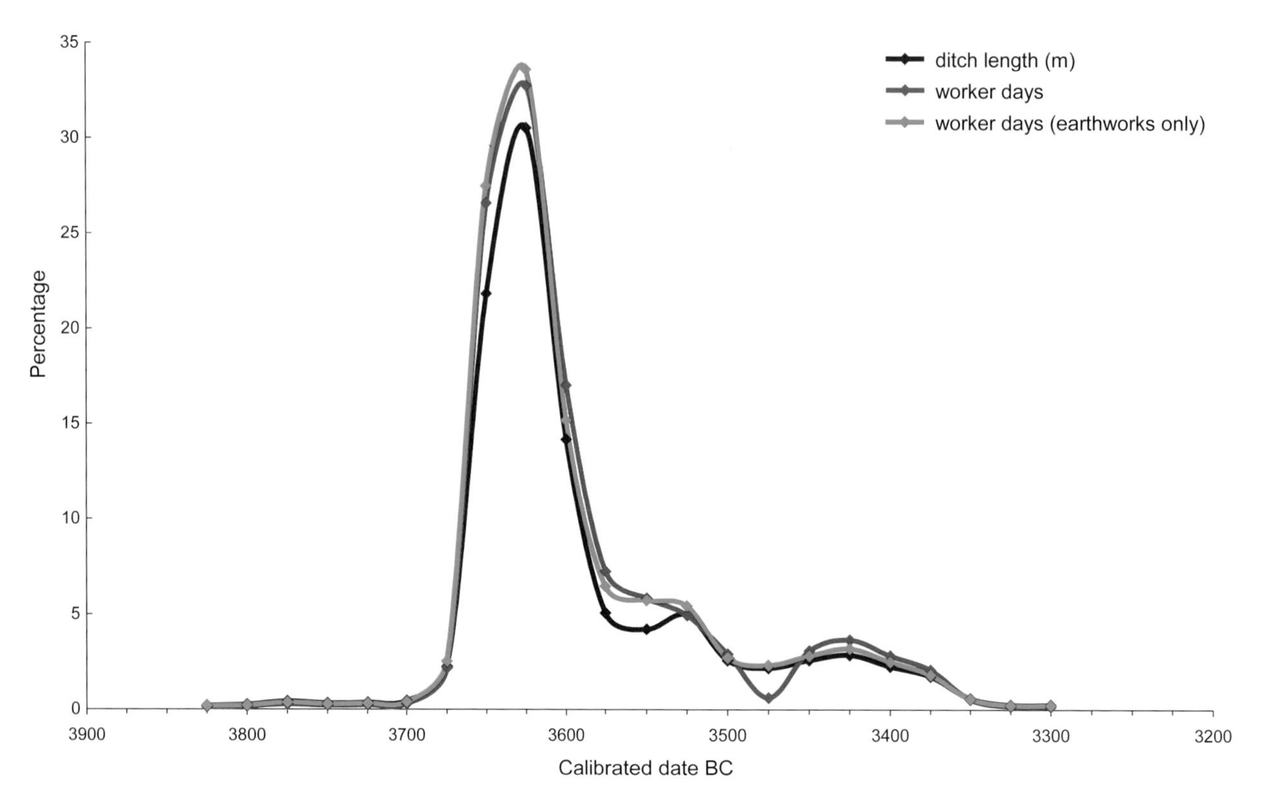

Fig. 14.19. Resource estimates for the construction of earthworks relating to the enclosures at Hambledon Hill (Mercer 2008b), Windmill Hill (Startin 1982b) and Haddenham (Evans and Hodder 2006) by 25-year period, compared with estimates based simply on ditch length. The red line includes estimates for timberwork at Hambledon Hill; the green line is based on earth-moving only.

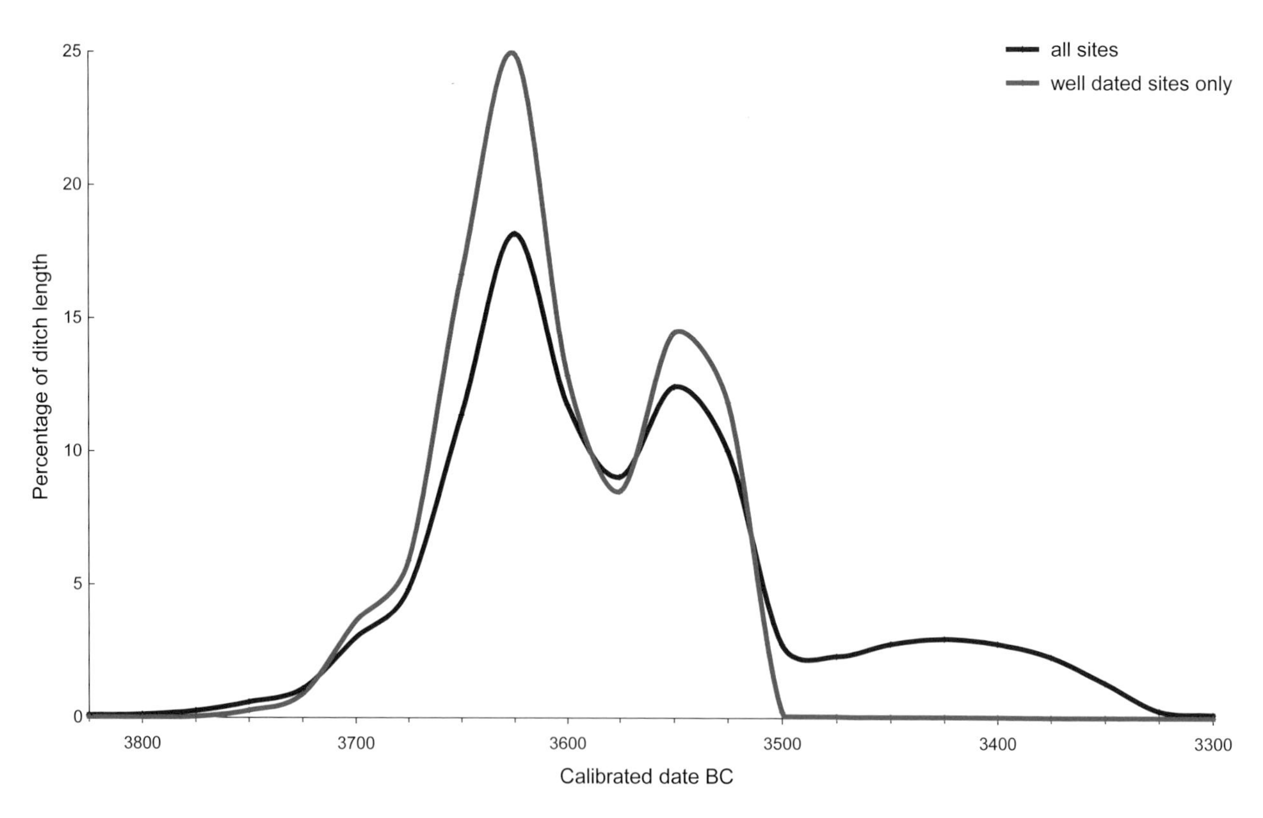

Fig. 14.20. Proportion of total ditch length excavated in each 25-year period for the circuits listed in Table 14.1. The red line includes circuits with estimated construction dates spanning less than a century; the blue line includes all the circuits.

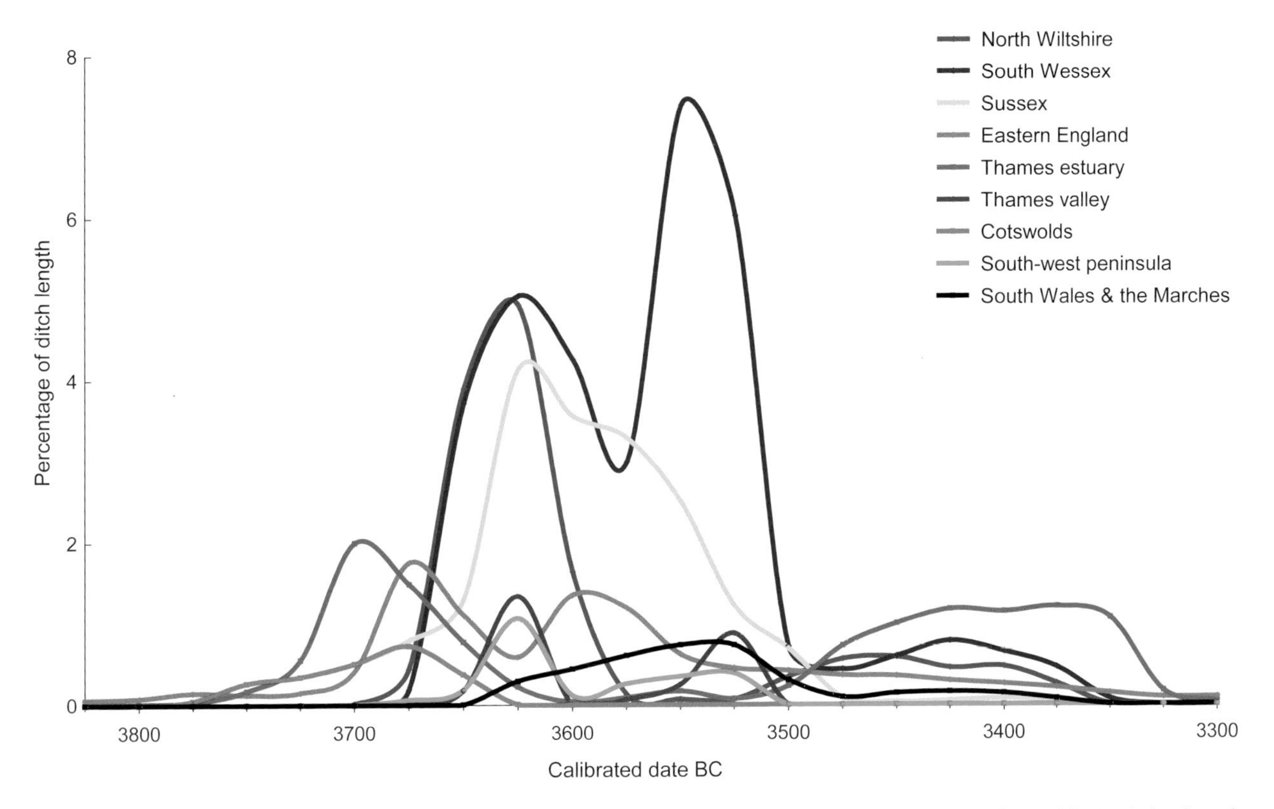

Fig. 14.21. Proportion of total ditch length excavated in each 25-year period for the circuits listed in Table 14.1, broken down by the regions covered in Chapters 3–11.

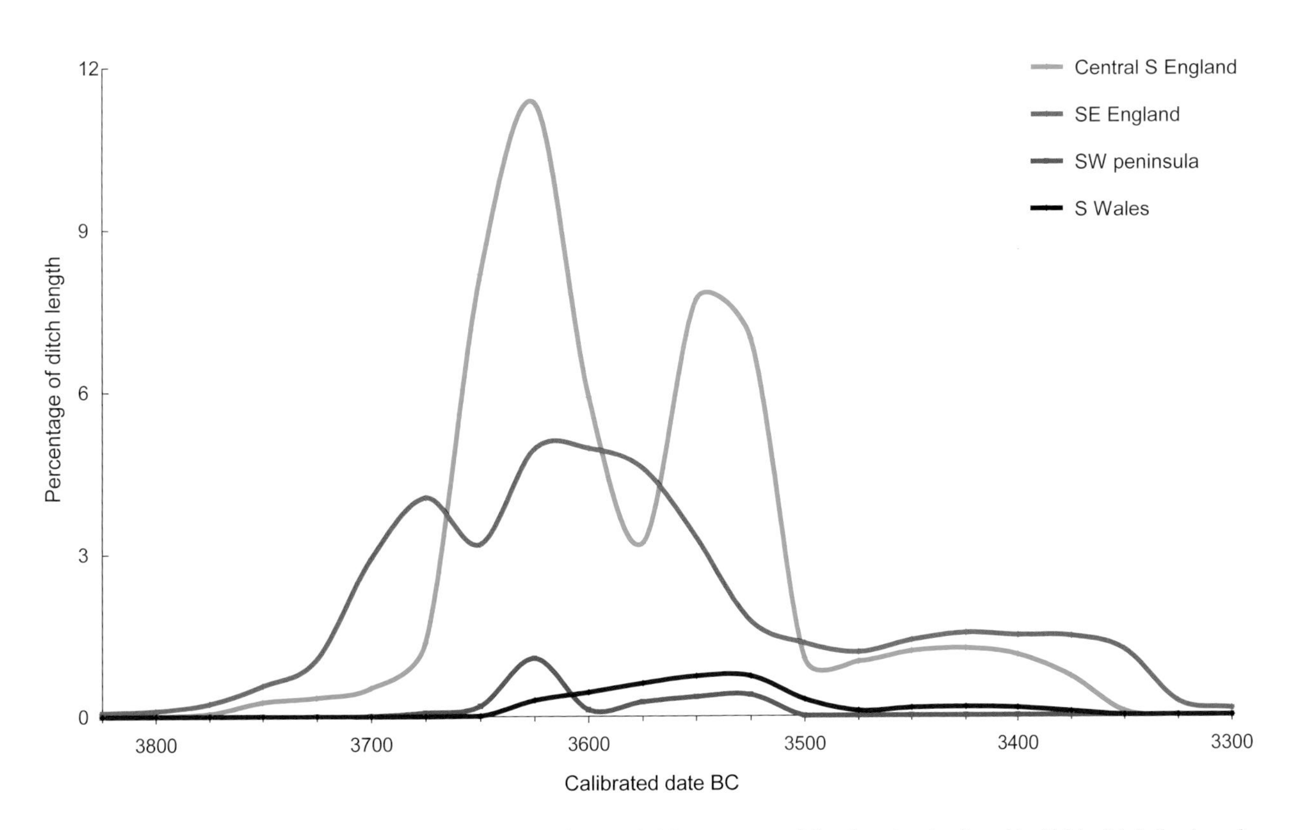

Fig. 14.22. Proportion of total ditch length excavated in each 25-year period for the circuits listed in Table 14.1, broken down by larger areas.

the excavations of the ditches (Fig. 14.19: green line). The estimate for the construction date of the Haddenham enclosure is so imprecise (Fig. 6.11: *start Haddenham*) that its resource estimate is spread so evenly across the time bands as to have little effect on the overall distribution. The estimate for the Haddenham palisade is omitted because the one date from that feature falls in the late third or early second millennium cal BC (Table 6.3: HAR-8094).

When these figures are compared with those calculated from simple estimates of the total lengths of the same circuits a very similar pattern emerges (Fig. 14.19: blue line). This much less sophisticated method thus seems to be a reliable proxy, at a coarse level, for resource estimates. The calculations have therefore been extended to include a much larger sample of earthworks for which the total ditch length can be reasonably estimated (Table 14.1). The proportion of total ditch length built in each twenty-five year period is shown for this larger sample in Fig. 14.20. A strongly bimodal pattern emerges, with the proportion of ditch length dug rising steeply from the second quarter of the 37th century and then falling sharply from *c.* 3625 cal BC to a low around 3575 cal BC. A second period of intensive construction followed in the middle decades of the 36th century cal BC. When the validity of this pattern is assessed by restricting the sample to those circuits with estimated construction dates spanning less than a century, an even stronger bimodal pattern emerges, confirming the legitimacy of the original analysis (Fig. 14.20). This cycle of resource expenditure cannot be explained as an artefact of the radiocarbon calibration curve. If we had sampled circuits which were really constructed in the first quarter of the 36th century cal BC, the methodology at our disposal would accurately estimate the date of sites constructed at this time (Bayliss *et al.* 2007a, 11–13). For example, the construction of Wayland's Smithy I occurred in *3610–3550 cal BC* (*83% probability*; Whittle *et al.* 2007b, fig. 4: *start_Wayland's Smithy I*) or *3545–3525* (*12% probability*), probably in *3590–3555 cal BC* (*67% probability*) or *3540–3535 cal BC* (*1% probability*). Figure 14.20 demonstrates that enclosure building caught on quickly and that within a generation or two there was a massive increase in the proportion of resources devoted to circuit construction. Intensive circuit building continued into the last quarter of the 36th century cal BC, although there was a noticeable reduction at the beginning of that century. Explanations are now required for the reduced effort expended on enclosure construction during the early decades of the 36th century cal BC. Building enclosures was still important to people at this time, although for whatever reason fewer resources were devoted to this task.

Regional trends, following the areas covered in the regional chapters of this volume, are illustrated in Fig. 14.21. It is apparent that there are not just variations in the expenditure of effort on circuit construction over time, but also spatial variations. For example, in the earliest phase, a much higher proportion of total construction occurred in the Thames estuary. As Chalk Hill shows, multiple circuits are part of the first manifestation of the enclosure idea. Construction in Wessex did not really get under way until the second quarter of the 37th century cal BC, but for the next 150 years effort was concentrated on the large enclosures of this region (Fig. 14.21). The resources expended on circuit construction in central-southern England are distributed in a strongly bimodal fashion (Fig. 14.22), mirroring the bimodality apparent in the overall expenditure of resources (Fig. 14.20) and accentuating the pattern evident for south Wessex (Fig. 14.21). The second peak of the distribution here is more pronounced than the earlier one, and may perhaps be synchronous with the greatest intensity of enclosure construction in south Wales and the Marches (Fig. 14.21).

In Wessex, the mid- to late 37th century cal BC saw considerable effort put into the construction of the large enclosures on Hambledon Hill and Windmill Hill, followed by a lull in the early 36th century cal BC when these sites remained in use but constructional activity was less intense. Taking those two sites as the largest of the reliably dated enclosures, it can also be noted that the biggest sites were not the earliest. In the second half of the 36th century cal BC, major new construction began again, at Maiden Castle and in the form of the inner Stepleton outwork at Hambledon Hill. This pattern of resource expenditure, however, is not entirely a product of the three big Wessex enclosures. Reliable estimates for the original size of the enclosures on Crickley Hill could not be included in this analysis because erosion and quarrying on the flanks of the spur make it impossible to know whether any of them originally extended along the south-east side (Fig. 9.2). Crickley was not large; if the circuits were all complete, the inner causewayed ditch would have been of similar length to that of the Stepleton enclosure on Hambledon Hill, and the outer causewayed ditch and the continuous ditch of similar length to that of the Etton enclosure. It is probable that the Crickley causewayed enclosure (both inner and outer circuits) was constructed on the first peak of constructional effort and that the continuous circuit there was built on the second. This may support the reality of the observed pattern, though uncertainties remain. For example, it is possible that the undated circuit at Robin Hood's Ball or the Rybury enclosure could fall in the suspected lull, although neither represents an investment of labour on the scale of the biggest Wessex enclosures.

Figure 14.22 does not show a similar pattern for other regions of southern Britain. That does not mean that this or similar cyclic patterns in the expenditure of effort were absent, only that none can currently be detected. To the east, the use of St Osyth seems to fall on one or other of the constructional peaks identified in Wessex, but here only the general currency of the site, not the individual circuits, has been dated. The other massive enclosure in eastern England, Haddenham, is not dated with sufficient precision to contribute here, but may represent another concentrated effort (as indeed argued by the excavators: Evans and Hodder 2006, 317). Generally, the enclosures in eastern England are not well dated, which obviously blurs any possible pattern. In the south-west, only the inner

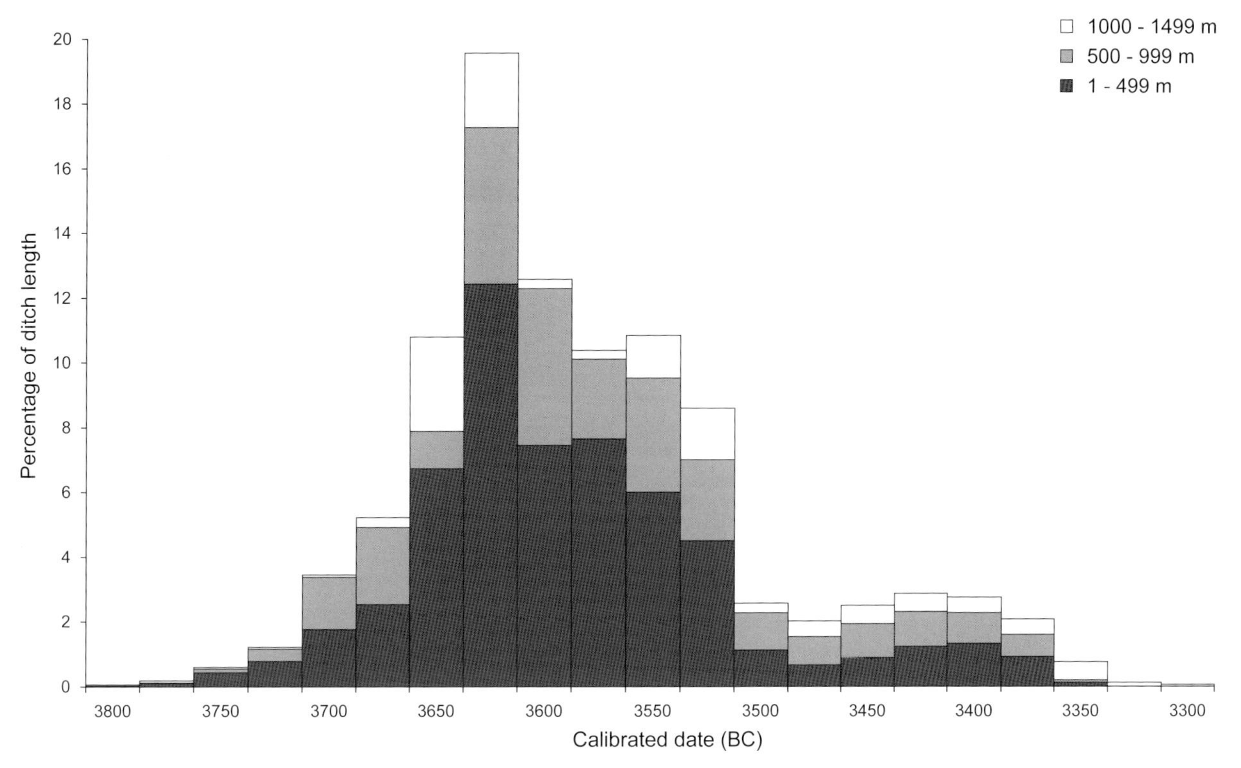

Fig. 14.23. Proportion of total ditch length excavated in each 25-year period for the circuits listed in Table 14.1, broken into categories by the ditch length of the dated circuits.

circuit at Hembury and the inner circuit at Raddon can be included in this analysis. The constructions of the outer circuit at Hembury and of the Helman Tor tor enclosure, however, probably both fall before *c.* 3650 cal BC. The outer enclosure (that is, the inner ramparts joining the two summits: see Chapter 10) at Carn Brea, if they form an outer circuit to the Neolithic complex there, would represent another major effort.

From the last quarter of the 36th century cal BC, much less effort was expended on the construction of new circuits, although some new earthworks were still built (Fig. 14.23). For example, the outer east cross dyke on Hambledon Hill was modified at the very end of the currency of causewayed enclosures in southern Britain (Fig. 14.10: *UB-4267*). Overall, 81% of the total effort on construction was expended between 3700–3500 cal BC, and 18% between 3500–3300 cal BC, most of the remainder falling in the last quarter of the 38th century cal BC.

Multiple circuits and multiple enclosures

Figure 14.24 shows the estimated construction dates, derived from the site-based models defined in Chapters 3–11, for the circuits of all enclosures in southern Britain with more than one dated circuit. As discussed above, UB-4267 from the outer east cross-dyke of the main enclosure on Hambledon Hill has been excluded from the model since this estimate appears to relate to an extension rather than the initial construction of this earthwork. For the causewayed enclosure on Crickley Hill and for the Northborough enclosure, strictly only *termini ante quos* are available for one of the circuits. The date estimates for both the eastern summit enclosure and for the inner ramparts at Carn Brea are shown in case the latter really form an outer Neolithic circuit at that site. It is evident that where multiple circuits have been dated, these are close in date if not precisely contemporary. Figure 14.25 shows the difference between the dates of both circuits where we have two dated circuits, or the period of construction (i.e. the difference between the first and the last dated circuit) where we have more than this. In all cases where there are two dated circuits, they could have been laid out and constructed as one enterprise. The exception, the circuits at Hembury, may be anomalous, because the construction of the inner circuit has been dated but only the destruction of the outer (Chapter 10). Alternatively, the circuits could have been constructed successively, but if so, the evidence suggests that this took place relatively rapidly, probably within a generation or two, and certainly within a single human lifespan.

More complex enclosures took longer to construct. Windmill Hill was built over a period of *5–75 years* (*95% probability*; Fig. 14.25: *period construction* (*Windmill Hill*)), probably within a period of *20–55 years* (*68% probability*). At Whitehawk, where four circuits have been dated with varying degrees of precision, construction took *20–145 years (95% probability*; Fig. 14.25: *period construction* (*Whitehawk*)), probably *45–110 years* (*68% probability*). In both cases, it is possible that the project was conceived and brought to completion within a single adult

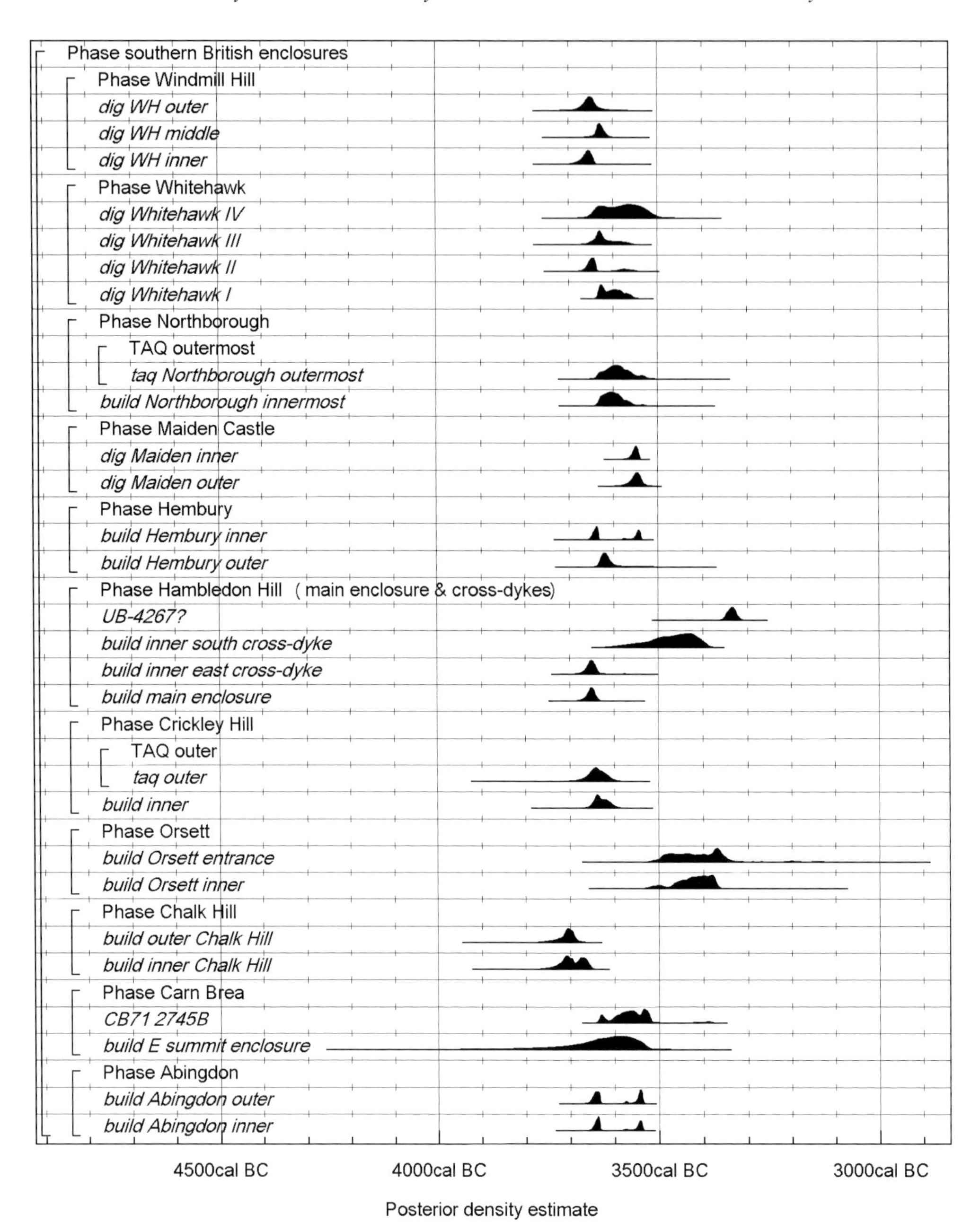

Fig. 14.24. Probability distributions of construction dates for circuits of causewayed and related enclosures from southern Britain which have more than one dated circuit. The format is identical to that for Fig. 14.1. The distributions are derived from the site-based models detailed in the captions to Figs 14.2–4.

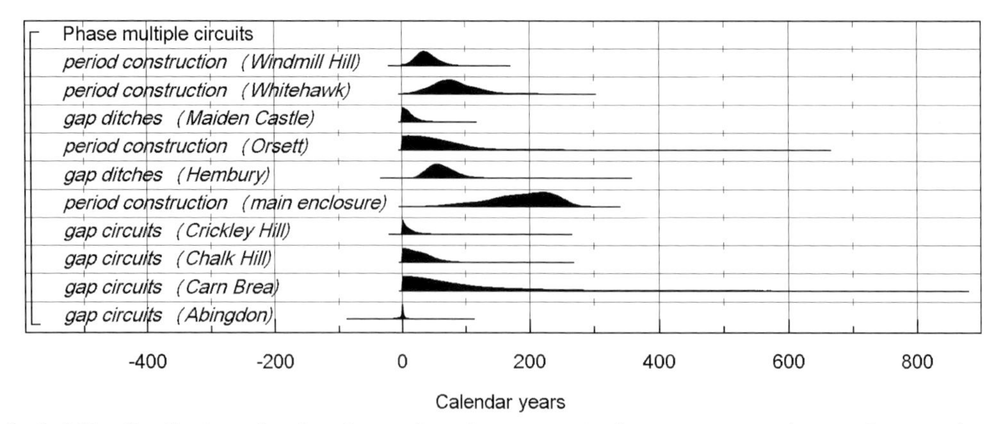

Fig. 14.25. Probability distributions showing the number of years required to construct enclosures from southern Britain with more than one dated circuit, calculated from the distributions shown in Fig. 14.24. 'Main enclosure' denotes the main enclosure on Hambledon Hill.

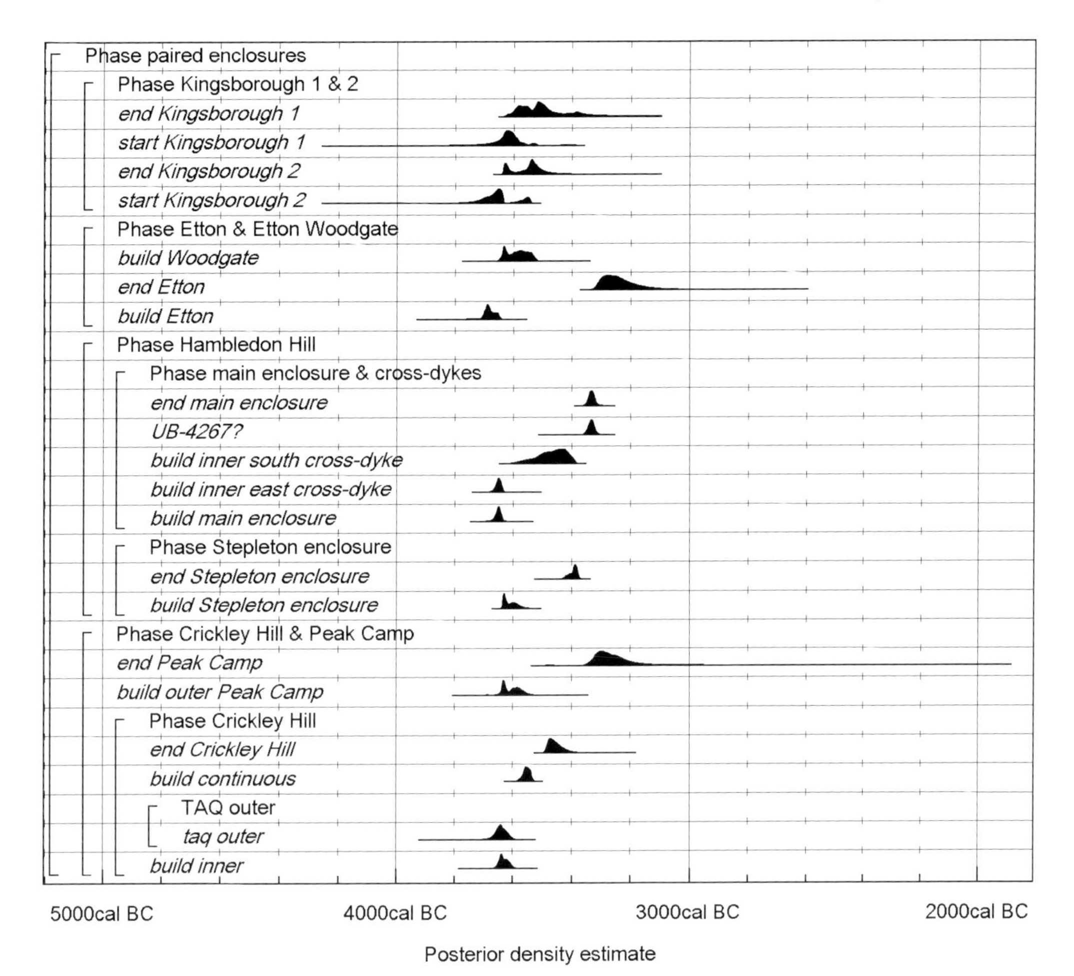

Fig. 14.26. Probability distributions for the construction and currency of pairs of enclosures from southern Britain which lie in close proximity. The format is identical to that for Fig. 14.1. The distributions are derived from the site-based models detailed in the captions to Figs 14.2–4.

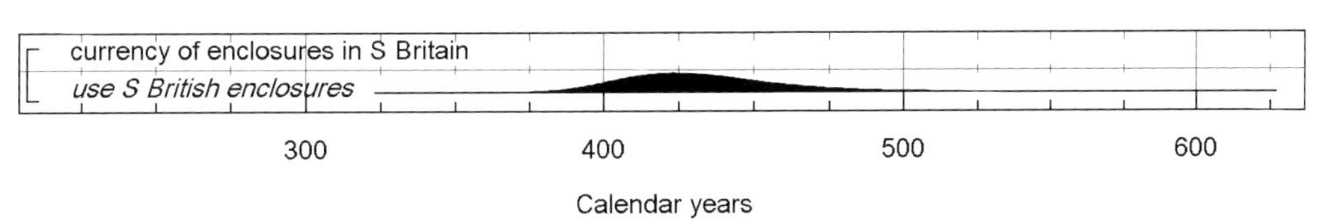

Fig. 14.27. Probability distribution for the number of years during which enclosures were in use in southern Britain, derived from the model defined in Figs 4.1–4.

lifetime. Such a tempo has significant social consequences and implications.

Much longer periods of construction are evidenced on Hambledon Hill. The question is whether this constitutes a similar phenomenon. If the cross-dykes are seen as effectively outer circuits (again excluding the probable modification of the inner east cross-dyke), the main enclosure took a substantial period to reach its final form, *85–270 years* (*95% probability*; Fig. 14.25: *period construction* (*main enclosure*)), probably *150–250 years* (*68% probability*). This estimate of the period of construction is realistic. Although the main enclosure and the inner east cross-dyke may be precisely contemporary (Fig. 14.24), the inner south cross-dyke, dated by UB-4268, an articulated cattle hock from beneath the bank (Table 4.2), was constructed substantially later.

If the outworks on the Stepleton spur also functioned as outer circuits, then this enclosure took *85–265 years* (*95% probability*; distribution not shown) to reach its final form, probably *110–135 years* (*12% probability*) or *155–245 years* (*56% probability*) – also a substantial period of time. Alternatively the Stepleton enclosure may have been conceived as a single circuit. The period of construction on Hambledon Hill suggests that it was significantly different from other sites. We have also already argued (Chapter 4) that the exceptionally extensive west-facing outworks late in the site sequence constitute a fundamental reorientation of the complex, transforming it from a causewayed

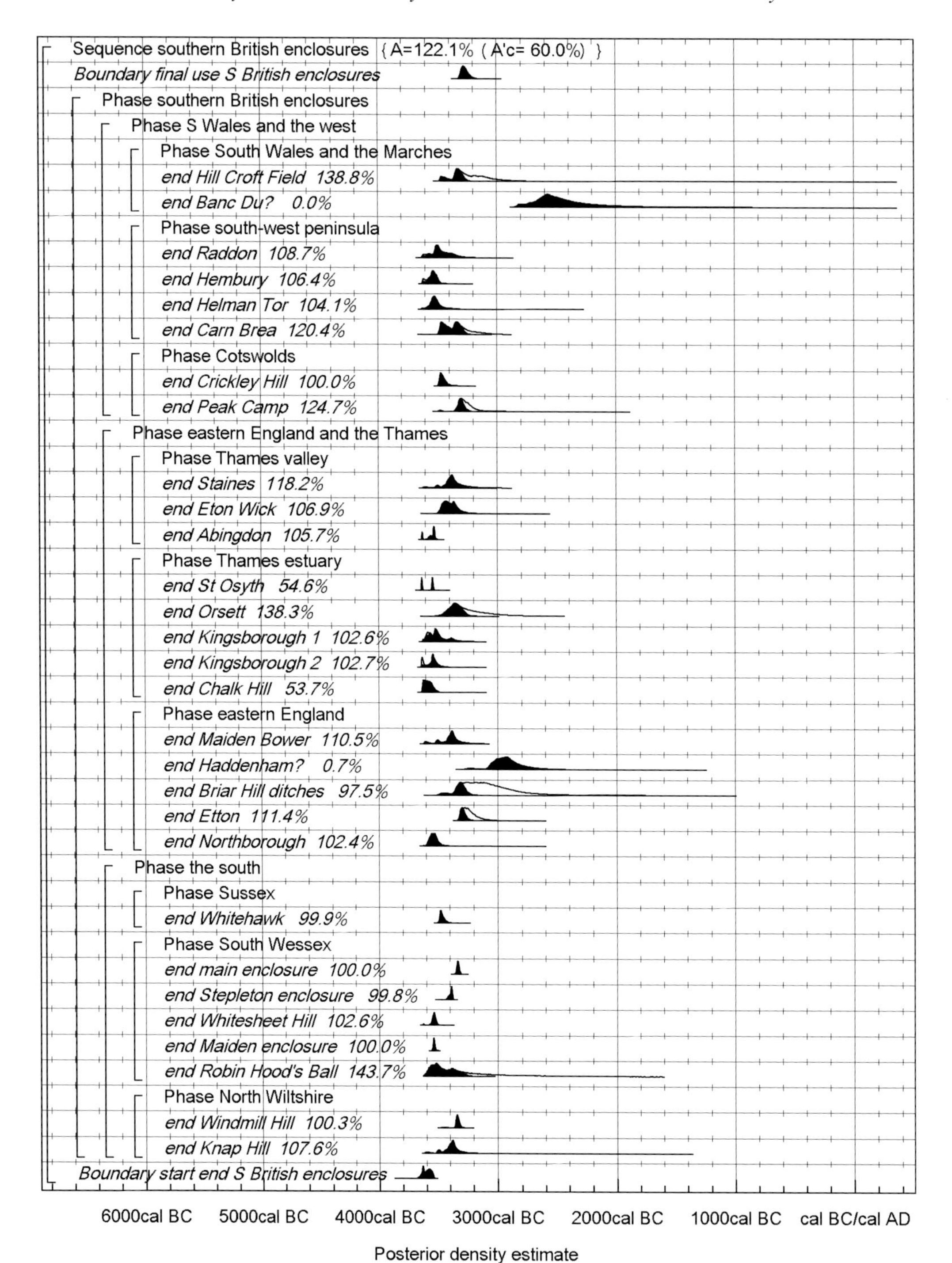

Fig. 14.28. Probability distributions for the dates of the end of causewayed and related enclosures in southern Britain. Distributions have been taken from the models defined in Chapters 3–11, as detailed in the captions to Figs 14.2–4. The format is identical to that for Fig. 14.1. The large square brackets down the left-hand side of the diagram, along with the OxCal keywords, define the overall model exactly.

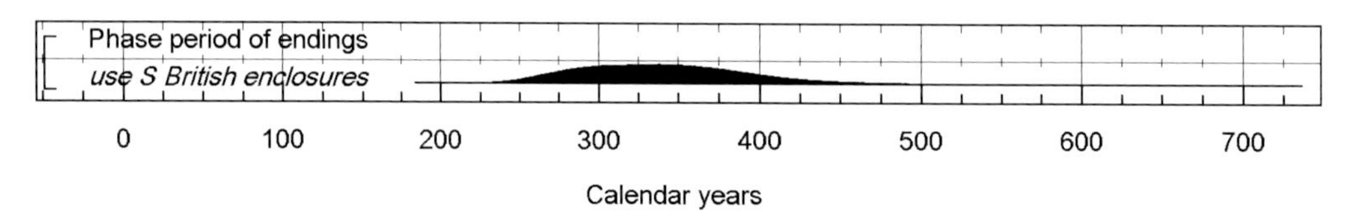

Fig. 14.29. Probability distribution for the number of years over which the primary use of causewayed and related enclosures in southern Britain ended, derived from the model shown in Fig. 14.28.

enclosure into something else. Once again, we have to deal with the implications of such a development for social relationships in the region.

Figure 14.26 shows the dates of construction and use for those enclosures which lie in such close proximity that they might have been conceived of as pairs. In all cases, the enclosures seem to have been constructed at different times. For example, the outer circuit at Peak Camp was probably built in the interval between the completion of both circuits of the causewayed enclosure and the inception of the continuous circuit at Crickley Hill (*73% probable*). It is almost certain (*more than 99% probable*) that the main enclosure at Hambledon Hill was constructed before the Stepleton enclosure there, and that Etton was initiated before Etton Woodgate. Kingsborough 2 is earlier than Kingsborough 1 (*71% probable*). In contrast, once built, these sites seem to have continued in concurrent use.

A similar trend may be apparent for the clusters of enclosures visible on Fig. 1.2. In East Sussex, the limited dating available for Combe Hill and Offham Hill, in addition to the rather more robust chronology available for Whitehawk (Fig. 14.2), may suggest a sequence of construction followed by contemporary use. In West Sussex, the tentative dating for Court Hill, Bury Hill and The Trundle is compatible with a similar pattern. The most convincing series are the three dated enclosures from the lower Welland valley, part of a wider cluster which embraces the lower Nene (Fig. 6.1), where again a sequence of construction followed by contemporary use is suggested (Fig. 14.3). Similarly, Windmill and Knap Hill, close to Rybury on the north Wiltshire downs, were built successively but were in use concurrently. Of the greater numbers in the upper Thames and the Cotswolds, only Abingdon, Crickley Hill and Peak Camp have been dated, and so the relationships are unknown.

The ending of enclosures

We have seen already that causewayed and related enclosures came to southern Britain in the late 38th century cal BC (Fig. 14.1: *start S British enclosures*) and continued in primary use until the decades around 3300 cal BC (Fig. 14.1: *end S British enclosures*) – over a period of *385–485 years* (*95% probability*; Fig. 14.27: *use S British enclosures*), probably of *400–455 years* (*68% probability*).

It is now time to consider when the enclosures, largely constructed in the 37th and 36th centuries cal BC, went out of use. This is more tricky. Defining endings raises several difficult questions. It could be argued that few such sites ever really had a definitive ending, because it can be in the nature of such earthworks to endure as visible traces, especially in prominent hilltop locations (in lower-lying locations the situation may often have been different), and people continued to use such places, perhaps both deliberately and coincidentally, and with varying degrees of intensity. Less frequented sites may still have carried considerable symbolic charge. The 'afterlife' of causewayed enclosures has already been discussed in these terms (Oswald *et al.* 2001, chapter 8). In the regional chapters, we have tried to demarcate a primary phase of use, defined partly by the nature of the ditch filling process and partly by associated deposition and material culture. Windmill Hill is a good case in point, with Peterborough and Beaker wares generally occurring from the upper secondary ditch fills upwards.[2] As discussed in Chapter 3, there was clearly continued use of the site from the late fourth millennium cal BC into the third, but the character of the use of the monument had changed. Other sites which were of much shorter duration included deliberately backfilled ditches, such as the case of the outer ditch at Maiden Castle, and ended within the currency of Bowl pottery.

In these terms, the endings discussed here relate to the substantial filling of the ditch circuits, particularly on unstable gravel and sand substrates, and the end of deposition associated with Bowl pottery. This is discussed in more detail on a site-by-site basis in the regional chapters. On this basis, a model for the period when the primary use of causewayed and related enclosures ended is shown in Fig. 14.28. The distributions for these endings have been taken from the site-based models defined in Chapters 3–11. As before, *end Banc Du* has poor agreement (A=38.1%) and so has been excluded from the model, and so does the ending of Haddenham (A=9.5%); this has also been excluded from the analysis. This model suggests that the primary use of the first enclosure ended in *3665–3540 cal BC* (*95% probability*; Fig. 14.28: *start end S British enclosures*), probably in *3645–3625 cal BC* (*20% probability*) or *3615–3555 cal BC* (*48% probability*). The first enclosure to go out of primary use did so whilst the period of intensive circuit construction (Fig. 14.7) was still underway (*99% probable*).

The last enclosure to go out of primary use did so in *3320–3195 cal BC* (*95% probability*; Fig. 14.28: *final use S British enclosures*), probably in *3305–3245 cal BC* (*68% probability*). This estimate encompasses the date for final use provided by the model for the overall currency of enclosures (Fig. 14.1), but is less precise as it depends on fewer data. Causewayed enclosures in southern Britain did not come to a sudden halt, but rather the period during which they went out of primary use spanned a period of *245–440 years* (*95% probability*; Fig. 14. 29: *disuse S British enclosures*), probably of *280–385 years* (*68% probability*). The staggered ending of the enclosure phenomenon stands in stark contrast to the swift tempo of its introduction. Different sites fell into disuse over a period of centuries, not the individual lifespans appropriate to the introduction of the phenomenon and the construction of most individual sites. Figure 14.30 shows the percentage of sites which went out of initial use in any given century. It is apparent that there is no single period when sites were more liable to go out of use. The overall pattern suggested when the endings of all sites are considered (except for Banc Du and Haddenham) is supported by the similar distribution produced when only the ten well dated sites (with endings estimated to within a century) are evaluated.[3]

The time when the first enclosure in a region went out of primary use may be varied. In most places, this happened in the 36th century cal BC, although in a few regions this may have happened over the succeeding centuries. There is no obvious spatial trend in this disuse, and the observed variation may as well relate to the number of well dated sites in a given region. In contrast, in most areas the last causewayed enclosure appears to have gone out of primary use in the 34th century cal BC. There may be a slight exception in eastern England, where activity may have continued for a few more generations (e.g. Fig. 14.28: *endEtton*). This trend might be even more apparent if Haddenham were included in the analysis. The imprecision of much of the dating in this region, however, must be acknowledged.

In relation to size and complexity of circuit layout, there are some signs of different trends. Figure 14.31 shows endings of enclosures by century against size, measured by total ditch length, and complexity as measured by numbers of circuits. It is apparent that both large and small enclosures could go out of use at any time within the span of the sequence of endings. Within this pattern, however, there may be a trend for smaller enclosures to come to an end earlier than larger ones. It is also apparent that both simpler and more complex enclosures could go out of use at any time within the span of the sequence of endings. Once more, however, there may be a tendency for more complex enclosures to endure in use after they were completed. This raises significant questions of the power of place and tradition.

The duration of enclosures

We turn now to the duration of enclosures, which can only be estimated once the start and end dates for each site have been established. As we have already seen, causewayed and related enclosures in southern Britain were in primary use for *385–485 years* (*95% probability*; Fig. 14.27: *use S British enclosures*), probably for *400–455 years* (*68% probability*). We can go on to look in more detail at the period of use of individual sites, as not all need have been in use for the entire currency of enclosures.

Figure 14.32 shows the probability distributions for the number of years in which the dated enclosures were in use. These distributions have been derived from the site-based models defined in Chapters 3–11. For a few sites, it has not been possible to estimate the period of use. At Bury Hill, for example, the only dated samples are from the ditch base and the initial silts, so that there is no indication from radiocarbon dating of how long activity continued at the site, although the absence of suitable samples from higher levels and the fact that ditches silted naturally without intervention argue for a short period of use followed by abandonment. Similar considerations apply at, among other sites, Kingsborough 2, Knap Hill and Offham Hill.

It is apparent that not all sites were in use for similar periods of time. To take examples from well dated sites where precise estimates of duration are possible, the large enclosure with three circuits at St Osyth may well have been in use for less than a generation (it is *91% probable* that this site was in use for less than 25 years). In contrast, it is *77% probable* that Windmill Hill was used for *300–350 years*. The use of St Osyth falls within the period of individual memory, while that of Windmill Hill probably extends beyond the span of active memory. The use of Chalk Hill (it is *83% probable* that Chalk Hill was in use for *50–125 years*) lies in the middle ground, within the span of memories which could have been transmitted between generations.

Figure 14.33 shows the proportion of dated sites which were used for different periods of time. The blue line, which includes all sites where we have been able to estimate durations of use, is anomalously smoothed and has a long tail, suggesting that some sites could have been used for many hundreds of years. This is almost certainly an artefact of radiocarbon dating, because, where there are insufficient measurements for the scatter on the radiocarbon dates to be evaluated, estimates of duration are imprecise and allow for longer periods of use than was the case in reality. For this reason, the analysis has been repeated using a sub-sample of 11 well dated sites where the duration has been estimated to within a span of 200 years at 95% probability.[4] This is the red line shown in Fig. 14.33. It can be seen that the tail of very long use beyond 400 years has disappeared. The peak constituted by a high proportion of sites going out of use within one or two generations of their construction is even more apparent from the subset of well dated sites. This analysis suggests that the primary use of *c.* 30% of sites lasted for less than 50 years. Approximately 80% of sites were used for less than 250 years, but a number of them were in use for more than 300 years.

Figures 14.34 and 14.35 show the duration of enclosures in southern Britain in relation to the complexity of their circuits and to area (using the same subset of 11 well dated sites). Both suggest similar, but not identical, trends. From Fig. 14.34 it is apparent that complex sites with up to three circuits accompanied less complex sites in rapid demise, over one or two generations. Whitehawk, with at least four circuits, is also to be found among those which lasted for less than 250 years. It is striking, however, that it is the more complex sites which tended to continue for 300 years or more. In relation to area of enclosure, it is apparent on Fig. 14.35 that it is not only the more complex but also the largest sites which tended to endure for longest (not just in terms of successive constructional activity but also in continuing use). Sites of varying sizes can be seen to end quite quickly, and Maiden Castle stands out as an extremely large enclosure with an extremely brief life.

It must be recognised that this analysis is based on a small number of sites, and so it is necessary to consider whether these trends are representative of the wider set of southern British enclosures. The large, complex enclosures which endured, shown on Figs 14.34 and 14.35, are Windmill Hill and the main enclosure on Hambledon Hill. From the larger sample of less well dated sites, Etton, a small, simple enclosure, seems to have continued for as long (or even longer). Potentially long-lived sites such as

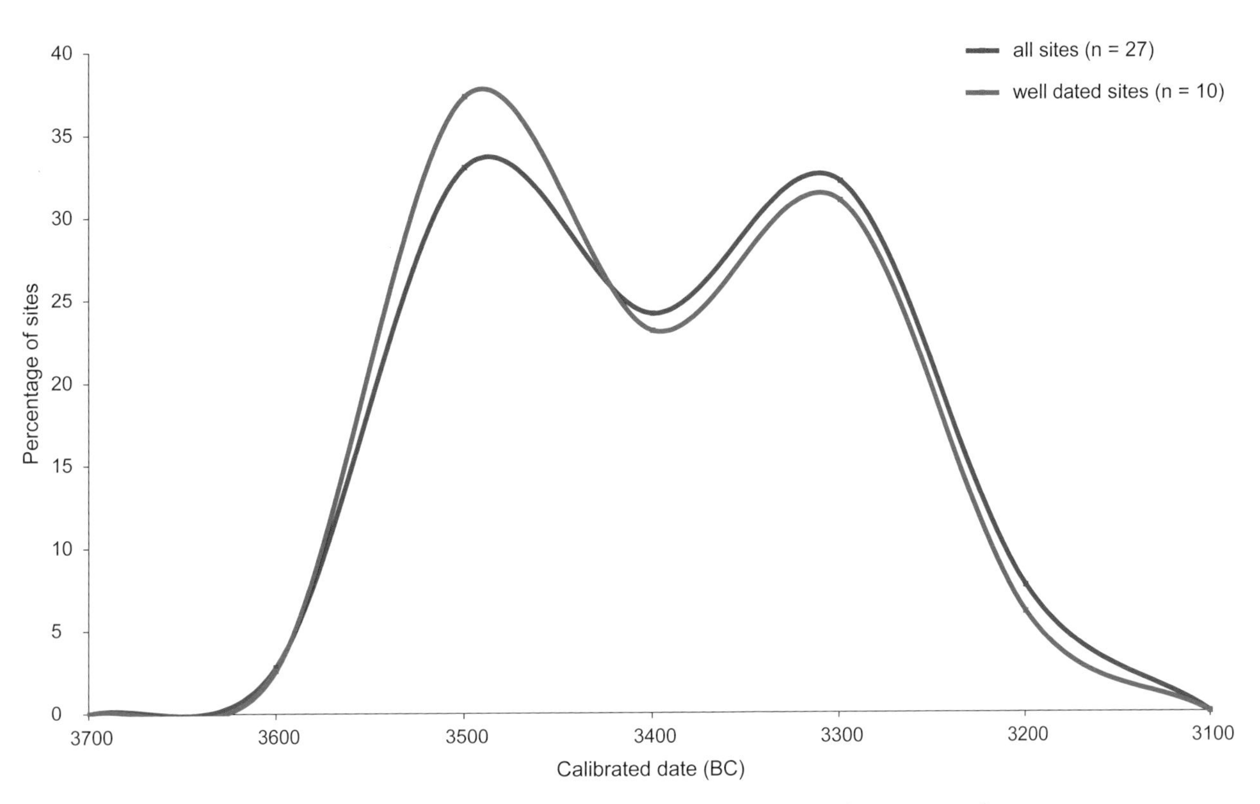

Fig. 14.30. Percentage of southern British enclosures going out of primary use by century.

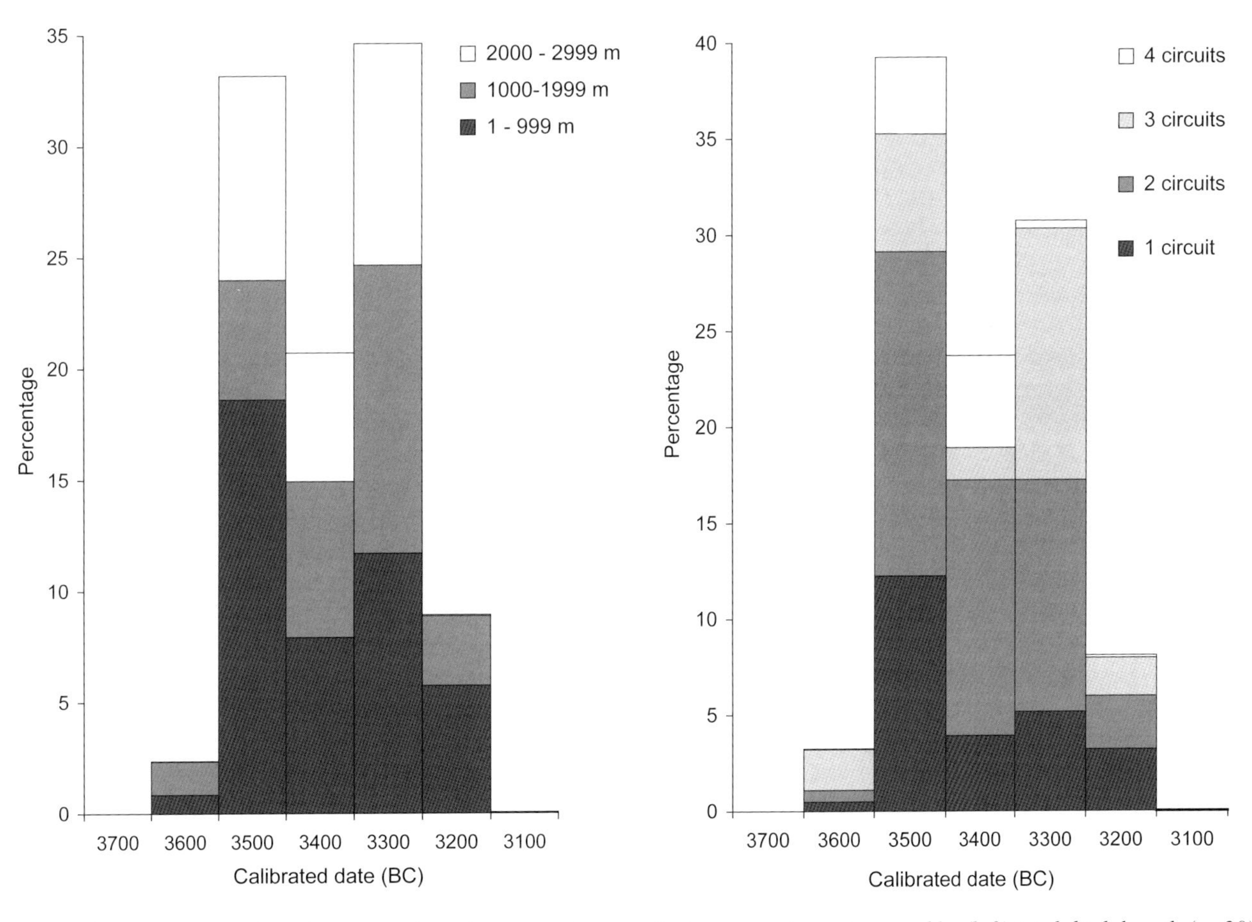

Fig. 14.31. Percentage of southern British enclosures going out of primary use by century and by (left) total ditch length (n=20) and (right) number of circuits (n=24).

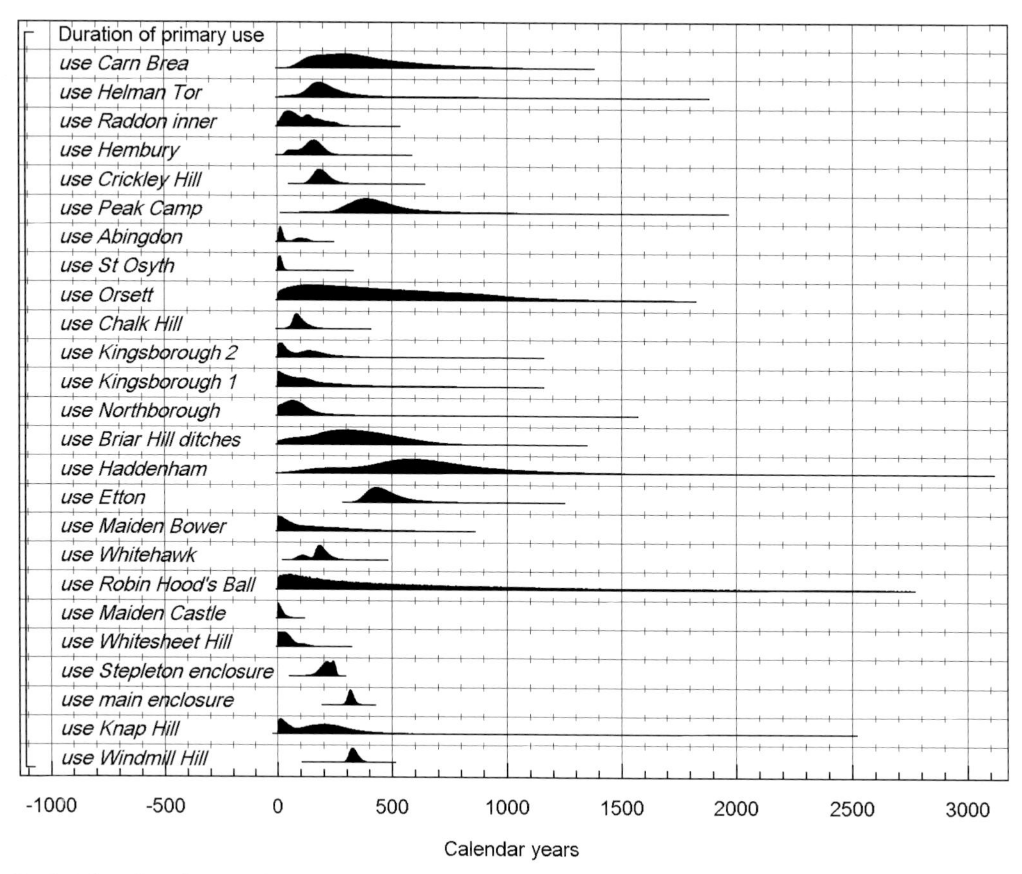

Fig. 14.32. Probability distributions for the number of years in which causewayed and related enclosures in southern Britain were in primary use, derived from the site-based models enumerated in the captions to Figs 14.2–4.

Haddenham (Fig. 6.12: *use Haddenham*) or Briar Hill (Fig. 6.23: *use Briar Hill ditches*) are extremely poorly dated, so that their apparent longevity may be spurious. The massive single-ditched enclosure at Haddenham was argued by its excavators to have been an undertaking of concentrated effort and relatively brief use (Evans and Hodder 2006a, 317). It is difficult to estimate the area of the enclosure at St Osyth, although this must have been over 5 ha, placing it among the larger sites (Oswald *et al.* 2001, fig. 4.23). That was probably of extremely brief duration (*less than 25 years at 91% probability*). Other large and complex sites are either unexcavated, like Fornham All Saints, or poorly dated, like The Trundle (Oswald *et al.* 2001, fig. 4.26). At the moment, therefore, neither size or complexity, nor a combination of the two, can be taken as reliable indicators of sites which endured. So what then was distinctive about Hambledon Hill and Windmill Hill on the one hand, and Etton on the other? This raises important questions, once again, about place and tradition. Was the maintenance of interest the same at Etton as in the Wessex examples, and was it the same in both of them? Was the cluster of enclosures around Etton equivalent to the concentration of effort and maintenance of interest in each of the two large Wessex sites?

The filling and recutting of enclosure ditches

The infilling of causewayed and related enclosure ditches would have resulted from an interplay between natural silting and human intervention, in the form of recutting, deposition and backfilling. The rate and character of natural silting would have been significantly affected by earthwork form and local topography, as well as by contemporary vegetation and land use. In the face of all these variables, it is difficult to assess rates of infill at particular monuments, especially given that some enclosure ditches may have been completely cleaned out; that deliberate backfilling may not always have been identified; that recuts, especially in loose rubble, may equally have escaped attention; and that the structure of banks and their proximity to the ditch edges can often be judged only uncertainly.

Many of the enclosure ditches considered here contained deep accumulations of the geological solid through which they were dug, sometimes occupying most of the depth of the ditch, whether chalk rubble, as at Windmill Hill (Figs 3.12–13), gravel, as at Abingdon (Fig. 8.15) or finer deposits, as in the two Kingsborough enclosures (Fig. 7.14). The Overton Down and Wareham Bog experimental earthworks, initiated in the early 1960s and subsequently excavated and recorded at fixed intervals, record the process and timescale of ditch silting on, respectively, chalk and sand (Bell *et al.* 1996). The silting of both ditches differs from that of causewayed enclosure ditches, especially in the case of Overton Down. It is worth summarising these differences and examining reasons for them to help to determine how far the experiments are applicable to the monuments under consideration here.

The fill of the Wareham Bog ditch remained mobile and unstable after 17 years, when approximately one-third of the original depth of the ditch (0.50 m out of 1.80 m) was filled with sand (Bell *et al.* 1996, fig. 14.1). For most of this period the silting was symmetrical, material from the bank starting to enter the ditch only in the last few years. It is easy to imagine the process continuing to almost fill the ditch, producing an end result similar to those seen in the gravels of, for example, Abingdon (Fig. 8.15) or the eastern arc of Etton (Fig. 6.31: sections B and C) before recuts were made. There is reason to think, however, that the process differed at both sites from that observed at Wareham. Delayed entry of material from the bank of Wareham earthwork into the ditch reflects its original construction, with a 1 m-wide berm between bank and ditch edge and a dumped bank conforming to the angle of rest of the sand. If the upcast had been closer to the ditch, as it may have been at Etton, where short-lived spoil heaps around the segments are envisaged rather than a regular, longer-lasting internal bank (Pryor 1998, 69; French 1998c, 320), it could have begun to enter the ditch sooner. In some segments in the east of the circuit, infill would have been accelerated by deliberate and repeated backfilling which often occupied between half and two-thirds of the ditch (French 1998c, 319–20; Pryor 1998, 68, 311). The completeness of turves in the phase 1A backfill of the eastern arc indicated that they had not been on the surface beside the ditch for more than a few years and probably less (French 1998c, 312, 315; Pryor 1998, 357).

At Abingdon the fills of both ditches were asymmetric from the first (Fig. 8.15), indicating little space between the bank, probably of simple dump construction, and the ditch, leading to the kind of silting effectively summarised in Avery's diagram (1982, fig. 9). Input from the bank from an early stage would surely have accelerated the process. In the outer ditch, block-like elements in dark, loamy layers derived from the interior near the base of the section (Fig. 8.15, lower) were seen as remnants of a collapsed turf revetment (Case 1956, 14). If so, there could have been an abrupt and massive inrush of gravel into the ditch, although there is the alternative possibility that the loamy layers were turves from the ditch edge, falling as it weathered back. In either case, infilling would have been rapid, since, if the loam bands have any seasonality, they suggest that over a metre of fill accumulated over only a few years.

The Tertiary and Drift deposits of Kingsborough are also mobile and unstable. The asymmetry of the fills of the inner ditch of Kingsborough 1 suggests a nearby inner bank and consequently accelerated infilling (Fig. 7.14: section A). Repeated slumping in the Kingsborough 2 fills (M. Allen *et al.* 2008, 242–4) is equally suggestive of rapid initial infill.

In all these cases, Wareham's one-third of depth in 17 years could, on the face of it, be an underestimate of the rate of infilling. To some extent this can be tested against the dating achieved in this project, especially when it comes to the first stage of apparently rapid, primary filling, derived from the ditch sides, with or without a contribution from the bank. The number of relevant enclosures is restricted because the upper or final parts of these fills have furnished samples suitable for dating less often than their lower parts. At Kingsborough 2, for example, all the datable samples (apart from a second millennium cal BC one from the top of the sequence) came from near the base of the primary fills (M. Allen *et al.* 2008, fig. 6).

At Abingdon, where there is no obvious sign of cleaning out or recutting until all the primary fills had accumulated, the estimates for both ditches are affected by the bimodality of all the dates from this monument (Figs 8.19–21). They are, however, compatible with a Wareham-like timescale: *0–35 years* (*95% probability*; Fig. 8.23: *recut B/inner*), probably *a decade* (*68% probability*) for the inner ditch in Trench B; *0–30 years* (*95% probability*; Fig. 8.23: *recut C/inner*), probably *0–15 years* (*68% probability*), for the inner ditch in Trench C; and *0–30 years* (*57% probability*; Fig. 8.23: *fill Abingdon outer*) or *45–125 years* (*38% probability*), probably *0–25 years* (*55% probability*) or *70–95 years* (*13% probability*) for the outer ditch.

At Kingsborough 1 the dates obtained span the primary fills, which occupy approximately one-third of the middle ditch (M. Allen *et al.* 2008, figs 3–4). They indicate accumulation over *0–285 years* (*95% probability*; Table 14.2; distribution not shown), probably over *0–130 years* (*68% probability*). This distribution is heavily skewed towards a shorter period of filling. This estimate could be compatible with the short duration of infill suggested by the Wareham experimental earthwork, the tail of the distribution towards a longer period of infill being a product of the small number of dates available. A slightly longer duration may be due to the partial cleaning out of the ditch while the primary fills were accumulating, visible in the truncation of contexts 2530, 2532 and 2533 (Fig. 7.14: section A). There is the impression that the middle ditch at Kingsborough 1 was maintained for a period then left to silt.

This effect is even more marked in the eastern arc at Etton, where repeated recutting and backfilling in the course of the extended use of the monument led to an interval of *165–250 years* (*14% probability*; Table 14.2; distribution not shown) or *280–510 years* (*81% probability*), probably *195–215 years* (*3% probability*) or *290–405 years* (*65% probability*) between the construction of the monument and the final phase 1C recut in its infilled ditch. Since the ditch was already largely infilled when the 1C recuts were made (Fig. 6.30: section B; Pryor 1998, figs 73–4), this interval may incorporate a period of stability before they were made. At Briar Hill equally numerous and complex recuts (Bamford 1985, figs 6–17) would be compatible with a similarly long span, although the potentially centuries-long duration of the site can be estimated only imprecisely (Chapter 6.3.1).

It is more often possible to date the accumulation of

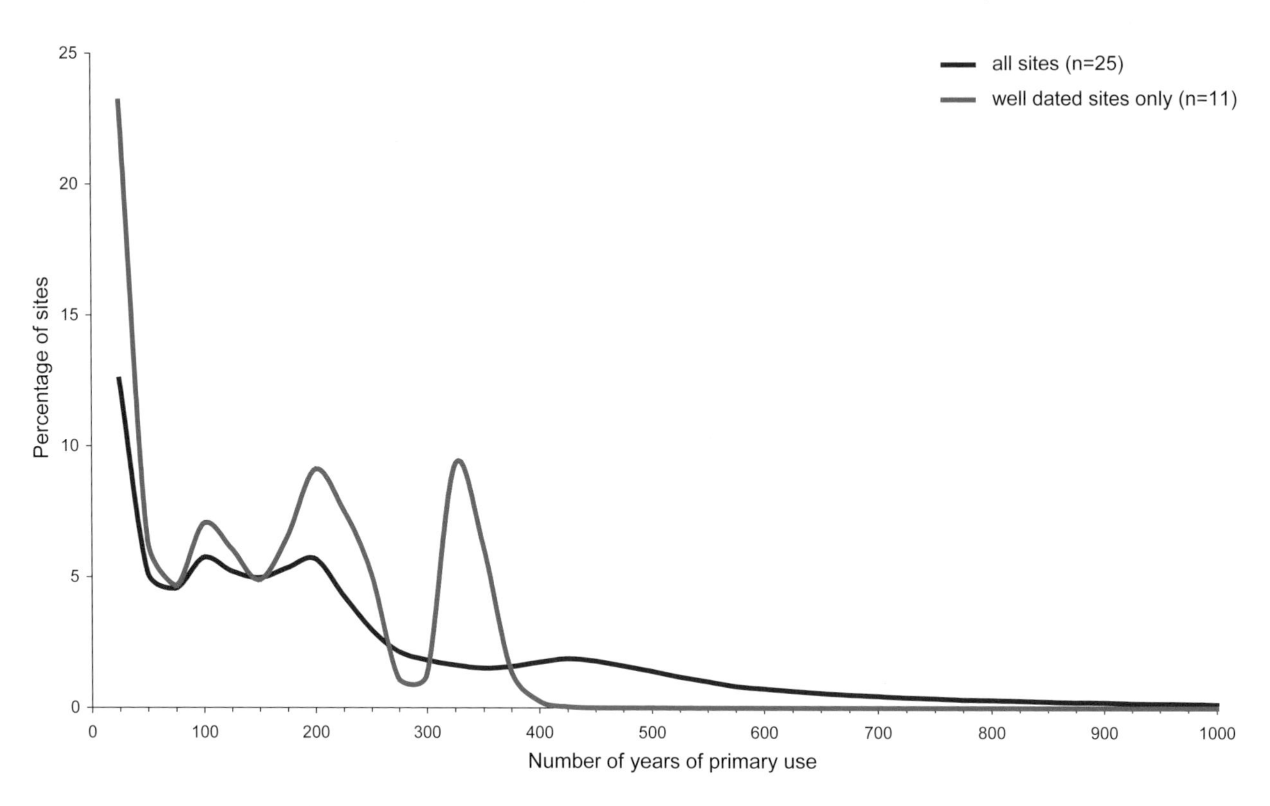

Fig. 14.33. Proportion of southern British enclosures which were used for different lengths of time (by 25-year period).

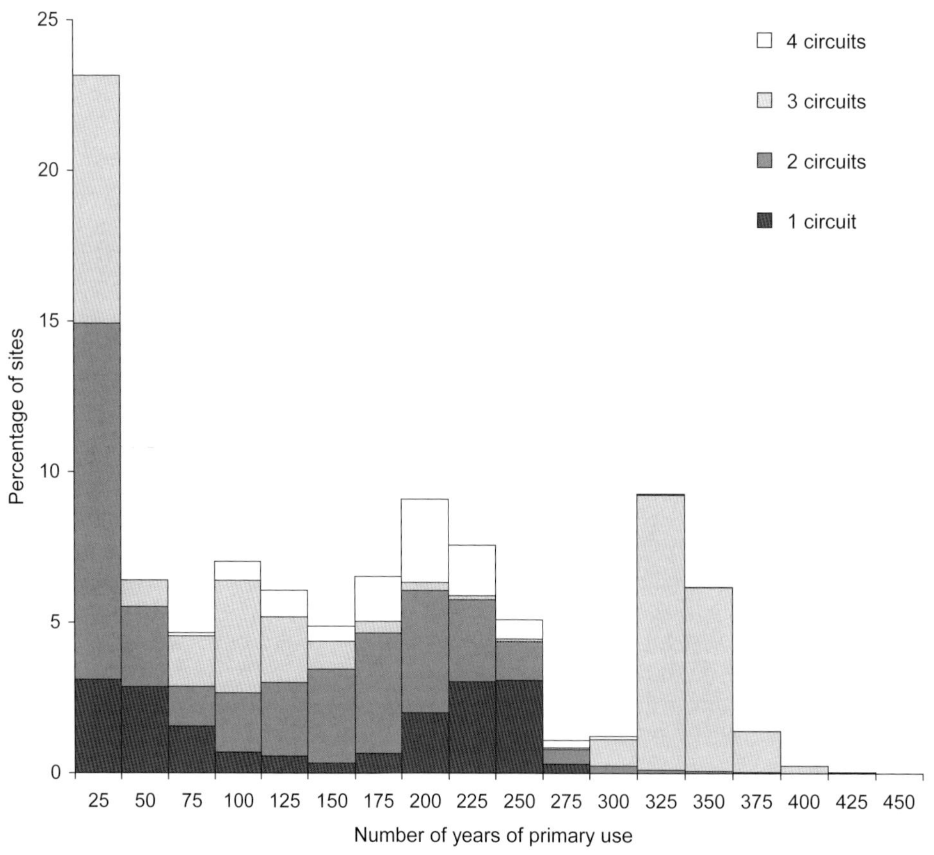

Fig. 14.34. Proportion of southern British enclosures which were used for different lengths of time (by 25-year period, and by number of circuits (n=11)).

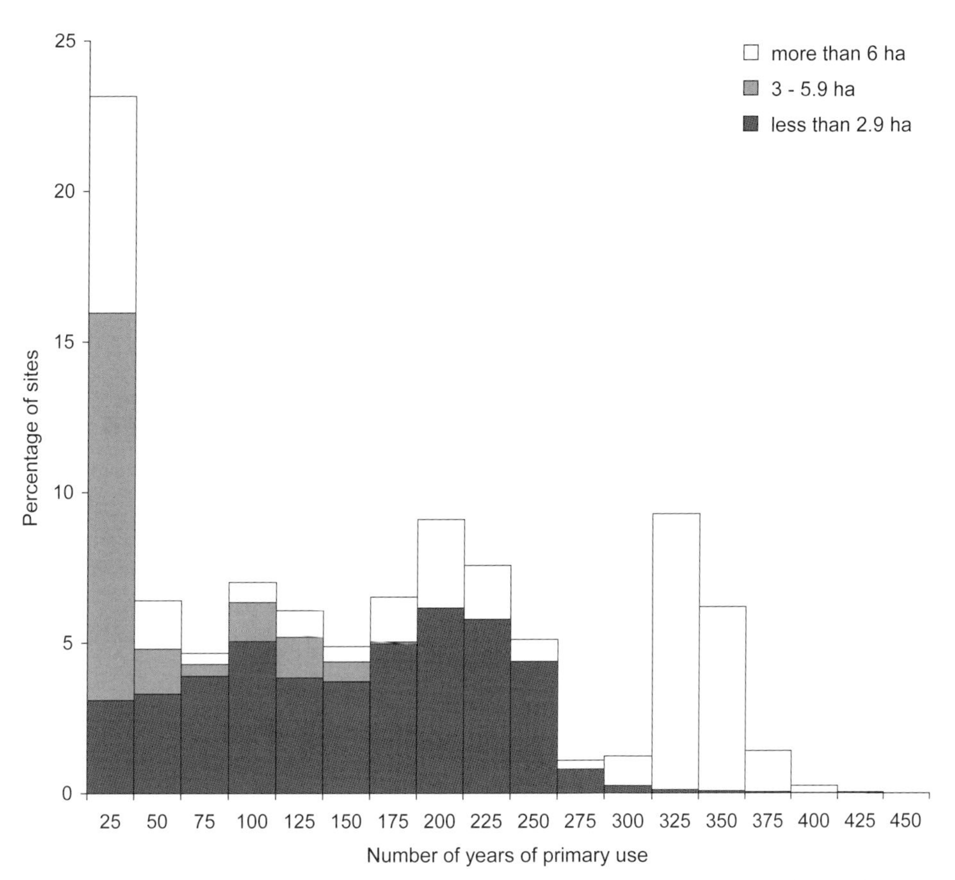

Fig. 14.35. Proportion of southern British enclosures which were used for different lengths of time (by 25-year period, and by estimated total area (n=11)).

primary fills on chalkland sites. Here, morphological and topographical dissimilarities between the Overton Down experimental earthwork and causewayed enclosure ditches are substantial.

1. The Overton Down earthwork was built on virtually level ground, while almost all the chalkland causewayed enclosures are on slopes, where infill could be accelerated by gravity.
2. Once the Overton earthwork was built, its builders went away, leaving it in undisturbed grassland, which colonised and stabilised both bank and ditch fill within about 15 years (Bell *et al.* 1996, fig. 14.2). An earthwork built in woodland, as many chalkland enclosures seem to have been, would not be surrounded by such a continuous matt of vegetation, leaving the bank and the ditch edges more prone to erosion and to disturbance in the course of subsequent visits, especially as livestock were periodically present.
3. This rapid colonisation of the Overton Down earthwork by grasses and herbs, combined with the earthwork's 1 m-wide berm, ensured that only a minimal amount of bank material entered the ditch before its symmetrical fills were stabilised, while the markedly asymmetric fills of some chalkland enclosures make it clear that bank material entered their ditches in some quantities (e.g. Figs 3.13, 3.23, 4.50).
4. The proportions of the experimental earthworks correspond roughly to those of enclosures built on mobile geologies, but less so to chalk-cut ones. The Overton Down ditch was dug with a depth:width ratio of approximately 1:1.5 which had weathered to 1:2.5 after some 30 years (Bell *et al.* 1996, fig 14.2). To take Hambledon as an example, the equivalent ratios for the extensively excavated ditches, where large numbers of sections should provide representative proportions, range from 1:1.7 for the Stepleton enclosure to 1:3.1 for the outer Stepleton outwork, with a mean of 1:2.4 (Mercer and Healy 2008, 747). If the Hambledon ditches were proportionately narrower after more than five millennia of weathering than the Overton Down one was after three decades, then their proportions would have been much narrower than Overton's when they were first dug. In consequence, the erosion of their sides will have filled the lower parts of the ditches more rapidly than the same process has at Overton. The profiles of other chalk-cut enclosure ditches suggest that they were originally of similar proportions.
5. There is occasionally evidence for timber bank structures, perhaps box frame ramparts, so that, as with the possible turf revetment of the outer bank at Abingdon, once these gave way or were destroyed, masses of bank material could enter ditches in a single event (having perhaps impeded natural fill processes up till then).

Table 14.2. Estimates of the period of primary infill from selected causewayed enclosure ditches.

Site and ditch	**Earlier parameter**	**Later parameter**	**Duration of infill**	***Posterior density estimate (probability in years)***	**Geology**
Abingdon inner	*build Abingdon inner* (Fig. 8.18)	*area B recut* (Fig. 8.19)	*recut B/inner* (Fig. 8.23)	*0–35 years (95%); 0–10 years (68%)*	Gravel
Abingdon inner	*build Abingdon inner* (Fig. 8.18)	*area C recut* (Fig. 8.20)	*recut C/inner* (Fig. 8.23)	*0–30 years (95%); 0–15 years (68%)*	Gravel
Abingdon outer	*build Abingdon outer* (Fig. 8.21)	*end Abingdon outer* (Fig. 8.21)	*fill Abingdon outer* (Fig. 8.23)	*0–30 years (57%)* or *45–125 years (38%); 0–25 years (55%)* or *70–95 years (13%)*	Gravel
Crickley continuous ditch	*UB-6397* (Fig. 9.10)	*UB-6396* (Fig. 9.10)	*fill Crickley continuous* (distribution not shown)	*10–125 years (95%); 15–75 years (68%)*	Limestone
Etton	*build Etton* (Fig. 6.33)	*GrA-29354* (Fig. 6.33)	*fill Etton* (distribution not shown)	*165–250 years (14%)* or *280–510 years (81%); 195–215 years (3%)* or *290–405 years (65%)*	Gravel
Hambledon main enclosure	*build main enclosure* (Fig. 4.14)	*HH76 1354* (Fig. 4.9)	*Hambledon main I fill* (distribution not shown)	*120–255 years (95%); 135–225 years (68%)*	Chalk
Hambledon main enclosure	*HH76 1354* (Fig. 4.9)	*OxA-7017* (Fig. 4.9)	*Hambledon main V fill* (distribution not shown)	*0–140 years (95%); 20–115 years (68%)*	Chalk
Hambledon Stepleton enclosure	*build Stepleton enclosure* (Fig. 4.11)	*ST80 1156* (Fig. 4.11)	*Stepleton first fill* (distribution not shown)	*85–195 years (95%); 105–165 years (68%)*	Chalk
Knap Hill	*build Knap Hill* (Fig. 3.20)	*OxA-15305* (Fig. 3.20)	*Knap Hill fill* (distribution not shown)	*0–215 years (95%); 0–110 years (68%)*	Chalk
Maiden Castle inner ditch	*dig Maiden inner* (Fig. 4.42)	*GrA-29109* (Fig. 4.42).	*Maiden Castle inner fill* (distribution not shown)	*0–30 years (95%); 0–20 years (68%)*	Chalk
Whitehawk ditch II	*dig Whitehawk II* (Fig. 5.7)	*R4100/143/W* (Fig. 5.7)	*Whitehawk II fill* (distribution not shown)	*0–140 years (95%); 5–30 years (16%)* or *70–125 years (52%)*	Chalk
Whitehawk ditch III	*dig Whitehawk III* (Fig. 5.8)	*OxA-14144* (Fig. 5.8)	*Whitehawk III fill* (distribution not shown)	*1–115 years (95%); 40–100 years (68%)*	Chalk
Whitehawk ditch I	*Dig Whitehawk I* (Fig. 5.6)	*OxA-14030* (Fig. 5.6)	*Whitehawk I fill* (distribution not shown)	*0–100 years (95%); 20–85 years (68%)*	Chalk

Site and ditch	Earlier parameter	Later parameter	Duration of infill	*Posterior density estimate (probability in years)*	Geology
Whitesheet Hill	*build Whitesheet Hill* (Fig. 4.26)	*GrA-30067* (Fig. 4.26)	*Whitesheet Hill fill* (distribution not shown)	*0–115 years* (95%); *0–55 years* (68%)	Chalk
Windmill inner ditch	*dig WH inner* (Fig. 3.9)	*GrA-25560* (Fig. 3.9)	*inner WH fill* (distribution not shown)	*165–190 years* (3%) or *275–355 years* (92%); *290–330 years* (68%)	Chalk
Windmill middle ditch	*dig WH middle* (Fig. 3.10)	*OxA-13714* (Fig. 3.10)	*middle WH fill* (distribution not shown)	*25–140 years* (72%) or *175–250 years* (23%); *45–130 years* (61%) or *200–225 years* (7%)	Chalk
Kingsborough 1 middle ditch	*start Kingsborough 1* (Fig. 7.15)	*GrA-29553* (Fig. 7.15)	*Kingsborough 1 fill* (distribution not shown)	*0–285 years* (95%); *1–130 years* (68%)	Drift deposits

These considerations go a long way to explain why the fill pattern of the Overton Down earthwork differs from those of most chalkland enclosure ditches. That fill pattern can be summarised as follows. Almost all of the 1.20 m of chalk rubble fill which occupied the ditch sides after 30 years (Bell *et al.* 1996, fig. 7.5) had already been in place two years after construction (Bell *et al.* 1996, fig. 14.2); virtually no rubble had accumulated on the centre of the ditch floor (almost certainly a product of the depth: width ratio); and after 20 years vegetation had spread over bank and ditch and a soil had begun to form (Bell *et al.* 1996, fig. 14.2). If current conditions persist, the present V-profile, with only some 0.10 m of fill on the centre-base of the ditch, could persist indefinitely.

In most chalkland causewayed enclosure ditches, rubble spanned the full width, rather than being concentrated at the sides, and, even at the centre, often occupied half or more of the surviving depth. This can be attributed to a less rapidly formed and less stabilising vegetation cover; to narrower proportions, seen strikingly in the 1.75 m of undifferentiated chalk rubble in the particularly deep and narrow ditch of Whitesheet Hill (Fig. 4.24); to the proximity and potential instability of banks, often accentuated by slope; and, at least in some cases, to repeated frequentation of the monuments.

The dating again provides information for those sites where there are sequences bracketing the rubble fills (Table 14.2). At Whitesheet Hill, the estimate for the accumulation of chalk rubble is *0–115 years* (*95% probability*; distribution not shown), probably *0–55 years* (*68% probability*), with the distribution heavily skewed towards a shorter period of infill. At Knap Hill, where there is similarly no sign of intervention in the rubble fills, the estimate is less precise – *0–215 years* (*95% probability*; distribution not shown), probably *0–110 years* (*68% probability*) – but could be comparably short as the distribution is strongly skewed towards a shorter duration. The shortest rubble accumulation was in the inner ditch at Maiden Castle, where the interval from the digging of the ditch to the deposition of the lowest 'midden' layer can be estimated as *0–30 years* (*95% probability*; distribution not shown), probably *0–20 years* (*68% probability*). It should be noted, as discussed in Chapter 4 and further below, that this layer at Maiden Castle may have been associated with the burning and collapse of the bank, which would have infilled the ditch faster than natural accumulation.

Relatively imprecise estimates for ditches I, II and III at Whitehawk and for the limestone rubble of the continuous ditch on Crickley Hill are of the same order as that for Knap Hill (Table 14.2). The exceptions are for the middle and inner ditches of Windmill Hill and for the main and Stepleton enclosures on Hambledon Hill. Estimates of the duration of primary filling in all four are surprisingly extended, at least a century and quite probably longer. This is implausible in the light of the considerations outlined above and of the estimates for other sites.

There is one obvious explanation, that the samples chosen to date the end of the accumulation of chalk rubble may have lain on stable surfaces, so that they could have significantly post-dated the underlying rubble deposits. They were *GrA-25560*, measured on an articulated bone sample from a bone deposit on the surface of the chalk rubble fill in the inner ditch of Windmill Hill (Fig. 3.12, lower: context 630); *OxA-13714*, measured on a rib from a 'bundle' in a bone deposit in a humic layer overlying the top of the chalk rubble in the middle ditch of Windmill Hill (Fig. 3.13, upper: context 411); *HH76 1354*, the mean of two measurements on articulating deer phalanges from an apparently dumped deposit overlying the top of the chalk rubble in the main enclosure on Hambledon Hill (Mercer and Healy 2008, fig. 3.29: layer 9a); and *ST80 1156*, the mean of two measurements on an articulated dog skeleton lying on the topmost, rather silty and comminuted, layer of chalk rubble fill (Mercer and Healy 2008, fig. 3.85: section D–D', interface of layers 3B and 2). Yet the upper limits of the Whitehawk estimates were similarly provided by dates from contexts succeeding the rubble fills, and these durations are much shorter. As at Etton, the extended durations at Hambledon and Windmill Hill probably reflect extended maintenance, with or without periods of stability and diminished intervention, undertaken before all the surviving primary fills accumulated. At Hambledon, the sections cited above show that rubble was removed from the two segments in question at least once, the ditch being cleared almost to the base, echoing the treatment of the inner ditch of Kingsborough 1. Cuts in chalk rubble are notoriously difficult to identify, and may be under-represented in the archaeological record, unlike interventions in the secondary silts of ditches, which are easier to recognise.

The main enclosure at Hambledon also provides a rare opportunity to estimate the rate of accumulation of secondary silts (e.g. Fig. 4.3, upper: layers 5, 5a, 5b). This much slower process seems to have been completely natural here; it can be estimated that approximately 0.30 m of secondary silt accumulated over *0–140 years* (*95% probability*; Table 14.2; distribution not shown), probably *20–115 years* (*68% probability*).

The intensity of deposition at enclosures

There is great variability in the density and composition of cultural material between the circuits of the same enclosure, as at Kingsborough 1 (M. Allen *et al.* 2008), Chalk Hill (Chapter 7), Maiden Castle (Sharples 1991a) or Windmill Hill (Whittle *et al.* 1999, figs 222–6). Variability in artefact density between monuments and between regions has also been demonstrated (C. Evans *et al.* 2006, table 12; Mercer 2006a, table 5.1). Both analyses, though conducted by different methods, suggest a gradient from generally low levels of deposition in the east (Great Wilbraham proving a signal exception) to higher ones in the Thames valley and yet higher ones in Wessex and, in Mercer's analysis, the south-west peninsula.

It is now possible to examine how far that pattern is a product of the varying durations of different sites as distinct from the behaviour of their users, and how far the material itself reflects the intensity of use of individual sites. To do this it is necessary to relate the estimated period of the primary use of a monument (the parameters assembled in Fig. 14.32) to estimates of the total amount of material deposited during that use (summarised in Tables 14.3–4). This is possible only for sites where a reasonably precise estimate of the duration of primary use is available; where the finds are contexted and quantified; and where the original extent of the monument can be estimated. Several of the sites employed by previous authors, including Haddenham, Great Wilbraham, Briar Hill, Orsett, Staines and Offham Hill, do not meet these criteria, especially the need for a relatively precise and robust estimate of duration.

A second major difference between this exercise and those of previous authors, in addition to spreading the assemblages over time, is that it employs only material from early Neolithic contexts (in the sixth and tenth columns of Table 14.3). This must have been deposited during the primary use of each site. In some cases there are major differences between these subtotals and the overall ones, as in the lithics from Windmill Hill and Chalk Hill, where there was substantial third and second millennium cal BC activity (Table 14.3). The results also differ from those presented for Hambledon Hill by Mercer and Healy (2008, table 11.4), since this deals with material from all contexts in all earthworks.

The exercise here is confined to Neolithic Bowl pottery and struck flint and chert, since these survive on all geologies. The excavated sample of each site was used to estimate the total assemblages. For ditches, the total length was estimated and the total assemblage extrapolated from the percentage of that length excavated. For other contexts, the total enclosed area was estimated and the total assemblage extrapolated from the percentage of the area excavated (Table 14.3). The results are necessarily approximate. The possibility that they are unreliable rises where only small, possibly unrepresentative, proportions of a site have been excavated (as indicated in the second column of Table 14.3). Furthermore, recovery and retention have not been even across all the sites included in the analysis. They were probably less than total in Leeds' excavations at Abingdon; and the totals for the excavations at Windmill Hill, including discarded material, were reconstructed from the paper archive of Keiller (Whittle *et al.* 1999, 26, 333). While sieving of one kind or another will have been practised in most recent excavations, it is generally difficult to determine its nature and extent. This is particularly significant for lithics, since the more sieving and flotation there are, the more microdebitage (chips with a maximum dimension <10 mm) will be recovered. In the two cases where chips have been separately quantified (Chalk Hill and Whitesheet Hill), they have been excluded from the totals, on the grounds that they were probably more fully recovered at these two sites than elsewhere.

For each site in Table 14.3, we have calculated the number of struck lithics and the number of Bowl pottery

Table 14.3. Excavated and estimated totals of Neolithic Bowl pottery and struck flint and chert from selected enclosures.

Site	% excavated	No. of Bowl sherds from all contexts		No. of Bowl sherds from early Neolithic contexts		No. of pieces of struck flint and chert from all contexts		No. of pieces of struck flint and chert from early Neolithic contexts		Notes
		Excavated	Estimated	Excavated	Estimated	Excavated	Estimated	Excavated	Estimated	
Eastern England										
Etton	Ditch 60% other 51%	2196	3785	1772	3785	6284	11798	1909	3580	Flint numbers from Middleton (1998). Sherd numbers approximate, calculated from information supplied by K. Gdaniec and M. Knight
Kingsborough 2	Ditch 18% other 60%	1141	5406	876	4827	143	549	57	317	From M. Allen *et al.* (2008)
Chalk Hill	Inner ditch 30% middle ditch 30% outer ditch 10%; other 22%	1228	7302	1210	7220	15003	68195	6675	30341	From Shand (2001); Gibson (2002a); Wilson (2002)
Thames valley										
Abingdon totals	Inner ditch 35% outer ditch 1% other 4%	5504	25914	5504	25914	5257	25100	4935	17050	From Case (1956); Case and Whittle (1982). Sherds numbers calculated on mean sherd weight of 7.5 g (C. Evans *et al.* 2006, 151) from weights given in publications. All finds from the ditch are taken as from early Neolithic contexts since there was very little later material in the ditch tops. Recovery and/or retention of finds are unlikely to have been complete in Leeds' excavations
Wessex										
Hambledon main enclosure	Ditch 18% other 14%	11052	69286	8754	54671	18090	111992	9254	56575	From Mercer and Healy (2008). Includes enclosure ditch and pits and other contexts within enclosure, excludes cross-dykes, south long barrow and western outwork
Hambledon Stepleton enclosure	Ditch 45% other 78%	9284	17019	7665	13719	12857	22263	7347	13962	From Mercer and Healy (2008).). Includes enclosure ditch and pits and other contexts within enclosure, excludes outworks
Whitesheet Hill	Ditch 1% other 1%	625	62500	611	61100	15972	1597200	15200	1520000	From Rawlings *et al.* (2004). Finds from the Piggott and Stone excavation are excluded because they are not quantified in the publication. Chips (flakes and fragments with a maximum dimension <10 mm) are excluded from the totals of struck flint and chert because, due to extensive sieving of pit contents, they amount to 23% of the material from non-ditch contexts and would reduce the comparability of the totals with those from other sites where chips were recovered on a far smaller scale or not at all
Maiden Castle	Inner ditch 1% Outer ditch 0.8% Other 2%	789	78950	789	78860	21437	765607	8127	290250	From Sharples (1991a). The larger assemblage from Wheeler's more extensive excavations has not been used because not all of it was available for quantification in the 1980s (e.g. Cleal 1991, 171)

Site	% excavated	No. of Bowl sherds from all contexts		No. of Bowl sherds from early Neolithic contexts		No. of pieces of struck flint and chert from all contexts		No. of pieces of struck flint and chert from early Neolithic contexts		Notes
		Excavated	Estimated	Excavated	Estimated	Excavated	Estimated	Excavated	Estimated	
Windmill Hill	Inner ditch 85% Middle ditch 30% Outer ditch 10% Other 2%	20814	83803	10357	62774	99889	443617	14681	110552	From Whittle *et al.* (1999, tables 1–51, 172–92). The totals of pottery from all contexts and of pottery and lithics from early Neolithic contexts in the Keiller and Smith excavations are taken from tables 1–51. Those of lithics from all contexts in the same excavations are taken from tables 191–2. Some quantities are approximate. Partly because they are derived from paper records of discarded artefacts (I. Smith 1965a, 29–30; Whittle *et al.* 1999, 333) The limits of early Neolithic ditch fills have been approximated from pottery and radiocarbon dates, or, failing these, by analogy with other segments
Knap Hill	Ditch 3% Other 2%	15	650	6	267	2786	112433	1346	49183	From Connah (1965). The material from the Cunningtons' earlier excavations is not included

sherds deposited per year of the primary use of the enclosure. This has been done by calculating the probability that it was in use for each 25-year band, multiplying this by the estimated total of struck lithics or Bowl pottery sherds from early Neolithic contexts (Table 14.3), and dividing this by the higher number of years limiting the band in question. The totals for each 25-year band of the duration of the use of the site are then added, to provide an estimate of the number of sherds or lithics deposited in each year of its use. For example, it is *79% probable* that Maiden Castle was in use for 0–25 years; we estimate that a total of 78,860 Bowl sherds were deposited during the primary use of this site. In the first 25 years of the use of Maiden Castle, 62,378 sherds (0.791 x 78,860) would have been deposited – 2,495 sherds per year (62,378 ÷ 25). The totals from similar calculations for the bands covering a duration of 26–50 years, 51–75 years, and so on, are then added together to provide the estimates of the numbers of sherds or struck lithics deposited per year (see below and Table 14.3).

The introduction of time into the estimates (Table 14.4) makes the quantity of material deposited at enclosures in Wessex far less uniformly rich, although most of the higher densities still occur in the region. This is not simply a matter of the availability and the quality of Chalk flint, since it applies to pottery as well as lithics, and both Hambledon enclosures have quite low frequencies of lithics.

It also demonstrates relatively high annual rates of deposition at the short-lived monuments of Abingdon and Maiden Castle. The result for Abingdon, of 666 Bowl sherds and 438 lithics per year, is probably representative, in that a substantial portion of the inner ditch was excavated, and may, if anything, be an underestimate, since in this, the oldest of the excavations used in the analysis, recovery and retention may not have been complete. The overall result for Maiden Castle, of 2806 Bowl sherds and 10,329 lithics per year, might seem questionable, in that the finds are quantified from only a very low proportion of the enclosure (Table 14.3). But there is reason to accept it because, although incomplete, the assemblage from Wheeler's more extensive excavations shows every sign of having been equally abundant. Although the artefacts from Wheeler's excavations were not quantified in the original report and are not all extant, the remnant of the Neolithic material reported by Cleal (1991) and Edmonds and Bellamy (1991) is so substantial as to be compatible with the densities estimated here from the Sharples material. Rims from 338 Neolithic Bowls survive from the Wheeler excavations, for example, alongside a total of 105 from 1985–6 (Cleal 1991, tables 132–3, microfiche).

Given only limited excavation, it is difficult to judge whether the high ceramic and lithic densities from Whitesheet Hill and the high lithic density from Knap Hill are to be taken at face value. The high Whitesheet densities are largely derived from a few prolific pits (Fig. 4.23), which may or may not be representative of the interior as a whole. At Knap Hill, the high lithic densities spring mainly from a dense knapping cluster encountered in one out of

Table 14.4. Quantities of Neolithic Bowl pottery and struck flint and chert deposited per year, based on the estimates in Table 14.3.

Site	***Posterior density estimate* (Fig. 14.32)**	**Bowl sherds per year (early Neolithic contexts only)**	**Lithics per year (early Neolithic contexts only)**	**No. of pieces of struck flint per Bowl sherd per year (early Neolithic contexts only)**
Eastern England				
Etton	*use Etton* *345–635 years (95% probability; 380–510 years (68% probability)*	8	8	1.0
Kingsborough 2	*use Kingsborough 2* *0–315 years (95% probability); 0–65 years (38% probability)* or *100–185 years (30% probability)*	74	5	0.1
Chalk Hill	*use Chalk Hill* *45–165 years (95% probability); 65–115 years (68% probability)*	70	294	4.2
Thames valley				
Abingdon	*use Abingdon* *0–40 years (57% probability)* or *65–145 years (38% probability); 0–30 years (54% probability)* or *85–110 years (14% probability)*	666	438	0.7
Wessex				
Hambledon main enclosure	*use main enclosure* *290–350 years (95% probability); 300–335 years (68% probability)*	166	171	1.0
Hambledon Stepleton enclosure	*use Stepleton enclosure* *165–255 years (95% probability); 195–250 years (68% probability)*	62	63	1.0
Whitesheet Hill	*use Whitesheet Hill* *1–125 years (95% probability); 1–55 years (68% probability)*	1445	35938	24.9
Maiden Castle	*use Maiden Castle* *1–50 years (95% probability); 1–20 years (68% probability)*	2806	10329	3.7
Windmill Hill	*use Windmill Hill* *180–200 years (1% probability)* or *290–390 years (94% probability); 305–350 years (68% probability)*	188	331	1.8
Knap Hill	*use Knap Hill* *1–460 years (95% probability); 1–65 years (23% probability)* or *115–280 years (45% probability)*	3	482	160.7

four narrow sections across the ditch (Connah 1965, fig. 2, table I). Again, it is difficult to tell how representative these are of the whole, although Maud Cunnington's discovery of clusters of 'flint chips' in her excavations of 1908–9 (Cunnington 1912, 61) suggests that Connah's concentration was not the only one.

Variable densities of lithics in part reflect an extra-domestic aspect to the industries of some enclosures. Maiden Castle is seen as a local focus of axehead production (Edmonds and Bellamy 1991, 227–8), and the industry of Offham Hill (excluded here for want of an estimate for the duration of its primary use) had an overall sherds:lithics ratio of 1:40 and an 'industrial' character in the sense of high frequencies of cortical flakes and low frequencies of cores and retouched pieces, with the connotation that cores may have been prepared on the site and removed elsewhere (James 1977). An industrial facies at Knap Hill is strongly suggested by the massive preponderance of primary over secondary flakes (Connah 1965, table I), even if Connah used the term 'primary' to include any flake with some dorsal cortex, as the absence of tertiary flakes from his totals suggests. Cortical flakes were, by contrast, rare at Whitesheet (unpublished data).

Leaving aside the exceptional quantities of lithics deposited at Maiden Castle and Whitesheet Hill, the estimated annual totals for the other sites amount to no more than the contents of one relatively artefact-rich pit. Even disregarding exceptionally large and rich pits like the Coneybury Anomaly (J. Richards 1990, 46, 213), single early to mid-fourth millennium cal BC pits, whether within enclosures or beyond them, have yielded totals such as 290 sherds and 427 lithics from pit 1A F350 on the Stepleton spur of Hambledon Hill (Mercer and Healy 2008, 286), 90 sherds and 249 lithics from pit 1096 at Middle Farm, Dorchester, Dorset (Butterworth and Gibson 2004, 15), and 147 sherds and 207 lithics from pit 146 at Kilverstone, Norfolk (Garrow *et al.* 2006, 27).

An estimated annual assemblage that is comparable in quantity with that from a pit that could have been dug and filled in less than a day by one or two people appears disproportionate to the size of the enclosures and to the workforce needed for their construction (see above). It is often clear, however, that deposition was not spread evenly over time. It was concentrated towards the end of primary use in the recuts in the inner ditch at Abingdon, the 'midden' layers of the inner ditch at Maiden Castle, the phase 1B and 1C deposits at Etton, above the ditch bases at Windmill Hill, and the phase VI deposits in both Hambledon enclosures. In other words, when these enclosures were built, with numbers of people gathered to undertake that work, little was placed in their ditches. It was only later that there came a change of practice (Sharples 1991a, 253), with the burial of artefacts and food remains on a more extensive scale.

The food remains provide a clue to the human scale of these later episodes. One of the young cows which dominate the faunal remains at Hambledon would have provided some 300 kg of meat, offal and fat, yet some of the phase VI recuts in the main enclosure, which seem to have been cut and filled in single events, contained the remains of two or three such animals in a single segment (Legge 2008, 543–4, 569). This points to gatherings of hundreds – many hundreds if several such consumption events took place simultaneously. The events in question may have included the building of some of the later outworks. If such events were rare, with the sites effectively abandoned for years on end, the relatively high densities from short-lived sites would contrast less than they appear to with low densities from longer-lived ones, since the assemblages from the longer-lived sites would have been concentrated in a few large-scale events rather than spread over centuries. The woodland environments in which most Wessex and Sussex enclosures were built and used could reflect occasional frequentation by people and their animals; the more open surroundings of sites in eastern England need not point to different patterns of use, simply to location of the monuments in different parts of the landscape. In this scenario, the estimate of *0–140 years* (*95% probability*), probably *20–115 years* (*68% probability*), for the apparently natural accumulation of phase V secondary silts in the main enclosure at Hambledon (Table 14.2), could correspond to an interval between large gatherings, one in which little cultural material was deposited in contrast to the quantities of artefacts and food remains piled into the subsequent phase VI slots (Mercer and Healy 2008, 56–7).

Violence at causewayed enclosures

In some of the regional chapters, particularly those covering more westerly areas of the country, we have come across evidence at causewayed and stone-walled tor enclosures for both violent episodes that must have involved significant numbers of people and violence relating to individual people. Beyond enclosures, most cases of violence are to individuals. How does the evidence from different contexts and for different kinds of violent encounter fit together, and are there any temporal and regional trends? This evidence can now be brought together (Figs 14.36–7).

The map (Fig. 14.37) shows that less than 20 percent of the dated enclosures overall have data of this kind. Within this sample, however, there is more evidence for major violent events at enclosures in the central and western parts of southern England, where almost half the dated enclosures have been the subject of attack. Thus the partial burning of posts in the palisade behind the outer and middle ditches at Orsett (Chapter 7) appears to stand rather on its own in the east, contrasting with several similar episodes farther west. At Staines an individual from the primary fill of the outer ditch (skull B) had both healed and unhealed wounds (Chapter 8; Fig. 14.36; Schulting and Wysocki 2005, table 2).

The scale of these collective events can be impressive. The burning in period 1B on the Shroton spur on Hambledon Hill appears over a 140-m length of ditch, very soon after the earthwork was built. A later episode of burning in period 2 in the inner Stepleton outwork can be traced over

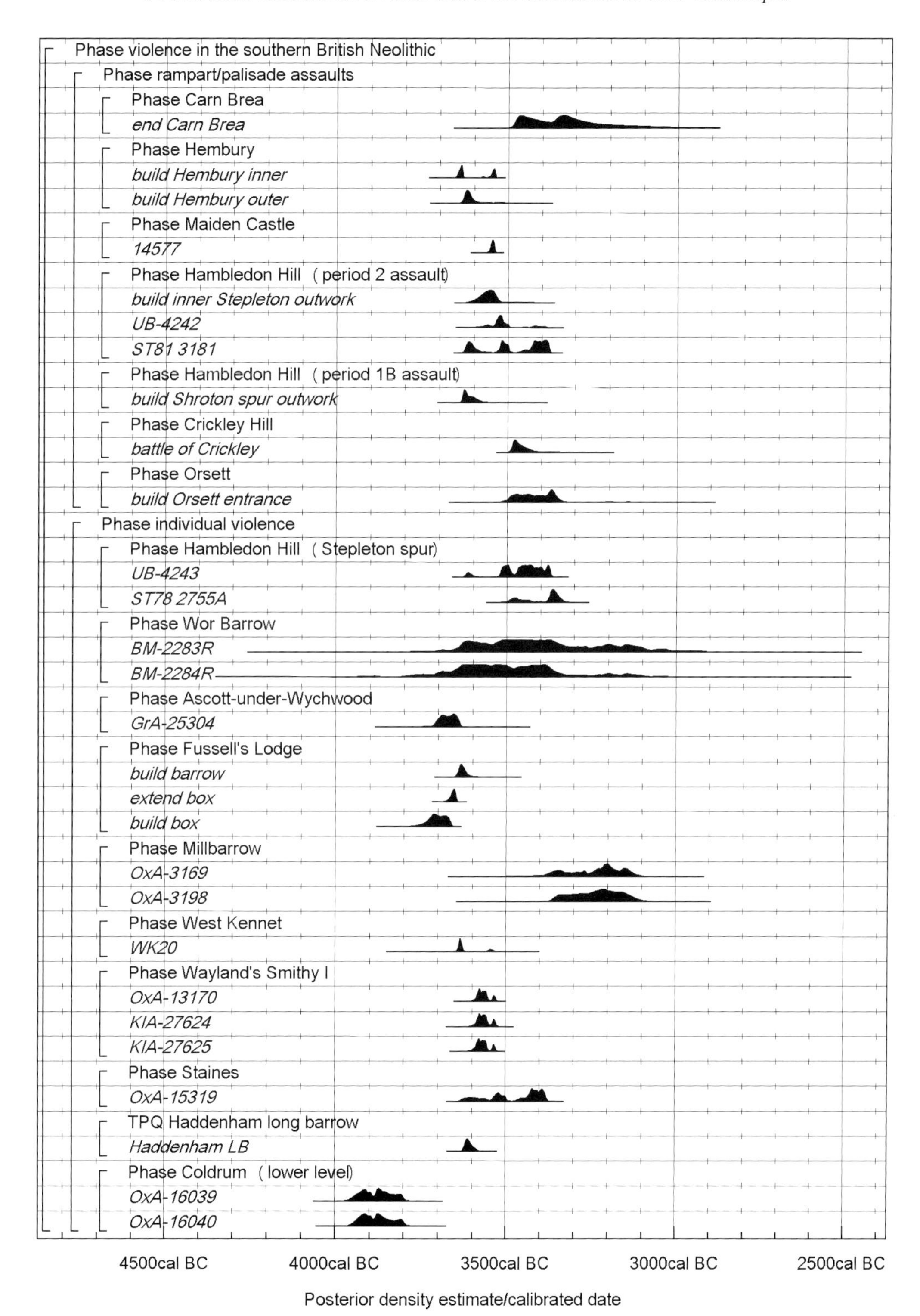

Fig. 14.36. Posterior density estimates for the dates of violent episodes in the early Neolithic of southern Britain. Distributions are derived from the site-based models enumerated in the captions to Figs 14.2–4, and additionally Bayliss et al. *(2007b, fig. 6) (West Kennet), Bayliss* et al. *(2007c, figs 3 and 5–7) (Ascott-under-Wychwood), Wysocki* et al. *(2007, fig. 10) (Fussell's Lodge), Figs 3.29–31 (Millbarrow), Whittle* et al. *(2007b, fig. 4) (Wayland's Smithy I), Figs 6.16–17 (Haddenham long barrow) and Fig. 7.27 (Coldrum).*

a 200-m length of ditch. This also occurred soon after the construction of the earthwork, as the burning was on the base of the ditch or over only a tiny amount of primary silting, and the earthwork appears to be unfinished. In both these cases, the burning appears to have destroyed a box-frame rampart constructed from oak uprights and hazel cladding, probably in the form of wattle panels or hurdles (Mercer and Healy 2008, fig. 3.99). Given the demonstrably short period between the construction of these earthworks and their burning, the question of whether they were built in

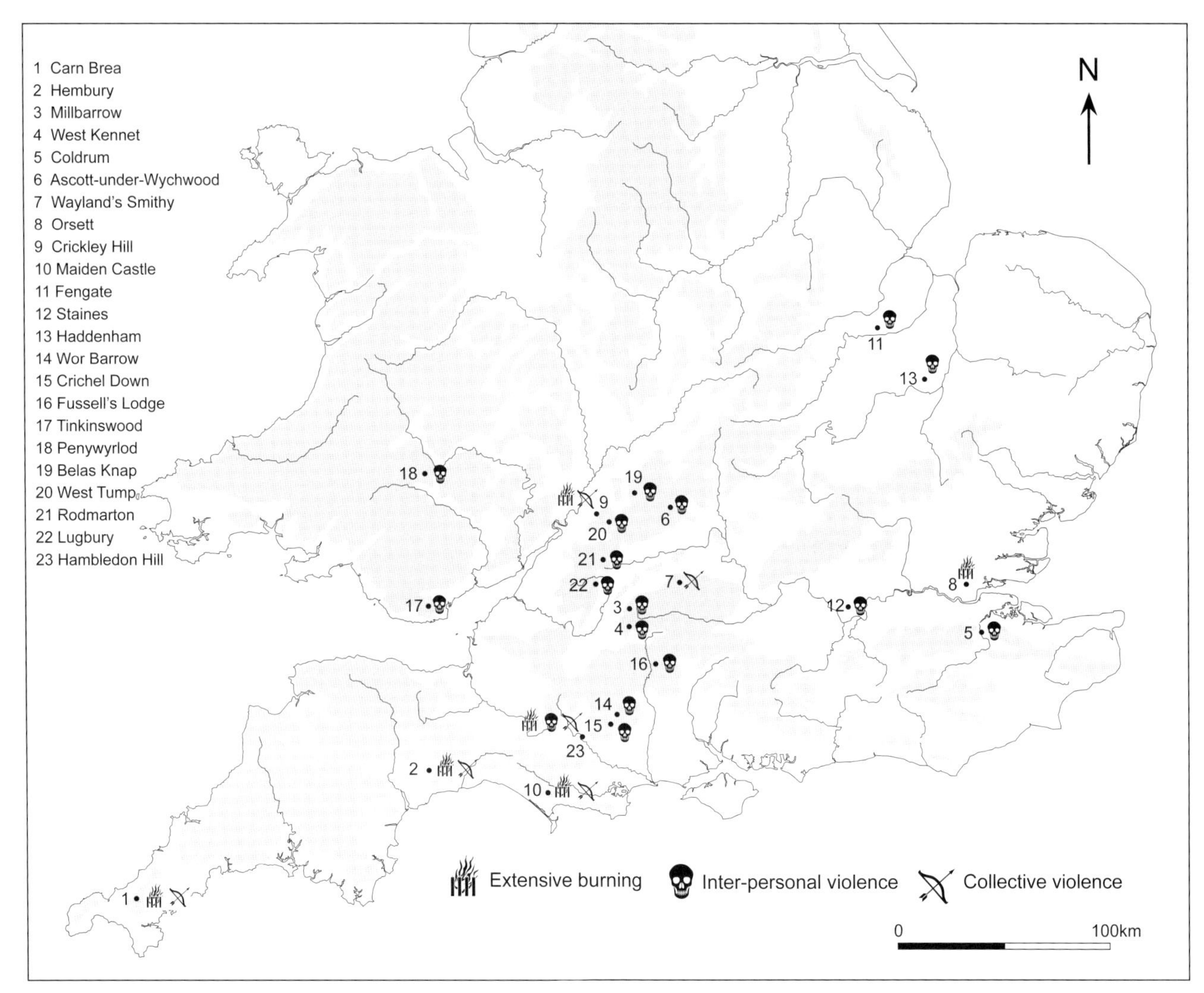

Fig. 14.37. Map of violent episodes in southern Britain in the fourth millennium cal BC. Note that inter-personal violence includes both cranial trauma and arrowhead wounds.

relation to an immediate threat has to be raised. An adult male buried on the base of the ditch of the burnt inner Stepleton outwork may have died in this conflict. A young man, buried in a pit with quantities of burnt material, may relate to the same event. Later on, in period 3, two young men died by arrowshot (Fig. 14.36: *UB-4243, ST78 2755A*). One of them lay on the base of the outer Stepleton outwork, and the other lay prone in the fill of the inner Stepleton outwork, above the base of the ditch (Figs 4.3, 14.36).

The episode which led to the deposition of nearly 400 arrowheads and extensive burning at Crickley Hill has been characterised as a battle: a violent assault (Chapter 9). The same seems to apply both at Hembury and at Carn Brea (Chapter 10), the latter with some 750 arrowheads in evidence as well as again extensive traces of burning. At Hembury there is a question of whether the burning events reflected in the inner and outer ditch circuits were exactly contemporary. Either the inner earthwork was constructed and then burnt soon after, to be followed by a repetition of the same sequence in the outer earthwork, or the inner earthwork stood for a while before being joined by the outer earthwork, with both then destroyed by fire at the same time. Our model for Hembury (Figs 10. 9–12) allows the possibility of two episodes of burning. There are numerous burnt arrowheads from the site (Chapter 10; Mercer 2006b). It is possible, though the evidence comes from much more restricted areas of excavation, that there were violent or dramatic events at Maiden Castle too, which could have produced the charcoal and scorching observed in the primary chalk rubble fills of the inner ditch, and the numbers of arrowheads recorded (Chapter 4; cf. Mercer 2006b). Given the very short timescale probably involved, this could again be seen as a case of anticipation of attack, though it may also have been the case that construction of enclosures aroused jealousies and tensions, and thereby precipitated attacks soon after. It is worth noting that, although the Carn Brea and Crickley Hill enclosures were respectively a stone wall and an almost continuous ditch with stone bank, Hembury, Maiden Castle and Orsett share the same kind of interrupted ditch circuit as other sites without evidence of attack. The outworks on Hambledon Hill also had interrupted ditches, but the evidence tends to suggest more continuous banks (Mercer and Healy 2008, figs 3.73, 3.81).

In terms of examples of individual deaths and violent encounters from other contexts, in the east there was an adult with arrowhead behind the sternum in the small mortuary deposit at Fengate (Chapter 6), and skulls with healed and unhealed wounds from the lower level of the chamber at Coldrum (Chapter 7). One of the five individuals from the Haddenham long barrow (Chapter 6) was associated with a leaf-shaped arrowhead, which in other instances can be shown to have been a cause of death. The dates for the deposits from which these remains were recovered at Coldrum and Haddenham are shown in Fig. 14.36; in these cases, the individuals themselves have not been directly dated and our estimates derive from samples in similar contexts.

Further west (Fig. 14.37), three individuals from Wayland's Smithy I might have met their deaths by arrowshot (Fig. 14.36: *OxA-13170, KIA-27624–5*; Whittle *et al.* 2007b); and the whole of the primary mortuary deposit might be related to some kind of massacre event (Whittle *et al.* 2007a). There was a leaf arrowhead 'in the region of the throat' of an adult male in the West Kennet long barrow, 'conceivably the cause of his death' (Fig. 14.36: *WK20*; Piggott 1962, 25). Another male, this time buried near the top of the primary fills of the ditch of Wor Barrow, in Cranborne Chase, had a leaf arrowhead among the ribs (Pitt Rivers 1898, pl. 251). Two antlers from the ditch base should predate this burial by only a short interval (Fig. 14.36: *BM-2283R, -2284R*). Elsewhere in Cranborne Chase, a leaf arrowhead was found among the ribs of an undated adult skeleton buried in a natural knoll on Crichel Down, (Piggott and Piggott 1944, 74–5). There was a probably healed wound on a skull from Millbarrow near Avebury (Schulting and Wysocki 2005, table 2); we have not been able to trace its exact context, and Fig. 14.36 shows estimates for the dates of individuals thought to be from the chamber (Chapter 3). Three skulls probably from the first deposits of the Fussell's Lodge long barrow (Wysocki *et al.* 2007; Michael Wysocki, pers. comm.) have healed wounds (Schulting and Wysocki 2005, table 2). Figure 14.36 follows the preferred model for the chronology of the barrow (Wysocki *et al.* 2007), although it should be noted that we have produced alternative models for the early history of this monument. In the eastern Cotswolds, one of the later individuals (B2) buried at Ascott-under-Wychwood died by arrowshot (Chapter 9; Benson and Whittle 2007; Bayliss *et al.* 2007c; Fig. 14.36: *GrA-25304*). More evidence comes from other chambered cairns in the Cotswolds, in the form of healed cranial wounds from Lugbury, Rodmarton, West Tump and Belas Knap (Schulting and Wysocki 2005, table 2); of these, only West Tump is dated, rather imprecisely (Fig. 9.24), but the crania in question have not been directly dated (Smith and Brickley 2006), and for these reasons we have not included this site in Fig. 14.36. Skulls with healed wounds have also been found at Hambledon Hill (Schulting and Wysocki 2005; McKinley 2008), one probably originally buried in the southern long barrow and the other from the phase VI slot in the main enclosure, but possibly redeposited; for these reasons, the dates of these contexts are not shown in Fig. 14.36. Further west again, in south Wales, there is evidence of individuals with both cranial wounds and arrowshot from Penywyrlod, and with cranial wounds from Tinkinswood (Chapter 11; Schulting and Wysocki 2005; Wysocki and Whittle 2000).

The greater number of samples showing evidence of violence affecting individuals from the west may be an artefact of the smaller number of large collective deposits of people in funerary constructions and the less frequent survival of bone in the eastern parts of the country. Whereas for enclosures we know that a significant number of sites in the east have been examined and there is not the kind of evidence for episodes of collective violence seen in the west, a significant number of early Neolithic human remains from other deposits in the east have not been examined. Overall, however, more than 350 skulls or crania have been examined from southern Britain and fewer than 9% show signs of trauma, healed or unhealed (Schulting and Wysocki 2005, 122). The wider significance of this evidence is discussed in Chapter 15.8.

14.3 Enclosures and other monuments in southern Britain

After the beginning of the Neolithic in Britain and Ireland, people began to make constructions with increasing frequency and of growing diversity: altering the earth, in Richard Bradley's phrase (1993). This cannot be seen as an absolute difference between the Mesolithic and Neolithic periods, since in the former people had built huts, shelters, platforms and possibly trackways, and had accumulated shell middens and dug pits in the ground – activities by no means confined to the latter stages of the Mesolithic (Allen and Gardiner 2002). After the start of the Neolithic, however, the number and scale of constructions and interventions of all kinds increase, ranging from shelters and houses, trackways and pits, to flint mine shafts and monuments. It is monuments above all which have figured in general characterisations of the nature of the Neolithic period, the assembly and application of labour for collective tasks of building on the one hand and the motivations for such enterprises on the other both being seen as distinctively new. There has been a general tendency to assume that such monumentality was a feature of the Neolithic from its beginning, though there have been signs in the recent literature of more discrimination (e.g. Cleal 2004; Healy 2004; J. Pollard 2004; Russell 2002; R. Bradley 2007; and see Whittle *et al.* 2007a), and some tendency, typological schemes of development notwithstanding, to assume that diverse forms of monuments co-existed.

This project has established that the distinctive form of monumentality represented by causewayed enclosures in southern Britain – involving conceptualising the generally circular enclosure of space, digging into the earth, piling upcast into banks, and on occasion building related timber structures such as palisades – probably began in the last quarter of the 38th century cal BC (Fig. 14.12). Did other forms of construction precede the building of causewayed

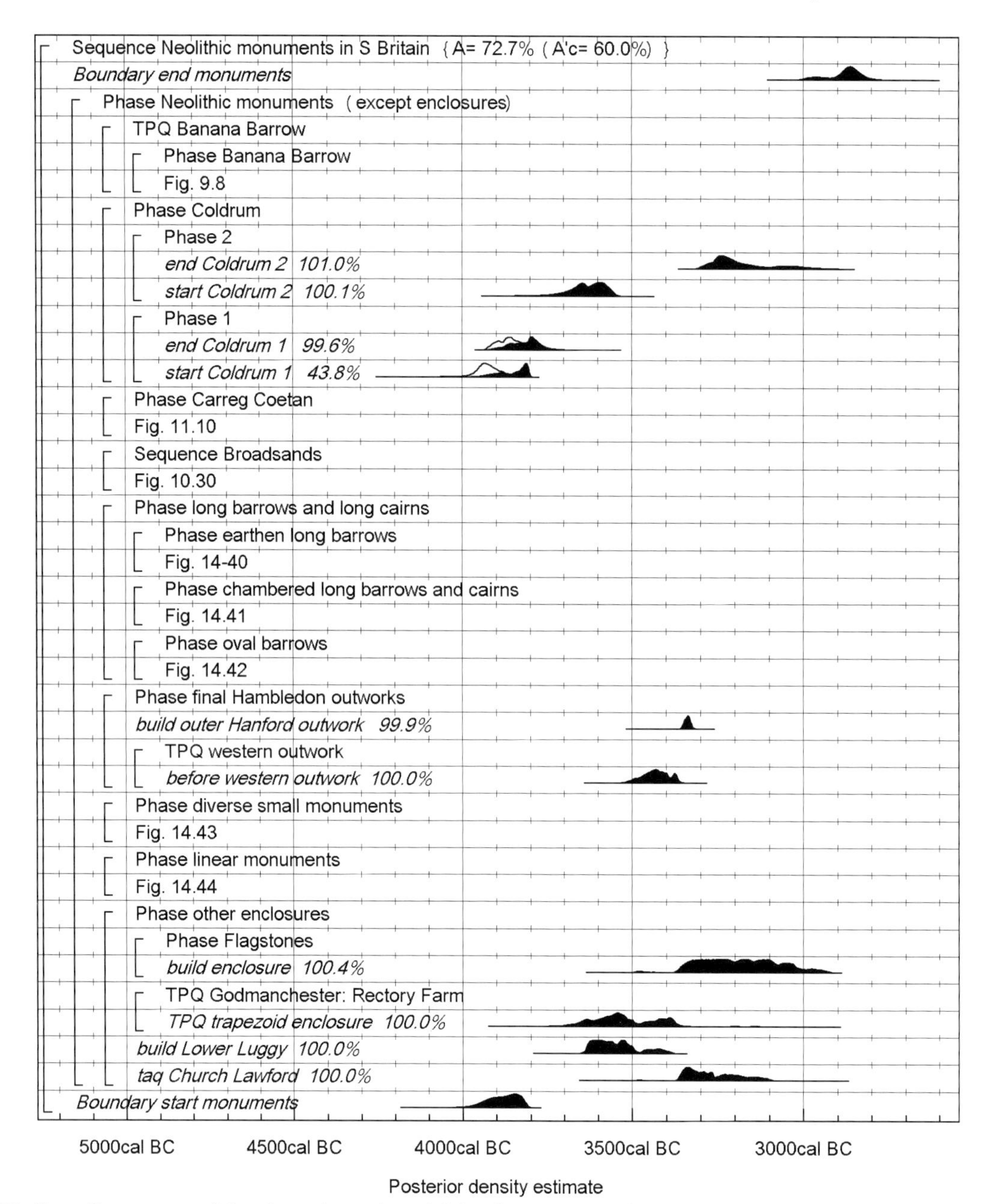

Fig. 14.38. Overall structure of the chronological model for the currency of early Neolithic monuments in southern Britain. The structures of the component sections of this model are shown in detail in Figs 9.8, 10.3, 11.10, and 14.40–2 and between the uniform phase boundaries of Figs 14.43–4 (although the posterior density estimates shown on these figures are not those relating to this model). Additional distributions have been taken from the models defined by Figs 4.7–13 (Hambledon Hill outworks), Fig. 4.48 (Flagstones), Fig. 6.15 (Godmanchester, Rectory Farm), Fig. 7.27 (Coldrum) and Fig. 11.15 (Lower Luggy and Church Lawford). The large square brackets down the left-hand side of Figs 14.38, 14.40–2, 9.8, 10.3 and 11.10, along with the OxCal keywords, define the overall model exactly.

enclosures? What forms did these take? What were the relative currencies of differing monument traditions? And what came after causewayed enclosures, and when?

Other monuments have been described and discussed in the regional chapters. Now is the time to examine them at a broader scale, in relation to the start and currency of causewayed and stone-walled tor enclosures in southern Britain. We have constructed five models to investigate the place of causewayed enclosures within the development of monumentality in the early Neolithic of southern Britain. None of these includes the dates from causewayed or tor enclosures themselves. First, an overall model which includes all other dated early Neolithic monumental constructions within our study areas has been built (Fig. 14.38), to determine whether enclosures were a primary feature of early Neolithic monumentality, and whether they were an ever-present component of it, or whether they were constructed and used for only part of the period. Then, three further broad categories of monument are presented: long barrows and cairns, along with oval barrows; diverse, small monuments, including ring ditches; and non-mortuary linear monuments, including

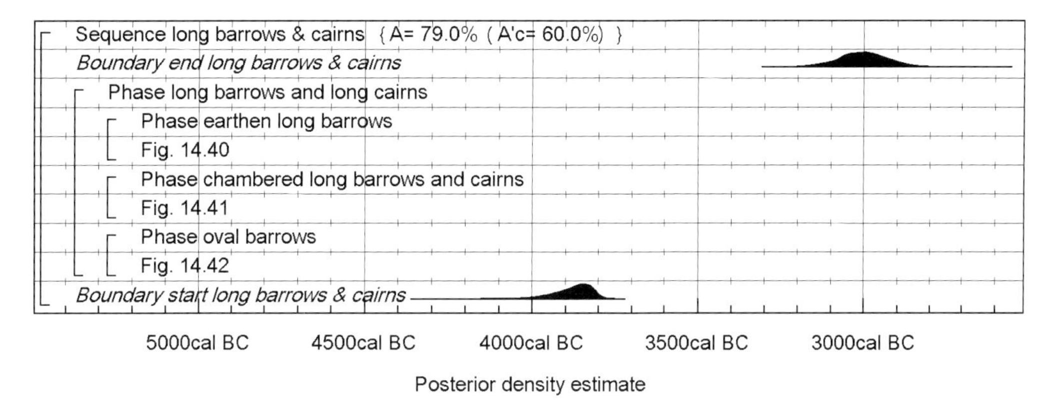

Fig. 14.39. Overall structure of the chronological model for the currency of long barrows and cairns in southern Britain. The component sections of this model are shown in detail in Figs 14.40–2. The large square brackets down the left-hand side of Figs 14.39–42, along with the OxCal keywords, define the overall model exactly.

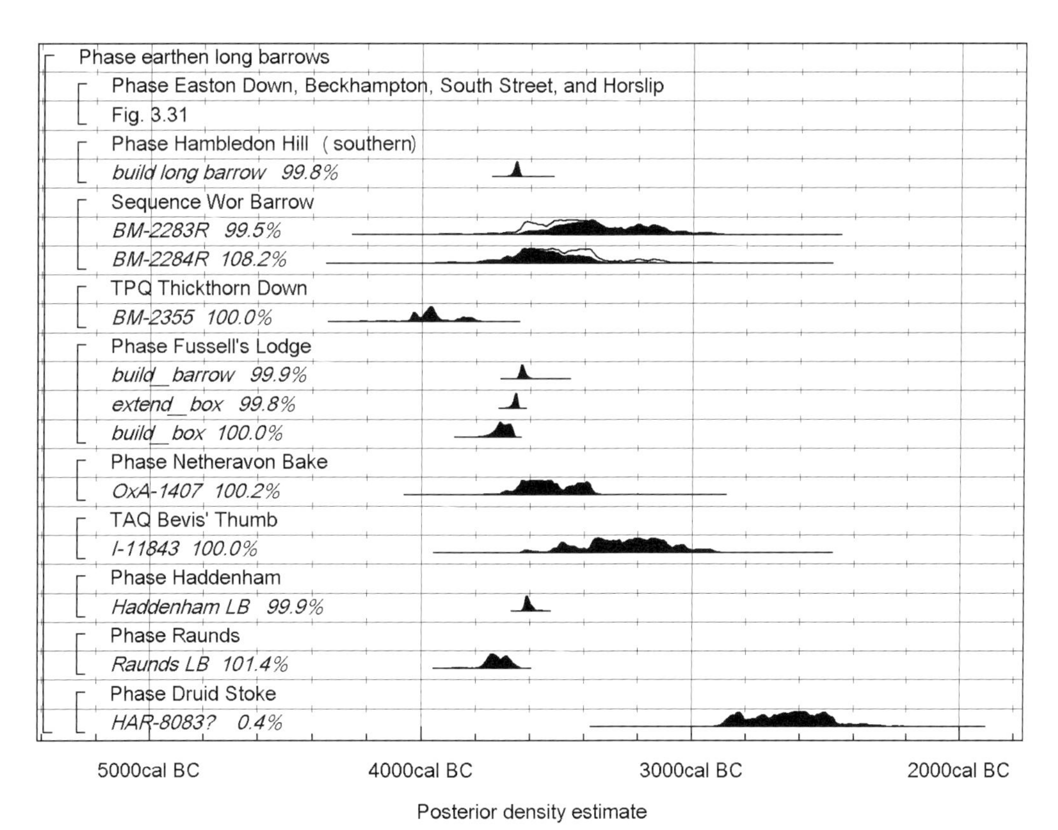

Fig. 14.40. Probability distributions of dates from earthen long barrows. The format is identical to that of Fig. 14.1. The structure of the component section of this model relating to Easton Down, Beckhampton, South Street and Horslip is shown in Fig. 3.31 (although the posterior density estimates shown on this figure are not those relating to this model). Other distributions have been taken from models defined in Figs 4.7–13 (Hambledon Hill), Wysocki et al. *(2007, fig. 10) (Fussell's Lodge), Figs 6.16–17 (Haddenham) and Figs 6.25–7 (Raunds). The overall structure of this model is shown in Fig. 14.39, and its other components in Figs 14.41–2.*

cursus monuments. Independent models to determine the currency of each of these traditions have been calculated (Figs 14.39–42, Fig. 14.43 and Fig. 14.44). An additional model has been constructed for long barrows and cairns, and oval barrows, in order to explore the currency of different architectural forms within this broad grouping (Fig. 14.45). The purpose of these models is to compare the currency of other Neolithic monument types with that of enclosures (Figs 14.45–6).

The overall form of the model for the construction and use of early Neolithic monuments in the areas of southern Britain where we have dated enclosures is shown in Fig. 14.38. Some of the components of the overall model have been taken from models defined in the regional chapters (although the posterior density estimates shown on these figures are not those relating to this model). For long barrows and cairns, and oval barrows, the components are defined in Figs 14.40–2, and for diverse, small monuments, and linear

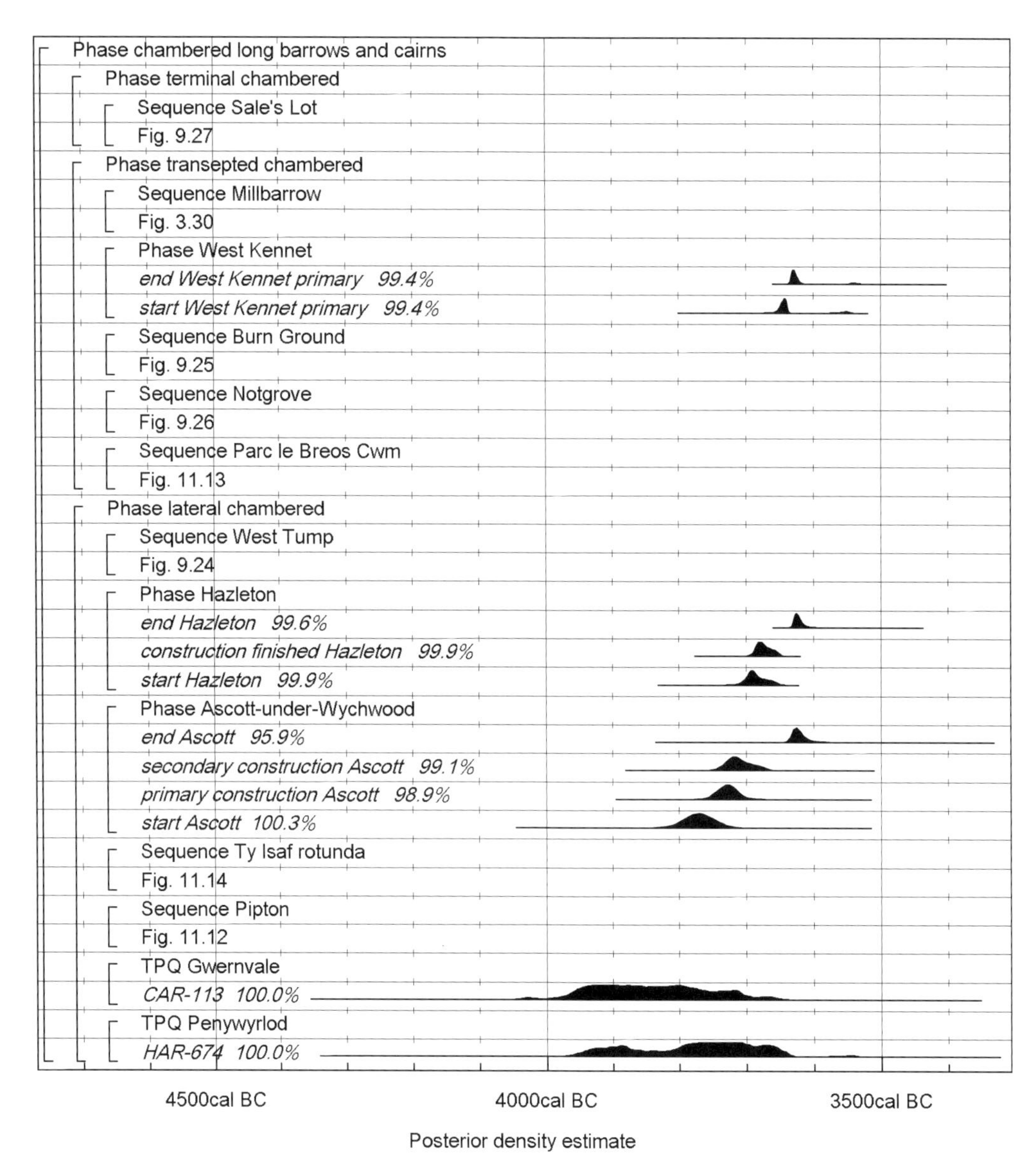

Fig. 14.41. Probability distributions of dates from chambered long barrows and cairns. The format is identical to that of Fig. 14.1. The structures of the component sections of this model are shown in Fig. 3.30 (Millbarrow), Figs 9.24–7 (West Tump, Burn Ground, Notgrove, and Sale's Lot), and Figs 11.12–14 (Pipton, Parc le Breos Cwm, and Ty Isaf) (although the posterior density estimates shown on these figures are not those relating to this model). Other distributions have been taken from models defined in Bayliss et al. *(2007b, fig. 6) (West Kennet), Meadows* et al. *(2007, figs 6–9) (Hazleton), and Bayliss* et al. *(2007c, figs 3 and 5–7) (Ascott-under-Wychwood). The overall structure of this model is shown in Fig. 14.39, and its other components in Figs 14.40 and 14.42.*

monuments, the components are defined within the phase boundaries shown in Figs 14.43–4 Many of the standardised likelihoods – that is to say, the dates for constructions and endings of individual monuments (Chapter 2.4.3) – have also been taken from models defined in the regional chapters; these are itemised in the captions to Figs 14.38–44.

The overall model suggests that the earliest monument in southern Britain was constructed in *3965–3810 cal BC* (*95% probability*; Fig. 14.38: *start monuments*), probably in *3915–3820 cal BC* (*68% probability*). Neolithic monumentality therefore began *70–250 years* before the first enclosure (*95% probability*; Fig. 14.47: *1st monument/1st enclosure*), probably *100–200 years* earlier (*68% probability*).

What form does this earliest monumentality take? Figure 14.38 shows the overall structure of a model for the currency of early Neolithic monuments in southern England. Our model includes 'classic' early Neolithic monuments such as long barrows and portal dolmens, but also modest, inconspicuous structures which are hard to classify, such as the Raunds avenue. The dates from the banana barrow on Crickley Hill are included, but only as *termini post quos* for the end of early Neolithic monuments (Fig. 14.38). The taphonomy of the dated material from this construction is uncertain, as indeed is its cultural affiliation (see Chapter 9). It remains an open question whether we regard this as a late Mesolithic or an early Neolithic construction. If we regard it as Neolithic

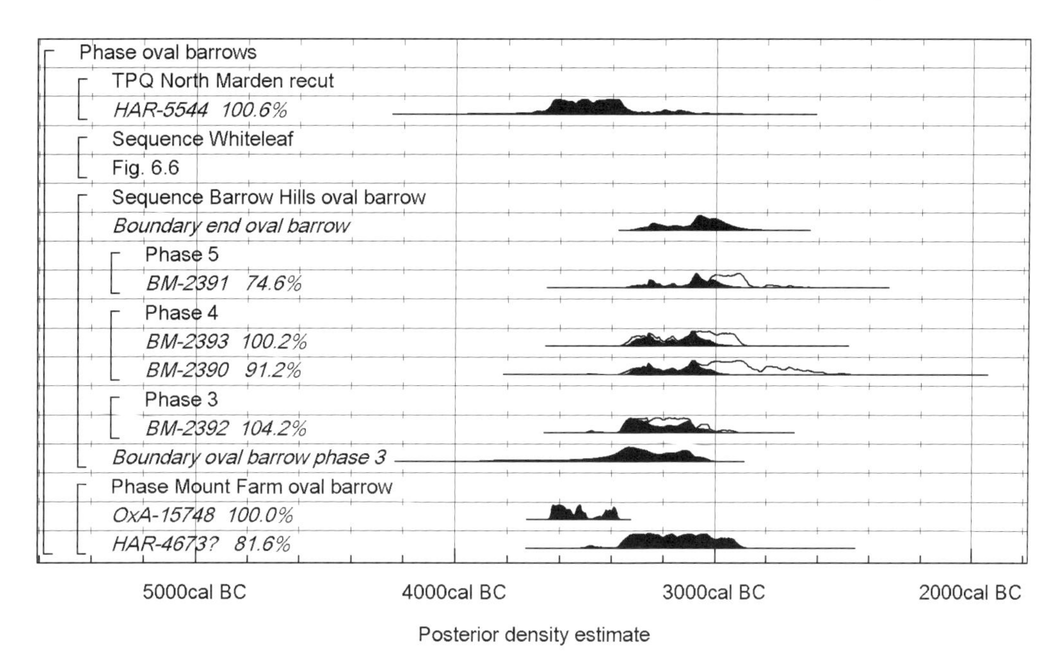

Fig. 14.42. Probability distributions of dates from oval barrows. The format is identical to that of Fig. 14.1. The structure of the component section of this model relating to Whiteleaf barrow is shown in Fig. 6.6 (although the posterior density estimates shown on this figure are not those relating to this model). The overall structure of this model is shown in Fig. 14.39, and its other components in Figs 14.40–1.

and the three consistent dates from it are not on residual samples, the effect would be to push the start of Neolithic monumentality slightly earlier. The early monument at Coldrum has been included in the model as a Neolithic construction (Fig. 14.38). Although the taphonomy of the dated material is poorly understood, there does seem to be a highly coherent group of radiocarbon dates on human remains, probably associated with the lower level of the stone box component of the monument, and perhaps thus its construction (see Chapter 7). If Coldrum forms part of the overall phase of early monumentality, then the weight of probability shifts to suggest a construction date for that site in the 39th rather than the later 40th century cal BC (compare Fig. 14.38 with Fig. 7.27). This simple arrangement may therefore stand at the beginning of the diverse tradition of stone-chambered monuments.

A model for the currency of the tradition of long barrows and cairns from the areas where we have dated causewayed enclosures is shown in Figs 14.39–42. This model estimates the start of the construction of monuments of this kind and the end of their use independently of the dates of all other early monuments. It suggests that this tradition began in *3995–3785 cal BC* (*95% probability*; Fig. 14.39: *start long barrows & cairns*), probably in *3910–3805 cal BC* (*68% probability*). It is *100% probable* that the first long barrow or cairn was constructed before the first enclosure (Fig. 14.47). The first long barrow or long cairn was built *50–275 years* before the first enclosure (*95% probability*; Fig. 14.47: *1st long barrow/1st enclosure*), probably *80–190 years* earlier (*68% probability*).

The practice of building long barrows and long cairns thus emerges before the first enclosures. The tradition was not uniform, since different types of barrows and cairns have long been recognised. A model for the currency of the varying forms of long barrow and cairn is given in Fig. 14.45. For each broad class, only a limited number of sites have been dated, and few have the precise chronologies that are now within reach (Bayliss and Whittle 2007). Some trends are, however, apparent. The first construction of chambered long cairns appears to have predated that of the first earthen long barrows (Fig. 14.45). It is, for example, *90% probable* that *start transepted* is before *start earthen*. Transepted long cairns may also have begun slightly earlier than lateral chambered cairns (*84% probable*). Caution at this stage is required, since the apparently early start for transepted cairns is entirely dependent on Burn Ground (Fig. 9.25). The number of dated terminal chambered cairns and oval barrows is so limited that it is impossible to place them reliably within the monument typology (although modifications to oval barrows at least appear to have continued to the end of the fourth millennium: Fig. 14.42). The terminally chambered monument at Sale's Lot appears to be relatively early within the tradition (Fig. 9.27). This contains a rotunda, which by association is also therefore relatively early, but it should be noted that the rotundae dated at Notgrove (Fig. 9.26) and Ty Isaf (Fig. 11.14) fall in the middle centuries of the fourth millennium cal BC. If not all rotundae are as early as has often been argued, we should also note that, on the basis of the single dated site of Carreg Coetan (Fig. 11.10; and see discussion of Poulnabrone in Chapter 12), neither are all portal dolmens.[5]

The establishment of new long barrows and cairns was a long-lived practice, spanning almost the whole of the fourth millennium cal BC (Fig. 14.39). Unlike enclosures, where new sites were established over a period of less than 200 years (*initiation S British enclosures*; Fig. 14.6), long barrows and cairns continued to be built into the last quarter of the fourth millennium (e.g. Millbarrow; Fig. 3.30). We can also bring in Wayland's Smithy here; the construction of its second, transepted phase probably dates to the 35th century cal BC, significantly later than, for example, the typologically very similar West Kennet long barrow which appears to have been built in the mid-37th century cal BC (Bayliss *et al.* 2007b; Whittle *et al.* 2007b). Were the circumstances surrounding the construction of these later examples the same as those of the initial examples in the same architectural form? Is there a conscious archaising here, and could such self-consciousness imply that the significance of these monuments had already substantively altered? There is a potentially significant contrast here between a more concentrated period of enclosure construction and a longer currency of barrow construction. The length of that currency makes it questionable whether enduring form was synonymous with unchanging meaning.

It is important not to confuse the currency of a monument tradition with the duration of use of individual sites. We have already seen that causewayed enclosures in southern Britain were used over a period of *385–485 years* (*95% probability*; Fig. 14.27: *use S British enclosures*), probably over a period of *400–455 years* (*68% probability*). Particular enclosures that were in use for this extended period of time were, however, the exception rather than the rule (Fig. 14.32). Only Etton, Windmill Hill and the enclosures on Hambledon Hill are strong candidates for having continued in use for more than 200 years, and a number of the others seem to have been in use for less than a human lifespan. Long barrows and cairns were constructed over a much longer period in the fourth millennium cal BC compared to enclosures (Fig. 14.46). On the basis of a small number of precisely dated sites (Whittle *et al.* 2007a, fig. 6), the dominant mode of their primary use may have been relatively brief: for up to a century but frequently less. On the basis of the extended series presented here, this trend may be robust, with perhaps only Notgrove (Fig. 9.26) and Pipton (Fig. 11.12) emerging as candidates for periods of use longer than 200 years.

A model for the chronology of a disparate collection of diverse, small monuments from the areas where causewayed enclosures have been dated in southern Britain is given in Fig. 14.43. Both the number of dated monuments and the precision of their chronologies are limited, but the model suggests that the earliest in this grouping dates to *3910–3535 cal BC* (*95% probability*; Fig. 14.43: *start diverse & small*), probably to *3770–3600 cal BC* (*68% probability*). It is *94% probable* that the first of these sites is later than the first long barrow or cairn, although it is only *66% probable* that the first of these sites is later than the first enclosure.

The Staines Road Farm ring ditch (see Chapter 8), and the very different monument of the Raunds turf mound in the Nene valley (see Chapter 6) are probably the earliest dated constructions within this grouping (Fig. 14.43). Form and associated artefacts suggest that the undated first phase of Horton in the middle Thames (see Chapter 8), and ring ditches associated with Mildenhall Ware at Brightlingsea, Essex, and Rainham, Greater London (see Chapter 7) may have been of comparable age. A diversity of form – encompassing among other features all manner of generally small circular and square ditches, other trenches and slots, a deep chalk shaft, various timber settings, inhumations, and depositions of artefacts, animal bones and other material – continued to be employed till at least the end of the fourth millennium cal BC. Apparently starting in the same period as the first hey-day of enclosure construction, a variety of generally much smaller, non-standardised, often funerary monuments continued to be built and used for much longer. Given that these constructions seem to have originated broadly at the same time as enclosures, they may have been part of the same social world, but operating on a more individual and more local level.

A model for the chronology of the varied linear monuments, as described in the regional chapters, from within the areas of southern Britain where we have dated causewayed enclosures is shown in Fig. 14.44. This form of construction is notoriously difficult to date due to the paucity of associated material of any kind (R. Bradley 1986; Barclay and Bayliss 1999). The model we have chosen to present in Fig. 14.44 excludes the luminescence ages for the two Eynesbury cursus monuments, and the problematic dating of the long mound at Raunds, for the reasons discussed in Chapter 6. Our model suggests that this type of construction first appeared in *3915–3545 cal BC* (*95% probability*; Fig. 14.44: *start linear monuments*), probably in *3795–3610 cal BC* (*68% probability*). This form of monument may have continued into the third millennium cal BC (Fig. 14.44). It should be noted that because of the very limited number of dated samples this model more closely relates to the construction of linear monuments than their use. It is therefore more comparable to the model for the establishment of new causewayed enclosures (Fig. 14.5) than to that for the currency of enclosures (Figs 14.1–4 and 14.27).

Although it is unclear from this model whether the first linear monument in southern Britain was constructed before or after the first enclosure, this ambiguity is largely a product of the imprecise dating of linear monuments as a whole.

At least when considering larger cursus monuments, it appears that the construction of individual examples of this form followed that of causewayed enclosures. In support of the primacy of enclosures, we can cite the excavated relationship between causewayed enclosure and cursus monument at Etton (Chapter 6), that between causewayed enclosure and long mound at Maiden Castle, and the air photographic evidence from Fornham All Saints (Chapter 6). The dated relationship of the Hambledon Hill enclosures and the Dorset cursus in Cranborne Chase (Chapter 4) is also compatible with this sequence. It is *90% probable* that the Dorset cursus was built after activity on Hambledon Hill had ceased, although the construction of the extensive phase 4 western outworks at Hambledon may have presaged

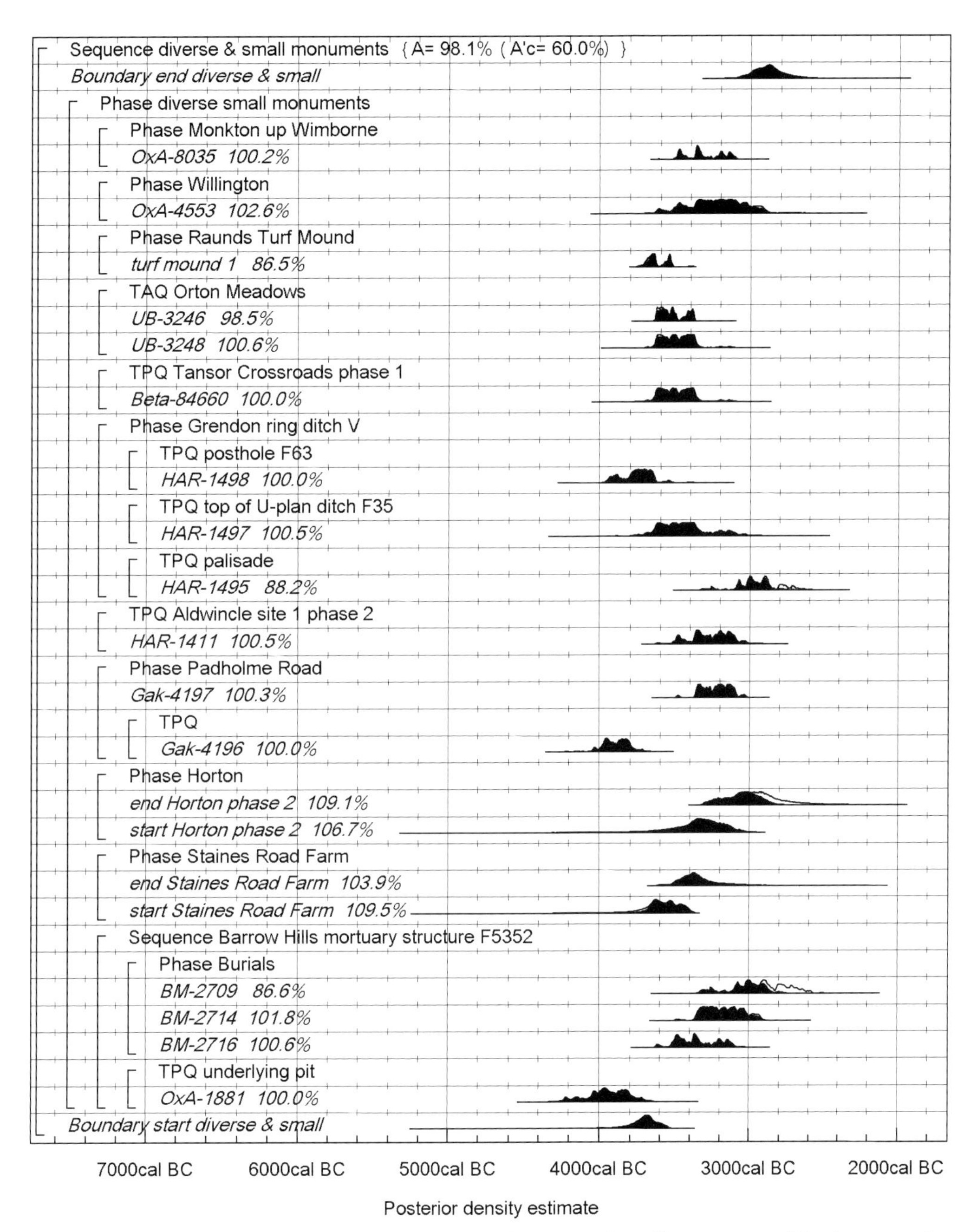

Fig. 14.43. Probability distributions of radiocarbon dates from diverse and small monuments. The format is the same as for Fig. 14.1. Some distributions have been taken from models defined in Figs 6.25–7 (Raunds) and Fig. 8.7 (Horton and Staines Road Farm). The model is defined exactly by the OxCal keywords and the brackets down the left-hand side of the diagram.

a shift in orientation towards the Chase (see discussion in Chapter 4). The dated relationship of the Abingdon enclosure and the Drayton cursus (Chapter 8) is less certain, although there is a sporting chance (*63% probable*) that in this case the cursus may have been earlier, if only by a generation or two. It may be that, after the period of intensive construction of causewayed enclosures was over, perhaps in the third quarter of the 36th century cal BC (Fig. 14.7), new major monumental undertakings were directed into extended linear form. The dating of the Drayton cursus may perhaps point to a short phase of overlap in the last quarter of the 37th and the first half of the 36th century cal BC, when people chose between accepted and new forms of construction. With regard to other enclosures (and see below), the trapezoidal enclosure at Godmanchester is stratigraphically earlier than the attached cursus (Chapter 6). The idea of linearity may, however, have its origins earlier than the building of the massive linear monuments. The shallow, discontinuous, 60 m-long Raunds avenue, probably dating to the 38th or 37th century cal BC (Fig. 14.44: *the avenue*), is the best southern British example at present,[6] and is not a classic ditched and banked cursus.

The final strand to consider is that of a handful of enclosures other than the causewayed and stone-walled tor enclosures of southern Britain. The dated examples in question, considered in the regional chapters, comprise

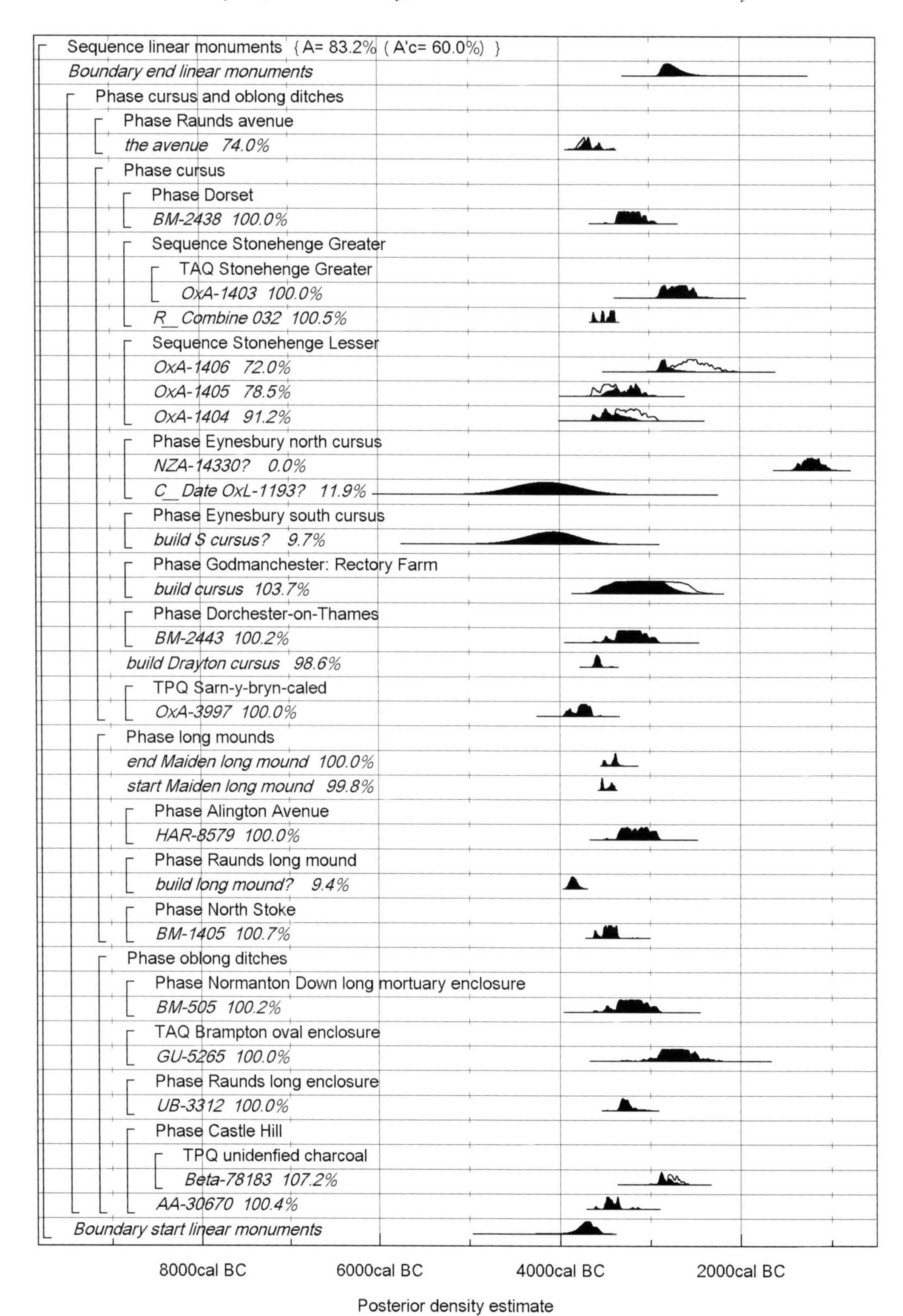

Fig. 14.44. Probability distributions of radiocarbon dates from linear monuments. The format is the same as for Fig. 14.1. Some distributions have been taken from models defined in Figs 4.41–5 (Maiden Castle), Fig. 6.13 (Eynesbury), Fig. 6.15 (Godmanchester, Rectory Farm), Figs 6.25–7 (Raunds) and Fig. 8.30 (Drayton). The model is defined exactly by the OxCal keywords and the brackets down the left-hand side of the diagram.

Godmanchester, Lower Luggy, Church Lawford and Flagstones (Fig. 14.38). As noted in Chapter 4, Flagstones is much more circular in form than any known causewayed enclosure, and comfortably post-dates the period of causewayed enclosure construction. The first phase of Stonehenge is an obvious point of comparison, both in terms of form and date (Cleal *et al.* 1995; Bayliss *et al.* 1997). As discussed in Chapter 6, there is nothing like the trapezoidal enclosure at Godmanchester anywhere else in southern Britain (or indeed beyond). It seems best to consider it as part of the considerable diversity of monumental construction that characterises the middle part of the fourth millennium cal BC. It belongs to an area of the country where the other, smaller monuments, if not the causewayed enclosures, show considerable variation in scale and layout. However impressive the size and complexity of its layout, and whatever arcane purposes this may have had, it was presumably the product of local or particular circumstances: an idea that did not catch on elsewhere. That may provide an interesting insight into the conditions of innovation. In comparison with causewayed enclosures and long barrows and cairns, perhaps there was insufficient authority for the idea to be legitimated and thus fully accepted elsewhere. The last two examples, Lower Luggy and Church Lawford, are also trapezoidal or sub-trapezoidal, though much smaller than Godmanchester. There are a number of other non-causewayed enclosures, such as Hill Croft Field in Herefordshire (Chapter 11) and Bury Hill in Sussex (Chapter 5), so we are not proposing a separate class or sub-group of trapezoidal enclosures We can see these two particular sites as further evidence of the diversity of construction in the mid-fourth millennium cal BC, and there must be many more like them waiting for a Neolithic date to be established by further fieldwork, Nymet Barton in Devon being one possibility (Chapter 10).

Our estimates for the currency of different monumental traditions in the early Neolithic of southern Britain are shown in Fig. 14.46. It is clear that causewayed and stone-walled enclosures are not the first monumental form to appear (*100% probable*). It is *87% probable* that the earliest form of monument is the long cairn (earthen long barrows appearing slightly later: Fig. 14.45). It is possible, however, that there may have been varied antecedents, such as we have seen at Coldrum, before more recurrent types were established. It is not clear whether other, diverse monument types appeared at the time when enclosures were built. We do not know whether the first diverse and small monument (as defined above) was constructed before the first enclosure (*34% probable*), nor whether the first linear monument was constructed before the first enclosure (*44% probable*). Enclosures could have formed part of a set of innovative constructions, all appearing in a concentrated horizon. Alternatively, new forms could have appeared sequentially. Until other monument types are dated to the resolution provided for enclosures here, we simply do not know. Their dates can be 'sucked in' to the currency of enclosures, or 'smeared' away (Baillie 1991). Furthermore, there may be sequence hidden within the broad monument typology considered here. We have already mentioned that discontinuous linear monuments, such as the Raunds avenue, may be earlier than more classic cursus monuments, and seen hints of temporal trends in the classification of long barrows and cairns (Fig. 14.45). Our analysis has relied on broad groupings, forced on us by the quality of dating available for monuments other than enclosures. More detailed consideration of trends and fashions in monument building through time must also await further research programmes of the kind presented here for enclosures.

14.4 Enclosures and the start of Neolithic activity in southern Britain

We come now to defining the place of enclosures in the scheme of things: the date of their appearance in relation to our estimates for the start of definably Neolithic activity across the regions covered in this study. This has been covered only partially in the regional chapters thus far, depending on local circumstances.

We have presented our chronologies so far in a series of defined regions, the extent of which varies, following the availability of dateable enclosures. This has not provided total coverage of southern Britain. We have not dated enclosures in Somerset, nor in Hampshire, parts of Berkshire, Surrey south of the Thames or Greater London. In looking for evidence of dated early Neolithic activity beyond enclosures, we have not searched those same areas, and so the Somerset Levels, a large tract of chalk downland in Hampshire and Berkshire, including the Isle of Wight, and the Weald, barely figure in our account so far.

Some of these lacunae are simply the product of a project designed in the first place to date early Neolithic enclosures. There is, of course, a good understanding of many aspects of sequence and development in the Somerset Levels (Coles and Coles 1986), and parts of Hampshire, including the Isle of Wight, the Berkshire downs and Surrey (e.g. RCHME 1979; Loader 2007; Cotton and Field 2004; Field and Cotton 1987). London may present a different situation. Although the city occupies a large area, there has now been substantial archaeological coverage, and a recent synthesis suggests, notwithstanding axehead finds from the river itself, the presence in the early Neolithic of extensive marshland and backswamp, probably very unfavourable for occupation (Wilkinson and Sidell 2007; Sidell and Wilkinson 2004). Analysis of over 1000 radiocarbon dates from the capital also shows very little dated Neolithic human activity (Meadows *et al.* forthcoming). The sands and gravels of the Weald have long been a prolific collecting ground, and the lithics leave no doubt of an early Neolithic presence (Gardiner 1984, fig. 3.2; Field and Cotton 1987, 77–79, 93, figs 4.7, 4.15), often on sites already used in the Mesolithic. Subsoil features, let alone monuments, remain elusive, however, and may have been scarce or absent.

We will now present the evidence for dated early Neolithic activity derived from sites other than enclosures region by region, starting in the south-east and moving westwards. For this purpose, we will use a slightly different regional division than in the earlier chapters (Fig. 14.48). This is to achieve a more balanced coverage, so that each region covers a reasonably large area and so that there is a reasonable number of dated samples available for each unit of analysis. The approach is entirely pragmatic. So here we will treat the middle Thames valley separately from the upper Thames valley, to reflect the considerable amount of development and archaeological research in this area, which allows a relatively refined picture of the early Neolithic to emerge in this region. We will also distinguish north Wessex (amalgamating north Wiltshire with Salisbury Plain) from south Wessex (i.e. the remainder of the Wessex

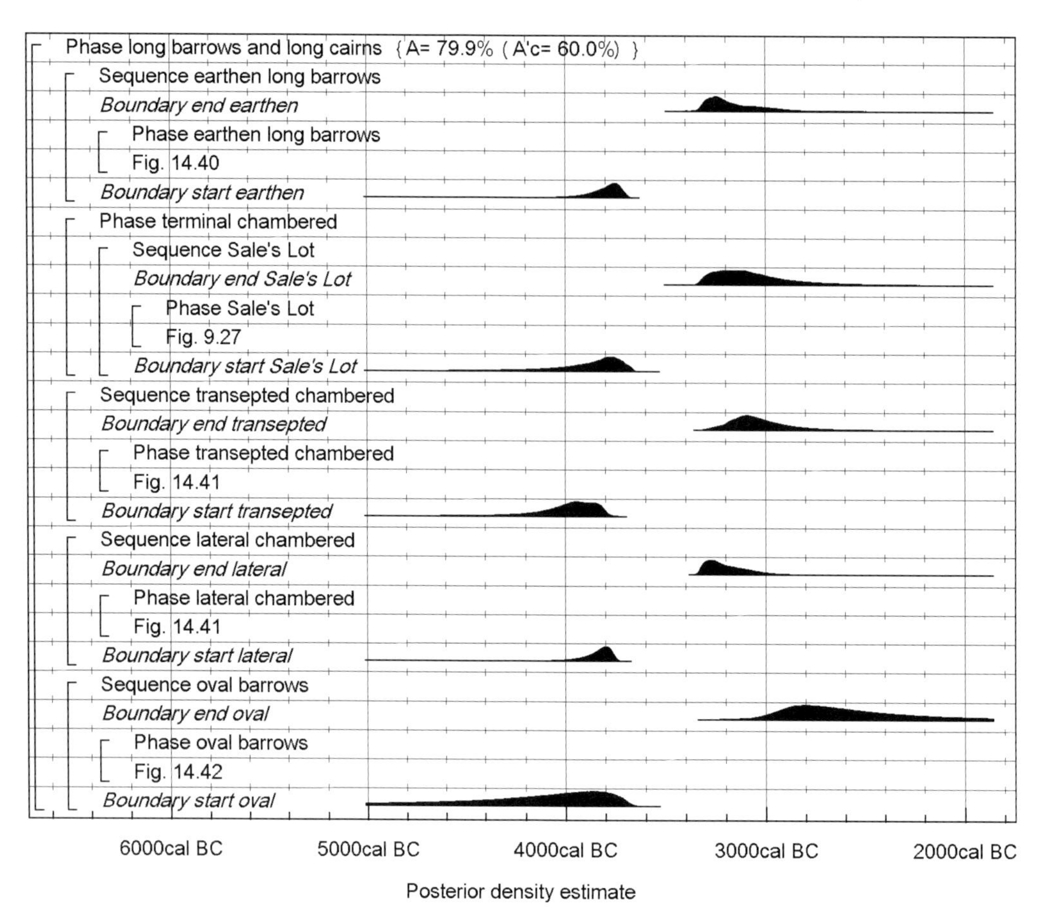

Fig. 14.45. Overall structure of the chronological model for the currency of types of long barrows, long cairns, and oval barrows in southern Britain. The structures of the component sections of this model are shown in detail in Figs 9.27 and 14.40–2 (although the posterior density estimates shown on these figures are not those relating to this model). The large square brackets down the left-hand side of these figures along with the OxCal keywords define the overall model exactly.

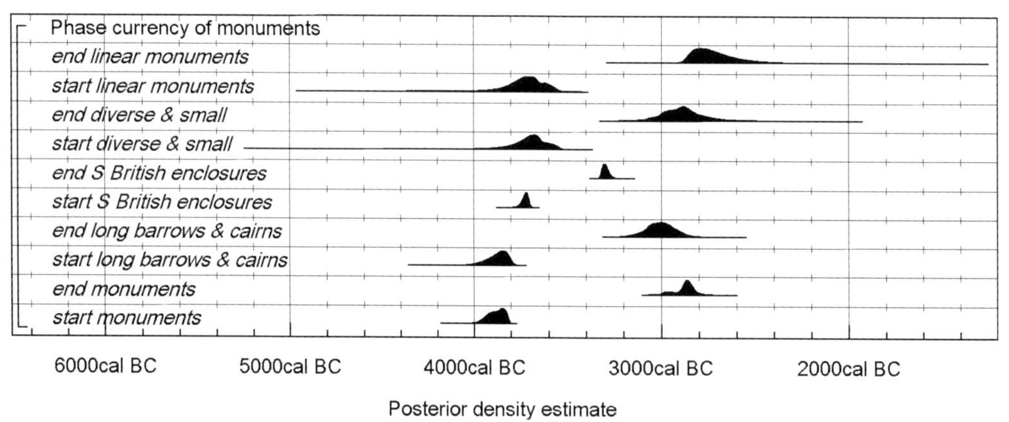

Fig. 14.46. Probability distributions of the currencies of enclosures (Figs 14.1–4), early Neolithic monuments overall (Figs 14.38, 14.40–2, 9.8, 10.3 and 11.10), long barrows (Figs 14.39–42), diverse and small monuments (Fig. 14.43), and linear monuments (Fig. 14.44).

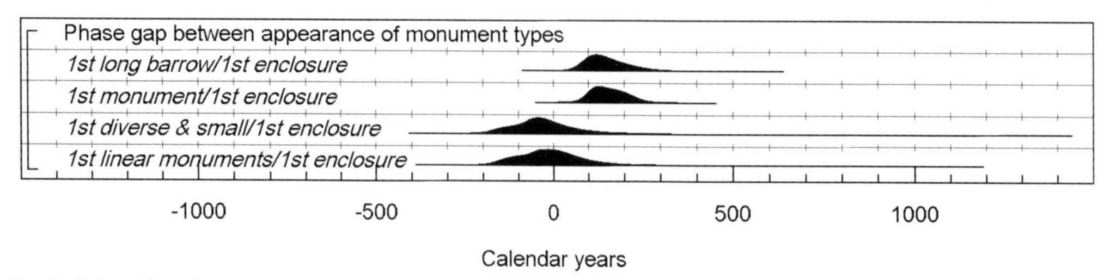

Fig. 14.47. Probability distributions showing the number of years between the first monument of a particular type and the first causewayed enclosure (derived from the distributions shown in Fig. 14.46).

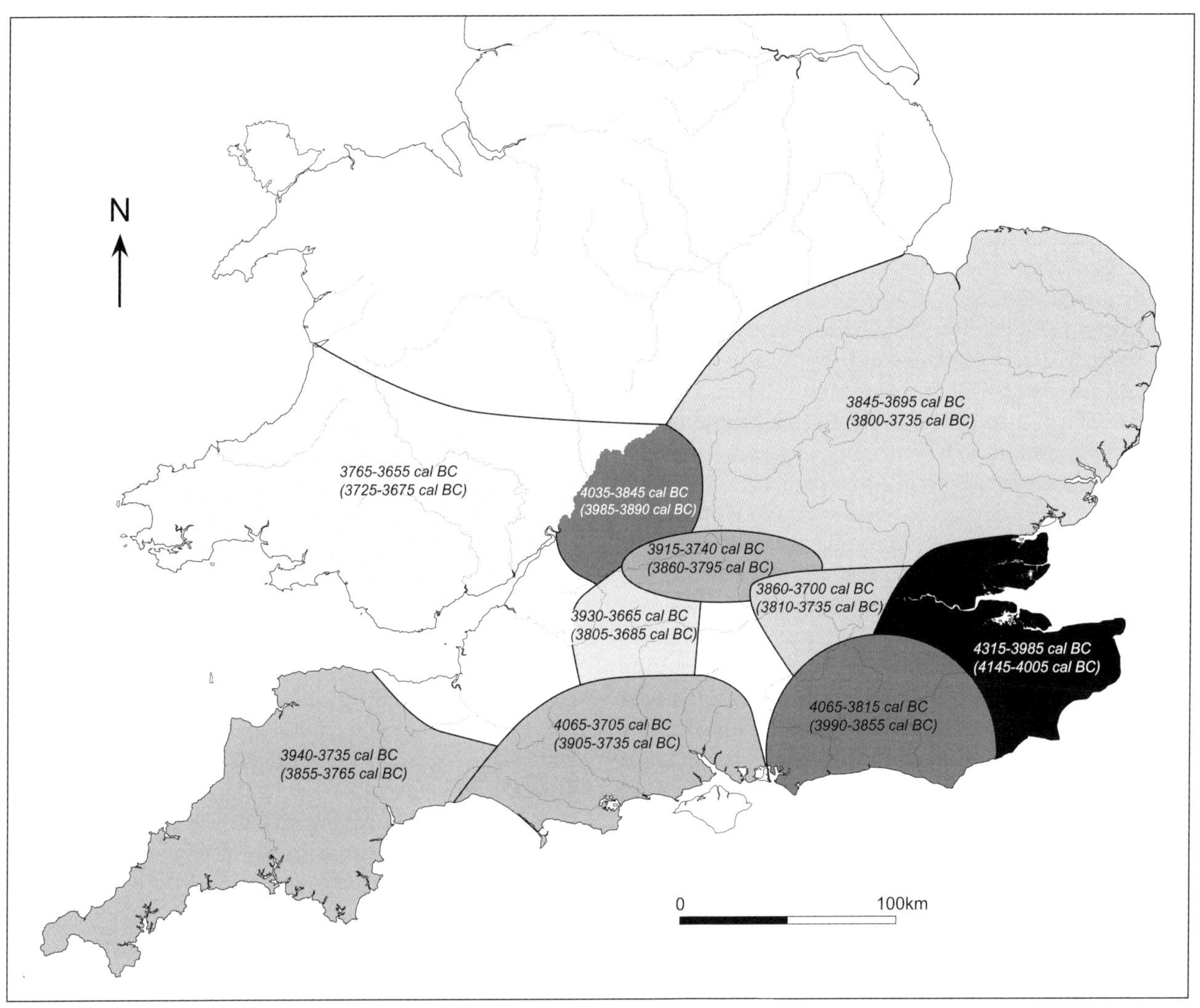

Fig. 14.48. Map showing date estimates for the start of Neolithic activity region by region in southern Britain, at 95% probability (68% probability in brackets).

area covered in Chapter 4). This expands the very small area covered in Chapter 3 to form a more viable unit for this analysis.

As we have seen in Chapter 2.2, scatter matters. In order to counteract the inescapable statistical scatter on a group of radiocarbon dates, it is necessary to model the statistical distribution of the dated activity. Failure to do this normally leads to an inaccurate assessment of the date of archaeological activity represented, with this seeming to start earlier, end later, and endure for longer than was actually the case (Buck *et al.* 1992; Bayliss *et al.* 2007a; 2008b; Bayliss 2009). For a statistical distribution to be implemented, it is necessary to define the end as well as the beginning of the period of archaeological activity. For the Neolithic, this presents a problem. The Neolithic began in southern Britain, but some of its innovations, most obviously farming, persist today. This is in contrast to the situation with causewayed enclosures, which were built, were in primary use for a period of time, and then went out of use. Defining the enclosure endings may not be unproblematic (see, for example, Chapter 3), but the enclosures are not still used for their original purpose. We still grow cereals.

We have a dilemma. The uniform-phase model which we have implemented here demands an ending, where archaeologically there is none. Pragmatically, again, we have deliberately defined our criteria for Neolithic activity to include certain types of artefacts and sites which have an early Neolithic currency. So, for example, one of the markers for the end of this phase is the end of the use of Bowl pottery and the beginning of the use of Peterborough Ware. Compromises have had to be made. Early dates on cereals and domesticated fauna have been included in these models, even where they are not known to occur in association with other material or features defined as diagnostically Neolithic, although their use continues beyond the end of the early Neolithic. If the radiocarbon age lies within the range of those associated with diagnostic artefacts or sites, it has been included (in fact, cases such as these represent less than 7 percent of our dataset); if it is later, it has not. We have been pragmatic here. It has seemed perverse to ignore very early dated occurrences of cereals. For example, we have used a date on cereal from Manor Way, Woolwich (Table 7.6: Beta-153983), even though we have no certain evidence that it was associated with other Neolithic material. These issues have already confronted us in modelling the introduction of Neolithic practices to Ireland (Chapter 12), where we have separated some of elements of the assemblage of Neolithic things and practices, and incorporated them in alternative models.

We have therefore included radiocarbon dates in our models for the early Neolithic in southern Britain, if the dated sample is directly associated with cultural material that we have defined as diagnostically Neolithic, or if it derives from a site whose architecture or form we have defined as diagnostically Neolithic, or if the sample itself is of material that we have defined as diagnostically Neolithic. Our criteria for definably early Neolithic activity include material culture (principally forms of Bowl pottery, leaf arrowheads and ground axeheads), domesticated plants and animals, and forms of architecture including all manner of constructions in earth, turf, chalk, gravel, timber and stone. Bowl pottery includes Carinated Bowl and the South-Western and Decorated styles. In contrast to the record from the other side of the North Sea, for example in the Rhine-Meuse estuary, where the first pots in sites like Hardinxfeld-Giessendam first appear in an otherwise hunter-gatherer milieu, to be joined gradually by other Neolithic elements (Louwe Kooijmans 2007), there is no hint in southern Britain of such material in late Mesolithic contexts or associations.

There is likewise no sign that leaf arrowheads were made in the late Mesolithic in southern Britain. Neolithic axeheads, of stone and flint, are of different forms to their Mesolithic counterparts, and were regularly finished by grinding or polishing – a technique only employed as far as we know, in the Mesolithic in Ireland (Cooney 2000a) and south Wales (David and Walker 2004). Generally in southern Britain neither the finished lithic artefact forms produced in the early Neolithic nor many of the materials employed (including deep-mined flint and rocks from remote sources) were current in the Mesolithic. There is no evidence for deep shafts being used for flint extraction in the southern British Mesolithic, and no certain evidence that the sources used for stone axehead manufacture in the Neolithic were in other than local use in the Mesolithic. There are, furthermore, precedents for these kinds of pots, projectile points and axeheads – as well as for flint mining – in continental Europe in the fifth millennium cal BC, even if there are also insular continuities in terms of core reduction and blade technology common to the late Mesolithic and early Neolithic in southern Britain.

Neither cereals nor sheep and goat were native to Britain, let alone Europe as a whole, and there is now genetic evidence that domesticated cattle derived from different populations to native aurochs (e.g. Bollongino and Burger 2007; Edwards *et al.* 2007); the situation with pigs may be comparable, though the currently available evidence can allow local domestication as well (Larson *et al.* 2007). Unlike in Ireland, where Ferriter's Cove provides the possibility of detecting an initial transfer of cattle into the island in a late Mesolithic context because there is no evidence of a native cattle population in the post-glacial period down to the start of the Neolithic, there is no reliable sign in Britain as a whole of domesticates in Mesolithic contexts. Finally, there is no evidence that Mesolithic people recurrently undertook the range of larger-scale buildings and diggings that go under the general label of monuments.

The rectangular timber houses found in Neolithic association are also both more substantial and of different form to anything in Mesolithic contexts in Britain. Known Mesolithic structures are small and rounded, and there are again continental precedents for rectangular houses in the fifth millennium cal BC in adjacent Europe. Some circular buildings have been dated to the fourth millennium cal BC in southern Britain (as at Penhale Round, Cornwall: Chapter 10), but we have only accepted them as certainly Neolithic for this analysis here where associated with other diagnostically early Neolithic material culture (as at Yarnton, Oxfordshire: Chapter 8).

In some of the regional chapters, the tables list radiocarbon dates with robust associations with diagnostic criteria for Neolithic activity separately from dates on other fourth millennium cal BC samples. There are certainly a number of dates in this latter category where there is good cause to suppose that the activity was indeed Neolithic in character. For example, some of the dated pits from Llandysul in south-west Wales (Chapter 11) are associated with diagnostic pottery and have been included in our model for the early Neolithic in south Wales and the Marches. Other dated pits there without diagnostic material associations, however, have not been included, although, as they are of the same general character and lack Mesolithic material, plausibly they are also Neolithic. As another example, burials in caves which are not associated with diagnostic Neolithic material culture and which simply have a fourth millennium cal BC date are not classed by us as Neolithic for the purpose of this analysis, although those with terrestrial isotopic dietary signatures probably were. In including dates in these models, our criteria, for both association and taphonomy, are deliberately severe. This is to ensure that our models estimate the dates for the assemblage of Neolithic things and practices which we have explicitly defined – it is not enough to take a fourth millennium date as indicating that an activity is Neolithic, as our objective is to independently determine the date of the early Neolithic

It is important to understand the difference between the range of Neolithic things and practices that the models presented here are dating and the Neolithic 'package' that has so often been discussed in the literature (see Chapter 1.5). For inclusion in the models, a radiocarbon date has to be associated with one diagnostic criterion. This means that we are estimating when Neolithic material and practices first appeared in an area; this is not necessarily the time when the entire economic and ideational scheme changed. Our models do not therefore assume that the entire range appeared together all at once. We will first examine the

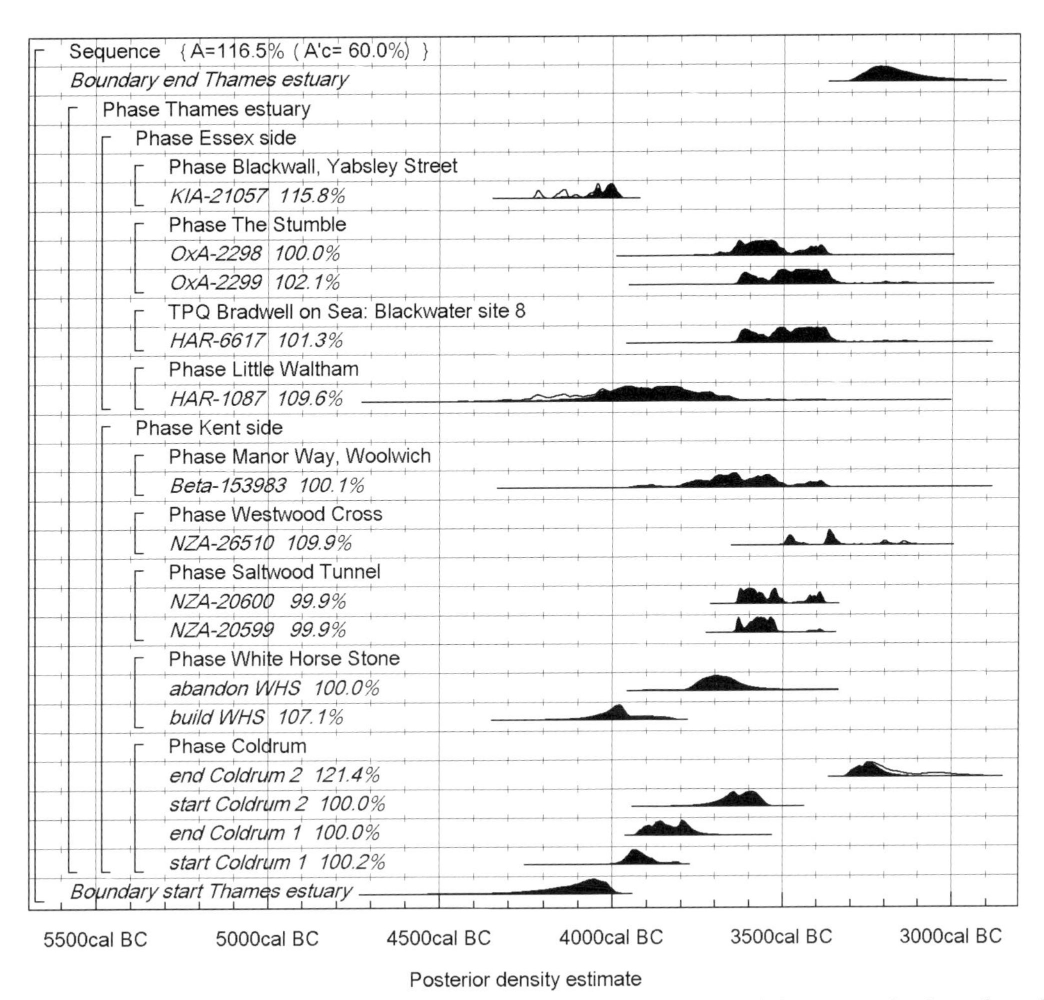

Fig. 14.49. Probability distributions of dates associated with diagnostically early Neolithic material culture from the Thames estuary (excluding those from enclosure sites). The format is the same as for Fig. 14.1. Distributions have been taken from the models defined in Fig. 7.26 (White Horse Stone) and Fig. 7.27 (Coldrum). The large square brackets down the left-hand side of the diagram, along with the OxCal keywords, define the overall model exactly.

appearance of the early Neolithic in southern Britain region by region, and then, to the limited extent that the data allow, consider whether different elements of the range were synchronous.

To sum up, the range of Neolithic things and practices employed to determine whether dates and sites are included in these models comprises:

- Cultivated cereals
- Animal domesticates
- Bowl pottery
- Typologically distinctive Neolithic lithics in the form of leaf arrowheads and ground axeheads
- Monuments
- Flint mines
- Rectangular timber buildings.

Regional evidence for the start of Neolithic activity other than enclosures

A model for the date of the early Neolithic in the Greater Thames estuary is shown in Fig. 14.49. Because the purpose of this analysis is to compare the date of the introduction of enclosures with the date of the introduction of other Neolithic things and practices, dates from enclosures are not included in this model. Key parameters from the site-based models for White Horse Stone (Fig. 7.26) and Coldrum (Fig. 7.27) have been included in this model as standardised likelihoods (see Chapter 2.3). This ensures that comparatively well dated sites with a greater number of calibrated radiocarbon dates do not bias the model. This analysis suggests that the Neolithic in the Greater Thames estuary started in *4315–3985 cal BC* (*95% probability*; Fig. 14.49: *start Thames estuary*), probably in *4145–4005 cal BC* (*68% probability*). This estimate is based on 15 likelihoods from nine sites (Table 14.5), associated with a range of Neolithic things and practices (Table 14.6).

The model for the chronology of the early Neolithic in Sussex has been presented in Chapter 5 (Figs 5.32–3). This suggests that the Neolithic in Sussex began in *4065–3815 cal BC* (*95% probability*; Fig. 5.32: *start Sussex Neolithic*), probably in *3990–3855 cal BC* (*68% probability*). This estimate is based on 27 radiocarbon dates from nine sites (Table 14.5), 17 of which are from deep flint mines (Table 14.6).

Table 14.5. Numbers of effective likelihoods included in the regional models for the early Neolithic in southern Britain. Likelihoods may derive from single radiocarbon dates, or from parameters in other models (these distil the information from large numbers of dates into a small number of distributions so that information from well dated sites does not bias the regional model).

Regions	No. of effective likelihoods	No. of effective calibrated radiocarbon dates	No. of effective parameters	No. of calibrated radiocarbon dates included in models producing effective parameters	No. of sites represented
Thames estuary	15	9	6	32	9
Sussex	27	27	-	-	9
Eastern England	38	29	9	54	26
Middle Thames	28	28	-	-	4
Upper Thames	27	26	1	5	8
N Wessex	24	13	11	62	15
S Wessex	17	13	4	36	10
Cotswolds	35	27	8	69	7
SW Peninsula	24	22	2	4	9
S Wales & Marches	41	41	-	-	14
Totals	**276**	**235**	**41**	**262**	**111**

Figure 6.50 shows the overall structure for the model for the chronology of the early Neolithic in eastern England, with component sections derived from the models shown in Figs 6.47–8. Estimated dates for the construction of some of the monuments have been taken from the site-based models and incorporated into this analysis as likelihoods. Distributions have been taken from the models shown in Figs 6.16 (Haddenham long barrow), Fig. 6.15 (Godmanchester, Rectory Farm), Fig. 6.33 (Etton cursus), and Figs 6.25–7 (Raunds). This analysis suggests that the Neolithic started in eastern England in *3845–3695 cal BC* (*95% probability*; Fig. 6.50: *start eastern Neolithic*), probably in *3800–3730 cal BC* (*68% probability*). This estimate is based on 38 likelihoods derived from 26 sites (Table 14.5), two thirds of which are associated with Bowl pottery (Table 14.6). It should be noted that the date estimates for the two cursus monuments at Eynesbury and for the Long Mound at Raunds have been excluded from this model for reasons discussed in Chapter 6.

A chronological model for the middle Thames valley is shown in Fig. 14.50. This is based on 28 radiocarbon dates, all of which are associated with Bowl pottery, from four sites. This model suggests that the Neolithic started in the middle Thames valley in *3860–3700 cal BC* (*95% probability*; Fig. 14.50: *start middle Thames Neolithic*), probably in *3810–3735 cal BC* (*68% probability*).

A model for the dating of the early Neolithic in the upper Thames valley is shown in Fig. 14.51. This model includes 27 likelihoods from eight sites, associated with a variety of Neolithic material and structures. This analysis suggests that the Neolithic started in the upper Thames valley in *3915–3740 cal BC* (*95% probability*; Fig. 14.51: *start upper Thames Neolithic*), probably in *3860–3795 cal BC* (*68% probability*).

Figure 14.52 shows the overall structure of a model for the early Neolithic in north Wessex, with component sections showing the dating of long barrows in the Avebury area given in Figs 3.30–1 (although the posterior density estimates shown on these figures are not those relating to this model). Other distributions have been taken from models defined by Wysocki *et al.* (2007, figs 9–11: Fussell's Lodge) and Bayliss *et al.* (2007b, figs 6–7: West Kennet). Overall, the model includes 24 likelihoods from 15 sites (Table 14.5). Fifteen of these likelihoods relate to long barrows, which reflects the amount of research on this monument type in this area (Table 14.6). In fact, the 15 likelihoods from long barrows derive from over 60 radiocarbon measurements and so the modelling approach adopted here alleviates the sampling bias which in actuality is much more severe. This analysis suggests that the Neolithic started in north Wessex in *3930–3665 cal BC* (*95% probability*; Fig. 14.52: *start north Wessex*), probably in *3805–3685 cal BC* (*68% probability*).

A chronological model for the early Neolithic of south Wessex is shown in Fig. 14.53. Distributions for activity on Hambledon Hill before the construction of the enclosure

Table 14.6. Numbers of effective likelihoods included in the regional models for the early Neolithic in southern Britain (excluding enclosures), showing the number of distributions associated with different early Neolithic things and practices. For each region, columns 3 to 10 total more than the number of effective likelihoods in column 2 because distributions may be associated with more than one element.

	No. of effective likelihoods	**Bowl pottery**	**Leaf arrowheads**	**Deep mines**	**Ground axeheads, flakes or fragments**	**Monuments**	**Rectangular structures**	**Cereals**	**Animal domesticates**
Thames estuary	15	9				4	2	6	2
Sussex	27	12	5	17		2			21
Eastern England	38	28	6		4	16		7	9
Middle Thames	28	27	14		18	5		13	27
Upper Thames	27	14	1		5	5	4	16	15
North Wessex	24	12	6		5	19		1	19
South Wessex	17	13	5		4	8		7	15
Cotswolds	35	29	21		13	29		4	34
SW peninsula	24	23	4		3	2	1	4	4
S Wales & Marches	41	28	10		9	28		8	16
Totals	**276**	**195**	**72**	**17**	**61**	**119**	**7**	**66**	**162**

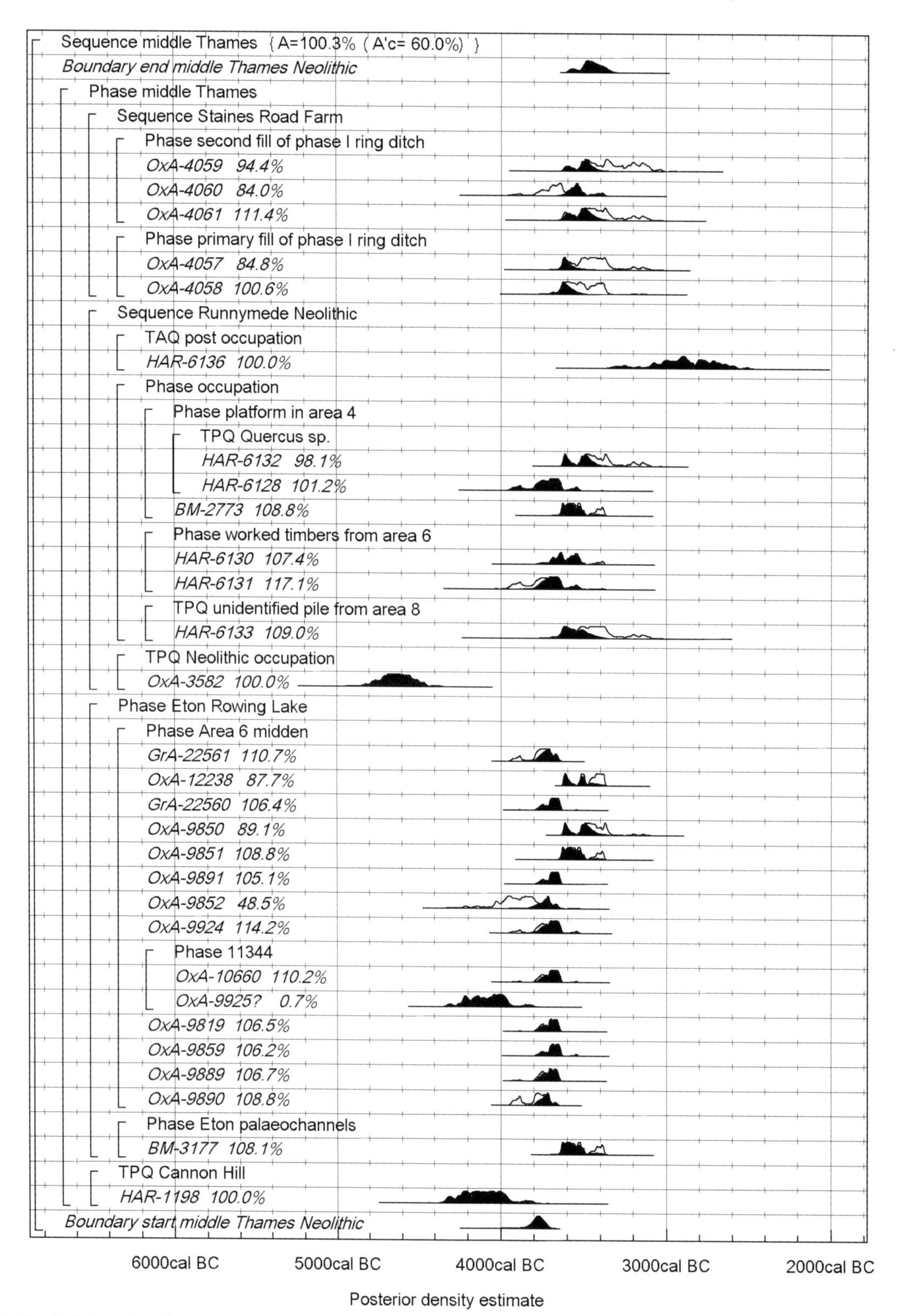

Fig. 14.50. Probability distributions of dates associated with diagnostically early Neolithic material culture from the middle Thames valley (excluding those from enclosure sites). The format is the same as for Fig. 14.1. The large square brackets down the left-hand side of the diagram, along with the OxCal keywords, define the overall model exactly.

complexes have been taken from the model defined in Figs 4.7–13. The date for the early Neolithic hearth in the Fir Tree Field shaft is taken from the model defined in Fig. 4.21, and the dates for the Maiden Castle long mound are derived from the model defined in Figs 4.34–7. Overall, the model includes 17 likelihoods, associated with a range of Neolithic practices, from 10 sites (Tables 14.5–6). This model suggests that the Neolithic started in south Wessex in *4065–3705 cal BC* (*95% probability*; Fig. 14.53: *start south Wessex*), probably in *3905–3735 cal BC* (*68% probability*).

We have presented a model for the chronology of

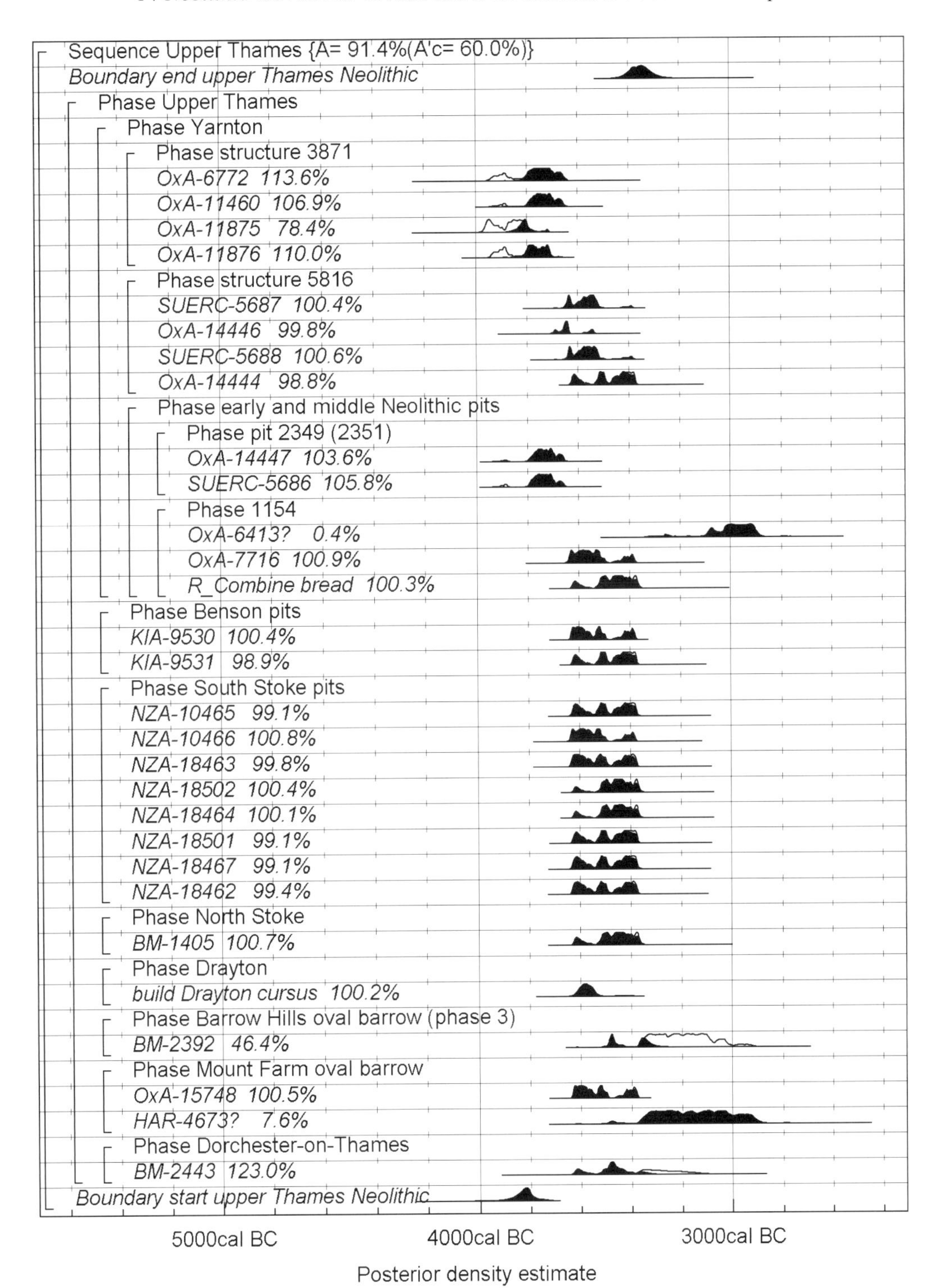

Fig. 14.51. Probability distributions of dates associated with diagnostically early Neolithic material culture from the upper Thames valley (excluding those from enclosure sites). The format is the same as for Fig. 14.1. The distribution for the Drayton cursus has been taken from the model defined in Fig. 8.30. The large square brackets down the left-hand side of the diagram, along with the OxCal keywords, define the overall model exactly.

the early Neolithic in the Cotswolds in Chapter 9 (Figs 9.29–30). This includes 35 likelihoods – 27 radiocarbon dates and parameters for the start and end of pre-cairn activity, and the use of the cairns and barrows at Ascott-under-Wychwood and Hazleton. These parameters have been taken from the models defined in Bayliss *et al.* (2007c, figs 5–7) and Meadows *et al.* (2007, figs 7–8). Twenty-nine of the likelihoods are associated with long barrows, despite the incorporation of parameters from Ascott-under-Wychwood and Hazleton which distil 69 radiocarbon dates into eight distributions. Unfortunately, no other Cotswold long cairn has enough radiocarbon dates for this approach to be practical, although collectively these dates are sufficiently numerous to unbalance the model. Of the 35 likelihoods for the model for this region, 29 are related to long cairns and barrows (Table 14.6). Nonetheless, on the

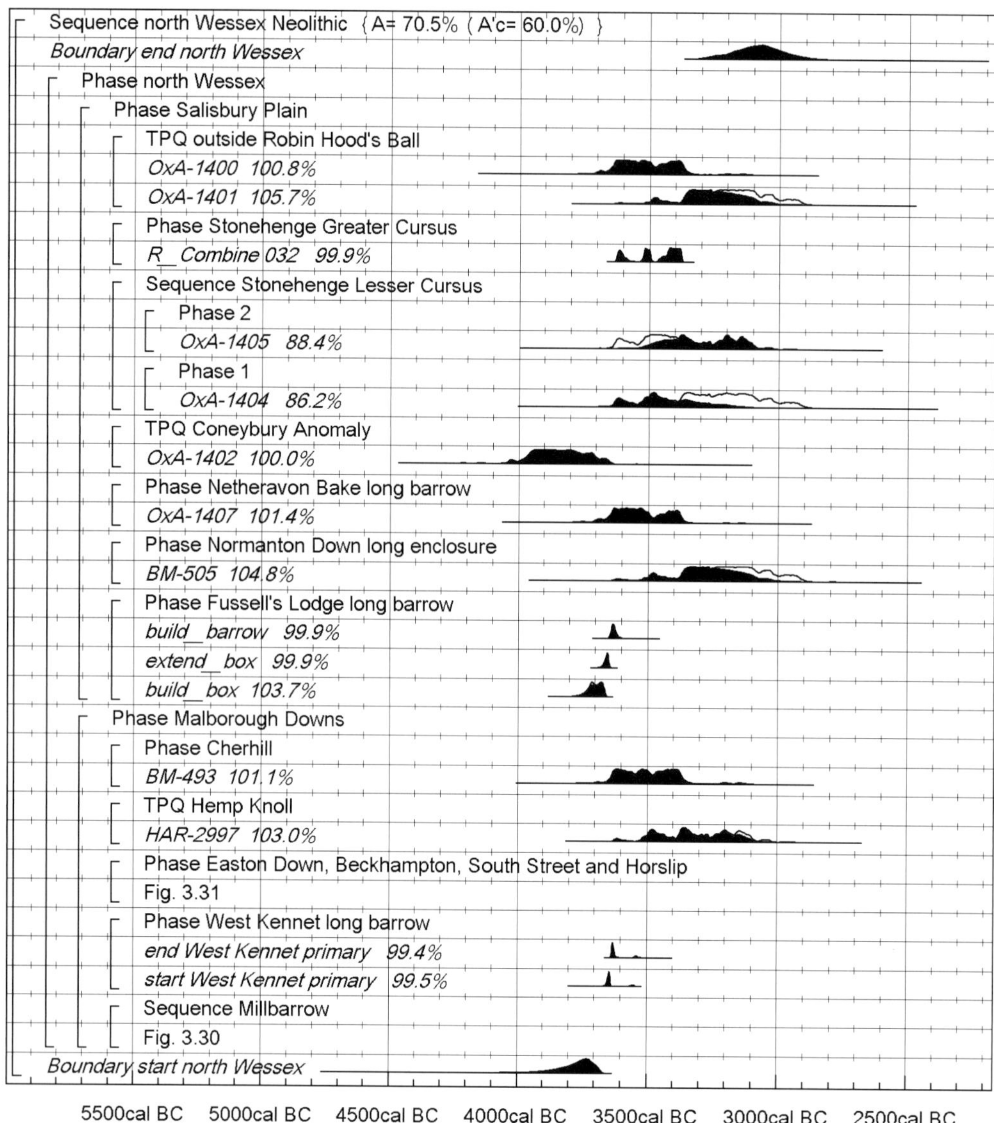

Fig. 14.52. Probability distributions of dates associated with diagnostically early Neolithic material culture from north Wessex (excluding those from enclosure sites). The format is the same as for Fig. 14.1. The structures of the components of this model relating to long barrows in the Avebury area are given in Figs 3.30–1 (although the posterior density estimates shown on these figures are not those relating to this model). Distributions have been taken from the models defined by Wysocki et al. *(2007, fig. 10) (Fussell's Lodge) and Bayliss* et al. *(2007b, fig. 6) (West Kennet). The large square brackets down the left-hand side of these diagrams, along with the OxCal keywords, define the overall model exactly.*

basis of the data currently available, our model suggests that the Neolithic in the Cotswolds began in *4035–3845 cal BC* (*95% probability*; Fig. 9.29: *start Cotswold Neolithic*), probably in *3985–3890 cal BC* (*68% probability*).

Figure 10.30 shows the chronological model for the early Neolithic in the south-west. This includes 24 likelihoods, as it is the boundaries for the use of Broadsands that are effective in the analysis. These distributions derive from nine sites. All are associated with the use of Bowl pottery. This model suggests that the Neolithic in the south-west peninsula began in *3940–3735 cal BC* (*95% probability*; Fig. 10.30: *start Neolithic settlement*), probably in *3855–3765 cal BC* (*68% probability*).

Finally, our model for the chronology of the early Neolithic of south Wales and the Marches is shown in Figs 11.10–11. It includes 41 radiocarbon dates, 28 of which are associated with long cairns, from 14 sites. This model suggests that the early Neolithic in this area began in *3765–3655 cal BC* (*95% probability*; Fig. 11.10: *start S Wales & Marches*), probably in *3725–3675 cal BC* (*68% probability*).

A model for the start of the Neolithic in the ten regions considered within southern Britain is shown in Fig. 14.54. This analysis treats the appearance of Neolithic activity over the whole of southern Britain as a process which once started continued until all areas had adopted at least one element of the Neolithic assemblage. It should be noted that this does not exclude a locally patchy adoption of Neolithic

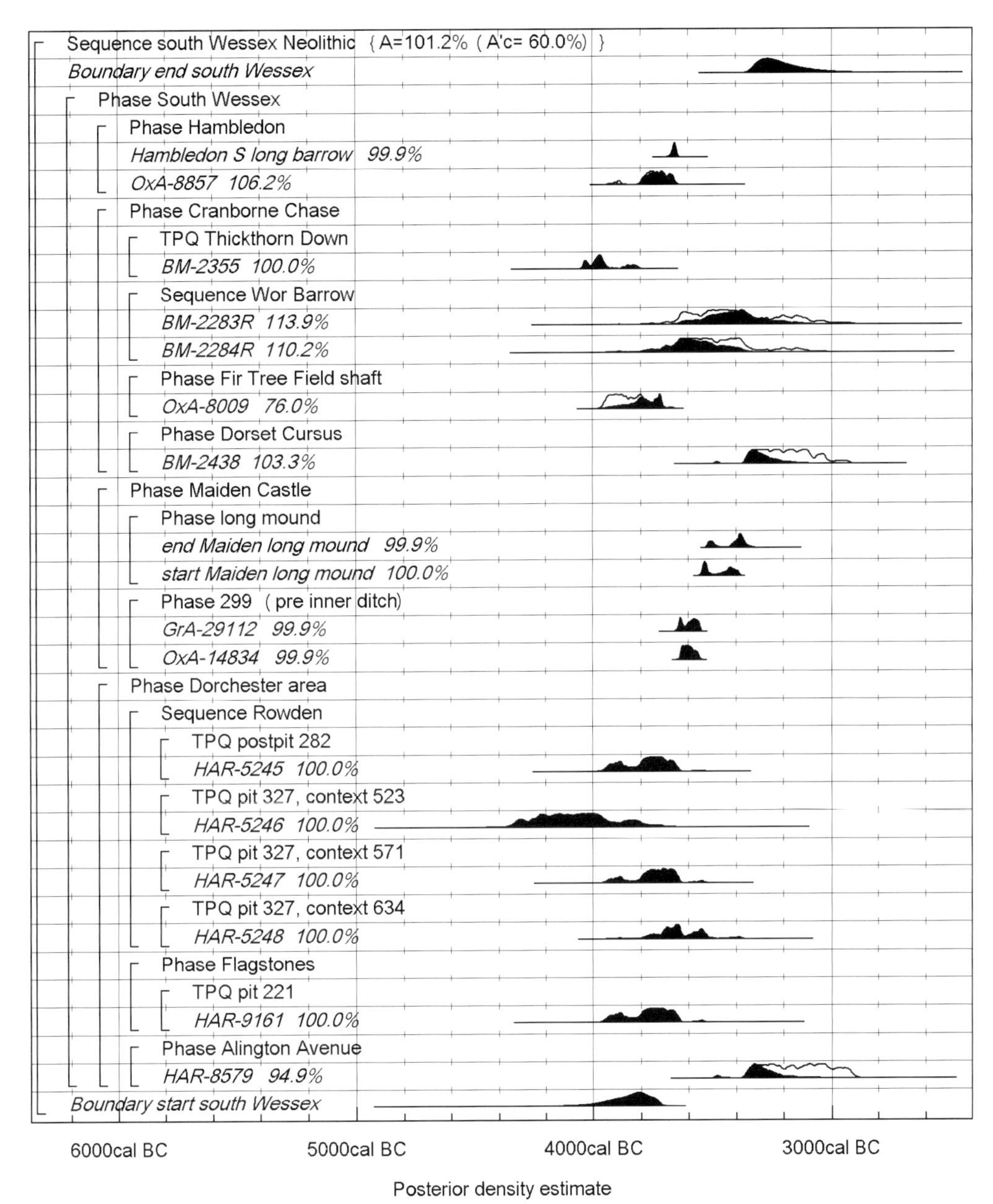

Fig. 14.53. Probability distributions of dates associated with diagnostically early Neolithic material culture from south Wessex (excluding those from enclosure sites). The format is the same as for Fig. 14.1. Distributions have been taken from the models defined by Figs 4.7–13 (Hambledon Hill), Fig. 4.21 (Fir Tree Field shaft) and Figs 4.41–5 (Maiden Castle). The large square brackets down the left-hand side of these diagrams, along with the OxCal keywords, define the overall model exactly.

things and practices. The regional estimates are based on a total of 276 likelihoods from 111 sites (Table 14.5).

Seventy percent of these distributions are associated with more than one element of the range of Neolithic things and practices (Fig. 14.55). This is almost certainly an underestimate since a number are from sites which are not yet fully published, so that the final tally of associations may be fuller. The three most frequent associations are with Bowl pottery (71%), animal domesticates (59%) and monuments (43%). Only a small proportion of dates (less than 7%) are associated solely with cultivation and animal husbandry without other components, and this may be reduced following the full publication of some of the sites concerned. When the composition of the sample is considered by region (Table 14.6) some significant differences appear. Sussex is the only area in the sample where there are dates from deep flint mines. The samples from north Wessex and the Cotswolds are heavily biased by dates from monuments, particularly long barrows and cairns. The samples from the middle Thames and the south-west peninsula are biased by disproportionate numbers of dates associated with Bowl pottery. In other areas, the samples are more varied. These differences may have a significant effect on the date estimates if different elements of the diagnostic Neolithic assemblage did not all appear at the same time.

Figure 14.54 suggests that the first appearance of Neolithic material and structures did not occur at the

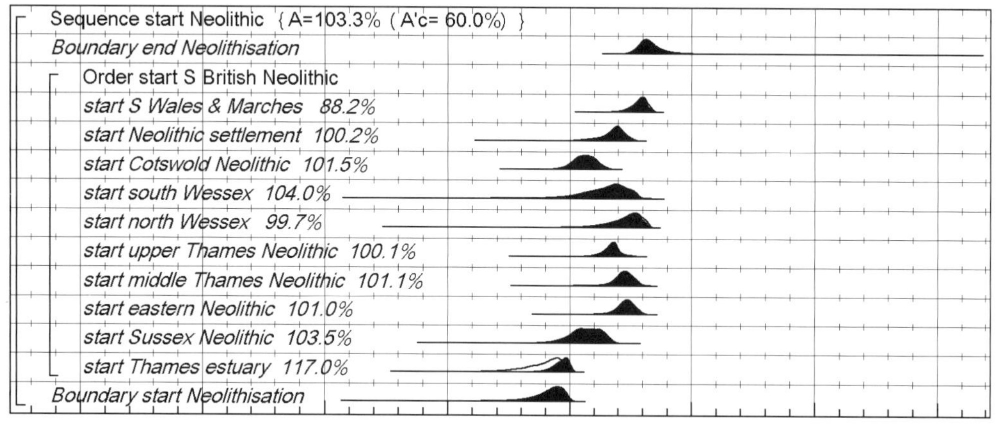

Fig. 14.54. Chronological model for the first Neolithic activity in southern Britain. Distributions for different regions have been taken from the models defined in Figs 14.49, 5.32–3, 6.50 and 6.47–8, 14.50, 14.51, 14.52 and 3.30–1, 14.53, 9.29–30, 10.30, and 11.10–11. The distribution 'start Neolithic settlement' is that for the south-west peninsula. The large square brackets down the left-hand side of the diagram, along with the OxCal keywords, define the overall model exactly.

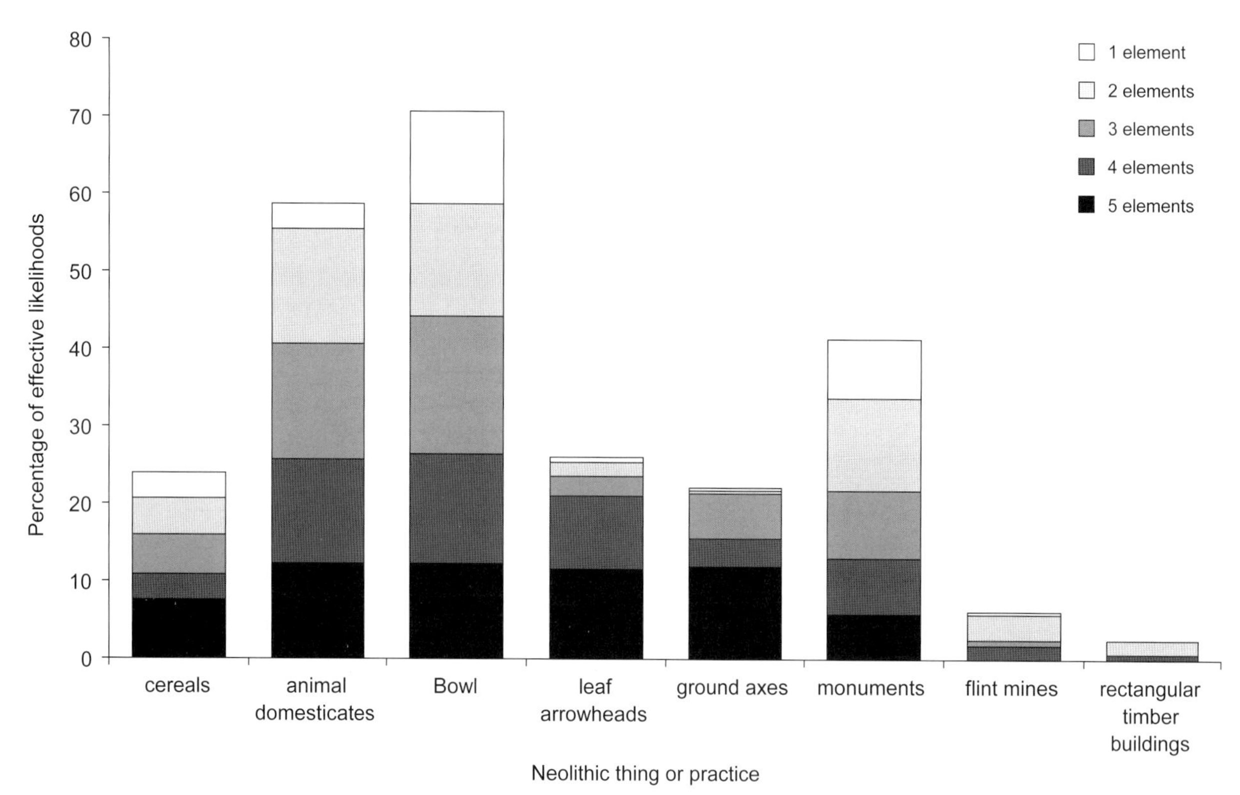

Fig. 14.55. Bar chart showing the proportions of the likelihoods (n=276) associated with different Neolithic things and practices included in the regional models for the early Neolithic of southern Britain.

same time across southern Britain. It is *91% probable* that the first diagnostic Neolithic activity in southern Britain occurred in the Greater Thames estuary. After this initial occurrence, Neolithic activity then appears, probably in the 40th century cal BC, in Sussex and the Cotswolds. In other areas, the first manifestation of diagnostic Neolithic things and practices is later: in the upper Thames valley, perhaps during the 39th century cal BC, and in a wide swathe across eastern England, the middle Thames valley, north and south Wessex and the south-west peninsula, over the following century or so. The first Neolithic activity in south Wales and the Marches does not seem to have appeared until the generations around 3700 cal BC.

This model suggests that it took an extended period for Neolithic practices to spread across southern Britain. It seems that it took *265–640 years* (*95% probability*; Fig. 14.56: *period of Neolithisation*), probably *310–475 years* (*68% probability*), from their first occurrence, probably

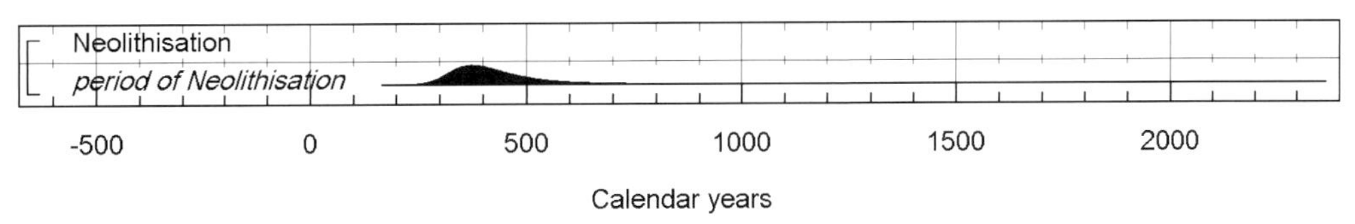

Fig. 14.56. The period during which the first Neolithic activity appeared across southern Britain, derived from the model shown in Fig. 14.54.

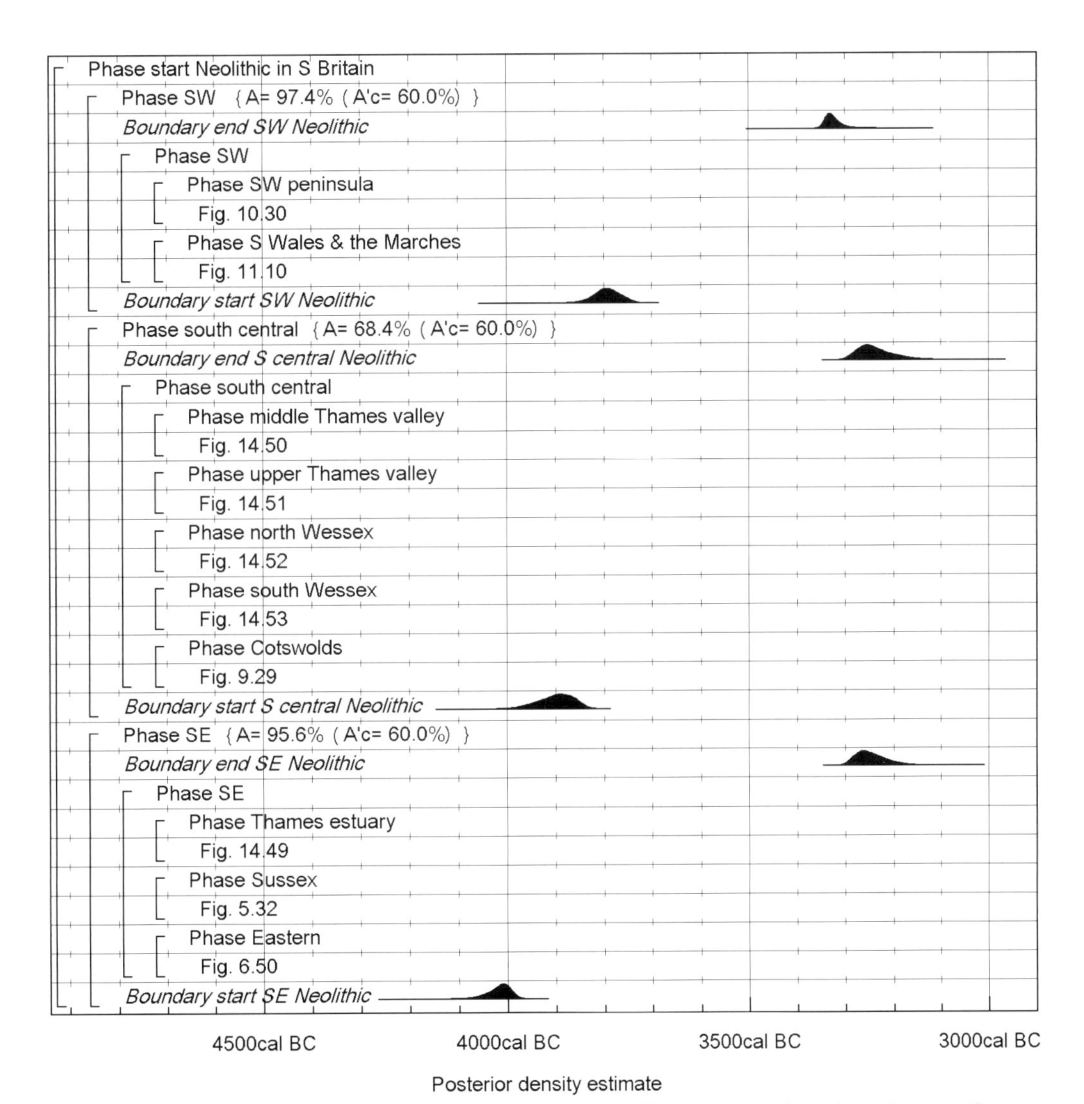

Fig. 14.57. Chronological model for the date of the early Neolithic in different areas of southern Britain. Component sections are shown between the uniform phase boundaries of the models defined in Figs 10.30, 11.10, 14.50–3, 9.29, 14.49, 5.32, and 6.50 (although the posterior density estimates shown on these figures are not those relating to this model). The large square brackets down the left-hand side of these diagrams, along with the OxCal keywords, define the overall model exactly.

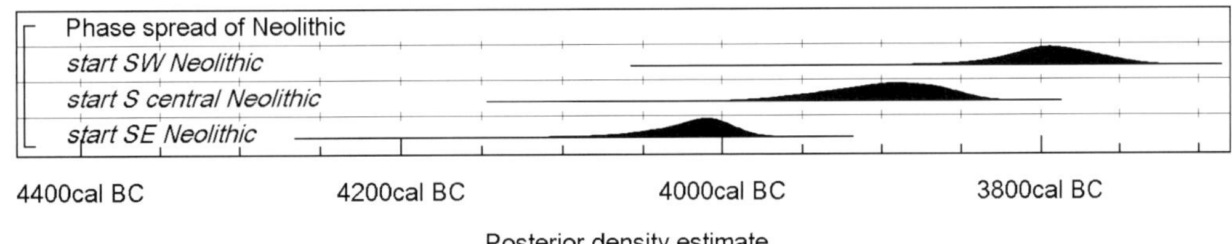

Fig. 14.58. Probability distributions of dates for the start of the early Neolithic in different areas of southern Britain, derived from the models shown in Fig. 14.57.

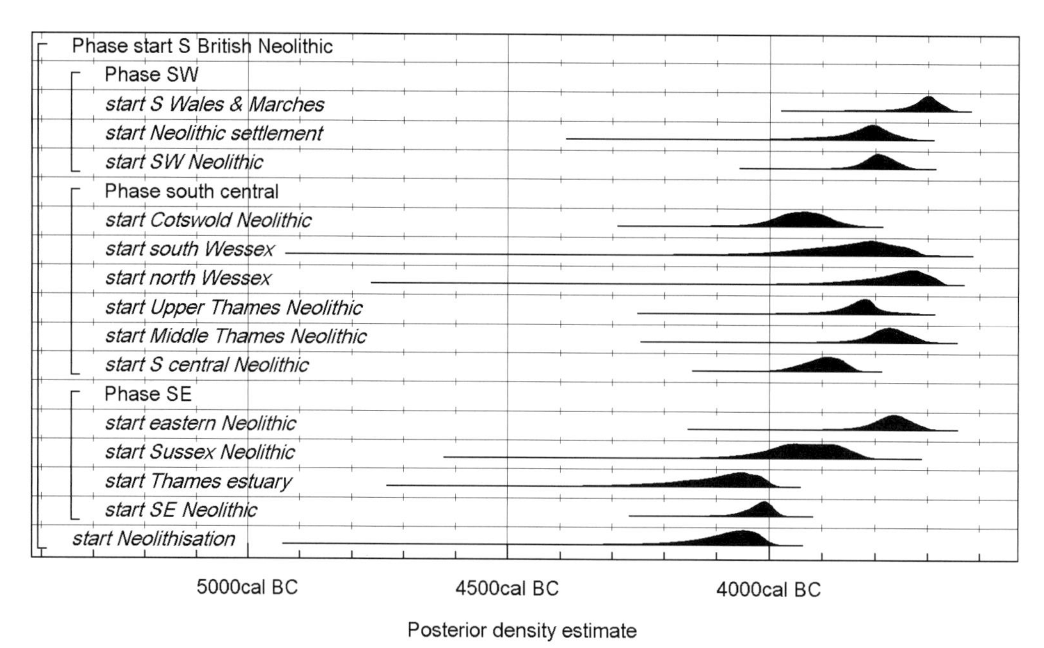

Fig. 14.59. Probability distributions of dates for the start of the early Neolithic in different areas of southern Britain, derived from the model shown in Fig. 14.57, and for the first Neolithic in the smaller regions utilised in the model shown in Fig. 14.54.

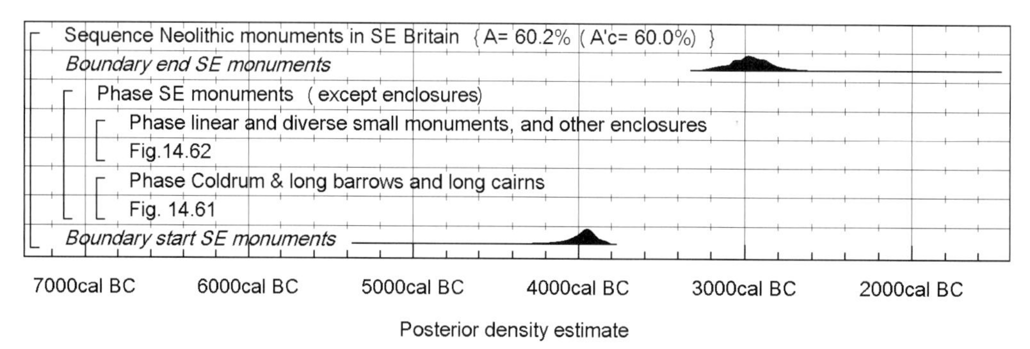

Fig. 14.60. Overall structure of the chronological model for early Neolithic monuments in south-east England. The component sections of this model are shown in detail in Figs 14.61–2. The large square brackets down the left-hand side of Figs 14.60–2, along with the OxCal keywords, define the overall model exactly.

in the Greater Thames estuary (*91% probable*), until their final appearance, very possibly in south Wales and the Marches (*61% probable*). This process began in *4235–3985 cal BC (95% probability*; Fig. 14.54: *start Neolithisation)*, probably in *4115–4010 cal BC (68% probability)* and was complete by *3765–3535 cal BC (95% probability*; Fig. 14.54: *end Neolithisation)*, probably by *3730–3635 cal BC (68% probability)*.

There are hints that the pace of this process may not have been constant throughout this period. In the first two centuries, Neolithic activity appears in only three regions; whereas in the next two centuries, it appears over the other seven. Once the initial idea was established, did the pace of its adoption increase? This raises two thorny questions.

The first is the question of foci or points of appearance. One possibility is that there was a single focus of first appearance, very probably in the Greater Thames estuary, which stood at the head of a subsequent process of spread outwards across southern Britain, probably next around 100 km into Sussex and more than 200 km into the Cotswolds. Another possibility, however, is that there were multiple foci or points of appearance, in Kent, Sussex and the Cotswolds, though not necessarily all at exactly the same time. Two of these areas are coastal and south-eastern, close to likely continental sources of contact or inspiration. But in this version the first appearance of things Neolithic in the Cotswolds is also early, and at some geographical remove from Kent and Sussex; around it are other areas where numbers of sites have been dated, although none appear as early as in the Cotswolds. Could this imply another point of origin by another route of introduction, say around the south-west peninsula and up the Severn estuary, or over shorter distances, up the rivers of Wessex? The difficulty in both cases is the lack of comparably early material in the areas between the Cotswolds and points south. We could perhaps get round this difficulty in two ways. We might invoke the regional gaps which we have not investigated (see above) as the possible way into the Cotswolds: thus along the Surrey and Berkshire Downs and swiftly across the upper Thames, with no visible trace left behind. Or

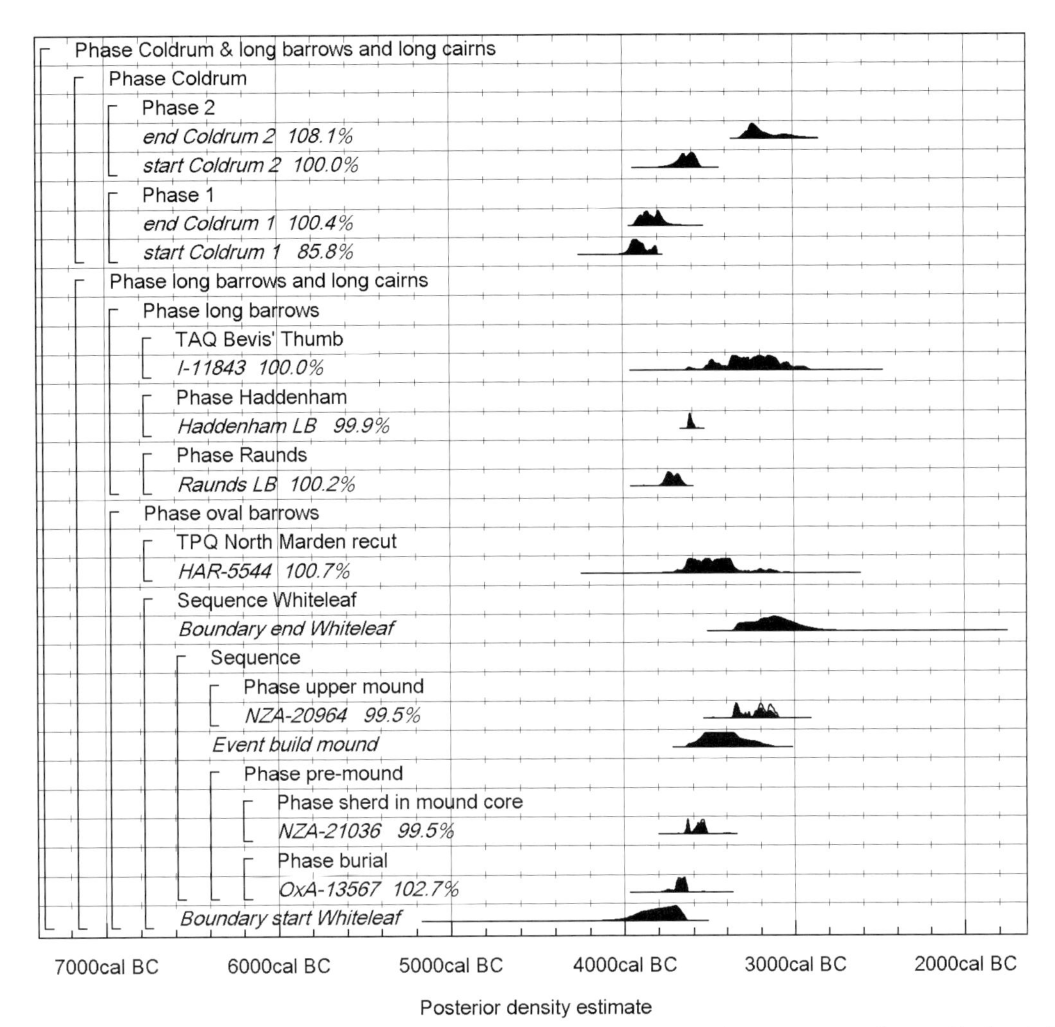

Fig. 14.61. Probability distributions of dates from Coldrum and long and oval barrows in south-east England. The format is identical to that of Fig. 14.1. Distributions have been taken from models defined in Fig. 7.27 (Coldrum), Figs 6.16–17 (Haddenham), and Figs 6.25–7 (Raunds). The overall structure of this model is shown in Fig. 14.60, and its other component in Fig. 14.62.

we could have recourse to that generalising theory about colonisation which notes the frequent recurrence of highly targeted moves; people (and normally not whole cultures) often colonise along reconnoitred or scouted routes, seeking to reach predetermined destinations and no others (e.g. Anthony 1990; and see further Chapter 15).

The second question is whether the models for the chronology of the early Neolithic are reliable. Compare Fig. 14.54, which shows estimates for the start of the Neolithic in different regions of southern Britain, with Fig. 14.15, which gives the date of the first dated enclosure in each region. The tick marks tell a tale – in Fig. 14.15 they mark generations, whereas in Fig. 14.54 they mark centuries. This project was designed to date causewayed and other enclosures. We therefore have reliable dates for an appreciable proportion of the known sites of that kind. In contrast, we have gathered as many as we could of the existing radiocarbon dates on early Neolithic contexts other than enclosures. This sample is neither designed nor random, but opportunistic. It depends upon the foci of past research, on the scale and circumstance of recent development, and on the ability of contract archaeologists in a given region to obtain radiocarbon dates. This is vividly illustrated by the model for the early Neolithic in the Greater Thames estuary (Fig. 14.49), where 37 of the 41 radiocarbon dates available have been obtained in the last five years! New information may change the picture presented here substantially.

Not only is the amount of information variable, but so too are its quality and its reflection of the types of early Neolithic practice present in a region. For example, all the radiocarbon dates included in the model for Sussex (Figs 5.32–3) were obtained before 1990. Among regions where the sample is dominated by dates from monuments (Table 14.6), there are both early date estimates for the first Neolithic, as in the Cotswolds, and late ones, as in south Wales and the Marches. In contrast, both regions where the samples are biased by disproportionate numbers of dates from pits and middens containing Bowl pottery, the middle Thames valley and the south-west peninsula, have produced later date estimates for the start of the Neolithic. In both cases, dates are available on samples

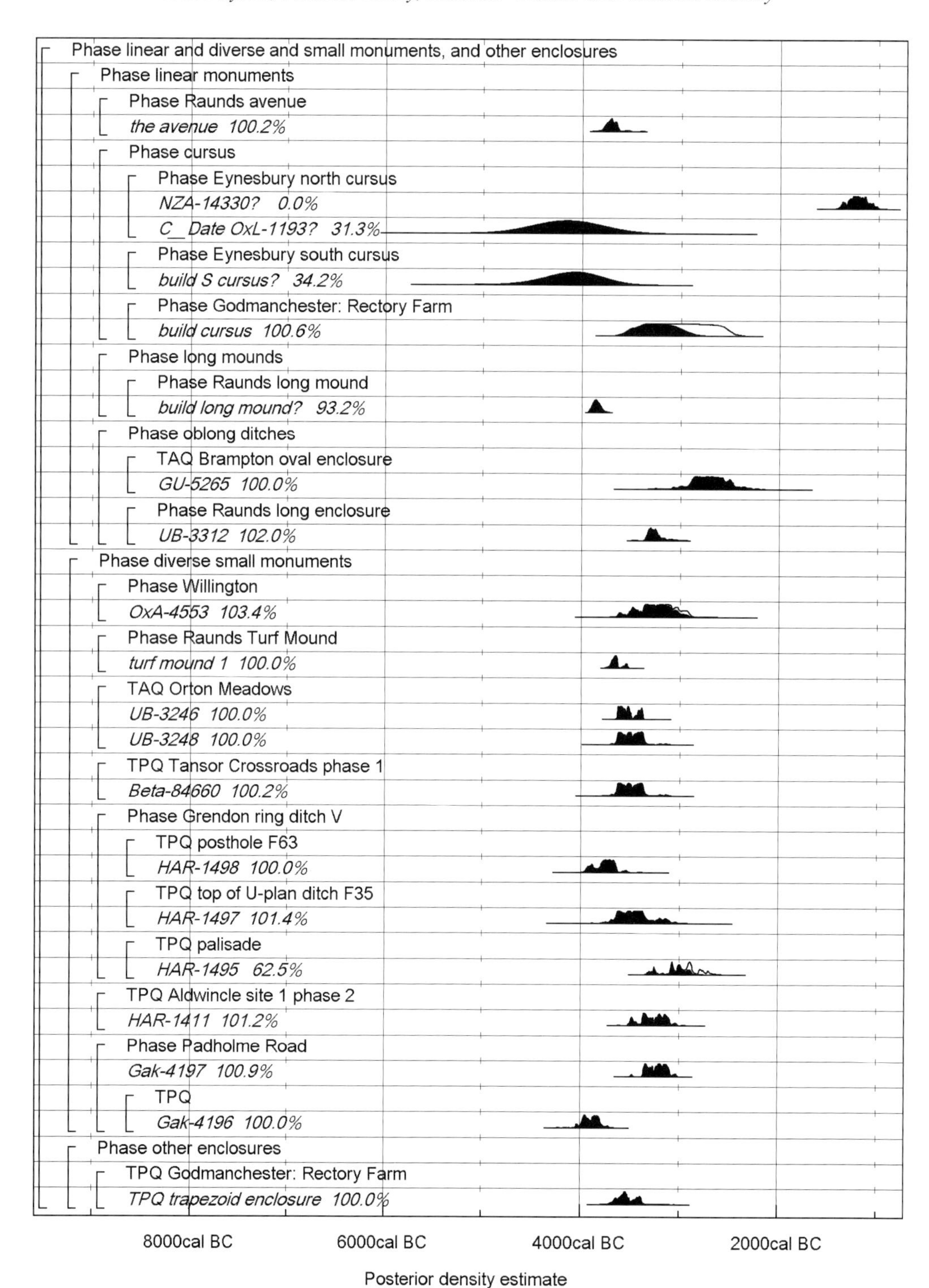

Fig. 14.62. Probability distributions of dates from linear and diverse small monuments, and other enclosures in south-east England. The format is identical to that of Fig. 14.1. Distributions have been taken from models defined in Fig. 6.13 (Eynesbury), Fig. 6.15 (Godmanchester, Rectory Farm) and Figs 6.25–7 (Raunds). The overall structure of this model is shown in Fig. 14.60, and its other component in Fig. 14.61.

associated with a range of Bowl pottery styles – but was there Neolithic activity before pottery was current? If so, it has not been dated. This would be surprising, at least in the south-west peninsula where a comparatively large number of radiocarbon dates have been obtained recently from a range of contexts both with and without pottery. In Sussex, pits and other small-scale activity are poorly represented, but a number of the flint mines have provided consistently early dates.

It is clear that the models for the chronology of the early Neolithic presented in this chapter are not as reliable as those relating to enclosures. To improve this position, first we need precise dating for a much larger sample of sites, where possible exploiting the potential of

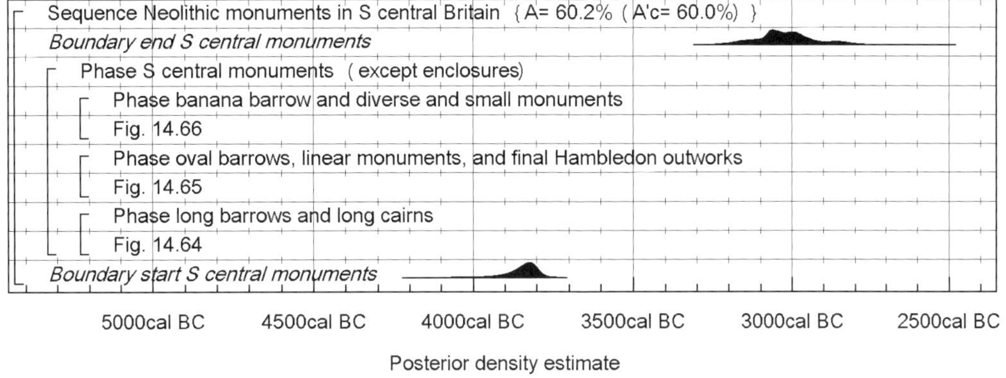

Fig. 14.63. Overall structure of chronological model for early Neolithic monuments in south-central England. The component sections of this model are shown in detail in Figs 14.64–6. The large square brackets down the left-hand side of Figs 14.63–6, along with the OxCal keywords, define the overall model exactly.

stratigraphy to provide informative prior information to constrain our models. This makes our wider chronologies much less reliant on the validity of our uninformative prior information (see Chapter 2.4.1 and 2.8). Second, new statistical methods currently in development may allow us to unpack the dating of the range of Neolithic activity considered here more reliably and produce more sophisticated spatio-temporal models (Karlsberg 2006; Blackwell and Buck 2003).

Meanwhile, we can build a number of alternative models to investigate the sensitivity of our chronologies for the early Neolithic in southern Britain to archaeological and mathematical assumptions.

First, we can aggregate the regions into larger areas, in order to provide a larger sample of data in each area, smoothing out possible idiosyncracies in the available regional data sets. We have aggregated the Greater Thames estuary, Sussex and eastern England (as south-east England); the middle Thames, the upper Thames, north Wessex, south Wessex and the Cotswolds (as south-central England); and the south-west peninsula and south Wales and the Marches (as south-west Britain). The chronological models for the early Neolithic in these areas are defined in Fig. 14.57. The date estimates for the first appearance of Neolithic things and practices are shown in Fig. 14.58. A simpler chronological progression is apparent. According to this model, it is *99% probable* that Neolithic things and practices first appeared in south-east England, followed by their appearance in south-central England, and then in south-west Britain. The spread of the phenomenon appears to occur at a relatively constant pace.

The estimates for the start of the Neolithic in these wider areas are compared with those for the smaller regions previously discussed in Fig. 14.59. The question is whether the area-based models are more reliable because they are based on a larger and more robust sample of data, with biases in the data smoothed out, or whether these larger areas mask subtleties in the process of Neolithisation. In Fig. 14.59, two potential variations stand out particularly. Does the start of the Neolithic in eastern England appear late, compared with the Thames estuary and Sussex, because of, say, a paucity of dates from Suffolk? By contrast, does the estimate for the start of the Neolithic in the Cotswolds appear early, compared with adjacent regions, because of the imbalance in dated contexts, which have been heavily biased towards long cairns and barrows? It can be noted that the estimate for the late start of the Neolithic in south Wales and the Marches, compared for example with the start in the adjacent south-west peninsula of England, also includes numerous samples from long cairns. At this stage of research, it is simply impossible to resolve these questions, and we therefore cannot say whether these variations are anomalies to be explained away or real patterns in a complex process of staggered starts.

We can now assess whether different elements of the assemblage of Neolithic things and practices appeared synchronously in the areas of southern Britain which we have just considered. Only for monuments and pottery are there sufficient data for independent analysis. Figures 14.60–2 define the model for the appearance of monuments (excluding causewayed enclosures) in south-east England. Figures 14.63–6 define the model for the appearance of monuments (excluding causewayed enclosures) in south-central England, and Figure 14.67 defines the model for the appearance of monuments (excluding causewayed and stone-walled enclosures) in south-west Britain. Figures 14.68–71 define the model for the chronology of Bowl pottery in south-east England; Figures 14.72–6 define a similar model for south-central England; and Figures 14.77–9 define the model for the currency of Bowl pottery in south-west Britain.

Figure 14.80 shows our estimates for the start of all Neolithic activity in each area (see Fig. 14.58), compared with the estimates for the first Neolithic monument and the first pottery in each area. All these models exclude the data from causewayed and tor enclosures, but they are not statistically independent. Our models for the start of the Neolithic (Fig. 14.57) include likelihoods associated with monuments, with pottery, and with other Neolithic activity (Table 14.6). Our models for early Neolithic monumentality include all likelihoods relating to monuments, including those which also have associated pottery. Equally, our models for the currency of Bowl pottery include all dates associated with this ceramic tradition, even those from

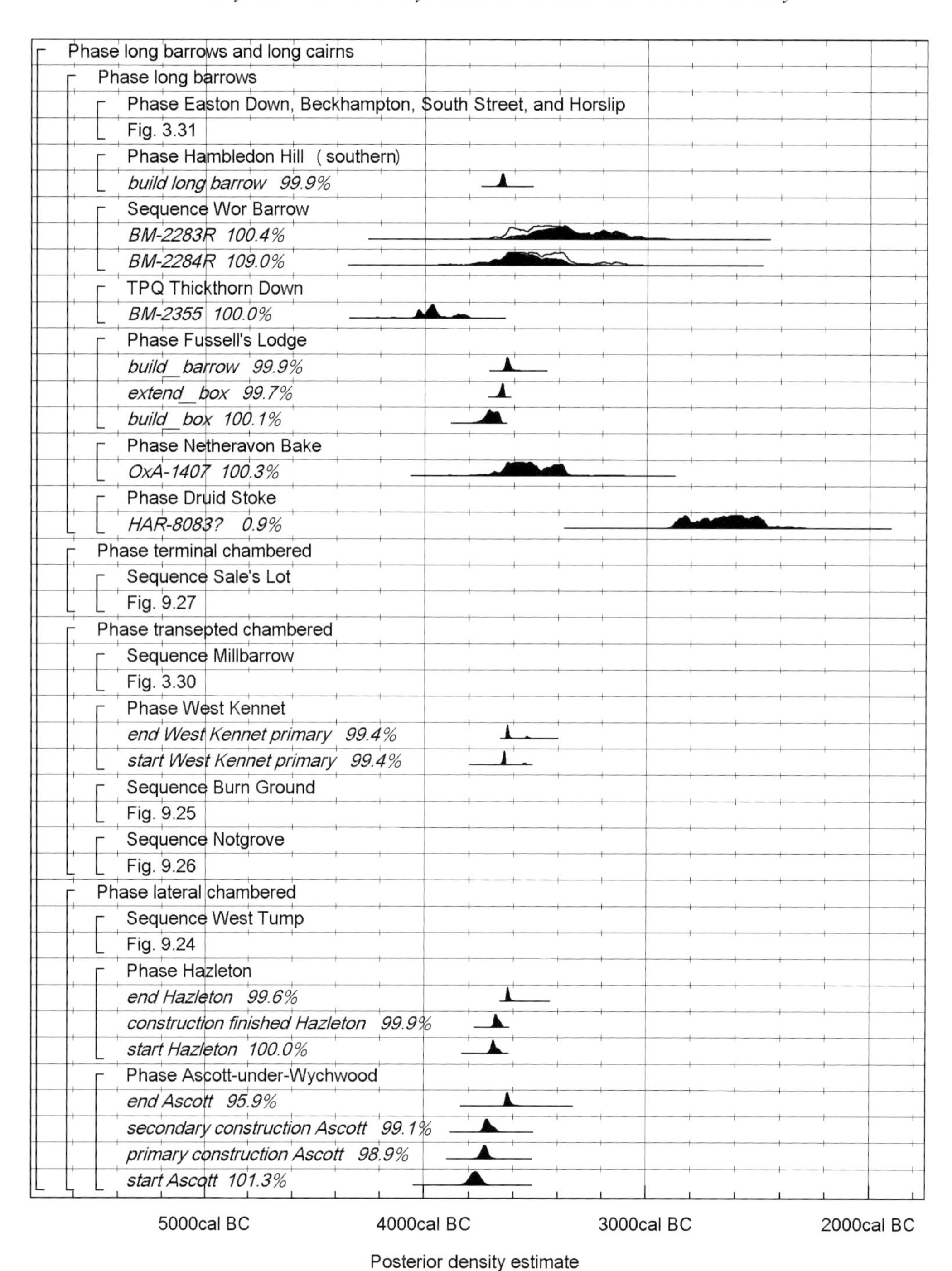

Fig. 14.64. Probability distributions of dates from long barrows and long cairns in south-central England. The format is identical to that of Fig. 14.1. The structure of the component sections of this component are shown in Figs 3.30–1 (long barrows in the Avebury area) and Figs 9.24–7 (West Tump, Burn Ground, Notgrove, and Sale's Lot) (although the posterior density estimates shown on these figures are not those relating to this model). Other distributions have been taken from models defined in Figs 4.7–13 (Hambledon Hill), Bayliss et al. *2007b, fig 6 (West Kennet), Meadows* et al. *2007, figs 6–9 (Hazleton), and Bayliss* et al. *2007c, figs 3 and 5–7 (Ascott-under-Wychwood). The overall structure of this model is shown in Fig. 14.63, and its other components in Figs 14.65–6.*

monuments. In some cases, however, when we divide dates into smaller categories, we no longer have sufficient data to assess realistically the scatter on the assemblage of dates. So, for example, our posterior density estimate for the start of monuments in south-west Britain (Fig. 14.67: *start SW monuments*) has an unrealistically long early tail.

We have seen that the first Neolithic in south-east Britain appeared in *4075–3975 cal BC* (*95% probability*; Fig. 14.57: *start SE Neolithic*), probably in *4035–3990 cal BC* (*68% probability*). The first monumental construction appeared in this area in *4155–3815 cal BC* (*95% probability*; Fig. 14.60: *start SE monuments*), probably in *4030–3885 cal BC* (*68% probability*). The first pottery appeared in south-east England in *4105–3975 cal BC* (*95% probability*; Fig.

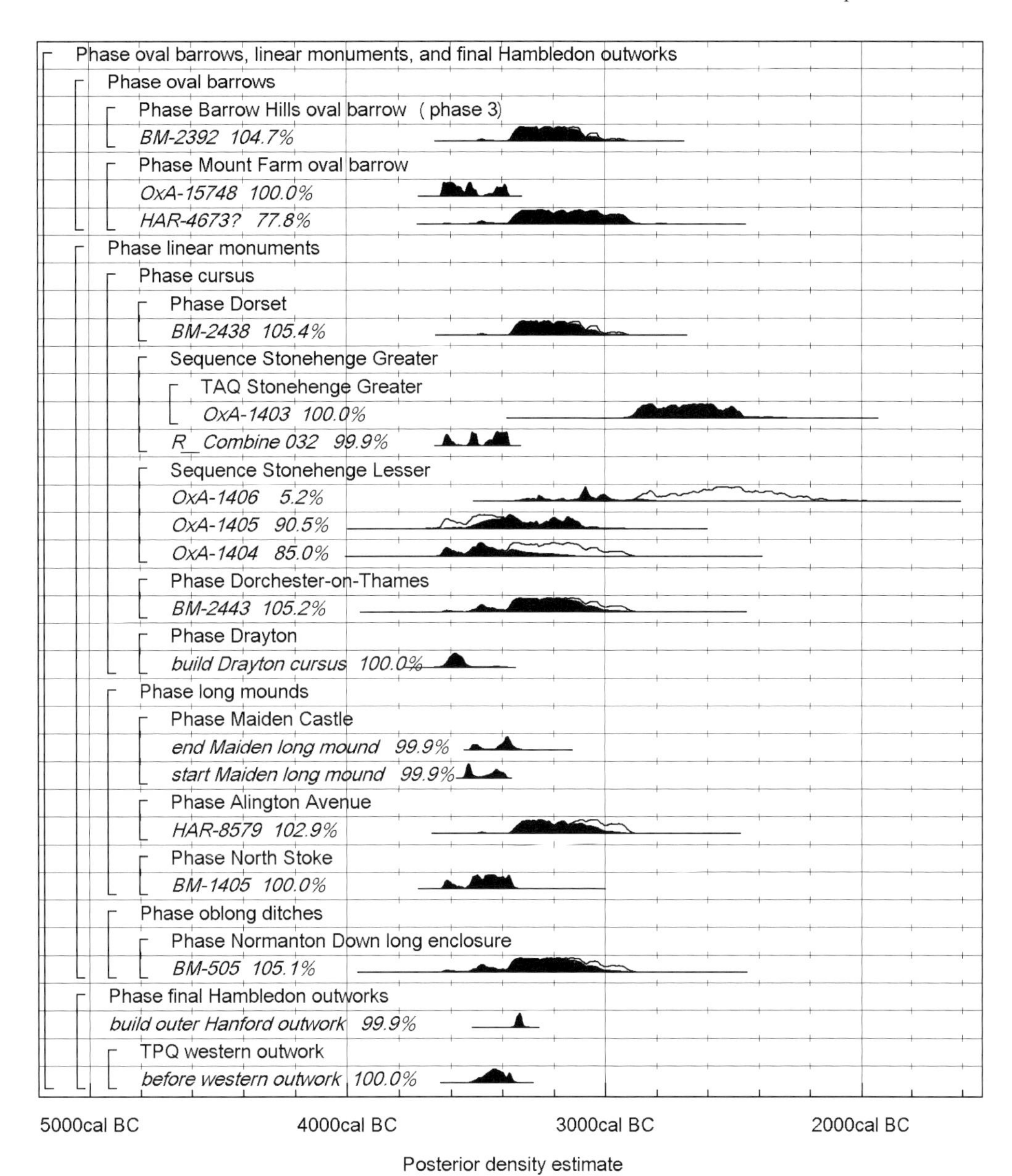

Fig. 14.65. Probability distributions of dates from oval barrows, linear monuments, and the final Hambledon outworks in south-central England. The format is identical to that of Fig. 14.1. Distributions have been taken from the model defined in Figs 4.7–13 (Hambledon Hill). The overall structure of this model is shown in Fig. 14.63, and its other components in Figs 14.64 and 14.66.

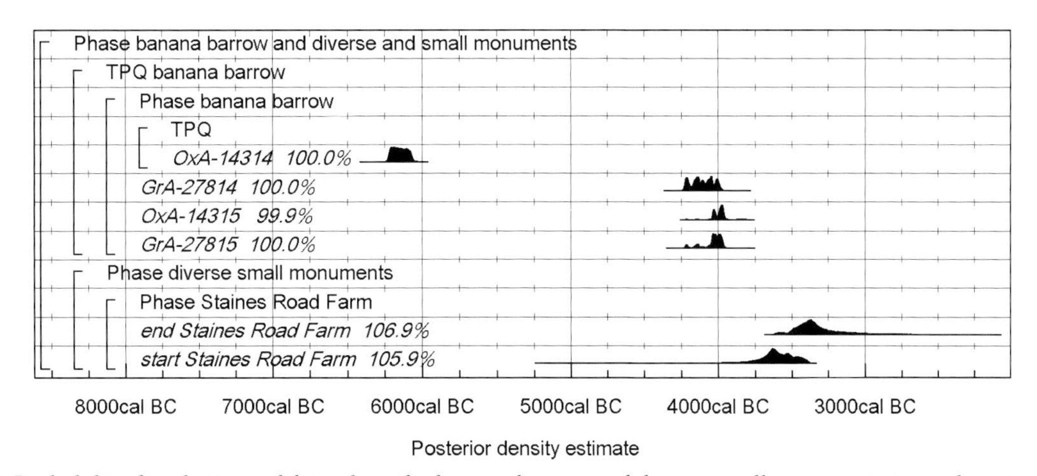

Fig. 14.66. Probability distributions of dates from the banana barrow and diverse small monuments in south-central England. The format is identical to that of Fig. 14.1. Distributions have been taken from model defined in Fig. 8.7 (Staines Road Farm). The overall structure of this model is shown in Fig. 14.63, and its other components in Figs 14.64–5.

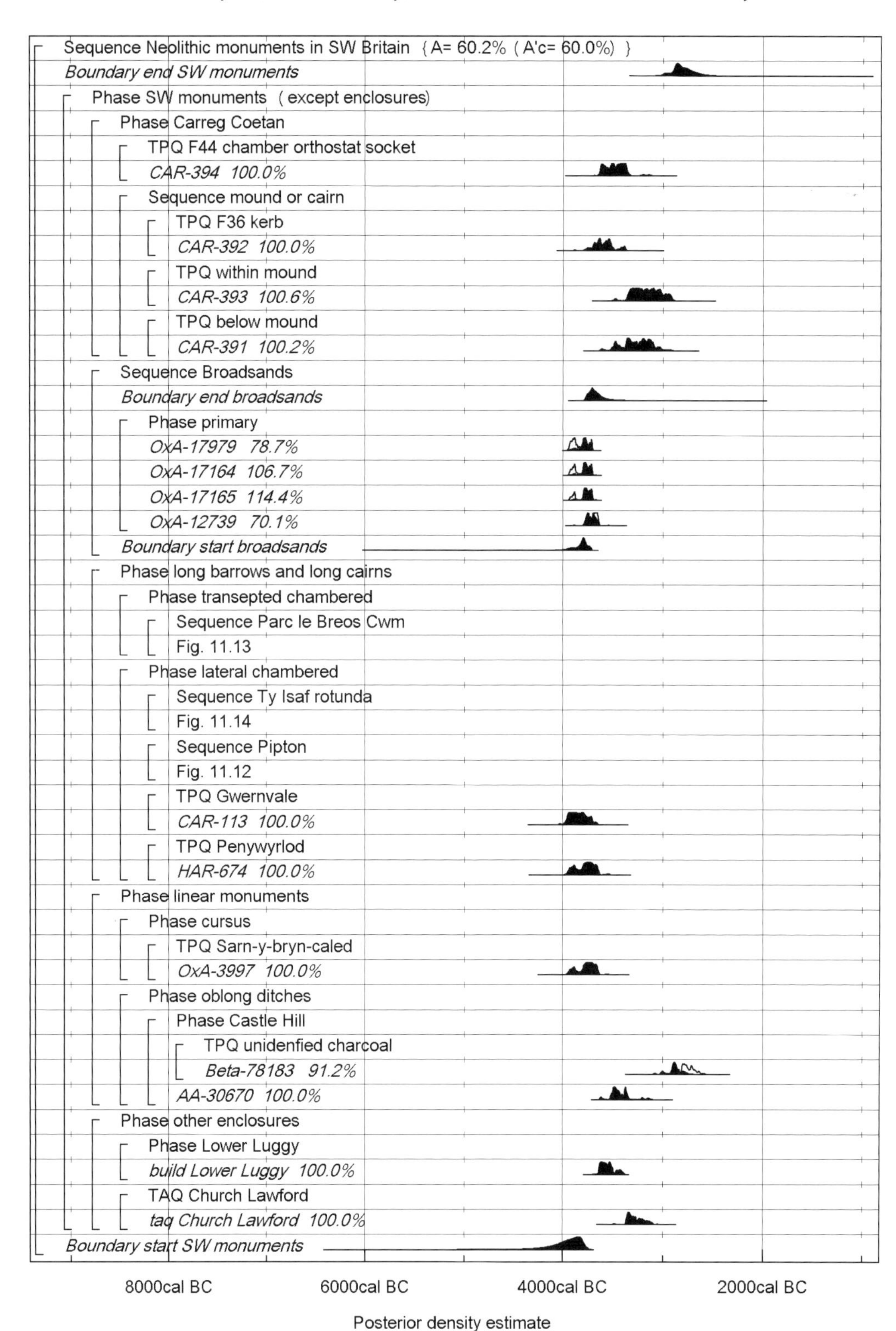

Fig. 14.67. Overall structure of the chronological model for the currency of early Neolithic monuments in south-west Britain. The component sections of this model are shown in detail in Figs 11.12–14 (Pipton, Parc le Breos Cwm, and Ty Isaf) (although the posterior density estimates shown on these figures are not those relating to this model). Distributions have been taken from the model defined in Fig. 11.15 (Church Lawford and Lower Luggy). The large square brackets down the left-hand side of the figures, along with the OxCal keywords, define the overall model exactly.

14.68: *start SE pots*), probably in *4055–3995 cal BC* (*68% probability*).

According to our models, the first Neolithic in south-central Britain appeared in *3975–3835 cal BC* (*95% probability*; Fig. 14.57: *start S central Neolithic*), probably in *3930–3855 cal BC* (*68% probability*). The first monumental construction appeared in this area in *3940–3765 cal BC* (*95% probability*; Fig. 14.63: *start S central monuments*),

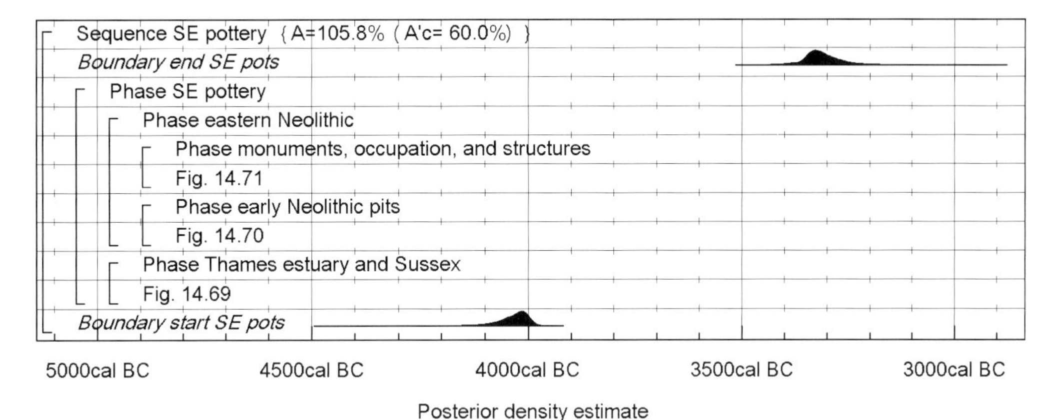

Fig. 14.68. Overall structure of the chronological model for the currency of Bowl pottery in south-east England. The component sections of this model are shown in detail in Figs 14.69–71. The large square brackets down the left-hand side of the figures, along with the OxCal keywords, define the overall model exactly.

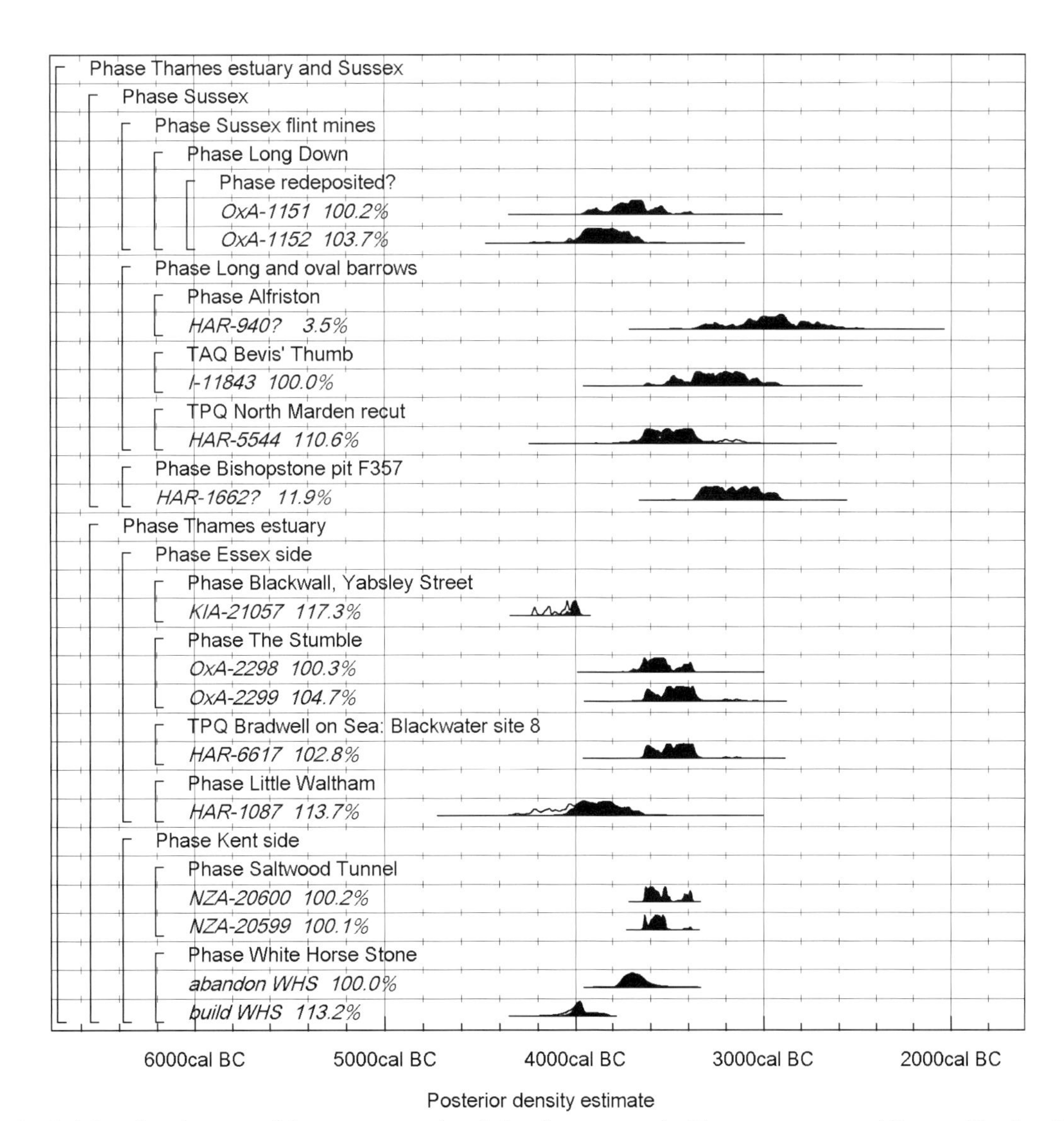

Fig. 14.69. Probability distributions of dates associated with Bowl pottery in the Thames estuary and Sussex. The distributions for White Horse Stone have been taken from the model defined in Fig. 7.26. The format is identical to that of Fig. 14.1. The overall structure of this model is shown in Fig. 14.68, and its other components in Figs 14.70–1.

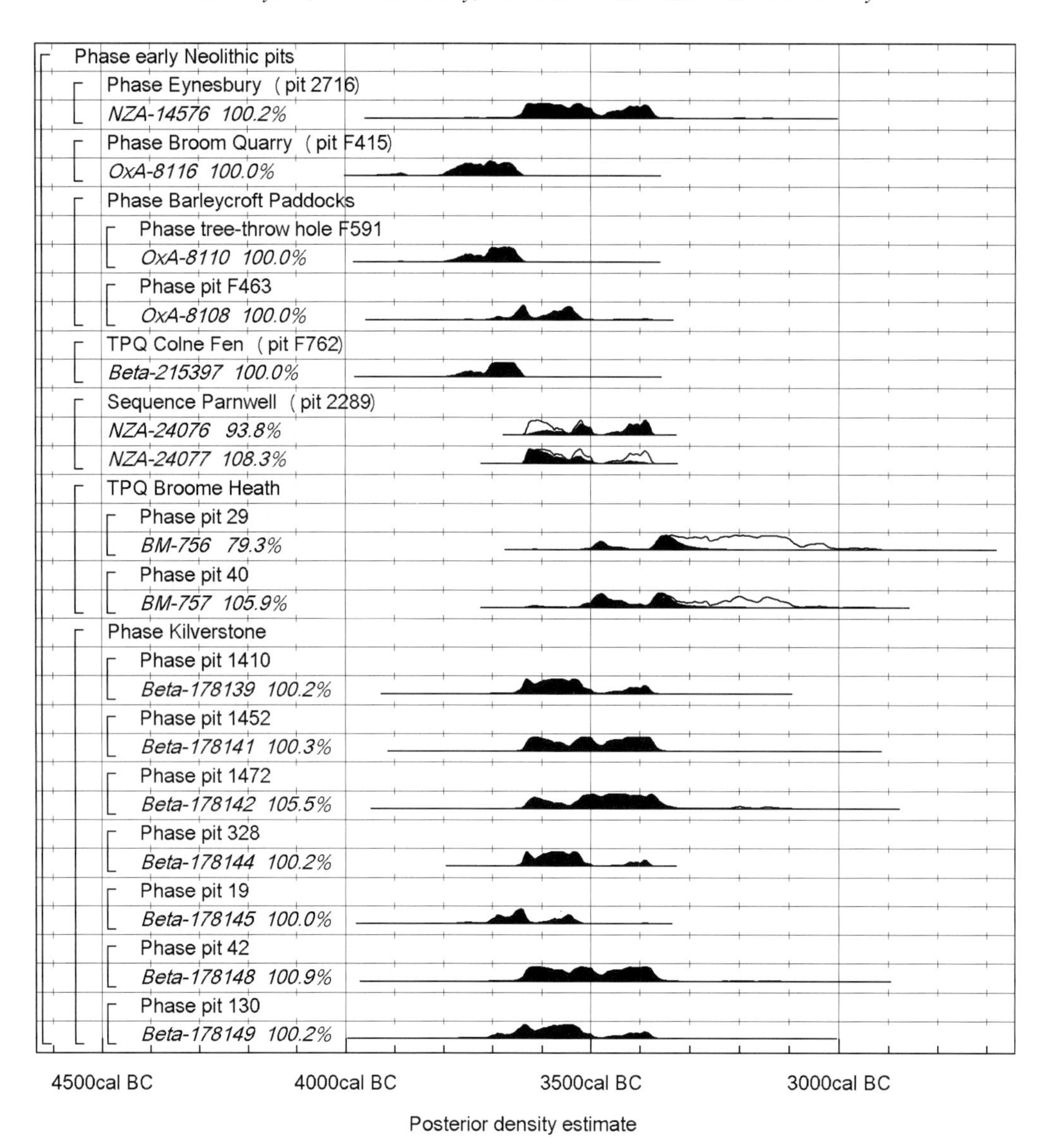

Fig. 14.70. Probability distributions of dates associated with Bowl pottery from pits in eastern England. The format is identical to that of Fig. 14.1. The overall structure of this model is shown in Fig. 14.68, and its other components in Figs 14.69 and 14.71.

probably in *3870–3790 cal BC* (*68% probability*). The first pottery appeared in south-central Britain in *3985–3830 cal BC* (*95% probability*; Fig. 14.72: *start S central pots*), probably in *3930–3850 cal BC* (*68% probability*).

The first Neolithic in south-west Britain, according to our models, appeared in *3855–3735 cal BC* (*95% probability*; Fig. 14.57: *start SW Neolithic*), probably in *3820–3760 cal BC* (*68% probability*). The first monumental construction appeared in this area in *4315–3735 cal BC* (*95% probability*; Fig. 14.67: *start SW monuments*), probably in *4030–3785 cal BC* (*68% probability*). The first pottery appeared in south-west Britain in *3820–3715 cal BC* (*95% probability*; Fig. 14.77: *start SW pots*), probably in *3785–3730 cal BC* (*68% probability*).

The number of years between the appearance of the first Neolithic things and practices and the appearance of the first pottery, area by area, is shown in Fig. 14.81. Pottery appeared in south-east England *−105–70 years* after the appearance of the first Neolithic (*95% probability*; Fig. 14.81: *start SE Neolithic/pots*), probably *−50–30 years* afterwards (*68% probability*). Pottery appeared in south-central England *−110–105 years* after the appearance of the first Neolithic (*95% probability*; Fig. 14.81: *start S central Neolithic/pots*), probably *−55–55 years* afterwards (*68% probability*). In south-west Britain, pottery appeared *−55–110 years* after the appearance of the first Neolithic (*95% probability*; Fig. 14.81: *start SW Neolithic/pots*), probably *−10–70 years* afterwards (*68% probability*).

These estimates for the gap between the appearance of pottery and the start of the Neolithic in an area can be negative, because in each case the precision of the estimates cannot determine that there is no possibility that the first pottery appeared before the first Neolithic (as our estimates for the start of the Neolithic include all the data associated with pottery in an area, this is obviously not possible!). This is because the models for the currency of Bowl pottery in

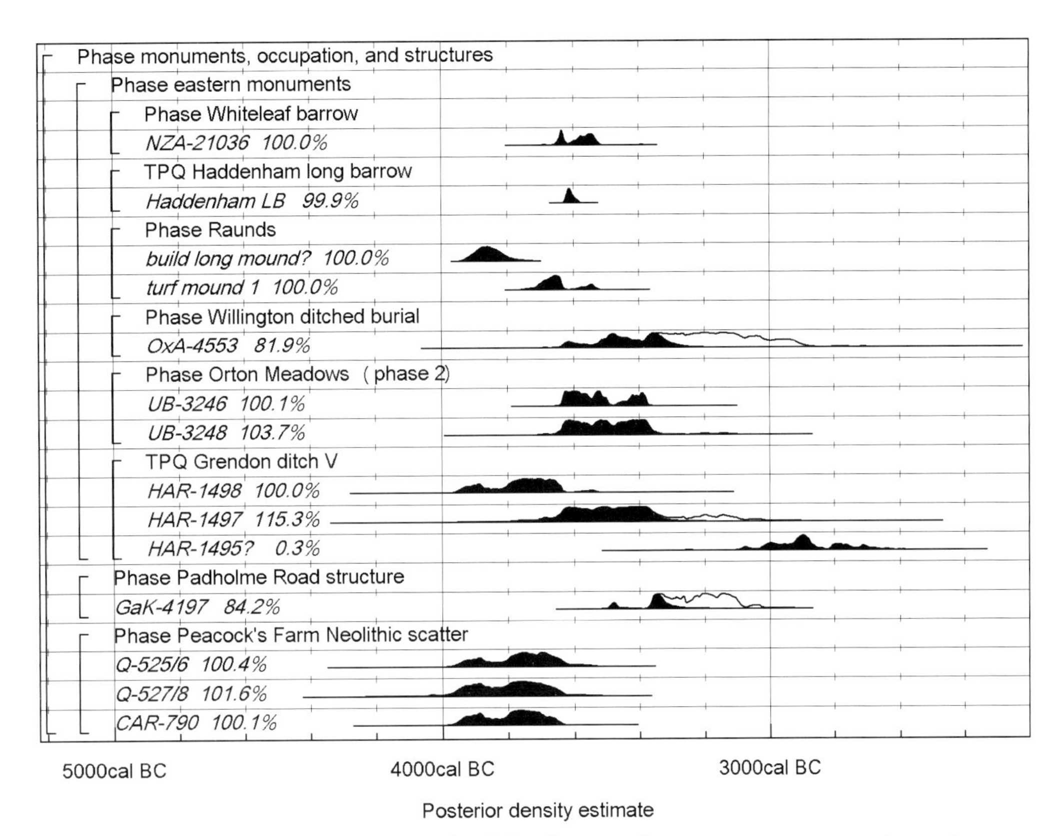

Fig. 14.71. Probability distributions of dates associated with Bowl pottery from monuments, occupation and structures in eastern England. The format is identical to that of Fig. 14.1. Distributions have been taken from models defined in Fig. 6.6 (Whiteleaf), Figs 6.16–17 (Haddenham long barrow), Figs 6.25–7 (Raunds), and Fig. 6.18 (Peacock's Farm). The overall structure of this model is shown in Fig. 14.68, and its other components in Figs 14.69–70.

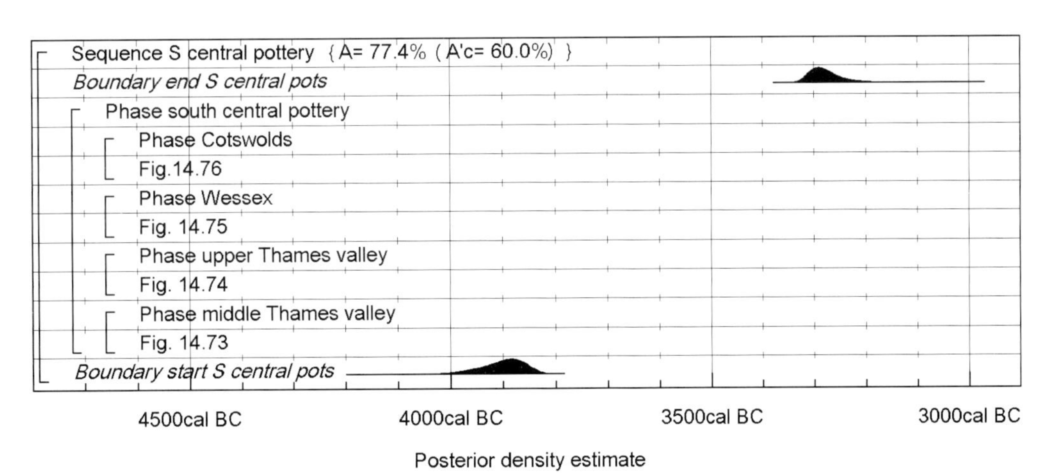

Fig. 14.72. Overall structure of the chronological model for the currency of Bowl pottery in south-central England. The component sections of this model are shown in detail in Figs 14.73–6. The large square brackets down the left-hand side of the figures, along with the OxCal keywords, define the overall model exactly.

each area rely on fewer data, and so the resultant posterior density estimates are less precise. Archaeologically, these distributions mean that pottery appeared in each area at a date very close to the first Neolithic – certainly within one or two generations, and very probably as a primary element of these innovations. There is a slightly greater possibility that pottery may have appeared in south-west Britain a generation or two after other elements, as this distribution has a larger probability of a real gap (Fig. 14.81). Given the available sample of dates, too much reliance should not be placed on this tentative trend. On this basis, therefore, we feel that any aceramic phase at the start of the southern British Neolithic is implausible.

The numbers of years between the appearance of the first Neolithic things and practices and the appearance of the first monument other than an enclosure, area by area,

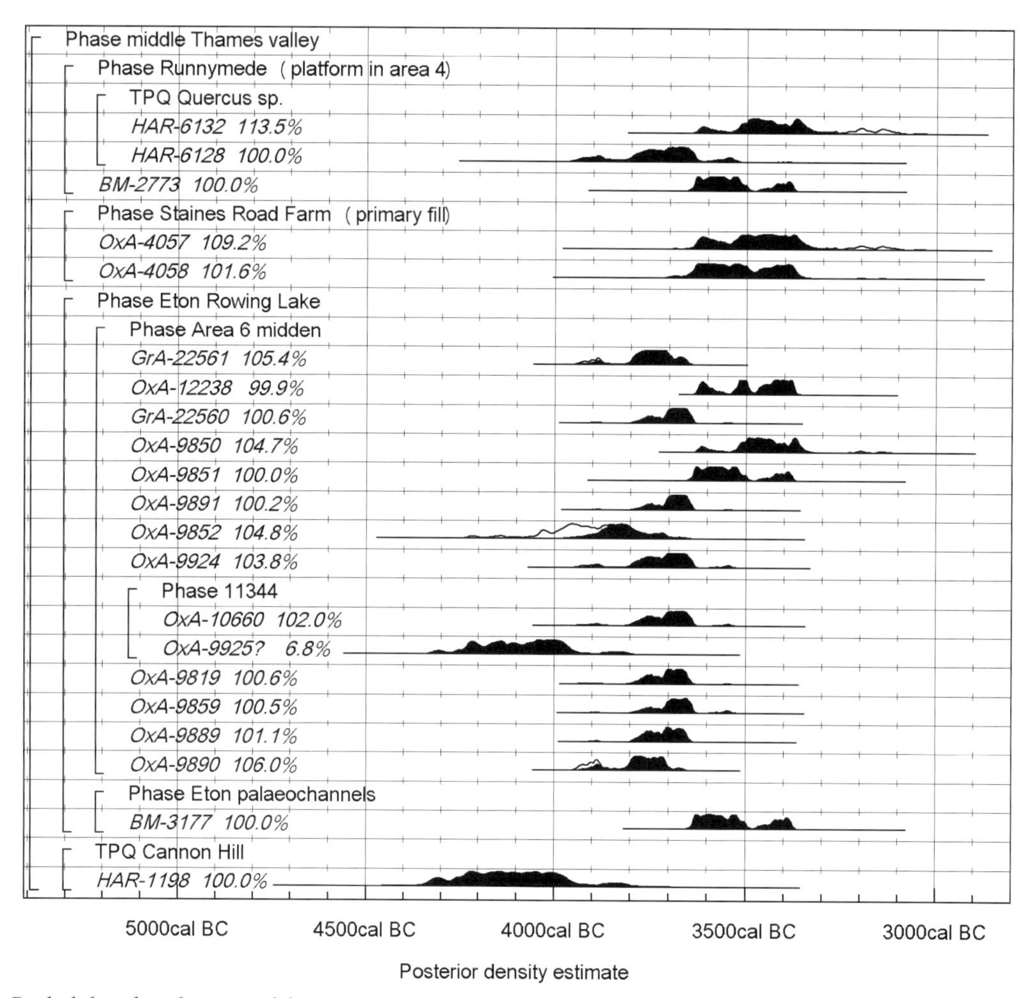

Fig. 14.73. Probability distributions of dates associated with Bowl pottery in the middle Thames valley. The format is identical to that of Fig. 14.1. The overall structure of this model is shown in Fig. 14.72, and its other components in Figs 14.74–6.

are shown in Fig. 14.82. The first monument appeared in south-east England −*155–215 years* after the appearance of the first Neolithic (*95% probability*; Fig. 14.82: *start SE Neolithic/monuments*), probably −*15–145 years* afterwards (*68% probability*). The first monument appeared in south-central England −*60–170 years* after the appearance of the first Neolithic (*95% probability*; Fig. 14.82: *start S central Neolithic/monuments*), probably *10–115 years* afterwards (*68% probability*). In south-west Britain, the first monument appeared −*535–75 years* after the appearance of the first Neolithic (*95% probability*; Fig. 14.82: *start SW Neolithic/monuments*), probably −*245–15 years* afterwards (*68% probability*).

In south-east and south-central England, it appears that monuments may not have formed a primary element of the first Neolithic activity, appearing several generations after that had begun (Fig. 14.82). The start of monumentality in south-west Britain must be later than the first appearance of the Neolithic there, since all the likelihoods relating to monuments are included in the more general model. The estimate for the start of monumentality in this area must therefore be anomalous. This seems to be because we have too few dates from too many monuments in this area to counteract the statistical scatter on our estimates for the use of each monument. In reality, the first monument in the south-west must have been contemporary with or only very slightly later than the first appearance of other Neolithic activity.

These estimates relate to monuments other than causewayed and stone-walled enclosures. The gaps between the earliest Neolithic and the first enclosure in our larger areas are shown in Fig. 14.83. Enclosures do not form an element of the first Neolithic in any of these areas, appearing two or three centuries after the start in south-east and south-central England, and perhaps a century or so later in south-west Britain. It should be noted that the interval shown in Fig. 14.83 for south-west Britain compares the start of Neolithic activity on the south-west peninsula and in south Wales and the Marches with the date of the first enclosure in the south-west peninsula (which is earlier than the first enclosure in south Wales and the Marches).

In more detail, the gaps between the earliest Neolithic and the first enclosure in each of our smaller regions are shown in Fig. 14.84. Here, we have compared the first enclosure in the middle and upper Thames with our estimated dates for the start of the Neolithic in both the

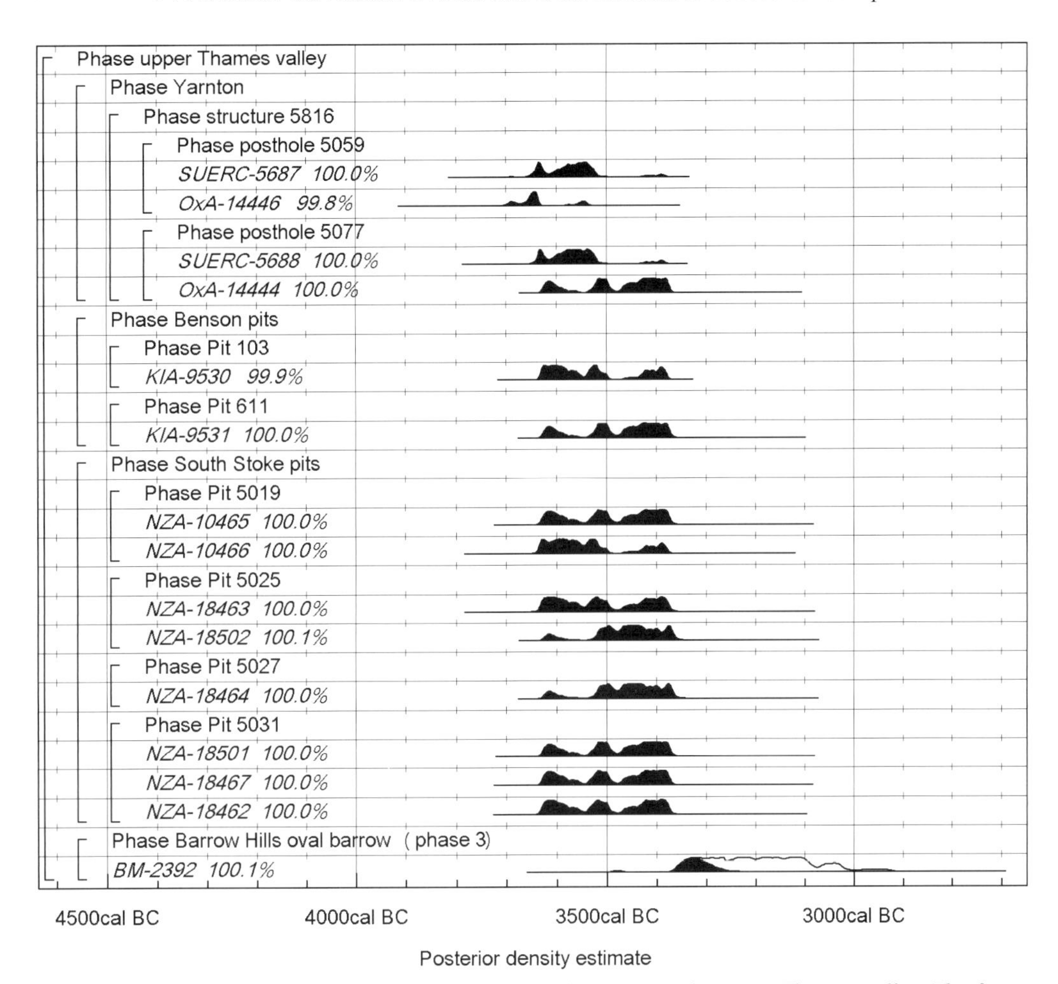

Fig. 14.74. Probability distributions of dates associated with Bowl pottery in the upper Thames valley. The format is identical to that of Fig. 14.1. The overall structure of this model is shown in Fig. 14.72, and its other components in Figs 14.73 and 14.75–6.

middle and upper Thames, and we have compared the date of the start of the Neolithic in north Wessex with the first enclosure in north Wiltshire. The estimates for the start of the Neolithic in south Wessex and the first enclosure in south Wessex are not strictly comparable as data from Salisbury plain are excluded from the former and included in the latter. Despite these slightly different definitions of the regions, the patterns shown are broadly valid. As enclosures come all at a rush, in regions where the Neolithic began comparatively early there was a gap of several centuries between the first Neolithic and the first enclosure. In other regions, where Neolithic activity appeared rather later, building enclosures may have begun perhaps three or four generations after the start of the Neolithic.

So, if neither monuments nor enclosures are elements of the first Neolithic in south-east and south-central England, do enclosures anywhere form primary elements of monumentality? The answer is no. Figure 14.85 shows the numbers of years between the first monument in each of our areas and the first enclosure (here again we have used the estimate for the start of enclosures in the south-west peninsula for this analysis because there are too few dated sites in south Wales and the Marches to provide an overall estimate for the wide south-west British area). In each of the areas considered, enclosures appeared at least two generations after the first monument. In the south-east, this interval was rather longer, probably more than a century. Nowhere, however, was the gap so long that memory of the first monument need have been lost by the time the first enclosure was built.

Is something of the tempo of change in Neolithic lives beginning to emerge out of these analyses? Compare the gap between the start of the Neolithic and the start of monumentality in an area (Fig. 14.82) with the gap between the start of monumentality and the first enclosure in the same area (Fig. 14.85). Could we see, from these estimates, major innovations as following a cycle measurable in lifetimes? We can also remember here the rhythm in the construction of enclosures themselves (Fig. 14.20), with a lull in the early 36th century cal BC, and perhaps a move to the construction of cursus monuments later in that century (Fig. 14.44), which might also conform to approximately the same temporal rhythm. If so, could this point towards important principles of seniority in the Neolithic worldview, or more generally towards the spans of active memory? So when the elders of the community, say, who had initiated

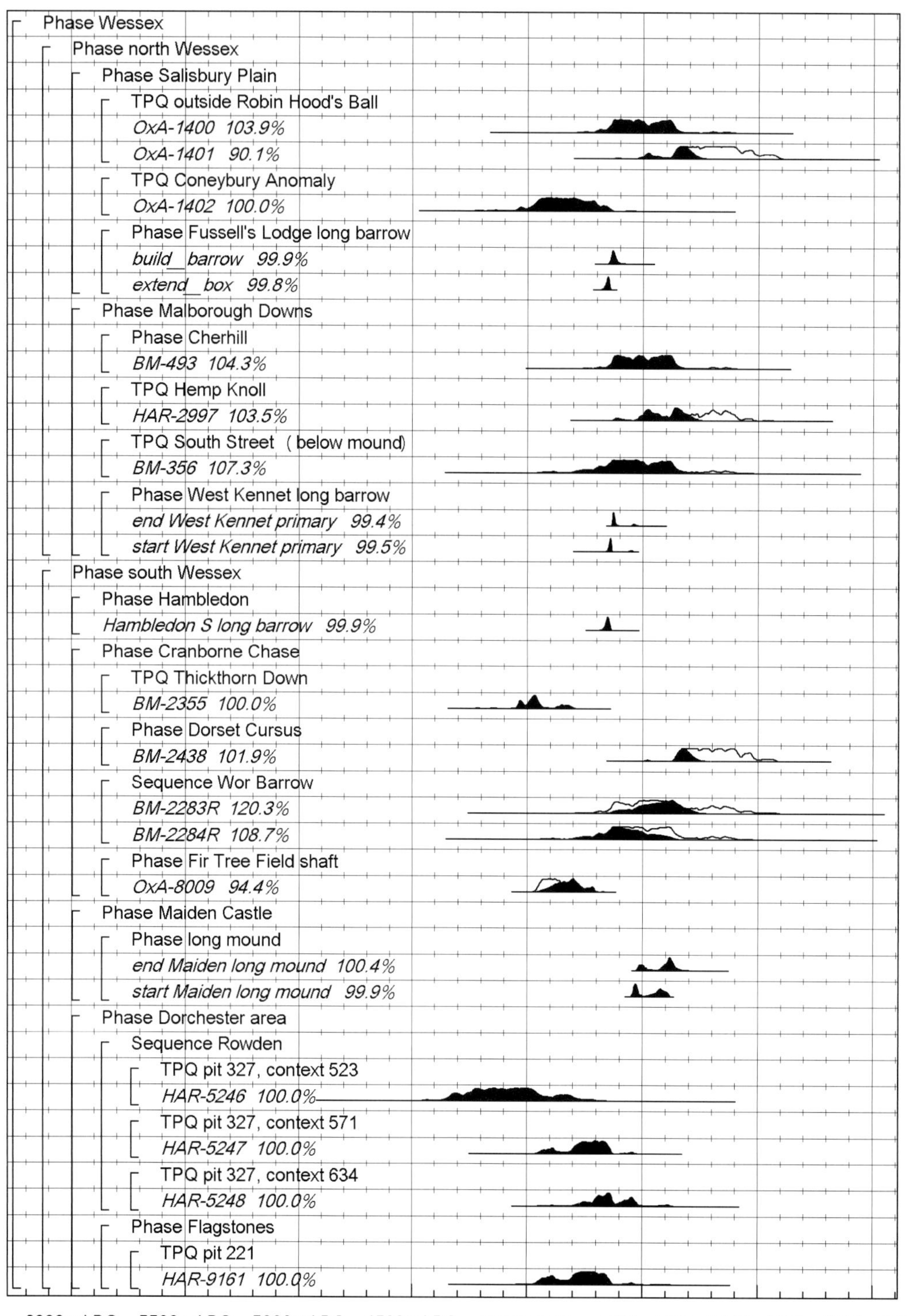

Fig. 14.75. Probability distributions of dates associated with Bowl pottery in Wessex. The format is identical to that of Fig. 14.1. Distributions have been taken from the models defined by Figs 4.7–13 (Hambledon Hill), Fig. 4.21 (Fir Tree Field shaft), Figs 4.41–5 (Maiden Castle), Wysocki et al. *(2007, fig. 10) (Fussell's Lodge), and Bayliss* et al. *(2007b, fig. 6) (West Kennet). The overall structure of this model is shown in Fig. 14.72, and its other components in Figs 14.73–4 and 14.76.*

new practices in their youth, came to the end of their days, did the memory of their achievements pass as their direct power over fresh events faded?

Finally, we consider the date when the early Neolithic ended in southern Britain. Our regional estimates for this transition vary substantially, spanning the latter half of the fourth millennium cal BC (compare, for example, *end Sussex Neolithic* (Fig. 5.32) with *end north Wessex* (Fig. 14.52)). This variability seems to be related to the composition of the dataset in each region, and hints that

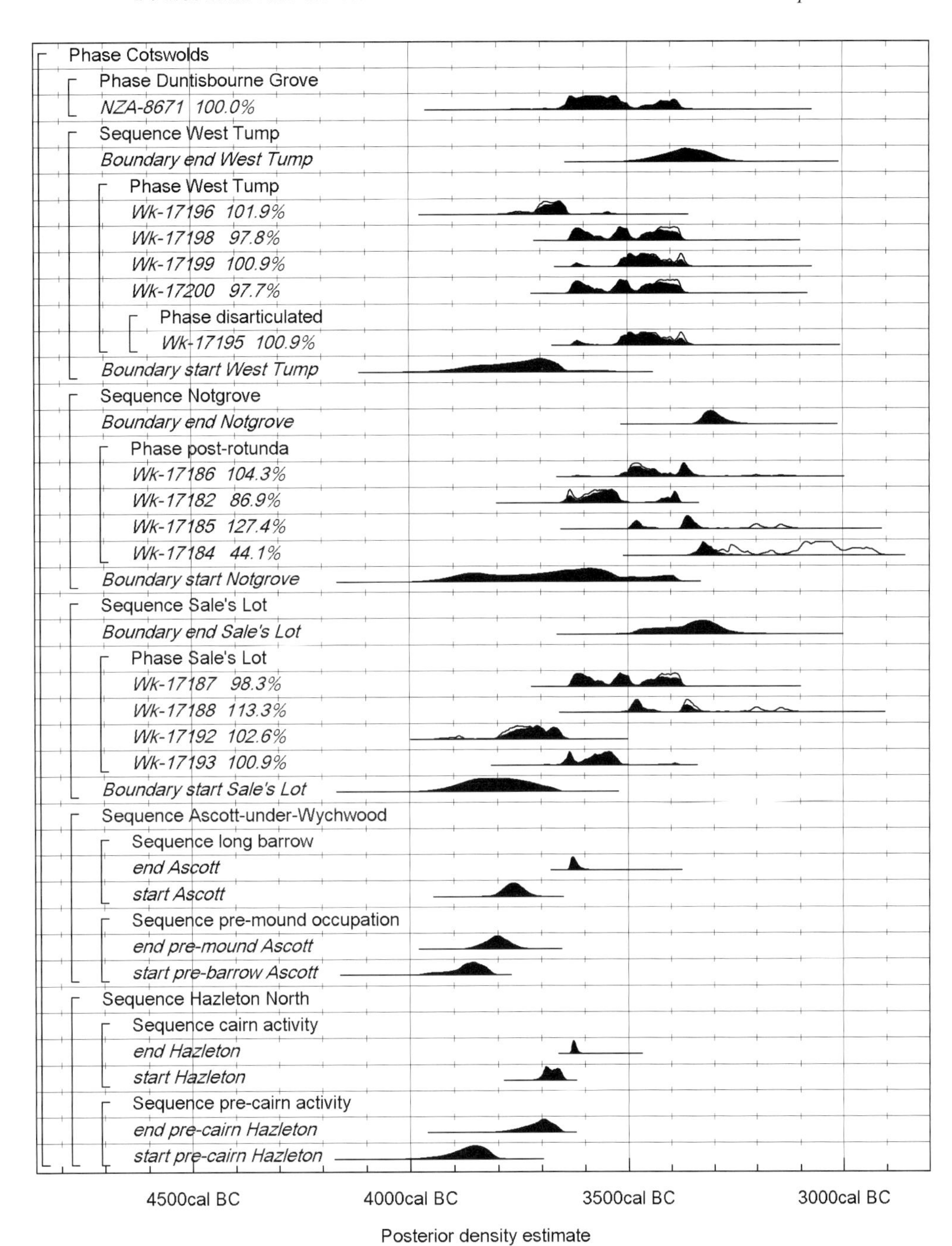

Fig. 14.76. Probability distributions of dates associated with Bowl pottery in the Cotswolds. The format is identical to that of Fig. 14.1. Distributions have been taken from the models defined by Meadows et al. *(2007, figs 6–9) (Hazleton) and Bayliss* et al. *(2007c, figs 3 and 5–7) (Ascott-under-Wychwood). The overall structure of this model is shown in Fig. 14.72, and its other components in Figs 14.73–5.*

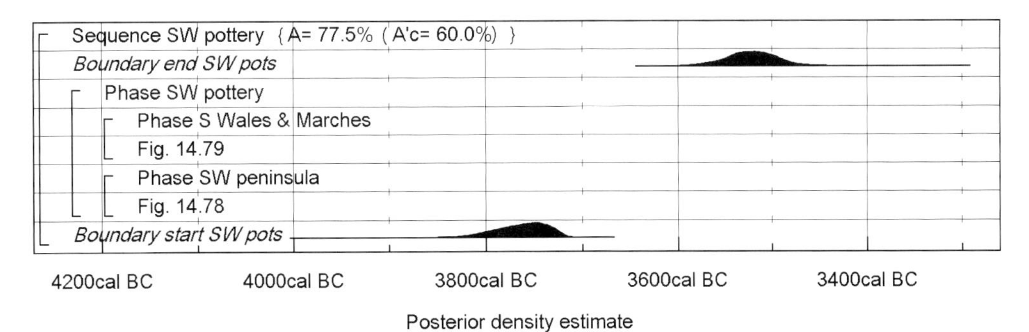

Fig. 14.77. Overall structure of the chronological model for the currency of Bowl pottery in south-west Britain. The component sections of this model are shown in detail in Figs 14.78–9. The large square brackets down the left-hand side of the figures, along with the OxCal keywords, define the overall model exactly.

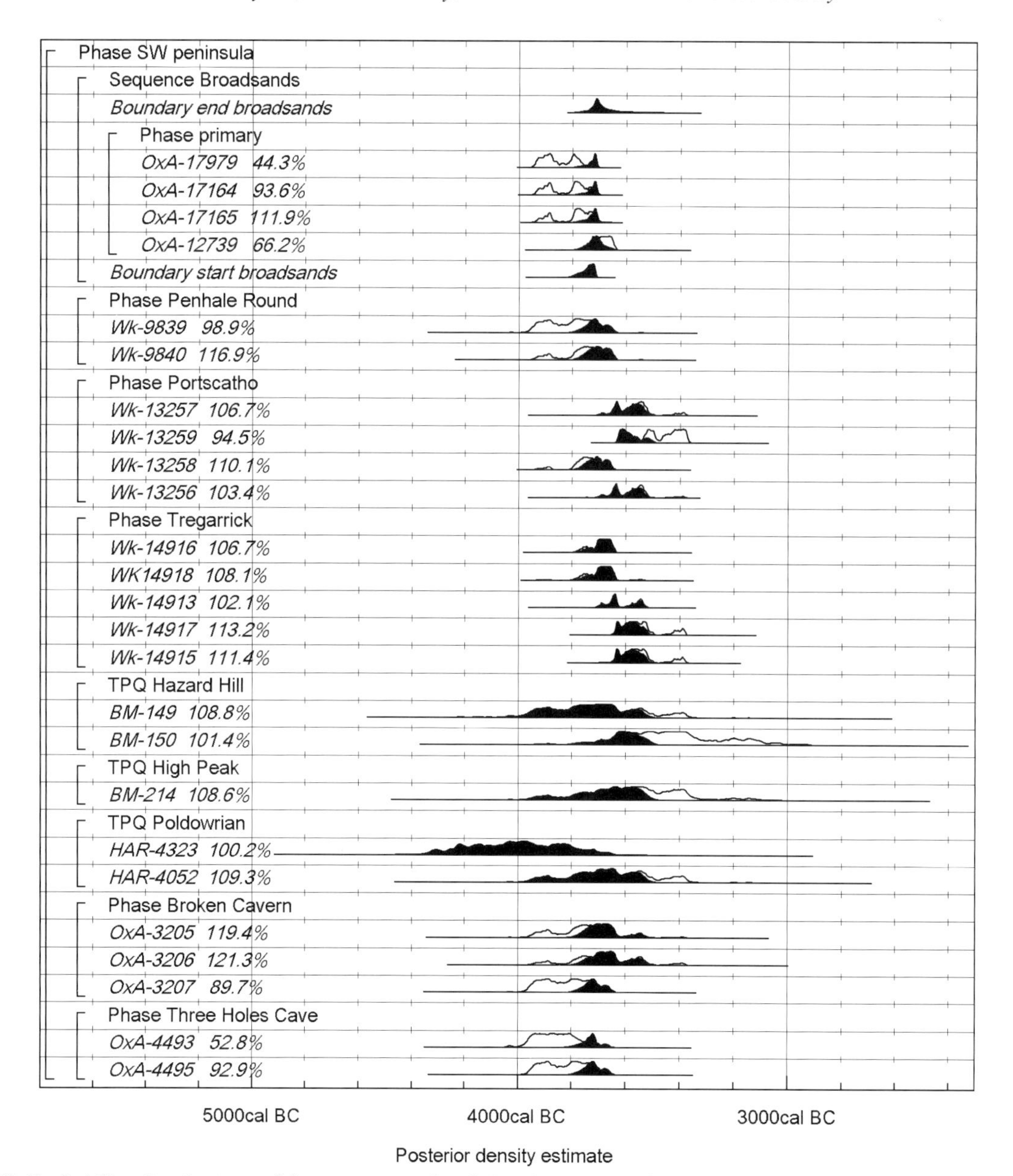

Fig. 14.78. Probability distributions of dates associated with Bowl pottery in the south-west peninsula. The format is identical to that of Fig. 14.1. The overall structure of this model is shown in Fig. 14.77, and its other component in Fig. 14.79.

different early Neolithic things and practices may have fallen out of favour at different times. This is apparent from Fig. 14.86, which shows the date when the early Neolithic ended in each of our larger areas, and the independent estimates for when the currency of Bowl pottery ended and when the monument types included in this study went out of primary use. It is clear that our date estimates for the 'end of the early Neolithic' are composite creations.

The end of the deposition of Bowl pottery in south-east and south-central England probably falls in the later part of the 34th or earlier part of the 33rd century cal BC (Fig. 14.86). The end of this tradition in south-west Britain, however, may be significantly earlier – ending in *3585–3465 cal BC* (*95% probability*; Fig. 14.77: *end SW pots*), probably in *3550–3490 cal BC* (*68% probability*). Table 14.6 shows that we have not dated fewer samples associated with Bowl pottery in south-west Britain than in the other areas, and so it is difficult to explain this difference as sampling bias. This unexpectedly early date for a change in ceramic fashion there may be an aspect of the distinct character of the Neolithic archaeology of the south-west peninsula (Chapter 10) and of parts of south Wales (e.g. Lynch 2000). In the south-west peninsula pottery use may even have diminished, given the scarcity there of Peterborough Ware and subsequently of Grooved Ware (Laidlaw and Mepham 1999, 44–5; Longworth and Cleal 1999).

The ends of the use of the monument types considered in this study in different areas of southern Britain are shown in Fig. 14.86. These agree in placing the end of the currency of these monument types in the first century or two of the third millennium cal BC. Again, not all kinds of monument may have ended at the same time. Linear monuments (Fig. 14.44), monuments that we have grouped as diverse and

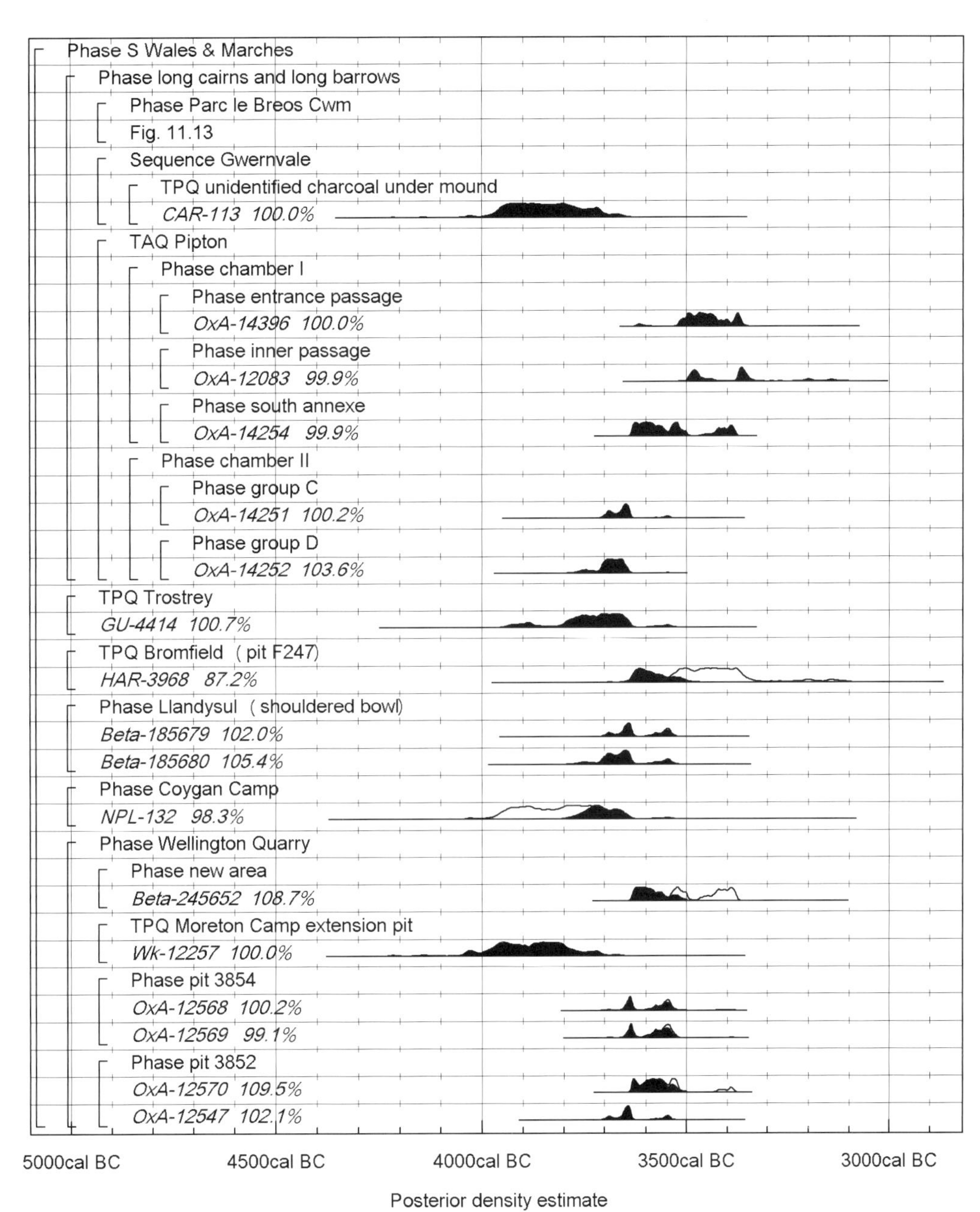

Fig. 14.79. Probability distributions of dates associated with Bowl pottery in south Wales and the Marches. The format is identical to that of Fig. 14.1. The component relating to Parc le Breos Cwm long cairn is shown in Fig. 11.13 (although the posterior density estimates shown on this figure are not those relating to this model). The overall structure of this model is shown in Fig. 14.77, and its other component in Fig. 14.78.

small (Fig. 14.43) and oval barrows (Fig. 14.42) seem to continue to be used into the third millennium. Long barrows and long cairns may have fallen out of favour a century or two earlier (Fig. 14.45). Causewayed and stone-walled enclosures themselves went out of primary use earlier still (Fig. 14.1). The only portal dolmen in southern Britain dated at the time of modelling, Carreg Coetan, may have been constructed around that time (Fig. 11.10).[7]

14.5 Patterns and development of early Neolithic material culture in southern Britain

The often large stratified artefact assemblages from causewayed enclosures have long provided a basis for the periodisation and classification of Neolithic material culture, for example by Piggott (1954). They have also made a major contribution to the interpretation of the uses of the enclosures, both as foci of consumption and exchange and as gathering places for perhaps widely scattered populations. The recognition in the inter-war period of pottery and axeheads of non-local origin at sites such as Hembury, Windmill Hill and Maiden Castle was a stimulus to their sourcing. Since then, all classes of artefact from enclosures have been the subject of study and analysis. This section concerns itself primarily with pottery and axeheads because they are less unevenly documented

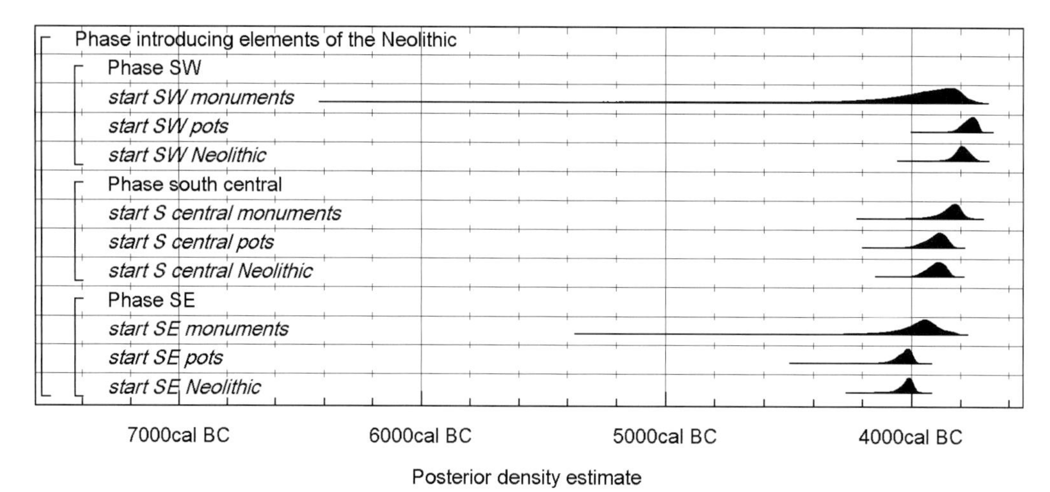

Fig. 14.80. Probability distributions of dates for the start of the early Neolithic, the appearance of pottery and the appearance of monuments in different areas of southern Britain, derived from the models shown in Fig. 14.57, 14.60–7 and 14.68–79.

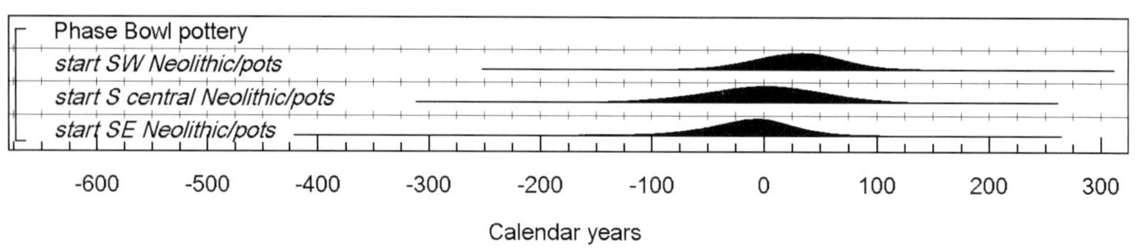

Fig. 14.81. Probability distributions showing the number of years between the appearance of the first Neolithic activity and the first pottery in an area of southern Britain (derived from the distributions shown in Fig. 14.80).

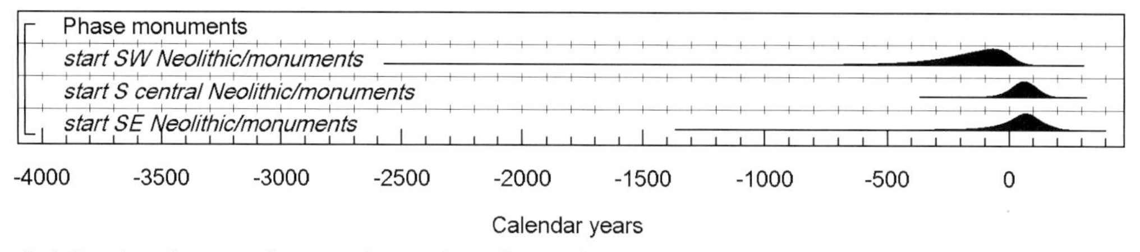

Fig. 14.82. Probability distributions showing the number of years between the appearance of the first Neolithic activity and the first monument in three areas of southern Britain (derived from the distributions shown in Fig. 14.80).

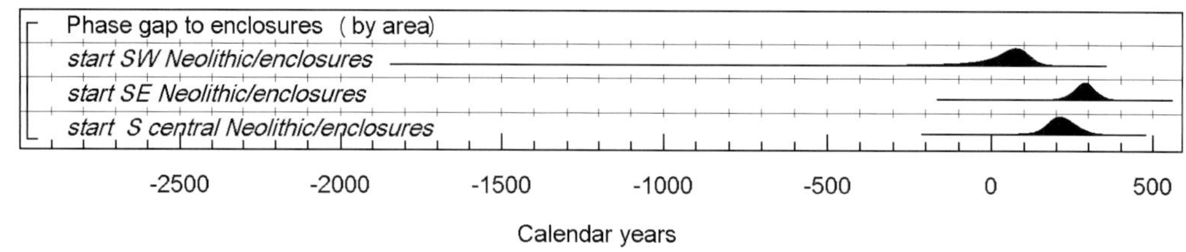

Fig. 14.83. Probability distributions showing the number of years between the appearance of the first Neolithic activity and the first causewayed or stone-walled enclosure in three areas of southern Britain (derived from the distributions shown in Figs 14.18 and 14.57).

across the gamut of enclosures and contexts beyond them than other artefact classes.

Bowl pottery

The date of the introduction of pottery into each broad area of our analysis of southern Britain is summarised in Fig. 14.80. Having earlier examined different components of the range of Neolithic things and practices, we can now investigate the chronology of different ceramic traditions. In the case of Carinated Bowl and other plain Bowl, the available numbers of dated contexts are so few that their chronologies are modelled across the whole of southern Britain (Figs 14.88, 14.90). This is unsatisfactory not only because of the small number of dates, many of which are *termini post quos*, but because pottery seems

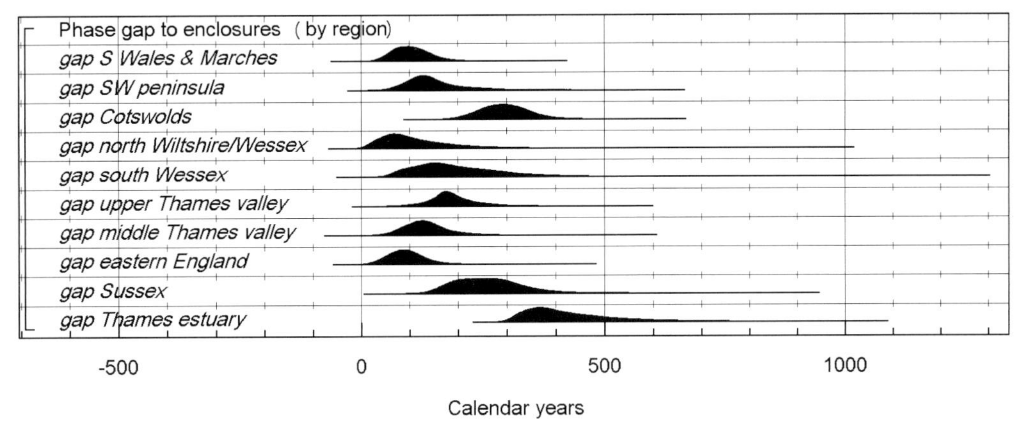

Fig. 14.84. Probability distributions showing the number of years between the appearance of the first Neolithic activity and the first causewayed or stone-walled enclosure in various regions of southern Britain (derived from the distributions shown in Figs 14.15 and 14.54).

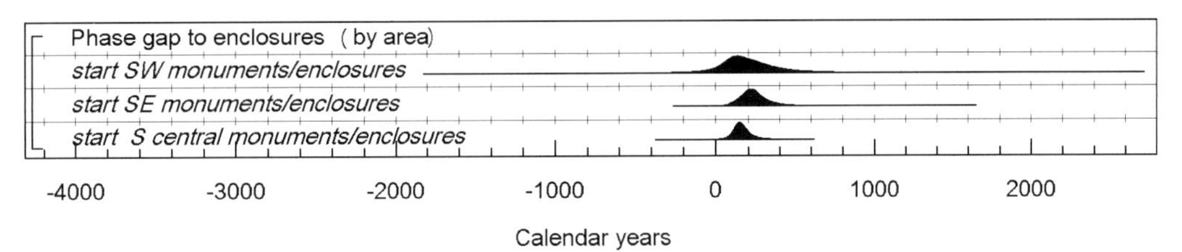

Fig. 14.85. Probability distributions showing the number of years between the appearance of the first monument and the first causewayed or stone-walled enclosure in various areas of southern Britain (derived from the distributions shown in Figs 14.18 and 14.80).

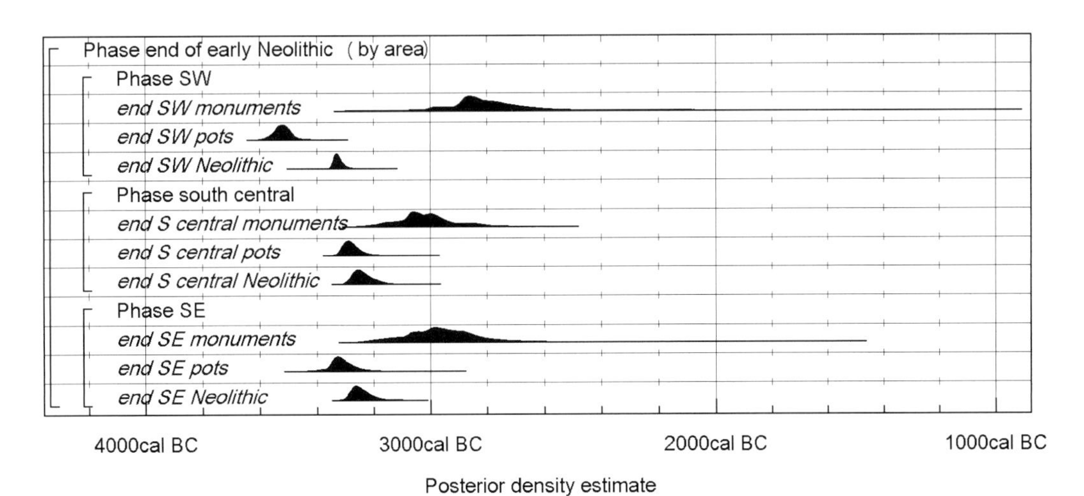

Fig. 14.86. Probability distributions of dates for the end of the early Neolithic, the end of the currency of Bowl pottery, and the final primary use of early Neolithic monuments in different areas of southern Britain, derived from the models shown in Fig. 14.57, Figs 14.60–7, and Figs 14.68–79.

to have come into use at different times in different areas of southern Britain (Fig. 14.80). Fewer sites are included in these analyses than in those for the overall currency of Bowl pottery in the same areas (Fig. 14.80) because some assemblages are so small and fragmentary as to defy finer classification and others are not yet fully analysed or published, so that their character sometimes remains uncertain.

Carinated Bowl. This term is employed to denote assemblages characterised by, although not always consisting completely of, open or neutral Bowls with a change in angle low on the body wall and with light simple or rolled-over rims and a fine finish (Fig. 14.87; Cleal 2004, 177–80). 'Carinated' is not used to encompass all shouldered vessels, as it is by some authors. The tradition is less frequent in the south of Britain than in the north of England, Scotland or Ireland. It occurs thinly through most of the study area, with the possible exception of Cornwall. Its contexts in southern Britain are often non- or pre-monumental (Table 14.7) – a very different situation

Table 14.7. Carinated Bowl pottery associated with the dates shown in Fig. 14.88.

Site	Subdivision	Illustrations or descriptions	Distribution	Notes
Little Waltham	Pit 251	Drury 1978, fig. 36	*HAR-1087*	
Yabsley Street		S. Coles *et al.* 2008, fig. 4	*KIA-20157*	
Orton Meadows	1st alignment	Mackreth forthcoming	UB-3248	Date for articulated burial in 2nd alignment provides *terminus ante quem* for pot in 1st alignment
Peacock's Farm	Scatter of Neolithic occupation material in peat	J. Clark *et al.* 1935, figs 12–13	*Q-525/6, Q-527/8, CAR-790*	
Barleycroft Paddocks	F591	C. Evans *et al.* 1999 (verbal description only)	*OxA-8110*	
Cannon Hill	Pit 1, layer 4. In single black layer with charcoal, struck flint (inc. leaf arrowhead and microlith), bone fragments, in a feature which was probably a solution pipe	Bradley *et al.* 1981, fig. 5: 1–9	*HAR-1198*	
South Street		Ashbee *et al.* 1979, fig 30: 1, 2	*BM-356*	
Rowden	Pit 327	P. Woodward 1991, fig. 52	*HAR-5248*	
Ascott-under-Wychwood	Pre-barrow midden	Barclay and Case 2007, figs 10.1–3	Between *start Ascott pre-barrow* and *end Ascott pre-barrow*	
Hazleton	Pre-cairn occupation	Smith and Darvill 1990, fig. 156	Between *start pre-cairn Hazleton* and *end pre-cairn Hazelton*	
Sweet Track		I. Smith 1976; Kinnes 1979b; Coles and Orme 1984a; Coles and Coles 1986, fig. 15	*Sweet Track*	
Broadsands		Radford 1958; Sheridan *et al.* 2008	Between *start broadsands* and *end broadsands*	
Gwernvale	F68	Britnell and Savory 1984, figs 38, 39, 43	*CAR-113*	

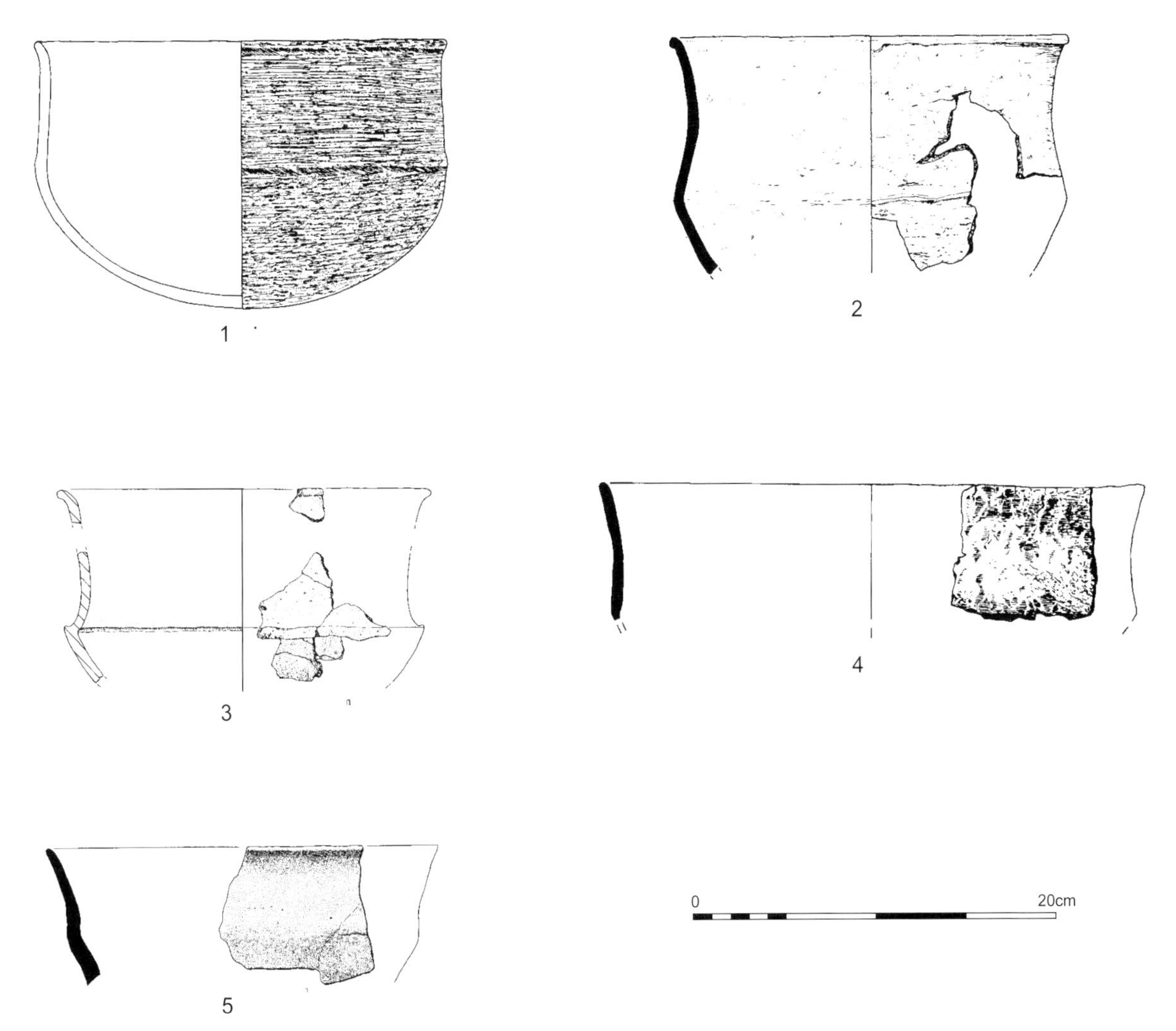

Fig. 14.87. Carinated Bowl pottery. 1 found in two heaps 1 m apart beside the Sweet Track, site R, after J. Coles et al. *(1973, 288–9); 2 from pit 327 at Rowden, after Woodward (1991, fig. 52); 3 from the pre-cairn occupation at Ascott-under-Wychwood, after Barclay and Case (2007, fig. 10.1); 4 found behind the head of a possibly female skeleton buried in a grave at Yabsley Street, Blackwall, after S. Coles* et al. *(2008, fig. 4); 5 from Lane Fox's (later Pitt Rivers') excavations in the Cissbury flint mines, after Barber* et al. *(1999, fig. 5.13).*

from farther north and west. The only indication of relation to an enclosure is in a brief description of the unpublished Chalk Hill pottery '. . . the assemblage contained a mixture of early Carinated Bowls (represented by fragmentary or residual material) with much larger quantities of Plain and shouldered Bowls', with relatively little decoration (Gibson and Leivers 2008, 252).

A model for the currency of Carinated Bowl in southern Britain is shown in Fig. 14.88. This estimates that the tradition first appeared in southern Britain in *4185–3975 cal BC* (*95% probability*; Fig. 14.88: *start CB S Britain*), probably in *4080–3990 cal BC* (*68% probability*). The tradition ended in southern Britain in *3715–3505 cal BC* (*95% probability*; Fig. 14.88: *end CB S Britain*), probably in *3685–3595 cal BC* (*68% probability*). The early date estimate for the introduction of this pottery type is entirely due to the date from Yabsley Street, Blackwall (Fig. 14.88: *KIA-20157*); no other dated assemblage from southern Britain need be earlier than 3800 cal BC.

Plain Bowl. Undecorated assemblages include some which do not correspond to even a broad definition of Carinated Bowl, their features including closed forms as well as open or neutral ones, bag-like, rounded or heavily shouldered profiles, some heavier rims, and coarser, thicker fabrics than those of much Carinated Bowl (Fig. 14.89). The assemblages and single vessels listed in Table 14.8 exclude indeterminate fragments. They fall into two main groups. Some could have been drawn from the undecorated component of Decorated assemblages, for example the single vessels placed in tomb chambers at Ascott-under-Wychwood (Barclay and Case 2007, fig. 10.4) and Hazleton (Smith and Darvill 1990, fig. 157: 33), or the relatively few sherds from the Etton Woodgate enclosure (Gdaniec 2005). Others are coherent assemblages of distinct, but not uniform, character. An obvious example is provided by over 400 vessels from Broome Heath, Norfolk, which lack decoration apart from rare fluting or rilling and are morphologically distinct from both local Decorated

Table 14.8. Plain Bowl pottery associated with the dates shown in Fig. 14.90.

Site	Sub-division	Illustrations or descriptions	Distribution
South-east			
Etton Woodgate	In ditches	Gdaniec 2005	Between *start Woodgate* and *end Woodgate*
Eynesbury	Pit 2716	Mepham 2004, fig. 17	*NZA-14576*
Gorhambury	In bedding trenches of structure	Neal *et al.* 1990, fig. 152: 1–4	*HAR-3484*
Padholme Road, Fengate	In bedding trenches of structure	Pryor 1974, fig. 6	*GaK-4197*
Broome Heath	Mainly in pits	Wainwright 1972, figs 25–34	*BM-756, BM-757*
South-centre			
Staines Road Farm	In first phase of ring ditch, and in second phase probably derived from first phase	P. Jones 2008	*OxA-4057, OxA-4058*
Gatehampton Farm, Goring	Ditch	T. Allen 1995, fig. 58: PRNs 4, 5, 6, 7, 8/104	Between *GrA-31358* and *BM-2835*
Ascott-under-Wychwood	Southern passage area	Barclay and Case 2007, fig. 10.4	Between *primary construction Ascott* and *end Ascott*
Cherhill		Evans and Smith 1983, fig. 23	*BM-493*
Coneybury Anomaly	In pit	J. Richards 1990, figs 28–31	*OxA-1402*
Fir Tree Field shaft	Hearth	French *et al.* 2007, fig. A4.7:P35	*OxA-8009*
Wor Barrow	Ditch	Cleal 1991, fig. 7.15: P175	*BM-2283R, BM-2284R*
Burn Ground	Near edge of blocking of S entrance to transverse chamber	Grimes 1960, fig. 30: upper	Before *end Burn Ground*
Hazleton	Lower fills of S chamber and passage	Smith and Darvill 1990, fig. 157:33	Between *construction finished* and *end Hazleton*
South-west			
Coygan Camp	In pit	Wainwright 1967	*NPL-132*
Parc le Breos Cwm	Multiple contexts, some sherds from pre-cairn surface	Whittle and Wysocki 1998, fig. 28: 5–7, possibly all one pot	Before *start Parc le Breos Cwm*

Table 14.9. Decorated Bowl pottery associated with the dates shown in Figs 14.92–9.

Site	Sub-division	South-Western element in assemblage	Illustrations or descriptions	Distribution
South-east				
Chalk Hill				Between *start Chalk Hill* and *end Chalk Hill*
Kingsborough 1			M. Allen *et al.* 2008, figs 7–8	Between *start Kingsborough 1* and *end Kingsborough 1*
Kingsborough 2			M. Allen *et al.* 2008, fig. 9	Between *start Kingsborough 2* and *end Kingsborough 2*
Orsett			Hedges and Buckley 1978, figs 32–35	Between *start Orsett* and *end Orsett*
Saltwood Tunnel				*NZA-20599, -20600*
St Osyth			Germany 2007, figs 44–48	Between *start St Osyth* and *end St Osyth*
The Stumble			N. Brown 1998, figs 78, 79	*OxA-2298, -2299*
Bury Hill	Both decorated sherds (drawings 4 and 5) described as from lower silts (Bedwin 1981, 82)		Bedwin 1981, fig. 7: 1–10	Between *build Bury Hill* and *end Bury Hill*
Offham Hill			Drewett 1977, fig. 11: 1, 2, 3, 5–12, 14, 19, 20	*burial 1*
Whitehawk			Ross Williamson 1930, pls V–VII; Curwen 1934a, figs 5–13, 23–40; Curwen 1936, figs 1–19	Between *build Whitehawk* and *end Whitehawk*
The Trundle			Curwen 1929b, pls VII–X; 1931, figs 10–14	*OxA-14009, OxA-14024*
Bevis' Thumb			Drewett 1981, 24	*I-11843*
Orton Meadows	2nd alignment			*UB-3248*
Barleycroft Paddocks	F463		C. Evans *et al.* 1999	*OxA-8108*
Briar Hill			Bamford 1985, figs 52–55	*build Briar Hill*
Etton			Pryor 1998, figs 175–201	Between *start Etton* and *end Etton*
Grendon	Area C ring ditch V		Gibson and McCormick 1985, figs 18–20	*HAR-1497, HAR-1498, HAR -1495?*
Haddenham enclosure			Gdaniec 2006, fig. 5.32: 1–6	Between *start Haddenham* and *end Haddenham*
Haddenham long barrow	Phase I, close to posthole of façade; Phase III		Knight 2006a, fig. 3.58:P1, P2, fig. 3.60)	*HAR-9173, HAR -9176, Haddenham LB*
Kilverstone			Garrow *et al.* 2006, figs 2.15–2.32	Between *start Kilverstone* and *end Kilverstone*
Maiden Bower			Piggott 1931, fig. 6; Matthews 1976, 8–9	Between *start Maiden Bower* and *end Maiden Bower*
Parnwell				*NZA-24076, -24077*
Whiteleaf			Childe and Smith 1954, figs 5–7	*NZA-21036*
South-central				
Abingdon			Avery 1982, Figs 14–19, Case 1956, figs 3–4	Between *start Abingdon* and *end Abingdon*
St Helen's Avenue, Benson			Pine and Ford 2003, fig. 10, fig. 11: 20–24	*KIA-9530, -9531*
Eton Wick			Ford 1993, microfiche	Between *start Eton Wick* and *end Eton Wick*
Fussell's Lodge	Under/in bone group A		Ashbee 1966, fig. 5: W1	Between *build_box* and *extend_box*
Fussell's Lodge	At proximal end of 'collapsed mortuary house'		Ashbee 1966, figs 5–6: W2–W9	*Build_barrow*
Hambledon Hill		Yes	I. Smith 2008a, figs 9.8, 9.9	Between *start Hambledon* and *end Hambledon*
Hazleton	Hearth on top of primary fill of S quarry		Smith and Darvill 1990, fig. 157:32	Between *start Hazleton* and *end Hazleton*
Hemp Knoll	Pits beneath barrow		M. Robertson-Mackay 1980, fig. 4: P1–P5	*HAR-2997*

Site	Sub-division	South-Western element in assemblage	Illustrations or descriptions	Distribution
Knap Hill		Yes	Connah 1965, fig. 6: 1–7	Between *start Knap Hill* and *end Knap Hill*
Pits outside Robin Hood's Ball		Yes	J. Richards 1990, 61	*OxA-1400, OxA-1401*
Peak Camp			Darvill 1981; 1982a	Between *start Peak Camp* and *end Peak Camp*
Runnymede Bridge			Needham 1991, figs 67–69	Between *start Runnymede occupation* and *end Runnymede occupation*
South Stoke			Timby *et al.* 2005, fig. 19: 1–11	*NZA-18463* to *NZA-18466, NZA -18502*
Staines			R. Robertson-Mackay 1987, figs 38–55	between *start Staines* and *end Staines*
West Kennet long barrow			Piggott 1962, fig. 10	between *start West Kennet primary* and *end West Kennet primary*
Windmill Hill		Yes	I. Smith 1965a, figs 14–29	Between *start Windmill Hill* and *end Windmill Hill*
South-west			Murphy and Evans 2005	
Cwm Meudwy, Llandysul				*Beta-185679, Beta-185680*
Ty Isaf	All chambers except IV (rotunda = chamber III)		Grimes 1939, fig. 6	Between *start Ty Isaf rotunda* and *end Ty Isaf rotunda*
Wellington Quarry			Jackson and Miller forthcoming	*OxA-12547, OxA-12568 to OxA -12570*
Bromfield	F247		Stanford 1982, fig. 5: 55–59	*HAR-3968*

assemblages and classic Carinated Bowl ones, although closer to the former (Wainwright 1972, figs 25–45; Herne 1988; Cleal 1992). At Broome Heath, the assemblage predates the enclosure by a substantial interval (Chapter 6), and, although miscellaneous plain wares are associated with other enclosures, none of these is a classic causewayed enclosure. They comprise the atypical, ill-defined circuit at Gatehampton Farm, Goring (Fig. 8.10), the incompletely enclosing ditches of Etton Woodgate (Fig. 6.35), and possibly the continuous enclosure in Hill Croft Field, Herefordshire, the pottery from which is so far (2009) unpublished. The pits at Broome Heath and an irregular hollow at Cherhill, Wiltshire (Evans and Smith 1983), are more typical of the contexts of this group of material.

A model for the currency of plain Bowl in southern Britain is shown in Fig. 14.90. This estimates that plain Bowl assemblages first appeared in southern Britain in *3970–3715 cal BC* (*95% probability*; Fig. 14.90: *start plain Bowl*), probably in *3855–3730 cal BC* (*68% probability*). They ceased to be deposited in southern Britain in *3475–3385 cal BC* (*8% probability*; Fig. 14.90: *end plain Bowl*) or *3375–3095 cal BC* (*87% probability*), probably in *3355–3210 cal BC* (*68% probability*). Although the category is composite, a couple of points can be made. In areas where Carinated Bowl occurs, other traditions were already present in the first quarter of the fourth millennium cal BC. The earlier assemblages probably include the 40 or so vessels at from the Coneybury Anomaly, singled out as distinctive by both Cleal (2004, 171–3) and Pailler and Sheridan (2009, 14–15), whether or not they reflect the north-west French connection suggested by the last two authors. This is so far dated only by a *terminus post quem*, measured on disarticulated animal bone (Fig. 14.90: OxA-1402); the probability that the deposit in question was dumped in a single event suggests, however, that the date may be close to the age of the assemblage, and the presence of articulated animal bone renders this verifiable (Chapter 4). If dates measured on bulk charcoal samples in the 1970s provide reliable *termini post quos*, then, in eastern England at least, some assemblages produced towards the end of the currency of Bowl pottery included those characterised by rounded forms, less emphatic rims than those of decorated assemblages, and rare rilling or fluting, as at Broome Heath and Padholme Road, Fengate (Fig. 14.90: *BM-756–7, GaK-4197).*

Decorated Bowl. Regional styles of Decorated Bowl were defined by Piggott (1954, 70–75) and adumbrated by I. Smith (1956) on the basis of a far smaller corpus of material than is now available. As more and more assemblages have been excavated, the Windmill style of north Wessex, the Abingdon style of the Thames valley, the Mildenhall style of East Anglia and the Whitehawk style of Sussex have tended to grade into each other, and Whittle's Decorated style, encompassing them all (1977b, 85–94), seems increasingly realistic. The assemblages are characterised by closed as well as neutral and sometimes open forms, both shouldered and unshouldered profiles, the former often with ledge-like shoulders, heavy rims, and

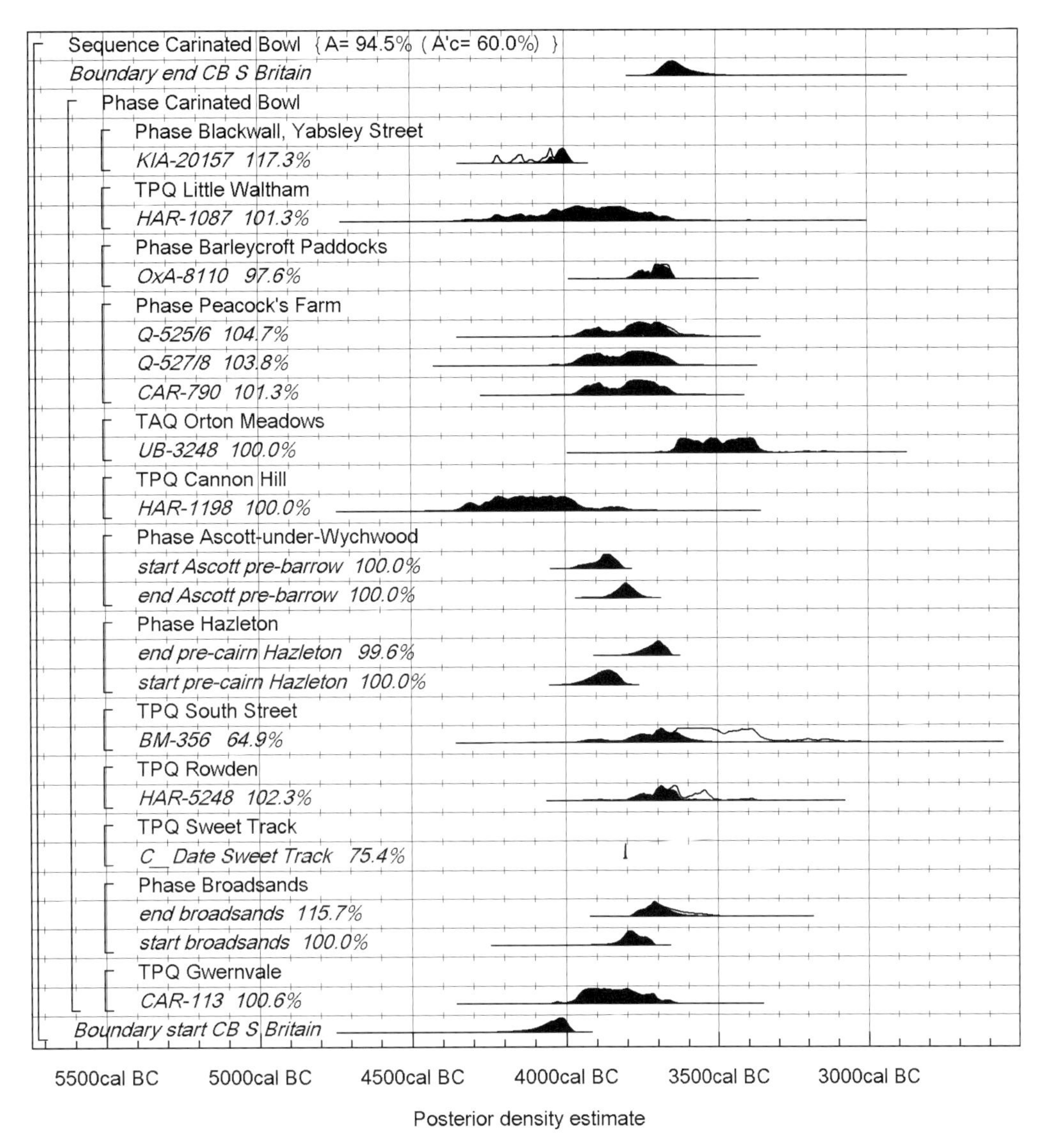

Fig. 14.88. Probability distributions of dates associated with Carinated Bowl pottery from southern Britain. The format is the same as for Fig. 14.1. Distributions have been taken from the models defined in Fig. 6.18 (Peacock's Farm) and Fig. 10.30 (Broadsands), and by Meadows et al. *(2007, figs 6–9) (Hazleton) and Bayliss* et al. *(2007c, figs 3 and 5–7) (Ascott-under-Wychwood). The large square brackets down the left-hand side of the diagram, along with the OxCal keywords, define the overall model exactly.*

decoration, generally linear and punctiform, on a minority of vessels (Fig. 14.91). This is classically the style found in causewayed enclosures, except in the south-west peninsula and adjoining areas, the only part of southern Britain from which it seems to be absent. There are numerous other occurrences, notably in pits.

In Wessex, where the distributions of Decorated and South-Western styles overlap, there is a particular diversity of assemblages, some combining elements of both. The largest such are from Hambledon Hill, in which there is a small Decorated element in a largely South-Western assemblage (I. Smith 2008a), and Windmill Hill where the Decorated element is dominant (I. Smith 1965a, 59–73; Zienkiewicz and Hamilton 1999, 286–7). In these cases, the relevant dates are included in the models for both the Decorated and South-Western styles, as indicated in Tables 14.9–10.

The overall structure of a model for the currency of Decorated Bowl in southern Britain is shown in Fig. 14.92. Since there are enough data to enable the currency of this tradition to be dated in different areas, the component section for south-east England is given in Figs 14.94–5, that for south-central England in Figs 14.97–8, and that for south-west Britain (in this case Wales and the Marches only) in Fig. 14.99. This model estimates that Decorated Bowl first appeared in southern Britain in *3745–3690 cal BC* (*95% probability*; Fig. 14.92: *start Decorated*), probably in *3730–3700 cal BC* (*68% probability*), and ended in southern Britain in *3315–3245 cal BC* (*95% probability*; Fig. 14.92: *end Decorated*), probably in *3305–3270 cal BC* (*68% probability*).

The model for the currency of Decorated Bowl in south-east England is given in Figs 14.93–5. This estimates that the tradition began in this area in *3780–3685 cal BC* (*95%

Table 14.10. South-Western style pottery associated with the dates shown in Figs 14.101–6.

Site	**Sub-division**	**Decorated element in assemblage**	**Gabbroic fabrics present**	**Drawings**	**Distribution**
South-central					
Knap Hill		Yes		Connah 1965, fig. 6: 1–7	Between *start Knap Hill* and *end Knap Hill*
Windmill Hill		Yes	Yes		Between *start Windmill Hill* and *end Windmill Hill*
Hambledon Hill		Yes	Yes	I. Smith 2008a, figs 9.1–9.9	Between *start Hambledon* and *end Hambledon*, gabbroic fabrics present from *Hambledon S long barrow*
Robin Hood's Ball			Yes	N. Thomas 1964a, fig. 4	Between *start Robin Hood's Ball* and *end Robin Hood's Ball*
Pits outside Robin Hood's Ball		Yes		J. Richards 1990, 61 (verbal description only)	*OxA-1400, OxA-1401*
Flagstones	Pits 221, 274			Cleal 1997, fig. 64: 14–16	*HAR-9161*
Maiden Castle			Yes	Cleal 1991, fig. 141:1, 2, 4, 5, 7; Wheeler 1943, figs 26–37	South-Western: from *start Maiden enclosure* to end *Maiden long mound*; gabbroic fabrics from *start Maiden enclosure* to *end Maiden enclosure*, with direct residue dates on sherds: *GrA-29111, 553; OxA-X-2135-46*
Thickthorn Down				Drew and Piggott 1936, pl. XXII: upper	*BM-2355*
Whitesheet Hill			Yes	Cleal 2004, fig. 9	South-Western between *start Whitesheet Hill* and *end Whitesheet Hill*; gabbroic fabrics between *start Whitesheet Hill* and *GrA-30067*
South-west					
Broken Cavern					*OxA-3205, OxA-3206, OxA-3207*
Carn Brea			Yes	Mercer 1981a, figs 66–74	Between *start Carn Brea* and *end Carn Brea*
Hazard Hill			Yes	Houlder 1963, fig. 7, upper	*BM-149, BM-150*
Helman Tor			Yes	Mercer 1997, figs 7–8	South-Western between *start Helman Tor* and *end Helman Tor*; gabbroic fabrics also *HT86 697*
Hembury			Yes	Liddell 1931, pl. XXVII; 1932, pl. XVIII; 1935, pls XXXVI, XXXVII	Between *start Hembury* and *end Hembury*
High Peak		South-Western	Yes	S. Pollard 1966, fig. 9: 1–7	*BM-214*
Penhale Round		South-Western	Yes		South-Western: *Wk-9839, Wk-9840*; gabbroic farbrics: *Wk-9839*
Poldowrian	Pit 106	South-Western		Smith and Harris 1982	*HAR-4323*
Portscatho		South-Western	Yes	Jones and Reed 2006, fig. 4	South-Western: *Wk-13256, Wk-13257, Wk-13258, Wk-13259*; gabbroic fabrics: *Wk-13256, Wk-13258, Wk-13259*
Raddon		South-Western	Yes		Between *start Raddon* and *end Raddon*
Tregarrick		South-western	Yes	Cole and Jones 2003, figs 4–5	South-Western: *WK-14913, Wk-14915 to Wk-14917*; gabbroic fabrics *Wk-14913, Wk-14915, Wk-14916, Wk-14917, Wk-14918*

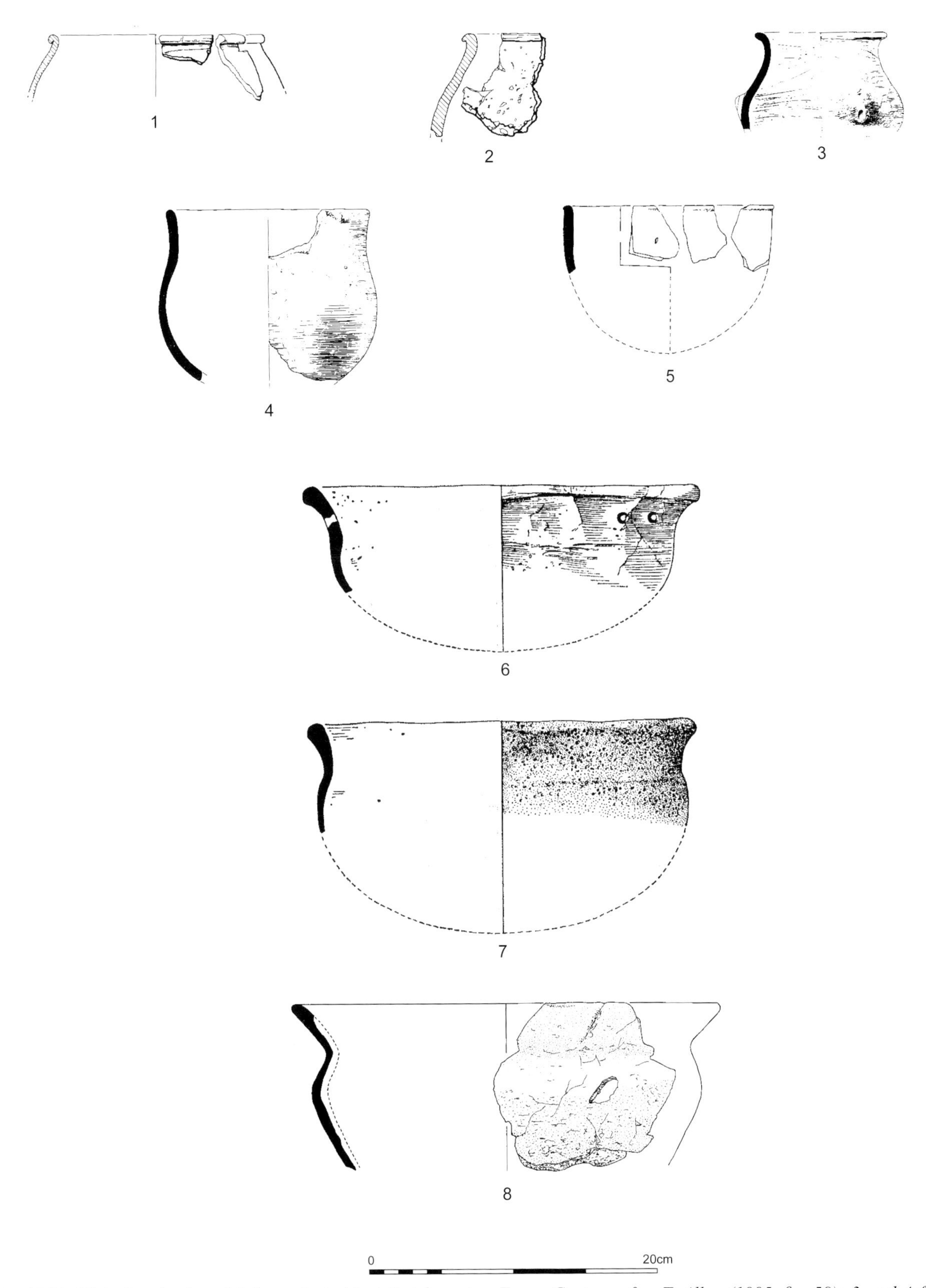

Fig. 14.89. Plain Bowls. 1 and 2 from ditch 46 at Gatehampton Farm, Goring, after T. Allen (1995, fig. 58); 3 and 4 from the Coneybury Anomaly after Cleal (1990a, fig. 29); 5 from layer 6a in the Fir Tree Field shaft, after French et al. *(2007, fig. A4.7); 6 and 7 from pit 40 at Broome Heath, after Wainwright (1972, fig. 28); 8 from Padholme Road, Fengate, after Pryor (1974, fig. 6).*

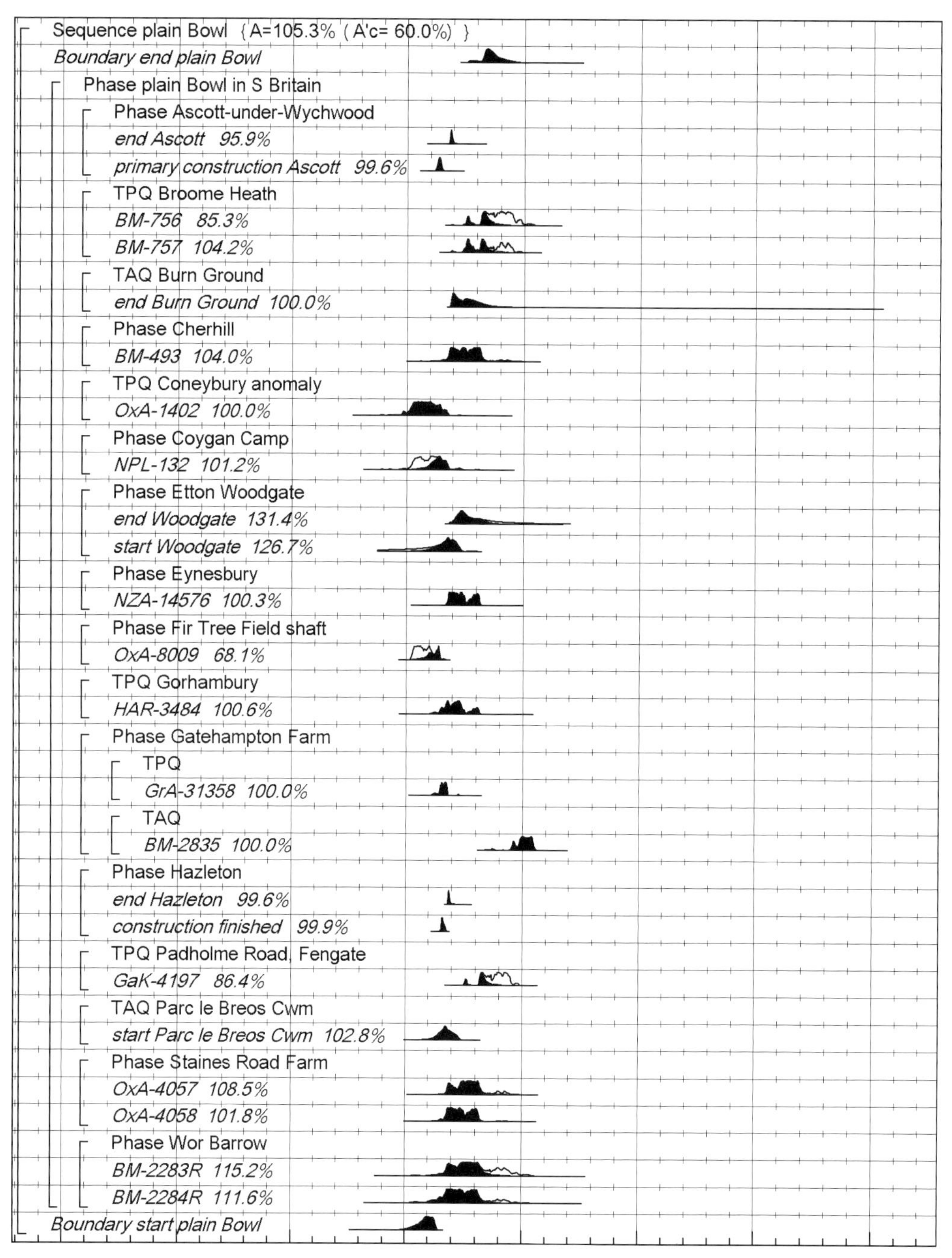

Fig. 14.90. Probability distributions of dates associated with plain Bowl pottery from southern Britain. The format is the same as for Fig. 14.1. Distributions have been taken from the models defined in Fig. 4.21 (Fir Tree Field shaft), Fig. 6.36 (Etton Woodgate), Fig. 9.25 (Burn Ground), and Fig. 11.13 (Parc le Breos Cwm) and by Meadows et al. *(2007, figs 6–9) (Hazleton) and Bayliss* et al. *(2007c, figs 3 and 5–7) (Ascott-under-Wychwood). The large square brackets down the left-hand side of the diagram, along with the OxCal keywords, define the overall model exactly.*

probability; Fig. 14.93: *start Decorated SE*), probably in *3745–3700 cal BC* (*68% probability*). In this area, the tradition ended in *3310–3185 cal BC* (*95% probability*; Fig. 14.93: *end Decorated SE*), probably in *3295–3225 cal BC* (*68% probability*).

The model for the currency of Decorated Bowl in south-central England is defined in Figs 14.96–8. This estimates that the tradition began in this area in *3770–3670 cal BC* (*95% probability*; Fig. 14.96: *start Decorated S central*), probably in *3735–3685 cal BC* (*68% probability*). In this area, the tradition ended in *3335–3245 cal BC* (*95% probability*; Fig. 14.96: *end Decorated S central*), probably in *3325–3285 cal BC* (*68% probability*).

The model for the currency of Decorated Bowl in south-west Britain (Wales and the Marches only) is defined in Fig. 14.99. Because dated occurrences of the tradition

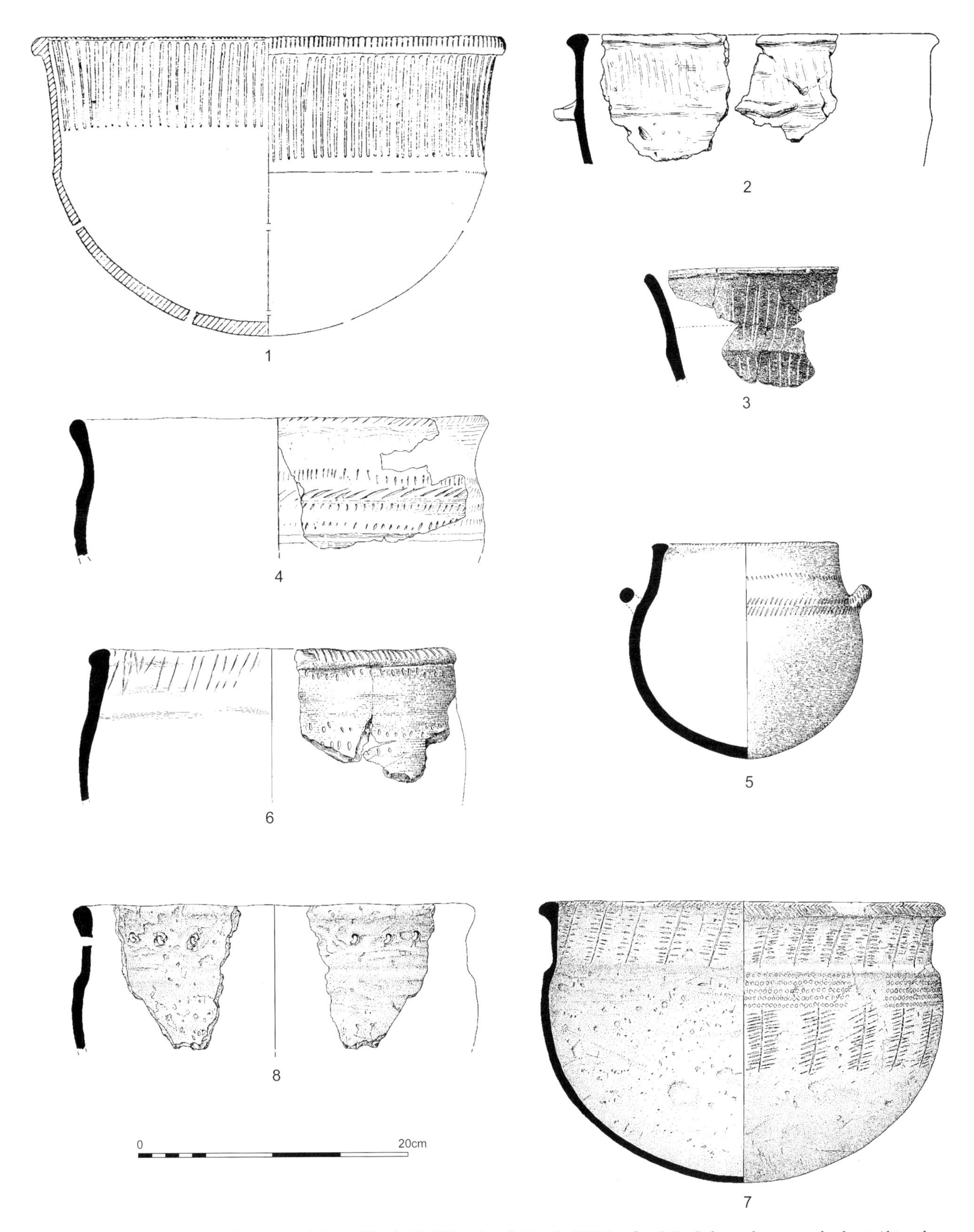

Fig. 14.91. Decorated Bowl pottery. 1 from Windmill Hill, after I. Smith (1965a, fig. 26); 2 from the inner ditch at Abingdon, after Avery (1982, fig.15); 3 from spit 5 in cutting VIII in ditch 3 at Whitehawk, after Curwen (1934a, fig. 5); 4 from segment 9 of the inner ditch of Kingsborough 1, after M. Allen et al. *(2008, fig. 8); 5 from the base of the SE butt of segment 1, and 6 from near the base of the same segment towards the NW butt at Etton, after Pryor (1998, figs 175, 177); 7 and 8 from pit cluster B at Kilverstone, after Garrow* et al. *(2006, fig. 2.16).*

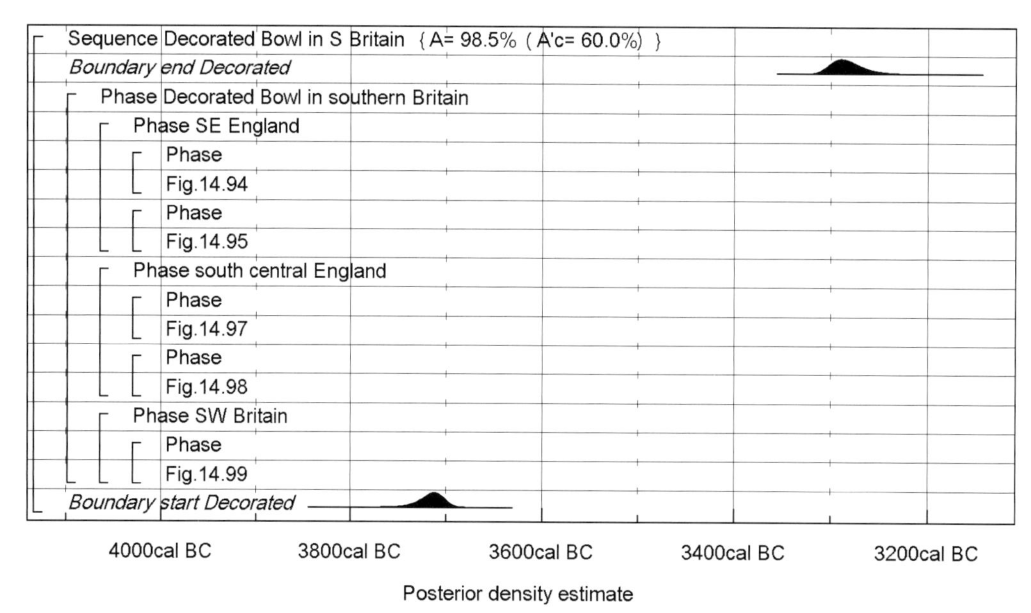

Fig. 14.92. Overall structure of the chronological model for the currency of Decorated Bowl pottery in southern Britain. The component sections of this model are shown in detail in Figs 14.94–5 and 14.97–8, and within the uniform phase boundaries of Fig. 14.99 (although the posterior density estimates shown on these figures are not those relating to this model). The large square brackets down the left-hand side of the figures, along with the OxCal keywords, define the overall model exactly.

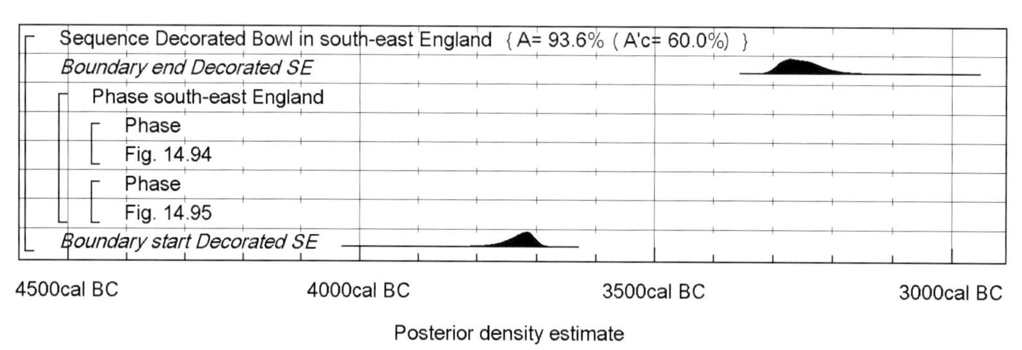

Fig. 14.93. Overall structure of the chronological model for the currency of Decorated Bowl pottery in south-east England. The component sections of this model are shown in detail in Figs 14.94–5. The large square brackets down the left-hand side of the figures, along with the OxCal keywords, define the overall model exactly.

are rare here, on the edge of its geographical range, the distributions have extremely long tails. The model estimates that Decorated Bowl first appeared in this area in *3985–3630 cal BC* (*95% probability*; Fig. 14.99: *start Decorated SW*), probably in *3770–3645 cal BC* (*68% probability*). In this area, the tradition ended in *3355–2965 cal BC* (*95% probability*; Fig. 14.99: *end Decorated SW*), probably in *3340–3185 cal BC* (*68% probability*).

South-Western. The South-Western style (or Hembury Ware) is distinguished by bag-shaped forms, simple rims, a variety of lugs, including horizontally perforated ones, and cordons. Shouldered or carinated forms and decoration are both rare (Fig. 14.100). It is the overwhelmingly dominant tradition in the south-west peninsula, occurring in all kinds of contexts, and is found in significant quantities in adjacent parts of Wessex. The assemblage from two pits predating the Flagstones enclosure, Dorset (Cleal 1997, fig. 64: 2–16), is here treated as a South-Western one (*contra* Cleal 2004, 173; Pailler and Sheridan 2009, 14). Typologically, the assemblage falls within the range of the South-Western style (Cleal 1997, 96–98), and even the one vessel that could be described as carinated (Cleal 1997, fig. 64: 8) can be matched among, for example, some of the rarer forms at Carn Brea (I. Smith 1981, fig. 68).

The overall structure of the model for the currency of South-Western style pottery in southern Britain is shown in Fig. 14.101, with its component sections given in Figs 14.102–3. This model estimates that South-Western style pottery first appeared in southern Britain in *3810–3690 cal BC* (*95% probability*; Fig. 14.101: *start South Western style*), probably in *3770–3705 cal BC* (*68% probability*). The tradition ended in southern Britain in *3340–3275 cal BC* (*95% probability*; Fig. 14.101: *end South Western style*), probably in *3335–3300 cal BC* (*68% probability*).

Gabbroic fabrics. It was recognised from the 1930s onwards that some of the finer South-Western style pots

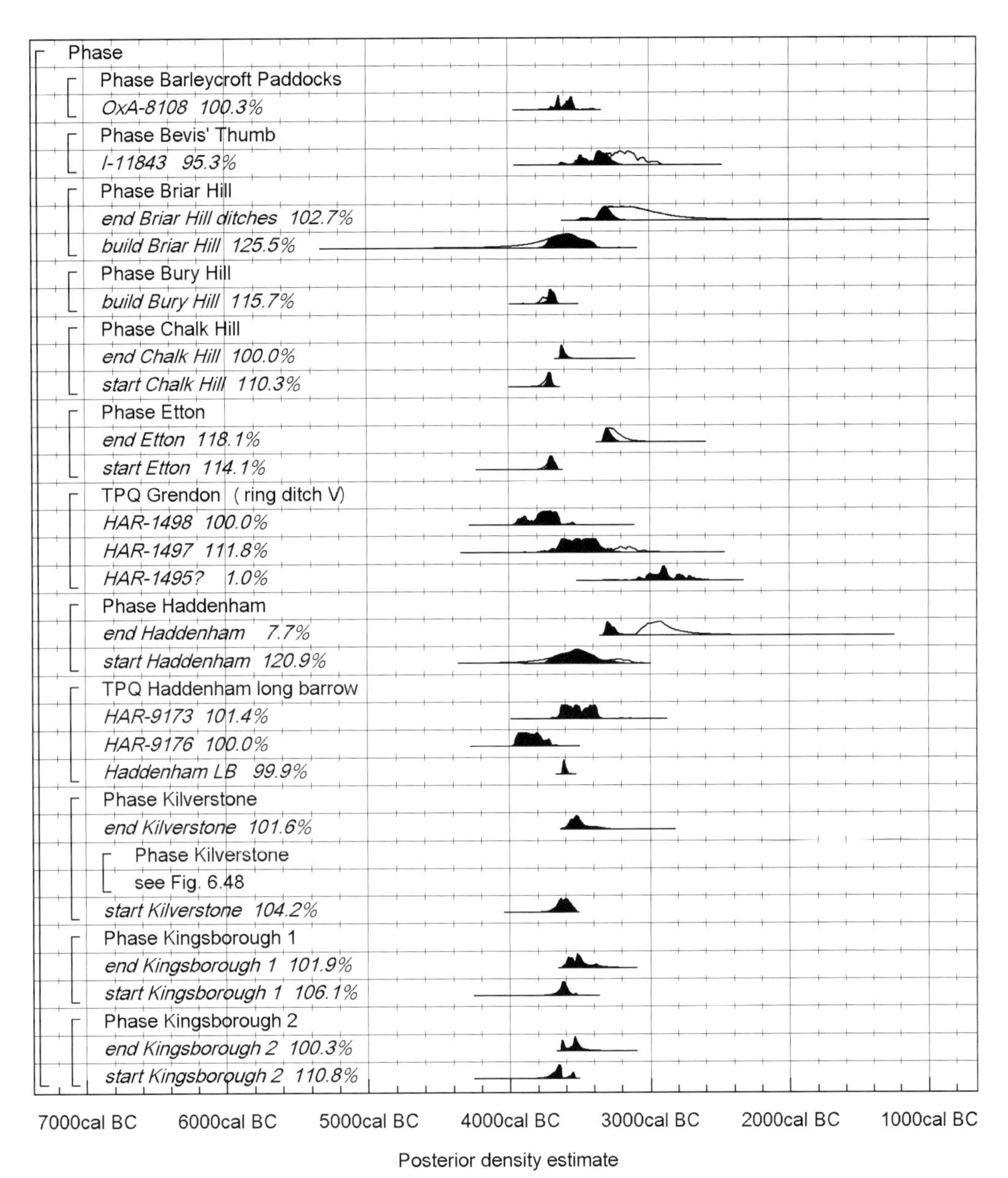

Fig. 14.94. Probability distributions of dates for Decorated Bowl pottery in south-east England. The sub-component of the model relating to pits at Kilverstone is shown in Fig. 6.48 (although the posterior density estimates shown on this figure are not those relating to this model). The format is identical to that for Fig. 14.1. Distributions have been taken from the models defined in Fig. 5.25 (Bury Hill), Fig. 6.33 (Etton), Fig. 6.23 (Briar Hill), Fig. 6.11 (Haddenham), Figs 6.16–17 (Haddenham long barrow), Fig. 7.21 (Chalk Hill), and Figs 7.15 and 7.17 (Kingsborough 1 and 2). The overall structure of this model is shown in Fig. 14.93, and its other component in Fig. 14.95.

at sites outside Cornwall were made of non-local clay, the temper in which resembled the material of stone axeheads, as at Hembury (Liddell 1935, 162–3) and Windmill Hill (I. Smith 1965a, 44). This was subsequently identified as gabbroic ware, the clay for which derives from the Lizard peninsula in south-west Cornwall (Peacock 1969). Progressive identifications have confirmed transport as far as Wessex but not beyond, the proportion in any assemblage diminishing eastward. A connection with causewayed enclosures is reinforced, since such fabrics tend to be present even in small assemblages from limited excavations, as at Robin Hood's Ball or Whitesheet Hill. It is surely significant that, of the dated assemblages including gabbroic fabrics listed in Table 14.10, non-enclosure contexts occur only in Cornwall and Devon, relatively close to the source. It is also noticeable that the gabbroic vessels found in Wessex enclosures tend to lie at the large end of the size range encountered at, for example, Carn Brea.

The overall structure of the model for the currency of gabbroic fabrics within South-Western style pottery is shown in Fig. 14.104, with its component sections given in Figs 14.105–6. This model estimates that gabbroic fabrics first appeared in *3800–3670 cal BC* (*95% probability*; Fig. 14.104: *start gabbroic*), probably in *3755–3685 cal BC* (*68% probability*). They ceased to be employed in the South-Western style in *3550–3415 cal BC* (*95%*

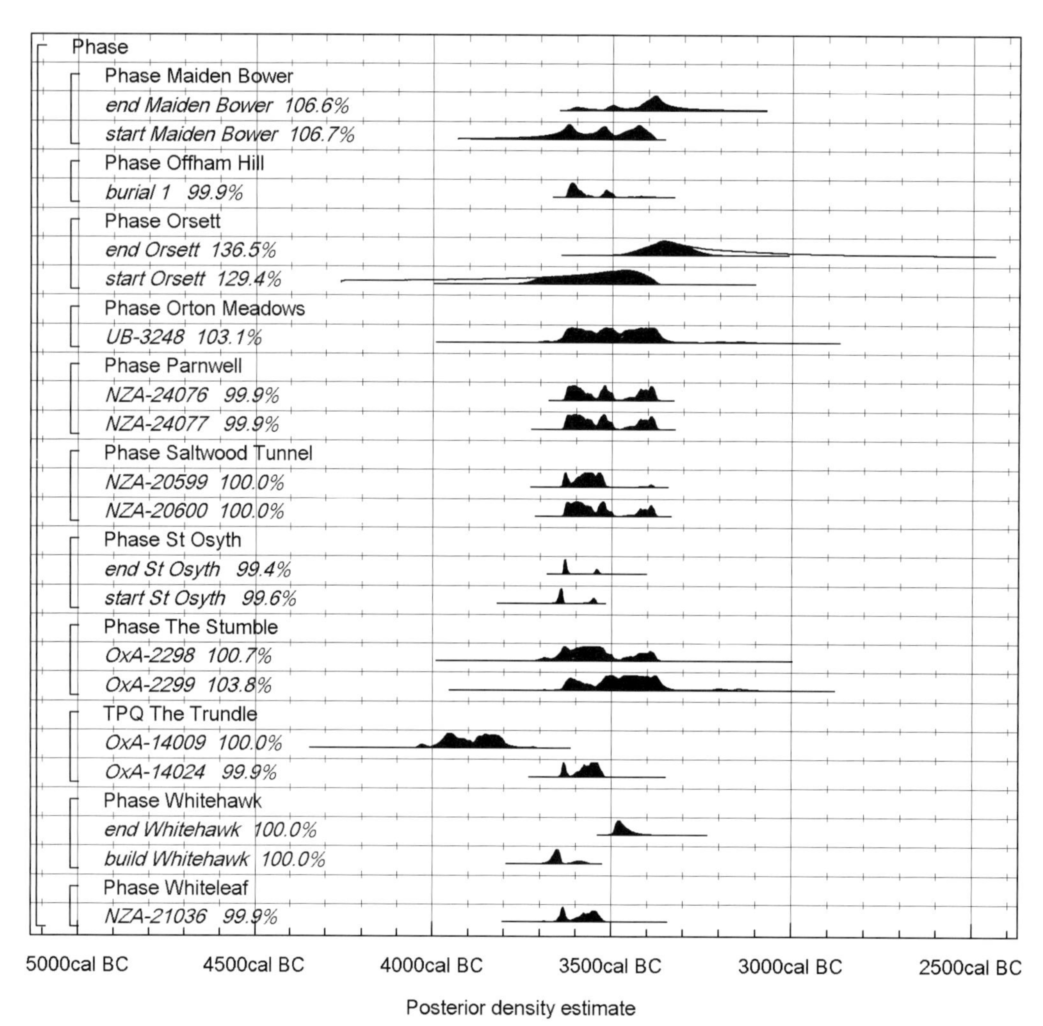

Fig. 14.95. Probability distributions of dates for Decorated Bowl pottery in south-east England. The format is identical to that for Fig. 14.1. Distributions have been taken from the models defined in Fig. 5.14 (Offham Hill), Figs 5.5–9 (Whitehawk), Fig. 6.4 (Maiden Bower), Fig. 7.10 (Orsett) and Fig. 7.6 (St Osyth). The overall structure of this model is shown in Fig. 14.93, and its other component in Fig. 14.94.

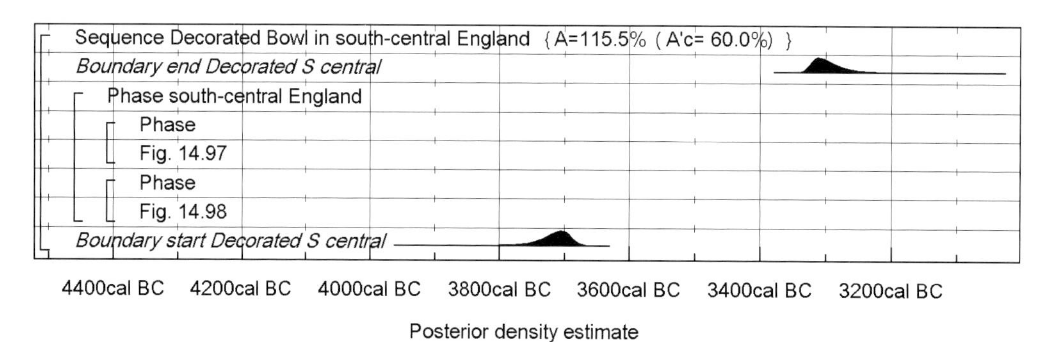

Fig. 14.96. Overall structure of the chronological model for the currency of Decorated Bowl pottery in south-central England. The component sections of this model are shown in detail in Figs 14.97–8. The large square brackets down the left-hand side of the figures, along with the OxCal keywords, define the overall model exactly.

probability; Fig. 14.104: *end gabbroic*), probably in *3545–3530 cal BC* (*10% probability*) or *3490–3440 cal BC* (*58% probability*). In this model, dates which are directly associated with gabbroic vessels are included as dates for the currency of this fabric. For sites where we have gabbroic pottery in stratified early Neolithic deposits, which have not been directly dated themselves, however, we have only concluded that this material must have been deposited after the site was established and before its primary use ended. Given the rarity of this type of material, this modelling approach allows for the fact that it reached the site at some time during its use, not necessarily during the whole period

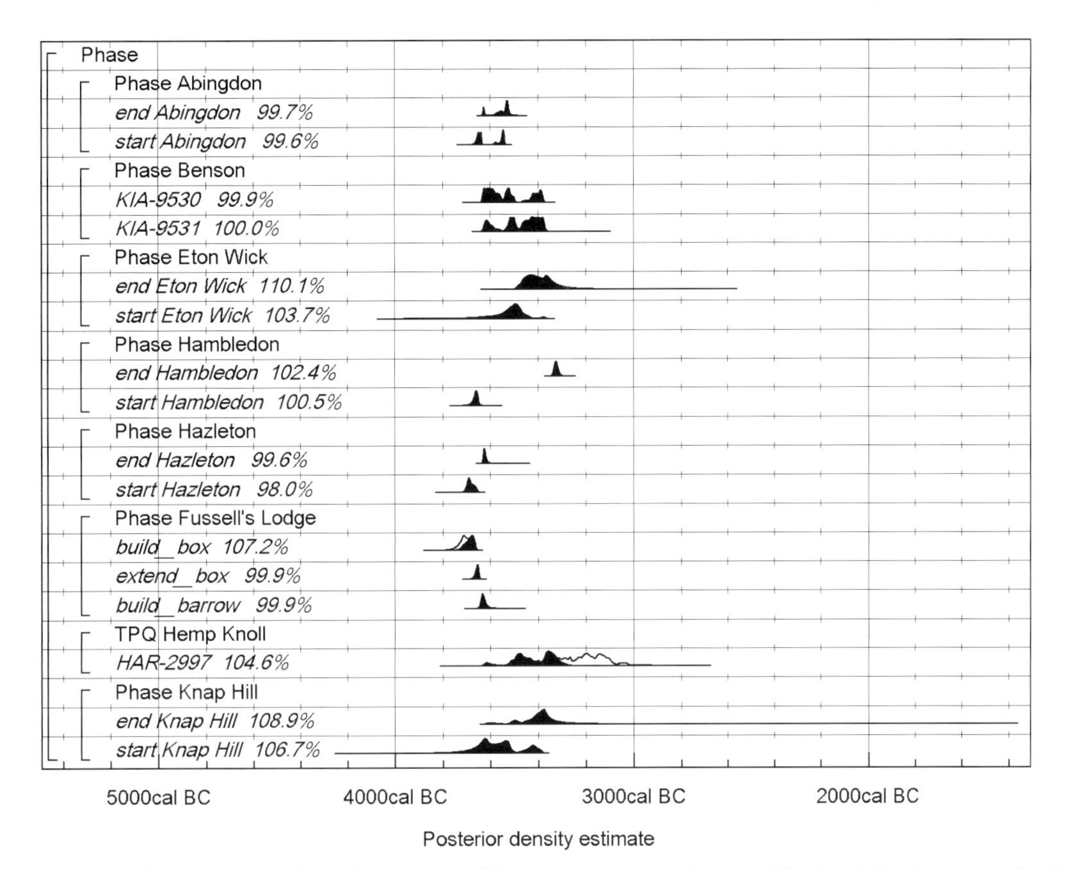

Fig. 14.97. Probability distributions of dates for Decorated Bowl pottery in south central England. The format is identical to that for Fig. 14.1. Distributions have been taken from the models defined in Fig. 3.25 (Knap Hill), Figs 4.7–13 (Hambledon Hill), Fig. 8.5 (Eton Wick), Figs 8.18–21 (Abingdon), and by Meadows et al. *(2007, figs 6–9) (Hazleton) and Wysocki* et al. *(2007, fig. 10) (Fussell's Lodge). The overall structure of this model is shown in Fig. 14.96, and its other component in Fig. 14.98.*

of this. This approach has also been used for modelling the chronology of the ground stone axeheads, which likewise occur in small numbers.

Figure 14.107 shows the currency of the different Bowl traditions in southern Britain. It is *99% probable* that Carinated Bowl appeared first, and *99% probable* that Decorated Bowl appeared after Carinated and some plain Bowl assemblages. It is *100% probable* that Carinated Bowl went out of use before the other types of Bowl pottery considered here. Decorated Bowl and plain Bowl went out of use more or less together in the decades around 3300 cal BC. It is *100% probable* that plain Bowl was in use before the disappearance of Carinated Bowl, and it is *99% probable* that Decorated Bowl had also appeared before the demise of pottery in the Carinated Bowl tradition. There was a probably fairly restricted period at the end of the 38th and in the earlier part of the 37th century cal BC when all three traditions were current. For example, the period between the introduction of Decorated Bowl and the disappearance of Carinated Bowl lasted for *1–215 years* (*95% probability*; Fig. 14.108: *end CB/start Decorated*), probably for *25–125 years* (*68% probability*).

Decorated Bowl appeared very quickly across much of southern Britain, beginning in the later part of the 38th century cal BC and ending in the latter part of the 34th or the 33rd century cal BC (Fig. 14.109). South-Western style pottery has a very similar currency (Fig. 14.110), although it seems to have begun a generation or two earlier than Decorated Bowl: *−35−100 years* (*95% probability*; Fig. 14.108: *South Western/Decorated*), probably *−10−55 years* (*68% probability*). In south-western Britain, the first pottery may have been in the South-Western style, although it is possible that ceramics in another tradition, Carinated or plain Bowl, may appear slightly earlier in this area. If there was earlier pottery in this area, the gap between it and the appearance of the South-Western style was very brief: only *−65−105 years* (*95% probability*; Fig. 14.111: *SW pots/South Western*), probably *−20−65 years* (*68% probability*). Gabbroic fabrics were probably used from the start of the South-Western style (Figs 14.110–11).

Figure 14.112 shows the dates of the first Neolithic things and practices in each area of southern Britain, along with the date of the first enclosure, the date of the first pottery and the date of the appearance of Decorated Bowl in each area. The appearances of South-Western Pottery and gabbroic fabrics are also shown. The first Neolithic things and practices including Carinated Bowl began in south-east England in the 41st century cal BC. Pottery and other early Neolithic things and practices, possibly including Plain, non-carinated, Bowl, spread to south-central England during the 40th and 39th centuries cal BC. It is apparent that the 38th century cal BC was a period of

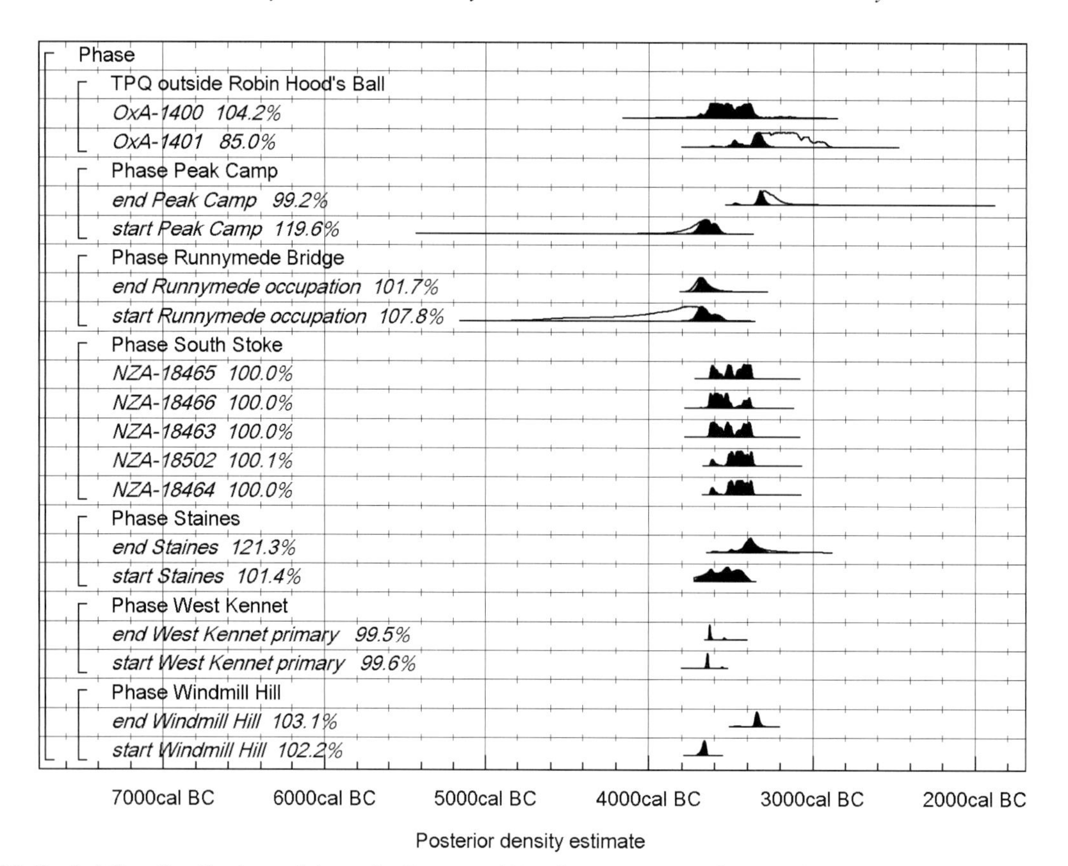

Fig. 14.98. Probability distributions of dates for Decorated Bowl pottery in south-central England. The format is identical to that for Fig. 14.1. Distributions have been taken from the models defined in Figs 3.8–11 (Windmill Hill), Fig. 8.3 (Staines), Fig 8.6 (Runnymede), Fig. 9.19 (Peak Camp) and by Bayliss et al. *(2007b, fig. 6) (West Kennet). The overall structure of this model is shown in Fig. 14.96, and its other component in Fig. 14.97.*

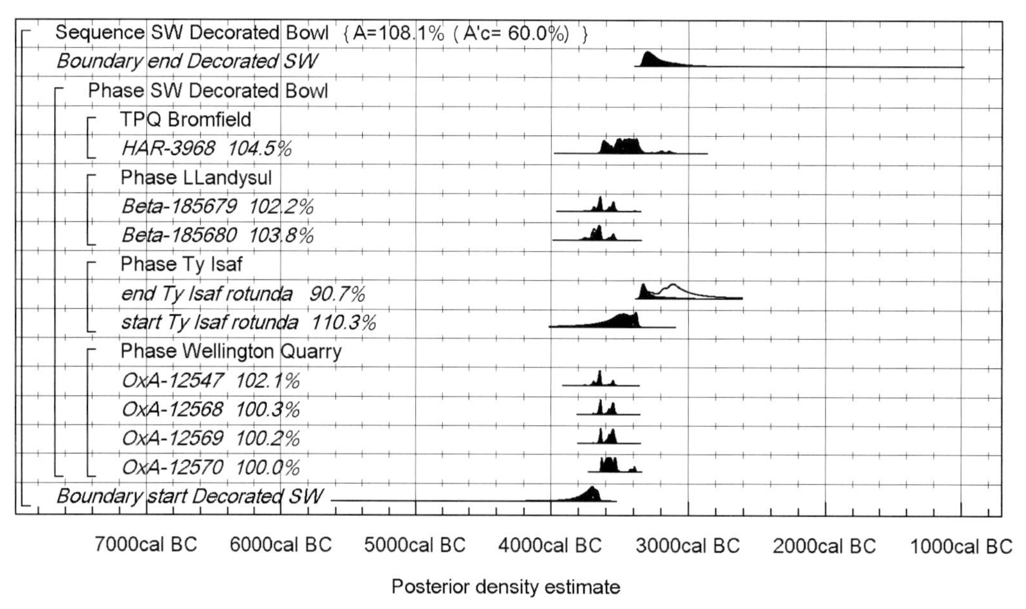

Fig. 14.99. Probability distributions of dates associated with Decorated Bowl pottery from south-west Britain. The format is the same as for Fig. 14.1. Distributions have been taken from the model defined in Fig. 11.14 (Ty Isaf). The large square brackets down the left-hand side of the diagram, along with the OxCal keywords, define the model exactly.

innovation. Neolithic things and practices spread to south-west Britain. During this century these included pottery, and the South-Western style together with gabbroic fabrics. Slightly later came the first enclosures in the south-west peninsula, and the first Decorated pottery in Wales and the Marches. Elsewhere, the last decades of the century saw the appearance of Decorated Bowl, and in south-east England at least, the first causewayed enclosures. The first

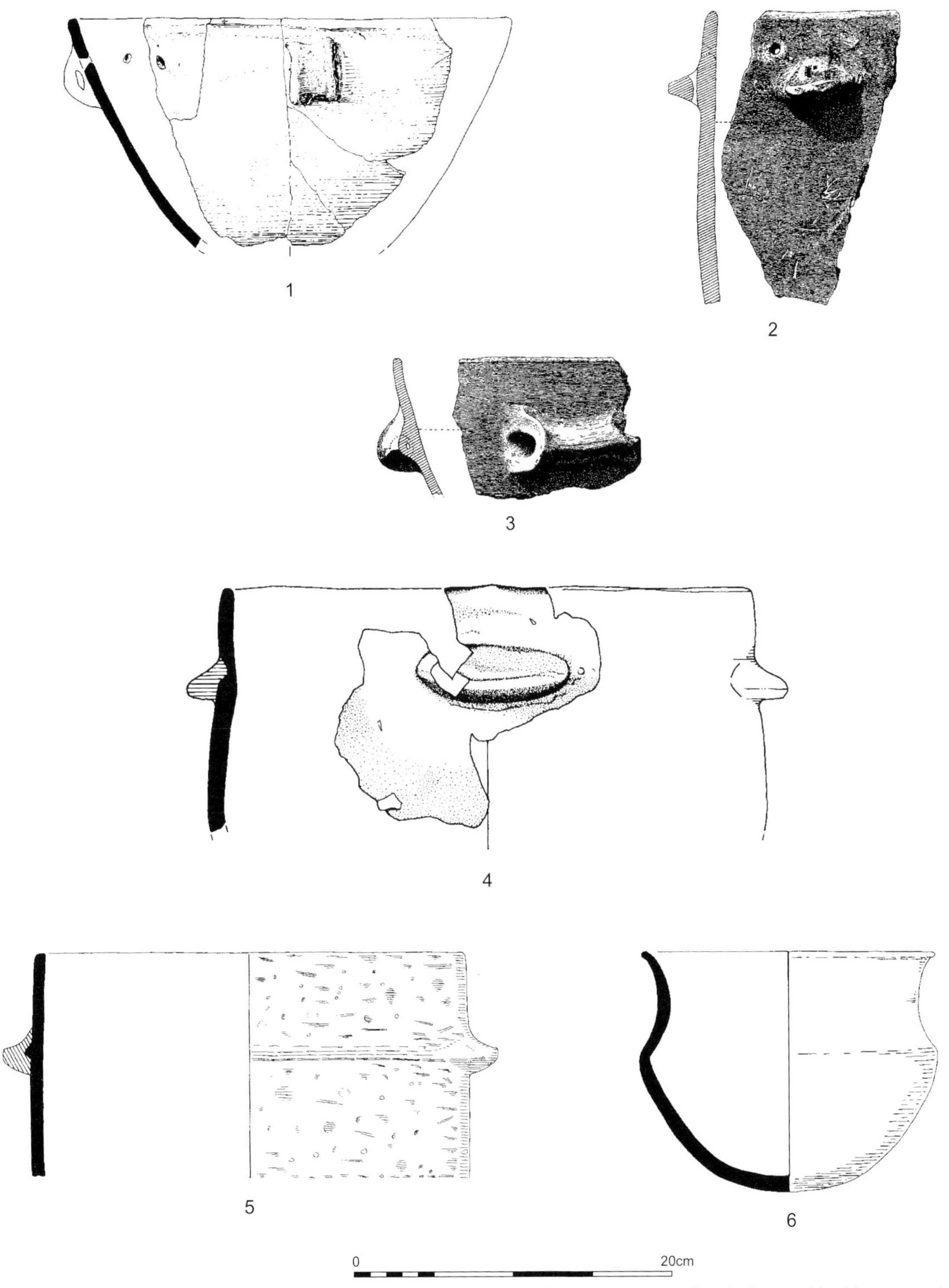

Fig. 14.100. South-Western style Bowls. 1 gabbroic ware vessel from a loam intercalated with the 'midden' layers in the inner ditch at Maiden Castle, after Cleal (1991, fig. 141), carbonised residue from this pot is dated by OxA-X-213-46 (Table 4.9; Fig. 4.42); 2 and 3 from Hembury, after Liddell (1931, pl. XXVII); 4 from pit 45 at Tregarrick Farm, after Cole and Jones (2003, fig. 5); 5 from Carn Brea, after I. Smith (1981, fig.72); 6 from Helman Tor, after I. Smith (1997, fig. 7); carbonised residue from this pot is dated by GrA-31319 and OxA-15631 (Table 10.3; Figs 10.21, 10.22: R_Combine HT86 697*).*

appearance of enclosures in south-central England may have been a few decades later.

The pattern of emergence of the different pottery traditions is summarised in Fig. 14.113, along with our estimate for the date of the first causewayed and related enclosures in southern Britain. The start of both the Carinated and plain Bowl traditions is earlier than the beginning of enclosures, but enclosures and Decorated Bowl appear at more or less the same time at the end of the 38th century cal BC. If there is any lag between these

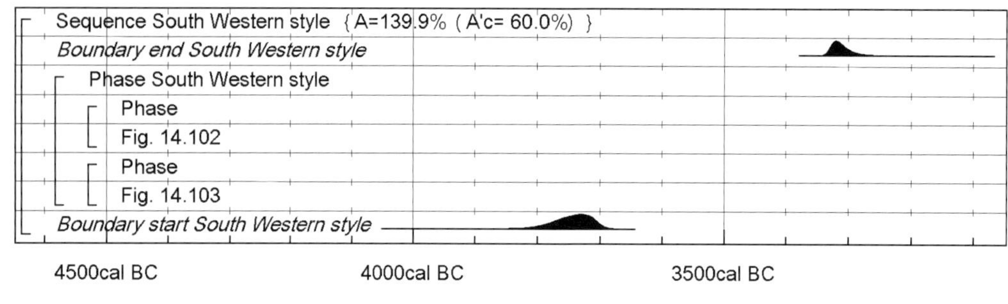

Fig. 14.101. Overall structure of the chronological model for the currency of South-Western style pottery in southern Britain. The component sections of this model are shown in detail in Figs 14.102–3. The large square brackets down the left-hand side of the figures, along with the OxCal keywords, define the overall model exactly.

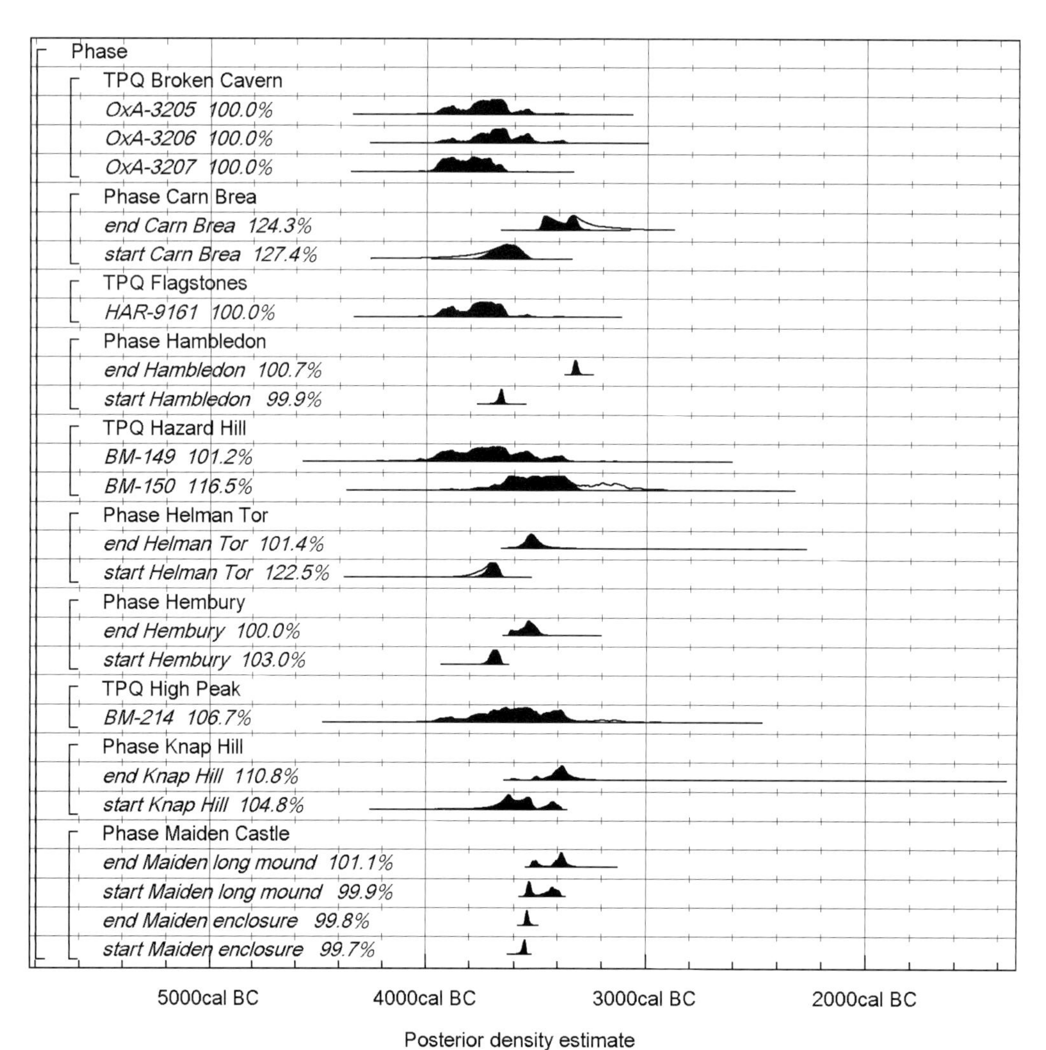

Fig. 14.102. Probability distributions of dates for South-Western style pottery in southern Britain. The format is identical to that for Fig. 14.1. Distributions have been taken from the models defined in Fig. 3.25 (Knap Hill), Figs 4.7–13 (Hambledon Hill), Figs 4.41–5 (Maiden Castle), Figs 10.9–12 (Hembury), Fig. 10.22 (Helman Tor), and Fig. 10.25 (Carn Brea). The overall structure of this model is shown in Fig. 14.101, and its other component in Fig. 14.103.

two phenomena, then Decorated Bowl may have appeared with the intensification of circuit construction, rather than with the first flush of enclosure (Fig. 14.108: *start enclosures/Decorated*; compare Fig. 14.14).

The chronological sequence of emergence of pottery styles in Fig. 14.113 conforms to several stratigraphic sequences. At the Ascott-under-Wychwood and Hazleton long cairns, Carinated Bowl assemblages sealed beneath

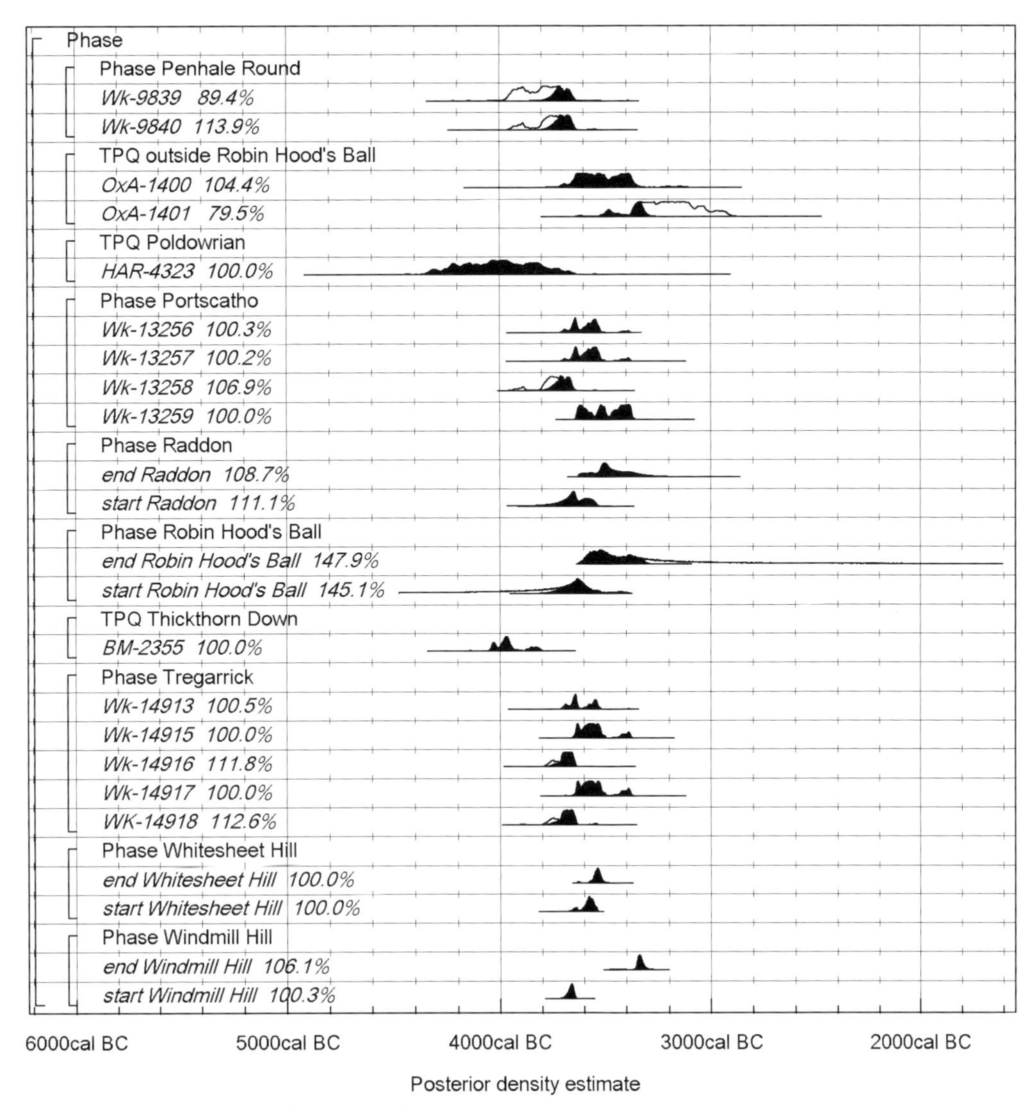

Fig. 14.103. Probability distributions of dates for South-Western style pottery in southern Britain. The format is identical to that for Fig. 14.1. Distributions have been taken from the models defined in Figs 3.8–11 (Windmill Hill), Fig. 4.26 (Whitesheet Hill), Fig. 4.51 (Robin Hood's Ball), and Fig. 10.16 (Raddon). The overall structure of this model is shown in Fig. 14.101, and its other component in Fig. 14.102.

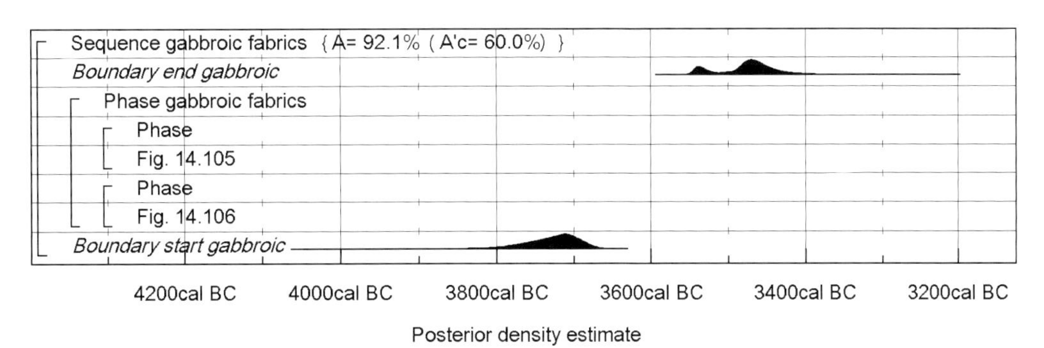

Fig. 14.104. Overall structure of the chronological model for the currency of gabbroic pottery fabrics in southern Britain. The component sections of this model are shown in detail in Figs 14.105–6. The large square brackets down the left-hand side of the figures, along with the OxCal keywords, define the overall model exactly.

the monuments (Barclay and Case 2007, figs 10.1–3; Smith and Darvill 1990, fig. 156) give way to plain vessels of different forms placed with the burials (Barclay and Case 2007, figs 10.1–3; Smith and Darvill 1990, fig. 157:33) and, at Hazleton, to a Decorated vessel in a hearth on top of the primary fill in the south quarry (Smith and Darvill 1990, fig. 157:33). In the Haddenham long barrow, an open, light-rimmed pot with a rounded profile of Carinated Bowl

Table 14.11. Stone axeheads relating to radiocarbon dates shown in Figs 14.114–17 and 14.119–21.

Rock type	Site	Sub-division	Comments and references	Artefact type	Distribution
Continental or possibly continental					
Jadeitite	Sweet Track		Clarke *et al.* 1985, fig. 3.31		*Sweet Track*
Distinctive hard, grey Palaeozoic Sandstone, ?from Ardennes or Scandinavia	Kingsborough 2		M. Allen *et al.* 2008, 262, fig. 11: B	Axehead	GrA-29557, OxA-14791
Attributed to Group I by Vin Davis or, tentatively, to a source in northern France by Roger Taylor	Raddon		Axehead of unusual triangular outline (Gent and Quinnell 1999b, fig. 16:1; Quinnell and Taylor 1999)	Axehead	Between *start Raddon* and *end Raddon*
NW tuffs					
VI	Abingdon	Inner ditch section C-II layer 3	Avery 1982, 40	Axehead flake	*GrA-30923, C2 (4) 36*
VI	Briar Hill		Bamford 1985, fig. 46: S2–S5		Between *build Briar Hill* and *end Briar Hill ditches*
VI	Etton	Pits and phases 1B and 1C in ditch. Also other contexts post-dating primary use of site	Pryor 1998, 257–68	Axehead, axehead fragments, axehead flakes	Between start Etton and *end Etton*
VI	Haddenham enclosure	On a small mound built on the base of segment	Evans and Hodder 2006, 253–7, 352–3, figs 5.14, 5.15, 5.31	Axehead fragment	Between *start Haddenham* and *end Haddenham*
VI	Kilverstone	Pit 1472	Garrow *et al.* 2006, 71	Axehead fragments	*Beta-178142*
VI	Padholme Road, Fengate		Pryor 1974, 12	Axehead flake	*Gak-4197*
VI	Parnwell	Pit 2289	L. Webley 2007	2 Axehead flakes	*NZA-24076, -24077*
VI	Peak Camp	Area II	Darvill 1981; 1982a	Axehead flake	Between *start Peak Camp* and *end Peak Camp*
VI	Staines	Inner ditch	R. Robertson-Mackay 1987, 118	Axehead fragment	Between *start Staines* and *end Staines*
VI	Windmill Hill	Inner Ditch XI spit 3, at 2 ft–base	J. Pollard 1999a, 64; Pollard and Whittle 1999, 340	2 axehead flakes	Between *dig WH inner* and *end WH inner*
cf VI	Wellington Quarry	Pits 3853, 3855	Jackson and Miller forthcoming	Axehead fragments	*OxA-12547*, *OxA-12568* to *OxA-12570*
XI	Windmill Hill	Middle Ditch, IIb, spit 5, at 3.5–5 ft (nearly on base)	J. Pollard 1999a, 47; Pollard and Whittle 1999, 340	?Axehead flake	Between *dig WH middle* and *end WH middle*
SW greenstones					
I	Windmill Hill	Outer Ditch IIIA, spit 3, at 2–2.5 ft	J. Pollard 1999a, 30; Pollard and Whittle 1999, 340	4 Axehead fragments	Between *dig WH outer* and *end WH outer*
I	Hambledon	S long barrow, LB3, SIII, layer 26, phase I	I. Smith 2008b, 632	Fragment	*Hambledon S long barrow*
IV	Carn Brea	Site J, in ditch outside enclosure wall	I. Smith 1981: S3	Axehead fragment	Between *start Carn Brea* and *end Carn Brea*
IV	Hambledon	Main enclosure, segment 4, layer 5, phase VI	I. Smith 2008a, 632	Axehead flake	Between *build main enclosure* and *end main enclosure*
IVa	Hembury		It is difficult to match the sectioned implements to those mentioned in Liddell's reports. This exercise follows I. Smith's conclusion that 'groups IVa and XVII appear to be securely dated here' (1979, 17)		Between *start Hembury* and *end Hembury*

Rock type	Site	Sub-division	Comments and references	Artefact type	Distribution
IVa	Maiden Castle	AOR 2335 from context 283, part of 280, fill of 2235, phase 2A; AOR 1572 from 324, fill of 325, phase 2D	1 from inner ditch, 1 from outer.	Axeheads	From *start Maiden enclosure* to end *Maiden enclosure*
XVI	Carn Brea	Site A1, amongst tumble from wall; site A1, in F13; site D layer 1B	I. Smith 1981, 158–9	Axehead fragments and flakes	Between *start Carn Brea* and *end Carn Brea*
XVI	Hambledon	Pit B F14 in central area	I. Smith 2008b, 631	Axehead	*HAR-9167*
XVI	Hambledon	Main enclosure, segment 3, layer 4, phase VI	I. Smith 2008b, 632	Axehead fragment	Between *build main enclosure* and *end main enclosure*
XVII	Hazard Hill	Hearth 7; pit 5	Houlder 1963, 26	Axehead	BM-149, BM-150
XVII	Helman Tor	Surface of Neolithic occupation layer; F166	Roe 1997	Axehead fragments	Between *start Helman Tor* and *end Helman Tor*
XVII	Hembury		It is difficult to match the sectioned implements to those mentioned in Liddell's reports. This exercise follows I. Smith's conclusion that 'groups IVa and XVII appear to be securely dated here' (1979, 17)	Axehead fragments	Between *start Hembury* and *end Hembury*
cf XVII	Hambledon	Main enclosure, segment 10, layer 6B, phase VI	I. Smith 2008b, 632	Joining axehead fragments	*OxA-8850*
cf XVII	Hambledon	Stepleton enclosure, segment 23, ST1, interface of layers 2 and 3, probably phase V	I. Smith 2008b, 632		Between *build Stepleton enclosure* and *end Stepleton enclosure*
Altered Amphibolite	Hambledon	Main enclosure, segment 8, layer 7, phase III; segment 9, layer 8, phase III; segment 10, layer 4, phase V	I. Smith 2008b, 632	Fragments probably from same axehead	Between *build main enclosure* and *end main enclosure*
Altered gabbro	Hambledon	S long barrow, LB3, SIII, layer 40, phase I; LB3, SIII, layer 21, phase III	I. Smith 2008b, 632	Flake and fragment, probably from same axe	*build long barrow*
Ungrouped greenstones	Carn Brea	Several contexts	I. Smith 1981, 159	Axehead fragments	Between *start Carn Brea* and *end Carn Brea*
Ungrouped greenstones	High Peak	Neo levels in trenches A and GA	S. Pollard 1966, 51	Axehead fragments	*BM-214*
Wales or Midlands?					
Banded tuff	Hambledon	Main enclosure, segment 7, layer 4, phase VI	I. Smith 2008b, 632	Axehead fragment	between *build main enclosure* and *end main enclosure*
N Wales					
VII	Etton	Pit F857	The only group VII even possibly from phase 1 (Pryor 1998, 264)	Axehead fragment	between *start Etton* and *end Etton*
S Wales					
VIII	Hambledon	Outer E cross-dyke, segment 5, layer 4, phase VI	I. Smith 2008b, 632	Axehead flake	Between *start Hambledon* and *end Hambledon*
cf VIII	Carn Brea	Site K, occupation surface at base of layer 2	I. Smith 1981, 159	Axehead fragment	Between *start Carn Brea* and *end Carn Brea*

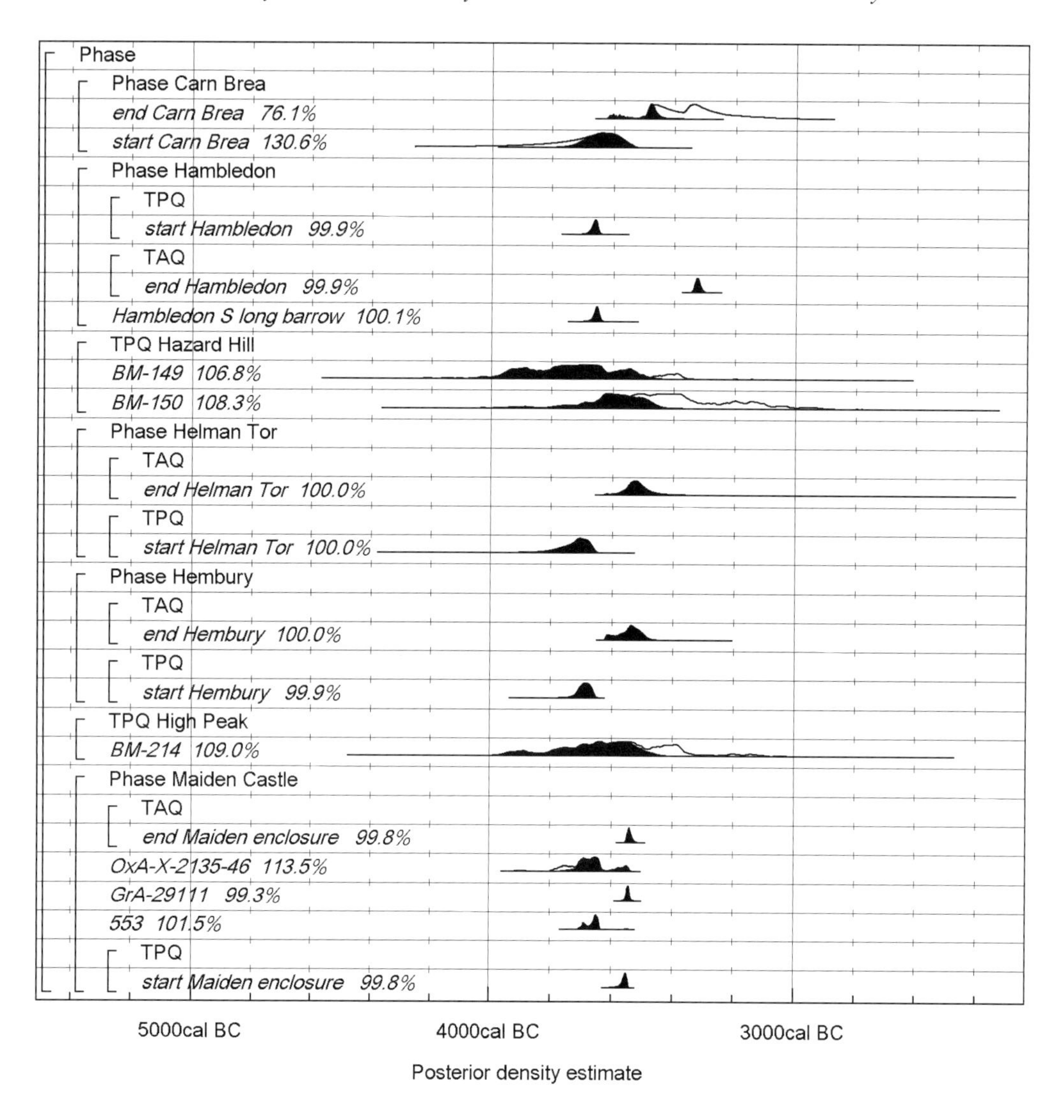

Fig. 14.105. Probability distributions of dates for gabbroic pottery fabrics in southern Britain. The format is identical to that for Fig. 14.1. Distributions have been taken from the models defined in Figs 4.7–13 (Hambledon Hill), Figs 4.41–5 (Maiden Castle), Figs 10.9–12 (Hembury), Fig. 10.22 (Helman Tor) and Fig. 10.25 (Carn Brea). The overall structure of this model is shown in Fig. 14.104, and its other component in Fig. 14.106.

affinities but with internal fluting (Knight 2006a, fig. 3.58: P1), placed close to a postpipe of the façade, was succeeded by sherds of a closed, heavy-rimmed, shouldered, Mildenhall style Decorated vessel (Knight 2006a, fig. 3.58: P2) outside the blocking of the main chamber. At Orton Meadows, Carinated Bowls in the first burial alignment were succeeded by heavier-rimmed bowls with fluting on the rim tops and the interior of the necks (Mackreth forthcoming). In the two Hambledon enclosure ditches, the frequency of decoration increased from bottom to top (I. Smith 2008a, table 9.11).

Given that Chalk Hill is among the earlier causewayed enclosures (Fig. 14.5), the Carinated Bowl element, seen as redeposited by Gibson and Leivers (2008, 252), might perhaps have been an integral part of the assemblage. At the other end of the timescale, the demonstration that Ebbsfleet Ware found near the base of the outer ditch at Windmill Hill in fact came from a later fourth or early third millennium cal BC recut (Chapter 3) removes the foundation of an argument that this tradition developed significantly earlier than the more elaborate varieties of Peterborough Ware (I. Smith 1966a, 474–8) and overlapped substantially with Decorated Bowl. The results of a Peterborough Ware dating programme undertaken by Peter Marshall, Ann Woodward and others are still pending (2011). In the meantime, it can be noted that the Welsh Peterborough Ware dates shown in Fig. 11.9 include a *terminus post quem* of *3340–2920 cal BC* (*95% probability*), probably of *3330–3215 cal BC* (*28% probability*) or *3180–3155 cal BC* (*4% probability*) or *3125–3010 cal BC* (*31% probability*) or *2980–2960 cal BC* (*4% probability*) or *2950–2940 cal BC* (*1% probability*), for a vessel of Ebbsfleet form accompanying a burial at Four Crosses, Powys (Table 11.4: *CAR-670*); and that the Etton dates include a measurement of *3350–3210 cal BC* (*95% probability*), probably of *3330–3275 cal BC* (*55% probability*) or *3265–3250 cal BC* (*13% probability*), on carbonised residue from an Ebbsfleet Ware sherd (Fig. 6.33; Table 6.8: *GrA-29353*).

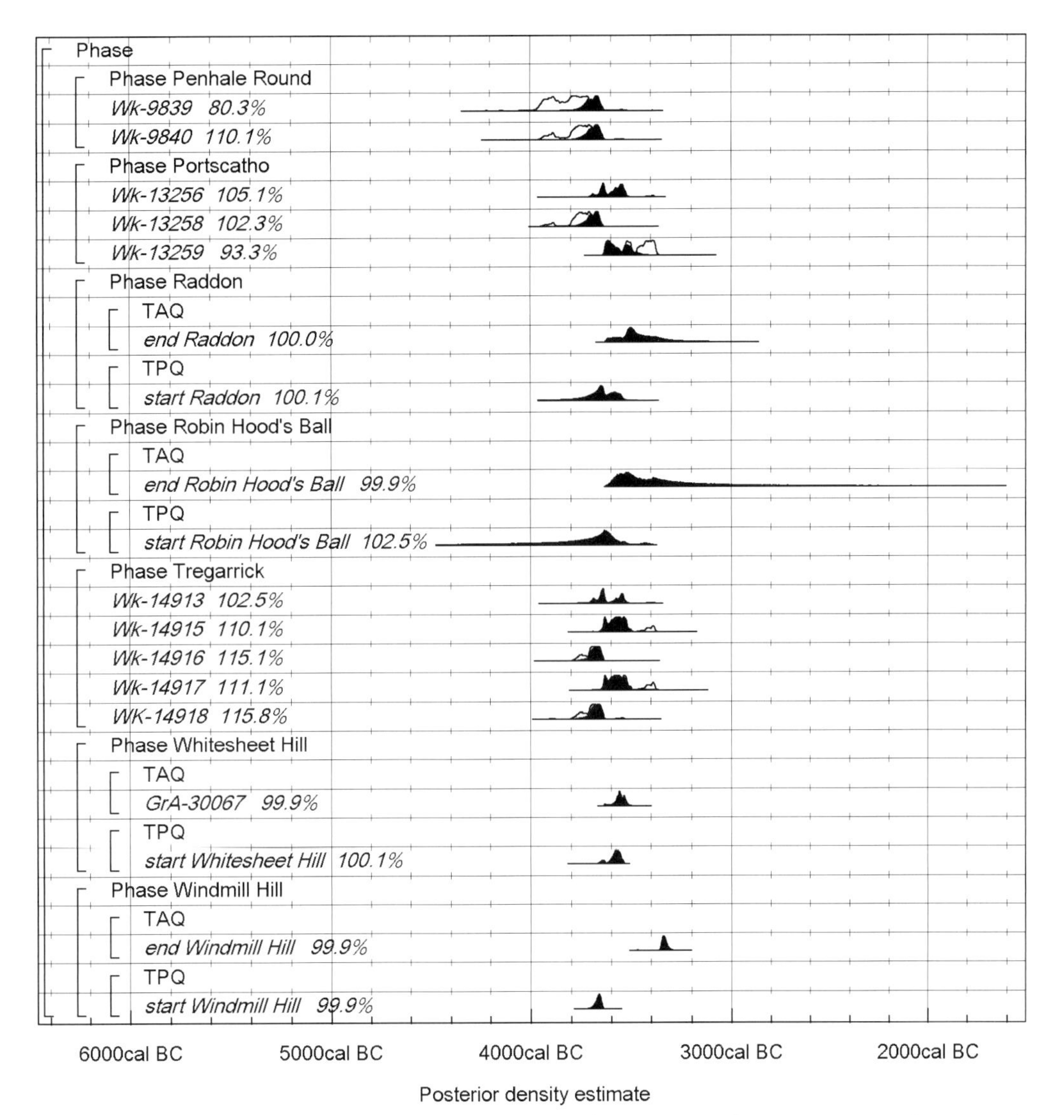

Fig. 14.106. Probability distributions of dates for gabbroic pottery fabrics in southern Britain. The format is identical to that for Fig. 14.1. Distributions have been taken from the models defined in Figs 3.8–11 (Windmill Hill), Fig. 4.26 (Whitesheet Hill), Fig. 4.51 (Robin Hood's Ball) and Fig. 10.16 (Raddon). The overall structure of this model is shown in Fig. 14.104, and its other component in Fig. 14.105.

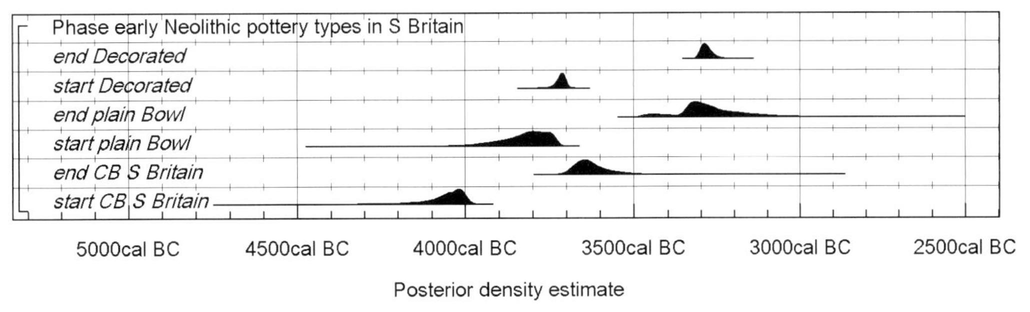

Fig. 14.107. Probability distributions for the currency of early Neolithic pottery types in southern Britain, derived from the models shown in Figs 14.88, 14.90 and 14.92 (and its component parts).

Axeheads

Stone axeheads, like gabbroic pottery fabrics, were recognised in the inter-war period as non-local imports at causewayed enclosures: artefacts brought from upland and mountainous areas to lowland England. The subsequent history of the identification of the implements and their sources is summarised, from different perspectives, by Grimes (1979) and Bradley and Edmonds (1993, 43–58). Many of the rocks in question have been assigned to petrological groups of varying homogeneity and validity (I–XXIV, listed by Clough, 1988, table 3). In general terms they range between two main kinds: fine-grained rocks that

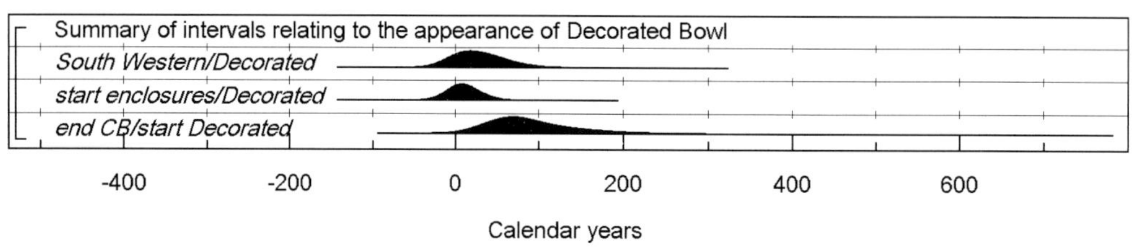

Fig. 14.108. Intervals between the end of the Carinated Bowl tradition and the appearance of Decorated Bowl, and between this and the appearance of causewayed enclosures and South-Western style pottery in southern Britain, derived from parameters calculated by the models shown in Figs 14.88, 14.1–4, 14.92 (and its component parts) and 14.101–3.

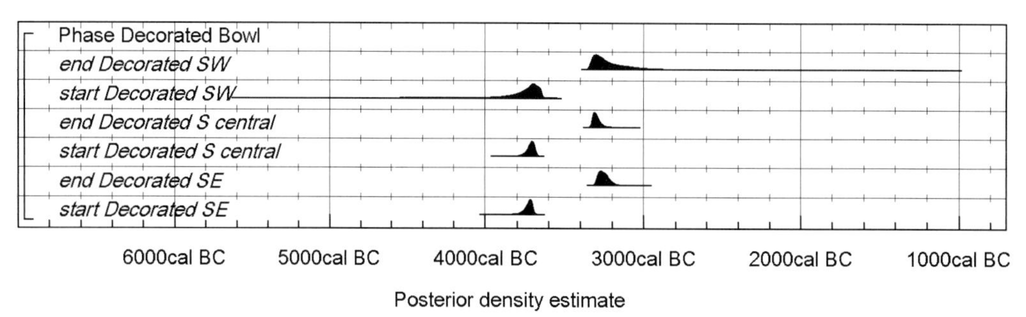

Fig. 14.109. Probability distributions for the currency of Decorated Bowl in different areas of southern Britain, derived from the models shown in Figs 14.93–5, 14.96–8 and 14.99.

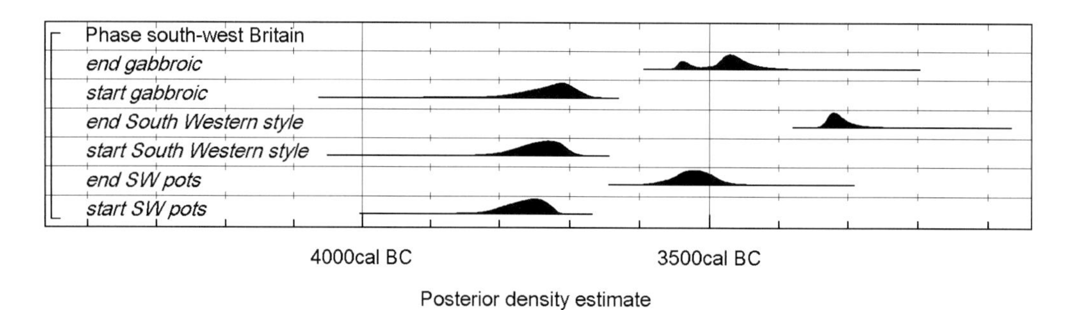

Fig. 14.110. Probability distributions for the currency of Bowl pottery, South-Western style pottery, and early Neolithic gabbroic fabrics in south-west Britain, derived from the models shown in Figs 14.77–9, 14.101–3 and 14.104–6.

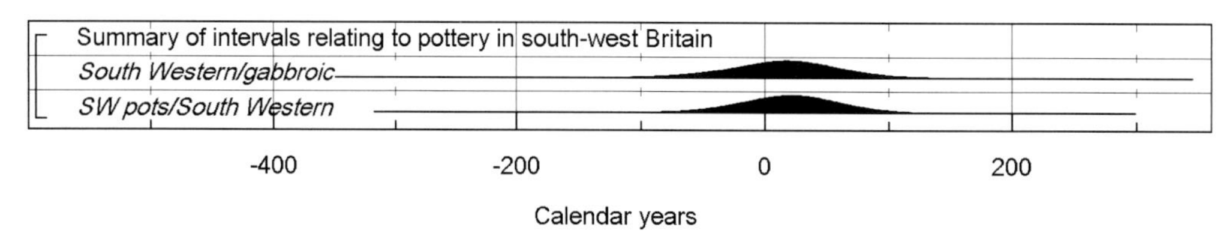

Fig. 14.111. Intervals between the first pottery in south-west Britain and the start of the South-Western style, and between this and the introduction of gabbroic fabrics in this tradition, derived from parameters calculated by the models shown in Figs 14.77–9, 14.101–3, and 14.104–6.

can be knapped like flint and coarser-grained rocks worked primarily by pecking and hammering. Of course, in reality, both methods of manufacture were used across a range of rock fabrics and textures. Extraction and working sites for the former are more readily identifiable by their relatively abundant debitage, as at Great Langdale in Cumbria, Graig Lwyd in Gwynedd, or Tievebulliagh and Rathlin Island in Co. Antrim. Comparable sites for the latter, many of which derive from the south-west peninsula, are elusive. This may be partly due to the lack of distinctive working debris; it is increasingly probable, however, that, at least in the case of the numerous implements attributed to petrologically diverse altered epidiorite rocks (Groups I, II, III, IV, XVI and XVII) that the main raw materials may have been collected as cobbles from beaches and perhaps other secondary deposits in Cornwall (P. Berridge 1993). Glacial erratics were also employed, both opportunistically and systematically, as in the case of Group VIII, where

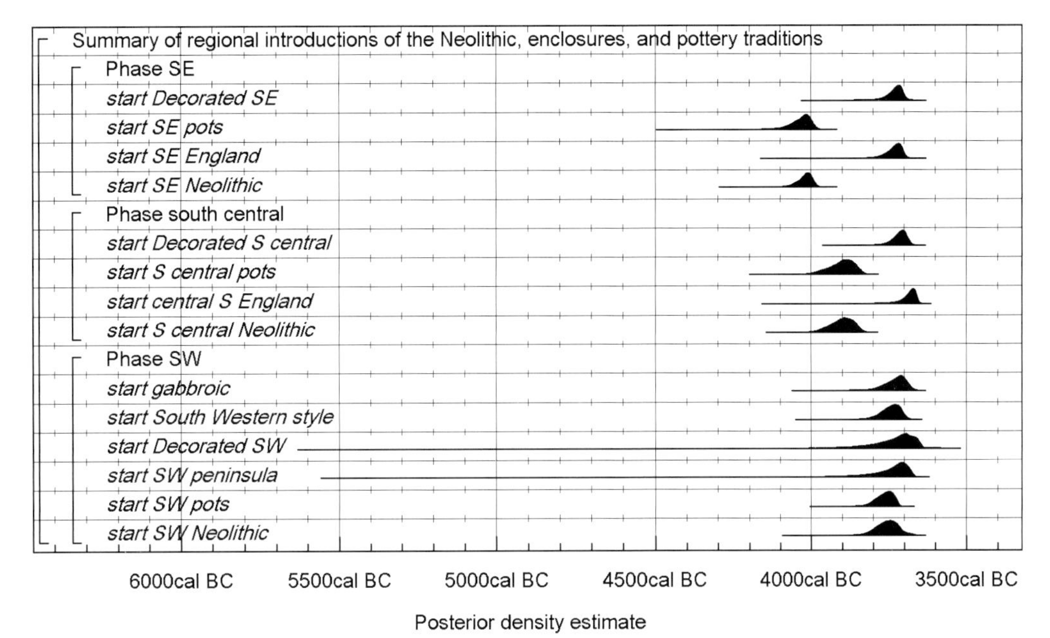

Fig. 14.112. Probability distributions of dates for the introduction of the earliest Neolithic things and practices (start SE Neolithic, start S central Neolithic, start SW Neolithic), causewayed or stone-walled tor enclosures (start SE England, start central S England, start SW peninsula), Bowl pottery (start SE pots, start S central pots, start SW pots), and Decorated Bowl pottery (start Decorated SE, start Decorated S central, start Decorated SW) in different areas of southern Britain, and of the South-Western style (start South Western style) and gabbroic fabrics (start gabbroic), derived from the models defined in Figs 14.57, 14.18, 14.68, 14.72, 14.77, 14.93, 14.96, 14.99, 14.101, and 14.104 (and their component parts if appropriate).

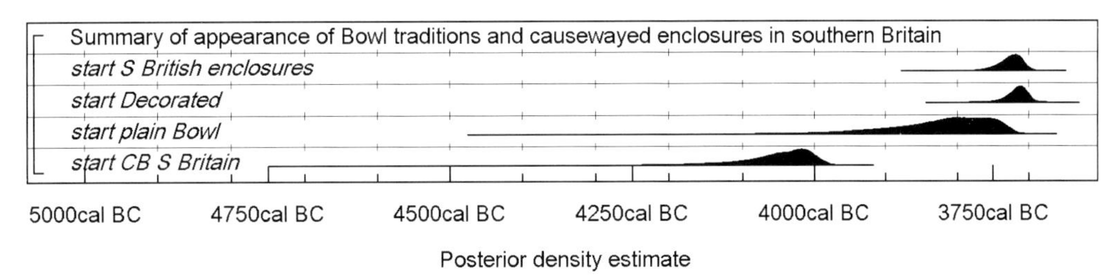

Fig. 14.113. Probability distributions of dates for the introduction of the different Bowl traditions and causewayed or related enclosures in southern Britain, derived from the models defined in Figs 14.1–4, 14.92 (and its component parts), 14.90 and 14.88.

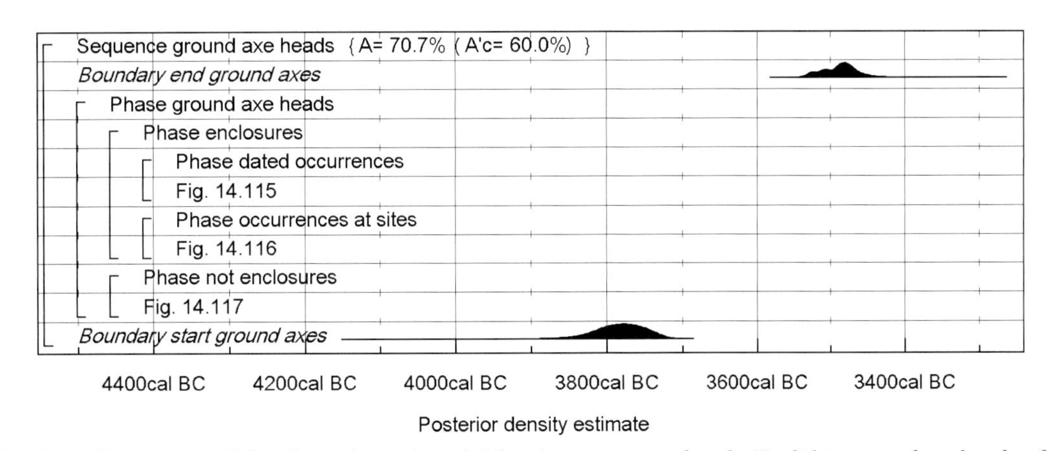

Fig. 14.114. Overall structure of the chronological model for the currency of early Neolithic ground axeheads of stone and distinctive flints in early Neolithic contexts in southern Britain. The component sections of this model are shown in detail in Figs 14.115–17. The large square brackets down the left-hand side of Figs 14.114–17, along with the OxCal keywords, define the overall model exactly.

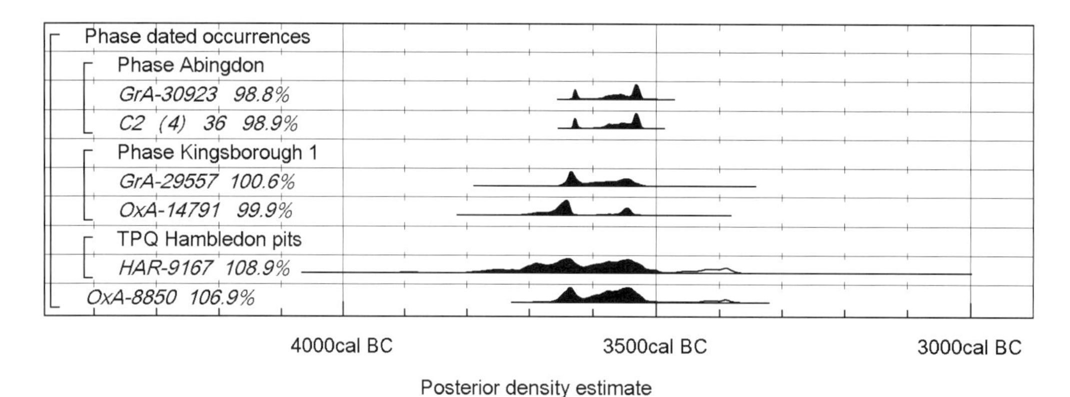

Fig. 14.115. Probability distributions of dates from enclosures directly associated with ground axeheads of stone and distinctive flints in early Neolithic contexts. The format is identical to that for Fig. 14.1. Distributions have been taken from the models defined in Figs 4.7–13 (Hambledon Hill), Figs 7.15 (Kingsborough 1), and Figs 8.18–21 (Abingdon). The overall structure of this model is shown in Fig. 14.114, and its other components in Figs 14.116–17.

erratic sources have been identified in Pembrokeshire (David and Williams 1995). While some of these sources were used locally by hunter-gatherer populations, their Neolithic use is marked by transport away from those sources, sometimes over substantial distances. Many petrological groups consist of relatively few implements. At the other end of the scale, Group VI axeheads, from the Great Langdale areas of central Cumbria, are by far the most numerous and have been found throughout northern, central and eastern Britain with scarcer examples in other areas (Clough and Cummins 1988, map 6). The next most numerous is Group I, which is concentrated south of the Trent-Severn line (Clough and Cummins 1988, map 2). There are also a small number of implements certainly or probably from continental sources, described below.

Neolithic flint axeheads, whether ground or flaked, are of forms distinct from Mesolithic ones and were made from a wide variety of flints, from both superficial and mined sources. Flint sourcing has progressed far enough to indicate that axeheads from the Sussex flint mines were transported into other regions (Craddock *et al.* 1983; forthcoming). Some flint axeheads stand out because they are made of material distinct from that of the rest of the industries in which they occur and distinct from the dark-coloured products of known flint mines. Depending on local circumstance, these may reflect careful selection of materials from nearby sources or transport over shorter or longer distances. Uneven levels of reporting mean that they will not always have been noted in publications. Where such distinctive flint axeheads can be pinpointed in the literature they are included in the models shown in Figs 14.114–18.

The vast majority of Neolithic stone and flint axeheads are stray finds, and only a fraction of the stratified samples are effectively dated. It is clear, too, that both continued to be made and used into at least the third millennium cal BC. Fiona Roe's list of over 20 stone axeheads, including those from north-western, south-western and Welsh sources, with Grooved Ware associations (1999, table 7.22) makes this point effectively. The use of a particular facies of the Langdale rock for Beaker period bracers (A. Woodward *et al.* 2006) suggests continued or resumed exploitation of this particular source into the late third or early second millennium cal. BC. The models shown in Figs 14.114–17, 14.118, 14.119–21, 14.122, 14.124–6, 14.127, 14.128, and 14.134–6 therefore include only artefacts stratified in early Neolithic contexts, these being listed in Tables 14.11 and 14.13. This is counter to Isobel Smith's assumption 'that surface finds probably relate to the main period of activity on the site in question' in her classic paper on stone axehead chronology (1979, 13), and it excludes many axeheads from superficial contexts on enclosures, some of which are probably of early Neolithic date. It is, however, the only secure way to proceed, given circumstances like those of Etton, where almost half of stone axehead finds post-date the primary use of the enclosure (phase 1) and there is a Peterborough Ware and Grooved Ware presence (Pryor 1998, 195–204, 262–3). At Carn Brea (Chapter 10) only those from the eastern summit enclosure are securely dated without question, and that from rampart 5 on site A3 is excluded, along with several unstratified examples from the site (see Chapter 10.5). Implements of south-western Groups IV, XVI and XVII and Welsh Group XIII from Wheeler's excavations at Maiden Castle, some of them from early Neolithic contexts, are reluctantly excluded because it is not possible from published sources to relate the petrological identifications to the implements described in the 1943 publication and hence to determine which were in early Neolithic contexts.

On this basis, a model for the currency of ground stone axeheads and distinctive flint axeheads from early Neolithic contexts in southern Britain is shown in Figs 14.114–17. Figure 14.115 shows the few measurements directly associated with the artefacts in enclosures. Figure 14.116 shows the more numerous instances where *termini post* and *ante quos* are provided for implements by start and end dates for individual earthworks or entire enclosures. Figure 14.117 shows dates of both kinds for implements from non-enclosure contexts. This suggests that the first example was deposited in *3850–3720 cal BC* (*95% probability*;

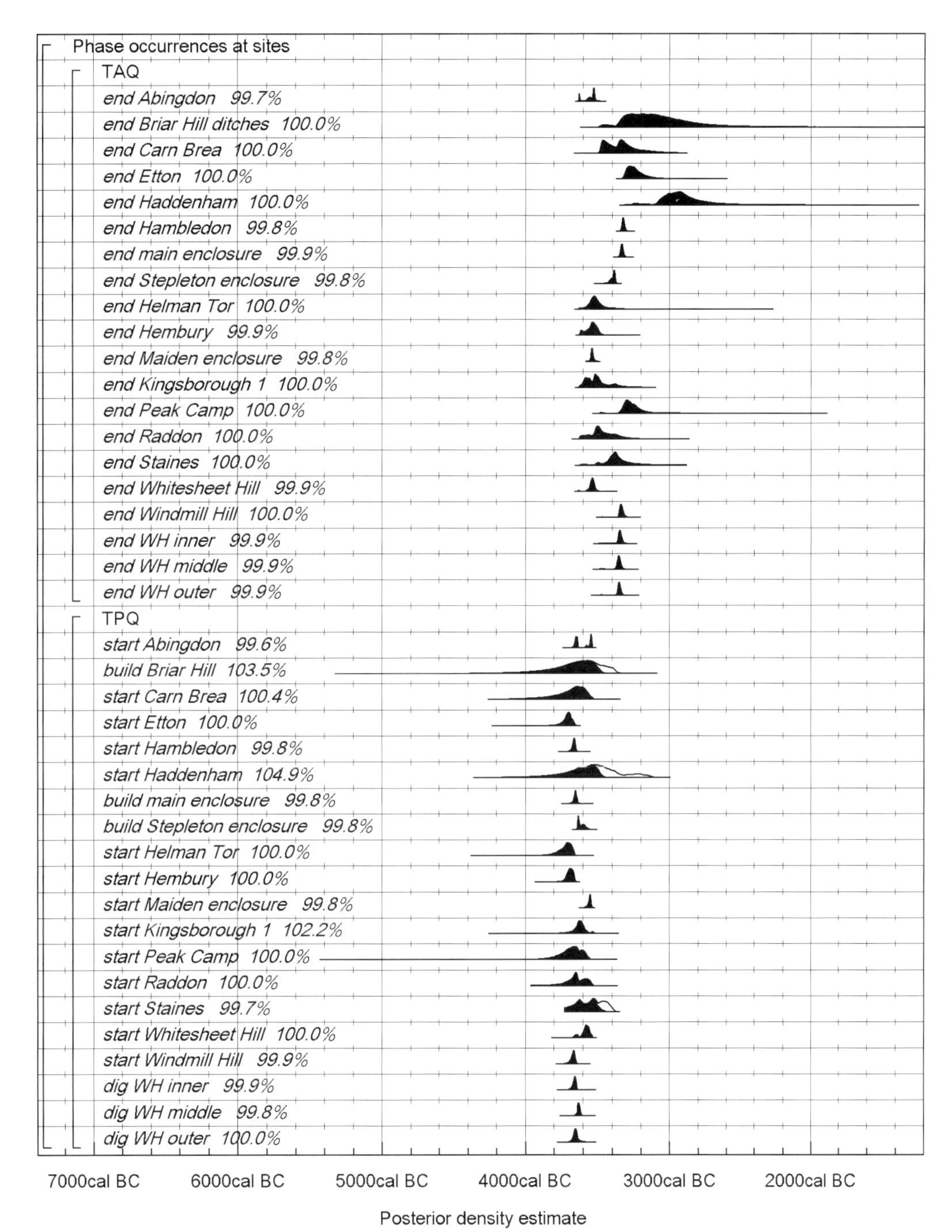

Fig. 14.116. Probability distributions of dates from enclosure sites with ground axeheads of stone and distinctive flints in early Neolithic contexts. The format is identical to that for Fig. 14.1. Distributions have been taken from the models listed in the captions to Figs 4.2–4. The overall structure of this model is shown in Fig. 14.114, and its other components in Figs 14.115 and 14.117.

Fig. 14.114: *start ground axes*), probably in *3810–3745 cal BC* (*68% probability*). In early Neolithic contexts in southern Britain, the practice ended in *3540–3440 cal BC* (*95% probability*; Fig. 14.114: *end ground axes*), probably in *3515–3460 cal BC* (*68% probability*).

Figure 14.118 shows a model for the chronology of the use of distinctive flints for polished axeheads in southern Britain. This material may have come from numerous sources, but there seems to have been a widespread preference for a creamy white to pale grey colour with inclusions which provide a marbled effect when polished. This obtains regardless of location. At Abingdon, on the upper Thames, 'creamy material with cherty inclusions' was used for polished axeheads (Avery 1982, 35); at Kingsborough 1, on Sheppey, a complete axehead is of 'light grey flint that has probably derived from a different source' (Butler and Leivers 2008, 257); a butt fragment from the Fir Tree Field shaft in Dorset is of 'an off-white coarse-grained cherty ?flint with traces of fossil inclusions which is likely to have been imported' (M. Green 2007c,

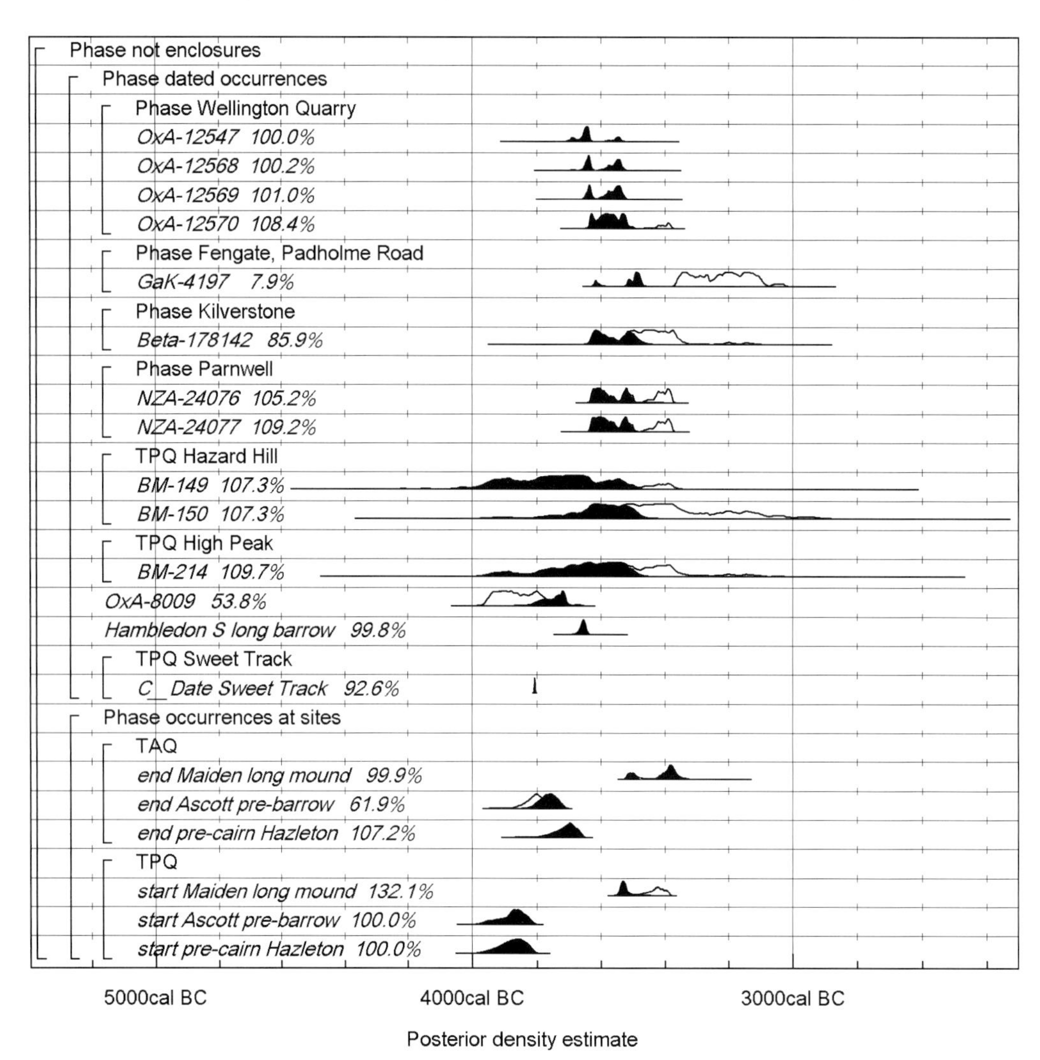

Fig. 14.117. Probability distributions of dates directly associated with ground axeheads of stone and distinctive flints in early Neolithic contexts, and from other sites where such axeheads have been found. The format is identical to that for Fig. 14.1. Distributions have been taken from the models defined in Figs 4.7–13 (Hambledon Hill), Fig. 4.21 (Fir Tree Field shaft) and Figs 4.41–5 (Maiden Castle), and from the models defined by Meadows et al. *(2007, figs 6–9) (Hazleton) and Bayliss* et al. *(2007c, figs 3 and 5–7) (Ascott-under-Wychwood). The overall structure of this model is shown in Fig. 14.114, and its other components in Figs 14.115–16.*

283); and at Hembury, in Devon, there is an 'opaque grey or white "Lincoln Flint" which is used exclusively for axes on this site and most of the pieces are burnt' (Liddell 1932, 178) It should be noted that while such flint can be found in Lincolnshire, it also occurs in superficial deposits elsewhere (e.g. Healy 1988, 33). These axeheads made of distinctive flint first appear in *4130–3755 cal BC* (*95% probability*; Fig. 14.118: *start different flint*), probably in *3940–3790 cal BC* (*68% probability*). They ceased to be deposited in early Neolithic contexts in southern Britain in *3575–3365 cal BC* (*95% probability*; Fig. 14.118: *end different flint*), probably in *3555–3480 cal BC* (*68% probability*).

A chronological model for the overall currency of ground stone axeheads from English and Welsh sources in early Neolithic contexts in southern Britain is given in Figs 14.119–21. Figure 41.120 shows measurements directly associated with implements from enclosures followed by *termini post* and *ante quos*. Figure 14.121 does the same for non-enclosure contexts. This model suggests that they first appeared in *3785–3650 cal BC* (*95% probability*; Fig. 14.119: *start stone axes*), probably in *3735–3710 cal BC* (*20% probability*) or *3700–3660 cal BC* (*48% probability*). In early Neolithic contexts in southern Britain, their deposition ceased in *3540–3440 cal BC* (*95% probability*; Fig. 14.119: *end stone axes*), probably in *3530–3520 cal BC* (*1% probability*) or *3515–3465 cal BC* (*67% probability*).

The main source areas of dated stone axeheads from southern Britain fall into three broad geographical zones: a north-western one comprising Great Langdale and adjacent deposits (Groups VI and XI), a south-western one comprising primarily Cornish sources (Groups I, IV, IVa, XVI, XVII and ungrouped greenstones), and a smaller Welsh one (Groups VII and VIII). They are examined separately in Figs 14.122, 14.124–6, and 14.127.

A chronological model for the currency of ground stone

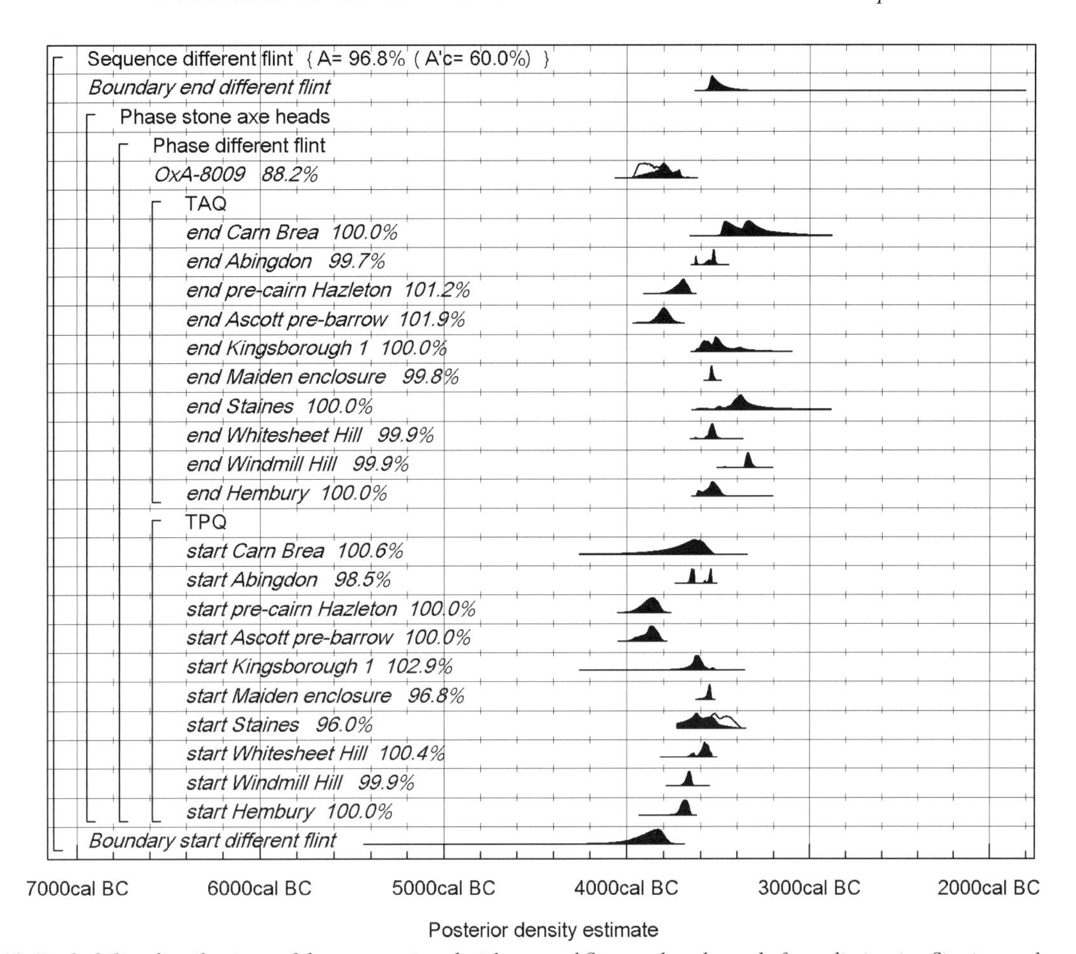

Fig. 14.118. Probability distributions of dates associated with ground flint axeheads made from distinctive flint in southern Britain. The format is the same as for Fig. 14.1. Distributions for enclosures have been taken from the models listed in the captions to Figs 4.2–4; other distributions have been taken from models defined in Fig. 4.21 (Fir Tree Field shaft), and by Meadows et al. *(2007, figs 6–9) (Hazleton) and Bayliss* et al. *(2007c, figs 3 and 5–7) (Ascott-under-Wychwood). The large square brackets down the left-hand side of the diagram, along with the OxCal keywords, define the model exactly.*

axeheads from north-western sources in early Neolithic contexts in southern Britain is shown in Fig. 14.122. This model suggests that they began to be deposited there in *3705–3540 cal BC* (*95% probability*; Fig. 14.122: *start NW axes*), probably in *3670–3630 cal BC* (*29% probability*) or *3610–3555 cal BC* (*39% probability*). In early Neolithic contexts in southern Britain, their deposition ceased in *3535–3370 cal BC* (*92% probability*; Fig. 14.122: *end NW axes*) or *3365–3315 cal BC* (*3% probability*), probably in *3510–3445 cal BC* (*68% probability*). It must be remembered that all the finds concerned are well removed from the source area, so that earlier associations may occur in the north of England. This southern currency is, however, consistent with the limited dating for the working of the Langdale outcrops (Fig. 14.123; Table 14.12). Those limitations are plural. Given the extent of the outcrop and its exploitation (Claris and Quartermaine 1989, fig. 2), the dates are thinly spread. Where samples are specified they were all bulk charcoal of several taxa and thus capable of including material of various ages, although centuries-old trees are unlikely to have grown on the mountain. They are therefore all interpreted as *termini post quos*.

The dated south-western implements include examples from the source area, and the slightly earlier date estimate for the start of the exploitation of these rocks may well reflect this. A chronological model for the currency in early Neolithic contexts from southern Britain of ground stone axeheads from sources in south-west England is shown in Figs 14.124–6. This model suggests that the exploitation of these sources began in *3810–3635 cal BC* (*86% probability*; Fig. 14.124: *start SW axes*) or *3615–3540 cal BC* (*9% probability*), probably in *3710–3645 cal BC* (*68% probability*). The deposition of axeheads from these sources in early Neolithic contexts in southern Britain ceased in *3555–3470 cal BC* (*95% probability*; Fig. 14.124: *end SW axes*), probably in *3540–3510 cal BC* (*68% probability*).

A chronological model for the currency in early Neolithic contexts from southern Britain of the three stratified and dated stone axeheads from sources in Wales is shown in Fig. 14.127. Unfortunately the small number of artefacts renders this of limited utility. It does suggest, however, that the Welsh sources were also exploited by the mid-fourth millennium cal BC, on the evidence of dates for Etton for Group VII and for Hambledon and Carn Brea for Group VIII and cf Group VIII respectively. Recent investigations on Graig Lwyd have yielded two dates which seem to relate

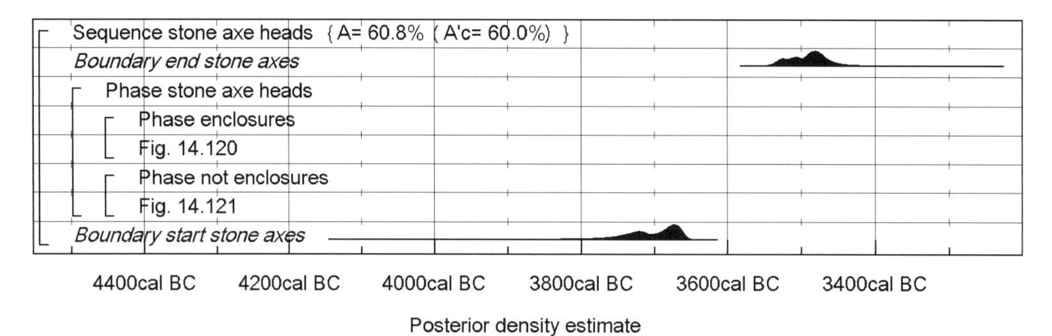

Fig. 14.119. Overall structure of the chronological model for the currency of early Neolithic ground stone axeheads in southern Britain. The component sections of this model are shown in detail in Figs 14.120–1. The large square brackets down the left-hand side of the figures, along with the OxCal keywords, define the overall model exactly.

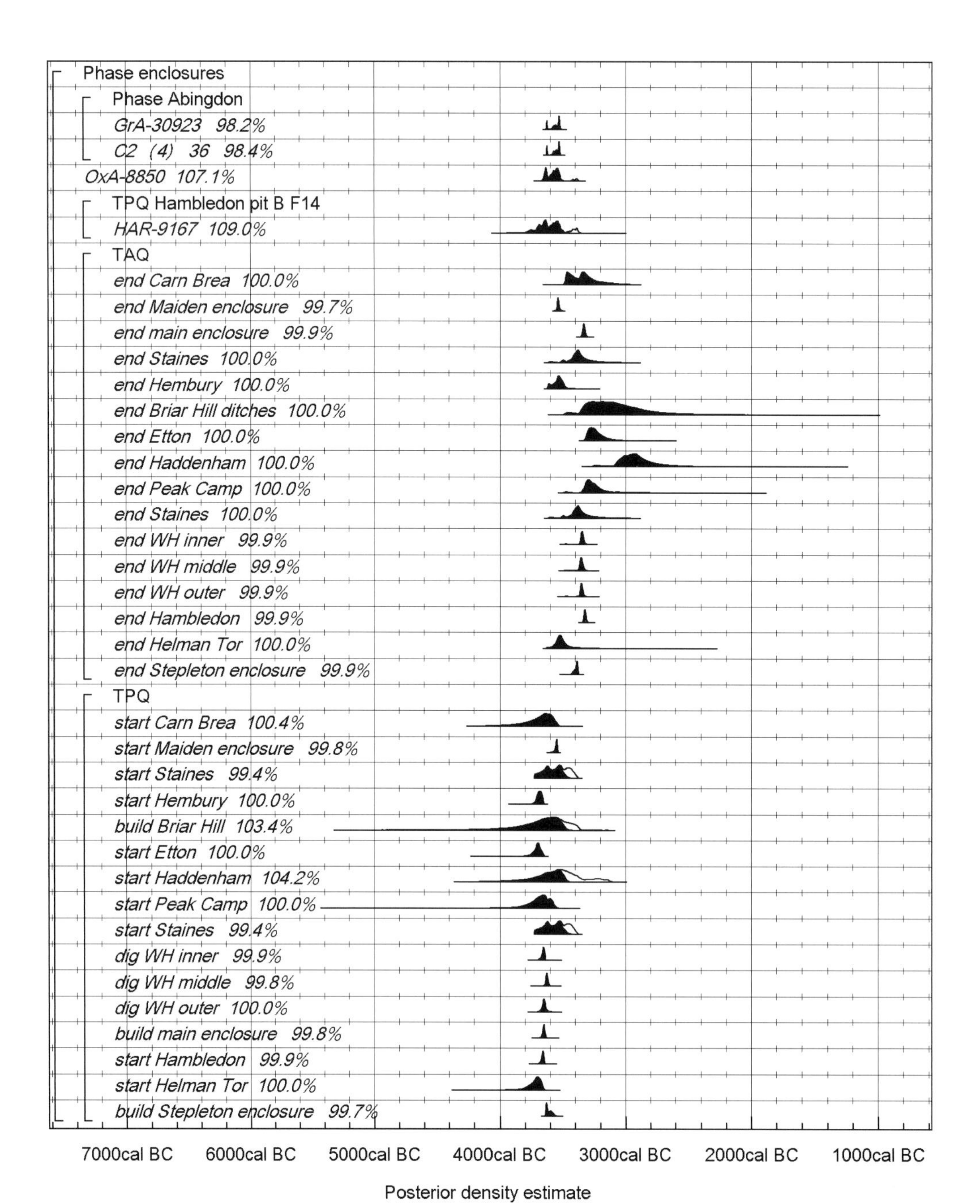

Fig. 14.120. Probability distributions of dates from enclosure sites with early Neolithic ground stone axeheads. The format is identical to that for Fig. 14.1. Distributions have been taken from the models listed in the captions to Figs 4.2–4. The overall structure of this model is shown in Fig. 14.119, and its other component in Fig. 14.121.

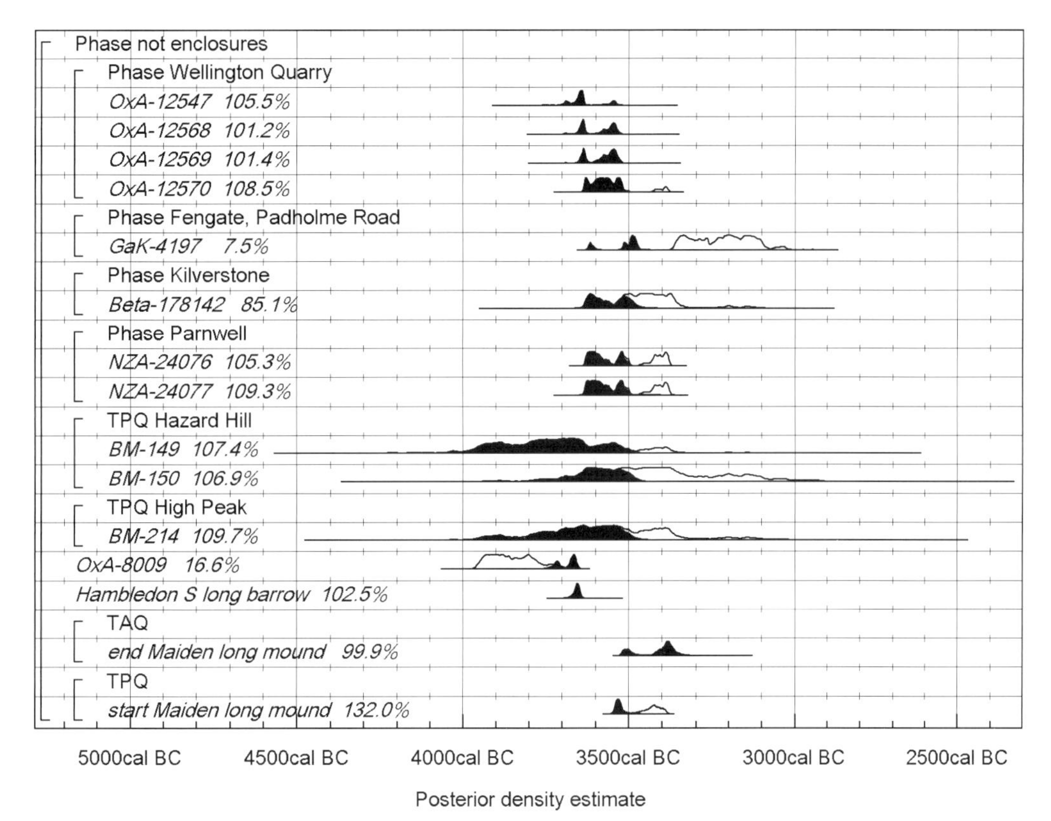

Fig. 14.121. Probability distributions of dates directly associated with early Neolithic ground stone axeheads, and from other sites where such axeheads have been found. The format is identical to that for Fig. 14.1. Distributions have been taken from the models defined in Figs 4.7–13 (Hambledon Hill), Fig. 4.21 (Fir Tree Field shaft) and Figs 4.41–5 (Maiden Castle). The overall structure of this model is shown in Fig. 14.119, and its other component in Fig. 14.120.

to extraction and working there (Table 14.12: Beta-128505, SWAN-1420; Williams and Davidson 1998). These too are *termini post quos*, and the more recent of them may relate to the late Neolithic exploitation evidenced by a Graig Lwyd axehead fragment and flakes in a third millennium cal BC pit within henge B at Llandygai, some 15 km away (Lynch and Musson 2001, 69–71, 120). Earlier local use is shown by evidence for working of the material at an early Neolithic house recently discovered at Parc Bryn Cegin, immediately next to Llandygai (Kenney and Davidson 2006; Kenney 2009).

The only indubitable continental import to be found in a dated context is an axehead of Alpine jadeitite from beside the Sweet Track in the Somerset Levels, for which the dendrochronological construction date for the track provides a *terminus post quem*, on the assumption that the track would have been there before the artefact could have been deposited from it (Fig. 14.128: *Sweet Track*). This artefact may already have been an heirloom when deposited, since quarrying at the source seems to have ceased by the end of the fifth millennium cal BC (Pétrequin *et al.* 2008, 269). If so, the same applies to the other jadeitite artefacts from Britain, including unstratified finds from the main enclosure on Hambledon Hill and from the possible enclosure at High Peak, Devon (I. Smith 2008b, 630). The Sweet Track date is shown with dates relating to two possibly continental imports: a fragmentary axehead of hard, grey Palaeozoic sandstone, perhaps from the Ardennes or Scandinavia, placed over a small group of animal bones in a segment butt at Kingsborough 2 (M. Allen *et al.* 2008, 244–5, 262) and a complete axehead from near the base of the outer ditch at Raddon which is variously attributed to Group I or, tentatively, to a source in northern France (Quinnell and Taylor 1999). Whatever its source, the fan-shaped outline of the implement, which has a pointed butt and a very wide blade, is exceptional (Gent and Quinnell 1999b, fig. 16:1). This and its green colour suggest an attempt to replicate a jadeitite axehead, some of which are of similar outline (Pétrequin *et al.* 2008, fig. 22.2). It is described as 'soft', in other words non-functional.

Jadeitite axeheads also reached Ireland, as did Group VI axeheads from Langdale, one example being found at Ballygalley, Co. Antrim, although not in a definitely early Neolithic context. Some ungrouped gabbros from Ireland may also be of British origin (Cooney and Mandal 1998, 105–10, 175–6). Antrim porcellanite axeheads were brought into Britain (Sheridan *et al.* 1992, fig. 6), as was Antrim flint and axeheads made of it (Saville 1999a). Neither is known from a stratified early Neolithic context, although there is a surface find of a flake from a porcellanite axehead from the same field as the Hazard Hill site in Devon (Clough and Cummins 1988, 161).

The Sweet Track provides a *terminus post quem* not only for the jadeitite axehead but for a flint one found beside it

Table 14.12. Radiocarbon dates from Great Langdale and Graig Lwyd.

Site	Laboratory number	Material	Context	Radiocarbon Age (BP)	$\delta^{13}C$ (‰)	Calibrated date range (cal BC) (95% confidence)
Langdale						
Langdale	BM-281	Unidentified bulk charcoal sample	Associated with implements and chippings, 90 cm below surface of peat	4680±135		3710–3020
Thunacar Knott	BM-676	Unidentified bulk charcoal sample	From layer of axe chippings (Bradley and Edmonds 1993, 80–81; Clough 1973)	4474±52		3360–2920
Stake Beck	OxA-2181	*Corylus avellana*, Pomoideae, *Quercus* and *Salix/Populus* charcoal. *Quercus* 20–75 years-old, remainder young wood	Surface of working floor, ?formed of dumps of material, seen as providing TAQ for site (Bradley and Edmonds 1993, 112–15)	4790±80	−25.5	3710–3360
Harrison Stickle trench 1	BM-2625	*Betula*, Pomoideae, *Quercus* and *Salix/Populus* charcoal. *Quercus* 20–75 years-old (mainly 20–35), remainder 3–25 yr	Associated with deposit of *in situ* debitage (Bradley and Edmonds 1993, 115–17)	4870±50	−25.3	3760–3530
Harrison Stickle trench 4	BM-2626	*Betula*, Pomoideae, *Corylus avellana*, and *Salix/Populus* charcoal, all 3–25 years-old	Associated with accumulation of debitage in natural hollow (Bradley and Edmonds 1993, 117–18)	4880±50	−24.8	4350–3960
Top Buttress site 95	BM-2628	*Betula*, Pomoideae, *Quercus* and *Salix/Populus* charcoal. *Betula* 3–25 yr, *Salix/Populus* 3–25 yr, *Quercus* 20–75 yr (mainly 20–35 yr)	1.30–1.40 m from surface, at base of sequence of *in situ* and dumped knapping deposits, stratified below BM-2627 (Bradley and Edmonds 1993, 126–9, fig. 6.13)	4760±50	−23.5	3650–3370
Top Buttress site 95	BM-2627	*Betula*, Pomoideae, *Quercus* and *Salix/Populus* charcoal. *Quercus* 20–75 yr (mainly 20–35 yr), *Betula* 3–75 yr (mainly 20–35 yr), *Salix/Populus* 3–25 yr, *Corylus avellana* 3–75 yr	0.40–0.50 cm from surface, near top of sequence of *in situ* and dumped knapping deposits, stratified above BM-2628 (Bradley and Edmonds 1993, 126–9, fig. 6.13)	6965±30		5980–5740
Thorn Crag	OxA-4212	Unspecified charcoal	Under flake-filled deposit	5080±90	−25.6	4050–3650
Graig Lwyd						
Site B, Trench 6, context 625/617	Beta-128505	Unspecified charcoal	Layer including Graig Lwyd flakes, from minimal exposure of deposits which 'may represent the stone scree layer exoloited for axe-making material' (Williams and Davidson 1998, 11–12)	4400±40		3310–2900
Cairn 67	SWAN-142	Unspecified charcoal flecks and lumps	From among tightly packed fresh, sharp Graig Lwyd flakes in clay sealed beneath a cairn (Williams and Davidson 1998, 18–19)	5330±90		4350–3960

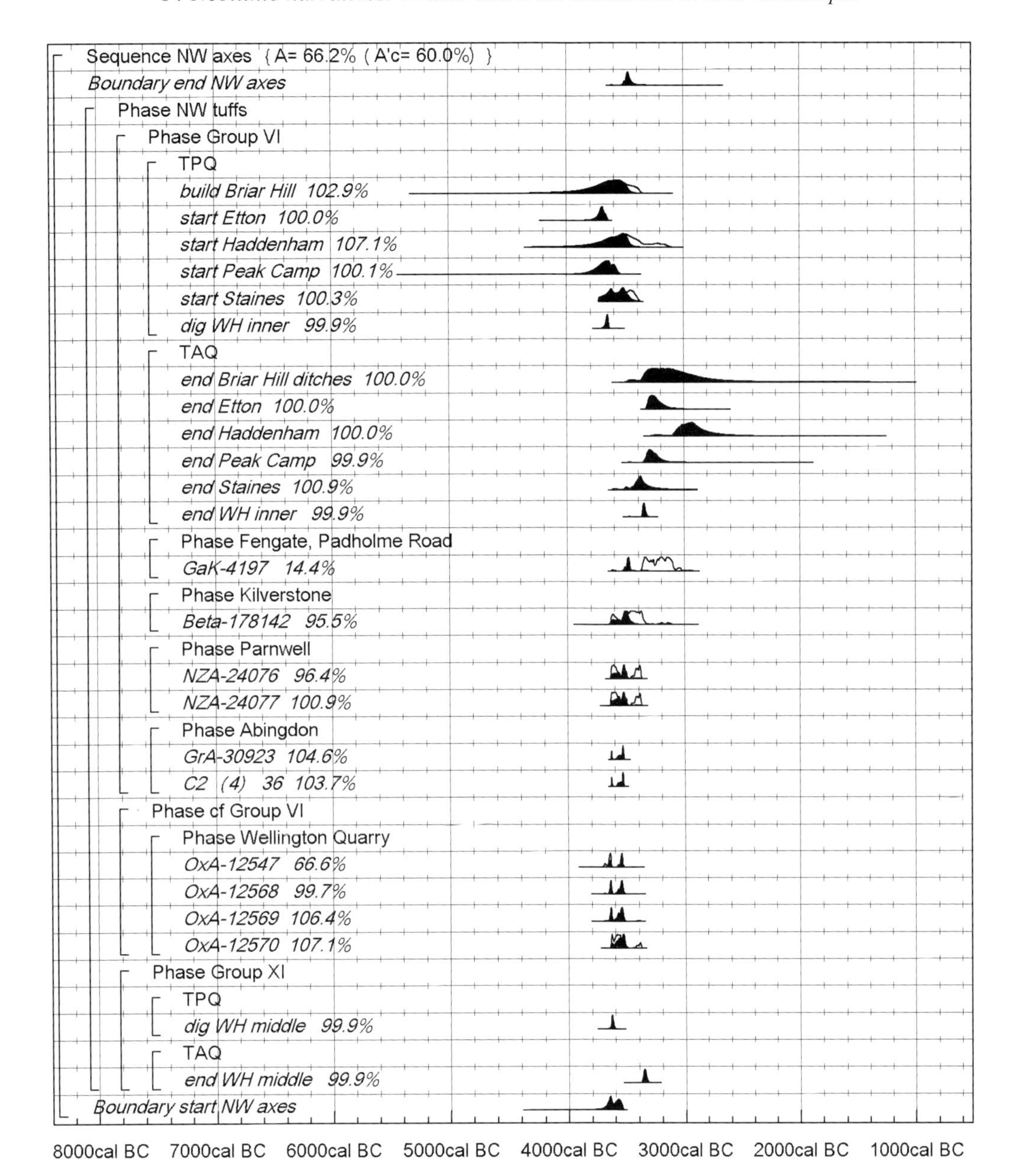

Fig. 14.122. Probability distributions of dates associated with early Neolithic ground stone axeheads from NW sources in southern Britain. The format is the same as for Fig. 14.1. Distributions have been taken from the models listed in the captions to Figs 4.2–4. The large square brackets down the left-hand side of the diagram, along with the OxCal keywords, define the model exactly.

(Coles and Coles 1986, pl. 28). The artefact is attributed to a South Downs source by trace element analysis (Craddock *et al.* 1983, sample no. 362) and is compatible with the 'Cissbury axe' form of those made at the mine sites (Holgate 1995c, fig. 12: 3–7; Barber *et al.* 1999, fig. 2.6). This accords with the early fourth millennium start for flint extraction in Sussex indicated by the available radiocarbon dates. An overall model for the chronology of the early Neolithic use of the Sussex flint mines is shown in Fig. 14.129. This suggests that they were worked from *4145–3805 cal BC* (*95% probability*; Fig. 14.129: *start Sussex flint mines*), probably from *4020–3855 cal BC* (*68% probability*). This period of activity ended in *3635–3340 cal BC* (*95% probability*; Fig. 14.129: *end Sussex flint mines*), probably in *3620–3475 cal BC* (*68% probability*).

Figure 14.130 compares start dates for the South Downs mines, axeheads of distinctive flint, and stone axeheads from British sources in the south of England. It is apparent that flint mining and axehead manufacture in Sussex occurred from the early years of the Neolithic. The selection of distinctive, unmined flints for polished axeheads had begun by the 39th century cal BC. Flints identical to those of the bulk of the industries in which they occur may well have been used for axeheads as early or earlier. We have simply not found any dated examples from before the currency of causewayed enclosures. Axeheads of

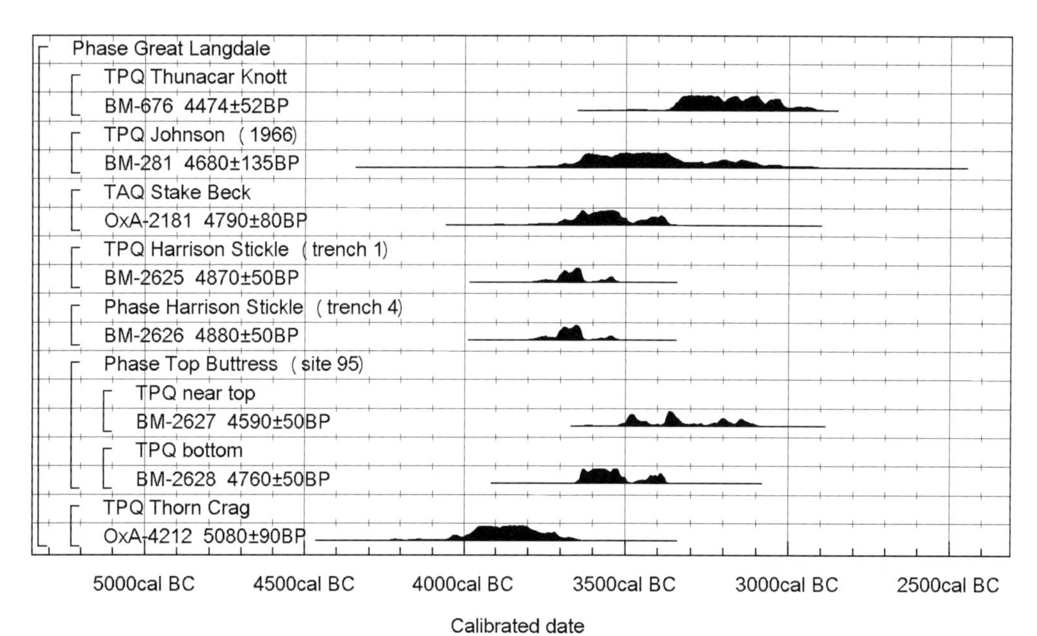

Fig. 14.123. Calibrated radiocarbon dates (Stuiver and Reimer 1993) from Great Langdale, Cumbria.

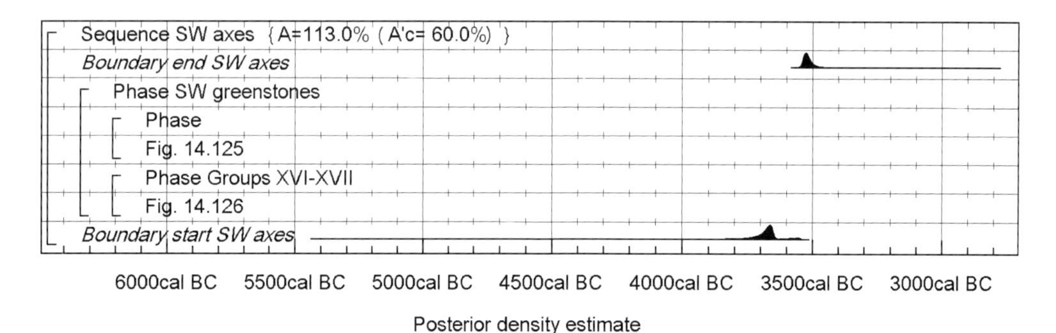

Fig. 14.124. Overall structure of the chronological model for the currency of early Neolithic ground stone axeheads from SW sources in southern Britain. The component sections of this model are shown in detail in Figs 14.125–6. The large square brackets down the left-hand side of the figures, along with the OxCal keywords, define the overall model exactly.

Table 14.13. Axeheads of distinctive flint relating to radiocarbon dates shown in Figs 14.114–17 and 14.118.

Site	Sub-division	Comment/reference	Artefact type	Prior distribution
South-east				
Kingsborough 1		M. Allen *et al.* 2008, fig. 10: 63, fig. 11:A	Axehead	Between *start Kingsborough 1* and *end Kingsborough 1*
South-central				
Staines		R. Robertson-Mackay 1987, 95	Axehead fragments and flakes	Between *start Staines* and *end Staines*
Abingdon		Avery 1982, 35	Axehead flakes	Between *start Abingdon* and *end Abingdon*
Ascott-under-Wychwood	Midden	Cramp 2007, 291, 292	Axehead flakes	Between *start Ascott pre-barrow* and *end Ascott pre-barrow*
Hazleton	Pre-cairn	Saville 1990, 154	Axehead flakes	Between *start pre-cairn Hazleton* and *end pre-cairn Hazleton*
Fir Tree Field	Hearth	French *et al.* 2007, fig. A4.2:3	Axehead fragment	*OxA-8009*
Whitesheet Hill		Rawlings *et al.* 2004, 160	Axehead flakes	Between *start Whitesheet Hill* and *end Whitesheet Hill*
Windmill Hill		I. Smith 1965a, 86, 102–3; J. Pollard 1999b, 330	Axeheads, fragments and flakes	Between *start Windmill Hill* and *end Windmill Hill*
South-west				
Carn Brea		Saville 1981, 138	Axehead fragments	Between *start Carn Brea* and *end Carn Brea*
Hembury		Liddell 1932, 178; 1935, 159	Axehead fragments and flakes	Between *start Hembury* and *end Hembury*

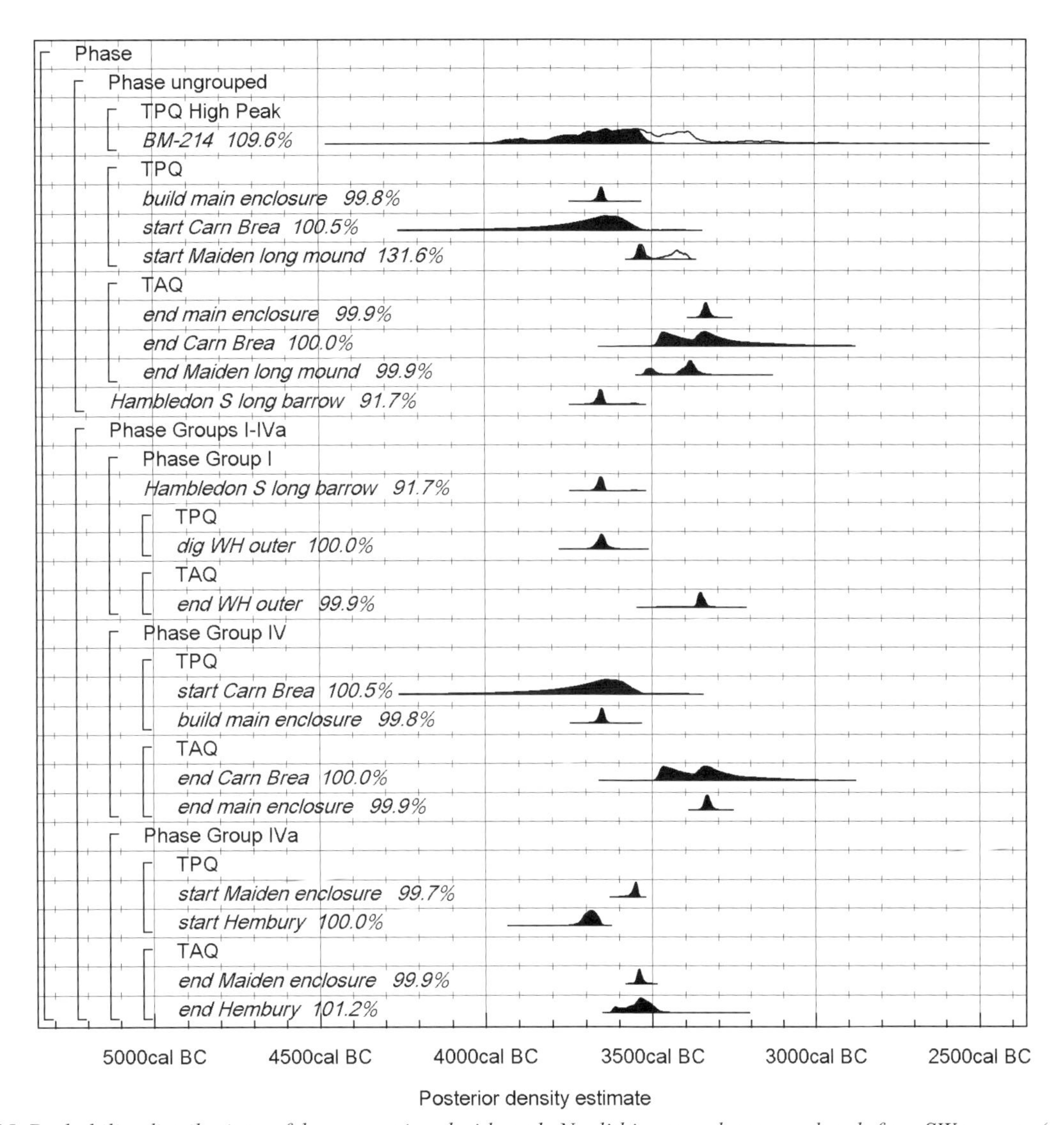

Fig. 14.125. Probability distributions of dates associated with early Neolithic ground stone axeheads from SW sources (ungrouped SW greenstones and Groups I, IV and IVa) in southern Britain. The format is identical to that for Fig. 14.1. Distributions have been taken from the models listed in the captions to Figs 4.2–4. The overall structure of this model is shown in Fig. 14.124, and its other component in Fig. 14.126.

distinctive flint and the imported continental jadeitites are the earliest dated ground axehead materials known from southern Britain, the insular stone sources coming into use in the 38th or 37th centuries cal BC. Figure 14.132 shows the intervals between the beginnings of these practices. The Sussex flint mines had been in use for a couple of centuries or so before the first ground stone axeheads from British sources came into circulation.

Figure 14.131 summarises the times when the main grouped English and Welsh stone sources began to be exploited. The first ground stone axeheads from insular sources appeared in southern Britain in the later 38th or earlier 37th century cal BC, including the products of both north-western and south-western sources. It is *81% probable* that the first axeheads from south-western sources were in use in southern Britain before the first from the north-west. This probably reflects the fact that the north-western sources lie outside the study area, so that their products may have been current earlier closer to the source. The south-western sources, on the other hand, however ill-defined, lie within the study area. Some of the dated enclosures are indeed so close to possible sources as to suggest that they were linked to their exploitation, notably Carn Brea and Group XVI, Helman Tor and Group XVII, and Hembury and Group IVa (Chapter 10).

The dates from early Neolithic contexts in Ireland containing Antrim porcellanite (group IX) are not modelled here. Its occurrence, however, in the Donegore and Magheraboy enclosures (Figs 12.5–9, and 12.15) and at sites such as the Ballygalley, Ballyharry and Monanny houses (Figs 12.22–7) indicates that, whatever the date of Magheraboy – discussed further below – the sources were being exploited by the 38th or early 37th century cal BC. Finds from court tombs and portal tombs (Sheridan *et al.* 1992, 406–7) also point to use in the fourth millennium, but provide little precision, given the state of the dating

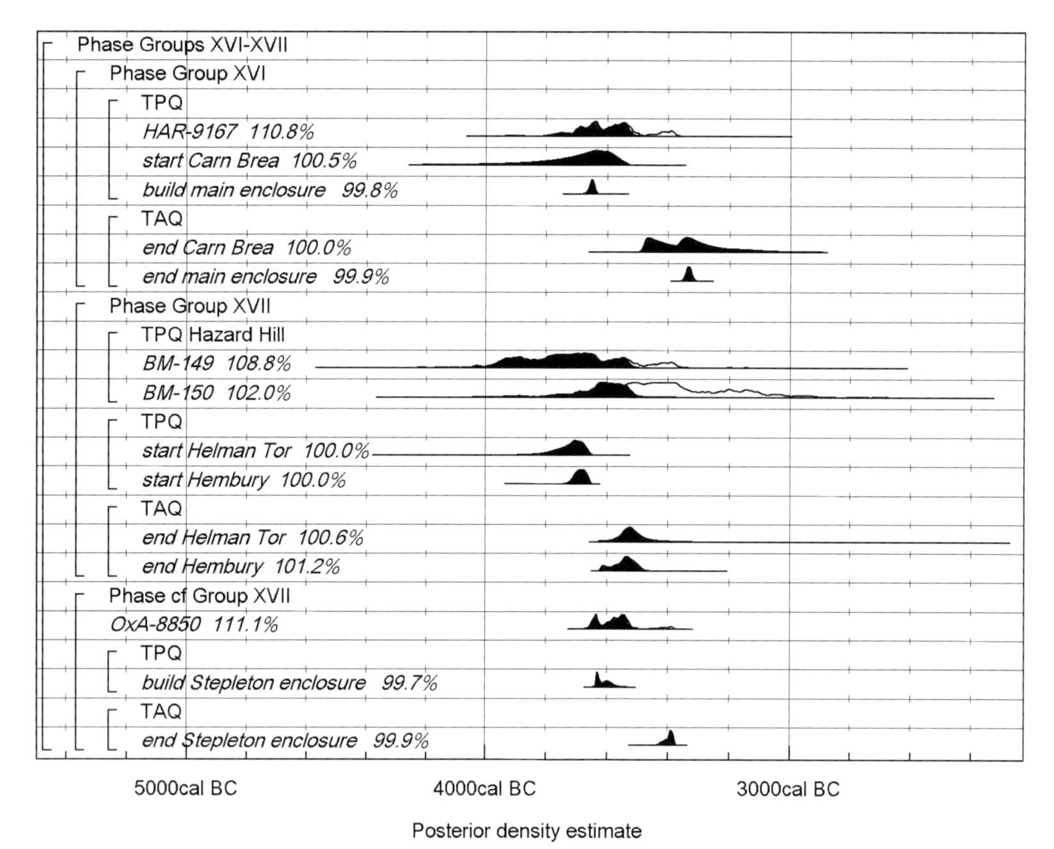

Fig. 14.126. Probability distributions of dates associated with early Neolithic ground stone axeheads from SW sources (ungrouped SW greenstones and Groups XVI and XVII) in southern Britain. The format is identical to that for Fig. 14.1. Distributions have been taken from the models listed in the captions to Figs 4.2–4. The overall structure of this model is shown in Fig. 14.124, and its other component in Fig. 14.125.

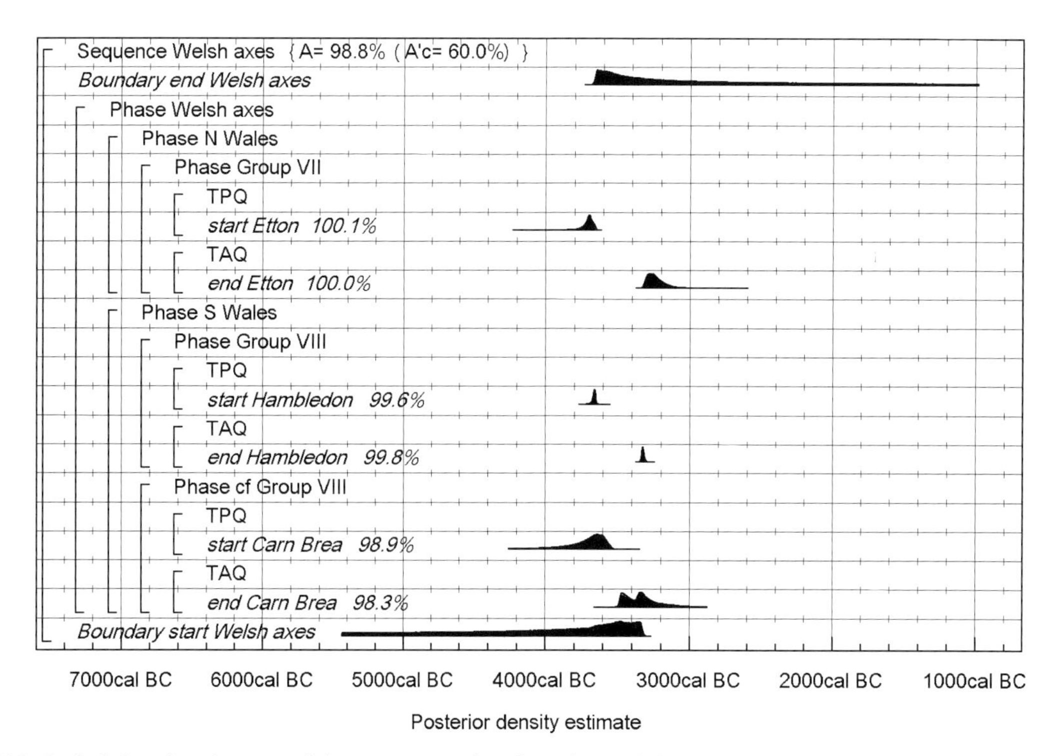

Fig. 14.127. Probability distributions of dates associated with early Neolithic ground stone axeheads from Welsh sources in southern Britain. The format is the same as for Fig. 14.1. Distributions have been taken from the models listed in the captions to Figs 4.2–4. The large square brackets down the left-hand side of the diagram, along with the OxCal keywords, define the model exactly.

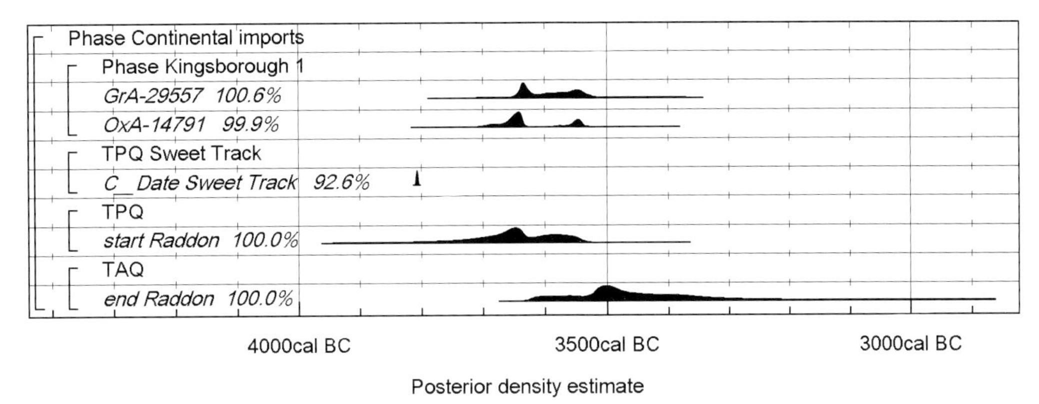

Fig. 14.128. Probability distributions of dates associated with certainly or possibly Continental ground stone axeheads in southern Britain. The distributions have been taken from the model defined in Figs 14.114–17.

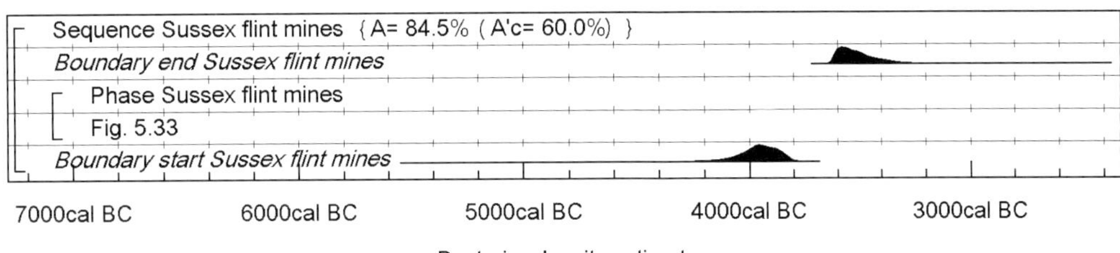

Fig. 14.129. Overall structure of the chronological model for the early Neolithic use of the Sussex flint mines. The component section of this model is shown in detail in Fig. 5.33 (although the posterior density estimates shown on this figure are not those relating to this model). The large square brackets down the left-hand side of these figures, along with the OxCal keywords, define the overall model exactly.

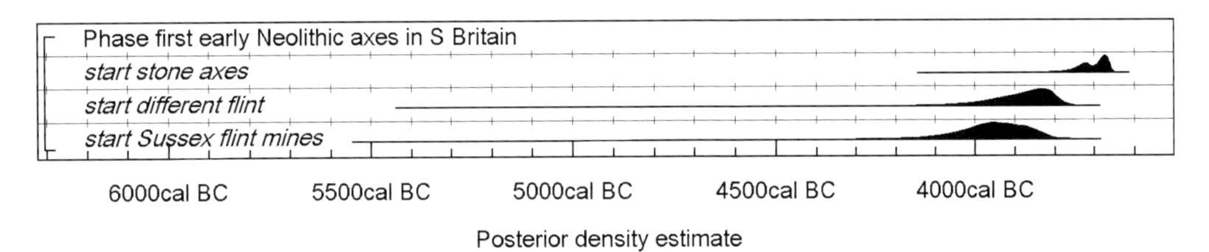

Fig. 14.130. Probability distributions of dates for the first ground stone axeheads in southern Britain, for the first ground axeheads made from distinctive flint, and for the beginnings of the Sussex flint mines, derived from the models defined in Figs 14.118, 14.119–21 and 14.129 (and its component part).

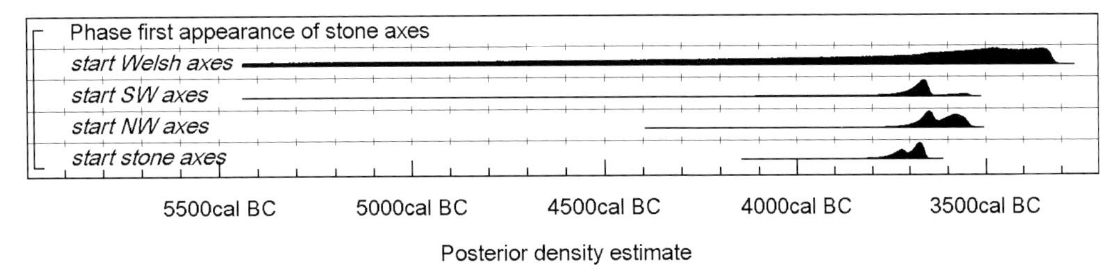

Fig. 14.131. Probability distributions of dates for the first appearance of ground stone axeheads from insular sources in southern Britain, derived from the models defined in Figs 14.127, 14.124–6, 14.122 and 14.119–21.

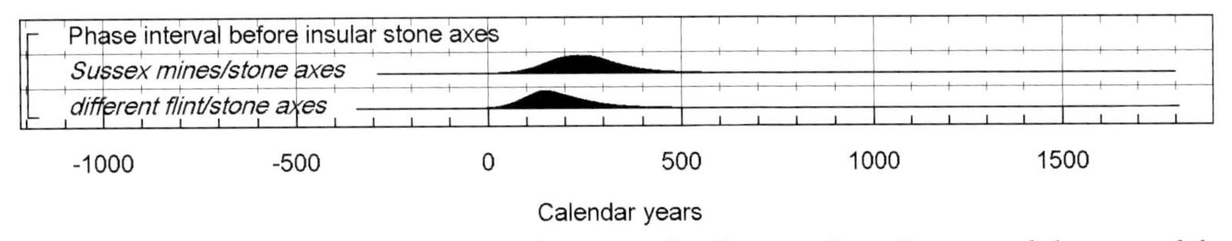

Fig. 14.132. Intervals between the first insular ground stone axeheads in southern Britain and the start of the Sussex flint mines and the first use of distinctive flint for ground axeheads, derived from the models defined in Figs 14.129, 14.118, and 14.119–21.

of these monument types (Chapter 12.3). On Lambay Island, dating at the source points to a fairly short period of porphyry exploitation for axehead production falling in the 38th or 37th centuries cal BC (Fig. 12.30).

The time when these various axehead types ceased to be deposited in early Neolithic contexts in southern Britain is shown in Fig. 14.133. None need have been deposited after the earlier 35th century cal BC, and the production of these objects may have declined at this time. It is noteworthy that stone axeheads are much scarcer than flint ones in Peterborough Ware associations but frequent (especially artefacts from south-western sources) in Grooved Ware ones (Bradley and Edmonds 1993, 55). Those authors' interpretations of different but contemporary sets of practices or ranked spheres of exchange might now be revised into a sequence of attenuation of exchange networks followed by their revival, accompanied by new meanings for the materials and objects themselves.

Things on the move

The models so far presented have made no allowance for the distances over which objects would have been transported. This is significant for the nature and scale of contact and exchange, and long-distance movement of artefacts may have occurred by several processes, or combinations of processes. Obvious examples include carriage by individuals in the course of fairly long journeys; hand-to-hand exchange over a series of short legs; and bulk transport, probably by water or pack animals. In the early Neolithic of southern Britain, stone axeheads and gabbroic pottery are the archaeologically visible commodities which were transported over the greatest distances. In the models which follow, non-local findspots are defined by an arbitrary limit of 75 km and dates from sites closer than this to the sources are excluded.

The model estimating the period during which ground axeheads from British sources were transported over distances of more than 75 km is shown in Figs 14.134–6. These include the flint axeheads from Carn Brea, where 'The flint type of which the axeheads are made is both varied and unidentifiable, and contrasts with the raw material otherwise exploited on the site. The implication is that these are imported implements' (Saville 1981, 138). The nearest sources of non-beach flint are in Devon (Newberry 2002). The model suggests that long-distance transport of insular stone axeheads began in *3725–3635 cal BC* (*95% probability*; Fig. 14.134: *start stone axe networks*), probably in *3680–3645 cal BC* (*68% probability*). This network declined in *3540–3440 cal BC* (*95% probability*; Fig. 14.134: *end stone axe networks*), probably in *3515–3460 cal BC* (*68% probability*).

A similar model, for the period during which gabbroic pottery fabrics were used for early Neolithic pots found more than 75 km from their source in southern Britain is shown in Fig. 14.137. This model suggests that gabbroic pottery was moved significant distances from *3805–3645 cal BC* (*95% probability*; Fig. 14.137: *start gabbroic import*), probably in *3715–3650 cal BC* (*68% probability*). This movement finished in *3555–3465 cal BC* (*95% probability*; Fig. 14.137: *end gabbroic import*), probably in *3550–3515 cal BC* (*68% probability*).

Figure 14.138 shows the period during which long-distance movement of objects is evidenced in the early Neolithic in southern Britain. It is apparent that these networks were probably established in the early 37th century cal BC, and that they may have shut down in the earlier 35th century cal BC. Earlier suggestions that exchange networks became more extensive from *c.* 3400 cal BC and that non-local stone axeheads occurred only late in the sequences at already well established enclosures (e.g. Bradley and Edmonds 1993, 40, 177) do not fit with an enlarged body of stratified and dated artefacts and a more precise chronology. Hambledon Hill provides a telling illustration: the primary silts of the south long barrow there, built in *3680–3635 cal BC* (*95% probability*; Fig. 4.10: *Hambledon S long barrow*), probably in *3665–3645 cal BC* (*68% probability*), included a sherd of gabbroic ware, a flake from an ungrouped south-western greenstone axehead, and a fragment of a Group I axehead (Mercer and Healy 2008, 143–4). Further gabbroic ware and south-western axehead fragments occurred within the primary use of the complex (Mercer and Healy 2008, tables 9.13, 10.2). Two pits are noteworthy. One in the main enclosure contained a Group XVI axehead and two gabbroic bowls (Mercer and Healy 2008, fig. 3.54). Another in the Stepleton enclosure lacked artefacts of south-western origin but contained a substantial early Neolithic assemblage (Mercer and Healy 2008, 292), together with charred fragments of *Erica vagans*, a heath which now grows only on the Lizard peninsula and in Northern Ireland (Austin *et al.* 2008). It is strongly suggestive of packing material and hence direct transport.

Group VI implements, dominant in eastern English enclosures, were found within the primary use, although above the initial silts, of Etton, Haddenham, Staines, Briar Hill, Peak Camp and Windmill Hill. Although they came into circulation in southern Britain later than those from south-western sources, they did so in *3705–3540 cal BC* (*95% probability*; Fig. 14.122: *start NW axes*), probably in *3670–3630 cal BC* (*29% probability*) or *3610–3555 cal BC* (*39% probability*), only slightly later than the start of enclosure building in *3765–3695 cal BC* (*95% probability*; Fig. 14.1: *start S British enclosures*), probably in *3740–3705 cal BC* (*68% probability*).

Figure 14.139 estimates the amount of time between the first appearance of stone axeheads from the south-west and Wales or gabbroic pottery near their sources, and the time when they were transported long distances (e.g. the difference between *start stone axes* and *start stone axe networks* in Figs 14.119 and 14.134). For both types of material the networks appear to have been established very quickly, probably within a generation or two; indeed, both may have circulated in a single network. This short interval applies only to sources in the south-west peninsula and Wales, since the north-western sources are well outside the study area.

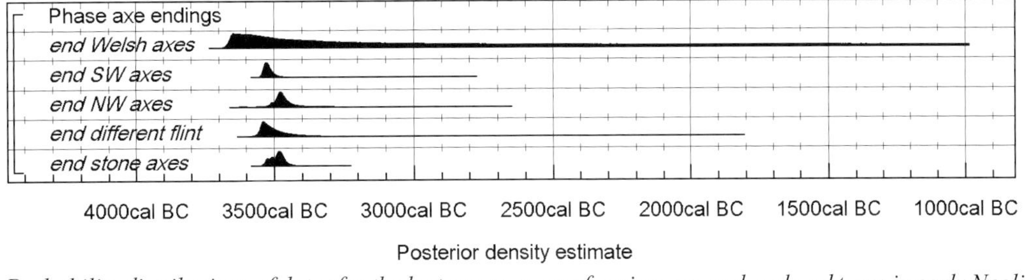

Fig. 14.133. Probability distributions of dates for the last appearance of various ground axehead types in early Neolithic contexts in southern Britain, derived from the models defined in Figs 14.118, 14.119–21, 14.122, 14.124–6 and 14.127.

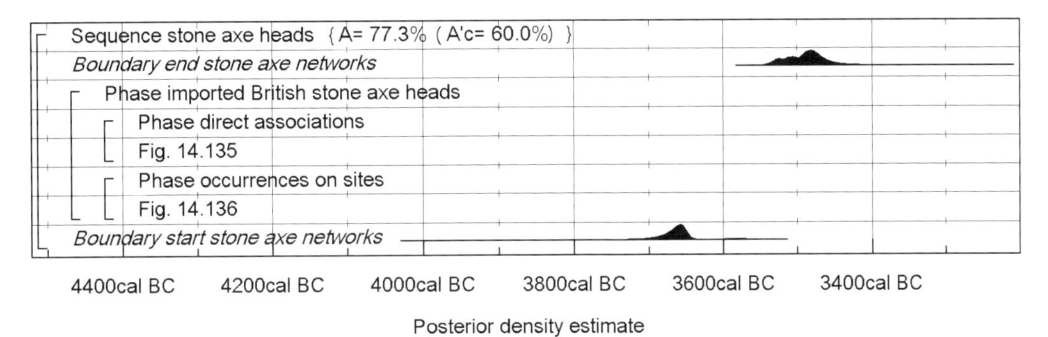

Fig. 14.134. Overall structure of the chronological model for the period when insular ground stone axeheads were transported distances of more than 75 km from their source in the early Neolithic. The component sections of this model are shown in detail in Figs 14.135–6. The large square brackets down the left-hand side of the figures, along with the OxCal keywords, define the overall model exactly.

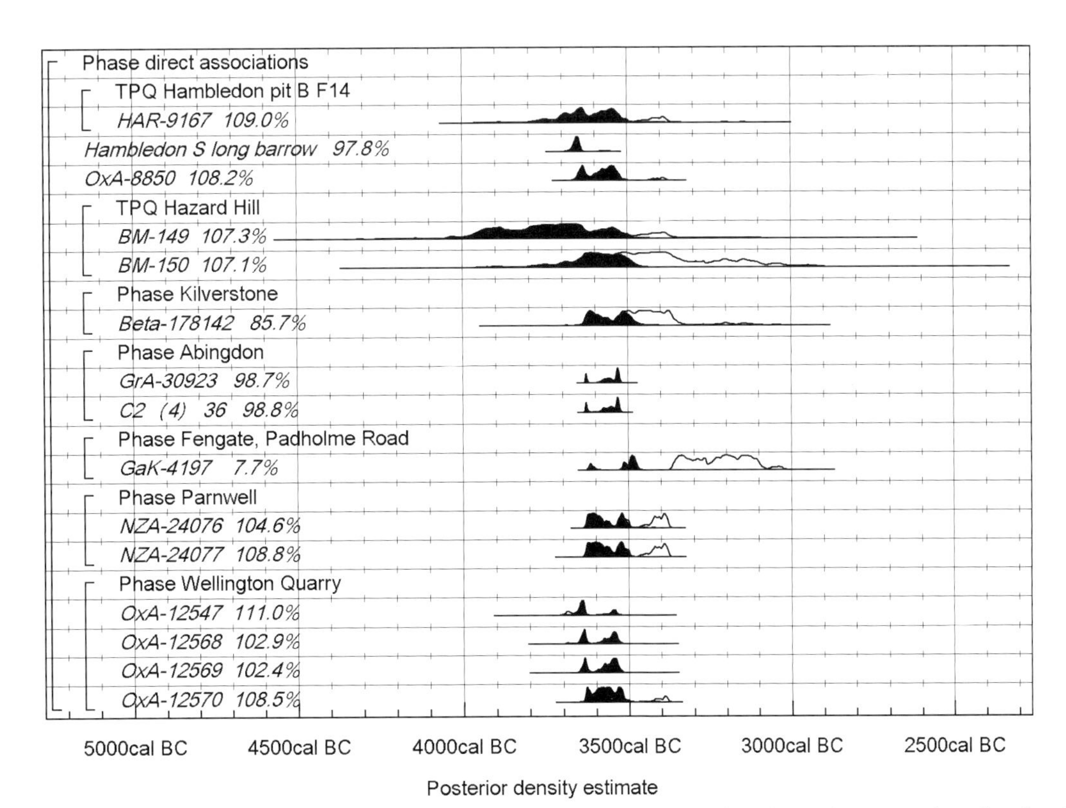

Fig.14.135. Probability distributions of dates from southern Britain associated with insular ground axeheads of stone or distinctive flint found more than 75 km from their source. The format is identical to that for Fig. 14.1. Distributions have been taken from the models defined in Figs 4.7–13 (Hambledon Hill) and Figs 8.18–21 (Abingdon). The overall structure of this model is shown in Fig. 14.134, and its other component in Fig. 14.136.

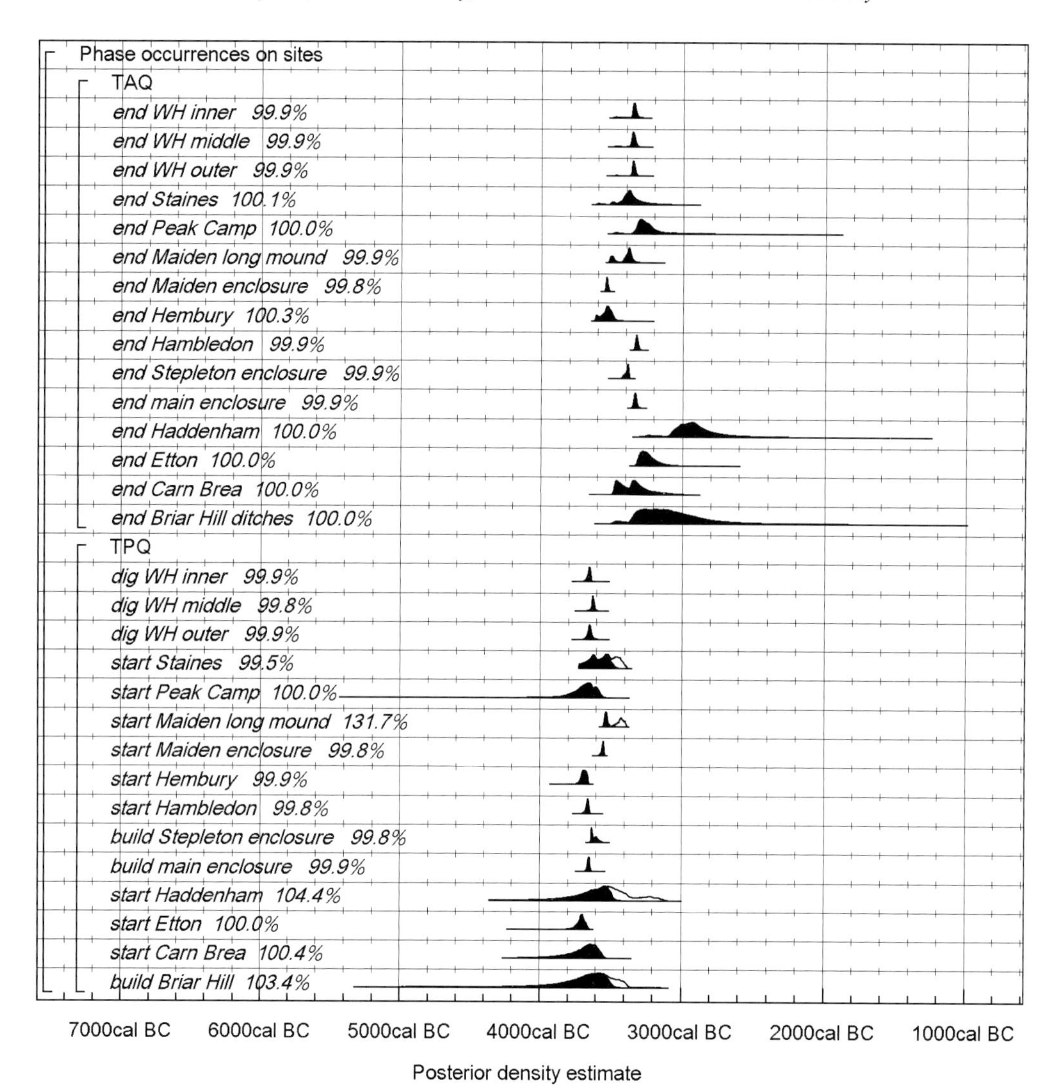

14.136. Probability distributions of dates from southern Britain associated with insular ground axeheads of stone or distinctive flint found more than 75 km from their source. The format is identical to that for Fig. 14.1. Distributions have been taken from the models listed in the captions to Figs 4.2–4. The overall structure of this model is shown in Fig. 14.134, and its other component in Fig. 14.135.

It is noteworthy that the Sussex enclosures do not figure at all in this. They lie outside the range of gabbroic wares; and the only stone object from an upland area is a fragment of granite without obvious sign of working, probably from Devon or Cornwall, found in the inner ditch at Offham (Drewett 1977, 218). The absence of stone axeheads marks them out from enclosures to the west, east and north and corresponds to a local scarcity of stone axeheads from all sources (Woodcock *et al.* 1988, fig. 4). The early establishment of the Sussex flint mines must be significant here. Some of the flint axeheads from the Sussex enclosures, both flaked and ground, are of the 'Cissbury' type made at the mines. There are examples from Whitehawk (Ross Williamson 1930, pl. XIII; Curwen 1936, fig. 320) and Bury Hill (Bedwin 1981, fig. 5), as well as the cache of three ground axeheads from Combe Hill (Drewett 1994, fig. 12). Four axeheads from Whitehawk have actually been attributed to South Downs sources by trace element analysis (Craddock *et al.* 1983, sample nos 699, 700, 703, 713). This tallies with the overlap between the use-lives of the mines and the enclosures and suggests that the mines and their products had considerable significance. Direct links between enclosures and particular groups of mines, like those proposed by Drewett *et al.* (1988, 60–2), may well have obtained, but are difficult to demonstrate on spatial grounds because the mines are concentrated on a block of downland between the two groups of Sussex enclosures, the only exception being the proximity of the Long Down mines to the probably Neolithic enclosure on Halnaker Hill (Fig. 5.1).The Sussex enclosures and their hinterland were, however, within the networks through which south-western and north-western artefacts were brought to lowland Britain, since axeheads from the South Downs reached not only the Somerset Levels, within the south-western network, but also East Anglia (Craddock *et al.* 1983, fig. 2), where axeheads from north-western sources are frequent (Clough and Cummins 1988, map 6).

While only three even possibly continental axeheads

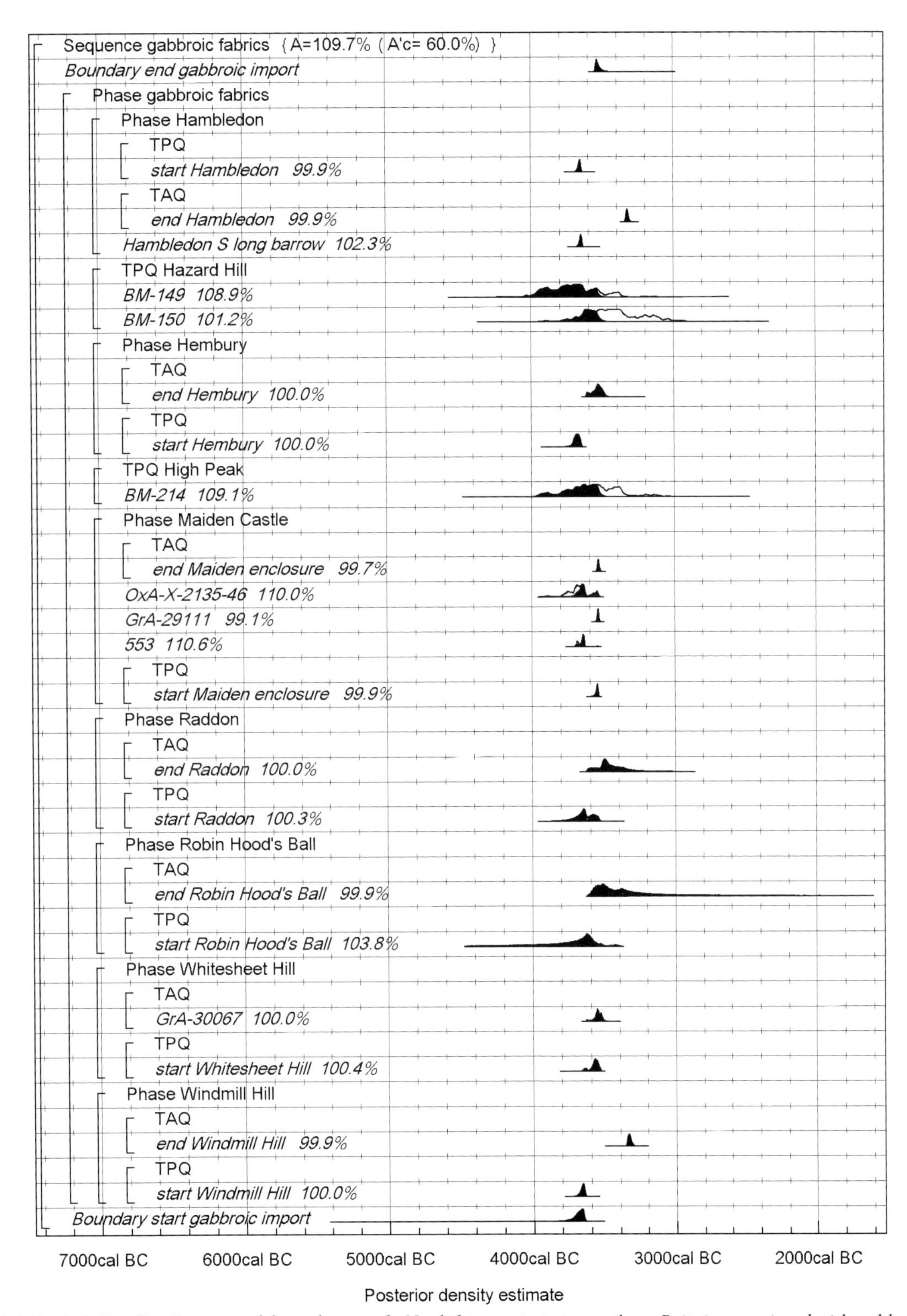

Fig. 14.137. Probability distributions of dates from early Neolithic contexts in southern Britain associated with gabbroic pottery fabrics found more than 75 km from the source. The format is the same as for Fig. 14.1. Distributions have been taken from the models listed in the captions to Figs 4.2–4. The large square brackets down the left-hand side of the diagram, along with the OxCal keywords, define the model exactly.

from Britain can be dated, they suggest that contacts may have been maintained after the 39th century cal BC deposition of the Sweet Track jadeitite axehead (Fig. 14.128). The impression of continued contact is reinforced by stray finds. Five products of the quarry and axehead-making site at Plussulien in Brittany have been found in southern England (Clough and Cummins 1988, map 10; Le Roux 1999, figs 59–60). Their source is seen as having been exploited from the late fifth millennium cal BC to the end of the third (Le Roux 2002, 107). This chronology

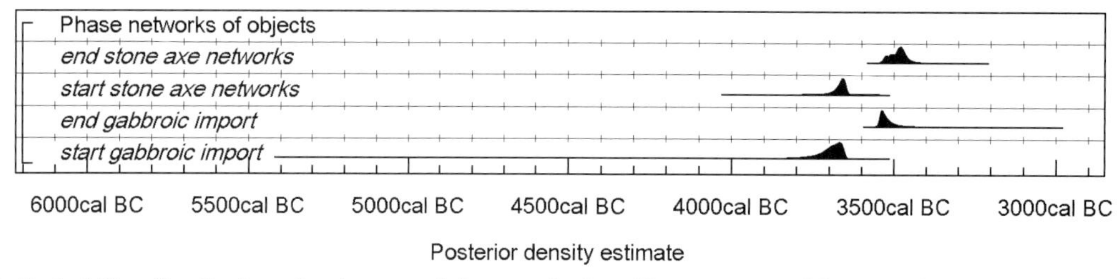

Fig. 14.138. Probability distributions for the period during which gabbroic pottery fabrics and insular stone axeheads were deposited in early Neolithic contexts in southern Britain, derived from the models defined in Figs 14.134–6 and 14.137.

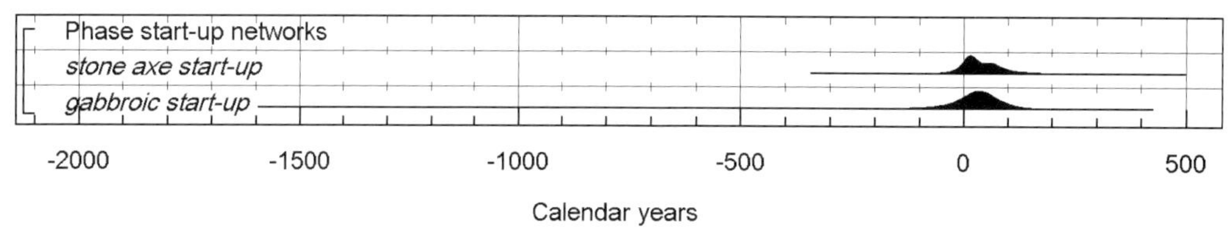

Fig. 14.139. Intervals between the first insular ground stone axehead in southern Britain and the start of long-distance axe movement, and between the first pottery in gabbroic fabrics and the start of its long-distance movement, derived from the models defined in Figs 14.119–21, 14.134–6, 14.104–6 and 14.137.

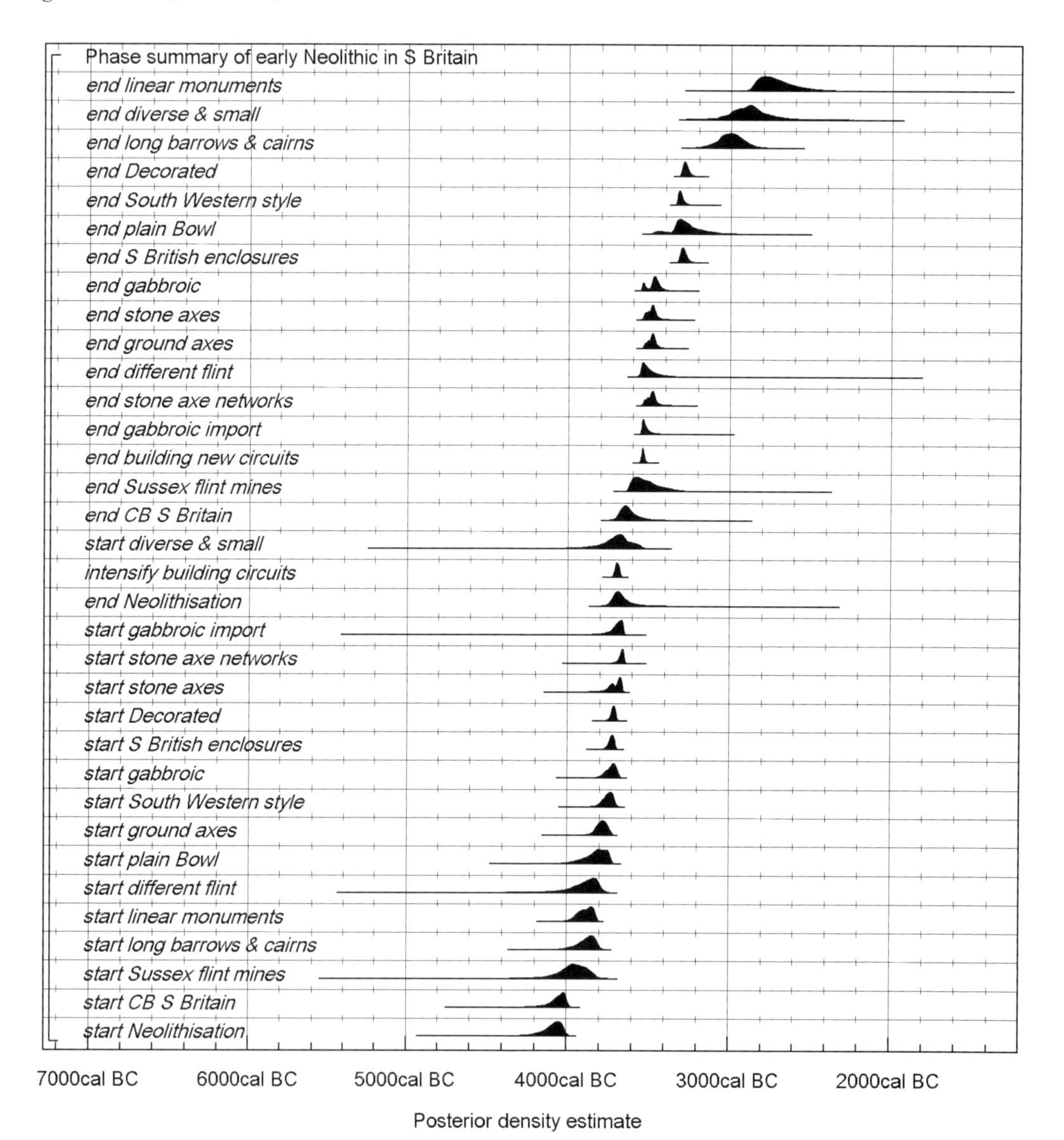

Fig. 14.140. Probability distributions of dates for entrances and exits of early Neolithic things and practices in southern Britain, taken from the models defined in Figs 14.1, 14.7, 14.39, 14.43, 14.44, 14.54, 14.88, 14.90, 14.92, 14.101, 14.104, 14.118, 14.119, 14.129, 14.134 and 14.137 (with their component parts where appropriate).

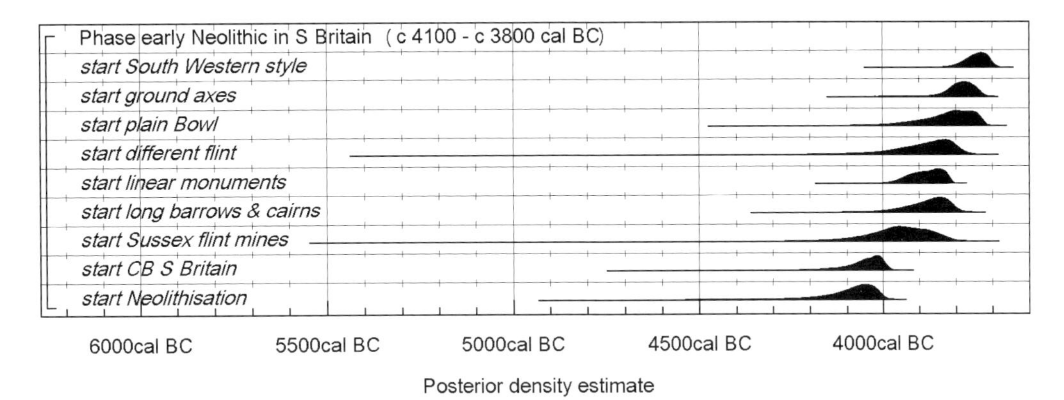

Fig. 14.141. Probability distributions of dates for entrances of early Neolithic things and practices in southern Britain (c. 4100–c. 3800 cal BC), taken from the models defined in Figs 14.39, 14.44, 14.54, 14.88, 14.90, 14.101, 14.118, and 14.129 (with their component parts where appropriate).

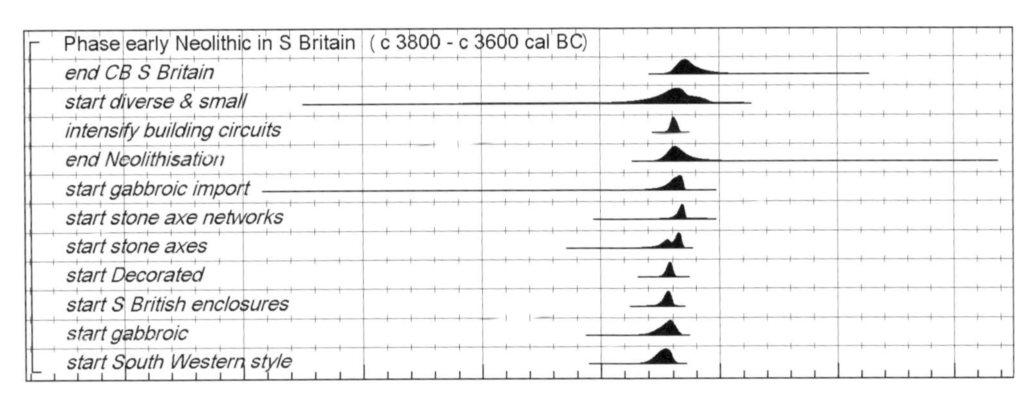

Fig. 14.142. Probability distributions of dates for entrances and exits of early Neolithic things and practices in southern Britain (c. 3800–c. 3600 cal BC), taken from the models defined in Figs 14.1, 14.7, 14.43, 14.54, 14.88, 14.92, 14.101, 14.104, 14.119, 14.134 and 14.137 (with their component parts where appropriate).

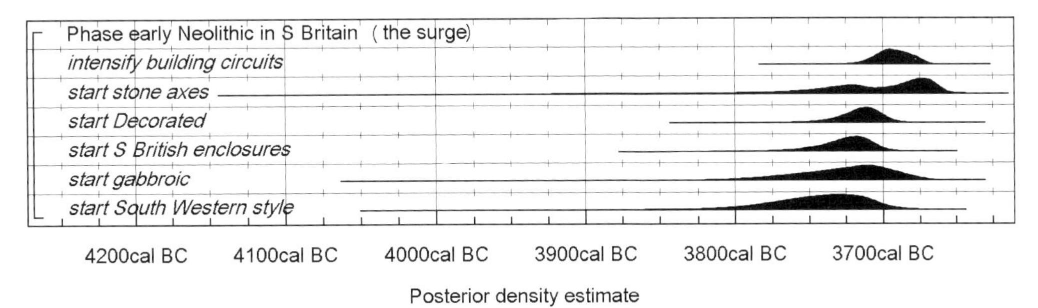

Fig. 14.143. Probability distributions of dates for the surge in innovative early Neolithic things and practices in southern Britain (c. 3750–c. 3675 cal BC), taken from the models defined in Figs 14.1, 14.7, 14.92, 14.101, 14.104 and 14.119 (with their component parts where appropriate).

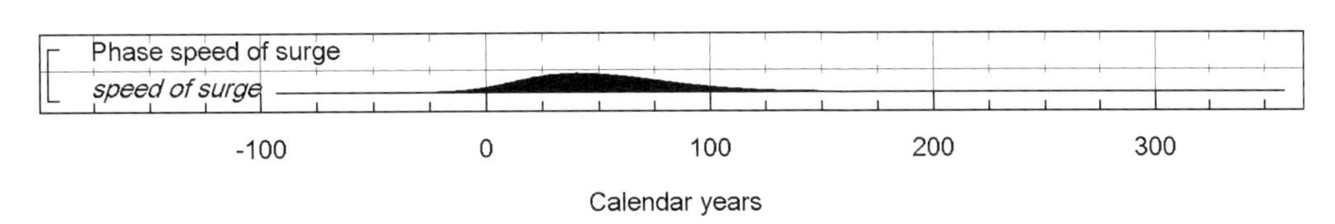

Fig. 14.144. Probability distribution of the period between the introduction of the South-Western style of pottery and the intensification of circuit construction at causewayed enclosures, marking the speed of the surge (derived from the distributions shown in Fig. 14.143).

is based on the contexts and typology of artefacts found elsewhere and on 22 radiocarbon dates measured on unidentified bulk charcoal samples from the workings, 14 of them from a stratified sequence (Le Roux 1999, 45–69). The excavator's difficulty in reconciling measurements and sequence, in which older results were sometimes stratified above younger ones (Le Roux 1999, 55–6), heightens the probability that some if not all of these measurements are *termini post quos* and suggests that exploitation may have started in the fourth rather than the fifth millennium, some time after dates for two small hearths at the base of the main sequence (95% confidence; 4940±115 BP; 3980–3380 cal BC; Gif-2682; and 4960±110 BP; 3990–3520 cal BC; Gif-2330; Le Roux 1999, fig. 15).

One of the English finds is an *hache à bouton*, likely on grounds of typology and association to date to the early third millennium cal BC (Le Roux 1999, 146–7; 2002, 111), but some or all of the remaining four could date back to the fourth millennium. Also relevant to the question of continental contact is the recognition of a group of very finely finished polished flint axeheads of a distinctive banded flint, again all stray finds, for which a Scandinavian source has been suggested, consonant with their predominantly east coast distribution (Saville 1999b; 2004a; Sheridan 1992, 208–10).

The long-distance transport of finished objects, in small quantities, was one end of a spectrum of exchange and transportation. Larger quantities of materials and artefacts were carried over shorter distances, in circumstances where one might envisage single-leg journeys and water-born or animal transport. The numbers of cattle slaughtered at some briefly and occasionally used Wessex enclosures must have been driven there. Those consumed at Hambledon, for example, did not reflect the complete cull of a sustainable herd, but were selected from their herds and brought there to be eaten (Legge 2008), and preliminary results of isotopic analysis of some of the cattle bone from Windmill Hill indicate that they were reared off the Chalk (Hege Usborne, pers. comm.). Cattle elsewhere may have travelled equally long distances. These animals also provide an obvious medium for the transport of relatively bulky and heavy loads. Both cattle and their putative loads may reflect the catchments of enclosures. Some detectable examples are noted here, although their appearance has not been formally modelled.

Nodular flint was carried into Cornwall from sources in Devon or farther away from at least the 37th century cal BC, given its use at Tregarrick Farm (Lawson-Jones 2003, 125), Helman Tor (Saville 1997), and Carn Brea (Saville 1981, 107–8), and into the Cotswolds, probably from the Wessex Chalk, as early as the 39th century cal BC, given its use in the pre-cairn occupation at Ascott-under-Wychwood (Cramp 2007, 291–2). The start of its transport into Wales (e.g. P. Bradley 1999, 50–1) is undated. Quern materials were also transported from an early stage. In the Cotswolds, fragments of May Hill gritstone formed part of the pre-tomb occupation deposit at Hazleton, some 40 km from the source, and a quern of the same material was built into the cairn at Burn Ground (Roe 2009, 27), although it is not clear at what stage in the probably long use-life of the monument (Fig. 9.25) it was inserted. In Wessex, Old Red Sandstone from the Mendips was transported over at least 40 km to Hambledon, where it was the main quern and rubber material of the main enclosure (Roe 2008, 634–5), and was present from the start of the sequence (Roe 2008, table 10.3). Non-local quern materials were also brought over relatively short distances to sites in the Thames valley, including the Staines causewayed enclosure and Eton Rowing Course (Roe 2009, 28–9).

The widespread use on the Wessex Chalk of pottery made of clay from Jurassic deposits to the north and west (Cleal 1995b) is another case of relatively short-distance, large-scale transport. At Hambledon vessels in this group of fabrics, from some 25–60 km away, and others from a non-Jurassic source to the south, some 30–40 km away, increased in frequency through the sequence (Mercer and Healy 2008, figs 3.67, 3.130), suggesting that, if they were brought by those frequenting the complex, its catchment may have expanded. In the south-west peninsula, up to half of the Hembury assemblage seems to be in a family of Carboniferous vein quartz fabrics originating near Raddon some 20 km to the west (Quinnell 1999, 48).

14.6 The southern British early Neolithic: an historical narrative

We are now in a position, for the first time, to attempt to write a narrative of the early Neolithic in southern Britain. This is summarised in Fig. 14.140. It is apparent that the pace of change is not constant through the centuries in question.

The first Neolithic things and practices probably appeared in southern Britain in the 41st century cal BC (Fig. 14.141). This initial Neolithic included at least the presence of Carinated Bowl. This first Neolithic presence, however, was probably not synchronous across southern Britain (Fig. 14.54), and may have spread generally outwards from the south-east corner of England. Other elements of the first centuries of the early Neolithic include flint mines in Sussex and, perhaps beginning slightly later, the first long barrows and long cairns, and the first linear monuments (though not yet 'classic' cursus monuments). At this time, probably during the course of the 39th century cal BC, plain Bowl assemblages without the diagnostic characteristics of Carinated Bowl appeared, and distinctive types of flint (not from the Sussex mines) were selected for the manufacture of ground axeheads. Here, we have not estimated independently the dates when cereals and domesticated animals were introduced (because of the current need to define the end as well as the beginning of a phase of activity in our models), but it is clear that they were both present in these early centuries – cereals from the substantial rectangular house at White Horse Stone in Kent (Chapter 7.6) and domesticated cattle, sheep and pig from the pre-barrow occupation at Ascott-under-Wychwood, Oxfordshire (Chapter 9.4).

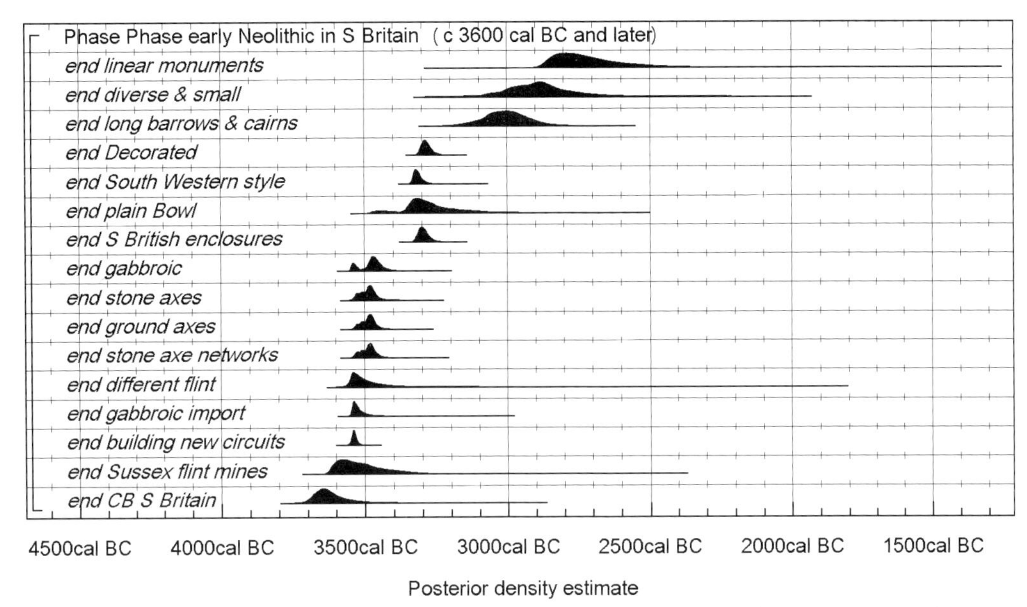

Fig. 14.145. Probability distributions of dates for exits of early Neolithic things and practices in southern Britain (c. 3600 cal BC and later), taken from the models defined in Figs 14.1, 14.7, 14.39, 14.43, 14.44, 14.88, 14.90, 14.92, 14.101, 14.104, 14.118, 14.119, 14.129, 14.134 and 14.137 (with their component parts where appropriate).

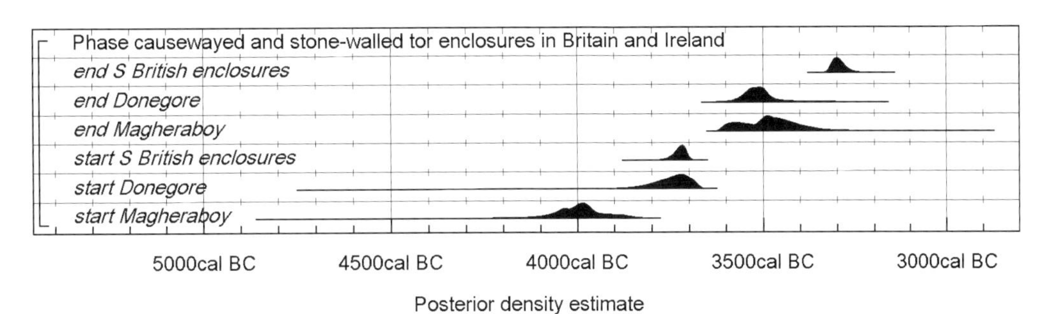

Fig. 14.146. Probability distributions of dates for the use of causewayed and related enclosures in Britain and Ireland, taken from the models defined in Figs 12.5–9, 12.15 and 14.1–4.

During the 38th century cal BC, the pace of change intensified markedly (Fig. 14.140). This is shown in Fig. 14.142, and in more detail in Fig. 14.143. Within the space of two or three generations (Fig. 14.144), the people of the south-west peninsula developed the South-Western style of pottery and began to exploit gabbroic clays; further east, people developed Decorated Bowl pottery and constructed the first causewayed enclosures. By this time, the first Neolithic things and practices had spread right across southern Britain, reaching south Wales and the Marches. As enclosure construction intensified during the early decades of the 37th century cal BC, long-distance networks for the movement of axeheads and gabbroic pottery were developed within Britain (in contrast to the network represented by the import of continental jadeitite, seen at the Sweet Track from the very end of the 39th or the very beginning of the 38th century cal BC). This startling array of innovation may have arisen within the span of an individual lifetime. It is hard to unpick causality within this veritable surge of change. Did the building and use of enclosures lead to the establishment of other new practices and the widening of social and material networks? Or did the changes of the 38th century cal BC produce the enclosure phenomenon? In the present state of knowledge, it is too close to call the answer, but we have dramatically narrowed the timeframe to the point where we need to consider the agency of two or three specific human generations.

Another uncertainty concerns the disparate collection of diverse and small monuments, the date estimate for the appearance of which is imprecise (Fig. 14.142). Some of these may have been first built and used as part of the surge of innovation of the later 38th into the earlier 37th century cal BC, or have been part of the intensifications of the mid-37th century cal BC. This uncertainty is important, because their small size stands in important contrast to the great collective goings-on witnessed at enclosures. Oval barrows too remain imprecisely dated but appear to fall in the second half of the fourth millennium cal BC (Fig. 14.42). So their apparent focus on individuals, at least in cases like Whiteleaf (Chapter 6.1.2) and Mount Farm (Chapter 8.6), may also stand in contrast to the collective focus of enclosures and long barrows.

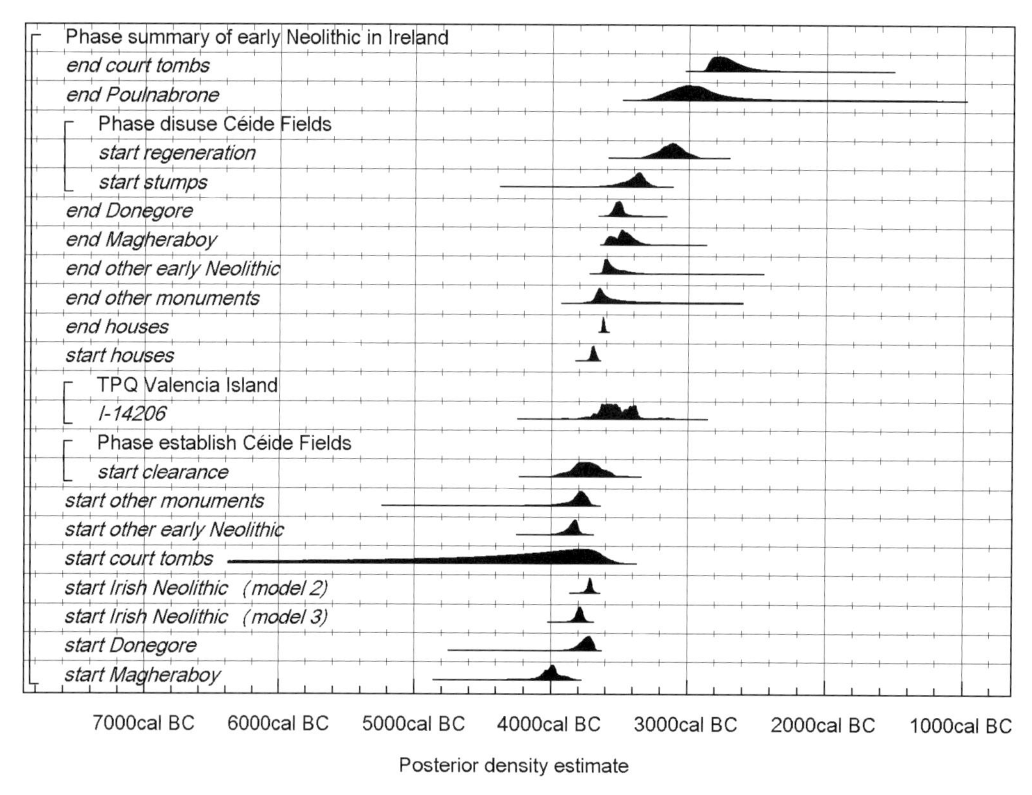

Fig. 14.147. Probability distributions of dates for entrances and exits of early Neolithic things and practices in Ireland, taken from the models defined in Figs 12.5, 12.15, 12.22, 12.30, 12.31, 12.32, 12.35, 12.37, 12.39, 12.54 and 12.56 (with their component parts where appropriate).

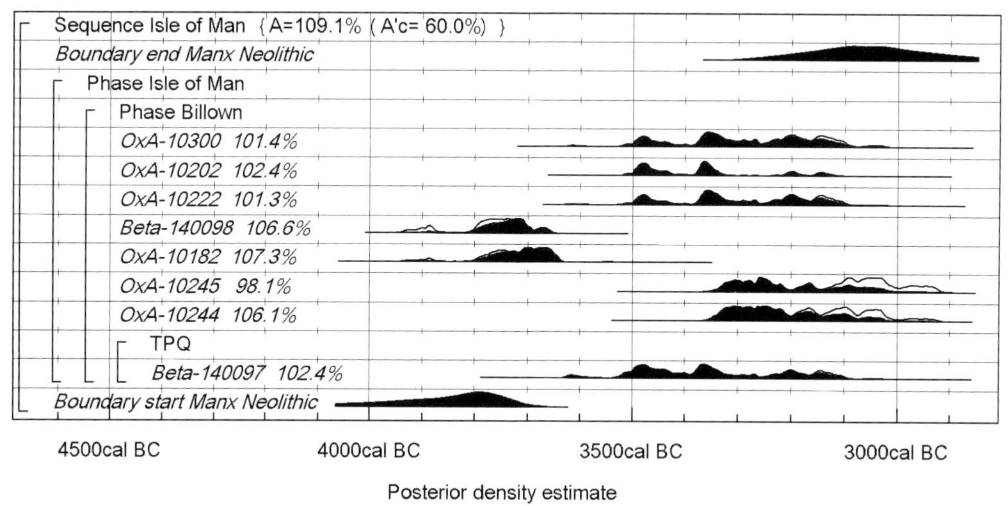

Fig. 14.148. Probability distributions of dates associated with diagnostically early Neolithic material culture from the Isle of Man. The format is the same as for Fig. 14.1. The large square brackets down the left-hand side of these diagrams, along with the OxCal keywords, define the overall model exactly.

This dynamic history continued. By the final quarter of the 37th century cal BC, enclosure construction was at its most intense across southern Britain (Fig. 14.20), but this was also a time when some at least of the long barrows and long cairns were ending (Bayliss and Whittle 2007). Was there a causal link between these events? In the earlier part of the 36th century cal BC, there was a slackening in the pace of enclosure circuit construction, before renewed efforts in the middle of the 36th century (Fig. 14.20), which constitute the last main bout of fresh enclosure building. Perhaps from the 36th century cal BC onwards, people started building the very different cursus monuments, as suggested by the dating evidence from Drayton (Chapter 8.6: where the problems of bimodality have been stressed) and Stonehenge (Chapter 4.4). In the generations around 3500 cal BC, as building new enclosures declined in

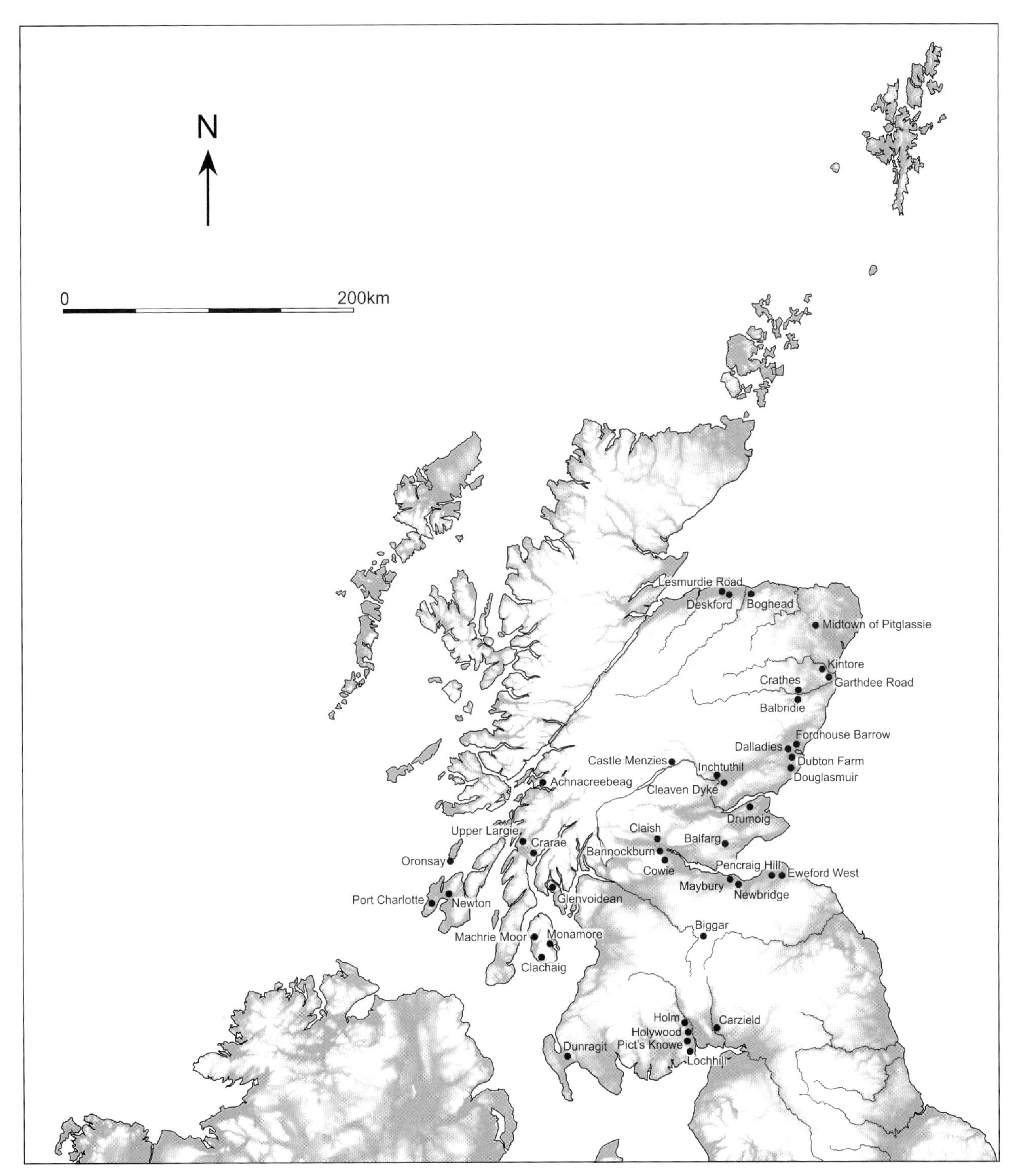

Fig. 14.149. Map of Scotland showing sites mentioned in the text.

fashion, it appears that the networks of movement of axeheads and gabbroic pottery also wound down (although at present our dating of these networks is too closely bound up with that for enclosures themselves for us to be entirely sanguine about the reliability of this picture). A single event, the battle of Crickley Hill, probably falling in the first half of the 35th century cal BC, may stand at the beginning of the end of the set of things and practices which we have put under the label of the early Neolithic.

Further endings and transformations followed. Decorated Bowl ceased to be deposited by around 3300 cal BC. Primary activity at even the most enduring of the causewayed enclosures also ended at this time (although this is partially a product of our definition of primary use as being associated with Bowl pottery!). The currency of South-Western style pottery also appears to have ended around this time, and probably also that of plain Bowl (Fig. 14.145). By this time too, it is probable that more cursus

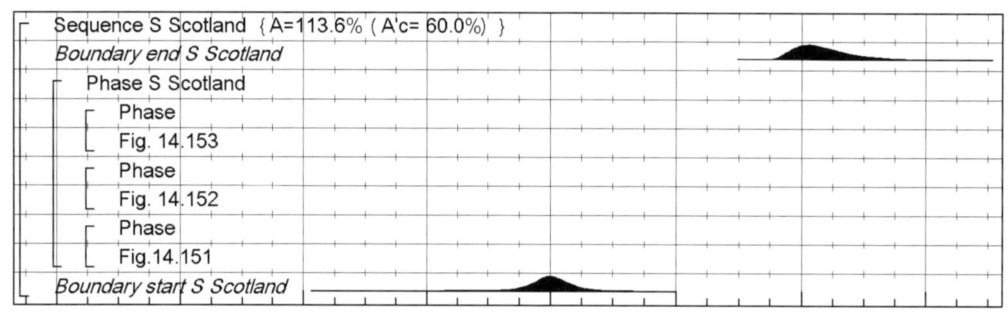

Fig. 14.150. Overall structure of the chronological model for early Neolithic activity in southern Scotland. The format is identical to that for Fig. 14.1. The components of the model are given in detail in Figs 14.151–3. The large square brackets down the left-hand side of Figs 14.150–3, along with the OxCal keywords, define the overall model exactly.

monuments had been constructed (Barclay and Bayliss 1999, figs 2.2 and 2.5). The start of Peterborough Ware has been largely beyond the reach of this project and awaits formal chronological modelling, but in South Wales and the Marches at least it seems to begin in the 34th or 33rd centuries cal BC (Fig. 11.19). Later still, around and after 3000 cal BC (Fig. 14.145), long barrows and long cairns, what we have defined as diverse and small monuments, and cursus monuments, all went out of primary use: the final demise of practices of by now varying antiquity.

14.7 The early Neolithic of Ireland, the Isle of Man and Scotland: a comparative framework

We can now begin to draw more strands together to contribute to a wider narrative still. First, we will compare our date estimates for enclosure construction in southern Britain with those for Magheraboy and Donegore in Ireland. Then we will summarise the models which we presented in Chapter 12 for the start and development of the early Neolithic in Ireland. Any reader happening to begin at this point in Chapter 14 is strongly advised to consult Chapter 12 before proceeding! After that, we will present a brief survey of evidence from the Isle of Man and a sample of available evidence from Scotland south of the Great Glen, before finally offering our preferred outline of a linked narrative for all these areas.

Ireland: a reprise of the argument so far

Figure 14.146 shows our date estimates for the construction and abandonment of the causewayed enclosures at Magheraboy and Donegore, in comparison with our estimated dates for the construction of the first causewayed enclosure in southern Britain as a whole and for the abandonment of the last enclosure in that area. Our date estimate for the establishment of the Donegore enclosure is compatible with the time when enclosures first appeared in southern Britain, and the end of its primary use, around 3500 cal BC, falls comfortably within the southern British pattern. Magheraboy stands apart from these trends, on the basis of our preferred model probably being built in the 40th century cal BC (Fig. 12.15). An alternative model presented in Chapter 12 pulls the site a little later, perhaps suggesting a construction date in the 39th century cal BC (Fig. 12.17), but as, argued there, that requires special pleading and is inconsistent with the criteria otherwise employed throughout this project; it also leaves Magheraboy in western Ireland out on its own as the earliest dated enclosure in the whole of Britain and Ireland. We can note that the end of Magheraboy's primary use does fit wider patterns, and that features within its interior date significantly later than the initiation of its enclosure ditch.

The matter does not have to be settled only within the bounds of Britain and Ireland. We will discuss wider European chronologies for the development of enclosures in Chapter 15, where the evidence for a range of ditched and palisaded constructions dated to before 4000 cal BC will be considered, which could have been the antecedents for the form of practice materialised at Magheraboy.

Whereas Donegore was discussed in its local and regional settings, in the same way that southern British enclosures were considered in the regional chapters, site by site, in the case of Magheraboy, the early estimate for its establishment necessitated a much wider review of the date for the early Neolithic in Ireland as a whole. Chapter 12.3 has set out a wide range of other evidence for early Neolithic things and practices in Ireland: rectangular timber houses, other occupations, domesticated fauna, the field systems at Céide Fields and elsewhere, court tombs, portal tombs, and other monuments (and, to constrain the end of the early Neolithic, we have considered the available dating evidence for Linkardstown burials and passage tombs, including the Mound of the Hostages, Tara).

We presented three alternative models for the chronology of the early Neolithic in Ireland, all excluding dates from the Donegore and Magheraboy enclosures. The first, which includes the assumption that court tombs and portal tombs belonged only within the early Neolithic, has very poor agreement and must be set aside. The second treats several elements of the model including court tombs, portal

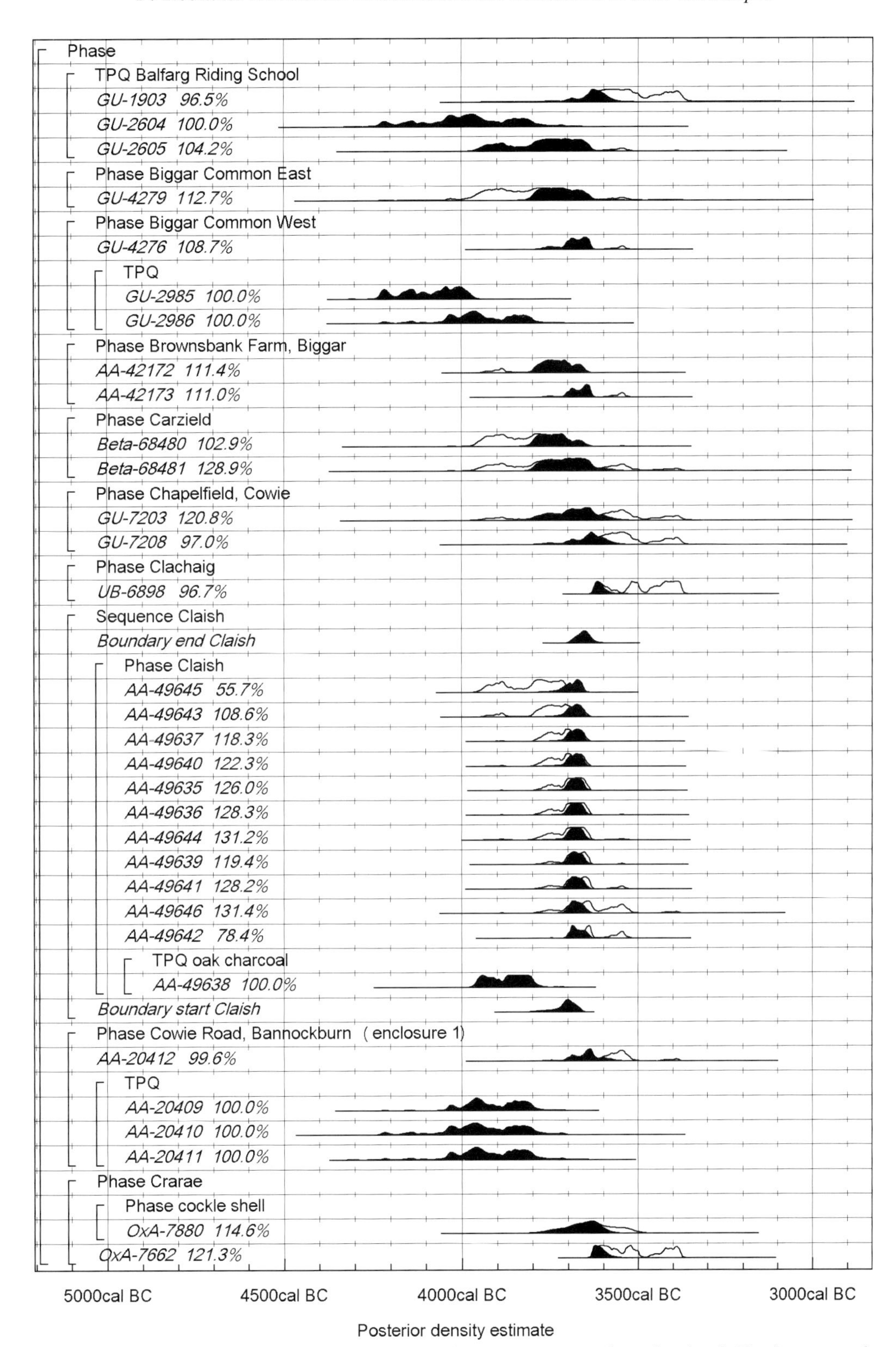

Fig. 14.151. Probability distributions of dates for early Neolithic activity in southern Scotland. The format is identical to that for Fig. 14.1. The overall structure of this model is shown in Fig. 14.150, and its other components in Figs 14.152–3.

tombs and domesticates simply as *termini ante quos* for the start of the early Neolithic, with only houses and other occupation in a uniformly distributed period of activity before the appearance of Linkardstown burials and passage tombs. In variants of the model, the removal of outlying dates for domesticates, including OxA-3869 from Ferriter's Cove, produced a date estimate for the start of the early Neolithic in Ireland in the later 38th century cal BC (Figs 12.54–5, 12.57). The third model puts all these elements (but excluding domesticates) within a single uniformly

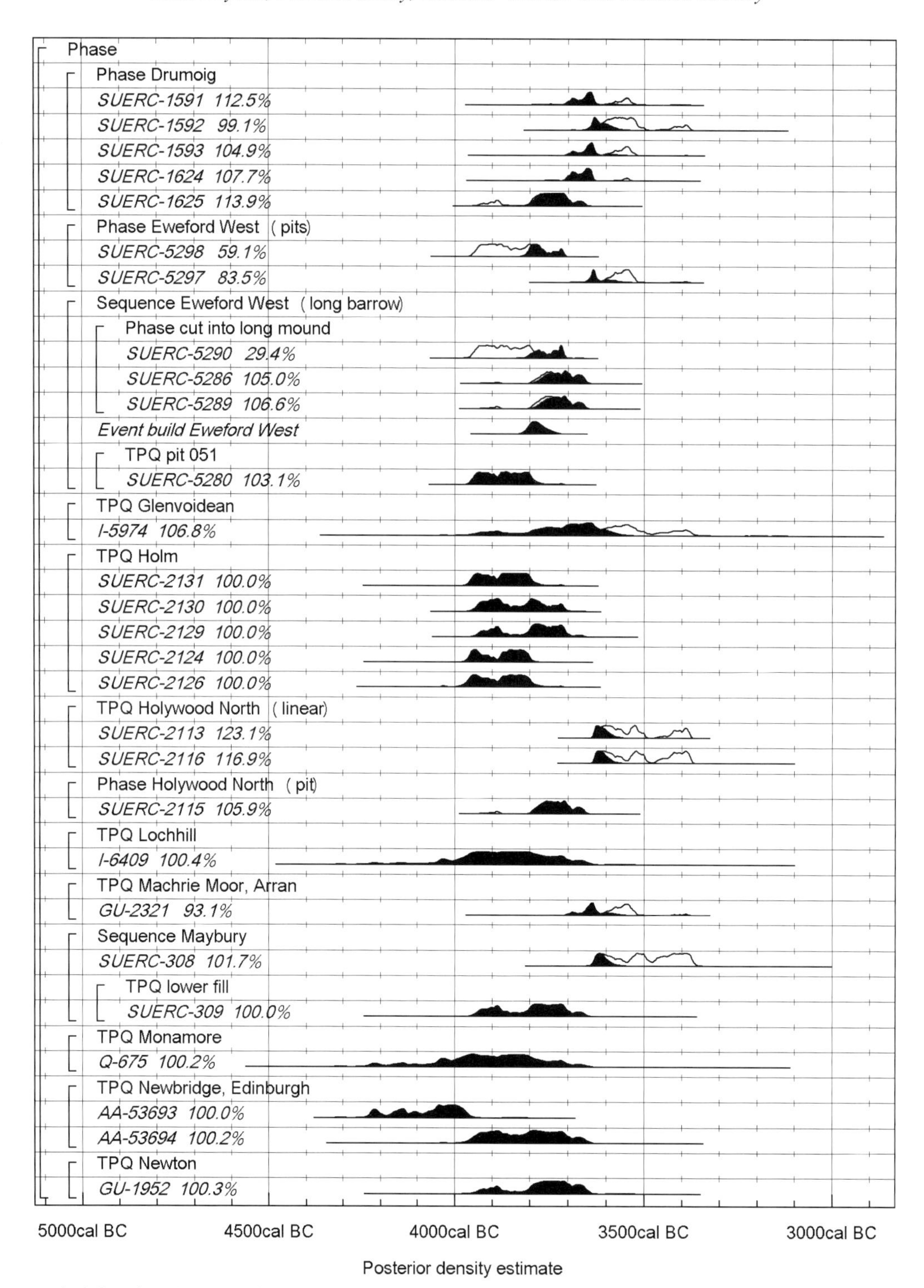

Fig. 14.152. Probability distributions of dates for early Neolithic activity in southern Scotland. The format is identical to that for Fig. 14.1. The overall structure of this model is shown in Fig. 14.150, and its other components in Figs 14.151 and 14.153.

distributed period of activity covering both the early, and selected elements of the middle, Neolithic in Ireland (incorporating again a sequence from rectangular houses and other early Neolithic occupation to Linkardstown burials to passage tombs; Figs 12.56–7). This produces a significantly earlier date estimate for the start of the early Neolithic in Ireland – in the earlier 38th century cal BC. Both of these models produce date estimates for the start of the Neolithic in Ireland that are significantly later than our estimate for the date at which Magheraboy was constructed.

Figure 14.147 provides a summary for the dates of different elements of the Irish Neolithic derived from the models described in Chapter 12. As things stand, and without special pleading, the enclosure at Magheraboy is stubbornly 200 years earlier than any other feature of the

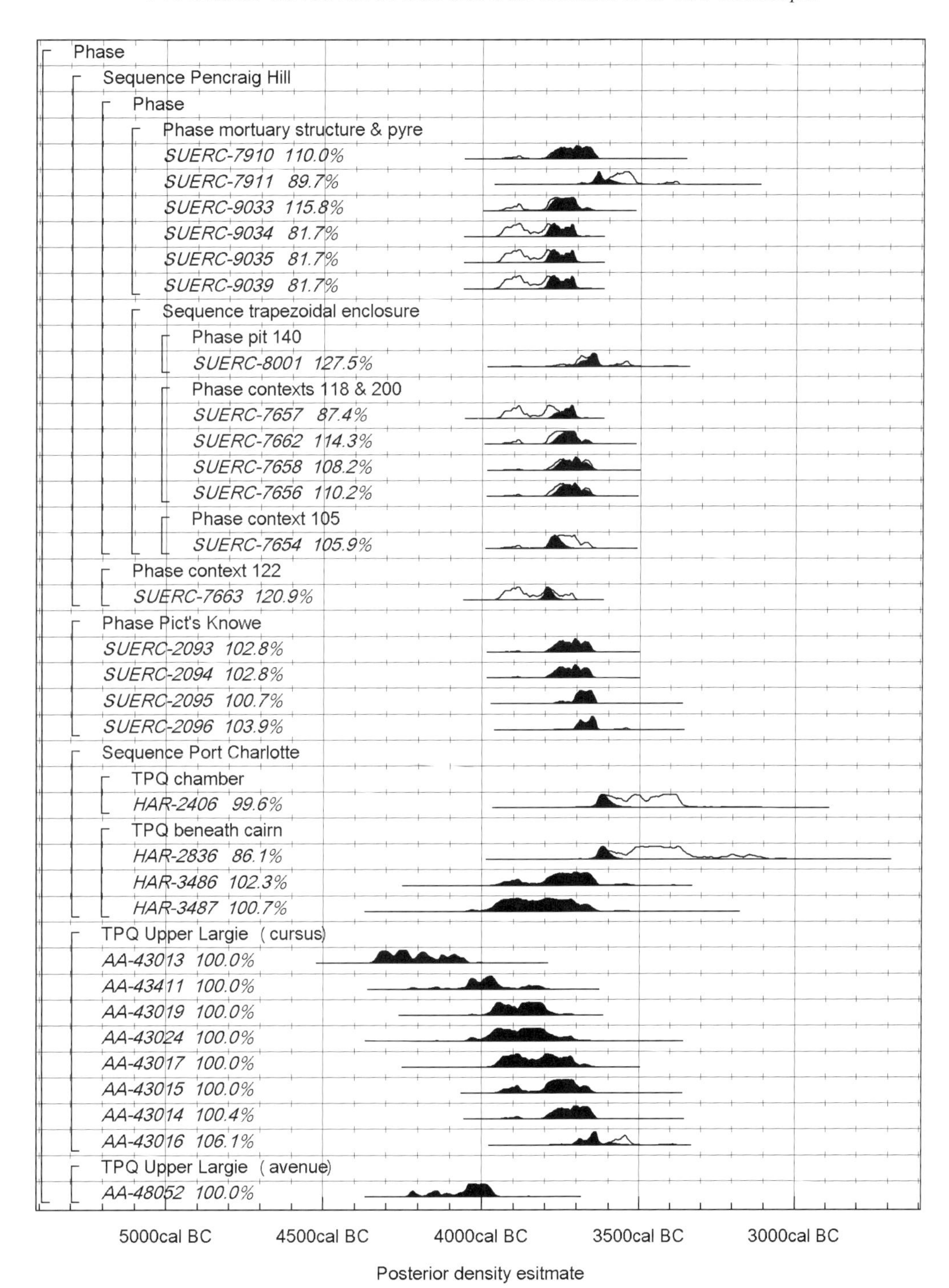

Fig. 14.153. Probability distributions of dates for early Neolithic activity in southern Scotland. The format is identical to that for Fig. 14.1. The overall structure of this model is shown in Fig. 14.150, and its other components in Figs 14.151–2.

early Neolithic so far reliably dated in Ireland. Various compromise options are discussed in Chapter 12, but none is convincing, and resolving this fundamental problem must be a priority for further research. Notwithstanding this issue, our analysis of the chronology of the early Neolithic in Ireland has highlighted some interesting trends. There is no compelling evidence that any other monument in Ireland was constructed before the second quarter of the fourth millennium cal BC, although the available dating evidence is of limited utility (Figs 12.31 and 12.35–6). The Céide field systems belong probably to the earlier to mid- fourth millennium cal BC, but not any earlier (Fig. 12.40). The rectangular houses stand out as belonging to a period of a century or less, in the late 38th into the later 37th century cal BC (Figs 12.28–9), rather later than the scarcer, larger Scottish halls, which began to be built in the earlier 38th century cal BC (Fig. 14.173). Depending on whether one favours model 3 or model 2, houses may have been a slightly later development within the start of the early Neolithic in Ireland or an integral feature of its very initiation respectively. In either model, we get a sense of the rapid tempo of development in Ireland. Our dating review was not able, however, to cover axehead production or the development of material networks in the way that was possible for southern Britain, and so our models are in this sense more limited. Nonetheless, unless further research manages to fill convincingly the gap between our current estimate for the construction date of the Magheraboy enclosure and the dates of other early Neolithic things and practices in Ireland, our date estimates as a whole suggest that the pace of Neolithisation in Ireland was swift – potentially court tombs, enclosures and other types of monuments, houses and other occupation, various forms of Bowl pottery, and cereals could all have appeared during the 38th century cal BC. On the basis of the published evidence, we do not find the suggestion that simple passage tombs may belong to the early years of the Neolithic in Ireland convincing (Sheridan 2003b; Sheridan *et al.* 2008; Pailler and Sheridan 2009). Uncertainty as to the original form of the disturbed monument at Broadsands in Devon, built in the later thirty-ninth or earlier thirty-eighth century cal BC (Fig. 10.30), reduces its worth as ammunition in this argument. Domesticated fauna may indicate sporadic contact with continental Europe from rather earlier, perhaps as early as the third quarter of the fifth millennium cal BC (Fig 12.43: *OxA-3869*).

The Isle of Man and Scotland south of the Great Glen

To consider the place of enclosures on an even wider basis, we will next bring in the Isle of Man and part of Scotland. This is obviously a selective exercise, since we have not been able to cover either north Wales or the rest of England in this study. Models for the chronology of the early Neolithic in the English Midlands (thus more or less coinciding with the northernmost distribution of causewayed enclosures in southern Britain) and the north of England, drawing on the existing corpus of radiocarbon dates, are currently being constructed by Seren Griffiths.[8] There is also currently fresh research on north Wales, led by the National Museum of Wales (Steve Burrow, pers. comm.), and there have been relevant contract archaeology projects near Bangor (e.g. Kenney 2009) and on Anglesey in recent times, among other examples. This is a substantial area of Britain as a whole to leave out of the current analysis, but it is beyond the remit of the current project, and we must be pragmatic and patient.

The Isle of Man. Lying in the middle of the northern part of the Irish Sea, the Isle of Man is of potentially great significance in the spread of Neolithic things and practices into western Britain and Ireland. There is so far, however, regrettably little that can be said about the chronology of the early Neolithic on Mann. None of the chambered tombs, discussed recently by Chris Fowler (2001; 2002), have radiocarbon evidence. The only relevant date in the list provided by Chiverrell *et al.* (1999) is OxA-2481 (4970±80 BP), on a marine limpet shell which calibrates to 3630–3070 cal BC (95% confidence) using the marine calibration dataset of Hughen *et al.* (2004) and a ΔR value of 5±40BP (Stuiver and Braziunas 1993). This sample was allegedly from below a cist at Port St Mary, on the southern end of the island, which contained human bone perhaps from three individuals (Swinnerton 1889). The court tombs of Cashtal yn Ard and King Orry's Grave point to communication with Ireland and south-west Scotland, as do the form and decoration of the local variant of Bowl pottery (Burrow 1997, 11–16; cf. Cooney 200a; Cummings 2009). From the north end of the island, the presence of cereal-type pollen has been claimed as far back as the start of Zone C in the pollen diagram from Ballachrink, radiocarbon dated to 4950–4680 cal BC (95% confidence; 5925±60 BP; AA-29337; Innes *et al.* 2003). Although other sites are mapped from around the Irish Sea (and beyond) with cereal-type pollen radiocarbon dated to the first half of the fifth millennium cal BC (Innes *et al.* 2003, fig. 1), including Machrie Moor on Arran (Robinson and Dickson 1988), the suggestion that this evidence relates to the cultivation of cereals presents considerable problems. It relies on the identification of 'cereal-type' pollen as indeed of cereal taxa, and the belief that there has been no contamination or stratigraphic intrusion in a particular location. At Ballachrink it seems that it is the identification of 'cereal-type' pollen with domesticated cereals that must be in error, as such pollen was found at several levels in the diagram and formed a coherent pollen zone (Innes *et al.* 2003, fig. 3). These instances of 'cereal-type' pollen are significantly earlier than any other indication of changed practice across the whole of Britain and Ireland, and so, for the present, it seems to us prudent not to accept such uncertain indications of cultivation in the face of the weight of other, more certain, strands of evidence.

That leaves the dating evidence from Billown itself, presented in Chapter 11. We have taken dates associated with diagnostic early Neolithic material and those on cereal grains themselves to suggest a period of early Neolithic activity at Billown. This began in *4040–3700 cal BC* (*95% probability*; Fig. 14.148: *start Manx Neolithic*), probably in *3905–3725 cal BC* (*68% probability*). This estimate is imprecise, because it based on very little evidence, our earliest dated samples probably falling in the 38th or 37th century cal BC. This period of activity on the site ended in *3240–2850 cal BC* (*95% probability*; Fig. 14.148: *end Manx Neolithic*), probably in *3170–2950 cal BC* (*68% probability*). Further dating of short-life material firmly associated with early Neolithic activity on Mann is obviously highly desirable.

Scotland south of the Great Glen. To complete our wider (but selective) sample of radiocarbon evidence for the start of the Neolithic in Britain and Ireland, we have gathered dates for the early Neolithic in Scotland south of the Great Glen. We have utilised the Historic Scotland database of radiocarbon dates (http://www.historic-scotland.gov.uk/index/heritage/archaeology/archaeology-techniques/radiocarbon-dating/), the datelist for northern Carinated Bowl given by Alison Sheridan (2007a, with references),

Table 14.14. Radiocarbon dates from sites in Scotland south of the Great Glen associated with diagnostic early Neolithic activity.

Laboratory Number	Description	Radiocarbon Age (BP)	$\delta^{13}C$ (‰)	Calibrated date range (cal BC) (95% confidence)	*Posterior density estimate (cal BC) (95% probability)*	References
Southern Scotland						
Balfarg Riding School, Fife						
GU-1903	Alder, hazel and ash charcoal from Context 8019B of Pit 8016 with plain Neolithic pottery bowls, of modified Carinated style	4765±85	−24.8	3710–3360	*3760–3740* (*1%*) or *3715–3550* (*94%*)	Barclay and Russell-White 1993, 160–1; Cowie 1993
GU-2604	Hazel, oak and willow charcoal from Context 8019B of Pit 8016 with plain Neolithic pottery, of modified Carinated style	5170±90	−25.4	4240–3770	*4240–3765*	Barclay and Russell-White 1993, 160–1; Cowie 1993
GU-2605	Oak charcoal from Context 8019B of Pit 8016 with plain Neolithic pottery bowls, of modified Carinated style	4950±90	−25.2	3960–3530	*3950–3635*	Barclay and Russell-White 1993, 160–1; Cowie 1993
Biggar Common (aka Biggar Common West), South Lanarkshire						
GU-4276	Hazel roundwood charcoal with small quantities of oak and alder charcoal from Sample Area 5,l from a charcoal spread (105) in an isolated spot with a concentration of Carinated Bowl sherds mixed with charcoal; possibly a food preparation area	4880±50		3770–3530	*3775–3630*	D.E. Johnston 1997, 240–3; Sheridan 2007a
GU-2985	Oak, hazel, birch and willow charcoal from a bonfire immediately under a non-megalithic long barrow with Carinated Bowl pottery and flint and chert artefacts	5250±50	−25.5	4240–3960	*4235–4190* (*13%*) or *4180–3965* (*82%*)	D.E. Johnston 1997, 240–3; Sheridan 2007a
GU-2986	Oak, hazel, and birch from a bonfire immediately under a non-megalithic long barrow with Carinated Bowl pottery and flint and chert artefacts	5150±70	−25.3	4230–3780	*4230–4200* (*2%*) or *4170–4125* (*3%*) or *4080–3770* (*90%*)	D.E. Johnston 1997, 240–3; Sheridan 2007a
Brownsbank Farm, Biggar, South Lanarkshire						
AA-42172	Single piece of hazel charcoal from pit (Feature 1), associated with Carinated Bowl pottery	4960±45	−25.9	3930–3640	*3795–3655*	Sheridan 2007a
AA-42173	Single piece of hazel charcoal from a second pit (Feature 2), associated with Carinated Bowl pottery	4865±45	−26.2	3710–3530	*3770–3625*	Sheridan 2007a
Carwood Hill (aka Biggar Common East), Biggar, South Lanarkshire						
GU-4279	Hazel charcoal from a spread of dense charcoal (103) in Area 2, near to shallow pits and containing large quantities of hazel kernel and early Neolithic pot sherds, probably Carinated Bowl. Deposition of carbonised material with kernels indicates an area of food processing, possibly associated with a fire and cooking	4990±110		4040–3530	*3810–3630*	Biggar Museum Trust 1993; Sheridan in D.E. Johnston 1997, 220; Sheridan 2007a
Carzield, Dumfries and Galloway						
Beta-68480	Bulk charcoal of mixed short-life species from a pit with Carinated Bowl pottery and cereal grains	5010±70		3970–3640	*3805–3655*	Sheridan 2007a; Brophy 2006
Beta-68481	Bulk charcoal of mixed short-life species from a pit with Carinated Bowl pottery and cereal grains	4920±110		3970–3380	*3805–3595*	Sheridan 2007a; Brophy 2006

Laboratory Number	Description	Radiocarbon Age (BP)	$\delta^{13}C$ (‰)	Calibrated date range (cal BC) (95% confidence)	*Posterior density estimate (cal BC) (95% probability)*	References
Chapelfield, Cowie, Stirling						
GU-7203	Bulk sample hazel charcoal from the final fill (350) of pit VII containing Carinated Bowl pottery. See GU-7208 from the basal fill	4860±100	−25.9	3940–3370	*3795–3580*	J. Atkinson 2002
GU-7208	Bulk sample hazel charcoal from a charcoal-rich layer forming the basal fill (440) of pit VII	4800±80	−26.0	3710–3370	*3765–3720 (5%)* or *3715–3560 (90%)*	J. Atkinson 2002
Clachaig, Arran, North Ayrshire						
UB-6898	Unburnt human cranium (sample D[2]) from Clyde cairn	4708±37	−22.0	3640–3370	*3635–3575*	Sheridan 2006b
UB-6897	Unburnt human cranium (sample C) from Clyde cairn. Excluded from models	3949±363	−21.0	3500–1490		Sheridan 2006b
Claish, Stirling						
AA-49645	Hazel charcoal bulk sample from post-pipe of post F30 in internal line 4, part of screen V, of timber hall. There is Carinated Bowl pottery in the timber hall as a whole	5000±50	−26.7	3960–3650	*3745–3650*	G. Barclay *et al.* 2002; Sheridan 2007a
AA-49643	Hazelnut shell bulk sample from layer of probably *in situ* burning in pit F19 within space C of timber hall	4950±50	−24.9	3930–3640	*3735–3645*	G. Barclay *et al.* 2002; Sheridan 2007a
AA-49637	Single hazelnut shell from F13, post of internal line 1 at end of screen (II) in timber hall	4935±40	−23.2	3800–3640	*3730–3645*	G. Barclay *et al.* 2002; Sheridan 2007a
AA-49640	Birch charcoal bulk sample from layer of *in situ* burning in pit F15 within space C of timber hall	4930±40	−26.0	3800–3640	*3730–3645*	G. Barclay *et al.* 2002; Sheridan 2007a
AA-49635	Hazelnut shell bulk sample from postpipe fill of F9, post in E wall of timber hall	4915±40	−28.3	3780–3630	*3720–3640*	G. Barclay *et al.* 2002; Sheridan 2007a
AA-49636	Hazelnut shell bulk sample from postpipe fill of F8, post in E wall of timber hall	4910±45	−22.5	3790–3630	*3720–3640*	G. Barclay *et al.* 2002; Sheridan 2007a
AA-49644	Hazelnut shell bulk sample from mid-fill of post F21 at N end of timber hall	4910±50	−25.0	3800–3630	*3720–3640*	G. Barclay *et al.* 2002; Sheridan 2007a
AA-49639	Hazelnut shell bulk sample from layer of *in situ* burning in pit F15 within space C of timber hall	4895±40	−24.0	3770–3630	*3710–3640*	G. Barclay *et al.* 2002; Sheridan 2007a
AA-49641	Emmer grain bulk sample from layer of *in situ* burning in pit F15 within space C of timber hall	4885±50	−25.0	3780–3530	*3715–3640*	G. Barclay *et al.* 2002; Sheridan 2007a
AA-49646	Hazelnut shell bulk sample from post-pipe of post F37, possibly secondary, in N wall of timber hall	4855±70	−27.1	3780–3380	*3715–3635*	G. Barclay *et al.* 2002; Sheridan 2007a
AA-49642	Hazelnut shell bulk sample from layer of probably *in situ* burning in pit F19 within space C	4845±40	−25.2	3710–3530	*3705–3635*	G. Barclay *et al.* 2002; Sheridan 2007a
AA-49638	Oak charcoal (?burnt stake) from F14, slot for screen II of timber hall	5080±40	−25.2	3970–3770	*3970–3785*	G. Barclay *et al.* 2002; Sheridan 2007a
Cowie Road, Bannockburn, Stirling						
AA-20412	Hazel charcoal from phase 2 fill of pit P25 of a pit-defined long mortuary enclosure Enclosure 1), 33 to 36m across with a rounded end, associated with Carinated Bowl pottery	4830±60		3710–3380	*3760–3740 (2%)* or *3715–3555 (93%)*	Rideout 1997, 37, 52–3; Sheridan 2007a

Laboratory Number	Description	Radiocarbon Age (BP)	$\delta^{13}C$ (‰)	Calibrated date range (cal BC) (95% confidence)	*Posterior density estimate (cal BC) (95% probability)*	References
AA-20409	Oak charcoal from the lower charcoal fill of pit P6 of a pit-defined long mortuary enclosure (Enclosure 1), 33 to 36 m across with a rounded end, associated with Carinated Bowl pottery	5130±60		4050–3780	*4050–3775*	Rideout 1997, 37, 52–3; Sheridan 2007a
AA-20410	Oak charcoal from the lower charcoal fill of pit P6 of a pit-defined long mortuary enclosure (Enclosure 1), 33 to 36 m across with a rounded end, associated with Carinated Bowl pottery	5145±80		4230–3760	*4230–4200 (2%)* or *4170–4125 (4%)* or *4120–4095 (1%)* or *4080–3755 (88%)*	Rideout 1997, 37, 52–3; Sheridan 2007a
AA-20411	Oak charcoal from the lower charcoal fill of pit P6 of a pit-defined long mortuary enclosure (Enclosure 1), 33 to 36 m across with a rounded end, associated with Carinated Bowl pottery	5135±70		4050–3770	*4160–4130 (1%)* or *4065–3755 (94%)*	Rideout 1997, 37, 52–3; Sheridan 2007a
Crarae, Argyll and Bute						
OxA-7662	Human phalanx from NN 1186.2, part of a small group of human bones and teeth at the east end of the middle segment of the burial chamber	4735±40	−21.5	3640–3370	*3640–3570*	Ashmore 2000; Schulting and Richards 2002b
OxA-7880	Cockle shell from sample NN 1161 which may refer to the construction/initial use phase of the monument. OxA-7880 Part of a large group of shells in the burial chamber, interpreted by the excavator as probably a foundation deposit	5230±55		3780–3490[i]	*3775–3575*	Ashmore 2000; Schulting and Richards 2002b
Drumoig, Cowbakie Hill and Craigie Hill, Fife						
SUERC-1591	Hazel charcoal from circular pit 171 associated with Carinated Bowl pottery	4850±45	−25.3	3710–3520	*3760–3740 (1%)* or *3715–3615 (89%)* or *3610–3560 (5%)*	Sheridan 2007a
SUERC-1592	Hazel charcoal from pit 176 associated with Carinated Bowl pottery	4775±45	−24.2	3650–3370	*3655–3560*	Sheridan 2007a
SUERC-1593	Hazelnut shell from circular feature 178 associated with Carinated Bowl pottery and leaf arrowhead	4835±45	−25.2	3710–3520	*3710–3560*	Sheridan 2007a
SUERC-1624	Hazel charcoal from probable cooking pit 2603 associated with Carinated Bowl pottery	4870±40	−25.8	3710–3530	*3760–3740 (2%)* or *3715–3625 (93%)*	Sheridan 2007a
SUERC-1625	Alder charcoal from shallow pit 2613 associated with Carinated Bowl pottery	4975±40	−25.8	3940–3650	*3800–3690 (87%)* or *3685–3660 (8%)*	Sheridan 2007a
Dunragit, Dumfries and Galloway						
SUERC-2103	Hazel charcoal believed to be associated with burning of oak post in cursus	4890±35		3720–3630		Sheridan 2007a
Eweford West, East Lothian						
SUERC-5290	Hazel charcoal from stakehole 216 on second mound phase of monument that ends as a non-megalithic long barrow/mortuary enclosure. Carinated Bowl pottery associated with this activity	5055±35	−25.2	3960–3710	*3805–3705*	Sheridan 2007a; Lelong and MacGregor 2007

Laboratory Number	Description	Radiocarbon Age (BP)	$\delta^{13}C$ (‰)	Calibrated date range (cal BC) (95% confidence)	*Posterior density estimate (cal BC) (95% probability)*	References
SUERC-5286	Alder charcoal from burnt timber screen set in trench 171 on second mound phase of monument that ends as a non-megalithic long barrow. Carinated Bowl pottery associated with this phase of activity	4950±35	−26.6	3800–3650	*3780–3650*	Sheridan 2007a; Lelong and MacGregor 2007
SUERC-5289	Hazel charcoal from stakehole 209 to W of timber screen on second mound phase of monument that ends as a non-megalithic long barrow. Carinated Bowl pottery associated with these activities	4960±35	−26.7	3900–3650	*3780–3655*	Sheridan 2007a; Lelong and MacGregor 2007
SUERC-5280	Cattle radius in large pit, no pottery; cut into first small mound of monument that ends as a non-megalithic long barrow	5065±35	−22.0	3970–3770	*3955–3795*	Sheridan 2007a; Lelong and MacGregor 2007
SUERC-5298	*Corylus* charcoal from pit 025, which contained Carinated Bowl pottery	5045±35	−26.70	3960–3710	*3815–3710*	Sheridan 2007a; Lelong and MacGregor 2007
SUERC-5297	*Corylus* charcoal from pit 019, which contained modified Carinated Bowl pottery	4800±35	−24.10	3660–3520	*3655–3555*	Lelong and MacGregor 2007
Glenvoidean, Bute, Argyll and Bute						
I-5974	Charcoal under the west slab of the main chamber	4860±115		3950–3360	*3945–3830 (13%)* or *3825–3570 (82%)*	Marshall and Taylor 1979
Holm, Dumfries and Galloway						
SUERC-2131	Oak charcoal 069 from *in situ* post in fill 198 of post-hole 115 of the post cursus. First of three posts within this posthole	5075±40	−24.8	3970–3770	*3965–3780*	Thomas 2007b; Sheridan 2007a
SUERC-2130	Oak charcoal 067 (Bag 2) from *in situ* post in fill 227 of post-hole 115 of the cursus. Third of three posts within this posthole	5025±40	−24.5	3960–3700	*3945–3710*	Thomas 2007b; Sheridan 2007a
SUERC-2129	Oak charcoal 067 (Bag 1) from same *in situ* post in fill 227 of post-hole 115 of the post cursus. Third of three posts within this posthole	5000±40	−25.5	3950–3660	*3945–3690*	Thomas 2007b; Sheridan 2007a
SUERC-2124	Oak charcoal 026 sealed in fill 073 of post-hole 075 of the post cursus	5095±35	−27.4	3980–3790	*3970–3890 (38%)* or *3885–3795 (57%)*	Thomas 2007b; Sheridan 2007a
SUERC-2126	Oak charcoal 030 sealed in fill 073 of post-hole 075 of the post cursus	5095±50	−25.6	3990–3770	*3990–3770*	Thomas 2007b; Sheridan 2007a
Holywood North, Dumfries and Galloway						
SUERC-2113	Oak charcoal 02 from fill 014 of post-hole 015 of post setting within ditch-defined cursus, cutting that for the large postpit 224 dated by SUERC-2116	4740±35	−26.2	3640–3370	*3640–3570*	Thomas 2007b; Sheridan 2007a
SUERC-2116	Oak charcoal 15 from layer 053 of large postpit 224 pre-dating cursus construction	4725±40	−25.1	3640–3370	*3640–3570*	Thomas 2007b; Sheridan 2007a
SUERC-2115	Hazelnut shell 09 in fill 135 of feature 102 within ditch-defined cursus, perhaps second of two postfills. Carinated Bowl pottery in lower and side fill of posthole	4960±35	−25.0	3900–3650	*3790–3655*	Thomas 2007b; Sheridan 2007a
Lochhill, Dumfries and Galloway						
I-6409	Wood from a plank from a mortuary structure under a chambered cairn. (Pot 'almost certainly' traditional Carinated Bowl: Sheridan 2007a, 491)	5070±105		4060–3640	*4055–3640*	Masters 1973

Laboratory Number	Description	Radiocarbon Age (BP)	$\delta^{13}C$ (‰)	Calibrated date range (cal BC) (95% confidence)	*Posterior density estimate (cal BC) (95% probability)*	References
Machrie Moor, Arran, North Ayrshire						
GU-2321	Mixed charcoal from pits with parts of six plain Neolithic pots including Carinated Bowls	4820±50	−25.5	3700–3510	*3710–3560*	Haggarty 1991
Maybury Business Park (Areas B and C), City of Edinburgh						
SUERC-308	Hazelnut shell from context 649 in upper fill of pit in Area B, with two sherds of Carinated Bowl pottery. Sheridan notes that sherds from Area B are small and it is not possible to be certain whether they represent 'traditional' Carinated Bowl pottery or 'modified Carinated Bowl'. The Area C pottery is 'traditional Carinated Bowl'	4710±55	−24.55	3640–3360	*3640–3565*	Sheridan 2007a
SUERC-309	Piece of hazel roundwood charcoal from primary fill 671 of same pit in Area B as provided SUERC-308 from context 649	4995±55	−25.57	3960–3650	*3945–3655*	Sheridan 2007a
Monamore, Arran, North Ayrshire						
Q-675	Charcoal from a hearth in the forecourt under the blocking of a chambered cairn	5110±110		4230–3650	*4230–4195 (2%)* or *4170–4125 (3%)* or *4120–4090 (2%)* or *4080–3655 (88%)*	MacKie 1966
Q-676	Charcoal from the top of a thick layer of deposits in the forecourt of a chambered cairn	4190±110		3080–2470		MacKie 1966
Newbridge, City of Edinburgh						
AA-53693	Oak charcoal possibly from post; Carinated Bowl pottery in fill of same feature	5235±55	−25.0	4240–3950	*4235–4185 (11%)* or *4180–3955 (84%)*	Sheridan 2007a
AA-53694	Oak charcoal possibly from post; Carinated Bowl pottery in fill of same	5010±75	−24.9	3970–3640	*3960–3655*	Sheridan 2007a
Newton, Islay, Argyll and Bute						
GU-1952	Alder, hazel and oak charcoal from Pit F3, a small pit with Carinated Bowl pottery, cut by possible fence lines, which were in turn earlier than pit F4 dated by GU-1951	4965±60	−27.4	3950–3640	*3945–3855 (18%)* or *3820–3640 (77%)*	Sheridan 2007a
Pencraig Hill, East Lothian						
SUERC-7910	Bone apatite from cremated human bone from fresh bodies burnt on pyre within mortuary structure of trapezoidal post-defined mortuary enclosure	4940±50	−27.9	3910–3630	*3785–3645*	Sheridan 2007a; Lelong and MacGregor 2007
SUERC-7911	Bone apatite from cremated human bone from fresh bodies burnt on pyre within mortuary structure of trapezoidal post-defined mortuary enclosure	4800±50	−27.7	3660–3380	*3695–3560*	Sheridan 2007a; Lelong and MacGregor 2007
SUERC-9033	Oak bark from collapsed pyre within mortuary structure of trapezoidal post-defined mortuary enclosure	4985±35	−28.0	3940–3660	*3800–3690 (93%)* or *3680–3665 (2%)*	Lelong and MacGregor 2007
SUERC-9034	Oak bark from collapsed pyre within mortuary structure of trapezoidal post-defined mortuary enclosure	5025±35	−29.2	3950–3700	*3800–3705*	Lelong and MacGregor 2007
SUERC-9035	Oak bark from collapsed pyre within mortuary structure of trapezoidal post-defined mortuary enclosure	5025±35	−28.0	3950–3700	*3800–3705*	Lelong and MacGregor 2007

Laboratory Number	Description	Radiocarbon Age (BP)	$\delta^{13}C$ (‰)	Calibrated date range (cal BC) (95% confidence)	*Posterior density estimate (cal BC) (95% probability)*	References
SUERC-9039	Oak bark from collapsed pyre within mortuary structure of trapezoidal post-defined mortuary enclosure	5025±35	−27.6	3950–3700	*3800–3705*	Lelong and MacGregor 2007
SUERC-8001	Hazel charcoal from N pit 140 at E end of N side of trapezoidal post-defined mortuary enclosure. Pit cuts E façade 114	4870±50	−25.1	3760–3530	*3715–3620 (94%)* or *3590–3570 (1%)*	Sheridan 2007a; Lelong and MacGregor 2007
SUERC-7657	Alder charcoal from basal fill 178 of corner posthole at junction of E façade and S long side of trapezoidal post-defined mortuary enclosure.	5015±35	−25.6	3950–3700	*3790–3700*	Sheridan 2007a; Lelong and MacGregor 2007
SUERC-7662	Alder charcoal from main fill 113 of E façade 114 of trapezoidal post-defined mortuary enclosure	4975±35	−25.1	3910–3650	*3780–3690 (90%)* or *3685–3660 (5%)*	Sheridan 2007a; Lelong and MacGregor 2007
SUERC-7658	Alder charcoal from main fill 113 of E façade 114 of trapezoidal post-defined mortuary enclosure	4945±35	−24.5	3800–3640	*3770–3655*	Sheridan 2007a; Lelong and MacGregor 2007
SUERC-7656	Hazel charcoal fragment from slot 199 behind of E façade 114 of trapezoidal post-defined mortuary enclosure	4955±35	−24.4	3800–3650	*3775–3660*	Sheridan 2007a; Lelong and MacGregor 2007
SUERC-7654	Hazel charcoal from main fill 105 of trench forming N side of trapezoidal post-defined mortuary enclosure. Carinated Bowl pottery and barley grains from this fill	4965±35	−27.8	3900–3650	*3800–3730*	Sheridan 2007a; Lelong and MacGregor 2007
SUERC-7663	Alder charcoal from rakeout of fire within possible structure on first phase of monument that ends as trapezoidal post-defined mortuary enclosure. No pottery in this phase	5025±35	−24.3	3950–3700	*3820–3755*	Sheridan 2007a; Lelong and MacGregor 2007
SUERC-7655	Alder charcoal from main fill 105 of trench forming N side of trapezoidal post-defined mortuary enclosure. Carinated Bowl pottery and barley grains from this fill	3835±35	−25.7	2470–2140		Sheridan 2007a; Lelong and MacGregor 2007
Pict's Knowe, Dumfries and Galloway						
SUERC-2093	Alder charcoal 2687 in fill of pit 6270 with Carinated Bowl pottery	4945±35	−26.9	3800–3640	*3785–3650*	Thomas 2007b; Sheridan 2007a
SUERC-2094	Alder charcoal 2491 in fill of a second pit 6471 with Carinated Bowl pottery	4945±35	−28.2	3800–3640	*3785–3650*	Thomas 2007b; Sheridan 2007a
SUERC-2095	Charred hazelnut shell 2655 (date 1) in fill of a third pit 6725 with Carinated Bowl pottery	4900±35	−24.4	3760–3630	*3765–3720 (8%)* or *3715–3635 (87%)*	Thomas 2007b; Sheridan 2007a
SUERC-2096	Hazel charcoal 2655 (date 2) in fill of a third pit 6725 with Carinated Bowl pottery	4875±35	−26.1	3710–3630	*3715–3630*	Thomas 2007b; Sheridan 2007a
Port Charlotte, Islay, Argyll and Bute						
HAR-2406	Charcoal from the chamber of Clyde chambered cairn. Sherds from 5 plain pots in the monument, but type not identified	4710±70		3650–3350	*3655–3560*	Sheridan 2007a
HAR-2836	Carbonised hazel nutshells and short-life species charcoal from occupation layer (PC78M104), with animal bones and flints under Clyde chambered cairn	4660±90	−25.2	3650–3100	*3660–3555*	Sheridan 2007a

Laboratory Number	Description	Radiocarbon Age (BP)	$\delta^{13}C$ (‰)	Calibrated date range (cal BC) (95% confidence)	*Posterior density estimate (cal BC) (95% probability)*	References
HAR-3486	Carbonised hazel nutshells and short-life species charcoal from occupation layer (PC79M405), with animal bones and flints under Clyde chambered cairn	4940±70	−26.4	3950–3630	*3945–3855 (14%)* or *3820–3630 (81%)*	Sheridan 2007a
HAR-3487	Carbonised hazel nutshells and short-life species charcoal from occupation layer (PC79M406), with animal bones and flints under Clyde chambered cairn	5020±90	−26.3	3990–3630	*3975–3645*	Sheridan 2007a
Upper Largie, Argyll and Bute						
AA-43013	Oak charcoal from post of cursus	5375±55		4350–4040	*4335–4050*	Sheridan 2007a
AA-43411	Oak charcoal from post of cursus	5175±55		4220–3800	*4230–4200 (2%)* or *4165–4125 (4%)* or *4075–3905 (74%)* or *3880–3795 (15%)*	Sheridan 2007a
AA-43019	Oak charcoal from post of cursus	5090±50		3990–3770	*3985–3765*	Sheridan 2007a
AA-43024	Oak charcoal from post of cursus	5090±75		4050–3700	*4040–4010 (3%)* or *4005–3705 (92%)*	Sheridan 2007a
AA-43017	Oak charcoal from post of cursus	5020±55		3970–3660	*3960–3695*	Sheridan 2007a
AA-43015	Oak charcoal from post of cursus	4975±50		3950–3650	*3945–3855 (18%)* or *3815–3650 (77%)*	Sheridan 2007a
AA-43014	Oak charcoal from post of cursus	4935±50		3900–3630	*3900-3875 (2%)* or *3805–3635 (93%)*	Sheridan 2007a
AA-43016	Oak charcoal from post of cursus	4840±50		3710–3520	*3715–3550*	Sheridan 2007a
AA-48052	Oak charcoal from post of avenue	5220±50		4230–3950	*4230–4195 (7%)* or *4175–3950 (88%)*	Sheridan 2007a
North-eastern Scotland						
Balbridie, Kincardine and Deeside						
OxA-1768	Flax from the destruction level of a timber hall associated with NE Carinated Bowl pottery	4940±70		3950–3630	*3790–3635*	Fairweather and Ralston 1993
OxA-1769	Crab apple from the destruction level of a timber hall associated with NE Carinated Bowl pottery	5010±90		3980–3630	*3815–3635*	Fairweather and Ralston 1993
OxA-1767	Oat grain from the destruction level of a timber hall associated with NE Carinated Bowl pottery	4820±80		3770–3370	*3780–3600*	Fairweather and Ralston 1993
GU-1828	Oak from the destruction level of a timber hall associated with NE Carinated Bowl pottery	5030±60	−24.9	3970–3660	*3960–3700*	Fairweather and Ralston 1993

Laboratory Number	Description	Radiocarbon Age (BP)	$\delta^{13}C$ (‰)	Calibrated date range (cal BC) (95% confidence)	*Posterior density estimate (cal BC) (95% probability)*	References
GU-1829	Oak from the destruction level of a timber hall associated with NE Carinated Bowl pottery	4785±150	−25.2	3950–3100	*3955–3595*	Fairweather and Ralston 1993
GU-1830	Oak from the destruction level of a timber hall associated with NE Carinated Bowl pottery	4970±75	−25.9	3960–3630	*3945–3650*	Fairweather and Ralston 1993
GU-1831	Oak from the destruction level of a timber hall associated with NE Carinated Bowl pottery	5015±125	−26.4	4050–3530	*4055–3630*	Fairweather and Ralston 1993
GU-1832	Oak from the destruction level of a timber hall associated with NE Carinated Bowl pottery	4970±70	−25.8	3960–3630	*3945–3650*	Fairweather and Ralston 1993
GU-1035	Oak charcoal from the destruction level BB77 F8/C3 of a timber hall associated with NE Carinated Bowl pottery	4840±165	−25.6	3980–3120	*3990–3590*	Fairweather and Ralston 1993
GU-1036	Oak charcoal from the destruction level BB77 F1/C9 of a timber hall associated with NE Carinated Bowl pottery	4740±135	−25.2	3790–3090	*3945–3855 (11%)* or *3825–3585 (84%)*	Fairweather and Ralston 1993
GU-1037	Oak charcoal from the destruction level BB77 F1/C1 of a timber hall associated with NE Carinated Bowl pottery	4930±80	−25.7	3950–3530	*3945–3850 (17%)* or *3845–3830 (1%)* or *3825–3635 (77%)*	Fairweather and Ralston 1993
GU-1038i	Oak from the destruction level BB77 F7/C6 of a timber hall associated with NE Carinated Bowl pottery	5160±100		4040–3700[ii]	*3990–3705*	Fairweather and Ralston 1993
GU-1038ii	Oak charcoal from the destruction level BB77 F7/C6 of a timber hall associated with NE Carinated Bowl pottery	5020±90	−26.5			Fairweather and Ralston 1993
GU-1421	Cereal grain bulk sample. No further contextual detail found	4745±160		3940–3020		G. Barclay *et al.* 2002
Boghead, Fochabers, Moray						
SRR-686	Charcoal from a black layer under NM round mound with much NE Carinated Bowl pottery	4898±60	−25.9	3800–3530	*3910–3875 (2%)* or *3805–3625 (93%)*	Burl 1984; Kinnes 1992b; G. Barclay *et al.* 2002; Noble 2006, 63
SRR-689	Charcoal from a black layer under burial mound with much NE Carinated Bowl pottery	4959±110	−28.5	3980–3520	*3980–3620*	Burl 1984; Kinnes 1992b; G. Barclay *et al.* 2002; Noble 2006, 63
SRR-683	Finely divided oak charcoal in sand infill of Pit 1 which was set in the old ground surface under the North Cairn	4950±180	−26	4230–3360	*4230–4200 (1%)* or *4170–4125 (1%)* or *4075–3565 (93%)*	Burl 1984
SRR-684	Large fragments of oak from layer XIII, debris on the old ground surface under North Cairn	4823±60	−24.7	3710–3380	*3760–3740 (1%)* or *3715–3540 (94%)*	Burl 1984
SRR-685	Finely divided oak charcoal under sand filling working hollow M, one of 15 hollows under the Cairn	5031±100	−26.4	4040–3630	*3995–3640*	Burl 1984

Laboratory Number	Description	Radiocarbon Age (BP)	$\delta^{13}C$ (‰)	Calibrated date range (cal BC) (95% confidence)	*Posterior density estimate (cal BC) (95% probability)*	References
Castle Menzies, Home Farm, Perth and Kinross						
OxA-9813	Oak charcoal from post of long mortuary structure	5130±40		4040–3800	*4040–4020 (3%)* or *3995–3890 (51%)* or *3885–3795 (41%)*	Sheridan 2007a
OxA-9987	Oak charcoal from post of long mortuary structure	5093±39		3980–3780	*3970–3795*	Sheridan 2007a
OxA-9816	Oak charcoal from post of long mortuary structure	5035±70		3980–3650	*3970–3690 (94%)* or *3680–3665 (1%)*	Sheridan 2007aa
OxA-9814	Oak charcoal from post of long mortuary structure	5010±40		3950–3690	*3945–3700*	Sheridan 2007a
Cleaven Dyke, Perth and Kinross						
GU-3911	Rotten oak charcoal in a small pit immediately underlying the bank of a bank barrow. See also GU-3912	5500±120	−26.6	4560–4040		Barclay and Maxwell 1998, 47
GU-3912	Rotten oak charcoal in a small pit immediately underlying the bank of a bank barrow. See also GU-3911	5550±130	−26.3	4690–4050		Barclay and Maxwell 1998, 47
Crathes, Warren Field, Aberdeenshire						
SUERC-4042	Short-life material. From timber hall, some from structural timbers, others from material sealed in pits or post holes. Structure as whole securely associated with Carinated Bowl pottery	5020±35		3950–3700	*3795–3705*	Sheridan 2007a
SUERC-4030	Short-life material. From timber hall, some from structural timbers, others from material sealed in pits or post holes	5005±35		3950–3700	*3790–3705*	Sheridan 2007a
SUERC-4043	Short-life material. From timber hall, some from structural timbers, others from material sealed in pits or post holes	4990±35		3940–3660	*3790–3705*	Sheridan 2007a
SUERC-4032	Short-life material. From timber hall, some from structural timbers, others from material sealed in pits or post holes	4990±40		3940–3660	*3790–3705*	Sheridan 2007a
SUERC-4038	Short-life material. From timber hall, some from structural timbers, others from material sealed in pits or post holes	4980±35		3930–3660	*3790–3705*	Sheridan 2007a
SUERC-4039	Short-life material. From timber hall, some from structural timbers, others from material sealed in pits or post holes	4975±35		3910–3650	*3790–3705*	Sheridan 2007a
SUERC-4033	Short-life material. From timber hall, some from structural timbers, others from material sealed in pits or post holes	4950±35		3800–3650	*3785–3695*	Sheridan 2007a
SUERC-4034	Short-life material. From timber hall, some from structural timbers, others from material sealed in pits or post holes	4945±35		3800–3640	*3785–3695*	Sheridan 2007a
SUERC-4041	Short-life material. From timber hall, some from structural timbers, others from material sealed in pits or post holes	4945±40		3800–3640	*3790–3695*	Sheridan 2007a
SUERC-4048	Oak charcoal. From timber hall, some from structural timbers, others from material sealed in pits or post holes	5235±35		4230–3960	*4230–4200 (7%)* or *4170–4125 (12%)* or *4120–4095 (3%)* or *4080–3965 (73%)*	Sheridan 2007a

Laboratory Number	Description	Radiocarbon Age (BP)	$\delta^{13}C$ (‰)	Calibrated date range (cal BC) (95% confidence)	*Posterior density estimate (cal BC) (95% probability)*	References
SUERC-4044	Oak charcoal. From timber hall, some from structural timbers, others from material sealed in pits or post holes	5205±35		4060–3950	*4225–4205 (1%)* or *4155–4130 (3%)* or *4060–3950 (91%)*	Sheridan 2007a
SUERC-4049	Oak charcoal. From timber hall, some from structural timbers, others from material sealed in pits or post holes	5065±35		3970–3770	*3960–3785*	Sheridan 2007a
Dalladies, Kincardine and Deeside						
I-6113	Wood (seemingly not oak) charcoal from a timber c 15cm in diameter from the SW end of the Phase 2 mortuary enclosure under a stone-revetted earthen long barrow. This measurement conflicts with SRR-289 from the same piece of wood	5190±105				Piggott 1972, 26
SRR-289	Charcoal from the NW end of the Phase 2 mortuary enclosure in an earthen long barrow	4660±50				Piggott 1972, 26
SRR-290	Charcoal from the NW end of the Phase 2 mortuary enclosure (context 30: VII: 71/1) in an earthen long barrow. It should be same date as SRR-289 from a comparable timber nearby	4540±60	−24.9			Piggott 1972, 26
Deer's Den, Kintore Bypass, Aberdeenshire						
OxA-8132	Single charred hazel nutshell from one of a concentration of pits, containing burnt bone, lithics and NE Carinated Bowl pottery	4945±40	−25.2	3800–3640	*3790–3650*	D. Alexander 2000; Sheridan 2007a
OxA-8133	Single charred hazel nutshell from one of a concentration of pits, containing burnt bone, lithics and NE Carinated Bowl pottery	4895±40	−24.7	3770–3630	*3765–3635*	D. Alexander 2000; Sheridan 2007a
Deskford, Leitchestown Farm, Moray						
AA-42986	Alder charcoal (deemed possibly residual by Sheridan 2007, 456) from basal pit fill 1043 with Carinated Bowl pottery in occupation site	5275±50		4250–3970	*4240–3975*	Sheridan 2007a
Douglasmuir, Friockheim, Angus						
GU-1210	Oak charcoal from a post pipe (DM79/T11/ F514/LO1), in a truncated post-hole forming part of end of post-hole enclosure	4855±55	−24.8	3750–3520	*3775–3565*	Kendrick 1995, 33
GU-1469	Oak charcoal from post-hole (DM80 BDD) of a post-hole enclosure. Approximate depth of post-hole 50–70 cm	4895±70	−24.6	3900–3520	*3935–3870 (5%)* or *3810–3615 (88%)* or *3605–3570 (2%)*	Kendrick 1995, 33
GU-1470	Oak charcoal from post-hole (DM80 BAV) of a post-hole enclosure. Taken from a depth of 75 cm of a post pipe	4900±65	−25.2	3900–3530	*3935–3870 (4%)* or *3810–3620 (91%)*	Kendrick 1995, 33
Dubton Farm, Brechin, Angus						
AA-39951	Short-life material from upper fill of large pit associated with food processing; modified Carinated Bowl pottery from this fill	4990±45		3950–3650	*3895–3875 (1%)* or *3825–3650 (94%)*	Sheridan 2007a; Cameron 2002

Laboratory Number	Description	Radiocarbon Age (BP)	$\delta^{13}C$ (‰)	Calibrated date range (cal BC) (95% confidence)	*Posterior density estimate (cal BC) (95% probability)*	References
Forest Road, Kintore, Aberdeenshire						
AA-52420	Salix sp. charcoal from feature ST 06, context 11008, burning episode in Phase III. ST06 is a rectilinear ditched long mortuary enclosure (or non-megalithic long barrow)	5040±50	−26.7	3970–3700	*3910–3720*	Sheridan 2007a; Cook and Dunbar 2008
SUERC-1367	Hazel charcoal from feature ST06, context 11006, Phase IIb. No pottery	5250±60	−26.4	4250–3950	*4240–3960*	Sheridan 2007a; Cook and Dunbar 2008
AA-52412	Oak charcoal from feature ST06, context 8264, Phases Ib–IV	5235±45	−26.3	4230–3960	*4230–4195* (*9%*) or *4175–3960* (*86%*)	Cook and Dunbar 2008
AA-52419	Oak charcoal from feature ST06, context 11008, Phase III burning episode. No pottery	5230±50	−25.1	4240–3950	*4230–4195* (*9%*) or *4175–3955* (*86%*)	Sheridan 2007a; Cook and Dunbar 2008
SUERC-1344	Oak charcoal from feature ST06, context 8705, Phases I–IV: ditch fill. Carinated Bowl pottery in same context	5195±45	−25.0	4220–3940	*4230–4200* (*3%*) or *4170–4125* (*5%*) or *4115–4095* (*1%*) or *4075–3940* (*85%*) or *3840–3815* (*1%*)	Cook and Dunbar 2008
SUERC-1371	Hazel charcoal from feature ST06, context 11009, Phase IV: fill of post-hole	5075±45	−26.3	3980–3710	*3865–3700*	Cook and Dunbar 2008
AA-52418	Oak charcoal from feature ST06, context 9961, Phase IV: ditch fill. Carinated Bowl pottery in same context	5080±50	−24.8	3980–3710	*3980–3760*	Sheridan 2007a; Cook and Dunbar 2008
SUERC-3627	Hazelnut shell, deemed residual, from feature O041, context 11274, in occupation with NE Carinated Bowl pottery	4840±40	−25.8	3700–3520	*3710–3615* (*94%*) or *3590–3570* (*1%*)	Sheridan 2007a; Cook and Dunbar 2008
SUERC-4128	Hazelnut shell (deemed residual), from feature O041, context 11274	4690±35	−26.2	3630–3360	*3635–3585*	Cook and Dunbar 2008
SUERC-1375	Alder charcoal from pit P21, context 11132, with NE Carinated Bowl	4835±40	−25.1	3700–3520	*3705–3615* (*92%*) or *3605–3570* (*3%*)	Sheridan 2007a; Cook and Dunbar 2008
SUERC-1324	Hazel charcoal from St 14, context 1501, with NE Carinated Bowl. St 14 is a hollow and stakeholes	4785±50	−26.1	3660–3370	*3695–3680* (*1%*) or *3665–3560* (*94%*)	Sheridan 2007a; Cook and Dunbar 2008
SUERC-1356	Barley grain from pit P14, context 9099. 2 saddle querns and burnt bone but no pottery	4755±45	−24.3	3650–3370	*3650–3570*	Cook and Dunbar 2008
SUERC-2654	Hazelnut shell, from pit P38, context 11338, with NE Carinated Bowl pottery and flint	4755±35	−25.1	3640–3370	*3645–3575*	Cook and Dunbar 2008
SUERC-2646	Wheat grain from pit P31, context 11139, with NE Carinated Bowl pottery	4740±35	−23.8	3640–3370	*3640–3575*	Cook and Dunbar 2008
SUERC-1355	Wheat grain from pit P14, context 9099. 2 saddle querns and burnt bone but no pottery	4735±110	−24.0	3710–3130	*3710–3570*	Cook and Dunbar 2008

Laboratory Number	Description	Radiocarbon Age (BP)	$\delta^{13}C$ (‰)	Calibrated date range (cal BC) (95% confidence)	*Posterior density estimate (cal BC) (95% probability)*	References
SUERC-1384	Birch charcoal from pit P50, context 11415, with NE Carinated Bowl pottery	4970±40	−26.2	3930–3650	*3755–3640*	Sheridan 2007a; Cook and Dunbar 2008
SUERC-1325	Hazel charcoal from pit P12, context 5504, with NE Carinated Bowl pottery	4865±50	−24.9	3750–3530	*3720–3615*	Sheridan 2007a; Cook and Dunbar 2008
SUERC-1323	Oak charcoal from feature St14, context 1501, with NE Carinated Bowl pottery. St 14 is a hollow and stakeholes	4855±40	−24.1	3710–3530	*3705–3625*	Cook and Dunbar 2008
SUERC-1374	Birch charcoal from feature P25, context 11131, a cremation pit, with NE Carinated Bowl pottery and flint	4895±45	−25.2	3780–3630	*3720–3630*	Sheridan 2007a; Cook and Dunbar 2008
SUERC-1376	Alder charcoal from pit P35, context 11315, with NE Carinated Bowl pottery and stone axe fragment	4965±40	−27.3	3910–3650	*3755–3640*	Sheridan 2007a; Cook and Dunbar 2008
Fordhouse Barrow, Dun, Angus						
OxA-8222	The 35 outer rings of a radially split oak plank used to build a mortuary structure in the phase 3B mound of a non-megalithic long barrow. Carinated Bowl associated with funerary activities linked with this structure	5035±40	−24.4	3960–3700	*3950–3755 (88%)* or *3745–3710 (7%)*	Ashmore 1999b; Sheridan 2007a
OxA-8223	The outer rings of a radially split oak plank used to build a mortuary structure in the phase 3B mound of a non-megalithic long barrow. Carinated Bowl associated with funerary activities linked with this structure	4920±45	−24.9	3800–3630	*3785–3635*	Ashmore 1999b; Sheridan 2007a
OxA-8224	Large fragments from an oak timber used to build a mortuary structure in the phase 3B mound of a non-megalithic long barrow. Carinated Bowl associated with funerary activities linked with this structure	4965±40	−26.4	3910–3650	*3915–3875 (6%)* or *3805–3650 (89%)*	Ashmore 1999b; Sheridan 2007a
Garthdee Road, Aberdeenshire						
SUERC-8607	Barley grain from occupation layer 49 in site with oval post-defined structure, pit and occupation layer, associated with Carinated Bowl pottery	4935±35	−25.9	3790–3640	*3780–3650*	Sheridan 2007a; Ashmore 2005
SUERC-8608	Barley grain from occupation layer 49 in site with oval post-defined structure, pit and occupation layer, associated with Carinated Bowl pottery	4925±35	−26.7	3790–3640	*3775–3645*	Sheridan 2007a; Ashmore 2005
SUERC-8609	Hazelnut shell from hearth 55 in oval post-defined structure, in site with pit and occupation layer, associated with Carinated Bowl pottery	4930±35	−26.5	3790–3640	*3775–3645*	Sheridan 2007a; Ashmore 2005
SUERC-8613	Barley grain from hearth 55 in oval post-defined structure, in site with pit and occupation layer, associated with Carinated Bowl pottery	4950±35	−27.0	3800–3650	*3790–3655*	Sheridan 2007a; Ashmore 2005
SUERC-8616	Barley grain from hearth 57 in oval post-defined structure, in site with pit and occupation layer, associated with Carinated Bowl pottery	4970±35	−27.5	3910–3650	*3800–3655*	Sheridan 2007a; Ashmore 2005
SUERC-8617	Hazelnut shell from hearth 57 in oval post-defined structure, in site with pit and occupation layer, associated with Carinated Bowl pottery	5020±35	−25.1	3950–3700	*3905–3855 (5%)* or *3850–3700 (90%)*	Sheridan 2007a; Ashmore 2005

Laboratory Number	Description	Radiocarbon Age (BP)	$\delta^{13}C$ (‰)	Calibrated date range (cal BC) (95% confidence)	*Posterior density estimate (cal BC) (95% probability)*	References
Inchtuthil, Perth and Kinross						
GU-2760	Burnt oak fencing timbers of a long mortuary enclosure	5160±70	−25.9	4230–3790	*4230–4200 (3%)* or *4170–4125 (4%)* or *4120–4095 (1%)* or *4080–3780 (87%)*	Barclay and Maxwell 1998, 35
GU-2761	Burnt oak fencing timbers of a long mortuary enclosure	5070±50	−25.8	3980–3710	*3970–3760 (94%)* or *3725–3710 (1%)*	Barclay and Maxwell 1998, 35
Lesmurdie Road, Elgin, Moray						
Poz-5483	Oak charcoal from lower fill F31/3 of pit 51, in occupation site, which has Carinated Bowl pottery in its upper fill	5025±35		3950–3700	*3945–3710*	Ashmore 2004b; Sheridan 2007a
Poz-5482	Hazel charcoal from lower fill F31/3 of pit 51, in occupation site, which has Carinated Bowl pottery in its upper fill	2500±30		790–510		Ashmore 2004b; Sheridan 2007a
Midtown of Pitglassie, Aberdeenshire						
GrA-34772	Cremated human bone fragment from shallow depression close to location of probable pyre, sealed beneath NM round cairn; associated with NE Carinated Bowl	4995±35		3940–3690	*3895–3875 (1%)* or *3815–3690 (92%)* or *3685–3660 (2%)*	Sheridan 2007b
GU-2014	Bulk wood charcoal (ash, alder, birch, beech, willow) forming a deposit on a NE Carinated Bowl in the main pit in the area surrounded by the ring-mound.	4935±105	−26.0	3970–3510	*3965–3615*	A. Shepherd 1996, 22; G. Barclay *et al.* 2002
GU-2049	Bulk wood charcoal (ash, alder, birch, beech, willow) from a deposit at the base of the ring-mound with NE Carinated Bowl pottery	4660±50	−25.3	3630–3350	*3640–3575*	A. Shepherd 1996, 22; G. Barclay *et al.* 2002

[1] Calibrated using the marine data of Hughen *et al.* 2004 and a ΔR value of 5±40 (Harkness 1993)
[2] Calibration of weighted mean of 5084±67 BP (T' =1.1; T'(5%) = 3.8, ν=1)

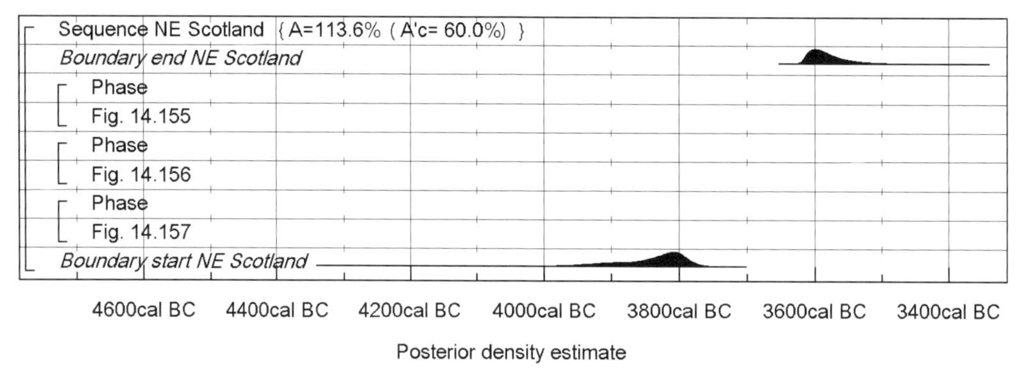

Fig. 14.154. Overall structure of the chronological model for early Neolithic activity in north-east Scotland. The format is identical to that for Fig. 14.1. The components of this model are given in detail in Figs 14.155–7. The large square brackets down the left-hand side of Figs 14.154–7, along with the OxCal keywords, define the overall model exactly.

and dates from such other recent publications as were available to us at the time of writing in 2009 (Lelong and MacGregor 2007; Cook and Dunbar 2008). This 'grab' sample incorporates the results from a wide range of research and contract archaeology projects, encompassing many of the shifts in emphasis in the archaeology of the Neolithic in Scotland that have taken place over recent years, summarised by Brophy (2006). Thus alongside a handful of determinations from western chambered cairns, generally few per site, often poorly contexted and regularly not on short-life material, there are increasing numbers of dates from eastern, lowland house sites, occupation sites, non-megalithic long barrows/mortuary enclosures, and linear monuments. Since this is an indicative exercise only, with no claims to completeness, we have chosen to exclude dates from north of the Great Glen, consciously here leaving aside the important but patchy radiocarbon dating evidence from the Western Isles, Caithness, and the Orkney and Shetland Islands; this decision also excludes the dates from the Oronsay middens.

We begin by presenting two models for the chronology of the first Neolithic things and practices in Scotland south of the Great Glen, covering respectively south and north-east Scotland. Both of these models include dates associated with all types of northern Carinated Bowl pottery, dates from early Neolithic monument types (long barrows and rectilinear mortuary enclosures, chambered cairns, non-megalithic round mounds, and linear constructions), dates from rectangular timber halls, and dates associated with other diagnostically Neolithic material, such as cereal grains and ground stone axeheads. Details of the dates included in the models presented here are given in Table 14.14 and the location of the sites mentioned is shown in Fig. 14.149.

Figure 14.150 shows the overall structure of the chronological model for early Neolithic activity in southern Scotland, here defined as land between the present English border and a line drawn roughly between the Tay at Perth, along Strathearn and past Tyndrum to Loch Etive (on whose north side lies the Achnacreebeag monument: Chapter 1.5). Figures 14.151–3 show the components of this model. The dates have been incorporated in the models on the same principles as those used throughout the rest of this volume. So, for example, the three dates from Balfarg Riding School (*GU-1903, -2604–5*: Fig. 14.151), all on bulk samples of charcoal which contained a component of wood which could have had a potentially significant age-offset (Table 14.14), have been treated as *termini post quos* for the end of early Neolithic activity in southern Scotland. In contrast, *GU-4279* from Biggar Common East (Fig. 14.151) has been included in the model as a sample on short-life material directly associated with the use of early Neolithic pottery, in this case probably traditional Carinated Bowl. The radiocarbon dates on the timber hall from Claish (G. Barclay *et al.* 2002) have been included in a component model for the chronology of that structure (for example, in the way that we have treated the dates from the Hazleton long cairn, elsewhere in this chapter). This ensures that a large number of radiocarbon dates from a single site do not unbalance the model. In effect, the twelve radiocarbon dates have been distilled into two parameters for the chronology of this site, which are effective in the overall chronological model for the early Neolithic in southern Scotland. Where appropriate, marine samples, such as the cockle shell at Crarae (*OxA-7880*; Fig. 14.151) have been calibrated using the marine dataset of Hughen *et al.* (2004) and a ΔR value of 5±40 BP (Stuiver and Braziunas 1993). Stratigraphic sequences have been included in the models for the long barrows/enclosures at Eweford West and Pencraig Hill (Figs 14.152–3; Lelong and MacGregor 2007), for the chambered cairn at Port Charlotte (Fig. 14.153; Sheridan 2007a), and a pit at Maybury (Fig. 14.152; Sheridan 2007a).

This model suggests that the early Neolithic began in southern Scotland in *3835–3760 cal BC* (*95% probability*; Fig. 14.150: *start S Scotland*), probably in *3815–3780 cal BC* (*68% probability*). This phase of activity ended in *3620–3535 cal BC* (*95% probability*; Fig. 14.150: *end S Scotland*), probably in *3610–3570 cal BC* (*68% probability*).

A similar model for the chronology of the early Neolithic in north-east Scotland is shown in Figs 14.154–7. Site-specific models for the timber halls at Balbridie and Crathes (Fairweather and Ralston 1993; Sheridan 2007a; H. Murray *et al.* 2009)[9] are similarly incorporated in this overall model (Fig. 14.155), so that the number of measurements from

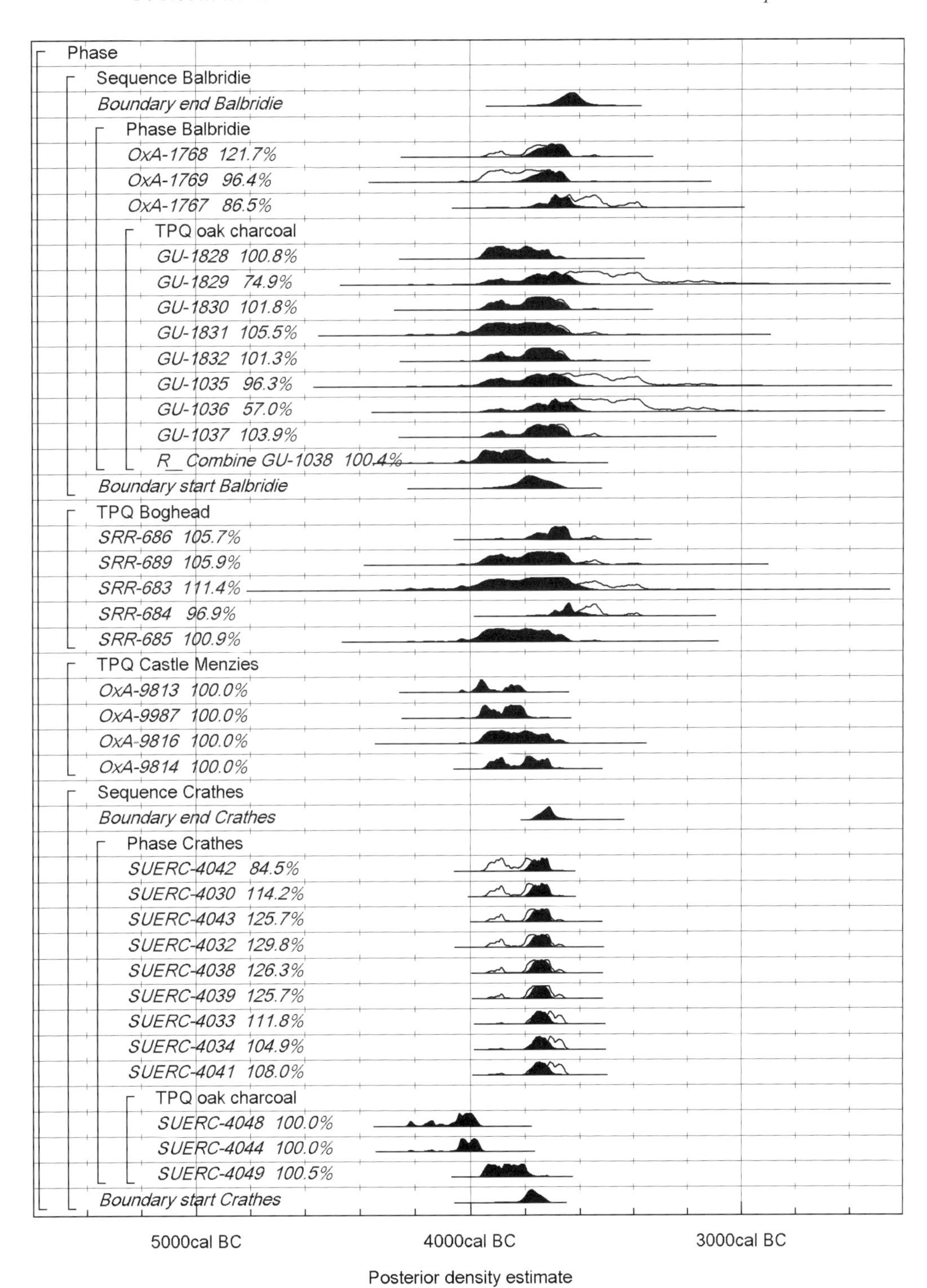

Fig. 14.155. Probability distributions of dates for early Neolithic activity in north-east Scotland. The format is identical to that for Fig. 14.1. The overall structure of this model is shown in Fig. 14.154, and its other components in Figs 14.156–7.

them does not unbalance the sample. A similar approach has also been taken for the pit site at Forest Road, Kintore, whose dating is exemplary (Cook and Dunbar 2008). Here *SUERC-1356*, for example, has been included in the model, as it is on a cereal grain from a pit with saddle querns, even though the pit did not contain any pottery. The stratigraphic sequence for the long barrow/enclosure at Forest Road, Kintore (Cook and Dunbar 2008), has also been included in the model (Fig. 14.156). Two dates on short-life samples have been included as *termini post quos* only: *AA-42986* from Deskford, which is deemed possibly residual (Sheridan 2007a, 456) and *SUERC-3627* from Forest Road, Kintore, which is deemed residual by the excavators (Cook and Dunbar 2008, 30). GU-3911 and -3912, two fifth millennium cal BC dates from a feature beneath the Cleaven Dyke, Perth and Kinross (Table 14.14), are not modelled because the interval between them and the building of the monument is too great to make them informative as *termini post quos*.

This model suggests that the early Neolithic began in

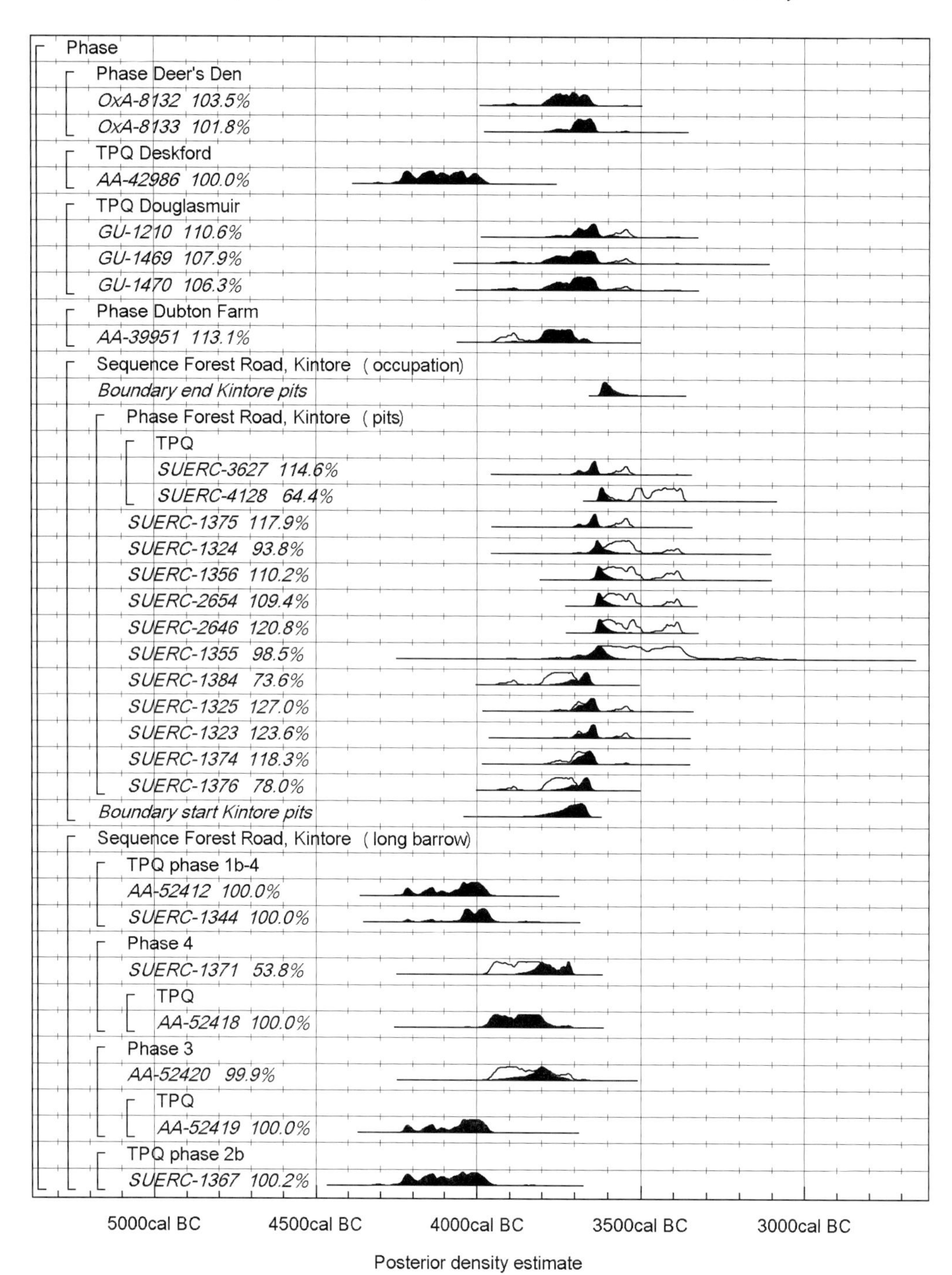

Fig. 14.156. Probability distributions of dates for early Neolithic activity in north-east Scotland. The format is identical to that for Fig. 14.1. The overall structure of this model is shown in Fig. 14.154, and its other components in Figs 14.155 and 14.157.

north-east Scotland in *3950–3765 cal BC* (*95% probability*; Fig. 14.154: *start NE Scotland*), probably in *3865–3780 cal BC* (*68% probability*). This phase of activity ended in *3625–3520 cal BC* (*95% probability*; Fig. 14.154: *end NE Scotland*), probably in *3615–3570 cal BC* (*68% probability*).

These models provide two independent estimates for the date when the first Neolithic things and practices appeared in different parts of Scotland. It is now time to investigate whether the different elements of the Neolithic appeared synchronously. Figure 14.158 shows the overall structure of a model for the chronology of all the variants of Carinated Bowl in Scotland south of the Great Glen. This includes all dates associated with traditional Carinated Bowl, North-East Carinated Bowl, and modified Carinated Bowl as defined by Sheridan (2007a). The components of this model are shown in Figs 14.160–4, without the surrounding uniform phase boundaries in Figs 14.163 and 14. 164 (although the posterior density estimates shown on these figures are not those relating to this model).

This model suggests that Carinated Bowl pottery first appeared in Scotland south of the Great Glen in *3825–3750*

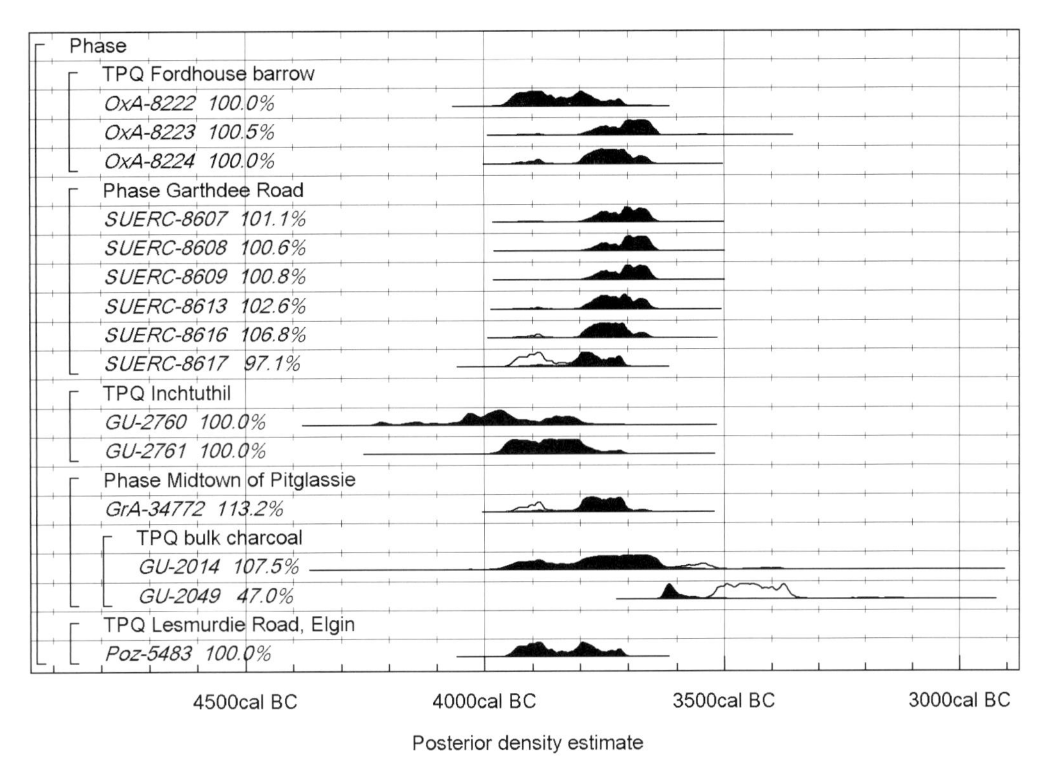

Fig. 14.157. Probability distributions of dates for early Neolithic activity in north-east Scotland. The format is identical to that for Fig. 14.1. The overall structure of this model is shown in Fig. 14.154, and its other components in Figs 14.155–6.

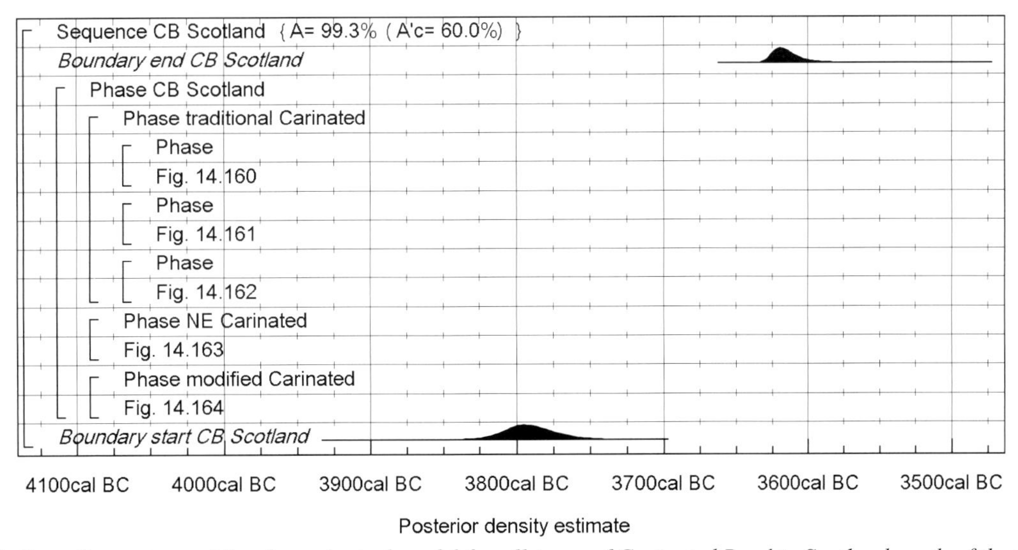

Fig. 14.158. Overall structure of the chronological model for all types of Carinated Bowl in Scotland south of the Great Glen. The format is identical to that for Fig. 14.1. The components of the model are given in detail in Figs 14.160–2 and between the uniform phase boundaries of the models shown in Figs 14.163 and 14.164 (although the posterior density estimates shown on these figures are not those relating to this model). The large square brackets down the left-hand side of these figures, along with the OxCal keywords, define the overall model exactly.

cal BC (*95% probability*; Fig. 14.158: *start CB Scotland*), probably in *3810–3775 cal BC* (*68% probability*). The currency of Carinated Bowl in this area ended in *3635–3590 cal BC* (*95% probability*; Fig. 14.158: *end CB Scotland*), probably in *3630–3605 cal BC* (*68% probability*).

Figure 14.159 shows the overall structure for the chronological model for the currency of traditional Carinated Bowl in Scotland south of the Great Glen, with the components given in Figs 14.160–2. This model suggests that traditional Carinated Bowl pottery first appeared in Scotland south of the Great Glen in *3825–3740 cal BC* (*95% probability*; Fig. 14.159: *start traditional Carinated*), probably in *3810–3765 cal BC* (*68% probability*). The currency of traditional Carinated Bowl in this area ended

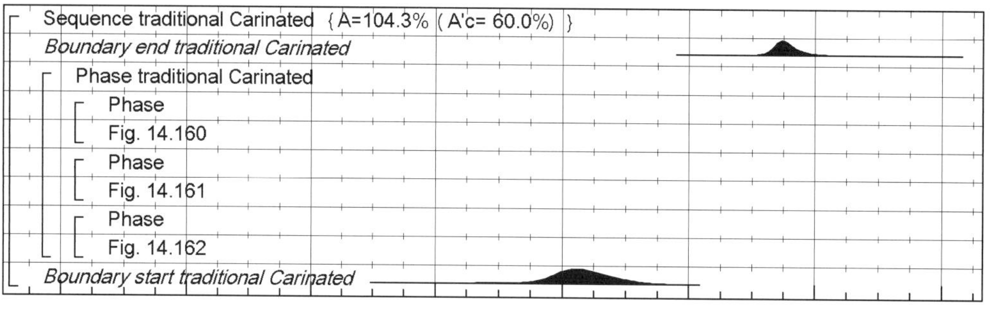

Fig. 14.159. Overall structure of the chronological model for traditional Carinated Bowl in Scotland south of the Great Glen. The format is identical to that for Fig. 14.1. The components of the model are given in detail in Figs 14.160–2. The large square brackets down the left-hand side of Figs 14.159–62, along with the OxCal keywords, define the overall model exactly.

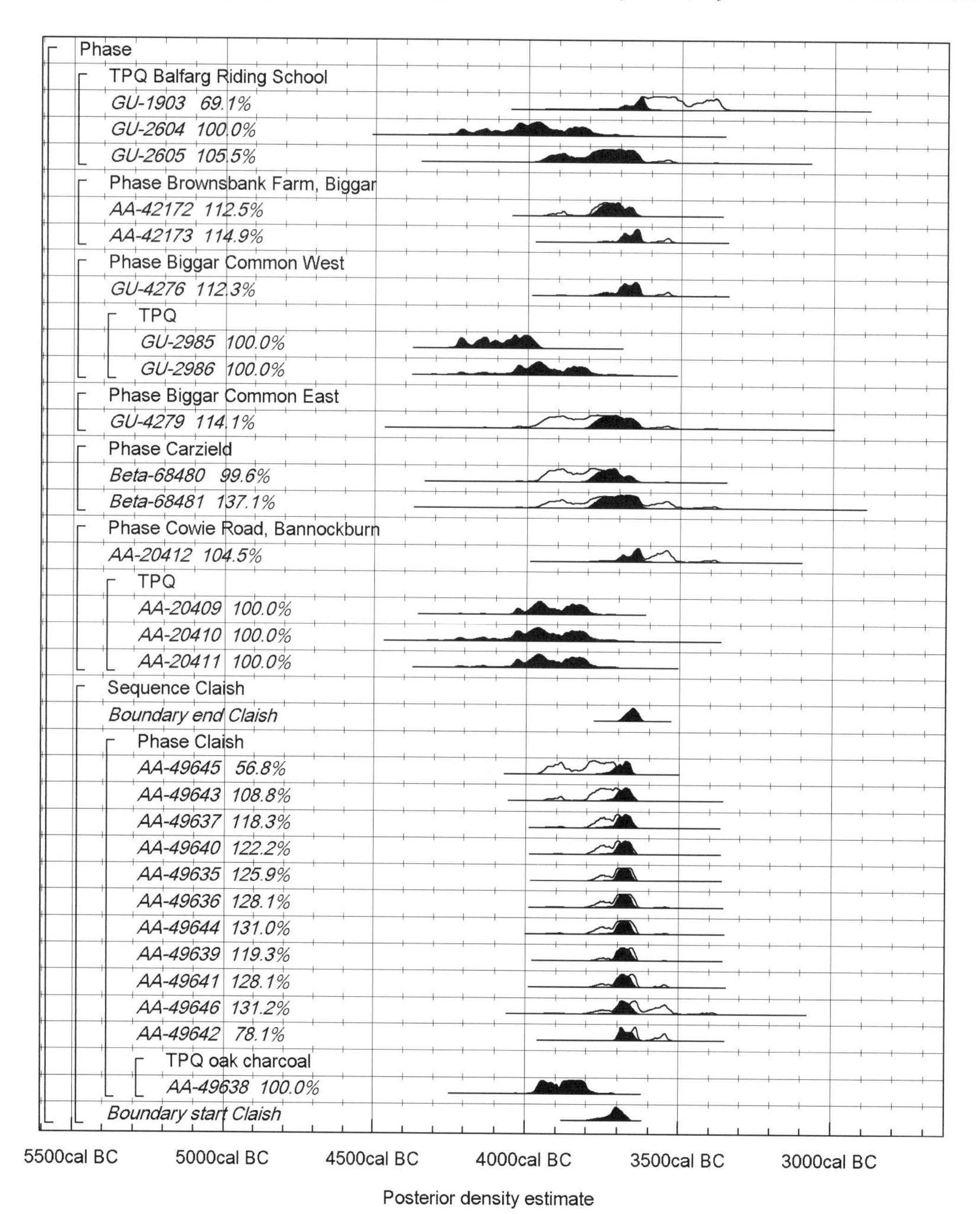

Fig. 14.160. Probability distributions of dates for samples associated with traditional Carinated Bowl in Scotland south of the Great Glen. The format is identical to that for Fig. 14.1. The overall structure of this model is shown in Fig. 14.159, and its other components in Figs 14.161–2.

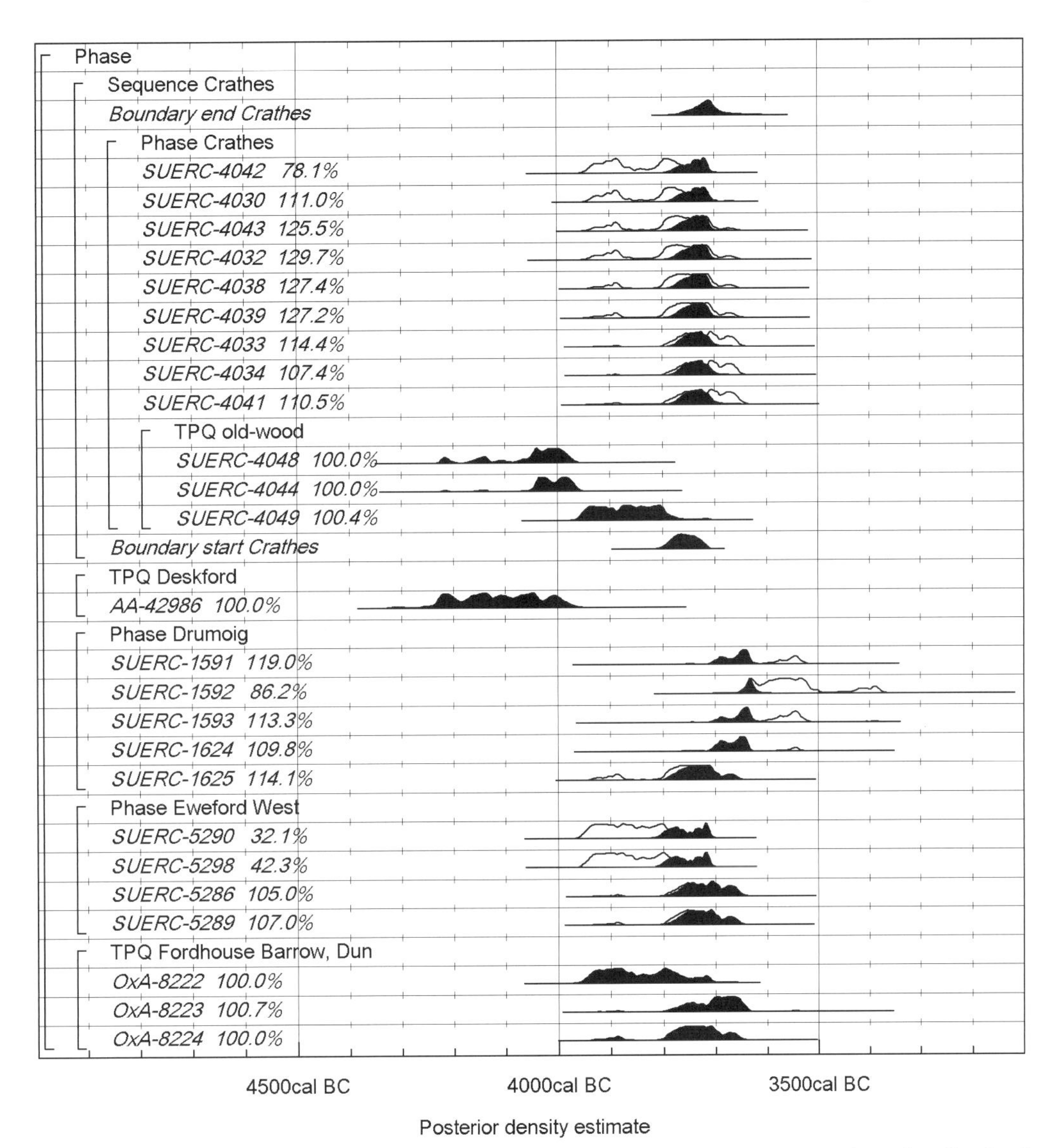

Fig. 14.161. Probability distributions of dates for samples associated with traditional Carinated Bowl in Scotland south of the Great Glen. The format is identical to that for Fig. 14.1. The overall structure of this model is shown in Fig. 14.159, and its other components in Figs 14.160 and 14.162.

in *3645–3595 cal BC* (*95% probability*; Fig. 14.159: *end traditional Carinated*), probably in *3635–3615 cal BC* (*68% probability*).

Figure 14.163 shows a model for the chronology of North-East Carinated Bowl pottery, in this case in a relatively restricted part of north-east Scotland between the rivers Dee and Spey. This model suggests that North-East Carinated Bowl pottery first appeared in Scotland south of the Great Glen in *4030–3725 cal BC* (*95% probability*; Fig. 14.163: *start NE Carinated*), probably in *3905–3770 cal BC* (*68% probability*). The currency of this variant of Carinated Bowl in this area ended in *3635–3420 cal BC* (*95% probability*; Fig. 14.163: *end NE Carinated*), probably in *3625–3540 cal BC* (*68% probability*). These estimates are imprecise – wider than those for traditional Carinated Bowl – because they depend on relatively few data, particularly once the large assemblage of dates from Balbridie is appropriately weighted in the model.

Figure 14.164 shows a chronological model for modified Carinated Bowl in Scotland south of the Great Glen, although it should be noted that data for this type of ceramic are severely restricted. This model suggests that modified Carinated Bowl pottery first appeared in Scotland south of the Great Glen in *4250–3650 cal BC* (*95% probability*; Fig. 14.164: *start modified Carinated*), probably in *3925–3690 cal BC* (*68% probability*). The currency of this variant of Carinated Bowl in this area ended in *3645–3110 cal BC* (*95% probability*; Fig. 14.164: *end modified Carinated*), probably in *3590–3390 cal BC* (*68% probability*).

The date estimates for the currency of all three variants of northern Carinated Bowl are shown in Fig. 14.165. All are consistent with the first appearance of the variants in the decades around 3800 cal BC.[10] On the available evidence, it is *86% probable* that North-East Carinated Bowl came into use slightly earlier than traditional Carinated Bowl, although this may be only the difference between the generation before 3800 cal BC and their children. This subtle trend needs to be confirmed by further dating of

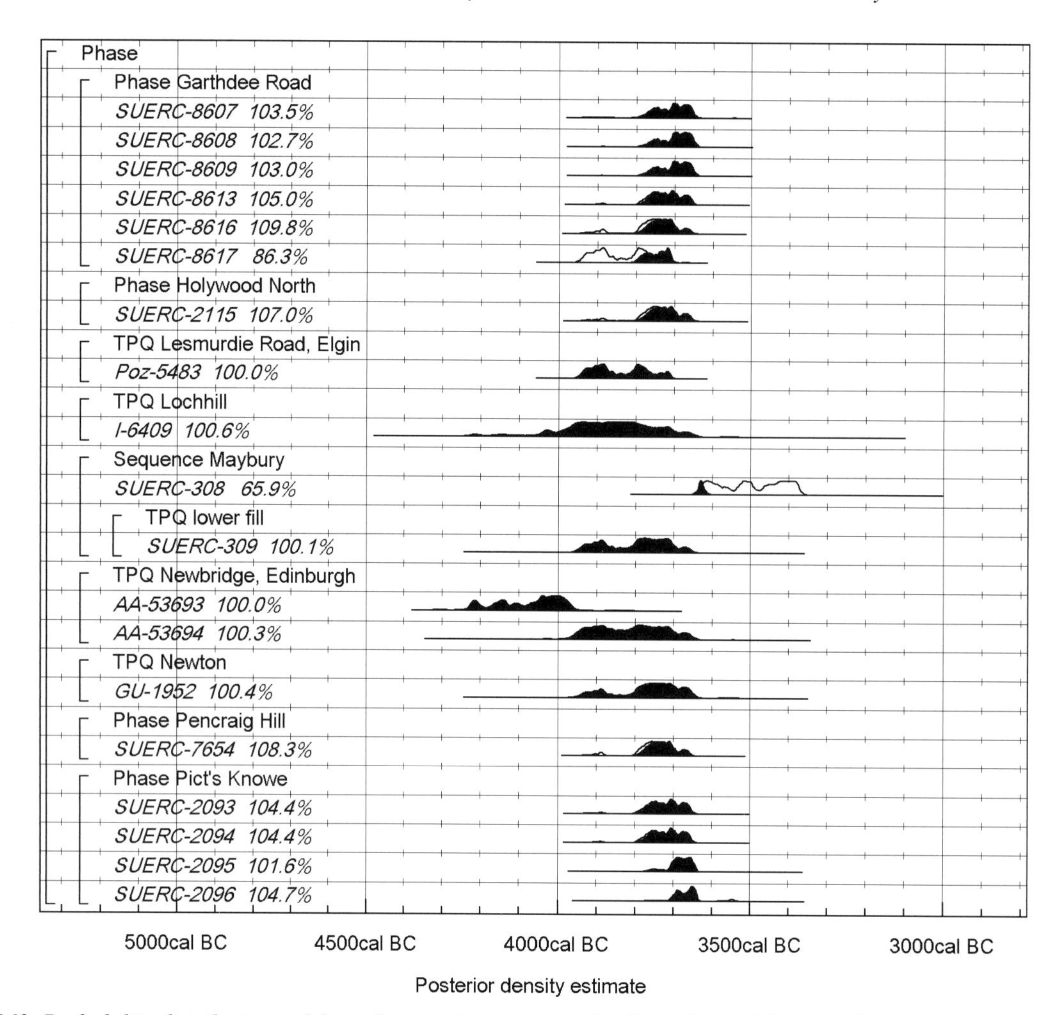

Fig. 14.162. Probability distributions of dates for samples associated with traditional Carinated Bowl in Scotland south of the Great Glen. The format is identical to that for Fig. 14.1. The overall structure of this model is shown in Fig. 14.159, and its other components in Figs 14.160–1.

North-East Carinated Bowl assemblages, as at present we may simply have too few dated sites effectively to deal with the scatter on the assemblage of calibrated dates for this pottery type. It is still perfectly possible that the introduction of all three variants of northern Carinated Bowl to Scotland was precisely contemporary. Modified Carinated Bowl is particularly poorly dated and must be a priority for further research. There are hints, however, in the existing dating, that this variant may begin a few generations later than the other two variants, and perhaps carry on in use into the 36th century cal BC (Fig. 14.165).

It is now time to consider the date of early Neolithic monuments in Scotland south of the Great Glen. The overall structure for a chronological model for their currency is given in Fig. 14.166, with the component parts relating to Scottish long barrows given in Fig. 14.168 and between the surrounding uniform phase boundaries of Fig. 14.167, the component for chambered cairns being given between the uniform phase boundaries of Fig. 14.169, and the component parts for linear monuments and non-megalithic round mounds in Figs. 14.170–1 (although the posterior density estimates shown on these figures are not those relating to this model). This model suggests that the first early Neolithic monument was constructed in Scotland in *3955–3785 cal BC* (*95% probability*; Fig. 14.166: *start Scottish monuments*), probably in *3920–3885 cal BC* (*14% probability*) or *3870–3795 cal BC* (*54% probability*). This phase of activity ended in *3620–3540 cal BC* (*95% probability*; Fig. 14.166: *end Scottish monuments*), probably in *3610–3570 cal BC* (*68% probability*).

A separate chronological model for the currency of Scottish long barrows and related forms is shown in Figs 14.167–8. This model does not include the three radiocarbon dates from Dalladies (Table 14.14; I-6113, SRR-289–90), since I-6113 and SRR-289 were from the same piece of wood and produced statistically significantly different radiocarbon measurements (T'=21.6; T'(5%)=3.8, ν=1) and SRR-290 from the same context has extremely low individual agreement when included in this model (A=2.3%), and may be anomalously young. In these circumstances, it appears prudent to exclude all these dates from the analysis. We have also included *I-6409* from Lochhill in this model, as it relates to the timber mortuary structure preceding a rebuild in stone (Masters 1973).

This model suggests that the first long barrow or variant form in Scotland south of the Great Glen was

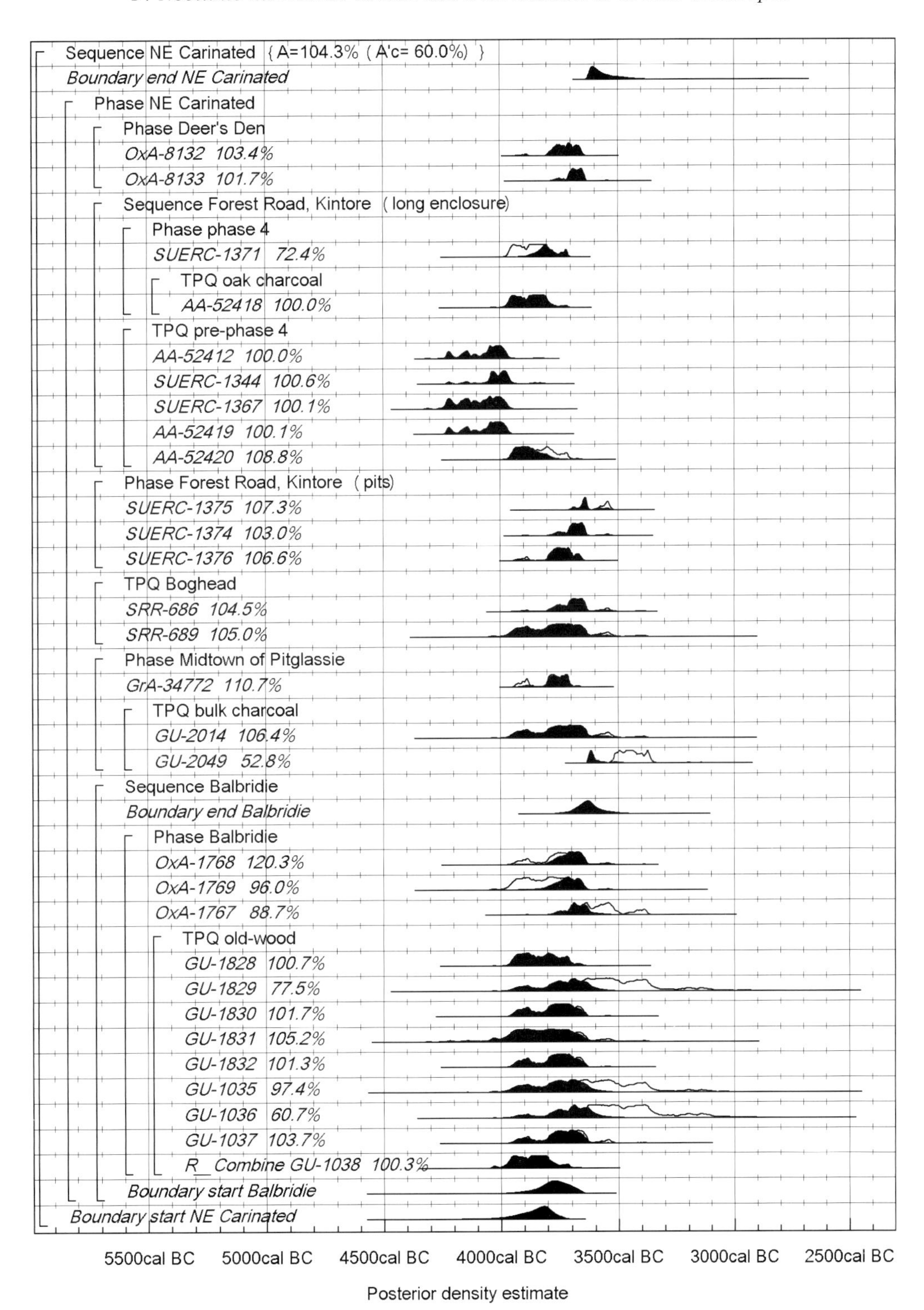

Fig. 14.163. Probability distributions of dates associated with North-East Carinated Bowl in Scotland south of the Great Glen. The format is the same as for Fig. 14.1. The large square brackets down the left-hand side of the diagram, along with the OxCal keywords, define the overall model exactly.

constructed in *3935–3750 cal BC* (*94% probability*; Fig. 14.167: *start Scottish long barrows*) or *3745–3735 cal BC* (*1% probability*), probably in *3840–3775 cal BC* (*68% probability*). This phase of activity ended in *3760–3620 cal BC* (*95% probability*; Fig. 14.167: *end Scottish long barrows*), probably in *3705–3640 cal BC* (*68% probability*).

A model for the currency of chambered cairns in this part of Scotland is shown in Fig. 14.169. Again, dates are scarce, and only three provide more than *termini post quos* for their contexts. On this scanty evidence, we estimate that this type of construction began in *4295–3495 cal BC* (*95% probability*; Fig. 14.169: *start Scottish chambered cairns*), probably in *3800–3560 cal BC* (*68% probability*). This phase of activity ended in *3625–3180 cal BC* (*95% probability*; Fig. 14.169: *end Scottish chambered cairns*),

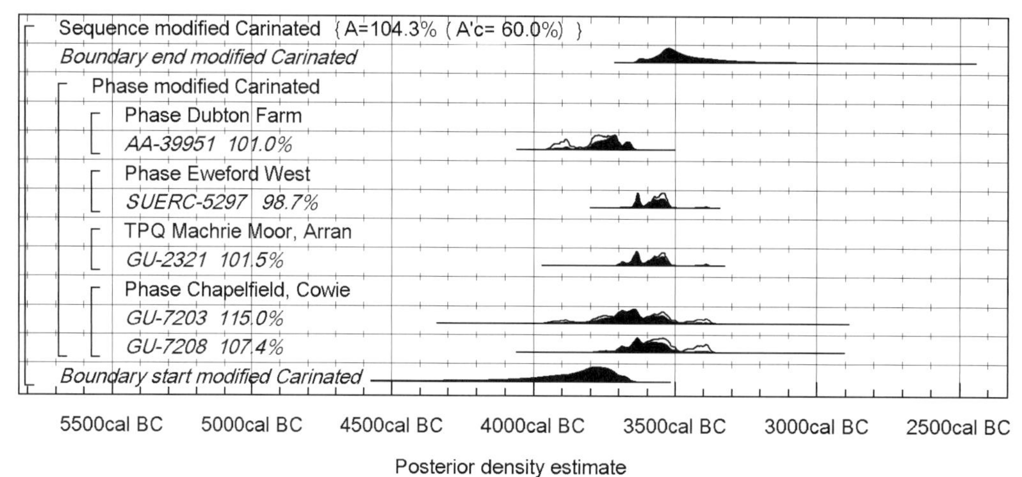

Fig. 14.164. Probability distributions of dates associated with modified Carinated Bowl in Scotland south of the Great Glen. The format is the same as for Fig. 14.1. The large square brackets down the left-hand side of the diagram, along with the OxCal keywords, define the overall model exactly.

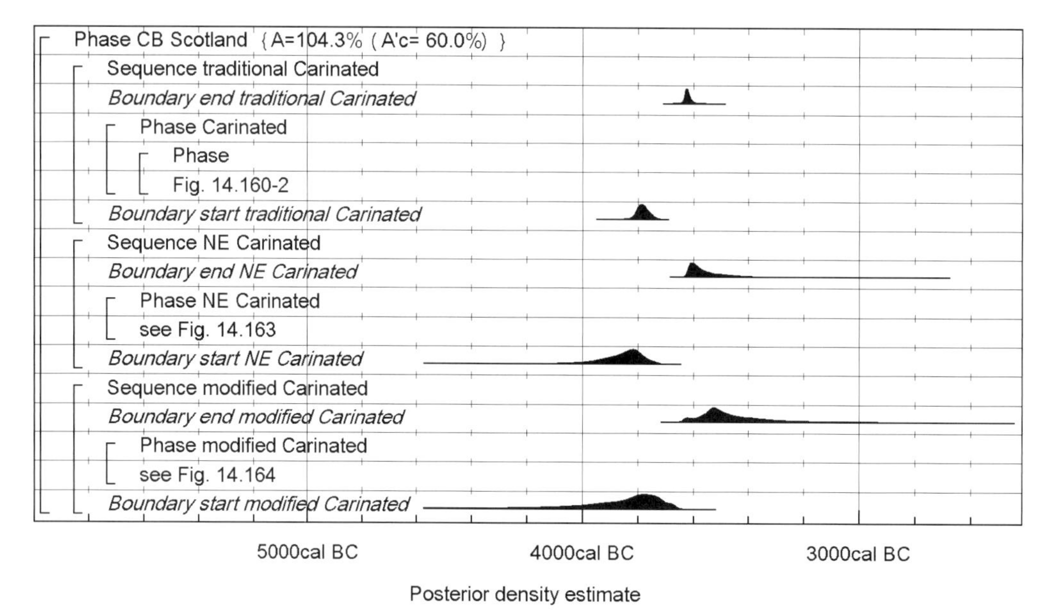

Fig. 14.165. Probability distributions for the currency of different types of Carinated Bowl in Scotland south of the Great Glen, derived from the models shown in Figs 14.159–62, 14.163, and 14.164.

probably in *3600–3555 cal BC* (*10% probability*) or *3525–3335 cal BC* (*58% probability*).

The dating of linear monuments in Scotland south of the Great Glen is known even less securely. Of the 29 calibrated radiocarbon dates shown on Fig. 14.170, only one is on short-life material. This calibrates to 3710–3380 cal BC (95% confidence; Table 14.14: AA-20412). This date and the even later *termini post quos* for the Holywood North monument provided by SUERC-2114 and SUERC-2116, provide the only firm dating for these monuments. This places them in the middle centuries of the fourth millennium cal BC. A date from the Dunragit cursus (Table 14.14: SUERC-2103) is excluded from our modelling here because the context and taphonomy of the sample remain uncertain pending full publication. If truly associated with the monument, it also supports a date in the middle rather the early centuries of the fourth millennium cal BC for these constructions. On the basis of the radiocarbon dates currently available (Fig. 14.170), there is no evidence that any of these monuments predate *c.* 3700 cal BC (*contra* J. Thomas 2006, 233), and some examples, such as that at Holywood North, may be a century or two later. An origin around 3700 cal BC for this monument tradition is compatible with their association with Carinated Bowl (and the chronologies presented for that pottery type here; Fig. 14.158), and allows the possibility that it was in some way a northern alternative to the practice of building enclosures further south (we are grateful to the anonymous referee for this suggestion). The claim that they represent ' "public architecture" as opposed to the more colossal *monumentality* of the long cairns and causewayed enclosures which developed after 3800 BC and 3650 cal BC respectively' (J. Thomas 2006, 233) cannot be supported.

The dating of non-megalithic round mounds (cf. Kinnes

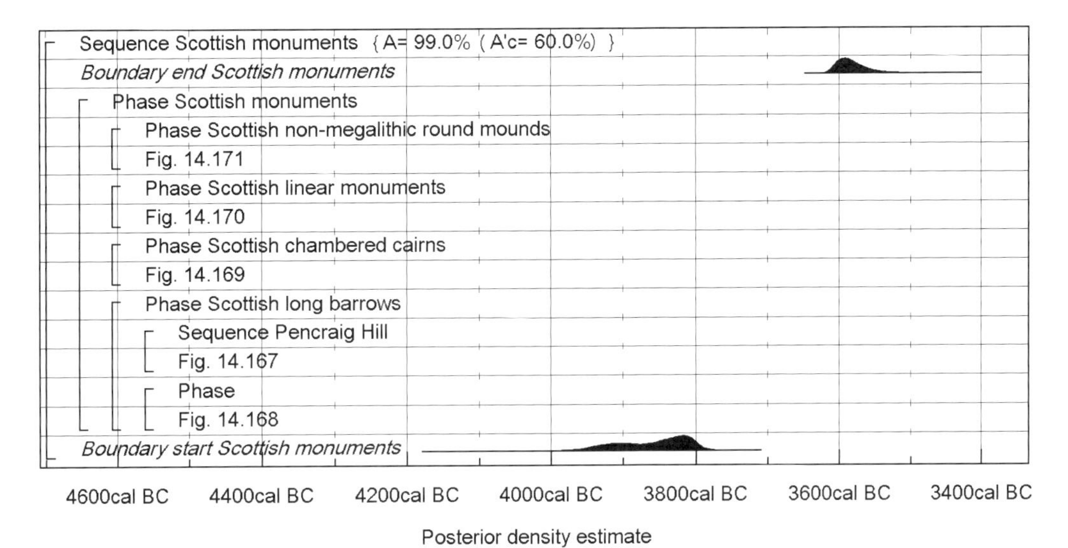

Fig. 14.166. Overall structure of the chronological model for early Neolithic monuments in Scotland south of the Great Glen. The format is identical to that for Fig. 14.1. The components of the model are given in detail in Figs 14.167–71 (without the surrounding boundaries in Figs 14.167 and 14.169) (although the posterior density estimates shown on these figures are not those relating to this model). The large square brackets down the left-hand side of Figs 14.166–71, along with the OxCal keywords, define the overall model exactly.

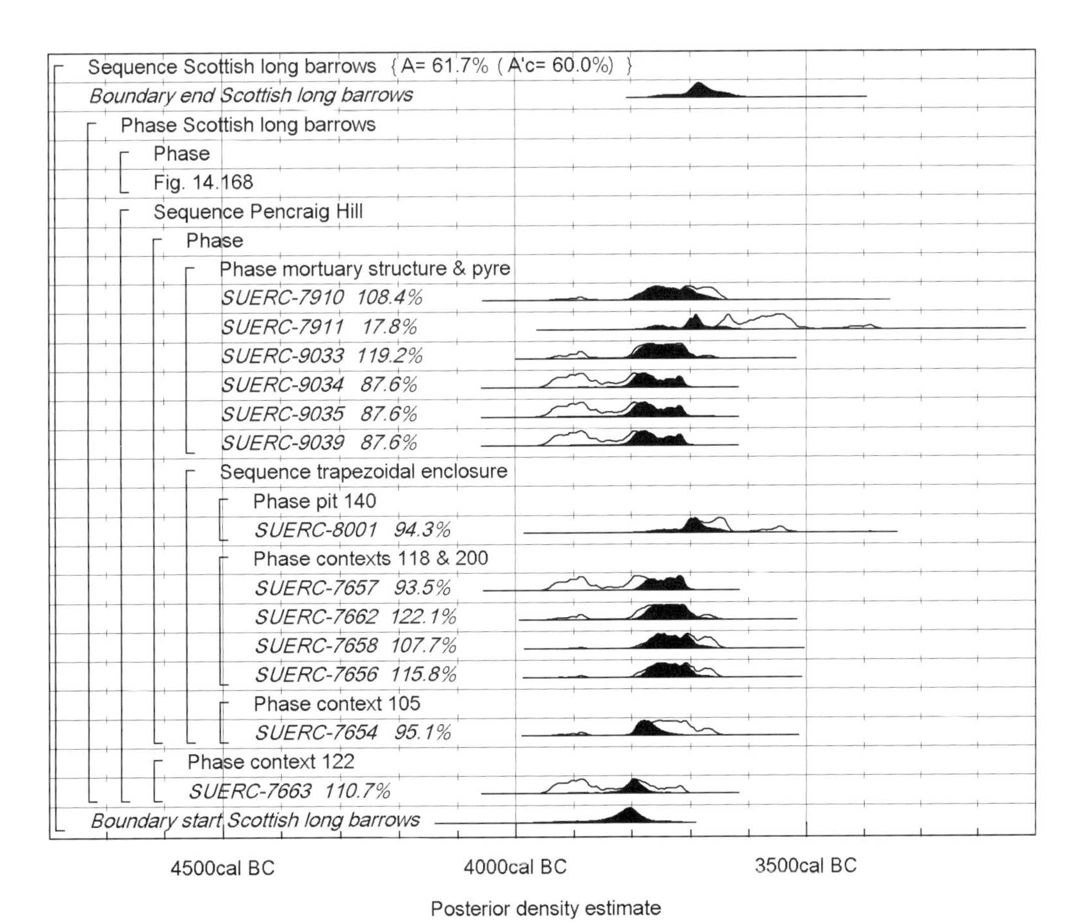

Fig. 14.167. Overall structure of the chronological model for early Neolithic long barrows in Scotland south of the Great Glen. The format is identical to that for Fig. 14.1. The component of the model is shown in detail in Fig. 14.168. The large square brackets down the left-hand side of Figs 14.167–8, along with the OxCal keywords, define the overall model exactly.

1992b) is even less secure – there being not a single date that is not a *terminus post quem*. For both of the dated sites, the latest date from beneath the mound provides a *terminus post quem* for construction of the mound. These are 3710–3380 cal BC (95% confidence; Table 14.14: SRR-684) for the mound at Boghead, and 3630–3350 cal BC

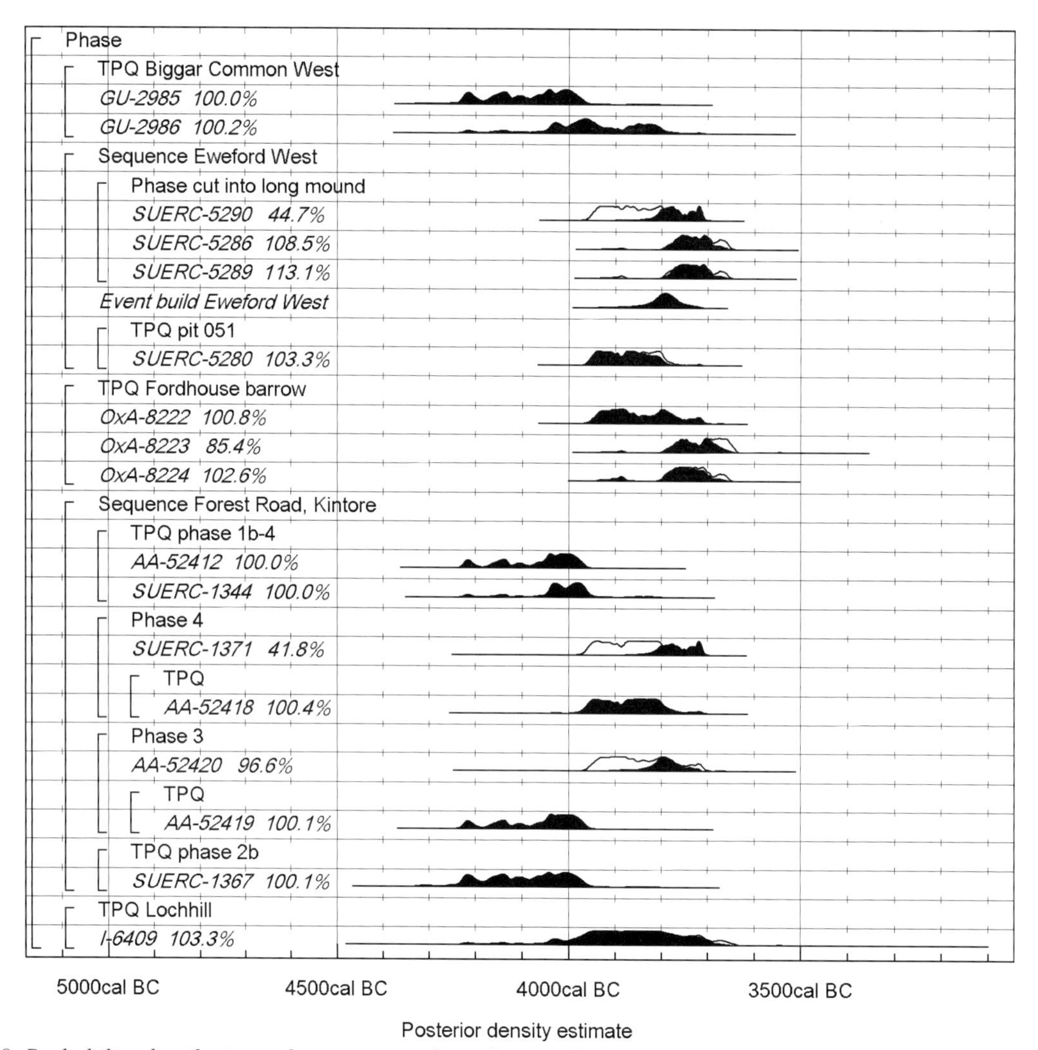

Fig. 14.168. Probability distributions of construction dates for samples associated with long barrows in Scotland south of the Great Glen. The format is identical to that for Fig. 14.1. The overall structure of this model is shown in Fig. 14.167.

(95% confidence; Table 14.14: GU-2049) for the mound at Midtown of Pitglassie. Again this monument type appears to fall in the middle centuries of the fourth millennium cal BC (Fig. 14.171).

Figure 14.172 shows a summary of our current chronology for early Neolithic monument types in Scotland south of the Great Glen. It is *77% probable* that the first Scottish long barrow predates the first chambered cairn, although given the limited sample of dates from chambered cairns it is difficult to say whether the stone chambered tradition really did follow on from the earthen and timber one. The dating of both the linear monuments and the non-megalithic round mounds currently leaves much to be desired, although such dating as exists at present would place these monuments in the middle centuries of the fourth millennium cal BC, along with Scottish chambered cairns, rather than with long barrows in the first centuries of the Scottish Neolithic.

Figure 14.173 shows a model for the chronology of rectangular timber halls in Scotland. Only three sites have dates: Balbridie, Claish and Crathes (at time of writing in early 2009, dates for fourth and fifth examples at Lockerbie Academy and Doon Hill[11] were still pending). In contrast to our approach to modelling these sites in estimating the date of the appearance of Neolithic things and practices (see above), this model treats all the dates from these timber halls as part of one continuous period of currency for the use of such structures. In this case, because we have exemplary series of dates from each of the structures, this is probably not the most realistic modelling approach. We have, however, adopted it so that our date estimates are directly comparable to those for Irish houses, where there are insufficient measurements from any one structure for a more sophisticated approach to be adopted. With these caveats, this model suggests that the currency of Scottish early Neolithic timber halls began in *3800–3705 cal BC* (*95% probability*; Fig. 14.173: *start Scottish houses*), probably in *3780–3725 cal BC* (*68% probability*). The currency of such halls ended in *3705–3630 cal BC* (*95% probability*; Fig. 14.173: *end Scottish houses*), probably in *3690–3645 cal BC* (*68% probability*).

It can be seen from Fig. 14.174 that the date estimates from the two approaches for modelling the chronology of early Neolithic timber halls in Scotland produce very similar results. The structures at the neighbouring sites of

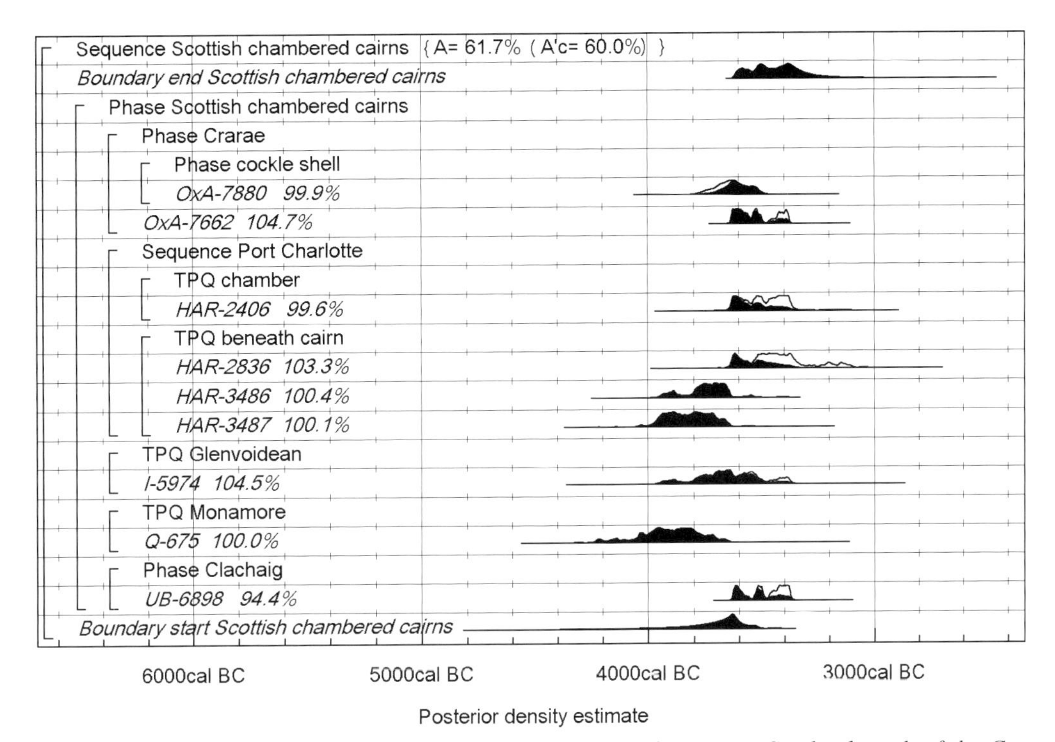

Fig. 14.169. Probability distributions of dates associated with chambered cairns in Scotland south of the Great Glen. The format is the same as for Fig. 14.1. The large square brackets down the left-hand side of the diagram, along with the OxCal keywords, define the overall model exactly.

Balbridie and Crathes seem to have been constructed in the first half of the 38th century cal BC. That at Crathes had probably gone out of use by the end of the century, but the structure at Balbridie seems to have been more enduring, standing until at least the middle of the 37th century cal BC. Claish, further south but with a strikingly similar ground plan to Balbridie (G. Barclay *et al.* 2002; Brophy 2007), is rather later, being constructed in the decades around 3700 cal BC, and being in use for around half a century.

A summary of our chronologies for the early Neolithic in Scotland south of the Great Glen is shown in Fig. 14.175. The first Neolithic things and practices arrived across lowland Scotland in the decades around 3800 cal BC.[12] Carinated Bowl, including both the traditional and North-East variants, was a component of this primary Neolithic activity. Monuments, specifically long barrows and variant forms, were also a primary component of this first Neolithic activity. Possibly a generation or two later came the first timber halls, and modified Carinated Bowl, during the course of the 38th century cal BC. The currencies of both halls and long barrows were relatively brief, probably ending in the first half of the 37th century cal BC. Around this time may come the first chambered cairns, linear monuments and non-megalithic round mounds, though the dating of none of these is entirely satisfactory. The end of both traditional and North-East variants of Carinated Bowl appears to fall in the last decades of the 37th century cal BC, although modified Carinated Bowl may continue in use during at least the 36th century cal BC. Our models for the general currency of Carinated Bowl include a disproportionate number of samples associated with traditional Carinated Bowl. Further dates on the other variants would be most welcome. Our dates for the end of the early Neolithic in this part of Scotland are heavily correlated with our date estimates for Carinated Bowl. There do not appear to be equivalents of southern Decorated Bowl in lowland Scotland, the nearest approximation being fluted linear decoration on some North-East Carinated Bowl (e.g. Sheridan 2007a, fig. 10). We also note Beacharra Ware in the west and Unstan Ware in the far north. Our date estimates may imply that Impressed Wares in Scotland followed on from modified Carinated Bowl.

14.8 Wider histories: the development of the early Neolithic in Britain and Ireland

We can now attempt to place causewayed and related enclosures on a much wider stage. Figure 14.176 provides a summary of the first appearance of Neolithic things and practices in the different parts of Britain and Ireland covered in this project. The Neolithic did not appear everywhere at once (Fig. 14.177) and the pace of its coming varied.

In south-east England, the first elements of the Neolithic appeared in the 41st and 40th centuries cal BC (Figs 14.176 and 14.57). Here, the first centuries of the Neolithic included Carinated Bowl, as at Yabsley Street, Blackwall (Fig. 14.49), with large rectangular timber houses, as at White Horse Stone (Fig. 7.26), monumental constructions such as the large megalithic chamber at Coldrum (Fig. 7.27), and flint mines in Sussex (Fig 5.33) appearing within a few generations. At White Horse Stone cereals were part of this first Neolithic with both wheat and

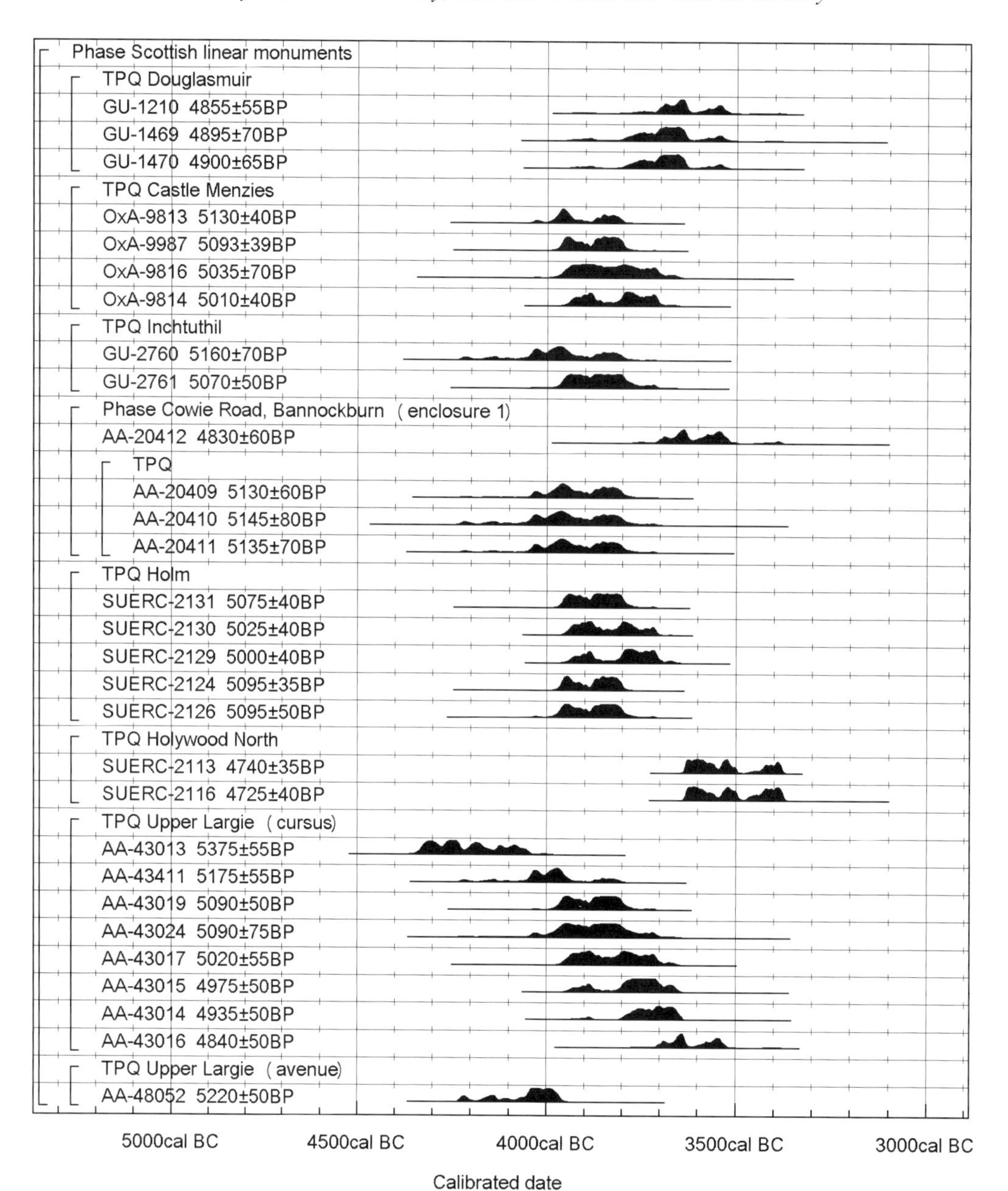

Fig. 14.170. Calibrated radiocarbon dates (Stuiver and Reimer 1993) for samples associated with linear monuments in Scotland south of the Great Glen.

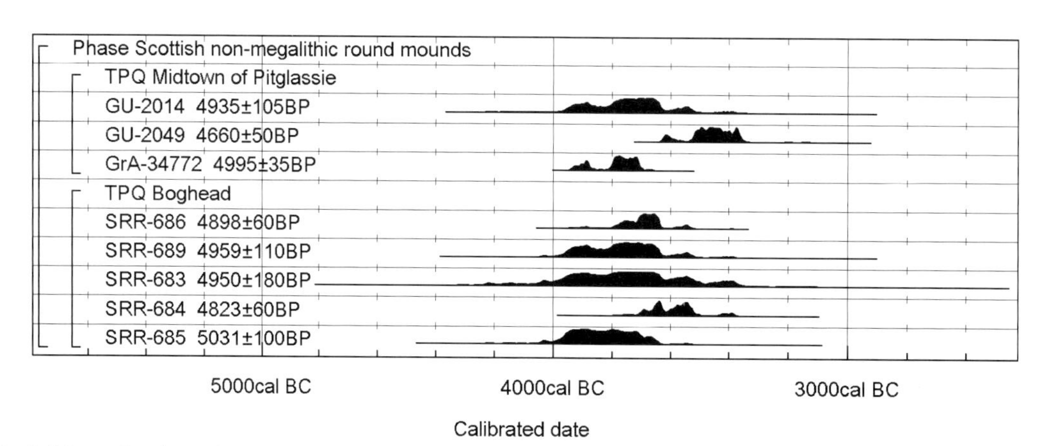

Fig. 14.171. Calibrated radiocarbon dates (Stuiver and Reimer 1993) for samples associated with non-megalithic round mounds in Scotland south of the Great Glen.

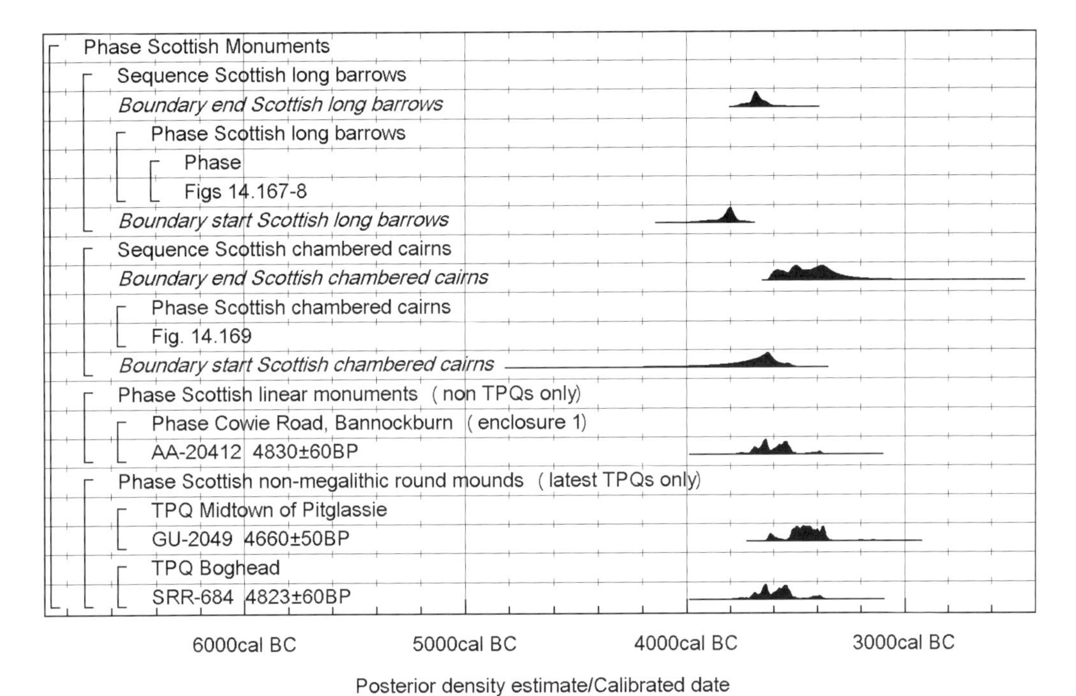

Fig. 14.172. Probability distributions for the currency of different types of early Neolithic monument in southern and north-east Scotland, derived from the models shown in Figs 14.167–8 and 14.169, and from selected calibrated dates shown on Figs 14.170–1.

unidentified cereal grains being directly dated to these earliest years of the British Neolithic (Table 7.6). Pottery was present from the beginning (Figs 14.80–1), although it may have been two or three generations before the first monument was constructed (Fig. 14.82). At this stage, we have no evidence for 'classic' early Neolithic monument types such as long barrows and causewayed enclosures, no certain evidence for other styles of Bowl pottery, no certain evidence for domesticated fauna (although a single cattle tooth from White Horse Stone (http://ads.ahds.ac.uk/catalogue/projArch/ctrl/bfw98/ may be such), and no evidence for the use of stone axeheads. Such absence of evidence is not evidence of absence, and it is salutary to note that three of the key sites have been investigated or dated only in the last five years, so that this picture may change substantially.

In south-central England, the first Neolithic things and practices appeared in the later 40th or early 39th century cal BC (Figs 14.176 and 14.57), *30–205 years (95% probability*; Fig. 14.178: *SE/S central*) after they appeared in south-east England, probably *80–165 years (68% probability*). Here, primary elements of the Neolithic included Carinated Bowl, cereals, and domesticated fauna (sheep, cattle and pig), as beneath the monuments at Ascott-under-Wychwood and Hazleton (Fig. 9.29). Beneath both, there were also small or ill-defined timber structures. The large rectangular timber house at Yarnton may date a few generations later, but also belongs to these first centuries of the Neolithic in this area (Fig. 8.27). Early occurrences of plain Bowl pottery and a non-local polished flint axehead, as at Fir Tree Field (Fig. 4.21), similarly belong to these centuries, but may not be evidence that these elements were absolutely primary in the appearance of the Neolithic in this area. At this stage, it is not clear whether long barrows form a primary element or whether they appear two or three generations later (Figs 14.80, 14.82). Sites such as Burn Ground (Fig. 9.27) certainly seem to have been constructed in the early centuries of the Neolithic in the Cotswolds. Causewayed enclosures, Decorated Bowl pottery and stone axeheads do not seem to have been part of this earliest phase in south-central England.

There is some evidence that this comparatively broad-scale analysis of the chronology of the earliest Neolithic in south-eastern Britain may be masking interesting regional variation (Fig. 14.54). Even within the areas considered, Neolithic things and practices may not have appeared all at once (*start Thames estuary* is more than a century earlier than *start eastern Neolithic*, for example: Fig. 14.54). The general trajectory of change from south-east to north-west across Britain may conceal a more complicated process. For example, *start Cotswold Neolithic* is rather earlier than might be expected if a rigid spatial trend is sought (Fig. 14.54). We have chosen to present our wider spatial analysis in the discussion here, because we are not entirely convinced that we yet have sufficient data to be sure that the more refined spatial analysis is reliable.

Figures 14.176–8 show that there was around a century between the first appearance of Neolithic things and practices in the south-east corner of England and their appearance in south-central England. It took this time for the new practices to spread over a distance of perhaps 100 km. In the decades around 3800 cal BC, the pace of change accelerated dramatically. Over a period of two or three generations, the first Neolithic things and practices appear

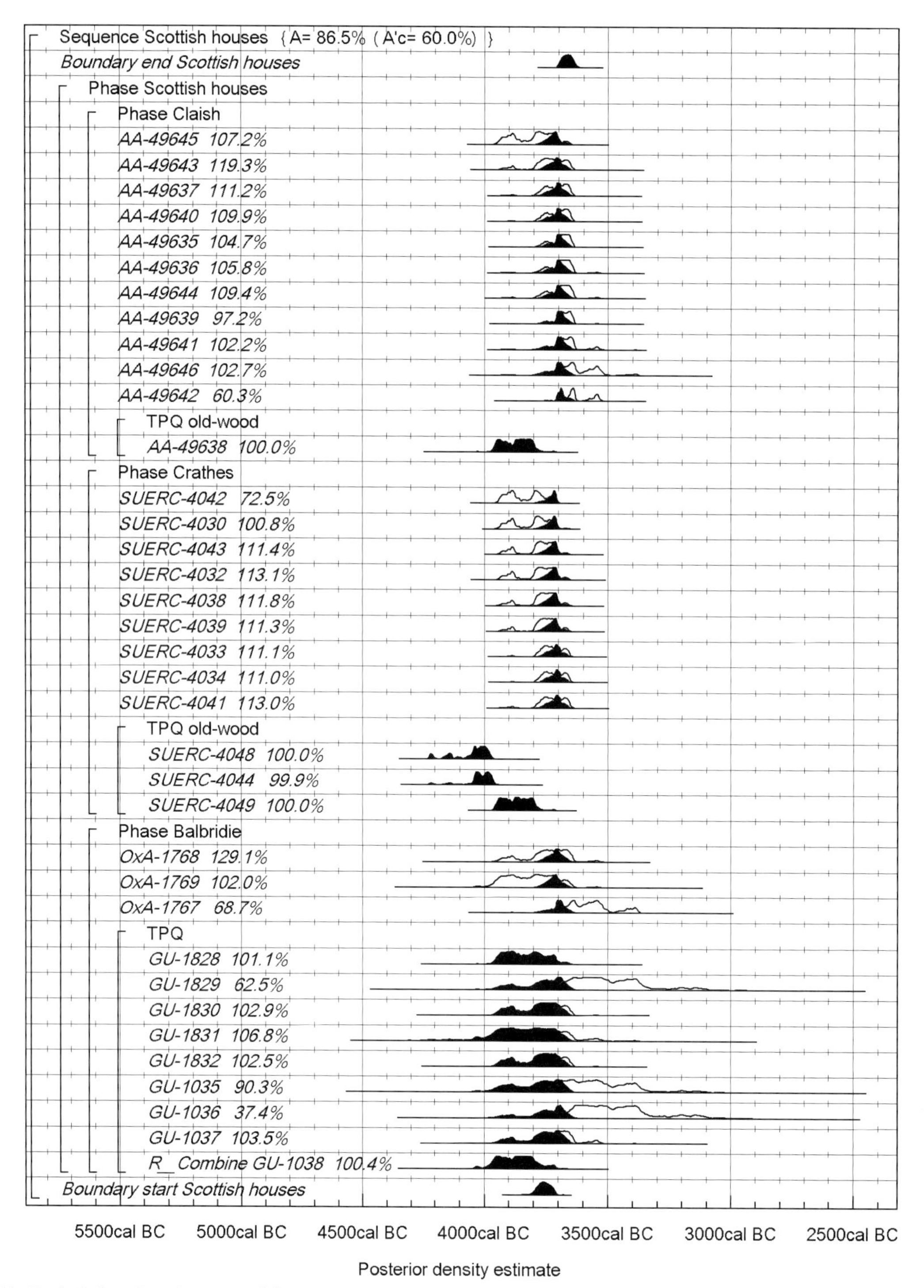

Fig. 14.173. Probability distributions of dates associated with rectangular timber halls from Scotland south of the Great Glen. The format is the same as for Fig. 14.1. The large square brackets down the left-hand side of the diagram, along with the OxCal keywords, define the overall model exactly.

over a very wide area, from southern Cornwall to north-east Scotland: a distance of some 600 km from the northern edge of what we have defined as south-central England to the Moray coast.[13] Was the character of this high-speed Neolithic the same as that of earlier centuries?

In south-west Britain, the first Neolithic things and practices appeared in the later 39th or earlier 38th century cal BC (Figs 14.176 and 14.57), *15–205 years (95% probability*; Fig. 14.178: *S central/SW*) after they appeared in south-central England, probably *55–150 years (68% probability*). Here, primary elements of the Neolithic included Carinated Bowl, as at Broadsands (Fig. 10.30), and probably South-Western style pottery (Figs 14.80–1). In this area, monuments are present from the very beginning, although enclosures (causewayed and stone-walled) are not (Fig. 14.83). Rectangular timber houses, like that at Penhale Round (Fig. 10.30), also belong to the initial Neolithic in the south-west, as do cereals and domesticated fauna, as

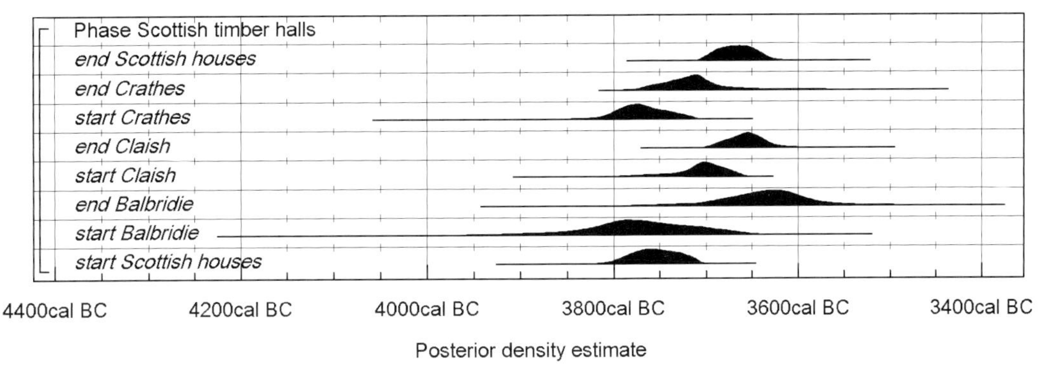

Fig. 14.174. Probability distributions of dates for the currency of early Neolithic timber halls in Scotland and for the construction and demolition of particular structures, taken from the models defined in Fig. 14.173, 14.150–3 and 14.154–7.

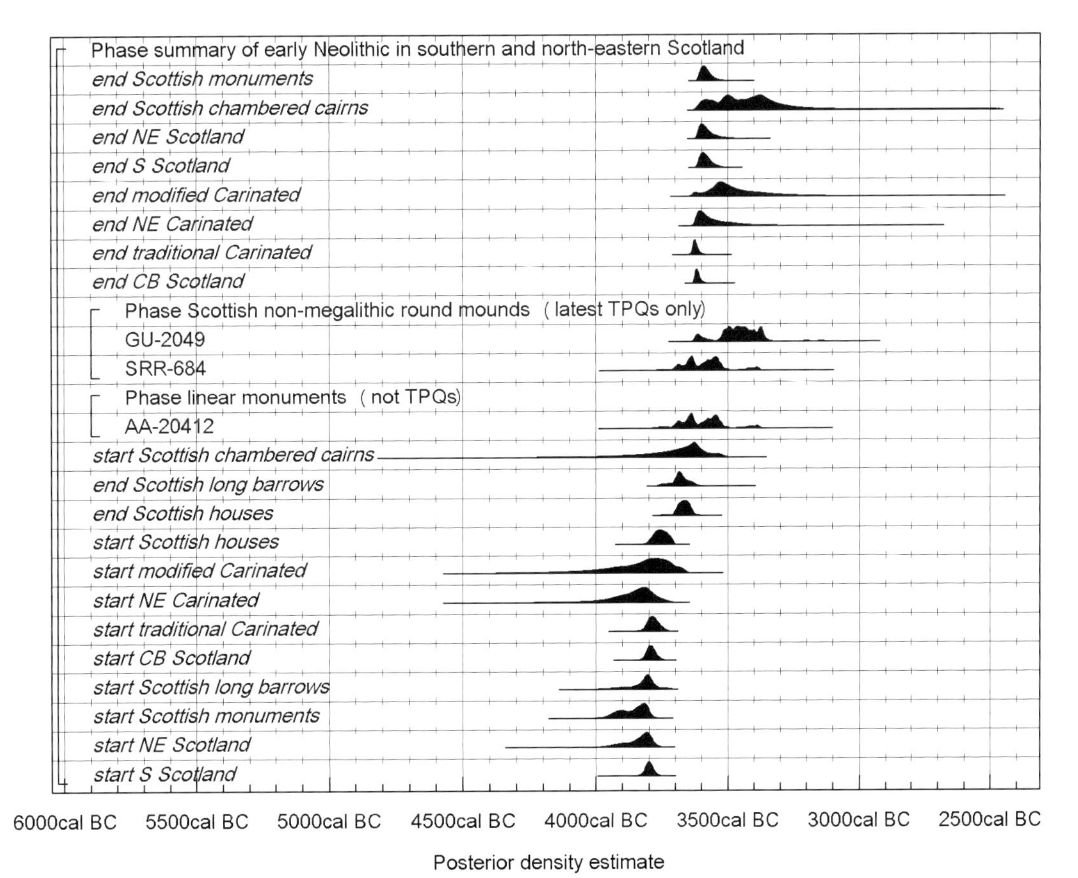

Fig. 14.175. Probability distributions of dates for entrances and exits of early Neolithic things and practices in southern and north-eastern Scotland, taken from the models defined in Figs 14.150, 14.154, 14.158, 14.159, 14.163, 14.164, 14.166, 14.167, 14.169 and 14.173 (with their component parts where appropriate), and from selected calibrated radiocarbon dates shown in Figs 14.170 and 14.171.

at Penhale Round and Broken Cavern respectively (Fig. 10.30). Ground stone axeheads, however, do not appear to be present in this earliest phase (Figs 14.119–21).

By this date, the decades around 3800 cal BC, a wider set of things and practices were included when the first Neolithic presence appeared in an area. We do not know which elements appeared with the first Neolithic on the Isle of Man, as the dating evidence is currently severely restricted (Fig. 14.148). Barley, plain Bowl pottery and ground stone axeheads were, however, present (Table 11.5).

Frankly, we do not know the date when the first Neolithic things and practices appeared in Ireland. The data are contradictory. On the one hand, we have a large and coherent series of dates which suggest the first appearance of the Neolithic in Ireland sometime within the 38th century cal BC (Fig 14.176). On the other, there is the dating of the causewayed enclosure at Magheraboy (Fig. 12.15), which is stubbornly 200 years earlier than the rest of the evidence. Magheraboy is not just a single monument with a potentially anomalous date, because the earliest contexts at that site bring with them an assemblage of other things and practices, comparable to those found in later centuries

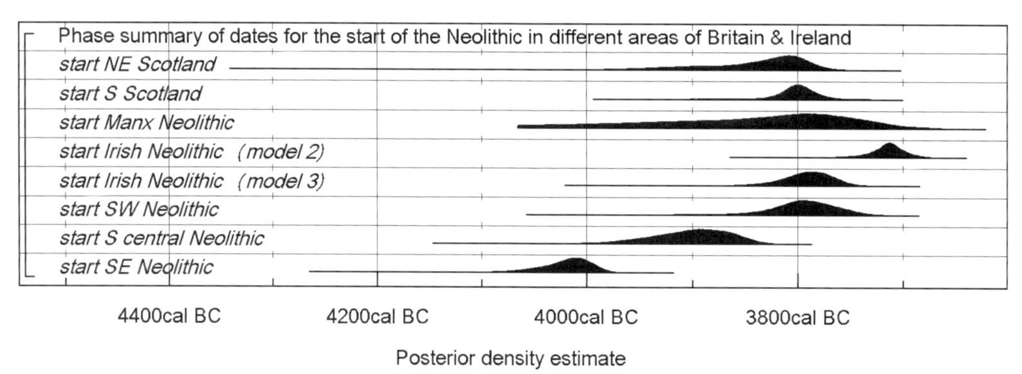

Fig. 14.176. Probability distributions of dates for the first appearance of early Neolithic things and practices in areas of Britain and Ireland, taken from the models defined in Figs 12.54, 12.56, 14.57, 14.148, 14.150 and 14.154 (with their component parts where appropriate).

in the early Neolithic in Ireland. We can now consider competing interpretations of this evidence in the light of the emerging picture of the process of Neolithisation across Britain and Ireland as a whole.

The spatial and time-transgressive trend evident for the appearance of the first Neolithic in Figs 14.176–7 in our view adds plausibility to the date estimate for the introduction of such practices into Ireland provided by model 3 (described in Chapter 12; Fig. 12.56). We suggest that model 2 (Fig. 12.54) may be biased by a disproportionate number of samples from the apparently short-lived house phenomenon in Ireland, and that a representative sample of dates on short-life samples firmly associated with the whole range of early Neolithic things and practices on the island would provide date estimates more in line with those currently provided by model 3. We note, for example, that the model for the chronology of other early Neolithic occupation in Ireland (Fig. 12.30) suggests that such activity begins in *4000–3700 cal BC* (*95% probability*; Fig. 12.30: *start other early Neolithic*), probably in *3840–3725 cal BC* (*68% probability*).

It is possible to shoehorn the existing dating for Magheraboy into this picture (Fig. 12.59) but it takes some forcing! The problem is that it is hard to interpret Magheraboy as the product of an early, different, episode of Neolithic contact up the west coast of Ireland, as has been argued for example for the very early domesticated fauna at Ferriter's Cove (e.g. Sheridan 2007a). The Carinated Bowl from the segmented ditch is in no way out of the ordinary for such assemblages in Ireland (Danaher 2007). The porcellanite axehead from the ditch also fits well in the wider spectrum of Group IX products. But this is at the heart of the Magheraboy problem, since there is no other evidence for the use of the Tievebulliagh and Rathlin Island sources so early, and we have already presented the evidence (this chapter, above) from elsewhere in western Britain for the appearance of exchange networks which involved the longer-range movement of stone axeheads at a substantially later date: from the first half of the 37th century cal BC (Fig. 14.134: *start stone axe networks*). In the light of all this, we consider that the special pleading that we fully acknowledge is required to coerce the Magheraboy dating into line with the rest of the early Neolithic in Ireland may be justified. This situation is obviously unsatisfactory and its resolution requires further research. Meanwhile we will go on with our discussion of Ireland favouring model 3, as the most plausible chronology for the appearance of the Neolithic there given the current contradictory nature of the evidence.

On this basis, the first century of the Neolithic in Ireland may include the presence of Carinated Bowl pottery (Table 12.4) and also the extraction of porphyry for axehead manufacture on Lambay Island (Fig. 12.30). Domesticated fauna were also certainly present (Fig. 12.42). It is possible that court tombs (Figs 12.23–4) and other monuments (Fig. 12.35) could start this early, although here we run up against the limitations of the available dating. The imprecision of our current date estimates also means that we cannot tell whether the establishment of the Céide Fields occurred right at the start of the Neolithic. At present, we have no certain instances of Carinated Bowl, porcellanite axeheads or cereals in Ireland before the appearance of rectangular timber houses, a tradition which clearly begins at least several generations after the start of the Neolithic in Ireland. The causewayed enclosure at Donegore may also have been established in the later 38th century cal BC, although again our dating is rather imprecise. On the basis of the published evidence, we do not accept the assertion that the passage tombs at Carrowmore have such early origins (Fig. 12.50). Portal tombs are almost entirely undated, but given our preferred interpretation of the varied dates now available from Poulnabrone (Fig. 12.31), these may now belong later in the fourth millennium cal BC.

In Scotland, a clearer pattern emerges. In southern Scotland (as defined above), the first Neolithic things and practices appeared within a generation of 3800 cal BC (Figs 14.150, 14.176). These included traditional Carinated Bowl, as at Brownsbank Farm, Biggar, cereals, as at Carzield, and long barrows, as at Eweford West. There is no evidence for North-East Carinated Bowl in this area, or for modified Carinated Bowl this early. Chambered cairns and linear monuments may belong to a slightly later period within the early Neolithic in the area. Only one timber hall has been dated in southern Scotland, the Claish structure

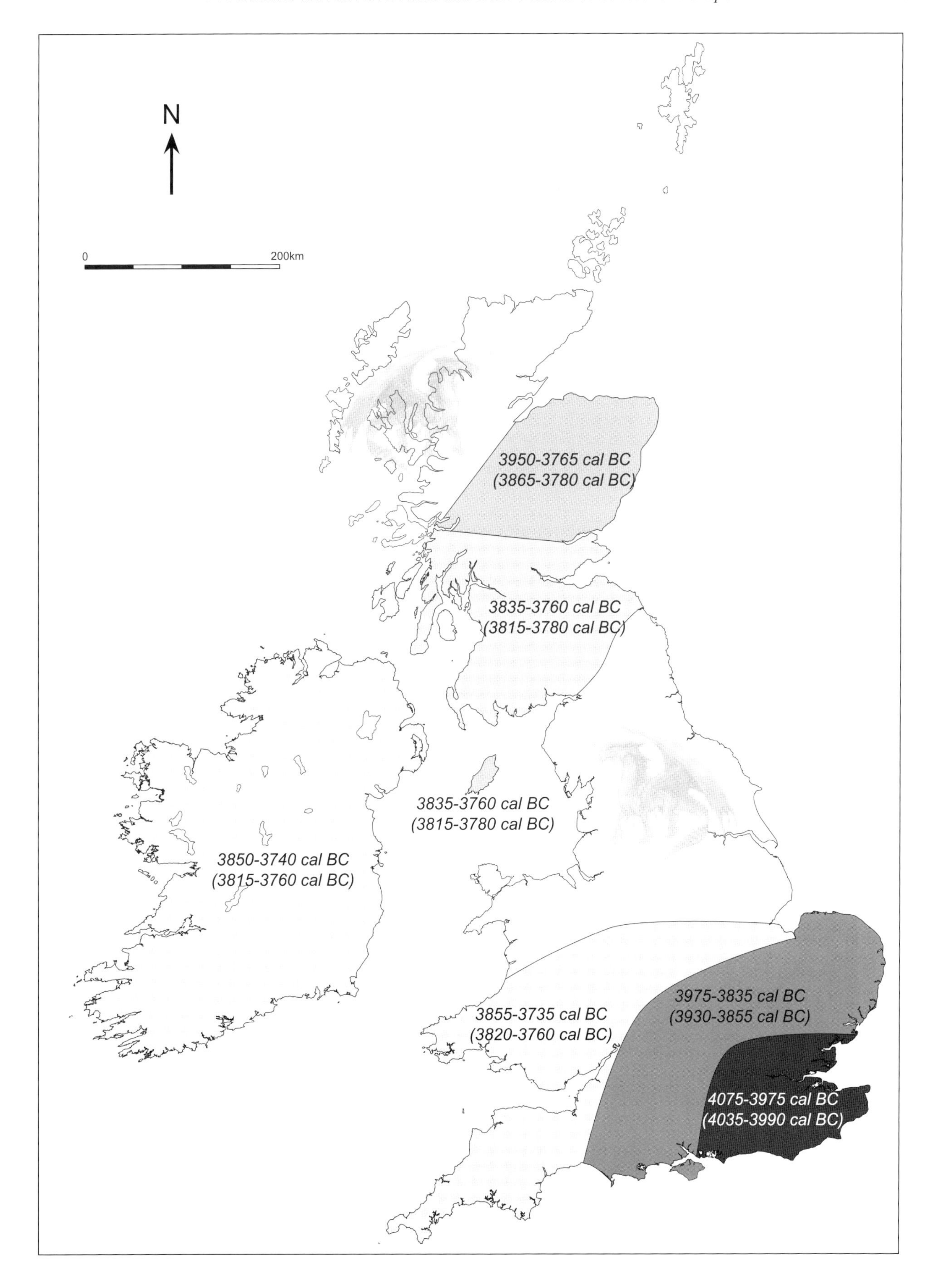

Fig. 14.177. Map showing date estimates for the start of Neolithic activity area by area across Britain and Ireland, at 95% probability (68% probability in brackets). Dragons lurk over areas not modelled in this study.

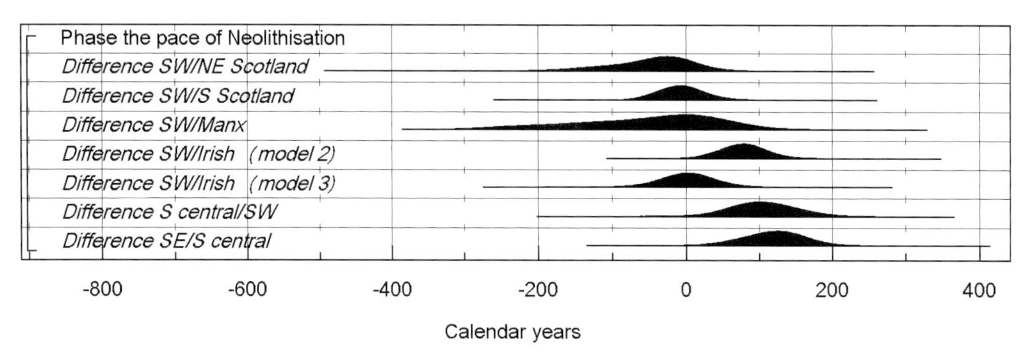

Fig. 14.178. Intervals between the appearance of the first Neolithic things and practices in different areas of Britain and Ireland, calculated from the distributions shown in Fig. 14.176.

not dating to the first generations of the Neolithic but belonging in the later part of the currency of such timber halls in Scotland (Fig. 14.174).

The first Neolithic appeared in north-east Scotland at very much the same time as it appeared farther south (Figs 14.154, 14.176 and 14.178), although there are fewer data and so our date estimate is less precise. Here, the first Neolithic included timber halls at Balbridie and Crathes, associated with North-East and traditional Carinated Bowl respectively. Wheat, barley, oats and flax were associated with the Balbridie hall, and barley was found in pits of similar date at Garthdee Road. Modified Carinated Bowl appears at this time at Dubton Farm, and a long barrow at Forest Road, Kintore, also dates to this primary phase. There is, however, no evidence that chambered cairns, linear monuments, or non-megalithic round mounds belong this early.

So were there differences between the elements of the Neolithic that appeared in south-east England in the century of so after *c.* 4050 cal BC, and those that appeared across a wide swathe of western and northern Britain, and in Ireland too, in the decades around 3800 cal BC? The presence or absence of different aspects of the Neolithic as part of the initial Neolithic activity in each of the areas considered in this analysis is shown in Fig. 14.179. Bearing in mind that the date of this first Neolithic varies across Britain and Ireland, some patterns emerge. Pottery appears to be an element of the primary Neolithic everywhere and, although the evidence is slightly more patchy, it is probable that cereals and domesticated fauna were too. Across the entire study area, except possibly the Isle of Man (Burrow 1997; Darvill 2004d, 40), it seems that Carinated Bowl formed at least a component of the earliest pottery assemblages.

There was thus a Neolithic 'package', but at first it was an accretive one (Fig. 14.179). In south-east England, where dated Neolithic elements are first perceptible, their appearance may be staggered, with perhaps both monuments and rectangular structures not appearing in the first generations. In south-central England, too, monuments may appear a generation or two after the first Neolithic practices. By the time the Neolithic spread to south-west Britain, Ireland, and Scotland south of the Great Glen, in the decades around 3800 cal BC, the 'package' had been assembled. In Ireland the dated cattle bone from a culturally Mesolithic context at Ferriter's Cove and the exceptionally early date of the Magheraboy enclosure stand apart from all our other estimates. If the former is regarded as a pre-Neolithic introduction (Chapter 12) and the latter held in suspense as meriting further investigation (Chapter 12 and above), then the other elements seem to be adopted all at once in Ireland, as in south-west Britain and Scotland south of the Great Glen. The exceptions are rectangular houses, which in both Ireland (in our preferred model 3) and Scotland (but not in the south-west peninsula) appear slightly after the first Neolithic things and practices, and polished stone axes, which everywhere may appear slightly later. Are these two bound up with the exchange networks which appear in all the three regions of southern Britain which we have examined in the decades when both enclosures and Decorated Bowl pottery appear?

Monumentality is not necessarily part of the first appearance of the Neolithic everywhere. In south-east and south-central England, the first monuments may have appeared two or three generations after the initial Neolithic (Fig. 14.82). In the 40th century cal BC, in south-east England, the first constructions were not necessarily of forms that later became recurrent. Elsewhere, as far as we can tell, long barrows and cairns (and timber variants on this idea: Sheridan 2006a), and court tombs in Ireland, may have been the first monuments to be built. Except possibly in Ireland, in all areas where they are present, causewayed and stone-walled enclosures were not among the first monuments. Rectangular timber structures may be part of the initial southern English Neolithic, or at least only a generation or two removed, although in Ireland and perhaps also in Scotland (where only three buildings are included in the analysis), houses appear to form concentrated horizons post-dating the first Neolithic presence.

Fig. 14.180 summarises the available dates for rectangular timber structures in Britain and Ireland. Further dating is under way for Lockerbie Academy in Dumfries and Galloway (Oliver Harris, pers. comm.), Doon Hill A (Ian Ralston, pers. comm.), Parc Bryn Cegin near Llandygai (Kenney and Davidson 2006),[14] Parc Cybi on Anglesey (Jane Kenney, pers. comm.), Horton in Berkshire (Pitts 2008; Alistair Barclay, pers. comm.), and Lismore Fields in

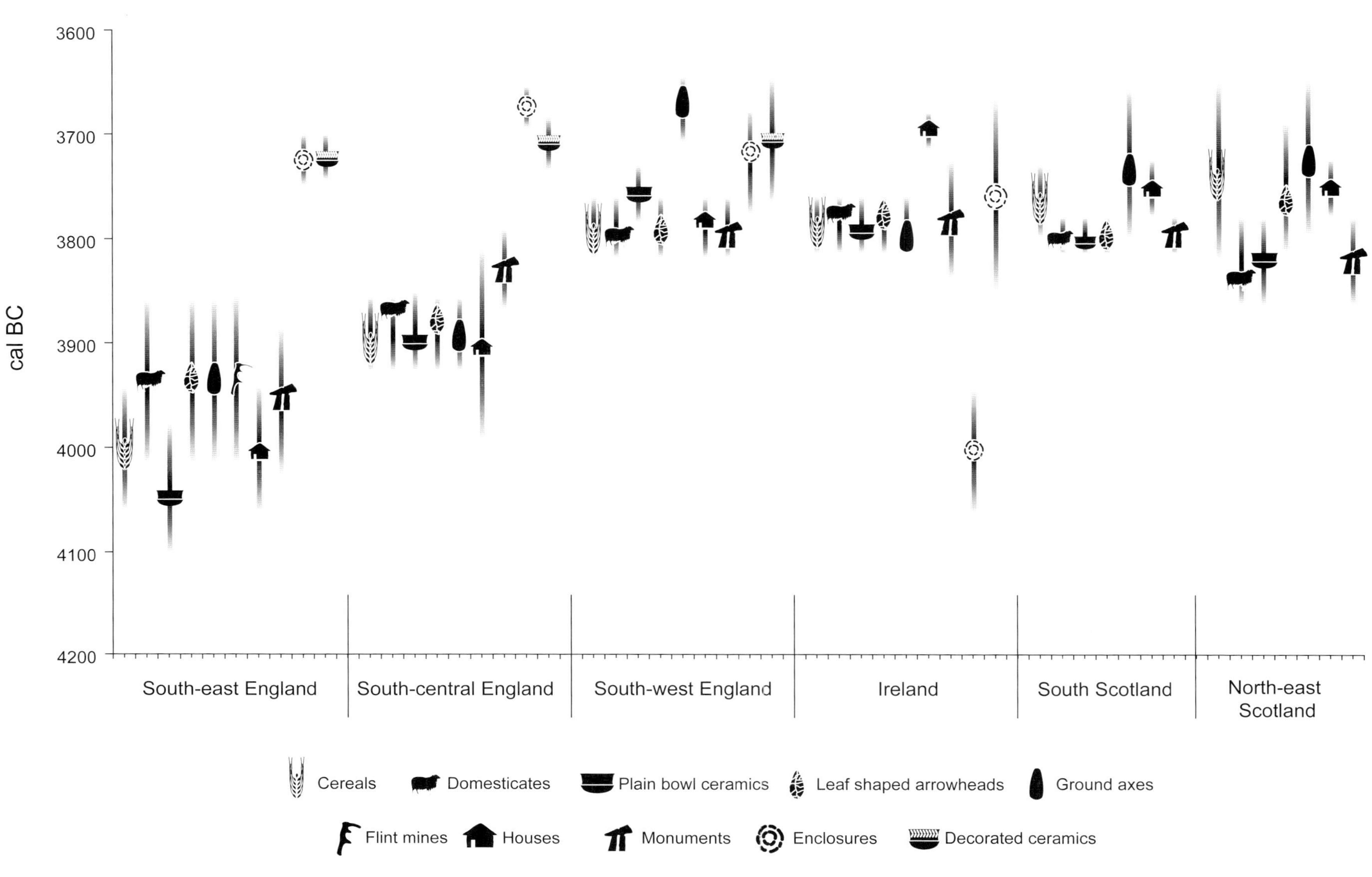

Fig. 14.179. Schematic diagram showing date estimates for the appearance of Neolithic things and practices across selected areas of Britain and Ireland.

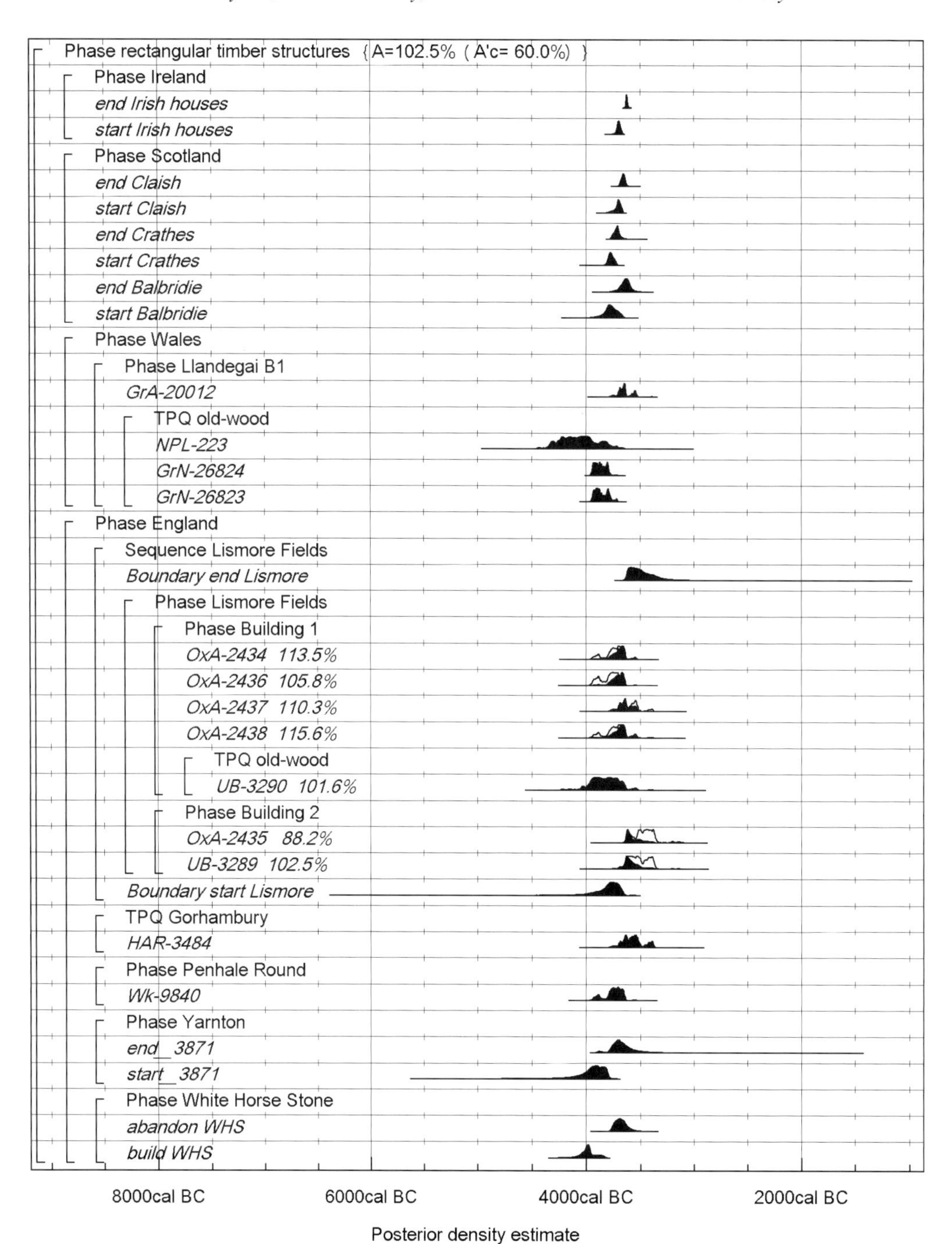

Fig. 14.180. Probability distributions of dates associated with rectangular timber structures in Britain and Ireland. The format is the same as for Fig. 14.1. Distributions have been taken from the models defined in Fig. 7.26 (White Horse Stone), Fig. 8.27 (Yarnton), Figs 12.22–7 (Irish houses), Figs 14.150–3 (Claish) and Figs 14.154–7 (Balbridie and Crathes). The large square brackets down the left-hand side of the diagram, along with the OxCal keywords, define the model exactly.

Derbyshire (Daryl Garton, pers. comm.), so that this picture will be refined in the near future. The existing Lismore Fields dates are listed in Table 14.15. The relatively few British buildings contrast with the numerous Irish ones in their larger size, many of them exceeding 20 m in length, while the Irish buildings cluster between 6 m and 14 m in length, with few outliers (Smyth 2006, fig. 5). The British buildings are of varying dates, ranging from the large timber hall at White Horse Stone, probably built in the 41st or 40th century cal BC, at the beginning of the Neolithic in Kent, to the even larger halls built in Scotland from the 38th century cal BC. The smaller Irish houses are different, apparently built and used in a restricted period of time between the decades around 3700 cal BC and *c.* 3625 cal BC (Figs 12.22–7). It is possible that the houses in north Wales and at Lismore Fields have more in common with the Irish tradition and fall within its currency.

In the decades around 3800 cal BC Neolithic things and practices first appeared over large areas of western and northern Britain and, we have suggested, in Ireland too

Table 14.15. Radiocarbon dates from rectangular structures at Lismore Fields, Derbyshire.

Laboratory Number	Description	Radiocarbon Age (BP)	$\delta^{13}C$ (‰)	Calibrated date range (cal BC) (95% confidence)	*Posterior density estimate (cal BC) (95% probability)*
Building I. Rectangular, 15.75 m by 5.35 m. Post built, some slots, 3 internal divisions					
OxA-2434	*Triticum* sp. grains from context 0089, postpipe, Building I	4930±70		3940–3530	*3810–3625 (92%)* or *3585–3530 (3%)*
OxA-2436	*Linum usitatissimum* seeds from context 0110, post-pipe, Building I	4970±70		3960–3630	*3910–3870 (2%)* or *3845–3630 (93%)*
OxA-2437	*Corylus* charcoal from context 0015, post-pipe, Building I	4840±70		3770–3380	*3765–3515*
OxA-2438	*Triticum* sp. grains and *Corylus* charcoal from posthole 0103 subsidence, Building I	4920±80		3950–3530	*3810–3615 (87%)* or *3610–3525 (8%)*
UB-3290	*Corylus, Fraxinus, Sorbus* and *Populus* charcoal from posthole 0138 subsidence, Building I	5024±126	−26.4	4050–3530	*4070–3625 (94%)* or *3585–3535 (1%)*
Building II. Rectangular, 7.7 m by 5.5 m. Post built, 1 internal division					
OxA-2435	*Corylus* and *Crataegus* charcoal from postpipe and subsidence below deliberate backfill in posthole 0238	4680±70		3640–3340	*3650–3395*
UB-3289	*Quercus* charcoal from postpipe below deliberate backfill in posthole 0275	4745±88	−25.7	3700–3350	*3705–3480 (88%)* or *3475–3400 (7%)*

(Fig. 14.176). In southern Britain the pace of change seems to have intensified markedly during the 38th century cal BC (Fig. 14.140). Was this also true elsewhere? Was this new Neolithic more dynamic than that which had come before? In Ireland, the enclosure at Donegore may have been constructed during the later 38th century cal BC or during the first decades of the 37th, and within a generation of 3700 cal BC came a veritable flood of houses (Fig. 14.181). In Scotland there is less evidence of innovation in the course of the 38th century; instead, the new practices all seem to have appeared at the same time, at the start of the century. Timber halls may be the exception (Fig. 14.181), as they may have been begun to be built a generation or so after the establishment of other Neolithic practices, although only three have so far been dated.

Figure 14.182 shows in greater detail the innovations witnessed by the generations of people who lived around 3700 cal BC. Although Donegore is imprecisely dated, it could be contemporary with the introduction of enclosures into southern Britain. This occurred at the same time as the emergence of Decorated Bowl and of gabbroic fabrics. Cleal (2004, 80) has already concluded that 'there is no evidence ... that Gabbroic Ware appears earlier than around the same time as the appearance of the causewayed and "tor" enclosures . . . . The occurrence of this true 'Ware' (i.e. style and fabric indicating a common source) is such a striking novelty that it suggests . . . a sizable shift in the way society was organised at around this time'. These innovations of the later 38th century were swiftly followed by further change in the succeeding decades. It is *90% probable* that the first enclosure in southern Britain predates the start of the Irish house phenomenon. This began around a generation later, at the time when intensive construction of enclosure circuits began (Fig. 14.183). This is also the time when extensive networks are first apparent within Britain, with the long-distance transport of stone axeheads and gabbroic pottery (Fig. 14.181). Full analysis and publication of Ballygalley, with its four houses, will clarify how far this phase relates to the various strands of evidence which have prompted the interpretation of the site as a redistribution centre for local and imported materials (D. Simpson 1996, 132). Their rapid appearance during the 37th century cal BC mirrors the first intensive period of causewayed enclosure construction in southern Britain (Fig 14.22). Were these contemporary phenomena linked? Did they both stem from similar changes in society on both sides of the Irish Sea which occurred during the 38th century cal BC?

If these practices had a common origin, they did not have a common demise. Figure 14.184 shows the dates when some of the traditions that had appeared in the early centuries of the Neolithic came to an end. Carinated Bowl pottery, at least its traditional and north-eastern variants, ceased to be made in Scotland in the decades just before

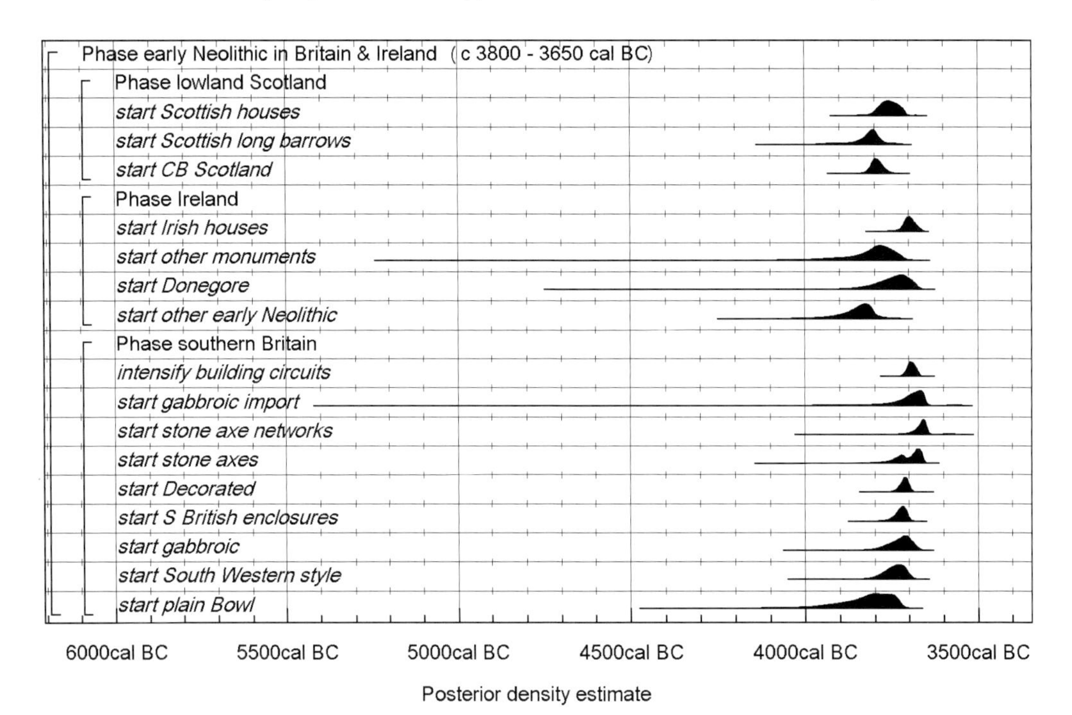

*Fig. 14.181. Probability distributions of dates for the appearance of novel things and practices in Britain and Ireland (*c. *3800–*c. *3650 cal BC), taken from the models defined in Figs 12.5, 12.22, 12.30, 12.35, 14.1, 14.7, 14.92, 14.101, 14.104, 14.119, 14.134, 14.137, 14.158, 14.167 and 14.173 (with their component parts where appropriate).*

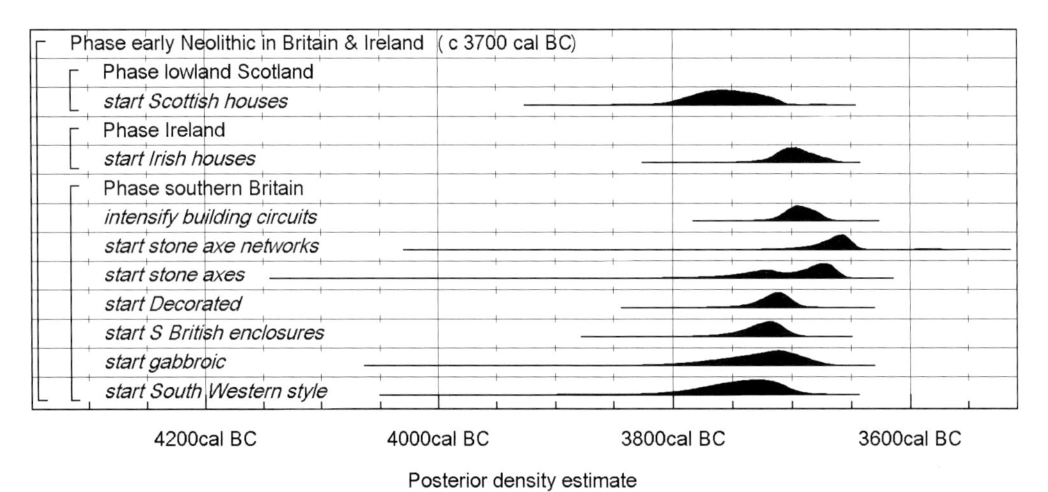

Fig. 14.182. Probability distributions of dates for the appearance of novel things and practices in Britain and Ireland in the decades around 3700 cal BC, taken from the models defined in Figs 12.5, 12.22, 14.1, 14.7, 14.92, 14.101, 14.104, 14.119, 14.134 and 14.173 (with their component parts where appropriate).

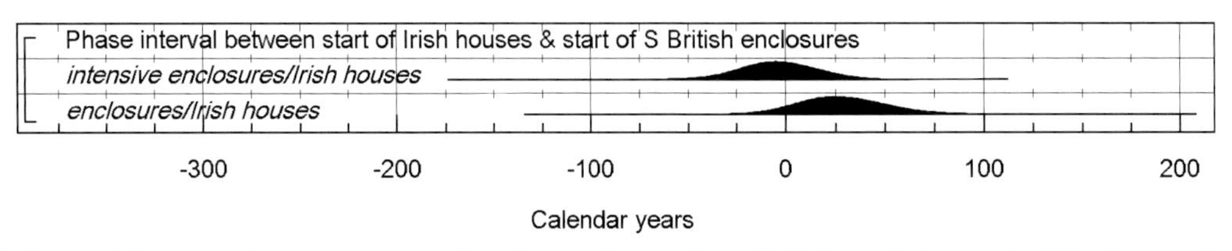

Fig. 14.183. Interval between the appearance of enclosures in southern Britain and the start of the house phenomenon in Ireland, derived from distributions shown in Figs 12.22, 14.1 and 14.7.

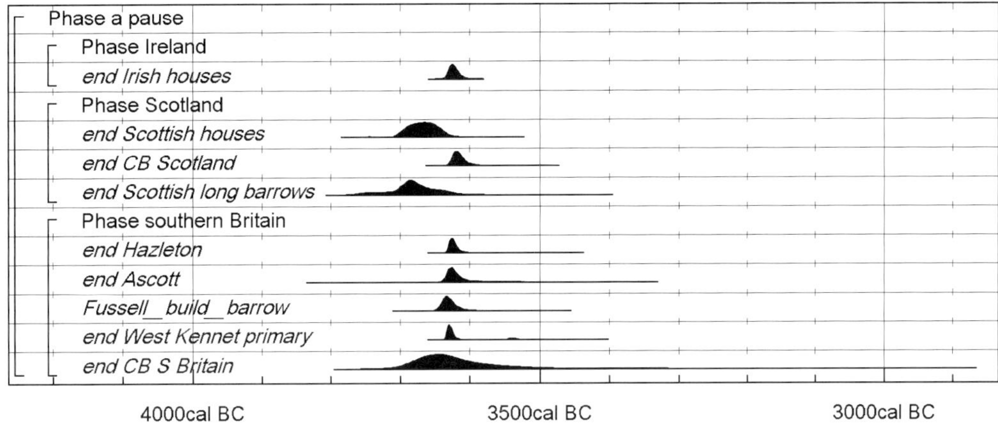

Fig. 14.184. Probability distributions showing the date when old practices ended during the 37th century cal BC, derived from models defined in Figs 12.22, 14.88, 14.158, 14.167, and 14.173 (and their component parts if appropriate), and by Bayliss et al. *(2007b, fig. 6) (West Kennet), Wysocki* et al. *(2007, fig. 10) (Fussell's Lodge), Meadows* et al. *(2007, figs 6–9) (Hazleton) and Bayliss* et al. *(2007c, figs 3 and 5–7) (Ascott-under-Wychwood).*

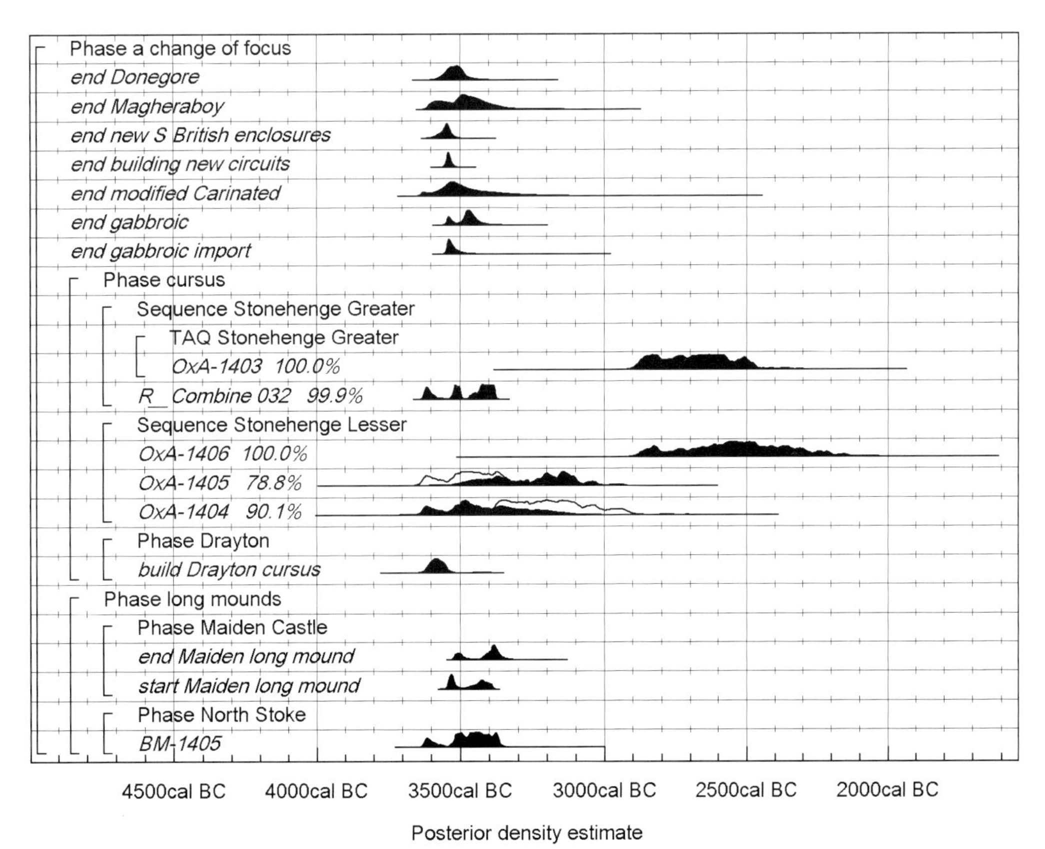

14.185. Probability distributions showing the change of focus in Neolithic activity in Britain and Ireland during the 36th century cal BC, derived from models defined in Figs 12.5, 12.15, 14.7, 14.4 4, 14.104, 14.118, 14.134, 14.137 and 14.164 (and their component parts if appropriate).

3600 cal BC, although modified Carinated Bowl may have been used rather longer (Fig. 14.165). Carinated Bowl in southern Britain also went out of use in the 37th century (Fig. 14.184). In the first half of that century, it seems that the construction and use of long barrows and related forms in Scotland ceased, giving this monument type a limited period of popularity there. Around the same time, the last of the Scottish timber halls was demolished (Fig. 14.184), giving this type of structure an even shorter currency.

The later decades of the 37th century also saw the closure of a number of the small sample of southern British long barrows which have currently been dated precisely

(Fig. 14.184). There is a contrast here. In Scotland long barrows were replaced by monuments of other types – chambered cairns and linear constructions among them. In southern Britain, despite these endings of particular monuments, the long barrow tradition continued to the end of the millennium (Fig. 14.46). In Ireland too, these decades at the end of the 37th century cal BC saw changes in practice. The rectangular house phenomenon dwindled as quickly as it had arisen and did not revive in the same form. The coincidence of these changes with the maximum input of resources into enclosure building in southern Britain (Fig. 14.20) may point to the displacement of old practices by a now fully developed system of large-scale aggregation and long-distance networks.

The peak of enclosure construction at the end of the 37th century was short-lived, and was succeeded by a lull in construction, at least in central southern England (Fig. 14.22). Unlike the Irish houses or the Scottish long barrows, however, the fortunes of enclosures revived and construction was again popular in the second half of the 36th century cal BC, although no new enclosures were founded after the middle of the century (Fig. 14.12: *end new S British enclosures*) and by 3500 cal BC over 80% of the construction effort had been expended. The ending of this second hey-day coincides with the abandonment of Donegore and Magheraboy in Ireland, perhaps the end of the currency of modified Carinated Bowl in Scotland, the demise of the long-distance transport of gabbroic pottery, and a decline in the long-distance transport of stone axeheads. Is this really the end of the world of the enclosures? Decorated Bowl continued to be used and the primary use of a very few enclosures persisted for another century or two (Etton, Windmill Hill, Hambledon Hill). But this continued use is the exception, not the rule. It is at this time that cursus monuments and bank barrows begin to be built. Although cursus monuments are later than enclosures in the few cases where there is a stratigraphic relationship between the two, a period of overlap during the 36th century cal BC, when both types of monument were being constructed, is suggested by the comparatively early date of the Drayton cursus (Fig. 14.185).

Otherwise, it is difficult to continue the narrative. The world of the second half of the fourth millennium – not the focus of this project – is still shrouded in uncertainty. We have not attempted to assemble the existing data or to model the chronology of things and practices which appear in this period, so that our endings stand alone without a comparable framework for successive developments.

14.9 Conclusion

In this chapter, we have attempted to tease out threads of chronology from the varied body of evidence for the early Neolithic in Britain and Ireland. This is the first attempt anywhere to use Bayesian statistical modelling of radiocarbon dates to produce a quantified, chronological narrative on such a scale. We have focused on causewayed and related enclosures, but have assembled the dating evidence for the preceding centuries of the Neolithic and proposed a detailed chronological framework. This structures the social context in which the enclosures emerge as a developed aspect of the insular Neolithic. Our dating of the enclosures themselves has revealed the tempo of the phenomenon – the pace of its introduction, the cycles of its popularity and the rhythms of its demise. Our chronologies for the time when enclosures came to an end are much fuzzier. We have not been able to invest the same effort to construct such detailed, quantified chronologies beyond 3500 cal BC, and so our understanding of the circumstances in which enclosures fell out of favour remains, comparatively, limited.

George Box (1979, 202) reminds us that 'all models are wrong, some models are useful'. The models presented in this chapter, and the data upon which they are based, are not of even quality. For enclosures, we have obtained a large series of new radiocarbon dates, chosen short-life samples and rigorously assessed the association between each sample and the context from which it was recovered. As importantly, wherever possible the samples have been selected around the chronological model (Bayliss and Bronk Ramsey 2004, 26), exploiting site stratigraphy to provide 'informative prior information' and refine the resultant date estimates. This approach has proven highly effective, both for recent excavations and, perhaps surprisingly, for sites where fieldwork took place as far back as the 1920s.

In our models we have routinely implemented a uniformly distributed phase of activity to counteract the statistical scatter on suites of radiocarbon dates. Although this 'uniformative prior information' component of our models is generally robust (Buck *et al.* 1992; Bayliss *et al.* 2007a, 14–17), it may not be appropriate if the archaeological activity in question is distributed very differently. For example, we have seen that more than 80% of the effort expended on enclosure construction was made between 3700 and 3500 cal BC, and less than 20% in the succeeding 200 years. The period of the construction of the circuits of causewayed enclosures is thus not uniformly distributed, but dramatically skewed towards the early centuries, with a much lower level of activity later (see above). In such circumstances, we may be able to use statistics such as the index of agreement to guide us in the selection of our models (see Chapter 2.4.4), and we must be very clear as to exactly what our models mean in archaeological terms. We have frequently employed sensitivity analyses (alternative models), to address issues such as these. 'All models are wrong' but, when several independent models give very similar results, it is implausible that they are *importantly* wrong (see, for example Fig. 14.109 which shows three independent models for the currency of Decorated Bowl in different areas of southern Britain which produce almost identical date estimates).

This project was designed to investigate enclosures. Our comparative models are reliant on the existing corpus of radiocarbon dates, which is of variable quality.

Our understanding of the chronology of enclosures is consequently much more robust than our models for the dating of other Neolithic things and practices. There is a large sample of well dated enclosures, and a high proportion of all known enclosures have been dated (Fig. 1.1). Our estimates for the currency of the phenomenon are therefore based on the sound foundation of explicitly quantified estimates for the dates when individual sites were used. In contrast, our models for the chronology of other elements of the Neolithic are a rag-bag mix of the good, the bad, and the downright hideous! There are large series of high-quality radiocarbon dates available, for example for short-life samples closely associated with Carinated Bowl in Scotland. The dating of some sites, such as the early Neolithic houses at Warren Field, Crathes, and Claish, is exemplary. For some problems, the collection of relatively small series of samples on a repeated basis has proved invaluable, such as for early Neolithic occupations from the south-west peninsula of England. In other instances, our models are highly provisional, because the available dates are few, or of low quality. For example, only a single radiocarbon date, of the 29 so far available from the many linear monuments in Scotland (Fig. 14.170), is from short-life material.

From this, it is clear that there can be nothing definitive about the chronologies presented here. They are our preferred interpretations, given the radiocarbon dates, contextual information, and statistical models available to us during this project. All will develop over the coming decades, and it is clear that there is much work to be done before our chronologies are as refined and robust as current methodologies now allow. So, we make no pretence that all our models are entirely right. Some of them will be *importantly* wrong (models 2 and 3 for the early Neolithic in Ireland are mutually contradictory and so cannot both be right!). Nonetheless, we feel that the scale of difference between the refined, quantitative chronologies which we have presented here and the impressionistic and fuzzy nature of previous frameworks cannot be exaggerated. Our new, more precise chronologies provide a structure which will enable prehistorians to trace sequences, where previously the unfoldings of past lives were compressed into one, to compare contemporary events and phenomena to reveal the diversity of choices made by past people, where in earlier research we have been unable to distinguish their voices, and to begin to unpick the varying tempos and scales of past change, where previously we were forced to dwell largely in the long-term. Chapter 15 will go on to explore why such differences matter.

Notes

1 Developments are underway which will enable alternative approaches to be adopted for the modelling of this data set, in particular the implementation of the trapezium distribution (Karlsberg 2006; Bronk Ramsey 2009a). These were not available at the time of writing.

2 In the case of one segment of the outer ditch at Windmill Hill, it is now clear that Ebbsfleet pottery quite low in the filling is due to a recut of considerable size (Chapter 3).

3 These are: Crickley Hill, Etton, Hambledon Hill main enclosure, the Stepleton enclosure, Whitehawk, Windmill Hill, Abingdon, Whitesheet, Maiden Castle and St Osyth.

4 These are: Crickley Hill, Hambledon Hill main enclosure, the Stepleton enclosure, Whitehawk, Windmill Hill, Abingdon, Whitesheet, Maiden Castle, St Osyth, Hembury and Chalk Hill.

5 Since this chapter was written, a handful of new dates on cremated bone from portal tombs/dolmens (note that we use these terms interchangeably) have been published (Kytmannow 2008, table 7.1). None of these suggest any earlier dating.

6 We have excluded the superficially early dates from the Raunds long mound (Chapter 6. 3) and the Eynesbury cursus monuments (Chapter 6.2) from the models for the reasons detailed in Chapter 6.

7 See Chapter 10, endnote 1, for details of Sperris and Zennor Quoits, for which dates have since been obtained.

8 In a PhD at Cardiff University, supervised by Alasdair Whittle and Alex Bayliss, and funded by the AHRC Collaborative Doctoral Awards scheme and English Heritage.

9 The final publication became available after our modelling.

10 The earlier tails on the estimates for *start NE Carinated* and *start modified Carinated* almost certainly arise from there being insufficient data in these models to fully account for the statistical scatter on the radiocarbon dates; see Chapter 2.2.

11 Oliver Harris and Ian Ralston, pers. comm.

12 Only the long tails of date estimates provided by models containing insufficient radiocarbon dates to effectively counteract their statistical scatter (see again Chapter 2.2) appear earlier than this; and even these distributions (e.g. *start Scottish monuments*; *start NE Carinated*; Fig. 14.175) are more likely to fall in the second half of the 38th century cal BC or later.

13 In contrast to the regional variation in date estimates for the start of the Neolithic in Southern Britain (Fig. 14.54), perhaps suggesting the potential for multi-focal beginnings there, no such variation is apparent in the wider analysis of Britain and Ireland (Fig. 14.176). The first Neolithic things and practices appear across wide areas in the decades around 3800 cal BC: only in Ireland (if model 2 is preferred) and South Wales and the Marches (Fig. 14.54) may they appear rather later.

14 See Chapter 11, endnote 4; the dates for this house are now available.

15 Gathering time: the social dynamics of change

Alasdair Whittle, Alex Bayliss and Frances Healy

> The concept of pre-history is one of the most ridiculous that can be imagined
>
> Lucien Febvre, *A new kind of history*, 1973, 35

15.1 Temporality and the dynamics of social change

On the basis of the explicit, quantified, probabilistic chronological models offered so far, we go on now to interpret what we have learned not only of the timing but also of the tempo and character of change, and thereby to explore the social dynamics of change.

More reliable timing allows us to sequence sites and events accurately. From a more confident sense of order, we can establish more reliably the connections, equivalences and contrasts, and better discriminate among the array of innovation, tradition, choice and agency. Timing enables tempo, a sense of the rate at which changes come, beyond the retentions and flow of time to which Tim Ingold (1993) refers. Timing and tempo together open up the possibility of seeking the underlying social dynamics of a shifting world. This chapter will develop interpretations to try to account for the timings, accelerating tempo and altering dynamics of this social world, and this will bring us to discussion of connections and networks, emulation and competition. It will attempt to give a connected and sequential commentary on the first centuries of the Neolithic in southern Britain and Ireland, going on from the narratives presented in Chapter 14, which will unite the debates about beginnings with what came after, and the discussion of individual features with a longer history. Both ends of this interpretive process unavoidably will be incomplete, since we have comparatively slight, and largely undated, evidence for late Mesolithic activity over most of these islands, on the one hand, and the middle part of the Neolithic has been beyond the remit of this project, on the other. But although the framework we have created here will be modified over the coming years, it allows us now to question many of our current understandings, and to offer new interpretations of the development of the first centuries of the Neolithic in southern Britain and Ireland, and further afield.

There is one important caveat. As Chapter 14 should have made clear, our own timetables are most reliable for causewayed enclosures in southern Britain; we have dated nearly 40 of these, many (though not all) with considerable precision. Our schedules for the development of other kinds of early Neolithic activity, including the beginnings of the period, are necessarily both less precise and at this stage less reliable. So the commentary that follows perforce is based on chronologies of varying precision. This produces a tension between the core of our own study, the wider British and Irish timescapes which we have sought to model, and the generally more informally modelled continental contexts which we also seek to pull in.

Beyond the details of this particular project lie wider issues about timescales and the dynamics of agency, social reproduction and change. We will conclude by reflecting on issues raised right from the start of the volume. If we can now offer greatly improved chronological resolution, we can begin to break down any sense that it is inevitably and unavoidably only the long-term which is open to investigation in these millennia, and start to break away from fuzzy prehistory. We will consider not only different kinds of timescale but also different kinds of agency, memory and cultural transmission that may have helped to condition the structures within which history unfolded. These come in the first place out of this particular study, but are shaped by reference to a much wider comparative literature, and they may serve also to illustrate what could now be possible in other studies.

15.2 Beginnings

Past positions and present possibilities

Few subjects have been as challenging as the question of the Mesolithic-Neolithic transition in Britain and Ireland. As noted in Chapter 1, opinion has tended to polarise around the opposed alternatives of colonisation and acculturation (e.g. Sheridan 2003a; 2003b; 2004; 2006a; 2007a; 2010; Pailler and Sheridan 2009; versus J. Thomas 2003; 2004a; 2004b; 2007a; 2008), and to some extent different processes have been sought in Britain and Ireland, acculturation having been the more favoured interpretation in Britain – for a while at least – and colonisation in Ireland (Cooney 2000a; 2003; 2007a). The style and character of the arguments of the leading British protagonists have been rather different. Alison Sheridan has proposed a succession of contacts and arrivals, with specified chronologies derived from visual inspection of radiocarbon dates from Britain and Ireland on the one hand, and from similarly constructed sequences for supposed continental source areas, backed up by ceramic and monumental typologies, on the other. Julian Thomas, in allowing for difference of process between Britain and Ireland (2008, 70), has nonetheless emphasised a very swift shift to domesticated plants and animals, pottery, timber architecture and polished stone tools *c.* 4000 cal BC, again based on visual inspection of radiocarbon dates, rapid initial change contrasting with 'the development of a fully agricultural landscape' over 'many generations' (2008, 80). Sheridan has proposed specific conditions in supposed continental source areas which prompted the movement of people (internal social disruptions in Brittany and Normandy; culture change and settlement expansion in northern France and Belgium), set against a claimed general lack of contact between offshore Mesolithic communities and the continent. Thomas, by contrast, has referred to material selections and recombinations, and to an array of subsistence, ideational and settlement factors, but without specifying particular reasons or motivations for the supposed timing of what he sees as rapid events *c.* 4000 cal BC. Sheridan presents a nuanced but short history, which gets the new folks ashore, as it were, then leaves them to their own devices, whereas Thomas offers a more general narrative, but for a longer story over several centuries.[1]

Other suggestions of a combination of processes have on the whole been less frequent (e.g. Whittle 2007a), but one variant, in terms of dominant and more active but numerically inferior colonists, can be noted. One of the most recent statements by Sheridan proposes 'small communities coming from the continent', and 'allows for the subsequent – and apparently rapid – acculturation of indigenous communities' (Pailler and Sheridan 2009, 1–2). There has been a strand of regional differentiation (back to at least Armit and Finlayson 1992; and see Piggott 1955) but proposals of the kind that there could have been more acculturation in the west and more colonisation in the east of Britain (Cummings and Whittle 2004, 88–91) have not been common. Debate remains very active; a recent example is a set of landscape perspectives (Finlayson and Warren 2010). How does all this look in the light of our models?

It is convenient to frame our own view in the first place with respect to the narrative interpretations of Sheridan, since she has made the most sustained efforts to define the chronological detail of the transition (summarised in Chapter 1.5). We have no serious disagreement with the episode of contact that appears to be represented by the Ferriter's Cove evidence. This leaves open the possibility, from at least as far back as the middle of the fifth millennium cal BC, of movement by boat up and down the western side of Britain and Ireland. (This need be no surprise in its own right, given the plentiful evidence from the north-west seaboard of Scotland for the movement of raw materials in the Mesolithic: Saville 2004b). At this date, the obvious source area for cattle and sheep is north-west France. The Ferriter's Cove situation is surely also significant with respect to the arguments about isolation. There is no evidence to suggest whether contact was established with the outside world from south-west Ireland, or the other way round. If the former, the general argument of Sheridan in support of colonisation as the contextually most likely process is weakened. We have no way of telling if other situations of this kind remain to be discovered (other domesticated fauna so far dated in Ireland probably relate to the later, more established beginning of the Neolithic in Ireland; Fig 12.42). Other contact finds can be cited from other situations in continental Europe, such as the Balkan clay seal found recently in a late Mesolithic context in northern Switzerland (Mauvilly *et al.* 2008), or Danubian imports into the Ertebølle world (Fischer 2002; Klassen 2004; Larsson 2007); the pair of domesticated cattle in a pit under Er Grah in the Morbihan, Brittany (Fig. 15.1), may also be another instance of initial contact (Tresset 2005a, 274–5; Tresset and Vigne 2006). In the light of these other cases, it seems an open question whether late Mesolithic communities in Britain were isolated or not. And the fact of contact does not appear to determine the shape of subsequent events and processes.

If we allow pre-Neolithic movement of domesticates, should we not also include in our models pre-Neolithic occurrences of cereal-type pollen? In Britain, these are often dated, as at Ballachrink, Isle of Man, to the earlier part of the fifth millennium cal BC, in contexts where there are other indicators of woodland disturbance (Chapter 11; Innes *et al.* 2003; Davey and Innes 2003); they have also been part of the discussion about LBK and even pre-LBK horticulture in the Alpine area and central Europe (Haas 1996; Lüning 2000). In the insular context, could these not be another 'bow-wave', an early form of experimentation with cereals and forest farming by, say, indigenous populations? We repeat the concerns raised in Chapter 14 (based on issues of identification, taphonomy and stratigraphy, and lack of corresponding archaeological evidence) and note the apparent absence of such occurrences closer to what we have identified as the start of the established Neolithic – thus in the second half of the fifth millennium cal BC – just at the point when one might suppose that a practice, allegedly widely established given the geographical range of its occurrences (Innes *et al.* 2003, fig. 1), would be further intensifying. Neither Sheridan nor Thomas has brought this phenomenon much into their accounts so far. Gabriel Cooney, who has confronted it (2007a, 548), is cautious, but open-minded. This problem remains open.

Our greatest disagreement with Sheridan rests in the

Fig. 15.1. The cattle pair in context e4 beside the Er Grah monument, Locmariaquer, Brittany. Left: view; right: detail. Photos: Jean-Denis Vigne.

matter of her claimed late fifth millennium cal BC movement from Brittany, bringing new people up the western coast of Britain as far north as Argyll in western Scotland, where they are represented in a tomb at Achnacreebeag. The interpretation can be challenged on several fronts.

In Brittany, recent work brings into doubt the proposed fifth millennium cal BC date of any such Breton strand. Sheridan (2010) suggests a currency of 4300/4200–4000 cal BC for late Castellic pottery in the Morbihan, which she considers related to the vessels from Achnacreebeag. But formal, Bayesian modelling of the relevant dates suggests that Castellic pottery did not go out of use there until *4120–3610 cal BC* (*95% probability*; *End*; Cassen *et al.* 2009, fig. 13, table 10), or until *4030–3770 cal BC* (*75% probability*).[2] Even if the Achnacreebeag pots do derive from the Castellic tradition, therefore, there is no necessary contradiction with the date estimate for the start of Neolithic things and practices in southern Scotland presented in Chapter 14.7 (*3835–3760 cal BC* (*95% probability*; Fig. 14.150: *start S Scotland*), probably *3815–3780 cal BC* (*68% probability*)). The supposed circumstances of internal social disruption in Brittany itself, claimed to have led to refugee boat people heading far north to escape them, can also be questioned, given how difficult it has been to establish reliable timings for the monuments of Brittany (Müller 1998; Cassen *et al.* 2009). Some pre-existing single menhirs were broken up and reset into substantial passage tombs such as La Table des Marchands and Gavrinis (Le Roux 1984; Cassen 2000; 2009), and the stone row adjacent to La Table des Marchands was dismantled (Fig. 15.2). But the dates of these events are not yet precisely established, and they could have many different explanations. These could include enhancement of new constructions by the incorporation of the old, which may or may not have been accompanied by social upheaval.

There are also doubts at the Argyll end of things. The Achnacreebeag monument lies in a today quite remote location on the north side of Loch Etive, on a narrow coastal strip backed by high hills (Fig. 15.3). It can be fitted without difficulty into local developments. The monument did not attract exceptional attention from Audrey Henshall, who assigned it to her Hebridean group (1972, 357–8), nor from its excavator Graeme Ritchie, who followed similar connections (1970; 1997, 74–6). Both its phases appear rather simple, a possibly closed cist in the centre of the cairn followed by the chamber inserted into the edge of the cairn and approached by a very short passage. This does not appear to constitute a highly distinctive monument

Fig. 15.2. View of La Table des Marchands and Le Grand Menhir Brisé, Locmariaquer, Brittany, under excavation. Photo: Serge Cassen.

(*pace* Sheridan 2010). The decorated Bowl pottery came from the second phase. Originally this was compared to the Beacharra style of decorated western Scottish Bowl pottery (Ritchie 1970; 1997; Sheridan 1995, 11, fig. 2.3), and wider reference too might be made to decorated Bowl traditions of the mid-fourth millennium cal BC in Ireland (Case 1961; Sheridan 1995). The decorative motif of inverted arcs is widespread. Although it does occur on Castellic pottery, it is also found in the repertoire of Irish passage tomb 'art' (most recently treated by Robin 2009). The bowl forms of the Achnacreebeag and various French pots are not identical, though admittedly similar. Neither phase of the Achnacreebeag monument has been radiocarbon dated (though Ritchie recorded charcoal from under the cairn (1970, 34), and this could and should be radiocarbon dated, if it survives).

Beyond these specific worries, we are struck by the lack of other evidence of this kind. Even if this was a small-scale arrival, we might reasonably expect some other signs of it up the west coast of Britain and around Ireland. In the early scenario, there should be a scatter of radiocarbon dates, falling into the centuries around 4000 cal BC, associated with Neolithic material of this kind from other sites, along the proposed migration route. Our detailed reviews of dates associated with early Neolithic things and practices in the south-west peninsula of Britain (Fig. 10.30), in south Wales and the Marches (Figs 11.10–11), and in Ireland (cf. Figs 12.54 and 12.56) have revealed no such evidence. More limited exercises reviewing comparable bodies of data from the Isle of Man (Fig. 14.148) and southern Scotland (Figs 14.150–3), similarly have revealed no evidence for Neolithic activity before the later 39th century cal BC. Recent, thorough, reviews of the evidence in north Wales

Fig. 15.3. View of the Achnacreebeag cairn, Loch Etive, Argyll and Bute, Scotland, under excavation. Photo: © RCAHMS.

and north-west England present similar patterns (Griffiths forthcoming). And, anyway, why should supposed Breton refugees have had to flee so far – all the way to remote Loch Etive, as far as we can discern ignoring Cornwall, south Wales, Ireland, south-west Scotland, and other points between?

If Achnacreebeag indeed had Breton connections, it could have resulted from a single, isolated contact without wider repercussions, and, on the evidence of the Breton chronology, could have occurred in the early fourth millennium cal BC rather than the late fifth.

The only other location specifically cited by Sheridan (2010) is the monument at Carreg Samson in south-west Wales (F. Lynch 1975). There are two issues here. Sheridan has classed this as a simple passage tomb, whereas we would rather see this as within the repertoire of portal tombs (though Frances Lynch (1976, 31) also sets it apart from them). She has claimed its one pot, a plain bowl of very simple form, as similar to Breton middle Neolithic forms, but it appears to us to fit well enough within insular Bowl styles. While portal tombs have often been claimed as an early form of monument (including by Cummings and Whittle 2004), on the basis partly of their simple architecture and partly of associated Bowl pottery (F. Lynch 1972; 1976), the three in western Britain which currently have radiocarbon dates (Carreg Coetan, Pembrokeshire, and now Zennor and Sperris Quoits, Cornwall) all fall in the mid- or late fourth millennium cal BC (Chapter 10, footnote 1; Chapter 11.4). The monument at Broadsands in Devon is also classified by Sheridan as a simple passage tomb, and is estimated to have been constructed in *3870–3710 cal BC* (*95% probability*; Fig. 10.30: *start broadsands*), probably in *3815–3740 cal BC* (*68% probability*). We do not see its simple form as easily categorisable, especially given its damaged state at the time of excavation, and the associated pottery is Carinated Bowl, and therefore from a very different tradition to that of Brittany. The monument belongs rather, in our view, to a diversity of early constructions found across southern Britain (and discussed further below). Because of our reading of sample associations, we have not accepted the claims for an early date (in the early fourth millennium cal BC) for the Carrowmore passage tombs in Co. Sligo (see again Chapters 12 and 14).

Generally, therefore, we can see no convincing evidence for a widespread migration from Brittany up the western coast of Britain in the early Neolithic, and certainly no evidence for any such movement in the last centuries of the fifth millennium BC.

In contrast, we are in broad, but not complete, agreement with the latest formulation by Sheridan (2010) of both the character and start date of the 'Carinated Bowl Neolithic' found widely across southern, eastern and northern Britain, and Ireland, but disagree in important details. Her description of novel pottery, lithics and lithic production sites including deep flint mines, timber structures, domesticates and various non-megalithic funerary structures accords in general with what we have also set out in the regional chapters and again in Chapter 14. Even if there are selection and recombination from continental sources, or what Thomas has previously called *bricolage* (J. Thomas 2003; 2008, 77), and while not every element of these innovations occurs together at every site, the extent of change is very striking.

One major question is the problematic nature of the date of the Magheraboy enclosure in Co. Sligo, which, on present evidence, may have been built in the 40th or 39th century cal BC (Fig. 12.15: *start Magheraboy*). Given that the Carinated Bowl Neolithic has also been labelled 'trans-Manche est', and that its affiliations (by whatever process) appear to lie broadly in an area between the Paris Basin and the Low Countries (Sheridan 2007a; 2010) and that the form of the enclosure itself at this date is echoed in the Paris Basin and eastwards (see below), it remains very surprising that the only potential early example of enclosure construction should occur so far west; we should keep in mind that up till now no causewayed enclosure has been discovered in Brittany or Normandy. Magheraboy keeps open, in a different way to mooted Breton and Norman connections, the possibility of small-scale arrivals on the west side of Ireland. If it really dates to the earliest fourth millennium cal BC, it may have been an event or experiment that did not have immediate major consequences, given the chronological gap till the better documented beginnings for the Neolithic in Ireland *c.* 3800 cal BC. We will come back to the site, and the possibility (discussed further in Chapter 14) that it could date somewhat later, in our discussion of beginnings in Ireland and western Scotland.

Our main divergence from Sheridan's scenario rests in the details of the dating of this phenomenon. In a previous account she saw its beginning in the 40th century cal BC, and strongly implied a more or less simultaneous spread, at least across England and Scotland (Sheridan 2007a). Her most recent interpretation is more cautious (Sheridan 2010). She refers to beginnings, still principally using visual inspection of radiocarbon dates, at *c.* 4000 cal BC, citing both Yabsley Street, Blackwall, and Coldrum, Kent (the single rim fragment from which is of unknown style). She characterises the phenomenon as a whole as 'arriving over much of Britain and most of Ireland within the first two centuries of the fourth millennium', going on to claim that 'the appearance was diaspora-like across wide areas of Britain and Ireland, rather than consisting of a primary point of colonisation in the south-east, followed by spread from that point' (Sheridan 2010).

Her more cautious view that the appearance of the Carinated Bowl Neolithic took two centuries can broadly apply to southern England, as we have shown in Chapter 14 (Figs 14.54 and 14.58), though the Carinated Bowl presence in south-west England is slight. But the latest account of Sheridan does not accord with the stadial spread across southern Britain proposed in Chapter 14, nor with the start dates of *c.* 3800 cal BC which we have proposed for Ireland, the Isle of Man and southern and north-eastern Scotland (Fig. 14.176). We have argued for a different kind of diaspora, perhaps spreading from an initial area of innovation in the south-east of England (although the current data could mask a more complex web of beginnings within southern England (compare Figs 14.54 and 14.58), and changing and accelerating in tempo as it extended to much of Britain and Ireland (Fig. 14.177). Our model also diverges from the generalising view of Thomas (2008) of very rapid initial change, which is implied to have taken place everywhere more or less simultaneously. This divergence serves not only to provide a very different chronology for the beginning of the Neolithic across Britain and Ireland, but also further to differentiate among the elements of innovation listed by Sheridan (2010). Timber houses and halls, for example, cannot now in our view simply be listed as an automatic or inevitable part of a package of novelties, since in both eastern Scotland and Ireland we can propose a very distinctive horizon for their occurrence, and this too has to be taken into account when interpreting the process of change at the beginning of the Neolithic in different parts of the offshore islands.

We agree in part with the characterisation of the proposed 'trans-Manche ouest' strand or strands of Sheridan (2007a; 2010). Carinated Bowl pottery is rare in the south-west and the South-Western style is dominant. Such difference requires explanation. We are less sure that it need be related specifically to sources in Normandy. Specific Norman origins for Broadsands are not proven. As for her third element of this 'trans-Manche ouest' strand, rotundae, a much later dating has been proposed in Chapter 9 (and see again Chapter 14). Sheridan (2010) has proposed arrival 'some time between 4000 and 3800' cal BC and 'during the first quarter of the fourth millennium'. The latter characterisation accords better with the models set out in Chapters 10 and 14, which suggest that the earliest Neolithic activity in the south-west peninsula probably began in the later 39th or earlier 38th century cal BC (Fig. 10.30: *start Neolithic settlement*).

A provisional scenario for initial colonisation

Taking both the factors discussed above and our proposed chronological framework into account, we can now offer our own story. The narrative of the Mesolithic-Neolithic transition need not be reduced to a single one. Though we are hampered by the continuing lack of good evidence for late Mesolithic activity in south-east England, which emerges as a major research priority for the future, and so far, individual sites such as Yabsley Street, Coldrum and White Horse Stone have provided positive evidence of only part of the range of innovations at the start of the Neolithic, we believe that the current evidence for earliest beginnings in the south-east of England, closest to the continent, coupled with the extent of innovations stressed above, probably does speak for some kind of initial colonisation. Dramatic new practice extends to the digging of deep flint mines in Sussex, most plausibly following established traditions of deep extraction, which go back in central Europe to the LBK in the sixth millennium cal BC (e.g. Eisele *et al.* 2003), and which were part of the activities of the Michelsberg culture in southern Belgium (see also Chapter 5.9).

The continental foreground: a brief survey

But why the 41st century cal BC, and why south-east England? A long time ago, one of us argued for a background of settlement expansion on the adjacent continent as the context from which newcomers from expanding populations budded off to colonise southern Britain as a whole (Whittle 1977b; cf. Case 1969). The original formulation got the chronology wrong, as it argued for change beginning in the earlier to mid-fifth millennium cal BC, in the post-LBK horizon. A later version, as chronology began to be revised (e.g. Kinnes and Thorpe 1986), suggested that an earlier date for the start of the British Neolithic would favour colonisation, but a later date acculturation (Whittle 1990a). That too looks doubtful. The spirit of explanation, however, in terms of change among Neolithic communities on the adjacent continent must still apply, even if a more subtle interpretation is now required. Sheridan has consistently made reference to this continental setting, especially to changes in Brittany, Normandy and a restricted area of northernmost France, as we have already seen, as well as to the movement of Alpine jadeitite axes (e.g. Sheridan 2010, and earlier references), but it is worth taking a broader if brief look at things, in order to evaluate as critically as possible the context from which colonisation of some kind into south-east England may have arisen.

The LBK and post-LBK longhouse world probably came to an end at some point in the middle of the fifth millennium cal BC. While the combination of typological series, stratigraphy, spatial developments and visual inspection of radiocarbon dates has suggested a precise chronology for the development of the LBK in the sixth millennium (Stehli 1994; Stäuble 2005; see also the dendrochronological evidence of wells: e.g. Koschik 2004), the chronology of fifth-millennium central Europe is still a matter of discussion because of conflicts between scientific dating and contextual analyses (Spatz 1999; Müller 2004; see also Dubouloz 2003 for the Paris basin). It is not possible to be precise about the continental chronology of much of the fifth millennium, since with the exception of the extensive dendrochronologies of the Alpine foreland beginning with the start of Neolithic settlement there *c.* 4300 BC (Schlichtherle 1997; Menotti 2004), sequences are very weak.

In spite of such difficulties, the mid-fifth millennium is a convenient starting point. Looking back, the LBK had appeared on parts of the Rhine perhaps between *c.* 5500 and 5300 cal BC (Gronenborn 1999; 2007a; Lüning 2000; Stäuble 2005), and was west of the Rhine, on the Aldenhovener Platte, in Dutch Limburg and parts of eastern southern Belgium perhaps from *c.* 5300 cal BC onwards (Louwe Kooijmans 2007; Crombé and Vanmontfort 2007); LBK or Rubané récent settlement perhaps appeared in the Paris basin of northern France in the very late sixth millennium cal BC (Allard 2007; Demoule 2007a).

The LBK, once seen as the classic colonisation fuelled by demographic growth, is now harder to characterise. There may have been both newcomers and local people involved from its inception (Gronenborn 1999; 2007a; Kind 1998; Lukes and Zvelebil 2008; Tillmann 1993), and isotopic analysis in particular has suggested what Detlef Gronenborn has called 'multi-tradition communities' (2007a, 84; see also Lukes and Zvelebil 2008). But in any one region opinion may remain divided. West of the Rhine, for example, Leendert Louwe Kooijmans is in no doubt of the reality of the intrusion of a fully formed way of life into the Graetheide (2007, 295; cf. Amkreutz *et al.* 2009), though some researchers only a little to the south in Belgian Hesbaye allow more complex interactions (Lodewijckx and Bakels 2009).

Perhaps within the blanket, so to speak, of shared culture in the LBK (cf. Robb and Miracle 2007), there were such divergences from region to region. There were certainly differences at a wider scale. The northern limits of the LBK and post-LBK world on the fringes of the north European plain did not alter much until the late fifth millennium cal BC; there was certainly contact with the Ertebølle world of the Baltic coast and southern Scandinavia, but without, so it would appear, Ertebølle identity being altered until the probably indigenous adoption of Neolithic things and practices perhaps just before or around 4000 cal BC (Fischer 2002; Klassen 2004; Hartz *et al.* 2007; Larsson 2007; Müller 2010a). The main changes observable within southern Scandinavian and northern German societies took place through the early phases of the TRB, with most of them estimated to have come later than *c.* 3800 cal BC (Müller 2009). Nor does LBK and post-LBK settlement appear to have spread beyond its initial extent in the southern Netherlands and Belgium, but on the evidence recovered by a series of deep excavations, especially in the Rhine-Meuse estuaries (Fig. 15.4), local communities only some 80–100 km distant maintained their own identity while gradually adopting elements of Neolithic things and practices through the fifth millennium cal BC: first pots, then pigs and cattle, and finally cereals (Louwe Kooijmans 2001a; 2001b; 2007). More established Neolithic practice and settlement are seen at a date estimated at *c.* 3600 cal BC at sites like Schipluiden in coastal Delfland (Louwe Kooijmans and Jongste 2006; Louwe Kooijmans 2009; see also Verhart 2000a). This important archaeological sequence is punctuated, rather than continuous, but it constitutes a process of indigenous change very close to south-east England.

In the Paris basin, opinion is divided on the process which brought the Rubané récent into existence (see Allard 2007). There was then a process of extension in the first half of the fifth millennium cal BC, principally to the west – and we still appear to have a rather hazy notion of the precise distribution of Cerny settlement, the cultural group at the end of this sequence in the middle part of the millennium, in relation to the Channel (Constantin *et al.* 1997; Demoule 2007b, 93). Extension to the west brought interaction with indigenous communities in north-west France, especially Brittany, themselves probably also in contact with or aware of Neolithic things, practices and ideas to the south, ultimately in the west Mediterranean (Marchand 2007; Scarre 2007a). Out of this contact appears to have emerged the first Breton Neolithic in the middle of the fifth millennium cal BC (Cassen *et al.* 2000; Cassen *et al.* 2009, fig. 13; Marchand 2007; Scarre 2007a).

These diverse transitions were variously accompanied by profound culture change, so there were complex processes at work. This is further complicated by the fact that the new cultural identities of the post-longhouse world – principally the northern Chasséen, Michelsberg and TRB cultural groupings – overlap geographically with both the areas of primary (or LBK and post-LBK) and secondary Neolithic settlement. This is a period of extensive change (Fig. 15.5), characterised recently in the case of the Chasséen and Michelsberg cultures as 'phénomène d'unification stylistique par interaction de différents groupes'[3] (Demoule *et al.* 2007b, 64). Just when this period begins, as already noted, has only been established to within a margin of a few centuries. Michelsberg culture chronology is central to this question. Typological study provided a probable sequence long ago (Lüning 1967; Biel *et al.* 1998), but precise dating has been more elusive. A combination of typological studies with the anchor of north Swiss-south German dendrochronologies strongly suggests that it must date from at least *c.* 4300 cal BC. Christian Jeunesse in particular (1998; Jeunesse *et al.* 2004; cf. Dubouloz 1998) has argued for slightly earlier beginnings in northern France, as early as *c.* 4500 cal BC, and this too emerges as another important objective for future formal modelling. A clearer picture is emerging from new dating programmes and intensive research on earthworks in northern Germany (Geschwinde and Raetzel Fabian 2009; Müller 2009). There it is now estimated that the Michelsberg culture started *c.* 4200 cal BC at the latest and lasted until *c.* 3500 cal BC. Secure samples stratified in ditches in Braunschweiger Land enclosures date the development from larger to smaller earthworks, which in central Germany are associated with Baalberge pottery. In southern Germany the Bruchsal and Heilbronn enclosures provide a clear picture of later Michelsberg developments, *c.* 3700 cal BC (Seidel 2008a).

So looking forward from the mid-fifth millennium cal BC, we can see not only cultural shifts of diverse kinds but also processes of change in settlement (Fig. 15.5). The demise of nucleated longhouse settlements was followed, except in the Alpine foreland, by a scarcity of identifiable house structures; by other markers of residence or marking of place, often characterised by aggregations of pits on the one hand and enclosures on the other; and by settlement rather more extensively distributed across the landscape. There may have been accompanying subsistence changes, perhaps especially in the location and intensity of cereal cultivation, though this is far from well understood, and nearly everywhere cattle seem particularly important (Auxiette and Hachem 2007; Bogucki 1993; 2000; Ebersbach 2002; Geschwinde/Raetzel-Fabian 2009; Pipes *et al.* 2009; Steppan 2003; Tresset 2000; 2003; 2005a). But there is also much variation in settlement

Fig. 15.4. Views of (top) Hardinxveld-Giessendam de Bruin and (below) Hardinxveld-Giessendam Polderweg under excavation. Photos: Leendert Louwe Kooijmans.

histories, and a very brief survey will serve to bring out the diverse nature of the continental foreground.

In southern Scandinavia, early Neolithic settlement was perhaps gradually established from around 4000 cal BC, mainly in the same coastal zones and immediate hinterlands used in the Ertebølle culture; more intense clearance and

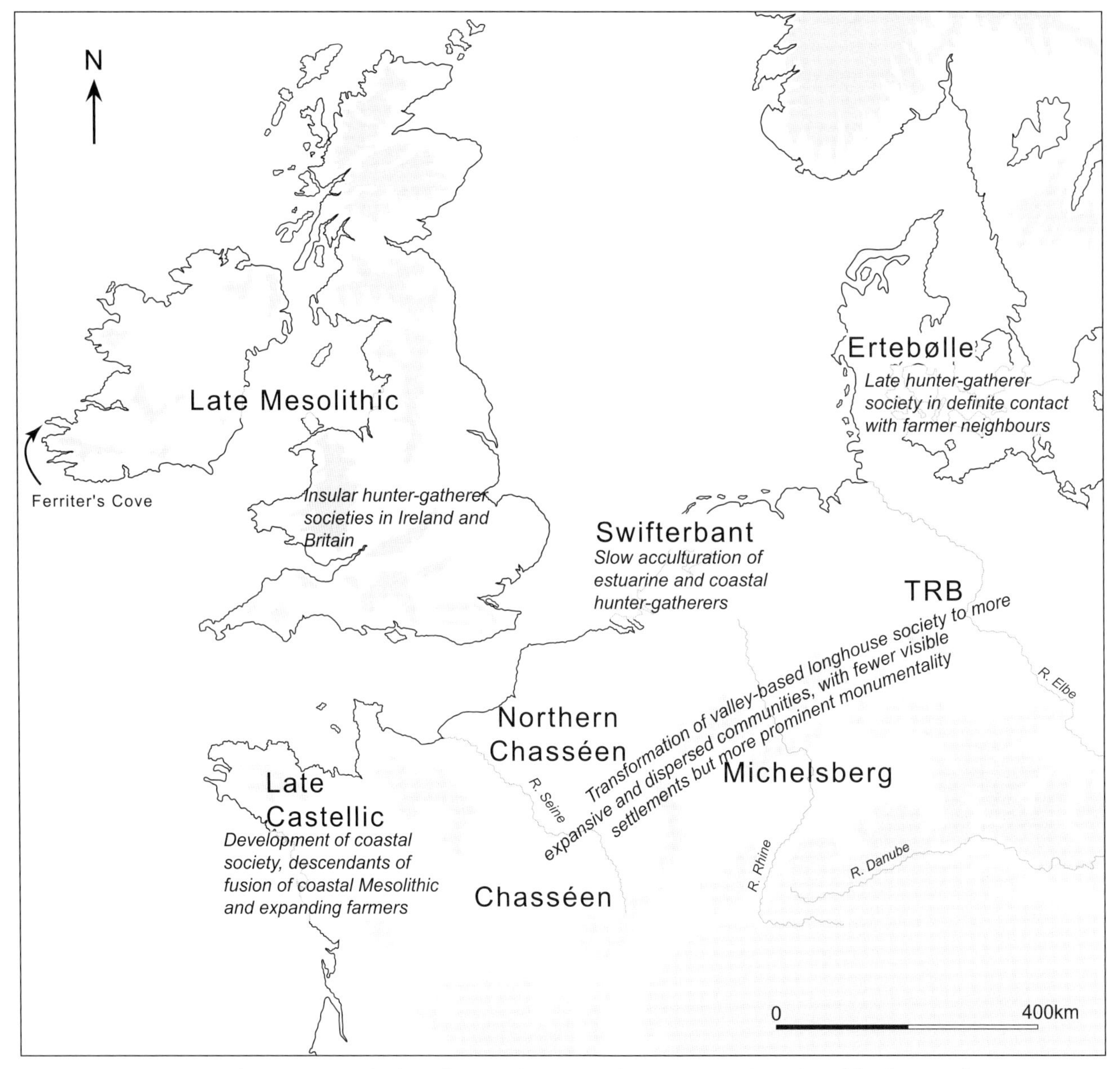

Fig. 15.5. Interpretive, schematic map of selected major features and processes in the cultural landscape of western Europe in the later fifth millennium cal BC.

more frequent monument building appear to belong to the end of the Early Neolithic and beginning of the Middle Neolithic, perhaps *c.* 3500 cal BC (Fischer 2002; Klassen 2004; Ebbesen 2007; Müller 2010a). The same trends may be true of the north European Plain, though Neolithic practices may have begun a little earlier (e.g. Hartz *et al.* 2007; Müller 2010b), and were linked to wider processes of TRB development to the south, in which settlement was normally dispersed and a variety of monuments including enclosures were constructed (Müller 2001; Meyer and Raetzel-Fabian 2006; Midgley 1992; 2005; 2008; Geschwinde and Raetzel-Fabian 2009; Klatt 2009). Overall, enclosures appeared *c.* 3500 cal BC in the northern TRB group contemporary with early megaliths, while non-earthen long barrows had been built since *c.* 3800 cal BC. In Lower Saxony and central Germany the Michelsberg expansion had already produced enclosures *c.* 4200 cal BC.

We can note, as an offshoot of the infill of the north European Plain, the probably late date – perhaps well after 4000 cal BC – at which clearance and monument building began in the northern provinces of the Netherlands, Drenthe and Friesland (Louwe Kooijmans *et al.* 2005; Fokkens 1998, 96–7). In coastal Delfland, further south, Schipluiden has a number of probably contemporary small neighbours in the earlier part of the fourth millennium cal BC (Louwe Kooijmans 2009). Further south again in the Low Countries, Louwe Kooijmans (2007, 297) has referred to Michelsberg expansion, 'remarkable changes' and even 'disruptions', from a date estimated at *c.* 4300 cal BC. It is worth quoting his account at some length:

> It seems that Neolithic society is restructured and that the basic unit shifts to a higher level, from the village in a segmentary society towards groups for which supra-

Fig. 15.6. Part of the enclosure ditch at Spiere-de Hel, West Flanders, Belgium, under excavation. Photo: Bart Vanmontfort.

> local enclosures have a central function, a development seen over wider tracts of western and northern Europe. It is in this stage, to be dated from 4300 cal BC onward, that the wide spaces between the restricted Neolithic enclaves in Belgium are filled in. Apparently both the Blicquy farmers and all final Mesolithic groups transformed into Michelsberg and changed to a new way of life. The Michelsberg complex also demonstrates an expansion towards the north, beyond the loess zone, into the Limburg Meuse Valley and the Münster Basin. This means a northern shift of the old agricultural frontier which must have had its effect on the local communities beyond (Louwe Kooijmans 2007, 297).

In a little more detail, Neolithic axes and adzes had been moved in numbers into the sandy lowlands of Belgium from the sixth into the fifth millennia cal BC (Verhart 2000b, figs 3–4). The enclosure at Spiere-de Hel in the middle Scheldt valley is a good example of Michelsberg settlement expanding within the loess belt of western Belgium (Fig. 15.6), beyond the much smaller enclaves of LBK and post-LBK settlement (Crombé and Vanmontfort 2007; Vanmontfort 2001; Vanmontfort *et al.* 2004). The construction of an enclosure is presumably, as noted above, a significant development in terms of local settlement dynamics, but the pollen evidence does not suggest extensive open ground (Vanmontfort *et al.* 2004, fig. 38) and there were few axes. The subsistence evidence suggests some cultivation, gathering and husbandry, especially of pig. The primary fill of the ditch suggests bank collapse, followed by recuts and gradual accumulation of material. Flint mines are suggested to be another central focus in a new 'hierarchised' settlement pattern (Crombé and Vanmontfort 2007, 268). On the sandy lowland beyond the loess, part of changes informally estimated in this case as 'most probably shortly before or after 4000 cal BC',[4] Michelsberg settlements are harder to find. They were perhaps smaller and more discrete than on the loess belt, and were possibly individually short-lived (Crombé and Vanmontfort 2007, 280); an important new research project on this area is now underway (Philippe Crombé, pers. comm.).

Other regions to the south, both in the Rhineland and in the Paris basin, show many of the same post-longhouse changes. Posthole-defined residential or domestic structures become much rarer, and ditched and palisaded enclosures are a recurrent feature. In some of the loess areas previously occupied by the LBK and its successors, Michelsberg settlement appears sparse (Zimmermann 2006b; 2006c), though in the Rhineland itself both pit sites and enclosures can be both substantial and locally abundant (e.g. Lüning 1967; Biel *et al.* 1998; Steppan 2003; Reiter 2005; Koch 2005; Meyer and Raetzel-Fabian 2006; Gronenborn 2007b). Some areas within the northern Chasséen-Michelsberg cultural complex, such as the Oise, Aisne, 'petite Seine', lower Marne and Yonne (e.g. Dubouloz *et al.* 1991; Lombardo *et al.* 1984) have quite dense distributions of enclosures. The complex enclosure at Bazoches-sur-Vesle, for example, in a side tributary of the Aisne, belongs to a valley landscape where enclosures occur every few kilometres, though it is not clear that these are all contemporary, nor where in the late fifth or early fourth millennium cal BC they may belong (Dubouloz *et al.* 1991; 1997; Dubouloz 1998). Some enclosure sites, on the basis of scattered or individual radiocarbon samples, not yet formally modelled, may not date much before *c.* 4000 cal BC, such as Boury-en-Vexin in the Oise (Lombardo *et al.* 1984). There is new evidence for other enclosures further north towards the Pas-de-Calais (Bostyn *et al.* 2006), and a recent discovery of a large, triple ditched enclosure, whose pottery appears to relate to the Groupe de Spiere, at Carvin 'Gare d'Eau', Pas-de-Calais, north-west of Douai (Cécile Monchablon, pers. comm.). There are other such enclosures in southern Belgium, as at Spiennes, and Spiere itself. Some of these sites are placed in the valley bottoms, like earlier longhouse settlement, and others on the valley sides or plateau edges, which may evoke in part a more extensive use of the landscape than in the longhouse system, and in part the possibility that some of these sites had a defensive role. A recent synthesis evokes things in these terms:

> Il pourrait s'agir, si elles n'avaient qu'une simple function défensive, d'une preuve de tensions émergentes face à

> des terres en raréfaction et à une démographie croissante; ou, à tout le moins, de la mise en place de systèmes idéologiques complexes chargés d'encadrer, par un ancrage manifeste dans le paysage, des communautés toujours plus dispersées dans l'espace (Demoule *et al.* 2007b, 69).[5]

Uninterrupted change or expansion may not characterise all regions. Sheridan (2010) has noted the proposed sequence in Normandy, where there was first settlement expansion estimated to belong to the second half of the fifth and early part of the fourth millennium cal BC, and then at a date informally estimated at *c.* 3800 cal BC, a significant phase of hiatus (Marcigny *et al.* 2007). Another local context not far away, in the lower Eure close to the Seine near Rouen, also suggests a landscape *c.* 4000 cal BC that was far from over-crowded. Occupation in the vicinity of the site of Louviers (Giligny 2005) probably goes back to the early fifth millennium cal BC Villeneuve-Saint-Germain group, but use of the marshy location itself dates to *c.* 4400–4300 cal BC and is associated with the Cerny group. More frequent occupation, of northern Chasséen cultural affiliation, dates to *c.* 4000–3800 cal BC. This was use of wet ground, for passage and discard, and perhaps not principally a settlement in its own right, but the pollen evidence again shows a still well wooded setting (Reckinger 2005), and the animal bones suggest a principal concern with cattle, but also some hunting (Tresset 2005b).

Rather further afield, even if it is probably too far away to be directly relevant to the beginning of the Neolithic in southern Britain, it is worth noting the abundant evidence for southern Chasséen settlement, including again occupation sites with pits, but rare structures, and enclosures (e.g. Thévenot 2005; Vaquer 1990). In the lower Rhône, intensive study between Valence and Orange, for example, has produced a picture in which 'l'économie et la société évoluent vers une occupation du sol plus dense et plus hiérarchisée'[6] (Demoule *et al.* 2007b, 66). Seasonal movements of animals between larger lowland and smaller upland sites have been proposed (Beeching 2003; Bréhard 2007).

In Brittany itself, it is hardly possible to follow such trends in the still scarce settlement evidence, and even the probably increasing numbers of monuments must stand as a very approximate proxy, most of them imprecisely dated (Marchand 2007; Scarre 2007a; Cassen 2009; with references). In central-west France, between the Loire and Gironde, enclosures become numerous from a date estimated to start probably in the first half of the fourth millennium cal BC, in the Néolithique récent of the region (Burnez and Fouéré 1999; cf. Cassen and Scarre 1997); possibilities of some dating to the Néolithique moyen, because of comparisons in form to those in the Paris basin and elsewhere, have not yet been confirmed (Burnez *et al.* 2001; Semelier 2007). The enclosures are the most obvious manifestation of a settlement infill much more marked than in the fifth millennium cal BC (Marchand 2007; Scarre 2007a).

The possible scale and nature of colonisation

So this wide range of evidence suggests various possibilities. There is much diversity, and there are so far unresolved questions of chronology. There is probably no compelling evidence for unmanageably populous landscapes along the breadth of the continent facing Britain, which might have generated large-scale population movement. On the other hand, there is no reason to exclude small-scale, piecemeal and perhaps episodic fissioning from continental communities, in a context to be generally characterised as one of change, which locally, as in western Belgium, appears to have been quite dramatic in terms of settlement expansion. Climate change has also increasingly been invoked as a causative or enabling factor (e.g. Gronenborn 2007a; 2007b; Strien and Gronenborn 2005; Bonsall *et al.* 2002; Tipping 2010), but we would like to see much greater precision in defining both claimed effects and their timings. The record in the Alpine foreland suggests a correlation between periods when Neolithic settlement is abundant and phases when lake levels were low and climate was warm and rather dry, and conversely between periods when Neolithic settlement appears more sparse and phases when lake levels were high and the climate was wet; these periods of higher water table are dated to 4000–3950 BC and 3700–3250 BC (this phase is composed of three successive events centred on *c.* 3600 BC, *c.* 3500 BC and *c.* 3350 BC) (Arbogast *et al.* 2006). Raised bogs in the north-east of the Netherlands also show a correlation between significant rises in atmospheric radiocarbon ($\Delta^{14}C$) and increasing wetness, at dates estimated at *c.* 4005–3935, 3665–3615, 3545–3485 cal BC and so on (Blaauw *et al.* 2004, table 1). It would be foolish to claim that there could be no effects on human activity from such shifts, given the subsistence and settlement changes in colder and wetter phases in the Alpine foreland, but on present timings they could prove to be more relevant say to the spread of enclosure construction across southern Britain than to the initial introduction of Neolithic things and practices, including cereal agriculture.

Can we refine a colonisation hypothesis any further? After all, previous recent versions have been based in large measure – apart from the arguments for timescales reviewed above – on the assertion of the isolation of Mesolithic Britain and Ireland from the continent and the scale of differences in material culture and other practices. It is hard to ignore the point of Thomas (2008), noted above, about material 'selection and recombination'. As Richard Bradley has put it (2007, 86):

> In principle, it should be possible to define the source, or sources, of any migrants through a close comparison between the material culture of Neolithic Britain and Ireland and its counterparts on the European mainland. Although there are a number of general similarities, particularly among the undecorated ceramics which are the earliest in these islands, attempts to define more exact links have so far failed. That is probably because the study area would have been accessible from so many different areas of Continental Europe.

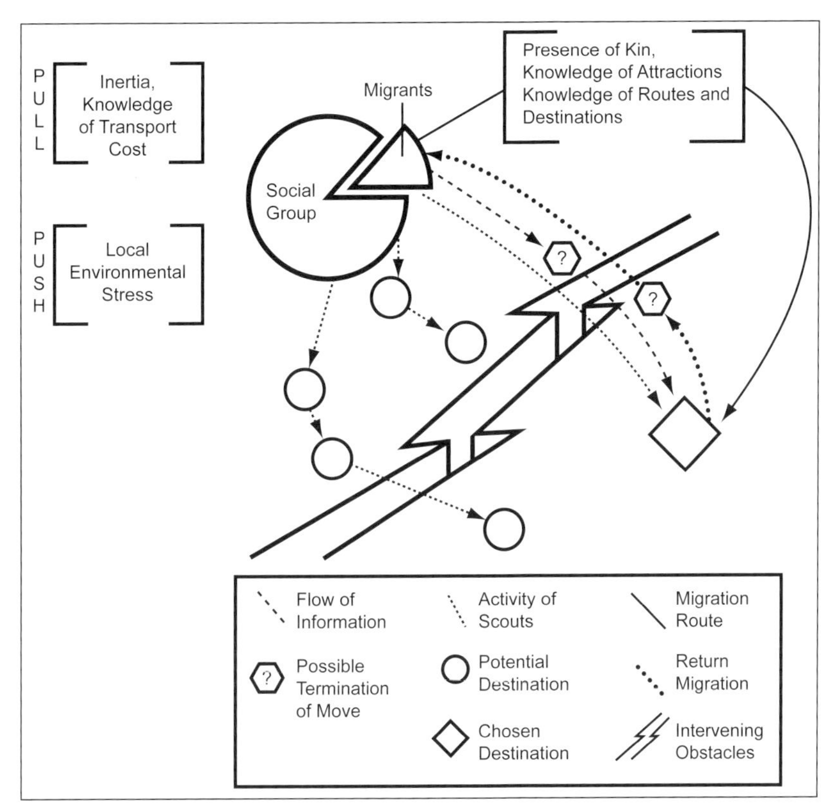

Fig. 15.7. A long-distance colonisation model: redrawn from David Anthony (1990).

The response of Sheridan (2007a, 468), while asserting the general affinity of Carinated Bowl pottery to the ceramic tradition of the Michelsberg culture, has been to evoke the likely existence of an exact or closer match in so far under-researched parts of northernmost France: in Nord-Pas de Calais and northern Picardie. So far, as it stands, that argument seems less than convincing. There remains little good evidence for the wholesale transference of continental cultural practices. If we look to the Michelsberg culture, for example, even close to north-east France, we only see partial overlap in the material repertoires. The enclosure site, noted above, of Spiere-de Hel in the middle Scheldt valley in Flanders – only a little over 100 km from the Kent coast, and rather less from the French border – is a good example. It is estimated to date to *c.* 4000 cal BC (Vanmontfort *et al.* 2004). Its pottery and flint assemblages include deep-necked jars and shouldered and even carinated bowls, and polished axes, scrapers and leaf-shaped arrowheads (e.g. Vanmontfort *et al.* 2004, figs 25–7 and 32–5), which would not look out of place in southern and eastern British assemblages of the earlier fourth millennium cal BC, but they also include other jar and bowl forms, and triangular points and long edge-retouched pieces, which certainly would.

Do we then revert to a notion of incomers from much more generalised source areas, as Bradley has proposed? There has been remarkably little theorising about the possible nature of colonisation in this British and Irish debate, despite the number of times the issue has been argued over. Perhaps only Humphrey Case (1969) really got to grips in detail with some of the basic issues, arguing that the conditions of exploration, by journeying individuals, and then subsequent initial establishment, in pioneering conditions by small groups, would have led to disruption of material traditions. That view was subsequently either criticised (e.g. R. Bradley 1984a, 9–14) or lost sight of altogether. A more general view of 'wave of advance' movement generated by demographic increase and proceeding by short steps at the frontier was proposed by Ammerman and Cavalli-Sforza (1984). Drawing on a much wider literature, David Anthony (1990; 1997; Fiedel and Anthony 2003; cf. Rouse 1986; Chapman and Hamerow 1997) has proposed a more general model for long-distance migration (Fig. 15.7), as opposed to short-distance migration akin to 'wave-of-advance' movement, in which 'in general, migration is most likely to occur when there are negative (push) stresses in the home region and positive (pull) attractions in the destination region, and the transportation costs between the two are acceptable' (Anthony 1990, 899). Push factors for long-distance migration are normally economic, often by people with 'focal' rather than broad-spectrum economies , though ideological and other factors are not to be discounted (Anthony 1990, 898–901). In agreement with the view of Case, colonisation is usually preceded by scouting, and where colonisation takes place is strongly contingent on where scouts happened to go (Anthony 1990, 902–3); 'migrants are not likely to move to areas about which they have no information' (Anthony 1990, 901). It is rare for whole cultures to move, and normal for budding off, fissioning and other kinds of selection to take place; 'cultures don't migrate; people do' (Anthony 1997, 27). 'A migration stream often flows from a highly restricted point of origin' and 'the pool

Table 15.1. Posterior density estimates for the appearance of selected Neolithic things and practices at various geographical scales, derived from the models in Chapter 14.

Study area	**Area within study area**	**Region within area**	**Parameter**	***Posterior density estimate (cal BC) (95% probability)***	***Posterior density estimate (cal BC) (68% probability)***
Southern England and Wales			Fig. 14.59: *start Neolithisation*	*4235–3985*	*4115–4010*
	South-east England		Fig. 14.57: *start SE Neolithic*	*4075–3975*	*4035–3990*
		Greater Thames estuary	Fig. 14.49: *start Thames estuary*	*4315–3985*	*4145–4005*
		Sussex	Fig. 5.32: *start Sussex Neolithic*	*4065–3815*	*3990–3855*
		Eastern England	Fig. 6.50: *start eastern Neolithic*	*3845–3695*	*3800–3730*
	South-central England		Fig. 14.57: *start S central Neolithic*	*3975–3835*	*3930–3855*
		Middle Thames valley	Fig. 14.50: *start middle Thames Neolithic*	*3860–3700*	*3810–3735*
		Upper Thames valley	Fig. 14.51: *start upper Thames Neolithic*	*3915–3740*	*3860–3795*
		North Wessex	Fig. 14.52: *start north Wessex*	*3930–3665*	*3805–3685*
		South Wessex	Fig. 14.53: *start south Wessex*	*4065–3705*	*3905–3735*
		Cotswolds	Fig. 9.29: *start Cotswold Neolithic*	*4035–3845*	*3985–3890*
	South-west Britain		Fig. 14.57: *start SW Neolithic*	*3855–3735*	*3820–3760*
		South-West peninsula	Fig. 10.30: *start Neolithic settlement*	*3940–3735*	*3855–3765*
		South Wales and the Marches	Fig. 11.10: *start S Wales & Marches*	*3765–3655*	*3725–3675*
Isle of Man			Fig. 14.148: *start Manx Neolithic*	*4040–3700*	*3905–3725*
Ireland (model 2)			Fig. 12.54; *start Irish Neolithic (model 2)*	*3750–3680*	*3730–3695*
Ireland (model 3)			Fig. 12.56; *start Irish Neolithic (model 3)*	*3850–3740*	*3815–3760*
Scotland S of Great Glen					
	S Scotland		Fig. 14.150: *start S Scotland*	*3835–3760*	*3815–3780*
	NE Scotland		Fig. 14.154: *start NE Scotland*	*3950–3765*	*3865–3780*

of potential migrants is kin-defined, often quite narrowly'; this narrow selection combined with innovation in new lands can lead to 'rapid stylistic change from what was in any case a narrowly defined pool of variability' (Anthony 1990, 903). Contact is usually maintained between colonisers in their new lands and their source areas, over considerable periods of time subsequently; 'migrations almost always move in two directions: the initial migration is followed by a counterstream moving back to the migrants' place of origin' (Anthony 1990, 897–8). In addition, migration streams can continue to operate in a given direction even though initial circumstances have changed (Anthony 1990, 904).

This scenario raises interesting possibilities. Should we think of potential cross-Channel movement at the very end of the fifth millennium cal BC as short-distance or long-distance? In favour of the latter is the planning normally required (and so well evoked by Case 1969) for moving across an ecological or cultural boundary (Anthony 1990, 902), which the Channel surely constitutes, and the fact that 'local moves would have only subtle effects on material culture' (Anthony 1990, 901), which should mean that we would find an uninterrupted continuation of Michelsberg culture practice in south-east England – which is clearly not the case. The review of continental settlement above may suggest possible specific economic motives, such as a desire for more land, but also a strong general sense of change and expansion. In this regard, the contemporaneity of many aspects of the south Scandinivian and northern German Neolithic sequence with the British early Neolithic is remarkable, despite the lack of shared material culture. An explanation is necessary and in both supra-regions this could well be due to processes in continental Europe.

If we cannot accurately pin down cause or causes, can we reflect further on the structure of this possible migration, as Anthony recommends (1990, 899)? There is no specific evidence so far for contact between the continent and late Mesolithic communities in south-east England, unlike the situation in the Dutch estuaries or the Ertebølle culture. One possibility would then be to regard the earliest Neolithic activity in south-east England as defined in this volume as just such a phase, as far back as the later 41st century cal BC (Fig. 14.54: *start Thames estuary*; Fig. 14.57: *start SE Neolithic*; Table 15.1). Continuation of the migration stream could have followed in the 40th century cal BC (e.g. Fig. 14.54: *start Sussex Neolithic*), as further scouting and then settling established new areas of Neolithic activity in central-southern England (e.g. Fig. 14.54: *start Cotswold Neolithic*), in what Anthony calls 'chain migration' (1990, 903). Continuing contact with source area or areas could well be symbolised in the flow of jadeitite axes into Britain, as Sheridan has argued (2010), though their origin was far from the immediate continental hinterland over the Straits of Dover. Indeed, we could even contemplate whether the putative migration stream was maintained until the 38th century cal BC, bringing first the idea of building long barrows and cairns and in the end the idea and practice of constructing enclosures.

We need to keep firmly in view the particularities of

this archaeological situation, while being guided by general migration theory of the kind discussed above. Though we do not have specific evidence of continental-insular pre-Neolithic contact in southern Britain, we do know (or think we know) that there were fifth millennium cal BC late Mesolithic communities (e.g. Jacobi 1978; Holgate 2003; Cotton 2004). Putative newcomers did not come into an empty land. Though we do not know when the Chestnuts monument was built in the Medway valley close to Coldrum (J. Alexander 1961), it may be significant that this was in a place with evidence of late Mesolithic activity, as was also the case at the middens of Ascott-under-Wychwood and Hazleton (Benson and Whittle 2007; Saville 1990). Similarity in settlement location around the fens may also suggest continuation of indigenous knowledge (Edmonds *et al.* 1999). So we could in fact envisage fusion and integration from a very early stage, from which perspective the attempt to keep colonisation and acculturation apart as separate processes might be to miss the character of this transformation entirely. Pottery, leaf arrowheads, deep flint mining, rectangular houses, cereals and domesticated animals could all be listed as innovations from the outside (though substantial houses were rare on the continent at this time, as at Beaumont, Puy-de-Dôme, or closer, at the large ditched and palisaded enclosure of Mairy, Ardennes: Demoule *et al.* 2007b; Marolle 1998), but how to dwell in the landscape may have been another matter. Tim Ingold (2000, chapter 8) has contrasted two forms of identity, one genealogical, based on origins, and the other relational, based on practice involving other people and things; the latter has proved a useful perspective in discussion of eastern Scotland (Warren 2004, 91) and can be adopted here as well. And there are early features, such as the construction and use of the stone monument at Coldrum, which are not easily linked to pre-existing practice on the immediately adjacent continent; though recent salvage excavation at Beaurieux in the Aisne valley has revealed two graves holding individuals, one with stones enhancing a wooden coffin, within a narrow enclosure 15 m long, and one or two other similar examples are known in the Marne and Yonne (Colas *et al.* 2007; Demoule *et al.* 2007b, 73; Thevenet 2008). The Coldrum construction may best be seen as the product of local circumstance.

Long-distance migration theory predicts continuing migration streams, as explored above. Sheridan has proposed small incoming communities (2010; Pailler and Sheridan 2009). Could we be dealing in fact with a very small-scale situation? What has not been brought into account so far is timescale. Where it has been possible to model the chronologies of selected long barrows and especially causewayed enclosures with some precision those often prove to be very short-lived: the product of specific generations. Could this also not be the case with the start of the Neolithic in south-east England? In this perspective, a different view of the range, structure, cause or causes, continuing contact, artefactual variability and continuing effects potentially involved (cf. Anthony 1990) would result. A small founder pool, operating say over only one or two generations, making a planned Channel crossing over its narrowest point and into the Greater Thames estuary, following from initial scouting, would be enough to initiate changes; motivation could be sought in the general conditions of change on the continent, but perhaps becomes a less central issue. A small-scale initial process, perhaps a rather low-key event in the grander continental scheme of things, would have allowed fusion and integration with indigenous population, which might otherwise be expected to have remained archaeologically visible in southern Britain into the early part of the fourth millennium cal BC.

The next steps

Over the following generations, the next steps were perhaps a further combination of 'chain migration' (Anthony 1990, 903) and acculturation as Neolithic things and practices spread gradually into south-central England, probably by the latter part of the 40th century cal BC (Fig. 14.58: *start S central Neolithic*), and then into south-west Britain by the second half of the 39th century cal BC (Fig. 14.58: *start SW Neolithic*; Table 15.1). This general spatio-temporal trend of Neolithic things and practices spreading westwards across southern Britain (Fig. 14.58), may mask a more nuanced, multi-focal story (Fig. 14.54), which unfortunately cannot be reliably revealed by the quality and quantity of our current data. Ascott-under-Wychwood and Hazleton have already been cited as places where early Neolithic middens were accumulated at spots in the landscape in which there had been Mesolithic activity, though we do not need to claim direct continuity; the Fir Tree Field shaft is another location with a similar succession. The construction of the Post and Sweet Tracks in the Somerset Levels in the very late 39th century cal BC, in an area of previous vegetational disturbance, could be another. Situations like these may suggest continued use of familiar, remembered places by an indigenous population. There is comparatively little sign of preceding Mesolithic activity on sites occupied in the early fourth millennium cal BC in the upper and middle Thames valley, though use of tree-throw holes, small pits, some middens and occupation spreads can be cited, as well as a large rectangular timber house at Yarnton (Hey and Barclay 2007). At Raunds in the Nene valley, the long mound was built at a confluence repeatedly visited during the Mesolithic, probably into the fifth millennium cal BC (Harding and Healy 2007, 47), and there is other Mesolithic activity in the wider area (Harding and Healy 2007, 47–8). There is evidence for Mesolithic activity on the southern chalk downland as a whole (Lawson 2007), but often at quite low densities, for example in north Wiltshire (McFadyen 2006, 131–4), and it has been suggested that Neolithic activity represents an infill of this kind of region (Whittle 1990b). A very different history, exemplified in the Fir Tree Field Shaft, may have been played out in Cranborne Chase to the south, with its numerous and abundant flint scatters spanning the whole of the Mesolithic (M. Green 2000, 20–8).

A postulated spread of Neolithic practices from the south-east would predict a slightly longer survival of late Mesolithic communities in both western and northern Britain. In the present state of evidence, this is hard to evaluate rigorously, and has anyway been beyond the remit of this project. There appears to be some preliminary support for this possibility in the radiocarbon dates for late Mesolithic activity at March Hill, Yorkshire, associated with rod microliths (Spikins 1999; 2002), and at South Haw, Yorkshire, with similar associations as well as with scalene triangles (Chatterton 2007). The evidence reviewed in Chapter 11 for the Gwent Levels in south-east Wales might also be compatible with a very early fourth millennium cal BC date for late Mesolithic activity, but so far inconclusively so. But clearly, many more such studies are needed.

Neolithic activity in south Wales and the Marches probably began in the generations around 3700 cal BC (Fig. 11.10: *start S Wales & Marches*), though the broader estimate for south-west Britain as a whole is closer to the generations around 3800 cal BC (Fig. 14.59: *start SW Neolithic*; Table 15.1). The two scales are revealing. On the one hand, the estimate for south Wales alone, based on fewer data, reminds us of the probable lag between initial events in the Greater Thames estuary and final establishment to the west. On the other hand, the broader-scale estimate for the time when the first Neolithic practices appeared in south-west Britain is comparable with those for the Isle of Man, Ireland (apart from Magheraboy in our preferred model 3) and southern and north-eastern Scotland (Figs 14.176–7, Table 15.1).

The closeness of these five date estimates is striking. It is legitimate to see them as connected (Fig. 15.8). They take our story on from a simple date estimate for the start of the Neolithic in south-west Britain. At the same kind of date, probably in the later 39th century cal BC, over the span of a few generations – perhaps of a single human lifetime – Neolithic things and practices were being established in south-west Britain, in north-eastern Scotland, and in southern Scotland. Perhaps a decade or two later, in the earlier 38th century cal BC, they appear in Ireland (model 3). Probably in this century they also appear in the Isle of Man (although the imprecision of our date estimate here reflects the particular paucity of data from the island). If our regional date estimate for the start of these practices in the south Wales and the Marches is reliable (and it is a small region with a consequently limited dataset), then the first Neolithic may have appeared here two or three generations later than elsewhere. After what appears to be a rather slow, perhaps piecemeal, spread across southern Britain, from the south-east, there is a significant gear-shift in the tempo of change: an impressive acceleration. As with all our estimates for the start of the Neolithic, we could wish for more radiocarbon dates on appropriate samples from individual sites, perhaps especially for Ireland, but the estimates for Scotland are based on a number of impressive recent projects, and should be reliable. What we have not been able to bring into account, being beyond the remit of the project, are estimates for the start of Neolithic activity in the Midlands, the north of England and north Wales, but preliminary modelling of newly available data, such as from the Milfield basin in north-east England (Johnson and Waddington 2008; Passmore and Waddington forthcoming), suggests provisionally that the same kind of date ranges will emerge (Griffiths forthcoming).

What kind of process applies at this point, and why now? Whereas the beginnings could have been the outcome of small-scale movements of newcomers from the continent and ensuing fusion with indigenous people, followed by a gradual spread across southern Britain, this marked acceleration from the later 39th century cal BC seems to demand a different explanation. Various possibilities present themselves. Given the areas involved, the apparent rate of spread increases significantly. Demographic expansion, spreading outwards by some kind of wave of advance, seems too simple, since the settlement record nowhere suggests an over-crowded landscape, and unrealistic, since the rates of demographic increase would have to have been unfeasibly high, as noted also for central and western Europe (Robb and Miracle 2007, 111). Perhaps some kind of critical mass, however, could have been achieved. Further filtered colonisation, including by boat, up and around the coasts of England and Scotland, is another possibility, and could have reflected ongoing social and other changes to the south. The early construction of long barrows/rectilinear mortuary enclosures in Scotland is a striking development compared with existing indigenous practice, and one that seems to have appeared early and rapidly in both southern and north-east Scotland (with examples from Eweford and Pencraig Hill in East Lothian, and Forest Road, Kintore, Aberdeenshire). Their existence marks a sharp break in regional terms, and one way to see these is to refer them to emerging monument traditions further south, to which we will return below.

Another interpretation, however, is of change now being accepted by indigenous communities and spreading rapidly through existing social networks. Perhaps again, both processes were at work, with chain migration, local acculturation, and continued contact with source areas (in this case now in southern Britain, as well as on the continent) all contributing to the situation. Perhaps the now local proximity of new worldviews and beliefs led to the acceleration in their uptake. And again, process or processes need not have been uniform everywhere. In eastern Scotland, for example, detailed study of the lithic industries of the fifth and fourth millennia suggests marked difference between late Mesolithic and early Neolithic traditions, in terms not only of forms, but also of production techniques and raw materials; moreover, many more early Neolithic sites have been found than late Mesolithic ones (Warren 2001; 2004; 2005). So it is far from clear here that any overall argument for direct continuity could plausibly be defended. Similar difficulties apply in Ireland, when late Mesolithic and early Neolithic lithic traditions are compared (Cooney 2007a). On the other hand, we can bear in mind the observation of far-reaching cultural realignments, as in the case of the Chasséen and Michelsberg cultures (Demoule *et al.* 2007b, 64), even where there is no need to evoke new population from the outside.

When comparisons of this kind are made, in terms of lithic traditions and overall settlement distribution, it is normally the case that generalised blocks of time are contrasted one with the other: an overall sense of the late Mesolithic versus a unified model of the early Neolithic. What is actually normally being compared is the outcome of centuries of early Neolithic activity, rather than the specifics of altering situations in, say, the 39th century cal BC or the 38th century cal BC. One intriguing example concerns the development of Carinated Bowl traditions in north-east Scotland. One view has been that the sequence begins with a traditional Carinated Bowl style, to be followed quite shortly by the variants of the North-East Carinated Bowl and modified Carinated Bowl styles (summarised by Sheridan 2007a). Our models suggest variation from the outset (Fig. 14.165). How does this view fit the possible processes mooted? Does it promote an idea of separate streams of migration? This seems unnecessarily complicated, from the general perspective offered above (Anthony 1990). Or would it not suit better a scenario in which existing regional identities were maintained, and transferred – quite subtly, given the muted differences between these styles – into the new medium of pottery? It is worth remembering the proximity of Balbridie and Crathes: on either side of the river Dee, the former with North-East Carinated and the latter with traditional Carinated Bowl pottery. Could there also be a similar story behind the different pottery in south-west England?

So, as far as possible in the present state of analysis, we need to try to track specific trajectories of change. Two further examples illustrate the possibilities. Beyond the area of our analysis in Chapter 14, it has been suggested that the continuation of late Mesolithic communities can be detected on smaller islands further offshore like Oronsay into the earlier fourth millennium cal BC, at a time when Neolithic activity was being established on the innermost islands, like Islay, and on the western mainland coast (Mithen *et al.* 2007, 518). Precise chronologies for these, potentially contemporary as well as adjacent, activities have the potential to shed further light on the dynamics of the transition. Secondly, and directly modelled in this project, there is the date of timber halls and houses. In southern and north-east Scotland, the large timber halls do not appear to belong to the first generations of the Neolithic, but rather to those of the children and grandchildren of the pioneers (Fig. 14.175). These substantial structures are probably not numerous, though more may well remain to be detected (Brophy 2007), and the use-lives of Balbridie, Crathes and Claish were relatively short (Fig. 14.173); all three were burned down, possibly deliberately (Brophy 2007). So here there is dramatic new practice, which occurs from place to place within southern and north-east Scotland, as new practices were becoming established. Was this a new idea brought by incomers, who did not have the resources to build until their economic base had been established? Or was it an innovation adopted by local people from what they had heard of (and possibly seen) through social networks extending southwards? Perhaps it will remain impossible to separate these possibilities, and the enduring significance of these buildings could have been to bring sizeable numbers of people together, perhaps of varying descent, for construction (cf. Startin 1978), use and perhaps also the spectacle of their death by fire (cf. Tringham 2005). But this practice only belonged to a restricted horizon, and cannot be used to generalise conditions in the early Neolithic as a whole in Scotland south of the Great Glen. It may evoke either acts of display by incomer communities, or a means of integration for people of varying history and descent. We cannot exclude either possibility in the current state of understanding, and it is possible that such enterprises in this kind of context could have had ambiguous meanings. One study of the construction of a ceremonial longhouse in lowland Papua New Guinea showed how the structure, built to repair an alliance, was conceived of differently by the two groups in question: outwardly a place of reconciliation for the builders, but a potentially hostile and threatening setting, given materials evoking dangerous substances, in the eyes of the others (Strathern and Stewart 1999).

Rectangular timber houses in Ireland were also built and used within a restricted timeframe (Fig. 15.9). These were in use, depending on our preferred interpretation, for either a century or so, or less than a century, from the late 38th century cal BC into the 37th century cal BC (Figs 12.22–7 and 12.28–9). In model 3, they belong a little after first beginnings, whereas in model 2 they follow closely on the start of the Neolithic in Ireland, more in line with the probable situation in Scotland. Models 2 and 3 cannot both be right, and given our inclination to favour model 3, the implications for the discussion here could be, first, that the process of first Neolithic beginnings in Ireland took a few generations, and secondly, that we cannot use evidence from the 37th century cal BC to infer conditions in the century or so before.

So we have offered a scenario and variants which we believe best fit the emerging chronology for the timing and successive appearance of the Neolithic over much of Britain and Ireland, beginning in south-east England probably in the 41st century cal BC, particularly the Greater Thames estuary, then spreading gradually, possibly piecemeal, into south-central England by the 40th century cal BC, and expanding thence much more rapidly, from the 39th century cal BC into the 38th century cal BC, into south-west Britain, Scotland south of the Great Glen, Ireland and the Isle of Man (Fig. 14.176). The appearance of Neolithic things and practices in the Midlands and northern England may belong to this period (Griffiths forthcoming), while in south Wales and the Marches these innovations may have appeared as late as the last decades of the 38th century or first decades of the 37th century cal BC (Fig. 14.54). Given the location of initial changes, and the range of material and other transformations, we think that this process was probably initiated by small, possibly fragmented or filtered groups from the adjacent continent, but it also seems very likely that indigenous communities were drawn into the process of change very soon, and perhaps even more or less from the outset. We could envisage indigenous people being attracted to the novelties, among others, of domesticated animals and fine artefacts, and thus rapidly drawn into the adoption of Neolithic things and practices; and the very momentum of new lifeways and beliefs in general, with their links to a wider world, could have attracted indigenous people to adopt the ways of incomers, now present in the same land. The pace of change appears to accelerate in the later 39th century cal BC, which may evoke a different combination of factors, perhaps involving principally a greater participation by indigenous communities in the areas around the regions of primary change. Taken at face value, it is hard to accommodate the very early dating of Magheraboy in this kind of scenario, and in terms of the colonisation theory reviewed above this would have been a very unusual, high-risk, and extremely long-distance migration. With the 'forcing' described and discussed in Chapter 14, however, it is perhaps possible – just – to accommodate the current dating of this site in the kind of narrative just offered. For the present, in the expectation of further dating of Magheraboy and other sites in Ireland, we shall have to leave this as a loose end, and perhaps also as a reminder that the story need not be single-stranded, as Alison Sheridan in particular has argued many times.

Alternative explanations

What then of the arguments for indigenous acculturation, set out in their purest form by Julian Thomas (1999; 2003; 2004a; 2004b; 2007a; 2008)? We have tried to accommodate perhaps his most fundamental point, that it is hard to find correspondence between material assemblages in Britain and plausible single source areas on the continent, with the model discussed above of initial, small-scale colonisation from a restricted source area. Further, with a longer and much more differentiated timescale now for change within the first centuries of the Neolithic in Britain and Ireland, diversity in monument traditions for example can much more easily be referred to development within the offshore islands, rather than to an eclectic and heterogeneous range of sources right across north-west Europe. We agree with his view, *contra* that of Sheridan, that there was probably more contact between late Mesolithic communities in southern Britain and Neolithic communities on the adjacent continent in the fifth millennium cal BC than currently meets the eye, but this is not for us the smoking gun that it represents for both Thomas and Sheridan, given the evidence from central and western Europe in the sixth and fifth millennia for the rather variable effects of proven contact between farmers and hunter-gatherers. We have also accommodated the case for the contribution of indigenous population to the whole process, but now in a much more specific set of scenarios.[7]

Over the past decade, the acculturation hypothesis has begun to look insufficiently supported by precise chronology, relying in latter statements on an assertion of rapid initial change followed by subsequent slow development. Neither part of that claim is now consistent with the patterns revealed in Chapter 14, and we go on below further to explore the pace of change in later centuries, especially in the 38th and 37th centuries cal BC. And the acculturation hypothesis has not so far adequately specified why change should have been initiated when it was – according to our models now, from the 41st century cal BC. Could we, however, not now run the sequence again, as it were, with the acculturation hypothesis as the dominant explanation of changes? Would this look more convincing if supported by a more precise timescale?

One way in might be by resort to the wider picture of continental change. Julian Thomas (1996) has proposed a gradual process of 'mesolithisation' of the primary Neolithic in central and western Europe, whereby elements of both an indigenous worldview and indigenous practice, including residential mobility and use of wild resources, would have been absorbed by primary Neolithic communities, resulting in the rather different character of post-Danubian cultures. A similar idea had already been proposed by continental archaeologists before radiocarbon dating was widely practised (e.g. Sangmeister 1960). This seems too simple. It reduces considerable diversity to a single idea. In particular, it is hard to show any clear or single trend to increased use of wild resources in the TRB-Michelsberg-Chasséen orbit. There was perhaps an earlier fifth millennium emphasis on wild animals in certain contexts, particularly mortuary ones (Sidéra 2000; 2003), and in probably mid-fifth millennium late Lengyel trapezoidal longhouse contexts in central Poland, at sites like Brześć Kujawski and Osłonki (Bogucki 2000), a very broad spectrum of resources were used. But cattle are dominant in the succeeding horizon further south in Poland at Bronocice (Pipes *et al.* 2009), and variously cattle and pig in northern French contexts of the later fifth and earlier fourth millennia (Arbogast 1994; 1998; Arbogast *et al.* 1991; Tresset 2000; 2003; 2005a; Tresset and Vigne 2006; 2007). The Alpine foreland trend is towards increased use of domesticates by the middle to later fourth millennium BC, after complex and shifting mixes of wild and tame in the faunal assemblages of the late fifth and earlier fourth millennia BC (e.g. Schibler *et al.* 1997a; 1997b; Ebersbach 2002). Changes in residential patterns are another matter. Certainly the end of the longhouse is a striking development, but on the one hand the longhouse system probably involved complex individual movements at varying scales (summarised in Whittle 2009), and on the other it is not clear at all that the later fifth millennium pattern of generally dispersed settlement, with large structures little visible archaeologically, combined with enclosures and other monuments as some kind of centralising or integrating place, should be referred to residentially mobile hunter-gatherers.

A different kind of shift and sequence could be proposed. This would involve a notion of social networks or some kind of communication and mutual awareness among later Mesolithic communities in Europe. There is now a discernible sequence in the transformations around the primary Neolithic of western and central Europe, region by region, and all, it could be argued, with substantial or dominant indigenous involvement. Things began to shift first in the Dutch estuaries, as described above, from around 5000 cal BC. The start of the Neolithic in Brittany began perhaps by the middle of the fifth millennium cal BC. The Neolithic sequence in the Alpine foreland begins around 4300 BC (Menotti 2004). Change in the Dutch estuaries was much more established by around 4000 cal BC, and came to the north European plain perhaps a little earlier, and about the same time to southern Scandinavia (Hartz *et al.* 2007; Larsson 2007; Müller 2009). Could there be a kind of domino effect in this sequence? There is no reason to suppose direct connection between the Dutch estuaries and Brittany. The Alpine foreland may seem remote and detached, though shells from the Atlantic coast are known in early fourth millennium BC contexts (Dieckmann *et al.* 1997), and the movement of Alpine jadeitite axes from the fifth millennium onwards also speaks for the possibility of long-range contact. There is much more reason to see a nexus of interaction from the Baltic to the Dutch estuaries, though the Swifterbant culture need not be seen simply as an offshoot of the Ertebølle culture. The convergence of transitions in the late fifth millennium cal BC, from the Rhine-Meuse estuary, if not also the Scheldt, round to the southern Baltic, would be one way to explain the indigenous initiation of new practice in south-east England in the 41st century cal BC. An alternative approach would be to accept the role of indigenous late Mesolithic communities on the northern European plain and in southern Scandinavia as the basis for further developments, but nonetheless to argue that agrarian societies to the south – the Michelsberg and late Lengyel phenomena – enhanced the clear cultural pressure on changing northern practices, and that the arrival of ideas through networks and individuals brought an end to Mesolithic lifestyle, both in Britain and southern Scandinavia.

So an argument can be constructed for convergence in the timings of 'going over'. This need not imply that the motivations for transformation were the same everywhere. Larsson (2007) has mooted the possibility for southern Scandinavia of a change in perception, conditioned by shifting environmental and physical conditions, such as sea level alterations and elm disease. But social relations could have been substantially different in these two regions. In southern Scandinavia there is convincing evidence from the Ertebølle culture for 'a social structure on par with the Neolithic societies to the south. They were incorporated in a widespread interregional network, with the exchange of exotic objects as symbols of social prestige within ranked societies' (Larsson 2007, 601). Indeed, Anders Fischer among others (2002; cf. Jennbert 1984) has proposed a model of late Ertebølle emulation and competition, with the supply of imported exotics making it harder and harder to 'obtain material symbols of power in the form of portable objects alone. Socially ambitious groups became engaged in the new economies, driven in significant part by social and ceremonial feasting' (Larsson 2007, 601). In southern Britain, however, the evidence is very different. Nothing in the late Mesolithic archaeology of lowland Britain, including in south-east England in particular (e.g. Cotton 2004; Cotton and Field 2004; Holgate 2003; Champion 2007), really suggests the kind of situation found on the shores of the Baltic, although all of the surviving sites here would have been inland (Shennan and Horton 2002) so that it remains theoretically possible that coastal occupation might have taken a form closer to the Baltic one. But instead, one might model residentially mobile, undifferentiated and small-scale communities. It could be tempting from such evidence for the late Mesolithic in southern Britain to think in terms of the values and worldview proposed for hunter-gatherers by Alan Barnard (2007; cf. Helms 2007, 488), in which sharing, deference to the will of the community, universal kin classification, primordial possession of the sacrosanct land, and harmonious natural equality were prominent – though there are obvious dangers in using such a scale of generalisation. Indeed, Julian Thomas (2007a, 431) has suggested that:

> Most hunter-gatherers consider that the landscape embodies vital forces and energies, which flow through patterns of reciprocity that link humans, animals, supernatural beings and places. Rather than a hostile environment, the landscape is one that provides for humans, within which animals are a kind of person who give up their flesh and energy, provided that they are treated with respect.

But such potential differences might be a more serious objection to the hypothesis of acculturation on its own than the perceived lack of contact with the continent. What overcomes the strength of this attitude in the adoption of, say, domesticated cattle?

Another difficulty from the perspective now of better timings is the claim for rapid initial change followed by gradual development (J. Thomas 2008). But could the acculturation hypothesis be adjusted to the different chronology of change which we now propose? In this view, things would begin in south-east England simply because that was the area closest to the continent. A process of substitution would ensue, with cattle favoured over deer, for example, and the novelty of cereals over traditional wild plants (J. Thomas 2004a; 2008, 67). Patterns of residence could have remained fluid and complex, with novel house structures embedded in seasonal, annual and lifetime cycles of movement through the landscape. Material culture changes, particularly the adoption of Carinated Bowl pottery and leaf arrowheads, would represent a 'new material language', 'a new 'technology of meaning'...clearly connected with memory, in that they brought clusters of associations and connotations to bear on social situations' (J. Thomas 1998, 154). Pottery would be to do primarily with the production, serving and storage of food (J. Thomas 1998, 154), though we could add the claim that carinated vessels do not work well for cooking (Starnini 2008). Thomas has further argued (1998, 154–5) that there is 'no indication that a single fixed or unified code of meaning underlay this repertoire, or that any one artefact had a single cultural signification stamped upon it', preferring a sense of meanings produced in 'rather localized and contingent ways' (J. Thomas 1998, 155). This last point is problematic. The pure acculturation hypothesis might work best if it were argued that the adoption of new material forms such as Carinated Bowl pottery and leaf arrowheads stood for relation to a wider sense of belonging, a new set of connections, reformulated as the wider world had changed. It therefore seems rather contradictory to insist to such a degree on 'localized and contingent' contexts, and pit depositions from the south of England to the north-east of Scotland, for example, seem to have much more in common than otherwise. Nonetheless, the pure acculturation hypothesis might proceed with a kind of rolling spread of new practice, accelerating according to the timetable proposed by this project from the 39th century cal BC. But in this case, would we not see more local divergence in the things and practices adopted?

Given how much remains to be understood, not only through further and better dating but also by more isotopic analysis, especially for provenance studies, and by genetic investigations, it is unwise to be dogmatic. We have not excluded acculturation from our preferred interpretations, but it now seems special pleading to rely on acculturation entirely. In some senses, the actual 'whodunnit' (Halstead 1996, 299) of the Mesolithic-Neolithic transition in Britain and Ireland may be less important than the sense of the scale and tempo of subsequent changes. Sheridan's various strands of migration do not cover this next stage, and Thomas has relied on a notion of gradual change. So we go on now to reflect on the implications of our proposed timetable for better understanding of what came between the Mesolithic-Neolithic transitions and the emergence of causewayed enclosures in southern Britain in the late 38th century cal BC. Neolithic things and practices having been got ashore, so to speak, and been distributed across Britain and Ireland, we will focus especially on three themes: settlement and subsistence, early monument building and use, and artefacts.

15.3 Land and living: faultlines and patterns

The categories of evidence for examining settlement and subsistence in the early Neolithic of Britain and Ireland are well known: houses and other timber structures; pits and various spreads and concentrations of occupation material; faunal and plant assemblages; suites of environmental data; more recently isotopic analyses; and so on (e.g. Darvill 1996c; Brophy 2007; Garrow *et al.* 2005; Smyth 2006; Schulting 2008). Probably most commentators would agree with the view of Tim Ingold (2000, chapter 8) that what is important in this situation is not tracking the descent of new practices but evaluating the style in which life was now lived: 'positions in the land are no more laid out in advance for persons to occupy, than are persons specified prior to taking them up. Rather, to inhabit the land is to draw it to a particular focus, and in so doing to *constitute* a place' (Ingold 2000, 149). This appears to have been accepted by supporters of both acculturation, prominently (e.g. J. Thomas 2007a, 430–5; 2008, 81), and colonisation, subtly (e.g. Warren 2004, 91, explicitly following Ingold). That said, there are familiar differences of opinion on specific features: between those who tend to see houses and other timber structures as the permanent residences of sedentary people and those who interpret the same features as the monumental constructions of people still in the process of transition, seeking to create places of assembly and new foci of emergent identity; between those who see pits as potentially the enduring residue of prolonged tenure of place and those who interpret them as marking the comings and goings of a population recurrently and to varying degrees on the move; and between those who see the presence of mixed farmers from the outset and those who claim much more gradual change.

These interpretive faultlines are no longer, by and large, absolute. Thus, as selected examples, Alison Sheridan (2010) has interpreted the large timber houses of lowland eastern Scotland as 'the communal residences of the first generation or two of settlers, built to offer security while their communities became established', constituting 'powerful statements of identity and presence in the landscape', and implying a 'significant degree of sedentism'; interestingly, however, she explicitly allows that other flimsier structures could suggest transhumance, with part of the community living in one place over the course of a year. For Kenny Brophy (2007, 89–90), the same large timber structures could better be seen as 'big houses', neither purely domestic nor isolated ritual structures, but central both physically and conceptually, with some but unproven possibilities of more temporary occupations round about them. Duncan Garrow (2010) has discussed the consequences of seeing pits and the depositions they contained, for example at Kilverstone in Norfolk, as the surviving, visible residues of much more permanent residence than often allowed, whereas Joshua Pollard has talked in terms of 'little sense of such rigid long-term commitment to place *through settlement*', suggesting timescales of perhaps only a few years, and periodic aggregations, often on a small scale, rather than 'long-term settlement' (1999c, 82, 85–8). In contrast to those who have argued for gradual, small-scale and perhaps largely symbolic adoption of cereal cultivation in the early Neolithic (e.g. Fairbairn 1999a), Amy Bogaard and Glynis Jones (2007) have found, on the basis of quantified analysis of both cereal and associated weed remains, no difference in the likely scale of cultivation between the LBK and the early Neolithic in Britain. And debate still continues on the implications of isotopic dietary analysis. Much of this argument has focused on the claimed shift from marine to terrestrial signatures between late Mesolithic and early Neolithic (more recently Milner *et al.* 2004; Richards and Schulting 2006; J. Thomas 2007a; Schulting 2008), but it is helpful to remember that Michael Richards, who has been prominent among those arguing for rapidly introduced dietary shift at the start of the Neolithic, has allowed some diversity of diet, proposed patterned variation between the mortuary populations of long barrows and causewayed enclosures respectively (M. Richards 2000), and suggested a possibly reduced role for plant products in general (M. Richards 2004, 89). For Ireland, Gabriel Cooney (2007a, 557) has allowed a 'variety of subsistence approaches'.

What has not been prominent in these varying debates is the question of timescales. This is not to claim that these are absent altogether, as seen above in the interpretations of both houses and diet. But there has been a general tendency, shared by most shades of opinion, to present a static sense of the first centuries of Neolithic in Britain and Ireland. One recent, rare exception explicitly cites and explores the period 3850–3650 cal BC in Dorset (Harris 2009). This section therefore has two aims: to draw attention to possible chronological patterns, trying to think above all of the context in which and from which causewayed enclosures emerged at the end of the 38th century cal BC, and in the light of possible trends, to offer some suggestions about the scale of activity in the landscape and the nature of production. Given the range of other changes seen as accelerating from the 38th into the 37th century cal BC (Figs 14.143 and 14.182), what does the evidence for land and living offer our understanding of the wider context? We will propose that it is so far difficult to find the same sense of continuing change in the domain of settlement as seen in other spheres, once Neolithic things and practices had been adopted, and this is ultimately very important in characterising the nature of the social dynamic in these first centuries. To some extent therefore we echo the emphasis by Julian Thomas (2008) on a contrast between the relatively rapid adoption of Neolithic ways and subsequent slower development. Whether this is the same in matters of production is less clear, however, and there may be some important hints of changes.

The models presented in Chapter 14 strongly suggest that most rectangular timber structures belonged to early stages of their regional sequences and were of comparatively short duration (Fig. 14.179). Neither timings nor durations were identical. Thus the structure at White Horse Stone began significantly earlier than the lowland Scottish halls, and those in turn began to be used earlier than the rectangular houses in Ireland, which flourished from the later 38th into the 37th century cal BC (Fig. 14.180). Gabriel Cooney (2007a, 557) has cautioned against seeing those 'just in terms of a complementary distribution with enclosures', though the parallel timings are certainly now very striking. Though the structure at White Horse Stone may have endured for several hundreds of years (Chapter 7.6), currently this appears exceptional as the dating evidence as a whole suggests relatively brief durations, impressively so in Ireland (Figs 12.22–8, 14.180). What we do not appear to be seeing is the persistence, by and large, of the practice of building rectangular timber structures, both large and small, right through the first centuries of the early Neolithic. Much of the effort involved in their construction may have been concentrated in the first generations of new styles of inhabitation of the land – land taking perhaps in some areas, or enhancement of existing practice in others.

The clues to changes through time in how people lived on the land are frustratingly scattered. On present evidence, the scale of things going on in the landscape was probably quite small in the period before the late 38th century cal BC. Even the 20m-long timber halls could have been put up by quite small workforces, or short-term aggregations if more hands were required. The setting out of the Sweet Track could also have been accomplished by a small number of people (Coles and Orme 1984a; 1984b). Generalising from the evidence presented in more detail in the regional chapters, there appear to be no large occupations before the late 38th century cal BC. Examples with reasonably secure dating from southern Britain include the structures at White Horse Stone and Yarnton, probably that at Penhale Round, the deposits in Area 6 at Eton, and the middens at both Ascott-under-Wychwood and Hazleton. Generalising in even more risky fashion, there is no compelling reason, as seemingly supported in recent, thorough regional reviews (e.g. Cotton and Field 2004; Hey and Barclay 2007; Lawson 2007), to see any great packing or density of occupation in the landscape, even at a local scale.

It is possible that occupation sites become more visible, and in some instances larger, over a longer timescale, probably from the 37th century cal BC onwards. It is striking in eastern England, for example, how the majority of the various eastern English pit sites discussed in Chapter 6 are associated with Mildenhall Ware, and with dates so far, as in limited fashion for Kilverstone, probably from the end of the 38th century cal BC onwards (Fig. 14.93: *start Decorated SE*). The Stumble and Runnymede may follow the same pattern, and in the upper Thames, the pit sites of Benson and South Stoke and the continuing use of Yarnton. It is not easy neatly to divide all the evidence in this way. Tregarrick in the south-west is a case in point, being probably early in the regional sequence but not certainly earlier than the enclosures of the south-west (Fig. 10.30). Perhaps the evidence so far is simply too scattered, but the issue of scale remains important. With the exceptions in East Anglia of pit sites like Kilverstone, Hurst Fen, Spong Hill, East Rudham, Eaton Heath and Broome Heath, there are still no convincingly large sites, and as far as those are concerned, the case for repeated, small-scale occupations – or even very short-term, social aggregations – is a strong one, spelled out particularly for Kilverstone (Garrow *et al.* 2005). There are some places in the landscape where significant concentrations of early Neolithic lithics were deposited, as at the possibly task-specific site of Honey Hill, Ramsey, Cambridgeshire (Edmonds *et al.* 1999). By and large, however, surface lithics of the period tend to be out-numbered, even swamped, by massive spreads of later material, as in the areas of Stonehenge (J. Richards 1990, 265–6, 271) and Avebury (Whittle *et al.* 2000, 148–51), and are often more circumscribed, as in the Maiden Castle area (R. Smith *et al.* 1997, 295–8).

So as a generalisation, we could propose that the appearance of causewayed and related enclosures in southern Britain does not correlate with any obvious increase in the numbers, size or density of dated occupation sites. As a working hypothesis, therefore, we could also propose that the social dynamic of change did not reside principally in the styles of residence on the land. But what of other aspects of inhabitation and tenure?

We have included cereals and domesticated animals among our criteria for the presence of Neolithic things and practices, but there is still much that we do not know. There have been long-running and still unresolved debates about the overall range and balance of subsistence resources used in the early Neolithic. One view has been that despite rapid initial changes, a mix of wild and domesticated resources was still in use for considerable periods of time, with cattle pre-eminent, reduced consumption of marine resources (if not some kind of taboo on them), and some cereal cultivation (J. Thomas 2008, 70–4); 'Early Neolithic diets will have been diverse, with particular persons, kin groups or communities having access to varied combinations of domesticated and wild resources according to location, time of year, social status and positions in networks of exchange and alliance' (J. Thomas 2008, 72).

A more general survey of early Neolithic 'foodways' (Schulting 2008) has noted plenty of hazelnuts, substantial amounts of charred grain, including emmer, einkorn, barley and bread wheat, and among the animals, numerous cattle alongside fewer sheep/goats and pigs, with wild game scarcer; even in the Coneybury Anomaly, where game is present, cattle provided far more meat than roe deer. In this view, at least some of the community would have been restricted in their mobility by the demands of cereal cultivation, and to some extent pig keeping; some animal-related transhumance may be implied in northern England and Scotland, and periodic concentrations of cattle are evidenced by the dung beetles and high phosphate levels at Etton (see Chapter 6) (Schulting 2008, 97). The Céide Fields in western Ireland (see Chapter 12) 'provide some sense of the potential scale of animal keeping', and isotopic analysis on probably slightly later material from the Orkneys may suggest close control of sheep, in the evidence for seaweed foddering of pregnant ewes in the run-up to lambing (Schulting 2008, 98; Balasse *et al.* 2005). Cattle could have been used for ploughing, other forms of traction, and as pack animals, and could have been the object of raiding (Schulting 2008, 99, 111). Lipid analysis has shown the widespread presence of dairy products (Copley *et al.* 2005; Copley and Evershed 2007).

Slight differences in isotopic data and caries rates from a series of sites in southern Britain allow 'local variations on a theme' (Schulting 2008, 96), to that extent agreeing with the otherwise rather different interpretation of Julian Thomas. Isotopic analysis has indicated a 'comprehensive shift' away from marine resources, at least in coastal areas (Schulting 2008, 95; cf. Schulting and Richards 2002a; 2002b; M. Richards *et al.* 2003), though questions of representativeness have been raised (Milner *et al.* 2004; cf. Richards and Schulting 2006). Perhaps what is minimally indicated is the end of the specialisation seen in some late Mesolithic diets (R. Hedges 2004). Isotopic analysis has also indicated variability between sites in southern Britain, such as the people buried in the long barrows at Parc le Breos Cwm, Hazleton, West Kennet, Hambledon Hill and Ascott-under-Wychwood (M. Richards 2000; R. Hedges *et al.* 2007b; 2008). The most notable variation in nitrogen isotope values has been seen at Hambledon Hill causewayed enclosure (M. Richards 2000; 2008), consistent with its likely role as a place of assembly of people potentially from far and wide, though the values reported from other enclosures in Chapter 13, admittedly on the basis of rather small samples, may hint at a more uniform picture. These values in general indicate a potentially high portion – at least 60% and sometimes as much as 80% – of the human dietary protein coming from animals, as meat and/or milk, assuming little or no intake of marine or freshwater fish (Hedges and Reynard 2007); this could translate into 'a meat intake of approximately 300g per person per day, or a milk intake of abut 3 litres, or a combination' (Hedges and Reynard 2007, 1248). However, there is much still to be understood about the relationships between faunal and human values in the trophic chain, and slight alterations in working assumptions serve to markedly reduce the contribution of human dietary protein from animals (potentially to 35–40%; Hedges and Reynard 2007, 1245–7). Even with the assumptions normally made, the contribution of cereal protein may be underrepresented, and 'a diet corresponding to the estimated high trophic level (75% of total protein from animal protein) may in fact be equivalent to 33% by weight of meat and 65% by weight of grain' (R. Hedges *et al.* 2008, 122). Glynis Jones has correspondingly pointed out that cereals may be consistently under-represented among charred plant remains (G. Jones 2000; Jones and Legge 2008).

Further isotopic work in the course this project (Julie Hamilton and Robert Hedges, Chapter 13) emphasises the extent to which variations in human stable isotope values are a product of variations in those of the animals which they ate (Fig. 13.1). In a small sample of sites, Windmill Hill stands out by the greater depletion of both animals and humans in both ^{13}C and ^{15}N, suggesting that, whatever the catchment of the enclosure, it was similar for bipeds and quadrupeds.

We can note in passing that few surveys of subsistence evidence at present incorporate the pollen story. This is mainly because there is a geographical disjunction between the varying sets of evidence: with enclosures and many of the relevant barrow sites in the south, in areas poor in pollen, and sites of pollen analysis in deeply stratified sequences often in the north and west, in areas of poorer bone preservation. The generalisation does not entirely hold true, as we have noted relevant pollen analyses on the edge of the Fens in East Anglia, the Thames estuary, the upper Thames valley and the Somerset Levels, but these are exceptions to a wider pattern of difference. Beyond this, there is a challenge now for palynologists to model *their* chronological frameworks more precisely (Blaauw and Christen 2005; Bronk Ramsey 2008), so that this evidence can be meaningfully related to our emerging archaeological narratives.

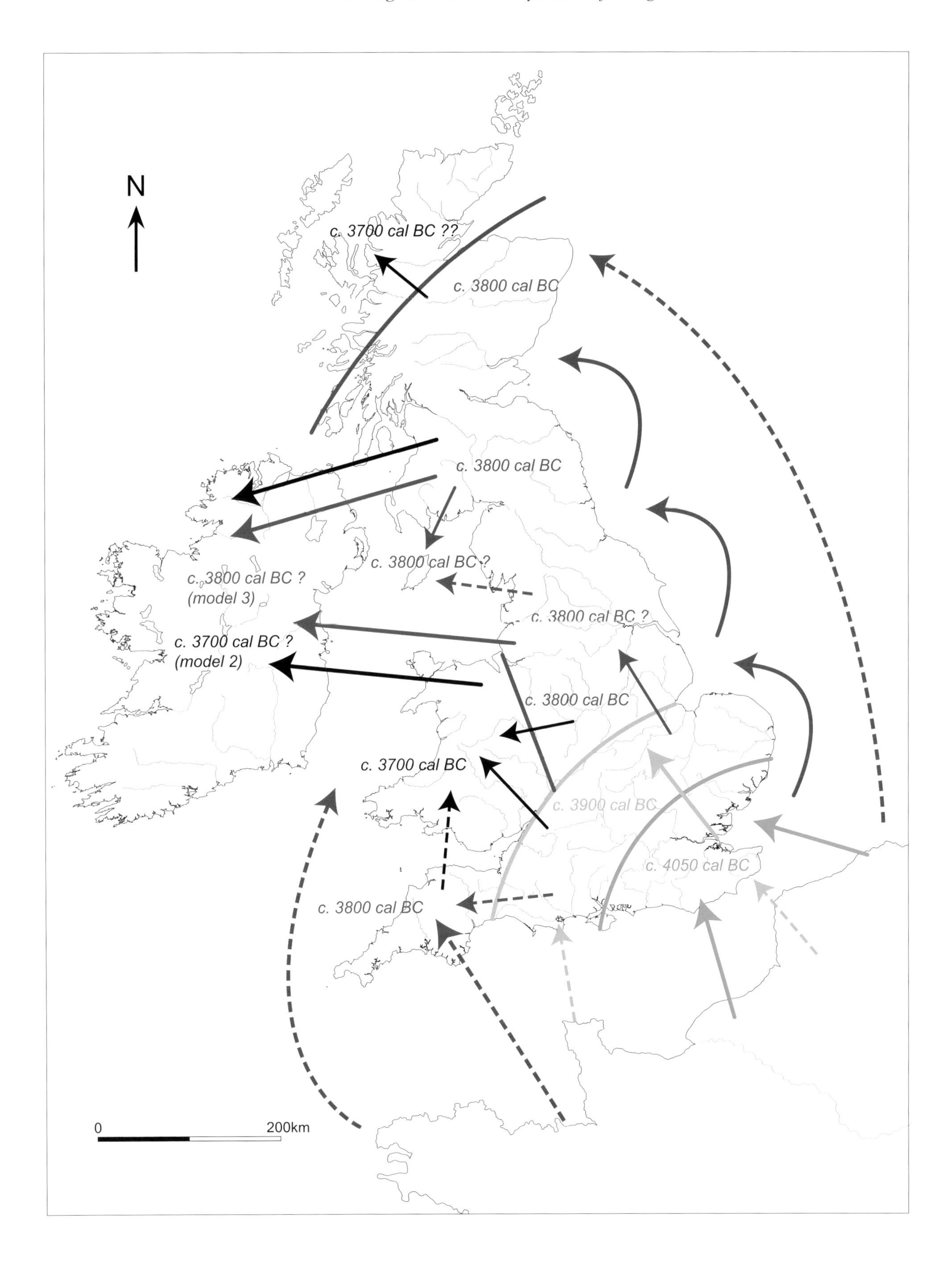

Fig. 15.8. Interpretive map of suggested dates, source areas and directions in the spread of Neolithic things and practices across Britain and Ireland. The colours denote contacts at different dates. Compare Fig. 14.176.

Fig. 15.9. House C at Monanny, Co. Monaghan, Ireland, under excavation, looking south-west. Photo: Irish Archaeological Consultancy Ltd.

What changes through time can we now detect? This is far from straightforward. The isotopic data from Ascott-under-Wychwood and Hazleton (R. Hedges *et al.* 2007b; 2008) come from individuals who probably lived during the 38th and 37th centuries cal BC (Bayliss *et al.* 2007c; Meadows *et al.* 2007). The values from the two sites, however, do not appear markedly different from the overall pattern already noted. Isotope values from Coldrum have yet to be published, but probably also conform to this pattern (Wysocki *et al.* in prep.). The occupation and midden underlying the long barrow at Ascott-under-Wychwood show the presence of domesticated animals in the 40th or 39th centuries cal BC, along with some wild game, including aurochs, red and roe deer and boar; among the domesticates. Although the sample size was small, cattle were roughly twice as numerous as pig, and sheep/goats were scarce, more or less matching the numbers of game (Mulville and Grigson 2007). Lipid analysis showed the presence of dairy fats, as well as products from ruminants and porcine animals (Copley and Evershed 2007). This single site appears to show an early establishment of patterns repeated in subsequent centuries, but given that the accumulation of the pre-barrow occupation and midden was not a single event (Bayliss *et al.* 2007c), it is hard yet again to get at the scale of things. Cereal cultivation could not definitely be shown here (without flotation), though there are cereals in the pre-cairn activity at Hazleton (Straker 1990), and they are attested at White Horse Stone (see Chapter 7.6).

Two sites which are potentially early, Coneybury Anomaly and Rowden (see Chapter 4.3–4), do hint at the scale of pre-enclosure consumption events. The contents of the Coneybury pit (Maltby 1990) have often been discussed for the presence of game, including roe and red deer, beaver and trout, but even here the much greater weight of beef compared with venison has recently been stressed (Legge 2008, 555). Some eight cattle appear to be represented (Maltby 1990), six in the subadult/young adult age range found predominantly at Hambledon Hill (Legge 2008, 555). Although it has been claimed that 'the bones from the Coneybury pit are evidently related to a brief and sumptuous slaughter event' (Legge 2008, 555), the temporality of deposition, as well as its timing, are not clear, since there was uneven body part representation and some of the pottery sherds appear weathered (Cleal 1990a). At Rowden, where there were also cereal remains, the most numerous bones came from pigs rather than cattle (Maltby 1991; Harris 2009, 116–17). Several animals may be represented, but it is possible that these accumulated over a period of time before deposition in a single event into the pit (Harris 2009, 117).

Many of the sites with isotopic data noted above belong to the 37th century cal BC or later. The settlement at Runnymede in the middle Thames is not demonstrably earlier (see Chapter 8.3). Here, cattle, predominantly young animals, were dominant over pigs and sheep by weight, game were scarce, and there were signs (from fragmentation, butchery patterns and burning) that cattle bone had been treated differently to that of smaller animals, suggesting their use principally for feasting rather than regular meals (Serjeantson 2006).

By definition now, evidence from causewayed enclosures belongs only from the late 38th century cal BC onwards. Anthony Legge (2008) has recently presented the animal bone evidence for Hambledon Hill, giving a picture of dominance by cattle. There was probably a non-resident cattle herd, from which mainly female cattle were culled, mostly subadult or young adult. Individual episodes of consumption, almost certainly involving animals taken alive to the site, can be identified in various contexts through many of the site phases, possibly involving some 100 beasts overall in the central area, and some 35–40 in the Stepleton complex, but probably only one or two animals in any one context, at least where most visible in the slots of the uppermost ditch fills of the central area. This presentation concentrates on consumption, played out in a series of events which periodically provided extravagant amounts of beef. It emphasises much less the nature of the live cattle herd, which might have in fact been constituted by any number of smaller herds at varying ranges from the site, and in which it can be inferred (*contra* Legge 2008, 544) that the possession of bulls was particularly important. So the general impression is of considerable concentrations of people in periodic assemblies (Legge 2008, 556), but the scale of cattle keeping out in the landscape remains much harder to quantify, given the substantial site timescale involved (see Chapter 4.1). Other patterns are also hard to read in terms of scale and intensity. Pigs were the second most numerous animals, slightly more frequent in the Stepleton enclosure, reinforcing other signs of its slightly different character (Mercer and Healy 2008, 326–37). Young sheep may have been culled in spring and autumn, though the sample was small (Legge 2008, 554), and sheep were generally culled across a wide rather than selective age range. Cereals may have arrived at the site in a semi-processed state, again implying its special character and periodic use (Legge 2008, 555; Jones and Legge 2008). The quantities were very substantial, suggesting a significant role for cultivated plant foods (Jones and Legge 2008, 476). Again, however, it is hard to quantify the scale of local or regional cultivation. If cleaned grain was being brought into the complex, its range is unknown. An exception to the import of cleaned grain is a massive emmer spikelet deposit from the Stepleton spur, which appears comparable to that from one of the Lismore Fields houses (Jones and Legge 2008, 474).

Further afield, there were cereal deposits at Balbridie, probably dating from the 38th and 37th centuries cal BC (Fig. 14.174). Other cereal finds of this sort of date from Garthdee Road and Forest Road, Kintore (Table 14.14) may suggest a well established practice of cereal cultivation, but again give little clue on their own to scale. Irish data (Monk 2000) are not demonstrably any earlier, finds from rectangular houses probably belonging to the late 38th into the later 37th centuries cal BC; similar finds from the interior of Magheraboy, along with sheep bones, probably date to no earlier than the 38th century cal BC (Table 12.2).

The potential symbolic significance of cattle can be traced back to at least the 38th century cal BC, in the form of the cattle skull laid on the old ground surface below the Ascott-under-Wychwood long barrow at a time judged to be that of construction (Benson and Whittle 2007, 225; Bayliss *et al.* 2007c). But just how large cattle and other herds were even in enclosure times is actually very hard to estimate. The recurrent emphasis on consumption of cattle at enclosures and other sites is certainly suggestive of a changing scale, though much of the impetus for this kind of social interaction could have resided in dealings with live animals: beasts and herds to admire and possess, to multiply and covet, and to acquire not only by patient breeding but also perhaps by raiding and theft. But what we need now for much greater clarity is a series of pre-enclosure sites, ideally dated to the 38th century cal BC and earlier. Did cattle herds take off in numbers as the first enclosures came to be constructed, or were they already there, part of the existing conditions in which the enclosure idea so dramatically flourished? Were they a major staple of the first centuries, or did they become more important along with the surge of other changes in the 38th century cal BC?

15.4 Building the world: monument sequences

Clearer patterns are beginning to emerge for the development of monuments and artefacts. With the varied constructions which we call monuments, we have suggested three important stages. First, there appears to be an initial phase in which monuments were scarce (sometimes without standardised forms), or absent; secondly, it appears that what can be seen as more typical long barrow and long cairn constructions (Fig. 15.10) became more common from around and after 3800 cal BC; and thirdly, this was followed around a century or so later – perhaps four generations – by the beginnings of the southern British enclosure tradition. The sequences in Ireland and Scotland need not be the same, and the challenges thrown up by Magheraboy have been extensively discussed. But the models which suggest start dates for the Neolithic in both Ireland and Scotland around 3800 cal BC include dates for constructions broadly allied to the long barrow and long cairn tradition, and are generally consistent with the trend suggested for southern Britain.

Our models do not agree with all other schemes in the

literature. We see no grounds to support the existence of very early passage tombs in the west of Ireland or indeed the west of Scotland (e.g. Fig. 12.50, and see above Chapter 15.2), and similarly, rotundae and oval barrows in the Cotswolds and elsewhere in southern Britain are not necessarily early types (e.g. Figs 9.26 and 11.14). There is also little – and so far ambiguous – evidence for a very early date for portal tombs in Ireland and western Britain (Figs 12.31 and 11.10), and we still have only a hazy notion of when court tombs were first built (Figs 12.32–4), beyond their general material associations and the stratigraphic relationship between rectangular timber house and court tomb at Ballyglass. But that still leaves considerable diversity in general, including such features as the timber or non-megalithic monuments of Ireland (e.g. Sheridan 2006a). Above all, we have now some better idea of the tempo of change, and that potentially brings new insights into the significance of pre-enclosure developments, and in turn into the setting in which enclosures themselves emerged.

Candidates for early constructions include Coldrum and the banana barrow at Crickley Hill; Burn Ground, Broadsands and the Post and Sweet Tracks are also candidates for relatively early dates, but appear much closer to *c.* 3800 cal BC. We have argued that the earliest human burials at Coldrum, probably from the 40th century cal BC onwards, date the construction of the substantial stone chamber in which they are deposited (Chapter 7.6). There is no primary association with human remains for the Crickley banana barrow, and its dating is uncertain (Fig. 9.8), though it definitely precedes the first enclosure there. The flint mines of Sussex, probably from at least the 40th century cal BC onwards (Figs 5.33–5) are another early kind of construction. If these enterprises offer different kinds of construction and assembly before *c.* 3800 cal BC, what is striking, apart from their apparent scarcity, is their diversity. The early Neolithic communities which we have sought to characterise began to undertake building and construction on a scale evidently neither practised nor perhaps imagined in the late Mesolithic.

That takes us back to the character of the beginning of the Neolithic in southern Britain. From the diversity suggested, it is hard to read off any particular continental cultural imprint, further reinforcing the suggestion made earlier in this chapter that both incomers and indigenous people were closely involved in the spread and development of Neolithic things and practices from early on in the process. The possible continental precedents are very scattered. The stone box at Coldrum is not easily paralleled, and the earlier literature on the site in fact sought wide antecedents, including in Scandinavia, north Germany and the Low Countries (Daniel 1950; Piggott 1935; J.H. Evans 1950; Jessup 1970). Chronologically, that now seems less probable, given the suggested date for the appearance of stone dolmens in southern Scandinavia *c.* 3600 cal BC, *after* an initial phase of earthen long barrows (Ebbesen 2007; Midgley 2008; Müller 1998), and the even later probable date for the appearance of Dutch hunebeds (Louwe Kooijmans *et al.* 2005). The other allowable area would then be Normandy or Brittany. The form of Broadsands is so simple that it is not easy either to categorise or to find specific comparanda for it. The long mound idea could go back to a variety of sources, from the Passy monuments of the Cerny culture in the Paris Basin, probably of the mid-fifth millennium cal BC (Demoule 2007a), to early TRB constructions in central Poland at a possibly similar or slightly later date (Midgley 2005; 2008). As already noted above, some framed and enclosed single graves are known in northern France, with early Michelsberg material associations – potentially late fifth millennium cal BC in date (Demoule 2007b). Likewise, long cairns in Normandy such as Vierville have now been dated to the late fifth millennium cal BC (Verron 2000; Sheridan 2010), and there are other, perhaps slightly earlier, elongated constructions in that area, as at Rots on the plain of Caen (Kinnes 1999). Mines can, however, be found in northern France and Belgium (Chapter 5.9).

Diversity in the first generations of the Neolithic in southern Britain is underlined by the simple grave at Yabsley Street, Blackwall (S. Coles *et al.* 2008; and see Chapter 7.3). Then perhaps by around 3800 cal BC, more established traditions of building cairns and barrows seem to have appeared. The sample of well dated constructions is still very small. To the five southern long barrows now formally modelled (Bayliss and Whittle 2007) can be added the Hambledon Hill long barrow (Mercer and Healy 2008; and see Chapter 4.1), the long barrow, turf mound and avenue at Raunds (Harding and Healy 2007; and see Chapter 6.3.2), and the Haddenham long barrow (Evans and Hodder 2006; and see Chapter 6.2.3). Burn Ground in the Cotswolds (Smith and Brickley 2006; and see Chapter 9.4) may belong towards the beginning of this suggested phase. Other less well dated southern British sites have been reviewed recently by Whittle *et al.* (2007a). The difficulties with Irish monument sequences have been stressed in Chapter 12, but some early Scottish constructions have good series of dates on short-life material, and have been modelled in Chapter 14.7 (Figs 14.150–3 and 14.154–7).

As this better dating evidence gradually accumulates, and in the effort for better understanding of the context in which enclosures were to emerge, older debates on the associations, meanings and social significance of these monumental traditions must be revisited. Taken on their own, the early monuments associated with human burials have been treated in oscillating ways. Already by 1950 (for other reviews see Darvill 2004a; Smith and Brickley 2009), Glyn Daniel was at pains to set aside an older concept to explain collective deposits, that of sacrifices to accompany dead chieftains to the beyond (Daniel 1950). In the 1970s, Colin Renfrew grouped southern long barrows and causewayed enclosures together to form a pre-chiefdom phase of social development, the emphasis here being on the relatively modest labour input required to construct individual barrows, and indeed individual enclosures (Renfrew 1973b). He saw barrows as 'territorial markers' (Renfrew 1976), and writing of megalithic tombs on the

Fig. 15.10. East Kennet long barrow, Marlborough Downs, north Wiltshire. Photos: (top) David Field; (lower) ©English Heritage. NMR.

Orkneys, he characterised them as the work of 'segmentary societies' principally on the basis of their dispersal across the landscape, such that each could be seen as at the centre of its own territory (Renfrew 1979). By the 1980s, ancestors came to the fore, first as legitimators of claims to land and resources (e.g. R. Bradley 1984a, 15–20), and then more generally as a kind of spiritual underpinning of the Neolithic way of life (e.g. Edmonds 1999). An ideological twist was offered in the view that overtly collective and egalitarian rites of disposal could have in fact masked much less equal power relations (Shanks and Tilley 1982). As well as ongoing technical discussions about the processes of formation and transformation involved in collective deposits, recent and current opinion reflects a range of possibilities, from commemoration of forebears in general (Barrett 1988) to dynastic arrangements in a competitive and sometimes violent social setting (Mercer 2006a; 2006b). Richard Bradley (2007, 50–9) has been careful to stress the extent of possible variation, including between Britain and Ireland. Access to interiors was perhaps restricted to a 'smaller group' than the totality of daily passers-by or of those who attended ceremonies at a site, though the presence of abundant remains allows the notion that 'the monuments stood for a wider community' (R. Bradley 2007, 52, 54); local variation 'may have been influenced by the status of particular individuals' (R. Bradley 2007, 55).

Although much attention has been given to sequences of development at individual sites (e.g. Kinnes 1992; Evans and Hodder 2006; R. Bradley 2007, 55–7), comparatively little detailed interpretation has been offered of change through time, other than at the scale of broad comparisons between earlier and later phases of the Neolithic. This is in contrast to the situation elsewhere, for example in Denmark, where it is possible to see a succession from early long barrows normally with just one or two people inhumed under or in them, to dolmens, from *c.* 3600 cal BC, with larger deposits in both closed and open chambers, and then to the numerous passage graves, perhaps in a concentrated horizon in the later fourth millennium cal BC, with their abundant and often compartmentalised human remains (Ebbesen 2007). Two exceptions, both dealing with the Orkneys, should be noted. Johannes Müller (1990) modelled the increasing labour force for monument construction, the centralisation processes, the opening of external networks, the opening of the landscape and a collapse at the end of the Neolithic. Chris Scarre (2007b, 53–5) has likewise proposed that increasing labour for monument construction reflects a progressive centralisation of political power across four phases of change through the Neolithic sequence as a whole; the precise chronology, however, is not specified.

A more focused approach came out of the pilot study on the Bayesian modelling of the chronology of southern long barrows (Bayliss and Whittle 2007). As well as indicating more precise timings and durations for individual monuments, this found little support for any notion of curated or ancestral bone; no material older than one or two generations seems to have been involved, and that potentially only at Hazleton and Fussell's Lodge (Meadows *et al.* 2007, 60; Wysocki *et al.* 2007, 81–2). The emphasis appears now to have been on the known and remembered dead, over spans of from one generation, as suggested for West Kennet (Bayliss *et al.* 2007b, fig. 6), to three to five, as at Ascott-under-Wychwood (Bayliss *et al.* 2007c, fig. 9). Given the initial indications of timing, Ascott-under-Wychwood in particular has been discussed in terms of a coming to terms with changing circumstances, especially the conceptual and psychological alterations in existence during the first two centuries of Neolithic practice, of small communities, turned in on themselves and principally conscious of their own identities, internal composition and categorisations (Whittle 2007b; cf. Whittle *et al.* 2007a). Perhaps this model too, which harks back to the egalitarian interpretive tradition in long barrow studies, now deserves to be challenged in the light of the wider emergent chronology.

If barrow construction became more frequent *c.* 3800 cal BC, that surely marks a significant shift. We do not know whether barrows and cairns came to be first built in substantial numbers with a great rush, as appears to be the case with enclosures a little later. But we should not then freeze the barrow phenomenon into a single frame. Judging simplistically from the sample of modelled southern long barrows, it could be that, whatever the precise rate at which the phenomenon took off, many of these constructions were being built already in the generations around 3800 cal BC – as probably indicated by Burn Ground, Ascott-under-Wychwood and Hazleton (Fig. 9.28). Importantly, they also continued to be developed and used in the 37th century cal BC, as the enclosure phenomenon rapidly got going – as variously indicated by Ascott-under-Wychwood, Hazleton and Fussell's Lodge. And there were major new constructions, as at West Kennet in the later 37th century cal BC, dating to the same time, whatever model for its interpretation is preferred (Wysocki *et al.* 2007), and as in the closing of the existing structures at Fussell's Lodge by the throwing up of the long barrow (Whittle *et al.* 2007a, fig. 6).

There could have been both difference and continuity between the barrow constructions of the pre-enclosure and enclosure horizons. Difference could rest in the details of architectural style and of the character of depositions. Thus the largest mound locally occurs at West Kennet, along with the spatial separation of chambers and passage, though Burn Ground appears to offer something very similar at an earlier date. West Kennet, however, also provides the greatest sense of categorisation of the dead, and Fussell's Lodge, if the third, preferred, model of its sequence is followed (Wysocki *et al.* 2007), may provide something intermediate between that and the collective deposits of Hazleton and Ascott-under-Wychwood, in the first half of the 37th century cal BC. In addition its outermost burials and latest deposits are one individual and another assemblage of parts of two individuals arranged to look like one individual, along with a cattle skull and a decorated pot. Continuity, however, can be sought in the generalities of these practices, from gathering up the remains – probably in many cases the corpses – of the freshly dead into purpose-built containers, to their marking and commemoration with substantial barrows and cairns. So practices may have altered subtly, and there may be significant difference between the accumulation of 21 people probably over three to five generations at Ascott-under-Wychwood and the deposition of over 40 people at West Kennet probably within one generation. But using and building barrows and cairns in southern Britain were not abandoned when enclosures started to be constructed, and so were evidently part and parcel of the same evolving worldview and social system. If so, a different perspective to that previously offered for Ascott-under-Wychwood may now be more appropriate. It is perhaps in the first two centuries or so of the Neolithic that people came to terms with changing circumstances, as putative incomers reacted to a new setting and new neighbours, and as indigenous people incorporated new ways of doing things. The pace of change may have quickened towards 3800 cal BC, and it may make most sense now to turn again to those models with elements at least of emulation, tension and competition in them, to best come to terms with the whole accelerating sequence from the 38th into the 37th century cal BC.

In this view, long barrows and long cairns can become markers again, but not perhaps as literal territorial markers as in the original formulation of that idea, since the evidence reviewed above for settlement and subsistence does not suggest urgent need for space as such, and because there was much variation within southern Britain in the frequency with which such constructions were built. If there were pressures on land and resources, we might expect them in areas like the middle and lower Thames and parts of East Anglia, where in fact barrows are comparatively infrequent. Rather barrows and cairns could have marked places and plural pasts important to both the self-definition of small communities and to their wider identity in relation to others. Perhaps it is time to be literal, and to collapse some of the subtle distinctions drawn between overt display and covert intentions, and to emphasise again the small numbers involved, which reduce even further with up-to-date analysis (Wysocki and Whittle 2000; Smith and Brickley 2009, 87–8). We seem stuck with a modern notion of the 'wider community', which does not adequately catch the nature or composition of a social landscape with disparate, dispersed and perhaps fluid groups in it. Some of these constructions could have been built to look back to very old pasts, as often mooted in long barrow studies, but given the times and distances involved, it is at least as likely that it was more immediate connections with contemporary or recent continental practices that were being invoked, and the deposition of the newly dead also places things firmly in the present rather than in an ancient past. Mary Helms (1998, 6–10), writing of hierarchical chiefdom societies, has stressed the associations of aristocrats with ancestors, and their role as affinal outsiders and thereby as inherently superior living ancestors. The argument in this chapter is not for emergent chiefdoms as such in the 38th century cal BC, but the importance of cosmological primacy at the heart of politics in kin-based society (Helms 1998, 11; 2007) would be one way to link our observations of the emergence of long barrows and cairns. It became important, over and over again, to deposit successive corpses or other human remains, each occasion perhaps the opportunity for overt display, in structures that themselves could have evoked a variety of cosmological distances beyond the immediate setting, thus fusing present and past. The potential rate at which such structures were built and used from the 38th into the 37th century cal BC in parts of southern Britain seems not only to underline the importance of this new practice, quite unlike anything that had gone before in the insular setting, but also strongly to suggest its competitive character.

It is hard to say at this stage whether the same overall sequence of monument development was followed in Ireland. Richard Bradley (2007, 59–62) has sketched a scheme to explain major differences between England and Ireland, relating the main ways in which the dead were deposited (with the emphasis in Ireland on cremation) to the manner in which residence was lived (more houses in Ireland) and the way in which structures came to an end (house burning in Ireland). In the light of the short chronology proposed for the use of rectangular houses in Ireland, and the wider uncertainties about the specific periods in which court tombs and other related monuments were constructed, it is wise to be cautious about this scenario. In addition, it may not capture sufficient of the variation evident in Ireland, with inhumations in some portal tombs, in caves, and in monuments like Parknabinnia (see Chapter 12.3).

In lowland southern and eastern Scotland, there may have been further difference. Things came in a rush, as it were, as 'mortuary' enclosures and long barrows appear to have been a feature of the early Neolithic landscape, at the same time as timber halls (Fig. 14.175). There was therefore no demonstrable lag between the establishment of Neolithic practices and the appearance of 'monuments' (Fig. 14.179). It is hard to tell the numbers of people deposited in constructions like those at Eweford West, Pencraig Hill or Forest Road, Kintore, though they may have been low (MacGregor and McLellan 2007, 23, 41; Cook and Dunbar 2008, 49). A simplistic reading of the evidence could suggest relatively few such monuments in the lowland setting, despite recent advances in recovery and understanding. This might seem similar to the early situation noted above for Denmark. It is hard at this stage therefore to read the same possibilities for a competitive increase in constructions in lowland Scotland as in parts of southern Britain. We will simply have to wait for further work on highland and western monuments in Scotland to reveal their main chronological trends.

15.5 Artefacts

Although the scope of interpretation of material culture has vastly increased in recent years, sufficient to attract the criticism that the term 'materiality' has become far too abstract (Ingold 2007b), the earliest Neolithic material in southern Britain and Ireland has been comparatively little discussed in its own right. Major effort has gone into establishing the order of things on the one hand (e.g. Herne 1988; Cleal 2004), and seeking the genealogies of descent and relationship on the other. Both are important, and a sense of connections is as significant in material culture as with monuments. But perhaps too many of the properties and associations of this early material have been overlooked. Andrew Herne wrote briefly some time ago (1988, 26) of the Carinated Bowl as unique material symbol, which 'must have affected [sic] radical changes in the cultural categories and symbolic boundaries that are built around the consumption of edible food'. Others like Alfred Gell (1998) have written in general terms of the 'technology of enchantment', and the ways in which objects can act as citations in fields or networks of relationships (A. Jones 2007, 81). But how might this actually have worked in the early Neolithic context? We concentrate here on pottery, leaf arrowheads and flaked, ground and polished stone and flint axes, though other aspects of flint working should also be kept in mind, to think about the circumstances of production, form, textures, and connotations of novelty and difference. Combined with the sequences modelled in this volume, this material can serve further to enhance the sense of dynamic change proposed here, both at the beginning of the Neolithic and especially from the 38th into the 37th century cal BC.

Pottery-making entailed a suite of unfamiliar skills, from the selection and preparation of clay and temper to the actual firing. The final stages of the process were transformations on a scale and of a nature not seen before in the insular setting. These could have been imbued with a level of mystique, even magic, similar to that attached to metalworking, another transformation by fire, in later periods. We know virtually nothing of the specific circumstances in which early pots were fired. Herne suggested (1988, 26) that potting could have been 'a carefully controlled procedure, one hedged around with formalized rules and practices, that both made the outcome symbolically safe and pragmatically successful'. The frequently high quality, in fabric, form and finish, of Carinated Bowls – at their best thin-walled, hard, and burnished – points to symbolic value.

New forms of arrowhead and axehead would, on the other hand, have been made by the application of familiar skills. But extra-functional qualities reached new levels (Fig. 15.11). The shallow, invasive flaking of many leaf arrowheads called for considerable skill and control and went beyond functional need, since many others were only marginally retouched (e.g. Middleton 1998, fig. 227) and an unknown number of early fourth millennium arrowheads may not have been retouched at all, on the evidence of an unretouched flake from beside the Sweet Track in the Somerset Levels, hafted in the same way as invasively flaked leaf arrowheads from nearby (J. Coles *et al.* 1973, 291). The elaborate finish of many leaf arrowheads could relate to their use in interpersonal conflict, with all its formal and informal rituals, from at least the 37th century cal BC (Fig. 14.36) and probably before. Whether or not this was the case, there was a change in archery itself. Single-piece arrowheads were rare in Britain before the start of the Neolithic, far more so than in north-west Europe. True *petit tranchet* arrowheads (in the sense of blade segments of symmetrical trapezoid outline with abrupt bilateral retouch) occasionally occur in late Mesolithic contexts (e.g. Holgate 1988b, 90) but are scarce overall; Stephen Green could list fewer than 300 from England and Wales against over 15,000 leaf arrowheads (1980, figs 31, 39; table VII.6). Furthermore, while there is a gradually increasing tally of Mesolithic bows and arrows from waterlogged contexts in Europe (e.g. Guilaine and Zammit 2005, 63–7), the few British examples were all made in the fourth millennium cal BC or later, on the evidence of radiocarbon dates, peat stratigraphy, arrowhead typology, or all three (Clark 1963; S. Green 1980, 170–83; Sheridan 1996). In this case absence of evidence is emphatically not evidence of absence, but it raises the possibility that archery may have become more frequent in Britain with the Neolithic.

Effort was also expended on the appearance and texture of axeheads. Not only did their form change, but far more time than invested in their original flaking was often devoted to grinding part or all of their surfaces, often beyond any improvement to the efficiency of the implement. Experiment suggests seven to nine hours of labour for an all-over-ground group VI axehead and up to three times as long for a flint one (Bradley and Edmonds 1993, 89; P. Harding 1987). While this had already been practised to some extent in Ireland and south Wales, its new frequency and ubiquity express a new belief that this was how the artefacts should be finished and how they should look and feel. As with arrowheads and other invasively retouched implements, 'the appearance of at least some of these objects may have at least as much to do with how they were perceived as how they were used' (Edmonds 1995, 45–6). An equally striking change in attitudes to axes is seen in the sinking of flint mines on the South Downs, probably from the 40th century cal BC (Chapter 5.9; Figs 14.129 and 5.33). This was the import not only of north-west European expertise but of a belief that it was worthwhile, even necessary, to win material for axeheads from below ground at considerable labour and risk. The powerful conceptual connotations and associations of mining and quarrying are explored by, among others, Barber *et al.* (1999, 61–7, 73), Topping (2004) and Edmonds (1995, 59–66). From the 39th century, too, visually distinctive flints from other, superficial sources were selected for axehead manufacture (Fig. 14.118).

All these artefacts may also have had other connotations of difference, linked to a sense of the distant and the exotic. As well as being associated with novel foodstuffs, pots could have been seen as coming from 'over there': for incomers and their direct descendants a visible and tangible link to areas of continental origin, and for indigenous people a symbol of novel affiliation with much wider social networks. It is clear that jadeitite axeheads were in circulation in Britain by around the end of the 39th century cal BC (Fig. 14.128), perhaps already with the status of old and valued heirlooms of continental descent (Pétrequin *et al.* 2008). The importance of the axe and the axehead is seen in Brittany in their representation on menhirs and in passage graves (Le Roux 1984).

These patterns of material novelty were not static. Ground stone axeheads from south-western sources came into use as Neolithic practices spread to the west, from at least the early 37th century cal BC (Fig. 14.124), an initial regional circulation expanding to an insular one after perhaps only a generation or two (Fig. 14.139). This formed part of a wider establishment of long-distance exchange networks, encompassing gabbroic pottery from the same area and axeheads from the north-west and other areas, which was established in the decades around 3700 cal BC (Fig. 14.138). Likewise, Decorated Bowl pottery was probably in use by the late 38th century cal BC (Fig. 14.92).

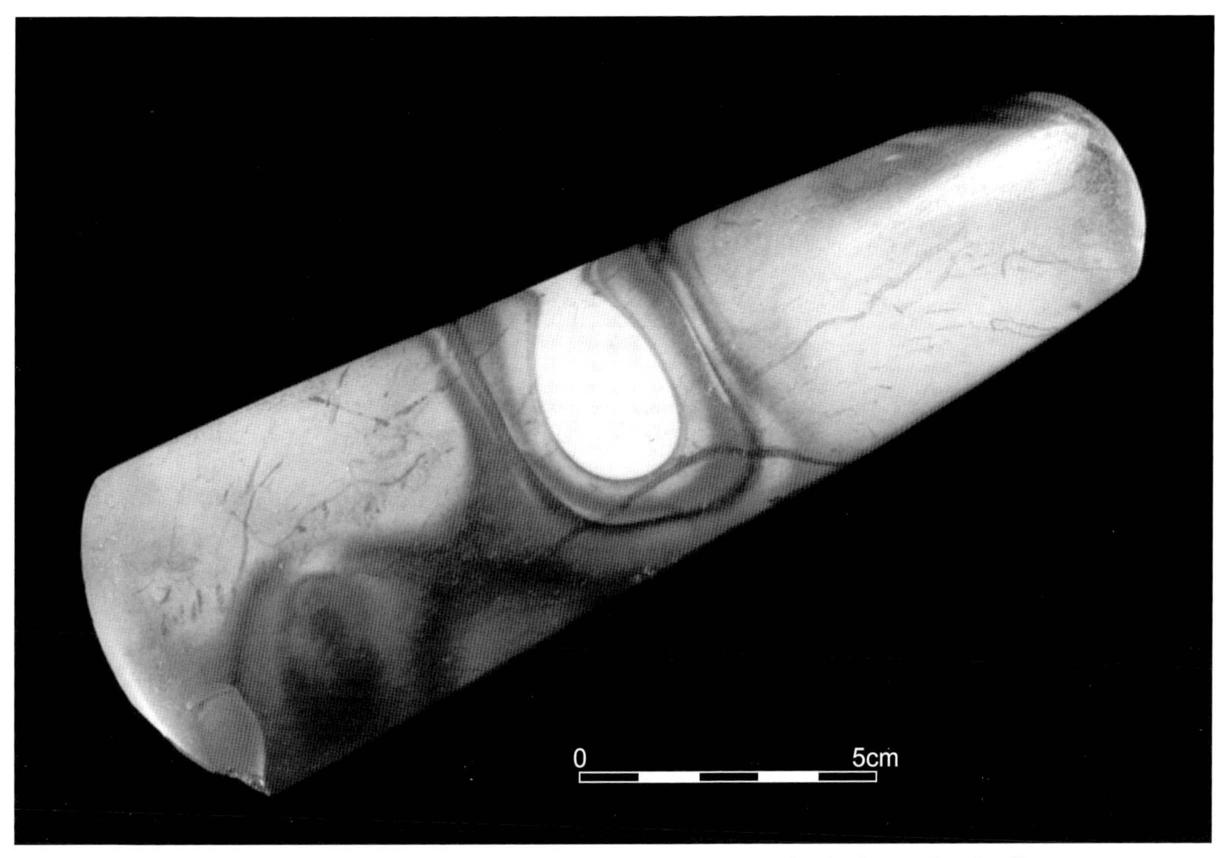

Fig. 15.11. The flint axehead from Bolshan Hill, Angus, Scotland. Photo: Alan Saville.

So in the run-up to and overlapping with the appearance of the first causewayed enclosures in southern Britain there were significant changes within the already established spectrum of material novelty and signification. Things moved further, and from a greater variety of sources, and some pottery was further enhanced by a rather limited range of linear and punctiform decoration, generally confined to rims, necks and shoulders.

Given its simplicity, it is perhaps understandable that rather little attention has been given to the potential significance of this decoration, though it would normally be assumed that the patterning applied to the upper parts and rims of pots acted as a visual symbol of some kind. Julian Thomas (1999, 101) has suggested that decoration was 'the product of unconsidered and routinised ways of working rather than an overt symbol of identity', 'drawing distinctions between persons, places and practices rather than large ethnic identities'. In a different context, study of increases in exterior decoration of serving vessels in the Puebloan south-west suggested a correlation with periods of increased social aggregation (B. Mills 2007). It is worth quoting a summary of trends (B. Mills 2007, 210):

> Across the northern Southwest, the first use of exterior designs and polychrome ceramics is during the Pueblo III period, which corresponds to a shift in settlement aggregation and open plaza spaces. With the transition to the more enclosed plazas of the Early Pueblo IV period, smaller and less visible exterior designs were used. The trend reversed itself with the use of larger plazas at later Pueblo IV period sites, where serving bowls with greater visual impact were used.

These trends (from roughly 1000 to 1400 AD) can be set in the context of the public performance of supra-household feasting, with all the senses actively at work, but especially visual perception of eye-catching things. The relative visibility of preparation and serving vessels is strongly suggested to correlate with the scale of participation in the sequence of feasting events (B. Mills 2007, 212); 'decorated bowls were focal points for the staging of consumption events' (B. Mills 2007, 234; cf. Blitz 1993).

In the southern British early Neolithic context, there is more than a chronological correlation between causewayed enclosures and Decorated Bowl pottery. The two have similar, although not identical, core distributions, excavated enclosures extending beyond the area where Decorated Bowl was current only in the south-west peninsula and Ireland. Among the 28 excavated causewayed enclosures which do coincide with the distribution of Decorated Bowl, the four which have yielded none are either sites with little or no Bowl pottery of any kind, despite reasonably extensive excavation, like Barkhale, or sites which have seen only very limited excavation, like Whitesheet Hill. Decorated wares seem to occur more consistently at causewayed enclosures than at other sites of the period, such as pit concentrations, hollows, treeholes and long barrows (Tables 14.8–9). Cleal has connected the variation in repertoire from site to site, especially enclosure sites, with a general sense of local identities (Cleal 1992). Perhaps decoration was simply one further elaboration of the enchantment of technology, without explicit meaning (cf. Bloch 1995; Miller 2008), and acted in a tactile as well as a visual way, as pots were handled and lifted: part of the 'framing' of ritual and other events (Miller 1985, 181).

The Puebloan analogy can only be suggestive rather than exact. But whereas it has proved difficult so far to find clear signs of intensification in settlement or subsistence in the run-up to the first appearance of causewayed enclosures in southern Britain in the late 38th century cal BC, it has been possible to offer models for development and change in monument building and material culture. These are important clues to the nature of society. This was far from static. The probable rate of change, apparently accelerated by the 38th century cal BC, combined with the character of both monuments and material culture, now more strongly suggests a dynamic and perhaps competitive social setting. If competition and emulation were significant factors, however, it does not appear from the currently available evidence in southern Britain that these were principally to do with land or resources, but rather a spectrum of other concerns, perhaps including identity, affiliation, descent, genealogical seniority, connectedness and prowess in general. There are no easily available labels for this kind of situation, beyond the familiar and very general terms of social evolutionary schemes, though the language in which we might further describe this social setting is discussed again below in relation to enclosures themselves. When enclosures appeared, they did not do so out of the blue, and in introducing further changes, they quickened already accelerating trends.

15.6 Enclosures: the significance of a history

When enclosures first came to be built in southern Britain, probably in the late 38th century cal BC (Fig. 14.1), there was a long history of similar practices behind them. That story, going back to the LBK of central and western Europe in the sixth millennium cal BC, has been authoritatively summarised at least twice in recent years (Andersen 1997; Meyer and Raetzel-Fabian 2006), and its individual components have been analysed and discussed many times over (for example, from a *much* longer list: Bertemes 1991; Biel *et al.* 1998; Daim and Neubauer 2005; Dubouloz *et al.* 1988; 1991; Gronenborn 2007b; Jeunesse 1996; Matuschik 1991; Mordant and Mordant 1988; Müller 2001; 2010a; Petrasch 1990; Trnka 1991; Whittle 1988b), so that there is no need to rehearse all the detail here. It is sufficient to stress the main outlines of development, and important to underline that it is inconceivable from this perspective that causewayed enclosures in southern Britain could have been an innovation completely independent of that continental background, though this central claim need not commit us to arguing for universal uniformity of practice and meaning.

The broad history is constituted by the first appearance of enclosures in central and western Europe in the sixth millennium cal BC, in the orbit of the LBK, followed by the *Kreisgrabenanlagen* or rondels of various cultural groups in the earlier fifth millennium cal BC of central Europe, with simpler layouts, including interrupted ditches, found sporadically to the west, including in the Paris basin, and succeeded in turn by a plethora of interrupted-ditch and palisaded forms, across a broad sweep of western and parts of central Europe, beginning variably in the later fifth millennium cal BC and continuing well on into the fourth millennium cal BC (Andersen 1997). There was probably no single history in detail, since there was considerable diversity from the LBK horizon onwards, but one can discern long-term shifts in association and role, first within the longhouse world of the LBK and its fifth millennium successors, and then from approximately the mid-fifth millennium cal BC within the rather different setting of the Michelsberg, northern Chasséen and TRB cultures that variously come after the Danubian tradition. Both LBK and post-LBK enclosures were closely associated with longhouses, the former either variously enclosing them, or marking their former presence, and the latter – the rondels – more formally set apart from, but often demonstrably still close to, longhouse settlements, and more formally, symmetrically and elaborately laid out than those of the sixth millennium. The causewayed enclosure or interrupted ditch system came into its own in the later fifth millennium and subsequently, and was associated, as already noted above in this chapter, with a much more dispersed pattern of settlement, and perhaps altered forms of subsistence practice.

Diversity is worth stressing, though it is hard to catch all the many variables of size, duration, sequence, association and practice. Some LBK enclosures were set around large concentrations of longhouses, though the ditch at Vaihingen in Baden-Württemberg silted up in later stages of the life of the settlement (Krause *et al.* 1998); Langweiler 8 on the Aldenhovener Platte came at the end of a long sequence of house construction, perhaps gathering up and marking the space formerly between longhouses or longhouse groupings (Boelicke *et al.* 1998; Lüning and Stehli 1994). Some LBK enclosures may have been laid out in stages, and separate ditch segments are already apparent at Rosheim in Alsace (Jeunesse 1996). In contrast, many rondels may have been laid out in a single episode to a carefully predetermined plan, and many of their ditches show signs of rapid silting, though with phases of recutting and some overall remodellings (Andersen 1997). Moreover, the signs from ceramic associations are already that this was probably a chronologically concentrated phenomenon (e.g. Trnka 2005; Neubauer 2005), and Bayesian modelling in the future might, one could predict, suggest a narrow horizon within the earlier fifth millennium cal BC. On the basis of radiocarbon dates from vertical stratigraphies, Petrasch (1990) has already postulated a narrow horizon of construction in the 48th century cal BC. Elaborate layouts, largely empty interiors, and significant orientations combine strongly to suggest a special character, and it is very tempting to see this as the manifestation of some kind of cult (one directed to sunrise has been suggested recently: Pásztor *et al.* 2008) which exploded across a significant area of central Europe, and perhaps equally rapidly lapsed again. Further west, at perhaps a roughly similar date or soon after, a large enclosure belonging to the Cerny group, and succeeding VSG houses, was constructed at Balloy les Réaudins in the Yonne valley of the Paris basin (Fig. 15.12), with some 60 ditch segments forming a single, oval circuit over 160 by 120 m in extent (Mordant 1992; 1997; Boureau 1997); mortuary enclosures are also found on the site, two famously directly overlying VSG houses. Finds in the ditch segments include pots, human skulls and deposits of animal bone (Mordant 1997). Other Cerny enclosures are known in the area of the Yonne-Seine confluence, including further lengths of interrupted ditches at Barbuise-Courtavant (Midgley 2005, fig. 12). Even earlier, in the Rubané récent of the Aisne valley, the single ditch circuit at Menneville had separate segments and enclosed seven longhouses (one of which intersected the ditch), with deposits in the ditch of both human and animal remains (Farruggia *et al.* 1996; Hachem *et al.* 1998).

So there was probably no single moment when the interrupted-ditch or causewayed enclosure idea came into being. The enclosure of L'Etoile, Somme, with its elongated ditch segments, and with 'epi-Rössen' or 'Rössen tardif' associations and probably to be placed in the middle of the fifth millennium cal BC, is also cited as relevant background (Jeunesse 1996; Bréart 1984). But then, according to current understanding of sequence and chronology, causewayed enclosures appear widely in the orbit of the Michelsberg and northern Chasséen cultures, and further afield, in the TRB (Fig. 15.13). Unfortunately, we do not yet know with certainty how rapid this process was. Following the standard relative chronology of Lüning (1967) for the Michelsberg culture, there appear to be plenty of enclosures in phases MKI–II. This span has recently been assigned, on the basis, one supposes, of visual inspection of radiocarbon dates, backed up by cultural connections to the Neolithic dendrochronologies of the Alpine foreland, to the period from 4200–4000 cal BC (Meyer and Raetzel-Fabian 2006, fig. 11; cf. Gronenborn 2010; Lichter 2010). It is to be noted again that an earlier start date for the Michelsberg culture, located in northern France, has been proposed, at *c.* 4500 cal BC (Jeunesse 1998; Jeunesse *et al.* 2004). While that issue is yet to be resolved, the clear current understanding is that early Michelsberg and corresponding early northern Chasséen enclosures belong to the late fifth millennium cal BC (Figs 15.14–19), and can be found quite widely from the Paris basin, as at Bazoches in a tributary of the Aisne, east to the Rhineland, as at sites like Miel, Mayen, Bruchsal 'Aue' (Reiter 2005), Ilsfeld (Seidel 2008b) and Urmitz, with examples known at least as far north as the Aldenhovener Platte, like Koslar 10 (Zimmermann 2006c; cf. Boelicke *et al.* 1979) and Inden 9 (Höhn 1997; Zimmermann 2006b).[8] The recent research of Michael Geschwinde and Dirk Fabian indicates that the whole northern fringe of the Lower Mountain Range possessed such enclosures *c.* 4200 cal BC and that Michelsberg enclosures were also present in some areas of central Germany (Geschwinde and Raetzel-Fabian 2009).

Also according to our current, imprecise chronologies, it is clear that not all causewayed enclosures belong this early. In the Rhineland, a couple have been assigned to MKIII/IV, estimated at 4000–3800/3700 cal BC, and then there, and to the east, a much larger number have been assigned to MKV, estimated at 3800/3700–3400 cal BC (Meyer and Raetzel-Fabian 2006, fig. 11; cf. Müller 2001), including substantial sites like Calden (Raetzel-Fabian 2000). Further to the north, the causewayed enclosures of Denmark, with one corresponding example in southern Sweden, belong only to the ENC–MNA1a–b phase, currently assigned to *c.* 3500–3200 cal BC on the basis of material associations and visual inspection of radiocarbon dates (Andersen 1997; Nielsen 2004). Southern Scandinavia thus follows a more linear path of monumental development, from early long barrows to early dolmens, with elaborated dolmens perhaps overlapping with the causewayed enclosures and passage graves perhaps concentrated in MN1b in the later fourth millennium cal BC (Nielsen 2004; Ebbesen 2007; Larsson 2008). In the Paris basin, interrupted-ditch enclosures may persist to the end of the complex of northern Chasséen and related cultural groupings at *c.* 3500 cal BC (Demoule *et al.* 2007b), but chronologies may not yet be refined enough (cf. Colas 2007) for as much precision as claimed further east. More recent fieldwork has found more enclosures to the north of the Paris basin, and closer to the Channel (e.g. Bostyn *et al.* 2006). In central-west France, as already noted above in this chapter, abundant enclosures probably belong to the fourth millennium cal BC rather than any earlier, but whether this regional tradition was flourishing before that of southern Britain remains for the present unclear. Further afield, southern Chasséen enclosures were in use from the later if not mid-fifth millennium cal BC (Vaquer 1990; Gandelin 2007; Beeching 1991; Demoule *et al.* 2007b).

As Christian Jeunesse has put it (1996, 258), 'Tout se passe comme si des pratiques encore faiblement codifiées dans les sociétés danubiennes acquéraient, avec le Néolithique récent, un caractère nettement plus stéréotypé'.[9] Although there is considerable diversity in size, layouts of ditch segments and palisades, site phasing and duration, these continental causewayed enclosures present recurrent themes: of bounding space in broadly similar ways, of marking presence by the deposition of material culture, animal bones and human remains, in ditches and interior pits, and of avoiding prolonged use for occupation or settlement. Thus, in terms of size, Urmitz, which bounds some 100 ha, is on a scale far greater than other Michelsberg enclosure (Boelicke 1978; Gronenborn 2007b), while the four closely placed circuits of Bazoches present a spatial complexity comparatively rarely seen across the whole Chasséen–Michelsberg–TRB orbit (Dubouloz *et al.* 1991; 1997). Both these examples may have gone through prolonged development, though

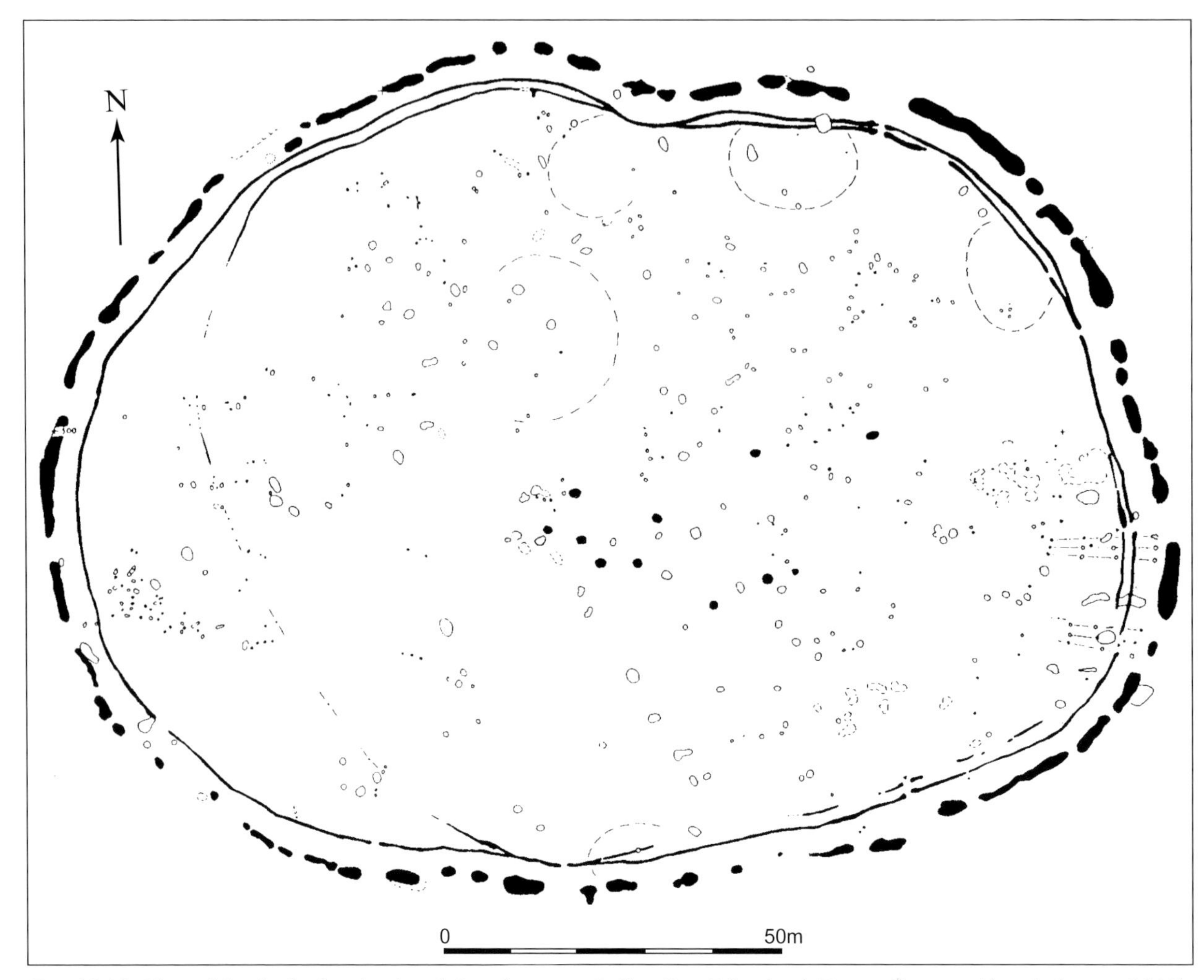

Fig. 15.12. Plan of the ditched and palisaded enclosure at Balloy 'Les Réaudins', Yonne, France. After Andersen (1997).

their duration has not been precisely established, while other enclosures appear to have been in use for much shorter periods of time. Recurrent are the practices of bounding space with at least one or two segmented ditch circuits, the ditch segments often aligned between multiple circuits, and normally backed by a more or less continuous palisade. Entrances may often best be marked by gaps or more formalised arrangements in the palisade circuits, and often by corresponding concentrations of deposition in adjacent ditch segments and ditch butt ends. Pottery, animal bone, and human remains are recurrent finds in ditches, often partial or fragmented. The deposit of whole animals at Boury-en-Vexin, Oise, is unusual (Lombardo *et al.* 1984; Meniel 1987), perhaps representing principally the deliberate slaughter of a whole herd of sheep (Rose-Marie Arbogast, pers. comm.); partial remains in lower layers of the ditch can be noted. Aurochs skulls spaced at intervals along the ditch circuits stand out at Bruchsal 'Aue' (Reiter 2005; Steppan 2003; Seidel 2008a). Human skulls and long bones are recurrent, but whole skeletons are not uncommon, particularly in central-west France (Semelier 2007). The substantial timber-framed buildings within the enclosure at Mairy, Ardennes (Marolle 1998), also stand out for their rarity. Much more common is the sporadic occurrence of pits, though these are occasionally present in more significant numbers, as within both phases of the (rather later) example of Sarup on Fyn (Andersen 1997). Finally, by way of this briefest of reminders – since the detailed literature is enormous – it is worth noting the work done in southern Chasséen contexts to establish the probable movement of both people and animals around the landscapes of the lower Rhône valley and elsewhere, across a range of sites from upland caves to lowland pit concentrations and enclosures (Beeching 2003; Gandelin 2007; Bréhard 2007).

It can therefore hardly be doubted that the general idea of enclosure construction and use in southern Britain was derived in some way from the adjacent European continent. Given the diversity apparent there, it is not necessary to argue for complete uniformity, because that never existed on the continent. Nor are the southern British causewayed enclosures identical with northern Chasséen or Michelsberg exemplars. In terms of layout alone, continental enclosures possess closely spaced ditch circuits, with aligned ditch segments, and backed by continuous palisades, far more often than is the case in southern Britain, though that combination does occur; Orsett is a case in point (Hedges and Buckley 1978; Fig. 7.8). But we need to go beyond

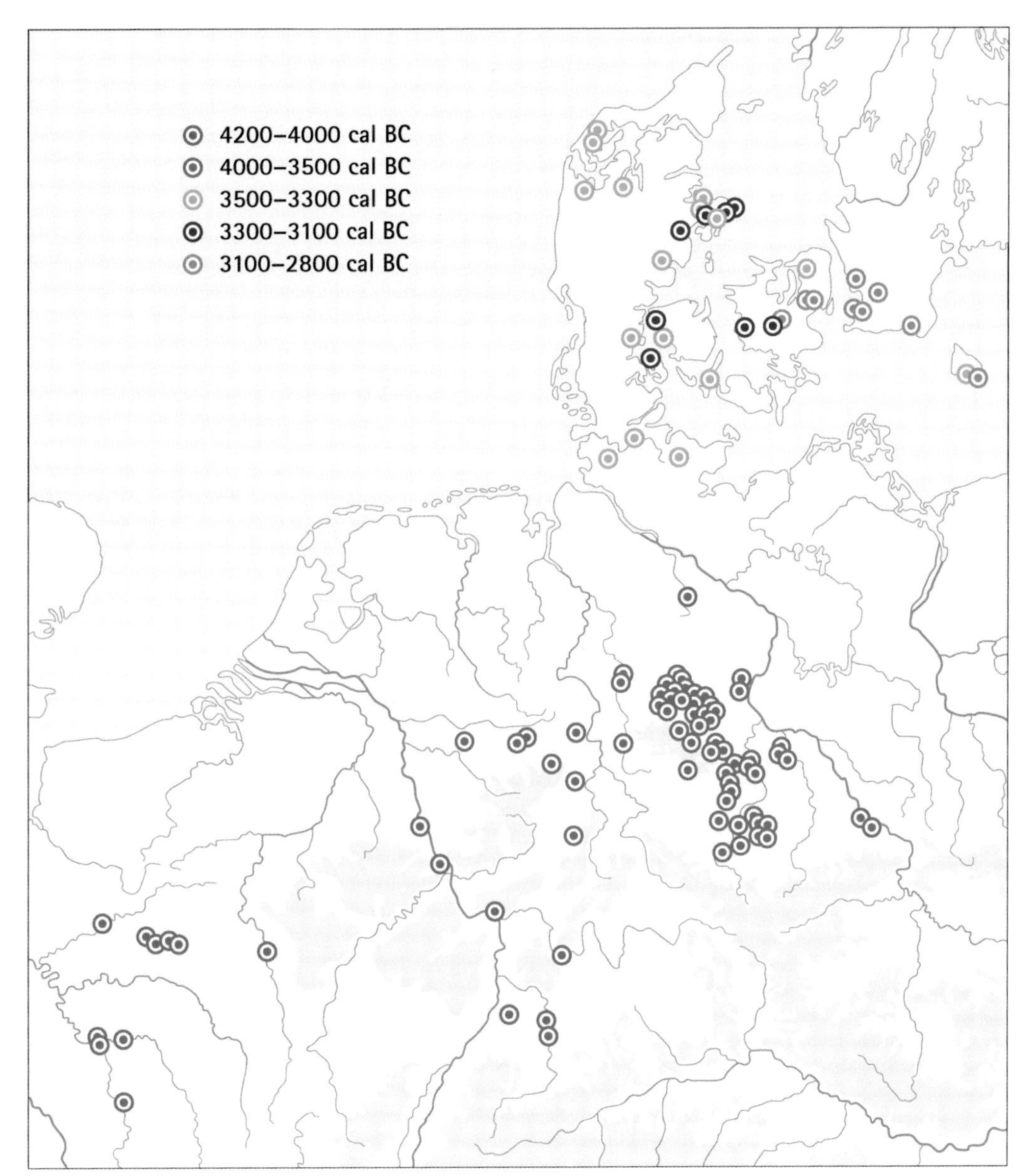

Fig. 15.13. Map of ditched enclosures from the Paris basin eastwards into Germany and southern Scandinavia, with informal date estimates from the late fifth to the early third millennia cal BC. From Müller (2010a).

the general links to ask what was adopted, imitated or emulated in the insular setting, and why at a particular date. It is clear that the longer enclosure tradition presented a powerful history: many, many generations back in the LBK, association with the great longhouses of the distant past, terrible killings at some (such as Asparn, Austria: Teschler-Nicola 1996), assembly and dramatic treatment of the dead at Herxheim (Zeeb-Lanz *et al*. 2009; Boulestin *et al*. 2009); and then the probable rush of great and elaborate rondel constructions. Those old doings might have attained the status of myth in the ongoing and still eventful performances of the enclosure tradition, across the range of impressive sites of recent history such as Noyen, Bazoches, Mairy, Boury, Urmitz, Bruchsal and a host of others. If links being made were to active continental practice, perhaps deepened by some kind of awareness of much older times, what was appealed to in the southern British case could have been an irresistible combination of myth and more active history (cf. Gosden and Lock 1998; Hodder 2006, chapter 6).

In the present state of information, it seems probable that the take-up of these ideas in southern Britain was principally to do with the acceleration of insular development. We cannot yet completely exclude the possibility of a fresh surge in continental enclosure construction from the 38th century cal BC, as hinted at in the synthesis of Meyer and Raetzel-Fabian (2006, fig. 11); if there was a cult-like quality to this, as we have argued earlier for rondels, that would perhaps explain the momentum of spread to and expansion within southern Britain. Nor can we completely exclude the possibility of further new arrivals in southern Britain. According to some of the colonisation theory reviewed above in this chapter, links with homelands are likely to have been maintained after initial movement, and it

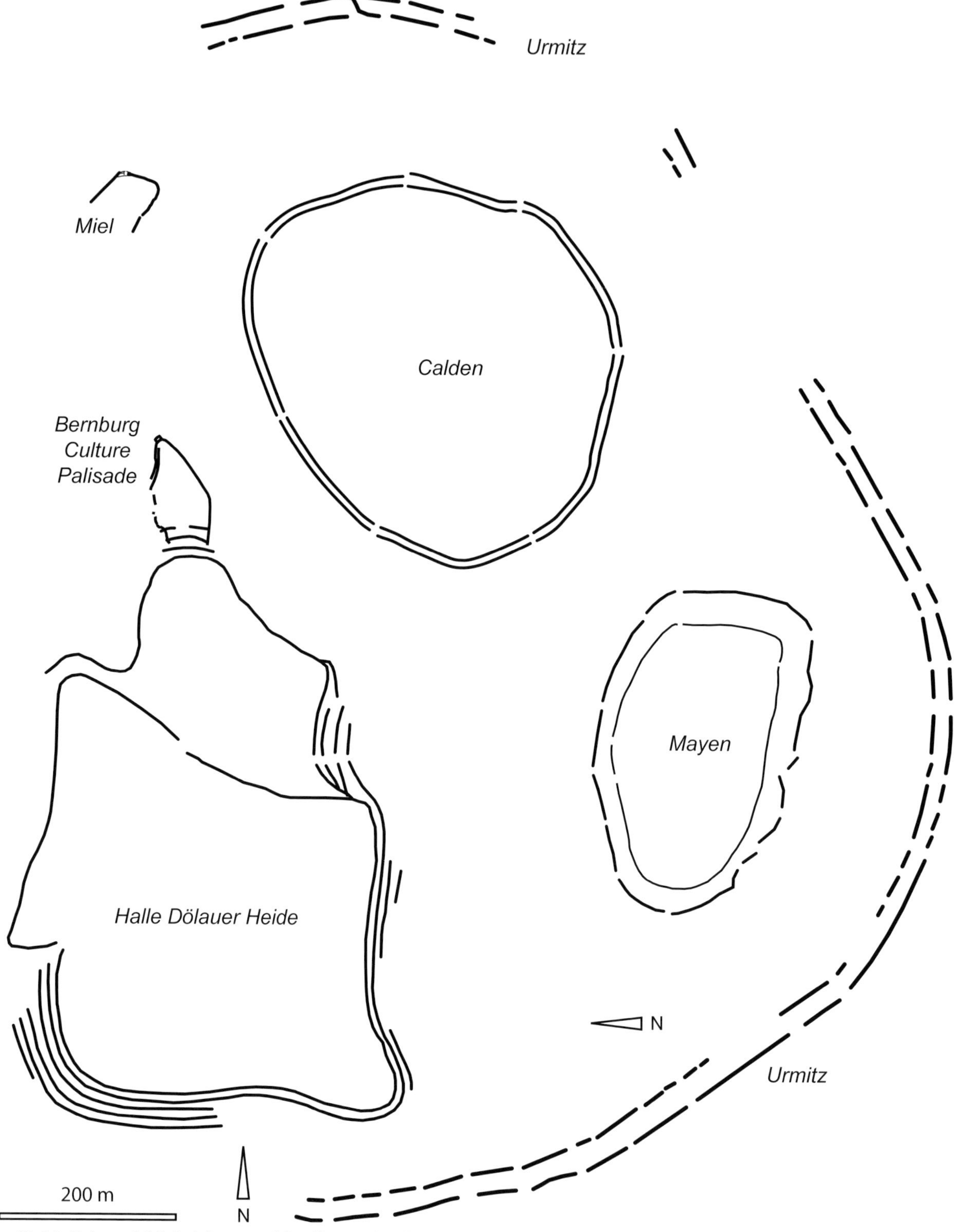

Fig. 15.14. Selected Michelsberg and Baalberge (Halle Dölauer Heide) enclosures, drawn to a common scale. After Meyer and Raetzel-Fabian (2006).

is not beyond the bounds of credibility that the appearance of enclosures in southern Britain is a manifestation of that. Against this idea, however, is a lack of other observable material change at this time which could be attributed to the outside; no one has suggested, for example, that the Decorated pottery style need relate to earlier fourth millennium continental inspiration. But in the context of continuing contact with the continent, seen also in the movement of jadeitite and other axeheads, communities, groups or organisers could have made more concerted and more dramatic use of distant things, whose impact as powerful innovation is well documented in anthropological

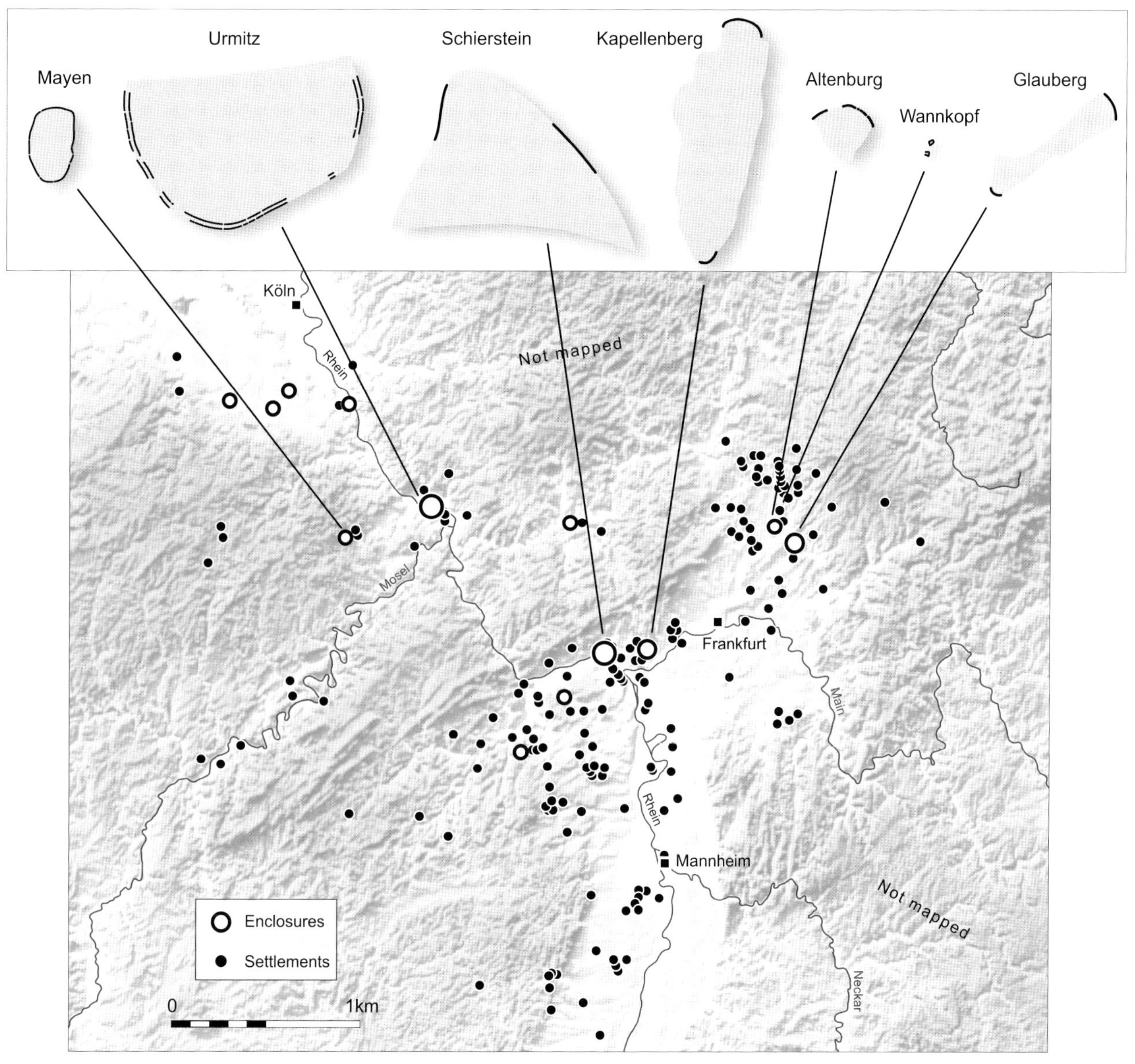

Fig. 15.15. Michelsberg enclosures and settlements in the middle Rhine and Rhine-Main area. After Gronenborn (2010).

case studies (e.g. Helms 1988; 1998). In her study of chiefdom societies, Mary Helms (1998, 11) suggests that:

> ...connections with cosmologically defined origins-related outside entities, including other kin groups or even other polities, are essential not only to the formal outward expression of hierarchy but also to its manifestations, however uneven, within society and that the dynamics of internal social inequality and political jockeying are expressed most vividly in reference to such contexts, too.

The likely power of a nexus of connections to the outside seems clear, and we have already emphasised the apparently dynamic nature of change in southern Britain in the run-up to the appearance of enclosures.

Both the continental and insular sequences underline the puzzle of why, if enclosures were already part of continental practice in the later fifth millennium, they were not adopted at the start of the Neolithic. We believe that appeals to the outside, to the 'distant', and the novel, and not excluding the powerfully ancient, are best seen from the insular context; *local* organisation was needed to put new ideas into practice: through example, through persuasion, and through mobilisation of labour. It is striking, however, that once again the first enclosures were probably built in south-east England, closest to the continent and potentially most open to or familiar with contemporary continental practice (Fig. 14.16). In a longer perspective, this was perhaps the second call on the outside, if the initiation of long barrows and cairns and related constructions was at least in part related to such concepts. If those had become established by *c.* 3800 cal BC and enclosures appear probably just before 3700 cal BC, this is in itself a further clue to the acceleration of change. Did those who brought in enclosures seek to trump existing barrow-related practice? Were the two kinds of monument in some kind of opposition?

In the present state of information, we are not inclined

Fig. 15.16. Views of the Michelsberg enclosure at Heilbronn-Klingenberg 'Schlossberg', before and under excavation; the ditch section is in the inner ditch. Photos: Ute Seidel.

to explain the increase in interrupted-ditch and causewayed enclosures on the continent and in southern Britain by reference to climate change. Detlef Gronenborn (2007b), reviewing the Michelsberg expansion and Rhineland sites including Bruchsal 'Aue', Bruchsal-Scheelkopf, Hetzenberg, Ilsfeld and Heidelberg-Handschuhsheim, draws attention to instances of peri-mortem violence and burning, and implies that these are causally related to 'the 37th c. B.C. crisis' (2007b, 20), the claimed climax of a trend to cooler and wetter conditions in southern central Europe from *c.* 4000 cal BC (2007b, 16; cf. Schibler *et al.* 1997b; Magny 2004; Arbogast *et al.* 2006). The local effects of climate shifts can be debated even in the Alpine foreland (Whittle 2003, chapter 6), but it is obviously unwise to ignore the possibility of wider effects which might have increased the chances of inter-group competition for resources. The general difficulty here is that, even with the chronological uncertainties noted above, it appears that the beginning of the main phase of the continental causewayed enclosure phenomenon comfortably precedes the climate changes in question, so that enclosures of this kind as a whole can hardly be 'explained' by climate change, and the instances of possible violence are spread between the 40th and 38th centuries cal BC, on informal inspection of

Fig. 15.17. Possible reconstructions of the circuits of the Michelsberg enclosure at Heilbronn-Klingenberg 'Schlossberg'. After Seidel (2010). Original drawing by S. Krisch, Tübingen; © Landesamt für Denkmalpflege Baden-Württemberg.

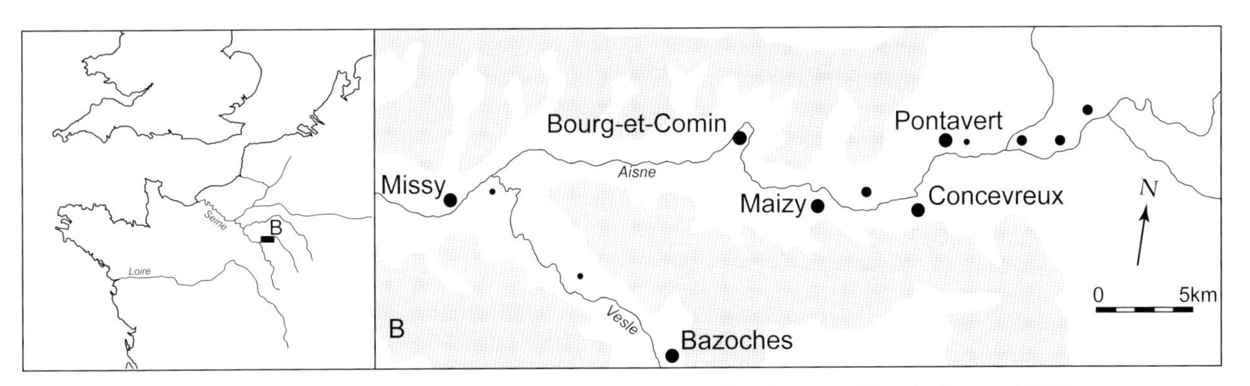

Fig. 15.18. Map of principal enclosures in the Aisne valley, France. After Andersen (1997).

radiocarbon dates, rather than concentrated in the 37th. Moreover, there may have been broad regional variations, with drier conditions mooted as characterising conditions further north in Europe 'around and after 4000 cal BC' (Gronenborn 2007b, 16).

Finally, it is worth noting again the relation between the continental enclosure history outlined above and the question of the dating of Magheraboy in western Ireland. If Magheraboy dates to very soon after 4000 cal BC, there would have been distant continental exemplars in existence, according to current understanding of chronologies, and probably closest in the Paris basin. So the wider history would allow its early date, as it were, but in turn that wider setting makes it all the more unusual at such a time, emphasised by the later dating of the enclosure at Donegore.

15.7 Enclosures in the making: places of innovation

So at a certain point in the southern British Neolithic sequence, dramatic new practices were initiated (Fig.

Fig. 15.19. Views of the enclosure at Bazoches, Aisne valley, under excavation. Photos: Jérôme Dubouloz, CNRS-INRAP.

15.23). We think that the circumstances of this innovation were probably competitive, with appeal deliberately made to things at a distance. Now, because we can trace genealogies of descent in the European enclosure tradition, it is easy to take this development for granted, but it is important to underline its novelty in the insular setting. Ian Hodder (1990, 260) referred to causewayed enclosures (and long barrows) as a 'monumental intervention in nature', and although the matter of attitudes to nature is perhaps an open question, this characterisation catches something of the change of scale seen in constructions from the late 38th century cal BC onwards. In another context, Tim Ingold (2006) has urged that we re-discover a capacity for astonishment, and that seems entirely appropriate here.

Enclosures had to be performed. In his discussion of the episodic, secret male initiation rites of the mountain Ok people of Papua New Guinea, Fredrik Barth noted that 'to assert a conception which is publicly compelling, can sometimes be far more precarious than other times' (1987, 61); in that context, 'a situation is created where the vision and commitment of a handful of senior men must be sufficiently strong to make it necessary for them to impose this ephemeral group identity on a vastly larger, ritually passive population which has no experience that calls for its conceptualization' (Barth 1987, 60). Faced with 'a receptive group of awed, attentive novices', the onus on the ritual expert is 'to make the mystery immanent, to spellbind himself and his novices with the experience' (Barth 1987, 44–5). The emphasis in the Ok case is on secrecy and episodic performance, at roughly ten-year intervals along the steps of initiation. That conditions the generation of variation, both through time and among neighbouring groups. How to do things may be held in the head of one person alone, and that not only places considerable emphasis on memory, given that 'most senior men had only fragmentary recollections of even the elementary initiations through which they had passed' (Barth 1987, 26), but also allows for plenty of creativity.

This comparison raises questions. It seems counter-intuitive to suppose that what went on at causewayed enclosures in southern Britain involved secret knowledge, given the scale of constructions and the probably large numbers of people involved. But in terms of *first* performances of the enclosure idea in a given region, as the practice spread, there may not have been prior knowledge among most of the participants of what precisely was to take place, even though individual elements – from digging to eating, or from material objects to their deposition – would have been familiar. So how did the practice actually get going? We have argued above that people with connections to the

Fig. 15.20. Aerial photos of Fornham All Saints, Suffolk, showing an angled cursus monument overlying two causewayed enclosures, looking north-west (above) and south-east (below). For the full plan, see Oswald et al. *(2001, fig. 4.25). Photos: © Suffolk County Council Archaeology Service.*

Fig. 15.21. The entry of guests into a funeral feast in the Torajan village of Banga, Indonesia. Photo: Brian Hayden.

continent both old and active brought it in, as a ploy in early Neolithic politics, to bolster their own position with awe-inspiring novelty. Were these people sufficient in number to materialise an enclosure by themselves, to lead, as it were, by example, or did they have to cajole and enchant followers and others, by performance on the one hand and enactment of things known only in myth and story?

There are several ways in which we could suppose that new participants or audiences could have been spellbound, once drawn in. First, it is probable that most enclosures were placed in new locations in the landscape. That is principally with respect to Mesolithic inhabitation; very few places of enclosure have signs of previous Mesolithic occupation. Perhaps that is just accident, but there is not the continuity (or is that too to be dismissed as fortuitous?) seen between pre-cairn Neolithic occupations and cairn constructions at sites like Gwernvale, Hazleton and Ascott-under-Wychwood (Britnell 1984; Saville 1990; Benson and Whittle 2007). There are also comparatively few signs of pre-enclosure early Neolithic activity directly on the spot at the majority of causewayed enclosures; the regional chapters give details (and the complications of interpretation) for, among others, Windmill Hill, Maiden Castle and Hambledon Hill (see also Mercer and Healy 2008, 53–4). There are of course several locations where long barrows are in varying degrees of proximity to enclosures, and in line with the discussion in section 15.4 it is probable that at least some pre-date the enclosure horizon. Those at Hambledon Hill are probably the physically closest, though it is not clear (*67% probable*; Table 4.4) that the southern long barrow there actually pre-dates the main enclosure, or at least predates it by much (Figs 4.10, 4.14, 4.17). The distinctions are not necessarily clear-cut, but many enclosures could have been deliberately sited to be in locations without visible or deep pasts, and to enchant by their freshness.

Secondly, however people were persuaded or motivated to contribute their labour, there would now have been bigger numbers involved than earlier. We cannot exclude the possibility of large gatherings preceding the formalisation of enclosures, as argued previously in general terms by John Barrett (1994), but the mobilisation of labour for enclosure construction is surely greater than that required for earlier building enterprises, even when site histories can be broken down into episodes of successive activity, for example at Windmill Hill (Chapter 3.1) or Hambledon Hill (Chapter 4.1); in some cases, for example at Maiden Castle (Chapter 4.3) and Abingdon (Chapter 8.5), it is probable that the mobilisation of labour was swift. There would have been a new kind of bodily consciousness for anyone involved in the construction of a ditch circuit, even if the experience of digging a single circuit need have been little different to that, say, of a substantial long cairn quarry, for example as at Hazleton and Ascott-under-Wychwood in the century before enclosures took off. This new kind of embodiment would have been accompanied by a potentially greater

Fig. 15.22. Perforated skull from the Michelsberg enclosure at Ilsfeld, Germany, and its reconstructed position in the ditch system. After Wahl (2000).

scale of sociality, with more people perhaps spending more time together on a single shared task than would regularly have been the case in day-to-day contexts. Nor should we forget the result of this shared labour in its own right. The phrase of Hodder quoted above gives major importance to ideas of the wild and nature, but we can equally place prime emphasis on the space, form and scale created by enclosures in themselves, and re-imagine the astonishment and enchantment of both builders and subsequent witnesses.

Once initiated, with demonstration of effective performances, it is easier to envisage the spread of the practice, with sufficient temporal intervals in the early years, combined with spatial separation, for diversity to be generated as in the Ok case noted above. Might the history of the spread of Neolithic things and practices, discussed above, also help in part to explain the differing distributions of enclosures in southern Britain? Could it be that in certain areas ritual experts, initiators and organisers, or people in general, chose to emphasise their remembered history in part by the frequency with which they made use of the enclosure idea? As presently recorded, there are three areas with particular concentrations of enclosures: on the Sussex downland, in the lower Welland and Nene valleys, and in the upper Thames catchment (Fig. 1.2). The Sussex enclosures are in an area where Neolithic activity goes back probably to

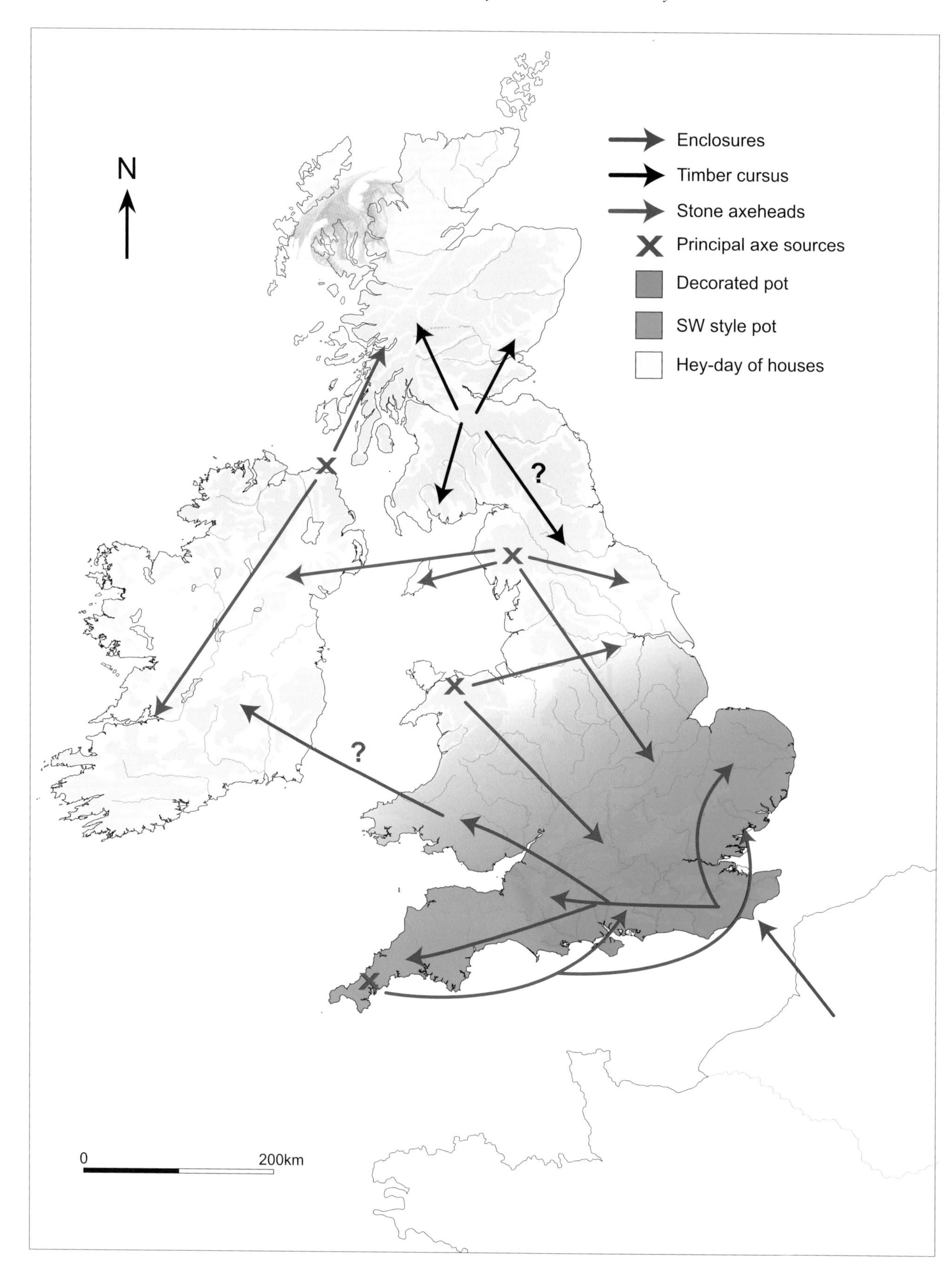

Fig. 15.23. Interpretive map of selected shared practices and networks forged in the generations around 3700 cal BC in Britain and Ireland. Compare Fig. 14.181.

the 40th century cal BC, while those of the upper Thames, flanking and overlapping with those of the Cotswolds, are directly adjacent to an area where Neolithic activity also goes back probably to the 40th century cal BC (Fig. 14.54: *start Sussex Neolithic* and *start Cotswold Neolithic*). The possible correlation with early beginnings is less clear, however, in the lower Welland-lower Nene case, and in general enclosures are found west of the East Anglian fens (Fig. 14.54: *start eastern Neolithic*; Chapter 6). There is, moreover, no particular concentration around the Greater Thames estuary itself, though numbers there have increased impressively in just the last few years (Chapters 1 and 7). There can be other ways to think about the differing distributions and site biographies within the dominant 150-year span of the enclosure idea, which we go on to discuss now in more detail.

15.8 Things that mattered: the generation of worldviews

Over the years there have been many general models of the meanings and significance of causewayed enclosures, many tending to agree with the summary view of Richard Bradley (2007, 74) that, despite diversity among sites, 'perhaps they were aggregation sites where public events took place'. These interpretations are summarised in Chapter 1.3. One of the most nuanced discussions stressed ambiguities and changes through time as well as diversity, suggesting among other themes the coming into existence of 'dominant locales' and (following Appadurai 1985) the practice of 'tournaments of value', involving the 'renegotiation of the value and significance attributed to objects obtained through a variety of social networks', and 'crucial for the reproduction of relations between dispersed communities' the provision of 'a bounded context in which a variety of practices that exposed the fabric of society could be undertaken and their interpretation controlled' (Edmonds 1993a, 108, 124–5). Although accounts of this kind regularly stress diversity, there are also many recurrent features, from styles of circuit construction, and the numbers of people implied, to the character of materials and residues found and the manner of their placing in the ground; communal construction, large-scale assembly, feasting, and patterned deposition of materials, food residues and remains of the human dead, are all parts of a canon of practice at causewayed enclosures widely accepted in Neolithic scholarship. Enclosures can be seen at one level as part of a repertoire of containers prevalent in the early Neolithic, which also includes pots, pits and barrows or cairns.[10] At the same time, interpretations of individual sites published over the last 20 years or so underline the diversity stressed in generalising accounts. Thus the report on Haddenham has emphasised a relatively brief but ongoing history of the mobilisation of labour, to create a 'great clearance', mimicking other aspects of woodland life (Evans and Hodder 2006); that on Hambledon Hill has recently stressed a 'frontier' position, the site aligned to others to its west and suggestive of 'quasi-political unity over long distances and equally quasi-political prominence for some sites as 'symbolic' of the social solidarity that they had come to represent'; attack and defence were prominent aspects of this world of the west (Mercer 2008a, 777; cf. Mercer 2006a; 2006b). Windmill Hill was seen to present a whole range of dominant concerns of early Neolithic society, arranged purposefully across its three circuits, to help people to create symbolic order (Whittle *et al.* 1999). The interpretation of Etton also underlined a spatial logic behind the character of deposition on either side of the single circuit, playing out domestic and funerary activity in periodic activity (Pryor 1998). Maiden Castle, finally, was seen as a locale for the negotiation of important but potentially dangerous rituals of social interaction, deliberately placed in an out-of-the-way setting (Sharples 1991a; cf. J. Evans *et al.* 1988).

What the present study adds above all is a sense of timing and tempo (cf. Bayliss *et al.* 2008b; Whittle and Bayliss 2007). We concentrate in the first place on the hey-day of the construction of causewayed enclosures over 150 years in the 37th century cal BC and the first half of the 36th century cal BC (Fig. 14.7). This overlaps with the ongoing history of the long barrow and long cairn tradition. We will then consider the later lives of those causewayed enclosures – and some long barrows and long cairns – which continued in use after the middle of the 36th century cal BC, from which time onwards cursus monuments were the next monumental innovation, at least in the south of Britain, and long barrows and long cairns continued to be used (Fig. 14.45). It is clear that we need to work at different scales, tacking between what is shared and what is particular to individual sites and parts of sites, and there is the opportunity now to consider both the timing of individual enclosures in the developing tradition and the overall tempo of the phenomenon as a whole. We will first reconsider some of the generalities already noted through the lens of temporality, before looking again at individual sites first presented in the regional chapters.

So far, the discussion may be seen as having taken enclosure form for granted. Some time ago, however, quoting the dictum of the French Symbolist poet Paul Valéry that projects are never finished, only abandoned, Christopher Evans proposed that we should think of 'prehistoric constructs as *projects*' (original italics), which were 'resolved (conceived) only through their construction'; 'given spatial qualities may only have been 'emergent' in the sequence of their construction' (C. Evans 1988b, 88). Questioning the application of notions of formal design, with particular reference to the Haddenham enclosure, he proposed that 'some aspects of the enclosure planning/layout…were not conceived in the initial stages, but *emerged* later in its construction/maintenance' (Evans 1988a, 130; original italics). The inner circuits of multiple constructions were proposed as probably the earliest features, a visual core from which subsequent concentric circuits were laid out (Evans 1988a; 1988b, 91). This view has since been quite widely followed in the literature on monuments in general (e.g. Barrett 1994; C. Richards 2004;

McFadyen 2007; discussed critically by Whittle 2006), and has been discussed again recently with reference to Hambledon Hill and other causewayed enclosures (Mercer 2006a, 69).

What emerges from the present study is something more complex. Clearly, some sites were modified over considerable periods of time, and in that sense were indeed ongoing projects. Hambledon Hill is probably at present the classic example, but we could add Crickley Hill, and perhaps Whitehawk, as well as Hembury and others. But the *initial* project at Hambledon, the construction of the inner main enclosure, and other examples like the first, interrupted circuits at Crickley, whether or not they were successive, present what Roger Mercer (2006a, 69) has called 'unitary conceptions': coherent, circular layouts, which appear at the level of precision achievable within the available modelling to be of a single date. The same probably applies to single-circuit enclosures like that at Etton – even though that was modified in subsequent phases. There is at least one example where the model of successive elaboration from an inner core can be supported: that of Windmill Hill, though the order was probably from inner to outer to middle, with the construction and primary use of the West Kennet long barrow in the probable interval between outer and middle circuits (Chapter 3.4; Fig. 3.28). In all these cases, and others, there seems little reason in fact to doubt the intention of enclosing space in predetermined form. That leaves other interesting issues, such as whether only the ritual experts involved in the first enclosure knew what they were about to do, such that form would have been *revealed* during and by the building process: a rather different perspective to that initiated by Christopher Evans. It is also worth reflecting on whether forms created were the same as forms planned or broadly agreed. Was, for example, the kidney-shaped layout seen at Haddenham, Briar Hill and the inner circuit at Windmill Hill, an on-the-spot compromise or shortening of the initial enterprise?

The brevity of many individual constructions rather than their lack of design can now be stressed. As discussed in Chapter 14, some were subsumed in longer histories. The longest-lasting enclosures now stand out as exceptions rather than the rule, and the development of Hambledon Hill, Windmill Hill, Crickley Hill/Peak Camp and Etton was different in each case. There were also episodes of construction within the medium-length histories of a century to a century and a half, as at Chalk Hill and Hembury, though the dating of the former was largely confined to one circuit. The enclosures of short duration, such as St Osyth, Abingdon and especially Maiden Castle, were not of the simplest form, nor the smallest. The three circuits at St Osyth were not directly dated; the two at Abingdon were either coeval or built within a few years of each other, as was probably also the case for the two closely spaced and impressively large circuits at Maiden Castle. Maiden Castle appears to belong to the latter end of the hey-day of causewayed enclosure construction. The models for both St Osyth and Abingdon are strongly bimodal. This suggests their construction in the 37th century cal BC on the one hand, but also allows it in the middle portion of the 36th century cal BC, which raises the intriguing possibility that the enclosures of the shortest duration tended to belong to the end of the tradition, either because events and fashions then moved on, or because circumstances at that point in the tradition required dramatic, brief performances.

Timing and tempo bring fresh perspectives to the business of assembly, first in the mobilisation of labour. This has been extensively discussed for Haddenham, the model proposed being one of a relatively short history of ongoing construction and modification, say over 50 years or fewer, involving a labour pool of hypothetically not more than 100 people working seasonally and a group of users suggested as '100–200 individuals or 10–40 residential/familial groups (or 3–7 'lineages')' (Evans and Hodder 2006, 328–9). Frustratingly, it was not possible to date that enclosure with any precision. Figure 4.18 presents estimates for the input of labour through the episodic history of Hambledon Hill. Apart from the late flourish probably in the 34th century cal BC involving the western outworks, the major input of labour was in the early phases of the site, in the first half of the 37th century cal BC. Roger Mercer has also proposed (2008b, 751) a '100 person' model, working perhaps in stints of 80 days a year over one or two years. While we need not impose any uniformity in the circumstances of construction, given all the other evidence for diverse practices, this order of magnitude would probably cover many other cases as well. As Mercer has commented (2008b, 751), this would not have been 'a major undertaking for a population of 1000 (100 families) who thought that it was important enough'. But we can now emphasise the increase in the overall tempo of construction during the course of the 37th century cal BC, with a lull at the turn of the century and a renewed burst of activity in the first part of the 36th century cal BC (e.g. Fig. 14.20; to all of which we return in section 15.10, in further discussion of Neolithic politics). We can also reflect on the difference in the social conditions of the mobilisation of labour compared with the 38th century cal BC. We would probably not normally think of 100 families or 1000 people behind the construction of an individual long barrow or long cairn, not least given the overall numbers in the Cotswolds, where estimates of barrow/cairn use-lives of 50 years' duration over a period of some 200 years suggested some 29 such monuments in operation at any one time (Whittle *et al.* 2007a, 137). So we are probably witnessing an increase – though one very hard to quantify – in the scale of labour mobilisation, and probably also an overall acceleration in the large-scale mobilisations through the 37th century cal BC. There need not be uniformity or regularity. The Windmill Hill area suggests difference from generation to succeeding generation, with first the modest enterprise of the inner ditch, then the crescendo of the construction of the great outer circuit, followed by the perhaps much more traditional and limited undertaking of the West Kennet long barrow (though still on a locally impressive scale), and finally capped by the task of intermediate demand required by the building of the middle circuit. A subsequent generation again may have built the much smaller enclosure on Knap Hill 8 km to the south (Fig. 3.32). Maiden Castle at the end of the hey-day of enclosure construction again offers intriguing possibilities of change. It encloses an area more or less the same as the main inner enclosure at Hambledon Hill, but its ditches were probably doubled right around the circuit, in contrast to Hambledon's, and would thus have required twice the effort of construction in a very short space of time.

The other aspect of assembly concerns what people did at enclosures once constructed. Here there are considerable challenges to interpretation, first since it is normal (and understandable) practice to infer the character of activity directly from the materials and residues to hand, and secondly because it is very difficult to scale the numbers of people present. Thus recurrently abundant (though varying) numbers of animal bones have often been taken to signify large-scale consumption (e.g. Whittle and Pollard 1998; 1999), and it is easy to move from that interpretation to the assumption that feasting was a dominant activity at such sites, and a goal in its own right. Other material such as lithics, including imported stone and flint axes, and pottery, is incorporated in such views either as by-product of temporary gatherings or as a sign of some (but limited) more prolonged occupation. An older view of course saw enclosures as seasonal places to deal with cattle management. Only rarely in more recent times have more specialised roles been suggested, the interpretation of Offham for example, where finds were in general very scarce, as a place to deal with the dead (Drewett 1977), standing out from the more common generalising views. What if, however, we have overlooked possible specific purposes? Should we go back to cattle kraals? To take just two examples, the presence of live cattle at Etton has been strongly suggested by beetle evidence, and at Northborough by phosphate analysis (Chapter 6.4). Some of the evidence for defence and attack, discussed further below, could be to do with cattle raiding. But then hilltop locations at least are not good places to keep cattle for any length of time, nor is the concentration of vulnerable herds in one place necessarily a better tactic than dispersal. Perhaps also smaller enclosures (like those say at Thornhill and Knowth in Ireland) might be expected to be a more common feature of the early Neolithic landscape in southern Britain if these cattle-oriented conditions were general.

Another possibility for a specific role could be that many enclosures were involved with treatment of the human dead and especially with subsequent mortuary and commemorative rites. We have already seen the presence of the dead at continental enclosures, and there are variable numbers of human remains in southern British examples, though the model of involvement with mortuary rites does not require consistent quantities. They are encountered, among others at Windmill Hill, Hambledon Hill, Maiden Castle, Whitehawk, Etton, Staines, and Abingdon (Chapters 3.1, 4.1 and 4.3, 5.1, 6.4.1 and 8.5). There are whole bodies and parts of bodies; on-site exposure has been suggested for Etton (Pryor 1998, 362), and for Hambledon Hill (McKinley 2008, 497–504). There, the human remains in general, like the animal bones from the site, were subject to damage from dogs and rodents, but the human material (as at Etton: Armour-Chelu 1998b; Pryor 1998, 362) was in general more weathered and degraded than the animal material; 23 finds of human bone, both articulated and disarticulated, also have cutmarks (McKinley 2008, 497–504). Some crania were deposited on their own, including on the base of the main enclosure ditch, and several have been noted as particularly weathered and worn; other contexts also suggest some curation of other bones (McKinley 2008; Mercer and Healy 2008, 759–60). Alongside the evidence for differential treatment, there are also links; at Windmill Hill, the femur of a human juvenile was inserted into a *Bos* humerus in the inner ditch (context 630: Whittle *et al.* 1999; Wysocki 1999; *contra* Pariat 2007, 122), and at Etton the excavator noted the resemblance between crania and upturned pots, for example in segment 7 (Pryor 1998, fig. 31, and 370).

So, without going into all the site detail, selected individuals and parts of bodies are deposited from time to time, often without apparent ceremony, in the non-ordinary context of the ditches (and sometimes other features) of enclosures. This raises the question of audience. What sort of gatherings did such depositions entail? Are we to suppose small, restricted groups of mourners – familiar perhaps from the modern perspective – or something on a much larger social scale, full of noise and public drama, involving many more people (cf. Parker Pearson 1992)? What, too, of the emotions aroused by such occasions (Metcalf and Huntington 1991, chapter 2)? Were these selected persons deposited without emotion, because removed from an ordinary social context, or did such a setting enhance the grief and anger of the occasion? The wider possibilities sit well with the conception of enclosures as places of collective labour and shared assembly, but the fact that we have not so far normally sought to attempt such a distinction in the character of mortuary or funerary activity underlines the problematic nature of burials at enclosures. It is noticeable that while the interim report on Hambledon Hill drew attention to the 'vast, reeking open cemetery' represented by the main enclosure (Mercer 1980, 63), discussion in the final report is much more muted on this theme, stressing social hierarchy and defence far more (Mercer and Healy 2008, 759–60; Mercer 2008a). And if personhood or identity was distributed, not confined conceptually to the singular body (C. Fowler 2004a; Whittle 2003), then we can also think not only about the body as redolent with meaning but also about human remains in general as a symbolic resource. Individual remains may work metonymically, part for whole, distributing identities and relations. It would now be an interesting programme systematically to date crania and other remains from primary contexts to see if curated, old material was brought into the enclosures.

Should we be content with the concept of simple

funerals, when we know from ethnographic studies that funerary rites may extend for years after a death, and that processes of forgetting (Forty and Küchler 1999) can be as important as chains of memory? In the case of the Bara people of Madagascar, burial is followed by gatherings and feasts, and eventual reburial. 'Death and burial are often shocking events that disrupt the normal flow of village activity. But the gathering and reburial events are experienced as an annual season of festivities…' (Metcalf and Huntington 1991, 116). Such gatherings are the biggest in Bara social existence, involving hundreds of people and the killing of up to a dozen cattle. But there are dangers as well, seen in wrestling, dancing and cattle riding, and there is a lurking fear of witchcraft. Fighting may result, and the gatherings end after a few days (Metcalf and Huntington 1991, 118–20).

Drawing on a wider range of examples from south-east Asia, Indonesia, Melanesia, Polynesia and the north American Northwest Coast, Brian Hayden has stated (2009, 29) that 'funeral feasts in traditional societies often constitute the single most important and costly event in the history of a family'. While noting other interpretations of excessively lavish feasts in terms of 'ideological cultural traditions' or with the need to impress the dead themselves, so that the ancestors will 'dispense fertility, wealth and success on their living descendants', he mainly promotes a view of the feast in 'transegalitarian' societies (notionally intermediate between egalitarian bands and stratified chiefdoms) as 'critical in obtaining political, social and economic advantages' (B. Hayden 2009, 30–1; see also Dietler and Hayden 2001). Funeral feasts in Indonesia, however, are concerned with more restricted goals (Fig. 15.21). They can occur long after a particular death, blurring the distinction between funeral and commemorative feasts. They can vary in scale, duration and size of audience, in Sulawesi from one–two nights with one pig and possibly one water buffalo, right up to the rare instance of 27 or more nights with more than 36 pigs and 16 water buffaloes (B. Hayden 2009, 32; Adams 2004). More than a thousand people can attend the more lavish events. Hayden stresses the ostentation, which may transgress normal egalitarian values, and the desire to invite and feed 'as many people from as large an area and as high rank as possible' (B. Hayden 2009, 33), which serves to create and cement alliances, marriage opportunities, openings for trade or exchange, and self-protection against the potential aggrandisement of others (B. Hayden 2009, 35–6). Finally, he underlines the sensuousness of feasts, their unusual foods, dramatic performances and symbolism, the emotions generated, the social closeness and intimacy generated (B. Hayden 2009, 38). 'Of all the pretexts that might be good for holding alliance or promotional feasts, funerals are probably the most suited' (B. Hayden 2009, 39), because of the emotional malleability and receptiveness of the participants.

Would such a specific role for causewayed enclosures work? It could encompass the human remains already noted, and many of the other finds including the animal bone assemblages. It could allow for differences within, for example, the Hambledon complex, with the Stepleton enclosure having an apparently more domestic role than the main enclosure (Mercer and Healy 2008). It might help to make partial sense of the relationship between causewayed enclosures and surrounding long barrows and long cairns; generally as already noted, the greatest concentrations of barrows/cairns coincide or are adjacent to the largest clusters of enclosures, though the lower Welland/lower Nene group is an exception to this pattern. And finally, the appearance of enclosures in the sequence could be seen as coming at a point when funeral and commemorative rites were becoming more elaborate and were taken into a wider domain, reflecting the putative competition already noted above. The relationship between Windmill Hill and West Kennet long barrow has already been noted. Other potentially similar relationships can be considered. At Hambledon Hill, for example, the excavated example of the two long barrows was one of the earliest elements of the complex (Table 4.4; Figs 4.14, 4.17), and was thus extant as enclosure construction continued. Nonetheless, the four barrow/cairn endings dated to the later 37th century cal BC – those of Ascott-under-Wychwood, Hazleton, Fussell's Lodge and West Kennet (Whittle *et al.* 2007a, fig. 9) – come strikingly at the point when enclosure construction was reaching its first peak (Fig. 14.20). So is this just coincidence, or were long barrows and long cairns at least temporarily or locally eclipsed as arenas where the dead and their spirits were set to rest?

Attractive though a specific or principal role like this might be, it does not seem to explain quite enough. It can be objected that it is difficult to separate funeral or commemorative feasts from a wider spectrum of public events of this kind (e.g. Dietler and Hayden 2001), and the particular goals inferred by Hayden may not be dominant over other motives including sorrow, closure, mourning, pacification of the dead and so on (e.g. M. Jones 2009; Hastorf 2009). And what of the other kinds of deposition, and the evidence for defence and attack? It is perhaps therefore safer to fall back on those more generalised and diverse kinds of role already frequently advocated for enclosures, as places of aggregation, negotiation and transformation (e.g. Edmonds 1993a; 1999; J. Thomas 1999; Evans and Hodder 2006; R. Bradley 2007; Mercer and Healy 2008). We could gloss these general themes further, by stressing the importance, given the sequence which we have been emphasising, of principles of seniority, prowess and affiliation. Seniority could sum up a thread running back into the first monuments, a desire to establish precedent and genealogical primacy, an urge to evoke the distant and the exotic, and sometimes the old, a compulsion to deal with the dead and the past, and a wish to be seen as innovative and creative. Prowess could evoke the ability to mobilise labour, the generosity to provide meat and other food in abundance, predicated probably on the capability to assemble and maintain large herds of cattle and other animals, and the capacity to defend oneself against the jealousies, predations and actual attacks of others.

Affiliation can speak for the provision of arenas to which people from far as well as near could be drawn, for the connections which brought in objects from distant sources, and for the fixing of these mixed identities in particular local places. It is important too to stress the opposites of these themes (cf. Barth 1987, chapter 9), to underline their importance. Thus assembly and aggregation imply dispersal and returning to much smaller groups; seniority incurs the risk of a lesser position; prowess carries the risk of limited success, scarcity or even failure; the killing of animals challenges their nurturing and accumulation as livestock; and affiliation may incur exclusions, enemies and violence. In the Bara mortuary domain, noted above, there are active concerns with notions of social order and vitality, and there are tensions between the two. Among components of order can be listed maleness, semen, bone, sterility and dying, and among the elements of vitality are femaleness, blood, flesh, fecundity and birth (Metcalf and Huntington 1991, 113–14). Maurice Bloch (1986; 1992) has also explored the inclusion of violence in acts of ritual which are otherwise seen to confer blessing and benefit to the participants.

This notion of opposites may help to outline some of the recurrent and dominant social and conceptual concerns of people in southern Britain from the late 38th century cal BC onwards. Can we go further? In the case of Windmill Hill, the character and distribution of finds within and around the three ditch circuits was taken to suggest the working through of a worldview or cosmology, with some kind of play between more abstract ideas of nature, the wild and the dead in the outer circuit and a more socialised world in the middle and inner circuits (Whittle *et al.* 1999). Contrasts have also been suggested between the different sides of Etton, and between circuit and interior (Pryor 1998); something similar has been mooted at Staines (P. Bradley 2004). Many of the elements of the Hambledon complex (e.g. Mercer and Healy 2008, 183–7, 337) could also be seen from this kind of cosmological perspective, in this instance with a more sacred core – or perhaps two cores – protected by a more profane exterior. There is no need, however, to insist that all such arenas had developed or recoverable cosmological schemes writ large upon them. It is entirely compatible with the notions of diversity and creativity discussed above that this should be an element more elaborated or more explicit in some sites than others, perhaps more often in the longer-lasting enclosures, though the dichotomy between the outer and inner ditches at both Abingdon and Maiden Castle can again be noted.

A more refined sense of timing and tempo should help our understanding of the scale of things, and we will concentrate here on deposition, connections and violence. The issue of feasting has already been raised, and the diversity of kinds of feasts and the scales of consumption is considerable (see above, and Dietler and Hayden 2001). Causewayed enclosures provide instances of both conspicuous consumption and acts of violence, so it may be legitimate to think of eating as in some cases a form of 'fighting with food'. That phrase derives from the study by Michael Young (1971) of Goodenough Island off the coast of New Guinea, where in a post-colonial setting instead of resorting to violence, people used competitive food exchange and festivals to shame enemies and offenders with gifts of pigs and yams. If this is too specific an analogy for fourth-millennium southern Britain, it is still important to be able to scale the nature of deposition, including food remains. Chapter 14.2 has stressed that the scale of deposition was often in fact quite modest. The most impressive deposits of cattle from Hambledon Hill come from slots cut into the largely silted main enclosure ditch, still within the primary use of the site, in the 34th century cal BC at the latest (Legge 2008); there are also impressive concentrations of material other than animal bones in the short-lived sites of Abingdon and Maiden Castle (Table 14.3), as well as at Whitesheet and Knap Hill. Nonetheless, it is rare for the primary levels of many causewayed enclosure ditches to be devoid of bone (as is, for example, normally the case with cursus ditches), as seen extensively in the large-scale excavations at Hambledon Hill and Etton (Legge 2008; Armour-Chelu 1998a), and even in the much more restricted 1988 excavations at Windmill Hill, confirming the wider pattern established by Keiller (Grigson 1999). That is not to require every ditch segment or every site to be the same; Offham and Combe Hill stand apart. But even if the remains of individual animals have been variously curated or exposed, and thereby dispersed, they nonetheless establish the recurrent killing of animals, normally cattle in the greatest numbers, a single beast of which could have provided meat for hundreds of people (Tresset 2000; Serjeantson 2006; Schulting 2008). So together the dating models and quantities of artefacts deposited provide perhaps on the one hand a relative sense of the frequency of visitation at enclosures through the 37th century cal BC and the first part of the 36th century cal BC, and on the other some indication of at least localised intensification of deposition towards the end of the use of enclosures.

Being connected was of central importance in the early Neolithic world. The Sussex mines were in use very early in the fourth millennium, their products reaching as far as Wessex and East Anglia, and other selected flints and continental jadeitites were also on the move well before enclosures (Figs 14.118 and 14.128). Chapter 14 has shown how the reach of exchange networks of south- and north-western stone axes extended during the first half of the 37th century cal BC (Fig. 14.140), more or less coinciding with the most active period of causewayed enclosure construction (Fig. 14.20). Those networks extended far to the east of the country, with Group VI axes at Etton and Haddenham, for example. The range of contacts visible through the phases of Hambledon Hill appears to extend with time (Chapter 4.1), though this trend cannot be traced as clearly at other sites. But it is striking that the axe networks are estimated in our models (e.g. Fig 14.144) to come to an end, or at least to decline substantially, *c.* 3500 cal BC, at the time when the construction of new enclosures had also come to an end. Axe sources like Langdale or Penmaenmawr show profuse traces of workings on the ground, but the investigations of the former have suggested rather episodic and individually small-scale exploitations (Bradley and Edmonds 1993; Edmonds 1993b; 1995).

Being connected was not necessarily the same as being identical, and it is worth underlining again the appearance of both the South-Western style of pottery and Decorated pottery during the latter half of the 38th century cal BC (Fig. 14.142). The patterns are revealingly mixed. Roger Mercer has suggested a contrast between 'a focus to the west' and a 'focus to the east', with the latter enclosures showing 'similar overall enclosive design but perhaps rather different layout, little evidence of violence, less apparent functional variety and different exchange linkages' (2006a, 72). Yet the layouts can be grouped into a number of tendencies which need not be divided neatly into western and eastern (R. Palmer 1976a), and while there are some broad regional tendencies within Decorated pottery, Ros Cleal (1992) has stressed the individualistic and eclectic assemblages at individual enclosures. Perhaps affiliation can be seen as a flexible and opportunistic strategy.

There was probably at times good cause for this. If the early Neolithic world was in part competitive, as we have suggested, it was from time to time also violent, seen at both inter-personal and group scales (Fig. 15.22; see also Fig. 14.37). As already indicated in Chapter 14.2, the key issues are scale and timing. It is very difficult to infer the nature and scale of violence from the individual instances. It is likely that there would have been many more wounds or trauma than those that appear on the skeleton (M. Smith and Brickley 2009). Examples of cranial trauma could be the result of ritualised violence, such as the one-to-one clubbing known among the Yanomamo of Amazonia (Schulting and Wysocki 2005; Chagnon 1968). Certainly some cranial traumas show healing, victims or participants having survived (Schulting and Wysocki 2005; M. Smith and Brickley 2009). In other individual instances, such as Individual B2 from Ascott-under-Wychwood long barrow in the Cotswolds, death appears to have been caused by ambush with bow and arrow, leading to a swift and painful end (Galer 2007; Knüsel 2007), but it is impossible to say more about the wider circumstances of this event. Was this just one unfortunate victim, or the only victim from a greater number who was given special subsequent treatment? Or was this simply a hunting accident? There is little sign of violence at Windmill Hill but one of the individuals in the primary deposit of the West Kennet long barrow has a leaf arrowhead at the neck, and is a likely victim, so we can at least say that in the period across which Windmill Hill was constructed there was some local violence. In Wayland's Smithy I, three out of the 14 individuals in the primary mortuary deposit, which probably formed over a very short period of time, are associated with leaf-shaped arrowheads, one of them actually with a flint tip lodged in the bone; and it is possible given the brevity of formation of the deposit and the imbalance between 11 men, two women and a child, that this reflects some kind of collective killing or massacre (Whittle *et al.* 2007b). Studies in the American South-West have suggested that mortuary deposits following massacres or raids are often characterised by sex imbalance, with females taken off as captives or having escaped earlier as refugees (Lowell 2007). It is of course impossible reliably to extrapolate the scale of the violent encounter from the number of victims deposited in any one place, but a simple reading of the evidence might suggest an episode at Wayland's Smithy involving at least tens of people.

Episodes of collective violence were more prevalent in the west, and a large proportion of the evidence for individual trauma so far known from the period also occurs in the west (Fig. 14.37; also stressed by Mercer 2006a; 2006b). Is there any discernible chronological pattern? Episodes of collective violence appear to be spread throughout the middle of the fourth millennium cal BC (Fig. 14.36), in line with the currency of causewayed enclosures. There were burnings at Hembury in the 37th century cal BC, successive episodes at Hambledon from the later 37th to the mid-36th century cal BC, where Maiden Castle also belongs (it is possible that the attacks at Maiden Castle and in period 2 in the inner Stepleton outwork were precisely contemporary), and then the probably 35th-century event at Crickley Hill and the probably late episodes at Orsett and Carn Brea. The mortuary deposit at Wayland's Smithy I, which may also reflect a wider scale of violence, probably formed in the earlier 36th century cal BC. The instances of inter-personal violence cited range from the early part of the fourth millennium cal BC (at Coldrum), well before the appearance of causewayed enclosures, to the closing centuries of the millennium (at Millbarrow) (Fig. 14.36).

The evidence suggests that inter-personal violence occurred throughout the early Neolithic in southern Britain. Clearly, this kind of evidence has been underestimated in many past interpretations of the Neolithic, including beyond Britain, but within the literature that has redressed the balance (including Carman and Harding 1999; Christensen 2004; Parker Pearson and Thorpe 2005) there are dramatic accounts which incline towards an extreme picture of sustained communal conflict (e.g. Keeley 1996; Golitko and Keeley 2007), driven in part by unsettled climate, as already discussed with reference to the Michelsberg sequence (e.g. Gronenborn 2007b). In some ethnographic situations there are claims of up to a 30% fatality rate among adult males due to inter-personal violence (Chagnon 1988, 986). Keeley (1996, 39) has claimed that 'the great majority of non-state societies were at war at least once every few years and many times each generation' (1996, 33) and that 'peace was a scarcer commodity for members of bands, tribes, and chiefdoms than for the average citizen of a civilized state' (1996, 39). This raises issues over much wider areas than we can go into here; other studies suggest that Neolithic societies are less violent than later state-organised systems (Peter-Röcher 2007). The southern British evidence – and indeed that from the rest of Britain and Ireland – suggests that violence was mainly episodic and recurrent, reflecting endemic rivalry and temporary tensions, likely to break out at any time between individuals, for all manner of prosaic and other reasons (among the Yanomamo, often starting because of sexual jealousies: Chagnon 1988, 986; see also Thorpe 2003). That characterisation may apply more widely, even back into the European Mesolithic, though among other instances in continental early Neolithic contexts we note the claim for the appearance of male archer-warriors in the early northern TRB (Brinch Petersen 2008). Perhaps we do not need to see different facets of early Neolithic sociality as fundamentally opposed. In wider terms, love and anger in one anthropological formulation very much go together (Overing and Passes 2000a; 2000b). People connected with others about whom they cared, in various senses of the word, but being thus connected and attentive to position and reputation, were also open to jealousy, competition and anger.

But with the appearance of causewayed enclosures in southern Britain and throughout their currency, came episodes of collective violence, on a bigger scale and of more dramatic character. The possible large-scale event reflected in the formation of the primary mortuary deposit at Wayland's Smithy I also belongs within this span. Is this because there is now a much larger sample of bigger archaeological sites, more extensively excavated, from which such evidence can emerge? Or did the practice of building and using causewayed and other enclosures go along with an increase in communal tensions, or indeed create them, as social networks intensified, more people who were not in regular contact were brought together, and desirables such as cattle and novel artefacts were assembled in perhaps greater quantities than ever before?

15.9 The hey-day of causewayed enclosures: a brief history

So now, having reviewed these general characterisations, and drawing on the sense of timing and tempo provided by the chronological models, we are in a position to sketch a brief but more site-specific narrative of the hey-day of causewayed enclosures in southern Britain and Ireland than was given in Chapter 14 (and see Fig. 15.23).

In Britain, things probably began quite slowly, in the east, in the late 38th century cal BC, like the first Neolithic practices some three centuries earlier (Table 15.2; Figs 14.15–16). The first enclosures were probably in the Greater Thames estuary, and perhaps for a generation or so Chalk Hill was either alone or one of very few sites of this kind in existence. The location is once again suggestive of the direction of continental links. The construction of Chalk Hill established the practice of large-scale, multiple circuits from the outset, and the tradition of abundant deposition in selected parts of the ditches, perhaps already the residue of more than just work party feasts (Dietler 1996; Schulting 2008, 107) but an extension of existing communal commensality. Kingsborough 2 may have followed, in the first generation or so of the 37th century cal BC, while Chalk Hill was still in use. There was clearly no rule book in operation, as its layout is simpler, and few artefacts were placed in the ditch (M. Allen *et al.* 2008, 244). Bury Hill in Sussex could fit in here (Fig. 5.31), its non-classic form also suggesting diversity in early layouts.

The pace began to quicken in the second quarter of the 37th century cal BC, with a scatter of sites along the south coast and its hinterland, like Whitehawk and Hembury, and possibly the first of the stone-walled tor enclosures in the far south-west (though their date estimates are imprecise), and the first of the enclosures in East Anglia, at Etton, and in Wessex, with the construction of the main enclosure at Hambledon Hill. Diversity also characterises this period, including some simple layouts such as Etton, though the initial plan at Hambledon was already on a considerable scale. It is possible that Hembury was built in anticipation of attack or at least attracted jealous attention very soon after it was constructed.

It is probable that relatively little time elapsed before the circuits at Whitehawk were multiplied, and further expansion took place at Hambledon Hill. These sites are far apart, but by the third quarter of the 37th century cal BC, other enclosures were appearing in coastal Essex, in Sussex, Wessex and now for the first time in the Cotswolds and the middle and upper Thames valley. So the gaps were closing, with more sites inland, and perhaps diversity and local aggrandisement were driven by emulation or at least awareness of others. Things were done differently in different places. The simple layout at Etton, for example, was kept going by recuts, and marked by unintensive deposition. An initially simple and small layout at Windmill Hill, however, was at the core of massive subsequent enlargement, each circuit probably following at an interval of a generation or so, with quite abundant deposition from the primary levels onwards. At Crickley Hill, either one circuit quickly followed another, or two were built more or less simultaneously. It was in this phase, probably between the 3640s and 3620s cal BC, that the primary use of some existing long barrows and long cairns came to an end, no longer perhaps – for one or other of the possible reasons discussed above – at the forefront, at least for the time being, of ritual attention. But we can note the continuation of the mainly eastern tradition of 'diverse and small' mortuary monuments, which had appeared at more or less the same time as enclosures themselves, or perhaps at the moment when enclosure construction was intensified (Fig. 14.142). Plenty of the evidence for inter-personal violence belongs to this period, but relatively little for larger encounters; the Hambledon Hill site phase 1b (second half of the 37th or the early 36th century cal BC) burning on the Shroton spur was probably extensive.

In the last quarter of the 37th century cal BC, enclosures appeared in south Wales and the Marches (Table 15.2), and the main overall distribution was established. There were limits to expansion northwards, in the southern Midlands, and the chronology of possible examples in north-east and north-west England and southern and eastern Scotland has yet to be established. At the turn of the century there appears to have been a lull in construction. The primary mortuary structure at Wayland's Smithy probably belongs to the early part of the 36th century cal BC, with its primary barrow probably set up two to three generations later, and the first part of the 36th century cal BC saw renewed construction of new enclosures, leading to further spatial infill; examples include probably Knap Hill and Maiden Castle, and possibly Abingdon (if it belongs to the later peak of its bimodal distribution). There was continued activity at Hambledon Hill (if not already in the late 37th century cal BC), and the initial circuit at Crickley Hill was replaced by the construction of the single, much less interrupted ditch, probably following the digging of adjacent Peak Camp. Some of the biggest depositions were made in this period. The evidence for large violent encounters seems to be confined to the largest sites: at Hambledon Hill and possibly at Maiden Castle. The burning in the inner Stepleton outwork at Hambledon in site phase 2 (mid-36th century cal BC) was once more extensive, again possibly of a circuit raised in anticipation of attack, as in site phase 1b (Chapters 4 and 14).

By the time the construction of new enclosures in southern Britain was on the wane, from the middle of the 36th century cal BC, different histories were being established. Enclosures had been in primary use for varying durations, from a generation or less to a century or more. Now only certain sites continued in active use: Hambledon Hill once more; Windmill Hill; Crickley Hill; and Etton. At this point the history of southern British monuments becomes more complicated, with the continuation of those enclosures, the periodic construction of long cairns (and in the west perhaps portal dolmens/tombs), and the initiation of cursus monuments. Before we turn to these developments in more detail, we need to confront the implications of the now more detailed history of the hey-day of southern British causewayed enclosures. We have stressed their appearance at a certain point in the overall sequence, their gradual but ever-accelerating establishment over three to four generations, followed by a lull, which was succeeded in turn by another generation or two of fresh construction. Variation can be seen now through the lens of these temporal and spatial trends, and from the perspective of individual site biographies (Fig. 15.24). Generalisations about the nature and meanings of activity at causewayed enclosures can now be set within a much more specific history. Having hinted at the evidence for competition in the period before enclosures, and at emulation on the one hand and various kinds of conflict on the other within their main period of use, what language should we use to characterise the social relations of these southern British cattle-keeping communities whose fluctuating ceremonial fortunes we have documented? And how can we use a more detailed history of enclosures to explore the different practices elsewhere in Britain and Ireland at this time?

The scarcity of causewayed enclosures in Ireland must speak for a different process. Their construction began at least as early as in southern Britain. Both Magheraboy and Donegore are very familiar, in terms of both layout and the nature of deposition, compared with the wider repertoire of forms and practices seen both in southern Britain and on the European continent. The same general models of their social role as special places of labour and assembly could be applied to them as elsewhere, and they could readily be envisaged as fitting into landscapes otherwise marked by the movement of artefacts, and, at least for a while, by the presence of houses. In this sense, at least some people in Ireland were connected to much wider social networks, whether this was primarily with Britain or with points beyond on the continent. Yet the very scarcity of these enclosures in Ireland underlines marked difference in the uptake of practices and traditions much more firmly established elsewhere. It might only have taken a small number of lineages or communities, say, to have tried out the innovation of marking place and identity in this way, but unlike elsewhere, for example first in south-east England and then beyond, the idea did not apparently catch on or spread widely in the island context of Ireland on the evidence presently available. Other ways of thinking and doing things prevailed.

By the same token, it is worth reflecting again also on the scarcity of enclosures in Britain north of the Midlands, though that is not to exclude the possibility of outliers being confirmed in due course in northern England and Scotland (see again Fig. 1.2, and Chapter 1.3; Oswald *et al.* 2001). Here again there must have been different processes and ways of thinking. This contrasts sharply with the different distributions of for example Carinated Bowl and stone axeheads, and those of the wider long cairn and long barrow distribution. While for Ireland we might have recourse to a notion of insular identity, perhaps for northern England and Scotland another kind of explanation now emerges from this dating study. Could it be that enclosures were most favoured in those areas of southern Britain which had had or maintained the strongest links with the European continent, from initial colonisation to subsequent migration streams? It remains a puzzling contrast that the long cairn/long barrow distribution left no such clear-cut marker. This suggestion also provides a rather passive explanation of the difference seen in northern England. But on a more active note, could it also be that linear timber monuments in Scotland were a northern equivalent of enclosures in the south (Fig. 15.23),[11] and could they be seen as an assertion of some kind of regional identity?

15.10 Early Neolithic politics: ritual experts and organisers?

There is a tension between top-down and bottom-up accounts of social change. Top-down narratives tend to enforce static, predetermined models, smoothing out variation and ignoring gaps in the evidence, while bottom-up constructions risk remaining fragmented, incomplete and missing the 'big picture'. Neither has been very systematically applied to the early Neolithic context in southern Britain. The early Neolithic has in fact attracted less detailed attention in large-scale social evolutionary modelling than the late Neolithic. Classically, for example, the labour input required for long barrows and causewayed

Table 15.2. Posterior density estimates for the building of causewayed and tor enclosures in southern Britain and Ireland, derived from the models defined in Chapters 3–12 as detailed in the captions to Figs 14.2–4, and the models defined in Figs 14.1–4, 14.5 and 14.7–10 (see Fig. 14.13 for an illustration showing the archaeological difference between these estimates).

Area	**Region**	**Site**	**Comment/explanation**	**Distribution**	***Posterior density estimate (cal BC) (95% probability)* or calibrated date range (cal BC)(95% confidence)**	***Posterior density estimate (cal BC) (68% probability)* or calibrated date range (cal BC)(68% confidence)**
Southern Britain as a whole				Fig. 14.1: *start S British enclosures*	*3765–3695*	*3740–3705*
				Fig. 14.5: *start new S British enclosures*	*3750–3685*	*3730–3700*
				Fig. 14.7: *intensify building circuits*	*3715–3670*	*3705–3680*
SE England		State of enclosure building in area		Fig. 14.18: *start SE England*	*3795–3685*	*3750–3700*
	Greater Thames estuary	First enclosure in region		Fig. 14.15: *Thames estuary*	*3710–3665*	*3700–3670*
		St Osyth		Fig. 7.6: *start St Osyth*	*3660–3630 (70%)* or *3565–3540 (25%)*	*3655–3635 (61%)* or *3555–3545 (7%)*
		Orsett		Fig. 7.10: *start Orsett*	*4180–3380*	*3815–3385*
		Kingsborough 2		Fig. 7.17: *start Kingsborough 2*	*3790–3630 (76%)* or *3615–3535 (19%)*	*3710–3635 (61%)* or *3565–3545 (7%)*
		Kingsborough 1		Fig. 7.15: *start Kingsborough 1*	*3780–3520*	*3660–3580*
		Chalk Hill		Fig. 7.21: *start Chalk Hill*	*3780–3680*	*3740–3690*
	Sussex	First enclosure in region		Fig. 14.15: *Sussex*	*3705–3650*	*3690–3660*
		Whitehawk		Fig. 5.5: *build Whitehawk*	*3690–3635 (73%)* or *3620–3560 (22%)*	*3675–3635 (67%)* or *3595–3585 (1%)*
		Offham Hill		Fig. 5.14: *burial 1*	*3635–3555 (66%)* or *3540–3490 (23%)* or *3435–3380 (6%)*	*3630–3585 (56%)* or *3525–3505 (12%)*
		Combe Hill	*Terminus ante quem* for inner ditch	Table 5.4: I-11613	3640–3010	3510–3110
		The Trundle	*Terminus post quem* for inner ditch)	Table 5.5: I-11614	3900–3370	3710–3520
			Terminus post quem for ditch 2	Table 5.5: OxA-14024	3650–3520	3640–3530
			Terminus post quem for spiral ditch	Table 5.5: I-11612	3940–3370	3710–3530
		Bury Hill		Fig. 5.31: *build Bury Hill*	*3775–3650*	*3760–3740 (7%)* or *3715–3660 (61%)*
		Court Hill		Fig. 5.28: *build Court Hill*	*3650–3530*	*3640–3620 (19%)* or *3605–3550 (49%)*
South-central England		Start of enclosure building in area		Fig. 14.18: *start central S England*	*3735–3645*	*3695–3655*
	South Wessex	First enclosure in region		Fig. 14.15: *south Wessex*	*3680–3640*	*3665–3645*
		Hambledon Hill		Fig. 4.7: *build main enclosure*	*3675–3630*	*3660–3640*
				Fig. 4.11: *build Stepleton enclosure*	*3640–3565*	*3640–3615 (42%)* or *3610–3585 (26%)*

Area	Region	Site	Comment/explanation	Distribution	***Posterior density estimate (cal BC) (95% probability)*** **or calibrated date range (cal BC)(95% confidence)**	***Posterior density estimate (cal BC) (68% probability)*** **or calibrated date range (cal BC)(68% confidence)**
		Whitesheet Hill		Fig. 4.26: *build Whitesheet Hill*	*3655–3630 (10%)* or *3610–3535 (85%)*	*3595–3550*
		Maiden Castle		Fig. 4.41: *start Maiden enclosure*	*3580–3535*	*3560–3540*
		Robin Hood's Ball		Fig. 4.51: *build Robin Hood's Ball*	*3640–3500 (91%)* or *3430–3400 (4%)*	*3635–3570*
	North Wiltshire	First enclosure in region		Fig. 14.15: *north Wiltshire*	*3685–3640*	*3670–3645*
		Windmill Hill		Fig. 3.15: *start Windmill Hill*	*3700–3640*	*3680–3650*
		Knap Hill		Fig. 3.25: *start Knap Hill*	*3765–3500 (78%)* or *3485–3380 (17%)*	*3660–3515 (63%)* or *3435–3415 (5%)*
	Eastern England	First enclosure in region		Fig. 14.15: *eastern England*	*3705–3650*	*3695–3660*
		Northborough		Fig. 6.39: *start Northborough*	*3700–3550*	*3645–3585*
		Etton Woodgate		Fig. 6.36: *build Woodgate*	*3645–3525*	*3640–3620 (16%)* or *3605–3540 (52%)*
		Etton		Fig. 6.33: *build Etton*	*3710–3645*	*3705–3670 (63%)* or *3665–3655 (5%)*
		Briar Hill		Fig. 6.21: *build Briar Hill*	*4170–3355*	*3745–3415*
		Haddenham		Fig. 6.11: *start Haddenham*	*3960–3125*	*3725–3365*
		Maiden Bower		Fig. 6.4: *start Maiden Bower*	*3775–3380*	*3660–3590 (23%)* or *3555–3505 (17%)* or *3475–3395 (28%)*
	Thames valley	First enclosure in region		Fig. 14.15: *Thames valley*	*3700–3605 (92%)* or *3585–3565 (2%)* or *3560–3540 (1%)*	*3660–3630*
		Abingdon		Fig. 8.22: *start Abingdon*	*3670–3630 (55%)* or *3585–3570 (3%)* or *3565–3535 (37%)*	*3655–3635 (42%)* or *3550–3540 (26%)*
		Gatehampton Farm	*Terminus post quem* for enclosure ditch	Table 8.4: GrA-31358	3760–3630	3710–3640
		Eton Wick		Fig. 8.5: *start Eton Wick*	*3720–3420 (94%)* or *3395–3365 (1%)*	*3560–3455*
		Staines		Fig. 8.3: *start Staines*	*3710–3400*	*3645–3600 (15%)* or *3570–3425 (53%)*
	Cotswolds	First enclosure in region		Fig. 14.15: *Cotswolds*	*3680–3615*	*3660–3630*
		Crickley Hill		Fig. 9.7: *start Crickley Hill*	*3705–3600*	*3670–3620*
		Peak Camp		Fig. 9.19: *start Peak Camp*	*3860–3555*	*3730–3585*

Area	Region	Site	Comment/explanation	Distribution	Posterior density estimate (*cal BC*) (*95% probability*) or calibrated date range (cal BC)(95% confidence)	Posterior density estimate (*cal BC*) (*68% probability*) or calibrated date range (cal BC)(68% confidence)
South-west Britain	South-west peninsula	Start of enclosure building in region		Fig. 14.18: *start SW peninsula*	*4020–3660*	*3780–3675*
		First enclosure in region		Fig. 14.15: *south-west peninsula*	*3705–3650*	*3695–3660*
		Hembury		Fig. 10.9: *start Hembury*	*3730–3650*	*3705–3665*
		Raddon		Fig. 10.16: *start Raddon*	*3820–3530*	*3700–3625 (42%)* or *3615–3550 (26%)*
		Helman Tor		Fig. 10.22: *start Helman Tor*	*3845–3650*	*3750–3665*
		Start Carn Brea		Fig. 10.25: *start Carn Brea*	*4040–3530*	*3755–3560*
	South Wales and the Marches	First enclosure in region		Fig. 14.15: *S Wales & the Marches*	*3645–3550*	*3640–3580*
		Hill Croft Field		Fig. 11.3: *build Hill Croft Field*	*3640–3500 (92%)* or *3415–3380 (3%)*	*3635–3620 (9%)* or *3605–3520 (59%)*
		Banc Du		Fig. 11.8: *build Banc Du*	*3645–3490 (84%)* or *3470–3400 (11%)*	*3640–3620 (7%)* or *3610–3515 (61%)*
Ireland		Donegore		Fig. 12.5: *start Donegore*	*3855–3665*	*3780–3685*
		Magheraboy		Fig. 12.15: *start Magheraboy*	*4115–3850*	*4065–3945*

enclosures was seen mainly as a foil for the much greater investments made in henges, Stonehenge and Silbury Hill (Renfrew 1973b). There have been one or two half-hearted attempts to evoke 'proto-chiefdoms' in the early Neolithic (e.g. Renfrew 1973b; compare Darvill 1979; and Ebbesen 2007, 48–50; Earle 1997), but none of the 20 criteria listed by Renfrew (1973b) – from 'ranked society' and 'redistribution of produce organized by the chief', 'a greater number of socioeconomic statuses', and 'pervasive inequality of persons or groups associated with permanent leadership', to 'more clearly defined territorial boundaries or borders', 'reduction of internal strife' and 'rise of priesthood' – seem obviously to apply to the early Neolithic situation in southern Britain. Nor does the 'organization and deployment of public labour' associated with large-scale schemes like irrigation works or the building of temples, temple mounds or pyramids, seem appropriate for early Neolithic times.

So is it largely a matter of more boldly applying more detailed evolutionary models? But which ones? Once we move from broad distinctions between Mesolithic and Neolithic 'modes of thought' based around contrasting attitudes to sharing versus accumulation, followership versus leadership, universal kin classification versus distinctions between kin and non-kin, and the land as sacrosanct versus people as sacrosanct (Barnard 2007; Helms 2007), what explanations should we adopt? And is this kind of distinction anyway sufficiently precise to encompass diversity among both hunter-gatherers and agriculturalists?

The notion of 'transegalitarian' societies has been applied to both complex hunter-gatherers and simple horticulturalists, as well as pastoral nomads:

> The term refers to societies that have characteristics intermediary between egalitarian bands at one end (with minimal private ownership and widespread sharing) and stratified chiefdoms at the other end. Transegalitarian societies therefore have ownership over resources and products, they have prestige goods and socioeconomic inequalities, but they lack the political stratification characteristic of true chiefdoms (B. Hayden 2009, 31).

Leaving aside the question of what a 'true' chiefdom may be (given that this is another area with immense variation: Drennan 1996; McIntosh 1999; cf. Pauketat 2007), this still leaves open an enormous amount of diversity. One tactic therefore might be to evoke more precise analogies within this broad evolutionary perspective (cf. R. Chapman 2008). For example, the distinction has been made in Melanesian ethnography between 'great men' and 'big men' (Godelier and Strathern 1991). Both are socially pre-eminent, but great men achieve this by involvement in restricted exchanges and ritual complexity, while big men are often seen as entrepreneurs, engaged in unequal or non-equivalent exchanges and not averse to warfare and violence; it is often supposed that, historically, big men systems emerged out of great men systems (Lemonnier 1991). Pierre Lemonnier

Fig. 15.24. The court tombs at Ballybriest, Co. Derry and Goward, Co. Down (above, left and right), and the portal tombs at Wateresk, Co. Down, and Gaulstown, Co. Waterford (below, left and right), Ireland. Photos: Vicki Cummings.

(1991) has discussed the relationship between warfare and large-scale ceremonial exchanges as two complementary forms of competition in which big men have a central role. Big men, if they do not actually start wars, are active and prominent in them, and exploit their consequences for their own advantage. They are crucial in peace-making, using talents for oratory, their connections and wealth to stop fighting and to organise compensation payments through ceremonial, non-equivalent (wealth for life) exchange (Lemonnier 1991, 8–11). So could we be thinking along these sorts of lines for the southern British case of the 37th to 36th centuries cal BC, with more dynamic organisers than simply the 'ritual experts' who guided initiation rituals among the small Ok communities of mountain New Guinea (Barth 1987)? Would this not bring alive in the southern British case the possibility of already genealogically senior people, competitive and restless, keen to innovate, to accumulate including by raiding and wider warfare if need be, but able also to make and temporarily keep the peace by holding large-scale gatherings and feasts? The accelerated or more concentrated timescales for enclosure construction which this study has presented would certainly be compatible with this kind of political manoeuvring.

But the problem of variation will not go away. Lemonnier himself cites (1991, 11–12) warfare and ensuing compensations in societies without big men. Polly Wiessner (2002) has emphasised, also using evidence from highland New Guinea, among the Enga, the capacity of egalitarian ideology and structures to curb the actions and scope of 'aggrandizers', through an ideology promoting access to resources, exchange with partners outside the clan, and the independence of segmentary lineages. So how could we be sure that causewayed enclosures are to do with organisers and aggrandisers in the first place?

If this approach seems doomed to chase from one kind of analogy to another, to be lost in an uncertain sea of variation, the bottom-up school appears largely to have avoided the problem altogether. The more recent literature on monuments has been much less explicit about social relations, concentrating on other themes such as experience, landscape setting, transformation and movement, and particularly at the scale of individual sites. But perhaps because of their more constrained features, long barrows and long cairns – and court tombs and portal tombs in Ireland – have continued to attract specific discussion in terms of families, kin groups, lineages and so on (e.g. J. Thomas 1987; Saville 1990; A. Powell 2005; Benson and Whittle 2007; M. Smith and Brickley 2009). Few of the many recent discussions of causewayed enclosures, however, have been explicit about the wider social relations involved in the many activities represented, though Roger Mercer (2006a, 74; 2008a), writing of western enclosures, has hinted at 'quasi-political prominence for some sites as 'symbolic' of the social solidarity that they had come to represent'.

Could the detailed timetables offered here not re-energise this task? They provide sequence, in the broadening from barrow and cairn construction to the building of enclosures, and in the shifting, often unstable biographies of individual examples of those arenas. This was a history in the making, rather than the inevitable arrival of types or stages, in which the decision to undertake and perform an enclosure was nowhere a foregone conclusion; southern Dorset, for example, only witnessed such an event right at the end of the period when causewayed enclosures were established, and large parts of the country were never to do so. Suppose, for example – though plenty of other scenarios could also apply – that some kind of 'big man' or 'great man' emerged in the area of Hambledon in the 3660s cal BC who believed in the power and reputation of enclosure. His descendants continued, periodically, with this practice, but his contemporaries in southern Dorset, and their descendants, did not, until, belatedly, and after the lull in constructions around the turn of the century brought on perhaps by general exhaustion, one of them decided to rejoin what was by now an old bandwagon…

Enclosures were preceded (and overlapped) by smaller monuments capable of being built by perhaps some 10,000 hours of labour, and which were normally to hold the remains of not more than 40 people, deposited over one to three–five generations. Using a 50-year span of primary use over a period of 200 years, there might have been 29 such monuments in contemporary use in the area of the Cotswolds. This probably does not speak for overall social hierarchy, though it could evoke a striving for seniority and local pre-eminence, as monument after monument was set up and used, as people creatively worked and reworked the architectural repertoire, and perhaps thought through a variety of descent modes. Kinds of descent are much more actively discussed for other parts of the Neolithic, for example the LBK. For that there is currently a dominant model of patrilocality and patrilineal descent (e.g. Eisenhauer 2003), though much more open arrangements than bounded corporate groups, including kindreds of bilateral descent, have also been mooted (Milisauskas 1986, 218; Whittle 2009, 254). Andrew Powell (2005, 22) has suggested that the architecture of court tombs and portal tombs projected 'idealized and formalized representations' of kinship and other local social relations, such that 'an ordered version of past kinship relations was distilled out of the complex web of descent and alliance, fusion and fission, of which the corporation constructing the tomb was the product, in order to portray its past in a way that legitimized the present'; architectural symmetries served to balance and control the past. Could the southern British case not also be characterised by diversity, with potentially strong contrasts between those mortuary architectures which emphasise opposition or difference (such as lateral chambered tombs), those which stress singularity (such as terminal chambered cairns), and those which effect complementarity (such as transepted chambered cairns)? Were these more prominent and contested issues among people living in central and western southern Britain?

But could we not see more in the architecture, both in its compartmentalisation and in its layout? Lateral chambered tombs in particular, with their careful symmetries and oppositions strongly suggest the possibility of separate descent groups. And were this so, it is striking that bilateral descent can be associated with short chains of social memory, which dissipate after three to four generations in a meshwork of complex relationships (Foxhall 1995; Forbes 2007, 136–41). This resonates with the short durations of the primary use of at least some southern British long barrows (Bayliss and Whittle 2007).[12] We do not need to force everything into the same mould, but could an idea of bilateral descent have been a dominant early trope in the domain of descent, to be succeeded or overlapped by the emergence of unilineal systems with longer chains of social memory? Is this succession expressed in the emergence of enclosures, the initial use of some of which persisted for 12 or more generations rather than the few generations of some long barrows and cairns? And does the reference to an older past argued for the architecture of Wayland's Smithy II probably in the second half of the 35th century cal BC (Whittle *et al.* 2007b, fig. 4) belong to this same kind of scenario?

The situation changes with the introduction of enclosures. We have discussed three scenarios, two specific and one general: the management of cattle; the elaboration of funerary or commemorative rites for the dead; and a general widening of social interaction as dispersed communities became more established. The very idea of enacting a version of the continental idea of enclosures may speak for the continuance of the urge for seniority and prominence. We might think in very broad terms for the very first enclosures of the kind of ritual experts described by Fredrik Barth (1987) in *Cosmologies in the making*, though thereafter, as the number of eye witnesses must have multiplied, it can hardly have been inherently secret knowledge that controlled the setting up of new enclosures; someone born in central southern England in say the 3680s cal BC could, if their life stretched to seven decades, have seen the building of as many as six enclosures, all within a few days' walking distance, say 75 km. In this regard, enclosures are ambiguous, since they may have created an opening or broadening of participation compared with the hidden worlds of barrow and cairn interiors, while at the same time presumably requiring organisers or promoters to galvanise or provoke action – and who knows if that still required the possession of secret knowledge? The elaboration of some sites may have been due to a desire both to emulate previous generations of builders and to out-do contemporaries in terms of what could be conceived possible.

There are other tensions. The mobilisation of labour is of key importance. With shortened timescales, and the 100-people model, the diversion of energy from other routine tasks is probably significantly less than previously envisaged in the literature, and any one episode of enclosure construction can be further broken down into individual circuits (as appropriate) and individual segments. As discussed above, it is not so much that construction was an endlessly ongoing project, but more that it was one that belonged to and required very specific, short-lived circumstances. To attract even a modest workforce over successive years for a single task of this kind might have required a balance between the persuasive powers of organisers and the communal will. Different participants may have sought or expected different rewards. The possibilities could evoke various of the ethnographic analogies already noted, from the big men whose action and reputation serve their community (Lemonnier 1991), to the communal brake on aggrandisers (Wiessner 2002). The general fragility and brevity of these comings together should perhaps be stressed the most. That these mobilisations took place from time to time and from place to place speaks for changing circumstances in the 37th and 36th centuries cal BC, but those eight generations probably saw not the establishment of more clearly demarcated power relations, but a shifting jostling for position within a historically derived idiom, open to individual or interest-group manipulation perhaps, but constantly subject to public or communal view and sanction. People who freely donated their labour could also walk away without constraint. A successful enclosure required not just labour but witnesses and participants, the largest assemblies perhaps attracting hundreds of people; gatherings can also quickly break up and disperse. Perhaps some of the violence seen at and around enclosures (principally more to the west than to the east) comes from internal dissension, *within* the constituencies of participants, rather than from external enemies, especially at or very soon after episodes of construction. Why were people in the west apparently more inclined to violence than those in the east?

The indications from ethnography are that people fight as much over such things as sex, gambling and reputation (Chagnon 1988; Thorpe 2003) as directly over resources. If cattle and ground stone axes were objects of desire in the early Neolithic, were these also the focus of competition? Are cattle and axes in a sense the cause as well as the symptom of causewayed enclosures? Although we have outlined new patterns in the chronological development of axe movements, we know so little of either sphere that it is unwise to be dogmatic. We know virtually nothing of rules and practices of ownership of cattle in the early Neolithic. Did particular families, kin groups or lineages accumulate the largest herds, and had this process begun before enclosures came to be built? We have already noted the slender clues of the cattle skull under the Ascott-under-Wychwood long barrow, probably of the 38th century cal BC, and the cattle skull in the final deposits at Fussell's Lodge, probably deposited in the 3650s or 3640s cal BC (Wysocki *et al.* 2007, fig. 10). Did the final arrangements at Fussell's Lodge suggest some kind of equivalence between selected, composite persons, decorated pottery and cattle? If two or three beasts could feed hundreds, perhaps any family or small group possessing cattle could potentially have laid on a feast, or contributed to one; the impression from the Hambledon cattle bones was of selected animals taken to the hill for slaughter (Legge 2008). The relative costs or consequences, however, must have varied depending on the size of herds, and possessors of more animals would certainly be at an advantage in competitive and recurrent circumstances. The incentives to raid cattle also come to mind (Schulting 2004). But if such conditions were widespread right across southern Britain – and cattle are encountered at Chalk Hill, Etton, Northborough and elsewhere in the east – we might expect more signs of inter-group violence in the east as well as in the west. So, were cattle more central to Neolithic subsistence strategies in western Britain than in the south-east? Or perhaps, the diverse, small monuments mainly of the east might speak for a less complicated descent world there, perhaps even the establishment of local social hierarchies, as seen in the contrasts between say West Kennet and Fussell's Lodge long barrows and the Whiteleaf oval barrow. Or again, even the older history of eastern connection with the European continent and the energy devoted in the west to building and bickering may be to do as much with matters of seniority and reputation as with straightforward measures of ownership and possession.

15.11 Elsewhere

If there are no easy labels for social developments in southern Britain from the 38th into the 37th and first half of the 36th centuries cal BC, their special character can be underlined by consideration of elsewhere in Britain and Ireland at these times (Figs 15.24–7).

We have already noted Richard Bradley's (2007) underlining of differences at a large scale between Britain and Ireland as wholes, which serve to relate the varying treatments of the body in death, by inhumation and cremation respectively, to the nature of residence in life, in house-poor and house-rich situations. In more detail, Chris Fowler (2001, 158; 2004b, 100) has referred to the variety of discourses about issues of identity, the body and death around the country as a whole. So were there absolute differences between southern Britain and the rest of Britain and Ireland, or equivalences despite differences in form, or just endless diversity from place to place and region to region?

It seems important to avoid any simple or absolute contrast between areas with and areas without enclosures. On the one hand, there are two proven examples in Ireland, and other potential candidates (Chapter 12), as there are also in north-east and north-west England, and southern and perhaps eastern Scotland. On the other hand, there are parts of southern Britain where enclosures were relatively rare, as in East Anglia east of the Fens. The late date and brief life of the Maiden Castle enclosure remind us, once again, that even *within* the main distribution of causewayed enclosures there were absences for much of their period of popularity. And not all southern enclosures were the same. There was also much else in common across Britain and Ireland, unsurprisingly given the processes argued above, including clearance sequences in pollen diagrams (e.g. K. Edwards 2004; Tipping *et al.* 2009), the use of cereals and domesticates, Bowl pottery, leaf arrowheads and polished stone axes, some other aspects of lithic technology, the building of rectangular timber houses, pit digging, and the construction of megalithic and non-megalithic mortuary structures. Linear monuments are found in Scotland, though claims for their very early dating are not securely based on short-life samples unequivocally associated with their construction and use, and they need in fact be no earlier in the north than in the south, in the present state of the evidence (Figs 14.44 and 14.170).

There are very few features which stand out as absolutely separate regional traits. Fields in western Ireland might be one candidate, alongside the predominantly southern British causewayed enclosures. Elsewhere it seems to be a question of overlap and difference of degree, with regional interaction persistently important (e.g. Cooney 2000a; G. Barclay 2004; Noble 2006; Waddington 1999; Passmore and Waddington forthcoming; Brophy and Barclay 2009). The distribution of the mainly Irish and western portal tombs or dolmens, for example, extends into the Cotswolds (Darvill 2004a); court tombs in Ireland overlap in style with western Scottish Clyde cairns, though regional styles can of course be found in the Hebrides and the Orkneys, and elsewhere. Likewise there are early regional variations within the Scottish Carinated Bowl tradition (see Chapter 14.7), but it is noticeable that the Carinated Bowl style probably comes to an end in Scotland soon after 3600 cal BC, not much later than the date of the more general end of that tradition further south, *c.* 3650 cal BC (Figs 14.88 and 14.158). And while the plethora of new sites in eastern Scotland, as outside Aberdeen and on the A1 east of Edinburgh (Cook and Dunbar 2008; Lelong and MacGregor 2007), serves to show that there is more to the Scottish early Neolithic sequence than what was earlier found on Orkney (G. Barclay 2004; Warren 2004), the Bowl pottery, pits, pyres and trapezoidal mounds do not seem wholly alien to or removed from features and practices in parts of eastern England.

What then are we to do with this rather blurred sense of both similarity and difference? We are not proficient with questions of either space or time. Using the boundaries of modern countries as cultural yardsticks is far too crude; any smaller scale for regions, although often implied, is normally poorly defined; but to refer everything to purely local agency, however, also seems inadequate. We are hampered, secondly, by inadequate chronologies. We can say little in detail, from the evidence reviewed in this volume, about the development of portal and court tombs in Ireland, or Clyde cairns in Scotland. So while we have been able to suggest a new view of the date of – and processes behind – the introduction of Neolithic things and practices in Ireland, Mann and Scotland, it remains very hard to follow subsequent developments in any detail. Did court tombs and Clyde cairns come with a rush in the 38th century cal BC, for example? Ballyglass follows the house underneath it, probably not earlier than the middle of the 37th century cal BC, but other specific clues like this are rare. At this stage we simply do not know, and we are back to fuzzy prehistory, which makes the more precise interpretations which we have sought in southern Britain more or less impossible, and comparisons between

Fig. 15.25. Eagle's Nest, Lambay Island, Co. Dublin. Excavation of porphyry (porphyritic andesite) for axehead production. Section shows build-up of porphyry debitage dating to the Early Neolithic; the quarried face is to the left of the photograph with a propped anvil stone in front of it. Photo: Gabriel Cooney.

the south and elsewhere for the time being extremely problematic.

One feature has been much better dated elsewhere: houses. Large timber halls were found in southern and eastern Scotland in the 38th century cal BC (Fig. 15.26); the longest-lasting example so far known, at Balbridie, persisted into the 37th century cal BC, as did the one constructed later at Claish (Fig. 14.174). In Ireland, rectangular houses were in use for a century or so, or less than a century, from the late 38th century cal BC into the later 37th century cal BC (Figs 12.22 and 12.28–9). In model 3 of Chapter 12, they belong a little after first beginnings, whereas in model 2 they follow closely on the start of the Neolithic. The Irish situation following model 3 is more in line with our current understanding of the situation in Scotland. As noted in section 15.2, models 2 and 3 cannot both be right, and our inclination was to favour model 3. So this possible framework gives interesting choices. It is difficult to argue that all houses are in some way the equivalent of enclosures, as implied for example by Sarah Cross (2003), since the Scottish halls probably precede the southern British causewayed enclosures, but they and at least some of the Irish rectangular houses could have been the venue for significant social gatherings, with feasting not excluded (though no compelling such animal bone assemblage has yet been published from a house site). What can be asserted if we follow model 3 is that, whereas in southern Britain, after a longer history of early Neolithic activity, communities went on to the more complex and at times extravagant activities seen at enclosures, in Ireland, relatively earlier in the sequence, sociality was focused on the house. The same may apply to the middle of England, on the basis of the dates from Lismore Fields, Derbyshire, and to north Wales, on the basis of dates from Llandygai. Further, the period of both phenomena was relatively brief, the heyday of southern enclosures lasting some eight generations, and that of Irish houses four or fewer. When creative innovation went on to produce cursus monuments in southern Britain, did attention shift in Ireland and Scotland to monumentalisation of a variety of tombs (Figs 15.24 and 15.27)? Is the relationship shown at Ballyglass, with court tomb overlying a dismantled rectangular house, typical of wider areas, and what interval was there between the two constructions there? Perhaps, as time went on, references to the past multiplied as much as practices in the present.

Of particular interest for the future would be more information from the area immediately to the north of the main distribution of southern British causewayed enclosures. How far north did one have to go, from well established and long-lived enclosure complexes like Crickley Hill/Peak Camp and Etton and its neighbours, before a different

Fig. 15.26. The timber hall at Warren Field, Crathes, Aberdeenshire, Scotland, under excavation. Photo: Murray Archaeological Services Ltd.

style of living was encountered? Rather than more abstract shufflings of the pack of regional diversities, concentrated research here could contribute much to our understanding of scales of social interaction.

15.12 Later histories: the pace and character of change

There came a time when a new kind of monument altogether came to be built: the cursus monument. Some of these appear directly to overlie causewayed enclosures, for example at the unexcavated Fornham All Saints (see again Fig. 15.20) and the excavated Etton examples. The date estimate for the end of the Etton causewayed enclosure lies in the later fourth millennium cal BC (Fig. 6.33). The long mound at Maiden Castle, whose linearity can surely be linked to the idea of cursus monuments and which also directly overlies the western circumference of the causewayed enclosure, is a little more precisely dated, belonging probably to the late 36th or 35th century cal BC (Fig. 4.56). The date estimate for the Dorset cursus is far from precise (Figs 4.19 and 4.58). The earliest examples are probably Stonehenge and Drayton (Fig. 14.185); locally, the greater Stonehenge cursus would follow Robin Hood's Ball, and depending on which of its peaks Abingdon falls, Drayton could follow or precede Abingdon (Chapter 8.6). Both events could fall in the mid-36th century cal BC, more or less coinciding with the end of the main period when causewayed enclosures were established.

So, causewayed enclosures flourished as the novel focus of large-scale, ceremonial activity for some eight generations, the success of the probably public performances waxing and waning through this timescape – with one pronounced lull in fresh construction and considerable variability from locality to locality. We have argued that the milieu was probably in various ways competitive, and possible signs of impressive but short-lived enclosure constructions and attendant assemblies may be a further clue to the nature of interaction in the mid-36th century cal BC. We know so little of cursus monuments that it is pointless to espouse any single interpretation, but the many existing views (see amongst others: Tilley 1994; C. Richards 1996; Barclay and Harding 1999; A. Barclay *et al.* 2003; Loveday 2006; J. Thomas 2007b; R. Bradley 2007) can all now be put into the preliminary outline of a more specific historical context. Whatever the precise circumstances, it is not difficult to envisage the creativity represented by cursus monuments (see again Barth 1987) as a product of continuing desire for innovation and difference. Thus, linearity now succeeds circularity, and movement and direction now rival activity in a single fixed spot. Though labour inputs may in many cases not have increased substantially, the new visual impact of cursus monuments was potentially stunning, and the experience of procession inside, outside

Fig. 15.27. Clyde cairns at Cairnholy, Dumfries and Galloway, Ardnadam, Argyll and Bute (above, left and right), Blasthill (Kintyre), Argyll and Bute, and Loch Nell, Argyll and Bute (below, left and right). Photos: Vicki Cummings.

or alongside these perhaps awe-inspiring, liminal places did away with or surpassed previous feasting and deposition in causewayed enclosures. Perhaps there were deliberately more arcane ideas at work now, with orientations and cosmological aspects possibly a significant dimension, with the setting, speculatively, a forum for the elaboration of abstract or more secret concepts of the past, ancestors, spirits, natural forces and the like: more easily controlled, and less open to direct contestation and rivalry than in the open and public arenas of causewayed enclosures. It was probably no accident that long barrows were incorporated into the Dorset cursus, or that one stands at the east end of the greater Stonehenge cursus.

The sequences now partially visible indicate, however, that this was no straightforward replacement, just as earlier causewayed enclosures were added to a repertoire of existing monumental constructions. This time, there is no evidence to suggest derivation from continental practice (though linear monuments did exist much earlier in northern France: Kinnes 1999). It has been suggested that this was an idea first developed in Scotland (e.g. J. Thomas 2006), but the vast majority of dates from Scottish linear monuments are on potentially old wood; those that are not give no clear primacy to northern development (Chapter 14.7). There is limited evidence for comparable monuments in Ireland, though for example there appears to be one to the east of and close to Newgrange (Smyth 2009). So at this stage it is impossible to see where the cursus idea first developed, or how quickly it was introduced, and if this was indeed an elaboration of, and in some kind of opposition to, causewayed enclosures, the first moves might just as well have been made in southern Britain. Indeed, eastern England provides a small number of possible antecedents in the form of rectilinear and elongated monuments which are poor in or devoid of cultural material, like cursus monuments and in comparable low-lying river valley locations to cursus monuments. Where these can be approximately dated, like the avenue at Raunds or the trapezoid enclosure at Godmanchester, they go back to the early or mid-fourth millennium cal BC. It is surely significant that a cursus was *appended* to the Godmanchester trapezoid enclosure, extending its original alignment, while two others were built *cutting across* the Etton and Fornham All Saints causewayed enclosures, as if superseding them (Chapter 6). It is noticeable that farther west in the upper Thames valley, with its numerous causewayed enclosures, there are also cursus monuments in numbers.

A perhaps more differentiated social landscape now came into being in southern Britain. If seniority was an important principle in earlier times, did cursus monuments come to subvert that from the mid-36th century cal BC onwards? Are we witnessing an increase simply in inter-group competition, or is there something more subtle by way of rivalry between say senior and junior clans or lineages? Alongside novel linear monuments, some of the old places of assembly continued in existence, and there was renewed conflict seen in the dramatic event of the battle of Crickley Hill in the 35th century cal BC (Fig. 9.20). Other old ways of doing things were still practised from time to time and place to place. Wayland's Smithy II probably also belongs to the 35th century cal BC (Whittle *et al.* 2007b, fig. 4), and Millbarrow probably even later (Fig. 3.30). Both use an architectural form which had been in favour at least two centuries earlier (Fig. 14.45), and could evoke a conscious archaising; neither is in an area with cursus monuments in the immediate vicinity, the downland edge close to Wayland's looking down on the Vale of the White Horse and the upper Thames valley beyond where linear constructions were probably by now a frequent sight, and Millbarrow out on the poorly known but perhaps little inhabited Lower Chalk north of Windmill Hill, with only the north face of the old enclosure in view; the stone avenues of the region were probably yet to be built (Gillings *et al.* 2008). There are further unanswered questions in the later history of long barrows. Few individual sites appear to have had a very long history of active use, though the rebuilding of Wayland's Smithy, and the start of secondary deposition in the chambers at West Kennet (Whittle *et al.* 2007b; Bayliss *et al.* 2007b), are counter-examples. And yet the tradition, indeed to some extent also like that of diverse and small monuments, persisted for a very long time. Did principles of descent endure more easily than the concerns of more public and political ritual?

Those causewayed enclosures still in use probably came to the end of their primary use at the end of the 34th century cal BC (Fig. 14.145). What continued at this point in southern Britain is unclear, and is getting beyond the reach of the present project, though it seems that no henges were yet constructed in the south. But it is striking how other things and practices come to an end from around this kind of date (Fig. 14.145), so there is every reason to suppose that change continued, even though the dynamics of the late fourth millennium have yet to be revealed. Further afield, there are also signs of ongoing change, for example in the further development of single burials in eastern parts of the country, as seen at Duggleby Howe in Yorkshire (Gibson and Bayliss 2009), and in the development of passage tombs in Ireland, but it is too soon to say whether these later-fourth millennium shifts are synchronous across Britain and Ireland or to predict whether they reflect broader or more regionalised trends.

15.13 Kinds of time and history

So now we have brought together the threads of our narrative, from the analyses presented in the regional chapters, and have attempted, in Ricoeur's terms (1980, 178), to elicit configuration from succession. This has been a study of the causewayed enclosures of southern Britain and their early Neolithic context, but the methodology could have been applied to any other archaeological field lacking either dendrochronology or documentary evidence providing finer chronological resolution than those offered by the scientific methods employed here. So what are the wider implications of what we have tried to achieve?

Timescales

As noted in Chapter 1, the long-term has been the default chronological perspective of many prehistorians. Partly this has been because of our inability to achieve finer chronological resolution routinely, so that in Mike Baillie's striking phrase (1991), all sorts of potentially disparate events and phenomena are 'sucked in and smeared', resulting in a kind of fuzzy prehistory in which the long-term has been seen as the safest, if over-general, option. 'Time perspectivism' is a clear example (see Chapter 1.1). That does not account for all recent discussions of time, in some of which notions like percolating time (Witmore 2007), assemblage (Lucas 2008) and landscape as time materialising (Bender 2002), attempt, at a theoretical level at least, to understand the ways in which things roll on from one moment – or appropriate time interval – to the next. Nor has the short-term been neglected, for example in recent discussions of house durations (Foxhall 2000) and generational or lifecourse cycles (Gilchrist 2000), but tellingly the most detailed studies are from later, quasi-historical periods, as in the analysis of house in classical and Hellenistic Greece (Foxhall 1995; 2000, 492). Even the event has received fresh attention, both as the appropriate scale for 'local, micro-scale, empirical detail...that has emerged as a characteristic of feminist epistemology' (Gilchrist 2000, 325) and as the hinge of structural change (Sewell 2005; Beck *et al.* 2007; Bolender 2010; and see Chapter 1). But while this opening up of more scales is highly welcome, it seems to be still the case for prehistoric studies that, on the one hand, the integration of different timescales is poorly argued and badly understood, and on the other, the long-term maintains its dominant interpretive role. Several examples were noted in Chapter 1. And this is puzzling, since as Robert Paynter has observed (2002, 97), 'the theoretical side of archaeology lost track of time just as the methodological side of archaeology was acquiring the ability to create absolute chronologies'. That comment on late twentieth century practice still seems to hold today.

It is worth briefly going back to the timescales of Braudel, because the notion of *longue durée* and related, general concepts of the long term have been so pervasive and influential in archaeology (Bailey 1981; Robb 2008). But though Braudel sets out his three timescales of *longue durée*, *conjoncture*, and *l'histoire événementielle* to dissect history into 'planes', of geographical time, social time and individual time (1975, 21), it is clear that – however much the general notion of *longue durée* has been picked up by prehistorians – his main interests are in the latter two scales. The scale of the *longue durée* serves in *The Mediterranean* to set the scene, and the significance of geography is always already social and socialised. This was pointed out some time ago by Ricoeur (1984, 209): '...everything he writes about is already part of a history of the Mediterranean...

geohistory is rapidly transformed into geopolitics...global history never ceases to come ashore...'. In one of his earlier papers, Ian Hodder did attack the validity of the long term as a separate plane, independently making many of the same points as Ricoeur; 'each event can be seen, not as the passive by-product of 'the environment', but as an active force in changing that environment (1987, 6). Few prehistorians have noted Ricoeur's critique (but see Borić 2003), and Hodder himself (2006) appears more recently to have inclined to a view of the long-term in the guise of very gradual, barely perceptible and incremental change.

Now this is not to write off a sense of the long-term. There are things that endure and things that change very, very slowly. The universe continues to expand; the earth rotates but gradually wobbles on its axis; ice sheets and glaciers slowly grind rock: all at long timescales hard for us to comprehend as humans, even if we can appreciate them as numbers. Climate may fluctuate over long timescales, though, as say with the end of the Younger Dryas, dramatic change can take place over just a few decades (Severinghaus *et al.* 1998); and population numbers may grow irreversibly but so slowly that any one human generation may be unaware of perceptible shifts, though people often seem to act – and again rapidly – on what they think they perceive as demographic 'pressures', rather than on scientifically measured and tested information (Ardener 1989). Within societies, ritual and styles of art (Bradley 1991, 210) and wider ideational structures (Hodder 1987, 7; 1990), may all also develop over long timescales beyond human consciousness (Giddens 1979, 326; Bourdieu 1990, 53; Gosden 1994, 112). But when this kind of notion of the long-term as slow change is taken to human history, it often seems to say very little. What does it tell us, for example, to state the long-term continuity of agriculture as the principal basis of subsistence from the early Holocene to the present? The statement is true, but very generalised. It would become more interesting if broken down in more detailed stages and trends, and then we could seek to break those down in turn, to examine them at even finer resolution. As Ricoeur has already noted (1984, 224), 'a long time can be a time without any present, and, so, without past or future as well. But then it is no longer a historical time, and the long time-span only leads back from human time to the time of nature'. He goes on (1984, 224):

> If the brief event can act as a screen hiding our consciousness of the time that is not of our making, the long time-span can, likewise, act as a screen hiding the time that we are.

It is worth remembering here the actual scales of Braudel's social and individual times; the latter are more or less self-evident (but see below), while the social time analysed in *The Mediterranean* is confined principally within two centuries, and often to specific decades, or runs of successive decades, within the sixteenth century in particular.

That Ricoeur should comment further (1984, 224) that '*all change enters the field of history as a quasi-event*' (original italics) seems particularly apposite. For him, the 'quasi-event' involves the unfolding of plot and character, and contributes to changes in fortune. Perhaps this leaves an ambiguity about slow, structural changes whose onset was not easily perceptible at any one time; population increase comes to mind as a possible example. But these only become relevant, as observed already for demography (Ardener 1989), when people act in response to real or imagined changes. Ricoeur partly qualified his position by noting (1984, 225) that 'it might perhaps even be said that with the brief event the episodic continues to dominate in plots that are nevertheless extremely complex, and that the long time-span gives precedence to the configuration'. It is hard to give up a notion of the shape of historical change: the 'collective destinies and general trends' of the title of Part Two of *The Mediterranean*. John Robb, for example, has set out (2007; see Chapter 1) his view, as a prehistorian, of the three major social trends in the Neolithic of the Mediterranean and wider areas of Europe, and we offer something of the same below by way of summary for Britain and Ireland. Since we have used Ricoeur extensively as a guide in this discussion, it is fitting to conclude it by one more quotation from *Time and narrative*. He finishes Volume 1 with these words (1984, 225):

> It reminds us that something happens to even the most stable structures. Something happens to them – in particular, they die out. That is why, despite his reticence, Braudel was unable to avoid ending his magnificent work with the description of a death, not, of course, the death of the Mediterranean but of Philip II.

So in our specific study of the early Neolithic in southern Britain and Ireland, we can reflect on the interpretative possibilities raised by the much more precise timescales for change which we have constructed. Both individual constructions and types of things and practices can now be assigned to individual centuries or portions of individual centuries, and even, when archaeology, sample availability and taphonomy, and radiocarbon calibration all combine favourably, to particular decades within individual centuries. Notable gains from this study are more precise timescales for the start of the gradual spread of Neolithic things and practices, beginning in south-east England probably in the 41st century cal BC (Fig. 14.58); its acceleration over much wider areas of western Britain, Ireland, the Isle of Man and Scotland in the late 39th century cal BC (Fig. 14.176); the emergence of monument building as regular practice probably by *c.* 3800 cal BC (Fig. 14.46); the further surge of innovation in the 38th century cal BC (Fig. 14.143); the appearance of enclosure construction in the late 38th century cal BC (Fig. 14.1); and the replacement of enclosures by cursus monuments as the novel style of building enterprise probably from the middle of the 36th century cal BC (Fig. 14.44). After slow beginnings, the tempo of major changes of this kind appears to be brisk, with intervals between major developments from a century and a half to well under a century – from several generations down to two or three. And these were not static horizons, as seen best in the period when most enclosures were constructed, which again has relatively slow beginnings, then an acceleration in the second and third quarters of the 37th century cal BC, followed by a lull in activity and then a final main burst of fresh building (Fig. 14.20). These 'collective destinies' break down further at the level of the biography of the individual site, which in turn inscribes a history specific not only to time but also to place. For all the activity engaged in enclosure construction across southern Britain as a whole, in any one decade in the second and third quarters of the 37th century cal BC or the first half of the 36th century cal BC there were plenty of areas where things were quiet.

There are of course continuities in the period we have covered. For example, styles of inhabitation of the land and ways of working stone may have had much in common from the fifth into the fourth millennia; the more precise history of early Neolithic pottery styles created by our study still suggests currencies in the order of two to four centuries; and long barrows, long cairns and related monuments were in use, over Britain and Ireland as a whole, from at least the 38th century cal BC to the 34th century cal BC, if not both earlier and later as well. We can also certainly echo John Robb (2007), and many other commentators, in suggesting longer-term trends in the development of the Neolithic, although our new chronologies allow us to trace the processes involved in much greater detail. For example, we have suggested that after the initial establishment of agricultural communities, their social relations became increasingly hierarchical through the middle part of the fourth millennium cal BC. In comparison to the scenario set out by John Robb (2007), our new chronologies bring forward significantly the emergence of more hierarchical social formations and accelerate substantially the pace of their development.

There are also, of course, still plenty of phases whose chronology still lacks the kind of precision we are seeking, such as: the late Mesolithic in Britain and Ireland as a whole; the end of the longhouse world on the adjacent European continent; the rate of spread of continental causewayed enclosures; the development of the first two or three centuries of the early Neolithic in both Britain and Ireland; or the nature and rate of change in the 35th and 34th centuries cal BC in southern Britain. So ours is at best a first step in an emerging narrative.

Lived history

So, perhaps the most important general finding of this project has been the realisation that it is possible to write about a remote past in terms of generations and decades: 'prehistory' is a term we could now abolish. But if enforced reliance on a fuzzy long term, on an inevitable recourse to coarse notions of the *longue durée*, should now be a thing of the past, the questions of links between parts of the narrative plot, of the possibility of multiple narratives, of the unfolding of changes of fortune, and of all the 'retentions and protentions' along the sliding line of time, must be faced by archaeologists concerned with the deep past as much as by historians of more recent periods. What can this study contribute to a sense of how people went on, how their lives unfolded in time (Fig. 15.28), beyond reducing that question to a series of single points in a merely linear chronology?

As ever, others have been here before us. The philosopher Rom Harré, for example, suggested a distinction between biological lifespan (from conception to death), social lifespan (from before birth to after death), and personal lifespan (a period of self-knowledge, from infancy to old age) (1991: see also Sofaer and Sofaer 2008).[13] Paul Ricoeur made his own distinctions (1984; cf. Gosden 1994, 54) between mortal time (which is personal), public time (which is collective), and human time (at the intersection of these other two). And there is of course a much wider and extensive literature on the nature of memory, including the character of social memory (among many others: Connerton 1990; Fentress and Wickham 1992; Forty and Küchler 1999). This has recently been fruitfully drawn upon in Neolithic and other studies, to suggest chains of remembering and forgetting, and varying senses of the past in the past (e.g. Edmonds 1999; Bradley 2002), and the possible link through memory between continental longhouse and insular long barrow or long cairn has already been a favourite of British Neolithic specialists for decades. But this burgeoning literature has tended to trade in generalities, and has not on the whole had the benefit of precise chronologies. Thus Richard Bradley (2002, 8) has asserted, from comparative literature, as already noted, a maximum 200-year span for unaltered oral traditions, which is then applied across the board to a number of Neolithic, Bronze Age and other early situations. Our own study can perhaps now offer useful refinement of these kinds of schema, and relate these to the kinds of chronological resolution now possible. This is important, because kinds and scales of memory are inescapably part of the nexus of structure and agency in which social existence unfolds. Not the least interesting facet of senses of time is their effect on action (Schieffelin 2002; James and Mills 2005).

In this study we have pragmatically used a generalised and heuristic notion of the duration of generations as 25 years. This was based on selected comparative studies (Helgason *et al.* 2003; Slatkin 2004; Whittle *et al.* 2007a). It could well be the case in some situations that generations were reckoned over a shorter timescale, and in many that they were thought of as even longer; one example is that of the grades within the male generation sets of the Borana Oromo, where dominant men operate within a concept of the ideal generation as 40 years, while lesser ones struggle to compete over longer scales (Megerssa and Kassam 2005). Whatever the extent of real variation in reckoning, the generation is a useful measure because on the one hand it fits comfortably within the notion of lifecycle or lifecourse and on the other easily encompasses the notion of event. Again we have no single measure for the span of either average or maximum lifetimes. Life tables for Neolithic Italy suggest average spans of little more than 40 years (Robb 2007, 40) – normally longer than a generation

– with only a very few people aged over 50 in any given small group (cf. Smith and Brickley 2009, 29). But we could also think of maximum lifetimes as say 60–70 years. As already stressed in relation to southern British long barrows (Whittle *et al.* 2007a), a seven-decades lifetime would encompass many of the successions of events and processes shown by the present study. It would not of course cover all changes. Someone born in say 3725 cal BC could have witnessed or heard about the first enclosure construction as a child, participated in further enclosure building as an adult, and lived long enough to transmit to the generation born in the middle part of the 37th century cal BC active memories of how things were done at the beginning. Those descendants could have lived through the lull in activity at the end of the 37th century cal BC, and into the resumption of construction in the first part of the 36th century cal BC. Memory transmitted through two maximum lifetimes – say five to six generations – would be the stuff of social or public time, and one that would be familiar in much later times to historians of say the fifteenth and sixteenth centuries AD (Elton 1974; Braudel 1975). And this seems to fit with the pulses or tempo of change that this volume has regularly revealed in the early Neolithic of southern Britain and Ireland. But why was this? Was there a sense simply of fading time, of inevitably choosing or drifting to do things differently as the visibility, authority and memory of preceding figures dwindled? Or was the early Neolithic sense of time more active in promoting innovation through an ongoing, creative concern for and use of the past? We have argued that long barrows and long cairns, enclosures themselves, and then in turn cursus monuments make varying reference to the past. The traditional position in Neolithic studies has been to look for the longest possible chains of memory, and while that might still apply, with qualification and reservations (because while form may refer to a deep past, internal architectural arrangements and those interred most certainly do not), to the introduction of long barrows and long cairns, it does not accord with our interpretation of the appearance of either enclosures or cursus monuments. Geographical distance – exotic things from far away – can substitute for temporal distance, and creative innovation can replace both.

The past was not confined to the individual lifetime or the span of transmission over a couple of lifetimes. Genealogies on the one hand and myth on the other evoke and often seek to control deeper pasts. The span of lineage reckoning can go back, especially in unilineal systems, a very long way: some 14–17 generations the case of the Tiv of west Africa (Bohannan 1952), and some 34 in the case of the Maori (J.G.D. Clark 1994). Other west African patrilineal systems regularly count 10–12 generations, and there are other examples, such as the Mututsi, who count six to eight generations (J.G.D. Clark 1994, 42–3). This gives a potential span, if generational reckoning were to be, perhaps crudely, turned into linear time, of well over a century to well over two centuries – or even more. In more detail, to take the Tiv case (Whittle 2003, chapter 5), while the general belief was that all the many Tiv were descended from one man, Tiv himself, the normal concern with descent was acted out in the closer setting of the lineage and territorial segment, consisting of some 200–1300 people. In that context, 'three fathers' is the normal range of individual genealogical memory of particular ancestors, beyond which more anonymous ancestors provide a genealogical charter to link back to Tiv himself (Bohannan 1952, 313). Both genealogy and more general ancestry can be seen as charters, to validate present social relationships, which in turn prove the genealogies (Bohannan 1952, 312, 315); the key criterion is consistency. It does not appear to be the case that the bones of forebears were much curated in the early Neolithic (see Chapter 15.10), and the alternative schema of bilateral descent, with often shorter lines traced, was also noted. But there is the potential in this field for one kind of active, if partial, social memory to operate over longer timescales. Counting of forebears, at a certain point, clearly merges into mythical time. The example of the central African Lugbara is a case in point (J. Middleton 1960; Whittle 2003). Mythic time has succession, but little sense of span, and even personal memory is probably often, perhaps normally, selective and creative (Bergson 1911; Bartlett 1932; Bloch 1998; Whittle 2003). Other ethnographies record the richness and variety of chronicles, stories, legends and moral tales that can merge into myth (Turner 1980; Ricoeur 1980), and these can be shown to be a basis for practical action, as among the western Apache (Basso 1984). The possible link between continental longhouses and insular long barrows and cairns comes once more to mind. We can now suggest that the minimum interval between the two was some seven centuries, but it is doubtful if the significance of the link was considered in this way. It is hard, however, to think of any other comparable example of the reach of mythic recall affecting action in the early Neolithic, and this discussion of longer scales of memory serves overall to underline the dominance of much shorter ones.

Total archaeology?

In the quotation which heads this chapter, Lucien Febvre goes on (1935, 35):

> A man who studies the period in which a certain type of Neolithic pottery was widespread is doing history in exactly the same kind of way as a man who draws a map of the distribution of telephones in the Far East in 1948. Both, in the same spirit, for the same ends, are devoting themselves to a study of the manifestations of the inventive genius of mankind, which differ in age and in yield, if you like, but certainly not in ingenuity.

The present study has included several types of pottery, but has gone far beyond those, to bring in, as part of the wider context of causewayed enclosures, a vast array of other activity: life in wooded landscapes; the comings and goings of occupation; pit digging; the keeping and the slaughter of cows; the movement and deposition of stone and flint axeheads; clearance; digging the earth to create enclosures,

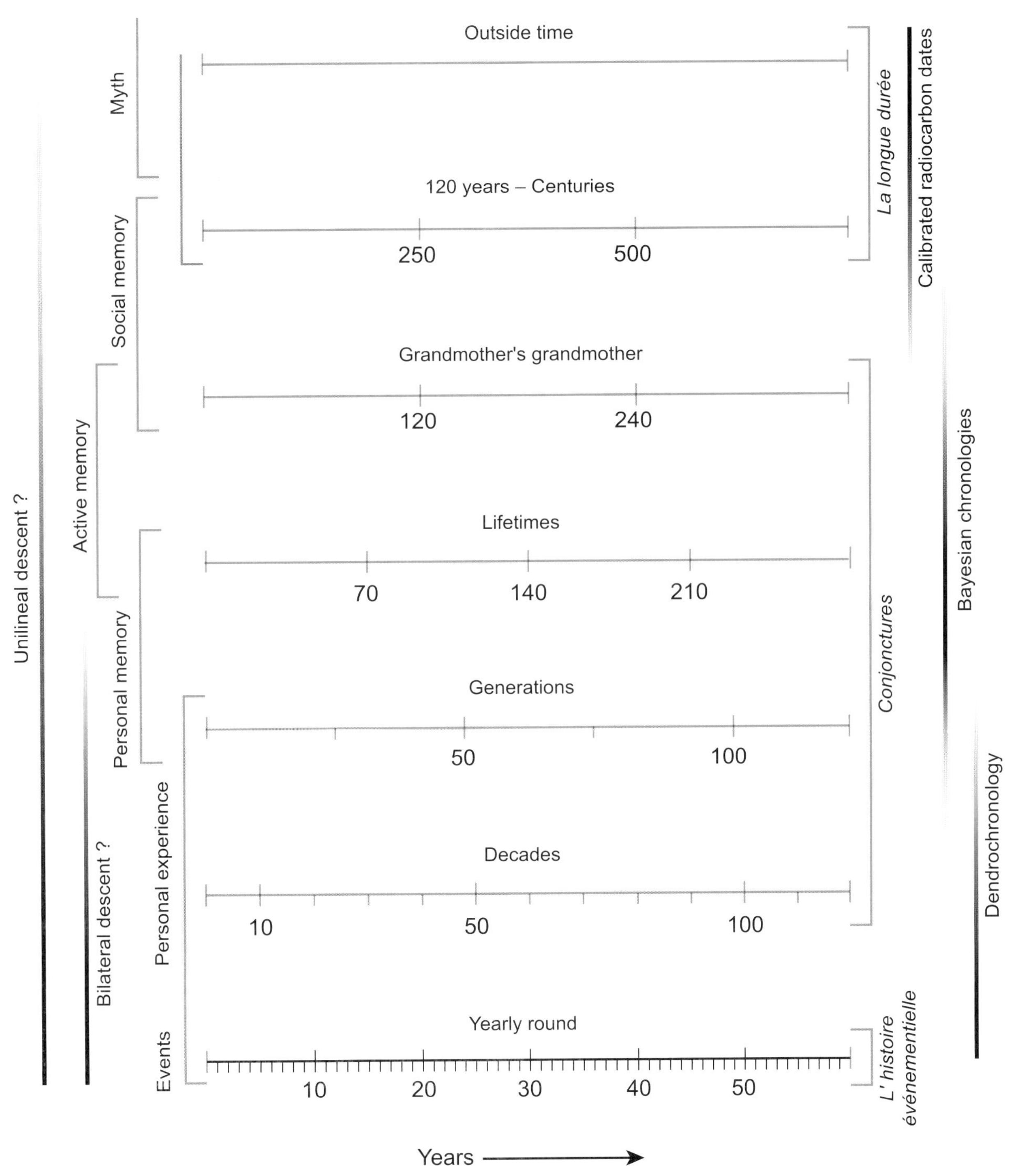

Fig. 15.28. Human timescales, experience and the transmission of memory.

mines and barrows; the building, use and burning of timber houses; the disposal of the dead; ambushes and battles; and assembly and social interaction. We have suggested several dimensions of the socialities through which this history was played out, from families, lineages, alliances and residence groups to wider communities and networks, some of them far afield; the dead are members of this meshwork, but normally as remembered forebears rather than distant or remote ancestors. We have been able to propose, from the finer chronological resolution now open to the discipline, a series of temporalities, with agency and structure playing out principally at the scale of generations, lifetimes and active social memory; the dead had a part at these scales, and occasionally something older comes in perhaps by way of myth and story. We have offered a complicated account, involving both new people and ideas from the outside and indigenous insular people and their existing practices and beliefs, and overall an accelerating tempo of change. We have suggested, within this intensifying sociality, the unfolding of a politics of emulation and competition, though there are no easily applicable or ready-made labels to characterise the diverse situations and relations encountered. Though there are also many aspects of the early Neolithic in southern Britain and Ireland which require much further research, and which this study has unavoidably investigated without the depth required, especially in the domains of settlement and subsistence, we claim to be offering radically new narratives.

What then should we call this kind of approach? It no longer seems adequate to retain the term 'prehistory', because of its baggage of fuzzy chronology. We have played with the notion of '(pre)history', but while attractive on paper, it is a limp and clumsy distinction when spoken. The French term 'protohistoire' (Daniel 1967) evokes the presence of texts which comment from the outside. Braudel used the term 'total history', designed to 'reconstruct the whole physical, intellectual and moral universe of each preceding generation' (Bintliff 1991, 12), and to catch the never-ending stream of being and events (Hodder 1987, 2), and there has also been talk of 'absolute history' (Paynter 2002, 95). Has the present study then been an exercise in 'total archaeology'? We can aspire to this, but do not claim that we have yet assembled enough detail in our narratives to justify using it. Mindful of Febvre's caution (1973, 35) 'not to underestimate the persistence of that old taboo which says, "You can only do history from texts" ', perhaps we can best conclude by underlining the hope that our kind of study, with narratives taken to the level of lifetimes, generations, decades, and even occasionally events, now begins to take the pre- out of prehistory. But what kind of history? Lucien Febvre saw any definition as a prison (1973, 31). Perhaps we can give the last word to him (1973, 31):

> A definition of history? Which history? I mean at what date and in what framework of civilization? Does history not vary, all the time, in its restless search for new techniques, new points of view, problems needing to be put more aptly? Definitions – do not the most precise definitions, the most carefully thought out and most meticulously phrased definitions run the risk of constantly leaving aside the best part of history?

Notes

1 As this volume was going to press, a marked and rapid increase in population density in Britain coincident with the appearance of cultigens around 6000 cal BP (3950 cal BC) has been claimed on the basis of summing calibrated radiocarbon dates (Collard *et al.* 2010, 267–8 and fig. 1). Further claims about spatio-temporal trends in population density, again based on summed probability distributions, have also been made (Collard *et al.* 2010, 268–9 and fig. 2). We have considerable concerns about the statistical validity of this approach, either for estimating the date of phases of activity in the past (Bayliss *et al.* 2007a, 9–11), or for estimating changes in past population (Surovell and Brantingham 2007), or for spatio-temporal modelling (cf. Buck *et al.* 2002; Nicholls and Nunn submitted). For example, apparent population concentrations in south-central England and southern Scotland in 6100–6000 cal BP (4050–3950 cal BC) appear to be artefacts of the inability of this statistical approach to counteract the scatter on groups of radiocarbon dates (see Chapter 2.2). We are also concerned about the very limited attempts to critically assess the radiocarbon dates included in this analysis (Collard *et al.* 2010, 867), especially as a substantial proportion are likely to include old-wood offsets which will systematically bias the sample towards older ages. In the absence of access to details of the dataset underlying this analysis, it is difficult to disentangle the effects of the statistical methodology employed, the sample of radiocarbon dates available, and the approach to assessing them on the results and conclusions produced.

2 These estimates are based on a complex model combining a total of 71 radiocarbon dates with site-based stratigraphy and archaeological periodisation (summarised in Cassen *et al.* 2009, fig. 11). Twenty-seven radiocarbon dates are associated with the Castellic cultural phase, although only nine of these were certainly made on short-lived material and at least one of these (AA-20403 from the Table des Marchands) appears to be residual, as it is earlier than a series of dates on stratigraphically earlier deposits. Although this model undoubtedly provides the most reliable dating for Castellic pottery available at present, there is certainly potential for refining this chronology. This could be done not only by obtaining further dates on short-lived samples clearly associated with diagnostic cultural material, but also by further investigation of the taphonomy and associations of the existing dated samples, and their potential for including old-wood offsets.

3 'A phenomenon of stylistic unification caused by the interaction of different groups'

4 Dating confirmed by the formal, if rather imprecise, estimate for the first activity in these mines of *4685–4250 cal BC* (*95% probability*; Fig. 5.38: *first NW European flint mines*), probably *4465–4320 cal BC* (*64% probability*) or *4290–4265 cal BC* (*4% probability*), presented in Chapter 5.9.

5 'It could, if the enclosures did not have just a simple defensive function, be to do with signs of emergent tensions in response to scarcer land and a growing population; or, at the least, with the establishment of complex ideological systems whose role was to embody, by a demonstrable rooting in the landscape, communities ever more dispersed in space.'

6 'economy and society evolve towards denser and more hierarchical settlement patterns.'

7 We can also note that, further afield, the situation in southern Scandinavia and the northern European Plain tends to point to the appearance of a new Neolithic ideology following acculturation processes at the Mesolithic–Neolithic transition (Klassen 2004; Müller 2010b). The aquatic resources of the Baltic had enabled internal processes in the Ertebølle culture, ending perhaps in a kind of pot-using, sedentary or semi-sedentary Mesolithic, which took in some domesticates but otherwise did not accept the new traits of southern Neolithic societies.

8 A new German-French project on the Michelsberg culture, 'Die Anfänge sozialer Komplexität: Erdwerke, Rohstoffnutzung und Territorialität im Neolithikum', financed by the Deutsche Forschungsgemeinschaft and the Agence Nationale de la Recherche, has been running since 2010.

9 'Everything happens as if practices just feebly codified in Danubian societies acquired, in the late Neolithic, a much more stereotyped character.'

10 A comparison we owe to Jonathan Last.

11 An idea we owe to Julian Thomas.

12 A suggestion we owe to Lin Foxhall.

Appendix: Some unanswered research questions for southern British enclosures

Frances Healy, Alasdair Whittle and Alex Bayliss

Work on the southern British regional chapters highlighted a number of site-specific questions relating to the enclosures, some of them previously aired, some of them, as far as can be seen, new. Many could be answered by targeted fieldwork. They are noted here, chapter-by-chapter, for ease of reference by those who will concern themselves with these sites in the future. Questions raised for the Isle of Man are included in Chapter 11, and for Ireland in Chapter 12.

North Wiltshire (Chapter 3)

Windmill Hill

Was there a fourth circuit at Windmill Hill? Discussion above (Chapter 15.7–9 and 15.12) suggested that the scale of the outer ditch took people to the limits of what they could conceive in the fourth millennium cal BC. It is worth remembering that there are other earthworks on the north side of the hill, outside the outer ditch, which were considered in the run-up to the 1988 excavations as possible candidates for outworks, perhaps to be compared to those known at other causewayed enclosures (Whittle *et al.* 1999). North-west and north-facing lynchets form an arc, running from the west side of the outer circuit around the north side of the hill, progressively farther away from that circuit until they merge into a linear earthwork which runs south-eastwards away from the site, while one lynchet continues around the hill for some distance to the south (McOmish 1999, fig. 15; Oswald *et al.* 2001, fig. 1.6). They are part of a field system in which vestigial transverse boundaries define small rectangular plots, the morphology suggesting a prehistoric or Romano-British origin (McOmish 1999, 16). Yet the pronounced curve of the terraces around the base of a hill is rare. On Fyfield and Overton Downs to the east and south-east, field systems of Bronze Age and later date are predominantly rectilinear (P. Fowler 2000, figs 2.1, 15.3), as they are on the rest of the Marlborough Downs (Gingell 1992, frontispiece, pls 1, 2, fig. 96). The same is true of the extensively surveyed field systems of Salisbury Plain (Bradley *et al.* 1994, fig. 10; McOmish *et al.* 2002, figs 1.17, 3.4, 3.9). This raises the possibility that the margin of the fields at Windmill Hill could have followed the line of an earlier earthwork. In the event, it was concluded that such earthworks at Windmill Hill were probably part of later field systems (McOmish 1999, 16), but it is worth keeping the question open, should any opportunity arise in the future to test this by excavation.

What were the extent of pit-digging and the character of pit contents within and beyond Windmill Hill? This project has contributed little further information. The intersecting pits outside the Windmill enclosure were not radiocarbon dated (Whittle *et al.* 2000), and this subject is one in need of further research.

What was the nature of later Neolithic and Early Bronze Age activity on Windmill Hill? Interpretations have ranged from appropriation of an already old monument by users of Beaker pottery as a means of legitimising newly acquired power (Bradley 1984, 79–81; Thomas 1999, 43–5, 123–5) to an argument that the monument was the disregarded backdrop to settlement episodes and barrow-building indistinguishable from the overall mosaic of activity across the landscape (Hamilton 1999b). It is difficult to imagine that substantial, well preserved earthworks would have lost all significance, especially within a major monument complex. Re-working of one segment, perhaps accompanied by the creation of a new entrance, around the turn of the fourth and third millennia cal BC and the placing of a burial in that same segment a thousand years later suggest that the enclosure retained a ceremonial role, although undoubtedly a changing and developing one (Whittle *et al.* 1999, 380). There is a good case for interrogating the evidence from these periods in the enclosure in conjunction with that from the flint scatter to the south (Whittle *et al.* 2000).

Knap Hill

Does the discovery of articulated bone in all three of Connah's cuttings through the bank indicate that the entire earthwork is underlain by freshly butchered bone, in turn indicating large-scale meat consumption very shortly before the enclosure was built?

Rybury

What are the date and function of the spurwork south of the Rybury enclosure (Fig. 3.27)?

South Wessex (Chapter 4)

Hambledon Hill

What was the nature and extent of earlier Neolithic activity over the unexcavated parts of the Hill, especially outside and between the enclosures?

Was there a further, outer, outwork on the Shroton spur?

Can the relation between the Stepleton and Hanford earthworks be better-defined? Investigation in and either side of the area where the outworks swing across the contours could clarify this.

What was the extent of Neolithic earthworks on the hillfort spur? The Iron Age ramparts may conceal even more extensive Neolithic earthworks than have been identified. The location of Neolithic entrances on the gentle slopes of the Shroton, Stepleton and Hanford spurs suggests that there may be another at the south-east angle of the hillfort spur.

Can environmental evidence from the hill itself be enhanced, at least to match advances in Cranborne Chase? If the technical difficulties could be overcome, a section at a location where a Neolithic earthwork is known to underlie Iron Age ones could yield sealed soils of both dates, as well as the potential for taking stratified sequences of mollusc samples through two sets of ditch fills.

Can the character, landuse history, and chronology of the apparent concentration of Neolithic settlement on the coastal plain to the south be elucidated? There is also the still untapped potential of the unpublished excavation of numerous pits, some with Bowl pottery in the South-Western style, at Moortown, on the lower Stour (Horsey and Jarvis 1984).

Can the prehistory of the Blackmoor Vale to the west of Hambledon Hill be elucidated? The area remains an archaeological and palaeoenvironmental blank, and with that blank persistent, understanding of the local human presence is one-sided. Its fluviatile deposits could provide a history of its human use, and might encapsulate stratified archaeological material. The Vale of Melksham stands in the same relation to Windmill Hill.

Whitesheet Hill

What is the date and function of the cross-ridge dykes and second enclosure, not to mention the enclosure preceding the hillfort (Fig. 4.22)?

Maiden Castle

How many Neolithic ditches are there at Maiden Castle?

What became of the spoil from the inner enclosure ditch? The chalk excavated from the outer enclosure ditch is likely to have been backfilled into it. The chalk excavated from the inner ditch has disappeared, and, at least in Trench I, it had done so by the time the long mound was built. Despite the restricted size of the trenches, and the presence of Iron Age features on and near the inner lip of the ditch, there are places where any surviving bank would have been visible (Sharples 1991a, figs 46–47). But there are no traces of any bank. One possibility is that the construction of the long mound over the circuits was accompanied by the obliteration of the above-ground earthwork and the incorporation of its mass into the long mound.

Was the Maiden Castle long mound built in stages, and was its central part a long barrow?

How did the one remaining apparently Neolithic burial in the area of the east end of the Maiden Castle long mound (skeletons Q2 and Q3) fit into the sequence?

How much use and re-working of Maiden Castle was there in the third and second millennia? Some features potentially of this age could not be tested in the course of the 1985–6 excavations or this project. In Wheeler's trench G, in the east hillfort entrance, a dense scatter of Beaker sherds (Wheeler 1943, 156, pl. XXIIIb) in the top of the inner enclosure ditch (Wheeler 1943, pl. XI: layer1) was associated with the fragmentary remains of two children (Skeletons GM1(a) and (b); Morant and Goodman 1943, 343–4), which, if they were not redeposited from Neolithic contexts, may suggest ceremonial use rather than occupation (Cleal 1991, 185). Sharples points out, too, that palisades in front of the original east hillfort entrance (Wheeler 1943, pl. CXIX: 'early palisades') were stratigraphically unrelated to the primary hillfort and may conceivably connect to activity of this period (1991a, 60).

Robin Hood's Ball

What is the date of the outer circuit at Robin Hood's Ball?

How did activity outside Robin Hood's Ball relate to the use of the enclosure?

Other sites

What was the date and nature of activity at Scratchbury? What was the date and nature of activity at South Cadbury and Ham Hill?

Sussex (Chapter 5)

Whitehawk

Does the external bank of ditch 2 incorporate a pre-existing long barrow? One of the segments excavated by Ross Williamson seems to change course around a conspicuous part of that bank: 'Curwen shows a length of bank to the north of this, adjacent to the ditch excavated in 1929. This is the only part of the second bank noted by him, so it must have been more prominent than the rest. Indeed, it is depicted on both plans as a long mound, measuring *c.* 16 m long and 9.5 m wide, and it is conceivable that it was an earlier feature incorporated into the bank and ditch' (RCHME 1995a, 17).

What are the date and stratigraphic relationships of enclosures 2a and 3a, identified by RCHME in 1993? Were they originally complete circuits, subsequently reworked into and partly overlain by later ones?

What are the date and stratigraphic relationships of the north-east tangential ditch?

Are there yet further circuits, perhaps corresponding to the fifth and sixth ditches observed by Curwen?

What is the date of the north-south row of pits or ditch segments on the racecourse to the south of the circuits, and does it relate to the complex?

The Trundle

Can The Trundle be more effectively dated?

How many circuits are there? How complete are they? How do they relate to each other?

Are the postholes surrounding segments of the second ditch and perhaps spiral ditch 2 contemporary with the segments or of Iron Age date, as suggested by Piggott (1954, 27)?

What was the Neolithic use of the areas within and between the ditches?

How many of the earthworks on the spurs to the west and north of The Trundle are part of the Neolithic complex rather than the Iron Age one?

Halnaker Hill

What is the date of Halnaker Hill?

Eastern England (Chapter 6)

The lower Nene and Welland

Why is there a cluster of causewayed enclosures here and how did its components relate to each other?

Uneven monument distribution

Is the apparent scarcity of Neolithic monuments east of the fens real or illusory? Could it be due to, for example, the presence of non-classic forms such as the Godmanchester trapezoid enclosure on the Great Ouse or some of the smaller monuments in the Nene valley?

What is the record of less fully investigated areas like most of Suffolk, the Coverloam of north-east Norfolk or the area north of the Welland?

Pit sites

Can adequate dating of extensive pit sites establish for how long they were used?

Can any chronological dichotomy be detected between extensive pit clusters and isolated pits and ephemeral contexts containing early Neolithic material? More extensive dating of features of both kinds at Barleycroft Farm, where different kinds of Bowl occur in different kinds of context, might be productive, as might dating of contexts with potentially early pottery, such as the hollow at the John Innes Centre.

The Greater Thames Estuary (Chapter 7)

St Osyth

Can the full plan of the St Osyth enclosure be established? Can more of the ditches be excavated and more datable samples obtained from ditch contexts?

Orsett

Can more be excavated of all parts of the enclosure to provide more datable samples from all three ditch circuits, the palisade and entrance features, and interior features?

Can other early Neolithic occupation sites in the vicinity be more precisely dated?

What was the date of the Springfield causewayed enclosure, the nearest neighbour to Orsett?

Kingsborough

Since more datable material exists from Kingsborough 1, but was not available at the time of sampling for this programme, can this be dated?

Burham

What was the date of the causewayed enclosure at Burham in the Medway valley, and how does it relate to the stone and timber constructions there?

Chalk Hill

Can any more of the inner, middle and tangential ditches be investigated to provide datable material for those circuits?

Does the large and elongated Nethercourt Farm feature nearby suggest the presence of *another* enclosure? Are the Kingsborough sites the only immediate neighbours around the Thames estuary?

Beyond the enclosures

Can other parts of Kent be further investigated? What of the Downs above Folkestone? What of the few known or suspected long barrows? What of the probable enclosure at Eastry? Are there really no cursus or other linear monuments in Kent?

Can more occupations be dated from both Essex and Kent? Can contexts sealed beneath or in alluvium, peat and brickearth be further exploited? Can the cropmark long barrows/long enclosures in both Essex and Kent be confirmed as Neolithic monuments?

The Thames Valley (Chapter 8)

Enclosures

What are the date and character of the ten known or probable causewayed enclosures in the middle and upper Thames which are so far uninvestigated?

Can Blewburton Hill above the valley be confirmed as a causewayed enclosure?

Has aerial survey been sufficiently extensive for all enclosures in the valley and along its sides to have been recognised? Can other forms of prospection be applied, including ones to sense remotely beneath alluvium?

Can anything further now be retrieved from Abingdon?

Can more be discovered of the character of Eton Wick and Gatehampton Farm?

Beyond the enclosures

Can concentrations of fifth millennium cal BC activity be located, for example along the palaeochannels of the middle Thames around Eton and Dorney?

What is the absolute date and character of the earliest Neolithic deposits at Runnymede?

Can the sequence of middens at Eton Rowing Lake be dated with greater precision?

More generally, can the potential of surfaces preserved beneath alluvium, unrivalled perhaps in any other area covered by this volume, be linked to further investigations of valley enclosures?

What is the detailed sequence of mortuary structures other than long barrows in the valley? Can we extend our understanding of valley-upland relationships?

Can we obtain more information on the transport of Chalk flint into the upper valley (already noted by Leeds in the 1920s) and the Cotswolds?

Can we obtain more precise dates for more cursus monuments in the Thames valley?

The Cotswolds (Chapter 9)

Crickley Hill

What was the nature and extent of fifth millennium cal BC activity here?

Can the chronology of the internal structures be elucidated?

What are the chronology and functions of the platform and shrine, the earlier stages of the long mound and the stone circle?

Peak Camp

Is there an inner earthwork and what is its date?

What are the nature and functions of the Area II ditch?

What other features lie in the interior?

Long barrows and cairns

What are the dates of The Crippets, Coberley and Briery long barrows, close to Crickley and Peak Camp? More broadly, can the existing archive for long cairns and barrows in the Cotswolds be further exploited to strengthen the chronologies outlined here?

The South-West (Chapter 10)

Enclosures

Can more be found of the enclosure at Membury?

Can more of the outer ditch be traced at Hembury? Can the features found between the Neolithic earthworks be further elucidated?

Can more of the circuits at Raddon be excavated?

Can the outer enclosures at both Helman Tor and Carn Brea be shown without question to belong to the same date as the tor enclosures?

There are various possible enclosures in the region, noted in the chapter, which need confirmation. And can anything still be done with what remains of High Peak?

Beyond the enclosures

What is the chronological relationship of causewayed enclosures and tor enclosures in the south-west to portal dolmens, long barrows, the Broadsands chambered monument, long 'mortuary' enclosures, entrance graves and cursus monuments?

The Marches, south Wales and the Isle of Man (Chapter 11)

Enclosures

How many of the Welsh causewayed enclosures are Neolithic? While the early Neolithic dates of the Banc Du and Womaston causewayed enclosures have been confirmed, the age of Norton remains uncertain following evaluation. This, and the first millennium cal BC date of Beech Court Farm, Ewenny, increase the desirability of obtaining secure dating for the possibly Neolithic causewayed enclosures at Corntown and Flemingston in south-east Wales and at Woolston in Shropshire. Dorstone Hill, in Herefordshire, would benefit from systematic analysis of the records and finds from the excavations of some time ago.

Beyond the enclosures

Is the Neolithic archaeology of Trostrey Castle, Monmouthshire, even half as significant as the interim statements tantalisingly suggest? This merits analysis and publication, with more effective dating, even if the entire story is only half as dramatic as the provisional accounts of monumental timber structures and other features indicate.

Can the dating of portal dolmens and related structures be improved, at least to the level of that of long barrows and cairns? Their age floats between typologically-based assertions of a very early fourth millennium cal BC date and the mid-fourth millennium *terminus post quem* for Carreg Coetan proposed in Chapter 11. Analysis and publication of Carreg Coetan would itself be an important gain, and might conceivably be accompanied by better dating, if the collection affords suitable samples. The inherent difficulty of finding such samples from monuments which could have remained accessible over long periods is, however, a problem here and elsewhere in Atlantic Britain.

Can settlement evidence, including that of lithic scatters, be analysed systematically and related to the monuments? While Banc Du is placed in its local context by the SPACES project, analysis of settlement evidence remains scant elsewhere, although that evidence is itself locally abundant.

Bibliography

Abbott, G.W. 1910. The discovery of prehistoric pits at Peterborough. *Archaeologia* 62, 333–52.

Adams, R. 2004. An ethnoarchaeological study of feasting in Sulawesi, Indonesia. *Journal of Anthropological Archaeology* 23, 56–78.

Adkins, K.P. and Adkins, P.C. 1984. A Neolithic cooking pit at Chigborough Farm, Little Totham. *Colchester Archaeological Group Annual Bulletin* 27, 33–43.

Adkins, K.P. and Adkins, P.C. 1992. A Neolithic settlement on the north bank of the river Blackwater. *Colchester Archaeological Group Annual Bulletin* 34, 15–43.

Adkins, R. and Jackson, R. 1978. *Neolithic stone and flint axes from the river Thames*. London: British Museum.

Aerts-Bijma, A.T., Meijer, H.A.J. and van der Plicht, J. 1997. AMS sample handling in Groningen. *Nuclear Instruments and Methods in Physics Research* B 123, 221–5.

Aerts-Bijma, A.T., van der Plicht, J. and Meijer, H.A.J. 2001. Automatic AMS sample combustion and CO2 collection. *Radiocarbon* 43(2A), 293–8.

Albone, J., Massey, S. and Tremlett, S. 2004. The national mapping programme in Norfolk, 2003–4. *Norfolk Archaeology* 44(3), 549–55.

Aldhouse-Green, S. 2000. *Paviland cave and the 'Red Lady': a definitive report*. Bristol: Western Academic & Specialist Press for the SCARAB Research centre of the University of Wales College, Newport, and the Friends of the National Museum of Wales.

Aldhouse-Green, S., Pettit, P. and Stringer, C. 1996. Holocene humans at Pontnewydd and Cae Gronw caves. *Antiquity* 70, 444–7.

Aldhouse-Green, S., Whittle, A., Allen, J.R.L., Caseldine, A.E., Culver, S.J., Day, M.H., Lundquist, J. and Upton, D. 1992. Prehistoric human footprints from the Severn estuary at Uskmouth and Magor Pill, Gwent, Wales. *Archaeologia Cambrensis* 141, 14–55.

Alexander, D. 2000. Excavation of Neolithic pits, later prehistoric structures and a Roman temporary camp along the line of the A96 Kintore and Blackburn Bypass, Aberdeenshire. *Proceedings of the Society of Antiquaries of Scotland* 130, 11–75.

Alexander, J. 1961. The excavation of the Chestnuts megalithic tomb at Addington, Kent. *Archaeologia Cantiana* 76, 1–57.

Allard, P. 2007. The Mesolithic-Neolithic transition in the Paris basin: a review. In A. Whittle and V. Cummings (eds), *Going over: the Mesolithic-Neolithic transition in north-west Europe*, 211–23. Oxford: Oxford University Press for The British Academy.

Allcroft, A.H. 1908. *Earthworks of England: prehistoric, Roman, Saxon, Danish, Norman and mediaeval*. London: MacMillan.

Allen, M.J. 1995. The prehistoric land-use and human ecology of the Malling–Caburn Downs. *Sussex Archaeological Collections* 133, 19–43.

Allen, M.J. 1997a. Landuse history: land molluscan evidence. In R.J.C. Smith, F. Healy, M.J. Allen, E.L. Morris, I. Barnes and P.J. Woodward, *Excavations along the route of the Dorchester by-pass, Dorset, 1986–8*, 166–84. Salisbury: Wessex Archaeological Trust.

Allen, M.J. 1997b. Environment and land-use: the economic development of the communities who built Stonehenge (an economy to support the stones). In B. Cunliffe and C. Renfrew (eds), *Science and Stonehenge*, 115–44. London: Proceedings of the British Academy 92.

Allen, M.J. 1997c. Landscape, land-use and farming. In R.J.C. Smith, F. Healy, M.J. Allen, E.L. Morris, I. Barnes and P.J. Woodward, *Excavations along the route of the Dorchester by-pass, Dorset, 1986–8*, 277–83. Salisbury: Wessex Archaeological Trust.

Allen, M.J. 2000. Soils, pollen and lots of snails. In M. Green, *A landscape revealed: 10,000 years on a chalkland farm*, 36–49. Stroud: Tempus.

Allen, M.J. 2002a. The chalkland landscape of Cranborne Chase: a prehistoric human ecology. *Landscapes* 13, 55–69.

Allen, M.J. 2002b. The land molluscs. In S.M. Davies, P.S. Bellamy, M.J. Heaton and P.J. Woodward, *Excavations at Alington Avenue, Fordington, Dorchester, Dorset, 1984–7*, 48–53. Dorchester: Dorset Natural History and Archaeological Society.

Allen, M.J. 2002c. Summary of landscape evolution. In S.M. Davies, P.S. Bellamy, M.J. Heaton and P.J. Woodward, *Excavations at Alington Avenue, Fordington, Dorchester, Dorset, 1984–7*, 185–96. Dorchester: Dorset Natural History and Archaeological Society.

Allen, M.J. 2005. Considering prehistoric environmental changes on the Marlborough Downs. In G. Brown, D. Field and D. McOmish (eds), *The Avebury landscape: aspects of the field archaeology of the Marlborough Downs*, 77–86. Oxford: Oxbow Books.

Allen, M.J. 2007. Land use and landscape development: the molluscan evidence. In C. French, H. Lewis, M.J. Allen, M. Green, R. Scaife and J. Gardiner, *Prehistoric landscape development and human impact in the upper Allen valley, Cranborne Chase, Dorset*, 151–89. Cambridge: McDonald Institute for Archaeological Research.

Allen, M.J. forthcoming. Radiocarbon dates from section 1 of the Channel Tunnel Rail Link, Kent. CTRL scheme-wide specialist report series, http://ads.ahds.ac.uk/catalogue/projArch/ctrl.

Allen, M.J. and Davis, B. 2009. A Middle neolithic pit in the West Kennet (Stone) Avenue, Avebury, 2005. *Wiltshire Archaeological and Natural History Magazine* 102, 12–21.

Allen, M.J. and Gardiner, J. 2000. *Our changing coast: a survey of the intertidal archaeology of Langstone harbour, Hampshire*. York: Council for British Archaeology.

Allen, M.J. and Gardiner J. 2002. A sense of time – cultural markers in the Mesolithic of southern England? In B. David and M. Wilson (eds), *Inscribed landscapes: marking and making place*, 139–53. Honolulu: University of Hawai'i Press.

Allen, M.J. and Gardiner, J. 2007. The Neolithic of the present day intertidal zone of Langstone Harbour, Hampshire. In J. Sidell and F. Haughey (eds), *Neolithic archaeology in the intertidal zone*, 59–70. Oxford: Oxbow Books.

Allen, M.J. and Green, M. 1998. The Fir Tree Field shaft; the date and archaeological and palaeo- environmental potential of a chalk swallowhole feature. *Proceedings of the Dorset Natural History and Archaeological Society* 120, 25–37.

Allen, M.J. and Hayden, C. forthcoming. White Horse Stone, Pilgrim's Way and Boarley Farm. In M.J. Allen, Radiocarbon dates from section 1 of the Channel Tunnel Rail Link, Kent. CTRL scheme-wide specialist report series, http://ads.ahds.ac.uk/catalogue/projArch/ctrl.

Allen, M.J., Hayden, C., Barclay, A. and Bayliss, A. 2005. Radiocarbon report for White Horse Stone, Kent. CTRL specialist report series, http://ads.ahds.ac.uk/catalogue/projArch/ctrl.

Allen, M.J., Leivers, M. and Ellis, C. 2008. Neolithic causewayed enclosures and later prehistoric farming: duality, imposition and the role of predecessors at Kingsborough, Isle of Sheppey, Kent, UK. *Proceedings of the Prehistoric Society* 74, 235–322.

Allen, M.J., Rhodes, E., Beavan, N. and Groves, C. 2004. Absolute dating. In C.J. Ellis, *A prehistoric ritual complex at Eynesbury, Cambridgeshire: excavation of a multi-period site in the Great Ouse valley, 2000–2001*, 60–7. Salisbury: Wessex Archaeological Trust.

Allen, T. 1995. *Lithics and landscape: archaeological discoveries on the Thames Water pipeline at Gatehampton Farm, Goring, Oxfordshire 1985–92*. Oxford: Oxford University Committee for Archaeology.

Allen, T., Barclay, A. and Lamdin-Whymark, H. 2004. Opening the wood, making the land: the study of a Neolithic landscape in the Dorney area of the middle Thames valley. In J. Cotton and D. Field (eds), *Towards a New Stone Age: aspects of the Neolithic in south-east England*, 82–98. York: Council for British Archaeology.

Allison, E. 2002. The shellfish. In G. Shand, *Excavations at Chalk Hill, near Ramsgate, Kent 1997–8: integrated assessment and updated research design*, 34. Unpublished document. Canterbury: Canterbury Archaeological Trust.

Ambers, J. 1996. Radiocarbon analyses from the Grime's Graves mines. In I. Longworth and G. Varndell, *Excavations at Grimes Graves Norfolk 1972–1976. Fascicule 5: mining in the deeper mines*, 100–8. London: British Museum Publications.

Ambers, J. 1998. Radiocarbon dating. In F. Pryor, *Etton: excavations at a Neolithic causewayed enclosure near Maxey, Cambridgeshire, 1982–87*, 349–50. London: English Heritage.

Ambers, J. 2003. The radiocarbon dating. Contribution in S. Ford and J. Pine, Neolithic ring ditches and Roman landscape features at Horton (1989 to 1996). In S. Preston (ed.), *Prehistoric, Roman and Saxon sites in eastern Berkshire: excavations 1989–1997*, 60–2. Reading: Thames Valley Archaeological Services Ltd.

Ambers, J. and Bowman, S. 1994. British Museum natural radiocarbon measurements XXII. *Radiocarbon* 36, 95–112.

Ambers, J. and Bowman, S. 1998. Radiocarbon measurements form the British Museum: datelist XXIV. *Archaeometry* 40, 413–35.

Ambers, J. and Bowman, S. 2003. Radiocarbon measurements from the British Museum: datelist XXVI. *Archaeometry* 45, 531–40.

Ambers, J. and Housley, R. 1995. Radiocarbon dating. In T. Allen, *Lithics and landscape: archaeological discoveries on the Thames Water pipeline at Gatehampton Farm, Goring, Oxfordshire 1985–92*, 112–13. Oxford: Oxford University Committee for Archaeology.

Ambers, J. and Housley, R. 1999. Radiocarbon dating. In A. Whittle, J. Pollard and C. Grigson, *The harmony of symbols: the Windmill Hill causewayed enclosure, Wiltshire*, 116–20. Oxford: Oxbow Books.

Ambers, J., Balaam, N.D., Bowman, S., Clark, A., Housley, R. and Sharples, N. 1991. Radiocarbon dates. In N. Sharples, *Maiden Castle: excavations and field survey 1985–6*, 102–5. London: English Heritage.

Ambers, J., Bowman, S. and Garwood, P., 1999. Appendix 2: radiocarbon dates from the Abingdon causewayed enclosure. In A. Barclay and C. Halpin, *Excavations at Barrow Hills, Radley, Oxfordshire. Volume I. The Neolithic and Bronze Age monument complex*, 337–9. Oxford: Oxford University Committee for Archaeology for the Oxford Archaeological Unit.

Ambers, J., Bowman, S., Garwood, P., Hedges, R. and Housley, R. 1999. Appendix 1: radiocarbon dating. In A. Barclay and C. Halpin, *Excavations at Barrow Hills, Radley, Oxfordshire. Volume I. The Neolithic and Bronze Age monument complex*, 330–7. Oxford: Oxford University Committee for Archaeology on behalf of the Oxford Archaeological Unit.

Ambers, J., Leese, M. and Bowman, S. 1986. Detection of bias in the background of vials used for scintillation counting. In M. Stuiver and R.S. Kra (eds), Proceedings of the twelfth international radiocarbon conference. *Radiocarbon* 28, 586–91.

Ambers, J., Matthews, K. and Bowman, S. 1987. British Museum natural radiocarbon measurements XX. *Radiocarbon* 29, 177–96.

Ambers, J., Matthews, K. and Bowman, S. 1989. British Museum natural radiocarbon measurements XXI. *Radiocarbon* 31, 15–32.

Ambers, J., Matthews, K. and Bowman, S. 1991. British Museum natural radiocarbon measurements XXII. *Radiocarbon* 33, 51–68.

Ambrose, S. 1990. Preparation and characterization of bone and tooth collagen for isotopic analysis. *Journal of Archaeological Science* 17, 431–51.

Ambrose, S. 1991. Effects of diet, climate and physiology on nitrogen isotope abundances in terrestrial foodwebs. *Journal of Archaeological Science* 18, 293–317.

Amkreutz, L., Vanmontfort, B. and Verhart, L. 2009. Diverging trajectories? Forager-farmer interaction in the southern part of the Lower Rhine area and the applicability of contact models. In D. Hofmann and P. Bickle (eds), *Creating communities: new advances in Central European Neolithic research*, 11–31. Oxford: Oxbow Books.

Ammerman, A.J. and Cavalli-Svorza, L.L. 1984. *The Neolithic transition and the genetics of populations in Europe*. Princeton: Princeton University Press.

Andersen, N. 1997. *Sarup volume 1. The Sarup enclosures*. Moesgaard: Jysk Arkæologisk Selskab.

Anon. 1965. Excavation and fieldwork in Wiltshire 1964. *Wiltshire Archaeological and Natural History Magazine* 60, 132–9.

Anon. 1977. Causewayed camps. *Current Archaeology* 58, 335–40.

Anon. 1990. Avebury: Windmill Hill. *Wiltshire Archaeological and Natural History Magazine* 83, 218–23.

Anon. 1997. Three Mesolithic houses discovered near Avebury. *British Archaeology* 28, 4.

Anon. 1999. Alton: Golden Ball Hill (SU 1270 6400). *Wiltshire Archaeological and Natural History Magazine* 92, 133.

Anthony, D. 1990. Migration in archeology: the baby and the bathwater. *American Anthropologist* 92, 895–914.

Anthony, D. 1997. Prehistoric migration as social process. In J. Chapman and H. Hamerow (eds), *Migrations and invasions in archaeological explanation*, 21–32. Oxford: British Archaeological Reports International Series.

Appadurai, A. 1985. Introduction: commodities and the value of things. In A. Appadurai (ed.), *The social life of things*, 3–63. Cambridge: Cambridge University Press.

ApSimon, A. 1969. An early Neolithic house in Co. Tyrone. *Journal of the Royal Society of Antiquaries of Ireland* 99, 165–8.

ApSimon, A. 1976. Ballynagilly and the beginning and end of the Irish Neolithic. In S.J. de Laet (ed.), *Acculturation and continuity in Atlantic Europe*, 15–38. Bruges: de Tempel.

ApSimon, A. 1986. Chronological contexts for Irish megalithic tombs. *Journal of Irish Archaeology* 3, 5–15.

Arbogast, R.-M. 1994. *Premiers élévages néolithiques du nord-est de la France*. Liège: ERAUL.

Arbogast, R.-M. 1998. Contribution de l'archéozoologie du site Michelsberg de Mairy (Ardennes) à l'étude de l'origine de la variabilité des faunes du néolithique récent du Nord de la France. In J. Biel, H. Schlichtherle, M. Strobel, and A. Zeeb (eds), *Die Michelsberger Kultur und ihre Randgebiete – Probleme der Entstehung, Chronologie und des Siedlungswesens*, 135–42. Stuttgart: Theiss.

Arbogast, R.-M., Hachem, L. and Tresset, A. 1991. Le Chasséen du Nord de la France: les données archéozoologiques. In A. Beeching, D. Binder, J.-C. Blanchet, C. Constantin, J. Dubouloz, R. Martinez, D. Mordant, J.-P. Thévenot and J. Vaquer (eds), *Identité du Chasséen*, 351–63. Nemours: Mémoires du Musée de Préhistoire de l'Ile de France 4.

Arbogast, R.-M., Jacomet, S., Magny, M. and Schibler, J. 2006. The significance of climate fluctuations for lake level changes and shifts in subsistence economy during the late Neolithic (4300–2400 B.C.) in central Europe. *Vegetation History and Archaeobotany* 15, 403–18.

Ardener, E. 1989. Social anthropology and population. In E. Ardener, *The voice of prophecy and other essays* (edited by M. Chapman), 109–26. Oxford: Blackwell.

Armit, I. and Finlayson, B. 1992. Hunter-gatherers transformed: the transition to agriculture in northern and western Europe. *Antiquity* 66, 664–76.

Armour-Chelu, M. 1991. The faunal remains. In N. Sharples, *Maiden Castle: excavations and field survey 1985–6*, 139–51. London: English Heritage.

Armour-Chelu, M. 1996. Comment [on OxA-1031]. In R.E.M. Hedges, R. Housley, P.B. Pettitt, C. Bronk Ramsey and G.J. van Klinken, Radiocarbon dates from the Oxford AMS system: *Archaeometry* datelist 21. *Archaeometry* 38, 193–4.

Armour-Chelu, M. 1998a. The animal bone. In F. Pryor, *Etton: excavations at a Neolithic causewayed enclosure near Maxey, Cambridgeshire, 1982–87*, 273–88. London: English Heritage.

Armour-Chelu, M. 1998b. The human bone. In F. Pryor, *Etton: excavations at a Neolithic causewayed enclosure near Maxey, Cambridgeshire, 1982–*7, 271–2. London: English Heritage.

Arneborg, J., Heinemeier, J., Lynnerup, N., Nielsen, H.L., Rud, N. and Sveinbjörnsdóttir, Á.E. 1999. Change of diet of the Greenland Vikings determined from stable carbon isotope analysis and ^{14}C dating of their bones. *Radiocarbon* 41, 157–68.

Arnold, C. 1987. Fridd Faldwyn: the Neolithic phase. *Archaeologia Cambrensis* 136, 39–42.

Arnold, J., Green, M., Lewis, B., and Bradley, R. 1988. The Mesolithic of Cranborne Chase. *Proceedings of the Dorset Natural History and Archaeological Society* 110, 117–25.

Ashbee, P. 1966. The Fussell's Lodge long barrow excavations 1957. *Archaeologia* 100, 1–80.

Ashbee, P. 1970. *The earthen long barrow in Britain*. London: Dent.

Ashbee, P. 1982. Mesolithic megaliths? The Scillonian entrance graves – a new view. *Cornish Archaeology* 21, 3–22.

Ashbee, P. 2005. *Kent in prehistoric times*. Stroud: Tempus.

Ashbee, P., Smith, I.F. and Evans, J.G. 1979. Excavation of three long barrows near Avebury, Wiltshire. *Proceedings of the Prehistoric Society* 45, 207–300.

Ashmore, P. J. 1996. A list of archaeological radiocarbon dates. *Discovery and Excavation in Scotland* 1, 122–8.

Ashmore, P. 1999a. Radiocarbon dating: avoiding errors by avoiding mixed samples. *Antiquity* 73, 124–30.

Ashmore, P.J. 1999b. A list of archaeological radiocarbon dates. *Discovery and Excavation in Scotland 1999*, 110–15.

Ashmore, P.J. 2000. A list of Historic Scotland archaeological radiocarbon dates. *Discovery and Excavation in Scotland 1996*, 136–42.

Ashmore, P. 2003. Terminology, time and space: labels, radiocarbon chronologies and a 'Neolithic' of small worlds'. In I. Armit, E. Murphy, E. Nelis and D. Simpson (eds), *Neolithic settlement in Ireland and western Britain*, 40–6. Oxford: Oxbow Books.

Ashmore, P. 2004a. Absolute chronology. In A.G. Shepherd and G.J. Barclay (eds), *Scotland in Ancient Europe: the Neolithic and Early Bronze Age of Scotland in their European context*, 125–36. Edinburgh: Society of Antiquaries of Scotland.

Ashmore, P.J. 2004b. A list of archaeological radiocarbon dates. *Discovery and Excavation in Scotland* 5, 155–73.

Ashmore, P.J. 2005. A list of archaeological radiocarbon dates. *Discovery and Excavation in Scotland* 6, 165–81.

Ashwin, T. 1996. Neolithic and Bronze Age Norfolk. *Proceedings of the Prehistoric Society* 62, 41–62.

Ashwin, T. 1998. Excavations at Salter's Lane, Longham, 1990: Neolithic and Bronze Age features and artefacts. *Norfolk Archaeology* 43, 1–30.

Ashwin, T. and Bates, S. 2000. *Excavations on the Norwich southern bypass, 1989–91. Part I: excavations at Bixley, Caistor St Edmund, Trowse, Cringleford and Little Melton.* Gressenhall: Archaeology and Environment Division, Norfolk Museums Service.

Atkinson, J.A. 2002. Excavation of a Neolithic occupation at Chapelfield, Cowie, Stirling. *Proceedings of the Society of Antiquaries of Scotland* 132, 139–92.

Atkinson, R.J.C. 1952. The Neolithic long mound at Maiden Castle. *Proceedings of the Dorset Natural History and Archaeological Society* 74, 36–8.

Atkinson, R.J.C., Piggott, C.M. and Sandars, N.K. 1951. *Excavations at Dorchester, Oxon.* Oxford: Department of Antiquities, Ashmolean Museum.

Austin, P., Hather, J. and Chisham, C. 2008. The wood charcoal. In R. Mercer and F. Healy, *Hambledon Hill, Dorset, England: excavation and survey of a Neolithic monument complex and its surrounding landscape*, 454–69. Swindon: English Heritage.

Auxiette, G. and Hachem, L. (avec la collaboration de E.-M. Giegl et M. Pruvost) 2007. Une histoire des bovinés durant les cinq millénaires précédant notre ère: l'exemple de la vallée de l'Aisne et de la Vesle (France). In *Les bovins: de la domestication à l'élévage, Colloque du Museum d'Histoire Naturelle 'Journée Bovins', 16 et 17 novembre 2006. Ethnozootechnie* 127–35.

Avery, M. 1982. The Neolithic causewayed enclosure, Abingdon. In H. Case and A. Whittle (eds), *Settlement patterns in the Oxford region: excavations at the Abingdon causewayed enclosure and other sites*, 10–50. London: Council for British Archaeology.

Avery, M. and Brown, D. 1972. Saxon features at Abingdon. *Oxoniensia* 37, 66–81.

Bailey, D.W. 1993. Chronotypic tension in Bulgarian prehistory: 6500–3500 BC. *World Archaeology* 25, 204–22.

Bailey, G.N. 1981. Concepts, time scales and explanations in economic prehistory. In A. Sheridan and G. Bailey (eds), *Economic archaeology*, 97–117. Oxford: British Archaeological Reports.

Bailey, G.N. 1983. Concepts of time in Quaternary prehistory. *Annual Review of Anthropology* 12, 165–92.

Bailey, G.N. 2007. Time perspectives, palimpsests and the archaeology of time. *Journal of Anthropological Archaeology* 26, 198–223.

Baillie, M.G.L. 1990. Checking back on an assemblage of radiocarbon dates. *Radiocarbon* 32, 361–6.

Baillie, M.G.L. 1991. Suck in and smear: two related chronological problems for the 90s. *Journal of Theoretical Archaeology* 12, 12–16.

Baker, E. and Mustoe, R. 1988. Goldington Bury Farm, Bedford, Bedfordshire. TL 0784 5044 TL 0784 5023. *South Midlands Archaeology* 18, 7–11.

Balaam, N.D., Corney, M., Dunn, C. and Porter, H. 1991. The surveys. In N. Sharples, *Maiden Castle: excavations and field survey 1985–6*, 37–42. London: English Heritage.

Balasse, M. Tresset, A., Dobney, K. and Ambrose, S.H. 2005. The use of isotope ratios to test for seaweed in eating in sheep. *Journal of the Zoological Society of London* 266, 283–91.

Ballin, T.B. 2009. *Archaeological pitchstone in northern Britain: characterization and interpretation of an important prehistoric source*. Oxford: Archaeopress.

Ballin, T.B. forthcoming. Struck flint from Irthlingborough, West Cotton and Stanwick *and* Overview of the lithic evidence. In J. Harding and F. Healy eds), *The Raunds Area Project. A Neolithic and Bronze Age Landscape in Northamptonshire Volume 2: Supplementary Studies*. Swindon: English Heritage.

Bamford, H.M. 1979. Briar Hill Neolithic causewayed enclosure second interim report, April 1976–October 1978. *Northamptonshire Archaeology* 14, 3–9.

Bamford, H.M. 1985. *Briar Hill: excavation 1974–1978*. Northampton: Northampton Development Corporation.

Bapty, I. 2007. *Lower Lugg archaeology and aggregates resource assessment.* Herefordshire Archaeology Report 226. Document prepared for English Heritage. Hereford: Herefordshire Archaeology.

Barber, A., Pannett, A., Fairburn, N., Cullen, K., Evans, D., Saunders, K. and Thorogood, S. 2006. Archaeological excavations along the Milford Haven to Aberdulais Natural Gas Pipeline 2006: a preliminary report. *Archaeology in Wales* 46, 87–99.

Barber, M. 1997. Landscape, the Neolithic, and Kent. In P. Topping (ed.), *Neolithic landscapes*, 77–85. Oxford: Oxbow Books.

Barber, M. 2004. 'Rubbishy pots instead of gold': a brief history of the Neolithic in the south east. In J. Cotton and D. Field (eds), *Towards a New Stone Age: aspects of the Neolithic in south-east England*, 1–11. York: Council for British Archaeology

Barber, M. 2005. Mining, burial and chronology: the West Sussex flint mines. In P. Topping and M. Lynott (eds), *The cultural landscape of prehistoric mines*, 94–109. Oxford and Oakville: Oxbow Books.

Barber, M., Field, D. and Topping, P. 1999. *The Neolithic flint mines of England.* Swindon: English Heritage.

Barclay, A. 2000. *Spatial histories of the Neolithic: a study of the monuments and material culture of central southern England.* Unpublished PhD thesis. Reading: Department of Archaeology, University of Reading.

Barclay, A. 2007. Connections and networks: a wider world and other places. In D. Benson and A. Whittle (eds), *Building memories: the Neolithic Cotswold long barrow at Ascott-under-Wychwood*, 331–44. Oxford: Oxbow Books.

Barclay, A. and Bayliss, A. 1999. Cursus monuments and the radiocarbon problem. In A. Barclay and J. Harding (eds), *Pathways and ceremonies: the cursus monuments of Britain and Ireland*, 11–29. Oxford and Oakville: Oxbow Books.

Barclay, A. and Case, H. 2007. The early Neolithic pottery and fired clay. In D. Benson and A. Whittle (eds), *Building memories: the Neolithic Cotswold long barrow at Ascott-under-Wychwood, Oxfordshire*, 263–81. Oxford: Oxbow Books.

Barclay, A. and Edwards, E. forthcoming. Earlier prehistoric pottery. CTRL scheme-wide specialist report series, http://ads.ahds.ac.uk/catalogue/projArch/ctrl.

Barclay, A. and Halpin, C. 1999. *Excavations at Barrow Hills, Radley, Oxfordshire. Volume I. The Neolithic and Bronze Age monument complex*. Oxford: Oxford University Committee for Archaeology on behalf of the Oxford Archaeological Unit.

Barclay, A. and Harding, J. (eds) 1999. *Pathways and ceremonies: the cursus monuments of Britain and Ireland.* Oxford and Oakville: Oxbow Books.

Barclay, A. and Hey, G. 1999. Cattle, cursus monuments and the river: the development of ritual and domestic landscapes in the upper Thames valley. In A. Barclay and J. Harding (eds), *Pathways and ceremonies: the cursus monuments of Britain and Ireland*, 11–29. Oxford and Oakville: Oxbow Books.

Barclay, A., Bradley, R., Hey, G. and Lambrick, G. 1996. The earlier prehistory of the Oxford region in the light of recent research. *Oxoniensia* 61, 2–20.

Barclay, A., Lambrick, G., Moore, J. and Robinson, M. 2003.

Lines in the landscape. Cursus monuments in the upper Thames valley: excavations at the Drayton and Lechlade cursuses. Oxford: Oxford Archaeology.

Barclay, G.J. 2004. '…Scotland cannot have been an inviting country for agricultural settlement': a history of the Neolithic in Scotland. In I.A.G. Shepherd and G.J. Barclay (eds), *Scotland in Ancient Europe: the Neolithic and Early Bronze Age of Scotland in their European context*, 31–44. Edinburgh: Society of Antiquaries of Scotland.

Barclay, G.J. and Maxwell, G.S. 1998. *The Cleaven Dyke and Littleour: monuments of the Neolithic in Tayside*. Edinburgh: Society of Antiquaries of Scotland.

Barclay, G.J. and Russell-White, C.J. 1993. Excavations in the ceremonial complex of the fourth to the second millennium BC at Balfarg/Balbirnie, Glenrothes, Fife. *Proceedings of the Society of Antiquaries of Scotland* 123, 43–210.

Barclay, G., Brophy, K. and MacGregor, G. 2002. Claish, Stirling: an early Neolithic structure in its context. *Proceedings of the Society of Antiquaries of Scotland* 132, 65–137.

Baring Gould, S., Burnard, R. and Enys, J.D. 1900. Exploration of the stone camp on St David's Head. *Archaeologia Cambrensis* 55 (series 5.7), 105–31.

Baring Gould, S., Burnard, R. and Enys, J.D. 1903. The exploration of Clegyr Voya. *Archaeologia Cambrensis* 58 (series 6.3), 1–11.

Barker, C.T. 1992. *The chambered tombs of south-west Wales*. Oxford: Oxbow Books.

Barker, G. and Webley, D. 1978. Causewayed camps and early Neolithic economies in central southern England. *Proceedings of the Prehistoric Society* 44, 161–86.

Barker, H. 1953. Radiocarbon dating: large-scale prepartion of acetylene from organic material. *Nature* 177, 631–2.

Barker, H. and Mackey, C.J. 1959. British Museum natural radiocarbon measurements I. *Radiocarbon* 1, 81–6.

Barker, H. and Mackey, C.J. 1960. British Museum natural radiocarbon measurements II. *Radiocarbon* 2, 26–30.

Barker, H. and Mackey, J. 1961. British Museum natural radiocarbon measurements III. *Radiocarbon* 3, 39–45.

Barker, H. and Mackey, J. 1963. British Museum natural radiocarbon measurements IV. *Radiocarbon* 5, 104–8.

Barker, H. and Mackey, J. 1968. British Museum natural radiocarbon measurements V. *Radiocarbon* 10, 1–7.

Barker, H., Burleigh, R. and Meeks, N. 1969a. New method for the combustion of samples for radiocarbon dating. *Nature* 221, 49–50.

Barker, H., Burleigh, R. and Meeks, N. 1969b. British Museum radiocarbon measurements VI. *Radiocarbon* 11, 278–94.

Barker, H., Burleigh, R. and Meeks, N. 1971. British Museum radiocarbon measurements VII. *Radocarbon* 13, 157–88.

Barnard, A. 2007. From Mesolithic to Neolithic modes of thought. In A. Whittle and V. Cummings (eds), *Going over: the Mesolithic-Neolithic transition in north-west Europe*, 5–19. Oxford: Oxford University Press for The British Academy.

Barnatt, J. 1982. *Prehistoric Cornwall: the ceremonial monuments*. Wellingborough: Turnstone Press.

Barnes, I. and Cleal, R.M.J. 1995. Neolithic and Bronze Age settlement at Weir Bank Stud Farm, Bray. In I. Barnes, W.A. Boismier, R.M.J. Cleal, A.P. Fitzpatrick and M.R. Roberts, *Early settlement in Berkshire: Mesolithic-Roman occupation sites in the Thames and Kennet valleys*, 1–51. Wessex Archaeological Report 6. Salisbury: Wessex Archaeology.

Barrett, J.C. 1988. The living, the dead and the ancestors: Neolithic and Early Bronze Age mortuary practices. In J.C. Barrett and I.A. Kinnes (eds), *The archaeology of context in the Neolithic and Bronze Age: recent trends*, 30–41. Sheffield: Department of Archaeology and Prehistory, University of Sheffield.

Barrett, J. and Bradley, R. 1991. The Cranborne Chase project and its publication. In J. Barrett, R. Bradley and M. Hall (eds), *Papers on the prehistoric archaeology of Cranborne Chase*, 1–10. Oxford: Oxbow Books.

Barrett, J. 1994. *Fragments from antiquity: an archaeology of social life in Britain, 2900–1200 BC*. Oxford: Blackwell.

Barrett, J.C., Bradley, R. and Green, M. 1991. *Landscape, monuments and society: the prehistory of Cranborne Chase*. Cambridge: Cambridge University Press.

Barth, F. 1987. *Cosmologies in the making: a generative approach to cultural variation in inner New Guinea*. Cambridge: Cambridge University Press.

Bartlett, F.C. 1932. *Remembering: a study in experimental and social psychology*. Cambridge: University Press.

Barton, N. and Roberts, A. 2004. The Mesolithic period in England: current perspectives and new research. In A. Saville (ed.), *Mesolithic Scotland and its neighbours*, 339–58. Edinburgh: Society of Antiquaries of Scotland.

Barton, R.N. 2000. The late-Mesolithic assemblages. In M. Bell, A. Caseldine and H. Neumann, *Prehistoric intertidal archaeology in the Welsh Severn estuary*, 39–48. York: Council for British Archaeology.

Barton, R.N., Berridge, P.J., Walker, M.J. and Bevins, R.E. 1995. Persistent places in the Mesolithic landscape: an example from the Black Mountain uplands of south Wales. *Proceedings of the Prehistoric Society* 61, 81–116.

Basso, K.H. 1984. "Stalking with stories": names, places, and moral narratives among the Western Apache. In E.M.Bruner (ed.), *Text, play and the story: the reconstruction of self and society*, 19–55. Washington, DC: American Ethnological Society.

Bates, M.R. and Whittaker, K. 2004. Landscape evolution in the lower Thames valley: implications for the archeology of the earlier Holocene period. In J. Cotton and D. Field (eds), *Towards a New Stone Age: aspects of the Neolithic in south-east England*, 50–70. York: Council for British Archaeology.

Batten, R., Gillespie, R., Gowlett, J.A.J. and Hedges, R.E. M. 1986. The AMS dating of separate fractions in archaeology. *Radiocarbon* 28, 698–701.

Bayes, T.R. 1763. An essay towards solving a problem in the doctrine of chances. *Philosophical Transactions of the Royal Society* 53, 370–418.

Bayliss, A. 1998. Some thoughts on using scientific dating in English archaeology and buildings analysis for the next decade. In J. Bayley (ed.), *Science in Archaeology: an agenda for the future*, 95–108. London: English Heritage.

Bayliss, A. 2007. Bayesian buildings: an introduction for the numerically challenged. *Vernacular Architecture* 38, 75–86.

Bayliss, A. 2009. Rolling out revolution: using radiocarbon dating in archaeology. *Radiocarbon* 51, 123–47.

Bayliss, A. and Bronk Ramsey, C. 2004. Pragmatic Bayesians: a decade integrating radiocarbon dates into chronological models. In C.E. Buck and A.R. Millard (eds), *Tools for constructing chronologies: tools for crossing disciplinary boundaries*, 25–41. London: Springer.

Bayliss, A. and Harry, R. 1997. The radiocarbon dating programme. In R. Harry and C. Morris, 'Excavations on the lower terrace, site C, Tintagel island, 1990–94'. *Antiquaries Journal* 77, 108–15.

Bayliss, A. and O'Sullivan, M. forthcoming. Interpreting chronologies for the Mound of the Hostages, Tara and its contemporary contexts in Neolithic and Bronze Age Ireland. In M. O'Sullivan, B. Cunliffe, G. Cooney and C. Scarre (eds), *Tara from the past to the future*. Bray: Wordwell.

Bayliss, A. and Tyers, I. 2004. Interpreting radiocarbon dates using evidence from tree rings. *Radiocarbon* 42, 939–46.

Bayliss, A. and Whittle, A. (eds) 2007. *Histories of the dead: building chronologies for five southern British long barrows. Cambridge Archaeological Journal* 17(1), supplement.

Bayliss, A. and Woodman, P.C. 2009. A new Bayesian chronology for Mesolithic occupation at Mount Sandel, Northern Ireland. *Proceedings of the Prehistoric Society* 75, 101–23.

Bayliss, A., Barclay, A., Lambrick, G. and Robinson, M. 2003a. Radiocarbon determinations. In A.J. Barclay, G. Lambrick, J. Moore and M. Robinson, *Cursus monuments in the upper Thames valley: excavations at the Drayton and Lechlade cursuses*, 180–5. Oxford: Thames Valley Landscapes Monograph.

Bayliss, A., Benson, D., Galer, D., Humphrey, L., McFadyen, L. and Whittle, A. 2007c. One thing after another: the date of the Ascott-under-Wychwood long barrow. *Cambridge Archaeological Journal* 17.1, supplement, 29–44.

Bayliss, A., Bronk Ramsey, C., Cook, G. and van der Plicht, J. 2007d. *Radiocarbon dates from samples funded by English Heritage under the Aggregates Levy Sustainability Fund 2002–4*. Swindon: English Heritage.

Bayliss, A., Bronk Ramsey, C., and McCormac, F.G. 1997. Dating Stonehenge. In B. Cunliffe and C. Renfrew (eds), *Science and Stonehenge*, 39–59. Oxford: Oxford University Press for The British Academy and.

Bayliss, A., Bronk Ramsey, C., van der Plicht, J. and Whittle, A. 2007a. Bradshaw and Bayes: towards a timetable for the Neolithic. *Cambridge Journal of Archaeology* 17.1, supplement, 1–28.

Bayliss, A., Groves, C., McCormac, F.G., Baillie, M.G.L., Brown, D. and Brennand, M. 1999. Precise dating of the Norfolk timber circle. *Nature* 402, 479.

Bayliss, A., Groves, C., McCormac, F.G., Bronk Ramsey, C., Baillie, M.G.L., Brown, D., Cook, G. T. and Switsur, R.V. 2003b. Dating. In P. Clark, *The Dover Bronze Age boat*, 250–5. London: English Heritage.

Bayliss, A., Healy, F., Bronk Ramsey, C., McCormac, F.G., Cook, G.T. and Harding, J., forthcoming a. Absolute chronology. In J. Harding and F. Healy (eds), *The Raunds Area Project. A Neolithic and Bronze Age Landscapes in Northamptonshire Volume 2: Supplementary Studies*. Swindon: English Heritage.

Bayliss, A., Healy, F., Bronk Ramsey, C., McCormac, F.G. and Mercer, R. 2008a. Interpreting Chronology. In R. Mercer and F. Healy, *Hambledon Hill, Dorset, England: excavation and survey of a Neolithic monument complex and its surrounding landscape*, 378–411. Swindon: English Heritage.

Bayliss, A., Healy, F., Shand, G., Weekes, J. and Whittle, A. forthcoming c. Chalk Hill radiocarbon dating. In P. Clark, G. Shand and J. Weekes, *The prehistoric landscapes of Chalk Hill, Ramsgate: archaeological excavations 1997–1998*. Canterbury: Canterbury Archaeological Trust.

Bayliss, A., McAvoy, F., Bronk Ramsey, C. and Cook, G. forthcoming b. Radiocarbon dating. In F. McAvoy, in preparation, Report on excavations at Rectory Farm, Godmanchester, Cambridgeshire.

Bayliss, A., McAvoy, F. and Whittle, A. 2007e. The world recreated: redating Silbury Hill in its monumental landscape. *Antiquity* 81, 26–53.

Bayliss, A., McCormac, F.G. and van der Plicht, J. 2004. An illustrated guide to measuring radiocarbon from archaeological samples. *Physics Education* 39, 137–44.

Bayliss, A., Pettitt, P. and Malim, T. 1996. The radiocarbon determinations. In T. Malim, 'The Cambridgeshire Dykes and Worsted Street'. *Proceedings of the Cambridge Antiquarian Society* 85, 95–8.

Bayliss, A., Popescu, E., Athfield-Beavan, N., Bronk Ramsey, C., Cook G.T. and Locker, A. 2004. The potential significance of dietary offsets for the interpretation of radiocarbon dates: an archaeologically significant example from medieval Norwich. *Journal of Archaeological Science* 31, 563–75.

Bayliss, A., Whittle, A. and Healy, F. 2008b. Timing, tempo and temporalities in the early Neolithic of southern Britain. *Analecta Praehistorica Leidensia* 40, 25–42.

Bayliss, A., Whittle, A. and Wysocki, M. 2007b. Talking about my generation: the date of the West Kennet long barrow. *Cambridge Archaeological Journal* 17.1, supplement, 85–101.

Beadsmoore, E., Garrow, D. and Knight, M. 2010. Refitting Etton: space, time and material culture within a causewayed enclosure in Cambridgeshire. *Proceedings of The Prehistoric Society* 76, 115–34.

Beavan, N. 2004. Chemistry: quality assurance. In C.J. Ellis, *A prehistoric ritual complex at Eynesbury, Cambridgeshire: excavation of a multi-period site in the Great Ouse valley, 2000–2001*, 65. Salisbury: Trust for Wessex Archaeology.

Beavan, N. and Sparks, R.J. 1998. Factors influencing the radiocarbon age of *Rattus exulans*. *Radiocarbon* 40, 601–13.

Beavan Athfield, N., Green, R.C., Craig, J., McFadgen, B. and Bickler, S. 2008. Influence of marine sources on ^{14}C ages: isotopic data from Watom Island, Papua New Guinea, inhumations and pig teeth in light of new dietary standards. *Journal of the Royal Society of New Zealand* 38, 1–23.

Beavan Athfield, N., MacFadgen, B. and Sparks, R.J. 1999. Reliability of bone gelatin AMS dating: *R. exulans* and marine shell radiocarbon dates from Pauatahanui midden sites in Wellington, N.Z. *Radiocarbon* 41, 119–26.

Beck, R.A. Jr., Bolender, D.J., Brown, J.A. and Earle, T.K. 2007. Eventful archaeology: the place of space in structural transformation. *Current Anthropology* 48, 833–60.

Beckett, J. and Robb, J.E. 2006. Neolithic burial taphonomy, ritual and interpretation in Britain and Ireland: a review. In R. Gowland and C. Knüsel (eds), *The social archaeology of funerary remains, 155–67*. Oxford: Oxbow Books

Bedwin, O. 1981. Excavations at the Neolithic enclosure on Bury Hill, Houghton, West Sussex, 1979. *Proceedings of the Prehistoric Society* 47, 69–86.

Bedwin, O. 1984. The excavation of a small hilltop enclosure on Court Hill, Singleton, West Sussex, 1982. *Sussex Archaeological Collections* 122, 13–22.

Bedwin, O. 1992. Prehistoric earthworks on Halnaker Hill, West Sussex, excavations 1981–1983. *Sussex Archaeological Collections* 130, 1–12.

Bedwin, O.R. and Aldsworth, F. 1981. Excavations at The Trundle, 1981. *Sussex Archaeological Collections* 119, 208–14.

Beeching, A. 1991. Sépultures, territoire et société dans le Chasséen meridional. In A. Beeching, D. Binder, J.-C. Blanchet, C. Constantin, J. Dubouloz, R. Martinez, D. Mordant, J.-P. Thévenot and J. Vaquer (eds), *Identité du Chasséen*, 327–41. Nemours: Mémoires du Musée de Préhistoire de l'Ile de France 4.

Beeching, A. 2003. Mobilité et société néolithiques dans les Alpes occidentales et la France méridionale. *Preistoria Alpina* 39, 175–87.

Bell, M. 1977. Excavations at Bishopstone, Sussex. *Sussex Archaeological Collections* 115, 1–299.

Bell, M. 2007a. Wetland-dryland relationships in the Severn Estuary and surroundings during the Mesolithic and Neolithic. In J. Sidell and F. Haughey (eds), *Neolithic archaeology in the intertidal zone*, 26–47. Oxford: Oxbow Books.

Bell, M. 2007b. *Prehistoric coastal communities: the Mesolithic in western Britain*. York: Council for British Archaeology.

Bell, M., Allen, J.R.L., Buckley, S., Dark, P. and Nayling, N. 2003. Mesolithic to Neolithic coastal change: excavations at Goldcliff East, 2003 and research at Redwick. *Archaeology in the Severn Estuary* 14, 1–26.

Bell, M., Allen, M.J., Smith, R.W. and Johnson, S. 2008. Molluscan and sedimentary evidence for the palaeoenvironmental history of Hambledon Hill and its surroundings. In R. Mercer and F. Healy, *Hambledon Hill, Dorset: excavation and survey of a Neolithic monument complex and its surrounding landscape*, 412–53. Swindon: English Heritage.

Bell, M., Caseldine, A. and Neumann, H. 2000. *Prehistoric intertidal archaeology in the Welsh Severn estuary*. York: Council for British Archaeology.

Bell, M., Fowler, P.J. and Hillson, S.W. (eds) 1996. *The experimental earthwork project, 1960–1992*. York: Council for British Archaeology.

Bender, B. 2002. Time and landscape. *Current Anthropology* 43, supplement, S103–12.

Bennett, F.J. 1913. Coldrum monument and exploration 1910. *Journal of the Royal Anthropological Institute of Great Britain and Ireland* 43, 76–85.

Benson, D. and Miles, D. 1974. *The upper Thames valley: an archaeological survey of the river gravels*. Oxford: Truexpress.

Benson, D. and Whittle, A. (eds) 2007. *Building memories: the Neolithic Cotswold long barrow at Ascott- under-Wychwood, Oxfordshire*. Oxford: Oxbow Books.

Benson, D.G., Evans, J.G. and Williams, G.H. 1990. Excavations at Stackpole Warren, Dyfed. *Proceedings of the Prehistoric Society* 56, 179–245.

Bentley, A. 2007. Mobility, specialisation and community diversity in the Linearbandkeramik: isotopic evidence from the skeletons. In A. Whittle and V. Cummings (eds), *Going over: the Mesolithic-Neolithic transition in north-west Europe*, 117–40. Oxford: Oxford University Press for The British Academy.

Berger, R., Harney, A.G. and Libby, W.F. 1964. Radiocarbon dating of bone and shell from their organic components. *Science* 144, 999–1001.

Bergh, S. 1995. *Landscape of the monuments. A study of the passage tombs in the Cúil Irra region*. Stockholm: Bureau for Archaeological Excavation, Central Board of National Antiquities.

Bergh, S. 2000. Transforming Knocknarea – the archaeology of a mountain. *Archaeology Ireland* 14, 14–18.

Bergh, S. 2002. Knocknarea: the ultimate monument: megaliths and mountains in Neolithic Cúil Irra, north-west Ireland. In C. Scarre (ed.), *Monuments and landscape in Atlantic Europe: perception and society during the Neolithic and Early Bronze Age*, 139–51. London: Routledge.

Bergson, H. 1911. *Matter and memory* (translated by N.M.Paul and W.S. Palmer, first published 1908). London: Allen and Unwin.

Berridge, G. 1983. An oval barrow (?) at Triffle, St Germans. *Cornish Archaeology* 22, 85–91.

Berridge, P.J. 1986. Mesolithic evidence from Hembury. *Proceedings of the Devon Archaeological Society* 44, 163–6.

Berridge, P. 1993. Cornish axe factories: fact or fiction? In N. Ashton and A. David (eds), *Stories in stone*, 45–56. London: Lithic Studies Society.

Berridge, P. and Roberts, A. 1986. The Mesolithic period in Cornwall. *Cornish Archaeo*logy 25, 7–34.

Berridge, P.J. and Simpson, S.J. 1992. The Mesolithic, Neolithic and early Bronze Age site at Bulleigh Meadow, Marldon. *Proceedings of the Devon Archaeological Society* 50, 1–18.

Berry, Sir J. 1929. Belas Knap long barrow, Gloucestershire; report of the excavations of 1929. *Transactions of the Bristol and Gloucestershire Archaeological Society* 51, 273–303.

Berry, Sir J. 1930. Belas Knap long barrow, Gloucestershire. Second report: the excavations of 1930. *Transactions of the Bristol and Gloucestershire Archaeological Society* 52, 123–50.

Bertemes, F. 1991. Untersuchungen zur Funktion der Erdwerke der Michelsberger Kultur im Rahmen des kupferzeitlichen Zivilisation. In J. Lichardus (ed.), *Die Kupferzeit als historische Epoche*, 441–64. Saarbrucken: Saarbrücker Beiträge zur Altertumskunde 55.

Bewley, B., Crutchley, S. and Grady, D. 2004. Aerial survey and its contribution to understanding the Neolithic of the south-east. In J. Cotton and D. Field (eds), *Towards a New Stone Age: aspects of the Neolithic in south-east England*, 71–5. York: Council for British Archaeology.

Biel, J., Schlichtherle, H., Strobel, M. and Zeeb, A. (eds) 1998. *Die Michelsberger Kultur und ihre Randgebiete – Probleme der Entstehung, Chronologie und des Siedlungswesens*. Stuttgart: Theiss.

Biggar Museum Trust 1993. Biggar Common (Biggar parish). Neolithic/Bronze Age artefact scatters. *Discovery and Excavation in Scotland 1993*, 87.

Bintliff, J. (ed.) 1991. *The Annales school and archaeology*. London: Leicester University Press.

Bird, D.G., Crocker, G. and McCracken, J.S. 1990. Archaeology in Surrey 1988–1989. *Surrey Archaeological Collections* 80, 201–27.

Bishop. S. 2010. Tarrant Launceston 15: another causewayed enclosure? *English Heritage Research News* 13, 28–9.

Blackwell, P.G. and Buck, C.E. 2003. The late glacial human reoccupation of north-west Europe: new approaches to space-time modelling. *Antiquity* 77, 232–9.

Blaauw, M. and Christen, J. A. 2005. Radiocarbon peat chronologies and environmental change. *Applied Statistics* 54, 805–16.

Blaauw, M., Heuvelink, G. B. M., Mauquoy, D., van der Plicht, J. and van Geel, B. 2003. A numerical approach to ^{14}C wiggle-match dating of organic deposits: best fits and confidence intervals. *Quaternary Science Reviews* 22, 1485–1500.

Blaauw, M., van Geel, B. and van der Plicht, J. 2004. Solar forcing of climatic change during the mid-Holocene: indications from raised bogs in the Netherlands. *The Holocene* 14, 35–44.

Blitz, J.H. 1993. Big pots for big shots: feasting and storage in a Mississippian community. *American Antiquity* 58, 80–96.

Bloch, M. 1986. *From blessing to violence: history and ideology in the circumcision ritual of the Merina of Madagascar*. Cambridge: Cambridge University Press.

Bloch, M. 1992. *Prey into hunter: the politics of religious experience*. Cambridge: Cambridge University Press.

Bloch, M. 1995. Questions not to ask of Malagasy carvings. In I. Hodder, M. Shanks, A. Alexandri, V. Buchli, J. Carmen, J. Last and G. Lucas (eds), *Interpreting archaeology: finding meaning in the past*, 212–15. London: Routledge.

Bloch, M.E.F. 1998. *How we think they think: anthropological approaches to cognition, memory and literacy*. Boulder: Westview.

Bocherens, H. and Drucker, D. 2003. Trophic level isotopic enrichment of carbon and nitrogen in bone collagen: case studies from recent and ancient terrestrial ecosystems. *International Journal of Osteoarchaeology* 13, 46–53.

Boelicke, U. 1978. Das neolitische Erdwerk Urmitz. *Acta Praehistorica et Archaeologica* 7/8, 73–121.

Boelicke, U., von Brandt, D., Gaffrey, J., Grünewald, C., Hilbert, K., Krüger, W., Kuper, W., Lüning, J., Orzschig, C., Seeher, J., Schwellnus, W., Stehli, P., Wolters, M. and Zimmermann, A. 1979. Untersuchungen zur neolithischen Beisedlung der Aldenhovener Platte VIII. *Bonner Jahrbucher* 179, 299–362.

Boelicke, U., von Brandt, D., Lüning, J., Stehli, P. and Zimmermann, A. 1988. *Der bandkeramische Siedlungsplatz Langweiler 8, Gemeinde Aldenhoven, Kreis Düren*. Köln: Rhienland-Verlag.

Bogaard, A. 2004. *Neolithic farming in central Europe*. London: Routledge.

Bogaard, A. 2005. 'Garden agriculture' and the nature of early farming in Europe and the Near East. *World Archaeology* 37, 177–96.

Bogaard, A. and Jones, G. 2007. Neolithic farming in Britain and central Europe: contrast or continuity? In A. Whittle and V. Cummings (eds), *Going over: the Mesolithic-Neolithic transition in north-west Europe*, 357–75. Oxford: Oxford University Press for The British Academy.

Bogucki, P. 1993. Animal traction and household economies in Neolithic Europe. *Antiquity* 67, 492–503.

Bogucki, P. 2000. How agriculture came to north-central Europe. In. T.D. Price (ed.), *Europe's first farmers*, 197–218. Cambridge: Cambridge University Press.

Bohannan, L. 1952. A genealogical charter. *Africa* 22, 301–15.

Bolender, D. (ed.) 2010. *Eventful archaeologies: new approaches to social transformation in the archaeological record*. Buffalo: State University of New York Press.

Bollongino, R. and Burger, J. 2007. Neolithic cattle domestication as seen from ancient DNA. In A. Whittle and V. Cummings (eds), *Going over: the Mesolithic-Neolithic transition in north-west Europe*, 165–87. Oxford: Oxford University Press for The British Academy.

Bonney, D. 1964. All Cannings: Rybury Camp. *Wiltshire Archaeological and Natural History Magazine* 59, 185.

Bonsall, C. 1978. The flint industry. In J. Hedges and D. Buckley, 'Excavations at a Neolithic causewayed enclosure, Orsett, Essex, 1975'. *Proceedings of the Prehistoric Society* 44, 255–9.

Bonsall, C., Macklin, M.G., Anderson, D.E. and Payton, R.W. 2002. Climate change and the adoption of agriculture in north-west Europe. *European Journal of Archaeology* 5, 9–23.

Boreham, S. 2006. Palaeoenvironmental studies. In C. Evans, M. Edmonds and S. Boreham, "Total archaeology' and model landscapes: excavation of the Great Wilbraham causewayed enclosure, Cambridgeshire, 1975–76'. *Proceedings of the Prehistoric Society* 72, 144–7.

Borić, D. 2003. "Deep time" metaphor: mnemonic and apotropaic practices at Lepenski Vir. *Journal of Social Archaeology* 3, 46–74.

Borić, D. 2008. First households and 'house societies' in European prehistory. In A. Jones (ed.), *Prehistoric Europe: theory and practice*, 109–42. Oxford: Blackwell.

Bostyn, F. and Lanchon, Y. 1992. *Jablines. Le Haut Château (Seine-et-Marne): une minière de silex au Néolithique*. Paris: Editions de la Maison des Sciences de l'Homme.

Bostyn, F. and Lanchon, Y. 1995. Jablines, 'le Haut-Château', Seine-et-Marne district. *Archaeologia Polonia* 33, 297–310.

Bostyn, F. and Lanchon, Y. 1997. The Neolithic flint mine at Jablines, 'Le Haut-Château' (Seine-et-Marne). In A. Ramos-Millán and M.A. Bustillo (eds), *Siliceous rocks and culture*, 271–91. Granada: Universidad de Granada.

Bostyn, F., Demolon, P., Frangin, E. and Séverin, C. 2006. Un sitte d'habitat du Néolithique moyen II à Lauwin-Planque (Nord): premiers résultats. In P. Duhamel (ed.), *Impacts interculturels au Néolithique moyen. Du terroir au territoire: sociétés et espaces*. 319–34. Dijon: 25ème supplément à la Revue Archéologique de l'Est.

Boulestin, B., Zeeb-Lanz, A., Jeunesse, C., Haack, F., Arbogast, R.-M. And Denaire, A. 2009. Mass cannibalism in the Linear Pottery culture at Herxheim (Palatinate, Germany). *Antiquity* 83, 968–82.

Bourdieu, P. 1990. *The logic of practice*. Stanford: Stanford University Press.

Boureau, C. 1997. L'enceinte de Balloy, "Les Réaudins" (Seine-et-Marne). In C. Constantin, D. Mordant and D. Simonin (eds), *La culture de Cerny: nouvelle économie, nouvelle société au Néolithique*, 93–110. Nemours: Édition de l'Association pour la Promotion de la Recherche Archéologique en Ile-de-France.

Bowden, M. 1984. *General Pitt Rivers: the father of scientific archaeology*. Salisbury: Salisbury and South Wiltshire Museum.

Bowman, S. 1990. *Radiocarbon dating*. London: British Museum.

Bowman, S. 1991. Radiocarbon chronology. In J.C. Barrett, R. Bradley and M. Green, *Landscape, monuments and society: the prehistory of Cranborne Chase*, 3–5. Cambridge: Cambridge University Press.

Bowman, S., Ambers, J. and Leese, M. 1990. Re-evaluation of British Museum radiocarbon dates issued between 1980 and 1984. *Radiocarbon* 32, 59–79.

Box, G.E.P. 1979. Robustness in scientific model building. In R.L. Launder and G.N. Wilkinson (eds), *Robustness in statistics*, 201–36. New York: Academic Press.

Bradley, P. 1999. The worked flint from the Dunn collection and the excavations. In A. Gibson, *The Walton Basin project: excavation and survey in a prehistoric landscape 1993–7*, 48–81. York: Council for British Archeology.

Bradley, P. 2004. Causewayed enclosures: monumentality, architecture, and spatial distribution of artefacts – the evidence from Staines, Surrey. In J. Cotton and D. Field (eds), *Towards a New Stone Age: aspects of the Neolithic in south-east England*, 115–23. York: Council for British Archaeology.

Bradley, R. 1969. The Trundle revisited. *Sussex Notes and Queries* 17, 133–4.

Bradley, R. 1970. The excavation of a Beaker settlement at Belle Tout, East Sussex, England. *Proceedings of the Prehistoric Society* 36, 312–79.

Bradley, R. 1982. Belle Tout – revision and reassessment. In P. Drewett, *The archaeology of Bullock Down, Eastbourne, East Sussex. The development of a landscape*, 62–71. Lewes: Sussex Archaeological Society.

Bradley, R. 1983. The bank barrows and related monuments of Dorset in the light of recent fieldwork. *Proceedings of the Dorset Natural History and Archaeological Society* 105, 15–20.

Bradley, R. 1984a. *The social foundations of Neolithic Britain.* London: Longman.

Bradley, R. 1984b. Regional systems in Neolithic Britain. In R. Bradley and J. Gardiner (eds), *Neolithic studies*, 5–14. Oxford: British Archaeological Reports.

Bradley, R. 1986. Radiocarbon and the cursus problem. In J.A.J. Gowlett and R.E.M. Hedges (eds), *Archaeological results from accelerator dating*, 139–41. Oxford: Oxford University Committee for Archaeology.

Bradley, R. 1990. *The passage of arms: an archaeological analysis of prehistoric hoards and votive deposits.* Cambridge: Cambridge University Press.

Bradley, R. 1991. Ritual, time and history. *World Archaeology* 23, 209–19.

Bradley, R. 1992. The excavation of an oval barrow beside the Abingdon causewayed enclosure, Oxfordshire. *Proceedings of the Prehistoric Society* 58, 127–42.

Bradley, R. 1993. *Altering the earth: the origins of monuments in Britain and continental Europe.* Edinburgh: Society of Antiquaries of Scotland.

Bradley, R. 1998a. *The significance of monuments: on the shaping of human experience in Neolithic and Bronze Age Europe.* London and New York: Routledge.

Bradley, R. 1998b. Ruined buildings, ruined stones: enclosures, tombs and natural places in the Neolithic of south-west England. *World Archaeology* 30, 13–22.

Bradley, R. 2000. *An archaeology of natural places.* London: Routledge.

Bradley, R. 2002. *The past in prehistoric societies.* London and New York: Routledge.

Bradley, R. 2007. *The prehistory of Britain and Ireland.* Cambridge: Cambridge University Press.

Bradley, R. and Chambers, R. 1988. A new study of the cursus complex at Dorchester-on-Thames. *Oxford Journal of Archaeology* 7, 271–89.

Bradley, R. and Edmonds, M. 1993. *Interpreting the axe trade.* Cambridge: Cambridge University Press.

Bradley, R. and Gordon, K. 1988. Human skulls from the river Thames, their dating and significance. *Antiquity* 62, 503–9.

Bradley, R., Entwistle, R. and Raymond, F. 1994. *Prehistoric land divisions on Salsibury Plain: the work of the Wessex Linear Ditches project.* London: English Heritage.

Bradley, R., Over, L., Startin, D.W.A. and Weng, R. 1981. The excavation of a Neolithic site at Cannon Hill, Maidenhead, Berkshire, 1974–75. *Berkshire Archaeological Journal* 68 (for 1975–6), 5–19.

Brady, C. 2009. A 'new' Neolithic enclosure at Rossnaree, Brú na Bóinne, Co Meath. *PAST* 62, 2–5.

Brainerd, G.W. 1951. The place of chronological ordering in archaeological analysis. *American Antiquity* 16, 301–13.

Brassil, K. and Gibson, A. 1999. A Grooved Ware pit and Bronze Age multiple inhumation at Hendre, Rhydymwyn, Flintshire. In R. Cleal and A. Macsween (eds), *Grooved Ware in Britain and Ireland*, 89–97. Oxford: Oxbow Books.

Braudel, F. 1975. *The Mediterranean and the Mediterranean world in the age of Philip II. Volume I* (translated by Siân Reynolds). London: Fontana/Collins.

Bréart, B. 1984. Le site néolithique du "Champ de Bataille" à L'Etoile (Somme): une enceinte à fossés interrompus. *Revue Archéologique de Picardie* 1984, 293–310.

Breen, T.C. 2003. Site 7, Cherryville. In I. Bennett (ed.), *Excavations 2001*, 180–1. Bray: Wordwell.

Bréhard, S. 2007. *Contribution archéozoologique à la connaissance de la fonction des grands sites de terrasse du Chasséen récent (début du 4e millénaire avant J.-C.) de la moyenne vallée du Rhône, dans leur contexte de Méditerranée nord-occidentale.* Unpublished PhD thesis, Muséum National d'Histoire Naturelle.

Brennand, M. and Taylor, M. 2003. The survey and excavation of a Bronze Age timber circle at Holme-next-the-Sea, Norfolk, 1988–9. *Proceedings of the Prehistoric Society* 69, 1–84.

Brennand, M., Clare, H. and Massey, S. 2002. Another causewayed enclosure from Norfolk. *PAST* 40, 7–8.

Brickley, M. and Thomas, R. 2004. The young woman and her baby or the juvenile and their dog: reinterpreting osteological material from a Neolithic long barrow. *Archaeological Journal* 161, 1–10.

Bridgland, D. 1994. *Quaternary of the Thames.* London: Chapman and Hall.

Brimble, L.J.F. 1948. *Trees in Britain, wild, ornamental and economic, and some relatives in other lands.* London: MacMillan and Co.

Brinch Petersen, E. 2008. Warriors of the Neolithic TRB-culture. In Z. Sulgostowska and A.J. Tomaszewski (eds), *Man –Millennia –Enviroment: studies in honour of Romuald Schild*, 33–8. Warsaw: Institute of Archaeology and Ethnology, Polish Academy of Sciences.

Brinch Petersen, E. and Meiklejohn, C. 2009. Late Mesolithic or early Neolithic burials? Examining the 'Tauber line'. In N. Finlay, S. McCartan, N. Milner. and C. Wickham-Jones (eds), *From Bann flakes to Bushmills: papers in honour of Professor Peter Woodman*, 165–74. Oxford: Oxbow Books.

Brindley, A.L. and Lanting, J.N. 1990. Radiocarbon dates for Neolithic single burials. *Journal of Irish Archaeology* 5, 1–7.

Brindley, A.L. and Lanting, J.N. 1992. Radiocarbon dates from the cemetery at Poulawack, Co. Clare. *Journal of Irish Archaeology* 6, 13–17.

Brindley, A.L. and Lanting, J.N. 1998. Radiocarbon dates for Irish trackways. *Journal of Irish Archaeology* 9, 45–67.

Brindley, A.L., Lanting, J.N. and Mook, W.G. 1983. Radiocarbon dates from the Neolithic burials at Ballintruer More, Co. Wicklow, and Ardchrony, Co. Tipperary. *Journal of Irish Archaeology* 1, 1–9.

Brindley, A.L., Lanting, J.N. and Mook, W.G. 1990. Radiocarbon dates from Irish fulachta fiadh and other burnt mounds. *Journal of Irish Archaeology* 5, 25–33.

Brindley, A.L., Lanting, J.N. and van der Plicht, J. 2005. Radiocarbon-dated samples from the Mound of the Hostages. In M. O'Sullivan, *Duma na nGiall: The Mound of the Hostages, Tara*, 281–98. Bray: Wordwell, in association with the UCD School of Archaeology.

Briscoe, G. 1956. Swale's Tumulus: a combined Neolithic A and Bronze Age barrow at Worlington, Suffolk. *Proceedings of the Cambridge Antiquarian Society* 50, 101–12.

Britnell, W.J. 1982. The excavation of two round barrows at Trelystan, Powys. *Proceedings of the Prehistoric Society* 52, 133–201.

Britnell, W.J. 1984. The Gwernvale long cairn, Crickhowell, Brecknock. In W.J. Britnell and H.N. Savory, *Gwernvale and Penywyrlod: two Neolithic long cairns in the Black Mountains of Brecknock*, 43–154. Cardiff: Cambrian Archaeological Association.

Britnell, W.J. and Savory, H.N. 1984. *Gwernvale and Penywyrlod: two Neolithic long cairns in the Black Mountains of Brecknock.* Cardiff: Cambrian Archaeological Association.

Broadmeadow, M.S.J. and Griffiths, H. 1993. Carbon isotope discrimination and coupling of CO_2 fluxes within forest canopies. In J.R. Ehleringer, A.E. Hall and G.D. Farquhar (eds), *Stable isotopes and plant water relations*, 109–29. San Diego: Academic Press.

Brock, F., Bronk Ramsey, C. and Higham, T. 2007a. Quality assurance of ultrafiltered bone dating. *Radiocarbon* 49, 187–92.

Brock, F., Higham, T. and Bronk Ramsey, C. 2007b. *Radiocarbon dating bone samples recovered from gravel sites*. Portsmouth: English Heritage.

Brock, F., Higham, T., Ditchfield, P. and Bronk Ramsey, C. 2010. Current pretreatment methods for AMS radiocarbon dating at the Oxford Radiocarbon Accelerator Unit (ORAU). *Radiocarbon* 52, 103–12.

Bronk, C.R. and Hedges, R.E.M. 1987. A gas ion source for radiocarbon dating. *Nuclear Instruments and Methods* B 29, 45–9.

Bronk, C.R. and Hedges, R.E.M. 1989. Use of the CO_2 source in radiocarbon dating by AMS. *Radiocarbon* 31, 298–304.

Bronk, C.R. and Hedges, R.E.M. 1990. A gaseous ion source for routine AMS radiocarbon dating. *Nuclear Instruments and Methods* B 52, 322–6.

Bronk Ramsey, C. 1995. Radiocarbon calibration and analysis of stratigraphy. *Radiocarbon* 36, 425–30.

Bronk Ramsey, C. 1998. Probability and dating. *Radiocarbon* 40, 461–74.

Bronk Ramsey, C. 2000. Comment on 'The use of Bayesian statistics for 14C dates of chronologically ordered samples: a critical analysis'. *Radiocarbon* 42, 199–202.

Bronk Ramsey, C. 2001. Development of the radiocarbon calibration program Oxcal. *Radiocarbon* 43, 355–63.

Bronk Ramsey, C. 2008. Deposition models for chronological records. *Quaternary Science Reviews* 27, 42–60.

Bronk Ramsey, C. 2009a. Bayesian analysis of radiocarbon dates. *Radiocarbon* 51, 337–60.

Bronk Ramsey, C. 2009b. Dealing with outliers and offsets in radiocarbon dating. *Radiocarbon* 51, 1023–45.

Bronk Ramsey, C. and Hedges, R.E.M. 1997. Hybrid ion sources: radiocarbon measurements from microgram to milligram. *Nuclear Instruments and Methods in Physics Research B* 123, 539–45.

Bronk Ramsey, C., Buck, C.E., Manning, S.W., Reimer, P. and van der Plicht, J. 2006. Developments in radiocarbon calibration for archaeology. *Antiquity* 80, 783–98.

Bronk Ramsey, C., Higham, T.F.G., Owen, D.C., Pike, A.W.G. and Hedges, R.E.M. 2002. Radiocarbon dates from the Oxford AMS system: *Archaeometry* datelist 31. *Archaeometry* 44 (3) Supplement 1, 1–149.

Bronk Ramsey, C., Higham, T.F., Bowles, A. and Hedges, R.E.M. 2004a. Improvements to the pre- treatment of bone at Oxford. *Radiocarbon* 46, 155–63.

Bronk Ramsey, C., Higham, T. and Leach, P. 2004b. Towards high precision AMS: progress and limitations. *Radiocarbon* 46, 17–24.

Bronk Ramsey, C., Pettitt, P.B., Hedges, R.E.M., Hodgins, G.W.L. and Owen, D.C. 2000a. Radiocarbon dates from the Oxford AMS system: *Archaeometry* datelist 29. *Archaeometry* 42, 243–54.

Bronk Ramsey, C., Pettitt, P.B., Hedges, R.E.M., Hodgins, G.W. and Owen, D.C. 2000b. Radiocarbon dates from the Oxford AMS system: *Archaeometry* datelist 30. *Archaeometry* 42, 459–79.

Bronk Ramsey, C., van der Plicht, J. and Weninger, B. 2001. 'Wiggle matching' radiocarbon dates. *Radiocarbon* 43, 381–9.

Brophy, K. 2006. Rethinking Scotland's Neolithic: combining circumstance with context. *Proceedings of the Society of Antiquaries of Scotland* 136, 7–46.

Brophy, K. 2007. From big houses to cult houses: early Neolithic timber halls in Scotland. *Proceedings of the Prehistoric Society* 73, 75–96.

Brophy, K. and Barclay, G. (eds) 2009. *Defining a regional Neolithic: evidence from Britain and Ireland.* Oxford: Oxbow Books.

Brothwell, D. 1965. Description of the bones. In I.F. Smith, *Windmill Hill and Avebury: excavations by Alexander Keiller, 1925–1939*, 138–40. Oxford: Clarendon Press.

Brothwell, D. 1971. Forensic aspects of the so-called Neolithic skeleton Q1 from Maiden Castle, Dorset. *World Archaeology* 3, 233–41.

Brothwell, D. 1999. Human remains. In A. Whittle, J. Pollard and C. Grigson, *The harmony of symbols: the Windmill Hill causewayed enclosure, Wiltshire*, 344–6. Oxford: Oxbow Books.

Brown, A. 1989. The social life of flint at Neolithic Hembury. *Lithics* 10, 46–9.

Brown, A. 1995. The Mesolithic and later flint artefacts. In T. Allen, *Lithics and landscape: archaeological discoveries on the Thames Water pipeline at Gatehampton Farm, Goring, Oxfordshire 1985–92*, 65–84. Oxford: Oxford University Committee for Archaeology.

Brown, N. 1988. A late Bronze Age enclosure at Lofts Farm, Essex, 1986. *Proceedings of the Prehistoric Society* 45, 249–302.

Brown, N. 1995. The Hullbridge survey 1982–1985, Neolithic to early Bronze Age pottery. In T.J. Wilknson and P.L. Murphy, *The archaeology of the Essex coast, volume I: the Hullbridge survey*, 128–31. Chelmsford: Essex County Council.

Brown, N. 1997. A landscape of two halves: the Neolithic of Chelmer valley/Blackwater estuary, Essex. In P.Topping (ed.), *Neolithic landscapes*, 88–98. Oxford: Oxbow Books.

Brown, N. 1998. Prehistoric pottery. In S. Wallis and M. Waughman, *Archaeology and the landscape in the lower Blackwater valley*, 132–41. Chelmsford: Essex County Council Archaeology Section.

Brown, N. forthcoming. The Stumble Neolithic pottery. In T.J. Wilkinson, P.L. Murphy and N. Brown, *The archaeology of the Essex coast, volume II: excavations at the prehistoric site of The Stumble*. Chelmsford: Essex County Council Historic Environment and Commerce.

Brown, N. and Ennis, T. 1999. Early Neolithic remains from Chadwell St Mary. *Essex Archaeology and History* 30, 258–9.

Brown, T.A., Nelson, D.E., Vogel, J.S. and Southon, J.R. 1988. Improved collagen extraction by modified Longin method. *Radiocarbon* 30, 171–7.

Buck, C. E. 2004. Bayesian chronological data interpretation: where now? In C.E. Buck and A.R. Millard (eds), *Tools for constructing chronologies: tools for crossing disciplinary boundaries*, 1–24. London: Springer.

Buck, C. E. and Bard, E. 2007. A calendar chronology for Pleistocene mammoth and horse extinction in North America based on Bayesian radiocarbon calibration. *Quaternary Science Reviews* 26, 2031–5.

Buck, C.E. and Christen, J.A. 1998. A novel approach to selecting samples for radiocarbon dating. *Journal of Archaeological Science* 25, 303–10.

Buck, C.E., Cavanagh, W.G. and Litton, C.D. 1996. *Bayesian approach to interpreting archaeological data.* Chichester: Wiley.

Buck, C.E., Christian, J.A. and James, G. N. 1999. BCal: an on-line Bayesian radiocarbon calibration tool. *Internet Archaeology* 7 (http://intarch.ac.uk/journal/issue7/buck/)

Buck, C.E., Christen, J.A., Kenworthy, J.B. and Litton, C.D. 1994a. Estimating the duration of archaeological activity using ^{14}C determinations. *Oxford Journal of Archaeology* 13, 229–40.

Buck, C.E., Kenworthy, J.B., Litton, C.D. and Smith, A.F.M. 1991. Combining archaeological and radiocarbon information: a Bayesian approach to calibration. *Antiquity* 65, 808–21.

Buck, C.E., Litton, C.D. and Scott, E.M. 1994b. Making the most of radiocarbon dating: some statistical considerations. *Antiquity* 68, 252–63.

Buck, C.E., Litton, C.D. and Smith, A.F.M. 1992. Calibration of radiocarbon results pertaining to related archaeological events. *Journal of Archaeological Science* 19, 497–512.

Buckley, D.G., Hedges, J.D., and Brown, N. 2001. Excavations at a Neolithic cursus, Springfield, Essex, 1979–85. *Proceedings of the Prehistoric Society* 67, 101–62.

Buckley, D.G., Major, H. and Milton, B. 1988. Excavation of a possible Neolithic long barrow or mortuary enclosure at Rivenhall, Essex, 1986. *Proceedings of the Prehistoric Society* 45, 77–91.

Buckley, J.D., Trautman, M.A. and Willis, E.H. 1968. Isotopes' radiocarbon measurements VI. *Radiocarbon* 10, 246–94.

Buckley, J.D. and Willis, E.H. 1970. Isotopes' radiocarbon measurements VIII. *Radiocarbon* 12, 87–189.

Buckley, J. and Valdes-Pages, C. 1981. Teledyne isotopes radiocarbon measurements XII. *Radiocarbon* 23, 329–44.

Bulard, A., Degros, J. and Tarrête, J. 1986. Premières fouilles sur le site néolithique d'extraction de silex du Haut Château à Jablines (Seine-et-Marne). *Revue Archéologique de l'Ouest*, supplément 1, 55–70.

Burchell, J.P.T. 1925. The shell mound industry of Denmark as represented at Lower Halstow, Kent. *Proceedings of the Prehistoric Society of East Anglia* 5, 73–8, 217–23.

Burchell, J.P.T. and Piggott, S. 1939. Decorated prehistoric pottery from the bed of the Ebbsfleet, Northfleet, Kent. *Antiquaries Journal* 19, 405–20.

Burenhult, G. 1980. *The archaeological excavation at Carrowmore, Co. Sligo, Ireland. Excavation seasons 1977–79.* Stockholm: Institute of Archaeology at the University of Stockholm.

Burenhult, G. 1984. *The archaeology of Carrowmore: environmental archaeology and the megalithic tradition at Carrowmore, Co. Sligo, Ireland.* Stockholm: Institute of Archaeology at the University of Stockholm.

Burenhult, G. 1998. *The Swedish archaeological excavations at Carrowmore, Co. Sligo, Ireland. Campaign season 1998. Excavation report. Tomb no. 51 (Listoghil).* (SMR Number SL014-20922). Unpublished document.

Burenhult, G. 2000. Carrowmore. In I. Bennett (ed.), *Excavations 1998: summary accounts of archaeological excavations in Ireland*, 180–3. Bray: Wordwell.

Burenhult, G. 2001. *The illustrated guide to the megalithic cemetery of Carrowmore, Co. Sligo.* Tjörnarp: Göran Burenhult.

Burenhult, G. 2003. The chronology of Carrowmore. In G. Burenhult and S. Westergaard (eds), *Stones and bones: formal disposal of the dead in Atlantic Europe during the Mesolithic-Neolithic interface 6000–3000 BC*, 66–9. Oxford: Archaeopress.

Burgess, C., Topping, P., Mordant, C. and Maddison, M. (eds) 1988. *Enclosures and defences in the Neolithic of western Europe.* Oxford: British Archaeological Reports.

Burl, H.A.W. 1984. Report on the excavation of a Neolithic mound at Boghead, Speymouth Forest, Fochabers, Moray, 1972 and 1974. *Proceedings of the Society of Antiquaries of Scotland* 114, 35–73.

Burleigh, R. 1972. Liquid scintillation counting of low levels of carbon-14 for radiocarbon dating. In M.A. Crook, P. Johnson and B. Scales (eds), *Liquid scintillation counting v2*, 139–46. London: Heyden.

Burleigh, R. 1976. Radiocarbon dates for flint mines. In F.H.G. Engelen (ed.), *Second international symposium on flint, 8–11 May 1975*, 89–91. Maastricht: Nederlandse Geologische Vereniging.

Burleigh, R. and Hewson, A. 1979. British Museum natural radiocarbon measurements XI. *Radiocarbon* 21, 339–52.

Burleigh, R. and Matthews, K. 1982. British Museum natural radiocarbon measurements XIII. *Radiocarbon* 21, 339–52.

Burleigh, R., Clutton-Brock, J., Felder, P.J. and Sieveking, G. 1977. A further consideration of Neolithic dogs with special reference to a skeleton from Grime's Graves, Norfollk, England. *Journal of Archaeological Science* 1, 353–66.

Burleigh, R., Hewson, A., and Meeks, N. 1976. British Museum natural radiocarbon measurements VIII. *Radiocarbon* 18, 16–42.

Burleigh, R., Ambers, J. and Matthews, K. 1984. British Museum natural radiocarbon measurements XVII. *Radiocarbon* 26, 59–74.

Burnez, C. and Fouéré, P. 1999. *Les enceintes néolithiques de Diconche à Saintes (Charente-Maritime): une périodisation de l'Artenac.* Paris: Mémoire de la Société Préhistorique Française 25.

Burnez, C., Louboutin, C. and Braguier, S. 2001. Les habitats néolithiques ceinturés du Centre-Ouest de la France. In J. Guilaine (ed.), *Communautés villageoises du Proche-Orient à l'Atlantique (8000–2000 avant notre ére)*, 205–20. Paris: Errance.

Burrow, S. 1997. *The Neolithic culture of the Isle of Man: a study of the sites and pottery.* Oxford: British Archaeological Reports.

Burrow, S. 1999. Neither east nor west: a social history of the Manx Neolithic. In P.J. Davey (ed.), *Recent archaeological research from the Isle of Man*, 27–38. Oxford: Archaeopress.

Burrow, S. 2006a. *The tomb-builders in Wales 4000–3000 BC.* Cardiff: National Museum of Wales.

Burrow, S. 2006b. *Catalogue of the Mesolithic and Neolithic collections in the National Museums and Galleries of Wales.* Cardiff: National Museum of Wales Books.

Burrow, S. and Darvill, T. 1997. AMS dating of the Manx Ronaldsway Neolithic. *Antiquity* 71, 412–19.

Burrow, S., Driver, T. and Thomas, D. 1999. Cornton Neolithic lithic scatter (SS926 765). *Archaeology in Wales* 39, 49.

Burrow, S., Driver, T. and Thomas, D. 2001. Bridging the Severn estuary: two possible earlier Neolithic enclosures in the Vale of Glamorgan. In T. Darvill and J. Thomas (eds), *Neolithic enclosures in Atlantic northwest Europe*, 91–100. Oxford: Oxbow Books.

Burstow, G.P. 1942. The Stone Age camp at Whitehawk. *Sussex County Magazine* 16(11), 314–19.

Butcher, S., Cameron, F., Curnow, P.E. and Pengelly, H. 1987. Romano-British features and material. In R. Robertson-Mackay, 'The Neolithic causewayed enclosure at Staines, Surrey: excavations 1961–63'. *Proceedings of the Prehistoric Society* 53, microfiche 1, 86–93, microfiche 2, 94–113.

Butler, A., Clay, P. and Thomas, J. 2002. A causewayed enclosure at Husbands Bosworth, Leicestershire. In G. Varndell and P. Topping (eds), *Enclosures in Neolithic Europe: essays on causewayed and non-causewayed sites*, 107–9. Oxford: Oxbow Books.

Butler, C. and Leivers, M. 2008. Flint. In M.J. Allen, M. Leivers, and C. Ellis, 'Neolithic causewayed enclosures and later prehistoric farming: duality, imposition and the role of predecessors at Kingsborough, Isle of Sheppey, Kent, UK'. *Proceedings of the Prehistoric Society* 74, 253–62.

Butterworth, C. and Gibson, C. 2004. Neolithic pits and a Bronze Age field system at Middle Farm, Dorchester. *Proceedings of the Dorset Natural History and Archaeological Society* 126, 15–25.

Byrne, G. 1990. Mayo. 1990:089. Rathlackan. Court tomb with associated pre-bog settlement. G166388. http://www.excavations.ie/.

Byrne, G. 1991. Rathlackan. Court tomb with associated pre-bog settlement. In I. Bennett (ed.), *Excavations 1990: summary accounts of excavations in Ireland*, 46. Bray: Wordwell.

Byrne, G. 1992. Mayo. 1992:147. Rathlackan. Court tomb with associated pre-bog settlement. G166388. SMR 007:01606. http://www.excavations.ie/.

Byrne, G. 1993. Mayo. 1993:177. Rathlackan. Court tomb with associated pre-bog settlement. G166388. SMR 007:01606. E000580 http://www.excavations.ie/.

Byrne, G., Warren, G., Rathbone, S., McIlreavy, D. and Walsh, P. 2009. Archaeological excavations at Rathlackan (E580): stratigraphic report. (http://www.heritagecouncil.ie/fileadmin/user_upload/INSTAR_Database/Neolithic_and_Bronze_Age_Landscapes_of_North_Mayo_Progress_Reports_6.pdf)

Cain, A.J. 1982. Subfossil mollusca. In H. Case and A. Whittle (eds), *Settlement patterns in the Oxford region: excavations at the Abingdon causewayed enclosure and other sites*, 47. London: Council for British Archaeology.

Callow, W.J., Baker, M.J. and Hassall, G.I. 1965. National Physical Laboratory radiocarbon measurements III. *Radiocarbon* 7, 156–61.

Callow, W.J., Baker, M.J. and Pritchard, D.H. 1963. National Physical Laboratory Radiocarbon measurements I. *Radiocarbon* 5, 34–8.

Callow, W.J. and Hassall, G.I. 1970. National Physical Laboratory Radiocarbon measurements VII. *Radiocarbon* 12, 181–6.

Cambridgeshire County Council, n.d. www.cambridgeshire.gov.uk/environment/planning/applications/major/mustfarm.

Cameron, K. 2002. The excavation of Neolithic pits and Iron Age souterrains at Dubton Farm, Brechin, Angus. *Tayside and Fife Archaeological Journal 8*, 19–76.

Camps, F.E., Chandra, H. and Dawes, J.D. 1987. Human bone. In R. Robertson-Mackay, 'The Neolithic causewayed enclosure at Staines, Surrey: excavations 1961–63'. *Proceedings of the Prehistoric Society* 53, microfiche 1, 6–20.

Carman, J. and Harding, A. (eds) 1999. *Ancient warfare: archaeological perspectives*. Stroud: Sutton.

Carruthers, W.J. and Thomas, R. 1991. The charcoal identifications. In P.J. Woodward, *The south Dorset ridgeway: survey and excavations 1977–84*, 111–4. Dorchester: Dorset Natural History and Archaeological Society.

Carstairs, P. 1986. An archaeological study of the Dorney area. *Records of Buckinghamshire* 28, 163–8.

Cartwright, C. 1977. The charcoals. In M. Bell, 'Excavations at Bishopstone, Sussex'. *Sussex Archaeological Collections* 115, 275–7.

Cartwright, C. 1978. Charcoal. In J. Hedges and D.G. Buckley, 'Excavations at a Neolithic causewayed enclosure, Orsett, Essex, 1975'. *Proceedings of the Prehistoric Society* 44, 293–4.

Cartwright, C. 1986. Charcoal identifications. In P.L. Drewett, 'The excavation of a Neolithic oval barrow at North Marden, West Sussex, 1982'. *Proceedings of the Prehistoric Society* 52, microfiche 24–5.

Cartwright, C. 1999. The charcoal assemblages. In A. Whittle, J. Pollard and C. Grigson, *The harmony of symbols: the Windmill Hill causewayed enclosure, Wiltshire*, 157–61. Oxford: Oxbow Books.

Case, H. 1956. The Neolithic causewayed camp at Abingdon, Berks. *Antiquaries Journal* 36, 11–30.

Case, H. 1961. Irish Neolithic pottery: distribution and sequence. *Proceedings of the Prehistoric Society* 27, 174–233.

Case, H. 1969. Neolithic explanations. *Antiquity* 43, 176–86.

Case, H. 1973. A ritual site in north-east Ireland. In G. Daniel and P. Kjærum (eds), *Megalithic graves and ritual: papers presented at the III Atlantic colloquium, Moesgård 1969*, 173–96. København: Jutland Archaeological Society.

Case, H. 1982a. Introduction. In H. Case and A. Whittle (eds), *Settlement patterns in the Oxford region: excavations at the Abingdon causewayed enclosure and other sites,* 1–8. London: Council for British Archaeology.

Case, H. 1982b. The linear ditches and southern enclosure, North Stoke. In H. Case and A. Whittle (eds), *Settlement patterns in the Oxford region: excavations at the Abingdon causewayed enclosure and other sites,* 60–75. London: Council for British Archaeology.

Case, H. and Whittle, A. (eds) 1982. *Settlement patterns in the Oxford region: excavations at the Abingdon causewayed enclosure and other sites*. London: Council for British Archaeology.

Caseldine, A. 2000. The vegetation history of the Goldcliff area. In M. Bell, A. Caseldine and H. Neumann, *Prehistoric intertidal archaeology in the Welsh Severn estuary*, 208–44. York: Council for British Archaeology.

Caseldine, A. and Griffiths, C.J. 2005. The charred plant remains. In K. Murphy and R. Evans, *Excavation of three ring-ditches and a prehistoric palisaded enclosure at Cwm Meudwy, Llandysul, Ceredigion, 2003*, 15. Unpublished client report. Llandeilo: Cambria Archeological Trust.

Caseldine, A., Druce, D. and Walker, M.J.C. 2001. Palaeoenvironmental assessment of samples from Beech Court Farm enclosure, Ewenny, Vale of Galmorgan. In Glamorgan-Gwent Archaeological Trust, *Beech Court Farm enclosure, Ewenny Quarry, Vale of Glamorgan: palaeoenvironmental assessment*, 5–9. Swansea: GGAT.

Caseldine, C.J., Coles, B.J., Griffith, F.M. and Hatton, J. 2000. Conservation or change? Human influence on the mid-Devon landscape. In T.P. O'Connor and R.A. Nicholson (eds), *People as an agent of environmental change*, 60–70. Oxford: Oxbow Books.

Caseldine, C., Thompson, G., Langdon, C. and Hendon, D. 2005. Evidence for an extreme climatic event on Achill Island, Co. Mayo, Ireland around 5200–5100 cal. yr BP. *Journal of Quaternary Science* 20, 169–78.

Cassen, S. 2000. Stelae reused in the passage graves of western France: history of research and sexualization of the carvings. In A. Ritchie (ed.), *Neolithic Orkney in its European context*, 233–46. Cambridge: McDonald Institute for Archaeological Research.

Cassen, S. (ed.) 2009. *Autour de la Table: explorations archéologiques et discourse savants sur des architectures mégalithiques à Locmariaquer, Morbihan (Tables des Marchands et Grand Menhir).* Nantes: Laboratoire de recherches archéologiques, CNRS and Université de Nantes.

Cassen, S. and Scarre, C. 1997. *Les enceintes néolithiques de La Mastine et Pied-Lizet (Charente-Maritime). Fouilles archéologiques et etudes paléoenvironmentales dans le marais poitevin (1984–1988)*. Chauvigny: Association des Publications Chauvinoises.

Cassen, S., Boujot, C. and Vaquero, J. 2000. *Eléments d'architecture. Exploration d'un tertre funéraire à Lannec er Gadouer (Erdeven, Morbihan). Constructions et reconstructions dans le Néolithique morbihannais. Propositions pour une lecture symbolique*. Chauvigny: Association des Publications Chauvinoises.

Cassen, S., Lanos, P., Dufresne, P., Oberlin, C., Delqué-Kolic, E. and Le Goffic, M. 2009. Datations sur site (Table des Marchands, alignement du Grand Menhir, Er Grah) et modélisation chronologiqie du Néolithique morbihannais. In S. Cassen (ed.), *Autour de la Table: explorations archéologiques et discours savants sur des architectures néolithiques á Locmariaquer, Morbihan (Table des Marchands et Grand Menhir)*, 737–68. Nantes: Laboratoire de recherches archéologiques, CNRS and Université de Nantes.

Caulfield, S. 1978. Neolithic fields: the Irish evidence. In H.C. Bowen and P.J. Fowler (eds), *Early land allotment in the British Isles*, 137–43. Oxford: British Archaeological Reports.

Caulfield, S. 1983. The Neolithic settlement of north Connaught. In T. Reeves-Smyth and F. Hamond (eds), *Landscape archaeology in Ireland*, 195–215. Oxford: British Archaeological Reports.

Caulfield, S. 1988. *Céide Fields and Belderrig guide*. Killala: Morrigan.

Caulfield, S., O'Donnell, R.G. and Mitchell, P.I. 1998. ^{14}C dating of a Neolithic field system at Céide fields, County Mayo, Ireland. *Radiocarbon* 40, 629–40.

Chagnon, N.A. 1968. *Yanomamo: the fierce people*. New York: Holt, Rinehart and Winston.

Chagnon, N. 1988. Life histories, blood revenge and warfare in a tribal population. *Science* 239, 985–91.

Chamberlain, A. 1996. More dating evidence for human remains in British caves. *Antiquity* 70, 950–3.

Champion, T. 2007. Prehistoric Kent. In J.H. Williams (ed.), *The archaeology of Kent to AD 800*, 67–132. Woodbridge: The Boydell Press and Kent County Council.

Chapman, A. 1985. Appendix 4: the construction of the Briar Hill earthworks: a work study. In H.M. Bamford, *Briar Hill: excavation 1974–1978*, microfiche 139–44. Northampton: Northampton Development Corporation.

Chapman, A. 1997. The excavation of Neolithic and medieval mounds at Tansor Crossroads, Northamptonshire 1995. *Northamptonshire Archaeology* 27, 3–50.

Chapman, J. and Hamerow, H. (eds) 1997. *Migrations and invasions in archaeological explanation*. Oxford: British Archaeological Reports International Series.

Chapman, R. 2008. Producing inequalities: regional sequences in later prehistoric southern Spain. *Journal of World Prehistory* 21, 195–260.

Chatterton, R. 2007. South Haw, northern England: an upland Mesolithic site in context. In C. Waddington and K. Pedersen (eds), *Mesolithic studies in the North Sea basin and beyond*, 69–80. Oxford: Oxbow Books.

Childe, V.G. 1931. The continental affinities of British Neolithic pottery. *Archaeological Journal* 88, 37–66.

Childe, V.G. and Smith, I.F. 1954. Excavation of a Neolithic barrow on Whiteleaf Hill, Bucks. *Proceedings of the Prehistoric Society* 20, 212–30.

Chiverrell, R.C., Davey, P.J., Gowlett, J.A.J. and Woodcock, J.J. 1999. Radiocarbon dates for the Isle of Man. In P.J. Davey (ed.), *Recent archaeological research from the Isle of Man*, 321–36. Oxford: Archaeopress.

Christen, J.A. 1994. Summarizing a set of radiocarbon determinations: a robust approach. *Applied Statistics* 43, 489–503.

Christen, J.A. and Litton, C.D. 1995. A Bayesian approach to wiggle-matching. *Journal of Archaeological Science* 22, 719–25.

Christen, J.A., Clymo, R. S. and Litton, C.D. 1995. A Bayesian approach to the use of ^{14}C dates in the estimation of the age of peat. *Radiocarbon* 37, 431–42.

Christensen, J. 2004. Warfare in the European Neolithic. *Acta Archaeologica* 75, 129–56.

Clapham, A.J. 2004. Waterlogged plant macrofossils. In C.J. Ellis, *A prehistoric ritual complex at Eynesbury, Cambridgeshire: excavation of a multi-period site in the Great Ouse valley, 2000–2001*, 81–7. Salisbury: Trust for Wessex Archaeology Ltd.

Claris, P. and Quartermaine, J. 1989. The Neolithic quarries and axe factory sites of Great Langdale and Scafell Pike: a new field survey. *Proceedings of the Prehistoric Society* 55, 1–25.

Clark, J.G.D. 1931. The flints. In E.C. Curwen, 'Excavations in the Trundle, Goodwood (second season) 1930'. *Sussex Archaeological Collections* 72, 137–41.

Clark, J.G.D. 1932. The curved flint sickle blades of Britain. *Proceedings of the Prehistoric Society of East Anglia* 7, 67–81.

Clark, J.G.D. 1934a. The flint implements. In E.C. Curwen, 'A late Bronze Age farm and a Neolithic pit-dwelling on New Barn Down, Clapham, Nr. Worthing'. *Sussex Archaeological Collections* 75, 164–6.

Clark, J.G.D. 1934b. A late Mesolithic settlement site at Selmeston, Sussex. *Antiquaries Journal* 14, 134–58.

Clark, J.G.D. 1936. The timber monument at Arminghall and its affinities. *Proceedings of the Prehistoric Society* 2, 1–51.

Clark, J.G.D. 1963. Neolithic bows from Somerset, England, and the prehistory of archery in north-west Europe. *Proceedings of the Prehistoric Society* 29, 50–98.

Clark, J.G.D. 1994. *Space, time, and man: a prehistorian's view*. Cambridge: Cambridge University Press.

Clark, J.G.D. and Godwin, H. 1962. The Neolithic in the Cambridgeshire Fens. *Antiquity* 36, 10–23.

Clark, J.G.D., Godwin, H., Godwin, M.E. and Clifford, M.H. 1935. Report on recent excavations at Peacock's Farm, Shippea Hill, Cambridgeshire. *Antiquaries Journal* 15, 284–319.

Clark, J.G.D., with Higgs, E.S. and Longworth, I.H. 1960. Excavations at the Neolithic site at Hurst Fen, Mildenhall, Suffolk (1954, 1957 and 1958). *Proceedings of the Prehistoric Society* 26, 202–45.

Clark, R.M. 1975. A calibration curve for radiocarbon dates. *Antiquity* 49, 251–64.

Clarke, A.F. 1982. The Neolithic of Kent: a review. In P. Leach (ed.), *Archaeology in Kent to AD 1500*, 25–30. London: Council for British Archaeology.

Clarke, C.P. and Lavender, N.J. 2008. *An early Neolithic ring-ditch and middle Bronze Age cemetery: excavation and survey at Brightlingsea, Essex*. Chelmsford: Essex County Council.

Clarke, D.L. 1973. Archaeology: the loss of innocence. *Antiquity* 47, 6–18.

Clarke, D.V., Cowie, T.G. and Foxon, A. 1985. *Symbols of power at the time of Stonehenge*. Edinburgh: National Museum of Antiquities of Scotland.

Clay, P. 1999a. A first causewayed enclosure for Leicestershire. *PAST* 32, 3–4.

Clay, P. 1999b. The Neolithic and Bronze Age of Leicestershire and Rutland. *Transactions of the Leicestershire Archaeological and Historical Society* 73, 1–18.

Cleal, R. 1990a. The prehistoric pottery [from the Coneybury anomaly]. In J.C. Richards, *The Stonehenge environs project*, 45–57. London: Historic Buildings and Monuments Commission.

Cleal, R. 1990b. The prehistoric pottery [from a pit on King Barrow Ridge]. In J.C. Richards, *The Stonehenge environs project*, 65–6. London: Historic Buildings and Monuments Commission.

Cleal, R. 1990c. The prehistoric pottery. In J.C. Richards, *The Stonehenge environs project*, 233–46. London: Historic Buildings and Monuments Commission.

Cleal, R. 1991. Earlier prehistoric pottery. In N. Sharples, *Maiden Castle: excavations and field survey 1985–6*, 171–85, microfiche M9:A4–E4. London: English Heritage.

Cleal, R. 1992. Significant form: ceramic styles in the earlier Neolithic of southern England. In N. Sharples and A. Sheridan (eds), *Vessels for the ancestors: essays on the Neolithic of Britain and Ireland in honour of Audrey Henshall*, 286–304. Edinburgh: Edinburgh University Press.

Cleal, R. 1993. Neolithic pottery. In S. Ford, 'Excavations at Eton Wick'. *Berkshire Archaeological Journal* 74, microfiche M1:E2–9.

Cleal, R. 1995a. The archacology of the early to middle Neolithic landscape. In R.M.J. Cleal, K.E. Walker and R. Montague, *Stonehenge in its landscape: twentieth-century excavations*, 473–6. London: English Heritage.

Cleal, R. 1995b. Pottery fabrics in Wessex in the fourth to second millennia BC. In I. Kinnes and G. Varndell (eds), *'Unbaked urns of rudely shape': essays on British and Irish pottery for Ian Longworth*, 185–94. Oxford: Oxbow Books.

Cleal, R. 1995c. Neolithic and Bronze Age pottery. In T. Allen, *Lithics and landscape: archaeological discoveries on the Thames Water pipeline at Gatehampton Farm, Goring, Oxfordshire 1985–92*, 85–8. Oxford: Oxford University Committee for Archaeology.

Cleal, R.M.J. 1997. Earlier prehistoric pottery. In R.J.C. Smith, F. Healy, M.J. Allen, E.L. Morris, I. Barnes and P.J. Woodward, *Excavations along the route of the Dorchester by-pass, Dorset, 1986–8*, 86–102. Salisbury: Wessex Archaeology.

Cleal, R.M.J. 2004. The dating and diversity of the earliest ceramics of Wessex and south-west England. In R. Cleal and J. Pollard (eds), *Monuments and material culture. Papers in honour of an Avebury archaeologist: Isobel Smith*, 166–92. East Knoyle: Hobnob Press.

Cleal, R. 2005. 'The small compass of a grave': early Bronze Age burial in and around Avebury and the Marlborough Downs. In G. Brown, D. Field and D. McOmish (eds), *The Avebury landscape: aspects of the field archaeology of the Marlborough Downs*, 115–32. Oxford: Oxbow Books.

Cleal, R. and Allen, M.J. 1994. Investigation of tree-damaged barrows on King Barrow Ridge and Luxenborough Plantation. *Wiltshire Archaeological and Natural History Magazine* 87, 54–84.

Cleal, R. and Pollard, J. (eds) 2004. *Monuments and material culture. Papers in honour of an Avebury archaeologist: Isobel Smith.* East Knoyle: Hobnob Press.

Cleal, R., Walker, K.E. and Montague, R. 1995. *Stonehenge in its landscape: twentieth-century excavations*. London: English Heritage.

Cleary, R. 1993. The later Bronze Age at Lough Gur: filling in the blanks. In E. Shee Twohig and M. Ronayne (eds), *Past perceptions: the prehistoric archaeology of south-west Ireland*, 114–20. Cork: Cork University Press.

Cleary, R. 1995. Later Bronze Age settlement and prehistoric burials, Lough Gur, Co. Limerick. *Proceedings of the Royal Irish Academy* 95C, 1–92.

Cleary, R. 2003. Enclosed Late Bronze Age habitation site and boundary wall at Lough Gur, Co. Limerick. *Proceedings of the Royal Irish Academy* 103C, 4–189.

Clifford, E.M. 1936. Notgrove long barrow, Gloucestershire. *Archaeologia* 86, 119–61.

Clifford, E.M. 1938. The excavation of the Nympsfield long barrow, Gloucestershire. *Proceedings of the Prehistoric Society* 4, 188–213.

Clipson, J. 1983. Flint report. In P.E. Leach, 'The excavation of a Neolithic causewayed enclosure on Barkhale Down, Bignor Hill, West Sussex'. *Sussex Archaeological Collections* 121, 20–1.

Clough, T.H.McK. 1973. Excavations on a Langdale axe chipping site in 1969 and 1970. *Transactions of the Cumberland and Westmorland Antiquarian and Archaeological Society* 73, 25–46.

Clough, T.H.McK. 1988. Introduction to the regional reports: prehistoric stone implements from the British Isles. In T.H.McK. Clough and W.A. Cummins (eds), *Stone axe studies volume 2. The petrology of prehistoric stone implements from the British Isles*, 1–11. London: Council for British Archaeology.

Clough, T.H.McK. and Cummins, W.A. (eds) 1988. *Stone axe studies volume 2. The petrology of prehistoric stone implements from the British Isles*. London: Council for British Archaeology.

Cloutman, E. 2006. Stratigraphy and pollen. In C. Evans and I. Hodder, *A woodland archaeology. Neolithic sites at Haddenham: the Haddenham project volume 1*, 203–7. Cambridge: McDonald Institute for Archaeological Research.

Cobb, C. 1991. Social reproduction and the longue durée in the prehistory of the midcontinental United States. In R. Preucel (ed.), *Processual and postprocessual archaeologies: multiple ways of knowing the past*, 162–82. Carbondale: Southern Illinois University Press.

Cody, E. 2002. *Survey of the megalithic tombs of Ireland. Volume VI, County Donegal*. Dublin: The Stationery Office.

Colas, C. 2007. Reconstitution des techniques de fabrication des céramiques des constructeurs d'enceinte du Néolithique moyen II en France septentrionale. In A. Agogué, D. Leroy and C. Verjux (eds), *Camps, enceintes et structures d'habitat néolithiques en France septentrionale*, 217–28. 27ème supplement à la Revue Archéologique du Centre de la France. Tours: Editions F.E.R.A.C.F.

Colas, C, Manolakakis, L. and Thevenet, C. 2007. Le monument funéraire Michelsberg ancien de Beaurieux 'la Plaine' (Aisne, France). In M. Besse (ed.), *Sociétés néolithiques: des faits archéologiques aux fonctionnements socio-économiques. Cahiers d'Archéologie Romande* 108, 329–34.

Cole, D. and Jones, A.M. 2003. Journeys to the rock: archaeological investigations at Tregarrick Farm, Roche, Cornwall. *Cornish Archaeology* 41–42, 107–43.

Coleman, J.C. 1947. Irish cave excavation. *Journal of the Royal Society of Antiquaries of Ireland* 77, 63–80.

Coles, B. 1998. Doggerland: a speculative survey. *Proceedings of the Prehistoric Society* 64, 45–81.

Coles, B. and Coles, J. 1986. *Sweet Track to Glastonbury*. London: Thames and Hudson.

Coles, B. and Coles, J. 1992. Passages of time. *Archäologische Mitteilungen aus Nordwestdeutschland* 15, 29–44.

Coles, J.M., Hibbert, F.A. and Orme, B.J. 1973. Prehistoric roads and tracks in Somerset, England: 3. The Sweet Track. *Proceedings of the Prehistoric Society* 39, 256–93.

Coles, J.M. and Orme, B.J. 1984a. Ten excavations along the Sweet Track (3200 bc). *Somerset Levels Papers* 10, 5–45.

Coles, J.M. and Orme, B.J. 1984b. A reconstruction of the Sweet Track. *Somerset Levels Papers* 10, 107–9.

Coles, S., Ford, S. and Taylor, A. 2008. An early Neolithic grave and occupation, and an early Bronze Age hearth on the Thames foreshore at Yabsley Street, Blackwall, London. *Proceedings of the Prehistoric Society* 74, 215–33.

Collard, M., Edinborough, K., Shennan, S. and Thomas, M.G. 2010. Radiocarbon evidence indicates that migrants introduced farming to Britain. *Journal of Archaeological Science* 37, 866–70.

Collet, H., Hubert, F., Joris, J.-P. and Toussaint, M. 2001. Spiennes: l'état des connaissances et bibliographie. Guide des sites préhistoriques et protohistoriques de Wallonie. *Vie Archéologique* (numéro special), 86–9.

Collins, A.E.P. 1957. Trial excavations in a round cairn on Knockiveagh, Co. Down. *Ulster Journal of Archaeology* 20, 8–28.

Collins, A.E.P. 1965. Ballykeel dolmen and cairn, Co. Armagh. *Ulster Journal of Archaeology* 28, 47–70.

Collins, A.E.P. 1976. Dooey's Cairn, Ballymacaldrack, Co. Antrim. *Ulster Journal of Archaeology* 39, 1–7.

Collins, A.E.P. 1978. Excavations on Ballygalley Hill, County Antrim. *Ulster Journal of Archaeology* 41, 15–32.

Collins, A.E.P. and Wilson, B.C.S. 1964. The excavation of a court cairn at Ballymacdermot, Co. Armagh. *Ulster Journal of Archaeology* 27, 3–22.

Collins, B. 1999. Macrofossil plant remains. In C. Mount, 'Excavation and environmental analysis of a Neolithic mound and Iron Age barrow cemetery at Rathdooney Beg, County Sligo, Ireland'. *Proceedings of the Prehistoric Society* 65, 365–7.

Connah, G. 1965. Excavations at Knap Hill, Alton Priors. *Wiltshire Archaeological and Natural History Magazine* 60, 1–23.

Connah, G. 1969. Radiocarbon dating for Knap Hill. *Antiquity* 43, 304–5.

Connerton, P. 1989. *How societies remember*. Cambridge: Cambridge University Press.

Constantin, C., Mordant, D. and Simonin, D. (eds) 1997. *La culture de Cerny: nouvelle économie, nouvelle société au Néolithique*. Nemours: Mémoires du Musée de Préhistoire d'Ile de France.

Cook, G.T., Bonsall, C., Hedges, R.E.M., McSweeney, K., Boroneant, V. and Pettitt, P.B. 2001. A freshwater diet-derived ^{14}C reservoir effect at the stone age sites in the Iron Gates gorge. *Radiocarbon* 43, 453–60.

Cook, M. and Dunbar, L. 2008. *Rituals, roundhouses and Romans: excavations at Kintore, Aberdeenshire, 2000–2006. Voulme 1: Forest Road.* Edinburgh: Scottish Trust for Archaeological Research.

Cooney, G. 1999. A boom in Neolithic houses. *Archaeology Ireland* 13(1), 13–16.

Cooney, G. 2000a. *Landscapes of Neolithic Ireland.* London: Routledge.

Cooney, G. 2000b. Recognising regionality in the Irish Neolithic. In A. Desmond, G. Johnson, M. McCarthy, J. Sheehan and E. Shee Twohig (eds), *New agendas in Irish prehistory: papers in commemoration of Liz Anderson*, 49–65. Bray: Wordwell.

Cooney, G. 2002. From Lilliput to Brobdignag: the traditions of enclosure in the Irish Neolithic. In G. Varndell and P. Topping (eds), *Enclosures in Neolithic Europe: essays on causewayed and non-causewayed sites*, 69–82. Oxford: Oxbow Books.

Cooney, G. 2003. Rooted or routed? Landscapes of Neolithic settlement in Ireland. In I. Armit, E. Murphy, E. Nelis and D. Simpson (eds), *Neolithic settlement in Ireland and western Britain*, 47–55. Oxford: Oxbow Books.

Cooney, G. 2005. Stereo porphyry: quarrying and deposition. In P. Topping and M. Lynott (eds), *The cultural landscape of prehistoric mines*, 14–29. Oxford and Oakville: Oxbow Books.

Cooney, G. 2007a. Parallel worlds or multi-stranded identities? Considering the process of 'going over' in Ireland and the Irish Sea zone. In A. Whittle and V. Cummings (eds), *Going over: the Mesolithic-Neolithic transition in north-west Europe*, 543–66. Oxford: Oxford University Press for The British Academy.

Cooney, G. 2007b. In retrospect: Neolithic activity at Knockadoon, Lough Gur, Co. Limerick, 50 years on. *Proceedings of the Royal Irish Academy* 107C, 215–25.

Cooney, G. 2008. Engaging with stone: making the Neolithic in Ireland and Western Britain. *Analecta Praehistorica Leidensia* 40, 203–14.

Cooney, G. and Grogan, E. 1994. *Irish prehistory: a social perspective.* Dublin: Wordwell.

Cooney, G. and Mandal, S. 1998. *The Irish stone axe project: monograph 1.* Bray: Wordwell.

Cooney, G., Mandal, S., O'Keeffe, E. and Warren, G. forthcoming. Earlier prehistory on Rathlin Island. In W. Forsythe and R. McConkey (eds), *Rathlin Island maritime archaeological survey*. Belfast: TSO.

Cooney, G., O'Sullivan, M. and Downey, L. 2006. *Repositioning Irish archaeology in the knowledge society*. Dublin: University College Dublin.

Coope, G.R. and Garrard, L.S. 1988. The petrological identification of stone implements from the Isle of Man. In T.H.McK. Clough and W.A. Cummins (eds), *Stone axe studies volume 2: the petrology of prehistoric stone implements from the British Isles*, 67–70. London: Council for British Archaeology.

Cooper, A. and Edmonds, M. 2007. *Past and present: excavations at Broom, Bedfordshire, 1996–2005*. Cambridge: Cambridge Archaeological Unit.

Copley, M.S., Mukherjee, A.J., Dudd, S.N., Straker, V., Payne, S. and Evershed, R.P. 2005. Dairying in antiquity III: evidence from absorbed lipid residues dating to the British Neolithic. *Journal of Archaeological Science* 32, 523–46.

Copley, M.S. and Evershed, R.P. 2007. Organic residue analysis. In D. Benson and A. Whittle (eds), *Building memories: the Neolithic Cotswold long barrow at Ascott-under-Wychwood, Oxfordshire*, 283–8. Oxford: Oxbow Books.

Copson, C. with Healy, F. 1997. Stone. In R.J.C. Smith, F. Healy, M.J. Allen, E.L. Morris, I. Barnes and P.J. Woodward, *Excavations along the route of the Dorchester by-pass, Dorset, 1986–8*, 133–6. Salisbury: Wessex Archaeology.

Corcoran, J.X.W.P. 1969. The Cotswold-Severn group. In T.G.E. Powell, J.X.W.P. Corcoran, F.M. Lynch and J.G. Scott (eds), *Megalithic enquiries in the west of Britain*, 13–104. Liverpool: Liverpool University Press.

Corlett, C. 2001. Neolithic housing development at Corbally, Co. Kildare. *Archaeology Ireland* 15(3), 4.

Corney, M. and McOmish, D. 2004. Survey. In M. Rawlings, M.J.

Allen and F. Healy, 'Investigation of the Whitesheet Down environs 1989–90: Neolithic causewayed enclosure and Iron Age settlement'. *Wiltshire Studies* 97, 146–8.

Cotton, J. 2004. Surrey's early past: a survey of recent work. In J. Cotton. G. Crocker and AA. Graham (eds), *Aspects of archaeology and history in Surrey: towards a research framework for the county*, 19–38. Guildford: Surrey Archaeological Society.

Cotton, J. and Field, D. (eds) 2004. *Towards a New Stone Age: aspects of the Neolithic in south-east England*. York: Council for British Archaeology.

Cowie, T.G. 1993. A survey of the Neolithic pottery of eastern and central Scotland. *Proceedings of the Society of Antiquaries of Scotland* 123, 13–41.

Cowley, L.F. 1960. Osseous remains [from Burn Ground]. In W.F. Grimes, *Excavations on defence sites, 1939–1945. I: mainly Neolithic–Bronze Age*, 70–2. London: HMSO.

Craddock, P.T., Cowell, M.R. and Hughes, M.J. forthcoming. The provenancing of flint axes by chemical analysis and the products of the Grime's Graves mines: a re-assessment. In I. Longworth, G. Varndell and J. Lech, *Excavations at Grime's Graves, Norfolk 1972–1976. Fascicule 6. Exploration and excavation beyond the deep mines*. London: British Museum Publications.

Craddock, P.T., Cowell, M.R., Leese, M.N. and Hughes, M.J. 1983. The trace element composition of polished flint axes as an indicator of source. *Archaeometry* 25, 135–63.

Cram, C.L. 1982. Animal bones. In M. Avery, 'The Neolithic causewayed enclosure, Abingdon'. In H. Case and A. Whittle (eds), *Settlement patterns in the Oxford region: excavations at the Abingdon causewayed enclosure and other sites*, 43–7. London: Council for British Archaeology.

Cramp, K. 2007. The flint. In D. Benson and A. Whittle (eds), *Building memories: the Neolithic Cotswold long barrow at Ascott-under-Wychwood, Oxfordshire*, 289–314. Oxford: Oxbow Books.

Crawford, O.G.S. and Keiller, A. 1928. *Wessex from the air*. Oxford: Clarendon Press.

Crombé, P. and Vanmontfort, B. 2007. The neolithisation of the Scheldt basin in western Belgium. In A. Whittle and V. Cummings (eds), *Going over: the Mesolithic-Neolithic transition in north-west Europe*, 263–85. Oxford: Oxford University Press for The British Academy.

Cross, S. 2003. Irish Neolithic settlement architecture – an appreciation. In I. Armit, E. Murphy, E. Nelis and D. Simpson (eds), *Neolithic settlement in Ireland and western Britain*, 195–202. Oxford: Oxbow Books.

Crowson, A. and Bayliss, A. 1999. Dating a burnt mound and its beakers at Northwold, Norfolk. In J. Evin, C. Oberlin, J. P. Daugas and J.F. Salles (eds), *Actes du 3ème congrès international <<Archaéologie et 14C>> Lyon, 6–10 Avril 1998*, 243–8. Revue d'Archéometrie Supplément 1999 et Société Préhistorique Française Mémoire 26.

Crutchley, S. 2005. Recent aerial survey work in the Marlborough Downs region. In G. Brown, D. Field and D. McOmish (eds), *The Avebury landscape: aspects of the field archaeology of the Marlborough Downs*, 34–42. Oxford: Oxbow Books.

Cuenca, C. 2006. Banbury, Banbury Booster 876F (SP45363868 to SP 45223490). *South Midlands Archaeology* 36, 35–9.

Cummings, V. 2009. *A view from the west:the Neolithic of the Irish Sea zone*. Oxford: Oxbow Books.

Cummings, V. and Fowler, C. 2004. The setting and form of Manx chambered cairns: cultural comparisons and social interpretations. In V. Cummings and C. Fowler (eds), *The Neolithic of the Irish Sea: materiality and traditions of practice*, 113–22. Oxford: Oxbow Books.

Cummings, V. and Whittle, A. 2004. *Places of special virtue: megaliths in the Neolithic landscapes of Wales*. Oxford: Oxbow Books.

Cummins, D. O., Delaney, G. F. G. and McAulay, I. R. 1960. Light collection in liquid scintillator cells. *Scientific Proceedings of the Royal Society of Dublin Series A*, 1, 21–6.

Cummins, W.A. 1979. Neolithic stone axes: distribution and trade in England and Wales. In T.H.McK. Clough and W.A. Cummins (eds), *Stone axe studies: archaeological, petrological, experimental and ethnographic*, 1–12. London: Council for British Archaeology.

Cummins, W.A. and Moore, W.R.G. 1988. The petrological identification of stone implements from the south-east midlands. In T.H.McK. Clough and W.A. Cummins (eds), *Stone axe studies volume 2. The petrology of prehistoric stone implements from the British Isles*, 41–4. London: Council for British Archaeology.

Cunnington, M.E. 1909. On a remarkable feature in the entrenchments of Knap Hill Camp, Wiltshire. *Man* 9, 49–52.

Cunnington, M.E. 1912. Knap Hill Camp. *Wiltshire Archaeological and Natural History Magazine* 37, 42–85.

Cunnington, M.E. 1929. *Woodhenge. A description of the site as revealed by excavations carried out there by Mr and Mrs B.H. Cunnington, 1926–7–8. Also of four circles and an earthwork enclosure south of Woodhenge*. Devizes: George Simpson & Co.

Curwen, E.C. 1929a. *Prehistoric Sussex*. London: Homeland Association.

Curwen, E.C. 1929b. Excavations in The Trundle, Goodwood, 1928. *Sussex Archaeological Collections* 70, 33–85.

Curwen, E.C. 1929c. Neolithic camp, Combe Hill, Jevington. *Sussex Archaeological Collections* 70, 209–11.

Curwen, E.C. 1930. Neolithic camps. *Antiquity* 4, 22–54.

Curwen, E.C. 1931. Excavations in The Trundle, Goodwood (second season) 1930. *Sussex Archaeological Collections* 72, 100–49.

Curwen, E.C. 1934a. Excavations at Whitehawk Camp, Brighton 1932–3. *Antiquaries Journal* 14, 99–113.

Curwen, E.C. 1934b. A late Bronze Age farm and a Neolithic pit-dwelling on New Barn Down, Clapham, Nr. Worthing. *Sussex Archaeological Collections* 75, 137–70.

Curwen, E.C. 1935. Whitehawk 1935 field-book. Manuscript. Department of Local History and Archaeology, Brighton Museum and Art Gallery.

Curwen, E.C. 1936. Excavations in Whitehawk Camp, Brighton, third season, 1935. *Sussex Archaeological Collections* 77, 60–92.

Curwen, E.C. 1946. *Plough and pasture*. London: Cobbett Press.

Curwen, E.C. 1954. *The archaeology of Sussex*. Second edition. London: Methuen and Co. Ltd.

Czernik, J. and Goslar, T. 2001. Preparation of graphite targets in the Gliwice Radiocarbon Laboratory for AMS ^{14}C dating. *Radiocarbon* 43, 283–91.

Daim, F. and Neubauer, W. (eds) 2005. *Zeitreise Heldenberg: Geheimnisvolle Kreisgräben. Niederösterreichische Landesausstellung 2005*. Horn and Vienna: Verlag Berger.

Danaher, E. 2003. *Ballincollig bypass road project: final report on archaeological excavation*. Drogheda and Cork: Archaeological Consultancy Services Ltd and Cork County Council.

Danaher, E. 2004. Symbolic enclosure: a tantalising Neolithic space in the north-west. *Archaeology Ireland* 18 (4), 18–21.

Danaher, E. 2007. *Monumental beginnings: the archaeology of the N4 Sligo inner relief road*. Dublin: National Roads Authority.

Danaher, E. 2009. An early Neolithic house at Barnagore, Co. Cork. *Journal of Irish Archaeology* 18, 1–16.

Danaher, E. and Cagney, L. 2005. *N4 Sligo inner relief road and county extension. Contract 1 – final report. Report on the archaeological excavation of an early Neolithic causewayed enclosure at area 2C, Magheraboy, Sligo*. Client report. Drogheda: Archaeological Consultancy Services Ltd.

Daniel, G. 1950. *The prehistoric chambered tombs of England and Wales*. Cambridge: Cambridge University Press.

Daniel, G. 1967. *The origins and growth of archaeology*. Harmondsworth: Penguin.

Darrah, R. 2006. Wood technology. In C. Evans and I. Hodder, *A woodland archaeology. Neolithic sites at Haddenham: the Haddenham project volume 1*, 118–30. Cambridge: McDonald Institute for Archaeological Research.

Darvill, T. 1979. Court cairns, passage graves and social change in Ireland. *Man* 14, 311–27.

Darvill, T. 1981. Excavations at the Peak Camp, Cowley: an interim report. *Glevensis. The Gloucester and District Archaeological Research Group Review* 15, 52–6.

Darvill, T. 1982a. Excavations at the Peak Camp, Cowley, Gloucestershire. *Glevensis. The Gloucester and District Archaeological Research Group Review* 16, 20–5.

Darvill, T. 1982b. *The megalithic chambered tombs of the Cotswold-Severn region*. Highworth: VORDA.

Darvill, T. 1984a. Neolithic Gloucestershire. In A. Saville (ed.), *Archaeology in Gloucestershire from the earliest hunters to the industrial age*, 80–112. Cheltenham: Cheltenham Art Gallery and Museums and the Bristol and Gloucestershire Archaeological Society.

Darvill, T. 1984b. *Birdlip bypass project – first report: archaeological assessment and field survey*. Bristol: Western Archaeological Trust.

Darvill, T.C. 1984c. A study of the Neolithic pottery form Gwernvale. In W.J. Britnell, 'The Gwernvale long cairn, Crickhowell, Brecknock'. In W.J. Britnell and H.N. Savory, *Gwernvale and Penywyrlod: two Neolithic long cairns in the Black Mountains of Brecknock*, 110–13. Cardiff: Cambrian Archaeological Association.

Darvill, T. 1986. Prospects for dating Neolithic sites and monuments in the Cotswolds and adjacent areas. In J.A.J. Gowlett and R.E.M. Hedges (eds), *Archaeological results from accelerator dating*, 119–24. Oxford: Oxford University Committee for Archaeology.

Darvill, T. 1987. *Prehistoric Britain*. London: Batsford.

Darvill, T. 1989. The circulation of Neolithic stone and flint axes: a case study from Wales and the mid-west of England. *Proceedings of the Prehistoric Society* 55, 27–43.

Darvill, T. 1990. Neolithic and Bronze Age pottery. In D.G. Benson, J.G. Evans, G.H. Williams, T. Darvill and A. David, 'Excavations at Stackpole Warren, Dyfed'. *Proceedings of the Prehistoric Society* 56, 208–22.

Darvill, T. 1996a. *Billown Neolithic landscape project, Isle of Man, 1995*. Bournemouth and Douglas: Bournemouth University and Manx National Heritage.

Darvill, T. 1996b. Billown, Isle of Man. *Current Archaeology* 13.6, 232–7.

Darvill, T. 1996c. Neolithic buildings in England, Wales and the Isle of Man. In T. Darvill and J. Thomas (eds), *Neolithic houses in northwest Europe and beyond*, 77–111. Oxford: Oxbow Books.

Darvill, T. 1997. *Billown Neolithic landscape project, Isle of Man, 1996*. Bournemouth and Douglas: Bournemouth University and Manx National Heritage.

Darvill, T. 1998. *Billown Neolithic landscape project, Isle of Man. Third report: 1997*. Bournemouth and Douglas: Bournemouth University and Manx National Heritage.

Darvill, T. 1999a. Billown Neolithic landscape project 1995–1997. In P. Davey (ed.), *Recent archaeological research on the Isle of Man*, 13–26. Oxford: British Archaeological Reports.

Darvill, T. 1999b. *Billown Neolithic landscape project, Isle of Man. Fourth report: 1998*. Bournemouth and Douglas: Bournemouth University and Manx National Heritage.

Darvill, T. 2000a. Neolithic Mann in context. In A. Ritchie (ed.), *Neolithic Orkney in its European context*, 371–85. Cambridge: McDonald Institute Monographs.

Darvill, T. 2000b. *Billown Neolithic landscape project, Isle of Man. Fifth report: 1999*. Bournemouth and Douglas: Bournemouth University and Manx National Heritage.

Darvill, T. 2001a. Neolithic enclosures in the Isle of Man. In T. Darvill and J. Thomas (eds), *Neolithic enclosures in Atlantic northwest Europe*, 155–70. Oxford: Oxbow Books.

Darvill, T. 2001b. *Billown Neolithic landscape project, Isle of Man. Sixth report: 2000*. Bournemouth and Douglas: Bournemouth University and Manx National Heritage.

Darvill, T. 2002. Billown Neolithic enclosures, Isle of Man. In G. Varndell and P. Topping (eds), *Enclosures in Neolithic Europe: essays on causewayed and non-causewayed sites*, 83–89. Oxford: Oxbow Books.

Darvill, T. 2003a. Billown and the Neolithic of the Isle of Man. In I. Armit, E. Murphy, E. Nelis and D. Simpson (eds), *Neolithic settlement in Ireland and western Britain*, 112–19. Oxford: Oxbow Books.

Darvill, T. 2003b. *Billown Neolithic landscape project, Isle of Man. Seventh report: 2002*. Bournemouth and Douglas: Bournemouth University and Manx National Heritage.

Darvill, T. 2004a. *Long barrows of the Cotswolds and surrounding areas*. Stroud: Tempus.

Darvill, T. 2004b. Soft-rock and organic tempering in British Neolithic pottery. In R.M.J. Cleal and J. Pollard (eds), *Monuments and material culture. Papers in honour of an Avebury archaeologist: Isobel Smith*, 193–206. East Knoyle: Hobnob Press.

Darvill, T. 2004c. *Billown Neolithic landscape project, Isle of Man. Eighth report: 2003*. Bournemouth and Douglas: Bournemouth University and Manx National Heritage.

Darvill, T. 2004d. Tales of the land, tales of the sea: people and presence in the Neolithic of Man and beyond. In V. Cummings and C. Fowler (eds), *The Neolithic of the Irish Sea: materiality and traditions of practice*, 46–54. Oxford: Oxbow Books.

Darvill, T. (ed.) 2005. *Stonehenge World Heritage Site: an archaeological research framework*. London and Bournemouth: English Heritage and Bournemouth University.

Darvill, T. 2006. Early prehistory. In N. Holbrook and J. Junca (eds), *Twenty-five years of archaeology in Gloucestershire: a review of new discoveries and new thinking in Gloucestershire, south Gloucestershire and Bristol 1979–2004*, 5–60. Kemble: Cotswold Archaeology and Bristol and Gloucestershire Archaeological Society.

Darvill, T. 2010. Tynwald Hill and the round mounds of the Isle of Man. In J. Leary, T. Darvill and D. Field (eds), *Round mounds and monumentality in the British Neolithic and beyond*, 53–71. Oxford: Oxbow Books.

Darvill, T. forthcoming. Neolithic communities: 4000–2000 BC.

In P. Davey (ed.), *A new history of the Isle of Man, volume II*. Liverpool: Liverpool University Press.

Darvill, T. and Fulton, A.K. 1998. *MARS. The Monuments at Risk Survey of England, 1995: main report*. Bournemouth and London: Bournemouth University School of Conservation Sciences and English Heritage.

Darvill, T.C. and Grinsell, L.V. 1989. Gloucestershire barrows: supplement 1961–1988. *Transactions of the Bristol and Gloucestershire Archaeological Society* 107, 39–105.

Darvill, T. and O'Connor, B. 2005. The Cronk yn How Stone and the rock art of the Isle of Man. *Proceedings of the Prehistoric Society* 71, 283–31.

Darvill, T. and Thomas, J. 2001. Neolithic enclosures in Atlantic northwest Europe: some recent trends. In T. Darvill and J. Thomas (eds), *Neolithic enclosures in Atlantic northwest Europe*, 1–23. Oxford: Oxbow Books.

Darvill, T. and Wainwright, G. 2002. SPACES – exploring Neolithic landscapes in the Strumble-Preseli area of southwest Wales. *Antiquity* 76, 623–4.

Darvill, T., Morgan Evans, D. and Wainwright, G. 2003. Strumble-Presceli Ancient Communities and Environment Study (SPACES): second report 2003. *Archaeology in Wales* 43, 3–12.

Darvill, T., Morgan Evans, D. and Wainwright, G. 2004. Strumble-Presceli Ancient Communities and Environment Study (SPACES): third report 2004. *Archaeology in Wales* 44, 104–9.

Darvill, T., Morgan Evans, D., Fyfe, R. and Wainwright, G. 2006. Strumble-Preseli Ancient Communities and Environment Study (SPACES): fourth report 2005. *Archaeology in Wales* 45, 17–23.

Darvill, T., Davies, R.V., Morgan Evans, D., Ixer, R.A. and Wainwright, G. 2007a. Strumble-Preseli Ancient Communities and Environment Study (SPACES): fifth report 2006. *Archaeology in Wales* 46, 100–7.

Darvill, T., Wainwright, G. and Driver, T. 2007b. Among tombs and stone circles on Banc Du. *British Archaeology* 92, 27–9.

Davey, P.J. (ed.) 1999. *Recent archaeological research on the Isle of Man*. Oxford: Archaeopress.

Davey, P. 2004. The Isle of Man: central or marginal in the Neolithic of the northern Irish Sea? In V. Cummings and C. Fowler (eds), *The Neolithic of the Irish Sea: materiality and traditions of practice*, 129–44. Oxford: Oxbow Books.

Davey, P. and Innes, J. 2003. The Early Neolithic and the Manx environment. In I. Armit, E. Murphy, E. Nelis and D. Simpson (eds), *Neolithic settlement in Ireland and western Britain*, 120–7. Oxford: Oxbow Books.

Davey, P. and Woodcock, J. 2003. Rheast Buigh, Patrick: middle Neolithic exploitation of the Manx uplands. In I. Armit, E. Murphy, E. Nelis and D. Simpson (eds), *Neolithic settlement in Ireland and western Britain*, 128–35. Oxford: Oxbow Books.

David, A. 1989. Some aspects of the human presence in west Wales during the Mesolithic. In C. Bonsall (ed.), *The Mesolithic in Europe*, 241–53. Edinburgh: John Donald.

David, A. 1999. Geophysical survey. In A. Whittle, J. Pollard and C. Grigson, *The harmony of symbols: the Windmill Hill causewayed enclosure, Wiltshire*, 17–23. Oxford: Oxbow Books.

David, A.E.U. 1990. *Palaeolithic and Mesolithic settlement in Wales with special reference to Dyfed*. Unpublished PhD thesis, University of Lancaster.

David, A. and Walker, E.A. 2004. Wales during the Mesolithic period. In A. Saville (ed.), *Mesolithic Scotland and its neighbours*, 299–337. Edinburgh: Society of Antiquaries of Scotland.

David, A. and Williams, G. 1995. Stone axe-head manufacture: new evidence from the Preseli Hills, west Wales. *Proceedings of the Prehistoric Society* 61, 433–60.

Davies, G.H. 1956. Maiden Bower near Dunstable. *Bedfordshire Archaeologist* 1, 98–101.

Davies, M. 1986a. Red Fescue Hole, Rhosili (SS 4266 8678). *Archaeology in Wales* 16, 34.

Davies, M. 1986b. Spurge Hole, Southgate (SS 5468 8730). *Archaeology in Wales* 16, 34.

Davies, O. 1937. Excavations at Ballyrenan, Co. Tyrone. *Journal of the Royal Society of Antiquaries of Ireland* 67, 89–100.

Davies, S.M., Bellamy, P.S., Heaton, M.J. and Woodward, P.J. 2002. *Excavations at Alington Avenue, Fordington, Dorchester, Dorset, 1984–7*. Dorchester: Dorset Natural History and Archaeological Society.

Davies, S.M., Woodward, P.J. and Ellison, A.B. 1991. The pottery. In P.J. Woodward, *The South Dorset ridgeway: survey and excavations 1977–84*, 96–101. Dorchester: Dorset Natural History and Archaeological Society.

Davis, R.V., Howard, H. and Smith. I.F.S. 1988. The petrological identification of stone implements from south-west England. In T.H.McK. Clough and W.A. Cummins (eds), *Stone axe studies volume 2. The petrology of prehistoric stone implements from the British Isles*, 14–20. London: Council for British Archaeology.

Davison, K., Dolukhanov, P.M., Sarson, G.R. and Shukurov, A. 2006. The role of waterways in the spread of the Neolithic. *Journal of Archaeological Science* 33, 641–52.

Dawes, J.D. 1987. Anatomical reports on the scattered human bone from the ditches O.D. 27 and 43, and ID 370 and the cremation and inhumation from the interior of the earthwork. In R. Robertson-Mackay, 'The Neolithic causewayed enclosure at Staines, Surrey: excavations 1961–63'. *Proceedings of the Prehistoric Society* 53, microfiche 12–20.

Dawson, M. 1993. Bedford southern bypass. *South Midlands Archaeology* 23, 7–12.

Dawson, M. 1996. Plantation Quarry, Willington: excavations 1988–1991. *Bedfordshire Archaeology* 22, 2–49.

Dawson, M. 2000. The Mesolithic interlude. In M. Dawson (ed.), *Prehistoric, Roman, and Post-Roman landscapes of the Great Ouse valley*, 46–50. London: Council for British Archaeology.

Dawson, T.E., Mambelli, S., Plamboeck, A.H., Templer, P.H. and Tu, K.P. 2002. Stable isotopes in plant ecology. *Annual Review of Ecology and Systematics* 33, 507–59.

Dean, J.S. 1978. Independent dating in archaeology. In M.B. Schiffer (ed.), *Advances in Archaeological Method and Theory, 1*, 223–65. New York: Academic Press.

Dee, M. and Bronk Ramsey, C. 2000. Refinement of graphite target production at ORAU. *Nuclear Instruments and Methods in Physics Research B* 172, 449–53.

Deetz, J. and Dethlefsen, E. 1965. The Doppler effect and archaeology: a consideration of the spatial aspects of seriation. *Southwestern Journal of Anthropology* 21, 196–206.

de Grooth, M.E.Th. 1997. The social context of Neolithic flint mining in Europe. In R. Schild and Z. Sulgostowska (eds), *Man and flint. Proceedings of the VIIth International Flint Symposium Warszawa-Ostrowiec Swietokrzyski September 1995*, 71–5. Warsaw: Institute of Archaeology and Ethnology.

Dehling, H. and van der Plicht, J. 1993. Statistical problems in calibrating radiocarbon dates. *Radiocarbon* 35, 239–44.

de Jong, A.F.M., Mook, W.G. and Becker, B. 1986. High-precision calibration of the radiocarbon time scale, 3930–3230 cal BC. *Radiocarbon* 28, 954–60.

de Jong, A.F.M., Mook, W.G. and Becker, B. 1989. Corrected calibration of the radiocarbon time scale, 3904–3203 cal BC. *Radiocarbon* 31, 201–5.

de Laet, S.J. 1982. *La Belgique d'avant les Romains*. Wetteren: Editions Universa.

Delaney, C.F.G. and McAulay, I.R. 1959. A radiocarbon dating system using scintillation techniques. *Scientific Procedings of the Royal Society of Dublin, Series A*, 1, 1–20.

Delibrias, M., Guillier, T. and Labeyrie, J. 1972. Gif natural radiocarbon measurements VII. *Radiocarbon* 14, 280–320.

Demoule, J.-P. 2007a. De l'Europe centrale au Bassin parisien (5200–4400). In J.-P. Demoule, R. Cottiaux, J. Dubouloz, F. Giligny, L. Jallot, L. Monolakakis, G. Marchand and I. Sénépart, *La révolution néolithique en France*, 42–59. Paris: La Découverte.

Demoule, J.-P. 2007b. L'origine des inegalités. In J.-P. Demoule, R. Cottiaux, J. Dubouloz, F. Giligny, L. Jallot, L. Monolakakis, G. Marchand and I. Sénépart, *La révolution néolithique en France*, 78–95. Paris: La Découverte.

Demoule, J.-P., Cottiaux, R., Dubouloz, J., Giligny, F., Jallot, L., Monolakakis, L., Marchand, G. and Sénépart, I. 2007a. *La révolution néolithique en France*. Paris: La Découverte.

Demoule, J.-P., Dubouloz, J. and Monolakakis, L. 2007b. L'émergence des premières sociétés complexes (4500–3500). In J.-P. Demoule, R. Cottiaux, J. Dubouloz, F. Giligny, L. Jallot, L. Monolakakis, G. Marchand and I.Sénépart, *La révolution néolithique en France*, 61–77. Paris: La Découverte.

Dennell, R. 1987. Accelerator dating: the first years reviewed. *Antiquity* 61, 137–8.

DeNiro, M.J. 1985. Postmortem preservation and alteration of *in vivo* bone collagen isotope ratios in relation to palaeodietary reconstruction. *Nature* 317, 806–9.

Desloges, J. 1986. Fouilles des mines silex sur le site néolithique de Bretteville-le-Rabet (Calvados). In Actes du Xe Colloque Interrégional sur le Néolithique. Caen 30 Septembre–2 Octobre 1983. *Revue Archéologique de l'Ouest* supplément 1, 73–101.

Desloges, J. 1990. Techniques d'acquisition de silex au néolithique, l'exemple de Bretteville-le-Rabet (Calvados). In *L'homme et l'industrie en Normandie du néolithique à nos jours: actes du congrès régional des sociétés historiques et archéologiques de Normandie, L'Aigle, 26–30 octobre 1988,* 147–57. Bulletin Spécial de la Société Archéologique et Historique de l'Orne. Alençon: Société Historique et Archéologique de l'Orne.

Desterbecq, D. 2005. *Résumé du rapport de fouille 2005. Synthèse des informations récoltées depuis 2002 sur les puits 79.1 and 79.2 à Petit-Spiennes*. Http://minesdespiennes.org/textes/synthesedesinformationsrecolteesdepuis2002.pdf.

Deumer, J.M., Gilot, E. and Capron, P.C. 1964. Louvain natural radiocarbon measurements II. *Radiocarbon* 6, 160–6.

de Valera, R. 1960. The court cairns of Ireland. *Proceedings of the Royal Irish Academy* 60C, 9–140.

de Valera, R. and O'Nulláin, S. 1964. *Survey of the megalithic tombs of Ireland: volume 2, Co. Mayo*. Dublin: The Stationery Office.

Dieckmann, B., Maier, U. and Vogt, R. 1997. Hornstaad-Hörnle, eine der ältesten jungsteinzeitlichen Ufersiedlungen am Bodensee. In H. Schlichtherle (ed.), *Pfahlbauten rund um die Alpen*, 15–21. Stuttgart: Theiss.

Dietler, M. 1996. Feasts and commensal politics in the political economy: food, power and status in prehistoric Europe. In P. Wiessner and W. Schiefenhövel (eds), *Food and the status quest: an interdisciplinary perspective*, 87–125. Providence: Berghahn.

Dietler, M. and Hayden, B. (eds) 2001. *Feasts: archaeological and ethnographic perspectives on food, politics and power*. Washington (DC): Smithsonian Institution Press.

Dimbleby, G.W. 1965. The buried soil under outer bank V and pollen analysis and charcoal identifications. In I.F. Smith, *Windmill Hill and Avebury: excavations by Alexander Keiller, 1925–1939*, 34–8. Oxford: Clarendon Press.

Dimbleby, G.W. and Evans, J.G. 1972. Broome Heath: the pre-enclosure environment. In G.J. Wainwright, 'The excavation of a Neolithic settlement on Broome Heath, Ditchingham, Norfolk'. *Proceedings of the Prehistoric Society* 38, 86–91.

Dimbleby, G.W. and Evans, J.G. 1974. Pollen and landsnail analysis of calcareous soils. *Journal of Archaeological Science* 1, 117–33.

Dines, H.G., Holmes, S.C.A. and Robbie, J.A. 1954. *Geology of the country around Chatham*. London: HMSO.

Dix, J. and Scaife, R. 2000. Location, geology and topography. In M.J. Allen and J. Gardiner, *Our changing coast: a survey of the intertidal archaeology of Langstone harbour, Hampshire*, 8–16. York: Council for British Archaeology.

Dixon, P. 1971. *Crickley Hill: third report 1971*. Cheltenham: Gloucestershire College of Art and Design.

Dixon, P. 1972a. Excavations at Crickley Hill. *Antiquity* 46, 49–52.

Dixon, P. 1972b. *Crickley Hill: fourth report 1972*. Cheltenham: Gloucestershire College of Art and Design.

Dixon, P. 1979. A Neolithic and Iron Age site on a hilltop in southern England. *Scientific American* 241, 142–50.

Dixon, P. 1981. Crickley Hill. *Current Archaeology* 76, 145–7.

Dixon, P. 1988a. The Neolithic settlements on Crickley Hill. In C. Burgess, P. Topping, C. Mordant and M. Maddison (eds), *Enclosures and defences in the Neolithic of western Europe*, 75–88. Oxford: British Archaeological Reports.

Dixon, P. 1988b. Crickley Hill 1969–1987. *Current Archaeology* 110, 73–8.

Dixon, P. 1994. *Crickley Hill. Volume 1. The hillfort defences*. Nottingham: Crickley Hill Trust and the Department of Archaeology, University of Nottingham.

Dixon, P. 2005. Thirty-five years at Crickley. *Current Archaeology* 200, 390–5.

Dixon, P. and Borne, P. 1977. *Crickley Hill and Gloucestershire prehistory*. Gloucester: Crickley Hill Archaeological Trust.

Dolan, B. and Cooney, G. 2010. Lambay lithics: the analysis of two surface collections from Lambay, Co. Dublin. *Proceedings of the Royal Irish Academy* 110C, 1–33.

Dolukhanov, P.M., Shukurov, A., Davison, K., Sarson, G., Gerasimenko, N.P., Pashkevich, G.A., Vybornov, A.A., Kovalyukh, N.N., Skripkin, V.V., Zaitseva, G.I. and Sapelko, T.V. 2009. The spread of the Neolithic in the south-east European plain: radiocarbon chronology, subsistence, and environment. *Radiocarbon* 51, 783–93.

Donahue, D.J., Beck, J.W., Biddulph, D., Burr, G.S., Courtney, C., Daman, P.E., Hatheway, A.L., Hewitt, L., Jull, A.J.T., Lange, T., Litton, N., Maddock, R., McHargur, L.R., O'Malley, J.M. and Toolin, L.J. 1997. Status of the NSF-Arizona AMS laboratory. *Nuclear Instruments and Methods in Physics Research B* 123, 51–6.

Dossin, J.M., Deumer, J.M. and Capron, P.C. 1962. Louvain Natural Radiocarbon Measurements I. *Radiocarbon* 4, 95–9.

Dowd, M. 2002. Kilgreany, Co. Waterford: biography of a cave. *Journal of Irish Archaeology* 11, 77–97.

Dowd, M. 2008. The use of caves for funerary and ritual practices in Neolithic Ireland. *Antiquity* 82, 305–17.

Down, A. and Welch, M. 1990. *Chichester excavations VII*. Chichester: Chichester: Chichester District Council.

Down, C. 1997. *The archaeological monitoring of groundworks at The Trundle, Singleton, West Sussex*. Chichester: Southern Archaeology.

Doyle, K., Grassman, B.A. and Weston, P. 2005. *Coxford Abbey Quarry, East Rudham, Norfolk. 'Strip, map & sample'. Archaeological excavation phase 1A*. Unpublished client report. Hertford: Archaeological Solutions Ltd.

Drennan, R. 1996. One for all and all for one: accounting for variability without losing sight of regularities in the development of complex society. In J.E. Arnold (ed.), *Emergent complexity: the evolution of intermediate societies*, 25–34. Ann Arbor: International Monographs in Prehistory.

Dresser, Q. 1985. University College Cardiff radiocarbon dates I. *Radiocarbon* 27, 338–85.

Drew, C.D. and Piggott, S. 1936. The excavation of long barrow 163a on Thickthorn Down, Dorset. *Proceedings of the Prehistoric Society* 2, 77–96.

Drewett, P. 1975a. The excavation of an oval burial mound of the third millennium B.C. at Alfriston, East Sussex, 1974. *Proceedings of the Prehistoric Society* 41, 119–52.

Drewett, P. 1975b. A Neolithic pot from Selmeston, East Sussex. *Sussex Archaeological Collections* 113, 193–4.

Drewett, P. 1977. The excavation of a Neolithic causewayed enclosure at Offham Hill, East Sussex, 1976. *Proceedings of the Prehistoric Society* 43, 201–42.

Drewett, P.L. 1978. Neolithic Sussex. In P.L. Drewett (ed.), *Archaeology in Sussex to AD 1500: essays for Eric Holden*, 23–9. London: Council for British Archaeology.

Drewett, P. 1981. A sample excavation at Bevis's Thumb, Compton, West Sussex. *University of London Bulletin of the Institute of Archaeology* 18, 22–4.

Drewett, P. 1982. *The archaeology of Bullock Down, Eastbourne, East Sussex. The development of a landscape*. Lewes: Sussex Archaeological Society.

Drewett, P.L. 1985. Neolithic pottery. In O. Bedwin and R. Holgate, 'Excavations at Copse Farm, Oving, West Sussex'. *Proceedings of the Prehistoric Society* 51, 220–1.

Drewett, P.L. 1986. The excavation of a Neolithic oval barrow at North Marden, West Sussex, 1982. *Proceedings of the Prehistoric Society* 52, 31–52.

Drewett, P. 1994. Dr V. Seton Williams' excavations at Combe Hill, 1962, and the role of Neolithic causewayed enclosures in Sussex. *Sussex Archaeological Collections* 132, 7–24.

Drewett, P. 2003. Taming the wild: the first farming communities in Sussex. In D. Rudling (ed.), *The archaeology of Sussex to AD 2000*, 39–46. Great Dunham: Heritage Marketing and Publications Ltd for the Centre for Continuing Education, University of Sussex.

Drewett, P. and Bedwin, O.R. 1981. Appendix: note on radiocarbon dates from Neolithic enclosures in Sussex. In O. Bedwin, 'Excavations at the Neolithic enclosure on Bury Hill, Houghton, West Sussex, 1979'. *Proceedings of the Prehistoric Society* 47, 86.

Drewett, P., Rudling, D. and Gardiner, M. 1988. *The south east to AD 1000*. London: Longman.

Driver, T. 1997. Norton: the first interrupted ditch enclosure in Wales? *Aerial Archaeology Research Group News* 15, 17–19.

Drury, P.J. 1978. *Excavations at Little Waltham 1970–71*. London and Chelmsford: Council for British Archaeology and Chelmsford Excavation Committee.

Dubouloz, J. 1998. Réflexions sur le Michelsberg ancien en Bassin parisien. In J. Biel, H. Schlichtherle, M. Strobel and A. Zeeb (eds), *Die Michelsberger Kultur und ihre Randgebiete – Probleme der Entstehung, Chronologie und des Siedlungswesens*, 9–20. Stuttgart: Theiss.

Dubouloz, J. 2003. Datation absolue du premier Néolithique du Bassin parisien: complément et relecture des données RRBP et VSG. *Bulletin de la Société Préhistorique Française* 100, 671–89.

Dubouloz, J., Hamard, D. and Le Bolloch, M. 1997. Composantes fonctionelles et symboliques d'un site exceptionnel: Bazoches-sur-Vesle (Aisne), 4000 ans av. J.-C. In A. Bocquet (ed.), *Espaces physiques, espaces sociaux dans l'analyse interne des sites du Néolithique à l'Âge du Fer*, 127–44. Paris: Éditions du Comité des Travaux Historiques et Scientifiques.

Dubouloz, J., Le Bolloch, M. and Ilett, M. 1988. Middle Neolithic enclosures in the Aisne valley. In C. Burgess, P. Topping, C. Mordant and M. Maddison (eds), *Enclosures and defences in the Neolithic of western Europe*, 209–26. Oxford: British Archaeological Reports.

Dubouloz, J., Mordant D. and Prestreau, M. 1991. Les enceintes "néolithiques" du Bassin parisien. Variabilité structurelle, chronologique et culturelle. Place dans l'évolution socio-économique du Néolithique regional. Modèles interprétatifs préliminaires. In A. Beeching, D. Binder, J.-C. Blanchet, C. Constantin, J. Dubouloz, R. Martinez, D. Mordant, J.-P. Thévenot and J. Vaquer (eds), *Identité du Chasséen*, 211–29. Nemours: Mémoires du Musée de Préhistoire de l'Ile de France 4.

Duller, G.A.T. 2004. Luminescence dating of Quaternary sediments: recent advances. *Journal of Quaternary Science* 19, 183–92.

Duller, G.A.T. 2008. *Luminescence dating: guidelines on using luminescence dating in archaeology*. Swindon: English Heritage.

Dunning, G.C. 1966. Neolithic occupation sites in east Kent. *Antiquaries Journal* 46, 1–25.

Dunning, G.C. 1976. Salmonsbury, Bourton-on-the Water, Gloucestershire. In D.W. Harding (ed.), *Hillforts: later prehistoric earthworks in Britain and Ireland*, 75–118. London: Academic Press.

Dunning, G.C. and Wheeler, R.E.M. 1931. A barrow at Dunstable, Bedfordshire. *Archaeological Journal* 88, 193–217.

Dyer, J. 1955. Maiden Bower near Dunstable. Part 1. *Bedfordshire Archaeologist* 1, 47–52.

Dyer, J. 1961. Maiden Bower. *Bedfordshire Magazine* 7, 320.

Dyer, J. 1962. Neolithic and Bronze Age sites at Barton Hill Farm, Bedfordshire. *Bedfordshire Archaeological Journal* 1, 1–24.

Dyer, J. 1964. A secondary Neolithic camp at Waulud's Bank, Leagrave. *Bedfordshire Archaeological Journal* 2, 1–15.

Dyson, L., Shand, G. and Stevens, S. 2000. Causewayed enclosures. *Current Archaeology* 168, 470–2.

Earle, T. 1997. *How chiefs come to power: the political economy in prehistory*. Stanford: Stanford University Press.

Ebbesen, K. 2007. *Danske dysser: Danish dolmens*. København: Attika.

Ebersbach, R. 2002. *Von Bauern und Rindern: eine Ökosystemanalyse zur Bedeutung der Rinderhaltung in bäuerlichen Gesellschaften als Grundlage zur Modellbildung im Neolithikum*. Basel: Schwabe.

Edmonds, M. 1993a. Interpreting causewayed enclosures in

the past and the present. In C. Tilley (ed.), *Interpretative archaeology*, 99–142. Oxford: Berg.

Edmonds, M. 1993b. Towards a context for production and exchange: the polished stone axe in earlier Neolithic Britain. In C. Scarre and F. Healy (eds), *Trade and exchange in prehistoric Europe*, 69–86. Oxford: Oxbow Books.

Edmonds, M. 1995. *Stone tools and society: working stone in Neolithic and Bronze Age Britain.* London: Batsford.

Edmonds, M. 1998. Polished stone axes and associated artefacts. In F. Pryor, *Etton: excavations at a Neolithic causewayed enclosure near Maxey, Cambridgeshire, 1982–87*, 260–8. London: English Heritage.

Edmonds, M. 1999. *Ancestral geographies of the Neolithic: landscapes, monuments and memory*. London and New York: Routledge.

Edmonds, M. 2006. The axe and the mound. In C. Evans and I. Hodder, *A woodland archaeology. Neolithic sites at Haddenham: the Haddenham project volume 1*, 352–3. Cambridge: McDonald Institute for Archaeological Research.

Edmonds, M. and Bellamy, P. 1991. The flaked stone. In N. Sharples, *Maiden Castle: excavations and field survey 1985–6*, 214–29. London: English Heritage.

Edmonds, M., Evans, C. and Gibson, D. 1999. Assembly and collection – lithic complexes in the Cambridgeshire fenlands. *Proceedings of the Prehistoric Society* 65, 47–82.

Edmonds, M. and Thomas, J.S. 1993. *Anglesey Archaeological Landscape Project: fourth interim report*. Lampeter: Saint David's University College.

Edwards, C.J., Bollongino, R., Scheu, A., Chamberlain, A., Tresset, A., Vigne, J.-D., Baird, J.F., Larson, G., Heupin, T.H., Ho, S.Y.W., Shapiro, B., Czerwinski, P., Freeman, A.R., Arbogast, R.-M., Arndt, B., Bartosiewicz, L., Benecke, N., Budja, M., Chaix, L., Choyke, A.M., Coqueugniot, E., Döhle, H.-J., Göldner, H., Hartz, S., Helmer, D., Herzig, B., Hongo, H., Mashkour, M., Özdogan, M., Pucher, E., Roth, G., Schade-Lindig, S., Schmölcke, U., Schulting, R., Stephan, E., Uerpmann, H.-P., Vörös, I., Bradley, D.G. and Burger, J. 2007. A mitochondrial history of the aurochs (*Bos primigenius primigenius*) in Europe. *Proceedings of the Royal Society* B, 274, 1377–85.

Edwards, D.A. 1978. The air photographs collection of the Norfolk Archaeological Unit, third report. *East Anglian Archaeology* 8, 87–105. Gressenhall: Norfolk Archaeological Unit.

Edwards, K.J. 2004. People, environmental impacts, and the changing landscapes of Neolithic and Early Bronze Age times. In I.A.G. Shepherd and G.J. Barclay (eds), *Scotland in Ancient Europe: the Neolithic and Early Bronze Age of Scotland in their European context*, 55–69. Edinburgh: Society of Antiquaries of Scotland.

Egging Dinwiddy, K. and Schuster, J. 2009. Thanet's longest excavation: archaeological investigations along the route of the Weatherlees-Margate-Broadstairs Wastewater Pipeline. In P. Andrews, K. Egging Dinwiddy, C. Ellis, E. Firth, A. Hutcheson, C. Philpotts, A. B. Powell and J. Schuster, *Kentish sites and sites of Kent: a miscellany of four archaeological excavations*, 64–9. Salisbury: Wessex Archaeology.

Eisele, K., Rind, M. and Sorcan, B. 2003. Ausgrabungen und Dokumentationen im neolithischen Hornsteinbergwerk von Abensberg-Arnhofen 2000 bis 2002. In M. Rind (ed.), *Wer andern eine Grube gräbt... Archäologie im Landkreis Kelheim*, Band 4, 42–51. Büchenbach: Dr. Faustus.

Eisenhauer, U. 2003. Jüngerbandkeramische Residenzregeln: Patrilokalität in Talheim. In J. Eckert, U. Eisenhauer and A. Zimmermann (eds), *Archäologische Perspektiven: Analysen und Interpretationen im Wandel. Festschrift für Jens Lüning zum 65. Geburtstag*, 561–73. Rahden: Marie Leidorf.

Ellis, C. 1986. The postglacial molluscan succession of the South Downs dry valleys. In G. de G. Sieveking and M.B. Hart (eds), *The scientific study of flint and chert*, 175–84. Cambridge: Cambridge University Press.

Ellis, C. 2004. *A prehistoric ritual complex at Eynesbury, Cambridgeshire: excavation of a multi- period site in the Great Ouse valley, 2000–2001*. Salisbury: Trust for Wessex Archaeology Ltd.

Elton, G. 1974. *England under the Tudors* (second edition). London: Methuen.

Engelhardt, B. and Binsteiner, A. 1988. Vorbericht über die Ausgrabungen 1984–1986 im neolitischen Feuersteinabbaurevier von Arnhofen. *Germania* 66, 1–28.

English Heritage 1998. *Dendrochronology: guidelines on producing and interpreting dendrochronological dates*. London: English Heritage.

Entwistle, R. and Bowden, M. 1991. Cranborne Chase: the molluscan evidence. In J. Barrett, R. Bradley and M. Hall (eds), *Papers on the prehistoric archaeology of Cranborne Chase*, 20–48. Oxford: Oxbow Books.

Eogan, G. 1984. *Excavations at Knowth, 1*. Dublin: Royal Irish Academy.

Eogan, G. 1986. *Knowth and the passage-tombs of Ireland*. London: Thames and Hudson.

Eogan, G. 1991. Prehistoric and early historic culture change at Brugh na Bóinne. *Proceedings of the Royal Irish Academy* 91C, 105–32.

Eogan, G. and Roche, H. 1997. *Excavations at Knowth, 2: settlement and ritual sites of the fourth and third millennia BC*. Dublin: Royal Irish Academy.

Eogan, G. and Roche, H. 1998. Further evidence for Neolithic habitation at Knowth, Co. Meath. *Riocht na Midhe* 9(4), 1–9.

Evans, C. 1988a. Excavations at Haddenham, Cambridgeshire: a 'planned' enclosure and its regional affinities. In C. Burgess, P. Topping, C. Mordant and M. Maddison (eds), *Enclosures and defences in the Neolithic of western Europe*, 127–48. Oxford: British Archaeological Reports.

Evans, C. 1988b. Acts of enclosure: a consideration of concentrically-organised causewayed enclosures. In J.C. Barrett and I. Kinnes (eds), *The archaeology of context in the Neolithic and Bronze Age: recent trends*, 85–96. Sheffield: Department of Archaeology and Prehistory.

Evans, C. 1988c. Monuments and analogy: the interpretation of causewayed enclosures. In C. Burgess, P. Topping, C. Mordant and M. Maddison (eds), *Enclosures and defences in the Neolithic of western Europe*, 47–73. Oxford: British Archaeological Reports.

Evans, C. and Hodder, I. 2006. *A woodland archaeology. Neolithic sites at Haddenham: the Haddenham project volume 1*. Cambridge: McDonald Institute for Archaeological Research.

Evans, C. and Knight, M. 2000. A Fenland delta: later prehistoric land-use in the lower Ouse reaches. In M. Dawson (ed.), *Prehistoric, Roman, and Post-Roman landscapes of the Great Ouse valley*, 89–106. York: Council for British Archaeology.

Evans, C. and Knight, M. 2001. The 'community of builders': the Barleycroft post alignments. In J. Brück (ed.), *Bronze Age landscapes: tradition and transformation*, 83–98. Oxford: Oxbow Books.

Evans, C. and Webley, L. 2003. *A delta landscape: the Over lowland excavations II*. Unpublished document. Cambridge: Cambridge Archaeological Unit.

Evans, C., Edmonds, M. and Boreham, S. 2006. 'Total archaeology' and model landscapes: excavation of the Great Wilbraham causewayed enclosure, Cambridgeshire, 1975–76. *Proceedings of the Prehistoric Society* 72, 113–62.

Evans, C., Appleby, G., Lucy, S. and Regan, R. forthcoming. *Prehistoric and Roman fen-edge communities at Colne Fen, Earith: the archaeology of the Lower Ouse valley, Volume I*. Cambridge: McDonald Institute for Archaeological Research.

Evans, C., Pollard, J. and Knight, M. 1999. Life in woods: tree-throws, 'settlement' and forest cognition. *Oxford Journal of Archaeology* 18, 241–54.

Evans, E.E. 1938. Doey's Cairn, Dunloy, County Antrim. *Ulster Journal of Archaeology* 1, 59–78.

Evans, E.E. 1939. Excavations at Carnanbane, County Londonderry: a double horned cairn. *Proceedings of the Royal Irish Academy* 45C, 1–12.

Evans, E.E. 1953. *Lyles Hill: a late Neolithic site in County Antrim*. Belfast: HMSO.

Evans, E.E. and Davies, O. 1935. Excvation of a chambered horned cairn, Browndod, Co. Antrim. *Proceedings of the Belfast Natural History and Antiquarian Society* 1935, 70–87.

Evans, J.G. 1966. Land mollusca from the Neolithic enclosure on Windmill Hill. *Wiltshire Archaeological and Natural History Magazine* 61, 91–2.

Evans, J.G. 1972. *Land snails in archaeology with special reference to the British Isles*. London and New York: Seminar Press.

Evans, J.G. 1981. Subfossil land-snail faunas from Grimes Graves and other Neolithic flint mines. In R.J. Mercer, *Grimes Graves, Norfolk. Excavations 1971–72: volume I*, 104–11. London: HMSO.

Evans, J.G. 1991. The environment. In N. Sharples, *Maiden Castle: excavations and field survey 1985–6*, 250–3. London: English Heritage.

Evans, J.G. and Rouse, A. 1991. The land mollusca. In N. Sharples, *Maiden Castle: excavations and field survey 1985–6*, 25. London: English Heritage.

Evans, J.G. and Smith, I.F. 1983. Excavations at Cherhill, North Wiltshire, 1967. *Proceedings of the Prehistoric Society* 49, 43–117.

Evans, J.G., Pitts, M.W. and Williams, D. 1985. An excavation at Avebury, Wiltshire, 1982. *Proceedings of the Prehistoric Society* 51, 305–10.

Evans, J.G., Limbrey, S., Máté, I. and Mount, R. 1993. An environmental history of the upper Kennet valley, Wiltshire, for the last 10,000 years. *Proceedings of the Prehistoric Society* 59, 139–95.

Evans, J.G., Rouse, A. and Sharples, N. 1988. The landscape setting of causewayed camps: recent work on the Maiden Castle enclosure. In J.C. Barrett and I. Kinnes (eds), *The archaeology of context in the Neolithic and Bronze Age: recent trends,* 73–8. Sheffield: Department of Archaeology and Prehistory.

Evans, J.H. 1950. Kentish megalithic types. *Archaeologia Cantiana* 63, 63–81.

Evens, E.D., Smith, I.F. and Wallis, F.S. 1972. The petrological identification of stone implements from south-western England. *Proceedings of the Prehistoric Society* 58, 255–75.

Evin, J., Marechal, J. and Marien, G. 1983. Lyon natural radiocarbon measurements IX. *Radiocarbon* 25, 59–128.

Fairbairn, A. 1999a. Charred plant remains. In A. Whittle, J. Pollard and C. Grigson, *The harmony of symbols: the Windmill Hill causewayed enclosure, Wiltshire*, 138–56. Oxford: Oxbow Books.

Fairbairn, A. 1999b. Palaeobotanical remains. In T. Darvill, *Billown Neolithic landscape project, Isle of Man. Fourth report: 1998*, 14–22. Bournemouth and Douglas: Bournemouth University and Manx National Heritage.

Fairbairn, A. 2000. Charred seeds, fruits and tubers. In A. Whittle, J.J. Davies, I. Dennis, A.S. Fairbairn and M. Hamilton, 'Neolithic activity and occupation outside Windmill Hill causewayed enclosure, Wiltshire: survey and excavation 1992–93'. *Wiltshire Archaeological and Natural History Magazine* 93, 168–75.

Fairweather, A.D. and Ralston, I. B.M. 1993. The Neolithic timber hall at Balbridie, Grampian region, Scotland: the building, the date, the plant macrofossils. *Antiquity* 67, 313–23.

Fallon, S.J., Guilderson, T.P. and Brown, T. A. 2007. CAMS/LLNL ion source efficiency revisited. *Nuclear Instruments and Methods in Physics Research B*, 259, 106–10.

Farrar, R.A.H. 1951. Archaeological fieldwork in Dorset in 1951. *Proceedings of the Dorset Natural History and Archaeology Society* 73, 85–115.

Farrar, R.A.H. 1957. A Neolithic pit at Sutton Poyntz, Weymouth. *Proceedings of the Dorset Natural History and Archaeological Society* 79, 112–13.

Farruggia, J.-P., Guichard, Y. and Hachem, L. 1996. Les ensembles funéraires rubanés de Menneville (Derrière le Village) (Aisne). *Actes du 18° Colloque Interrégional sur le Néolithique, Dijon, 1991,* 119–74.

Febvre, L. 1973. *A new kind of history: from the writings of Febvre.* (Edited by P. Burke, translated by K. Folca.) London: Routledge and Kegan Paul.

Fentress, J. and Wickham, C. 1992. *Social memory*. Oxford: Blackwell.

Fiedel, S.J. and Anthony, D.W. 2003. Deerslayers, pathfinders and Icemen: origins of the European Neolithic as seen from the frontier. In M. Rockman and J. Steele (eds), *Colonization of unfamiliar landscapes: the archaeology of adaptation*, 144–68. London: Routledge.

Field, D. 1997. The landscape of extraction. In P. Topping (ed.), *Neolithic landscapes*, 55–67. Oxford: Oxbow Books.

Field, D. 2004. Sacred geographies in the Neolithic of south-east England. In J. Cotton and D. Field (eds), *Towards a New Stone Age: aspects of the Neolithic in south-east England*, 154–63. York: Council for British Archaeology.

Field, D. 2008. *Use of land in central southern England during the Neolithic and early Bronze Age*. Oxford: British Archaeological Reports.

Field, D. and Cotton, J. 1987. Neolithic Surrey: a survey of the evidence. In J. Bird and D.G. Bird (eds), *The archaeology of Surrey to 1540*, 71–96. Guildford: Surrey Archaeological Society.

Field, L.F. 1939. Castle Hill, Newhaven. *Sussex Archaeological Collections* 80, 263–8.

Field, N.H., Matthews, C.L. and Smith, I.F. 1964. New Neolithic sites in Dorset and Bedfordshire, with a note on the distribution of Neolithic storage pits in Britain. *Proceedings of the Prehistoric Society* 30, 352–81.

Finlayson, B. and Warren, G.M. (eds) 2010. *Landscapes in transition*. Oxford and London: Oxbow Books and Council for British Research in the Levant (Levant Supplementary Series 8).

Firman, R.J. 1994. Crickley Hill: the geological setting and its archaeological relevance. In P. Dixon, *Crickley Hill. Volume 1. The hillfort defences*, 11–24. Nottingham: Crickley Hill Trust and the Department of Archaeology, University of Nottingham.

Firth, A. 2000. Development-led archaeology in coastal environments: investigations at Queenborough, Motney Hill and Gravesend in Kent, UK. In K. Pye, K. Allen and J.R.L. Allen (eds), *Coastal and estuarine environments: sedimentology, geomorphology and geoarchaeology*, 403–17. London: Geological Society.

Fischer, A. 2002. Food for feasting? An evaluation of explanations of the neolithisation of Denmark and southern Sweden. In A. Fischer and K. Kristiansen (eds), *The Neolithisation of Denmark: 150 years of debate*, 343–93. Sheffield: J.R. Collis Publications.

Fishpool, M. 1999. Land mollusca. In A. Whittle, J. Pollard and C. Grigson, *The harmony of symbols: the Windmill Hill causewayed enclosure, Wiltshire*, 127–38. Oxford: Oxbow Books.

Fitzpatrick, A.P. 1992. Westhampnett bypass excavations. *PAST* 13, 1–2.

Fitzpatrick, A.P. 1997. *Archaeological excavations on the route of the A27 Westhampnett bypass, West Sussex, 1992. Volume 2: the Late Iron Age, Romano-British, and Anglo-Saxon cemeteries*. Salisbury: Wessex Archaeology.

Fitzpatrick, A.P., Powell, A.B. and Allen, M.J. 2008. *Archaeological excavations on the route of the A27 Westhampnett Bypass, West Sussex, 1992. Volume 1: Late Upper Palaeolithic–Anglo-Saxon*. Wessex Archaeology Report 21. Salisbury: Trust for Wessex Archaeology Ltd.

Fitzpatrick, A.P., Butterworth, C.A. and Grove, J. 1999. *Prehistoric and Roman sites in east Devon: the A30 Honiton to Exeter improvement DBFO, 1996–9*. Salisbury: Wessex Archaeology.

Fleming, A. 2005. Megaliths and post-modernism: the case of Wales. *Antiquity* 79, 921–32.

Focken, U. 2004. Feeding fish with diets of different ratios of C3- and C4-plant-derived ingredients: a laboratory analysis with implications for the back-calculation of diet from stable isotope data. *Rapid Communications in Mass Spectrometry* 18, 2087–92.

Focken, U. and Becker, K. 1998. Metabolic fractionation of stable carbon isotopes: implications of different proximate compositions for studies of the aquatic food webs using $\delta^{13}C$ data. *Oecologia* 115, 337–43.

Fokkens, H. 1998. *Drowned landscape: the occupation of the western part of the Frisian-Drentian plateau, 4400 BC–AD 500*. Assen: Rijksdienst voor het Oudheidkundig Bodemonderzoek.

Foley, C. 1988. Only an old pile of stones. Creggandevesky court tomb, Co Tyrone. In A. Hamlin and C. Lynn (eds), *Pieces of the past: archaeological excavations by the Department of the Environment for Northern Ireland 1970–1986*, 3–5. Belfast: HMSO.

Forbes, H. 2007. *Meaning and identity in a Greek landscape: an archaeological ethnography*. Cambridge: Cambridge University Press.

Ford, S. 1986. A newly-discovered causewayed enclosure at Eton Wick, near Windsor, Berkshire. *Proceedings of the Prehistoric Society* 52, 319–20.

Ford, S. 1993. Excavations at Eton Wick. *Berkshire Archaeological Journal* 74, 27–36.

Ford, S. and Pine, J. 2003. Neolithic ring ditches and Roman landscape features at Horton (1989 to 1996). In S. Preston (ed.), *Prehistoric, Roman and Saxon sites in eastern Berkshire: excavations 1989–1997*, 13–85. Reading: Thames Valley Archaeological Services Ltd.

Ford, S. and Taylor, K. 2004. Neolithic occupation at Cippenham, Slough, Berkshire. In J. Cotton and D. Field (eds), *Towards a New Stone Age: aspects of the Neolithic in south-east England*, 99–104. York: Council for British Archaeology.

Ford, W.J. 2003. The Neolithic complex at Charlecote, Warwickshire. *Transactions of the Brimingham and Warwickshire Archaeological Society* 107, 1–39.

Forsythe, W. and Gregory, N. 2007. A Neolithic logboat from Greyabbey Bay, Co Down. *Ulster Journal of Archaeology* 66, 6–13.

Forty, A. and Küchler, S. (eds) 1999. *The art of forgetting*. Oxford and New York: Berg.

Fowler, C. 2001. Personhood and social relations in the British Neolithic with a case study from the Isle of Man. *Journal of Material Culture* 6, 137–63.

Fowler, C. 2002. Body parts: personhood and materiality in the earlier Manx Neolithic. In Y. Hamilakis, M. Pluciennik and S. Tarlow (eds), *Thinking through the body: archaeologies of corporeality*, 47–69. New York: Kluwer/Plenum.

Fowler, C. 2004a. *The archaeology of personhood: an anthropological approach*. London: Routledge.

Fowler, C. 2004b. In touch with the past? Monuments, bodies and the sacred in the Manx Neolithic and beyond. In V. Cummings and C. Fowler (eds), *The Neolithic of the Irish Sea: materiality and traditions of practice*, 91–102. Oxford: Oxbow Books.

Fowler, P.J. 2000. *Landscape plotted and pieced: landscape history and local archaeology in Fyfield and Overton, Wiltshire*. London: Society of Antiquaries of London.

Fox, A. 1963. Neolithic charcoal from Hembury. *Antiquity* 37, 228–9.

Foxhall, L. 1995. Monumental ambitions: the significance of posterity. In N. Spencer (ed.), *Time, tradition and society in Greek archaeology: bridging the 'Great Divide'*, 132–49. London: Routledge.

Foxhall, L. 2000. The running sands of time: archaeology and the short term. *World Archaeology* 31, 484–98.

Framework Archaeology 2006. *Landscape evolution in the middle Thames valley: Heathrow Terminal 5 excavations volume 1, Perry Oaks*. Oxford and Salisbury: Framework Archaeology.

Fredengren, C. 2007. Lake settlement project – from the deep waters. *Antiquity* 81, http://www.antiquity.ac.uk/ProjGall/fredengren/index.html

Fredengren, C. 2009. Lake-platforms at Lough Kinale – memory, reach and place: a Discovery programme Project in the Irish midlands. In S. McCartan, R. Schulting, G. Warren and P. Woodman (eds), *Mesolithic horizons: volume 2*, 882–6. Oxford: Oxbow Books.

Fredengren, C. 2010. Lough Kinale: the archaeology of lake and lakeshore. In C. Fredengren, A. Kilfeather and I. Stuijts, *Lough Kinale: studies of an Irish lake*, 129–66. Bray: Wordwell.

Freeman, S., Bishop, P., Bryant, C., Cook, G., Dougans, D., Ertunc, T., Fallick, A., Ganeshram, R., Maden, C., Naysmith, P., Schnabel, C., Scott, M., Summerfield, M. and Xu, S. 2007. The SUERC AMS laboratory after 3 years. *Nuclear Methods & Instruments in Physics B*, 259, 66–70.

French, C.A.I. 1994. *The archaeology along the A605 Elton–Haddon bypass, Cambridgeshire*. Fenland Archaeological Trust Monograph 2. Peterborough and Cambridge: Fenland Archaeological Trust and Cambridgeshire County Council.

French, C. 1998a. The relict palaeochannel systems in the

vicinity of the causewayed enclosure. In F. Pryor, *Etton: excavations at a Neolithic causewayed enclosure near Maxey, Cambridgeshire, 1982–87*, 5–7. London: English Heritage.

French, C. 1998b. Description of illustrated sections. In F. Pryor, *Etton: excavations at a Neolithic causewayed enclosure near Maxey, Cambridgeshire, 1982–87*, 51–66. London: English Heritage.

French, C. 1998c. Soils and sediments. In F. Pryor, *Etton: excavations at a Neolithic causewayed enclosure near Maxey, Cambridgeshire, 1982–87*, 311–31. London: English Heritage.

French, C. 1998d. Molluscs from the enclosure ditch. In F. Pryor, *Etton: excavations at a Neolithic causewayed enclosure near Maxey, Cambridgeshire, 1982–87*, 333–5. London: English Heritage.

French, C. 2003. *Geoarchaeology in action: studies in soil micromorphology and landscape evolution*. London and New York: Routledge.

French, C. 2005. Discussion and conclusions. In C. French and F. Pryor, *Archaeology and environment of the Etton landscape*, 163–71. Peterborough: Fenland Archaeological Trust.

French, C. 2006. Micromorphological analysis. In C. Evans and I. Hodder, *A woodland archaeology. Neolithic sites at Haddenham: the Haddenham project volume 1*, 39–41, 78–81. Cambridge: McDonald Institute for Archaeological Research.

French, C., Lewis, H., Allen, M.J., Green, M., Scaife, R. and Gardiner, J. 2007. *Prehistoric landscape development and human impact in the upper Allen valley, Cranborne Chase, Dorset*. Cambridge: McDonald Institute for Archaeological Research.

French, C., Lewis, H., Allen, M.J., Scaife, R.G. and Green, M. 2003. Archaeological and palaeo-environmental investigations of the upper Allen valley, Cranborne Chase, Dorset (1998–2000): a new model of earlier Holocene landscape development. *Proceedings of the Prehistoric Society* 69, 201–34.

French, C. and Pryor, F. 1992. *The south-west Fen Dyke survey project 1982–86*. Peterborough: Fenland Archaeological Trust.

French, C. and Pryor, F. 2005. *Archaeology and environment of the Etton landscape*. Peterborough: Fenland Archaeological Trust.

Froom, F.R. 1972a. A Mesolithic site at Wawcott, Kintbury. *Berkshire Archaeological Journal* 66, 23–44.

Froom, F.R. 1972b. Some Mesolithic sites in south-west Berkshire. *Berkshire Archaeological Journal* 66, 11–22.

Fry, M. 2000. *Coití: logboats from Northern Ireland*. Belfast: Environment and Heritage Service, Department of the Environment.

Funnell, J. D. 1996. *Resistivity survey at Whitehawk Neolithic causewayed enclosure*. London: Ancient Monuments Laboratory, English Heritage.

Gale, J.D. 1986. *Leaf arrowheads: the evidence from Crickley Hill and its wider implications*. Unpublished BA dissertation, Department of Archaeology, University of Nottingham.

Gale, R. 1991a. Charred wood. In N. Sharples, *Maiden Castle: excavations and field survey 1985–6*, 125–9. London: English Heritage.

Gale, R. 1991b. The environment and agricultural economy: charcoal identifications. In N. Sharples, *Maiden Castle: excavations and field survey 1985–6*, microfiche M6:C6–D10. London: English Heritage.

Gale, R. 1999. Charcoal. In T. Gent and H. Quinnell, 'Excavation of a causewayed enclosure and hillfort on Raddon Hill, Stokely Pomeroy'. *Proceedings of the Devon Archaeological Society* 57, 58–9.

Gale, R. 2002. The charcoal. In N. Page, *A477(T) Sageston-Redberth bypass: excavation of a Neolithic occupation site 2001*, 31–5. Unpublished client report. Llandeilo: Cambria Archeological Trust.

Gale, R. 2008. Charcoal. In M.J. Allen, M. Leivers and C. Ellis, 'Neolithic causewayed enclosures and later prehistoric farming: duality, imposition and the role of predecessors at Kingsborough, Isle of Sheppey, Kent, UK'. *Proceedings of the Prehistoric Society* 74, 274–7.

Galer, D. 2007. The human remains. In D. Benson and A. Whittle (eds), *Building memories: the Neolithic Cotswold long barrow at Ascott-under-Wychwood, Oxfordshire*, 189–220. Oxford: Oxbow Books.

Gandelin, M. 2007. *Les enceintes chasséennes de Villeneuve-Tolosane et Cugnaux dans leur contexte du Néolithique moyen européen*. Unpublished PhD thesis, École des Hautes Études en Sciences Sociales, Toulouse.

Gardiner, J. 1984. Lithic distributions and settlement patterns in central southern England. In R. Bradley and J. Gardiner (eds), *Neolithic studies*, 15–40. Oxford: British Archaeological Reports.

Gardiner, J.P. 1988. *The composition and distribution of Neolithic surface flint assemblages in central southern England*. Unpublished PhD thesis, University of Reading.

Gardiner, J. 1990. Flint procurement and Neolithic axe production on the South Downs: a re-assessment. *Oxford Journal of Archaeology* 9, 119–40.

Gardiner, J. 1991. The [earlier Neolithic] flint industries in the study area. In J.C. Barrett, R. Bradley and M. Green, *Landscape, monuments and society: the prehistory of Cranborne Chase*, 31. Cambridge: Cambridge University Press.

Gardiner, J. 2001. Catalogue of surviving flintwork from the Worthing group of mines. In M. Russell, *Rough quarries, rocks and hills: John Pull and the Neolithic flint mines of Sussex*, 202–23. Oxford: Oxbow Books.

Garrow, D. 2006. *Pits, settlement and deposition during the Neolithic and early Bronze Age in East Anglia*. Oxford: British Archaeological Reports.

Garrow, D. 2010. The temporality of materials: occupation practices in Eastern England during the 5th and 4th millennia BC. In B. Finlayson and G.M Warren (eds), *Landscapes in transition*, 208–18. Oxford and London: Oxbow Books and Council for British Research in the Levant (Levant Supplementary Series 8).

Garrow, D., Beadsmoore, E. and Knight, M. 2005. Pit clusters and the temporality of occupation: an earlier Neolithic site at Kilverstone, Thetford, Norfolk. *Proceedings of the Prehistoric Society* 71, 139–57.

Garrow, D., Lucy, S. and Gibson, D. 2006. *Excavations at Kilverstone, Norfolk: an episodic landscape history*. Cambridge: Cambridge Archaeological Unit.

Garwood, P. 1999. Radiocarbon dating and the chronology of the monument complex. In A. Barclay and C. Halpin, *Excavations at Barrow Hills, Radley, Oxfordshire. Volume I. The Neolithic and Bronze Age monument complex*, 293–309. Oxford: Oxford University Committee for Archaeology on behalf of the Oxford Archaeological Unit.

Gdaniec, K. 2005. The ceramic assemblage [from the Etton Landscape sites]. In C. French and F. Pryor, *Archaeology and environment of the Etton landscape*, 67–71. Peterborough: Fenland Archaeological Trust.

Gdaniec, K. 2006. The pottery assemblage [from the causewayed enclosure]. In C. Evans and I. Hodder, *A woodland archaeology. Neolithic sites at Haddenham: the Haddenham project volume 1*, 299–306. Cambridge: McDonald Institute for Archaeological Research.

Gelfand, A.E. and Smith, A.F.M. 1990. Sampling approaches to calculating marginal densities. *Journal of the American Statistical Association* 85, 398–409.

Gell, A. 1992. *The anthropology of time: cultural constructions of temporal maps and images*. Oxford: Berg.

Gell, A. 1998. *Art and agency: an anthropological theory*. Oxford: Clarendon Press.

Gent, T.H. and Quinnell, H. 1999a. Salvage recording on the Neolithic site at Haldon Belvedere. *Proceedings of the Devon Archaeological Society* 57, 77–104.

Gent, T.H. and Quinnell, H. 1999b. Excavation of a causewayed enclosure and hillfort on Raddon Hill, Stokely Pomeroy. *Proceedings of the Devon Archaeological Society* 57, 1–75.

Geophysical Surveys of Bradford 1989. *Report No 89/38*. Bradford: Geophysical Surveys of Bradford.

Geophysical Surveys of Bradford 1993. *Whitehawk Camp, Brighton.* Report Number 93/118. Bradford: Geophysical Surveys of Bradford.

Geophysical Surveys of Bradford 1995. *Whitesheet Hill, Wiltshire. Survey no. 92/95*. Bradford: Geophysical Surveys of Bradford.

Germany, M. 2003. A causewayed enclosure at St Osyth, Essex. *PAST* 44, 9–10.

Germany, M. 2007. *Neolithic and Bronze Age monuments and middle Iron Age settlement at Lodge Farm, St Osyth, Essex: excavations 2000–3*. Chelmsford: Essex County Council Historic Environment and Commerce.

Geschwinde, M. and Raetzel-Fabian, D. 2009. *Eine Fallstudie zu den jungneolithischen Erdwerken am Nordrand der Mittelgebirge*. Rahden: Marie Leidorf.

Gibson, A. 1994. Excavations at the Sarn-y-Bryn-Caled cursus complex, Welshpool, Powys, and the timber circles of Great Britain and Ireland. *Proceedings of the Prehistoric Society* 60, 143–223.

Gibson, A. 1995a. The Neolithic and Bronze Age archaeology of Grendon in its setting. In D. Jackson, 'Archaeology at Grendon Quarry, Northamptonshire part 2: other prehistoric, Iron Age and later sites excavated in 1974–75 and further observations between 1976–80'. *Northamptonshire Archaeology* 26, 27–30.

Gibson, A. 1995b. A review of Peterborough Ware in Wales. In I. Kinnes and G. Varndell (eds), *'Unbaked urns of rudely shape': essays on British and Irish pottery for Ian Longworth*, 24–39. Oxford: Oxbow Books.

Gibson, A. 1998. Neolithic pottery from Ogmore, Glamorgan. *Archaeologia Cambrensis* 147, 56–67.

Gibson, A. 1999. *The Walton Basin project: excavation and survey in a prehistoric landscape 1993–7*. York: Council for British Archeology.

Gibson, A. 2000. Survey and trial excavation at a newly discovered long barrow at Lower Luggy, Berriew, Powys. *Studia Celtica* 34, 1–16.

Gibson, A. 2002a. The pottery, Neolithic and early Bronze Age. In G. Shand, *Excavations at Chalk Hill, near Ramsgate, Kent 1997–8. Integrated assessment and updated research design*, 13–15. Unpublished document. Canterbury: Canterbury Archaeological Trust.

Gibson, A. 2002b. Earlier prehistoric funerary and ritual sites in the upper Severn valley. *Montgomeryshire Collections* 90, 1–30.

Gibson, A. 2003. A newly discovered Neolithic enclosure at Lower Luggy, Berriew, Powys. *PAST* 45, 1–2.

Gibson, A. 2006. Excavations at a Neolithic enclosure at Lower Luggy, near Welshpool, Powys, Wales. *Proceedings of the Prehistoric Society* 72, 163–91.

Gibson, A. forthcoming. The Neolithic pottery from Cross Roads and St Richards Road, Deal. Prepared for the Canterbury Archaeological Trust.

Gibson, A. and Bayliss, A. 2009. Recent research at Duggleby Howe, North Yorkshire. *Archaeological Journal* 166, 39–78.

Gibson, A. and Kinnes, I. 1997. On the urns of a dilemma: radiocarbon and the Peterborough problem. *Oxford Journal of Archaeology* 16, 65–72.

Gibson, A. and Leivers, M. 2008. Neolithic pottery. In M.J. Allen, M. Leivers and C. Ellis, 'Neolithic causewayed enclosures and later prehistoric farming: duality, imposition and the role of predecessors at Kingsborough, Isle of Sheppey, Kent, UK'. *Proceedings of the Prehistoric Society* 74, 245–53.

Gibson, A. and McCormick, A. 1985. Archaeology at Grendon Quarry, Northamptonshire, part 1: Neolithic and Bronze Age sites excavated in 1974–5. *Northamptonshire Archaeology* 20, 23–66.

Gibson, A. and Musson, C. 1990. A cropmark enclosure and a sherd of later Neolithic pottery from Brynderwen, Llandyssil, Powys. *Montgomeryshire Collections* 78, 11–15.

Gibson, A.M. and Simpson, D. 1987. Lyle's Hill, Co. Antrim. *Archaeology Ireland* 1(2), 72–5.

Giddens, A. 1979. *Central problems in social theory.* London: MacMillan.

Gilchrist, R. 2000. Archaeological biographies: realizing human lifecycles, -courses and -histories. *World Archaeology* 31, 325–8.

Giligny, F. (ed.) 2005. *Un site Néolithique Moyen en zone humide: Louviers "La Villette" (Eure)*. Rennes: Documents Archéologiques de l'Ouest.

Gilks, W.R., Richardson, S. and Spiegelhalther, D.J. 1996. *Markov Chain Monte Carlo in practice.* London: Chapman and Hall.

Gillespie, R. 1989. Fundamentals of bone degradation chemistry: collagen is not 'the way'. *Radiocarbon* 32, 239–46.

Gillespie, R. 2002. Neolithic house at Gortaroe, Westport, Co. Mayo. *Archaeology Ireland* 16(1), 7.

Gillespie, R., Gowlett, J.A., Hall, E.T. and Hedges, R.E.M. 1984a. Radiocarbon measurement by accelerator mass spectrometry: an early selection of dates. *Archaeometry* 26, 15–20.

Gillespie, R., Gowlett, J.A., Hall, E.T., Hedges, R.E.M. and Perry, C. 1985. Radiocarbon dates from the Oxford AMS system: *Archaeometry* datelist 2. *Archaeometry* 27, 237–46.

Gillespie, R., Hedges, R.E.M. and Wand, J.O. 1984b. Radiocarbon dating of bone by Accelerator Mass Spectrometry. *Journal of Archaeological Science* 11, 165–70.

Gillespie, R., Hedges, R.E.M. and Humm, M.J. 1986. Routine AMS dating of bone and shell proteins. *Radiocarbon* 28, 451–6.

Gillespie, R., Hedges, R.E.M. and White, N.R. 1983. The Oxford radiocarbon accelerator facility. *Radiocarbon* 25, 729–37.

Gillings, M., Pollard, J., Wheatley, D. and Peterson, R. 2008. *Landscape of the megaliths: excavation and fieldwork on the Avebury monuments, 1997–2003*. Oxford: Oxbow Books.

Gilman, P. (ed.) 1989. Excavations in Essex 1988. *Essex Archaeology and History* 20, 157–71.

Gilman, P. (ed.). 1991. Excavations in Essex 1990. *Essex Archaeology and History* 22, 148–61.

Gilot, E. 1997. *Index général des dates Lv. laboratoire du carbone*

14 de Louvain/Louvain-la-Neuve. Liège-Louvain: Studia Praehistorica Belgica.

Gilot, E., Ancion, N. and Capron, P.C. 1966. Louvain natural radiocarbon measurements IV. *Radiocarbon* 8, 248–55.

Gingell, C.J. 1992. *The Marlborough Downs: a later Bronze Age landscape and its origins*. Devizes: Wiltshire Archaeological and Natural History Society in co-operation with the Trust for Wessex Archaeology.

Glamorgan-Gwent Archaeological Trust Ltd. 2001. *Beech Court Farm enclosure, Ewenny Quarry, Vale of Glamorgan: palaeoenvironmental assessment*. GGAT Report 2001/001, Project A609, Excavation 398, prepared for Minimax Ltd.

Godelier, M. and Strathern, M. (eds) 1991. *Big men and great men: personifications of power in Melanesia*. Cambridge: Cambridge University Press.

Godwin, H. 1978. *Fenland: its ancient past and uncertain future*. Cambridge: Cambridge University Press.

Godwin, H. and Willis, E.H. 1961. Cambridge University natural radiocarbon measurements III. *Radiocarbon* 3, 60–76.

Godwin, H. and Willis, E.H. 1962. Cambridge University natural radiocarbon measurements V. *Radiocarbon* 4, 57–70.

Golitko, M. and Keeley, L. 2007. Beating ploughshares back into swords: warfare in the Linearbandkeramik. *Antiquity* 81, 332–42.

Gonfiantini, R., Rozanski K. and Stichler, W. 1990. Intercalibration of environmental isotope measurements: the program of the International Atomic Energy Agency. *Radiocarbon* 32, 369–74.

Gosden, C. 1994. *Social being and time*. Oxford: Blackwell.

Gosden, C. and Lock, G. 1998. Prehistoric histories. *World Archaeology* 30, 2–12.

Goslar, T., Czernik, J. and Goslar, E. 2004. Low-energy 14C AMS in Poznan Radiocarbon Laboratory, Poland. *Nuclear Instruments and Methods in Physics Research B*, 223–224, 5–11.

Gosselin, F. 1986. Un site préhistorique d'exploitation du silex à Spiennes (Ht) au lieu-dit 'Petit- Spiennes'. *Vie Archéologique* 22, 33–160.

Gossip, J. and Jones, A.M. 2007. *Archaeological investigations of a later prehistoric and a Romano-British landscape at Tremough, Penryn, Cornwall*. Oxford: Archaeopress.

Goves, C. 2004. Dendrochronology. In C.J. Ellis, *A prehistoric ritual complex at Eynesbury, Cambridgeshire: excavation of a multi-period site in the Great Ouse valley, 2000–2001*, 60–1. Salisbury: Trust for Wessex Archaeology Ltd.

Gowen, M. 1988. *Three Irish gas pipelines: new archaeological evidence in Munster*. Dublin: Wordwell.

Gowen, M. and Tarbett, C. 1988. A third season at Tankardstown. *Archaeology Ireland* 2(4), 156.

Gowen, M. and Tarbett, C. 1989. Tankardstown South. Neolithic/ Bronze Age. In I. Bennett (ed.), *Excavations 1988: summary accounts of archaeological excavations in Ireland*, 24–6. Dublin: Wordwell.

Gowen, M. and Tarbett, C. 1990. Tankardstown South. In I. Bennett (ed.), *Excavations 1989: summary accounts of archaeological excavations in Ireland*, 38–9. Dublin: Wordwell.

Gowlett, J.A.J., Hedges, R.E.M., Law, I.A. and Perry, C. 1986. Radiocarbon dates from the Oxford AMS system: *Archaeometry* datelist 4. *Archaeometry* 28, 206–21.

Gowlett, J.A.J., Hedges, R.E.M., Law, I.A. and Perry, C. 1987. Radiocarbon dates form the Oxford AMS system: *Archaeometry* datelist 5. *Archaeometry* 29, 125–55.

Graves-Brown, P. 1998. Ewenny, Beech Court Farm prehistoric enclosure (SS 9040 7660). *Archaeology in Wales* 38, 111–12.

Green, B. 1988. The petrological identification of stone implements from East Anglia: second report. In T.H.McK. Clough and W.A. Cummins (eds), *Stone axe studies, volume 2. The petrology of prehistoric stone implements from the British Isles*, 36–40. London: Council for British Archaeology.

Green, H.S. 1980. *The flint arrowheads of the British Isles*. Oxford: British Archaeological Reports.

Green, H.S., Bull, E., Campbell, E., Coles, G. and Currant, A. 1986. Excavations at Little Hoyle (Longbury Bank), Wales, in 1984. In D.A. Roe (ed.), *Studies in the Upper Palaeolithic of Britain and northwest Europe*, 99–119. Oxford: British Archaeological Reports.

Green, M. 2000. *A landscape revealed: 10,000 years on a chalkland farm*. Stroud: Tempus.

Green, M. 2007a. Fir Tree Field shaft. In C. French, H. Lewis, M.J. Allen, M. Green, R. Scaife and J. Gardiner, *Prehistoric landscape development and human impact in the upper Allen valley, Cranborne Chase, Dorset*, 76–82. Cambridge: McDonald Institute for Archaeological Research.

Green, M. 2007b. Monkton-up-Wimborne Late Neolithic pit circle/shaft complex (MUW 97). In C. French, H. Lewis, M. Allen, M. Green, R. Scaife and J. Gardiner, *Prehistoric landscape development and human impact in the upper Allen valley, Cranborne Chase, Dorset* , 114–22. Cambridge: McDonald Institute for Archaeological Research.

Green, M. 2007c. Lithics from the shaft. In C. French, H. Lewis, M. Allen, M. Green, R. Scaife and J. Gardiner, *Prehistoric landscape development and human impact in the upper Allen valley, Cranborne Chase, Dorset* , 280–5. Cambridge: McDonald Institute for Archaeological Research.

Greenfield, E. 1960. A Neolithic pit and other finds from Wingham, East Kent. *Archaeologia Cantiana* 74, 58–72.

Griffith, F.M., 1985. Some newly discovered ritual monuments in mid Devon. *Proceedings of the Prehistoric Society* 51, 310–15.

Griffith, F.M. 1994. Changing perceptions of the context of prehistoric Dartmoor. In F.M. Griffiths (ed.), 'The archaeology of Dartmoor: perspectives from the 1990s'. *Proceedings of the Devon Archaeological Society* 52, 85–99.

Griffith, F.M. 2001. Recent work on Neolithic enclosures in Devon. In T. Darvill and J. Thomas (eds), *Neolithic enclosures in Atlantic northwest Europe*, 66–77. Oxford: Oxbow Books.

Griffiths, S. forthcoming. *Chronological modelling of the Mesolithic/Neolithic transition in Britain*. Unpublished PhD thesis, Cardiff University.

Grigson, C. 1982a. Sexing Neolithic cattle skulls and horncores. In B. Wilson, C. Grigson and S. Payne (eds), *Ageing and sexing animal bones from archaeological sites*, 24–35. Oxford: British Archaeological Reports.

Grigson, C. 1982b. Porridge and pannage: pig husbandry in Neolithic England. In S. Limbrey and M. Bell (eds), *Archaeological aspects of woodland ecology*, 297–304. Oxford: British Archaeological Reports.

Grigson, C. 1984. The domestic animals of the earlier Neolithic in Britain. In G. Nobis (ed.), *Die Anfänge des Neolithikums vom Orient bis Nordeuropa. IX. Der Beginn der Haustierhaltung in der 'Alten Welt'*, 205–20. Köln: Bohlau.

Grigson, C. 1999. The mammalian remains. In A. Whittle, J. Pollard and C. Grigson, *The harmony of symbols: the Windmill Hill causewayed enclosure, Wiltshire*, 164–252. Oxford: Oxbow Books.

Grimes, W.F. 1933. Priory Farm Cave, Monkton, Pembrokeshire. *Archaeologia Cambrensis* 88, 88–100.

Grimes, W.F. 1936. The megalithic monuments of Wales. *Proceedings of the Prehistoric Society* 2, 106–39.

Grimes, W.F. 1939. The excavation of Ty-Isaf long cairn, Brecknock. *Proceedings of the Prehstoric Society* 5, 119–42.

Grimes, W.F. 1960. *Excavations on defence sites, 1939–1945. I: Mainly Neolithic–Bronze Age*. London: HMSO.

Grimes, W.F. 1979. The history of implement petrology in Britain. In T. Clough and W. Cummins (eds), *Stone axe studies*, 1–4. London: Council for British Archaeology.

Grogan, E. 1991. Appendix. Radiocarbon dates from Brugh na Bóinne. In G. Eogan, 'Prehistoric and early historic culture change at Brugh na Bóinne'. *Proceedings of the Royal Irish Academy* 91C, 126–32.

Grogan, E. 2004. The implications of Irish Neolithic houses. In I.A.G. Shepherd and G.J. Barclay (eds), *Scotland in Ancient Europe: the Neolithic and Early Bronze Age of Scotland in their European context*, 103–14. Edinburgh: Society of Antiquaries of Scotland.

Grogan, E. 2005. *The North Munster project, volume 2: the prehistoric landscape of north Munster*. Bray: Wordwell.

Grogan, E. and Eogan, G. 1987. Lough Gur excavations by Séan P. Ó Ríordáin: further Neolithic and Beaker habitations on Knockadoon. *Proceedings of the Royal Irish Academy* 87C, 299–506.

Gronenborn, D. 1999. A variation on a basic theme: the transition to farming in southern Central Europe. *Journal of World Prehistory* 13, 123–210.

Gronenborn, D. 2007a. Beyond the models: 'Neolithisation' in Central Europe. In A. Whittle and V. Cummings (eds), *Going over: the Mesolithic-Neolithic transition in north-west Europe*, 73–98. Oxford: Oxford University Press for The British Academy.

Gronenborn, D. 2007b. Climate change and sociopolitical crises: some cases from Neolithic central Europe. In T. Pollard and I. Banks (eds), *War and sacrifice: studies in the archaeology of conflict*, 13–32. Leiden and Boston: Brill.

Gronenborn, D. 2010. 'Hauptlingstümer' – Zentren politischer Landschaften. *Archäologie in Deutschland* 3, 2010, 32–5.

Grootes, P.M., Nadeau, M.J. and Rieck, A. 2004. ^{14}C-AMS at the Leibniz-Labor: radiometric dating and isotope research. *Nuclear Instruments and Methods in Physics Research B*, 223–224, 55–61.

Groves, C. 2003. Dendrochronology. In M. Brennand and M.Taylor, 'The survey and excavation of a Bronze Age timber circle at Holme-next-the-Sea, Norfolk, 1988–9'. *Proceedings of the Prehistoric Society* 69, 31–6.

Guilaine, J. and Zammit, J. 2005. *The origins of war: violence in prehistory.* Oxford: Backwell.

Gwynn, A.M., Mitchell, G.F. and Stellfox, A.W. 1942. The exploration of some caves near Castletownroche, Co. Cork. *Proceedings of the Royal Irish Academy* 48B, 371–90.

Haas, J.N. 1996. Pollen and plant macrofossil evidence of vegetation change at Wallisellen-Langachermoos (Switzerland) during the Mesolithic-Neolithic transition 8500 to 6500 years ago. *Dissertationes Botanicae* 167 (Berlin).

Hachem, L. 2009. Élevage, chasse et société dans le Néolithique français : exemples dans le Danubien du Nord de la France. In J.-P. Demoule (ed.), *La révolution Néolithique dans le monde*, 197–213. Paris: Inrap/Universcience, Éditions CNRS.

Hachem, L., Guichard, Y., Farruggia, J.-P., Dubouloz, J. and Ilett, M. 1998. Enclosure and burial in the earliest Neolithic of the Aisne valley. In M. Edmonds and C. Richards (eds), *Understanding the Neolithic of north-western Europe*, 127–40. Glasgow: Cruithne Press.

Haggarty, A. 1991. Machrie Moor, Arran: recent excavations at two stone circles. *Proceedings of the Soiety of Antiquaries of Scotland* 121, 51–94.

Håkansson, S. 1968. University of Lund radiocarbon dates I. *Radiocarbon* 10, 36–54.

Håkansson, S. 1981. University of Lund radiocarbon dates XIV. *Radiocarbon* 23, 384–403.

Hall, D. 1985. Survey work in eastern England. In S. Macready and F.H. Thompson (eds), *Archaeological field survey in Britain and abroad*, 25–44. London: Society of Antiquaries of London.

Hall, D. 1996. *The Fenland Project number 10: Cambridgeshire survey, the Isle of Ely and Wisbech.* Cambridge: Cambridgeshire Archaeological Committee.

Hall, D. and Coles, J. 1994. *Fenland survey: an essay in landscape and persistence.* London: English Heritage.

Hall, D. and Hutchings, J.B. 1972. The distribution of archaeological sites between the Nene and the Ouse valleys. *Bedfordshire Archaeological Journal* 7, 1–16.

Halpin, E. 1995. Excavations at Newtown, Co. Meath. In E. Grogan and C. Mount (eds), *Annus Archaeologiae: archaeological research 1992*, 45–54. Dublin: Organisation of Irish Archaeologists.

Halstead, P. 1996. The development of agriculture and pastoralism in Greece: when, how, who and what? In D. Harris (ed.), *The origins and spread of agriculture and pastoralism in Eurasia*, 296–309. London: University College, London.

Hamilton, J., Hedges, R.E.M. and Robinson, M.A. 2009. Rooting for pigfruit: pig feeding in Neolithic and Iron Age Britain compared. *Antiquity* 83, 998–1011.

Hamilton, M. 1999a. Pottery. Part 2: late Neolithic and Bronze Age. In A. Whittle, J. Pollard and C. Grigson, *The harmony of symbols: the Windmill Hill causewayed enclosure, Wiltshire*, 292–317. Oxford: Oxbow Books.

Hamilton, M. 1999b. Secondary use of causewayed enclosures in the region and beyond: Peterborough Ware, Beaker pottery and round barrows. In A. Whittle, J. Pollard and C. Grigson, *The harmony of symbols: the Windmill Hill causewayed enclosure, Wiltshire,* 373–5. Oxford: Oxbow Books.

Hamilton, M. and Aldhouse-Green, S. 1998. Ogmore-by-Sea (SS 861 756 to SS 861 751). *Archaeology in Wales* 38, 113–16.

Hamilton, W. D., Bayliss, A., Bronk Ramsey, C., Meadows, J. and van der Plicht, H. 2007. Radiocarbon dating. In M. Germany, *Neolithic and Bronze Age monuments and middle Iron Age settlement at Lodge Farm, St Osyth, Essex: excavations 2000–3*, 95–102. Chelmsford: Essex County Council Historic Environment and Commerce.

Hanson-James, N. 1993. *An investigation of the Neolithic central area on Crickley Hill.* Unpublished BA dissertation, University of Nottingham.

Hardiman, M.A., Fairchild, J.E. and Longworth, G. 1992. Harwell radiocarbon measurements XI. *Radiocarbon* 34, 47–70.

Harding, A.F. with Lee, G.E. 1987. *Henge monuments and related sites of Great Britain.* Oxford: British Archaeological Reports.

Harding, J. 2003. *Henge monuments of the British Isles*. Stroud: Tempus.

Harding, J. 2005. Rethinking the great divide: long-term structural history and the temporality of event. *Norwegian Archaeological Review* 38, 88–101.

Harding, J. and Healy, F. 2007. *The Raunds Area project: a Neolithic and Bronze Age landscape in Northamptonshire.* Swindon: English Heritage.

Harding, P. 1987. An experiment to produce a ground flint axe. In

G. de G. Sieveking and M. Newcomer (eds), *The human uses of flint and chert*, 37–42. Cambridge: Cambridge University Press.

Harding, P. 1990a. Lithics [from the Coneybury Anomaly]. In J.C. Richards, *The Stonehenge Environs project*, 43–5. London: Historic Buildings and Monuments Commission.

Harding, P. 1990b. The comparative analysis of four stratified flint assemblages and a knapping cluster. In J.C. Richards, *The Stonehenge Environs project*, 213–25. London: Historic Buildings and Monuments Commission for England.

Harding, P. and Gingell, C. 1986. The excavation of two long barrows by F. de M. and H.F.W.L. Vatcher. *Wiltshire Archaeological and Natural History Magazine* 80, 7–22.

Harkness, D.D. 1983. The extent of the natural ^{14}C deficiency in the coastal environment of the United Kingdom. Journal of the European Study Group on Physical, Chemical and Mathematical Techniques Applied to Archaeology. *PACT* 8 (IV.9), 351–64.

Harkness, D.D. and Wilson, H.W. 1972. Some applications in radiocarbon measurements at the Scottish Research Reactor Centre. In T.A. Rafter and T. Grant-Taylor (eds), *Proceedings of the 8th International Radiocarbon Dating Conference, Lower Hutt, New Zealand*, 209–23. Wellington: Royal Society of New Zealand.

Harkness, D.D. and Wilson, H.W. 1973. Scottish Universities Research and Reactor Centre radiocarbon measurements I. *Radiocarbon* 15, 554–65.

Harman, M. 1992. Human bone from F3003. In A. Whittle, R.J. Atkinson, R. Chambers, R. Thomas and N. Thomas, 'Excavations in the Neolithic and Bronze Age complex at Dorchester-on-Thames, Oxfordshire'. *Proceedings of the Prehistoric Society* 58, 153.

Harré, R.1991. *Physical being: a theory for a corporeal psychology*. Oxford: Blackwell.

Harris, O. 2006. Agents of identity: performative practice at the Etton causewayed enclosure. In D. Hofmann, J. Mills and A. Cochrane (eds), *Elements of being: mentalities, identities and movements*, 40–9. Oxford: British Archaeological Reports.

Harris, O. 2009. Making places matter in early Neolithic Dorset. *Oxford Journal of Archaeology* 28, 111–23.

Hart, S.C., Gehring, C.A., Selmants, P.C. and Deckert, R.J. 2006. Carbon and nitrogen elemental and isotopic patterns in macrofungal sporocarps and trees in semiarid forests of the south–western USA. *Functional Ecology* 20, 42–51.

Hartnett, P.J. 1951. A Neolithic burial from Martinstown, Kiltale, Co. Meath. *Journal of the Royal Society of Antiquaries of Ireland* 81, 19–23.

Hartz, S., Lübke, H. and Terberger, T. 2007. From fish and seal to sheep and cattle: new research into the process of neolithisation in northern Germany. In A. Whittle and V. Cummings (eds), *Going over: the Mesolithic-Neolithic transition in north-west Europe*, 567–94. Oxford: Oxford University Press for The British Academy.

Hastorf, C.A. 2009. Comments. In B. Hayden, 'Funerals as feasts: why are they so important?' *Cambridge Archaeological Journal* 19, 43–4.

Haughey, F. 2007. Searching for the Neolithic while it may be found: research in the inter-tidal zone of the London Thames. In J. Sidell and F. Haughey (eds), *Neolithic archaeology in the intertidal zone*, 86–94. Oxford: Oxbow Books.

Hauzeur, A. 2006. The raw material procurement as implied cause of interregional network: diachronic examples in the LPC of the middle Mosel. In P. Allard, F. Bostyn and A. Zimmermann (eds), *Contribution des matériaux lithiques dans la chronologie du Néolithiqie ancien et moyen en France et dans les régions limitrophes. Actes de la Xième session de l'EAA, Lyon, Septembre 2004. Groupe thématique II: interprétation des données*, 15–27. Oxford: British Archaeological Reports.

Hawkes, J. 1934. Aspects of the Neolithic and Chalcolithic periods in Western Europe. *Antiquity* 8, 24–42.

Hawkes, J. 1935. The place of origin of the Windmill Hill culture. *Proceedings of the Prehistoric Society* 1, 127–9.

Hawkes, J. 1938. The significance of channelled ware in Neolithic western Europe. *Archaeological Journal* 95, 126–73.

Hayden, B. 2009. Funerals as feasts: why are they so important? *Cambridge Archaeological Journal* 19, 29–52.

Hayden, C. forthcoming. The prehistoric landscape at White Horse Stone, Aylesford, Kent. CTRL integrated site report series, http://ads.ahds.ac.uk/catalogue/projArch/ctrl.

Haynes, C.V. 1967. Bone organic matter and radiocarbon dating. In *Radioactive dating and methods of low-level counting*, 163–7. Vienna: IAEA.

Hazzledine Warren, S., Piggott, S., Clark, J.G.D., Burkitt, M.B. Godwin, H. and Godwin, M.E. 1936. Archaeology of the submerged land-surface of the Essex coast. *Proceedings of the Prehistoric Society* 11, 178–210.

Healey, E. and Green, H.S. 1984. The lithic industries. In W.J. Britnell, 'The Gwernvale long cairn, Crickhowell, Brecknock'. In W.J. Britnell and H.N. Savory, *Gwernvale and Penywyrlod: two Neolithic long cairns in the Black Mountains of Brecknock*, 113–32. Cardiff: Cambrian Archaeological Association.

Healy, F. 1983. Neolithic and later material from a shaft at Brampton. *Norfolk Archaeology* 38 (3), 363–74.

Healy, F. 1984a. Farming and field monuments: the Neolithic in Norfolk. In C. Barringer (ed.), *Aspects of East Anglian prehistory (twenty years after Rainbird Clarke)*, 77–140. Norwich: Geo Books.

Healy, F. 1984b. Recent finds of Neolithic Bowl pottery in Norfolk. *Norfolk Archaeology* 39, 65–82.

Healy, F. 1986. The excavation of two Early Bronze Age round barrows on Eaton Heath, Norwich, 1969–70. In A.J. Lawson, *Barrow excavations in Norfolk, 1950–82*, 50–8. Gressenhall: Norfolk Archaeological Unit.

Healy, F. 1988. *The Anglo-Saxon cemetery at Spong Hill, North Elmham. Part VI: occupation during the seventh to second millennia BC*. Gressenhall: Norfolk Archaeological Unit.

Healy, F. 1991. Appendix 1. Lithics and pre-Iron Age pottery. In R.J. Silvester, *The Fenland Project Number 4: the Wissey Embayment and the Fen Causeway, Norfolk*, 116–39. East Anglian Archaeology 52. Gressenhall: Norfolk Archaeological Unit.

Healy, F. 1996. *The Fenland project number 11. The Wissey embayment: evidence for pre-Iron Age settlement accumulated prior to the Fenland project*. Gressenhall: Field Archaeology Division, Norfolk Museums Services.

Healy, F. 1997a. Site 3. Flagstones. In R.J.C. Smith, F. Healy, M.J. Allen, E.L. Morris, I. Barnes and P.J. Woodward, *Excavations along the route of the Dorchester by-pass, Dorset, 1986–8*, 27–48. Salisbury: Wessex Archaeology.

Healy, F. 1997b. Antler picks. In R.J.C. Smith, F. Healy, M.J. Allen, E.L. Morris, I. Barnes and P.J. Woodward, *Excavations along the route of the Dorchester by-pass, Dorset, 1986–8*, 157. Salisbury: Wessex Archaeology.

Healy, F. 1997c. Settlement. Neolithic and Bronze Age. In R.J.C. Smith, F. Healy, M.J. Allen, E.L. Morris, I. Barnes and P.J. Woodward, *Excavations along the route of the Dorchester by-pass, Dorset, 1986–8*, 283–91. Salisbury: Wessex Archaeology.

Healy, F. 1997d. Communal monuments and burials. Neolithic and Bronze Age. In R.J.C. Smith, F. Healy, M.J. Allen, E.L. Morris, I. Barnes and P.J. Woodward, *Excavations along the route of the Dorchester by-pass, Dorset, 1986–8*, 295–9. Salisbury: Wessex Archaeology.

Healy, F. 2004. Hambledon Hill and its implications. In R.M.J. Cleal and J. Pollard (eds), *Monuments and material culture. Papers in honour of an Avebury archaeologist: Isobel Smith*, 15–38. East Knoyle: Hobnob Books.

Healy, F. 2006. Pottery deposition at Hambledon Hill. In A. Gibson (ed.), *Prehistoric pottery: some recent research*, 11–37. Oxford: British Archaeological Reports.

Healy, F. and Jacobi, R. 1984. The beginnings? In F. Healy, 'Farming and field monuments: the Neolithic in Norfolk', in C. Barringer (ed.), *Aspects of East Anglian prehistory (twenty years after Rainbird Clarke)*, 79–84. Norwich: Geo Books.

Heaton, T.H.E. 1999. Spatial, species, and temporal variations in the C-13/C-12 ratios of C-3 plants: implications for palaeodiet studies. *Journal of Archaeological Science* 26, 637–49.

Hedges, J. 1980. The Neolithic in Essex. In D.G. Buckley (ed.), *Archaeology in Essex to AD 1500*, 26–39. London: Council for British Archaeology.

Hedges, J. 1982. Fields Farm, Layer de la Haye TL 978 194. *Essex Archaeology and History* 14, 114.

Hedges, J. and Buckley, D.G. 1978. Excavations at a Neolithic causewayed enclosure, Orsett, Essex, 1975. *Proceedings of the Prehistoric Society* 44, 219–308.

Hedges, R.E.M. 1981. Radiocarbon dating with an accelerator: review and preview. *Archaeometry* 23, 1–18.

Hedges, R.E.M. 2004. Isotopes and red herrings: comment on Milner *et al.* and Lidén *et al. Antiquity* 78, 34–7.

Hedges, R.E.M. and Law, I.A. 1989. The radiocarbon dating of bone. *Applied Geochemistry* 4, 249–53.

Hedges, R.E.M. and Reynard, L.M. 2007. Nitrogen isotopes and the trophic level of humans in archaeology. *Journal of Archaeological Science* 34, 1240–51.

Hedges, R.E.M., Bronk, C.R. and Housley, R.A. 1989a. The Oxford Accelerator Mass Spectrometry facility: technical developments in routine dating. *Archaeometry* 31, 99–114.

Hedges, R.E.M., Chen Tiemei, and Housley, R. A. 1992a. Results and methods in the radiocarbon dating of pottery. *Radiocarbon* 34, 906–15.

Hedges, R.E.M., Housley, R.A., Bronk, C.R. and van Klinken, G.J. 1991. Radiocarbon dates from the Oxford AMS system: *Archaeometry* datelist 16. *Archaeometry* 33, 279–96.

Hedges, R.E.M., Housley, R.A., Bronk, C.R. and van Klinken, G.J. 1992c. Radiocarbon dates from the Oxford AMS system: *Archaeometry* datelist 14. *Archaeometry* 34, 141–60.

Hedges, R.E.M. Housley, R.A., Bronk Ramsey, C. and van Klinken, G.J. 1993. Radiocarbon dates from the Oxford AMS system: *Archaeometry* datelist 16. *Archaeometry* 35, 147–67.

Hedges, R.E.M., Housley, R.A., Bronk Ramsey, C. and van Klinken, G.J. 1994. Radiocarbon dates from the Oxford AMS system: *Archaeometry* datelist 18. *Archaeometry* 36, 337–74.

Hedges, R.E.M., Housley, R.A., Bronk, C.R. and van Klinken, G.J. 1995. Radiocarbon dates from the Oxford AMS system: *Archaeometry* datelist 20. *Archaeometry* 37, 417–30.

Hedges, R.E.M., Housley, R.A., Law. I.A. and Bronk, C.R. 1989b. Radiocarbon dates from the Oxford AMS system: *Archaeometry* datelist 9. *Archaeometry* 31, 207–34.

Hedges, R.E.M., Housley, R.A., Law, I.A. and Bronk, C.R. 1990. Radiocarbon dates from the Oxford AMS system: *Archaeometry* datelist 10. *Archaeometry* 32, 101–8.

Hedges, R.E.M., Housley, R.A., Law, I.A. and Perry, C. 1988a. Radiocarbon dates from the Oxford AMS system: *Archaeometry* datelist 7. *Archaeometry* 30, 155–64.

Hedges, R.E.M., Housley, R.A., Law, I.A., Perry, C. and Gowlett, J.A.J. 1987. Radiocarbon dates from the Oxford AMS system: *Archaeometry* datelist 6. *Archaeometry* 29, 289–306.

Hedges, R.E.M., Housley, R.A., Law, I.A., Perry, C. and Hendy, E. 1988b. Radiocarbon dates from the Oxford AMS system: *Archaeometry* datelist 8. *Archaeometry* 30, 291–305.

Hedges, R.E.M., Housley, R., Pettitt, P.B., Bronk Ramsey, C. and van Klinken, G.J. 1996. Radiocarbon dates from the Oxford AMS system: *Archaeometry* datelist 21. *Archaeometry* 38, 181–207.

Hedges, R.E.M., Housley, R.A., Ramsey, C.B and van Klinken, G.J. 1997. Radiocarbon dates from the Oxford AMS system: *Archaeometry* datelist 24. *Archaeometry* 39, 445–71.

Hedges, R.E.M., Humm, M.J., Foreman, J., Klinken, G.J. van and Bronk, C.R. 1992b. Developments in sample combustion to carbon dioxide, and in the Oxford AMS carbon dioxide ion source system. *Radiocarbon* 34, 306–11.

Hedges, R.E.M., Pettitt, P.B., Bronk Ramsey, C., and Van Klinken, G.J. 1998. Radiocarbon dates from the Oxford AMS system: *Archaeometry* datelist 26. *Archaeometry*, 40, 437–55.

Hedges, R.E.M., Clement, J.G.C., Thomas, D.L. and O'Connell, T.C. 2007a. Collagen turnover in the adult femoral mid-shaft: modeled from anthropogenic radiocarbon tracer measurements. *American Journal of Physical Anthropology* 133, 808–16.

Hedges, R.E.M., Saville, A. and O'Connell, T. 2008. Characterizing the diet of individuals at the Neolithic chambered tomb of Hazleton North, Gloucestershire, England, using stable isotopic analysis. *Archaeometry* 50, 114–28.

Hedges, R.E.M., Stevens, R.E. and Pearson, J.A. 2007b. Carbon and nitrogen stable isotope compositions of animal and human bone. In D. Benson and A. Whittle (eds), *Building memories: the Neolithic Cotswold long barrow at Ascott-under-Wychwood, Oxfordshire*, 255–62. Oxford: Oxbow Books.

Helbaek, H. 1952. Early crops in southern England. *Proceedings of the Prehistoric Society* 18, 194–233.

Helgason, A., Hrafnkelsson, B., Gulcher, J.R., Ward, R. and Stefánsson, K. 2003. A populationwide coalescent analysis of Icelandic matrilineal and patrilineal genealogies: evidence for a faster evolutionary rate of mtDNA lineages than Y chromosomes. *American Journal of Human Genetics* 72, 1370–88.

Helms, M.W. 1988. *Ulysses' sail: an ethnographic odyssey of power, knowledge, and geographical distance.* Princeton: Princeton University Press.

Helms, M.W. 1998. *Access to origins: affines, ancestors and aristocrats.* Austin: University of Texas Press.

Helms, M.W. 2007. House life. In R.A. Beck, Jr. (ed.), *The durable house: house society models in archaeology*, 487–504. Carbondale: Center for Archaeological Investigations, Southern Illinois University.

Hemp, W.J. 1929. Belas Knap long barrow, Gloucestershire. *Transactions of the Bristol and Gloucestershire Archaeological Society* 51, 261–72.

Hencken, H. O'Neill. 1932. *The archaeology of Cornwall and Scilly*. London: Methuen & Co. Ltd.

Hencken, H. O'Neill. 1935. A cairn at Poulawack, Co. Clare. *Journal of the Royal Society of Antiquaries of Ireland* 95, 191–222.

Henshall, A. 1972. *The chambered tombs of Scotland: Volume Two*. Edinburgh: Edinburgh University Press.

Henshall, A. 1978. Manx megaliths again: an attempt at structural analysis. In P.J. Davey (ed.), *Man and environment in the Isle of Man*, 171–6. Oxford: British Archaeological Reports.

Herity, M. 1982. Irish decorated Neolithic pottery. *Proceedings of the Royal Irish Academy* 82C, 249–404.

Herity, M. 1987. The finds from Irish court tombs. *Proceedings of the Royal Irish Academy* 87C, 103–281.

Herne, A. 1988. A time and a place for the Grimston bowl. In J.C. Barrett and I.A. Kinnes (eds), *The archaeology of context in the Neolithic and Bronze Age: recent trends*, 9–29. Sheffield: Department of Archaeology and Prehistory, University of Sheffield.

Herring, P. and Kirkham, G. forthcoming. A bank cairn at Rough Tor, Bodmin Moor, Cornwall.

Herring, P. and Thomas N. 1988. *Kit Hill archaeological survey*. Truro: Cornwall Archaeological Unit.

Hey, G. 1997. Neolithic settlement at Yarnton, Oxfordshire. In P. Topping (ed.), *Neolithic landscapes*, 99–111. Oxford: Oxbow Books.

Hey, G. and Barclay, A. 2007. The Thames valley in the late fifth and early fourth millennium cal BC: the appearance of domestication and the evidence for change. In A. Whittle and V. Cummings (eds), *Going over: the Mesolithic-Neolithic transition in north-west Europe*, 399–422. Oxford: Oxford University Press for The British Academy.

Hey, G., Bayliss, A. and Boyle, A. 1998. Iron Age inhumation burials at Yarnton, Oxfordshire. *Antiquity* 73, 551–62.

Hey, G., Dennis, C. and Mayes, A. 2007. Archaeological investigations on Whiteleaf Hill, Princes Risborough, Buckinghamshire, 2002–6. *Records of Buckinghamshire* 47(2), 3–80.

Hey, G., Mulville, J. and Robinson, M. 2003. Diet and culture in southern Britain: the evidence from Yarnton. In M. Parker Pearson (ed.), *Food, culture and identity in the Neolithic and early Bronze Age*, 79–88. Oxford: British Archaeological Reports.

Higginbotham, E. 1977. Excavations at Woolley Barrows, Morwenstow. *Cornish Archaeology* 16, 10–16.

Higham, T.F.G. and Hogg, A.G. 1997. Evidence for late Polynesian colonisation of New Zealand: University of Waikato radiocarbon measurements. *Radiocarbon* 39, 149–92.

Higham, T. F. G., Jacobi, R. M. and Bronk Ramsey, C. 2006. AMS radiocarbon dating of ancient bone using ultrafiltration. *Radiocarbon* 48, 179–95.

Hillam, J., Groves, C.M., Brown, D.M., Baillie, M.G., Coles, J.M. and Coles, B.J. 1990. Dendrochronology of the English Neolithic. *Antiquity* 64, 210–20.

Hillam, J., Morgan, R.A. and Tyers, I. 1987. Sapwood estimates and the dating of short ring sequences. In R.G.Ward (ed.), *Applications of tree-ring studies: current research in dendrochronology and related areas*, 165–85. Oxford: British Archaeological Reports.

Hingley, R. 1996. Prehistoric Warwickshire: a review of the evidence. *Transactions of the Birmingham and Warwickshire Archaeological Society* 100, 1–24.

Hinton, P. 2004. Plant remains. In M. Rawlings, M.J. Allen and F. Healy, 'Investigation of the Whitesheet Down environs 1989–90: Neolithic causewayed enclosure and Iron Age settlement'. *Wiltshire Studies* 97, 177–9.

Hoare, R.C. 1812. *The ancient history of south Wiltshire*. London: William Miller.

Hobley, B. 1971. Neolithic storage hollows and an undated ring-ditch at Baginton, Warwickshire. *Transactions of the Birmingham and Warwickshire Archaeological Society* 84, 1–6.

Hodder, I. 1987. The contribution of the long term. In I. Hodder (ed.), *Archaeology as long-term history*, 1–8. Cambridge: Cambridge University Press.

Hodder, I. 1990. *The domestication of Europe*. Oxford: Blackwell.

Hodder, I. 1992. The Haddenham causewayed enclosure – a hermeneutic circle. In I. Hodder, *Theory and practice in archaeology*, 213–40. London: Routledge.

Hodder, I. 1999. *The archaeological process: an introduction*. Oxford: Blackwell.

Hodder, I. 2006. *Çatalhöyük: the leopard's tale. Revealing the mysteries of Turkey's ancient 'town'*. London: Thames and Hudson.

Hogg, A.G., Lowe, D.J. and Hendy, C. 1987. Waikato date list 1. *Radiocarbon* 29, 263–301.

Höhn, B. 1997. Das Michelsberger Erdwerk Inden 9, Gem. Jülich, Kr. Düren. In J. Lüning (ed.), 'Studien zur neolithischen Besiedlung der Aldenhovener Platte und ihre Umgebung'. *Rheinische Ausgrabungen* 43, 473–598.

Holden, E. 1951. Earthworks on Court Hill. *Sussex Notes and Queries* 13, 183–5.

Holden, E. 1973. The possible remains of a Neolithic causewayed camp on Offham Hill. *Sussex Archaeological Collections* 111, 109–10.

Holgate, R. 1981. The Medway megaliths and Neolithic Kent. *Archaeologia Cantiana* 97, 221–34.

Holgate, R. 1987. Neolithic settlement patterns at Avebury, Wiltshire. *Antiquity* 61, 259–63.

Holgate, R. 1988a. *Neolithic settlement of the Thames basin*. Oxford: British Archaeological Reports.

Holgate, R. 1988b. The flints. In G. Lambrick, *The Rollright Stones: megaliths, monuments and settlement in the prehistoric landscape*, 85–90. London: Historic Buildings and Monuments Commission for England.

Holgate, R. 1995a. GB4 Harrow Hill near Findon, West Sussex. *Archaeologia Polona* 33, 347–50.

Holgate, R. 1995b. GB 6 Long Down near Chichester, West Sussex. *Archaeologia Polona* 33, 350–2.

Holgate, R. 1995c. Neolithic flint mining in Britain. *Archaeologia Polona* 33, 133–61.

Holgate, R. 1996. Essex c. 4000–1500 BC. In O. Bedwin (ed.), *The archaeology of Essex. Proceedings of the 1992 Writtle Conference*, 15–25. Chelmsford: Essex County Council Planning Department.

Holgate, R. 2003. Late Glacial and Post-glacial hunter-gathers in Sussex. In D. Rudling (ed.), *The archaeology of Sussex to AD 2000,* 29–38. Great Dunham: Centre for Continuing Education, University of Sussex.

Holgate, R. and Start, D. 1985. A Neolithic pit at Remenham, near Henley-on-Thames, Berkshire. *Berkshire Archaeological Journal* 72, 1–7.

Hollos, D.B. 1999. *The long mound sequence at Crickley Hill*. Draft PhD thesis to be presented at the University of Nottingham.

Holmes, S.C.A. 1981. *Geology of the country around Faversham*. Memoir of the Geological Survey, Great Britain. London: HMSO.

Horne, B. 1996. Will the real Neolithic please stand up? *Manshead* 36, 22–39.

Horne, P.D., MacLeod, D. and Oswald, A. 2002. The seventieth causewayed enclosure in the British Isles? In G. Varndell and P. Topping (eds), *Enclosures in Neolithic Europe: essays on causewayed and non-causewayed sites*, 115–20. Oxford: Oxbow Books.

Houlder, C.H. 1963. A Neolithic settlement on Hazard Hill, Totnes. *Proceedings of the Devon Archaeological Society* 21, 2–30.

Housley, R.A. 1991. AMS techniques. In N. Sharples, *Maiden Castle: excavations and field survey 1985–6*, microfiche M3: C1–C2. London: English Heritage.

Hubert, F. 1980. Mesvin, 'Sans Pareil', Gem. und Kr. Mons, Prov. Hainault. In G. Weisgerber (ed.), *5000 Jahre Feuersteinbergbau: die Suche nach dem Stahl der Steinzeit*, 428–9. Bochum: Deutsches Bergbau-Museum.

Hughen, K.A., Baillie, M.G.L., Bard, E., Beck, J.W., Bertrand, C.J.H., Blackwell, P.G., Buck, C.E., Burr, G.S., Cutler, K.B., Damon, P.E., Edwards, R.L., Fairbanks, R.G., Friedrich, M., Guilderson, T.P., Kromer, B., McCormac, G. Manning, S., Bronk Ramsey, C., Reimer, P.J., Reimer, R.W., Remmele, S., Southon, J.R., Stuiver, M., Talamo, S., Taylor, F.W., van der Plicht J. and Weyhenmeyer, C.E. 2004. Marine04 marine radiocarbon age calibration, 0–26 cal kyr BP. *Radiocarbon* 46(3) 1059–86.

Hughes, G. and Crawford, G. 1995. Excavations at Wasperton, Warwickshire, 1980–1985. *Birmingham and Warwickshire Archaeological Society Transactions* 99, 9–45.

Hughes, G. and Woodward, A. 1995. A ring ditch and Neolithic pit complex at Meole Brace, Shrewsbury. *Transactions of the Shropshire Archaeological and Historical Society* 70, 1–21.

Hughes, J. 2005. Two Neolithic structures in Granny townland, County Kilkenny. In J. O'Sullivan and M. Stanley (eds), *Recent archaeological discoveries on national road schemes 2004: archaeology and the National Roads Authority*, 25–35. Dublin: National Roads Authority.

Hummler, M. 2005. Before Sutton Hoo: the prehistoric settlement (c. 3000 BC to AD 550). In M. Carver, *Sutton Hoo: a seventh-century princely burial ground and its context*, 391–458. London: British Museum Press.

Hurtrelle, J. and Piningre, J.-F. 1978. Datation radiocarbone du Cerny des Sablins à Etaples (Pas-de-Calais). *Bulletin de la Société Préhistorique Française* 75(3), 83–6.

Ilett, M. and Hachem, L. 2001. Le village néolithique de Cuiry-lès-Chaudardes (Aisne, France). In J. Guilaine (ed.), *Communautés villageoises du Proche-Orient à l'Atlantique (8000–2000 avant notre ère)*, 171–86. Paris: Errance.

Ingold, T. 1993. The temporality of the landscape. *World Archaeology* 25, 152–74.

Ingold, T. 2000. *The perception of the environment: essays in livelihood, dwelling and skill*. London: Routledge.

Ingold, T. 2006. Rethinking the animate, re-animating thought. *Ethnos* 71, 9–20.

Ingold, T. 2007a. *Lines: a brief history*. London: Routledge.

Ingold, T. 2007b. Materials against materiality. *Archaeological Dialogues* 14, 1–16.

Innes, J.B., Blackford, J.J. and Davey, P.J. 2003. Dating the introduction of cereal cultivation to the British Isles: early paleoecological evidence from the Isle of Man. *Journal of Quaternary Science* 18, 603–13.

Institute of Archaeology Sussex Archaeological Field Unit 1987. *The Trundle, west Sussex: a geophysical survey of the proposed British Telecom Goodwood radio station*. Unublished manuscript.

International Study Group 1982. An inter-laboratory comparison of radiocarbon measurements in tree rings. *Nature* 298, 619–23.

Jackson, D.A. 1976. The excavation of Neolithic and Bronze Age sites at Aldwincle, Northants, 1967–71. *Northamptonshire Archaeology* 11, 12–70.

Jackson, D. 1995. Archaeology at Grendon Quarry, Northamptonshire, part 2: other prehistoric, Iron Age and later sites excavated in 1974–75 and further observations between 1976–80. *Northamptonshire Archaeology* 26, 3–32.

Jackson, J.W. 1943. Animal bones. In R.E.M. Wheeler, *Maiden Castle, Dorset*, 360–71. London: Society of Antiquaries of London.

Jackson, R. and Miller, D. forthcoming. *Wellington Quarry, Herefordshire (1986–96): investigations of a landscape in the Lower Lugg valley*. Oxford: Oxbow Books.

Jacobi, R.M. 1978. The Mesolithic in Sussex. In P.L. Drewett (ed.), *Archaeology in Sussex to AD 1500*, 15–22. London: Council for British Archaeology.

Jacobi, R. 1979. Early Flandrian hunters in the south-west. *Proceedings of the Devon Archaeological Society* 37, 48–93.

Jacobi, R. 1980. The early Holocene settlement of Wales. In J.A. Taylor (ed.), *Culture and environment in prehistoric Wales*, 131–206. Oxford: British Archaeological Reports.

Jacobi, R.M. 1982. Later hunters in Kent: Tasmania and the earliest Neolithic. In P.E. Leach (ed.), *Archaeology in Kent to AD 1500*, 12–24. London: Council for British Archaeology.

Jacomet, S., Leuzinger, U. and Schibler, J. 2004. *Die jungsteinzeitliche Seeufersiedlung Arbon/Bleiche 3: Umwelt und Wirtschaft*. Thurgau: Departement für Erziehung und Kultur des Kantons Thurgau.

James, B. 1977. The flint industry. In P. Drewett, 'The excavation of a Neolithic causewayed enclosure at Offham Hill, East Sussex, 1976'. *Proceedings of the Prehistoric Society* 43, 211–18.

James, W. and Mills, D. 2005. *The qualities of time: anthropological approaches*. Oxford: Berg.

Jay, M. and Richards, M.P. 2006. Diet in the Iron Age cemetery population at Wetwang Slack, East Yorkshire, U.K.: carbon and nitrogen stable isotope evidence. *Journal of Archaeological Science* 33, 653–62.

Jay, M. and Richards, M.P. 2007. British Iron Age diet: stable isotopes and other evidence. *Proceedings of the Prehistoric Society* 73, 169–90.

Jelgersma, S. 1979. Sea-level changes in the North Sea basin. In E. Oele, R.T. Schüttenhelm and A.J. Wiggers (eds), *The Quaternary history of the North Sea*, 233–48. Uppsala: University of Uppsala.

Jennbert, K. 1984. *Den produktiva gåvan: tradition och innovation i Sydskandinavien för omkring 5300 år sedan*. Lund: Gleerup.

Jessup, R.F. 1937. Excavations at Julliberrie's Grave, Chilham, Kent. *Antiquaries Journal* 17, 122–37.

Jessup, R.F. 1939. Further excavations at Julliberrie's Grave, Chilham. *Antiquaries Journal* 19, 260–81.

Jessup, R.F. 1970. *South east England*. London: Thames and Hudson.

Jeunesse, C. 1996. Les enceintes à fossés interrompus du Néolithique danubien ancien et moyen et leurs relations avec le Néolithique récent. *Archäologisches Korrespondenzblatt* 26, 251–61.

Jeunesse, C. 1998. Pour une origine occidentale de la culture de Michelsberg? In J. Biel, H. Schlichtherle, M. Strobel and A. Zeeb (eds), *Die Michelsberger Kultur und ihre Randgebiete – Probleme der Entstehung, Chronologie und des Siedlungswesens*, 29–46. Stuttgart: Theiss.

Jeunesse, C., Lefranc, P. and Denaire, A. 2004. *Groupe de Bischheim, origine du Michelsberg, genèse du groupe d'Entzheim*. Zimmersheim: Cahiers de l'Association pour la Promotion de la Recherche Archéologique en Alsace.

Johnson, B. and Waddington, C. 2008. Prehistoric and Dark Age settlement remains from Cheviot Quarry, Milfield Basin, Northumberland. *Archaeological Journal* 165, 107–264.

Johnson, N. and Rose, P. 1984. Helman Tor (CCRA report 1983–4). *Cornish Archaeology* 23, 186.

Johnson, N. and Rose, P. 1994. *Bodmin Moor: an archaeological survey. Volume 1: the human landscape to c. 1800*. London: English Heritage.

Johnston, D.A. 1997. Biggar Common, 1987–93: an early prehistoric funerary and domestic landscape in Clydesdale, South Lanarkshire. *Proceedings of the Society of Antiquaries of Scotland* 127, 185–253.

Johnston, D.E. 1956. A Romano-British site near Bedford. *Bedfordshire Archaeology* 1, 92–7.

Jones, A. 2007. *Memory and material culture*. Cambridge: Cambridge University Press.

Jones, A. 2008. How the dead live. In J. Pollard (ed.), *Prehistoric Britain*, 177–201. Oxford: Blackwell.

Jones, A.M. and Reed, S.J. 2006. By land, sea and air: an early Neolithic pit group at Portscatho, Cornwall, and consideration of coastal activity during the Neolithic. *Cornish Archaeology* 45, 1–30.

Jones, A.M. and Taylor S. 2001. Discoveries along the St Newlyn East to Mitchell pipeline. *Cornish Archaeology* 39–40, 161–6.

Jones, A.M. and Thomas, C. 2010. Bosiliack and a reconsideration of entrance graves. *Proceedings of the Prehistoric Society* 76, 271–96.

Jones, C. 2004. *The Burren and the Aran Islands: exploring the archaeology*. Cork: The Collins Press.

Jones, C. 2007. *Temples of stone: exploring the megalithic tombs of Ireland.* Cork: The Collins Press.

Jones, C. in preparation. Excavation of a court tomb at Parknabinnia, Co. Clare.

Jones, G. 2000. Evaluating the importance of cultivation and collecting in Neolithic Britain. In A.S. Fairbairn (ed.), *Plants in Neolithic Britain and beyond*, 79–84. Oxford: Oxbow Books.

Jones, G. 2005. Garden cultivation of staple crops and its implications for settlement location and continuity. *World Archaeology* 37, 164–76.

Jones, G. and Legge, A. 1987. The grape (*Vitis vinifera* L.) in the Neolithic of Britain. *Antiquity* 61, 452–5.

Jones, G. and Legge, A.J. 2008. Evaluating the role of cereal cultivation in the Neolithic: charred plant remains from Hambledon Hill. In R. Mercer and F. Healy, *Hambledon Hill, Dorset: excavation and survey of a Neolithic monument complex and its surrounding landscape*, 469–76. Swindon: English Heritage.

Jones, M. 2009. Comments. In B. Hayden, 'Funerals as feasts: why are they so important?' *Cambridge Archaeological Journal* 19, 42–3.

Jones, N.W. 2010. Womaston Neolithic causewayed enclosure, Powys: survey and excavation 2008. *Archaeologia Cambrensis* 158, 19–42.

Jones, P. 2008. *A Neolithic ring ditch and later prehistoric features at Staines Road Farm, Shepperton*. Godalming: Surrey County Archaeological Unit.

Jope, M. 1965. Faunal remains. 2. Frequencies and ages of species. In I.F. Smith, *Windmill Hill and Avebury: excavations by Alexander Keiller, 1925–1939*, 142–5. Oxford: Clarendon Press.

Jordan, D., Haddon-Reece, D. and Bayliss, A. 1994. *Radiocarbon dates from samples funded by English Heritage and dated before 1981*. London: English Heritage.

Karlsberg, A.J. 2006. *Flexible Bayesian methods for archaeological dating*. Unpublished PhD thesis, University of Sheffield.

Keeley, L. 1996. *War before civilization*. New York and Oxford: Oxford University Press.

Keevill, G. 1992. Northampton, King's Heath; Whitelands. *South Midlands Archaeology* 22, 42–4.

Keiller, A. 1934. Excavation at Windmill Hill. In *Proceedings of the First International Congress of Prehistoric and Protohistoric Sciences, London, August 1–6 1932*, 135–8. Oxford: Oxford University Press.

Keith, A. 1913. Report on the human remains found by F.J. Bennett, Esq., FGS, in the central chamber of a megalithic monument at Coldrum, Kent. *Journal of the Royal Anthropological Institute of Great Britain and Ireland* 43, 86–100.

Kelleher, H. 2009. *Tullahedy, Co. Tipperary Neolithic enclosure and settlement*. In I. Bennett (ed.), *Excavations 2006*, 516–8. Wordwell: Bray.

Kendall, H.G. 1914. Flint implements from the surface near Avebury: their classification and dates. *Proceedings of the Society of Antiquaries of London* (2nd series) 26, 73–85.

Kendall, H.G. 1919. Windmill Hill, Avebury and Grime's Graves: cores and choppers. *Proceedings of the Prehistoric Society of East Anglia* 3, 104–8, 192–9.

Kendall, H.G. 1922. Scraper-core industries of north Wilts. *Proceedings of the Prehistoric Society of East Anglia* 3, 515–41.

Kendall, H.G. 1923. Excavations conducted on the NE side of Windmill Hill. In *Report of the Earthworks Committee: accounts, reports of the council and of the congress for the year 1922*, 25–26. London: Congress of Archaeological Societies/Society of Antiquaries of London.

Kendrick, J. 1995. Excavation of a Neolithic enclosure and an Iron Age settlement at Douglasmuir, Angus. *Proceedings of the Society of Antiquaries of Scotland* 125, 29–67.

Kenney, J. 2009. Recent excavations at Parc Bryn Cegin, Llandygai, near Bangor, north Wales. *Archaeologia Cambrensis* 157, 9–142.

Kenney, J. and Davidson, A. 2006. Neolithic houses – and more besides – at Llandygai. *Current Archaeology* 203, 592–7.

Kenny, J. 1994. *Archaeological investigation: Trundle Triangle car park*. Chichester: Chichester District Archaeological Unit.

Kenward, R. 1982. A Neolithic burial enclosure at New Wintles Farm, Eynsham. In H. Case and A. Whittle (eds), *Settlement patterns in the Oxford region: excavations at the Abingdon causewayed enclosure and other sites*, 51–4. London: Council for British Archaeology.

Keynes, J.M. 1923. *A tract on monetary reform*. London: Macmillan.

Kiely, J. 2003. A Neolithic house at Cloghers, Co. Kerry. In I. Armit, E. Murphy, E. Nelis and D. Simpson (eds), *Neolithic settlement in Ireland and western Britain*, 182–7. Oxford: Oxbow Books.

Kiely, J. and Dunne, L. 2005. Recent archaeological excavations in the Tralee area. In M. Connolly (ed.), *Past kingdoms: recent archaeological research, survey and excavation in County Kerry*, 40–64. Tralee: The Heritage Centre.

Kigoshi, K. and Endo, K. 1962. Gakushuin natural radiocarbon measurements I. *Radiocarbon* 4, 84–94.

Kigoshi, K. and Endo, K. 1963. Gakushuin radiocarbon measurements II. *Radiocarbon* 5, 109–71.

Kind, C.-J. 1998. Komplexe Wildbeuter und frühe Ackerbauern. Bemerkungen zur Ausbreitung der Linearbandkeramik im südlichen Mitteleuropa. *Germania* 76, 1–24.

Kinnes, I. 1978. The earlier prehistoric pottery. In J. Hedges and

D. Buckley, 'Excavations at a Neolithic causewayed enclosure, Orsett, Essex, 1975'. *Proceedings of the Prehistoric Society* 44, 259–368.

Kinnes, I. 1979a. *Round barrows and ring ditches in the British Neolithic*. London: Department of Prehistoric and Romano-British Antiquities, British Museum.

Kinnes, I.A. 1979b. Description of the Neolithic bowl. In J.M. Coles and B.J. Orme, 'The Sweet Track: Drove site'. *Somerset Levels Papers* 5, 52–4.

Kinnes, I. 1988. The cattleship Potemkin: reflections on the first Neolithic in Britain. In J.C. Barrett and I. Kinnes (eds), *The archaeology of context in the Neolithic and Bronze Age: recent trends*, 2–8. Sheffield: Department of Archaeology and Prehistory.

Kinnes, I. 1991. The Neolithic pottery. In S. Needham, *Excavation and salvage at Runnymede Bridge, 1978: the Late Bronze Age waterfront site*, 157–61. London: British Museum Press.

Kinnes, I. 1992a. *Non-megalithic long barrows and allied structures in the British Neolithic*. London: British Museum.

Kinnes, I. 1992b. Balnagowan and after: the context of non-megalithic mortuary sites in Scotland. In N. Sharples and A. Sheridan (eds), *Vessels for the ancestors: essays in honour of Audrey Henshall*, 83–103. Edinburgh: Edinburgh University Press.

Kinnes, I. 1998. The pottery. In F. Pryor, *Etton: excavations at a Neolithic causewayed enclosure near Maxey, Cambridgeshire, 1982–87*, 161–214. London: English Heritage.

Kinnes, I. 1999. Longtemps ignorées: Passy-Rots, linear monuments in northern France. In A. Barclay and J. Harding (eds), *Pathways and ceremonies: the cursus monuments of Britain and Ireland*, 148–54. Oxford: Oxbow Books.

Kinnes, I. and Pryor, F. 1998. Fired clay. In F. Pryor, *Etton: excavations at a Neolithic causewayed enclosure near Maxey, Cambridgeshire, 1982–87*, 269–70. London: English Heritage.

Kinnes, I. and Thorpe, I.J. 1986. Radiocarbon dating: use and abuse. *Antiquity* 60, 221–3.

Kirkham, G. 2005. Prehistoric linear ditches on the Marlborough Downs. In G. Brown, D. Field and D. McOmish (eds), *The Avebury landscape: aspects of the field archaeology of the Marlborough Downs*, 149–55. Oxford: Oxbow Books.

Klassen, L. 2004. *Jade und Kupfer: Untersuchungen zum Neolithisierungsprozess im westlichen Ostseeraum unter besonderer Berücksichtigung der Kulturenentwicklung Europas 5500–3500 BC*. Aarhus: Aarhus University Press.

Klatt, S. 2009. Die neolithischen Einhegungen im westlichen Ostseeraum. In T. Terberger (ed.), *Neue Forschungen zum Neolithikum im Ostseeraum*, 7–134. Rahden: Marie Leidorf.

Knapp, A.B. (ed.) 1992. *Archaeology, Annales, and ethnohistory*. Cambridge: Cambridge University Press.

Knight, M. 2006a. Pottery [from the long barrow]. In C. Evans and I. Hodder, *A woodland archaeology. Neolithic sites at Haddenham: the Haddenham project volume 1*, 158–61. Cambridge: McDonald Institute for Archaeological Research.

Knight, M. 2006b. The F.534 pottery. In C. Evans and I. Hodder, *A woodland archaeology. Neolithic sites at Haddenham: the Haddenham project volume 1*, 279. Cambridge: McDonald Institute for Archaeological Research.

Knight, M. 2006c. Prehistoric pottery. In C. Evans, M. Edmonds and S. Boreham, ' "Total archaeology" and model landscapes: excavation of the Great Wilbraham causewayed enclosure, Cambridgeshire, 1975–76'. *Proceedings of the Prehistoric Society* 72, 134–9.

Knüsel, C. 2007. The arrowhead injury to Individual B2. In D. Benson and A. Whittle (eds), *Building memories: the Neolithic Cotswold long barrow at Ascott-under-Wychwood*, 218–20. Oxford: Oxbow Books.

Koch, R. 2005. *Das Erdwerk der Michelsberger Kultur auf dem Hetzenberg bei Heilbronn-Neckargartach.* Stuttgart: Theiss.

Koschik, H. (ed.) 2004. *Der bandkeramische Siedlungsplatz von Erkelenz-Kückhoven. I. Untersuchungen zum bandkeramischen Siedlungsplatz Erkelenz-Kückhoven, Kreis Heinsberg (Grabungskampagnen 1989–1994). Archäologie*. Köln: Rheinland Verlag.

Krause, R., Arbogast, R.-M., Hönschiedt, S., Lienemann, J., Papadopoulos, S., Rösch, M., Sidéra, I., Smettan, H.-W., Strien, H.-C. and Welge, K. 1998. Die bandkeramischen Siedlungsgrabungen bei Vaihingen an der Enz, Kreis Ludwigsburg (Baden-Württemberg). Ein Vorbericht zu den Ausgrabungen von 1994–1997. *Bericht der Römisch-Germanischen Kommission* 79, 5–105.

Kromer, B., Rhein, M., Bruns, M., Schoch-Fischer, B., Münnich, K.-O., Stuiver, M. and Becker, B. 1986. Radiocarbon calibration data for the 6th to the 8th millennia BC. *Radiocarbon* 28, 954–60.

Kromer, B., Manning, S. W., Kuniholm, P. I., Newton, M. W., Spurk, M. and Levin, I. 2001. Regional $^{14}CO_2$ offsets in the troposphere: magnitude, mechanisms, and consequences. *Science* 294, 2529–32.

Kytmannow, T. 2008. *Portal tombs in the landscape: the chronology, morphology and landscape setting of portal tombs in Ireland, Wales and Cornwall.* Oxford: Archaeopress.

Lacaille, A.D. and Grimes, W.F. 1955. The prehistory of Caldey. *Archaeologia Cambrensis* 104, 85–165.

Lacaille, A.D. and Grimes, W.F. 1961. The prehistory of Caldey. Part 2. *Archaeologia Cambrensis* 110, 30–70.

Laidlaw, M. 1999. Pottery [from Long Range]. In A. Fitzpatrick, C.A. Butterworth and J. Grove, *Prehistoric and Roman sites in east Devon: the A30 Honiton to Exeter imporvement DBFO, 1996–9*, 148–52. Salisbury: Wessex Archaeology.

Laidlaw, M. and Mepham, L. 1999. Pottery [from Castle Hill]. In A. Fitzpatrick, C.A. Butterworth and J. Grove, *Prehistoric and Roman sites in east Devon: the A30 Honiton to Exeter imporvement DBFO, 1996–9*, 43–51. Salisbury: Wessex Archaeology.

Lamdin-Whymark, H. 2003. Fairford, Horcott Pit, SU 14329873. *Transactions of the Bristol and Gloucestershire Archaeological Society* 121, 277.

Lancaster University Archaeology Unit 1992. *Billown Quarry, Malew, Isle of Man: archaeological work and investigations*. Limited circulation printed report.

Lane Fox, A.H. 1876. Excavations in Cissbury Camp, Sussex: being a report of the exploration committee of the Anthropological Institute for the year 1975. *Journal of the Anthropological Institute* 5, 357–90.

Lanting, J.N. and Brindley, A.L. 1996. Irish logboats and their European context. *Journal of Irish Archaeology* 7, 85–95.

Lanting, J.N. and Brindley, A.L. 1998. Dating cremated bone: the dawn of a new era. *Journal of Irish Archaeology* 10, 1–8.

Lanting, J.N. and van der Plicht, J. 1994. ^{14}C AMS: pros and cons for archaeology. *Palaeohistoria* 35/36, 1–12.

Lanting, J.N., Aerts-Bijma, A.T. and van der Plicht, J. 2001. Dating of cremated bones. *Radiocarbon* 43, 249–54.

Larson, G., Albarella, U., Dobney, K., Rowley-Conwy, P., Schibler, J., Tresset, A., Vigne, J.-D., Edwards, C.D., Schlumbaum, A., Dinu, A., Bălăçsescu, A., Dolman, G., Tagliacozzo, A., Manaseryan, N., Miracle, P., van Wijngaarden-Bakker, L.,

Massetti, M., Bradley, D.G and Cooper, A. 2007. Ancient DNA, pig domestication, and the spread of the Neolithic into Europe. *Proceedings of the National Academy of Science* 104, 15276–81.

Larsson, L. 2007. Mistrust traditions, consider innovations? The Mesolithic-Neolithic transition in southern Scandinavia. In A. Whittle and V. Cummings (eds), *Going over: the Mesolithic-Neolithic transition in north-west Europe*, 595–616. Oxford: Oxford University Press for The British Academy.

Larsson, L. 2008. Ritual structures in south Scandinavian prehistory. *Proceedings of the Prehistoric Society* 74, 193–214.

Last, J. 1999. Out of line: cursuses and monument typology in eastern England. In A. Barclay and J. Harding (eds), *Pathways and ceremonies: the cursus monuments of Britain and Ireland*, 86–97. Oxford: Oxbow Books.

Last, J. 2005. Life by the river: a prehistoric landscape at Grendon, Northamptonshire. *Proceedings of the Prehistoric Society* 71, 333–60.

Lavender, N. 1995. Brightlingsea, ring ditch at Moverons Pit (TM 070 183). In P.J. Gilman and A. Bennett (eds), 'Archaeology in Essex 1994'. *Essex Archaeology and History* 26, 242.

Lavender, N. 1996. Brightlingsea, ring ditch at Moverons Pit (TM 070 183). In P.J. Gilman and A. Bennett (eds), 'Archaeology in Essex 1994'. *Essex Archaeology and History* 27, 266.

Law, I.A. and Hedges, R.E.M. 1989. A semi-automated bone pretreatment system and the pretreatment of older and contaminated samples. In A. Long, R.S. Kra and D. Srdoc (eds), Proceedings of the 13th International ^{14}C Conference, *Radiocarbon* 31(3), 247–53.

Lawson. A.J. 2007. *Chalkland: an archaeology of Stonehenge and its region.* East Knoyle: Hobnob Press.

Lawson-Jones, A. 2003. The flint. In D. Cole and A.M. Jones, 'Journeys to the rock: archaeological investigations at Tregarrick Farm, Roche, Cornwall'. *Cornish Archaeology* 41–42, 123–31.

Leach, A.L. 1918. Flint working sites on the submerged land surface (submerged forest) bordering the Pembrokeshire coast. *Proceedings of the Geological Association* 29(2), 46–64.

Leach, P.E. 1983. The excavation of a Neolithic causewayed enclosure on Barkhale Down, Bignor Hill, West Sussex. *Sussex Archaeological Collections* 121, 11–30.

Leaf, C.S. 1934. Report on the excavation of two sites in Mildenhall Fen. *Proceedings of the Cambridge Antiquarian Society* 35, 106–27.

Lech, J. 1997. Remarks on prehistoric flint mining and flint supply in European archaeology. In A. Ramos-Millán and M.A. Bustillo (eds), *Siliceous rocks and culture*, 611–37. Granada: Universidad de Granada.

Lee, F. 2006. Human skeletal remains. In C. Evans and I. Hodder, *A woodland archaeology. Neolithic sites at Haddenham: the Haddenham project volume 1*, 140–53. Cambridge: McDonald Institute for Archaeological Research.

Leech, R. 1977. *The upper Thames valley in Gloucestershire and Wiltshire*. Bristol: Committee for Rescue Archaeology in Avon, Gloucestershire and Somerset.

Leeds, E.T. 1922. Further discoveries of the Neolithic and Bronze Ages at Peterborough. *Antiquaries Journal* 2, 220–37.

Leeds, E.T. 1927. A Neolithic site at Abingdon, Berkshire. *Antiquaries Journal* 7, 438–64.

Leeds, E.T. 1928. A Neolithic site at Abingdon, Berkshire (second report). *Antiquaries Journal* 8, 461–77.

Leeds, E.T. 1929. The Neolithic site at Abingdon. *Antiquaries Journal* 9, 37.

Legge, A.J. 1981. Aspects of cattle husbandry In R. Mercer (ed.), *Farming practice in British prehistory*, 169–81. Edinburgh: Edinburgh University Press.

Legge, A.J. 2008. Livestock and Neolithic society at Hambledon Hill. In R. Mercer and F. Healy, *Hambledon Hill, Dorset: excavation and survey of a Neolithic monument complex and its surrounding landscape*, 536–86. Swindon: English Heritage.

Leivers, M. 2008. Worked and utilised stone. In M.J. Allen, M. Leivers, and C. Ellis, 'Neolithic causewayed enclosures and later prehistoric farming: duality, imposition and the role of predecessors at Kingsborough, Isle of Sheppey, Kent, UK'. *Proceedings of the Prehistoric Society* 74, 262.

Lelong, O. and MacGregor, G. 2007. *The lands of ancient Lothian: interpreting the archaeology of the A1*. Edinburgh: Society of Antiquaries of Scotland.

Lemonnier, P. 1991. From great men to big men: peace, substitution and competition in the Highlands of New Guinea. In M. Godelier and M. Strathern (eds), *Big men and great men: personifications of power in Melanesia*, 7–27. Cambridge: Cambridge University Press.

Leon, B. 2005. Mesolithic and Neolithic activity on Dalkey Island – a reassessment. *Journal of Irish Archaeology* 14, 1–21.

Leone, M. 1978. Time in American archaeology. In C.L. Redman, M.J. Berman, E.V. Curtin, W.T. Langhorne, N.M. Versaggi and J.C. Wanser (eds), *Social archaeology: beyond subsistence and dating*, 25–36. London: Academic Press.

Le Roux, C.-T. 1984. A propos des fouilles de Gavrinis (Morbihan): nouvelles données sur l'art mégalithique armoricain. *Bulletin de la Société Préhistorique Française* 81, 240–45.

Le Roux, C.-T. 1999. *L'outillage de pierre polie en métadolérite du type A. Les ateliers de Plussulien (Côtes d'Armor): production et diffusion au Néolithique dans la France de l'ouest et au delà.* Travaux du Laboratoire 'Anthropologie, Préhistoire et Quaternaire armoricains' 43. Rennes: Université de Rennes I.

Le Roux, C.-T. 2002. Plussulien et la diffusion des haches polies armoricaines. In J. Guilaine (ed.), *Matériaux, productions, circulations du Néolithique à l'Age du Bronze*, 101–14. Paris: Errance.

Lévi-Strauss, C. 1966. *The savage mind.* London: Weidenfeld and Nicholson.

Lewis, C. 2005. My time. *Current Archaeology* 196, 198–9.

Lewis, J. 2000. The Neolithic period. In MoLAS, *The archaeology of Greater London. An assessment of archaeological evidence for human presence in the area now covered by Greater London*, 63–80. London: Museum of London.

Lewis, J.M. 1974. Excavations at Rhos-y-clegyrn prehistoric site, St Nicholas, Pembs. *Archaeologia Cambrensis* 123, 13–42.

Lewis, M.P. 1992. *The prehistory of coastal south-west Wales 7500–3600 BP: an interdisciplinary palaeoenvironmental and archaeological investigation.* Unpublished PhD thesis, University of Wales, Lampeter.

Lewis, J.S.C. and Welsh, K. 2004. Perry Oaks – Neolithic inhabitation of a west London landscape. In J. Cotton and D. Field (eds), *Towards a New Stone Age: aspects of the Neolithic in south-east England,* 105–9. York: Council for British Archaeology.

Lichter, C. 2010. Michelsberger Erdwerke. *Archäologie in Deutschland* 3, 2010, 20–1.

Liddell, D.M. 1930. Report on the excavations at Hembury Fort, Devon, 1930. *Proceedings of the Devon Archaeological Society* 1.2, 39–63.

Liddell, D.M. 1931. Report on the excavations at Hembury Fort, Devon: second season 1931. *Proceedings of the Devon Archaeological Society* 1.3, 90–120.

Liddell, D.M. 1932. Report on the excavations at Hembury Fort, Devon, third season 1932. *Proceedings of the Devon Archaeological Society* 1.4, 162–90.

Liddell, D.M. 1935. Report on the excavations at Hembury Fort, Devon, 4th and 5th seasons 1934 and 1935. *Proceedings of the Devon Archaeological Society* 2.3, 135–75.

Lindley, D.V. 1985. *Making decisions* (second edition). London: Wiley.

Liversage, D. 1968. Excavations at Dalkey Island, Co. Dublin. *Proceedings of the Royal Irish Academy* 66C, 52–223.

Liversage, G.D. 1958. An island site at Lough Gur. *Journal of the Royal Society of Antiquaries of Ireland* 88, 67–81.

Loader, R.D. 2007. The Wootton Quarr Archaeological Survey. In J. Sidell and F. Haughey (eds), *Neolithic archaeology in the intertidal zone*, 48–58. Oxford: Oxbow Books.

Lobb, S. 1995. Excavations at Crofton causewayed enclosure. *Wiltshire Archaeological and Natural History Magazine* 88, 18–25.

Lodewijckx, M. and Bakels, C. 2009. Frontier settlements of the LBK in central Belgium. In D. Hofmann and P. Bickle (eds), *Creating communities: new advances in Central European Neolithic research*, 32–49. Oxford: Oxbow Books.

Logue, P. 2003. Excavations at Thornhill, Co. Londonderry. In I. Armit, E. Murphy, E. Nelis and D. Simpson (eds), *Neolithic settlement in Ireland and western Britain,* 149–55. Oxford: Oxbow Books.

Lombardo, J.L., Martinez, R. and Verret, D. 1984. Le site chasséen du Culfroid à Boury-en-Vexin dans son contexte historique et les apports de la stratigraphie de son fossé. *Revue Archéologique de Picardie* 1–2, 269–84.

Longin, R. 1971. New method of collagen extraction for radiocarbon dating. *Nature* 230, 241–2.

Longworth, I.H. 1979. The Neolithic and Bronze Age pottery. In G.J. Wainwright, *Mount Pleasant, Dorset: excavations 1970–1971*, 75–124. London: Society of Antiquaries of London.

Longworth, I.H. and Cleal, R. 1999. Grooved Ware gazetteer. In R. Cleal and A. Macsween (eds), *Grooved Ware in Britain and Ireland*, 177–206. Oxford: Oxbow Books.

Longworth, I.H. and Kinnes, I.A. 1980. *Sutton Hoo excavations 1966, 1968–70*. London: British Museum.

Longworth, I. and Varndell, G. 1996. The Neolithic pottery. In S. Needham, *Refuse and disposal at area 16, east Runnymede*, 100–5. London: British Museum Press.

Louwe Kooijmans, L. 1974. *The Rhine-Meuse delta. Four studies on its prehistoric occupation and Holocene geology*. Leiden: Brill.

Louwe Kooijmans, L.P. (ed.) 2001a. *Hardinxveld-Giessendam, Polderweg. Een jachtkamp uit het Laat-Mesolithicum, 5500-5000 v. Chr*. Amersfoort: Rapportage Archeologische Monumentenzorg 83.

Louwe Kooijmans, L.P. (ed.) 2001b. *Hardinxveld-Giessendam, De Bruin. Een jachtkamp uit het Laat-Mesolithicum en het begin van de Swifterbant-cultuur, 5500–4450 v. Chr*. Amersfoort: Rapportage Archeologische Monumentenzorg 85.

Louwe Kooijmans, L.P. 2007. The gradual transition to farming in the Lower Rhine Basin. In A. Whittle and V. Cummings (eds), *Going over: the Mesolithic-Neolithic transition in north-west Europe*, 287–309. Oxford: Oxford University Press for The British Academy.

Louwe Kooijmans, L.P. 2009. The agency factor in the process of Neolithisation – a Dutch case study. *Journal of Archaeology in the Low Countries* 1-1, 27–54.

Louwe Kooijmans, L.P. and Jongste, P.B.F. (eds) 2006. *Schipluiden, a Neolithic settlement on the Dutch North Sea coast, 3600–3400 cal BC*. Leiden: Analecta Praehistorica Leidensia 37/38 (2005–2006).

Louwe Kooijmans, L.P., van der Broeke, P.W., Fokkens, H. and van Gijn, A.L. (eds) 2005. *The prehistory of the Netherlands*. Amsterdam: Amsterdam University Press.

Loveday, R. 1989. The Barford ritual complex: further excavations (1972) and regional perspective. In A. Gibson (ed.), *Midlands prehistory: some recent and current researches into the prehistory of central England*, 51–84. Oxford: British Archaeological Reports.

Loveday, R. 2006. *Inscribed across the landscape: the cursus enigma*. Stroud: Tempus.

Lowe, J.J. and Walker, M.J.C. 2000. Radiocarbon dating the last glacial-interglacial transition (^{14}C ka BP) in terrestrial and marine records: the need for new quality assurance protocols. *Radiocarbon* 42, 53–68.

Lowell, J.C. 2007. Women and men in warfare and migration: implications of gender imbalance in the Grasshopper region of Arizona. *American Antiquity* 72, 95–123.

Lucas, G. 2005. *The archaeology of time*. London: Routledge.

Lucas, G. 2008. Time and the archaeological event. *Cambridge Archaeological Journal* 18, 59–65.

Lukes, A. and Zvelebil, M. 2008. Inter-generational transmission of culture and LBK origins: some indications from eastern-central Europe. In D. Bailey, A. Whittle and D. Hofmann (eds), *Living well together? Settlement and materiality in the Neolithic of south-east and central Europe*, 139–50. Oxford: Oxbow Books.

Lüning, J. 1967. Die Michelsberger Kultur: ihre Funde in zeitlicher und räumlicher Gliederung. *Bericht der Römisch-Germanischen Kommission* 48, 1–350.

Lüning, J. 2000. *Steinzeitliche Bauern in Deutschland: die Landwirtschaft im Neolithikum*. Bonn: Habelt.

Lüning, J. and Stehli, P. 1994. *Die Bandkeramik im Merzbachtal auf der Aldenhovener Platte*. Bonn: Habelt.

Lyman, R.L. and Harpole, J.L. 2002. A.L. Kroeber and the measurement of Time's Arrow and Time's Cycle. *Journal of Anthropological Research* 58, 313–38.

Lynch, A. 1988. Poulnabrone – a stone in time. *Archaeology Ireland* 2(3), 105–7.

Lynch, A. 1990. Comment. In R.E.M. Hedges, R.A. Housley, I.A. Law and C.R. Bronk, 'Radiocarbon dates from the Oxford AMS system: *Archaeometry* datelist 10'. *Archaeometry* 32, 101–8.

Lynch, A.H., Hamilton, J. and Hedges, R.E.M. 2008. Where the wild things are: aurochs and cattle in England. *Antiquity* 82, 1025–1039.

Lynch, A. and Ó Donnabhain, B. 1994. Poulnabrone portal tomb. *The Other Clare* 18, 5–7.

Lynch, F. 1972. Portal dolmens in the Nevern valley. In F.M. Lynch and C.B. Burgess (eds), *Prehistoric man in Wales and the west: essays in honour of Lily F. Chitty*, 67–84. Bath: Adams & Dart.

Lynch, F. 1975. Excavations at Carreg Samson, Mathry, Pembrokeshire. *Archaeologia Cambrensis* 124, 15–35.

Lynch, F. 1976. Towards a chronology of megalithic tombs in Wales. In G.C. Boon and J.M. Lewis (eds), *Welsh Antiquity*, 63–79. Cardiff: National Museum of Wales.

Lynch, F. 1984. Discussion [of the Neolithic pottery]. In W.J. Britnell, 'The Gwernvale long cairn, Crickhowell, Brecknock'. In W.J. Britnell and H.N. Savory, *Gwernvale and Penywyrlod: two Neolithic long cairns in the Black Mountains of Brecknock*, 106–10. Cardiff: Cambrian Archaeological Association.

Lynch, F. 1986. Excavation of a kerb circle and ring cairn on

Cefn Caer Euni, Merioneth. *Archaeologia Cambrensis* 135, 81–120.

Lynch, F. 1993. *Excavations in the Brenig Valley: a Mesolithic and Bronze Age landscape in north Wales*. Bangor: Cambrian Archaeological Association.

Lynch, F. 2000. The earlier Neolithic. In F. Lynch, S. Aldhouse-Green and J.L. Davies, *Prehistoric Wales*, 42–78. Stroud: Sutton Publishing.

Lynch, F., Aldhouse-Green, S. and Davies, J.L. 2000. *Prehistoric Wales*. Stroud: Sutton Publishing.

Lynch, F. and Musson, C. 2001. A prehistoric and early medieval complex at Llandegai, near Bangor, north Wales. *Archaeologia Cambrensis* 150, 17–142.

Maby, J.C. 1950. Ancient charcoals. In R. Musson, An excavation at Combe Hill camp near Eastbourne, August 1949. *Sussex Archaeological Collections* 89, 115.

MacGregor, G. and McLellan, K. 2007. A burning desire to build: excavations at Eweford West and Pencraig Hill (3950–3380 BC). In O. Lelong and G. MacGregor, *The lands of ancient Lothian: interpreting the archaeology of the A1*, 15–45. Edinburgh: Society of Antiquaries of Scotland.

MacKie, E.W. 1966. New excavations on the Monamore Neolithic chambered cairn, Lamlash, Isle of Arran, in 1961. *Proceedings of the Society of Antiquaries of Scotland* 97, 1–34.

Mackreth, D.F. forthcoming. Prehistoric burial sites and finds in Orton Meadows, Peterborough.

Macphail, R. 1990. The soils. In A. Saville, *Hazleton North, Gloucestershire, 1979–82: the excavation of a Neolithic long cairn of the Cotswold-Severn group*, 223–7. London: Historic Buildings and Monuments Commission for England.

Macphail, R. 1999. Soils. In A. Whittle, J. Pollard and C. Grigson, *The harmony of symbols: the Windmill Hill causewayed enclosure, Wiltshire*, 121–26. Oxford: Oxbow Books.

Macpherson-Grant, N. 1969. Two Neolithic bowls from Birchington, Thanet. *Archaeologia Cantiana* 84, 249–50.

Magilton, J. 1998. Sussex's first henge? *Sussex past and present. The Sussex Archaeological Society Newsletter* 84, 4–5.

Magny, M. 2004. Holocene climate variability as reflected by mid-European lake-level fluctuations and its probable impact on prehistoric human settlements. *Quaternary International* 113, 65–79.

Maitland Howard, M. 1965. The molluscan fauna from outer bank and ditch V. In I.F. Smith, *Windmill Hill and Avebury: excavations by Alexander Keiller, 1925–1939*, 38–40. Oxford: Clarendon Press.

Malim, T. 1999. Cursuses and related monuments of the Cambridgeshire Ouse. In A. Barclay and J. Harding (eds), *Pathways and ceremonies: the cursus monuments of Britain and Ireland*, 77–85. Oxford and Oakville: Oxbow Books.

Malim, T. 2000. The ritual landscape of the Neolithic and Bronze Age along the middle and lower Ouse valley. In M. Dawson (ed.), *Prehistoric, Roman, and Post-Roman landscapes of the Great Ouse valley*, 57–88. London: Council for British Archaeology.

Mallory, J.P. 1993. A Neolithic ditched enclosure in Northern Ireland. In J. Pavúk (ed.), *Actes du XIIe congrès international des Sciences Préhistoriques et Protohistoriques. Bratislava, 1–7 septembre 1991. Volume 2*, 415–18. Bratislava: Institut Archéologique de l'Académie Slovaque des Sciences, Nitra.

Mallory, J.P. and Hartwell, B. 1984. Donegore Hill. *Current Archaeology* 92, 271–4.

Mallory, J.P. and McNeill, T. E. 1991. *The archaeology of Ulster from colonization to plantation*. Belfast: Institute of Irish Studies, Queen's University Belfast.

Mallory, J.P., Nelis, E. and Hartwell, B. forthcoming. *Excavations on Donegore Hill, Co. Antrim*. Bray: Wordwell.

Malone, C. 1989. *The English Heritage book of Avebury*. London: Batsford and English Heritage.

Maltby, M. 1990. Animal bones [from the Coneybury Anomaly]. In J.C. Richards, *The Stonehenge environs project*, 57–61. London: Historic Buildings and Monuments Commission.

Maltby, M. 1991. The animal bones. In P.J. Woodward, *The South Dorset Ridgeway: survey and excavations 1977–84*, 105–6. Dorchester: Dorset Natural History and Archaeological Society.

Maltby, M. 2002. Animal bones from prehistoric features. In S.M. Davies, P.S. Bellamy, M.J. Heaton and P.J. Woodward, *Excavations at Alington Avenue, Fordington, Dorchester, Dorset, 1984–7*, 53–5. Dorchester: Dorset Natural History and Archaeological Society.

Maltby, M. 2004. Animal bones. In M. Rawlings, M.J. Allen and F. Healy, Investigation of the Whitesheet Down environs 1989–90: Neolithic causewayed enclosure and Iron Age settlement. *Wiltshire Studies* 97, 167–71.

Maltby, M. 2007. Animal bone from the Fir Tree Field Shaft and associated pits. In C. French, H. Lewis, M.J. Allen, M. Green, R. Scaife and J. Gardiner, *Prehistoric landscape development and human impact in the upper Allen valley, Cranborne Chase, Dorset*, 295–9. Cambridge: McDonald Institute for Archaeological Research.

Mandal, S. 1997. Striking the balance: the roles of petrography and geochemistry in stone axe studies in Ireland. *Archaeometry* 39, 289–308.

Mandal, S. 2007. Petrolographical report on stone objects found in archaeological investigations relating to the Sligo Inner Relief Road. In E. Danaher, *Monumental beginnings: the archaeology of the N4 Sligo inner relief road*, CD for Area 2C. Dublin: National Roads Authority.

Mann, W.B. 1983. An international reference material for radiocarbon dating. *Radiocarbon* 25, 519–27.

Manning, C. 1985. A Neolithic burial mound at Ashleypark, Co. Tipperary. *Proceedings of the Royal Irish Academy* 85C, 61–100.

Mant, A.K. 1987. Knowledge acquired from post-war exhumations. In A. Boddington, A.N. Garland and R.C. Janaway (eds), *Death, decay and reconstruction: approaches to archaeology and forensic science*, 65–80. Manchester: Manchester University Press.

Marchand, G. 2007. Neolithic fragrances: Mesolithic-Neolithic interactions in western France. In A. Whittle and V. Cummings (eds), *Going over: the Mesolithic-Neolithic transition in north-west Europe*, 225–42. Oxford: Oxford University Press for The British Academy.

Marcigny, C., Ghesquière, E. and Desloges, J. 2007. *La hache et la meule: les premiers paysans du Néolithique en Normandie (6000–2000 avant notre ère)*. Le Havre: Muséum d'Histoire Naturelle du Havre.

Mariotti, A. 1983. Atmospheric nitrogen is a reliable standard for natural 15N measurements. *Nature* 303, 685–7.

Markham, M. 2000. *Provenance studies of British prehistoric greenstone implements using non- destructive analytical methods*. Unpublished PhD thesis, Open University.

Marolle, C. 1998. Le site Michelsberg des "Hautes Chanvières" avec bâtiments et enceinte à Mairy, Ardennes – France. In J. Biel, H. Schlichtherle, M. Strobel and A. Zeeb (eds), *Die Michelsberger Kultur und ihre Randgebiete – Probleme der Entstehung, Chronologie und des Siedlungswesens*, 21–9. Stuttgart: Theiss.

Marshall, A. 1995. Salmonsbury. In B. Rawes (ed.), 'Archaeological review no. 19, 1994'. *Transactions of the Bristol and Gloucestershire Archaeological Society* 113, 185–6.
Marshall, D.N. and Taylor, I.N. 1979. Excavation of the chambered cairn at Glenvoidean, Isle of Bute. *Proceedings of the Society of Antiquaries of Scotland* 108, 1–39.
Marshall, P.D. 2008. Appendix XVI: radiocarbon dates. In J. Kenney, *Recent excavations at Llandygai, near Bangor, north Wales: full excavation report*, 186–204. Gwynedd Archaeological Trust Report No. 764.
Marshall, P.D., Hamilton, W.D., Woodward, A. and Beamish, M. forthcoming. A precise chronology for Peterborough Ware?
Martin, E.A. 1981. The barrows of Suffolk. In A.J. Lawson, E.A. Martin and D. Priddy, *The barrows of East Anglia*, 64–88. Gressenhall, Bury St Edmunds and Chelmsford: Norfolk Archaeological Unit, Suffolk County Council and Essex County Council.
Martin, E.A. 1982. When is a henge not a henge? *Proceedings of the Suffolk Institute of Archaeology and History* 35, 141–3.
Martin, E.A. 1989. The Neolithic. In D. Dymond and E. Martin (eds), *An historical atlas of Suffolk*, 36–7. (Second edition.) Ipswich: Suffolk County Council, Environment & Transport and Suffolk Institute of Archaeology and History.
Martin, P. 2001. *Was Maiden Castle defended in the Neolithic?* Unpublished BSc. dissertation, University of Bournemouth.
Masters, L. 1973. The Lochhill long cairn. *Antiquity* 47, 96–100.
Matthews, C.L. 1976. *Occupation sites on the Chiltern Ridge: excavation at Puddlehill and sites near Dunstable, Bedfordshire – Part I: Neolithic, Bronze Age and Early Iron Age*. Oxford: British Archaeological Reports.
Matuschik, I. 1991. Grabenwerke des Spätneolithikums in Süddeutschland. *Fundberichte aus Baden-Württemberg* 16, 27–55.
Mauvilly, M., Jeunesse, C. and Doppler, T. 2008. Ein Tonstempel aus der spätmesolithischen Fundstelle von Arconciel/La Souche (Kanton Freiburg, Schweiz). *Quartär* 55, 151–7.
Mays, S. 1998. *The archaeology of human bones*. London: Routledge.
McAulay, I.R. and Watts, W.A. 1961. Dublin radiocarbon dates I. *Radiocarbon* 3, 26–38.
McAvoy, F. 2000. The development of a Neolithic monument complex at Godmanchester, Cambridgeshire. In M. Dawson (ed.), *Prehistoric, Roman, and Post-Roman landscapes of the Great Ouse valley*, 51–6. York: Council for for British Archaeology.
McCartan, S.B. 1994. A later Mesolithic site at Rhendoo, Jurby. *Proceedings of the Isle of Man Natural Hitory and Antiquarian Society* 10, 88–117.
McCartan, S.B. 1999. The Manx Early Mesolithic: a story set in stone. In P.J. Davey (ed.), *Recent archaeological research on the Isle of Man*, 5–11. Oxford: British Archaeological Reports.
McCartan, S.B. 2000. The utilisation of island environments in the Irish Mesolithic: agendas for Rathlin Island. In A. Desmond, G. Johnson, M. McCarthy, J. Sheehan and E. Shee Twohig (eds), *New agendas in Irish prehistory: papers in commemoration of Liz Anderson*, 15–30. Bray: Wordwell.
McCartan, S., Schulting, R., Warren, G. and Woodman, P. (eds) 2009. *Mesolithic horizons*. Oxford: Oxbow Books.
McClatchie, M., Whitehouse, N., Schulting, R., Bogaard, A. and Barratt, P. 2009. Cultivating societies: new insights into agriculture in Neolithic Ireland. In M. Stanley, E. Danaher and J. Eogan, (eds), *Dining and dwelling*, 1–8. Dublin: National Roads Authority.
McColl, L.J. 2006. *Issues of contemporaneity in palaeoenvironmental and archaeological records*. Unpublished PhD thesis, University of Sheffield.
McConway, C. 2000. *Tullahedy, Co. Tipperary Neolithic landscape*. In I. Bennett (ed.), *Excavations 1998*, 203–4. Wordwell: Bray.
McCormac, F.G. 1992. Liquid scintillation counter characterisation, optimisation, and benzene purity correction. *Radiocarbon* 34, 37–45.
McCormac, F.G., Bayliss, A., Baillie, M.G.L. and Brown, D.M. 2004. Radiocarbon calibration in the Anglo-Saxon period: AD 495–725. *Radiocarbon* 46, 1123–5.
McCormac, F.G., Bayliss, A., Brown, D.M., Reimer, P.J. and Thompson, M.M. 2008. Extended radiocarbon calibration in the Anglo-Saxon Period, AD 395–485 and AD 735–805. *Radiocarbon* 50, 11–17.
McCormac, F.G., Kalin, R.M. and Long, A. 1993. Radiocarbon dating beyond 50,000 years by liquid scintillation counting. In J.E. Noakes, F. Schönhofer and H.A. Polach (eds), *Liquid scintillation spectrometry 1992*, 125–33. Tucson, Arizona: Radiocarbon.
McErlean, T., McConkey, R. and Forsythe, W. 2002. *Strangford Lough: an archaeological survey of the maritime cultural landscape*. Belfast: Blackstaff Press.
McFadyen, L. 2006. Landscape. In C. Conneller and G. Warren (eds), *Mesolithic Britain and Ireland: new approaches*, 121–38. Stroud: Tempus.
McFadyen, L. 2007. Making architecture. In D. Benson and A. Whittle (eds), *Building memories: the Neolithic Cotswold long barrow at Ascott-under-Wychwood, Oxfordshire*, 348–54. Oxford: Oxbow Books.
McIntosh, S.K. (ed.) 1999. *Beyond chiefdoms: pathways to complexity in Africa*. Cambridge: Cambridge University Press.
McKeown, S.A. 1999. Charred wood remains. In P. Woodman, E. Anderson and N. Finlay, *Excavations at Ferriter's Cove, 1983–95: last foragers, first farmers on the Dingle Peninsula*, 104–6, 214–17. Bray: Wordwell.
McKinley, J. 2008. Human remains. In R. Mercer and F. Healy, *Hambledon Hill, Dorset: excavation and survey of a Neolithic monument complex and its surrounding landscape*, 477–521. Swindon: English Heritage.
McManus, C. 2004. Mullaghbuoy. In I. Bennett (ed.), *Excavations 2002: summary accounts of archaeological excavations in Ireland*, 7–8. Bray: Wordwell.
McNabb, J., Felder, P.J., Kinnes, I. and Sieveking, G. 1996. An archive on recent excavations at Harrow Hill, Sussex. *Sussex Archaeological Collections* 134, 21–37.
McOmish, D. 1999. A new earthwork survey. In A. Whittle, J. Pollard and C. Grigson, *The harmony of symbols: the Windmill Hill causewayed enclosure, Wiltshire*, 14–17. Oxford: Oxbow Books.
McOmish, D. 2005. Bronze Age land allotment on the Marlborough Downs. In G. Brown, D. Field and D. McOmish (eds), *The Avebury landscape: aspects of the field archaeology of the Marlborough Downs*, 133–6. Oxford: Oxbow Books.
McOmish, D., Field, D. and Brown, G. 2002. *The field archaeology of the Salisbury Plain training area*. Swindon: English Heritage.
McQuade, M., Molloy, B. and Moriarty, C. 2009. *In the shadow of the glen: archaeological excavations along the N8 Cashel to Mitchelstown Road Scheme*. Dublin: National Roads Authority.
McSparron, C. 2003. The excavation of a Neolithic house and

other structures at Enagh, County Derry. *Ulster Journal of Archaeology* 62, 1–13.

McSparron, C. 2008. Have you no homes to go to? *Archaeology Ireland* 85, 18–21.

Meadows, J. 2003. *Dating Briar Hill: interpreting controversial radiocarbon results from the Neolithic causewayed enclosure at Briar Hill, Northamptonshire*. Portsmouth: English Heritage.

Meadows, J., Barclay, A. and Bayliss, A. 2007. A short passage of time: the dating of the Hazleton long cairn revisited. *Cambridge Archaeological Journal* 17.1, supplement, 45–64.

Meadows, J., Marshall, P. and Sidell, J. forthcoming. *Absolute dating: a regional review for London: volume I (physical and chemical methods)*.

Megerssa, G. and Kassam, A. 2005. The 'rounds' of time: time, history and society in Borano Oromo. In W. James and D. Mills (eds), *The qualities of time: anthropological approaches*, 251–65. Oxford: Berg.

Mein, A. G. 1992. Excavations at Trostrey Castle, Usk, Gwent. *Archaeology in Wales* 32, 11–14.

Mein, A.G. 1994. Trostrey Castle, Trostrey. *Archaeology in Wales* 36, 48–50.

Mein, A.G. 1996. Trostrey Castle, Trostrey. *Archaeology in Wales* 36, 64–6.

Mein, A.G. 2002. Trostrey Castle, Trostrey. *Archaeology in Wales* 42, 107–10.

Mein, A.G. 2003. Neolithic mortuary ritual at Trostrey, Monmouthshire [and] Trostrey Castle, Trostrey. *Archaeology in Wales* 43, 65–9, 107–10.

Mellars, P. and Dark, P. 1998. *Star Carr in context: new archaeological and palaeoecological investigations at the early Mesolithic site of Star Carr, north Yorkshire*. Cambridge: McDonald Institute for Archaeological Research.

Meniel, P. 1987. Les dépôts animaux du fossé chasséen de Boury-en-Vexin. *Revue Archéologique de Picardie* 1–2, 3–26.

Menotti, F. (ed.) 2004. *Living on the lake in prehistoric Europe: 150 years of lake-dwelling research*. London and New York: Routledge.

Mepham, L. 2004. Pottery. In C.J. Ellis, *A prehistoric ritual complex at Eynesbury, Cambridgeshire: excavation of a multi-period site in the Great Ouse valley, 2000–2001*, 28–32. Salisbury: Wessex Archaeological Trust.

Mercer, R.J. 1980. *Hambledon Hill: a Neolithic landscape*. Edinburgh: Edinburgh University Press.

Mercer, R.J. 1981a. Excavations at Carn Brea, Illogan, Cornwall, 1970–1973: a Neolithic fortified complex of the third millennium bc. *Cornish Archaeology* 20.

Mercer, R.J. 1981b. *Grimes Graves, Norfolk. Excavations 1971–72: volume I*. London: HMSO.

Mercer, R.J. 1984. Everley Water Meadow, Iwerne Stepleton, Dorset. *Proceedings of the Dorset Natural History and Archaeological Society* 106, 110–11.

Mercer, R.J. 1985. A Neolithic fortress and funeral center. *Scientific American* 252(3), 94–101.

Mercer, R.J. 1986. The Neolithic in Cornwall. *Cornish Archaeology* 25, 35–80.

Mercer, R.J. 1987. A flint quarry in the Hambledon Hill Neolithic enclosure complex. In G. de G. Sieveking and M.H. Newcomer (eds), *The human uses of flint and chert: papers from the fourth International Flint Symposium*, 160–3. Cambridge: Cambridge University Press.

Mercer, R.J. 1988. Hambledon Hill, Dorset, England. In C. Burgess, P. Topping, C. Mordant and M. Maddison (eds), *Enclosures and defences in the Neolithic of western Europe*, 89–106. Oxford: British Archaeological Reports.

Mercer, R.J. 1990. *Causewayed enclosures*. Princes Risborough: Shire Publications.

Mercer, R.J. 1997. The excavation of a Neolithic enclosure complex at Helman Tor, Lostwithiel, Cornwall. *Cornish Archaeology* 36, 5–61.

Mercer, R.J. 1999. The origins of warfare in the British Isles. In J. Carman and A. Harding (eds), *Ancient warfare*, 143–56. Stroud: Sutton Publishing Ltd.

Mercer, R.J. 2001. Neolithic enclosed settlements in Cornwall: the past, the present and the future. In T. Darvill and J. Thomas (eds), *Neolithic enclosures in Atlantic northwest Europe*, 43–9. Oxford: Oxbow Books.

Mercer, R.J. 2003. The early farming settlement of south western England in the Neolithic. In I. Armit, E. Murphy, E. Nelis and D. Simpson (eds), *Neolithic settlement in Ireland and western Britain*, 56–70. Oxford: Oxbow Books.

Mercer, R. 2004. Enclosures and monumentality and the Mesolithic-Neolithic continuum. In R.M.J. Cleal and J. Pollard (eds), *Monuments and material culture. Papers in honour of an Avebury archaeologist: Isobel Smith*. East Knoyle: Hobnob Press, 39–46.

Mercer, R.J. 2006a. The first known enclosures in southern Britain: their nature, function and role, in space and time. In A. Harding, S. Sievers and N. Venclová (eds), *Enclosing the past: inside and outside in prehistory*, 69–75. Sheffield: J.R.Collins Publications.

Mercer, R.J. 2006b. By other means? The development of warfare in the British Isles 3000–500 BC. *Journal of Conflict Archaeology* 2, 119–51.

Mercer, R. 2008a. Hambledon among other causewayed enclosures. In R. Mercer and F. Healy, *Hambledon Hill, Dorset: excavation and survey of a Neolithic monument complex and its surrounding landscape*, 772–7. Swindon: English Heritage.

Mercer, R. 2008b. The nature of Neolithic enclosure construction at Hambledon Hill. In R. Mercer and F. Healy, *Hambledon Hill, Dorset: excavation and survey of a Neolithic monument complex and its surrounding landscape*, 744–53. Swindon: English Heritage.

Mercer, R. and Healy, F. 2008. *Hambledon Hill, Dorset: excavation and survey of a Neolithic monument complex and its surrounding landscape*. Swindon: English Heritage.

Metcalf, P. and Huntington, R. 1991. *Celebrations of death: the anthropology of mortuary ritual* (second edition). Cambridge: Cambridge University Press.

Meyer, M. and Raetzel-Fabian, D. 2006. Neolithische Grabenwerke in Mitteleuropa: ein Überblick. *www.jungsteinSITE.de*, 15. Dezember 2006, 1–54.

Middleton, J. 1960. *Lugbara religion: ritual and authority among an East African people*. London: Oxford University Press.

Middleton, R. 1998. Flint and chert artefacts. In F. Pryor, *Etton: excavations at a Neolithic causewayed enclosure near Maxey, Cambridgeshire, 1982–87*, 215–50. London: English Heritage.

Middleton, R. 2006a. The lithic assemblage [from the dyke-side investigations]. In C. Evans and I. Hodder, *A woodland archaeology. Neolithic sites at Haddenham: the Haddenham project volume 1*, 44–55. Cambridge: McDonald Institute for Archaeological Research.

Middleton, R. 2006b. The lithic assemblage [from test-pit investigations]. In C. Evans and I. Hodder, *A woodland archaeology. Neolithic sites at Haddenham: the Haddenham project volume 1*, 58–61. Cambridge: McDonald Institute for Archaeological Research.

Middleton, R. 2006c. The struck flint [from the long barrow]. In C. Evans and I. Hodder, *A woodland archaeology. Neolithic sites at Haddenham: the Haddenham project volume 1*, 161–71. Cambridge: McDonald Institute for Archaeological Research.

Middleton, R. 2006d. Struck flint [from the causewayed enclosure]. In C. Evans and I. Hodder, *A woodland archaeology. Neolithic sites at Haddenham: the Haddenham project volume 1*, 282–98. Cambridge: McDonald Institute for Archaeological Research.

Midgley, M. 1992. *TRB culture: the first farmers of the North European Plain*. Edinburgh: Edinburgh University Press.

Midgley, M. 2005. *The monumental cemeteries of prehistoric Europe*. Stroud: Tempus.

Midgley, M.S. 2008. *The megaliths of northern Europe*. London: Routledge.

Mielke, J.E. and Long, A. 1969. Smithsonian Institution radiocarbon measurements V. *Radiocarbon* 11, 163–82.

Milisauskas, S. 1986. *Early Neolithic settlement and society at Olszanica*. Ann Arbor: University of Michigan.

Miller, D. 1985. *Artefacts as categories: a study of ceramic variability in Central India*. Cambridge: Cambridge University Press.

Miller, D. 2008. *The comfort of things*. Cambridge: Polity Press.

Mills, B.J. 2007. Performing the feast: visual display and suprahousehold commensalism in the Puebloan Southwest. *American Antiquity* 72, 210–39.

Mills, J. 2006. *Modes of movement: Neolithic and Bronze Age human mobility in the Great Ouse, Nene and Welland river valleys*. Unpublished PhD thesis, Cardiff University.

Milner, N., Craig, O., Bailey, G., Pedersen, K. and Andersen, S. 2004. Something fishy in the Neolithic? A re-evaluation of stable isotope analysis of Mesolithic and Neolithic coastal populations. *Antiquity* 78, 9–22.

Mitchell, A.F. 1974. *A field guide to the trees of Britain and northern Europe*. London: Collins.

Mitchell, A. 1978. *A field guide to the trees of Britain and northern Europe* (second edition). London: Collins.

Mitchell, F. 1990. Early Bronze Age fulachts on Valencia Island. In V. Buckley (ed.), *Burnt offerings: international contributions to burnt mound archaeology*, 24–31. Dublin: Wordwell.

Mitchell, G.F. 1989. *Man and environment in Valencia Island*. Dublin: Royal Irish Academy.

Mithen, S. 2003. *After the ice: a global human history 20,000–5000 BC*. London: Weidenfeld and Nicholson.

Mithen, S., Pirie, A., Smith, S. and Wicks, K. 2007. The Mesolithic-Neolithic transition in western Scotland: a review and new evidence from Tiree. In A. Whittle and V. Cummings (eds), *Going over: the Mesolithic-Neolithic transition in north-west Europe*, 511–41. Oxford: Oxford University Press for The British Academy.

Molleson, T.I. 1986. New radiocarbon dates for the occupation of Kilgreany Cave, County Waterford. *Journal of Irish Archaeology* 3, 1–3.

Molloy, K. and O'Connell, M. 1987. The nature of the vegetational changes at about 5,000 BP, with particular reference to the elm decline: fresh evidence from Connemara, western Ireland. *New Phytologist* 106, 203–20.

Molloy, K. and O'Connell, M. 1991. Palaeoecological investigations towards the reconstruction of woodland and land-use history at Lough Sheeauns, Connemara, western Ireland. *Review of Palaeobotany and Palynology* 67, 75–113.

Molloy, K. and O'Connell, M. 1995. Palaeoecological investigations towards the reconstruction of environment and land-use changes during prehistory at Ceide Fields, western Ireland. *Probleme der Küstenforschung im südlichen Nordseegebiet* 23, 187–225.

Money, J.H. 1960. Excavation at High Rocks, Tunbridge Wells, 1954–1956. *Sussex Archaeological Collections* 98, 173–222.

Money, J.H. 1962. Excavations at High Rocks, Tunbridge Wells, 1954–1956: supplementary note. *Sussex Archaeological Collections* 100, 149–50.

Monk, M. 1993. People and environment: in search of farmers. In E. Shee Twohig and M. Ronayne (eds), *Past perceptions: the prehistoric archaeology of south-west Ireland*, 35–52. Cork: Cork University Press.

Monk, M. 2000. Seeds and soils of discontent: an environmental archaeological contribution to the nature of the early Neolithic. In A. Desmond, G. Johnson, M. McCarthy, J. Sheehan and E. Shee Twohig (eds), *New agendas in Irish prehistory: papers in commemoration of Liz Anderson*, 67–87. Bray: Wordwell.

Mook, W.G. 1986. Business meeting: recommendations/resolutions adopted by the twelfth international radiocarbon conference. *Radiocarbon* 28, 799.

Mook, W.G. and Streurman, H.J. 1983. Physical and chemical aspects of radiocarbon dating. In W.G. Mook and H.T. Waterbolk (eds), *Proceedings of the first international symposium ^{14}C and Archaeology*, 31–55. *PACT* 8.

Mook, W.G. and Waterbolk, H.T. 1985. *Radiocarbon dating. Handbooks for archaeologists 3*. Strasbourg: European Science Foundation.

Moore, D.G. 2003. Neolithic houses in Ballyharry townland, Islandmagee, Co. Antrim. In I. Armit, E. Murphy, E. Nelis and D. Simpson (eds), *Neolithic settlement in Ireland and western Britain*, 156–63. Oxford: Oxbow Books.

Moore, D.G. 2004. Hostilities in early Neolithic Ireland: trouble with the new neighbours – the evidence from Ballyharry, County Antrim. In A. Gibson and A. Sheridan (eds), *From sickles to circles: Britain and Ireland at the time of Stonehenge*, 142–54. Stroud: Tempus.

Moore, D.G. 2009. *N2 Finglas-Ashbourne Road Scheme: report on archaeological excavation of site 5, Kilshane, Co. Dublin*. Unpublished report, Cultural resource Development Services Ltd.

Moore, W. and Williams, J. 1975. A later Neolithic site at Ecton, Northampton. *Northamptonshire Archaeology* 10, 3–30.

Moorey, P.R.S. 1982. A Neolithic ring-ditch and Iron Age enclosure at Newnham Murren, near Wallingford. In H. Case and A. Whittle (eds), *Settlement patterns in the Oxford region: excavations at the Abingdon causewayed enclosure and other sites*, 55–9. London: Council for British Archaeology.

Morant, G.M. and Goodman, C.N. 1943. Human bones. In R.E.M. Wheeler, *Maiden Castle, Dorset*, 337–60. London: Society of Antiquaries of London.

Mordant, D. (ed.) 1992. *Balloy, "Les Réaudins": enceinte du Néolithique, culture de Cerny*. Dammaine-les-Lys: Conseil Général de Seine-et-Marne, Service du Patrimoine.

Mordant, D. 1997. Le complexe des Réaudins à Balloy: enceinte et nécropole monumentale. In C. Constantin, D. Mordant and D. Simonin (eds), *La culture de Cerny: nouvelle économie, nouvelle société au Néolithique*, 449–79. Nemours: Édition de l'Association pour la Promotion de la Recherche Archéologique en Ile-de-France.

Mordant, C. and Mordant, D. 1988. Les enceintes néolithiques de la Haute-Vallée de la Seine. In C. Burgess, P. Topping, C. Mordant and M. Maddison (eds), *Enclosures and defences in the Neolithic of western Europe*, 231–54. Oxford: British Archaeological Reports.

Mordant, C. and Mordant, D. 1992. Noyen-sur-Seine: a mesolithic waterside settlement. In B. Coles (ed.), *The wetland revolution in prehistory*, 55–64. Exeter: WARP and The Prehistoric Society.

Morgan, R. 2006a. Structural timbers and roundwood [the long barrow]. In C. Evans and I. Hodder, *A woodland archaeology. Neolithic sites at Haddenham: the Haddenham project volume 1*, 104–18. Cambridge: McDonald Institute for Archaeological Research.

Morgan, R. 2006b. Tree-ring results [the long barrow]. In C. Evans and I. Hodder, *A woodland archaeology. Neolithic sites at Haddenham: the Haddenham project volume 1*, 177–87. Cambridge: McDonald Institute for Archaeological Research.

Morris, E.L. 2004. Pottery. In C. Butterworth and C. Gibson, 'Neolithic pits and a Bronze age field system at Middle Farm, Dorchester'. *Proceedings of the Dorset Natural History and Archaeological Society* 126, 20.

Mount, C. 1999. Excavation and environmental analysis of a Neolithic mound and Iron Age barrow cemetery at Rathdooney Beg, County Sligo, Ireland. *Proceedings of the Prehistoric Society* 65, 337–71.

Mudd, A., Williams, J. and Lupton, A. 1999. *Excavations alongside Ermin Street, Gloucestershire and Wiltshire. The archaeology of the A419/A417 Swindon to Gloucester road scheme*. Oxford: Oxford Archaeological Unit.

Müldner, G. and Richards, M.P. 2005. Fast or feast: reconstructing diet in later medieval England by stable isotope analysis. *Journal of Archaeological Science* 32, 39–48.

Müldner, G. and Richards, M.P. 2007. Stable isotope evidence for 1500 years of human diet at the city of York, UK. *American Journal of Physical Anthropology* 133, 682–97.

Müller, J. 1990. Arbeitsleistung und gesellschaftliche Leistung bei Megalithgräbern. Das Fallbeispiel Orkney. *Acta Praehistorica et Archaeologica* (Berlin) 22, 9–35.

Müller, J. 1996. The use of correspondence analysis for different kinds of data categories: domestic and ritual Globular Amphorae sites in Central Germany. *Analecta Praehistorica Leidensia* 28, 217–22.

Müller, J. 1998. Die absolutchronologische Datierung der europäischen Megalithik. In B. Fritsch, M. Monte, I. Matuschik, J. Müller and C. Wolf (eds), *Tradition und Innovation. Prähistorische Archäologie als historische Wissenschaft. Festschrift für Christian Strahm*, 63–106. Rahden: Marie Leidorf.

Müller, J. 1999. Zur Radiokarbondatierung des Jung- bis Endneolitikums und der Frühbronzezeit im Mittelelbe-Saale Gebiet (4100–1500 v. Chr.). *Bericht der Römisch-Germanischen Kommission* 80, 25–56.

Müller, J. 2001. *Soziochronologische Studien zum Jung- und Spätneolithikim im Mittelelbe-Saale-Gebiet (4100–2700 v. Chr.). Eine sozialhistorische Interpretation prähistorischer Quellen*. Rahden: Marie Leidorf.

Müller, J. 2002. Zur Belegungsabfolge des Gräberfeldes von Trebur: Argumente der typologieunabhängigen Datierungen. *Prähistorische Zeitschrift* 77, 148–58.

Müller, J. 2009. Neolithische Monumente und neolithische Gesellschaften. In H.-J. Beier, E. Classen, T. Doppler and B. Ramminger (eds), *Neolithische Monumente und neolithische Gesellschaften*. *Varia Neolithica* 6, 7–16.

Müller, J. 2010a. Dorfanlagen und Siedlungssysteme: die europäische Perspektive: Südosteuropa und Mitteleuropa. In Badisches Landesmuseum (ed.), *Jungsteinzeit in Umbruch: die "Michelsberger Kultur" und Mitteleuropa vor 6000 Jahren*, 250–7. Karlsruhe: Badisches Landesmuseum.

Müller, J. 2010b. Early pottery in the North – a southern perspective. *Bericht der Römisch-Germanischen Kommission* 89.

Mullins, C. 2000. Castlefarm. Prehistoric complex. In I. Bennett (ed.), *Excavations 1998: summary accounts of archaeological excavations in Ireland*, 101–2. Bray: Wordwell.

Mulville, J. and Grigson, C. 2007. The animal bones. In D. Benson and A. Whittle (eds), *Building memories: the Neolithic Cotswold long barrow at Ascott-under-Wychwood, Oxfordshire*, 237–53. Oxford: Oxbow Books.

Murphy, K. 1992. Plas Gogerddan, Dyfed: a multi-period burial and ritual site. *Archaeological Journal* 149, 1–38.

Murphy, K. 2003. Cwm Meudwy, Llandysul (SN 405 419). *Archaeology in Wales* 43, 92–4.

Murphy, K. and Evans, R. 2005. Excavation of three ring-ditches and a prehistoric palisaded enclosure at Cwm Meudwy, Llandysul, Ceredigion, 2003. Unpublished client report. Llandeilo: Cambria Archeological Trust.

Murphy, K. and Evans, R. 2007. Excavation of Neolithic pits, three ring-ditches and a palisaded enclosure at Cwm Meudwy, Llandysul, Ceredigion, 2003. *Archaeologia Cambrensis* 155, 23–48.

Murphy, P. and Brown, N. 1999. Archaeology of the coastal landscape. In L.S. Green (ed.), *The Essex landscape: in search of its history. The 1996 Cressing Conference*, 11–19. Chelmsford: Essex County Council.

Murray, A.S. and Wintle, A.G. 2000. Luminescence dating of quartz using an improved single-aliquot regenerative-dose protocol. *Radiation Measurements* 32, 57–73.

Murray, H.K., Murray, J.C. and Fraser, S.M. 2009. *A tale of unknown unknowns: a Mesolithic pit alignment and a Neolithic timber hall at Warren Field, Crathes, Aberdeenshire*. Oxford: Oxbow Books.

Murray, L.J. 1999. *A zest for life: the story of Alexander Keiller*. Wootton Bassett: Morven Books.

Museum of London Archaeology Service 1999. *Tollgate ARC TLG 98 Archaeological Excavation Interim Report*, http://ads.ahds.ac.uk/catalogue/projArch/ctrl.

Musson, R. 1950. An excavation at Combe Hill camp near Eastbourne, August 1949. *Sussex Archaeological Collections* 89, 105–16.

Mustoe, R.S. 1988. Salvage excavation of a Neolithic and Bronze Age ritual site at Goldington, Bedford: a preliminary report. *Bedfordshire Archaeology* 18, 1–5.

Nadeau, M.J., Schleicher, M., Grootes, P.M., Eerlenkeuser, H., Gottdang, A., Mous, D.J.W., Sarnthein J.M. and Willkomm, H. 1997. The Leibniz-Labor AMS facility at the Christian-Albrechts University, Kiel, Germany. *Nuclear Instruments and Methods in Physics Research B*, 123, 22–30.

Nadeau, M.J., Grootes, P.M., Schleicher, M., Hasselberg, P., Rieck, A. and Bitterling, M. 1998. Sample throughput and data quality at the Leibniz-Labor AMS facility. *Radiocarbon* 40 239–45.

Naylor, J.C. and Smith, A.F.M. 1988. An archaeological inference problem. *Journal of The American Statistical Association* 83, 588–95.

Naysmith, P., Scott, E.M., Cook, G.T., Heinemeier, J., van der Plicht, J., Van Strydonck, M., Bronk Ramsey, C., Grootes, P.M. and Freeman, S.P.H.T. 2007. A cremated bone intercomparison study. *Radiocarbon* 49, 403–8.

Neal, D.S., Wardle, A. and Hunn, J. 1990. *Excavation of the Iron Age, Roman and Medieval settlement at Gorhambury, St Albans*. London: English Heritage.

Needham, S. 1991. *Excavation and salvage at Runnymede Bridge, 1978: the Late Bronze Age waterfront site.* London: British Museum Press.

Needham, S. 1996. Chronology and periodisation in the British Bronze Age. *Acta Archaeologica* 67, 121–40.

Needham, S. 2000. *The passage of the Thames: Holocene environment and settlement at Runnymede. Runnymede Bridge research excavations, volume 1.* London: British Museum Press.

Needham, S. 2005. Transforming Beaker culture in north-west Europe: processes of fusion and fission. *Proceedings of the Prehistoric Society* 71, 171–217.

Needham, S., Bronk Ramsey, C., Coombs, D., Cartwright, C. and Pettitt, P. 1997. An independent chronology for British Bronze Age metalwork: the results of the Oxford radiocarbon accelerator programme. *Archaeological Journal* 154, 55–107.

Needham, S. and Trott, M.R. 1987. Structure and sequence in the Neolithic deposits at Runnymede. *Proceedings of the Prehistoric Society* 53, 479–98.

Nelis, E. 2003. Donegore Hill and Lyles Hill, Neolithic enclosed sites in Co. Antrim: the lithic assemblages. In I. Armit, E. Murphy, E. Nelis and D. Simpson (eds), *Neolithic settlement in Ireland and western Britain*, 203–17. Oxford: Oxbow Books.

Nelis, E. 2004. Neolithic flint-work from the north of Ireland: some thoughts on prominent tool types and their production. In A. Gibson and A. Sheridan (eds), *From sickles to circles: Britain and Ireland at the time of Stonehenge*, 155–75. Stroud: Tempus.

Nelson, D. E. 1991. A new method for carbon isotopic analysis of protein. *Science* 251, 552–4.

Neubauer, W. 2005. Am Fusse des Heldenbergs. Die dreifache Kreisgrabenanlage Glaubendorf 2. In F. Daim and W. Neubauer (eds), *Zeitreise Heldenberg. Geheimnisvolle Kreisgräben*, 52–7. Horn-Wien: Verlag Berger.

Newberry, J. 2002. Inland flint in prehistoric Devon: sources, tool-making quality and use. *Proceedings of the Devon Archaeological Society* 60, 1–36.

Newman, C. 1997. *Tara: an archaeological survey.* Dublin: Royal Irish Academy for the Discovery Programme.

Newman, R. and Radford, E.L. 1930. Foreword to the report on the excavations at Hembury Fort. In D. Liddell, 'Report on the excavations at Hembury Fort, Devon, 1930'. *Proceedings of the Devon Archaeological Society* 1.2, 39.

Niblett, R. 2001. A Neolithic dugout from a multi-period site near St Albans, Herts, England. *The International Journal of Nautical Archaeology* 30, 155–95.

Nicholls, G. and Jones, M. 2001. Radiocarbon dating with temporal order constraints. *Applied Statistics* 50**,** 503–21.

Nicholls, G. and Nunn, P. submitted. On building and fitting a spatio-temporal change-point model for settlement and growth at Bourewa, Fiji Islands. *Applied Statistics* (pre-print at http://arxiv.org/abs/1006.5575).

Nicholls, R.J., Dredge, A. and Wilson, T. 2000. Shoreline change and fine-grained sediment input: Isle of Sheppey coast, Thames estuary, UK. In K. Pye and J.R.L. Allen (eds), *Coastal and estuarine environments: sedimentology, geomorphology and geoarchaeology*, 305–15. London: Geological Society Special Publication 175.

Nickel, C. 1997. Menschliche Skelettreste aus Michelsberger Fundzusammenhängen. *Bericht des Römisch-Germanischen Kommission* 78, 29–195.

Nielsen, P.O. 2004. Causewayed camps, palisade enclosures and central settlements in the Middle Neolithic in Denmark. *Journal of Nordic Archaeological Science* 14, 19–33.

Noakes, J.E., Kim, S.M. and Stipp, J.J. 1965. Chemical and counting advances in liquid scintillation age dating. In E.A. Olsson and R.M. Chatters (eds), *Proceedings of the sixth international conference on radiocarbon and tritium dating*, 68–92. Washington DC: Pullman.

Noble, G. 2006. *Neolithic Scotland: timber, stone, earth and fire.* Edinburgh: Edinburgh University Press.

Noe-Nygaard, N., Price, T.D. and Hede, S.U. 2005. Diet of aurochs and early cattle in southern Scandinavia: evidence from ^{15}N and ^{13}C stable isotopes. *Journal of Archaeological Science* 32, 855–71.

Nowakowski, J. 1993. Archaeology along the hard shoulder – the Indian Queens project. *Cornish Archaeology* 32, 146–51.

Nowakowski, J. 1998. *A30 project, Cornwall – archaeological investigations along the route of the Indian Queens bypass 1992–1994. Assessment and updated project design.* Unpublished document. Truro: Cornwall County Council.

O'Connell, M. and Molloy, K. 2001. Farming and woodland dynamics in Ireland during the Neolithic. *Proceedings of the Royal Irish Academy* 101B (1–2), 99–128.

O'Connell, T.C. and Hedges, R.E.M. 1999. Isotopic comparison of hair and bone: archaeological analyses. *Journal of Archaeological Science* 26, 661–5.

O'Connell, T.J. and O'Neill, N. 2009. A fixed abode: Neolithic houses in County Carlow. In M. Stanley, E. Danaher and J. Eogan (eds), *Dining and dwelling*, 85–97. Dublin: National Roads Authority.

O'Connor, E. 2008. Fragments from the past: the prehistory of the M3 in County Meath. In J. O'Sullivan and M. Stanley (eds), *Roads, rediscovery and research*, 83–94. Dublin: National Roads Authority.

O'Connor, T.P. 1977a. Appendix I: the human skeletal remains. In P. Drewett, 'The excavation of a Neolithic causewayed enclosure at Offham Hill, East Sussex, 1976'. *Proceedings of the Prehistoric Society* 43, 228–9.

O'Connor, T.P. 1977b. Appendix II: animal skeletal material. In P. Drewett, 'The excavation of a Neolithic causewayed enclosure at Offham Hill, East Sussex, 1976'. *Proceedings of the Prehistoric Society* 43, 229–31.

O'Donnell, R.G. 1997. *The establishment of a radiocarbon dating facility at University College Dublin and its application to a study of palaeoecological material from Céide Fields and the North Mayo blanket bog.* Unpublished PhD thesis, National University of Ireland.

O'Donovan, E. 2003. 438. Kishoge. Prehistoric house. 30423 23212. 01E0061. In I. Bennett (ed.), *Exavations 2001: summary accounts of archaeological excavations in Ireland*, 125–6. Bray: Wordwell.

O'Donovan, E. 2004. A Neolithic house at Kishoge, Co. Dublin. *Journal of Irish Archaeology* 12/13, 1–27.

Ó Floinn, R. 1992. A Neolithic cave burial in Limerick. *Archaeology Ireland* 6(2), 19–21.

O'Kelly, M.J. 1958. A horned cairn at Shanballyedmond, Co. Tipperary. *Journal of the Cork Historical and Archaeological Society* 63, 37–72.

O'Kelly, M.J. 1969. Radiocarbon dates for the Newgrange passage grave, Co. Meath. *Antiquity* 43, 140.

O'Kelly, M.J. 1972. Further radiocarbon dates from Newgrange, Co. Meath. *Antiquity* 46, 226–7.

O'Kelly, M.J. 1982. *Newgrange: archaeology, art and legend.* London: Thames and Hudson.

Olding, F. 2000. *The prehistoric landscapes of the eastern Black Mountains*. Oxford: British Archaeological Reports.

Olivier, L.C. 2001. Duration, memory and the nature of the archaeological record. In H. Karlsson (ed.), *It's about time: the concept of time in archaeology*, 61–70. Göteborg: Bricoleur Press.

Olsson, I.U. 1970. The use of oxalic acid as a standard. In I.U. Olsson (ed.), *Radiocarbon variations and absolute chronology: Nobel symposium, 12th Proceedings*, 17. New York: Wiley.

Olsson, I.U. 1979. Radiometric dating. In B.E. Berglund (ed.), *Palaeohydrological changes in the temperate zone in the last 15,000 years: sub-project B, lake and mire environments, Project guide, v 2, Specific methods: Dept Quaternary Geology*, 1–38. Lund: University of Lund.

O'Neil, H.E. 1966. Sale's Lot long barrow,Withington, Gloucesteshire, 1962–1965. *Transactions of the Bristol and Gloucestershire Archaeological Society* 85, 5–35.

O'Neil, T. 2005a. *N4 Sligo inner relief road and county extension. Contract 1 – final report. Report on the archaeological excavation of an early Medieval enclosure and early Neolithic enclosure ditch with associated features at Area 2B, Magheraboy, Sligo*. Client report for Sligo Borough and County Council. Drogheda: Archaeological Consultancy Services Ltd.

O'Neil, T. 2005b. Zone 1 (ditch segments). In E. Danaher and L. Cagney, *N4 Sligo inner relief road and county extension. Contract 1 – final report. Report on the archaeological excavation of an early Neolithic causewayed enclosure at Area 2C, Magheraboy, Sligo*, 79–82. Client report for Sligo Borough and County Council. Drogheda: Archaeological Consultancy Services Ltd.

Ó Néill, J., Donaghy, E, and Sloan, B. 2004. *Investigations at Ballyharry Farm, Ballyharry, Co. Antrim AE/04/02, Data Structure Report no. 27*. Unpublished report for the Centre for Archaeological Fieldwork, Queen's University, Belfast, on behalf of the Environment and Heritage Service, Northern Ireland.

Ó Nualláin, S. 1972. A Neolithic house at Ballyglass near Ballycastle, Co. Mayo. *Journal of the Royal Society of Antiquaries of Ireland* 102, 49–57.

Ó Nualláin, S. 1983. Irish portal tombs: topography, siting and distribution. *Journal of the Royal Society of Antiquaries of Ireland* 113, 75–105.

Ó Nualláin, S. 1998. Excavation of the smaller court-tomb and associated hut sites at Ballyglass, County Mayo. *Proceedings of the Royal Irish Academy* 98C, 125–75.

Ó Nualláin, S., Greene, S.A. and Rice, K. forthcoming. *Excavation of the centre-court tomb and underlying house site at Ballyglass, Co. Mayo*. Dublin: Department of Archaeology, University College Dublin.

Ó Ríordáin, S. 1954. Lough Gur excavations: Neolithic and Bronze Age houses on Knockadoon. *Proceedings of the Royal Irish Academy* 56C, 297–459.

Österholm, I. and Österholm, S. 1984. The kitchen middens along the coast of Ballysadare Bay. In G. Burenhult, *The archaeology of Carrowmore. Environmental archaeology and the megalithic tradition at Carrowmore, Co. Sligo, Ireland*, 326–45. Stockholm: Institute of Archaeology, University of Stockholm.

Östlund, H.G. 1957. Carbon dioxide proportional counting for natural radiocarbon measurements. *Arkiv för Kemi* 12, 69–78.

Östlund, H.G. 1959. Stockholm natural radiocarbon measurements II. *Radiocarbon* 1, 35–441.

Östlund, H.G. and Engstrand, L.G. 1963. Stockholm natural radiocarbon measurements V. *Radiocarbon* 5, 203–27.

O'Sullivan, A. 2001. *Foragers, farmers and fishers in a coastal landscape: an intertidal archaeological survey of the Shannon estuary.* Dublin: Discovery Programme.

O'Sullivan, A. and Breen, C. 2007. *Maritime Ireland: an archaeology of coastal communities*. Stroud: Tempus.

O'Sullivan, M. 2005. *Duma na nGiall: The Mound of the Hostages, Tara*. Bray: Wordwell, in association with the UCD School of Archaeology.

Oswald, A., Dyer, C. and Barber, M. 2001. *The creation of monuments: Neolithic causewayed enclosures in the British Isles*. Swindon: English Heritage.

Otlet, R.L. 1977. Harwell radiocarbon measurements II. *Radiocarbon* 19, 400–23.

Otlet, R.L. 1979. An assessment of laboratory errors in liquid scintillation methods of ^{14}C dating. In R. Berger and H.E. Suess (eds), *Proceedings of the Ninth International Radiocarbon Conference*, 256–67. Los Angeles: University of California Press.

Otlet, R.L. and Evans, G.V. 1983. Progress in the application of miniature gas counters to radiocarbon dating of small samples. In W.G. Mook and H.T. Waterbolk (eds), *Proceedings of the First International Symposium ^{14}C and Archaeology. PACT* 8, 213–22. Strasbourg: Council of Europe.

Otlet, R.L. and Polach, H.A. 1990. Improvements in the precision of radiocarbon dating through recent developments in liquid scintillation counters. In W.G. Mook and H.T. Waterbolk (eds), *Proceedings of the Second International Symposium: ^{14}C and Archaeology. PACT* 29, 225–38. Strasbourg: Council of Europe.

Otlet, R.L. and Warchal, R.M. 1978. Liquid scintillation counting of low-level ^{14}C. In M.A. Crook and P. Johnson (eds), *Liquid scintillation counting* 5, 201–18. London: Heyden.

Otlet, R.L., Huxtable, G., Evans, G.V., Humphreys, D.G., Short, T.D. and Conchie, S.J. 1983. Development and operation of the Harwell small counter facility for the measurement of ^{14}C in very small samples. *Radiocarbon* 25, 565–75.

Otlet, R.L., Huxtable, G. and Sanderson, D.C.W. 1986. The development of practical systems for ^{14}C measurement in small samples using miniature counters. *Radiocarbon* 28, 603–14.

Otlet, R.L., Walker, A.J., Hewson, A.D. and Burleigh, R. 1980. ^{14}C interlaboratory comparison in the UK: experiment design, preparation, and preliminary results. *Radiocarbon* 22, 936–46.

Overing, J. and Passes, A. 2000a. Preface. In J. Overing and A. Passes (eds), *The anthropology of love and anger: the aesthetics of conviviality in Native Amazonia*, xi–xiv. London: Routledge.

Overing, J. and Passes. A. 2000b. Introduction: conviviality and the opening up of Amazonian anthropology. In J. Overing and A. Passes (eds), *The anthropology of love and anger: the aesthetics of conviviality in Native Amazonia*, 1–30. London: Routledge.

Oxford Archaeological Unit 1995. *Tollgate Cropmark Complex, Gravesham, Kent. Archaeological Evaluation Report TIS no. 192/84-10411*. http://ads.ahds.ac.uk/catalogue/projArch/ctrl.

Oxford Archaeological Unit 2000. White Horse Stone. A Neolithic longhouse. *Current Archaeology* 168, 450–2.

Page, N. 2001. A477 Sageston-Redberth bypass (SN 082 038). *Archaeology in Wales* 41, 124.

Page, N. 2002. *A477(T) Sageston-Redberth bypass. Excavation of a Neolithic occupation site 2001*. Unpublished client report. Llandeilo: Cambria Archeological Trust.

Pailler, Y. and Sheridan, A. 2009. Everything you always wanted to know about...la néolithisation de la Grande-Bretagne et de l'Irlande. *Bulletin de la Société Préhistorique Française* 106, 1–32.

Palmer, C. and Jones, M. 1991. Plant resources. In N. Sharples, *Maiden Castle: excavations and field survey 1985–6*, 129–39. London: English Heritage.

Palmer, R. 1976a. Interrupted ditch enclosures in Britain: the use of aerial photography for comparative studies. *Proceedings of the Prehistoric Society* 42, 161–86.

Palmer, R. 1976b. Causewayed enclosure at Crofton (Great Bedwyn). *Wiltshire Archaeological and Natural History Magazine* 70/71, 124–5.

Palmer, R. and Oswald, A. 2008. The field survey. In R. Mercer and F. Healy, *Hambledon Hill, Dorset: excavation and survey of a Neolithic monument complex and its surrounding landscape*, 15–39. Swindon: English Heritage.

Palmer, S.C. 2003. King's Newnham, Warwickshire: Neolithic, Bronze Age and Iron Age excavations along a gas pipeline in 1990. *Transactions of the Brimingham and Warwickshire Archaeological Society* 107, 41–74.

Palmer, S.C. forthcoming. *Neolithic, Bronze Age, Iron Age, Romano-British and Anglo-Saxon excavations on the Transco Churchover to Newbold Pacey gas pipeline in 1999.* Warwick: Warwickshire Museum Field Services.

Pariat, J.-G. 2007. *Des morts sans tombe? Le cas des ossements humains en contexte non sépulcral en Europe temperée entre les 6e et 3e millénaires av. J.-C.* Oxford: British Archaeological Reports.

Parker, A. 1999. The pollen and sediments of Daisy Banks Fen. In A. Barclay and C. Halpin, *Excavations at Barrow Hills, Radley, Oxfordshire. Volume I. The Neolithic and Bronze Age monument complex*, 254–74. Oxford: Oxford University Committee for Archaeology on behalf of the Oxford Archaeological Unit.

Parker, A.G., Goudie, A.S., Anderson, D.E., Robinson, M.A. and Bonsall, C. 2002. A review of the mid-Holocene elm decline in the British Isles. *Progress in Physical Geography* 26, 1–45.

Parker Pearson, M. 1992. Tombs and monumentality in southern Madagascar: preliminary results of the central Androy survey. *Antiquity* 66, 941–8.

Parker Pearson, M. and Thorpe, I.J.N. (eds) 2005. *Warfare, violence and slavery in prehistory.* Oxford: British Archaeogical Reports.

Parker Pearson, M., Cleal, R., Marshall, P., Needham, S., Pollard, J., Richards, C., Ruggles, C., Sheridan, A., Thomas, J., Tilley, C., Welham, K., Chamberlain, A., Chenery, C., Evans, J., Knüsel, C., Linford, N., Martin, L., Montgomery, J., Payne, A. and Richards, M. 2007. The age of Stonehenge. *Antiquity* 81, 617–39.

Passmore, D.G. and Waddington, C. forthcoming. *Archaeology and environment in Northumberland. Till-Tweed Studies Volume II.* Oxford: Oxbow Books.

Pásztor, E., Barna, J.P. and Roslund, C. 2008. The orientation of *rondels* of the Neolithic Lengyel culture in central Europe. *Antiquity* 82, 910–24.

Pauketat, T.R. 2007. *Chiefdoms and other archaeological delusions.* Plymouth: Altamira Press.

Pavlů, I. 2002. *Life on a Neolithic site. Bylany – situational analysis of artefacts.* Prague: Institute of Archaeology, Czech Academy of Sciences.

Payne, G. 1880. Celtic remains discovered at Grovehurst, Milton. *Archaeologia Cantiana* 13, 122–6.

Paynter, R. 2002. Time in the valley: narratives about rural new England. *Current Anthropology* 43, supplement, S85–101.

Pazdur, A. and Pazdur, M.F. 1986. Aparatura pomiarowa Laboratorium C-14 w Gliwicach. Doswiadczenia konstrukcyjne i eksploatacyjne (Equipment C-14 laboratory in Gliwice. Construction and exploitation experiences). *Zeszyty Naukowe Politechnikiki Śląskiej, Seria Matematyka-Fizyka, Zesz. 46, Geochronometria 1*, 55–69.

Pazdur, A., Awsiuk, R., Bluszcz, A., Pazdur, M.F., Walanus, A. and Zastawny, A. 1982. Gliwice radiocarbon dates VII. *Radiocarbon* 24, 171–81.

Pazdur, M.F. 1992. Chronologie de la minière de silex néolithique de Jablines. In F. Bostyn and Y. Lanchon, *Jablines, le Haut-Château (Seine-et-Marne). Une minière de silex au Néolithique*, 233–4. Paris: Editions de la Maison des Sciences de l'Homme.

Pazdur, M.F., Awsiuk, R., Bluszcz, A., Halas, S., Pazdur, A., Walanus, A. and Zastawny, A. 1979. Preliminary results of the study of isotopic fractionation during chemical purification of carbon dioxide for radiocarbon dating. *Radiochemical and Radioanalytical Letters* 39, 157–6.

Peacock, D.P.S. 1969. Neolithic pottery production in Cornwall. *Antiquity* 43, 145–9.

Peacock, D., Cutler, L. and Woodward, P. 2010. A Neolithic voyage. *International Journal of Nautical Archaeology* 39, 116–24.

Pearson, A. 2003. *Beech Court Farm enclosure, Ewenny, Vale of Glamorgan: post-excavation summary. GGAT Project A835.* Swansea: Glamorgan Gwent Archaeological Trust.

Pearson, G.W. 1984. *The development of high precision ^{14}C measurement and its application to archaeological time-scale problems.* Unpublished PhD thesis, Queen's University, Belfast.

Pearson, G.W. 1987. How to cope with calibration. *Antiquity* 61, 98–103.

Pearson, G.W. and Stuiver, M. 1986. High-precision calibration of the radiocarbon timescale. 500–2500 BC. *Radiocarbon* 28, 839–62.

Pearson, G.W., Pilcher, J.R., Baillie, M.G.L., Corbett, D.M. and Qua, F. 1986. High-precision ^{14}C measurements of Irish oaks to show the natural ^{14}C variations from AD 1840 to 5210 BC. *Radiocarbon* 28, 911–34.

Peglar, S. 2006. The Ouse channel Flandrian sequence. In C. Evans and I. Hodder, *A woodland archaeology. Neolithic sites at Haddenham: the Haddenham project volume 1*, 26–9. Cambridge: McDonald Institute for Archaeological Research.

Peglar, S. and Waller, M. 1994. The Ouse channel, Haddenham. In M. Waller, *The Fenland project, number 9: Flandrian environmental change in Fenland*, 47–84. Cambridge: Cambridgeshire Archaeological Committee.

Percival, J. 1931. Grain. In D. Liddell, 'Report on the excavations at Hembury Fort, Devon: second season 1931'. *Proceedings of the Devon Archaeological Society* 1.3, 180.

Percival, S. 2002. Prehistoric pottery. In J.W. Percival, 'Neolithic and Bronze Age occupation in the Yare valley: excavations at Three Score Road, Bowthorpe, 1999–2000'. *Norfolk Archaeology* 44(1), 76–9.

Percival, S. 2003. Prehistoric pottery. In D. Robertson, 'A Neolithic and early Saxon settlement: excavations at Yarmouth Road, Broome, 2001'. *Norfolk Archaeology* 44, 236–8.

Percival, S. 2004. Pottery. In M. Whitmore, 'Excavations at a Neolithic site at the John Innes Centre, Colney, 2000'. *Norfolk Archaeology* 44(4), 422–6.

Perkins, D. 1998. *A gateway island.* Unpublished PhD thesis. University College, London.

Perkins, D. 2004. Oval barrows on Thanet. In J. Cotton and D. Field (eds), *Towards a New Stone Age: aspects of the Neolithic in south-east England*, 76–81. York: Council for British Archaeology.

Petchey, F. and Higham, T.F.C. 2000. Bone diagenesis and radiocarbon dating of fish bones at the Shag River Mouth site, New Zealand. *Journal of Archaeological Science* 276, 135–50.

Peter-Röcher, H. 2007. *Gewalt und Krieg im prähistorischen Europa: Beiträge zur Konfliktforschung auf der Grundlage archäologischer, anthropologischer und ethnologischer Quellen*. Bonn: Habelt.

Petersen, F.F. and Healy, F. 1986. The excavation of two round barrows and a ditched enclosure on Weasenham Lyngs, 1972. In A.J. Lawson, *Barrow excavations in Norfolk, 1950–82*, 70–103. Gressenhall: Norfolk Archaeological Unit.

Peterson, R. 2003. *Neolithic pottery from Wales: traditions of construction and use*. Oxford: British Archaeological Reports.

Petrasch, J. 1990. Mittelneolithische Kreisgrabenanlagen in Mitteleuropa. *Bericht der Römisch-Germanischen Kommission* 71, 407–564.

Pétrequin, P., Errera, M., Pétrequin, A. and Allard, P. 2006. The Neolithic quarries of Mont Viso, Piedmont, Italy: initial radiocarbon dates. *Journal of European Archaeology* 9, 7–30.

Pétrequin, P., Sheridan, A., Cassen, S., Errera, M., Gauthier, E., Klassen, L., Le Maux, N. and Pailler, Y. 2008. Neolithic Alpine axeheads, from the Continent to Great Britain, the Isle of Man and Ireland. *Analecta Praehistorica Leidensia* 40, 261–79.

Pettitt, P. 2000. The Paviland radiocarbon dating programme: reconstructing the chronology of faunal communities, carnivore activity and human occupation. In S. Aldhouse-Green, *Paviland Cave and the 'Red Lady': a definitive report*, 63–71. Bristol: Western Academic & Specialist Press.

Phillips, D. and Gregg, J.W. 2003. Source partitioning using stable isotopes: coping with too many sources.*Oecologia* 136, 261–9. (http://www.epa.gov/wed/pages/models/stableIsotopes/isosource/isosource.htm)

Philp, B. 1973. *Excavations in West Kent 1960–1970*. Dover: Kent Archaeological Rescue Unit.

Piggott, S. 1929. Neolithic pottery and other remains from Pangbourne, Berks., and Caversham, Oxon. *Proceedings of the Prehistoric Society of East Anglia* 6, 30–9.

Piggott, S. 1931. The Neolithic pottery of the British Isles. *Archaeological Journal* 88, 67–158.

Piggott, S. 1932. The Mull Hill Circle, Isle of Man, and its pottery. *Antiquaries Journal* 12, 146–57.

Piggott, S. 1934. The Neolithic pottery. In E.C. Curwen, 'A late Bronze Age farm and a Neolithic pit-dwelling on New Barn Down, Clapham, Nr. Worthing'. *Sussex Archaeological Collections* 75, 162–4.

Piggott, S. 1935. A note on the relative chronology of the English long barrows. *Proceedings of the Prehistoric Society* 1, 115–26.

Piggott, S. 1937. Neolithic pottery from Hackpen, Avebury. *Wiltshire Archaeological and Natural History Magazine* 48, 90–1.

Piggott, S. 1943. Introductory [to 'Neolithic and early Bronze Age pottery']. In R.E.M. Wheeler, *Maiden Castle, Dorset*, 137–44. London: Society of Antiquaries.

Piggott, S. 1952. The Neolithic camp on Whitesheet Hill, Kilmington parish. *Wiltshire Archaeological and Natural History Magazine* 54, 404–10.

Piggott, S. 1954. *Neolithic cultures of the British Isles*. Cambridge: Cambridge University Press.

Piggott, S. 1955. Windmill Hill – east or west? *Proceedings of the Prehistoric Society* 20, 96–101.

Piggott, S. 1959. The radio-carbon dates from Durrington Walls. *Antiquity* 33, 289–90.

Piggott, S. 1962. *The West Kennet long barrow: excavations 1955–56*. London: HMSO.

Piggott, S. 1965. Alexander Keiller 1889–1955. In I.F. Smith, *Windmill Hill and Avebury. Excavations by Alexander Keiller 1925–1939*, xix–xxii. Oxford: Clarendon Press.

Piggott, S. 1972. The excavation of the Dalladies long barrow, Fettercairn, Kincardineshire. *Proceedings of the Society of Antiquaries of Scotland* 104, 23–47.

Piggott, S. and Piggott, C.M. 1944. Excavation of barrows on Crichel and Launceston Downs, Dorset. *Archaeologia* 90, 47–80.

Pilcher, J.R., Baillie, M.G.L., Schmidt, B. and Becker, B. 1984. A 7,272-year tree-ring chronology for western Europe. *Nature* 312, 150–2.

Pine, J. and Ford, S. 2003. Excavations of Neolithic, late Bronze Age, early Iron Age and early Saxon features at St Helen's Avenue, Benson, Oxfordshire. *Oxoniensia* 68, 131–78.

Piningre, J.-F., Bostyn, F. and Couppé, J., with Constantin, C. and Delibrias, G. 1991. L'atelier de taille du silex des Sablins à Etaples (Pas-de-Calais). *Gallia Préhistoire* 33, 83–135.

Pipes, M.-L., Kruk, J., Makowicz-Poliszot, D. and Milisauskas, S. 2009. Funnel Beaker animal husbandry at Bronocice. *Archaeologia Baltica* 12, 31–45.

Pitt Rivers, A.H.L.-F. 1898. *Excavations in Cranborne Chase near Rushmore, on the borders of Dorset and Wiltshire 1893–1896, Vol. IV*. London: Harrison and Sons.

Pitts, M. 1980. A gazetteer of Mesolithic finds on the West Sussex coastal plain. *Sussex Archaeological Collections* 118, 153–62.

Pitts, M. 2006. News. *British Archaeology* 91, 6–8.

Pitts, M. 2008. Rare house continues first farmers debate. *British Archaeology* 102, 9.

Pitts, M. 2009. Isle of Man house is one of Britain's first. *British Archaeology* 108, 9.

Pitts, M.W. and Jacobi, R.M. 1979. Some aspects of change in flaked stone industries of the Mesolithic and Neolithic in southern Britain. *Journal of Archaeological Science* 6, 163–77.

Pitts, M. and Whittle, A. 1992. The development and date of Avebury. *Proceedings of the Prehistoric Society* 58, 203–12.

Polach, H.A. 1972. Cross checking of the NBS oxalic acid and secondary laboratory radiocarbon dating standards. In T.A. Rafter and T. Grant-Taylor (eds), *Proceedings of the 8th International Radiocarbon Dating Conference, Lower Hutt, New Zealand*, 688–717. Wellington: Royal Society of New Zealand.

Pollard, J. 1998. *Excavations at Over: late Neolithic occupation (sites 3 and 4). CAU Report 281*. Unpublished document. Cambridge: Cambridge Archaeological Unit.

Pollard, J. 1999a. The Keiller excavations. In A. Whittle, J. Pollard and C. Grigson, *The harmony of symbols: the Windmill Hill causewayed enclosure, Wiltshire*, 24–72. Oxford: Oxbow Books.

Pollard, J. 1999b. Flint. In A. Whittle, J. Pollard and C. Grigson, *The harmony of symbols: the Windmill Hill causewayed enclosure, Wiltshire*, 318–37. Oxford: Oxbow Books.

Pollard, J. 1999c. "These places have their moments": thoughts on settlement practice in the British Neolithic. In J. Brück and M. Goodman (eds), *Making places in the prehistoric world*, 76–93. London: University College London Press.

Pollard, J. 2004. A 'movement of becoming': realms of existence in the early Neolithic of southern Britain. In A.M. Chadwick (ed.), *Stories from the landscape: archaeologies of inhabitation*, 55–69. Oxford: British Archaeological Reports.

Pollard, J. 2005. Memory, monuments and middens. In G. Brown, D. Field and D. McOmish (eds), *The Avebury landscape: aspects of the field archaeology of the Marlborough Downs*, 103–14. Oxford: Oxbow Books.

Pollard, J. and Cleal, R.M.J. 2004. Dating Avebury. In R. Cleal and J. Pollard (eds), *Monuments and material culture. Papers in honour of an Avebury archaeologist: Isobel Smith*, 120–9. East Knoyle: Hobnob Press.

Pollard, J. and Hamilton, M. 1994. Recent fieldwork at Maiden Bower. *Bedfordshire Archaeological Journal* 21, 10–18.

Pollard, J. and Healy, F. (eds) 2008. Neolithic and early Bronze Age. In C.J. Webster (ed.), *The archaeology of south west England: south west archaeological research framework and research agenda,* 75–101. Taunton: Somerset County Council.

Pollard, J. and Reynolds, A. 2002. *Avebury: the biography of a landscape*. Stroud: Tempus.

Pollard, J. and Robinson, D. 2007. A return to Wodhenge: the results and implications of the 2006 excavations. In M. Larsson and M. Parker Pearson (eds), *From Stonehenge to the Baltic: living with cultural diversity in the third millennium BC*, 159–68. Oxford: Archaeopress.

Pollard, J. and Whittle, A. 1999. Stone other than flint. In A. Whittle, J. Pollard and C. Grigson, *The harmony of symbols: the Windmill Hill causewayed enclosure, Wiltshire*, 338–41. Oxford: Oxbow Books.

Pollard, S.H. 1966. Neolithic and Dark Age settlements on High Peak, Sidmouth, Devon. *Proceedings of the Devon Archaeological Society* 23, 35–59.

Pollard, S.H. 1967. Radiocarbon dating, Neolithic and Dark Age settlements on High Peak, Sidmouth, Devon. *Proceedings of the Devon Archaeological Society* 25, 41–2.

Possnert, G. 1984. AMS with the Uppsala EN tandem accelerator. *Nuclear Instruments and Methods in Physics Research B*, 233, 159–61.

Possnert, G. 1990. Radiocarbon dating by accelerator technique. *Norwegian Archaeological Review* 23, 30–7.

Powell, A.B. 2005. The language of lineage: reading Irish court tomb design. *European Journal of Archaeology* 8, 9–28.

Powell, R. 1977. A triple ring ditch at Maxey. *Durobrivae* 5, 12–3.

Power, C. 1999. Human remains. In P. Woodman, E. Anderson and N. Finlay, *Excavations at Ferriter's Cove, 1983–95: last foragers, first farmers on the Dingle Peninsula*, 102–3. Bray: Wordwell.

Prendergast, D.M. 2000. The problems raised by small charcoal samples for radiocarbon analysis. *Journal of Field Archaeology* 27, 237–9.

Price, T.D., Bentley, R.A., Lüning, J., Gronenborn, D and Wahl, J. 2001. Human migration in the Linearbandkeramik of central Europe. *Antiquity* 75, 593–603.

Priddy, D. 1988. Excavations in Essex 1987. *Essex Archaeology and History* 19, 260–71.

Privat, K.L. and O'Connell, T.C. 2002. Stable isotope analysis of human and faunal remains from the Anglo-Saxon cemetery at Berinsfield, Oxfordshire: dietary and social implications. *Journal of Archaeological Science* 29, 779–90.

Pryor, F. 1974. *Excavation at Fengate, Peterborough, England: the first report*. Toronto: Royal Ontario Museum.

Pryor, F. 1978. *Excavation at Fengate, Peterborough, England: the second report*. Toronto: Royal Ontario Museum.

Pryor, F. 1980. *Excavation at Fengate, Peterborough, England: the third report*. Northampton and Toronto: Northamptonshire Archaeological Society and Royal Ontario Museum.

Pryor, F. 1984. *Excavation at Fengate, Peterborough, England: the fourth report*. Northampton and Toronto: Northamptonshire Archaeological Society and Royal Ontario Museum.

Pryor, F. 1985a. The flints. In F. Pryor, C. French, D. Crowther, D. Gurney, G. Simpson, G. Taylor and M. Taylor, *The Fenland project No. 1: archaeology and environment in the lower Welland valley*, 151–63. Peterborough: Fenland Archaeological Trust.

Pryor, F. 1985b. Prehistoric features. In F. Pryor, C. French, D. Crowther, D. Gurney, G. Simpson, G. Taylor and M. Taylor, *The Fenland project No. 1: archaeology and environment in the lower Welland valley*, 59–88. Peterborough: Fenland Archaeological Trust.

Pryor, F. 1985c. Discussion. In F. Pryor, C. French, D. Crowther, D. Gurney, G. Simpson, G. Taylor and M. Taylor, *The Fenland project No. 1: archaeology and environment in the lower Welland valley*, 298–312. Peterborough: Fenland Archaeological Trust.

Pryor, F. 1987. Etton 1986: Neolithic metamorphoses. *Antiquity* 61, 78–81.

Pryor, F. 1988. Etton, near Maxey, Cambridgeshire; a causewayed enclosure on the fen edge. In C. Burgess, P. Topping, C. Mordant and M. Maddison (eds), *Enclosures and defences in the Neolithic of western Europe*, 107–26. Oxford: British Archaeological Reports.

Pryor, F. 1993. Excavations at site 11, Fengate, Peterborough, 1969. In W.G. Simpson, D. Gurney, J. Neve and F. Pryor, *Fenland Project 7: Excavations in Peterborough and the Lower Welland Valley 1960–69,* 127–40. East Anglian Archaeology 61. Peterborough: Fenland Archaeological Trust.

Pryor, F. 1995. Abandonment and the role of ritual sites in the landscape. *Scottish Archaeological Review* 9/10, 96–109.

Pryor, F. 1998. *Etton: excavations at a Neolithic causewayed enclosure near Maxey, Cambridgeshire, 1982–87*. London: English Heritage.

Pryor, F. 2001. *The Flag Fen basin: archaeology and environment of a fenland landscape*. London: English Heritage.

Pryor, F., Cleal, R. and Kinnes, I. 1998. Discussion of the Neolithic and earlier Bronze Age pottery. In F. Pryor, *Etton: excavations at a Neolithic causewayed enclosure near Maxey, Cambridgeshire, 1982–87*, 209–13. London: English Heritage.

Pryor, F., French, C., Crowther, D., Gurney, D., Simpson, G., Taylor, G. and Taylor, M. 1985. *The Fenland project No. 1: archaeology and environment in the lower Welland valley*. Peterborough: Fenland Archaeological Trust.

Pryor, F., French, C. and Taylor, M. 1985. An interim report on excavations at Etton, Maxey, Cambridgeshire. *Antiquaries Journal* 65, 275–311.

Pryor, F. and Kinnes, I. 1982. A waterlogged causewayed enclosure in the Cambridgeshire Fens. *Antiquity* 56, 124–6.

Pugh, G. 1998. Abingdon Multiplex (SU48709654). *South Midlands Archaeology* 28, 84.

Purcell, A. 2000. Corbally, Brownstown and Silliot Hill, Co. Kildare. In I. Bennett (ed.), *Excavations 1998: summary accounts of archaeological excavations in Ireland*, 103–4. Bray: Wordwell.

Purcell, A. 2002. Excavation of three Neolithic houses at Corbally, Kilcullen, Co. Kildare. *Journal of Irish Archaeology* 11, 31–75.

Pye, W.R. 1967. Dorstone Hill. *Transactions of the Woolhope Naturalists' Field Club* 39(1), 157.

Pye, W.R. 1968. Dorstone Hill. *Transactions of the Woolhope Naturalists' and Field Club* 39(2), 362.

Pye, W.R. 1969. Dorstone Hill. *Transactions of the Woolhope Naturalists' Field Club* 39(3), 475.

Pye, W.R. 1975. Fron Ddyrys. *Archaeology in Wales* 15, 40.

Pye, W.R. 1976. Fron Ddyrys. *Archaeology in Wales* 16, 29.

Quinnell, H. 1999. Pottery. In T. Gent and H. Quinnell, 'Excavation of a causewayed enclosure and hillfort on Raddon Hill, Stokely Pomeroy'. *Proceedings of the Devon Archaeological Society* 57, 38–53.

Quinnell, H. 2002. Early Neolithic pottery. In D. Cole and A.M. Jones, 'Journeys to the rock: archaeological investigations at Tregarrick Farm, Roche, Cornwall'. *Cornish Archaeology* 41–42, 113–21.

Quinnell, H. and Taylor, R. 1999. Stone artefacts and rock fragments. In T.H. Gent and H. Quinnell, 'Excavation of a causewayed enclosure and hillfort on Raddon Hill, Stokely Pomeroy'. *Proceedings of the Devon Archaeological Society* 57, 53–6.

Radford, C.A.R. 1958. The chambered tomb at Broadsands, Paignton. *Proceedings of the Devon Archaeological Exploration Society*, 5, 147–68.

Raemaekers, D. 1999. *The articulation of a 'New Neolithic': the meaning of the Swifterbant culture for the process of Neolithisation in the western part of the European plain (4900–3400 BC).* Leiden: University of Leiden.

Raetzel-Fabian, D. 2000. *Calden: Erdwerk und Bestattungsplätze des Jungneolithikums. Architektur–Ritual–Chronologie*. Bonn: Habelt.

Raftery, B. 1974. A prehistoric burial at Baunogenasraid, Co. Carlow. *Royal Irish Academy Proceedings* C, 277–312.

Raftery, B. 1996. *Trackway excavations in the Mountdillon bogs, Co. Longford, 1985–1991*. Dublin: Department of Archaeology, University College Dublin.

Raftery, J. 1973. A Neolithic burial mound at Ballintruer More, Co. Wicklow. *Journal of the Royal Society of Antiquaries of Ireland* 103, 214–19.

Rahtz, P. and ApSimon, A. 1962. Neolithic and Beaker sites at Downton, near Salisbury, Wiltshire. *Wiltshire Archaeological and Natural History Magazine* 58, 116–41.

Ralph, E.K., Michael, H.N. and Han, M.C. 1973. Radiocarbon dates and reality. *MASCA Newsletter* 9, 1–20.

Rawes, B. 1991. A prehistoric and Romano-British settlement at Vineyards farm, Charlton Kings, Gloucesteshire. *Transactions of the Bristol and Gloucestershire Archaeological Society* 109, 25–89.

Rawlings, M., Allen, M.J. and Healy, F. 2004. Investigation of the Whitesheet Down environs 1989–90: Neolithic causewayed enclosure and Iron Age settlement. *Wiltshire Studies* 97, 144–96.

Ray, K. 1998. Bury Down, Lanreath: investigations in 1994. *Cornish Archaeology* 33, 227–8.

Ray, K. 1994. Bury Down, Lanreath: investigations in 1994. *Cornish Archaeology* 33, 227–8.

Ray, K. 2001. Early enclosures in south-east Cornwall. In T. Darvill and J. Thomas (eds), *Neolithic enclosures in Atlantic northwest Europe*, 50–65. Oxford: Oxbow Books.

Ray, K. 2007. The Neolithic in the West Midlands: an overview. In P.Garwood (ed.), *The undiscovered country: the earlier prehistory of the West Midlands*, 51–78. Oxford: Oxbow Books.

RCHME 1960. *A matter of time: an archaeological survey of the river gravels of England, prepared by the Royal Commission on Historical Monuments (England)*. London: HMSO.

RCHME 1970. *An inventory of historical monuments in the county of Dorset. Volume three: central Dorset*. London: HMSO.

RCHME 1976. *Ancient and historical monuments of the county of Gloucestershire, volume 1: Iron Age and Romano-British monuments in the Gloucestershire Cotswolds*. London: HMSO.

RCHME 1979. *Long barrows in Hampshire and the Isle of Wight*. London: HMSO.

RCHME 1995a. *A survey of earthworks at Whitehawk Camp, Brighton, East Sussex*. Cambridge: RCHME.

RCHME 1995b. *A causewayed enclosure and the Trundle Hillfort on St Roche's Hill, Singleton, West Sussex: an earthwork survey by the Royal Commission on the Historical Monuments of England*. Cambridge: RCHME.

RCHME 1996. *Hambledon Hill, Child Okeford, Hanford and Iwerne Courtney or Shroton, Dorset. NMR numbers ST 81, SW 10 and 17. Request survey June–September 1996*. Cambridge: RCHME.

Reckinger, F. 2005. La séquence palynologique. In F. Giligny (ed.), *Un site Néolithique Moyen en zone humide: Louviers "La Villette" (Eure)*, 29–33. Rennes: Documents Archéologiques de l'Ouest.

Reed, S.J. 1999. Radiocarbon dating. In T. Gent and H. Quinnell, 'Excavation of a causewayed enclosure and hillfort on Raddon Hill, Stokely Pomeroy'. *Proceedings of the Devon Archaeological Society* 57, 59–61.

Rees, S. 1992. *A guide to ancient and historic Wales: Dyfed*. London: HMSO.

Reide, F., Edinborough, K., and Thomas, M. 2009. Tracking Mesolithic demography in time and space and its implications for explanations of culture change. In P. Crombé, M. Van Strydonck, J. Sergant, M. Boudin and M. Bats (eds), *Chronology and evolution within the Mesolithic of north-west Europe: proceedings of an international meeting, Brussels, May 30th – June 1st 2007*, 177–94. Newcastle Upon Tyne: Cambridge Scholars Publishing.

Reimer, P.J., Baillie, M.G.L., Bard, E., Bayliss, A., Beck, J.W., Bertrand, C.J.H., Blackwell, P.G., Buck, C.E., Burr, G.S., Cutler, K.B., Damon, P.E., Edwards, R.L., Fairbanks, R.G., Friedrich, M., Guilderson, T.P., Hogg, A.G., Hughen, K.A., Kromer, B., McCormac, F.G., Manning, S., Bronk Ramsey, C., Reimer, R.W., Remmele, S., Southon, J.R., Stuiver, M., Talamo, S., Taylor, F.W., van der Plicht, J. and Weyhenmeyer, C.E. 2004. IntCal04 terrestrial radiocarbon age calibration, 0–26 cal kyr BP. *Radiocarbon* 46, 1029–58.

Reiter, S. 2005. *Die beiden Michelsberger Anlagen von Bruchsal 'Aue' und 'Scheelkopf': zwei ungleiche Nachbarn*. Stuttgart: Theiss.

Renfrew, C. 1973a. *Before civilization*. London: Cape.

Renfrew, C. 1973b. Monuments, mobilization and social organization in neolithic Wessex. In C. Renfrew (ed.), *The explanation of culture change: models in prehistory*, 539–58. London: Duckworth.

Renfrew, C. 1976. Megaliths, territories and populations. In S.J. de Laet (ed.), *Acculturation and continuity in Atlantic Europe*, 198–220. Brugge: de Tempel.

Renfrew, C. 1979. *Investigations in Orkney*. London: Society of Antiquaries.

Reynolds, P. 1993. Experimental reconstruction. In D.W. Harding, I.M. Blake and P.J. Reynolds, *An Iron Age settlement in Dorset: excavation and reconstruction,* 93–113. Edinburgh: Department of Archaeology, University of Edinburgh.

Reynolds, P. 1995. The life and death of a posthole. In L. Shepherd (ed.), *Interpreting stratigraphy 5: proceedings of the 5th stratigraphy conference*, 21–5. Norwich: Norfolk Archaeological Unit.

Rhodes, E. 2004. OSL methods and measurement; the south cursus sequence; the north cursus. In C.J. Ellis, *A prehistoric ritual complex at Eynesbury, Cambridgeshire: excavation of a multi-period site in the Great Ouse valley, 2000–2001*, 61–5. Salisbury: Trust for Wessex Archaeology.

Richards, C. 1996. Henges and water: towards an elemental understanding of monumentality and landscape in Late Neolithic Britain. *Journal of Material Culture* 1, 313–36.

Richards, C. 2004. Labouring with monuments: constructing the dolmen at Carreg Samson, south- west Wales. In V. Cummings and C. Fowler (eds), *The Neolithic of the Irish Sea: materiality and traditions of practice*, 72–80. Oxford: Oxbow Books.

Richards, C. (ed.) 2005. *Dwelling among the monuments: the Neolithic village of Barnhouse, Maeshowe passage grave and surrounding monuments at Stenness, Orkney*. Cambridge: McDonald Institute for Archaeological Research.

Richards, J.C. 1990. *The Stonehenge environs project*. London: Historic Buildings and Monuments Commission for England.

Richards, M.P. 2000. Human consumption of plant foods in the British Neolithic: direct evidence from bone stable isotopes. In A.S. Fairbairn (ed.), *Plants in Neolithic Britain and beyond*, 123–35. Oxford: Oxbow Books.

Richards, M.P. 2004. The early Neolithic in Britain: new insights from biomolecular archaeology. In I.A.G. Shepherd and G.J. Barclay (eds), *Scotland in Ancient Europe: the Neolithic and Early Bronze Age of Scotland in their European context*, 83–90. Edinburgh: Society of Antiquaries of Scotland.

Richards, M.P. 2008. Stable isotope values. In R. Mercer and F. Healy, *Hambledon Hill, Dorset: excavation and survey of a Neolithic monument complex and its surrounding landscape*, 522–7. Swindon: English Heritage.

Richards, M.P. and Hedges, R.E.M. 1999. Stable isotope evidence for similarities in the types of marine foods used by late Mesolithic humans at sites along the Atlantic coast of Europe. *Journal of Archaeological Science* 26, 717–22.

Richards, M.P. and Schulting, R.J. 2006. Against the grain? A response to Milner *et al.* (2004). *Antiquity* 80, 444–58.

Richards, M.P., Schulting, R.J. and Hedges, R.E.M. 2003. Sharp shift in diet at onset of Neolithic. *Nature* 425, 366.

Ricoeur, P. 1980. Narrative time. *Critical Inquiry* 7(1), 169–90.

Ricoeur, P. 1984. *Time and narrative* (volume 1). (Translated by K. McLaughlin and D. Pellauer.) Chicago and London: University of Chicago Press.

Rideout, J.S. 1997. Excavation of Neolithic enclosures at Cowie Road, Bannockburn, Stirling, 1984–5. *Proceedings of the Society of Antiquaries of Scotland* 127, 29–68.

Ritchie, J.N.G. 1970. Excavation of the chambered cairn at Achnacreebeag. *Proceedings of the Society of Antiquaries of Scotland* 102, 31–55.

Ritchie, G. 1997. Monuments associated with burial and ritual in Argyll. In G. Ritchie (ed.), *The archaeology of Argyll*, 67–94. Edinburgh: Edinburgh University Press.

Robb, J. 2007. *The early Mediterranean village: agency, material culture and social change in Neolithic Italy.* Cambridge: Cambridge University Press.

Robb, J. 2008. Introduction [to special section on time and change in archaeological interpretation]. *Cambridge Archaeological Journal* 18, 57–9.

Robb, J. and Miracle, P. 2007. Beyond 'migration' versus 'acculturation': new models for the spread of agriculture. In A. Whittle and V. Cummings (eds), *Going over: the Mesolithic-Neolithic transition in north-west Europe,* 99–115. Oxford: Oxford University Press for The British Academy.

Roberts, A. 1995. Digging and delving in the diluvium: past and present work in the caves of South Devon. *Torquay Natural History Society Transactions and Proceedings* 22, 47–64.

Roberts, A. 1996. Comments. In R.E.M. Hedges, P.B. Pettit, C. Bronk Ramsey and G.J. van Klinken, 'Radiocarbon dates fom the Oxford AMS system: *Archaeometry* datelist 22'. *Archaeometry* 38, 397–9.

Robertson, D. 2003. A Neolithic and early Saxon settlement: excavations at Yarmouth Road, Broome, 2001. *Norfolk Archaeology* 44, 222–50.

Robertson-Mackay, M.E. 1980. A 'head and hooves' burial beneath a round barrow, with other Neolithic and Bronze Age sites, on Hemp Knoll, near Avebury, Wiltshire. *Proceedings of the Prehistoric Society* 46, 123–76.

Robertson-Mackay, R. 1962. The excavation of the causewayed camp at Staines, Middlesex. *Archaeological Newsletter* 7, 131–4.

Robertson-Mackay, R. 1965. The primary Neolithic settlement in southern England; some new aspects. In *Atti del VI Congresso Internazionale delle Scienze Preistoriche e Protoistoriche, Roma 1962: II Communicazioni, sezione I–IV*, 319–23. Rome: UISPP.

Robertson-Mackay, R. 1987. The Neolithic causewayed enclosure at Staines, Surrey: excavations 1961–63. *Proceedings of the Prehistoric Society* 53, 23–128.

Robertson-Mackay, R. nd (internal evidence suggests a finalisation date *c.* 1985). Staines, Surrey. The Neolithic causewayed enclosure. Photocopy of typescript with ms annotations, prepared as a monograph which was later condensed into an article for publication (Robertson-Mackay 1987). National Monuments Record, Swindon: AA 051785/2A PT3 PC1; box 00692, box location 3e 5XI (4a).

Robertson-Mackay, R., Blackmore, L., Hurst, J.G., Jones, P., Moorhouse, S. and Webster, L. 1981. A group of Saxon and medieval finds from the site of the Neolithic causewayed enclosure at Staines, Surrey, with a note on the topography of the area. *Transactions of the London and Middlesex Archaeological Society* 32, 107–31.

Robin, G. 2009. *L'architecture des signes: l'art pariétal des tombeaux néolithiques autour de la mer d'Irlande.* Rennes: Presses Universitaires de Rennes.

Robins, P. 1998. Mesolithic sites at Two Mile Bottom, near Thetford, Norfollk. In N. Ashton, F. Healy and P. Pettitt (eds), *Stone Age archaeology: essays in honour of John Wymer*, 205–10. Oxford: Oxbow Books.

Robinson, D.E. and Dickson, J.H. 1988. Vegetational history and land use: a radiocarbon-dated pollen diagram from Machrie Moor, Arran, Scotland. *New Phytologist* 109, 223–51.

Robinson, M. 1991. Neolithic and late Bronze Age insect assemblages. In S.P. Needham, *Excavation and salvage at Runnymede Bridge, 1978: the late Bronze Age waterfront site*, 277–326. London: British Museum Press.

Robinson, M. 1998. Insect assemblages. In F. Pryor, *Etton: excavations at a Neolithic causewayed enclosure near Maxey, Cambridgeshire, 1982–87*, 337–50. London: English Heritage.

Robinson, M. 2000a. Coleopteran evidence for the elm decline, Neolithic activity in woodland, clearance and the use of the landscape. In A.S. Fairbairn (ed.), *Plants in Neolithic Britain and beyond*, 27–36. Oxford: Oxbow Books.

Robinson, M. 2000b. Neolithic and late Bronze Age insect assemblages. In S.P. Needham, *The passage of the Thames: Holocene environment and settlement at Runnymede. Runnymede Bridge research excavations, volume 1*, 146–67. London: British Museum Press.

Robinson, M. 2000c. Further considerations of Neolithic charred cereals, fruit and nuts. In A.S. Fairbairn (ed.), *Plants in Neolithic Britain and beyond*, 85–90. Oxford: Oxbow Books.

Robinson, M. 2004. Insect remains from Neolithic long barrow 2589. In C.J. Ellis, *A prehistoric ritual complex at Eynesbury, Cambridgeshire: excavation of a multi-period site in the Great Ouse valley, 2000–2001*, 79–80. Salisbury: Trust for Wessex Archaeology Ltd.

Roe, F.E.S., 1997. Stone axes and rubbers. In R.J. Mercer, 'The excavation of a Neolithic enclosure complex at Helman Tor, Lostwithiel, Cornwall'. *Cornish Archaeology* 36, 53–4.

Roe, F. 1999. Stone axes. In A. Barclay and C. Halpin, *Excavations at Barrow Hills, Radley, Oxfordshire. Volume I. The Neolithic and Bronze Age monument complex*, 228–33. Oxford: Oxford University Committee for Archaeology for the Oxford Archaeological Unit.

Roe, F. 2008. Worked stone other than axes and adzes. In R. Mercer and F. Healy, *Hambledon Hill, Dorset: excavation and survey of a Neolithic monument complex and its surrounding landscape*, 632–40. Swindon: English Heritage.

Roe, F. 2009. Corn grinding in southern England: what can the querns tell us? In K. Brophy and G. Barclay (eds), *Defining a regional Neolithic: the evidence from Britain and Ireland*, 26–34. Oxford: Oxbow Books.

Roe, F.E.S. and Edmonds, M. 1991. Axes. In N. Sharples, *Maiden Castle: excavations and field survey 1985–6*, 280–1, microfiche M9:A4–E4. London: English Heritage.

Ross Williamson, R.P. 1930. Excavations in Whitehawk Neolithic camp, near Brighton. *Sussex Archaeological Collections* 71, 56–96.

Rouse, I. 1986. *Migrations in prehistory: inferring population movement from cultural remains*. New Haven and London: Yale University Press.

Rouse, A. and Rowland, S. 1999. Small vertebrates. In A. Whittle, J. Pollard and C. Grigson, *The harmony of symbols: the Windmill Hill causewayed enclosure, Wiltshire*, 253–6. Oxford: Oxbow Books.

Rowley-Conwy, P. 2004. How the West was lost: a reconsideration of agricultural origins in Britain, Ireland and southern Scandinavia. *Current Anthropology* 45, S83–S113.

Rozanski, K., Stichler, W., Gonfiantini, R., Scott, E.M., Beukens, R.P., Kromer, B. and van der Plicht, J. 1992. The IAEA ^{14}C intercomparison exercise 1990. *Radiocarbon* 34, 506–19.

Rudebeck, E. 1996. Heroes and tragic figures in the transition to the Neolithic: exploring images of the human being in archaeological texts. *Journal of European Archaeology* 4, 55–86.

Rudling, D. (ed.) 2002. *Downland settlement and land-use: the archaeology of the Brighton bypass*. London: Institute of Archaeology, University College London.

Russell, M. 1996. Discussion. In M. Russell and D. Rudling, 'Excavations at Whitehawk Neolithic enclosure, Brighton, East Sussex, 1991–1993'. *Sussex Archaeological Collections* 134, 56–60.

Russell, M. 1997. NEO-'realism?': an alternative look at the Neolithic chalkland database of Sussex. In P. Topping (ed.), *Neolithic landscapes*, 69–76. Oxford: Oxbow Books.

Russell, M. 2001a. *The early Neolithic architecture of the south Downs*. Oxford: British Archaeological Reports.

Russell, M. 2001b. *Rough quarries, rocks and hills: John Pull and the Neolithic flint mines of Sussex*. Oxford: Oxbow Books.

Russell, M. 2002. *Monuments of the British Neolithic: the roots of architecture*. Stroud: Tempus.

Russell, M. 2004. The treachery of images: deconstructing the early Neolithic monumental architecture of the South Downs. In J. Cotton and D. Field (eds), *Towards a New Stone Age: aspects of the Neolithic in south-east England*, 168–76. York: Council for British Archaeology.

Russell, M. and Rudling, D. 1996. Excavations at Whitehawk Neolithic enclosure, Brighton, East Sussex, 1991–1993. *Sussex Archaeological Collections* 134, 39–61.

Russell-White, C.J. 1995. The excavation of a Neolithic and Iron Age settlement at Wardend of Durris, Aberdeenshire. *Proceedings of the Society of Antiquaries of Scotland* 125, 9–27.

Ryan, M.F. 1973. The excavation of a Neolithic burial mound at Jerpoint West, Co. Kilkenny. *Proceedings of the Royal Irish Academy* 73 C, 107–27.

Ryan, M. 1980. Prehistoric burials at Clane. *Journal of the Kildare Archaeological Society* 16, 108–11.

Ryan, M. 1981. Poulawack, Co. Clare: the affinities of the central burial structure. In D. Ó Corráin (ed.), *Irish antiquity: essays and studies presented to Professor M.J. O'Kelly*, 134–46. Cork: Tower Books.

Sangmeister, E. 1960. Zur kulturellen und zeitlichen Stellung der Rössener Kultur. In F. Eckstein (ed.), *Theoria: Festschrift für W.-H. Schuchardt*, 199–207. Baden-Baden: Grimm.

Savage, R. 1988. *Village, fortress, shrine: Crickley Hill Gloucestershire 3500 BC–AD 500*. Cheltenham: Crickley Hill Archaeological Trust.

Saville, A. 1978. Excavations at Icomb Hill, Gloucesteshire. *Transactions of the Bristol and Gloucestershire Archaeological Society* 96, 27–31.

Saville, A. 1979. Further excavations at the Nympsfield chambered tomb, Gloucestershire, 1974. *Proceedings of the Prehistoric Society* 45, 53–91.

Saville, A. 1981. The flint and chert artefacts. In R.J. Mercer, 'Excavations at Carn Brea, Illogan, Cornwall, 1970–1973: a Neolithic fortified complex of the third millennium bc'. *Cornish Archaeology* 20, 101–52.

Saville, A. 1982. Carrying cores to Gloucestershire: some thoughts on lithic resource exploitation. *Lithics* 3, 25–8.

Saville, A. 1984. Palaeolithic and Mesolithic evidence for Gloucestershire. In A. Saville (ed.), *Archaeology in Gloucestershire from the earliest hunters to the industrial age*, 59–79. Cheltenham: Cheltenham Art Gallery and Museums and the Bristol and Gloucestershire Archaeological Society.

Saville, A. 1985. The flints. In S. Trow, 'An interrupted-ditch enclosure at Southmore Grove, Rendcomb, Gloucestershire'. *Transactions of the Bristol and Gloucestershire Archaeological Society* 103, 19–22.

Saville, A. 1990. *Hazleton North, Gloucestershire, 1979–82: the excavation of a Neolithic long cairn of the Cotswold-Severn group*. London: Historic Buildings and Monuments Commission for England.

Saville, A. 1997. The flint and chert artefacts. In R.J. Mercer, 'The excavation of a Neolithic enclosure complex at Helman Tor, Lostwithiel, Cornwall'. *Cornish Archaeology* 36, 39–52.

Saville, A. 1999a. A cache of flint axeheads and other flint artefacts from Auchenhoan, near Campbeltown, Kintyre, Scotland. *Proceedings of the Prehistoric Society* 65, 83–123.

Saville, A. 1999b. An exceptional polished flint axe-head from Bolshan Hill, near Montrose, Angus. *Tayside and Fife Archaeological Journal* 5, 1–6.

Saville, A. 2002. Lithic artefacts from Neolithic causewayed enclosures: character and meaning. In G. Varndell and P. Topping (eds), *Enclosures in Neolithic Europe: essays on causewayed and non-causewayed sites,* 91–105. Oxford: Oxbow Books.

Saville, A. 2004a. A polished flint axehead from near Hayscastle, Pembrokeshire, Wales and its typological context. In R. Cleal and J. Pollard (eds), *Monuments and material culture. Papers in honour of an Avebury archaeologist: Isobel Smith*, 225–30. East Knoyle: Hobnob Press.

Saville, A. 2004b. The material culture of Mesolithic Scotland. In A. Saville (ed.), *Mesolithic Scotland and its neighbours: the early Holocene prehisotory of Scotland in its British and Irish context, and some northern European perspectives*, 185–220. Edinburgh: Society of Antiquaries of Scotland.

Saville, A. 2008. The flint and chert artefacts. In R. Mercer and F. Healy, *Hambledon Hill, Dorset: excavation and survey of a Neolithic monument complex and its surrounding landscape*, 648–743. Swindon: English Heritage.

Savory, H.N. 1956. The excavation of the Pipton long cairn, Brecknockshire. *Archaeologia Cambrensis* 105, 7–39.

Savory, R.N. 1980. The Neolithic in Wales. In J.A. Taylor (ed.), *Culture and environment in prehistoric Wales*, 207–31. Oxford: British Archaeological Reports.

Scaife, R. 2001. Flag Fen: the vegetation and environment. In F. Pryor, *The Flag Fen basin: archaeology and environment of a fenland landscape*, 351–81. London: English Heritage.

Scaife, R. 2005. Palynological analyses of the valley peat deposits at Southorpe. In C. French and F. Pryor, *Archaeology and environment of the Etton landscape*, 12–14. Peterborough: Fenland Archaeological Trust.

Scaife, R. 2008. Pollen. In M.J. Allen, M. Leivers and C. Ellis, 'Neolithic causewayed enclosures and later prehistoric farming: duality, imposition and the role of predecessors at Kingsborough, Isle of Sheppey, Kent, UK'. *Proceedings of the Prehistoric Society* 74, 269–71.

Scarre, C. 2007a. Changing places: monuments and the Neolithic transition in western France. In A. Whittle and V. Cummings (eds), *Going over: the Mesolithic-Neolithic transition in north-west Europe,* 243–61. Oxford: Oxford University Press for The British Academy.

Scarre, C. 2007b. *The megalithic monuments of Britain and Ireland.* London: Thames and Hudson.

Scharff, R. F., Ussher, R. J., Cole, G.A. J., Newton, E. T., Dixon A.F. and Westropp T. J. 1906. The exploration of the caves of County Clare. Being the second report from the committee appointed to explore Irish caves. *Transactions of the Royal Irish Academy* 33B, 1–76.

Schibler, J., Hüster-Plogmann, H. Jacomet, S., Brombacher, C., Gross-Klee, E. and Rast-Eicher, A. 1997a. *Ökonomie und Ökologie neolithischer und bronzezeitlicher Ufersiedlungen am Zürichsee*. Zürich: Monographien der Kantonsarchäologie Zürich.

Schibler, J., Jacomet, S., Hüster-Plogmann, H. and Brombacher, C. 1997b. Economic crash in the 37th and 36th centuries cal. BC in Neolithic lake shore sites in Switzerland. *Anthropozoologica* 25/26, 553–70.

Schieffelin, B.B. 2002. Marking time: the dichotomizing discourse of multiple temporalities. *Current Anthropology* 43, supplement, S5–17.

Schlichtherle, H. 1997. Neolithische und bronzezeitliche Häuser in den Feuchtbodensiedlungen Südwestdeutschlands. In H. Beck and H. Steuer (eds), *Haus und Hof in ur- und frühgeschichtlicher Zeit*, 86–136. Göttingen: Vandenhoeck & Ruprecht.

Schulting, R.J. 1998. *Slighting the sea: the Mesolithic-Neolithic transition in north-west Europe*. Unpublished PhD thesis, Department of Archaeology, University of Reading.

Schulting, R. 2000. New AMS dates from the Lambourn long barrow and the question of the earliest Neolithic in southern England : repacking the Neolithic package? *Oxford Journal of Archaeology* 19, 25–35.

Schulting, R.J. 2004. An Irish Sea change: some implications for the Mesolithic-Neolithic transition. In V. Cummings and C. Fowler (eds), *The Neolithic of the Irish Sea: materiality and traditions of practice*, 22–8. Oxford: Oxbow Books.

Schulting, R. 2008. Foodways and social ecologies from the early Mesolithic to the early Bronze Age. In J. Pollard (ed.), *Prehistoric Britain*, 90–120. Malden MA and Oxford: Blackwell.

Schulting, R. and Richards, M. 2000. The use of stable isotopes in studies of subsistence and seasonality in the British Mesolithic. In R. Young (ed), *Mesolithic lifeways: current research from Britain and Ireland*, 55–65. Leicester: School of Archaeological Studies, University of Leicester.

Schulting, R.J. and Richards, M.P. 2002a. Finding the coastal Mesolithic in southwest Britain: AMS dates and stable isotope results on human remains from Caldey Island, south Wales. *Antiquity* 76, 1011–25.

Schulting, R.J. and Richards, M.P. 2002b. The wet, the wild and the domesticated: the Mesolithic-Neolithic transition on the west coast of Scotland. *European Journal of Archaeology* 5, 147–89.

Schulting, R.J. and Wysocki, M. 2005. 'In this chambered tumulus were found cleft skulls . . .': an assessment of the evidence for cranial trauma in the British Neolithic. *Proceedings of the Prehistoric Society* 71, 107–38.

Scott, E.M. 2003. The third international radiocarbon intercomparison (TIRI) and the fourth international radiocarbon intercomparison (FIRI) 1990–2002: results, analyses, and conclusions. *Radiocarbon* 45, 135–408.

Scott, E.M., Long, A. and Kra, R.S. (eds) 1990. Proceedings of the international workshop on intercomparison of radiocarbon laboratories. *Radiocarbon* 32, 253–397.

Scull, C.J. 1990. Excavation and survey at Watchfield, Oxfordshire, 1983–89: an interim report. *Oxoniensia* 55, 42–54.

Scull, C.J. 1992. Excavation and survey at Watchfield, Oxfordshire, 1983–92. *Archaeological Journal* 149, 124–281.

Scull, C. and Bayliss, A. 1999. Radiocarbon dating and Anglo-Saxon graves. In U. von Freeden, U. Koch and A. Wieczorek (eds), *Völker an Nord- und Ostsee und die Franken. Akten des 8. Sachsensymposiums in Mannheim vom 7. bis 11. September1997*, 39–50. Bonn: Habelt.

Sealy, J.C., Van der Merwe, N.J., Lee Thorp, J.A. and Lanham, J.L. 1987. Nitrogen isotope ecology in southern Africa: implications for environmental and dietary tracing. *Geochimica et Cosmochimica Acta* 51, 2707–17.

Seidel, U. 2008a. *Michelsberger Erdwerke im Raum Heilbronn.* Stuttgart: Theiss.

Seidel, U. 2008b. Das Michelsberger Erdwerk von Ilsfeld 'Ebene'. In U. Seidel, *Michelsberger Erdwerke im Raum Heilbronn*, 71–182. Stuttgart: Theiss.

Seidel, U. 2010. Kultbau, Marktort oder Fluchtburg? *Archäologie in Deutschland* 3, 2010, 22–5.

Semelier, P. 2007. *Ossements humains et enceintes néolithiques: l'exemple du centre-ouest de la France*. Unpublished PhD thesis, L'Université Bordeaux 1.

Serjeantson, D. 1998. *Review of environmental archaeology in southern Britain. Neolithic and early Bronze Age (4000–1500 bc): the development of agriculture and animal husbandry. The animal bones*. Unpublished report for English Heritage. London and Southampton: Ancient Monuments Laboratory, English Heritage and Faunal Remains Unit, University of Southampton.

Serjeantson, D. 2006. Food or feast at Neolithic Runnymede?. In D. Serjeantson and D. Field (eds), *Animals in the Neolithic of Britain and Europe*, 113–34. Oxford: Oxbow Books.

Severinghaus, J.P., Sowers, T., Brook, E.J., Alley, R.B. and Bender, M.L. 1998. Timing of abrupt climate change at the end of the Younger Dryas interval from thermally fractionated gases in polar ice. *Nature* 391, 142–6.

Sewell, W.H. Jr. 2005. *The logics of history: social theory and social transformation*. Chicago: University of Chicago Press.

Shand, G. 1998. A Neolithic causewayed enclosure in Kent. *PAST* 29, 1.

Shand, G. 2001. *Archaeological excavations at Chalk Hill, Ramsgate Harbour approach road 1997/8*. Client Report. Canterbury: Canterbury Archaeological Trust Ltd.

Shanks, M. and Tilley, C. 1982. Ideology, symbolic power and ritual communication: a reinterpretation of Neolithic mortuary practices. In I. Hodder (ed.), *Symbolic and structural archaeology*, 129–54. Cambridge: Cambridge University Press.

Shanks, M. and Tilley, C. 1987. *Social theory and archaeology*. Oxford: Polity Press.

Sharples, N. 1986. Maiden Castle project 1985: an interim report. *Proceedings of the Dorset Natural History and Archaeological Society* 107, 111–19.

Sharples, N. 1987. Maiden Castle project 1986: an interim report. *Proceedings of the Dorset Natural History and Archaeological Society* 108, 53–61.

Sharples, N. 1991a. *Maiden Castle: excavations and field survey 1985–6*. London: English Heritage.

Sharples, N. 1991b. *English Heritage Book of Maiden Castle*. London: Batsford and English Heritage.

Sharples, N. n.d. *Maiden Castle: excavations 1985, 1986. Archive report*. Unpublished document. Dorset County Museum 1992.91.26.1.645/1.

Sharples, N. and Clark, A. 1991. Interpretation [of the radiocarbon dates]. In N. Sharples, *Maiden Castle: excavations and field survey 1985–6*, 129–39. London: English Heritage.

Shee Twohig, E. 1990. *Irish megalithic tombs*. Luton: Shire Archaeology.

Shennan, I. 1994. Coastal evolution. In M. Waller, *The Fenland project, number 9: Flandrian environmental change in Fenland*, 47–84. Cambridge: Cambridgeshire Archaeological Committee.

Shennan, I. and Horton, B. 2002. Holocene land- and sea-level changes in Great Britain. *Journal of Quaternary Science* 17, 511–26.

Shennan, I., Lambeck, K., Horton, B., Innes, J., Lloyd, J., McArthur, J., Purcell, T. and Rutherford, M. 2000. Late Devensian and Holocene records of relative sea-level changes in northwest Scotland and their implications for glacio-hydro-isostatic modelling. *Quaternary Science Reviews* 19, 1103–35.

Shennan, I., Peltier, W.R., Drummond, R., and Horton, B. 2002. Global to local scale parameters determining relative sea-level changes and the post-glacial isostatic adjustment of Great Britain. *Quaternary Science Reviews* 21, 397–408.

Shennan, S. 1988. *Quantifying archaeology*. Edinburgh: Edinburgh University Press.

Shennan, S.J., Healy, F. and Smith, I.F. 1985. The excavation of a ring-ditch at Tye Field, Lawford, Essex. *Archaeological Journal* 142, 150–215.

Shepherd, A.N. 1996. A Neolithic ring-mound at Midtown of Pitglassie, Auchterless, Aberdeenshire. *Proceedings of the Society of Antiquaries of Scotland* 126, 17–51.

Shepherd, N. 1995. Bedford southern bypass (TL0446–0950). *South Midlands Archaeology* 25, 2–7.

Sheridan, A. 1992. Scottish stone axeheads: some new work and recent discoveries. In N. Sharples and A. Sheridan (eds), *Vessels for the ancestors: essays on the Neolithic of Britain and Ireland in honour of Audrey Henshall*, 194–212. Edinburgh: Edinburgh University Press.

Sheridan, A. 1995. Irish Neolithic pottery: the story in 1995. In I. Kinnes and G. Varndell (eds), *'Unbaked urns of rudely shape': essays on British and Irish pottery for Ian Longworth*, 3–22. Oxford: Oxbow Books.

Sheridan, A.J. 1996. The oldest bow . . . and other objects. *Current Archaeology* 149, 188–90.

Sheridan, A. 2001. Donegore Hill and other Irish Neolithic enclosures: a view from outside. In T. Darvill and J. Thomas (eds), *Neolithic enclosures in Atlantic northwest Europe*, 171–89. Oxford: Oxbow Books.

Sheridan, A. 2003a. French connections I: spreading the marmites thinly. In I. Armit, E. Murphy, E. Nelis and D. Simpson (eds), *Neolithic settlement in Ireland and western Britain*, 3–17. Oxford: Oxbow Books.

Sheridan, A. 2003b. The chronology of Irish megalithic tombs. In G. Burenhult (ed.), *Stones and bones: formal disposal of the dead in Atlantic Europe during the Mesolithic-Neolithic interface 6000–3000 BC*, 69–99. Oxford: British Archaeological Reports.

Sheridan, A. 2004. Neolithic connections along and across the Irish Sea. In V. Cummings and C. Fowler (eds), *The Neolithic of the Irish Sea: materiality and traditions of practice*, 9–21. Oxford: Oxbow Books.

Sheridan, A. 2005. Les éléments d'origine bretonne autour de 4000 av. J.-C. en Écosse: témoignages d'alliance, d'influence, de déplacement, ou quoi d'autre? In G. Marchand and A. Tresset (eds), *Unité et diversité des processus de néolithisation de la façade atlantique de l'Europe (6e–4e millénaires avant notre ère)*, 25–37. Paris: Mémoire 36 de la Société Préhistorique Française.

Sheridan, A. 2006a. A non-megalithic funerary tradition in early Neolithic Ireland. In M. Meek (ed.), *The modern traveller to our past: Festschrift in honour of Ann Hamlin*, 24–31. Rathfriland: DPK.

Sheridan, A. 2006b. The National Museums Scotland radiocarbon dating programmes: results obtained during 2005/6. *Discovery and Excavation in Scotland* 7, 204–6.

Sheridan, A. 2007a. From Picardie to Pickering and Pencraig Hill? New information on the 'Carinated Bowl Neolithic' in northern Britain. In A. Whittle and V. Cummings (eds), *Going over: the Mesolithic-Neolithic transition in north-west Europe*, 441–92. Oxford: Oxford University Press for The British Academy.

Sheridan, A. 2007b. Radiocarbon dates arranged through National Museums Scotland during 2006/7. *Discovery and Excavation in Scotland* 8, 220–1.

Sheridan, A. 2010. The Neolithisation of Britain and Ireland: the 'big picture'. In B. Finlayson and G.M. Warren (eds), *Landscapes in transition*, 89–105. Oxford and London: Oxbow Books and Council for British Research in the Levant (Levant Supplementary Series 8).

Sheridan, J.A., Cooney, G. and Grogan, E. 1992. Stone axe studies in Ireland. *Proceedings of the Prehistoric Society* 58, 389–416.

Sheridan, A., Schulting, R., Quinnell, H. and Taylor, R. 2008. Revisiting a small passage tomb at Broadsands, Devon. *Proceedings of the Devon Archaeological Society* 66, 1–26.

Shore, J.S., Bartley, D.D. and Harkness, D.D. 1995. Problems encountered with the ^{14}C dating of peat. *Quaternary Science Reviews* 14, 373–83.

Shotton, F.W, Blundell, D.J. and Williams, R.E.G. 1967. Birmingham University radiocarbon dates I. *Radiocarbon* 9, 35–7.

Sidell, J. and Wilkinson, K. 2004. The central London Thames: Neolithic river development and floodplain archaeology. In J. Cotton and D. Field (eds), *Towards a New Stone Age: aspects of the Neolithic in south-east England*, 38–70. York: Council for British Archaeology.

Sidell, J., Thomas, C. and Bayliss, A. 2007. Validating and improving archaeological phasing at St Mary Spital, London, UK. *Radiocarbon* 42, 593–610.

Sidéra, I. 2000. Animaux domestiques, bêtes sauvages et objets en matières animales du Rubané au Michelsberg. De l'économie aux symboles, des techniques à la culture. *Gallia Préhistoire* 42, 107–94.

Sidéra, I. 2003. De l'usage des produits de la chasse pour différencier des hommes. Fonctions votive et sociale de la chasse au Néolithique ancien et moyen du Bassin Parisien. In P. Chambon and J. Leclerc (eds), *Les pratiques funéraires néolithiques avant 3500 av. J.-C. en France et dans les régions limitrophes. Saint-Germain-en-Laye 15–17 juin 2001*, 91–8. Paris: Société Préhistorique Française.

Sieveking, G. de G. 1960. Ebbsfleet: Neolithic sites. *Archaeologia Cantiana* 74, 192–3.

Silvester, R.J. 1991. *The Fenland project number 4: the Wissey embayment and the fen causeway, Norfolk*. Gressenhall: Norfolk Archaeological Unit.

Simpson, D. 1993. Ballygalley. *Current Archaeology* 134, 60–2.

Simpson, D. 1995. The Neolithic settlement at Ballygalley, Co. Antrim. In E. Grogan and C. Mount (eds), *Annus archaeologiae. Archaeological research* 1992, 37–44. Dublin: Organisation of Irish Archaeologists.

Simpson, D. 1996. Ballygalley houses, Co. Antrim, Ireland. In T. Darvill and J. Thomas (eds), *Neolithic houses in northwest Europe and beyond*, 123–32. Oxford: Oxbow Books.

Simpson, D., Conway, M. and Moore, D.G. 1990. The Neolithic settlement site at Ballygalley, Co. Antrim. Excavation 1989, interim report. *Ulster Journal of Archaeology* 53, 40–9.

Simpson, D., Conway, M. and Moore, D.G. 1995. Ballygalley (Croft Manor). Neolithic-Bronze Age settlement/industrial site. D374075. SMR 35:54. In I. Bennett (ed.), *Excavations 1994. Summary of archaeological excavations in Ireland*, 3–4. Bray: Wordwell.

Simpson, D. and Gibson, A. 1989. Lyle's Hill. *Current Archaeology* 114, 214–5.

Simpson, W.G. 1981. Excavations in field OS 124, Maxey, Cambridgeshire. *Northamptonshire Archaeology* 16, 34–64.

Simpson, W.G. 1985. Excavations at Maxey, Bardyke Field, 1962–63. In F. Pryor, C. French, D. Crowther, D. Gurney, G. Simpson, G. Taylor and M. Taylor, *The Fenland project no. 1: archaeology and environment in the lower Welland valley*, 245–64. Peterborough: Fenland Archaeological Trust.

Simpson, W.G. 1993. The excavation of a late Neolithic settlement at Barholm, Lincolnshire. In W.G. Simpson, D. Gurney, J. Neve and F. Pryor, *Fenland project 7: excavations in Peterborough and the lower Welland valley 1960–69*, 7–28. Peterborough: Fenland Archaeological Trust.

Simpson, W.G., Gurney, D.A., Neve, J. and Pryor, F. 1993. *The Fenland project number 7: excavations in Peterborough and the lower Welland valley 1960–1969*. Peterborough: Fenland Archaeological Trust.

Slatkin, M. 2004. A population-genetic test of founder effects and implications for Ashkenazi Jewish diseases. *American Journal of Human Genetics* 75, 282–93.

Slota, P.J., Jull, A.J.T., Lirick, T.W. and Toolin, L.J. 1987. Preparation of small samples for ^{14}C accelerator targets by catalytic reduction of CO. *Radiocarbon* 29, 303–6.

Smith, A.G. and Cloutman, W.E. 1988. Reconstruction of Holocene vegetation history in three dimensions at Waun-Fignen-Felen, an upland site in south Wales. *Philosophical Transactions of the Royal Society of London B* 322, 159–219.

Smith, A.G., Pearson, G.W. and Pilcher, J.R. 1970. Belfast radiocarbon dates I. *Radiocarbon* 12, 285–90.

Smith, A.G., Pearson, G.W. and Pilcher, J.R. 1971. Belfast radiocarbon dates III. *Radiocarbon* 13, 103–25.

Smith, A.G., Pearson, G.W. and Pilcher, J.R. 1973. Belfast radiocarbon dates V. *Radiocarbon* 15, 212–28.

Smith, A.G., Pearson, G.W. and Pilcher, J.R. 1974. Belfast radiocarbon dates VII. *Radiocarbon* 16, 269–76.

Smith, A.G., Whittle, A., Cloutman, E.W. and Morgan, L.A. 1989. Mesolithic and Neolithic activity and environmental impact on the south-east fen-edge in Cambridgeshire. *Proceedings of the Prehistoric Society* 55, 207–49.

Smith, G. 1990. A Neolithic long barrow at Uplowman Road, Tiverton. *Proceedings of the Devon Archaeological Society* 48, 15–26.

Smith, G. and Harris, D. 1982. The Excavation of Mesolithic, Neolithic and Bronze Age settlements at Poldowrian, St Keverne, 1980. *Cornish Archaeology* 21, 23–62.

Smith, G.H. 1989. Evaluation work at the Druid Stoke megalithic monument, Stoke Bishop, Bristol, 1983. *Transactions of the Bristol and Gloucestershire Archaeological Society* 107, 27–37.

Smith, I.F. 1954. Neolithic pottery from the submerged landscape of the Essex coast (Part II). *Institute of Archaeology 10th Annual Report*, 28–33.

Smith, I.F., 1956. *The decorative art of Neolithic ceramics in south-eastern England and its relations*. Unpublished PhD thesis, University of London, Institute of Archaeology.

Smith, I.F. 1959. Excavations at Windmill Hill, Avebury, Wilts, 1957–8. *Wiltshire Archaeological and Natural History Magazine* 57, 149–62.

Smith, I.F. 1965a. *Windmill Hill and Avebury: excavations by Alexander Keiller, 1925–1939*. Oxford: Clarendon Press.

Smith, I.F. 1965b. Neolithic pottery from Rybury Camp. *Wiltshire Archaeological and Natural History Magazine* 60, 127.

Smith, I.F. 1965c. Excavation of a bell barrow, Avebury G55. *Wiltshire Archaeological and Natural History Magazine* 60, 24–46.

Smith, I.F. 1966a. Windmill Hill and its implications. *Palaeohistoria* 12, 469–81.

Smith, I.F. 1966b. Description and catalogue of the Neolithic and Bronze Age pottery. In P. Ashbee, 'The Fussell's Lodge long barrow excavations, 1957'. *Archaeologia* 100, 18–23.

Smith, I.F. 1971. Causewayed enclosures. In D. Simpson (ed.), *Economy and settlement in Neolithic and early Bronze Age Britain and Europe*, 89–112. Leicester: Leicester University Press.

Smith, I.F. 1974. The Neolithic. In C. Renfrew (ed.), *British prehistory: a new outline*, 100–36. London: Duckworth.

Smith, I.F. 1976. The pottery. In J.M. Coles and B.J. Orme, 'The Sweet Track: railway site'. *Somerset Levels Papers* 2, 63–4.

Smith, I.F. 1979. The chronology of British stone implements. In T. Clough and W. Cummins (eds), *Stone axe studies*, 13–22. London: Council for British Archaeology.

Smith, I.F. 1981. Stone artefacts and the Neolithic pottery. In R.J. Mercer, 'Excavations at Carn Brea, Illogan, Cornwall, 1970–1973: a Neolithic fortified complex of the third millennium bc'. *Cornish Archaeology* 20, 153–85.

Smith, I.F. 1983. Pottery. In P.E. Leach, 'The excavation of a Neolithic causewayed enclosure on Barkhale Down, Bignor Hill, West Sussex'. *Sussex Archaeological Collections* 121, 17–20.

Smith, I.F. 1991. Round barrows Wilsford cum Lake G51–G54: excavations by Ernest Greenfield in 1958. *Wiltshire Archaeological and Natural History Magazine* 84, 11–39.

Smith, I.F. 1997. The Neolithic pottery. In R.J. Mercer, 'The excavation of a Neolithic enclosure complex at Helman Tor, Lostwithiel, Cornwall'. *Cornish Archaeology* 36, 29–37.

Smith, I.F. 2008a. The pottery from the hilltop excavations of 1974–82. In R. Mercer and F. Healy, *Hambledon Hill, Dorset, England: excavation and survey of a Neolithic monument complex and its surrounding landscape*, 587–613. Swindon: English Heritage.

Smith, I.F. 2008b. Stone axes and adzes. In R. Mercer and F. Healy, *Hambledon Hill, Dorset, England: excavation and survey of a Neolithic monument complex and its surrounding landscape*, 630–2. Swindon: English Heritage.

Smith, I.F. and Darvill, T.C. 1990. The prehistoric pottery. In A. Saville, *Hazleton North, Gloucestershire, 1979–82: the excavation of a Neolithic long cairn of the Cotswold-Severn group*, 141–52. London: Historic Buildings and Monuments Commission for England.

Smith, I.F. and Simpson, D. 1966. Excavation of a round barrow on Overton Hill, North Wiltshire. *Proceedings of the Prehistoric Society* 32, 122–55.

Smith, M.J. and Brickley, M.B. 2004. Analysis and interpretation of flint toolmarks found on bones from West Tump long barrow, Gloucestershire. *International Journal of Osteoarchaeology* 14, 18–33.

Smith, M. and Brickley, M. 2006. The date and sequence of use of Neolithic funerary monuments: new AMS dating evidence from the Cotswold Severn region. *Oxford Journal of Archaeology* 25, 335–56.

Smith, M. and Brickley, M. 2009. *People of the long barrows: life, death and burial in the earlier Neolithic*. Stroud: The History Press.

Smith, R. 1984. The ecology of Neolithic farming systems as exemplified by the Avebury region of Wiltshire. *Proceedings of the Prehistoric Society* 50, 99–120.

Smith, R.J.C., Healy, F., Allen, M.J., Morris, E.L., Barnes, I. and Woodward, P.J. 1997. *Excavations along the route of the Dorchester by-pass, Dorset, 1986–8*. Salisbury: Wessex Archaeology.

Smith, W.G. 1894. *Man the primaeval savage: his haunts and relics from the hill-tops of Bedfordshire to Blackwall*. London: Edward Stanford.

Smith, W.G. 1904a. Early man. In H.A. Doubleday and W. Page (eds), *The Victoria history of the counties of England. A history of Bedfordshire: volume I*, 145–74. Westminster: Archibald Constable and Company Limited.

Smith, W.G. 1904b. *Dunstable: its history and surroundings. The Homeland Library III*. London: the Homeland Association for the Encouragement of Touring in Great Britain.

Smith, W.G. 1915. Maiden Bower, Bedfordshire. *Proceedings of the Society of Antiquaries of London* (second series) 27, 143–61.

Smyth, J. 2006. The role of the house in early Neolithic Ireland: some new approaches. *Journal of European Archaeology* 9, 225–57.

Smyth, J. 2007. *Neolithic settlement in Ireland: new theories and approaches*. Unpublished PhD thesis, University College Dublin.

Smyth, J. (ed.) 2009. *Brú na Bóinne World Heritage Site Research Framework*. The Heritage Council: Kilkenny.

Smyth, J. 2011. The house and group identity in the Irish Neolithic. *Proceedings of the Royal Irish Academy* 111C, 1–31.

Smyth, J. forthcoming. Tara in pieces – change and continuity at the turn of the 3rd millennium BC. In M. O'Sullivan, B. Cunliffe, G. Cooney and C. Scarre (eds), *Tara from the past to the future*. Bray: Wordwell Press.

Snashall, N. 1997. *The Neolithic shrine at Crickley Hill*. Unpublished BA dissertation, University of Nottingham.

Snashall, N. 1998. *The interior of the Neolithic enclosures at Crickley Hill*. Unpublished MA dissertation, University of Nottingham.

Snashall, N. 2002. *The idea of residence in the Neolithic Cotswolds*. Unpublished PhD thesis, Department of Archaeology and Prehistory, University of Sheffield.

Sofaer, J. and Sofaer, J. 2008. The authenticity of ambiguity: writing the Dis/interest project. In D. Arnold and J. Sofaer (eds), *Biographies and space*, 168–193. London: Routledge.

Soffe, G. and Clare, T. 1988. New evidence of ritual monuments at Long Meg and Her Daughters, Cumbria. *Antiquity* 62, 552–7.

Somerville, E. 2003. Sussex: from environmental change to landscape history. In D. Rudling (ed.), *The archaeology of Sussex to AD 2000*, 235–46. Great Dunham: Heritage Marketing and Publications Ltd for the Centre for Continuing Education, University of Sussex.

Southon, J. and Roberts, M. 2000. Ten years of sourcery at CAMS/LLNL – evolution of a Cs ion source. *Nuclear Instruments and Methods in Physics Research B*, 172, 257–61.

Spatz, H. 1999. *Das mittelneolithische Gräberfeld von Trebur, Kreis Groß-Gerau*. Materialien zur Vor- und Frühgeschichte von Hessen 19. Wiesbaden: Landesamt für Denkmalpflege Hessen.

Spikins, P.A. 1999. *Mesolithic northern England: environment, population and settlement*. Oxford: British Archaeological Reports.

Spikins, P.A. 2002. *Prehistoric people of the Pennines: reconstructing the lifestyles of Mesolithic hunter-gatherers on Marsden Moor*. Leeds: West Yorkshire Archaeology Service.

Sponheimer, M., Robinson, T., Ayliffe, L., Roeder, B., Hammer, J., Passey, B., West, A., Cerling, T., Dearing, D. and Ehleringer, J. 2003. Nitrogen isotopes in mammalian herbivores: hair δ15N values from a controlled feeding study. *International Journal of Osteoarchaeology* 13, 80–7.

Stanford, S.C. 1982. Bromfield, Shropshire – Neolithic, Beaker and Bronze Age sites, 1966–70. *Proceedings of the Prehistoric Society* 48, 279–320.

Starnini, E. 2008. Material culture traditions and identity. In D.W.

Bailey, A. Whittle and D. Hofmann (eds), *Living well together? Settlement and materiality in the Neolithic of south-east and central Europe*, 101–7. Oxford: Oxbow Books.

Startin, W. 1978. Linear Pottery Culture houses: reconstruction and manpower. *Proceedings of the Prehistoric Society* 44, 143–59.

Startin, W. and Bradley, R. 1981. Some notes on work organisation and society in prehistoric Wessex. In C. Ruggles and A. Whittle (eds), *Astronomy and society in Britain during the period 4000–1500 BC*, 289–96. Oxford: British Archaeological Reports.

Startin, W. 1982a. The labour force involved in constructing the [Abingdon] causewayed enclosure. In H. Case and A. Whittle (eds), *Settlement patterns in the Oxford region: excavations at the Abingdon causewayed enclosure and other sites*, 49–50. London: Council for British Archaeology.

Startin, W. 1982b. Prehistoric earthmoving. In H. Case and A. Whittle (eds), *Settlement patterns in the Oxford region: excavations at the Abingdon causewayed enclosure and other sites*, 143–55. London: Council for British Archaeology.

Stäuble, H. 2005. *Häuser und absolute Datierung der Ältesten Bandkeramik*. Bonn: Habelt.

Steele, J. 2010. Radiocarbon dates as data: quantitative strategies for estimating colonization front speeds and event densities. *Journal of Archaeological Science* **37**, 2017–30.

Stehli, P. 1994. Chronologie der Bandkeramik im Merzbachtal. In J. Lüning and P. Stehli (eds), *Die Bandkeramik im Merzbachtal auf der Aldenhovener Platte*, 79–191. Bonn: Habelt.

Steier, P. and Rom, W. 2000. The use of Bayesian statistics for ^{14}C dates of chronologically ordered samples: a critical analysis. *Radiocarbon* 42, 183–98.

Stenhouse, M.J. and Baxter, M.S. 1979. The uptake of bomb ^{14}C in humans. In R. Berger and H.E. Suess (eds), *Radiocarbon dating*, 324–41. Berkeley: University of California Press.

Stenhouse, M.J. and Baxter, M.S. 1983. ^{14}C dating reproducibility: evidence from routine dating of archaeological samples. *PACT* 8, 147–61.

Steppan, K. 2003. *Taphonomie – Zoologie – Chronologie – Technologie – Ökonomie. Die Säugertierreste aus dem jungsteinzeitlichen Grabenwerken in Bruchsal/Landkreis Karlsruhe*. Stuttgart: Theiss.

Stevens, R., Lister, A. and Hedges, R. 2006. Predicting diet, trophic level and palaeoecology from bone stable isotope analysis: a comparative study of five red deer populations. *Oecologia* 149, 12–21.

Stone, J.F.S., Piggott, S. and Booth, A. St J. 1954. Durrington Walls, Wiltshire: recent excavations at a ceremonial site of the early second millennium BC. *Antiquaries Journal* 34, 155–77.

Stone, J.F.S. 1947. The Stonehenge cursus and its affinities. *Archaeological Journal* 104, 7–19.

Strachan, D. 1996. Cropmark of a possible long mortuary enclosure north of Rose Cottage, Chadwell St. Mary. *Essex Archaeology and History*, 27, 305–7.

Straker, V. 1990. Carbonised plant macrofossils. In A. Saville, *Hazleton North, Gloucestershire, 1979–82: the excavation of a Neolithic long cairn of the Cotswold-Severn group*, 215–18. London: Historic Buildings and Monuments Commission for England.

Strathern, A. and Stewart, P. 1999. Dangerous woods and perilous pearl shells: the fabricated politics of a longhouse in Pangia, Papua New Guinea. *Journal of Material Culture* 5, 69–89.

Strien, H.-C. and Gronenborn, D. 2005. Klima- und Kulturwandel während des mitteleuropäischen Altneolithikums (58./57–51./50. Jahrhundert v. Chr.). In D. Gronenborn (ed.), *Klimaveranderung und Kulturwandel in neolithischen Gesellschaften Mitteleuropas, 6700–2200 v. Chr.*, 131–49. Mainz: Verlag des Römisch-Germanischen Zentralmuseums.

Stuckenrath, R. and Mielke, J.E. 1972. Smithsonian Institution radiocarbon measurements VII. *Radiocarbon* 14, 401–12.

Stuckenrath, R. and Mielke, J.E. 1973. Smithsonian Institution radiocarbon measurements VIII. *Radiocarbon* 15, 388–424.

Stuiver, M. and Becker, B. 1993. High-precision decadal calibration of the radiocarbon time scale, AD 1950–6000 BC. *Radiocarbon* 35, 35–66.

Stuiver, M. and Braziunas, T.F. 1993. Modeling atmospheric ^{14}C influences and ^{14}C ages of marine samples to 10,000 BC. *Radiocarbon* 35, 137–89.

Stuiver, M. and Kra, R.S. 1986. Editorial comment. *Radiocarbon* 28(2B), ii.

Stuiver, M. and Pearson, G.W. 1986. High-precision calibration of the radiocarbon timescale, AD 1950–2500 BC. *Radiocarbon* 28, 805–38.

Stuiver, M. and Polach, H.A. 1977. Reporting of 14C data. *Radiocarbon* 19, 355–63.

Stuiver, M. and Reimer, P.J. 1986. A computer program for radiocarbon age calculation. *Radiocarbon* 28, 1022–30.

Stuiver, M. and Reimer, P.J. 1993. Extended ^{14}C data base and revised CALIB 3.0 ^{14}C age calibration program. *Radiocarbon*, 35, 215–30.

Stuiver, M., Reimer, P.J., Bard, E., Beck, J.W., Burr, G.S., Hughen, K.A., Kromer, B., McCormac, F.G., van der Plicht, J. and Spurk, M. 1998b. INTCAL98 radiocarbon age calibration, 24,000–0 cal BP. *Radiocarbon* 40, 1041–84.

Stuiver, M., Reimer, P.J. and Braziunas, T.T. 1998a. High-precision radiocarbon age calibration for terrestrial and marine samples. *Radiocarbon* 40, 1127–51.

Stukeley, W. 1743. *Abury, a temple of the British druids*. London: printed for the author and sold by W. Innys, R. Manby, B. Dod and J. Brindley.

Suess, H.E. 1967. Bristlecone pine calibration of the radiocarbon time scale from 4100 BC to 1500 BC. In *Radiocarbon dating and methods of low level counting*, 143–51. Vienna: International Atomic Energy Agency.

Sumner, H. 1913. *The ancient earthworks of Cranborne Chase*. London: Chiswick Press.

Surovell, T.A. and Brantingham, P.J. 2007. A note on the use of temporal frequency distributions in studies of prehistoric demography. *Journal of Archaeological Science* 34, 1868–77.

Sutcliffe, A.J. and Zeuner, F.E. 1958. Excavations in the Torbryan Caves, Devonshire: I. Tornewton Cave. *Proceedings of the Devon Archaeological Exploration Society* 5, 127–46.

Swinnerton, F. 1889. The early Neolithic cists and refuse heap at Port St Mary. *YN Liaar Mannigah* 1, 241–4.

Switsur, V.R. 1981. Cambridge University natural radiocarbon measurements XV. *Radiocarbon* 23, 81–93.

Switsur, R. 1994. Radiocarbon dating. In M. Waller (ed.), 'The Fenland Project, Number 9: Flandrian environmental change in Fenland'. *East Anglian Archaeology* 70, 27–34.

Switsur, V.R. and West, R.G. 1973. Cambridge University natural radiocarbon measurements XII. *Radiocarbon* 15, 534–44.

Switsur, V.R. and West, R.G. 1975. Cambridge University natural radiocarbon measurements XIV. *Radiocarbon* 17, 301–12.

Switsur, V.R, Hall, M.A. and West, R.G. 1970. Cambridge University natural radiocarbon measurements IX. *Radiocarbon* 12, 590–8.

Sykes, N. 2004. Neolithic and Saxon animal bone. In C.J. Ellis,

A prehistoric ritual complex at Eynesbury, Cambridgeshire: excavation of a multi-period site in the Great Ouse valley, 2000–2001, 87–91. Salisbury: Trust for Wessex Archaeology Ltd.

Tamers, M.A. 1965. Routine carbon-14 dating using liquid scintillation techniques. In R.M. Chatters and E.A. Olson (eds), *Radiocarbon and tritium dating: Proceedings of the Sixth International Conference on Radiocarbon and Tritium Dating Washington D.C.*, 53–67. Pullman, WA: Clearinghouse for Federal Science and Technology Information.

Tarrête, J. 1989. Extraire et façonner. In C. Goudineau and J. Guilaine (eds), *De Lascaux au Grand Louvre: archéologie et histoire en France*, 140–3. Paris: Editions Errance.

Taylor, A. 1981. Appendix II. The barrows of Cambridgeshire. In A.J. Lawson, E.A. Martin and D. Priddy, *The barrows of East Anglia*, 108–20. Gressenhall, Bury St Edmunds and Chelmsford: Norfolk Archaeological Unit, Suffolk County Council and Essex County Council.

Taylor, M. 1998. Wood and bark from the enclosure ditches. In F. Pryor, *Etton: excavations at a Neolithic causewayed enclosure near Maxey, Cambridgeshire, 1982–87*, 115–59. London: English Heritage.

Taylor, R.E. 1995. Radiocarbon dating: the continuing revolution. *Evolutionary Anthropology: Issues, News, and Reviews* 4, 169–81.

Teschler-Nicola, M. 1996. Anthropologische Spurensicherung–Die traumatischen und postmortalen Veränderungen an den linearbandkeramischen Skelettresten von Asparn/Schletz. In *Rätsel um Gewalt und Tod vor 7000 Jahren: eine Spurensicherung*, 47–64. Asparn a.d. Zaya: Museum für Urgeschichte.

Thevenet, C. 2007. De pierre ou de bois: coffre et architecture de la sépulture 10 du monument Michelsberg de Beaurieux (Aisne, France). In P. Moinat et P. Chambon (eds), *Les cistes de Chamblandes et la place des coffres dans les pratiques funéraires du Néolithique moyen occidental.* Actes du colloque de Lausanne, 12–13 mai 2006. *Cahiers d'Archéologie Romande* 110, Lausanne, et *Mémoires de la Société Préhistorique Française* 43, Paris, 143–53.

Thévenot, J.-P. 2005. *Le camp de Chassey (Chassey-le-Camp, Saône-et-Loire): les niveaux néolithiques du rampart de "la Redoute"*. Dijon: Revue Archéologique de l'Est, supplément 25.

Thomas, D. 1992. Nant Hall Road, Prestatyn (SJ 070 832). *Archaeology in Wales* 32, 59.

Thomas, D. 1993. Nant Hall Road, Prestatyn (SJ 070 832). *Archaeology in Wales* 33, 50.

Thomas, J. 1984. A tale of two polities. In R. Bradley and J. Gardiner (eds), *Neolithic studies*, 161–76. Oxford: British Archaeological Reports.

Thomas, J. 1987. Relations of production and social change in the Neolithic of north-west Europe. *Man* 22, 405–30.

Thomas, J. 1991. *Rethinking the Neolithic*. Cambridge: Cambridge University Press.

Thomas, J. 1996. The cultural context of the first use of domesticates in central and north-west Europe. In D. Harris (ed.), *The origins and spread of agriculture and pastoralism in Eurasia*, 310–22. London: University College, London.

Thomas, J. 1998. Some problems with the notion of external symbolic storage, and the case of Neolithic material culture in Britain. In C. Renfrew and C. Scarre (eds), *Cognition and material culture: the archaeology of symbolic storage*, 149–56. Cambridge: McDonald Institute for Archaeological Research.

Thomas, J. 1999. *Understanding the Neolithic*. London: Routledge.

Thomas, J. 2001. Neolithic enclosures: reflections on excavations in Wales and Scotland. In T. Darvill and J. Thomas (eds), *Neolithic enclosures in Atlantic northwest Europe*, 132–43. Oxford: Oxbow Books.

Thomas, J. 2003. Thoughts on the 'repacked' Neolithic Revolution. *Antiquity* 77, 67–74.

Thomas, J.S. 2004a. Materiality and traditions of practice in Neolithic south-west Scotland. In V. Cummings and C. Fowler (eds), *The Neolithic of the Irish Sea: materiality and traditions of practice*, 174–84. Oxford: Oxbow.

Thomas, J.S. 2004b. Recent debates on the Mesolithic-Neolithic transition in Britain and Ireland. *Documenta Praehistorica* 31, 113–30.

Thomas, J. 2006. On the origins and development of cursus monuments in Britain. *Proceedings of the Prehistoric Society* 72, 229–41.

Thomas, J. 2007a. Mesolithic-Neolithic transitions in Britain: from essence to inhabitation. In A. Whittle and V. Cummings (eds), *Going over: the Mesolithic-Neolithic transition in north-west Europe*, 423–39. Oxford: Oxford University Press for The British Academy.

Thomas, J. (ed.) 2007b. *Place and memory: excavations at the Pict's Knowe, Holywood and Holm Farm, Dumfries and Galloway, 1994–8.* Oxford: Oxbow Books.

Thomas, J. 2008. The Mesolithic-Neolithic transition in Britain. In J. Pollard (ed.), *Prehistoric Britain*, 58–89. Malden MA and Oxford: Blackwell.

Thomas, J., Marshall, P., Parker Pearson, M., Pollard, J., Richards, C., Tilley, C. and Welham, K. 2009. The date of the Greater Stonehenge Cursus. *Antiquity* 83, 40–53.

Thomas, K. 1996. A contribution to the environmental history of Whitehawk Neolithic enclosure. In M. Russell and D. Rudling, 'Excavations at Whitehawk Neolithic enclosure, Brighton, East Sussex, 1991–1993'. *Sussex Archaeological Collections* 134, 51–6.

Thomas, K.D., 1977. Appendix IV: the land mollusca from the enclsoure on Offham Hill. In P. Drewett, 'The excavation of a Neolithic causewayed enclosure at Offham Hill, East Sussex, 1976'. *Proceedings of the Prehistoric Society* 43, 234–9.

Thomas, K.D. 1981a. Land snail assemblages. In O.R. Bedwin and F. Aldsworth, 'Excavations at The Trundle, 1981'. *Sussex Archaeological Collections* 119, 211–13.

Thomas, K.D. 1981b. The land mollusca. In O. Bedwin, 'Excavations at the Neolithic enclosure on Bury Hill, Houghton, West Sussex, 1979'. *Proceedings of the Prehistoric Society* 47, 84–5.

Thomas, K.D. 1982. Neolithic enclosures and woodland habitats on the south downs in Sussex, England. In M. Bell and S. Limbrey (eds), *Archaeological aspects of woodland ecology*, 147–70. Oxford: British Archaeological Reports.

Thomas, K.D. 1983a. Land snail assemblages. In O. Bedwin and F.G. Aldsworth, 'Excavations at The Trundle, 1981'. *Sussex Archaeological Collections* 119, 211–13.

Thomas, K.D. 1983b. Mollusc analysis of samples from the ditch-fill of trench II. In P.E. Leach, 'The excavation of a Neolithic causewayed enclosure on Barkhale Down, Bignor Hill, West Sussex'. *Sussex Archaeological Collections* 121, 28–30.

Thomas, K.D. 1984. The environment of the Court Hill enclosure. In O. Bedwin, 'The excavation of a small hilltop enclosure on Court Hill, Singleton, West Sussex, 1982'. *Sussex Archaeological Collections* 122, 19–21.

Thomas, K.D. 1992. Evidence of past environments and land-use at Halnaker Hill from a study of the land molluscs. In O. Bedwin, 'Prehistoric earthworks on Halnaker Hill, West Sussex, excavations 1981–1983'. *Sussex Archaeological Collections* 130, 8–10.

Thomas, K.D. 1994. Evidence for the environmental setting of the Neolithic enclosure at Combe Hill, East Sussex. In P. Drewett, 'Dr V. Seton Williams' excavations at Combe Hill, 1962, and the role of Neolithic causewayed enclosures in Sussex'. *Sussex Archaeological Collections* 132, 17–19.

Thomas, N. 1956. A Neolithic pit on Waden Hill, Avebury. *Wiltshire Archaeological and Natural History Magazine* 56, 167–71.

Thomas, N. de L.W. 1964a. The Neolithic causewayed camp at Robin Hood's Ball, Shrewton. *Wiltshire Archaeological and Natural History Magazine* 59, 1–27.

Thomas, N. 1964b. A gazetteer of Neolithic and Bronze Age sites and Antiquities in Bedfordshire. *Bedfordshire Archaeological Journal* 2, 16–22.

Thorpe, I.J.N. 2001. Danish causewayed enclosures – temporary monuments? In T. Darvill and J. Thomas (eds), *Neolithic enclosures in Atlantic northwest Europe*, 190–203. Oxford: Oxbow Books.

Thorpe, I.J.N. 2003. Anthropology, archaeology and the origin of warfare. *World Archaeology* 35, 145–65.

Thurnam, J. 1860. Examination of barrows on the downs of North Wiltshire in 1853–57. *Wiltshire Archaeological and Natural History Magazine* 6(18), 317–36.

Tilley, C. 1994. *A phenomenology of landscape: places, paths and monuments*. Oxford: Berg.

Tilley, C. and Bennett, W. 2001. An archaeology of supernatural places: the case of West Penwith. *Journal of the Royal Anthropological Institute* 7, 335–62.

Tillmann, A. 1993. Kontinuität oder Diskontinuität? Zur Frage einer bandkeramischen Landnahme im südlichen Mitteleuropa. *Archäologische Informationen* 16, 157–87.

Timby, J., Stansbie, D., Norton, A. and Welsh, K. 2005. Excavations along the Newbury reinforcement pipeline: Iron Age–Roman activity and a Neolithic pit group. *Oxoniensia* 70, 203–307.

Time Team 2005. http://www.channel4.com/history/timeteam/2005_north_found.html.

Timoney, M.A. 1984. The hut sites on Knocknarea mountain. In G. Burenhult, *The archaeology of Carrowmore. Environmental archaeology and the megalithic tradition at Carrowmore, Co. Sligo, Ireland*, 216–318. Stockholm: Institute of Archaeology at the University of Stockholm.

Tingle, M. 1999. Flint and chert. In T.H. Gent and H. Quinnell, 'Excavation of a causewayed enclosure and hillfort on Raddon Hill, Stokely Pomeroy'. *Proceedings of the Devon Archaeological Society* 57, 29–37.

Tingle, M. 2000. Excavations at Membury, East Devon. July 1998 and March 2000. Privately circulated.

Tingle, M. 2006. Excavations of a possible causewayed enclosure and Roman site at Membury 1986 and 1994–2000. *Proceedings of the Devon Archaeological Society* 64, 1–52.

Tipping, R. 2010. The case for climatic stress forcing choice in the adoption of agriculture in the British Isles. In B. Finlayson and G.M Warren (eds), *Landscapes in transition*, 66–76. Oxford and London: Oxbow Books and Council for British Research in the Levant (Levant Supplementary Series 8).

Tipping, R., Bunting, M.J., Davies, A.L., Fraser, S., McCulloch, R. and Murray, H. 2009. Modelling land use around an early Neolithic timber 'hall' in north east Scotland from high spatial resolution pollen analyses. *Journal of Archaeological Science* 36, 140–9.

Tobin, R. 2002. 630. Corbally. Neolithic houses. 01E0299. In I. Bennett (ed.), *Excavations 2001: summary accounts of archaeological excavations in Ireland*, 185–7. Bray: Wordwell.

Todd, M. 1984a. Excavations at Hembury, Devon, 1980–3: a summary report. *Antiquaries Journal* 64, 251–68.

Todd, M. 1984b. Hembury (Devon): Roman troops in a hillfort. *Antiquity* 58, 171–4.

Todd, M. 2002. The cross-dyke at Hembury. *Proceedings of the Devon Archaeological Society* 60, 207–10.

Tomalin, D. forthcoming. Pottery and fired clay from Irthlingborough, West Cotton and Stanwick, with an overview of the ceramic evidence. In J. Harding and F. Healy (eds), *The Raunds Area Project. A Neolithic and Bronze Age Landscapes Northamptonshire Volume 2: Supplementary Studies*. Swindon: English Heritage.

Topp, C. 1962. The portal dolmen of Drumanone, Co. Roscommon. *Bulletin of the Institute of Archaeology, London* 3, 38–46.

Topping, P. 2004. The South Downs flint mines: towards an ethnography of prehistoric flint extraction. In J. Cotton and D. Field (eds), *Towards a New Stone Age: aspects of the Neolithic in south-east England*, 177–90. York: Council for British Archaeology.

Topping, P. 2005. Shaft 27 revisited: an ethnography. In P. Topping and M. Lynott (eds), *The cultural landscape of prehistoric mines*, 63–93. Oxford: Oxbow Books.

Toussaint, M., Collet, H. and Jadin, I. 2010. Datations radiocarbones d'ossements humains du site minier néolithique de Spiennes (Mons, Hainaut) : première approche. *Notae Praehistoricae* 30, 73–80.

Trautman, M.A. and Willis, E.H. 1966. Isotopes Inc radiocarbon measurements V. *Radiocarbon* 8, 161–203.

Tresset, A. 2000. Early husbandry in Atlantic areas. Animal introductions, diffusion of techniques and native acculturation at the north-western margin of Europe. In J. Henderson (ed.), *The prehistory and early history of Atlantic Europe*, 17–32. Oxford: British Archaeological Reports.

Tresset, A. 2003. French connections II: of cows and men. In I. Armit, E. Murphy, E. Nelis and D. Simpson (eds), *Neolithic settlement in Ireland and western Britain*, 18–30. Oxford: Oxbow Books.

Tresset, A. 2005a. La place changeante des bovins dans les bestiaires du Mésolithique final et du Néolithique d'Armorique et des régions adjacentes. In G. Marchand and A. Tresset (eds), *Unité et diversité des processus de néolithisation de la façade atlantique de l'Europe (6e–4e millénaires avant notre ère)*, 271–86. Paris: Mémoire 36 de la Société Préhistorique Française.

Tresset, A. 2005b. Elevage, chasse et alimentation carnée. In F. Giligny (ed.), *Un site Néolithique Moyen en zone humide: Louviers "La Villette" (Eure)*, 249–62. Rennes: Documents Archéologiques de l'Ouest.

Tresset, A. and Vigne, J.-D. 2006. Le depot d'animaux de la structure e4: une illustration de la symbolique des bovines à la charnière du Mésolithique et du Néolithique bretons? In C.-T. Le Roux, Y. Lecerf and J.-Y. Tinévez, ' Monuments mégalithiques à Locmariaquer (Morbihan: le long tumulus d'er Grah et son environnement'. *Gallia Préhistoire,* 38th supplement, 123–45.

Tresset, A. and Vigne, J.-D. 2007. Substitution of species, techniques and symbols at the Mesolithic-Neolithic transition in Western Europe. In A. Whittle and V. Cummings (eds), *Going over: the Mesolithic-Neolithic transition in north-west*

Europe, 189–210. Oxford: Oxford University Press for The British Academy.

Tringham, R. 2005. Weaving house life and death into places: a blueprint for a hypermedia narrative. In D. Bailey, A. Whittle and V. Cummings (eds), *(un)settling the Neolithic*, 98–111. Oxford: Oxbow Books.

Trnka, G. 1991. *Studien zu mittelneolithischen Kreisgrabenanlagen*. Wien: Verlag der Österreichischen Akademie der Wissenschaften.

Trnka, G. 2005. Kreise und Kulturen – Kreisgrabenanlagen in Mitteleuropa. In F. Daim and W. Neubauer (eds), *Zeitreise Heldenberg. Geheimnisvolle Kreisgräben*, 10–18. Horn-Wien: Verlag Berger.

Trow, S. 1985. An interrupted ditch enclosure at Southmore Grove, Rendcomb, Gloucestershire. *Transactions of the Bristol and Gloucestershire Archaeological* Society 103, 17–22.

Trudell, S.A., Rygiewicz, P.T. and Edmonds, R.L. 2004. Patterns of nitrogen and carbon stable isotope ratios in macrofungi, plants and soils in two old-growth conifer forests. *New Phytologist* 164, 317–35.

Turner, V. 1980. Social dramas and stories about them. *Critical Inquiry* 7(1), 141–68.

Ubelaker, D.H., Buchholz, B.A. and Stewart, J.E.B. 2006. Analysis of radiocarbon in different skeletal and dental tissue types to evaluate date of death. *Journal of Forensic Science* 51, 484–8.

Underwood, D. 1996. The worked flint. In M. Russell and D. Rudling, Excavations at Whitehawk Neolithic enclosure, Brighton, East Sussex, 1991–1993. *Sussex Archaeological Collections* 134, 49–50.

van der Merwe, N.J. and Medina, E. 1991. The canopy effect, carbon isotope ratios and foodwebs in Amazonia. *Journal of Archaeological Science* 18, 249–59.

van der Plicht, J. 1993. The Groningen radiocarbon calibration program. *Radiocarbon* 35, 231–7.

van der Plicht, J., Wijma, S., Aerts, A.T., Pertuisot, M.H. and Meijer, H.A.J. 2000. Status report: the Groningen AMS facility. *Nuclear Instruments and Methods in Physics Research B* 172, 58–65.

Vandeputte, K., Moens, L. and Dams, R. 1996. Improved sealed-tube combustion of organic samples to CO_2 for stable isotope analysis, radiocarbon dating and percent carbon determinations. *Analytical Letters* 29, 2761–73.

van Klinken, G., Richards, M. and Hedges, R.E.M. 2000. An overview of causes for stable isotopic variations in past European human populations: environmental, ecophysiological, and cultural effects. In S. Ambrose and M. Katzenberg (eds), *Biogeochemical approaches to paleodietary analysis*, 39–63. New York: Kluwer Academic.

van Klinken, G., van der Plicht, J. and Hedges, R.E.M. 1994. Bone $^{13}C/^{12}C$ ratios reflect (palaeo-) climatic variations. *Geophysical Research Letters* 21, 445–8.

van Nedervelde, J. 1977. Nanna's Cave (SS 1458 9697). *Archaeology in Wales* 17, 24.

Vanmontfort, B. 2001. The Group of Spiere as a new stylistic entity in the Middle Neolithic Scheldt basin. *Notae Praehistoricae* 21, 139–43.

Vanmontfort, B., Geerts, A.-I., Casseyas, C., Bakels, C.C., Buydens, C., Damblon, F., Langohr, R., Van Neer, W. and Vermeersch, P.M. 2004. De Hel in de tweede helft van het 5de millenium v.Chr. Een midden-Neolithische enclosure te Spiere (prov. West-Vlaanderen). *Archeologie in Vlaanderen* 8, 9–77.

Van Strydonck, M., Boudin, M., Hoefens, M. and de Mulder, G. 2005. ^{14}C-dating of cremated bones – why does it work? *Lunula* 13, 3–10.

Van Strydonck, M., Ervynck, A., Boudin, M., Van Bos, M. and De Wilde, R. 2009. The relationship between ^{14}C content, $\delta^{13}C$ and $\delta^{15}N$ values in bone collagen and the proportion of fish, meat and plant material in the diet: a controlled feeding experiment. In P. Crombé, M. Van Strydonck, J. Sergant, M. Boudin and M. Bats (eds), *Chronology and evolution within the Mesolithic of north-west Europe: proceedings of an international meeting, Brussels, May 30th–June 1st 2007*, 541–55. Newcastle upon Tyne: Cambridge Scholars Publishing.

Van Strydonck, M., Nelson, D.E., Crombé, P., Bronk Ramsey, C., Scott, E.M., van der Plicht, J. and Hedges, R.E.M. 1999. What's in a ^{14}C date? In J. Evin, C. Oberlin, J.P. Daugas and J.F. Salles (eds), *Actes du 3ème congres international 'Archaeologie et ^{14}C', Lyon, 6–10 Avril 1998. Revue d'Archeometrie Supplément 1999* et *Société Préhistorique Française Memoire* 26, 433–48.

Vaquer, J. 1990. *Le Néolithique en Languedoc occidental*. Paris: Éditions du CNRS.

Varndell, G. and Topping, P. (eds) 2002. *Enclosures in Neolithic Europe: essays on causewayed and non-causewayed sites*. Oxford: Oxbow Books.

Vatcher, F. de M. 1961. The excavation of the long mortuary enclosure on Normanton Down, Wilts. *Proceedings of the Prehistoric Society* 27, 160–73.

Verhart, L.B.M. 2000a. *Times fade away: the neolithization of the southern Netherlands in an anthropological and geographical perspective*. Leiden: Faculty of Archaeology, Leiden University.

Verhart, L. 2000b. The transition from Mesolithic to Neolithic in a Dutch perspective. *Notae Praehistoricae* 20, 127–32.

Verheyleweghen, J. 1966. Le néolithique minier belge. Son origine et ses relations culturelles. *Palaeohistoria* 12, 529–57.

Verrill, L. 2006. *Later prehistoric environmental marginality in western Ireland: multi-proxy investigations*. Unpublished PhD thesis, University of Edinburgh.

Verron, G. 2000. *La préhistoire de la Normandie*. Rennes: Ouest-France Université.

Vogel, J.C. and Marais, M. 1971. Pretoria radiocarbon dates I. *Radiocarbon* 13, 378–94.

Vogel, J.C. and van der Plicht, J. 1993. Calibration curve for short-lived samples, 1900–3900 BC. *Radiocarbon* 35, 87–91.

Vogel, J.C. and Waterbolk, H.T. 1967. Groningen radiocarbon dates VII. *Radiocarbon* 9, 107–55.

Vogel, J.C. and Waterbolk, H.T. 1972. Groningen radiocarbon dates X. *Radiocarbon* 14, 6–110.

Vogel, J.C., Fuls, A. and Vissier, E. 1986. Pretoria radiocarbon dates III. *Radiocarbon* 28, 1133–72.

Vogel, J.C., Fuls, A., Visser, E. and Becker, B. 1993. Pretoria calibration curve for short-lived samples, 1930–3350 BC. *Radiocarbon* 35, 73–85.

Vogel, J.S., Nelson, D. and Southon, J.R. 1987. ^{14}C background levels in an accelerator mass spectrometry system. *Radiocarbon* 29, 323–33.

Vogel, J.S., Southon, J.R., Nelson, D.E. and Brown, T.A. 1984. Performance of catalytically condensed carbon for use in AMS. *Nuclear Instruments and Methods in Physics B*, 5, 289–93.

Vyner, B. 2001. Clegyr Boia: a potential Neolithic enclosure and associated monuments on the St David's peninsula, southwest Wales. In T. Darvill and J. Thomas (eds), *Neolithic enclosures in Atlantic northwest Europe*, 78–90. Oxford: Oxbow Books.

Waddington, C. 1999. *A landscape archaeological study of the*

Mesolithic-Neolithic in the Milfield basin, Northumberland. Oxford: Archaeopress.
Waddington, C. 2001. Breaking out of the morphological straitjacket: early Neolithic enclosures in northern Britain. *Durham Archaeological Journal* 16, 1–13.
Wadell, J. 1998. *The prehistoric archaeology of Ireland.* Galway: Galway University Press.
Wahl, J. 2000. Kult, Kannibalismus und Sonderbestattung. Die schwierige Deutung vorgeschichtlicher Skelettreste. In H.-P. Kuhnen (ed.), *Morituri: Menschenofer, Todgeweihte, Strafgerichte*, 29–38. Trier: Rheinisches Landesmuseum Trier.
Wainwright, G.J. 1967. *Coygan Camp: a prehistoric, Romano-British and Dark Age settlement in Carmarthenshire.* Cardiff: Cambrian Archaeological Association.
Wainwright, G.J. 1972. The excavation of a Neolithic settlement on Broome Heath, Ditchingham, Norfolk. *Proceedings of the Prehistoric Society* 38, 1–97.
Wainwright, G.J. 1973. The excavation of prehistoric and Romano-British settlements at Eaton Heath, Norwich. *Archaeological Journal* 130, 1–43.
Wainwright, G.J. and Cunliffe, B.W. 1985. Maiden Castle: excavation, education and entertainment? *Antiquity* 59, 97–100.
Wainwright, G. J. and Longworth, I.H. 1971. *Durrington Walls: excavations 1966–1968.* London: Society of Antiquaries of London.
Wakely, J. 2006. Other marks. In C. Evans and I. Hodder, *A woodland archaeology. Neolithic sites at Haddenham: the Haddenham project volume 1*, 147–9. Cambridge: McDonald Institute for Archaeological Research.
Walker, A.J. and Otlet, R.L. 1985. Harwell Radiocarbon measurements IV. *Radiocarbon* 27, 74–94.
Walker, A.J. and Otlet, R.L. 1988. Harwell radiocarbon measurements VI. *Radiocarbon* 30, 297–317.
Walker, A.J., Keyzor, R.S. and Otlet, R.L. 1988. Harwell radiocarbon measurements VII. *Radiocarbon* 30, 319–40.
Walker, A.J., Williams, N. and Otlet, R.L. 1990. Harwell radiocarbon measurements VIII. *Radiocarbon* 32, 165–96.
Walker, A.J., Young, A.W. and Otlet, R.L. 1991. Harwell radiocarbon measurements X. *Radiocarbon* 33, 87–113.
Walker, J. 1999. Late twelfth and early thirteenth century aisled buildings: a comparison. *Vernacular Architecture* 30, 21–53.
Walker, M. 1999. Pollen analysis. In A. Whittle, J. Pollard and C. Grigson, *The harmony of symbols: the Windmill Hill causewayed enclosure, Wiltshire*, 161–3. Oxford: Oxbow Books.
Walker, M.J.C., Bryant, C., Coope, G.R., Harkness, D.D., Lowe, J.J. and Scott, E.M. 2001. Towards a radiocarbon chronology of the Late-Glacial: sample selection strategies. *Radiocarbon* 43, 1007–21.
Wallace, P.F. 1977. A prehistoric burial cairn at Ardcrony, Nenagh, Co. Tipperary. *North Munster Archaeological Journal* 19, 3–20.
Waller, M. 1994. *The Fenland project, number 9: Flandrian environmental change in Fenland.* Cambridge: Cambridgeshire Archaeological Committee.
Waller, M. and Alderton, A. 1994. Peacock's Farm. In M. Waller, *The Fenland project, number 9: Flandrian environmental change in Fenland*, 118–24. Cambridge: Cambridgeshire Archaeological Committee.
Wallis, S. and Waughman, M. 1998. *Archaeology and the landscape in the lower Blackwater valley.* Chelmsford: Essex County Council Archaeology Section.
Walsh, F. 2004. N2 *Carrickmacross-Aclint road re-alignment: site 110 Monanny 1. Post-excavation assessment and updated project design.* Dún Laoghaire: Irish Archaeological Consultancy Ltd.
Wand, J.O., Gillespie, R. and Hedges, R.E.M. 1984. Sample preparation for accelerator-based radiocarbon dating. *Journal of Archaeological Science* 11, 159–63.
Ward, A. 1987. Cefn Bryn, Gower. *Archaeology in Wales* 27, 39–40.
Ward, G.K. and Wilson, S.R. 1978. Procedures for comparing and combining radiocarbon age determinations: a critique. *Archaeometry* 20, 19–31.
Warren, G.M. 2001. Marking space? Stone tool deposition in Mesolithic and early Neolithic Eastern Scotland. In M. Zvelebil and K. Fewster (eds), *Ethnoarchaeology and hunter-gatherers: pictures at an exhibition*, 91–100. Oxford: British Archaeological Reports.
Warren, G.M. 2004. The start of the Neolithic in Scotland. In I.A.G. Shepherd and G.J. Barclay (eds), *Scotland in Ancient Europe: the Neolithic and Early Bronze Age of Scotland in their European context*, 91–102. Edinburgh: Society of Antiquaries of Scotland.
Warren, G. 2005. *Mesolithic lives in Scotland.* Stroud: Tempus.
Warren, G. 2007. Radiocarbon dates from Belderrig, Co.Mayo. August 2007 Graeme Warren http://www.ucd.ie/t4cms/bdg_dates_outline_june_2007_web.pdf
Warren, G.M. 2009a. Times of change: the Mesolithic and Mesolithic-Neolithic transition in northwest Ireland. In P. Crombé, M. Van Strydonck, J. Sergant, M. Boudin and M. Bats (eds), *Chronology and evolution within the Mesolithic of north-west Europe: proceedings of an international meeting, Brussels, May 30th–June 1st 2007*, 635–52. Newcastle Upon Tyne: Cambridge Scholars Publishing.
Warren, G. 2009b. Belderrig: a 'new' later Mesolithic and Neolithic landscape in northwest Ireland. In N. Finlay, S. McCartan, N. Milner and C. Wickham-Jones (eds), *From Bann Flakes to Bushmills*, 143–52. Oxford: Prehistoric Society/Oxbow Books.
Warren, G., Little, A. and Stanley, M. 2009. A late Mesolithic lithic scatter from Corralanna, Co. Westmeath and its place in the Mesolithic landscape of the Irish midlands. *Proceedings of the Royal Irish Academy* 109C, 1–35.
Warrilow, W., Owen, G. and Britnell, W. 1986. Eight ring-ditches at Four Crosses, Llandysilio, Powys, 1981–85. *Proceedings of the Prehistoric Society* 52, 53–87.
Waterbolk, H.T. 1971. Working with radiocarbon dates. *Proceedings of the Prehistoric Society* 37(2), 15–33.
Waterman, D.M. 1965. The court cairn at Annaghmare, Co. Armagh. *Ulster Journal of Archaeology* 28, 3–46.
Waterman, D.M. 1978. The excavation of a court cairn at Tully, County Fermanagh. *Ulster Journal of Archaeology* 41, 3–14.
Watson, A. 2006. (Un)intentional sound? Acoustics and Neolithic monuments. In C. Scarre and G. Lawson (eds), *Archaeoacoustics*, 11–22. Cambridge: McDonald Institute for Archaeological Research.
Webley, D.P. 1958. A 'cairn cemetery' and secondary Neolithic dwelling on Cefn Cilsanws, Vaynor (Breckn). *Bulletin of the Board of Celtic Studies* 18(1), 79–88.
Webley, D.P. 1976. How the west was won: prehistoric land-use in the Southern Marches. In G.C. Boon and J.M. Lewis (eds), *Welsh antiquity: essays mainly on prehistoric topics presented to H.N. Savory upon his retirement as Keeper of Archaeology*, 19–35. Cardiff: National Museum of Wales.

Webley, L. 2007. A fen-edge landscape at Parnwell, Peterborough: prehistoric, Roman and Saxon activity. *Proceedings of the Cambridge Antiquarian Society* 96, 79–114.

Weir, D.A. 1999. Pollen analysis and Mollusca. In C. Mount, 'Excavation and environmental analysis of a Neolithic mound and Iron Age barrow cemetery at Rathdooney Beg, County Sligo, Ireland'. *Proceedings of the Prehistoric Society* 65, 355–65.

Wessex Archaeology 2003. *Holocene coastal environments, human activity and sea-level rise: archaeological investigations of three sites in the Mid-Thames estuary* (by C. Ellis and R.G. Scaife, based on reports and contributions by R.G. Scaife, N.G. Cameron, M. Godwin and M.J. Allen). Unpublished text. Salisbury: Wessex Archaeology.

West, S. 1990. *West Stow, Suffolk: the prehistoric and Romano-British occupations*. Bury St Edmunds: Suffolk County Council Planning Department.

Western, A.C. 1982. Charcoals. In M. Avery, The Neolithic causewayed enclosure, Abingdon. In H. Case and A.W.R. Whittle (eds), *Settlement patterns in the Oxford region: excavations at the Abingdon causewayed enclosure and other sites*, 49. London: Council for British Archaeology.

Wheeler, R.E.M. 1943. *Maiden Castle, Dorset*. London: Society of Antiquaries.

White, G.M. 1934. Prehistoric remains from Selsey Bill. *Antiquaries Journal* 14, 40–52.

Whitehouse, N.J., McClatchie, M., Barratt, P., Schulting, R., Mclaughlin, R. and Bogaard, A. 2010. INSTAR – Cultivating Societies. *Archaeology Ireland* 24(2), 16–19.

Whitmore, M. 2004. Excavations at a Neolithic site at the John Innes Centre, Colney, 2000. *Norfolk Archaeology* 44, 406–31.

Whittle, A. 1977a. Earlier Neolithic enclosures in north-west Europe. *Proceedings of the Prehistoric Society* 43, 329–48.

Whittle, A.W.R. 1977b. *The earlier Neolithic of southern England and its continental background*. Oxford: British Archaeological Reports.

Whittle, A. 1988a. *Problems in Neolithic archaeology*. Cambridge: Cambridge University Press.

Whittle, A. 1988b. Contexts, activities, events – aspects of Neolithic and Copper Age enclosures in Neolithic central and western Europe. In C. Burgess, P. Topping, C. Mordant and M. Maddison (eds), *Enclosures and defences in the Neolithic of western Europe*, 1–19. Oxford: British Archaeological Reports.

Whittle, A. 1990a. Prolegomena to the study of the Mesolithic-Neolithic transition in Britain and Ireland. In D. Cahen and M. Otte (eds), *Rubané et Cardial*, 209–27. Liège: Etudes et Recherches Archéologiques de l'Université de Liège 39.

Whittle, A. 1990b. A model for the Mesolithic-Neolithic transition in the upper Kennet valley, north Wiltshire. *Proceedings of the Prehistoric Society* 56, 101–10.

Whittle, A. 1993. The Neolithic of the Avebury area: sequence, environment, settlement and monuments. *Oxford Journal of Archaeology* 12, 29–53.

Whittle, A. 1994. Excavations at Millbarrow chambered tomb, Winterbourne Monkton, north Wiltshire. *Wiltshire Archaeological and Natural History Magazine* 87, 1–53.

Whittle, A. 1996. *Europe in the Neolithic: the creation of new worlds*. Cambridge: Cambridge University Press.

Whittle, A. 1997a. Moving on and moving around: Neolithic settlement mobility. In P. Topping (ed.), *Neolithic landscapes*, 15–22. Oxford: Oxbow Books.

Whittle, A. 1997b. *Sacred mound, holy rings. Silbury Hill and the West Kennet palisade enclosures: a later Neolithic complex in north Wiltshire*. Oxford: Oxbow Books.

Whittle, A. 1999. The Neolithic period, *c.* 4000–2500/2200 BC: changing the world. In J. Hunter and I. Ralston (eds), *The archaeology of Britain*, 58–76. London: Routledge.

Whittle, A. 2003. *The archaeology of people: dimensions of Neolithic life*. London: Routledge.

Whittle, A. 2005. Lived experience in the Early Neolithic of the Great Hungarian Plain. In D. Bailey, A. Whittle and V. Cummings (eds), *(un)settling the Neolithic*, 64–70. Oxford: Oxbow Books.

Whittle, A. 2006. The temporality of enclosure. *Journal of Iberian Archaeology* 8, 15–24.

Whittle, A. 2007a. The temporality of transformation: dating the early development of the southern British Neolithic. In A. Whittle and V. Cummings (eds), *Going over: the Mesolithic-Neolithic transition in north-west Europe*, 377–98. Oxford: Oxford University Press for The British Academy.

Whittle, A. 2007b. Building memories. In D. Benson and A. Whittle (eds), *Building memories: the Neolithic Cotswold long barrow at Ascott-under-Wychwood*, 361–4. Oxford: Oxbow Books.

Whittle, A. 2009. The people who lived in longhouses: what's the big idea? In D. Hofmann and P. Bickle (eds), *Creating communities: new advances in Central European Neolithic research*, 249–63. Oxford: Oxbow Books.

Whittle, A. and Bayliss, A. 2007. The times of their lives: from chronological precision to kinds of history and change. *Cambridge Archaeological Journal* 17, 21–8.

Whittle, A. and Cummings, V. (eds) 2007. *Going over: the Mesolithic-Neolithic transition in north-west Europe*. Oxford: Oxford University Press for The British Academy.

Whittle, A. and Pollard, J. 1998. Windmill Hill causewayed enclosure: the harmony of symbols. In M. Edmonds and C. Richards (eds), *Understanding the Neolithic of north-western Europe*, 231–47. Glasgow: Cruithne Press.

Whittle, A. and Pollard, J. 1999. The harmony of symbols: wider meanings. In A. Whittle, J. Pollard and C. Grigson, *The harmony of symbols: the Windmill Hill causewayed enclosure, Wiltshire*, 381–90. Oxford: Oxbow Books.

Whittle, A. and Wysocki, M. 1998. Parc le Breos Cwm transepted long cairn, Gower, West Glamorgan: date, contents and context. *Proceedings of the Prehistoric Society* 64, 139–82.

Whittle, A., Atkinson, R.J.C., Chambers, R. and Thomas, N. 1992. Excavations in the Neolithic and Bronze Age complex at Dorchester-on-Thames, Oxfordshire. *Proceedings of the Prehistoric Society* 58, 143–201.

Whittle, A., Barclay, A., Bayliss, A., McFadyen, L., Schulting, R. and Wysocki, M. 2007a. Building for the dead: events, processes and changing worldviews from the thirty-eighth to the thirty-fourth centuries cal BC in southern Britain. *Cambridge Archaeological Journal* 17.1, supplement, 123–47.

Whittle, A., Bayliss, A. and Wysocki, M. 2007b. Once in a lifetime: the date of the Wayland's Smithy long barrow. *Cambridge Archaeological Journal* 17.1, supplement, 103–21.

Whittle, A., Bayliss, A. and Healy, F. 2008. The timing and tempo of change: examples from the fourth millennium cal BC in southern England. *Cambridge Archaeological Journal* 18.1, 65–70.

Whittle, A., Davies, J.J., Dennis, I., Fairbairn, A.S. and Hamilton, M. 2000. Neolithic activity and occupation outside Windmill Hill causewayed enclosure, Wiltshire: survey and excavation 1992–93. *Wiltshire Archaeological and Natural History Magazine* 93, 131–80.

Whittle, A., Pollard, J. and Grigson, C. 1999. *The harmony of symbols: the Windmill Hill causewayed enclosure, Wiltshire.* Oxford: Oxbow Books.

Whittle, A., Rouse, A.J. and Evans, J.G. 1993. A Neolithic downland monument in its environment: excavations at the Easton Down long barrow, Bishops Cannings, north Wiltshire. *Proceedings of Prehistoric Society* 59, 197–239.

Wiessner, P. 2002. The vines of complexity: egalitarian structures and the institutionalization of inequality among the Enga. *Current Anthropology* 43, 233–69.

Wilde, W.R. 1857. *A descriptive catalogue of the antiquities of stone, earthen and vegetable materials in the Museum of the Royal Irish Academy*. Dublin: Royal Irish Academy.

Wilkinson, K. and Sidell, J. 2007. London, the backwater of Neolithic Britain? Archaeological significance of Middle Holocene river and vegetation change in the London Thames. In J. Sidell and F. Haughey (eds), *Neolithic archaeology in the intertidal zone*, 71–85. Oxford: Oxbow Books.

Wilkinson, K. and Straker, V. 2008. Neolithic and early Bronze Age environmental background. In C.J. Webster (ed.), *The archaeology of South West England. South West Archaeological Research Framework Resource Assessment and Research Agenda*, 63–74. Taunton: Somerset County Council.

Wilkinson, T.J. and Murphy, P.L. 1995. *The archaeology of the Essex coast, volume I: the Hullbridge survey*. Chelmsford: Essex County Council.

Wilkinson, T.J., Murphy, P.L. and Brown, N. forthcoming. *The archaeology of the Essex coast, volume II: excavations at the prehistoric site of The Stumble*. Chelmsford: Essex County Council.

Williams, A. 1952. Clegyr Boia, St David's (Pemb.): excavation in 1943. *Archaeologia Cambrensis* 102, 20–47.

Williams, B.B. 1986. Excavations at Altanagh, County Tyrone. *Ulster Journal of Archaeology* 49, 33–88.

Williams, D.F. 1997. A note on the petrology of some Neolithic pottery from Helman Tor, Lanlivery, Cornwall. In R.J. Mercer, 'The excavation of a Neolithic enclosure complex at Helman Tor, Lostwithiel, Cornwall'. *Cornish Archaeology* 36, 37–9.

Williams, D.N., Dorling, P. and Preece, N. 2006. *Hill Croft Field, Bodenham: an archaeological evaluation*. Unpublished report produced by Herefordshire Archaeology.

Williams, J. Ll. and Davidson, A., with Flook, R., Jenkins, D.A., Muckle, P., and Roberts, T. 1998. Survey and excavation at the Graiglwyd Neolithic axe-factory, Penmaenmawr. *Archaeology in Wales* 38, 3–21.

Williams, R.E.G. and Johnson, A.S. 1976. Birmingham University radiocarbon dates X. *Radiocarbon* 18, 249–67.

Willis, E.H., Tauber, H. and Münnich, K.O. 1960. Variations in the atmospheric radiocarbon concentration over the past 1300 years. *Radiocarbon* 2, 1–4.

Willock, E.H. 1936. A Neolithic site on Haldon. *Proceedings of the Devon Archaeological Society* 2.4, 255–63.

Willock, E.H. 1937. A further note on the Neolithic site on Haldon. *Proceedings of the Devon Archaeological Society* 3.1, 33–43.

Wilson, T. 2002. The lithics. In G. Shand, *Excavations at Chalk Hill, near Ramsgate, Kent 1997–8: integrated assessment and updated research design*, 23–6. Unpublished document. Canterbury: Canterbury Archaeological Trust.

Witmore, C.L. 2007. Landscape, time, topology: an archaeological account of the southern Argolid, Greece. In D. Hicks, G. Fairclough and L. McAtackney (eds), *Envisioning landscape: situations and standpoints in archaeology and heritage*, 194–224. Walnut Creek, CA: Left Coast Press.

Witts, G.B. 1881. Description of the long barrow, called 'West Tump', in the parish of Brimpsfield, Gloucestershire. *Transactions of the Bristol and Gloucestershire Archaeological Society* 5, 201–11.

Wohlfarth, B. and Possnert, G. 2000. AMS Radiocarbon measurements from the Swedish varved clays. *Radiocarbon* 42, 323–33.

Wood, W. 1996. Faunal remains. In M. Russell and D. Rudling, 'Excavations at Whitehawk Neolithic enclosure, Brighton, East Sussex, 1991–1993'. *Sussex Archaeological Collections* 134, 51.

Woodcock, A. 2003. The archaeological implications of coastal change in Sussex. In D. Rudling (ed.), *The archaeology of Sussex to AD 2000*, 1–16. Great Dunham: Heritage Marketing and Publications Ltd for the Centre for Continuing Education, University of Sussex.

Woodcock, A.G., Kelly, D.B. and Woolley, A.R. 1988. The petrological identification of stone implements from south-east England. In T.H.McK. Clough and W.A. Cummins (eds), *Stone axe studies volume 2. The petrology of prehistoric stone implements from the British Isles*, 21–33. London: Council for British Archaeology.

Woodman, P. 1976. The Irish Mesolithic/Neolithic transition. In S.J. de Laet (ed.), *Acculturation and continuity in Atlantic Europe: Proceedings of the 4th Atlantic Colloquium*, 296–307. Bruges: de Tempel.

Woodman, P. 1978a. *The Mesolithic in Ireland: hunter-gatherers in an insular environment*. Oxford: British Archaeological Reports.

Woodman, P. 1978b. A re-appraisal of the Manx Mesolithic. In P.J. Davey (ed.), *Man and environment in the Isle of Man*, 119–39. Oxford: British Archaeological Reports.

Woodman, P. 1981. The postglacial colonisation of Ireland: the human factors. In D. Ó Corráin (ed.), *Irish antiquity*, 93–110. Cork: Tower Books.

Woodman, P. 1992. Excavations at Mad Man's Window, Glenarm, Co. Antrim: problems of flint exploitation in east Antrim. *Proceedings of the Prehistoric Society* 58, 77–106.

Woodman, P. 1997. Killuragh cave. In I. Bennett (ed.), *Excavations 1996: summary accounts of archaeological excavations in Ireland*, 67–8. Bray: Wordwell.

Woodman, P. 2000. Getting back to basics: transitions to farming in Ireland and Britain. In T.D. Price (ed.), *Europe's first farmers*, 219–59. Cambridge: Cambridge University Press.

Woodman, P.C. 2009. Challenging times: reviewing Irish Mesolithic chronologies. In P. Crombé, M. Van Strydonck, J. Sergant, M. Boudin and M. Bats (eds), *Chronology and evolution within the Mesolithic of north-west Europe: Proceedings of an international meeting, Brussels, May 30th–June 1st 2007*, 195–216. Newcastle: Cambridge Scholars Publishing.

Woodman, P., Anderson, E. and Finlay, N. 1999. *Excavations at Ferriter's Cove, 1983–95: last foragers, first farmers on the Dingle Peninsula*. Bray: Wordwell.

Woodman, P., Finlay, N. and Anderson, E. 2006. *The archaeology of a collection: the Keiller-Knowles collection of the National Museum of Ireland.* Bray: Wordwell in association with the National Museum of Ireland.

Woodman, P. and McCarthy, M. 2003. Contemplating some awful(ly) interesting vistas: importing cattle and red deer into prehistoric Ireland. In I. Armit, E. Murphy, E. Nelis and D. Simpson (eds), *Neolithic settlement in Ireland and western Britain*, 31–9. Oxford: Oxbow Books.

Woodman, P., McCarthy, M. and Monaghan, N. 1997. The Irish

Quaternary Fauna project. *Quaternary Science Reviews* 16, 129–59.

Woodward, A. 1992. Neolithic pottery. In S. Cracknell and M.W. Bishop, 'Excavations at 25–33 Brook Street, Warwick, 1973'. *Transactions of the Brimingham and Warwickshire Archaeological Society* 97, 26–7.

Woodward, A., Hunter, J., Ixer, R., Roe, F., Potts, P.J., Webb, P.C., Watson, J.S. and Jones, M.C. 2006. Beaker age bracers in England: sources, function and use. *Antiquity* 80, 530–43.

Woodward, P.J. 1991. *The South Dorset Ridgeway: survey and excavations 1977–84*. Dorchester: Dorset Natural History and Archaeological Society.

Woodward, P.J., Davies, S.M. and Graham, A.H. 1993. *Excavations at the old Methodist chapel and Greyhound Yard, Dorchester, 1981–84*. Dorchester: Dorset Natural History and Archaeology Society.

Woodward, P.J., Staines, S., Evans, J.G., Rouse, A., Bellamy, P. and Edmonds, M. 1991. The landscape survey. In N. Sharples, *Maiden Castle: excavations and field survey 1985–6*, 9–36. London: English Heritage.

Wymer, J.J. (ed.) 1977. *Gazetteer of Mesolithic sites in England and Wales*. London: Council for British Archaeology.

Wymer, J.J. 1986. A further Neolithic pit on Bunker's Hill, Witton. *Norfolk Archaeology* 39, 315–22.

Wymer, J.J. and Brown, N.R. 1995. *Excavations at North Shoebury: settlement and economy in south-east Essex 1500 BC–AD 1500*. Chelmsford: Essex County Council Planning Department Archaeology Section.

Wymer, J.J. and Healy, F. 1996. Neolithic and Bronze Age activity and settlement at Longham and Beeston with Bittering. In J.J. Wymer, *Barrow excavations in Norfolk 1984–88*, 28–53. Gressenhall: Norfolk Archaeological Unit.

Wymer, J.J. and Robins, P.A. 1994. A long blade flint industry beneath Boreal peat at Titchwell, Norfolk. *Norfolk Archaeology* 42, 13–37.

Wysocki, M. 1999. Inner ditch, Trench F, immature femur 6422 inserted into *Bos* humerus in bone deposit 630. In A. Whittle, J. Pollard and C. Grigson, *The harmony of symbols: the Windmill Hill causewayed enclosure, Wiltshire*, 346. Oxford: Oxbow Books.

Wysocki, M. and Whittle, A. 2000. Diversity, lifestyles and rites: new biological and archaeological evidence from British earlier Neolithic mortuary assemblages. *Antiquity* 74, 591– 601.

Wysocki, M., Bayliss, A. and Whittle, A. 2007. Serious mortality: the date of the Fussell's Lodge long barrow. *Cambridge Archaeological Journal* 17.1, supplement, 65–84.

Wysocki, M., Griffiths, S., Hedges, R.E.M., Higham, T., Fernandez-Jalvo, Y. and Whittle, A. in preparation. Coldrum: dating, dietary analysis and taphonomy of the human remains from a Medway megalithic monument.

Xu, S., Anderson, R., Bryant, C, Cook, G.T., Dougans, A., Freeman, S., Naysmith, P., Schnable, C. and Scott, A.E.M. 2004. Capabilities of the new SUERC 5MV AMS facility for ^{14}C dating. *Radiocarbon* 46, 59–64.

Yates, A. 2000a. Ewenny, Beech Court Farm prehistoric enclosure (SS 904 766). *Archaeology in Wales* 40, 89.

Yates, A. 2000b. *Beech Court Farm enclosure, Ewenny quarry, Ewenny, Vale of Glamorgan: archaeological field evaluation stage 1b internal trenches*. GGAT Report 2000/038, Project A609, Excavation 398. Swansea: Glamorgan-Gwent Archaeological Trust.

Yates, A. 2002. *A prehistoric enclosure at Beech Court Farm, Ewenny quarry, Ewenny, Vale of Glamorgan, June 1998–Present*. Unpublished client report. Swansea: Glamorgan-Gwent Archaeological Trust.

Young, M.W. 1971. *Fighting with food: leadership, values and social control in a Massim society*. Cambridge: Cambridge University Press.

Young, R. 1987. *Lithics and subsistence in north-eastern England: aspects of the prehistoric archaeology of the Wear Valley, Co Durham, from the Mesolithic to the Bronze Age*. Oxford: British Archaeological Reports.

Zeeb-Lanz, A., Arbogast, R.-M., Haack, F., Haidle, M.N., Jeunesse, C., Orschiedt, J., Schimmelpfennig, D. and van Willingen, S. 2009. The LBK settlement with pit enclosure at Herxheim near Landau (Palatinate). First results. In D. Hofmann and P. Bickle (eds), *Creating communities: new advances in Central European Neolithic research*, 202–19. Oxford: Oxbow Books.

Zienkiewicz, L. 1999. Pottery. Part 1: early Neolithic including Ebbsfleet. In A. Whittle, J. Pollard and C. Grigson, *The harmony of symbols: the Windmill Hill causewayed enclosure, Wiltshire*, 258–92. Oxford: Oxbow Books.

Zienkiewicz, L. and Hamilton, M. 1999. Pottery. In A. Whittle, J. Pollard and C. Grigson, *The harmony of symbols: the Windmill Hill causewayed enclosure, Wiltshire*, 257–317. Oxford: Oxbow Books.

Zimmermann, A. 2006a. Production and demand of flint artefacts in the Bandkeramik of western Germany. In P. Allard, F. Bostyn and A. Zimmermann (eds), *Contribution des matériaux lithiques dans la chronologie du Néolithique ancien et moyen en France et dans les régions limitrophes. Actes de la Xième session de l'EAA, Lyon Septembre 2004. Groupe thématique II: interprétation des données*, 80–3. Oxford: British Archaeological Reports.

Zimmermann, A. 2006b. Aldenhovener Platte, Inden 9, Gde Geuenich, Kreis Düren. Michelsberger Erdwerk. In. J. Kunow and H.-H. Wegner (eds), *Urgeschichte im Rheinland. Jahrbuch 2005 des Rheinischen Vereins für Denkmalpflege und Landschaftschutz,* 283–4. Köln: Verlag des Rheinischen Vereins für Denkmalpflege und Landschaftschutz.

Zimmermann, A. 2006c. Aldenhovener Platte, Koslar 10, Gde Jülich, Kreis Düren. Grabenanlage der Michelsberger Kultur. In. J. Kunow and H.-H. Wegner (eds), *Urgeschichte im Rheinland. Jahrbuch 2005 des Rheinischen Vereins für Denkmalpflege und Landschaftschutz,* 284–5. Köln: Verlag des Rheinischen Vereins für Denkmalpflege und Landschaftschutz.

Zondervan, A. and Sparks, R.J. 1997. Development plan for the AMS facility at the Institute of Geological and Nuclear Sciences, New Zealand. *Instruments and Methods in Physics Research B* 123, 79–83.

Zondervan, A., Poletti, M., Purcell, C., and Sparks, R.J. 2007. Accelerator and beamline upgrades at the AMS facility of GNS Science, New Zealand. *Instruments and Methods in Physics Research B*, 259, 47–9.

Zvelebil, M. and Rowley-Conwy, P. 1984. Transition to farming in northern Europe: a gatherer-hunter perspective. *Norwegian Archaeological Review* 17, 104–27.

Zvelebil, M. and Rowley-Conwy, P. 1986. Foragers and farmers in Atlantic Europe. In M. Zvelebil (ed.), *Hunters in transition*, 67–93. Cambridge: Cambridge University Press.

Index

Page numbers for principal passages relating to a topic are shown in **bold**, page numbers for illustrations relating to a topic are shown in *italics*